# The Center of the Sunlit Sky

## The Nitartha Institute Series

*published by Snow Lion Publications*

Nitartha Institute was founded in 1996 by The Dzogchen Ponlop Rinpoche, under the guidance of Khenchen Thrangu Rinpoche and Khenpo Tsültrim Gyamtso Rinpoche, the leading contemporary teachers of the Karma Kagyü tradition of Tibetan Buddhism. The Institute, under the aegis of Nitartha *international,* aims to fully transmit the Buddhist tradition of contemplative inquiry and learning; it offers Western students training in advanced Buddhist view and practice, as taught by the Karma Kagyü and Nyingma lineages of Tibet.

The Institute is pleased to ally with Snow Lion Publications in presenting this series of important works offering a wide range of graded educational materials that include authoritative translations of key texts from the Buddhist tradition, both those unique to the Kagyü and Nyingma lineages and those common to the wider scope of Indo-Tibetan Buddhism; modern commentaries by notable lineage scholar-practitioners; manuals for contemplative practice; and broader studies that deepen understanding of particular aspects of the Buddhist view. The initial releases are from the Kagyü tradition and will be followed by publications from the Nyingma tradition.

This publication is an Intermediate Level Nitartha book.

# The Center of the Sunlit Sky

## *Madhyamaka in the Kagyü Tradition*

Karl Brunnhölzl

*Including a Translation of Pawo Rinpoche's Commentary on the Knowledge Section of Śāntideva's* The Entrance to the Bodhisattva's Way of Life (Bodhicaryāvatāra)

Snow Lion Publications
ITHACA, NEW YORK ✦ BOULDER, COLORADO

Snow Lion Publications
P.O. Box 6483
Ithaca, NY 14851 USA
(607) 273-8519
www.snowlionpub.com



Printed in Canada on acid-free recycled paper.

ISBN 1-55939-218-5

Cataloging-in-Publication Data is available from the Library of Congress.

*Contents*

Much ado about nothing.
William Shakespeare

"O young lady, who gave you this self-confidence of yours?"
"The Elder himself imparted it to me, because this self-confidence of mine would not have arisen if the Elder had not questioned me."
From T*he Sūtra of the Prophecy of the Young Lady Excellent Moon*

Breathe the form of Madhyamaka—open sky
Feel the sound of Madhyamaka—roaring silence
Open up to the touch of Madhyamaka—letting go
Be thrilled by the taste of Madhyamaka—equality's variety
Get soaked within the scent of Madhyamaka—freedom innate

Resistance is liberation
No point in fighting
You are all surrounded by yourself

Give up the surroundings
Don't defend your
headquarters

And conquer the
citadel
of

self-surrender

# *Acknowledgments*

THIS BOOK would never have come into existence were it not for The Dzogchen Ponlop Rinpoche telling me in his usual, seemingly casual way, "You should write an introduction on Madhyamaka for your translation of Pawo Rinpoche's commentary on the *Bodhicaryāvatāra.*" At first, I took this remark as a joke. However, Rinpoche kept coming back to this idea. He even became very specific about what such an introduction should include and which texts should be consulted, so I could not but start taking this project more seriously. It rapidly grew from a mere introduction into quite an extensive volume of its own, partly because Rinpoche, at each of our meetings over the years, added topics to be included. Thus, my sincere gratitude and respect go to The Dzogchen Ponlop Rinpoche for his original idea and his continuous inspiration and guidance throughout the entire project. Even greater is the kindness and skillfulness of Khenchen Tsultrim Gyamtso Rinpoche, who for many years has guided Western students through the world of Tibetan Buddhist scriptures with their various philosophical systems and terminologies. Without him, I would not have much of a clue about the intricacies of the Buddhist teachings and their practical application. Further thanks go to Acharya Lama Tenpa Gyaltsen, who helped with many questions about translation. I am also very grateful to all the Western scholars, particularly Prof. Lambert Schmithausen and Dr. Klaus-Dieter Matthes, who opened my eyes to the richness and profundity of both the Sanskrit language and the Yogācāra tradition.

Sincere thanks go to Sidney Piburn and Jeff Cox from Snow Lion Publications for their readiness to publish this text. Tracy Davis and Steve Rhodes deserve thanks and praise for being very meticulous and caring editors. My heartfelt gratitude is also extended to Mette Harboe and Carmen Rumbaut for their untiring diligence in accomplishing the first volunteer phase of editing, in terms of English as well as content. They are both to be commended for offering many helpful suggestions and insights, as are Linda Patrik and Jirka Hladis. Thanks to Julia Martin for her assistance with the bibliographic research in Vienna and Stephanie Johnston for preparing the charts. Regarding the financial side, I would like to express my deep gratitude to a dear friend and anonymous benefactor who alleviated my task of self-sponsoring, and to Nitartha Institute for assistance during the final phase of the project. I would also like to thank the Tsadra Foundation for funding the preparation of the index. Last but not least, I am very grateful to all the people in Europe, Asia, and North America who contributed to the text through their discussions with me and/or by providing food and shelter while I was working all over the globe on this nomad project.

In particular, I feel very pleased and honored that this book marks the beginning of the *Nītārtha Institute Series* as an expression of the activities of the Nītārtha Institute (under the direction of The Dzogchen Ponlop Rinpoche). This series is designed as a timely attempt to present the scriptural traditions of both the Kagyü and Nyingma schools of Tibetan Buddhism to a wider Western audience.

Over the years, I have had the good fortune to be able to sip a few random drops from the vast ocean of the Buddhist teachings, but I no doubt lack the attainments of a true scholar. I never completed the traditional three-year meditation retreat, so I have no realization either. And not being a native speaker of either English, Tibetan, or Sanskrit, I do not have sufficient command of any of these languages. In brief, there isn't anything to qualify me to write a book like this. In doing so, I have only tried to comply with the wish of The Dzogchen Ponlop Rinpoche. It lies in the nature of such a project that there is no certainty that it will benefit anybody else. What is certain, though, is that I myself learned a lot during the writing process, for which I am extremely grateful. So, if there is anything in what follows that sounds good, makes sense, and serves as an antidote to suffering, may it be enjoyed as coming from realized masters and scholars who know what they are talking about. Everything else, including all mistakes, can safely be said to be mine.

May this book serve as a contributing cause for the enlightened activity of H. H. the Seventeenth Gyalwang Karmapa Urgyen Trinlay Dorje that swiftly and unimpededly embraces all sentient beings without exception. May it in particular assist in sustaining the pure scholarly tradition of the Karma Kagyü lineage as it was initiated and upheld by all the Karmapas as a means to liberate beings from ignorance and suffering.

Brabrand, on the vast plains of Jutland, Denmark,
on a completely ordinary day in December 2003

# *Foreword*

*Entering the Way of the Bodhisattva* is one of the most influential and inspiring texts in Buddhist history. Renowned for its poetry, it presents some of the most profound teachings of the Buddhist philosophical tradition in a lucid and simple style, combining the view of emptiness with direct instructions for contemplative practices of compassion.

The author of the *Bodhicaryāvatāra*, as the text is titled in its original Sanskrit, is Śāntideva, a great eighth-century Indian master from Nālandā University.[1] The treatise is a very practical guide for those aspiring to actualize the practices of the six pāramitās, or perfections: generosity, discipline, patience, exertion, meditation, and superior knowledge or prajñā.

Buddhist practitioners in India and Tibet have expounded, studied, and practiced the *Bodhicaryāvatāra* in an unbroken tradition until today. Over the centuries, great Buddhist masters of India and Tibet composed numerous commentaries and instructions on the text. Many masters not only wrote about this famous book, but also continuously taught this text to their students. One such master is the most renowned wandering hermit Patrul Rinpoche, who taught this text at Dzogchen Shri Singha Shedra of the Dzogchen Monastery, and later at his retreat area in the Dzachu region of eastern Tibet. Indeed, this text addresses timeless issues, which are of critical importance to anyone who is seriously engaged in spiritual pursuits, and contemporary masters continue to write about it and teach it to their students.

The *Bodhicaryāvatāra* is presented in ten main topics or chapters: 1) Benefits of Bodhicitta; 2)Purification; 3) Embracing Bodhicitta; 4) Awareness; 5) Vigilance; 6) Patience; 7) Perseverance; 8) Meditation; 9) Wisdom (prajñā); and 10) Dedication.

The exposition of the Madhyamaka, or the Middle Way philosophy, in the ninth chapter is one of the classic presentations of this profound view and forms the basis for elucidating the śūnyatavāda, or teachings on emptiness, as taught by Nāgārjuna, the founder of the Middle Way school.

One of the most detailed and complete commentaries on the *Bodhicaryāvatāra* is the *Ocean of the Dharma of the Great Vehicle*[2], composed by Pawo Tsuklak Trengwa (1504–1566). He was a great teacher of the Kagyü lineage of Tibet and was one of the two most important students of the Eighth Karmapa, Mikyö Dorje (1507–1554), a great scholar and meditation master who wrote over thirty volumes of commentaries and instructions on Buddhist sūtras and tantras.

The Kagyü lineage is rich in intellectual studies, especially in the areas of philosophy and logic, as well as in its tradition of practice instructions, famed for their directness. Teachers in this tradition use a balanced approach to lead students along the "middle way," a distinctive method of the Kagyü lineage. Through study, combined with practice pursuant to these instructions, one may develop the wisdom that is the basis for transcending the neurotic confusion of saṃsāra.

The scholarly tradition of the Kagyü lineage expanded rapidly during the time of the Seventh, Eighth, and Ninth Karmapas. The author of this text, Pawo Rinpoche, lived during the peak of this period, and played a very important role in clarifying the intentions of Karmapa Mikyö Dorje and enriching the view of the Kagyü Madhyamaka school. His contribution to Kagyü scholarship was thus very important, and his writings are still studied today at different Kagyü shedras, including the main seat of His Holiness the Karmapa, Tsurphu, in Tibet, and at Karma Shri Nalanda Institute in Rumtek, Sikkim, India.

The *Bodhicaryāvatāra* is one of the few Indian Buddhist texts for which the original Sanskrit has survived. It was first translated into Tibetan from Sanskrit in the eighth century. Now, in the twenty-first century, we are especially fortunate to have many different translations of the root verses in English, as well as translations of portions of some commentaries.

I am delighted to present *The Center of the Sunlit Sky,* which includes a translation of the commentary by Pawo Tsuklak Trengwa on the chapter of the *Bodhicaryāvatāra* on "Wisdom." A special feature of this first publication in the Nitartha Institute Series is an extensive introductory presentation of Madhyamaka in the Kagyü tradition by Dr. Karl Brunnhölzl.

Karl Brunnhölzl is a highly qualified translator, interpreter, and teacher. This excellent translation and comprehensive introduction to Madhyamaka in the Kagyü tradition reflect his knowledge, wisdom, and extensive experience studying and presenting these materials for many years. In particular, he has studied Tibetan language and Buddhist philosophy and logic with Very Venerable Khenchen Tsultrim Gyamtso Rinpoche and myself, as well as with many other teachers. He has also translated numerous Tibetan texts into English and German. Karl has been one of the key translators and teachers at the Nitartha Institute.

This book gives, for the first time in a Western publication, a comprehensive presentation of the unique Kagyü view of Madhyamaka. While going into great detail in his presentation of the view, Karl is still careful to address Madhyamaka within a context of meditation. Special features of his detailed treatment include a discussion of Shentong in relation to Madhyamaka and a detailed consideration of differences between Kagyü and Geluk understandings of this philosophy as highlighted in the works of Mikyö Dorje and Tsongkhapa. In sum, this is a pioneering effort to make Kagyü scholarship on Madhyamaka philosophy known to a wider audience.

I am grateful to have had the opportunity to teach the ninth chapter of *Bodhicaryāvatāra* at Nitartha Institute Europe. Karl prepared the translation of this chapter for my class, along with that of the commentary by Pawo Tsuklak Trengwa, and assisted with translation during my teaching. At that time, Karl and I discussed how important it would be to write an extensive introduction to this chapter when published in English. I am delighted by Karl's remarkable accomplishment. He has not only presented us with a wonderful translation, but also an outstanding introduction that truly elucidates the view of Śāntideva through the teachings of the great Kagyü Madhyamaka masters.

May this translation contribute to the genuine effort to transplant pure dharma in the West. May this book awaken the wisdom heart of all beings and through this, may countless sentient beings benefit.

In the dharma,

Dzogchen Ponlop Rinpoche
Nalanda West
Seattle, Washington
May, 2004

1 Nālandā University was one of the greatest institutions of higher learning in human history. It reached its zenith during the first millennium and by the seventh century encompassed hundreds of buildings and upwards of 10,000 students and faculty. The university was home to the renowned Buddhist scholars of that time, including Nāgārjuna, Āryadeva, Śāntarakṣita, Padmasambhava and Candrakīrti. It was destroyed in the 12th and 13th centuries.

2 བྱང་ཆུབ་སེམས་དཔའི་སྤྱོད་པ་ལ་འཇུག་པའི་རྣམ་པར་བཤད་པ་ཐེག་ཆེན་ཆོས་ཀྱི་རྒྱ་མཚོ་ཟབ་རྒྱས་མཐའ་ཡས་པའི་སྙིང་པོ། *(byang chub sems dpa'i spyod pa la 'jug pa'i rnam par bshad pa theg chen chos kyi rgya mtsho zab rgyas mth'a yas pa'i snying po).*

# *Preface*

GIVEN THE NUMBER OF STUDIES on Madhyamaka in general and the quantity of translations of Madhyamaka texts into Western languages, one might well wonder what the point of yet another book on this topic, with yet another translation of the ninth chapter of the *Bodhicaryāvatāra*,[1] might be. The brief answer to this is that, despite the extensive materials on Madhyamaka that are currently available in the West, the overall picture of this Buddhist system in India and Tibet is not nearly complete. A number of issues call for an attempt to fill in some gaps. First, with a few exceptions, the majority of books or articles on Madhyamaka by Western—particularly North American—scholars is based on the explanations of the Gelugpa school of Tibetan Buddhism.[2] Deliberately or not, many of these Western presentations give the impression that the Gelugpa system is more or less equivalent to Tibetan Buddhism as such and that this school's way of presenting Madhyamaka (especially with respect to its Consequentialist[3] branch) is the standard or even the only way to explain this system,[4] which has led to the still widely prevailing assumption that this is actually the case. From the perspective of Indian and Tibetan Buddhism in general, nothing could be more wrong. In fact, the peculiar Gelugpa version of Madhyamaka is a minority position in Indo-Tibetan Buddhism, since its uncommon features are neither found in any Indian text nor accepted by any of the other Tibetan schools.[5] Thus, the current situation in the West in no way represents the richness of Madhyamaka views that existed in India and are still transmitted in all four major Tibetan Buddhist schools. Specifically, there is no general outline of the Madhyamaka view as presented in the Kagyü school of Tibetan Buddhism in any Western language.[6]

However, I would like to make it clear at the outset that this book is not about sectarianism or which view is the better one. Rather, it should be regarded as an attempt to shed some light on more facets of the living Indo-Tibetan Buddhist tradition and to introduce them to a wider Western audience. As the Buddha himself always said, it is up to us which teachings we personally find most convincing and helpful for our lives.

In addition, there is a rather common cliché that the followers of the Kagyü school just chant rituals or sit in caves and three-year retreats to practice meditation and lack any scholarly tradition. By presenting materials from a number of mainly Karma Kagyü sources, I attempt to show that there definitely *is* a rich scholarly and scriptural tradition in this school and to offer a glimpse of it.

Marpa's scholarly accomplishment, resulting from his twenty-one years of studying with many masters in India, is still evident in his numerous translations contained in the Tibetan Buddhist canon, in both *Kangyur*[7] and *Tengyur*.[8] Not widely known is that Milarepa studied intensively with Marpa before he set off for his solitary retreats. His familiarity with advanced Buddhist terminology and concepts can be seen in many of his vajra songs. Starting with Gampopa[9] (1079–1153), the school's early masters wrote mainly works that focus on meditation practice. Before Gampopa met his principal teacher, Milarepa, he was already an accomplished master in the Kadampa[10] tradition, well known for its rigorous educational training. He composed numerous texts on Mahāmudrā, and his *Jewel Ornament of Liberation*[11] is held in high esteem by all Tibetan traditions. The First Karmapa Tüsum Khyenba[12] (1110–1193) studied extensively for about two decades with most of the greatest masters of his time, including Chaba Chökyi Senge[13] and Patsab Lotsāwa,[14] before he became Gampopa's student. The Second Karmapa Karma Pakshi (1206–1283) wrote many—now lost—volumes, including a text on valid cognition.[15] The Third Karmapa Rangjung Dorje[16] (1284–1339) greatly contributed to the corpus of practice-oriented works, mainly through his famous *Profound Inner Reality*,[17] but he also wrote a number of more scholarly works, such as his *Distinction between Consciousness and Wisdom*,[18] a treatise on Buddha nature,[19] and a recently rediscovered commentary on Nāgārjuna's *Praise to the Dharmadhātu.* The Fourth Karmapa Rölpay Dorje[20] (1340–1383) was a prolific writer on logic and reasoning.

The Sixth Karmapa Tongwa Tönden[21] (1416–1453) studied extensively with the great Sakya master Rongtön Sheja Künrig[22] (1367–1449). From this time onward, throughout Tibet, the Karmapas established a number of major Kagyü monastic colleges (*shedra*),[23] the main ones being Tagbo Legshay Ling[24] and Satam Nyinje Ling.[25] According to Jamgön Kongtrul's *Treasury of Knowledge*,[26] initially, the sources for the exegetical system of the sūtra texts in the Kagyü lineage are for the most part to be found in the Sakya tradition, specifically in the explanations of Rongtön. The Karma Kagyü school's independent exegetical tradition with regard to the great sūtra texts started with the Seventh Karmapa's[27] (1454–1506) *Ocean of Texts on Reasoning*[28] and his commentary on *The Ornament of Clear Realization.* This exegetical tradition reached its culmination in the extensive works of the Eighth Karmapa Mikyö Dorje[29] (1507–1554), who wrote commentaries on four of the five traditional topics of sūtra studies[30] as well as a number of independent treatises on both sūtras and tantras, over thirty volumes all together. The Ninth Karmapa Wangchug Dorje[31] (1556–1603), in addition to his famous three major texts on Mahāmudrā[32] and other works on tantra, wrote both brief and extensive commentaries on the five topics of sūtra.[33] Also the Fourteenth and Fifteenth Karmapas, Tegchog Dorje (1798–1868) and Kakyab Dorje (1871–1922), were accomplished scholars, both involved in the nonsectarian Rime[34] movement in Eastern Tibet; they composed numerous texts. Other great scholars in the Karma Kagyü school who wrote their own commentaries and treatises on both sūtras and tantras include the Fifth and Sixth Shamarpas, Göncho Yenla[35] (1525–1583) and Chökyi Wangchug[36] (1584–1630), the First Karma Trinlayba Choglay Namgyal[37] (1456–1539), the Second Pawo Rinpoche Tsugla Trengwa[38] (1504–1566), Tagbo Dashi Namgyal[39] (1512–1587), the Eighth Situpa Chökyi Jungnay[40] (1699–1774), and Jamgön Kongtrul Lodrö Taye[41] (1813–1899), one of the main figures in the Rime movement.[42]

The flourishing of this well-established scholarly tradition was somewhat weakened after the time of the Ninth Karmapa as a result of almost all its colleges being closed down by the Central Tibetan government. The most important exception to this was the college at Palpung[43] Monastery in eastern Tibet, founded by the Eighth Situpa in 1727. Nevertheless, most of the classical Kagyü scriptures continue to be studied and transmitted to the present day. Unfortunately, during the Chinese takeover of Tibet, many of these texts became lost and were only partly rediscovered in recent years. In 1981, the Sixteenth Karmapa Rangjung Rigbay Dorje[44] (1924–1981) reestablished the school's tradition of monastic colleges by founding the Karma Śrī Nālandā Institute at his seat-in-exile in Rumtek (India). Since this time, an increasing number of Kagyü colleges have been opened in India and Nepal. In addition, since the early 1990s, Nītārtha International under the direction of The Dzogchen Ponlop Rinpoche is involved in preserving (on electronic media), editing, and republishing all the major texts of the Karma Kagyü lineage, starting with its "eight great texts of sūtra and tantra"[45] plus their main commentaries. More recently, Thrangu Rinpoche's Vajra Vidya Institute in Sarnath, India, has also become involved in editing and republishing the Karma Kagyü scriptural inheritance. In the West, the eight great texts are gradually being translated into English and German and studied at Nītārtha Institute in Canada and Germany.

There is still widespread misunderstanding about what Madhyamaka is and is not, even—or maybe particularly—among Buddhists. These misconceptions are mostly accompanied by a great deal of resistance to what is often assumed to be merely dry intellectual gymnastics. There are strong concerns as to whether the Madhyamaka approach has any practical value at all or is just outright nihilism. It seems that there are two main reasons for this attitude. In general, to put it mildly, we do not appreciate it when our treasured and often unconscious ways of looking at the world are brought into daylight and questioned, but this is precisely what Madhyamaka does, relentlessly and thoroughly. Furthermore, especially in the West, there are hardly any instructions on how to actually work with this approach in a personal rather than just a theoretical way, nor much instruction on why this might be to our benefit.

In other words, in order to appreciate Madhyamaka, we first need to understand how this approach can provide us a chance to vividly notice our rigid ways of viewing ourselves and the world. We may then acknowledge how this literally narrow-minded outlook causes our many problems and our suffering.[46] It is crucial to see that Madhyamaka is not just another philosophical trinket that we add on top of all the sophisticated conceptual garbage of which we have already too much anyway. Madhyamaka is not about adding more intellectual headaches, but loosening up and letting go of everything that gives us headaches in the first place. When we first look at the jungle of Madhyamaka refutations of all kinds of belief systems, they might seem quite alien and complicated. However, all these views simply mirror the fixations and complications that we foster in our own minds. Thus, what makes things complicated is not Madhyamaka itself but our inflexible and discursive mind. Actually, Madhyamaka is not at all about *doing* something complex, new, or particular but about *undoing* in a very basic and profound sense. When we start to realize this, we might discover some genuine interest and even delight in unraveling the convoluted web of our ingrained patterns. It is these patterns that prevent us from fundamentally relaxing our minds, finding relief from mental afflictions,[47] and being more kind toward ourselves and others, with whom we share the same basic problems. Thus, from a practical point of view, it is not Madhyamaka's business to refute the strange belief systems of other schools and people, most of whom lived hundreds of years ago in quite different cultures and societies. Rather, we may consider these views as examples that can help us with finding out about our own beliefs and how they cause us trouble. Consequently, as Buddhist practitioners, it is a matter of applying the Madhyamaka approach first and foremost to our own mental entrenchments and trying to come out into the open.

As for Śāntideva's *Bodhicaryāvatāra*, there surely exist numerous translations of the whole text (both from the Tibetan and the Sanskrit) and especially its ninth chapter on knowledge.[48] The commentaries on which these translations rely are some of the classic Indian commentaries (mostly Prajñākaramati's *Bodhicaryāvatārapañjikā*), various commentaries from the Tibetan Gelugpa school, a single Sakya commentary,[49] and a single Nyingma commentary.[50] In a study on a few selected verses from the eighth and ninth chapters of the text, Williams (1998a) offers some glimpses into a variety of commentaries from all four schools. So far, though, there is no translation of a Kagyü commentary on Śāntideva's famous ninth chapter into any language. Thus, the purpose of the present study is to address these issues in the following ways.

The first part of this book is an attempt to give a general and systematic outline of Madhyamaka (and more specifically of its Consequentialist branch) in terms of ground, path, and fruition that is based on the original Indian texts and their understanding in the Tibetan Kagyü tradition. Throughout my research, I have always tried to directly rely on the main Indian Madhyamaka sources,[51] in either the Sanskrit originals (if available) or their Tibetan translations. As for the Tibetan commentaries on these texts, my presentation rests primarily on the two major Madhyamaka commentaries in the Karma Kagyü tradition. The teachers of this school say that if one wants to know how Madhyamaka in general and the Consequentialist system in particular is presented in the Karma Kagyü lineage, these are the two texts to study:

- The first is a large commentary on Candrakīrti's *Entrance into Centrism* by the Eighth Karmapa Mikyö Dorje, called *The Chariot of the Tagbo Siddhas.*[52] It is not only a commentary on this one major work by Candrakīrti. By referring to a wide range of other Centrist texts as well, it treats all the crucial issues in Madhyamaka in general. In particular, the Karmapa's text includes and extensively comments on the entire long section in Candrakīrti's *Lucid Words* (his other main work) that defends Buddhapālita and criticizes Bhāvaviveka, thus leading to the later distinction between Autonomists and Consequentialists.

- The second text is an equally voluminous commentary on Śāntideva's *Entrance to the Bodhisattva's Way of Life* by one of the Eighth Karmapa's major disciples, Pawo Rinpoche Tsugla Trengwa. It is called *Exposition of The Entrance to the Bodhisattva's Way of Life, the Essence of the Immeasurable, Profound, and Vast Ocean of the Dharma of the Great Vehicle.* As well as being a detailed commentary on Śāntideva's text, it preserves many of the Eighth Karmapa's general explanations on Madhyamaka.

In the Kagyü tradition in general, both commentaries are the earliest and most detailed presentations of Madhyamaka and considered the standard works on this subject. They were written at a time when the debate about the novel interpretation of the Madhyamaka system by Je Tsongkhapa Lobsang Tragba[53] (1357–1419) was still in full swing. However, Karmapa Mikyö Dorje's text in particular not only is a reaction to the position of Tsongkhapa and his followers but addresses most of the views on Madhyamaka that were current in Tibet at the time, including the controversial issue of "Shentong-Madhyamaka." More important, it presents a Madhyamaka view that is not just a philosophical system but a view whose primary focus is its efficiency in serving as the basis and means for liberation and Buddhahood. The Karmapa's work is distinctly Kagyü in that it amply illuminates the connection of Madhyamaka with Mahāmudrā and the siddha tradition, in terms of both view and practice. The text quotes such Indian mahāsiddhas as Saraha, Tilopa, and Nāropa, as well as the great Kagyü yogis of

Tibet, such as Milarepa, Gampopa, Götsangba,[54] Jigden Sumgön,[55] and the First Sangye Nyenba Rinpoche Dashi Baljor,[56] who was the Eighth Karmapa's main teacher and a great siddha. This approach is in itself an "online," direct oral instruction that is imparted simultaneously to reading the written commentary. One may struggle in the midst of all these Madhyamaka arguments and refutations, and then suddenly there is a yogic song, which cuts through all these philosophical complexities right on the spot with a fresh breeze of nonconceptual ease. In this way, the Eighth Karmapa's commentary is quite unique and at the same time extremely profound.

In addition, I draw from three other Kagyü sources on Madhyamaka. The first two are by the famous Drugba Kagyü master Künkhyen Padma Karpo[57] (1527–1596) who, in terms of his Madhyamaka view, is considered to be a Consequentialist. These texts include

- his commentary on *The Entrance to the Bodhisattva's Way of Life*, called *The Lamp for the Middle Path,* and
- *An Illumination of Three Centrist Scriptural Systems, Called The Chariot That Establishes the Definitive Meaning*, which comments on Nāgārjuna's *Fundamental Verses on Centrism*, Candrakīrti's *Entrance into Centrism*, and Milarepa's vajra song called *True Expression of Centrism.*[58]

The final source is a later—and sometimes quite different—presentation of Madhyamaka, which is found in

- several chapters (mainly 6.3, 7.2, and 7.3) in Jamgön Kongtrul Lodrö Taye's *Treasury of Knowledge.*

Based on the groundwork of these scriptures, I try to explore the relevance of the Madhyamaka system for the Buddhist practitioner. Here, the emphasis does not lie on unraveling the details of its logic or searching for a philosophy behind it (others have already done that extensively). Rather, my focus is on the practical application and efficacy of this approach when used as a spiritual tool to train our minds in a way that is not just theoretical or intellectual but as personal as it can get. This means that its teachings and methods are explicitly intended as a way of life that permeates our whole being in order to put an end to our own and others' suffering.

Finally, as a scriptural example for such an approach, the ninth chapter of the *Bodhicaryāvatāra* is presented in the light of a translation of Pawo Tsugla Trengwa's commentary.

As for the general approach to studying, presenting, and practicing Madhyamaka and the above materials, a few remarks about methodology seem necessary here. The traditional Indian and Tibetan way of explaining Buddhist texts is to combine scholarly methods with an account of the experiential relevance of the material as mind training for the practitioner. This represents an attempt to avoid both mere dry scholasticism unrelated to one's experiences in life and mere blind faith or some sort of "emotional spirituality" that is not grounded in its proper scriptural background and critical analysis. When one speaks of faith in Buddhism, this explicitly means well-informed trust that is born from a thorough and proper investigation of the teachers and the teachings in which this trust is to be put.

Such a combined approach implies that the style and terminology of the presentation may vary considerably. Thus, especially for people with little or no background in the Buddhist scholarly tradition, some issues may seem inaccessible at first. Apart from terminology, however, the main reason for this seeming inaccessibility lies in the nature of the subjects that Madhyamaka addresses, which are often not easily digestible. Another reason is the specific ways in which Centrists analyze and communicate, which are usually very different from our ordinary ways of thinking and speaking. In addition, almost all Indian and Tibetan texts and their commentaries were originally written by highly learned scholars for other scholars who were all very familiar with the relevant materials and their background as well as the technical terms and difficult key points. Consequently, these texts are usually terse in the extreme, come with a plethora of complicated technical terms, and mainly use examples that come from Indian or Tibetan culture and thus often do not ring any bells for us. Hence, both nonscholars and Buddhist practitioners who are unfamiliar with all the terms and details often become overwhelmed by such presentations and quickly lose interest in them. To be sure, in order to remedy that problem, I am far from advocating any oversimplification or superficial popularization that would dilute profound issues. However, I think there is a lot in Madhyamaka that can be conveyed pretty straightforwardly and shown to be practically relevant to most people without reliance on complicated terminology.

Whenever I study and teach these materials, I regularly encounter the fact that mere translations of Indian and Tibetan texts are usually not the best way to communicate their contents, judging by the reactions of many people who are exposed to such translations. Even if—or especially when—these translations are precisely correct, they can even turn into the most counterproductive way of communicating what the texts say. However, it usually helps a lot to paraphrase and elaborate on the classic texts and to furnish contemporary examples that illustrate the salient points equally well or even better. Therefore, here too, I mainly choose this approach in presenting material from such texts. This means that Western scholars will not always find the precise source for each paraphrase of certain passages from the texts that I use in my presentation.[59] They may also miss all the technical details of the standard critical apparatus.[60] Some might even consider this way of working with texts to be completely unscientific, since the personal and practical relevance of the material is addressed too.

So, what to do? Going through this book will certainly require some effort from readers at times. However, they might want to consider that, for a long time, Western philosophies, cultures, and societies have cultivated a split between intellect and experience, body and mind, and the two poles of being "objective" (or "scientific") and "subjective" (that is, "experiential" or even "emotional"). However, this split is really only a Western invention. Like most Indian (or Asian) spiritual approaches, the Buddhist path does not regard these aspects as contradictory per se, nor does it favor one side over the other. Naturally, our approach to Buddhism in general—and Madhyamaka in particular—depends entirely on what we are looking for. Are we interested in it merely as an external object of philosophical, historical, or other study, or are we interested in it as an aid for training and transforming our minds, that is, the inner subject that studies and experiences all this? Even in the latter case, most of us will usually just follow the natural tendencies of our dualistic minds and vote for either a more intellectual approach or a more experiential one, while discarding or avoiding the other. However, why not use both? Who says that we always have to live in the square box of an either/or world?

Buddhism explicitly uses all facets of our minds. If we want to be a Buddha, which is nothing other than experiencing the full potential of our minds, we do not have to—and in fact should not—deny or neglect our personal experiences, our emotions, our intellectual sharpness, or any other part of our existence. In principle, everything can be used as part of the path to mental freedom. If we try to avoid or discard certain aspects of our minds, we just deprive ourselves of our innate mental richness and reduce the number of tools that we can skillfully employ in order to end our own and others' suffering. In a way, the whole Madhyamaka project is about getting our minds unstuck and letting go of preconceived ideas, narrow-mindedness, and thinking in terms of black and white. Training the mind in this way of leaving all constrictions behind is what enables us to relax and widen our perspective in a fundamental manner. Specifically, in Buddhism, sharpening our intelligence through intellectual analysis and working with our emotional experiences at the same time are clearly regarded as mutually supporting and reinforcing each other. In this vein, we might consider widening our approach toward what we may regard as the only or correct method of treating the topic of Madhyamaka. Thus, our intent to reach the state of liberation from suffering could eventually evolve into a process of not only reading or talking about the theory of Madhyamaka, but having it come alive as our personal exercise in such mind training.

# *Introduction*

Among Buddhists, when the issue of study and reasoning in Buddhism comes up, one often does not have to probe very deeply to encounter resistance to study in general and reasoning or logic in particular. This approach is apparent in statements such as: "Study and logic is only for intellectual people." "It has nothing to do with me as a person." "It only creates more thoughts." "I had enough of that in school." "I just want to meditate and make my own experiences." "I'd rather take the path of devotion." "Who cares about the views of different people and schools in India two thousand years ago?" But is it fair to portray Madhyamaka as being only of historical, intellectual relevance or as merely an abstract philosophy that has nothing to do with the personal experience of modern people? What could there be in Buddhist conceptual analysis—and especially in the Madhyamaka approach to it—that is relevant and worthwhile for Buddhist practitioners even today?

In 1973, the great Western Buddhologist Edward Conze addressed the issue whether Buddhist texts in general and the *Prajñāpāramitā sūtras* (the source of Madhyamaka) in particular are still "up-to-date" for a "modern Western audience," weaving in some remarks that will continue to guarantee him a top rank in the category of "not being politically correct" also today:

> Finally one could also treat them as *spiritual* documents which are still capable of releasing spiritual insights among people separated from their original authors by two thousand years and vast disparities in intellectual and material culture. There is, however, a certain absurdity about interpreting spiritual matters in the abstract and in general terms, since everything depends on concrete conditions and the actual persons and their circumstances. Some will regard this literature as rather strange and alien, and may long for something more homespun. They will, I hope, allow me to retort with a remark that so endeared me to my students at Berkeley. Asked what Buddhism should do to become more acceptable to Americans, I used to enumerate with a smile a few concessions one might perhaps make respectively to the

> feminist, democratic, hedonistic, primitivistic and anti-intellectual tendencies of American society. Though in the end I invariably recovered my nerve and reminded my listeners that it is not so much a matter of the Dharma adjusting itself to become adaptable to Americans, but of Americans changing and transforming themselves sufficiently to become acceptable to the Lord Buddha.[61]

In brief, the sole aim of all Buddhist teachings is to help us realize the true nature of our minds. Thus, apart from certain outer cultural forms, there is no point in trying to alter the essential core of the means to remedy our mental afflictions in order to make it more palatable to the various fashionable whims triggered by these very afflictions. Rather, the main point of Buddhist studies is always to connect with the teachings personally by applying them to the individual experiences in our own mind. In Buddhism, we do not study in order to follow a curriculum or pursue a career but because we intend to learn how to tame our minds, see things as they are, and gain freedom from suffering. Moreover, when we engage in studying Buddhism, what is processed is our very mind. Since the materials are tailored to address the mind, plenty of emotional and intellectual reactions are sure to be triggered by this process of the mind working with its contents and being worked on by them. All of these reactions can and should be acknowledged, watched, and processed as they appear. This is nothing other than practice—mindfully dealing with our experiences.

Most people seem to believe that studying means creating more thoughts. However, this is just like the initial experience of having more thoughts when we start to practice the meditation of calm abiding. That this seems to be the case is only because we never took the time to really look at our thoughts before and thus remained unaware of their sheer number and rapid flow. Looking at them just shows us the perpetual rush hour in our minds, so it is only a matter of whether we notice this constant stream or are busily carried away by it. Thus, when we study Buddhism—and especially when we use analysis through reasoning—our thoughts about reality that are initially very massive and solid are chopped into "smaller" and "lighter" concepts. We observe that these concepts are more numerous, but actually the overall quantity of "thought mass" stays the same. The advantage of gradually processing our rigid and clumsy ideas by first noticing and then deconstructing them is that it is much easier to deal with our concepts once they become more flexible and subtle. In this way, we gradually approach a nonconceptual direct realization of the nature of our mind in which all concepts are absent.

This process can be compared to melting a big block of ice. If we take a large chunk out of the freezer and just let it sit there, it takes much longer for it to melt into water than if we chop it into small pieces, since each one of these pieces will melt much more quickly. In the same way, when our hard, solid concepts in cyclic existence—which are often as painful and unyielding as some jagged chunks of ice—get broken down into their underlying assumptions, they can dissolve more easily into the gentle and soothing waters of nirvāṇa. Moreover, if we try to deal with our massive and largely unconscious thought patterns merely by striving to attain some peaceful or blissful state through calming the mind in meditation, this will have no lasting effect on the deeply rooted habitual belief systems that govern our actions in the world. The lord of yogis, Milarepa, sang in one of his vajra songs:

> Don't be attached to the pool of calm abiding,
> But let the foliage of superior insight burst into open bloom.

The Buddha always emphasized a three-step approach to practicing his teachings: listening (studying), reflecting, and meditating. He did not say, "Listen and then meditate." However, it is exactly the middle stage of reflection that is often missing in the practice of Buddhists. As students of Buddhism, we are required to first gain sufficient access to the relevant information about Buddhist theory and practice through both scriptures and oral instructions. Following that, the material has to be investigated and integrated into our own personal understanding. Finally, meditation serves as the means to familiarize ourselves with this understanding on increasingly deeper levels until it becomes a spontaneous living experience in every situation.

Thus, it is at the step of reflection that reasoning in general—and Madhyamaka reasoning in particular—comes into play. Here, reflection does not mean just pondering something in a vague way but employing systematic and rigorous techniques of reasoning to gain thorough and incontrovertible certainty about the key issues of the Buddhist path. The Buddha himself said that his teachings should not be accepted out of unquestioning belief or because people of high rank propagate them. Rather, the teachings should be scrutinized carefully, in much the same way gold is analyzed for its purity. This means that, in Buddhism, true and reliable confidence can arise only through a well-founded personal understanding of the proper reasons that something works and is trustworthy. Otherwise, it is just some kind of assumption or blind faith that can easily be lost when doubts appear.

Looking at the widespread dislike of reasoning and logic on the one hand and our everyday approach to the world on the other hand, we will probably be surprised when we have to acknowledge that we actually make daily use of reasoning and logic even though we may not always be aware of it. As Dharmakīrti begins his *Drop of Reasoning*:

> Since correct knowledge precedes the accomplishment of all purposes of persons, it is taught [here]. Correct knowledge is twofold: perception and inference.

All our sciences and much of our professional and private lives are based not only on direct observation but also on reasoning. Consciously or unconsciously, we usually act in one way or another because we know the connection between certain actions and the results we want to achieve or to avoid. We are not just acting randomly. Farmers plant seeds and cultivate them in a specific way in order to have a good harvest. Architects build skyscrapers based on mathematical calculations. Parents tell their children not to touch the hot stove, because it hurts. Besides that, our favorite question is always "why?" and we usually are not satisfied until the answer makes good sense. So we use and live with reasoning and logic all the time, but when we hear these words, we wince and run.

From a Buddhist point of view, our human mental world is a highly conceptual one. Pure, immediate experience unaccompanied by conceptual processing hardly ever happens. Since we deal with the world through thoughts and concepts most of the time anyway, we might as well make use of them in an intelligent way on our Buddhist path, rather than regarding our thoughts as something to get rid of and deliberately excluding our intellect from our practice. In Buddhism, being intelligent and inquisitive is not a crime. It is also not a question of being either exclusively intellectual or exclusively devoted, with—we hope—lots of blissful experiences. There is nobody but ourselves to restrict the range of skillful means that we may beneficially apply as practitioners. Being skillful as well as developing higher insight and wisdom are certainly two major focuses on the Buddhist path, and both obviously require some intelligence and refined mental activity.

If incontrovertible certainty about the foundations of the Buddhist path and its fruition has not been achieved, it may be problematic to engage in meditation. Jamgön Kongtrul Lodrö Taye says in his *Treasury of Knowledge* that trying to meditate without study and reflection is like trying to climb a mountain without hands and feet. The Tibetan word *gomba* (sgom pa), usually translated as "meditation," means "to cultivate, train or familiarize." If there is no clarity or certainty about what to familiarize with even on a conceptual level, what are we going to cultivate or familiarize ourselves with? In fact, our meditation/familiarization will lack a clear and proper object. Without such an object, it is more than likely that doubts will arise during such "meditation" and afterward. If we carry around unresolved questions about Buddhist practice and theory, wondering what we are actually doing, we have only two real options: either go back and try to resolve our doubts by gaining certainty through convinced insight or eventually drop the whole enterprise. Once our initial enthusiasm has faded, it becomes increasingly difficult to sustain the motivation for continuous practice without being basically convinced about what we are doing, especially when encountering unfavorable circumstances. That this is not merely a theoretical scenario is, unfortunately, amply illustrated by a number of even longtime Buddhist practitioners who finally give up their practice due to such doubts (which is not to say, of course, that this is the only reason for that to happen).

The practical approach to gaining incontrovertible conceptual certainty is called analytical meditation or superior insight. Starting with the most basic Buddhist notions, such as the four reminders that turn the mind away from cyclic existence, this kind of meditation may be applied throughout the whole path. For example, when we reflect on the precious and rare opportunity of human existence or on impermanence, there is no point in trying to convince ourselves of these things by just repeating "My life is precious" or "Everything is impermanent" like a mantra. Rather, it is important to come up with some good reasons that this is the case. This process is, of course, supported by more systematic scriptural material, but there is a definite sense that we must apply personal investigation and mentally process these statements from various angles by connecting them to our own experience.

This is even more important with such key Buddhist notions as the lack of a personal self and the lack of any real identity of phenomena. Tackling these topics in order to make them personally relevant to our lives cannot be accomplished without some degree of personal investigation by honestly looking into our own views of the world and being willing to question them. Some of the most radical and challenging ways to do this are no doubt contained in the Madhyamaka teachings.

## What Is Madhyamaka?

A typical Madhyamaka answer to the question "What is Madhyamaka?" would state what it is not: It is not a philosophy, not a religion, not a doctrine, not a historical school of thought, not a belief system, not a linguistic theory or analysis, not a psychotherapy, not agnosticism, not nihilism, not existentialism, nor is it an intellectual mind game of some people in India and Tibet who had too much spare time and just wanted to tease others.

So, what is it then? When we use the word *Madhyamaka*, we first have to be clear about whether we are referring to a view, a meditation system, a spiritual path, its fruition, or the ultimate nature of all phenomena, including our mind. The most fundamental meaning of Madhyamaka is this last one. This ultimate nature is the fundamental ground within which Madhyamaka view, meditation, and conduct evolve. The essential characteristic of such view, meditation, and conduct is that they are all aimed at nothing but realizing this nature. Madhyamaka fruition is then the direct and incontrovertible experience of this ultimate reality within our own mind.

Now, what can we say about this fundamental Madhyamaka? Basically, there are two kinds of answers that are pointedly illustrated in Pawo Rinpoche's commentary on *The Entrance to the Bodhisattva's Way of Life*:

> [Some] consider merely not giving an answer as the ultimate actuality. This is certainly a case of giving those who understand the meaning of Centrism a good chance for a laugh. . . . Therefore, it is explained that when Mañjuśrī asked Vimalakīrti about the meaning of the actual, the genuine answer [in this case] was to not give an answer.[62] However, when one naïve being does not give an answer to the question of another one, how could these two cases ever be comparable? You should know the difference between a bodhisattva in his last existence who dwells under the bodhi tree and [someone like] Devadatta sitting under a nimba tree. If you think, "These are comparable," then ask about genuine [reality] in front of an ox and you will get the final answer that you wish for.[63]

Thus, ultimately, from the point of view of the true nature of phenomena itself and for such highly realized beings as Mañjuśrī and Vimalakīrti who directly experience it in meditative equipoise, there is nothing that could be said about it, since its very essence is that all discursiveness and its reference points[64] have dissolved. As Nāgārjuna's *Fundamental Verses on Centrism* says:

> Peace is the utter peace of all observed objects
> And the utter peace of discursiveness.
> At no time did the Buddha teach
> Any dharma to anybody.[65]

Conventionally and from the perspective of beings who have not yet realized this ultimate nature, however, this does not mean that nothing can be said about the view and the methods that gradually lead to the direct realization of this nature as an incontrovertible experience. *The Fundamental Verses* says:

> Without reliance on conventions,
> The ultimate cannot be taught.
> Without realization of the ultimate,
> Nirvāṇa cannot be attained.[66]

In other words, ordinary language is the container for the nectar of wisdom: The entire range of Buddhist notions related to ground, path, and fruition are but indications whose only purpose is to lead beings to mental freedom and not to trap them in just another conceptual cocoon. Thus, whatever might be said about Madhyamaka and whatever aspects of it we practically apply must be understood as being merely like a pointing finger that makes us look in a certain direction (or rather no direction). However, this finger should not be mistaken for what it points to. As it is said, "Do not mistake the finger pointing to the moon for the moon itself." Thus, it is on the basis of their minds directly realizing ultimate reality—the moon of the actual Madhyamaka—and for the sake of others realizing this too that Centrist masters set out to point with their scriptural, verbal, and physical fingers to this orb free from center or edge.

On the conventional level, in the great vehicle of Buddhism, Madhyamaka as a "school" is regarded as the second major system beside the Yogācāra (Yoga Practice)[67] school. Madhyamaka is not just something that was made up by Centrist masters such as Nāgārjuna. Rather, it has a firm basis in the teachings of Buddha Śākyamuni. This refers not only to the *Prajñāpāramitā sūtras* but also to many other sūtras from the first and third turnings of the wheel of dharma.[68] During the second century CE, Nāgārjuna formulated these teachings in a systematic fashion that embedded their basic message of emptiness in a rigorous system of reasoning.[69] However, Nāgārjuna never referred to himself as a "Mādhyamika," nor did he consider himself the founder of a new school or a system called "Madhyamaka." He just used the term "discussion of emptiness."[70] In fact, his approach is a system to get rid of all systems, including itself. Nāgārjuna's basic concern was to free the teachings of the Buddha from all superimpositions and denials, his main target being the scholastic systems of Abhidharma within Buddhism. It was only later when Bhāvaviveka[71] started to talk about Madhyamaka as a distinct view that Nāgārjuna began to be regarded as the founder of this "new" school, whose followers were also called "Proponents of the Lack of Nature." Over the following centuries, there were many debates in India and Tibet about the correct understanding of Nāgārjuna's presentation, which led to different streams within the Madhyamaka school. In this book, its system is explained as it was understood by the "early Centrists"[72] in Tibet. In general, this refers to the ways in which Centrism was presented in Tibet before Tsongkhapa, which are based on the Indian treatises on Centrism and the oral teachings of the numerous Indian masters with whom Tibetans had direct contact during this time.[73] More specifically, the Eighth Karmapa Mikyö Dorje identifies the lineages that come from Atīśa (982–1054) and Patsab Lotsāwa[74] (born 1055) as "the early Tibetan tradition of Consequentialism." This tradition of teaching Centrism continues to the present day in most parts of the Kagyü, Nyingma, and Sakya schools of Tibetan Buddhism.

## An Extreme Middle

To find out what the whole project of Madhyamaka is about, it is helpful to look first at the Sanskrit word itself. In the West, *Madhyamaka* is usually translated as "middle way," but the word "way" does not have any correlate in either the Sanskrit term nor its Tibetan equivalent *uma*.[75] *Madhya* means "middle or center," *ma* is an emphasizing affix, and *ka*[76] refers to anything that deals with or expresses this middle, be it texts, philosophical systems, or persons. (The latter are mostly called "Mādhyamika," however.) Thus, Madhyamaka means "that which deals with (or proclaims) the very middle/center." The corresponding Tibetan term *uma* usually also refers to "the very middle." Some masters, such as the Eighth Karmapa Mikyö Dorje, interpret the syllable *ma* as a negative and thus take the whole term to mean that there is not (*ma*) even a middle (*u*) between the extremes. This interpretation may not strictly conform with Tibetan grammar, but its meaning surely has a basis in the scriptures. *The Sūtra of the King of Meditative Concentration* declares:

> Both existence and nonexistence are extremes.
> Purity and impurity are extremes too.
> Therefore, having left behind both extremes,
> The wise do not abide even in a middle.[77]

*The Sūtra Requested by Crown Jewel* states:

> The perfection of knowledge[78] is free from extremes and also does not abide in a middle.[79]

*The Kāśyapa Chapter Sūtra* says:

> This so-called cyclic existence is an extreme. This "nirvāṇa" is a second extreme. What is the middle between these two extremes is not to be analyzed, not to be shown, without appearance, without cognition: Kāśyapa, this is called "the middle way, the perfect discrimination of phenomena."
>
> The center is without form, unseen, nonabiding, nonappearing, and without a location.[80]

Here, this center is furthermore explained as being equivalent to ultimate reality and suchness.

Nāgārjuna states in his *Fundamental Verses on Centrism*:

> Where there is neither beginning nor end,
> Where should there be a middle?[81]

In his *Song of Looking at the Expanse of Dharmas*, Atīśa says:

> If the middle is completely released from extremes,
> Since there are no extremes, there is also no middle.
> The view that is without middle and extremes
> Is the perfect view.[82]

*The Treasury of Knowledge* quotes the Sixth Shamarpa Chökyi Wangchug's *Collected Reasonings*:

> Under analysis, neither middle nor end is found,
> And one does not dwell even in a middle.
> All claims will dissolve.
> There is neither beginning nor end, and a center is not observed.
> There are no positions and no philosophical systems.
> At this point, this is the great center.[83]

In his commentary, Pawo Rinpoche agrees:

> When clinging has been purified, finally, even a mere middle cannot be observed. All views have completely vanished.[84]

> One might wonder, "Is there actually a middle between these two extremes?" If there are no extremes, where should there be a middle? . . . When all kinds of grasping that superimpose or deny existence, nonexistence, a middle, and so on have subsided, . . . this is called "seeing or realizing identitylessness."[85]

Thus, the actual Madhyamaka per se does not refer to a middle way between two extreme views (such as thesis and antithesis) in the sense of trying to find a synthesis or keeping some sort of balance between such extremes as existence and nonexistence or permanence and annihilation.[86] It is also not some definable or identifiable middle in relation or opposition to any extremes, since—in the Centrist view—such a middle would only serve as another reference point and thus as a further extreme. Nor does it primarily indicate the middle way between extreme forms of practice or lifestyle, such as ascetism and indulgence in sense pleasures, which was taught by the Buddha in other contexts.[87] Of course, such a practical middle way may very well be one of the expressions of the Madhyamaka view and realization, but Madhyamaka itself goes much further.

The whole point of Madhyamaka is what is called "complete freedom from any extremes." Extremes in the Madhyamaka sense refer not only to polarities or notions that are extreme in a very obvious way, but to any kind of reference point whatsoever. In fact, "extreme" is just another word for reference point. It is important not to misunderstand the freedom from all reference points as just another reference point or theory, a more sophisticated philosophical point of view, or some mere utter blankness. Rather, the actual Madhyamaka stands for the unobstructed, supple, and relaxed openness of a mind in which all impulses of grasping at something have completely dissolved. As Nāgārjuna's *Sixty Stanzas on Reasoning* says:

> By taking any standpoint whatsoever,
> You will be snatched by the cunning snakes of the afflictions.
> Those whose minds have no standpoint
> Will not be caught.
>
> If there were a standpoint,
> There would be desire and freedom from desire.
> However, great beings without a standpoint
> Do not have desire, nor are they free from desire.
>
> Those whose minds are not moved,
> Not even by a flicker of a thought about "complete voidness,"
> Have crossed the horrifying ocean of existence
> That is agitated by the snakes of the afflictions.[88]

## Madhyamaka Travels: The Complicated Road to Simplicity

When talking about Madhyamaka as the practical path or soteriological approach to this ultimate freedom from all reference points, what is most important is the underlying motivation and purpose of teaching and traveling this path. Especially at points when our minds get weary of all the reasonings, when nothing seems to make sense, and when we wonder why we got into this in the first place, it is helpful to remember this. If we just look at the complex techniques of deconstructive analysis and reasoning in which Centrists engage, it is easy to lose track of what this rigorous dismantling of everything is good for. Essentially, just as in the case of all other teachings of the Buddha, the only thing that Centrists are genuinely concerned about is to help sentient beings to overcome suffering and its causes and to reach the irreversible liberation of Buddhahood (which is nothing other than the ultimate Madhyamaka described earlier). Thus, what lies at the heart of the Madhyamaka approach is not a mere view but a bodhisattva's motivation to free all beings from suffering.

In the Centrist approach, the root cause of suffering is identified as the clinging that takes oneself and other phenomena to be real in just the way they appear. Different from that, the luminous space of our mind's true nature is essentially free from all discursiveness and reference points. In itself, this space is basic awareness which unfolds as an unceasing natural display of its own. Through its vividness, we may momentarily become unaware of its actual nature and get caught up in its mere appearance. Being lost in the flux of mind's display without an awareness of its spacious nature leads to a fundamental fear of just allowing its free flow. There is some urge to feel grounded and safe within the stream of this infinite expanse, so we try to hold on to something within it or freeze it altogether. Imagine sitting on a sunny beach and looking at the ocean's large rolling waves, feeling relaxed and serene just from watching the play of this moving vastness. However, if you were to fall into this ocean and get washed away by its huge waves, your state of mind would be far from spacious and relaxed. Most probably, you would not think that the waves are just a superficial movement on the surface of the deep, still waters of the ocean and that their nature is nothing but freely flowing water. Rather, you would be helplessly carried away by the power of these waves. You would panic and desperately try to find something to hold on to, which would only bring you closer to drowning. This is the situation of sentient beings in saṃsāra.

In the ocean of mind, there is no fixed point to stand on, so all we do as mistaken beings is hold on to our initial impulse of trying to grasp at such a fixed point. This impulse of grasping itself becomes our first reference point, called "me." It is, in a sense, a very basic self-justification for our existence. To adapt the famous words of Descartes, we seem to say, "I grasp, therefore I am." This first, central reference point of "me" naturally leads to its counterpart of "other" and all further ones, such as subject, object, inside, outside, good, bad, and so on. Gradually, these reference points become more and more solidified through additional layers of conceptual paint and glue. Finally, we have managed to convince ourselves of the hard-and-fast reality of our magnificent work of art—this self-spun sophisticated cocoon that ensnares us—to such a degree that we feel it is the most natural thing in the world and hold on to it for dear life. We have completely lost track of where we started and of the fact that this construction is entirely homemade. Within this castle in the sky, we feel attraction to those of its very real-looking parts that affirm ourselves, while giving rise to aversion toward its other parts. This emotional polarity calls for action: trying to obtain or keep what we feel attracted to and to avoid or get rid of what we feel aversion to. As the karmic fruits of such actions, we then experience the various types of happiness and suffering in cyclic existence. During this continuous process, every single aspect of it just adds up to and solidifies our cocoon even more. Thus, in the double sense of the word, we keep spinning in what is called cyclic existence.

Since, according to Centrists, the main cause of suffering is our basic clinging to reference points, it is this cause that we have to dissolve in order to obtain freedom from its result: suffering. Thus, whatever is taught in Centrism is based on precisely this motive and constantly points to what might happen once our cocoon unravels. For Centrists, apart from just being tools to the end of liberating sentient beings from their pains, there is no intrinsic value or purpose in philosophy, reasoning, refuting other people's positions, or even meditation altogether. Candrakīrti says in his *Entrance into Centrism*:

> The analyses in [Nāgārjuna's] treatise were not performed out of attachment to debate.
> [Rather,] true reality has been taught for the sake of complete release.
> It may well be that in the process of explaining true reality
> The scriptures of others become ruined, but there lies no fault in this.[89]

In the end, Madhyamaka refers to the actual direct experience of a nonreferential state of mind that is utterly free from all discursiveness obscuring the seeing of mind's true nature. So when Centrists talk about freedom from discursiveness, it means not only freedom from extreme or wrong ideas but complete absence of any coarse, subtle, conscious, or unconscious ideas, thoughts, or mental images whatsoever (obviously, this does not mean some kind of coma). At the most subtle level, this means to be free from even the most deeply ingrained tendencies within the mental flux of ordinary sentient beings, such as our instinctive "gut feeling" of being individuals who are different from others and the appearance of subject and object as being distinct. Of course, we cannot affect such deep levels of mind with mere conceptual reasoning, but Centrists regard the path to mental freedom as a gradual process of stripping off the many layers of our cocoon of obscurations. Conceptual analysis is used as the initial remedy, but it is only a technique that points beyond both obscurations and their remedies (including this very analysis), that is, beyond the entire realm of reference points altogether, no matter whether we call them bondage and cyclic existence or liberation and nirvāṇa.

Reasoned analysis is refined more and more through the threefold approach of studying, reflecting, and meditating. In other words, coarse concepts are counteracted with more subtle concepts, which are in turn dissolved by even more refined ones. Meditation basically means becoming familiar with such insights and thus letting them sink in to the deeper levels of the mind that will become more and more accessible and prominent as we proceed along the path. Finally, we will be able to let go of even the most subtle referential threads of the cocoon. Thus, reasoned analysis does not end up in some blank nothingness but eventually gives way to relaxing the mind on a profound level and just resting with crisp wakefulness in its natural, uncontrived state beyond words, concepts, and reference points. It is in this way that *Madhyama* is utter freedom from discursiveness and *Madhyamaka* is the view or teaching that points to this freedom. As Nāgārjuna begins his *Praise to the Vajra of Mind*:

> I prostrate to my own mind
> That eliminates mind's ignorance
> By dispelling the web of mental events
> Through this very mind.

## Sharpening the Mind, Opening the Heart

So far, we have seen what is dissolved on the Madhyamaka path and what is finally attained. What is the driving force that allows us to actually work with our delusion? What is the main mental factor that brings about freedom? It is called *prajñāpāramitā*, the perfection of knowledge. As their name suggests, the *Prajñāpāramitā sūtras*—on which the Madhyamaka system is based—deal extensively with such knowledge.[90] Conventionally speaking, this involves two aspects: emptiness as the object to be realized by prajñāpāramitā and the wisdom of prajñāpāramitā as the subject that realizes emptiness. Ultimately, there is no difference between these two aspects of subject and object. However, in terms of cultivating the realization of this unity of the ultimate subject and object on the path, the sūtras do not address only the object, or emptiness. In a more hidden way, they also lay out the gradual subjective process of realizing emptiness, that is, how knowledge is perfected in the mind. This means a detailed description of what happens in the minds of bodhisattvas when they progress through the various levels of realizing emptiness that finally culminate in perfect Buddhahood.[91] Thus, the texts always refer to "the perfection of knowledge (or wisdom)"; they never say "the perfection of emptiness" or "the perfection of the nature of phenomena." Of course, by definition, there is nothing to be perfected in emptiness or the true nature of the mind anyway. However, there surely is a lot to be perfected in our awareness of this nature. So the perfection of knowledge means perfecting not the ultimate object to be realized but the realization of this object.

During what is experienced as the mental paths and bhūmis of refining and uncovering the perfection of knowledge, this perfection itself is something that is completely beyond all reification,[92] inconceivable, and inexpressible. However, as mentioned before, other than just becoming mute about it, it is still possible to compassionately and skillfully point to just that which is beyond everything one could say or think about it. In *The Sūtra of Vast Display*, right after having become the Awakened One, Buddha Śākyamuni is reported to have uttered the following verse:

> I have found a nectarlike dharma,
> Profound, peaceful, free from discursiveness, luminous, and unconditioned.
> Whoever I would teach it to could not understand it.
> Thus, I shall just stay silent in the middle of the forest.[93]

How can we understand that the Buddha first expressed the utter futility of teaching others what he had realized and then engaged in doing precisely this for forty-five years, until the end of his life? Essentially, enlightenment is inexpressible and inconceivable, but it is not inaccessible. Possessing this insight as well as the infinite compassion and capacity to actually show others how to reach mental freedom, the Buddha taught what cannot be taught.

Again, it should be kept in mind that verbal or other indications are nothing but a pointing finger and not that to which this finger points. We cannot experience the taste of delicious food simply by talking or hearing about it. Still, we might become inspired to engage in preparing such food and then relish it. In the same way, we might become inspired to make some effort to experience the taste of enlightenment while not mistaking the words for their referents. Otherwise, if there is nothing to be said anyway, what would be the point of twenty-one huge volumes of *Prajñāpāramitā sūtras* in the Buddhist canon, all the detailed Madhyamaka scriptures, or the teachings of the Buddha in general?

Usually, Centrists—and particularly Consequentialists—are known for their refusal to make any statements about what happens when all obscurations have finally dissolved. The reason for this is that they try to avoid fueling our ever-active impulse to get hooked on anything that is presented to us as just another reference point. In particular, as we journey on the Buddhist path and thus refine our understanding, our reference points seem to become ever more sophisticated, up to the most sophisticated reference point of thinking that we are without reference point. Hence, the Centrist approach is adamant in taking away our good old mental toys while strictly refusing to provide new toys, not even very nice ones such as "Buddhahood," "enlightenment," "Dharmakāya," or "freedom from discursiveness."

This is why Centrist texts so often deny that Buddhahood, wisdom, and the three enlightened bodies exist and that a Buddha possesses wisdom. However, these are not categorical statements that wisdom and so on absolutely do not exist in any way and under all circumstances. Rather, such explanations should be understood in the same noncommital way that all Centrist negations are employed. For example, from the refutation of arising it does not necessarily follow that one asserts nonarising or anything else instead. Also, when Centrists deny that a sprout arises, they do so in order to stop our clinging to the notion that such arising is really existent. It does not mean that they try to refute or stop the activity of farming as such.

Likewise, the Centrist denial that wisdom and Buddhahood exist has a number of purposes. It serves as a means to put an end to the fixation that wisdom and Buddhahood are really established, since it is not only our getting hooked on worldly things that has to be dissolved but also the grasping at supramundane phenomena in terms of the Buddhist path and fruition. Thus, such denial is not a teaching that wisdom and Buddhahood are inert things or utter nothingness after everything has been annihilated. Nor is the denial of the existence of wisdom to be taken as an affirmation that wisdom is not established, since all thinking in terms of existence, nonexistence, and so on is nothing but being trapped in reification; that is to say, it is exactly what is to be relinquished. If even ordinary things cannot be seen as fitting into such categories as existent, nonexistent, and so on, how should these dualistic notions ever apply to the very means or the result of eliminating precisely these dualistic notions? Furthermore, the teaching that wisdom does not exist implies that subject and object are never found as separate entities within the nature of all phenomena. Since a Buddha realizes the expanse that is primordially without the duality of subject and object, a Buddha does not possess any wisdom in the sense of a realizer that engages in an object as something to be realized. Still, the three enlightened bodies, the four or five wisdoms, nonreferential compassion, and enlightened activity do function as dynamic processes, but they cannot be solidified or pinned down in any way. The detailed explanations of these factors in Centrist texts are meant as conventional descriptions that in themselves point to nonreferential openness-awareness.

Thus, Centrist masters thoroughly prepare the ground by continually making it clear that our tendency to grasp at everything—be it mundane or supramundane—is our fundamental problem and that we must be constantly aware of it. It is against this background that a number of positive statements in the scriptures clearly indicate that freedom or enlightenment is not mere extinction. The final perfection of knowledge or wisdom manifests as a living and compassionate awareness of the nature of all phenomena in which all reference points—including those of emptiness as an object and knowledge as a subject—have vanished altogether. This wisdom is neither a mere negation of everything nor just emptiness. It is the luminous and open expanse of the true nature of mind which is aware of its own fundamental state.[94] *The Prajñāpāramitā Sūtra in Eight Thousand Lines* says:

> "The mind is no-mind. The nature of the mind is luminosity." . . . ". . . does one find or observe existence or non-existence in this no-mindness?" "No, venerable Subhūti." . . . "What is this no-mindness?" "Venerable Śāriputra, no-mindness is unchanging and nonconceptual."[95]

*The Sūtra Requested by Crown Jewel* declares:

> O son of good family, the knowledge of bodhisattvas is the source of wisdom. It is the source of merit. It is the source of studying. It is the source of qualities. It is the source of dharma. It is the source of the power of retention and self-confidence. It is the source of individual perfect awareness. It is the source of being endowed with the supreme of all aspects of qualities and wisdom. O son of good family, this is the completely pure engagement in the perfection of knowledge of bodhisattvas.[96]

Nāgārjuna's *Praise to the Expanse of Dharmas* reads:

> Imagine that a garment that may be purified by fire
> Becomes contaminated by various stains at some point.
> When it is put into a fire,
> Its stains are burned, but the garment is not.[97]
>
> Likewise, luminous mind
> Has the stains of desire and so forth.
> The fire of wisdom burns its stains,
> But not luminous true reality.
>
> All the many sūtras spoken by the Victor
> That teach emptiness
> Make the afflictions subside,
> But they do not weaken the basic element.[98]

Rāhulabhadra begins his *Praise to the Perfection of Knowledge*:

> O perfection of knowledge, you are unspeakable, inconceivable, and inexpressible.
> You have not arisen and do not cease—your nature is that of space.
> You are the sphere of personally experienced wisdom.
> I bow to you, Mother of the Victors of the three times.

Bhāvaviveka's *Heart of Centrism*[99] declares that this highest cognition is real but that it has no object or content. It can be experienced but cannot be described in words; it can only be suggested. His *Lamp of Knowledge* says:

> Since [true reality] is without discursiveness, it is peace. Since it is peace, it is the sphere of nonconceptual wisdom. Since it is the sphere of nonconceptual wisdom, it cannot be known through something else. Since words do not apply to that which cannot be known through something other [than this wisdom], the very nature of true reality is perfectly beyond the superimpositions of words.[100]

Candrakīrti says in his *Lucid Words*:

> The ultimate is not known due to something other. It is peace. It is what the noble ones[101] are aware of as that which is to be personally experienced [by them]. . . . This is not consciousness.[102]
>
> Once stainless nondual wisdom has been manifested . . . through the power of personal realization . . . , one will be released.[103]

His autocommentary on *The Entrance into Centrism* states:

> The ultimate of the Buddhas is this very nature. It is ultimate reality by virtue of its very undeceptiveness. Still, all of them have to personally experience it on their own.[104]

*The Entrance into the Supreme Knowledge of Centrism* declares:

> In this natural state of primordial nonarising,
> There is nothing to be negated and nothing to be affirmed.
> Nirvāṇa and nonnirvāṇa
> Are without difference in the natural state of nonarising.
>
> This is not even nonarising as such,
> Because arising things do not exist.
> The seeming does not exist, the ultimate does not exist,
> Buddhas do not exist, sentient beings do not exist,
>
> Views do not exist, something to be meditated on does not exist,
> Conduct does not exist, and results do not exist:
> The actuality of this is what is to be cultivated.

Let this mind free from thoughts rest in its own peace.

Without identifying something, without being distracted,
Without characteristics, and luminous—thus meditate.[105]

The Eighth Karmapa Mikyö Dorje says in his *Chariot of the Tagbo Siddhas*:

I certainly do not say that there is no difference between wisdom (the cognizance that has changed state) and consciousness ([the cognizance that] has not [so changed]).[106]

Pawo Rinpoche's commentary on *The Entrance to the Bodhisattva's Way of Life* explains:

Once clinging in terms of superimposition and denial has come to an end in such a way, just this empty and luminous nature of phenomena in which there is nothing to be removed or to be added is the fundamental state of phenomena. This is expressed as primordial nirvāṇa as such.[107]

Thus, it is seen that the expanse of dharmas[108] is not an object of speech, reflection, and expression. It is for just this [type of seeing] that the conventional terms "penetrating the nature of phenomena" and "beholding ultimate reality" are used. The conventional term "personally experienced wisdom" is then used for the very knowledge that does not observe the characteristics of the reference points of subject and object.[109] Thus, the nature of phenomena is not seen through apprehending a subject and an object. Rather, if one knows that subject and object are not observable, one engages in the nature of phenomena.[110]

Because one has engaged in emptiness through devoted interest on [the paths of] accumulation and junction, emptiness—which is, like space, without any difference—is realized on the path of seeing in a manner of being omnipresent. Through the power of eliminating adventitious stains on the paths of meditation, every aspect of the qualities intrinsic to emptiness is revealed. [This is] as if one were to fathom the extents and special features of every [instance of] space exactly as they are, starting from the space of the limitless realms of sentient beings down to the [space] that is enclosed by the fibrils of the split tip of a hair. Finally, it is as if one were to simultaneously and fully comprehend in one single moment the entirety of the element of space

> that is included in the three times and beyond unity and multiplicity. Likewise, in one single moment, one simultaneously and fully comprehends the entirety of the expanse of dharmas (or emptiness) exactly as it is. It is beyond unity and multiplicity and has always been intrinsic to all Buddhas, bodhisattvas, hearers, solitary realizers, and sentient beings; to all the five aggregates; the eighteen constituents; the twelve sources; and to all the factors to be relinquished or to be attained. In dependence on the worldly seeming level, [this final realization is described by] saying, "Perfect Buddhahood is attained."[111]

Yet Buddhahood is in no way a self-sufficient or self-indulgent state, since its wisdom-space radiates the living warmth of infinite and spontaneous compassion. Realizing the nature of one's own mind means seeing the nature of everybody's mind. The more clearly Buddhas and bodhisattvas experience the shining of the true heart of all beings, the more clearly they realize the suffering of these beings that comes from cloudlike ignorance within the clear sky of their minds. Seeing through the illusory nature of both this ignorance and the ensuing unnecessary suffering, Buddhas and bodhisattvas cannot help doing everything they can to wake up and comfort their fellow beings, just as we would try to wake up people who show all the signs of having a terrible nightmare and soothe them by telling them that it was just a dream. Furthermore, Pawo Rinpoche declares:

> Thus, by gaining power over and becoming very skilled in the dependent origination of the collections of causes for the entirety of cyclic existence and nirvāṇa, compassion for the assembly of sentient beings who do not realize this in the same way wells up unbearably. [However,] at this point, there is nothing to be observed as either oneself or sentient beings. To the same extent that great compassion increases, also this very [realization] that, primordially, nothing can be observed as sentient beings, what is not sentient beings, suffering, happiness, and so on grows and increases. This is the ultimate seeing that is like the orb of the sun. When it becomes stable and increases in such a way, great compassion—which is like the light rays of the sun—will grow even more than before. [Beings with such realization] do not behold sentient beings, but great compassion still flowers in them. They do not behold themselves either, but they still lend their support to all sentient beings. They do not behold anything to be attained whatsoever, but they still establish beings in great enlightenment. Just as there is no place whatsoever to go to beyond space, they do not behold anybody who would go somewhere beyond, but they still display [the activity of] liberating sentient beings from cyclic existence. . . .

> Hence, just as skillful physicians exert themselves for the sake of the diseased, one makes one-pointed efforts for the sake of those who are ignorant since beginningless time because of various [ways of] having reference points. [Ignorant beings] only exert themselves for the causes of suffering and then angrily look at the results [of this]. They burden themselves with their own sufferings by plunging into a swamp that they stirred up themselves, and then they have no clue what to do. Just as [people outside the swamp] know that this swamp in which these naïve beings are drowning is shallow and small, one fully comprehends the nature of cyclic existence through knowing true reality. Thus, one is released from both the extremes of attachment to and fear of swamp-like cyclic existence. Through knowing that one moreover has the ability to pull sentient beings out [of this swamp], one will manage to remain in cyclic existence for the sake of others as long as space exists. This is the direct result of having meditated on emptiness.[112]

Part 1 of this book provides an overview of the transmission of Madhyamaka from India to Tibet and presents this system in terms of ground, path, and fruition. Further chapters are devoted to the Autonomist-Consequentialist distinction, the controversial issue of a "Shentong-Madhyamaka," the distinction between expedient and definitive meaning, and a brief sketch of the major differences between the Eighth Karmapa's and Tsongkhapa's interpretations of Centrism. Part 2 consists of a brief introduction to Śāntideva's *Entrance to the Bodhisattva's Way of Life* (focusing mainly on its ninth chapter on knowledge) and a translation of Pawo Rinpoche's commentary on this chapter.

# PART ONE

## *The General Presentation of Madhyamaka in the Kagyü Tradition*

# 1

# *The Transmission of Madhyamaka from India to Tibet and Its Relation to Vajrayāna and Mahāmudrā*

IN HIS INTRODUCTION TO *The Chariot of the Tagbo Siddhas*, the Eighth Karmapa gives a very detailed account of three distinct Indian transmissions of Madhyamaka that are continued in the Tibetan Kagyü lineage. In his presentation of these lineages, the Karmapa does not merely show the richness of transmission. He clearly explains not only that the final purport of Madhyamaka is no different from the main Kagyü teachings of Mahāmudrā and the Six Dharmas of Nāropa, but that Madhyamaka view and meditation are the indispensable basis that underlies the entire range of practices in this school. The Karmapa's interest in doing so is not just to establish some philosophical or theoretical consistency on the levels of sūtra and tantra. His essential concern is more important: to give clear specifications as to how Madhyamaka is crucial in all practices so that they actually function as practical tools to definitely liberate the mind from all obscurations.[113] Again, the heart that brings the Madhyamaka approach to life is not a mere view but a bodhisattva's motivation to free all beings from suffering. In tune with this basic thrust of classic Madhyamaka, the Eighth Karmapa's foremost concern throughout his commentary is one of ultimate versus pedagogic, not ultimate versus conventional. He focuses on whether the view's orientation is soteriological as opposed to philosophical. In other words, his concern is about what is useful for liberation rather than what may be an elegant theory or a philosophical system that is coherent from a conventional perspective. Thus, when he refutes some views of other Tibetan masters or their attacks on the Mahāmudrā system of the Kagyü school, he does so not for polemical reasons or simply to streamline his own position and point out the philosophical inconsistencies of others. Rather, his essential criterion is whether a view can serve as a soteriologically efficient basis for the Buddhist path. Since this is the most important issue in Madhyamaka, the relevant points from the Karmapa's introduction will be included in the following discussion.

The origin of the approach that later came to be called Madhyamaka can be clearly traced back to the sūtras of Buddha Śākyamuni himself. Thus, it is not at all a later invention or even a contradiction of what are sometimes called the Buddha's "original" teachings. Even in the Pāli canon, there are numerous statements that accord with Madhyamaka in both words and meaning. We often find the negation of both extremes of a dilemma and even the fourfold negation (tetralemma) that is so characteristic of Madhyamaka. In his *Fundamental Verses*, Nāgārjuna refers to the *Kaccāyanagottasutta*:[114]

> Through his knowledge of entities and nonentities,[115]
> In the instruction for Kātyāyana,
> The Victor has refuted
> Both [their] existence and nonexistence.[116]

The *Acelakāśyapasutta* spells out the typical fourfold negation of arising by saying that suffering is not produced from itself, nor from something other, nor from both, nor from neither. Rather, it is said to come about through dependent origination, which in itself is not characterized by any of these four extremes.[117]

The Pāli canon contains several references to the fourteen undecided questions[118] that follow the structure of the tetralemma. The Buddha refused to agree to any of these questions when they were put to him by the mendicant Vacchagotta. For example:

> Gotama denies that . . . the Tathāgatha passes to another existence after death here, . . . does not pass to another existence after death here, (that) he both does and does not pass to another existence after his death here, (and that the Tathāgata) neither passes nor does not pass to another existence after his death here.[119]

The Buddha also explained the purely soteriological reasons for such a denial:

> To hold that the world is eternal, or to hold that it is not, or to agree of any other of the propositions you adduce, Vaccha, is the thicket of theorizing, the wilderness of theorizing, the bondage . . . the tangle and the shackles of theorizing, attended by ill, distress, perturbation and fever; it conduces not to aversion, passionlessness, tranquillity, peace, illumination and Nirvāṇa. This is the danger I discern in these views, which makes me scorn them all.[120]

Both the dialectic structure and the content of these fourteen questions have their exact parallels in Nāgārjuna's *Fundamental Verses*[121] and other texts.[122] Also in the *Brahmajālasutta* (*Dīgha Nikāya*), the Buddha discards all theories, views, and speculations as dogmatic narrow-mindedness (*diṭṭhivāda*) and refuses to be drawn into their net (*jāla*).[123]

Even the crucial notion of emptiness can be found in the Pāli canon. For example, the Buddha prophesies about future monks:

> The monks will no longer want to hear and study the suttāntas taught by the Thus-Gone One that are so very deep in meaning, supramundane, and related to emptiness (*suññatā-patisaṃyuttā*). Instead, they will only listen to the mundane suttāntas taught by disciples and composed by poets, which are artistic and embellished with beautiful words and syllables.[124]

Ānanda asked the Buddha:

> Lord, it is said that the world is empty (*suñña*), the world is empty. But Lord, in what respect is the world called empty?

The Buddha answered:

> Ānanda, since it is empty of identity or anything pertaining to identity, therefore it is said that the world is empty.[125]

There is further mention of emptiness by referring to the mind when attaining nirvāṇa upon the cessation of afflictions and ordinary consciousnesses.[126] In the collection of songs of realization of Theravādin nuns, the *Therīgāthā*, the female arhat Uttamā proclaims that she has attained emptiness and signlessness upon entering nibbāna.[127]

As is well known, the *Prajñāpāramitā sūtras* are the teachings of the Buddha that are most directly related to Madhyamaka. However, there are many other sūtras that also serve as the scriptural bases of this system. These include *The Jewel Mound*[128] collection (specifically *The Kāśyapa Chapter Sūtra* and *The Sūtra of the Meeting of Father and Son*),[129] *The Sūtra of the White Lotus of Genuine Dharma*,[130] *The Sūtra of the King of Meditative Concentration*, *The Sūtra of the Arrival in Laṅka*,[131] and *The Sūtra That Unravels the Intention.*[132] Thus, Madhyamaka as a later system is definitely based on all levels of the sūtras of the Buddha. It can well be considered as a logical and systematized continuation of many of the most crucial elements in his teachings.

The generally accepted beginning of Madhyamaka as a formalized system is attributed to Nāgārjuna in the second century. According to the Eighth Karmapa Mikyö Dorje, Nāgārjuna, his main disciple Āryadeva, Aśvaghoṣa[133] (both second/third century), and Śāntideva (eighth century) are called "the Centrists of the model texts,"[134] since no other Centrists ever denied that they were Centrists or disputed their texts. The debate that led to the later Tibetan division of Centrists into Autonomists and Consequentialists[135] started in the sixth century with Bhāvaviveka, who criticized the way in which Buddhapālita, who lived early in that century, had commented on Nāgārjuna's *Fundamental Verses on Centrism.* Candrakīrti (sixth/seventh century) extensively defended Buddhapālita's presentation and rebutted Bhāvaviveka's critique of the latter. Thus, he is regarded as the actual founder of the Consequentialist system, since he presented it in such a thorough way. Many later Centrists, such as Jñānagarbha (seventh century), Śāntarakṣita (eighth century), Kamalaśīla (740–795), Haribhadra (eighth century), and Prajñākaramati (tenth century), exhibited some positions that vary slightly from Candrakīrti's approach. Atīśa (982–1054) seems to have mostly—but not exclusively—followed Candrakīrti's approach. However, in India throughout this time, there was no notion of distinct subschools among Centrists, and, with maybe a single late exception, even the names Autonomists and Consequentialists were not used in Indian texts.[136] In particular, there is no evidence that the Consequentialist approach was generally considered any better than the Autonomist one. Rather, the texts of those Centrists who later came to be labeled Autonomists enjoyed great and widespread esteem. In fact, all these masters differed only in the methodology through which the correct view of the ultimate in one's mind is best communicated to and generated in others. They do not show the slightest difference in their position on ultimate reality, since all of them are fully qualified Centrists. Otherwise, if they differed with regard to the ultimate, it would follow that either the Autonomist or the Consequentialist view is not Centrism, since there are no multiple true natures of phenomena.

The Eighth Karmapa says that, in Tibet, some people mistakenly claim that certain Centrists, such as Candrakīrti, do have a higher view and realization and a better philosophical system than certain others, such as Bhāvaviveka. However, if this were the case, the latter would not be Centrists at all, since for someone who has not fully realized the actual meaning of Centrism, the expressions "Centrism" and "Centrist" remain nothing but mere names. Furthermore, since the Buddha taught in accordance with individual disciples' various mental abilities, there surely appear distinctions in terms of the expedient and definitive meanings within the other three philosophical systems in Buddhism. However, in the context of Centrism as its fourth and highest philosophical system,[137] the Buddha taught only the final definitive meaning. Since there is no distinction between expedient and definitive meaning in the Centrist teachings themselves, how could any Centrists have higher or lower views?

During the first four hundred years of Buddhism in Tibet, Centrism was transmitted mainly from an Autonomist perspective. This is primarily because many of the leading Indian masters during the early spread of Buddhism to Tibet, such as Śāntarakṣita and Kamalaśīla, followed this approach.[138] Thus, the majority of Madhyamaka texts to be translated into Tibetan during the first period of translation were either by Nāgārjuna or by Autonomists.[139] As mentioned earlier, to a certain extent Atiśa's transmission was an exception here. However, certainly up through his time, there was no clear differentiation of distinct Madhyamaka "schools" headed by Bhāvaviveka and Candrakīrti, and their approaches were evidently studied side by side. As for early Tibetan masters after Atiśa, Ngog Lotsāwa Loden Sherab[140] (1059–1109) is said to have followed the Autonomist approach. It is also known that Chaba Chökyi Senge (1109–1169) strictly adhered to Autonomist reasonings and completely denied the use of consequences.[141] He is moreover said to have defeated the Kashmiri Consequentialist Jayānanda in debate. Atiśa's disciples Dromtönpa Gyalway Jungnay[142] (1005–1064) and Nagtso Lotsāwa Tsultrim Gyalwa[143] (born 1011), as well as several Kadampa masters such as Potowa[144] (1031?–1105), are said to have been early Tibetan Consequentialists. However, a systematic translation and propagation of the major Consequentialist scriptures, especially those of Candrakīrti, started only with Patsab Lotsāwa Nyima Tra (born 1055). After that, it still took a few more centuries before all Tibetan schools more or less unanimously regarded the Consequentialist system as the supreme Centrist approach, a position held to this day.

## I. The Two Lineages of the Indigenous and Unique Transmissions of the Kagyü Tradition[145]

### a. The Lineage from Nāropa[146]

This transmission starts, of course, with the Buddha and continues with Avalokiteśvara, Mañjuśrī, and Vajrapāṇi. From Nāgārjuna it was passed on to Āryadeva, Candrakīrti,[147] Mātaṅgī, Tilopa (988–1069), Nāropa (1016–1100), Marpa (1012–1097), Milarepa (1040–1123), Gampopa (1079–1153), the First Karmapa Tüsum Khyenba (1110–1193), Drogön Rechen[148] (1088–1158), Bomtragba,[149] the Second Karmapa Karma Pakshi (1206–1283), Orgyenba (1230–1309), the Third Karmapa Rangjung Dorje (1284–1339), Gyalwa Yungdönba[150] (1284–1365), the Fourth Karmapa Rölpay Dorje (1340–1383), the Second Shamarpa Kachö Wangbo[151] (1350–1405), the Fifth Karmapa Teshin Shegba[152] (1384–1415), Ratnabhadra, the Sixth Karmapa Tongwa Tönden (1416–1453), Jampel Sangbo[153] and the First Gyaltsab Paljor Töndrub[154] (1427–1489), the Seventh Karmapa Chötra Gyamtso, Nyemo Goshri Göncho Öser[155] and Jetsün Reba Chenbo (1505-1569)[156] up through the Eighth Karmapa Mikyö Dorje. After him, this transmission continues in the commonly known way within the Kagyü tradition.[157]

## b. The Lineage from Maitrīpa

Maitrīpa (1012–1097) realized that the Madhyamaka taught by Saraha the Elder, Saraha the Younger (Śavaripa), Nāgārjuna, and Candrakīrti has the same meaning and taught it in this way to others. From Maitrīpa, this lineage was passed on to Marpa, Milarepa, and Gampopa. After Gampopa, it continues in the same way as the lineage from Nāropa above.

Maitrīpa's cycle of Centrist teachings is known as "the twenty-five dharma works of mental nonengagement."[158] His *Ten Verses on True Reality* says:

> Those who wish to know true reality
> [See] that it is neither with aspect nor without aspect.
> Not adorned with the guru's instructions,
> The middle is only middling.[159]

Maitrīpa's student, the late Indian Centrist Sahajavajra (eleventh/twelfth century), says in his commentary[160] that "with aspect" and "without aspect" in this verse refer to the views of all Aspectarians and Non-Aspectarians,[161] who do not realize true reality. The definitive meaning of true reality is the lack of nature. It accords with the explanations on dependent origination by Centrist masters such as Nāgārjuna, Āryadeva, and Candrakīrti. "The guru" is Bhagavatī—the perfection of knowledge—as well as these Centrist masters. "The middle" is the nature of true reality which accords with their explanations: It is the unity of arising and nonarising, of dependent origination and emptiness. Any kind of "middle" that is understood as some remainder after having negated certain specifics is not correct; it is "only middling." Thus, Maitrīpa's explanation of Centrism fully accords with the above masters.[162]

In Tibet, three distinct ways of fulfilling the intended meaning of this "Madhyamaka of mental nonengagement" have developed:

1. the practice that focuses on the profound and luminous Madhyamaka of the Mantra vehicle
2. the practice that focuses on the profound Madhyamaka of the Sūtras
3. the practice that focuses on "the Madhyamaka of False Aspectarian Mere Mentalism"[163]

Marpa and Milarepa transmitted and accomplished the entirety of the first two practices. Gampopa specifically focused on the second practice and widely propagated it. He was praised by the Buddha in *The Sūtra of the King of Meditative Concentration* as the one who would later spread the teachings of this sūtra—the Madhyamaka. These specific sūtra-based instructions of Gampopa were given the name of Mahāmudrā, a term that primarily comes from the tantras. The great translator and scholar Gö Lotsāwa Shönu Pal[164] (1392–1481) says in his *Blue Annals*:

> Tagbo Rinpoche produced an understanding of Mahāmudrā in those beginners who had not obtained initiation. This is the system of the Prajñāpāramitā.[165]

Here the Eighth Karmapa Mikyö Dorje says that when the Madhyamaka view of this system dawns in one's mind stream, this is called "the manifestation of ordinary mind"[166] or "the manifestation of the Dharma Body."[167] When one realizes that the bearers of the nature of phenomena, such as sprouts and thoughts, are not established as anything other than this nature of phenomena, one refers to this realization using the conventional expression of "thoughts appearing as the Dharma Body."

The view and meditation of this Mahāmudrā system as inseparable from Centrism are said to be very necessary in order to eliminate remaining latencies of discursiveness and the impregnations of negativity[168] at the time when extremely pleasant experiences of the Vajrayāna's wisdom of the unity of bliss and emptiness arise in one's mind. Even a partial dawning of the view and meditation of this Mahāmudrā in the mind serves as the supreme panacea for the referential grasping at what is held to be inferior (such as seeming reality and adventitious stains) or superior (such as ultimate reality or the nature of phenomena). Without such a remedy, just like medicine turning into poison, the view and meditation of the freedom from discursiveness would turn into a view and meditation that are themselves nothing but discursiveness.

That this specific sūtra-based Mahāmudrā system is not just an invention of the Kagyüpas in Tibet is demonstrated by the following passages from Indian treatises. In his *Entrance into True Reality*, Jñānakīrti (eighth/ninth century) says:

> As for those of highest capacities among the persons who exert themselves in the pāramitās, when they perform the meditations of calm abiding and superior insight, even at the stage of ordinary beings, this grants them the true realization characterized by having its origin in Mahāmudrā. Thus, this is the sign of irreversible [realization]. . . .
>
> All these results are accomplished through the meditation of the nondual training in Mahāmudrā. As the *Prajñāpāramitā sūtras* extensively say:
>
>> Those who wish to train in the grounds of hearers should listen to just this prajñāpāramitā . . . and should practice the yoga of just this prajñāpāramitā.

> The same is said there for [those who wish to train] "in the grounds of solitary realizers" and "in the grounds of Buddhas." Another name of Mother Prajñāpāramitā is Mahāmudrā, because it is the very nature of nondual wisdom.[169] . . .
>
> Hence, the Blessed One's teaching on the meditation of nondiscursiveness is for the purpose of entering nondiscursiveness, that is, the meditation of the nondual training in Mahāmudrā.[170]

Both *The Treasury of Knowledge*[171] and *The Blue Annals*[172] cite parts of these sections from Jñānakīrti's text and agree that this Mahāmudrā system

> is clearly explained in Sahajavajra's *Commentary on The Ten Verses on True Reality* as the wisdom of suchness that has the three characteristics of its nature being pāramitā, according with the secret mantra, and its name being "Mahāmudrā."[173]

In his *Commentary on The Sublime Continuum*, Gö Lotsāwa relates this statement to the corresponding passages in Sahajavajra's commentary.[174] These read:

> Since this master [Maitrīpa] gives a summarized explanation of the pith instructions of pāramitā that accord with the mantra system, through the very being of the nature of phenomena that bears the name "prajñāpāramitā" . . . , he first pays his respect to the very nature of the three enlightened bodies.[175]

and

> The gist of this is:
>
> By not abiding on the side of the remedy
> And not being attached to true reality either,
> There is no wish for a result of anything whatsoever.
> Therefore, it is known as Mahāmudrā.
>
> Here, "Mahāmudrā" refers to the pith instructions on the true reality of Mahāmudrā, that is, thoroughly knowing the true reality of entities.[176]

The text further says:

> The pith instructions of pāramitā are the definite realization of Madhyamaka that is adorned with the pith instructions of the guru. This is

> the ultimate emptiness, the spontaneously present prajñā endowed with the supreme of all aspects . . .[177]
>
> Some express this as "the wisdom of true reality, Mahāmudrā."[178]

Right after the above statement on Sahajavajra's commentary, *The Blue Annals* continues:

> Therefore, the Mahāmudrā of the Prajñāpāramitā of the Lord Gampopa was described by Lord Götsangba as being a doctrine of Maitrīpa. The Mahāmudrā which belongs to the path of the tantra was also expounded by Lord Gampopa to his "inner" disciples.

*The Commentary on the Difficult Points of The Wheel of Time, Called Padminī* says:

> "Mahāmudrā [the Great Seal]" is she who gives birth to all Thus-Gone Ones appearing in the past, future, and present, that is, Prajñāpāramitā. Since she seals bliss through the nonabiding nirvāṇa[179] . . . , she is the seal. Since she is superior to karmamudrā and jñānamudrā and free from the latent tendencies of cyclic existence, she is great.[180]

Thus, the explicit teaching of this Mahāmudrā is the Madhyamaka of emptiness free from discursiveness as taught in the sūtra system. Ultimately, Maitrīpa's key notion of "mental nonengagement" or "mental disengagement" is nothing but the subjective side of what is called "freedom from discursiveness." The only way in which the mind can engage in this "object"—the absence of discursiveness—is precisely by not engaging in or fueling any discursiveness, thus letting it naturally settle on its own accord. In other words, the absence of reference points can be realized only by a nonreferential mind, since this is the only perceptual mode that exactly corresponds to it. This is stated many times in the sūtras. For example, *The Prajñāpāramitā Sūtra in Seven Hundred Lines*[181] says:

> Not abiding in anything whatsoever, this is the meditation on the perfection of knowledge. Not thinking about anything and not cognizing anything whatsoever, this is the meditation on the perfection of knowledge.

*The Prajñāpāramitā Sūtra in Eight Thousand Lines* agrees:

> This meditation on the perfection of knowledge means not meditating on any phenomenon.[182]

*The Sūtra Requested by Ocean of Intelligent Insight*[183] states:

> Do not mentally engage in phenomena.
> Completely abandon doing anything further.
> Realize all phenomena
> As equality in true reality.
>
> What is taught is application of mindfulness
> Without mindfulness or something to be mentally engaged.

Atīśa says in his *Centrist Pith Instructions*:

> For example, if you rub two sticks [against each other], fire comes forth. Through this condition, the two sticks are burned and become nonexistent. Thereafter, the fire that has burned them also subsides by itself. Likewise, once all specifically characterized and generally characterized phenomena are established as nonexistent [through knowledge], this knowledge itself is without appearance, luminous, and not established as any nature whatsoever. Thus, all flaws, such as dullness and agitation, are eliminated. In this interval, consciousness is without any thought, does not apprehend anything, and has left behind all mindfulness and mental engagement. For as long as neither characteristics nor the enemies and robbers of thoughts arise, consciousness should rest in such a [state].[184]

Pawo Rinpoche clarifies what mental nonengagement means:

> Its meaning is to rest one-pointedly on the focal object [of meditation], without being distracted by other thoughts. If this [one-pointed resting] were stopped, all meditative concentrations would stop. Therefore, in general, "mental nonengagement" has the meaning of not mentally engaging in any object other than the very focus of the [respective] meditative concentration. In particular, when focusing on the ultimate, [mental nonengagement] has the meaning of letting [the mind] be without even apprehending this "ultimate." However, this should not be understood as being similar to having fallen asleep.[185]

Sahajavajra's *Commentary on The Ten Verses on True Reality* agrees:

> In this context, "mental nonengagement" is not like closing your eyes and, just like [inanimate things, such as] a vase or a woolen cloth, not

> seeing anything at all. Here, there is no complete absence of mental engagement.[186]

In a very similar way, in both his commentary on *The Dhāraṇī of Entering Nonconceptuality* and his *Stages of Meditation*,[187] Kamalaśīla repeatedly elaborates on this clear distinction between "mental nonengagement" and "the complete absence of mental engagement"[188] (such as fainting, deep sleep, or just utter dullness), which is obviously not the point of meditating in order to realize ultimate reality. In the context of analytical meditation, he also emphasizes the need for discriminating analysis to precede mental nonengagement, since the ultimate cannot be realized without this step of analysis.

The Eighth Karmapa says that, implicitly, this system of Mahāmudrā also teaches the profound actuality of both sūtras and tantras, that is, the ordinary and extraordinary ultimate Heart of the Blissfully Gone Ones.[189] With this in mind, Gampopa, Pamo Truba[190] (1110–1170), Jigden Sumgön (1143–1217), and many others have said that "the treatise of our Mahāmudrā is this *Treatise of the Sublime Continuum of the Great Vehicle*[191] composed by the Blessed One Maitreya." Götsangba Gönbo Dorje said that the initiators of this dharma of Mahāmudrā are both the Great Brahman Saraha and Nāgārjuna. Saraha taught Mahāmudrā from the side of affirmation, while Nāgārjuna taught it from the side of negation. *The Blue Annals* says:

> This [system] that is known as "the glorious Tagbo Kagyü" is not a lineage of [mere] words. Rather, it is a lineage of the actuality [behind these words]. "Actuality" refers to the lineage of realization of the stainless Mahāmudrā. The guru from whom one receives this realization of Mahāmudrā is stated to be one's root guru.[192]

In his *Treasure Vault of Mahāmudrā*,[193] Padma Karpo gives a highly detailed account of all the main sources of the Mahāmudrā system and its relation to Madhyamaka, the sūtras, and the tantras. On the basis of this, he clearly invalidates all attacks by other Tibetans, such as that Mahāmudrā is not found in the sūtras or that it is equal to the quietist Chinese Hvashang Mahāyāna approach[194] as it is reported to have been refuted in the debate at Samye[195] by Kamalaśīla.

Karmapa Mikyö Dorje states that, in addition to the Kagyü lineage, many others in Tibet taught this dharma system of Mahāmudrā. For example, it is contained in the teachings called *The Pacification of Suffering*[196] that the Indian master Padampa Sangye[197] brought to Tibet. In particular, we have the Mahāmudrā transmissions to the great bodhisattva Tropu Lotsāwa Jambay Bal[198] (1173?–1225) by many Indian scholars and siddhas, such as Mitrayogin[199] and the great Kashmiri Paṇḍita Śākyaśrībhadra (1140s–1225) who visited Tibet from 1204-

1213. The portion of the Mahāmudrā teachings that was later transmitted to the great translators Jamba Lingba,[200] Gö Lotsāwa Shönnu Bal, Trimkang Lochen,[201] and others when the great Bengali Paṇḍita Vanaratna (1385–1468) visited Tibet three times[202] also belongs to this type of Mahāmudrā system.[203]

## II. The Lineage from Atīśa

This second transmission from Nāgārjuna via Āryadeva, Candrakīrti,[204] and the Elder and Younger Vidyākokila[205] reached Atīśa (982–1054). It continued with Dromtönpa (1005–1064),[206] Chen Ngawa Tsultrim Bar[207] (1033/38–1103), and Jayülwa[208] (1075–1138). Then Gampopa received it from the latter and many other Kadampa masters. An alternative lineage went from Atīśa via the Kadampa masters Potowa (1031?–1105) and Sharawa[209] (1070–1141) directly to the First Karmapa. After him, the lineage continues as above.

Here, the Eighth Karmapa addresses the issue of whether the Madhyamaka teachings called Mahāmudrā that were transmitted by Maitrīpa and the Madhyamaka teachings transmitted from Atīśa are the same dharma system. In terms of the true reality that they teach, there is no difference, but they differ in their approach to realizing this actuality. In Atīśa's lineage, one determines true reality through conceptual examination and analysis. Then, one rests in meditative equipoise through the knowledge that entails a small degree of clear appearance with regard to the aspect of a nonimplicative negation.[210] In Maitrīpa's system, just as a fire dies once its wood has been consumed, one determines the nature of this examining and analyzing knowledge itself through seeing that it is baseless and without root. Then one rests in meditative equipoise in that which does not involve any sense of negation or affirmation whatsoever.

Gampopa had perfected the view and the meditations of calm abiding and superior insight in the Madhyamaka context according to the Kadampa system when he came to Milarepa. When Gampopa offered his realization to him, Milarepa said, "As for the aspect of calm abiding in your practice, however good all of this may be, it does not go beyond being a cause for rebirth in the higher realms of saṃsāra. As for the aspect practice of superior insight, all of this entails the danger of divergence into the four deviations from emptiness.[211] It may well serve as a remedy for some portions of reification, such as clinging to real existence. However, since it is not able to cut through the entirety of clinging to extremes, there is the danger that the whole complex of this excellent view and meditation itself could turn into cognitive obscurations. Hence, if one is fettered, there is no difference between being fettered by an iron chain and being fettered by a golden chain." Later, Gampopa said about this, "If I had not met the great master Milarepa, I would have risked rebirth as a long-lived god." Thus, Gampopa combined the systematic and analytical approach of the Kadampa teachings with the mainstream Kagyü instructions on Mahāmudrā, which led to him being called "the one who united the two streams of Kadampa and Mahāmudrā."

## III. The Lineage from Patsab Lotsāwa Nyima Tra

This lineage was transmitted from Nāgārjuna[212] to Candrakīrti and then to his direct disciple Mañjuśrīkīrti. It continued with Devacandra[213] (tenth century), the Brahman Ratnavajra[214] (tenth/eleventh century), Parahita (eleventh century), Mahāsumati[215] ( eleventh/twelfth century), and Patsab Lotsāwa (born 1055), who studied in Kashmir for twenty-three years. He invited the Paṇḍita Kanakavarman to Tibet, translated many Madhyamaka treatises, and propagated Candrakīrti's system. Apart from Kanakavarman, in translating, he collaborated with a number of other Indian Paṇḍitas, such as Mahāsumati, Jayānanda, Tilakakalaśa, Muditāśrī, and Sūkṣmajana. Later, the First Karmapa Tüsum Khyenba extensively studied Madhyamaka with Patsab Lotsāwa.[216] From the Karmapa, the lineage continues as above.

Again, the question arises as to whether this Madhyamaka system and the Madhyamaka teachings that were transmitted from Atīśa are an identical dharma system. The Eighth Karmapa says that not only are they identical, but even their terminologies are alike. Still, in the system transmitted from Patsab Lotsāwa, the predominant approach is to determine the Centrist view through inferences that result from studying it. Then, through supreme knowledge in meditative equipoise, one rests within the meaning to be validated that has been determined through such inference. In Atīśa's system, one determines the view through all kinds of reasoned awareness that result from the triad of study, reflection, and meditation. Then, through supreme knowledge in meditative equipoise, the mind rests in a nonreferential manner within the object to be validated that has been determined in such a way. One might wonder how the systems of Patsab Lotsāwa and Atīśa differ as to cultivating the view and meditation of Madhyamaka. In terms of the teachings themselves, there is no difference. However, the difference lies in the greater or lesser propensities of vigor and knowledge of the individuals who dedicatedly apply themselves to the true reality of Madhyamaka. Still, it is not absolutely impossible that followers of Patsab may cultivate the view and meditation in accordance with Atīśa's system. Likewise, it is not ruled out that followers of Atīśa may cultivate the view and meditation according to the system of Gampopa.

As for the reading transmission and the tradition of scriptural exegesis of Madhyamaka as these were known in Tibet during the time of Karmapa Mikyö Dorje, down to Patsab Lotsāwa, they are as indicated in the three transmission lineages above. After Patsab, they continue with Shang Tangsagba,[217] Drom Wangchug Tragba,[218] Sherab Dorje,[219] the two brothers Dentsül and Tragden,[220]

**OVERVIEW OF THE MADHYAMAKA LINEAGES TRANSMITTED IN THE KARMA KAGYÜ SCHOOL**

*(as presented by the Eighth Karmapa Mikyö Dorje)*

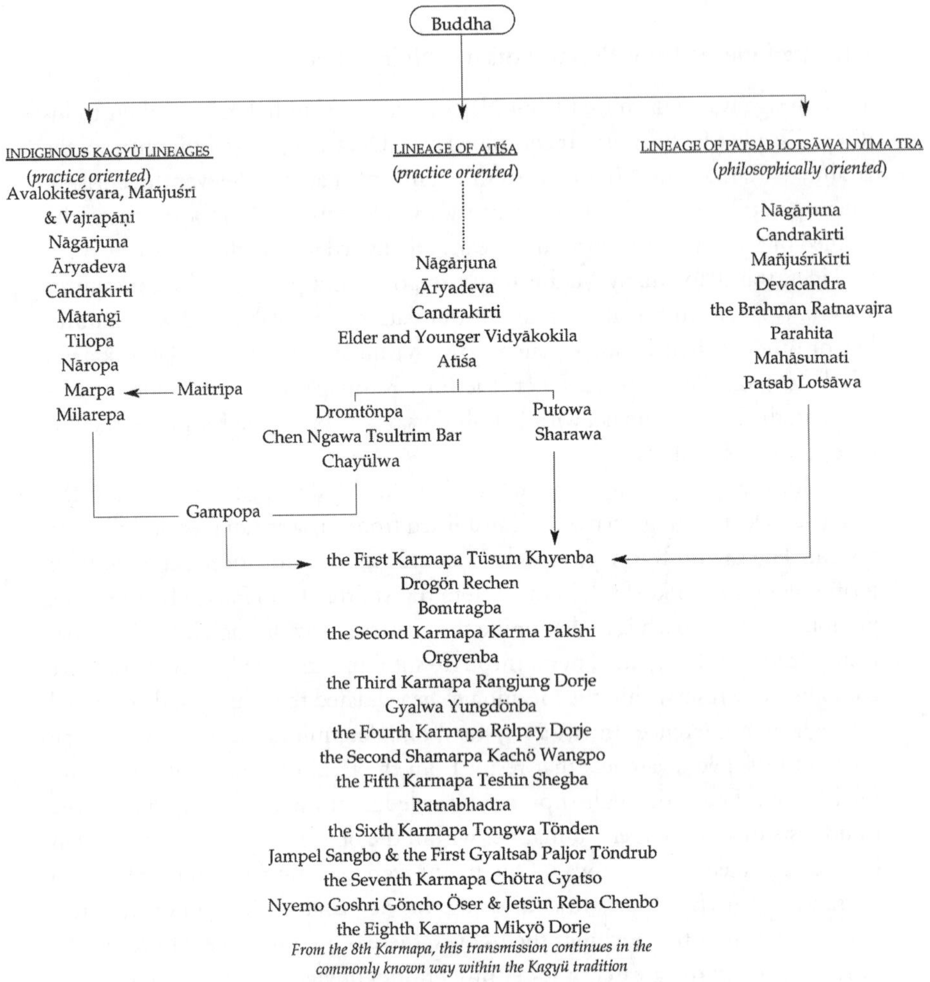


*Adapted from Nitartha Institute: 1997 - Madhyamika lineage chart of 8th Karmapa, Mikyö Dorje by The Dzogchen Ponlop Rinpoche*

Deway Lha,[221] Jotsün Uraba,[222] Sherab Pal,[223] Darma Sherab,[224] Pangdön Sherab Rinchen,[225] Sönam Senge,[226] Pangdön Samten Sangbo,[227] Pangdön Shönnu Samten,[228] Tangnagba,[229] Dashi Senge,[230] Shönnu Sangbo,[231] Sekangba Chötra,[232] Thangsagba Shönnu Gyaltsen,[233] Gyal Morongba Chenbo,[234] Jamchen Rabjamba Sangyay Phel,[235] Bumtra Sumba,[236] and the First Karma Trinlayba. It was from the latter that the Eighth Karmapa received this transmission. After him, it continues in the usual lineage of the Kagyü tradition.

As mentioned before, Karmapa Mikyö Dorje identifies the two lineages that come from Patsab Lotsāwa and Atīśa as "the early tradition of Consequentialists" in Tibet. He says that even before, but especially after, the beginning of "the new tradition of Consequentialists" (Tsongkhapa's novel interpretation of the Consequentialist system), the proponents of this earlier tradition had became as rare as stars in daylight. He specifically mentions the great translator Kyabcho Balsangbo,[237] the great Rendawa Shönnu Lodrö,[238] Dagtsang Lotsāwa,[239] and the great tulkus of the Tagbo Kagyü together with some of their realized yogic disciples.[240]

There remains the question of whether there is a dharma system of Madhyamaka in the mantra vehicle that is different from the dharma system of Madhyamaka as taught by Nāgārjuna and his spiritual heirs. The Eighth Karmapa declares that there is no difference between the mantra vehicle and Nāgārjuna's Centrism from the point of view of freedom from reference points. This means that once the objects of negation—clinging to extremes and clinging to reference points—have been relinquished, there is nothing whatsoever to be affirmed. However, the luminous wisdom mind that is explained in the sūtras and the luminous wisdom mind explained in the tantras are not the same. If they were just the same, either the tantric path would be indispensable as the means to realize the luminous mind as explained in the sūtras, or the tantric path would be superfluous for realizing the luminous mind as explained in the tantras, since the same could be accomplished through the sūtra path alone. Moreover, the luminous mind in the sūtras and the luminous mind in the tantras are explained to be mutually exclusive in the sense of not coexisting. *The Prajñāpāramitā Sūtra in Eight Thousand Lines* says:

> As for the mind, it is no-mind. The nature of the mind is luminosity.[241]

According to Mikyö Dorje, the basis that is intended by this statement is the luminous mind as it is explained in the tantras. The purpose of saying that the actual nature of the mind (the six or eight consciousnesses) is luminosity is to understand that one attains the Buddhahood of the sūtra approach through the path of the sūtras. Thus, the above quotation refers to the nondual wisdom mind that "is without the mind that consists of apprehender and apprehended." The luminous mind of the tantras resides in all sentient beings in an unmanifest way. However, when it is about to become manifest, gradually all eight consciousnesses, including their nature, completely vanish, until finally the luminous mind as described in the tantras dawns. Thus, in the Kagyü lineage, in talking about Buddhahood in the sūtras and tantras, the same names are used for the ground based on which Buddhahood is accomplished, the path that accomplishes it, and the fruition that is accomplished. These names are "the Heart of the Blissfully

Gone Ones," "mind," and "luminosity," each one in terms of ground, path, and fruition. However, what is labeled by these terms is not the same in the sūtras and tantras. Therefore, it is explained that the accomplishment of sūtric Buddhahood does not cover the attainment of tantric Buddhahood, whereas the accomplishment of tantric Buddhahood incorporates sūtric Buddhahood. This is the unmistaken vital dharma-eye of all sūtras and tantras.

One might wonder, "Is the Heart of the Blissfully Gone Ones not also taught in the sūtras?" It surely is taught, but only as a mere name. Since its full scope does not fit into the minds of the disciples of the sūtra system, it is taught in a way that is not to be taken literally. On the other hand, in the tantras, it is taught both in this way and in a manner that is to be taken literally. In the sūtras, the tantric meaning is taught implicitly in a hidden manner, but the sūtric path does not operate with Buddha nature as it is taught in the tantras. Rather, on the basis of the six or eight consciousnesses, the sūtric path causes the relinquishment of the two obscurations and the gathering of the two accumulations, which leads to attaining sūtric Buddhahood. Therefore, in the sūtras, Buddha nature is explained as being unconditioned. On this basis of it being unconditioned, it is sometimes further interpreted as an entity and sometimes as an empty nonentity. With the first way of interpretation in mind, Dölpopa[242] and others have interpreted Buddha nature as an unconditioned entity that is permanent, lasting, and unchanging. Thinking of the second way of interpretation, the great translator Ngog Lotsāwa interpreted Buddha nature as emptiness in the sense of a nonimplicative negation, while Āryavimuktisena and Haribhadra[243] have explained the expanse of dharmas (that is, the disposition that is the foundation for accomplishing the perfections) as emptiness.

There are further distinctions between the Madhyamaka of the sūtras and the tantras. The vajra vehicle contains the path of means—certain techniques for utilizing the central channel[244]—that serves to determine the freedom from reference points. This path is absent in the Madhyamaka system of the sūtra approach. In particular, there is a difference as to whether both the view of the emptiness that is intrinsically free from reference points yet endowed with the supreme of all aspects and the wisdom that leads to the realization of this view can dawn for beginners through their mastery of certain secret essential points without the need to make any mental effort. Furthermore, there is a distinction as to the basis on which one cuts through reference points, that is, whether certain distinct features of the central channel are utilized as such a basis. Finally, in the Vajrayāna, one identifies the bearers of the nature of phenomena—all of seeming reality—with the name of a specific bearer of this nature: the designation "the nature of phenomena which is ultimate reality." Through this, one can attain from these bearers of the ultimate nature the result that consists in a change of their state into the enlightened bodies and wisdoms that are the unity of the two realities.

In general, there is not only a common view and purport in Madhyamaka, Mahāmudrā, and Vajrayāna, but it is emphasized again and again that a thorough understanding of Madhyamaka is crucial for the effectiveness of Vajrayāna and Mahāmudrā practices. No matter how many of these practices we may perform, none of them qualifies as Vajrayāna or Mahāmudrā—even if outwardly they are performed in a technically perfect way—if they lack the three indispensable features of the renunciation of cyclic existence, the altruistic motivation of the mind of enlightenment, and the view of emptiness. Tagbo Dashi Namgyal's well-known *Moonbeams of Mahāmudrā* says:

> No matter whether this is based on analytical meditation or resting meditation, it is in any case of great importance to find out the view of emptiness. Any view and meditation that lack this [view] cannot cut through the root of [cyclic] existence.[245]

> No matter which progressive stages of meditation in the sūtras, tantras, or pith instructions you look at, at first, when the [correct] view is searched for, discriminating knowledge is indispensable. . . . And yet, having analyzed through discrimination, finally the very [process of] discrimation itself comes to rest, ushering in nonconceptual [wisdom].[246]

What makes us thoroughly ascertain the correct view of emptiness is none other than the Madhyamaka system. In fact, the presentations in the tantras and the Mahāmudrā texts employ terms such as "emptiness," "freedom from discursiveness," and "nonarising" all the time but usually do not elaborate on them much, because they take it for granted that persons who have arrived at these advanced practices have gone through a prior training in the view of emptiness. Here, the importance of Madhyamaka lies in its being a prerequisite and constant aid for the practices of Vajrayāna and Mahāmudrā. This means not only that we must have done our homework by familiarizing ourselves with the view of nonreferentiality before engaging in these practices. More important, the uncompromising Madhyamaka way of dealing with our clinging and mental reference points plays an important role in the experiential process of letting go of even the most subtle layers of fixating and what is fixated on along the path, be it grasping at impure objects, pure objects, or the subjects that perceive such objects.

Without going into the details, I will highlight a few issues to illustrate the process of undoing mental fixation. One of the central notions in Vajrayāna is what is called unity, such as the unity of appearance and emptiness, the unity of clarity and emptiness, the unity of bliss and emptiness, and the unity of awareness and emptiness. Obviously, without an understanding of each factor in these four pairs, there is no way one can grasp the meaning of their unity. Here, unity does not at all refer to two distinct phenomena or features that are separate at first and later joined through meditation. Rather, it refers to natural inseparability that can be split up only conceptually, not experientially. For example, the unity of appearance and emptiness is to be understood in precisely the way *The Heart Sūtra*[247] teaches it:

> Form[248] is emptiness, emptiness is also form. Emptiness is no other than form and form is no other than emptiness.

If we do not understand the oneness of appearance and emptiness and then engage in, for example, deity visualizations, we will inevitably cling to the real existence of these deities, just as we do with ordinary appearances. Or, we might try to annihilate or "emptify" ordinary, "impure" appearances through the mantra *Oṃ svabhāva śuddhaḥ sarvadharmāḥ svabhāva śuddho 'haṃ* and then replace them with the "real" and "pure" appearances of mandalas and deities (see also the four deviations from emptiness above).

The explicit purpose of deity yoga is to serve as a remedy that reverses our clinging to ordinary appearances. This is not accomplished through working only with the objective side of our experiences by replacing a bad movie with a better one, that is, replacing impure appearances with pure appearances. Rather, the main focus lies on the subjective side, that is, mind itself as the projector of all these movies. This means that the mind realizes all pure and impure appearances, including the mind itself, as being illusionlike—appearing while not really existing. The crucial point is that this realization must be applied equally to the very mind that realizes it. To experience the unity of appearance and emptiness in terms of both the perceiver and the perceived, the visualization practice of divine appearances must be constantly imbued with the view of their emptiness. However, if there is any clinging to the real existence of mandalas and deities, to their characteristics (their shapes, colors, or mere luminous clarity) or to the wisdom mind that meditates on all this, then the basic problem of clinging is not remedied. Rather, it becomes even more solidified by grasping at something "pure" instead of something "impure." As Milarepa said above, this kind of calm abiding only leads to rebirth as a god in higher realms of saṃsāra. Moreover, it lacks the aspect of superior insight. The starting and main point of superior insight in visualization practice is to look at the empty nature of all these forms that appear in the mind as well as at the looking mind itself.

Also, when the visualization is dissolved at the end of the session, this is not meant to annihilate the deities and their mandalas. Rather, it is a training in letting go of even our divine and pure objects of focus and then resting the mind in its uncontrived nature free from all reference points. At the end of this phase of completion, we arise again as the deity, and the next meditation session starts anew with emptiness and the mandala appearing from within it. Thus, we alternate between the creation stage,[249] in which appearance is emphasized, and the completion stage,[250] in which emptiness is emphasized. The first important purpose of this alternating between appearance and emptiness is to remedy the clinging to both of these. Dissolving the visualization is a technique that remedies the clinging to its real existence, while its reappearance from emptiness is a technique to remedy the clinging to some blank state without appearance. In actual fact, however, appearances and emptiness cannot be separated, as the empty nature of appearances is intrinsic to them. So the second important purpose of meditating on the stages of creation and completion is to train in the nondiscriminatory experience of the inseparable unity of appearance and emptiness, which is possible only on the basis of not clinging to either facet of this unity. In this way, we become familiar with the true nature of mind without getting stuck in either its luminous or its empty aspect. Śākya Chogden[251] says:

> If there were not the way in which nondual wisdom is empty of nature
> That is elucidated by the texts of Consequentialists and Autonomists,
> What would relinquish our clinging to profound luminous wisdom's
> reality
> And our conceptions of being attached to magnificent deities?[252]

The necessity for a background in the Madhyamaka view is also highly evident in the teachings on Mahāmudrā. In general, Centrist texts are regularly quoted and notions such as "emptiness," "freedom from discursiveness and reference points," and "neither arising nor ceasing" abound. In particular, among the well-known four yogas of Mahāmudrā,[253] the second is so named because, with the vision of emptiness predominating, it is the realization that mind and all other phenomena do not arise, abide, or cease and are free from any discursiveness and reference points. The third yoga refers to realizing the equality of mind and appearances, cyclic existence and nirvāṇa, empty and not empty, and so on, all being of "one taste" in that they lack a nature of their own. The fourth yoga is the level of nothing to meditate on, no meditator, and no meditation, neither anything to be realized nor any realization.

In particular, an experiential familiarity with the Madhyamaka approach is crucial for the stages of Mahāmudrā insight meditation, when mind is investigated in its various expressions of stillness and movement. The instructions for these analytical meditations are very concise, but they often follow exactly the lines of more detailed Madhyamaka analyses. It is true that, in Mahāmudrā analysis, the emphasis lies on directly and nonconceptually looking at the mind, but obviously this is not accomplished right away. Naturally, beginners start investigating in a conceptual way. In this context, any resultant conceptual insight into emptiness is helpful only if it eventually proves to be conducive to the immediate kind of introspection. Hence, such insight is an obstacle if one clings to an intellectual understanding of emptiness. However, the same is true for the Madhyamaka approach, which indeed starts on the more intellectual plane but constantly points to and facilitates direct experience and insights into emptiness (this is what is meant by "experiential familiarity," mentioned above). In both the Madhyamaka and the Mahāmudrā approaches, one must gradually let go of conceptual understanding, reification, and hanging on to any reference point at all.

Thus, without being aware of the actual thrust of the Mahāmudrā investigations of mind and appearances, we might either try to skip them altogether or just go through the motions and think, "Of course, I know that my mind has no color and shape." When we do not personally engage in scrutinizing our mind from different aspects and angles within the states of both stillness and movement, we just keep getting caught up in the experiences that rush through this mind. In this way, we completely miss the point of such an analysis as an active process from our own side to eradicate misperceptions and approach the liberating insight into the true nature of the experiencing mind itself. As the Ninth Karmapa's famous Mahāmudrā text *The Ocean of Definitive Meaning* says:

> Some may wonder, "It is fine to demonstrate right from the start that this mind can neither be watched nor seen, but beyond that, what is the point in investigating [whether it has a] color and so on?" It is precisely because sentient beings do not realize that mind—which lacks a nature—definitely does not have such [color and so forth] that they, since time without beginning, take what they call "me" and "I" to be something real. Based on that, attachment, aversion, and ignorance arise, and thus they wander in cyclic existence, the ocean of suffering. In order to put an end to that, you [must] probe into the depths of your own mind, the main root of cyclic existence, through investigating, examining, and analyzing [it]. Thus, through determining it to be empty and without identity, it is certain that you see the unmistaken actuality of the basic nature. Through being certain that mind lacks a nature, you realize that the mistakenness of clinging to any identity of cyclic existence is without reality. By the force of that, you are certain that all phenomena are empty. Consequently, your attachment to all worldly pursuits is put to an end, and the root of reification, the cause

> of cyclic existence, is cut through. Therefore, there is good reason for investigating the mind.[254]

Tagbo Dashi Namgyal's *Great Manual for Guidance in Mahāmudrā, Called Elucidating Natural True Reality* agrees:

> You might wonder, "Is it not sufficient to embrace whatever appears in the mind with mindfulness from the very start, without needing gradual steps of guidance?" Such might suffice for the rare few whose karmic disposition is of the instantaneous type. However, in [all] other cases, unless one is led through the gradual steps of guidance, doubts about the root of mind and appearances are not resolved, and the certainty that entails the experience of seeing [one's] nature will not dawn. Hence, although there may be other [kinds of] mindfulness, things will not work out [as they should], since there is no self-aware mindfulness.[255]

The same master's *Moonbeams of Mahāmudrā* frequently quotes Madhyamaka texts as its sources besides the words of the great siddhas of Mahāmudrā and states:

> For the most part, these instructions . . . appear to have the same essential points as the progressive stages of meditation in the sūtra approach as [found in] *The Prajñāpāramitā Pith Instructions*,[256] Kamalaśīla's three-volume *Stages of Meditation*,[257] and Atīśa's *Centrist Pith Instructions*.[258]

> First, one analyzes [the mind] through discriminating knowledge. It is explained that, through this, the very [process of] discrimination itself comes to rest, upon which nonconceptual wisdom dawns.[259]

> Here, the way of determining the nature of the mind is similar to the determination of personal identitylessness in the sūtra approach. . . . Likewise, the way of determining thoughts and appearances is similar to the determination of phenomenal identitylessness in the sūtra approach.[260]

> However excellent a meditation in which insight has not arisen may be, it is nothing more than one of the various kinds of mundane meditations of non-Buddhists or ordinary Buddhists. Other than that, if such [meditation] does not even qualify as a meditation of the lower [Bud-

dhist] vehicles, it is needless to mention that it does not qualify as a meditation of the great vehicle, such as Madhyamaka or, particularly, Mahāmudrā. For that reason, it is very important to seriously engage in the meditation of insight.[261]

2

# *The Middle from Beginning to End*

MADHYAMAKA IS MOST GENERALLY CLASSIFIED as the actual Madhyamaka (that which is to be communicated) and the verbal Madhyamaka (the means to communicate this actuality). The actual Madhyamaka is presented as threefold:

1) Madhyamaka ground: the unity of the two realities. The two realities are seeming reality and ultimate reality. On the level of seeming reality, conventionally speaking, all phenomena are nothing but mere collections of causes and conditions. Our labels that emerge based on these phenomena are just superimposed, conventional designations that are coined in an interdependent way. Ultimately, however, phenomena are not to be found as any of the extremes of our mental reference points, such as existing, not existing, arising, or ceasing. They are also free from abiding in a so-called middle. Thus, it is the nature of all these fleeting phenomena to appear while not having any identifiable nature of their own, very much like rainbows or reflections in a mirror. This is the unity of the two realities.

2) Madhyamaka path: the unity of the seeming mind of enlightenment and the ultimate mind of enlightenment, or the unity of means and knowledge. Through understanding the modes of being of the two realities in this way, bodhisattvas realize that seeming reality consists of phenomena that are merely nominal. Since all phenomena are free from arising and so on, they are realized to be free from all mistaken superimpositions. The unity of the seeming mind of enlightenment and the ultimate mind of enlightenment is to train in the illusionlike means to accomplish the benefit of oneself and others while constantly being immersed in the knowledge that realizes the nature of all phenomena. This means developing dependently originating and illusionlike great compassion for countless dependently originating and illusionlike sentient beings who have all been our loving mothers at some point in the infinite round of cyclic existence. Motivated by this compassion, bodhisattvas train in the illusionlike and spacelike two accumulations of merit and wisdom that comprise the six or ten perfections.[262]

3) Madhyamaka fruition: the unity of the Dharma Body and the Form Bodies. The fruition of this training is as follows: Through having reached the culmination of the most lucid appearance of the ultimate mind of enlightenment, all afflictive, cognitive, and meditational obscurations including their latent tendencies are eliminated and all mental reference points have vanished. This is the perfect accomplishment of one's own welfare: the Dharma Body. Through having arrived at the culmination of the most lucid appearance of the seeming mind of enlightenment, the perfect accomplishment of the welfare of others—the Form Bodies—is attained. This accomplishment for others means complete mastery of enlightened activity that manifests from the perspective of all countless sentient beings to be trained until the end of time and space. The unity of these two kinds of enlightened bodies means that, while the Dharma Body never moves away from its natural state of luminous spaciousness, the Form Bodies manifest as the effortless and spontaneous activities of enlightened body, speech, and mind (such as turning the wheel of dharma) that are naturally in perfect harmony with every single sentient being.

The verbal Madhyamaka as the means to express this threefold actuality of ground, path, and fruition are the teachings of the Buddha and the treatises of the great Mādhyamika masters such as Nāgārjuna. These treatises comment on the words of the Buddha in two ways. First, they comment on the intentions of "the Madhyamaka scriptures of the ordinary vehicles," that is, the teachings of mainly the expedient meaning that were spoken with certain intentions. Through this, they help practitioners realize that there are no internal contradictions in the words of the Buddha and that his words cannot be invalidated through reasoning. In this way, the students' trust and confidence in the Buddha as the Omniscient One become irreversible and increase further and further. Second, these treatises comment on the ultimate actuality that is expressed by "the Madhyamaka scriptures of the extraordinary great vehicle," which are the teachings of the definitive meaning that do not entail any other intentions or implications. Thus, the texts generate confidence in the definitive meaning in those who are suitable for it and provide for their relief from all obscurations on the great paths and grounds of bodhisattvas.

As for the persons who are called Centrists, there are two levels. Those on the first level uphold the Centrist view by following master Nāgārjuna and understand the meaning of the texts that say that all phenomena are without nature. Centrists on the second level are described by Candrakīrti as those in whose mental continua the realization of Centrism has dawned and whose realization is in concordance with the realization of the noble ones of all three vehicles. For bodhisattvas, this realization begins on the path of seeing of the great vehicle. Thus, noble bodhisattvas are those who are able to rest in meditative equipoise within the nature of phenomena through having cultivated the specific knowledge of this path in meditation. In general, this means that all those noble ones of the second level—learners and nonlearners—who rest in meditative equipoise within the nature of phenomena are the actual Centrists. Those among these noble ones who abide within the phase of subsequent attainment[263] and thus engage in various activities on the level of seeming reality as well as all ordinary beings who uphold the Centrist view without having directly realized it are called "Centrists who follow common worldly consensus."

Thus, as for upholding the Madhyamaka view and having realized it, there are four possibilities. There are (1) people who uphold the Madhyamaka view and in whose continua its realization has not arisen, (2) those in whose continua its realization has arisen and who do not uphold the Madhyamaka view, (3) those for whom both are the case, and (4) those for whom neither is the case.

Among these, the second possibility might require some explanation. According to Karmapa Mikyö Dorje, there surely are cases of bodhisattvas who have realized the actuality of Madhyamaka but who—for the sake of training certain kinds of beings to be trained—do not uphold the view of Madhyamaka. However, it is impossible that they do not uphold the final intended meaning of this view, because it is impossible for the noble ones of the great vehicle to say something mistaken about the view and the accomplishment of the two realities, since they have directly realized ultimate reality. Then, there are also beings such as the noble ones among the hearers and solitary realizers who indeed have accomplished the actual Madhyamaka, since its realization has been born in them. However, they do not uphold the view of Madhyamaka, since their insight has not properly engaged in the scriptural system of Centrism. Therefore, their minds have not been trained in the conventions of Centrist view and accomplishment. The only exceptions to this are those noble ones among the hearers and solitary realizers who have the highest capacities. For, once the basic nature of Madhyamaka just as it is has been realized through the path, the self-confidence of the knowledge that grows from this path cannot be subdued. This knowledge that arises in meditation is at the same time the means to unmistakenly express the actual Madhyamaka of the basic nature. Once such knowledge has been developed, there is not the slightest difficulty in teaching others the actuality that is experienced by it.

Another example of one who has realized the actual Madhyamaka while not upholding its view is an ordinary being in whose mind stream the realization of Madhyamaka may arise through the power of cultivating the exemplary wisdom and the two stages of creation and completion in the Vajrayāna. Of course, this person does not know how to express the Madhyamaka view. Nevertheless, there are cases of such Vajrayāna practitioners who have not been trained in the conventional terms of Madhyamaka and who still display the power to explain the

Madhyamaka view, debate about it, and even compose treatises on it. All this is the result of removing blockages in the free flow of nāḍī, prāṇa, and bindu. And even for ordinary beings in whom the realization of the actual Madhyamaka has not yet arisen, it is possible that a moment of self-confident knowledge could emerge that causes them to propound the Madhyamaka view just as it is. Through this, they may rise as indisputable guides who in the middle of an ocean of opponents can eliminate all kinds of wrong views. Such can happen through the power of intense devotion to the guru and the three jewels or through the force of overwhelming compassionate accumulations of merit that are motivated by the mind of enlightenment for the sake of all beings.

In general, however, all who uphold and proclaim what is called "the Madhyamaka view"— whether they are noble beings in whom realization has arisen or ordinary beings in whom it has not—do so only for the sake of putting an end to the wrong views of others, that is, solely from the perspective of those who entertain such views and suffer through them. Thus, when Centrists "uphold" the view of Madhyamaka and present its ground, path, and fruition, they never put this forward as a system of their own in which they believe. The reason is that they simply do not present anything whatsoever as their own system and that "upholding this view" refers to nothing but the process of helping other people to free themselves from clinging to any kind of view or system. In this way, something that looks like a Madhyamaka "system" or "school" can only emerge in the dialogues that Centrists may have with others. This also explains why all Madhyamaka texts mainly consist of refutations of the positions of others. The reason for all these refutations lies not in mere sophistry or nihilism on the part of Centrism, but in the fact that all conceptual constructions are by their nature incapable of really capturing phenomena and their nature, be it on the seeming or the ultimate level. Rather, they only obscure our direct perception of how things really are and thus lead to mistaken actions and suffering.

## *Madhyamaka Ground*

### What Is Reality?

The ground of the Madhyamaka system is the correct view on the two realities. As *The Sūtra of the Meeting of Father and Son* says:

> Without having learned this from others,
> The Knower of the World distinguished these two realities.
> The one is the seeming and the other the ultimate—
> There is no other third reality.

In general, the Sanskrit word *satya* can mean both "truth" and "reality." In the context of the two "realities" in Centrism, this term refers to realities in the sense that what is experienced in some way by someone is that person's individual reality, no matter how delusive this experience might be from the perspective of others. It is like when we say that someone "lives in a different reality." We do not mean that this person does not live on this planet but that her or his view or perception of things is not the same as ours. This is even more obvious in people who go insane and live completely in their own world, not because they went to some "Crazy Disney World" located somewhere else but because the entire experiential framework of their minds has changed. In Centrism, reality is understood in an experiential or perceptual sense and not ontologically as some hard-and-fast "real existence" in a substantial, independent, or absolute manner. Rather, this notion of real existence is precisely what Centrists keep denying. So for them, "realities" refer to different types of experiences of individual beings, without there being some independent reality somewhere. In other words, Centrists would not say, "The truth is out there." This means that seeming reality does not exist apart from the minds of the ordinary sentient beings whose experience it is. Likewise, ultimate reality is not some absolute or transcendent given. It does not exist anywhere other than in the minds of noble ones who rest in meditative equipoise within the nature of phenomena. The manifold expressions of seeming reality in different beings are usually compared to the various dream experiences of different sleepers. None of the episodes in their dreams has any correlate in any real outer reality, but at the time of dreaming, everything that is experienced is subjectively completely real. Ultimate reality is compared to waking up from the dream and realizing that none of the events in one's dream ever happened as anything other than a mere appearance in one's own mind. As Candrakīrti says in his *Entrance into Centrism*:

> It is through the perfect and the false seeing of all entities
> That the entities that are thus found bear two natures.
> The object of perfect seeing is true reality,
> And false seeing is seeming reality.[264]

As a simplified analogy, consider the well-known computerized pictures with three-dimensional effects (called "Magic Eye" and the like). If we look at one of these two-dimensional pictures and do not focus on any of its details but basically look through it, the picture appears as a completely different three-dimensional image. Nothing new is added to the two-dimensional picture itself when the three-dimensional image is seen, and there is also no other spatial reality behind this flat sheet of paper. The only thing that has changed is the way of looking at it. However, this is precisely what makes all the difference. Since we can experience substantial changes in our perception in such a simple way, how can we rule out even more dramatic expansions of our minds, if we work in a systematic and all-encompassing manner on our way of seeing the world?

Since the two realities refer to experiences or perceptions, they are not just some abstract conceptual or formal truths (such as "one plus one equals two"). Also, when we see a table or hear a sound, we would not think of this as seeing or hearing a "truth," nor would we conceive the perceiving consciousness itself as a "truth." Rather, we refer to both the objects and the perceiving subject as some kind of reality that we perceive or experience. As Broido rightly says:

> Truth is a property of sentences (relativized to contexts) or, philosophically, a property of propositions, but in any case not a property of cognitions or cognitive states or appearances or experiences or "things." It is only with a very great sense of strain that an English-speaker can say of a visual object or experience that it is true or false. . . . Given this strain and the resulting confusion it is not surprising that many Western accounts of the satyas are unintelligible.[265]

Moreover, in terms of the Buddhist path, mere "truths" do not have any liberating power per se; only realizations that have been fully integrated into one's mind as experiential realities have such power. For example, it is widely accepted that smoking is hazardous to one's health, but all smokers who have tried to quit know equally well that it takes much more than just this truth to actually change addictive patterns.

Thus, the two realities are not understood merely as general truths (of course, they are also formally true) but as the individual realities that are experienced by either the mistaken minds of sentient beings or the unmistaken wisdom minds of noble ones.[266] These realities encompass both the objective and the subjective sides of experience. The objects that we see, hear, and so forth, including the various kinds of consciousness that perceive these objects, are our reality; and what the nobles ones perceive is "their" reality.

Therefore, in Centrism, the distinction of the two realities is not an ontological one but primarily epistemological. This means that we are not talking about two separate sets of reality that independently and objectively exist in two different realms called saṃsāra and nirvāṇa. Rather, the two realities refer to just what is experienced by two different types of beings with different types and scopes of perception. More important still, since the overall purport of the teachings of the Buddha is liberation from cyclic existence, the presentation of the two realities and their relation is nothing but a means to this end. Since this presentation is used as a pedagogical tool for accomplishing liberation, the actual contrast between the two realities is soteriological in nature. The dividing line is drawn between what is delusive or seeming in the sense of being unreliable when seeking for liberation from cyclic existence and what is genuine or ultimate in the sense of being reliable as the appropriate basis for such liberation. As Pawo Rinpoche says:

> [The seeming] is not a stable reality, because it does not withstand analysis and because it does not appear as an object of the meditative equipoise of the noble ones. . . . [The ultimate] is "genuine," because it is essential for those who wish for liberation and undeceiving with respect to the result, which is Buddhahood.[267]

The presentation of the difference between seeming and ultimate reality together with the ensuing activities on a seeming path are regarded as the means to achieve the direct realization of what is called ultimate reality. Nāgārjuna says in his *Fundamental Verses*:

> Without reliance on conventions,
> The ultimate cannot be taught.
> Without realization of the ultimate,
> Nirvāṇa cannot be attained.[268]

Thus, the presentation of the two realities is in itself an aspect of the bodhisattvas' skill in means, but within this educational approach, neither of these two realities is "better" or more real than the other. The reason for this is that all presentations and practical applications of these two can only happen within the framework of seeming reality itself, since they only need to be taught to those who have an essentially dualistic state of mind. As such, these two cannot but be mutually dependent and dualistic, since it is impossible to talk about, reflect on, or meditate on the one without the other. Likewise, there is no way to proceed on the path to "the ultimate" without using and eventually letting go of seeming reality. On the other hand, within the meditative equipoise of those who directly perceive what is called ultimate reality, all reference points of a dualistic mind have completely subsided. Thus, any arguments about what is seeming, ultimate, real, or false are by definition simply irrelevant to this perceptual perspective. *The Sūtra That Teaches the Unity of the Nature of the Expanse of Dharmas*[269] says:

> O Mañjuśrī, when the expanse of dharmas is taken as the source of valid cognition, there is neither seeming reality nor ultimate reality.

Pawo Rinpoche states:

> It is for the native nature of all phenomena, the very expanse of dharmas just as it is, . . . that the conventional term "ultimate reality" is used. . . . This is what abides as the actual nature of all phenomena. It is the object of the profound meditative equipoise of noble ones. Therefore, it is presented as a stable reality in dependence on the seeming. [However,] it is not [such a stable reality] independently through its nature, because the Buddhas themselves behold neither real nor delusive phenomena.[270]

> It is definitely stated that all phenomena have one single reality and that just this that is called "real" or "delusive" is not observed. Nevertheless, in order for naïve beings[271] to be able to leave their fear behind, the provisional presentation of subject and object is [given as] something that leaves the status quo of mere common worldly consensus as it is. Thus, naïve beings are guided by using the conventional term "seeming reality."[272]

Candrakīrti says in his *Lucid Words*:

> What is taught as arising and such in terms of dependent origination does not concern the nature of the objects of the uncontaminated wisdom of those free from the blurred vision[273] of basic ignorance. Rather, it is [taught] with respect to the objects of the consciousnesses of those whose eyes of intelligent insight are affected by the blurred vision of basic ignorance.[274]

> We teach the delusiveness of entities with regard to seeming reality as a remedy against [the beliefs of] worldly people who cling to this [delusiveness] as being real. However, the noble ones who have accomplished what is to be accomplished do not see anything that is delusive or not delusive. Moreover, for those who have realized the delusiveness of all phenomena, do karma and cyclic existence exist? They do not observe any phenomenon as either existent or non-existent.[275]

From the perspective of the meditative equipoise of noble ones who realize the ultimate, experientially there is only "one reality." However, it may be conceived or designated in various ways when these noble ones engage in their activities in order to help others so that they too may realize this reality. *The Sixty Stanzas on Reasoning* states:

> That nirvāṇa is the sole reality

Is what the Victors have declared.[276]

Atīśa's *Entrance into the Two Realities* declares:

The ultimate is just a single one.
Others assert it to be twofold.
The nature of phenomena is not established as anything whatsoever,
So how could it be two or three and such?[277]

## No Ground for the Two Realities

In general, there are various presentations of the two realities in the different Buddhist philosophical systems up through the Autonomists. All their presentations agree on the following general points (Autonomists doing so just conventionally) about ultimate reality: (1) it cannot be invalidated through reasoning, (2) it withstands analysis, (3) it abides ultimately as an undeceiving nature, and (4) it is the object of an unmistaken subject. Seeming reality is defined as the opposite of this.

As for Consequentialists, one looks in vain for their own special presentation of the two realities. Rather, when they dispel the mistakenness in the minds of those who uphold philosophical systems, they do so by simply putting an end to wrong views through demonstrating the inconsistencies of any position in terms of an actually or substantially existing ultimate. When Consequentialists describe what is to be adopted and rejected by giving their own presentations of seeming reality, they do not use specific new terms to establish a system of their own that explains this process. Rather—both in terms of everyday life and the Buddhist path—they engage in what is to be adopted and rejected in a way that is adjusted to the conventions of "correct" and "false" as these accord with common worldly consensus without analysis. To support this approach, they point to the Buddha, who taught the two realities in accordance with such conventions merely for the sake of helping worldly beings to finally realize true reality:

> The world disputes with me, but I do not dispute with the world. Whatever is asserted as existent in the world, that I assert as existent too. Whatever is asserted as nonexistent in the world, that I assert as nonexistent too.[278]

When Centrists talk about common worldly consensus or the perspective without analysis, they usually make a distinction between ordinary people whose minds have not been altered by philosophical views and people whose minds have been so altered. Common worldly consensus is then identified as what is consensus among those who have not been affected in this sense. However, it is obvious that there is no single universal set of things about which there is common consensus in the world, even when leaving aside philosophical views in a strict sense. There are an endless number of regional or social views or consensus on almost all issues, and in the end, majority vote or custom in a given society or group is what determines the local sets of consensus. Thus, the famous Tibetan master Gendün Chöpel (1903–1951) said that, basically, there is nobody whose mind is not affected by some sort of view. The only difference concerns what kind of view. Some people are affected by the views of their parents or their social group; others may be affected by certain religious, scientific, or political theories. In light of this, it seems impossible to pinpoint anything as common worldly consensus among people who are not affected by a view, since such people simply seem to be nonexistent. Thus, such consensus does not refer to certain social conventions, scientific theories, or commonly held views that people more or less consciously agree on.

Can we find another way to determine the type of common consensus that is unaffected by views? It is hard to draw a sharp line here, but according to Centrists like Candrakīrti, Śāntarakṣita, and Gendün Chöpel, this common consensus refers to our direct nonconceptual experiences and sense perceptions. Conceptual cognitions, except for merely labeling what we experience in this way, represent for the most part the kind of consciousness that is already affected by some view. Candrakīrti is reported to have pointed to his robe and said, "If you ask me what this is, I would say this is Candrakīrti's robe. If you ask me what the building behind me is, I would say it is Nālandā University. Other than that, I have nothing to say."

Thus, common worldly consensus in the Centrist sense primarily refers to the very basic things that we perceive and label by taking them for granted, usually without even thinking about them, such as that we eat when we feel hungry, that fire burns, that water flows downhill, that there is a world of people out there who are different from ourselves, and that we want to be happy and avoid suffering. These appearances of seeming reality are what determine our ordinary behavior. If they are not analyzed, they seem to be there and—mostly—function as we expect them to. Usually, our bodies are still there when we wake up in the morning and function in the same way as yesterday. Then, we feed them and take the same road to the same place where we have been working for many years. However, as soon as we start to analyze these appearances for what they really are, they start to lose their characteristics and functions, because we step out of our familiar frame of reference within which these appearances manifest and operate. This is also obvious from modern science: For example, according to quantum physics, there are no such things as matter, roads, cars, or bodies, so who or what is driving home after an exciting day in the quantum lab? On the other hand, subjectively, we do not live our lives by behaving as quantum fields or the like. We do not relish quarks and energy waves but eat pancakes and drink coffee. Thus, one could say that common worldly consensus is mainly that which we take for granted in our everyday transactions and which functions accordingly as long as it is not questioned.

In more technical terms, the Eighth Karmapa says that "worldly" refers to all mental activities under the sway of afflictive and cognitive obscurations through which the dualistic appearances of apprehender and apprehended on the level of seeming, worldly reality are imagined, as well as all thoughts and expressions in dependence on this imagining that are used by those who experience dualistic appearances. On this level of the worldly seeming, the conventions of everything in both the world and the treatises that is already consensus or suitable to become some consensus are called "the conventions of the worldly seeming." As Śāntideva says:

> Thus, two kinds of world are seen:
> The one of yogins and the one of common people.
> Here, the world of common people
> Is invalidated by the world of yogins.
>
> Also the yogins, due to differences in insight,
> Are overruled by successively superior ones.[279]

The Centrist presentation of the two realities is in no way established as a Centrist system of its own. Rather, such descriptions are used as mere labels. When they are analyzed, neither a defining characteristic nor an example of ultimate reality can be found. Thus, all that is left on the side of Consequentialists in their communications with others are mere nominal definienda that give the impression of being defined by certain defining characteristics. However, since such names are also empty of a nature of their own, ultimate emptiness is even beyond being an object of the wisdom of noble ones. So how could anybody find a nature that makes up or defines this emptiness?

One might argue with the Consequentialists' refusal to take a position regarding the ultimate by saying, "As was said above, the defining characteristics of ultimate reality are that it (1) cannot be invalidated through reasoning, (2) withstands analysis, (3) abides ultimately as an undeceiving nature, and (4) is the object of an unmistaken subject. So, ultimately speaking, is there such a phenomenon or not? If there is, you Consequentialists are realists.[280] If there isn't, the presentation of the two realities is meaningless." The Eighth Karmapa responds that Consequentialists do not claim that, ultimately, there is an ultimate reality that is endowed with such defining characteristics, since they also do not claim that, ultimately, there is a seeming reality that has the opposite defining characteristics. The reason for this is that both realities are just presented in mutual dependence. Moreover, it is not only impossible to establish an ultimate reality with such defining characteristics through any valid cognition whatsoever, but the notion of such an ultimate reality can also be invalidated through reasoning. Thus, the two realities are primordially natural emptiness in which all flux of mental reference points is completely absent, be these subject or object, defining characteristics, definiendum, and example; or valid cognition, what is to be validated, and the result of validation. All presentations of the inexpressible and inconceivable that are made from the perspective of ordinary beings by conventionally referring to "ultimate reality" are nothing but a futile attempt to write words onto space. However, the Buddha and Nāgārjuna explain that such expositions are still given for the sake of dispelling the wrong ideas of those who misconceive the two realities as something that has characteristics (such as real existence) versus something that is the fundamental nature of knowable objects. Particularly, if no presentation of ultimate reality is provided, profound true reality as it actually is will not be realized. The sūtras say:

> If the ultimate did not exist, pure conduct would be meaningless and the appearance of Thus-Gone Ones would be pointless. Since the ultimate exists, bodhisattvas should be skilled in the ultimate.

In summary, nonnominal, profound, and ultimate emptiness that is the actual object of the wisdom of noble ones is free from either withstanding or not withstanding analysis. As such, it is beyond expression. On the other hand, the nominal[281] emptiness that is the object of a correct reasoning consciousness is surely not something that can withstand analysis. Nevertheless, Centrists apply names such as "ultimate reality" or "emptiness" to that which is essentially without name and constitutes true reality. Thus, since they use such illustrating designations, one cannot say that Centrists are unable to conventionally express this ultimate reality. As will be explained further, this is an essential point in Centrism.

## The Detailed Explanation of the Two Realities

The essential points on the two realities having been elucidated, the ground now seems properly prepared for a slight elaboration on this conventional distinction.

### *The Meaning of the Terms*

The Sanskrit term for "the seeming" is *saṃvṛti* (Tib. kun rdzob), which literally means "to completely cover, conceal, or obscure." This is also given as its main sense in the twenty-fourth chapter of Candrakīrti's *Lucid Words*, in which he lists three meanings of this term:

1) Seeming means *completely obscuring*, since ignorance completely blocks the true reality of things.
2) The seeming bears this name because it is *mutually dependent* and thus not independently or truly existent. This includes everything that is merely established in dependence on something else (such as something being long and short respectively) as well as all that originates in dependence on various causes and conditions.
3) Seeming also refers to *signs and symbols*, that is, to worldly conventions and expressions. This not only refers to language or conventional terms but encompasses all objects of expression, means of expression, knowing consciousnesses, and knowable objects.[282]

*The Treasury of Knowledge* reports two more meanings:

4) Bhāvaviveka's *Blaze of Reasoning* says that "the seeming refers to the *complete diversification* of all entities, such as forms."[283]
5) The seeming is *make-believe* or *pretense*. As Haribhadra says, "It is seeming, because it does not withstand the force of analysis."[284]

Thus, seeming reality (*saṃvṛtisatya*) is called seeming because basic ignorance obscures the seeing of true reality. It is still called a reality, because naïve beings take it to be real and because it functions in accordance with how it is perceived until true reality is realized. This is the only way in which it is undeceiving for sentient beings.

The Sanskrit term for the ultimate is *paramārtha* (Tib. don dam). *Parama* (Tib. dam pa) means "supreme or ultimate," and *artha* means "object, purpose, or actuality." Bhāvaviveka's *Blaze of Reasoning* lists three different ways in which the compound of these two words can be read in Sanskrit:

> 1) Since it is an object and ultimate, it is the ultimate object. (2) Or, [it may be read as] "the object of the ultimate": Since it is the object of ultimate nonconceptual wisdom, it is the object of the ultimate. (3) Or, it [can be understood as] "that which is in accordance with the ultimate object": Since the ultimate object exists in the knowledge that is in approximate accordance with the realization of this ultimate object, it is that which is in accordance with the ultimate object.[285]

The first way to understand this means that both *parama* and *artha* refer only to the object—emptiness—as opposed to the subject that realizes it.[286] The second alternative means that *parama* refers to the subject (wisdom) and *artha* to the object (emptiness).[287] The third option indicates a reasoning consciousness that cognizes ultimate reality not directly but inferentially.[288] The majority of Autonomists seem to favor the second way of reading *paramārtha,* while not denying the first. Consequentialists usually follow Candrakīrti's *Lucid Words,* which confirms the first reading:

> Since it is both an object and ultimate, it is the ultimate object. Since just this is real, it is ultimate reality.[289]

Thus, ultimate reality (*paramārthasatya*) is called ultimate because it is the ultimate sphere of nonconceptual wisdom in the meditative equipoise of noble ones. It is called reality because it is undeceiving in all aspects.[290] Pawo Rinpoche says:

> It is called "object" because one engages in the fundamental nature in dependence on the seeming and because it is what is to be strived for. It is "supreme" because it is essential for those who wish for liberation and undeceiving with respect to the result, which is Buddhahood. Thus, it is a term for [such] a common locus.[291]

### *Painting the Sky: A Description of Their Defining Characteristics*

Here, the general definition of reality is "that which is undeceiving." Thus, seeming reality is defined as that which is undeceiving on the seeming level. In Centrism, this refers to those phenomena that are found without analysis, that is, from the perspective of the false perception of ordinary sentient beings that is distorted by basic ignorance. In other words, these are all phenomena that are fabricated and superimposed through the reference points of imagination, speech, and expression. The Eighth Karmapa emphasizes that this seeming reality is neither something separate from the basic ignorance that imagines it nor is it this very ignorance itself. Candrakīrti says in his *Entrance into Centrism*:

> Since ignorance obscures its true nature, this is the seeming.
> The Sage has declared that seeming reality
> Is that which is fabricated and appears as real through this [ignorance].
> Thus, fabricated entities are the seeming.[292]

To be more precise, seeming reality is characterized by afflicted ignorance.[293] This is the type of ignorance that is contained within the twelve links of dependent origination and is the cause of cyclic existence. One may wonder why the seeming is presented as a reality at all, since it is what appears from an intrinsically distorted perspective. In general, it is just on the conventional level and provisionally that Centrists speak of it as a reality in order to guide ordinary beings. The first reason to present it as a reality is in terms of subjective experience, because worldly people take seeming appearances to be really existing just as they appear. The second reason lies in worldly empiricism, because causes and results appear to function in an unmistaken way from the perspective of provisional reasoning, that is, as long as the notions of cause and result themselves are not questioned. However, seeming reality is clearly not an objective or stable reality, because it does not withstand analysis and because it does not appear as an object of the meditative equipoise of the noble ones.

In general, ultimate reality is that which is ultimately undeceiving. In Centrism, this refers to that which is perceived through nonconceptual self-aware wisdom from the perspective of the perfect perception of noble ones in meditative equipoise. Again, ultimate reality is in no way established as something that is different or independent from the meditative equipoise of noble ones. There is also no meditative equipoise of noble ones apart from this ultimate reality. Such meditative equipoise is not to be understood as a perception of *something* or of just one single ultimate object, such as *the* emptiness or *the* ultimate. Rather, it is more like a simultaneous panoramic awareness of the true nature of all phenomena. In this, there is no duality of subject and object and no restriction through focusing on some particular object. As such, it is completely unfabricated. Thus, nonreferential wisdom sees the nonreferential nature of phenomena beyond imagination and expression. The way in which this wisdom sees is called "without seeing," since it does not see in the same manner as ordinary beings do. It does not see anything as they perceive and label it. *The Concise Prajñāpāramitāsūtra*[294] says:

> Beings usually speak of "seeing the sky."
> Examine this point of how you see the sky!
> The Buddha taught that the seeing of phenomena is just like this.

In his *Entrance into the Two Realities*, Atīśa agrees:

> In the very profound sūtras,
> It is said that nonseeing is to see this.
> Here, there is no seeing and no seer,
> No beginning and no end, just peace.
>
> Entities and nonentities are left behind.
> It is nonconceptual and nonreferential.

> . . .
> It is inexpressible, unobservable,
> Unchanging, and unconditioned.
> When it is realized by yogins,
> Afflictive and cognitive obscurations are relinquished.[295]

Jñānagarbha's *Distinction between the Two Realities* says:

> It is not suitable to abide
> As an entity corresponding to its appearance.
> It does not appear in any way whatsoever
> For any entity of consciousness.[296]

His autocommentary explains:

> The ultimate does not abide as it appears, since it does not even appear for the knowledge of the Omniscient One. Therefore, the sūtras say:
>
> > Not seeing anything at all is to see true reality.[297]

Bhāvaviveka's *Heart of Centrism* says:

> Its character is neither existent, nor nonexistent,
> Nor [both] existent and nonexistent, nor neither.
> Centrists should know true reality
> That is free from these four possibilities.[298]

By definition, ultimate reality cannot be taught or demonstrated. As *The Sūtra of Engaging in the Two Realities*[299] says:

> Devaputra, ultimate reality cannot be taught. Why is that? Ultimately, all such phenomena as the one who teaches, what is taught, and the basis on which this is taught are utterly unborn. One is not able to explain utterly unborn phenomena through utterly unborn phenomena.

Therefore, it is said that the ultimate cannot be an object of cognition. When the formations of mind or mental events merge with the ultimate, all of them are naturally and completely at peace, and none of them has any chance to stir for even a single moment. As Śāntideva's *Entrance to the Bodhisattva's Way of Life* says:

> The ultimate is not the sphere of cognition.
> It is said that cognition is the seeming.[300]

Karmapa Mikyö Dorje explains that this mode of being is the vital point of the definitive meaning of all sūtras and tantras and nothing other than the "Mahāmudrā of mental nonengagement that is beyond cognition" that was transmitted from Saraha and Śavaripa to Marpa and Milarepa.

There is no contradiction between, first, the explanation that the ultimate is taken as the object of the wisdom of noble ones and, second, the teaching in some sūtras and treatises that it is not the sphere of cognition. The ultimate can be said to be seen by nonconceptual wisdom in terms of negative determination:[301] The very fact that nothing whatsoever is to be seen is not seen as anything at all. On the other hand, the ultimate is not seen in terms of any positive determination,[302] that is, by any dualistic consciousness in the manner of a knowable object and a subject that knows this object. This means that not seeing any reference points is expressed as seeing their actual nature. It is similar to the following example: Imagine some people who are in doubt as to whether they can write letters onto space or not. Through their not "seeing"—that is, their not finding—any possibility of being able to write in this way, they "see" in the sense of understanding that they are not able to write in such a way. As in the case of seeming reality, one might argue that such an ultimate reality cannot have the status of a reality on the grounds that it is not established as anything at all. Ultimately, that is true, but provisonally, ultimate reality is taught in order to guide sentient beings in accordance with the conventions of logic and reasoning.

When not analyzed, seeming reality refers to the plain presence of mere appearances that can be satisfying only as long as they are left unquestioned. When slightly analyzed, seeming reality is just the assembly of interdependent causes and conditions. Since we engage in what is without any real nature through our conventions of thinking and expression, it is "mere nominality," "mere conventionality," "mere imagination," and "mere superimposition." All these terms serve as synonyms for seeming reality. When thoroughly analyzed, all phenomena are in themselves nothing but the complete primordial peace of reference points and characteristics. It is not that they become free from reference points through the vision of the noble ones, through reasoned analysis, or through emptiness. The phenomena that are found from the perspective of a mind without analysis and with slight analysis are called seeming reality. That which is "found" (in the manner of nonseeing) through thorough analysis and the meditative equipoise of noble ones is called ultimate reality or emptiness. It is also named suchness, because it never changes into anything else. It is "the true end,"[303] because it is seen as what is unmistaken. It is designated as "signlessness," since it is the cessation of all reference points and characteristics. It is "the expanse of dharmas," because it is the cause for the dharma qualities of the noble ones.[304]

In brief, the difference between seeming reality and ultimate reality is whether a perceived object is ultimately deceiving or undeceiving and whether the corresponding subject perceives this object in a way that is essentially mistaken or unmistaken. Thus, the main criterion for distinguishing the two realities lies in the dissimilar modes of perception of the minds of ordinary beings and noble ones.

In general, seeming reality is not an object that is known or seen from the perspective of nonconceptual wisdom minds, while ultimate reality is not an object that can be known from the perspective of mistaken minds. Thus, actually, there is no common basis or ground for a division into two realities. However, *The Treasury of Knowledge* says that, from the perspective of no analysis, one may take "just that which can be known" as the basis for distinguishing the two realities. As *The Sūtra of the Meeting of Father and Son* says:

> What can be known is nothing but just these two realities.

In his commentary on *The Ornament of Clear Realization*, called *The Noble One Resting at Ease*, the Eighth Karmapa provisionally suggests "phenomena's nature" as the basis for classifying the two realities. In this way, he distinguishes between two types of nature: phenomena's ultimate nature and their seeming nature. However, he also makes it very clear that this is just conventional verbiage:

> Here, this nature that is [called] "phenomena's own nature" has to be classified as the two realities. As for the ultimate, just in terms of convenient conventional expressions, [one may say,] "All phenomena do not have a nature. Therefore, they are empty of nature. This is their [ultimate] nature or entity." [In actual fact,] however, there are many points to be disputed and examined even with respect to this mere [statement]. As for the seeming—exemplified by something like a pillar—[the fact] that just this appearing aspect of a pillar possesses the function to support a beam and so on is presented as its [seeming] nature.[305]

From the various perspectives of the individuals who are the knowers of what can be known, there are not only two realities. Strictly speaking, within seeming reality, there are as many realities as there are beings. In a sense, we all live in our own world, since nobody has any experiences that are exactly the same as those of others. In Centrism, there is no such thing as collective experience that is really shared with others. However, that everybody has different experiences does not mean that there is some actual reality out there that exists independently of individual perceptions and is just seen in different ways. This understanding is not even uniquely Buddhist, as precisely the same is suggested by modern Western cognitive science and biology, which, for example, gained many detailed insights into how differently various animals perceive what we call the world.

How then could we define a general outer reality that is independent of individual perception? If we just go by majority vote, compared to the number of animals and the many ways that they perceive "the world," the reality that corresponds to our more or less "common" human perception is a hopeless candidate. We have no basis for establishing our perception as more valid than or superior to other beings'. In fact, as science tells us, in one way or another, all animals have much sharper senses than humans. So it is only our conceptual mind that might entitle us to claim superiority or validity of cognition. According to Buddhism, however, conceptual mind is essentially mistaken in that it mixes up mental images with their seemingly real referents. In brief, the entirety of the infinite realities of perceived objects and perceiving subjects within cyclic existence is actually delusive.

Take, for example, a person like Joseph Stalin, who was seen by many as a cruel dictator and murderer. Others regarded him as a great politician and war hero. Still others may have perceived him as a friend, many as their enemy. His children saw him as their father, his wife as her husband, and his parents as their child. Mosquitos or tigers experienced him as a source of delicious food, the bacteria in his body as their abode or universe, and his dog as its master. So who among them is "correct" about Mr. Stalin?

Still, when Buddha Śākyamuni appeared in this world and taught the dharma, he did so in a human body. Accordingly, he gave his instructions on the basis of human perceptions and conceptions and thus presented the common human way of seeing the world as conventionally real. It was only in comparison with this human perspective that he presented other beings' way of seeing as "unreal"—that is, unreal for human beings, but not from the conventional perspective of these other beings themselves. Thus, from the human perspective, conventionally, a river is said to be real as water, and the eye consciousness that perceives it as water is said to be undeceiving. Judging from this perspective, other ways of seeing this river, such as when it is said that hungry ghosts experience it as a stream of pus and blood or gods as nectar, are then conventionally unreal and deceiving. However, in no way does this mean that the human way of seeing the world is per se any more real or better than the perspective of any other being.

As for ultimate reality, it is impossible to say whether the experiences of ultimate reality in the meditative equipoises of different noble beings are the same or individually distinct, since it is the very nature of such meditative equipoise to be free from all reference points. Thus, experientially, the question of being one or many simply does not apply on this level. If different noble beings in meditative equipoise were to have exactly the same experience, it would absurdly follow that all these noble beings have one and the same mind. How then could there be different noble beings in the first place? Moreover, if they have the same mind, either they would have to progress on the path simultaneously in exactly the same way or, since they all experience in the same way—no matter whether they are called arhats, bodhisattvas, or Buddhas—there would be no progressive stages at all for different beings on the path. Conversely, if their experiences were different, then there would be as many ultimate realities as there are noble beings. This would mean that the ultimate would be multiple and thus not be the ultimate or final nature of phenomena. Or, one might wonder which one of all these many ultimate realities actually is ultimate reality. In addition, this contradicts the numerous statements that there is only a single ultimate reality.

### *Are the Two Realities One or Different?*

What is the relationship between the two realities themselves? It is a highly debated issue whether they are one or different. That this is not just academic hairsplitting will be clear from what the Eighth Karmapa says below about how this question applies to such expressions as "the equality of cyclic existence and nirvāṇa" and "thoughts being the Dharma Body," which serve as pith instructions for meditation practice.

The classic scriptural reference for the two realities being neither one nor different is *The Sūtra That Unravels the Intention.* This text lists four flaws that would follow if the two realities were one:

1) Just as ordinary beings perceive seeming reality, they would see ultimate reality at the same time. Thus, while still ordinary beings, they would be liberated without effort and achieve nirvāṇa or Buddhahood.
2) The defining characteristics of seeming reality and ultimate reality would be mutually inclusive. From this, it would follow that, for example, the emptiness of a desirable object is also an object of desire and thus a cause for suffering rather than its remedy.
3) Just as there is no diversity in the ultimate nature of all conditioned phenomena of seeming reality, there would be no diversity among conditioned phenomena.
4) Yogic practitioners would not have to seek for an ultimate reality beyond conditioned entities as they appear to the senses or as they are conceived by the thinking mind.

If the two realities were different, this would entail the following four flaws:

1) Those who see ultimate reality would not be liberated from cyclic existence, since the experience of seeming reality would be completely unaffected by seeing ultimate reality. Thus, they would not achieve nirvāṇa or Buddhahood.
2) Ultimate reality would not be the true nature of the conditioned entities of seeming reality, just as a vase is not the true nature of a piece of cloth.
3) The mere identitylessness or lack of nature of conditioned entities would not be their ultimate character, since these two are completely unrelated.
4) Afflicted phenomena and purified phenomena—in other words, mental states of basic ignorance with their delusive appearances and the nonconceptual wisdom that realizes emptiness—would simultaneously exist within the continua of noble beings, such as Buddhas, since realizing emptiness would not have eliminated ignorance.[306]

*The Treasury of Knowledge* says that, conventionally and without further analysis, the two realities may be said to be one in nature but different isolates.[307] This means that their nature is one but they appear as something different for the conceptual mind. Ultimately, they are inexpressible as "one" or "different." Pawo Rinpoche states that all presentations of the two realities as being one or different—whether in terms of nature or isolates—cannot but be construed in a way that is tied down to the conventions of dialectics. Centrism, however, does not present these conventional terms (such as "isolates") as parts of a system of its own. Moreover, he quotes the concluding verse from the previously cited chapter of *The Sūtra That Unravels the Intention*:

> The defining characteristic of the conditioned realms and the ultimate
> Is their defining characteristic of freedom from being one and different.
> Those who think of them in terms of oneness and difference
> Have not mentally engaged them in a proper way.

Thus, the Buddha declared that it is an improper approach to conceptualize phenomena that are free from being one or different as being one or different. Karmapa Mikyö Dorje and Padma Karpo agree in that the two realities are not even conventionally one or different. The Karmapa argues that the question of being one or different can only apply to the level of common worldly consensus that presupposes really existing things. In general, if things really exist, they can only exist in such a way that they are either one or different. Otherwise, they simply do not exist at all. In the Centrist system, however, just like all other phenomena, the two realities are not conceived or expressed as something that really exists. Thus, how could Centrists think of them as one or different?

When seen from the perspective of the minds of ordinary beings, the two realities are not one either, because ultimate reality does not appear for these beings.

They are also not different, because ordinary beings do not perceive two distinct realities. Furthermore, they cannot be expressed as being the same or different, since they are mutually dependent: They are delusive as opposed to undelusive. In general, what depends on something else cannot be the same as what it depends on, because it is contradictory for one thing to be both that which depends on something and that on which it depends. What is mutually dependent also cannot be different: If a phenomenon is dependent on something else, this is precisely the fact that makes it something that is not established on its own or by itself in the first place. Since this one phenomenon is not findable on its own, there is nothing that could be different from its counterpart or anything else. Thus, there is not even something to depend on something other. On the other hand, if what is dependent on something other is established in itself, there is no possibility that it is—and also no need for it to be—dependent on anything else.

Also, when seen from the perspective of the meditative equipoise of noble ones, the two realities are not one either, because the diversity of seeming reality does not appear in such equipoise. They are also not different, because the noble ones in meditative equipoise do not perceive two distinct realities. If they were to perceive seeming reality too, this would mean that they would have the appearance of something that they would take to be not empty. Thus, they would not be free from the characteristics of conditioned phenomena and the bondage of clinging to them. However, without release from these, the state of a noble being, nirvāṇa, and Buddhahood are completely impossible. Thus, if the two realities do not even appear as two in the meditative equipoise of noble ones, what point is there in talking about their hypothetical attributes, such as their being one or different?

The two realities are also not contradictory or mutually exclusive in the sense that the more powerful one of them is able to obstruct or cancel out the other, thus rendering it powerless. They are not two separately existing entities and also not just two ways of seeing the same thing. Rather, seeming reality appears only in the mistaken minds of ordinary beings and does not appear from the perspective of wisdom. The opposite is true for ultimate reality. Thus, it is not that two contradictory phenomena or realities interfere with each other in a single location or mind. This is just as there is no mutual perceptual or object-related interference between the existence of, for example, purple mice for a certain person who is drunk and the nonexistence of such mice for everybody else.

When we look at this from the point of view of a single object, it becomes obvious that the two realities are neither the same nor different. For example, a table is not its emptiness, and the table's emptiness is not the table. Otherwise, seeing the table with one's visual consciousness would mean seeing emptiness. Or, it would follow that noble ones in meditative equipoise still see tables and the like when resting in the realization of emptiness. There is also no common locus for a table and its emptiness; that is, there isn't something that is both. On the other hand, one cannot extract a table's emptiness from the table, put it right next to the table, and perceive two distinct objects. Nor can the table's emptiness be found as something different within the table itself. The same principle applies to all ordinary phenomena. *The Sūtra That Unravels the Intention* gives many examples of this, such as that we cannot separate pepper and its hotness or gold and its color. Likewise, we would not say that the hotness of pepper is the pepper or that the color of a piece of gold is that piece of gold.

In terms of Buddhist practice, Karmapa Mikyö Dorje emphasizes that such statements in the Kagyü lineage as "Thoughts are the Dharma Body," "Saṃsāra is nirvāṇa," and "Afflictions are wisdom" are taught with the intention that, ultimately, the two realities do not exist as different things. However, such phrases are not meant to establish that thoughts and the Dharma Body, saṃsāra and nirvāṇa, and so on are one in nature with the understanding that the two components of such pairs are two actual and distinct entities or realities. The reason for this is as follows: To negate that thoughts and the Dharma Body, and so on, are ultimately different implies also the negation that they are one in nature. This means that if there are no two actually existing and distinct phenomena to have a connection with each other in the first place, one cannot establish a connection of oneness in nature between such nonexistents. As Gampopa says:

> Make firm your resolve
> That this connate consciousness is wisdom.
> Once you gain certainty about this, you see true reality.
>
> Make firm your resolve
> That these thoughts that emerge from the mind
> Are the ultimate.
> Once you experience this, you see your heart.
>
> Make firm your resolve
> That these imputed tendencies that appear and resound
> Are the Dharma Body.
> Once you attain realization of this, you see what is real.[308]

Pamo Truba declares:

> The waves of affliction and clinging to a self
> Are the wisdom of the Buddhas of the three times.
> The darkness of thoughts and ignorance

Is great luminosity free from discursiveness.
The blaze of the three poisons of the afflictions
Is the wisdom mandala of the Victors.[309]

Such statements may indeed sound as if the two realities—thoughts and the Dharma Body, and so on—were one in nature. However, only those who have the tendency to solidify and reify everything can take the two realities, saṃsāra and nirvāṇa, thoughts and the Dharma Body, and such to be real entities and then label them good or bad, high or low, and so on. The above quotations merely indicate that all phenomena are equal in that they have not even the slightest nature of their own. They all have the same mode of being, which is that they are without nature and are just suchness in which there is no difference or otherness. Thus, these teachings do not say that a saṃsāra and a nirvāṇa that exist separately as actual things are one in nature. Moreover, this very same expression that all phenomena are one or equal in that they are without nature is used over and over in the Buddha's own words that teach the profound definitive meaning, such as the *Prajñāpāramitā sūtras. The Jewel Casket Sūtra*[310] says:

There is not the slightest difference to be made between afflictions and Buddha qualities.

*The Great Drum Sūtra*[311] agrees:

Mind and enlightenment
Are not seen as two.
What is the defining characteristic of enlightenment
Is also the defining characteristic of mind.

That such statements have to be taken literally is made clear in the system of Nāgārjuna, who was prophesied by the Buddha as the one who would elucidate the definitive meaning of Madhyamaka. His *Fundamental Verses* says:

What is the nature of the Thus-Gone One
Is the nature of beings.
The Thus-Gone One is without nature,
And all beings are without nature.

There is not the slightest difference
Between cyclic existence and nirvāṇa.
There is not the slightest difference
Between nirvāṇa and cyclic existence.[312]

The Eighth Karmapa does not deny the possibility that, based on the explicit words of the above statements, some people might misconceive the two realities, thoughts and the Dharma Body, and so on as having one nature in the sense of an ultimately existing nature of all things. On the other hand, once those who are the fully qualified recipients of such teachings realize the actual meaning of these explicit words, they will be released from all thoughts that the two realities are one or different in terms of an actual nature. The reason for this is that the meaning of the dharma cannot be understood through reliance on mere words. Rather, teaching and practicing the dharma always have to be grounded in the four reliances.[313] Thus, there is no way that people with a proper understanding could mistake the explicit words of teachings such as Gampopa's *Answers to the Questions of Tüsum Khyenba*:

> Connate mind as such is the Dharma Body.
> Connate appearances are the light of the Dharma Body.[314]

Tragba Gyaltsen[315] (1147–1216), the third supreme head of the Sakya school, puts this even more dramatically:

> The hells' ground of burning iron
> Is the Akaniṣṭha of true reality.
> The fiery suffering of heat and cold
> Is the Dharma Body free from discursiveness.
> The views of non-Buddhist forders[316]
> Are the Madhyamaka of true reality.[317]

*The Seven Points of Mind Training*, transmitted from Atīśa and the Kadampa lineage in all four schools of Tibetan Buddhism, says:

> Seeing delusion as the four enlightened Bodies is the unsurpassable protection through emptiness.[318]

As for the unity of the two realities, Padma Karpo's *Illumination of Three Centrist Scriptural Systems* says:

> From the perspective of the basic nature, . . . the nature of phenomena, the fundamental nature or [just] the nature, nothing can be posited as anything. Therefore, this [actuality] is labeled "emptiness," "lack of nature," or "dependent origination." Since this is not established as anything whatsoever, it is suitable that anything emerges from it. If it were established as any [real] nature, since it is impossible for

> a [real] nature to change into something other, it would not be suitable that something other than this [real nature] appears, just as charcoal does not turn white [even] if it is washed with milk. Whatever appears from the aspect of phenomenal expression does not affect [this ultimate] nature, just as space [seems to] fluctuate in various ways, such as clouds, dusty winds, sunlight, darkness, and moonlight. Therefore, we have the twofold classification into the ultimate when looking at the unchanging fundamental nature and into the seeming when looking at the fluctuations of [its] radiance. Since both parts of such a classification are of the same taste in that they have the nature of lacking any nature, nobody is able to distinguish them as something different. Therefore, they are called "inseparable" or a "unity," very much like ice and water. Thus, one should understand that, just as ground and fruition are not discerned as two, ground and path as well as path and fruition are inseparable.[319]

Just as water is the inseparable nature of ice, ultimate reality is the nature of seeming reality. They are neither the same nor different. Needing to quench one's thirst in the midst of a glacier, one would not discard the ice and search for water elsewhere. One would need only to melt the ice. In the same way, we do not have to dump seeming reality and import ultimate reality from somewhere else beyond our world. Rather, it is only through realizing the unity of the two realities that the icy glaciers of seeming reality can melt into the soothing waters of ultimate reality. At the same time, this unity is the unity of appearance and emptiness and the unity of wisdom and emptiness.

## *Seeming Divisions of the Seeming*

### Seeming Reality and Mere Seeming

To account for the difference between what appears to ordinary beings and to the noble ones in subsequent attainment, Candrakīrti's autocommentary on *The Entrance into Centrism* distinguishes between "seeming reality" and the "mere seeming" among seeming appearances in general.[320] As explained earlier, the first is what appears for ordinary beings in whose minds the ignorance of clinging to real existence has not dissolved. This is not the same as what appears during the subsequent attainment of noble ones in whose minds such ignorance has subsided. Thus, what appears for them during this phase is called the "mere seeming."

From the perspective of a Buddha, seeming phenomena do not appear under any circumstances. As far as ordinary beings and other noble beings such as bodhisattvas are concerned, it is in terms of whether they are affected by afflicted or unafflicted ignorance that the Buddha spoke about "seeming reality" and the "mere seeming." Unafflicted ignorance is an equivalent for the cognitive obscurations, that is, the latent tendencies of clinging to reality plus the clinging to the fact that phenomena lack reality and are illusionlike. Since the noble ones are affected only by this unafflicted type of ignorance, for them there is just a mere appearance of delusive phenomena—the "mere seeming"—which is a natural occurrence on their paths. Such mere seeming appearances emerge only during the states of subsequent attainment of the noble ones, but not during their meditative equipoise. For them, all that is perceived as real and solid through the clinging of ordinary beings is not real, because they perceive no such real phenomena in meditative equipoise and are fully and instantaneously aware that everything that appears to them during subsequent attainment is delusive, like an illusion or a reflection. Such appearances are deceiving for ordinary beings, but for the noble ones they are mere fictions that originate in dependence upon fictitious causes and conditions. Thus, what is seen by them under the influence of unafflicted ignorance is not considered seeming reality but the mere seeming.

The actual nature of this mere seeming—emptiness—is the ultimate that is seen from the perspective of the meditative equipoise of noble ones. Buddhas do not see the undeceiving ultimate as anything else, but the clinging of ordinary beings observes nothing but the deceiving phenomena of seeming reality. Since both afflicted and unafflicted ignorance—the causes for seeming reality and the mere seeming—have ceased in Buddhas, the results of these causes—seeming appearances—have subsided too.

### Worldly Seeming and Yogic Seeming

The "worldly seeming" refers to the sphere of so-called common worldly people. From the Buddhist point of view, these are of two kinds: average individuals who are not engaged in philosophical systems and non-Buddhists who are engaged in various philosophical systems. Thus, the worldly seeming encompasses both the seeming reality of ordinary beings as described above plus the realms of various non-Buddhist philosophical and scientific theories.

As for Buddhist yogic practitioners, there are many types, as classified by the four Buddhist philosophical systems, the five paths, or the ten grounds of bodhisattvas. The "yogic seeming" ranges from what is found through conventional cognitions from the perspective of slight analysis, such as subtle impermanence, up through the appearances and realizations during the subsequent attainment of noble hearers, solitary realizers, and bodhisattvas. In particular, for Centrists, the yogic seeming begins with a conceptual understanding of emptiness that comes from studying and continues with more experiential insights through reflection and analytical meditation. Finally, there is the true realization of the nature of phenomena, which arises in nonconceptual and nondualistic meditative equipoise. Thus, the Centrist yogic seeming does not refer only to the realizations of advanced practitioners; it encompasses all levels of relating to and practicing the Centrist teachings on emptiness. This yogic seeming is also designated as "the analytic seeming," "the seeming connected to a reasoning consciousness of noble ones," and "the Centrist seeming." The way in which the yogic seeming is communicated is partly by conventions about which there is already immediate common worldly consensus. To account for the particulars of the Buddhist path, yogic practitioners also rely on the conventions in the words of the Buddha that may serve as a basis for common consensus among them, such as the causes and results of cyclic existence and liberation, the presentations of grounds and paths, the mental factors to be relinquished and their remedies, and the specific ways in which meditative equipoise and subsequent attainment appear.

**Correct and False Seeming**

This distinction pertains only to what appears to ordinary beings. Here, Centrists differentiate between perceptions that are based on unaffected and affected sense faculties. *The Entrance into Centrism* says:

> False seeing is asserted to be twofold:
> [Perceptions through] clear sense faculties and defective sense faculties.
> The consciousnesses of those with defective sense faculties
> Are asserted as false in comparison to consciousnesses based on sound sense faculties.
>
> What is apprehended by the six undamaged sense faculties
> Is what the world cognizes.
> This is real in terms of the world.
> The rest is presented as false in terms of the world.[321]

Atīśa's *Entrance into the Two Realities* states:

> The seeming is asserted as twofold:
> The false one and the correct one.
> The first is twofold: [appearances such as floating] hairs or [double] moons
> As well as the conceptions of inferior philosophical systems.
>
> These arising and ceasing phenomena,
> Only satisfying when not examined
> And being able to perform functions,
> Are asserted as the correct seeming.[322]

As these verses indicate, the distinction between correct perception and false perception within the seeming is made only from the perspective of ordinary beings. From the perspective of the wisdom of noble ones and Centrist reasoning, illusory cows and "actual" cows are equally unreal or delusive. This was demonstrated by Candrakīrti in a very practical manner when he drew a picture of a cow on a wall, milked it, and thus produced "actual milk" from this drawn cow. On another occasion, he bumped into a pillar at Nālandā University. This caused great laughter among his friends, who said, "Hey, you just ran into that pillar—what happened to your view of emptiness?" Candrakīrti just waved his hand through the pillar and answered, "Which pillar?" There is no doubt that Centrists deny any reliable criteria or valid cognitions to establish something as correct and something other as false among seeming appearances. It is only to reflect common worldly consensus that they call perceptions that result from unaffected sense faculties "correct." What is perceived through unaffected sense faculties is real for worldly beings, since, from their perspective, it appears as real, they cling to it as real, and it is conventionally undeceiving. Thus, it is only in comparison to such worldly "correctness" that other perceptions that result from affected sense faculties are called "false." The same applies to the respective objects of such perceptions. However, as is said in the above quotations, both correct and false seeming are just two varieties of false seeing and its objects.

What is perceived through affected sense faculties is considered to be false or nonexistent even by worldly beings based on their notions of what is correct perception. Thus, it is not even a part of seeming reality, let alone any ultimate existence. Here, a distinction is made between inner and outer conditions that affect the sense faculties and result in mistaken perceptions. Inner conditions for mistakenness are, for example, blurred vision due to cataracts, or perceptual distortions from taking drugs. Outer conditions include the causes of a mirage or an echo. In Buddhism, "sense faculties" include the nonphysical "mental sense faculty," which is basically the moment of consciousness that immediately precedes and triggers the next moment of consciousness. This is seen as the sense faculty of the mental consciousness as opposed to the sense consciousnesses. When it is affected, for example, by the condition of sleep, this results in dream experiences. In the waking state, the main condition for the mistakenness of the mental consciousness consists in flawed inferential cognitions. These are based either on everyday wrong views, such as believing in really existing outer objects, or on the wrong views that are established by various Buddhist and non-Buddhist realists in their philosophical systems, such as an eternal self, a primal cosmic substance, or infinitesimal particles. Such notions are not found or used within ordinary worldly consensus and thus not considered as the correct seeming.

Centrists compare those who entertain such kinds of views with people who have no natural skill at climbing trees but attempt it by letting go of the tree's lower branches and simultaneously reaching for its higher branches. In this way, rather than getting higher up, they just fall through the space between the branches and crash to the ground. In the same way, through their intention to find true reality, realists of all kinds try to go beyond worldly conventions but do not realize actual reality. Rather, they fall into the extremes of permanence and extinction that lie in between. Therefore, they deviate from both realities. *The Entrance into Centrism* explains:

> Those who are outside the path of venerable noble Nāgārjuna
> Do not possess the means for peace.
> They deviate from [both] seeming reality and true reality.
> Since they deviate from the two realities, there is no liberation to be accomplished.[323]

In his autocommentary, Candrakīrti says that what is cognized by affected sense faculties, such as a hallucination, does not fall under the category of seeming reality. Again, seeming reality is understood as only that which is taken to be real by ordinary sentient beings, since the criteria for what is seemingly real are general worldly perception and consensus. There is no worldly consensus that appearances such as illusions or mirages perform the same functions as ordinary things. Likewise, the imputations of philosophers do not serve as bases for our conventional everyday transactions. The mere fact that some persons perceive something that nobody else perceives, or that they have their own private notions about things that are not shared by others, does not turn these into "seeming realities." Rather, on the mere conventional level, they are invalidated through the perceptions and ideas that most other people have and that serve as the bases for their everyday transactions. Therefore, such "private" appearances and notions are called the "false seeming." However, this does not constitute a third reality besides seeming reality and ultimate reality nor a third category of existents, since such appearances are not real or existent for either ordinary beings with unaffected sense faculties or noble ones.

The way in which this distinction between "correct" and "false" is presented shows clearly that it is again not something that is asserted by the Centrists themselves. The Eighth Karmapa mentions the view of certain Tibetan doxographers who say that one of the features that distinguishes Autonomists and Consequentialists is that the Autonomists assert this distinction between correct and false within seeming reality, while the Consequentialists do not assert it. There are also some people who say that this distinction exists as part of the Consequentialists' own system too. Finally, there are those who say that it does not even conventionally exist in the Consequentialist system. However, all of these positions are unjustified for the following reasons. Even the Autonomist system does not acknowledge the slightest difference, in terms of their being correct or false, between appearances during the daytime and appearances in a dream or between two dream appearances. Therefore, what need is there to mention whether there is such a distinction in the Consequentialists' own system? On the other hand, if this classification as correct or false in terms of common worldly consensus were not even presented on the conventional level, this would contradict verses VI.24 and VI.25 from Candrakīrti's *Entrance into Centrism* cited above. Like Consequentialists, Autonomists also make this distinction not as part of their own system but only in accordance with common worldly consensus. This is clearly expressed by Autonomist masters such as Bhāvaviveka, Jñānagarbha, and Śāntarakṣita.[324]

To summarize, in their own context, seeming appearances in general may be differentiated as follows: "Seeming reality" or the "correct seeming" is only that which is correctly perceived and labeled by ordinary beings according to their standards of correct and false. What is wrongly perceived or labeled according to these standards is the "false seeming." The illusionlike appearances during the subsequent attainment of noble ones are the "mere seeming." Thus, both the false seeming and the mere seeming are mere seeming appearances, but they do not fall under the category of seeming reality. The false seeming is not considered to be real even by ordinary beings, whereas the way in which noble ones perceive the mere seeming as unreal has nothing in common with the way that ordinary beings perceive. Furthermore, to distinguish between the sphere of all non-Buddhists—whether engaged in any philosophical systems or not—and the specific practices, experiences, and realizations on the various Buddhist paths, one speaks about the "worldly seeming" and the "yogic seeming."

However, none of these distinctions is to be taken as a hard-and-fast category that is established in any way or more real than the others. Rather, all of them are merely descriptive, much as when one describes different appearances in a dream. From the perspective of the waking state, there is not the slightest difference in terms of their reality between the appearances of a mirage and water in a dream. Hence, all conventional classifications and descriptions of seeming appearances should not make us forget that all such appearances, from ordinary forms up through a Buddha's omniscience, are just illusionlike. As the *Prajñāpāramitā sūtras* say:

> I declare that all phenomena including nirvāṇa—and even if there were any phenomenon more supreme than that—are illusionlike and dreamlike.[325]

### *Dividing Space: Divisions of the Ultimate*

Of course, there can be no divisions of the actual nature of the ultimate. However, in terms of a terminological classification, "nominal ultimate reality" is distinguished from "nonnominal (or actual) ultimate reality." The first is what is approximately concordant with ultimate reality. On the subject side, it is a reasoning consciousness about emptiness that fulfills the criteria of inferential valid cognition. On the object side, it is the emptiness that is characterized as a nonimplicative negation. Such can be regarded as a reality, since it is undeceiving from the perspective of analytical reasoning. It is, however, only a partial freedom from reference points. For example, the nonimplicative negation "nonarising" that negates arising still involves the notion of nonarising. As Śāntideva says, such notions must be let go too:

> Through familiarity with the latent tendencies of emptiness,
> The latent tendencies of entities will be relinquished.
> Through familiarity with "utter nonexistence,"
> These too will be relinquished later on.
>
> Once neither entities nor nonentities
> Remain before the mind,
> There is no other mental flux [either].
> Therefore, it is utter nonreferential peace.[326]

The actual and complete freedom from all reference points, such as arising, nonarising, existence, and nonexistence, is called nonnominal ultimate reality. *The Treasury of Knowledge* reminds us to be aware that all the various avenues of analyzing the two realities in Centrist treatises are solely dealing with nominal ultimate reality. Actual ultimate reality is by definition completely inaccessible to any conceptual analysis.[327]

In terms of the object to be negated, nominal ultimate reality is further classified as personal identitylessness and phenomenal identitylessness.[328] In terms of defining characteristics, it can be divided into the three "doors to liberation": emptiness, signlessness, and wishlessness[329] (sometimes a fourth door, nonapplication,[330] is added). Among these, it is emptiness in particular that is further classified in various ways in different scriptures.[331]

In conclusion, one may wonder whether the phenomena that are contained in the two realities exist as knowable objects. In terms of the Centrists' own system, when such phenomena are analyzed and not found, obviously this question is pointless. And when Centrists talk about these phenomena without analysis, they do not describe them in such a way as to say that certain ones among them exist as correct knowable objects and certain others do not. However, when speaking about phenomena in adaptation to the common worldly consensus of others, without analysis, Centrists in general say that all phenomena contained in the two realities are suitable to be known as mental objects. As for those Centrists who are beyond worldly experiences, in order to guide disciples and without analysis, they just repeat what is the common worldly consensus of those who say that knowable objects accord with dependent origination and are illusionlike. Again, it is only from the perspective of such people that these Centrists say this. As for the illusionlike "mere seeming" that originates under the influence of unafflicted ignorance (the phenomena included in that aspect of the seeming which is the consensus of noble ones within the context of the presentation of the two realities as just something mutually dependent), these Centrists would say that, conventionally, the phenomena of this mere seeming correctly exist as knowable objects. All other phenomena do not exist as correct knowable objects of unmistakenness. They include all phenomena of seeming reality that originate from and are affected by afflicted ignorance as well as all appearances and ideas of those who are affected by incidental causes for mistakenness, such as visual objects for people with blurred vision or notions about a permanent self.

### *A Critical Analysis of Some Other Tibetan Views on the Two Realities in Centrism*

Other Tibetan masters, such as Tsongkhapa and his followers, give the following definitions of the two realities. The definition of seeming reality is "what is found through conventional valid cognition" or "what is found from the perspective of conventional consciousness without examination." The definition of ultimate reality is "what is found through the valid cognition of a reasoning consciousness" or "what is found from the perspective of the final reasoning consciousness." Through such definitions, they claim to represent the intention of the well-known verse from *The Entrance into Centrism*:

> It is through the perfect and the false seeing of all entities
> That the entities that are thus found bear two natures.
> The object of perfect seeing is true reality,
> And false seeing is the seeming reality.[332]

To analyze the phrase "the perspective of conventional consciousness without examination" in the above definition of seeming reality, Pawo Rinpoche asks whether "examination" refers to a thorough and precise examination of things or just to their superficial examination by distinguishing them through labels and names. If it means thorough examination, then any kind of precise analytical reflection and its findings—such as reflecting on subtle atomic particles and finding that they do not exist—would not belong to seeming reality. If "examination" refers to the second option, then mere labeling consciousnesses and what is labeled by them would not be included in seeming reality. Furthermore, does the term "conventional" here refer to the cognitive mode of a consciousness that conceives of and works with conventions or to the mere fact that something is a convention? In the first case, consciousness during deep sleep and while fainting as well as in the meditative absorption without discrimination[333] would not be included in seeming reality. In the second case, it would follow that ultimate reality too is seeming reality.

As for the phrase "what is found from the perspective of the final reasoning consciousness," it just exposes clinging to the positions of realists. The reason is as follows: All that seems to appear as form and such is nothing but delusive appearance, or various dependently originating assemblages. Our mental grasping takes these fleeting phenomena as existing in just the way they appear. In accordance with such clinging and under the influence of certain causes and conditions, an ensuing subjective consciousness of them appears. In this way, our fundamental error lies precisely in mistaking this process for "having found something." However, a hypothetical something that is found through Centrist reasoning is absolutely impossible. Consequently, something that is not found—as the counterpart of what is found—cannot be set up through Centrist reasoning either.

So the actual clinging to phenomenal identity is precisely this belief of naïve beings that they find an object through a subject—that is, consciousness—that cognizes it. In order to dissolve such grasping, identitylessness is taught by means of the two realities. Pawo Rinpoche concludes that to use phrases such as "what is found from the perspective of consciousness" in the definitions of the two realities even with regard to the actual ultimate, that is, when it is necessary to remove all clinging to something that can be found, just shows one's lack of confidence in emptiness. In particular, a phenomenon "that is found from the perspective of the final reasoning consciousness" is utterly impossible, since the Buddha himself said:

> Abiding in the heart of enlightenment, I do not fathom any phenomenon whatsoever.

The people who use the above definitions might say then, "Granted, it is impossible to find something from the perspective of final reasoning. Nevertheless, we label precisely the fact of not finding anything as 'the ultimate.'" From a certain point of view, it may be fine to formulate the definition of the ultimate as "not finding anything from the perspective of reasoning," but when one wants to explain that there is *nothing* to be found, what is the point of still using the words "what is found" in the above definition of ultimate reality? In actual fact, however, how could "not finding anything" be the ultimate, since "finding something" and "not finding anything" are nothing but reference points, and it is asserted that the ultimate is freedom from reference points? Furthermore, phrases such as "what is found through conventional valid cognition" and "objects of a perception that is aware of outer referents" are just drawn from the conventions of dialectics. In the context of Centrism, they are completely out of place. As *The Entrance into the Two Realities* clearly says:

> Perceptual and inferential cognition—
> These two are accepted by Buddhists.
> Only narrow-minded fools say
> That emptiness is realized by these two.

and

> Perceptual and inferential cognition are useless.
> It is just for the sake of refuting non-Buddhist opponents
> That the learned ones have promoted them.
>
> The learned master Bhavya said
> That the scriptures are clear about
> [The ultimate] being realized neither through
> Conceptual nor nonconceptual consciousnesses.[334]

Some people might still argue, "In Candrakīrti's *Entrance into Centrism,* the line 'the entities that are thus found bear two natures'[335] teaches that something is found from the perspective of reasoning." The verse that contains this line teaches only that there are two modes of apprehending the vast variety of all entities: perfect seeing and false seeing. However, it does not teach that something is found from the perspective of reasoning or consciousness.

In general, there are many positions on ultimate reality, such as asserting it as a nonimplicative negation, saying that it is an implicative negation, or stating it in an affirmative way as something permanent and stable. However, each of these presentations implies a certain purpose. For example, in a certain situation, the ultimate may be explained as a nonimplicative negation in order to remove an opponent's clinging to it being established in a certain way. In another situation, it may be explained as an implicative negation in order to dispel the clinging to it being a nonimplicative negation. At other times, it may also be described as something permanent and stable that is not empty of qualities in order to remedy the clinging that the ultimate is just a nonexistent. Hence, it should be clear that all these explanations do not really contradict each other. However, if they are propounded in any way that involves clinging to them, they are a far cry from the ultimate, for a negation is just an imputation by a mind that clings to nonexistence, and an affirmation is an imputation by a mind that clings to existence. In the light of the actual nature of phenomena, all clinging—no matter to what—is simply mistaken.

"Nonimplicative negation" is just a technical term used in the explanations of philosophical systems. It does not refer to anything other than what ordinary worldly people understand by nonexistence. Therefore, if the ultimate were a nonimplicative negation, in terms of the dichotomous categories of existence and nonexistence, it would mean nonexistence. If it were an implicative negation, or something affirmative in the sense of a permanent and stable ultimate, then in terms of the dichotomous categories of existence and nonexistence, it would mean existence. However, it is obvious that neither the category of existence nor that of nonexistence applies to the ultimate. Nor can the ultimate be both an existent and a nonexistent. Clinging to existence is the view of permanence, and clinging to nonexistence is the view of extinction. Those who look at phenomena as existent or nonexistent do not see the utter peace that is actually to be looked at. The Buddha himself said that to have views in terms of entities or nonentities means not to see the true reality in his teaching. Moreover, the Buddha has refuted existence, nonexistence, and both again and again. When analyzed, afflicted seeming appearances are not established either as existent or as nonexistent. Hence, this is all the more the case for the ultimate. In addition, no matter whether the seeming is believed to exist by its nature or to not exist at all, in neither case could it be relinquished. As for the ultimate, it cannot be either an entity or a nonentity, since both entities and nonentities are conditioned in the sense of being mentally imputed and mutually dependent. Consequently, if the ultimate were an entity or a nonentity, it would follow that it too was conditioned. This is clearly stated in Nāgārjuna's *Fundamental Verses*:

> How could nirvāṇa be
> Both an entity and a nonentity?
> Nirvāṇa is unconditioned.
> Entities and nonentities are conditioned.[336]

The Buddhas—whether they abide in front of us or have passed into nirvāṇa—do not abide in any of the four extremes of existence, nonexistence, both, or neither. Existence and nonexistence are nothing but extremes, and any clinging to either of them is just a mental state of entertaining fancies. However, from the perspective of seeing actual reality, no fancies are at work.

Still, Pawo Rinpoche says, there are some commentaries by later Tibetans (such as Tsongkhapa and his followers) who cannot accept that the seeming is not something that exists by its nature. Thus, they keep saying that "the seeming is not nonexistent, while the ultimate is not existent" and that a particular phenomenon "is not nonexistent on the seeming level, while it is not existent on the ultimate level." Such tortuous statements come down to nothing but the wrong view that the mistaken appearances of the seeming exist by their nature and that the ultimate is nothing whatsoever, just like the horns of a rabbit.

Others are afraid of emptiness as the state in which all discursiveness and reference points are at utter peace and think that something ultimate must definitely be established. Hence, they express their clinging to some established ultimate reality by claiming the opposite of the above: that "the seeming is not existent, while the ultimate is not nonexistent." Pawo Rinpoche compares them to people who insist that medicine has to be mixed with poison before it can be administered. He says that if such ways of explanation were suitable, they would be readily accepted by non-Buddhist schools too. For example, materialistic hedonists could then well say, "Former and later lifetimes are not existent, while the present personal self is not nonexistent." Others would say, "Buddhist liberation is not existent, while it is not the case that liberation is nonexistent for non-Buddhists." All these positions would be just as suitable as saying, "The seeming is not existent, while the ultimate is not nonexistent."

### *The Definite Number of Two Realities and the Purpose of Understanding Them*

As explained earlier, the main purpose for distinguishing the two realities is primarily soteriological. This is also the criterion that determines their number. In this vein, seeming or conventional reality is presented in order to teach the accumulation of merit. What results from this is the accumulation of wisdom, the realization of ultimate reality free from conventions. Thus, since enlightenment depends on the gathering of these two accumulations, the realities are presented as two in number. *The Fundamental Verses* says:

> Those who do not understand
> The division of these two realities
> Do not understand the profound true reality
> Of the Buddha's teaching.
>
> Without reliance on conventions,
> The ultimate cannot be taught.
> Without realization of the ultimate,
> Nirvāṇa will not be attained.[337]

Āryadeva's *Four Hundred Verses on the Yogic Practice of Bodhisattvas* states:

> First, one should explain
> Whatever is pleasant to specific people.
> There is no way that someone who is repelled
> Can be a suitable receptacle for the genuine dharma.

> Just as barbarians cannot understand
> Through any other language [than their own],
> So the world cannot understand
> Except through the worldly.[338]

*The Entrance into Centrism* says:

> Conventional reality is what serves as the means.
> Ultimate reality is what results from the means.[339]

This also indicates the benefit of comprehending and working with the two realities. If one does not understand them and their relationship, the true nature of phenomena will not be realized. On the other hand, if one understands the two realities, there will be no confusion about the unmistaken meaning of the teachings of the Buddha. Through being skilled in understanding and working with the display of seeming reality, one will be fully aware of the aspect of means—that is, all the points that are to be adopted or rejected for the sake of liberation—and will practice them accordingly. Through realizing ultimate reality, one will proceed to the great "nonabiding nirvāṇa" that is both naturally pure and pure of all adventitious stains. *The Treasury of Knowledge* quotes early Tibetan masters:

> Through appearances, one does not reject the path of karma.
> Through their being empty, clinging does not arise.
> The unity of the two realities is the middle path.[340]

Other people give different reasons that the two realities are definitely two in number. They say that this is because there are definitely two kinds of objects (those that withstand analysis and those that do not). Furthermore, they relate the two realities to two types of cognition (mistaken and unmistaken) or two types of persons (those in cyclic existence and those in nirvāṇa). However, something that withstands final Centrist analysis is impossible. That which withstands temporary analysis is called the "worldly and yogic correct seeming," but only in comparison with the false seeming. However, since the two Form Bodies also belong to the correct seeming, it would follow that they are objects of mistaken cognitions. Moreover, according to the intention of such scriptures as the *Aṅgulimālīyasūtra*,[341] the nirvāṇa of the lesser vehicle[342] is not the ultimate. Thus, it would follow that those who achieve it are in a mistaken mental state. In brief, by adducing the above reasons, it is not possible to satisfactorily account for the realities being definitely two in number.

One might wonder, though, whether there is a definite number of two or four realities in Buddhism, since the Buddha also taught that all phenomena are included in the four realities of the noble ones. However, these were taught for specific purposes and thus are of expedient meaning. In terms of the definitive meaning, the first two realities of suffering and its origin do not exist by nature, and the reality of the path is finally left behind like a boat after one has crossed a river. Therefore, they are not truly real as such. Also, the seeming is of a delusive nature and thus not real. Therefore, all phenomena are primordially natural great cessation, or nonabiding nirvāṇa. This is the ultimate and only reality. However, in terms of the final definitive meaning, neither real nor delusive is taught. As *The Sūtra Requested by Brahmāviśeṣacinti*[343] says:

> Look, Brahmā, when I dwell in the heart of enlightenment, I do not know "real" and "delusive."

*The Sūtra of the Meditative Concentration of the Wisdom Seal of the Thus-Gone Ones*[344] declares:

> Some speak here about four realities.
> When residing in the heart of enlightenment,
> Not even a single reality is seen to be established.
> So how could there be four?

Practically speaking, most misconceptions about the Buddhist teachings have their root in the two realities' not being properly understood and distinguished. Moreover, many statements in the scriptures may seem to be contradictory or paradoxical if they are not seen in the proper context of the two realities. As Edward Conze puts it:

> The thousands of lines of the Prajñāpāramitā can be summed up in the following two sentences: 1). One should become a Bodhisattva (or, Buddha-to-be), i.e., one who is content with nothing less than all-knowledge attained through the perfection of wisdom for the sake of all beings. 2). There is no such thing as a Bodhisattva, or as all-knowledge, or as a "being," or as the perfection of wisdom, or as an attainment. To accept these contradictory facts is to be perfect.[345]

It is not just a matter of "accepting contradictory facts," however, but rather of gaining a thorough understanding of each of the two realities, because then there are no contradictions at all. However, if the two perspectives of these realities are mixed, or if one of them is mistakenly used as an argument to negate the other, everything becomes very confusing. Moreover, this opens the way for all kinds of wrong ideas and conduct, such as "Everything is empty, so what does anything matter?" "All phenomena are primordial nirvāṇa, so everything is just pure and fine." "Since there are no positive or negative actions, I can do whatever I like." "Things cannot be empty, because we all experience a common world and the workings of cause and effect." The two realities are taught precisely in order to avoid falling into these extremes of either total nonexistence or solid existence, because both notions lead to wrong actions and ensuing suffering. As a rule, it may be said that as long as we experience afflictive emotions and suffering (as the expressions of a dualistic mental framework), we are right in the middle of seeming reality, no matter what we might wish for or pretend. In this situation, it does not help at all to deny or cover this experiential reality with a misunderstood conceptual overlay of emptiness or ultimate reality. In other words, as long as our experiences are bound to seeming reality, our mental development and our actions have to be carried out within this framework too. No matter how lofty our theories or understanding may be, as long as we experience ourselves as distinct persons and as subject to the causes and results of our actions, there is no way to ignore such causes and results. Moreover, to do so would prevent us from using seeming reality in an appropriate way, which is the only way to actually transcend it. As Bhāvaviveka's *Jewel Lamp of Centrism* says:

> In order to guide beginners,
> A method is taught,
> Comparable to the steps of a staircase,
> That leads to perfect Buddhahood.
>
> Ultimate reality is only to be entered
> Once we have understood seeming reality.[346]

Thus, as a Centrist, while practicing or behaving in the context of seeming reality, it is only for the sake of the result—liberation from suffering—that one adopts the things to be adopted and abandons the things to be abandoned on this level. At this time, one does not simultaneously analyze one's actions for their ultimate reality in order to invalidate them. Moreover, to do so would just take one back to square one, since the same analysis—when applied to the sufferings and difficulties that one still experiences on the seeming level—would equally annul the very problems that got one started on the path. But as we all know, it does not help to analyze our miseries away. In addition, ultimately or when analyzed, not practicing on this nonexistent path is as empty as practicing. If a person is happy this way—not suffering and not doing anything about it—that is surely fine. However, if we still feel uncomfortable—or feel even more uncomfortable—after having analyzed everything to zero, we might want to get back to good old conventional reality and do something about it. Śāntideva says:

Merit in relation to illusionlike Victors
Is just the same as in the case of real entities.
. . .

No matter whether on the seeming or the actual level,
According to the scriptures, this has a result,
Just as worshipping a real Buddha
Will yield a [real] result.

"Without sentient beings, whose is the result?"
This is true, but we still strive on the level of ignorance.
For the sake of completely pacifying suffering,
You should not spurn this ignorance in terms of the result.

Self-centeredness—the cause for suffering—
Increases through the ignorant belief in a self.
You might say, "You cannot put an end to this,"
But it is better to meditate on identitylessness.[347]

*The Heart Sūtra* states:

> There is no attainment and no nonattainment. Therefore, Śāriputra, since bodhisattvas have no attainment, they rely on the perfection of knowledge and abide in it. In their minds, there are no obscurations and no fear. By leaving behind all mistakenness, they reach the final nirvāṇa.

Thus, to apply the unity of the two realities is to pay complete attention to our mental, verbal, and physical actions in the experiential context of seeming reality, while constantly imbuing and lightening—not annihilating—this process with a good dose of awareness of ultimate reality. "To lighten" may well be understood here in two senses: not being so heavy-handed with ourselves and others, as well as bringing more light into this world. The better we understand the two realities and their relationship, the more this will enhance our practice of combining wisdom and skill in means. As Padmasaṃbhava says:

Our view is as high as the sky,
And our conduct is as fine as barley flour.

## The Emptiness of Emptiness

### *Freedom Is the Nature of Not Having a Nature*

By now, we should be familiar with the standard Centrist phrase "all phenomena lack a nature." On the other hand, it is said that "emptiness is the nature of all phenomena." Surely, this is not meant to be left standing as an outright contradiction, nor should it allow for emptiness to be misconceived as a "real core" of things.[348] Therefore, it is obvious that Centrists use the terms "nature" and "entity" in two different ways.[349] To epitomize this distinction, one could say, "The nature of phenomena is that they do not have a nature." Buddhists in general and Centrists in particular reject essentialism, but once this is made clear, they seem to have no problem with employing essentialist terms. Thus, to say that "phenomena lack a nature" refers to their lack of a nature in the sense of some real, identifiable, intrinsic "own-being" that exists independently. Such a nature is the primary target that is refuted in Centrism. On the other hand, when emptiness is called "the nature of all phenomena," this designation is only justified on the mere conventional level in light of the following three aspects: the nature of phenomena is not produced newly through any of these phenomena, it is always unmistaken, and it does not change into something else when it finally is fully realized. Thus, it is only from such a conventional perspective that this "nature" is said to be unfabricated and not dependent on anything else. As *The Fundamental Verses* states:

> It is not reasonable that a nature
> Originates from causes and conditions.
> A nature that originates from causes and conditions
> Would be a nature that is produced.
>
> How could a "produced nature"
> Be suitable as a nature?
> Natures are unfabricated
> And not dependent on anything else.[350]

Taking the five aggregates (such as form) as examples, *The Sūtra of Vimalakīrti's Instructions* states:

> Form itself is empty. Form does not become empty through being destroyed, but it is the nature of form to be empty. . .[351]

As "the emptiness of emptiness" and "the emptiness of the nature" among the twenty emptinesses described below explicitly teach, emptiness is no exception to being empty. In other words, emptiness as "the nature of all phenomena" just indicates the lack of nature of all phenomena, including emptiness itself. Thus, what is called ultimate reality is just the fact that seeming reality does not exist by its nature. In this way, the very lack of any nature is the unmistaken nature of both realities. However, a nature that is established in any way—be it by a nature of its own or the lack thereof—is not suitable as the nature of either of the two realities.

In brief, all phenomena are empty of a nature of their own, which is conventionally called their nature. As Nāgārjuna's *Seventy Stanzas on Emptiness* declares:

> The eye is empty of an identity of its own.
> It is also empty of any other identity.
> [Visible] form is empty in the same way.
> Also the remaining sources are alike.[352]

*The Entrance into Centrism* says:

> Since it is its nature,
> The eye is empty of an eye.
> In the same way ears, nose, tongue,
> Body, and also mind are to be interpreted.
>
> Since it is its nature,
> [Visible] form is empty of [visible] form.
> Sound, smell, taste, tangible objects,
> And also phenomena are just like that.[353]

What is said here is that the eye and all other phenomena lack a nature in the sense that they are empty of a nature of their own and that this is their nature. That the eye is empty of a nature of its own does not mean that the eye is empty of a nature that is something other than the very eye itself, as Candrakīrti's autocommentary explicitly clarifies:

> Here, one speaks about emptiness [as the fact] that the eyes and so on [are empty] of these very eyes and so on. This makes it completely clear that [this is] the emptiness of a nature, whereas it is not an emptiness of one not existing in an other, [such as] "the eye is empty, since it lacks an inner agent" or "it is empty of the nature of apprehender and apprehended."[354]

As usual, however, such formulations of phenomena being empty of themselves or lacking a nature are not presented as the results of reasoned analysis that are established in any way through the Centrists' own system. It is only in order to accord with the kind of analysis that is common consensus for others that emptiness is said to be the nature of all phenomena in the above sense of being unfabricated and not dependent on anything else. Thus, this "nature" that is expressed in such a way does not have any nature itself, nor is it established as any nature. This is the intention that is contained in the above verses. They are formulated by superimposing this notion of "nature" onto the lack of a nature for the sake of counteracting the common notion of an independent, intrinsic, and real nature that ordinary beings entertain. In actual fact, there is no nature of the two realities that is established in any way at all. Therefore, the Buddha said that all phenomena are neither empty nor nonempty, neither existent nor nonexistent, neither unarisen nor not unarisen. It is just with the intention to counteract specific wrong views of different beings that some Centrists have taught that there is a nature of phenomena, while others said that there is no such nature. Some explained that this nature is emptiness and some that it is not emptiness. Others said that entities exist, and still others stated that entities do not exist. However, in the Centrists' own presentation of the two realities, such reference points as to whether a nature of anything exists or not are never put forward on any level.

Some people interpret this term "nature" in a mistaken way, saying, "Since the seeming nature of fire, for example, is dependently originated, it is not suitable as its nature. On the other hand, since its ultimate nature is not dependently originated, it is suitable as its nature." However, neither of the two realities is something static, but they are both presented in a way that is based on the process of dependent origination. The nature of seeming reality is delusive dependent origination, and it is in comparison to this that the nature of ultimate reality—undelusive dependent origination—is justified as its nature. *The Treasury of Knowledge* explains emptiness as signifying the unity of identitylessness and dependent origination. In the word "emptiness," "empty" means nonexistence, and what does not exist is any identity of persons or phenomena; *-ness* stands for dependent origination, or the apparent conditioning of phenomena. One might wonder then, "Does emptiness as the nature of phenomena exist?" From the perspective of the noble ones, since it is beyond speech, thought, and expression, what could be said about it? However, from the perspective of the seeming, that is, the world of dependent origination, one cannot say that it does not exist. If one took the position that emptiness does not exist, it would be pointless for bodhisattvas to train in the path of the six perfections in order to realize this emptiness.

This is explained by using three technical terms: the basis of emptiness, the object of negation, and the basis of negation:

a) The basis of emptiness (all that bears the nature of being empty) is all phenomena.
b) The object of negation (that of which phenomena are empty) is any personal and phenomenal identity.
c) The basis of negation (that which is empty of these objects of negation) is all phenomena.

This formulation implies that the basis of emptiness, the object of negation, and the basis of negation are identical. Thus, the way in which phenomena are empty is that all phenomena are empty of themselves; they are empty of any real nature or identity of their own. For example, let's take the appearance of a table as the basis of emptiness, that is, as that which has the nature of being empty. When analyzed, this seemingly real appearance of a table has no findable real identity as a table (the object of negation). For, "the table" exists only as a conceptual construct through our having lumped together the distinct data of our five sense perceptions into some imaginary whole. Apart from what we perceive through our senses, there is no table. And these sensory data themselves are not a table either, since they are nothing but color, shape, texture, and so on. Moreover, they also lack any real or inherent existence, since they are merely a series of ephemeral, flickering appearances without any identifiable core. In this way, the basis of negation is the mere appearance of a table. In summary, the table is empty of (being) a table.

This is why it is said that all phenomena are empty of themselves: When analyzed through reasonings that analyze for the ultimate, there is no phenomenon that is established as this given phenomenon itself. However, emptiness does not mean that phenomena are not empty when not analyzed and then become empty when analyzed with reasoning. Emptiness is not some kind of spiritual atom bomb that evaporates our world. Nor do we meditate on phenomena that are actually nonempty as being empty, thus producing some conceptually fabricated emptiness. Likewise, it is not the case that phenomena are nonempty as long as the wisdom of the noble ones has not arisen and then become empty once it has arisen. Nor does emptiness refer to something that existed before and then becomes nonexistent later, such as a candle flame that later dies out. Also, emptiness does not mean that phenomena are empty of an object of negation that is something other than these very phenomena, such as a vase being empty of water. Nor does emptiness mean that something is utterly nonexistent, like the horns of a rabbit. All of these notions are mistaken emptinesses, since they are not empty of their own nature and thus represent various kinds of mentally contrived emptiness, emptiness in the sense of extinction, or limited emptiness. Therefore, they are not suitable as the foundation for the path to liberation nor as the remedy for the two obscurations.

In the midst of all the technicalities, reasonings, and concepts related to emptiness, it is important not to lose sight of the essential point of all this. The fundamental concern of Centrists is liberation from cyclic existence and attainment of Buddhahood. Thus, emptiness is not some sophisticated philosophical or metaphysical concept, nor is it just some kind of metalanguage. Rather, its real and only significance is that the realization of what it actually refers to is the single suitable foundation for achieving these goals of liberation and omniscience. Primordially, all phenomena—from the everyday objects of our senses up to the most subtle level of Buddha wisdom—are not established as any kind of reference point, such as existent, nonexistent, real, delusive, empty, or nonempty. It is just this fact that is conventionally labeled as "emptiness," "true reality," "suchness," and so on. In terms of labeling, there is nothing more to it. However, the direct realization of the actuality to which the label "emptiness" points is precisely what serves as the path to liberation and the remedy for the two obscurations. As *The Fundamental Verses* says:

> What is dependent origination
> Is explained as emptiness.
> It is a dependent designation
> And in itself the middle path.[355]

Since both afflictive and cognitive obscurations originate from clinging to really existing things, yogic practitioners put an end to all such clinging once they realize that all phenomena are primordially free from all discursiveness and reference points. To rest in meditative equipoise within the actual native state of all phenomena—all phenomena being empty of a nature of their own—is the remedy for all obscurations. It is the sun that outshines the darkness of mistaken views and the cure that eliminates the poison of reification. Emptiness is the quintessence of the Buddha's teaching and the supreme cause for gaining mastery over the five inexhaustible spheres of adornment of all Blissfully Gone Ones: enlightened body, speech, mind, qualities, and activity.

### *Elaborations on Simplicity*

This simple emptiness has been elaborated into a number of classifications of emptiness in the scriptures. Of course, there are no divisions in emptiness, but such classifications are made from various points of view and for specific purposes.

To begin, emptiness may be classified as twofold:

1) "emptiness of analyzing all aspects" that is limited and arrived at through mental analysis and

2) "emptiness endowed with the supreme of all aspects."

Pawo Rinpoche quotes Mañjuśri:

> The emptiness of analyzing all aspects
> Is without a core, just like a banana tree.
> The emptiness endowed with the supreme of all aspects
> Will never be like that.

When one thoroughly analyzes what phenomena's own nature is, that nature is emptiness. Thus, in having no core, all phenomena are similar to a banana tree.[356] However, the emptiness endowed with the supreme of all aspects lies completely beyond the sphere of analysis. And no matter how it might be analyzed, it is not and does not become like the first emptiness, a bare emptiness of inherent nature. This is because the unity of wisdom and emptiness never changes into anything other than just this unity.

What this latter emptiness is endowed with are all excellent remedial qualities, such as the six perfections. Thus, it is both emptiness and that which makes one attain unsurpassable Buddhahood. In *The Sublime Continuum*,[357] illustrated through the example of a group of painters drawing the king's portrait, this emptiness is explained as the full manifestation of the Dharma Body. *The Sūtra Requested by Crown Jewel* gives an extensive description of this emptiness:

> Donning the armor of great love and grounded in great compassion, [the bodhisattva] practices meditative stability that manifests in the form of the emptiness endowed with the supreme of all aspects. Here, one may wonder, "What is this emptiness endowed with the supreme of all aspects?" It is that in which [the perfections of] generosity, ethics, patience, vigor, meditative stability, knowledge, and means are complete. It is that in which great love, compassion, joy, and equanimity are complete.[358] In it, engagement in the wisdom of reality is complete. The mind of enlightenment—considering sentient beings—is complete. The application of [a bodhisattva's] intention and supreme intention is complete. Generosity, pleasant speech, beneficial activity, and consistency [in words and deeds][359] are complete. Mindfulness and alertness are complete. The four applications of mindfulness, the four correct exertions, the four limbs of miraculous powers, the five faculties, the five powers, the seven branches of enlightenment, and the eightfold path of noble ones[360] are complete in it. Calm abiding and superior insight are complete too. Giving, being tamed, perfect control, and certainty are complete. Shame and embarrassment are

complete. It is not endowed with negative dharmas and is endowed with all positive dharmas. It is continuously blessed with the mode of being of Buddhas. It is perfectly embraced by the blazing mode of being of the dharma. It is endowed with the all-encompassing mode of being of the spiritual community. It is blessed by beholding all sentient beings. It is exquisitely embellished by the full accomplishment of Buddha bodies. It consummately entails melodious Buddha speech. It is endowed with the equality of the meditative concentration of Buddhas. It possesses the miraculous powers and the individual perfect awarenesses of Buddhas. It is perfectly embraced by the force of the ten powers, dwells in the four fearlessnesses, and is in accordance with the eighteen unique qualities of Buddhas; that is, it is not mixed with the vehicles of hearers and solitary realizers. In it, afflictions together with their affiliations with latent tendencies are eliminated. It is not separated from the wisdom of supernatural knowledge. It is the reliance of all sentient beings and entails the four reliances. It includes the equality of mundane and supramundane phenomena. It is without blame, since it fully matures all sentient beings. It is skillful in guiding them and eliminates all sufferings of sentient beings. In it, all afflictions are purified. It has crossed the stream [of cyclic existence], and all clinging is severed in it. It is utter natural peace and not disquieted in the midst of karma and afflictions. It is equanimity through the nature of phenomena. It observes all Buddhadharmas. It is inert by its own specific characteristic. It is courageous in granting blessings. Its intrinsic state is to be disengaged while constantly engaged in the activities of Buddhas. It is composure through utter peacefulness. It is the constant effort to mature sentient beings. This is called "the emptiness endowed with the supreme of all aspects." . . . If it does not exhibit one of these aspects, it is not the emptiness endowed with the supreme of all aspects. At the point when the aspects of all Buddhadharmas are fully complete and visible and when there is no coexistence with any afflicted agitations or discursiveness of focusing on characteristics, this is the emptiness endowed with the supreme of all aspects.[361]

In his *Stages of Meditation*, Kamalaśīla emphasizes the meditative cultivation of this emptiness, since—unlike a bare emptiness—it leads to perfect Buddhahood.[362] Mikyö Dorje agrees that this emptiness is the great perfection of knowledge. Pawo Rinpoche's commentary clearly says that the emptiness that is taught in the *Prajñāpāramitā sūtras* and commented on by Nāgārjuna is this "emptiness endowed with the supreme of all aspects." The reason is that this emptiness completely forsakes all reference points and thus connects one with all the qualities of the five paths, the ten grounds, and the final result of Buddhahood.

There is another twofold classification of emptiness:

1) emptiness associated with stains and
2) emptiness without stains.

As *The Distinction between the Middle and Extremes* says:

> As for afflicted phenomena and purified phenomena,
> [One] is associated with stains and [the other] is without stains.
> Its purity is considered in the same way
> As the element of water, gold, and space are pure.[363]

The second chapter of *The Sūtra of the Arrival in Laṅka* lists seven emptinesses:

> Mahāmati, in brief, emptiness is sevenfold: the emptiness of defining characteristics, the emptiness of the nature of entities, the emptiness of possibility, the emptiness of impossibility, the emptiness of all phenomena being inexpressible, the great emptiness of the ultimate wisdom of noble ones, and the emptiness of one [not existing in] an other. . . . This emptiness of one [not existing in] an other, Mahāmati, is very inferior, and you should abandon it.[364]

Among these, it is only the emptiness of defining characteristics that qualifies as the ultimate emptiness of Centrists.

In terms of the bearers of the true nature of phenomena, the sūtras even speak about sixteen, eighteen, or twenty kinds of emptiness. *The Prajñāpāramitā Sūtra in One Hundred Thousand Lines*[365] and the revised edition of *The Prajñāpāramitā Sūtra in Twenty-five Thousand Lines*[366] list all these twenty emptinesses. Based on this, Āryavimuktisena and Haribhadra have ascertained their total number as twenty. *The Prajñāpāramitā Sūtra in Eight Thousand Lines* and the tantras speak about sixteen emptinesses. Thus, Maitreya's *Distinction between the Middle and Extremes*, Dignāga's *Summary of Prajñāpāramitā*,[367] and other texts list sixteen emptinesses. Needless to say, all these enumerations are merely explained in terms of the seeming in order to remedy certain concepts, wrong views, and clingings of different disciples on various stages of the path.

**The Twenty Emptinesses**

In his *Chariot of the Tagbo Siddhas*, the Eighth Karmapa follows the explanation of Candrakīrti that presents twenty emptinesses.[368] In general, these can be condensed into the two identitylessnesses. Thus, the twenty emptinesses are asserted as the path of the great vehicle, since they teach phenomenal identitylessness as the remedy for cognitive obscurations in detail.

1) *The emptiness of the internal* means that the six sense faculties of eye, ear, nose, tongue, body, and mind are empty of any nature of their own. To lack any nature of their own is their very nature.
2) *The emptiness of the external* indicates the same for the six objects of these six faculties, such as forms and sounds.
3) *The emptiness of the internal and the external* means that both the inner sense faculties and their outer objects are without nature.
4) *The emptiness of emptiness* clarifies that emptiness itself is also empty of a nature of its own. The purpose of explaining this fourth emptiness is to put an end to the clinging that emptiness itself is established as anything in any way. In *The Sūtra Requested by Kāśyapa*, the Buddha warned against holding on to or solidifying emptiness in any way:

> "Kāśyapa, those who conceptualize emptiness by focusing on it as emptiness I explain as those who fall away from this teaching. Kāśyapa, those who have views about the person that are as big as Mount Meru are better off than those who proudly entertain views about emptiness. Why is this? Kāśyapa, as emptiness means to emerge from all views, I declare that those who have views about this very emptiness are incurable. Kāśyapa, it is as follows: For example, if you give a diseased person medicine and this medicine cures the entire disease but stays in the person's stomach and does not come out again, Kāśyapa, what do you think? Will this person be released from disease?" "O Blessed One, this person will not [be released]. If this medicine cures all of the [original] disease but stays in the stomach and does not come out again, the person will develop a very severe stomach disease." The Blessed One said, "Kāśyapa, in the very same way, as emptiness is the only way to emerge from all views, I declare that those who have views about this very emptiness are incurable."

Nāgārjuna's *Praise to the Supramundane* says:

> In order to relinquish all imagination,
> You taught the nectar of emptiness.
> However, those who cling to it
> Are also blamed by you.[369]

The siddha Saraha is also quite outspoken about this in his statement that those who cling to the existence of things are as stupid as cattle, while those who cling to emptiness are even worse.

5) *The emptiness of the great* refers to the lack of an intrinsic nature of the whole universe, which consists of the outer surroundings and the sentient beings that live in them.
6) *The emptiness of the ultimate* refers to nirvāṇa's absence of a nature of its own. Nirvāṇa is considered the ultimate supreme purpose to be achieved by sentient beings. However, the Buddha taught it to be empty too in order to put an end to the wrong notions of nirvāṇa being existent, nonexistent, both, or neither. This emptiness of the ultimate refers to the natural nirvāṇa or the nonabiding nirvāṇa. It does not refer to the nirvāṇas with remainder[370] or without remainder[371] in the vehicles of hearers and solitary realizers.
7) *The emptiness of conditioned phenomena* refers to the emptiness of everything in the three realms of existence that originates from causes and conditions and entails arising, abiding, and ceasing.
8) *The emptiness of unconditioned phenomena* is the lack of an intrinsic nature of everything that is without arising, abiding, and ceasing.
9) *The emptiness of what is beyond extremes* means that the middle way, which is free from the two extremes of permanence and extinction and so on, is itself empty of being beyond all extremes.
10) *The emptiness of that which is without beginning and end* refers to the emptiness of cyclic existence, which is without beginning and end because it is free from coming from somewhere or going somewhere. Its emptiness is that it is empty of being without beginning and end.
11) *The emptiness of what is not rejected* refers to what is to be adopted. In general, flaws are to be rejected, and what has no flaws designates what is to be adopted. The latter are the purified phenomena, that is the two accumulations of merit and wisdom. That these are empty of being something that is not rejected is the emptiness of what is not rejected.
12) As for *the emptiness of the primordial nature*,[372] the very nature of phenomena is that they have no nature. It is nothing but their lack of any nature that is labeled their "nature." This nature is not something that was made by the noble ones or the Buddhas. Rather, the nature of all phenomena is primordially empty emptiness. Thus, phenomena are not made empty through emptiness or anything else; they are just naturally empty. However, this empty nature of phenomena is also not established as any nature whatsoever. In fact, the nature of phenomena itself lacks any nature, and this is what is called "the emptiness of the primordial nature." In terms of the basis of emptiness, as for their meaning, there is no difference between this "emptiness of the primordial nature" and "the emptiness of emptiness." However,

these two are explained separately in order to put an end to two aspects of clinging: clinging to emptiness as being emptiness and clinging to emptiness as being the actual nature of phenomena. The essential point for both these emptinesses is that the Buddha taught emptiness as the remedy for viewing all phenomena as nonempty, solidly existing things. If this remedial emptiness itself were not empty of a nature of its own as well, or if it had the nature of being an identifiable and actually existing nature, which reifying view could be more enormous than that? This is precisely the situation that is referred to as the antidote turning into poison. The Karmapa gives a further analogy for the detrimental effect of clinging to emptiness: If water is all that one has to extinguish a fire and then this water itself turns into a blazing fire, there is no means left to extinguish the fire.

13) *The emptiness of all phenomena* means that each single phenomenon within the entire spectrum of conditioned and unconditioned phenomena is without a nature of its own.
14) *The emptiness of specifically characterized phenomena*[373] refers to the lack of a nature of the entire range of specifically characterized phenomena, starting with form up through omniscience.
15) As for *the emptiness of the unobservable*,[374] what is unobservable are the three times. The past has ceased already, the future has not yet arisen, and the present moment cannot be found when analyzed for a beginning, a middle, or an end. However, to consider what is not observable in this way as having the nature of being unobservable is an error. Thus, the emptiness of the unobservable means that the unobservable three times lack the nature of being unobservable.
16) *The emptiness of the nature of nonentities*[375] means that all phenomena originate from infinite interdependent causes and conditions and thus lack any intrinsic nature of being a real collection that is set up by anything in any way.

After this explanation of sixteen emptinesses in the above-mentioned *Prajñāpāramitā sūtras*, there follows a description of four more emptinesses that summarize them.

17) *The emptiness of entities*[376] is the emptiness of the five aggregates.
18) *The emptiness of nonentities*[377] refers to the emptiness of all unconditioned phenomena, such as space and nirvāṇa.
19) *The emptiness of self-entity*[378] means that there is no nature of the self-entity of all phenomena. It is the nature of phenomena—emptiness—that is explained as their "self-entity," since it was never produced through the seeing of the wisdom of the noble ones. That this empty self-entity too is empty of itself is expressed as "the emptiness of self-entity."

20) As for *the emptiness of other-entity*,[379] Candrakīrti's autocommentary on *The Entrance into Centrism* gives three reasons that emptiness can be called "other-entity." First, conventionally, emptiness is not established as any nature whatsoever. In actual fact, however, emptiness abides all the time as the supreme true reality of all things, whether Buddhas appear or not. In this respect, it is other than the phenomena of the seeming that bear this nature, since they do not exist all the time. Second, since emptiness is what is to be realized by ultimate supreme wisdom, it is other than the things of the seeming that are not what is realized by this wisdom. Third, emptiness is beyond cyclic existence. Thus, it exists "on the other side" of it. The seeming, however, is not beyond cyclic existence.[380] Thus, the highest reality or the suchness that is completely unchanging and has the defining characteristic of emptiness is "the emptiness of other-entity."

In the context of these last two emptinesses, the single emptiness that is the basic nature of all phenomena is expressed in two different ways by using the conventional terms *self-entity* and *other-entity*. However, again, both of these emptinesses are not established as any entities of their own. In order to determine this single emptiness, first, it is taught that the self-entity of this emptiness lies in its being a natural emptiness that is not produced by the noble ones. Consequently, the emptiness of such a self-entity is that it is empty of being this natural, unproduced emptiness. Second, this very same emptiness may also be called other-entity or supreme entity. However, while using such a formulation in order to comply with some systems that are the common consensus of others, it is clearly determined that the very nature of such an other-entity is also nothing but emptiness.

The way in which these twenty emptinesses are related to the different levels of the path are presented in Haribhadra's commentary *Illumination of The Ornament of Clear Realization*.[381] The first three pertain to the phase of engagement through devoted interest.[382] The fourth is related to the level of the supreme dharma.[383] The following seven (5–11) correspond to the seven impure grounds of bodhisattvas, and the next three sets of two (12–17) to the three pure grounds respectively. The last three emptinesses (18–20) pertain to the Buddha ground. They are associated with Buddhahood, because the first is the foundation for relinquishing the afflictive obscurations including their latent tendencies; the second is the foundation for relinquishing the cognitive obscurations including their latent tendencies; while the last has the sense of self-existence.[384] When explained in this way, during the phase of engagement through devoted interest, the corresponding emptinesses are the objects that are realized through the valid cognition of a reasoning consciousness, or the objects that are realized through a consciousness that is approximately concordant with yogic valid perception.[385]

Those emptinesses that relate to the grounds of bodhisattvas explain what is realized through the corresponding levels of yogic valid perception. On the Buddha ground, none of these twenty bearers of emptiness is observable as anything whatsoever by the wisdom of omniscience.

In some scriptures, one finds references to "eighteen emptinesses." However, these are not a different set of emptinesses. With the exception of numbers (17) and (20), they are the same as those in the preceding enumeration.

**The Sixteen Emptinesses**

In general, when one speaks about "the sixteen emptinesses," this can refer to one of two slightly differing sets of sixteen. The first set consists of the sixteen emptinesses as they were described in the enumeration of twenty emptinesses above. The second set is found in Maitreya's *Distinction between the Middle and Extremes* and other texts.[386] The following is a presentation of this second list.

The first four emptinesses are related to seeming reality:

1) *The emptiness of the internal* is the lack of nature of the six sense faculties.
2) *The emptiness of the external* is the lack of nature of the six objects of these faculties.
3) *The emptiness of the internal and the external* is the emptiness of any physical bases of these two, such as the sense organs[387] and outer matter.
4) *The emptiness of the great* refers to the lack of nature of the whole universe, including the inanimate surroundings and all sentient beings who live in them.

The next two emptinesses correspond to ultimate reality:

5) *The emptiness of emptiness* refers to the emptiness of the wisdom that directly sees that the first four emptinesses are empty.[388]
6) *The emptiness of the ultimate* refers to the way in which this wisdom sees emptiness as the perfect actual mode of being of all phenomena. This mode of being is called the ultimate because it is undeceiving. That this ultimate is not established as a nature of its own is "the emptiness of the ultimate."

The bases of emptiness of the next eight emptinesses are taught for particular purposes, because the eight phenomena that are the bearers of these emptinesses are related to the practice of bodhisattvas:

7) *The emptiness of conditioned phenomena* is the emptiness of the conditioned positive phenomena of the path.
8) *The emptiness of unconditioned phenomena* means the emptiness of the uncon-

ditioned positive phenomena of nirvāṇa.

9) *The emptiness of what is beyond extremes* refers to the emptiness of the middle way that bodhisattvas practice in order to benefit limitless sentient beings.
10) *The emptiness of what is without beginning and end* is the emptiness of a bodhisattva's practice of not giving up cyclic existence in order to not abandon sentient beings.
11) *The emptiness of what is not rejected* means the emptiness of rendering all that is positive inexhaustible within the nirvāṇa without remainder through dedications and the perfection of power.
12) *The emptiness of the primordial nature* refers to the emptiness of cultivating the bodhisattva's primordial nature—the naturally abiding disposition[389] that is naturally pure and also empty of adventitious stains—in order to purify it from these stains.
13) *The emptiness of specifically characterized phenomena* means the emptiness of the major and minor marks of a Buddha.
14) *The emptiness of all phenomena* refers to the emptiness of all the qualities of a Buddha, such as the ten powers, the four fearlessnesses, and the eighteen unique qualities.

The first four of these last eight emptinesses refer to what bodhisattvas have in common with hearers and solitary realizers. The last four refer to the uncommon features of practicing the great vehicle.[390] The key for bodhisattvas to engage in the great vehicle in a fully qualified way is the realization of emptiness. How is that? The word "bodhisattva" denotes a being who is courageous enough to generate the mind of enlightenment and strive for Buddhahood for the sake of all sentient beings. Bodhisattvas are said to be courageous, because they are not afraid of three things: the infinite number of sentient beings to be liberated, the infinite time it takes to liberate them, and the great hardships they have to go through in order to help these beings. Considering this overwhelming task, how can bodhisattvas be so brave or—as one would say nowadays—unrealistic? Even with great compassion and a lot of goodwill, as long as they take cyclic existence to be real, there is no way that they could reasonably entertain the hope of ever accomplishing the liberation of infinite beings or lightheartedly take upon themselves all the difficulties that such a project involves. Thus, it is precisely because bodhisattvas are fundamentally "un-realistic"—not taking things as real altogether—that they can bear whatever appears and work with it. On the other hand, if cyclic existence is not realized as being empty, it is impossible not to become weary of both its many sufferings and all the effort it takes to liberate one's fellow beings. Consequently, one will reject cyclic existence and abandon sentient beings.

Through the realization that cyclic existence is just an illusion, a bodhisattva's own experiences and perceptions are completely unaffected by all samsaric defects, just as a lotus has its roots in the muddy ground of a pond but rises above the water as an immaculate flower. However, emotionally, bodhisattvas are not at all unaffected by seeing the states of sentient beings who—unlike themselves—still take this illusion of cyclic existence to be real and thus are under its sway. In a way, this is the same as when we watch the usual bad news on television and are aware that none of it is really happening on our screen. Still, what we see might very well trigger compassion in us for those who are going through the actual experiences that we are seeing. So in itself, what we see there is not our own experience, and—unlike the people whose actual experience it is—we are not under its control. Rather, it is still we who have the remote control and can flip through the channels (unfortunately, this does not mean that we are in full control of that process . . .). Likewise, since bodhisattvas are not under the control of what happens to others in cyclic existence, they have no problem in staying and working within what appears to others as samsaric reality. However, realizing emptiness is not at all a dull, numb, or undifferentiated blank state of mind in which nothing goes on anymore. In fact, in terms of bodhisattvas' own experience, it is said that it is their greatest joy to help other beings who suffer, so they enter cyclic existence with the same delight as when we plunge into the refreshing waters of a cool lake on a hot summer day.

Finally, there are the last two emptinesses that summarize the preceding fourteen:

15) *The emptiness of nonentities* is presented in terms of the two objects of negation—imaginary persons and phenomena—being negated.
16) *The emptiness of the nature of nonentities* is presented from the perspective that the persons and phenomena in terms of the nature of phenomena[391] exist as the remainder after the negation of the above two objects of negation.[392]

Again, these last two emptinesses are not self-sufficient emptinesses that differ in any way from the other fourteen. Rather, they are just further divisions by way of conceptual isolates. The purpose of presenting them separately is to eliminate the two extremes of superimposition and denial with respect to each individual basis of emptiness. Therefore, the last two emptinesses are added for the sake of understanding that the elimination of the extremes of superimposition and denial must cover all fourteen preceding emptinesses. These two extremes mean neither mistakenly superimposing existence onto imaginary persons and phenomena nor categorically denying the persons and phenomena in terms of the nature of phenomena.

When we compare the two above presentations of (A) twenty emptinesses and

(B) sixteen emptinesses, in addition to slightly varying orders of enumeration,[393] there are a number of differences in content and emphasis. Roughly speaking, one could say that (A) presents emptiness more from a general point of view or in terms of it being the object to be realized. On the other hand, (B) often emphasizes the emptiness of the path as the process of realizing emptiness and of the mind that travels on this path, that is, the subjective aspect that cultivates and realizes emptiness. These tendencies show in that certain bases of emptiness are more or less dissimilar in (A) and (B).

In the enumeration of sixteen emptinesses, the emptiness of the internal and the external (B3) does not refer to the sum of internal sense faculties and external objects but specifically to their physical bases. The emptiness of emptiness (B5) does not refer to emptiness in general or to emptiness as the object to be realized; it emphasizes that also the subjective side—the wisdom mind that realizes emptiness—is empty. The same goes for the emptiness of the ultimate (B6), as it refers to the subjective mode of realizing the ultimate, in which the emptiness of "subjective" wisdom and the emptiness of "objective" emptiness are undifferentiable. Emptinesses (B9) through (B12) all highlight certain aspects of the practice of bodhisattvas: The emptiness of what is beyond extremes (B9) does not just refer to the emptiness of the middle way itself but makes it clear that the actual practice of this middle way is empty as well. The emptiness of what is without beginning and end (B10) not only indicates the emptiness of cyclic existence but also shows that the ongoing compassionate activity within this empty cyclic existence by a bodhisattva who has realized its emptiness is empty too. The emptiness of what is not rejected (B11) means that all activities on the path to provide for and to ensure the inexhaustible qualities and activities of a Buddha are empty. As for the emptiness of the primordial nature (B12), the basis of this emptiness is not the empty nature of all animate and inanimate phenomena in general. Rather, it is the practice of uncovering the true nature of sentient beings' mind, or Buddha nature, which is called their "naturally abiding disposition."[394] No doubt also this practice of revealing our Buddha nature is no exception to being empty. The bases of the emptiness of specifically characterized phenomena (B13) are not all such phenomena but only the excellent major and minor characteristics of a Buddha. Finally, the basis of the emptiness of all phenomena (B14) does not refer to the entirety of all phenomena in general but is limited to all the enlightened qualities of Buddhahood.

In conclusion, the Eighth Karmapa says that in reference to the "sixteen emptinesses" in Centrism, their definitive meaning is the interpretation as given by Candrakīrti in the above enumeration of twenty emptinesses. This is because in Centrism all phenomena are empty of a nature of their own.

## The Two Types of Identitylessness

### *Lost Identity*

The contemporary Tibetan master Dzongsar Khyentse Rinpoche said in one of his talks, "Some people are afraid that, in Buddhism, they would lose their ego. That is true, but you can tell them that they don't have to worry, it will come back." This statement is surely good for a laugh, but—as we will soon see—at the same time it profoundly illuminates the basic problem.

On a slightly more serious note, I am afraid a few words on the translation of the Sanskrit term *nairātmya* (Tib. bdag med) as "identitylessness" are unavoidable. Nowadays, in English translations, a persistent, common worldly consensus of rendering this term as "selflessness" or "egolessness" has developed. If one disregards the relatively superficial flaw that the word "selflessness" usually refers to something completely different (an altruistic attitude or behavior) from what *nairātmya* means, the above renderings may be acceptable as common worldly consensus when used in a more casual context. Such translations not only entail a number of major problems when used in a more strict philosophical sense, but are in fact obstacles to a correct and deeper understanding of the meaning of *nairātmya* as one of the most central topics in Centrism.

Originally, the Sanskrit word *ātman* meant "breath."[395] In non-Buddhist Indian philosophy, it came to primarily indicate the ultimate true essence of each individual sentient being—one's "true self," "soul," or "pure spirit." Notwithstanding other varying features, all schools that assert this ātman agree that it is permanent, singular, independent, and really existent. It is what has to be liberated from the illusions of cyclic existence. In Buddhist philosophy, the term is not limited to an eternal individual soul but refers to the general notion of a singular, permanent, and independent entity or identity that really exists by its own nature.

This notion is precisely what Centrists negate. They distinguish two types of the lack of such an ātman: the lack of a personal ātman and the lack of an ātman of all other inner and outer phenomena. For example, Centrists speak of the nonexistence or the lack of an ātman of a table. Now, the English terms "self" and "ego" refer solely to a person's being or individuality; they are never used in relation to inanimate things. Thus—except in modern-day "Buddhist hybrid English"—one would normally never speak of the "self of a table," much less the "ego of a table." Both linguistically and in terms of meaning, it is more appropriate to speak of analytically seeking and not finding any real identity of a table. The same goes for a real identity of a person. This is clearly expressed in Candrakīrti's commentary on Āryadeva's *Four Hundred Verses*:

> "Identity" (*ātman*) refers to a nature (*svabhāva*) of entities that does not

> dependend on anything other. The nonexistence of this is identitylessness (*nairātmya*). Through classifying it in terms of phenomena and persons, it is understood as twofold: "phenomenal identitylessness" and "personal identitylessness." The "person" is what is imputed in dependence on the five aggregates. . . . "Phenomena" are the entities that are called "aggregates," "sources," and "constituents."[396]

Thus, in order to cover this meaning of *nairātmya*, the terms "personal identitylessness" and "phenomenal identitylessness" were chosen.[397] From this explanation, it should also be clear that "identitylessness" in general is an equivalent of emptiness. The lack of a real identity and the lack of a real nature refer to the same basic fact. Hence, what is explicitly described in detail through the various presentations of emptiness above refers mainly to phenomenal identitylessness, while personal identitylessness is implicitly included in these emptinesses.

Specifically, as for "personal identitylessness," there is no clear distinction in ordinary Western thinking between "self," "ego," and "person." In addition, various psychological and philosophical schools use a great many different definitions for each of these terms. Hence, by using expressions such as "the self of a person," "the ego of a person," or "personal self," it is very difficult, if not impossible, to understand the striking difference between the two terms "identity" and "person" as they are used in Buddhist philosophy. As a consequence, the crucial point of precisely identifying the actual target of the Buddhist refutation of a real personal identity is likely to be missed. For, the conventional notion of a person who performs various functions on the seeming level is never questioned. *The Entrance into Centrism* says:

> Although he is free from the views about a real personality,[398]
> The Buddha taught "me" and "mine."
> In the same way, all entities are certainly without nature,
> But he taught the expedient meaning that they "exist."[399]

Thus, in terms of personal identitylessness, the object of negation through Centrist reasoning is the idea that a person really exists in an independent way through his or her own nature. This notion is precisely what the deeply ingrained instinctive impulse of believing in ourselves as single individuals holds on to. That this impulse is largely unconscious just makes it all the more effective and powerful.

According to Centrists, the clinging to a personal identity is in turn based on the even more fundamental grasping for a real identity of phenomena in general. This means that as long as we take things in general to be real, we will always pick out one or more among them and cling to it as something real, taking it either in itself to be our imagined personal identity or as something that supports or reinforces this sense of identity. Thus, the two kinds of identity are very closely interconnected.[400] Nāgārjuna's *Precious Garland* says:

> As long as the clinging to the aggregates exists
> For that long there is also [the clinging to] "me."
> Through this identification with "me,"
> Again, there is karma and thus, again, rebirth.[401]

So how is the term "identity" used here? On the one hand, "personal identity" is a mere imputation on the basis of the five aggregates that lacks any nature. Through beginningless fundamental ignorance and in dependence on the five aggregates, we presume a nature of a person that serves as the particular foundation or continuity for our actions and experiences. In more technical terms, such a person is seen as the underlying basis for karmic actions and their results. This is the imaginary referent object of the clinging to "I" and "me," which is continuously present in all sentient beings who possess basic ignorance. In other words, it is just what we fancy when we think, "This is me." It may also be called "the experiencer," "the individual," and so on.

"Phenomenal identity" refers to the assumed real existence of all phenomena on the basis of which such a personal identity is ascribed or that seem to be under its control (such as one's own body and mind) as well as to all other objects, such as other beings or inanimate forms. In dependence on the material elements and our mind, we cling to a real nature of phenomena such as visible forms and the various consciousnesses experiencing them. We take some phenomena to exist as the objective entities that give rise to others—our subjective consciousnesses—which apprehend them. In brief, to cling to phenomenal identity means to cling to the real existence of all material and mental phenomena that are other than what we regard as our personal identity.

This description of the two types of identity may give rise to a number of questions. We might think that we do not really see ourselves or phenomena as having such hard-and-fast identities. And even if we did, what is wrong with experiencing ourselves as "me" and phenomena as real and different from this "me"? Why did the Buddha teach identitylessness? And why should we try to get rid of some identity that we obviously never had in the first place? In other words, why is it such a big issue in Buddhism to negate the two identities?

When we look a bit closer into our habitual ways of referring to ourselves, such as in ordinary language and thinking, we discover a number of obvious inconsistencies and contradictions that show the underlying fundamental confusion. Sometimes we label and treat some or all aspects of our individual five aggregates as constituting an "I," while at other times we rather regard them as something related to this "I." The funny thing is that usually nobody seems to be aware of this, let alone bothered by it. For example, we tend to say such things as "my legs," thus making—and experiencing—a clear distinction between "me" and these legs that are "mine." We do not think, "I am my legs." We clearly feel that "me" is something more than just legs. Still, we say, "I am walking," though what actually moves are the legs or maybe the whole body. However, we wouldn't say, "My legs walk" or "My body walks." Now, if it is really "me" and not just my legs walking, does that mean that my mind or my feelings walk too? Similarly, we say, "I am sick," "I have a headache," and also "My head aches." So who or what aches here or is sick, the head or me? Usually, we consider our head and ourselves as different, so what harm does it do to "me" if my head aches? And how is this different from anybody else's head aching, which is equally different from "me"? Another typical example is to say both "my mind" and "I think" or "I feel." So, again, is it my mind that thinks and feels, or is it "me"? If the mind were "me" or the self, it would be a contradiction to call it "mine"; this would be as impossible as something being both me and my car. To take yet another instance, what do we really mean when we say, "I wash myself"? Does the "I" wash the "I," does the mind wash the body, or does just one hand wash the other parts of the body? So sometimes we regard our mind as "me" and the body as "mine," and sometimes it is the other way around. We might think of "myself" being located somewhere in the upper body or in the head and then consider the feet as "my feet." Or, we see the head as "mine" and the rest of the body as "me." Usually, the "I" feels to be inside "my skin" and sees this skin as something outer that still belongs to this "I." Occasionally, we even feel "out of our minds" altogether.

No doubt, we can easily come up with a zillion more examples of such highly inconsistent talking and thinking. So how does all this nonsense come about? The main reason for such inconsistencies is that we are constantly shifting the object or basis to which we are referring when we say "I," "me," and "mine." In fact, this very shifting of what we regard as "me" and "mine" points in itself to the fact that there is no such thing as a stable and unchanging "me." As long as we do not question all of this, it seems to be a completely natural and convenient way of dealing with ourselves and our world, and it usually works just fine. However, faced with the simple question "Who am I?," we all have a very hard time coming up with a clear answer or definition of exactly who or what we are. The more we think about this, the more difficult it is to pinpoint something. In fact, it is not at all clear what this "I" or "me" really is, evidently not even to "ourselves." So, if we do not question it, our self seems to be the most obvious and close thing we can imagine. However, as soon as we search for it, other than running into further inconsistencies, there is nothing to be found. It is like trying to catch a rainbow in space.

Of course, one might say, "Well, all of this is just conventional talk, so why make it into a problem?" From one point of view, nothing could be truer, and if we were to leave it as nothing but conventional discourse, also from the Centrist point of view, there would in fact be no problem whatsoever. But the crucial point here is that it is not really this notion of "me" or some personal identity as such that is considered the root of cyclic existence. Rather, the problem lies with our instinctive subjective clinging to such a vague personal identity, which is in turn based on the even more fundamental clinging to phenomenal identity. This basic impulse of experiencing everything from the perspective of "I" and "me" seems to be the most natural thing in the world and usually goes completely unquestioned. For example, we may go to a shopping mall and look at some nice, expensive watches. If the shop owner drops one of these watches and it breaks, we are not really too worried. We might even be relieved and think, "I'm glad it wasn't mine." However, if we receive this very watch as a birthday present and it breaks, our reaction is surely not that detached. Yet it is the same watch and the same thing that happened to it. We might watch a multicar crash on the news and not waste many thoughts on all those wrecked cars (though one would hope we would on the people who drove them). But how do we feel if we detect a small scratch on our own car? Where is this "mine" that seems to make all the difference and causes us suffering? Is "mine" the same as the Swiss watch? Or is "mine" different from it? Is "mine" inside the watch or outside of it? When searched for, it is nowhere to be found. However, according to the Buddha, it is precisely this tendency to experience everything in terms of "me" and "mine" that makes us feel distinct from others, develop attraction and aversion, and act these emotions out, which in turn causes all our well-known miseries. As Dharmakīrti's *Commentary on Valid Cognition* says:

> If there is a self, consciousness about others [arises].
> From the aspects of self and others, clinging and aversion [result].
> Then, through our close connection with these,
> All flaws come forth.[402]

To be sure, there is no problem in just thinking or saying, "I am Kim," "I walk," "This is my car," and so on. As good Buddhists, we might even have tried to go through all these painful Madhyamaka reasonings to disprove a single and unchanging self and understand that there is no such thing. However—and now we come back to Dzongsar Khyentse Rinpoche's words—our actual hang-up is that we constantly keep thinking and acting *as if* we really were independent and single individuals with our own case history or personal file. This shows in our impulses to protect this somebody from what he or she does not like and chase after what he or she feels attracted to. This is how we find ourselves in the middle of the rat race of cyclic existence. The spontaneous, natural ease with which this functions is illuminated by an anecdote about a great siddha who remained in advanced meditative equipoise for many years. During all this time, he stayed in the hut that belonged to him and his wife. When he finally rose from his meditation, the first thing he asked his wife was, "Where is my dinner?" She just answered, "If this is all that came out of your meditative equipoise, you'd better go right back and practice some more."

In general, when asked, most of us would agree that we are not permanent or completely independent. However, when we are directly reminded of our impermanence in ways that we cannot ignore, such as getting gray hairs, falling ill, being in a car accident, or facing death, we usually become very upset. Likewise, if asked, we would surely say that our left big toe is not our personal self, but when it hurts or when we even lose it, we do not at all regard ourselves as separate from this toe. Thus, one very effective meditation on personal identitylessness is to consider how it affects our individual sense of identity to imagine losing, one by one, all our body parts. In addition, we can ask ourselves, at what point in this process of losing our limbs do we still feel like the same person whom we believe we are now, in full possession of all our body parts? Do we change in our existence as John or Mary when we lose one finger, or does that take several limbs? What if just our torso and head were left? And when do we cease to exist as a person altogether? The same contemplation can be applied to losing our relatives, our friends, our possessions, and certain features of our mind, as with senility. Such meditations might sound strange, but in practice they are excellent and powerful tools for learning something about ourselves and our attachments in a personal way that is quite different from mere theoretical speculations about a hypothetical self. At the same time, they also work on our concepts of regarding our body and mind as well as all other phenomena as real and distinct entities, such as seeing the collection of many body parts as a single "body"; taking the diversity of our momentarily changing feelings, thoughts, and perceptions to be one "mind"; or regarding an assemblage of various wooden or metal parts as a "chair" or a "car."

Thus, the fundamental reason that the precise identification of these two kinds of clinging to an identity—personal and phenomenal—is considered so important is again soteriological. Through first uncovering our clinging and then working on it, we become able to finally let go of this sole cause for all our afflictions and sufferings. Thus, the actual object of negation of reasoning in the context of knowledge through study and reflection is nothing more than this instinctive mistaken mode of cognition that takes the two kinds of identity to be really existent. This very same tendency to reify where there is nothing to be reified is also what must be let go of in meditation practice. In more technical terms, it is the object of negation of the path of yogic valid perception that arises from meditation. In this way, such innate clinging is the actual object of negation of both reasoning and the path. *The Entrance into Centrism* says:

First, we cling to our self, saying "me,"
Then we develop attachment to things, saying "this is mine."

Through mentally seeing that afflictions and mistakes without exception
Originate from the views about a real personality
And realizing that the self is the object of these [views],
Yogic practitioners negate a self[403]

When we analyze the object of negation in Centrist reasoning, it should be clear that the two kinds of identity have no possible existence as actual objects that are to be negated. It is impossible for any phenomenon to exist as a permanent, singular, and independent personal identity. Likewise, a phenomenon that is really established through an intrinsic nature of its own is not possible either. However—and this cannot be repeated too often—the actual target in the context of negating the two kinds of identity is the clinging to these identities on the subject side. In other words, the object of negation is a mistaken cognition, a wrong conception that apprehends something nonexistent as existent. Since there is no actual object of negation on the objective side, there never was anything objective to be relinquished. So "negating an identity" is just another expression for the process of letting go of our subjective clinging to imaginary identities. Of course, from the Centrist point of view, this clinging itself is not something real either. However, as long as there is an individual mistaken notion of an object, there is also the notion of a subject. Consequently, with the realization that an object is illusory, the subject that held on to it dissolves naturally. On the other hand, if there were an object of negation that was established as an actual object, we would not be able to relinquish it anyway, no matter how hard we tried. For no one can successfully negate something that actually exists or, for that matter, prove the existence of something that does not actually exist.

Thus, for Buddhist reasoning and meditation to be soteriologically efficient, it is crucial to acknowledge that their actual target lies not at the level of the apprehended objects—the notions of a real personal or phenomenal identity—but at the level of the apprehending subject—the largely unconscious and instinctive clinging to such identities. Again, the reason that this clinging needs to be tackled is that it is the initial spark that triggers the blaze of desire for some phenomena and aversion to others, eventually spreading into the wildfire of samsaric distress. For example, desire arises from thinking that "I" need something or someone. Hatred arises when people harm us and we think that they harmed "me." Pride is based on the thought that "I" am better than others. We experience jealousy or envy because we think that some persons, possessions, qualities, or honors should be "mine." As for unawareness or ignorance, it is often a hazy state of mind. However, it also shows clearly and most fundamentally in this very sense of "me" and "mine," which in turn is the basis for the arising of "my" other mental afflictions. Further, more active expressions of ignorance are the thought "I don't care" and the refusal to look at how things really are.

Fundamentally speaking, it is impossible to tackle our subjective experiences and our clinging right away. We cannot stop this initial impulse of grasping by simply telling ourselves, "Just don't cling." Nor does it help to think, "I will not give rise to mental afflictions anymore." Yet, whenever we think "me" or "mine," this always refers to some object, sometimes our body and sometimes our mind, that we mistakenly call "me" and "mine." That is why Madhyamaka works via the demonstration and realization that there are no such identities to be grasped in the first place. There is nothing that could serve as a reference point for our clinging and our afflictions. It is only upon clearly seeing this that we can finally relax and let go of holding on to what is not there.

This is similar to what happens if someone mistakes a water hose with a zigzag pattern in the garden for a snake. There never was a snake in this hose in the first place, but due to the misconception of a snake this person will panic, start to tremble and sweat, and run away. So there is a whole chain reaction of mistaken—and completely unnecessary—cognitive, emotional, physical, and verbal actions and reactions, but they are all due to the initial mistaken notion of a snake. What would somebody else do to help that person calm down? Surely there is no point in administering tranquilizers, doing psychotherapy against fear of snakes, or merely trying to soothe the person by saying, "Don't be afraid. Just relax, take it easy." And even if these methods were to help for a while, the next time the person would encounter that hose (or a similar one), the same drama would unfold again. So other people would point out that there never was a snake, but just a hose. Still, just having this pointed out by somebody else is also not sufficient. The person who is afraid has to arrive at her own certainty that there was no snake, is no snake, and will be no snake in that hose. Such certainty can only be gained through this person's own examination of the hose, thus seeing that it lacks any characteristics of an actual snake. Only then can the person finally relax and maybe even laugh about the whole event. Thus, it is only through the personal realization that there is no object to justify the fear which is experienced that the experiencer—the perceiving subject—can let go of the clinging to the existence of a snake and be relieved of the ensuing suffering. Another example for this kind of misconception are patients who wander from one doctor's office to another, deeply convinced that they have a tumor, despite the evidence from countless tests and examinations that they do not. As *The Commentary on Valid Cognition* says:

> Without invalidating its object,
> One is not able to relinquish this [clinging to identity].[404]

To return once more to the initial statement that people are afraid to lose their ego in Buddhism, is it really frightening or maybe just boring to realize identitylessness? Do we have to give up all of our individuality or personality and become some lifeless enlightened clone or zombie? As was shown, we don't lose anything, since we realize that we never had any real identity in the first place. Rather, there is only a lot to gain—freedom from suffering—by letting go of what ties us down and makes us suffer: our clinging and grasping to something that does not exist anyway. When we realize that there is nothing to lose and nobody to be harmed, we can relax and let go of the idea that we have something to lose, and let go of our attempts to hold on to or protecting this something. Usually, we are afraid that without our sense of "me" and real things we would not be able to live our lives in an organized way. In fact, however, such grasping to real things and a real "me" makes everything quite heavy, complicated, and clumsy. In addition, it uses up a lot of our energy that could be spent in more joyful and beneficial ways. So when we stop this misguided use of our mental potential, we have free access to the whole scope of its dynamic vitality. The true qualities of the nature of our mind can shine forth unimpededly, and life may become a playful dance of appearances. And we don't have to wait until enlightenment for this to happen, since such effects show during all phases of the path in accordance with how much we loosen our tight grip on "us" and our solid world.

There actually are situations in ordinary life that might give us a glimpse that not apprehending a personal or phenomenal identity is a joyful state of mind. Imagine you start to play a musical instrument. At the beginning, everything is very clumsy; you have to think a lot and coordinate your mind, your fingers, the instrument, and the notes, and they all seem separate and disconnected. But once you are trained to a certain degree, you might become completely absorbed in the process of making music, "losing yourself" in your playing. You don't think of or experience yourself as a particular person or a player; there is not even a sense of "me" anymore. Likewise, you don't perceive the instrument, the fingers, and your mind as different or separate things. Still, or—from the Buddhist point of view—because of that, this does not mean that there is nothing going on or that this situation is depressing. On the contrary, it is an alive and joyful state of mind. Everything flows together in a playful and lighthearted dance. In fact, the less you think about yourself—or anything else, for that matter—the better you can play and the more the instrument, the melody, and the player become one.

Technically speaking, personal identitylessness and phenomenal identitylessness are taught in order to liberate all beings from both afflictive and cognitive obscurations. Personal identitylessness is taught mainly to liberate hearers and solitary realizers. In addition, phenomenal identitylessness is taught for the sake of bodhisattvas attaining omniscience. One might wonder, "If there is no self, does that mean that there is also nothing that is 'mine'?" Obviously, if there is no agent, there is nothing to be acted upon either, just as there is no vase if there is no potter to produce it. Thus, without "me," there is nothing that is "mine" or "other." And if visible forms and so on are not observed, there are also no thoughts of attachment and aversion. Therefore, when the aggregates are seen as being empty of a self and what is related to such a self, nobody sees anything that could be cyclic existence. This is called liberation. *The Precious Garland* says:

> The aggregates that originate from the clinging to "me"
> And the clinging to "me" are actually delusive.
> How could there be a real arising
> Of something whose seed is delusive?
>
> When one sees that the aggregates are thus not real,
> The clinging to "me" will be relinquished.
> Once this clinging to "me" has been relinquished,
> The aggregates will not originate anymore.[405]

Āryadeva's *Four Hundred Verses on the Yogic Practice of Bodhisattvas* says:

> If one sees that objects are without identity,
> The seed of existence ceases.[406]

*The Entrance into Centrism* says:

> Because there is no object without agent,
> Therefore, what is mine does not exist without a self.
> Consequently, yogins regard a self and what is mine as empty
> And thus are completely released.[407]

Therefore, by not grasping at cyclic existence, hearers and solitary realizers pass into nirvāṇa. As for bodhisattvas, they realize both identitylessnesses completely, but because of their great compassion they continue to assume various forms of seeming existence that merely appear for the benefit of others.

### *Phenomenal Identitylessness*

Two types of phenomenal identitylessness may be distinguished:

1) the innate type, which comes from the instinctive clinging to phenomenal identity
2) the imaginary type, which is superimposed through philosophical systems

The innate phenomenal identity refers to the object of the instinctive misconception of ordinary worldly beings who naturally see each phenomenon as having a real and specific nature of its own. "Phenomena" includes everything from form up to omniscience. In other words, this term encompasses the entirety of the five aggregates, the twelve sources, and the eighteen constituents, including all phenomena of nirvāṇa.

The imaginary phenomenal identity is based on the innate clinging to the real existence of phenomena in general. It refers to all kinds of speculative superimpositions of phenomenal entities that are described by different philosophical and scientific schools, such as that it is the nature of phenomena to be permanent or impermanent, that they consist of infinitesimal atomic particles, or, that they are made up of smallest moments of mind.

The Eighth Karmapa says that most expressions of the general clinging to a real nature of all phenomena exist merely from the perspective of ordinary worldly mistakenness and its conventions. This category includes most of the words in the Buddha's teachings, which are employed as mere conventions from the perspectives of particular disciples. The terminology of these teachings is either expressed in terms of common worldly consensus or is suitable to become some sort of common consensus. In addition, there are the conventions of those who cling to some particular identity of phenomena. These are the conceptual imputations by Buddhists and non-Buddhists that are neither common worldly consensus nor something spoken by the Buddha. They do not exist even on the conventional level and include non-Buddhist notions such as all knowable objects being included in six, sixteen, or twenty-five categories;[408] notions common to some Buddhists and non-Buddhists, such as infinitesimal atomic particles; and Buddhist notions, such as hidden but real outer referents, a real, nondual, and self-aware other-dependent nature, a ground consciousness, a permanent and unconditioned Buddha nature that is adorned with all the major and minor marks, or an imaginary personal self that is established through conventional valid cognition.

Of course, most people will object here that the Buddha indeed spoke about a ground consciousness and the other Buddhist notions above. Karmapa Mikyö Dorje's answer is that, in general, when the Buddha spoke on the level of no analysis, conventionally, one can distinguish between an expedient meaning and a definitive meaning in his words.[409] On this conventional level, such terms as "ground consciousness" are of expedient meaning that entails a certain intention and is meant to guide disciples toward liberation. Still, some Buddhists might cling to these expressions as presenting something real, since they were spoken by the Buddha. However, the Buddha's intention was to communicate something on the conventional level, and it is precisely on this conventional level that such terms do not carry any definitive meaning. The main reason for this is that they do not even represent common worldly consensus but just imputations arrived at through philosophical speculation. For example, the notion of a ground consciousness was mainly introduced to explain how karmic actions are stored and ripen into their results, even over many lifetimes. Centrists question the necessity of such a storehouse consciousness as the basis for karma, but not the mere dependently originating operation of karmic cause and effect on the seeming level. As such, this operation definitely is a part of common worldly consensus. Likewise, it is said that self-awareness is necessary for having a memory. Again, the mere fact of remembering is common worldly consensus and thus not disputed in Centrism, but it is denied that there is some further really existent basis for memory, be it self-awareness or anything else.

On the other hand, everything that the Buddha said on the level of analysis—all the presentations within the setting of the two realities—is solely of definitive meaning. Nothing of what he taught on the level of analysis is of expedient meaning. In brief, both on the level of the seeming and the ultimate reality, any hypothetical, real nature of any phenomenon from form up through omniscience in general as well as all superimpositions of such a nature are natural emptiness. This is the supreme essential pith of the Centrist teachings.

In the general context of explaining the view, among the two types of identitylessness, phenomenal identitylessness is usually ascertained first for the following reasons:[410]

First, the coarse form of phenomenal identitylessness is the negation of real existence (its object of negation). Certain degrees of understanding coarse phenomenal identitylessness are common to both Buddhists and non-Buddhists. Thus, in general, it is easier for everybody to start with phenomenal identitylessness than personal identitylessness, which is extraneous to non-Buddhist systems.

Second, after one has determined that all phenomena are empty of a nature of their own, it is implicitly established that a so-called personal identity that we impute through innate ignorance onto our five aggregates is also empty of a nature of its own. For it is realized that all possible bases for the mistaken view of a personal identity are without nature.

In this way, the realization of phenomenal identitylessness relinquishes the two obscurations. Therefore, phenomenal identitylessness is said to be the primary one among the two types of identitylessness.

### *Personal Identitylessness*

Personal identitylessness is the unique, distinctive feature of the followers of Buddhist philosophical systems. Obviously, there are also many non-Buddhists who possess various degrees of realizing coarse phenomenal identitylessness as well as those whose beliefs entail following a course of positive ethical conduct. Therefore, the actual difference between non-Buddhist and Buddhist views lies in the acceptance versus the denial of a real identity of the person.

As with phenomenal identity, there are two types of a hypothetical personal identity:

1) the subtle, innate personal identity, which is the object of the innate clinging to it
2) the coarse, imaginary personal identity, which is imputed through philosophical systems

The so-called innate personal identity or self refers to the object of "the innate views about a real personality." Here, "a real personality" refers to a really existing self that is somehow related to the five aggregates, which are in themselves momentarily impermanent and collections of many parts. "The views about it" may simply be classified as two: the clinging to "me" and to "mine." Usually, however, they are explained as twenty in number. These consist of four different possible ways of relating each of the five aggregates to a personal self. To take the aggregate of form[411] as an example, these four are as follows:

a) the view that form is the self
b) the view that the self by nature possesses form
c) the view that the self by nature exists in form
d) the view that form by nature exists in the self

The same applies to the remaining four aggregates, thus resulting in a total of twenty such misconceptions. These misconceptions are called views, but in the context of the innate clinging to a personal identity, they are to be understood more as the various natural expressions of our instinctive, gut-level impulse of experiencing ourselves as distinct beings. This originates from the beginningless habituation of taking the five aggregates as reference points for thinking "I," "me," and "mine." This habituation naturally exists in all sentient beings, and in a sense one could call it a kind of survival instinct, since it leads to our efforts of sustaining what we see as "me" and protecting it from harm. Thus, neither this clinging nor its object—"I" or "me"—depends on any imputation through philosophical or other belief systems. When not analyzed, the personal identity or "self" that is the object of the innate views about a real personality can be said to nominally exist on the mere conventional level, because the clinging to "I" and "mine" is experientially present in all sentient beings and shows through their verbal expressions and behaviors.

The so-called "imaginary personal identity or self is based on the innate clinging to a personal identity, but it is not naturally present in all beings. Rather, it is what is newly imputed in various ways through studying, reflecting on, or meditating on the conceptual superimpositions in different views or philosophical systems. This may be seen as a real self, an individual true identity or the core of the person, such as a permanent, self-sufficient, and single ātman or the various theories about an "ego" in Western psychology. The clinging to such imaginary personal identities is called "the imaginary views about a real personality." The objects of these views are nothing but labels by certain people and schools. They are not common worldly consensus. Therefore, they do not exist either as conventions that appear in common for everybody or as parts of seeming reality. Karmapa Mikyö Dorje lists three general types of an imaginary personal identity:

a) imputations of a personal identity that is either something other than or the same as the five aggregates, such as an eternal, single, and autonomous self as advocated by most non-Buddhist Indian schools, or the position of some of the Highly Venerated Ones[412] who say that the aggregates or the mind itself are the self
b) the imputation that the self is neither the same as nor different from the aggregates, as it is upheld by the followers of Vātsīputra[413]
c) Tsongkhapa's assertion of a personal self that is established through conventional valid cognition and serves as the support for the continuity of karmic actions and their results, that is, the personal self that is imputed onto the aggregates and not mingled with the personal self that is understood as the object of negation of reasoning.

When expressed on the conventional level, the assumed, innate personal identity that is the object of our innate clinging is just a label applied in dependence on the five aggregates, such as saying, "I am Ben." This is not different from calling a collection of different parts a "car." Centrism does not at all negate that this plain convention exists on the seeming level without analysis. On the level of analysis, however, what Centrism does negate on the level of both seeming and ultimate reality is that there is something really existing by its own nature to which this label "I" refers. The reasons for this object of our innate clinging to a personal identity being negated are as follows: All afflictions and problems originate on the basis of the views about a real personality, which constitute the subjective mental states of clinging to an innate personal identity. In addition, the wisdom in the meditative equipoise of noble ones does not see any such innate identity even on the conventional level.

On the other hand, any "imaginary personal identity" is categorically negated on both the level of no analysis and the level with analysis, as well as on both levels of reality. For, let alone ultimate reality, such an imaginary personal identity does not even fall under seeming reality, since it does not accord with any of the common conventions of either worldly people or noble ones. As for the impact of the imaginary views about a personal identity (which take imaginary personal identities as their objects), in addition to being mistaken in themselves, they intensify and solidify the innate views about a personal identity as well. Furthermore, if one clings to any kind of imaginary personal identity or self, one will not travel the path to liberation and omniscience through the middle way that relinquishes the two extremes.

When considering the many imputations and technicalities in the views that are refuted in Centrist texts, one might come up with the following objection: "As was said, the fundamental cause of cyclic existence is the innate clinging to a personal identity or self. However, Centrist texts do not state any reasonings to negate the self that is the object of this innate clinging. Is it not unreasonable to exclusively reason against all kinds of imaginary types of self, when the actual cause of samsaric suffering is the innate clinging to a self?" There is no problem here, since the object of the innate clinging to a personal identity—whether this is considered to be a self, a real personality, an individual, or a sentient being—is not the object of negation as long as it is just accepted as a mere convention on the level of no analysis, such as saying, "I walk" or "I meditate." Such a mere conventional label "I" as it is used in our everyday transactions is not negated in Centrism, because—just as with all other conventions—it is neither possible nor necessary to negate it. All conventions are mere agreements to put certain tags or symbols on certain appearances, so what is there to negate? In other words, there is no reason for not calling a house a house. This name is as good as any other name, such as *maison* in French or *casa* in Italian, but since English-speaking people have agreed on *house*, there is no reason for them not to communicate with this label. Otherwise, one would have to negate all naming altogether. Thus, there is no need to negate such conventional labels as "I" and "house," since—as bare labels—they do no harm and in fact assist us in accomplishing our worldly transactions.

On the other hand, in the context of negation through analysis, the reasonings that negate the first three types of an imaginary personal identity also function as reasonings to negate any innate personal identity. For, any notion of an innate self does not lie beyond the three ways of analysis through reasoning that cover these three types of imaginary self. Moreover, these reasonings negate the entirety of all objects onto which both the innate and imaginary views about a real personality can possibly grasp. Therefore, it is not the case that Centrist texts fail to negate the innate type of a personal identity.

In general, if one does not realize that all kinds of personal identity are empty of a nature of their own, one is not able to realize phenomenal identitylessness in an exhaustive way. In other words, if personal identitylessness is not fully realized, there is no complete realization of phenomenal identitylessness either.

### *Are the Two Identitylessnesses One or Different?*

In general, all phenomena lack both a personal and a phenomenal identity. More specifically, the question of the existence of a personal identity primarily applies to such phenomena as our body and mind, as it is pretty obvious for most people that such inanimate things as tables and houses do not have a personal self. Thus, in Centrism, inanimate things are addressed primarily in terms of their lack of real existence, or phenomenal identitylessness. As was said earlier, holding on to a personal identity with respect to body and mind is based on regarding body and mind as really existent. In the same way, other phenomena may also serve as additional reference points for sustaining our clinging to a personal self that per se primarily focuses on our psychophysical continuum. Therefore, both types of identitylessness apply to all phenomena. They just differ in their specific objects of negation. Since the object of negation in the case of personal identitylessness is an "I" or "self," this identitylessness is formulated as the inverse of its particular object of negation, that is, "personal identity." In terms of phenomenal identitylessness, what is to be negated is "real existence," or a real "phenomenal identity". Consequently, this identitylessness is also presented from the perspective of reversing its specific object of negation. In this way, both identitylessnesses are conceptual specifications that are the inverses of their respective objects of negation.

Thus, technically speaking and on the mere conventional level, the two identitylessnesses can be said to be one in nature and different isolates. The reasons for this are as follows: Since all phenomena are equally without identity, they cannot be differentiated in the slightest through their entities. Consequently, any kind of assumed personal identity is just a specific instance among hypothetical identities of phenomena in general. For example, a phenomenon such as a book may serve as a basis for attributing certain features to it, yet there is nothing in it that can be apprehended as a really existing thing. However, if the appearance of this book is identified as such a basis for attribution in the context of mere temporary designation, the "personal identitylessness" of this book may be understood as its lack of an identity of its own. The book's phenomenal identitylessness means that there is no book that is really established. These two facts—that an own identity of the book is not established and that the book is not established as something that really exists—are undifferentiable in nature. They can only be separated in a conceptual way by referring to different objects of negation.

### *The Purpose of Teaching Two Identitylessnesses*

Here, one may wonder, "If the two identitylessnesses are undifferentiable in nature, why is it necessary to distinguish between them? Moreover, if personal identitylessness is an instance of phenomenal identitylessness, it should be sufficient to teach only phenomenal identitylessness. Also, if the purpose to be accomplished—liberation and omniscience through the elimination of the two obscurations—is already fulfilled through one's realizing the teaching on phenomenal identitylessness, it seems pointless to speak as well about personal identitylessness."

The reasons for explaining both identitylessnesses are as follows: The Buddha taught personal identitylessness primarily in order to take care of those with the disposition of the lesser vehicle. Thus, this identitylessness serves to gradually introduce those of lesser capacities to the teachings. Furthermore, it is the stepping-stone for the liberation of those who have the dispositions of hearers and solitary realizers. There is a definite necessity to teach personal identitylessness to those with these dispositions, because release from cyclic existence is not possible if this identitylessness is not taught and cultivated accordingly. However, hearers and solitary realizers are not suitable vessels for the extensive teachings on the identitylessness of all phenomena in the continua of infinite sentient beings. For their goal of personal liberation from cyclic existence, it is sufficient to explicitly teach them only personal identitylessness (which is, however, based on and implicit in phenomenal identitylessness). Thus, even if phenomenal identitylessness were explicitly and fully taught to them, for the time being, they would neither need it nor benefit from it. Therefore, they are taught only personal identitylessness, they meditate on it, and they realize it completely. On the other hand, phenomenal identitylessness is taught extensively in order to take care of bodhisattvas as those who have the disposition of the great vehicle. Since it is the goal of bodhisattvas to attain omniscience and work for the welfare of all other beings, it is for this purpose that they are mainly taught phenomenal identitylessness. As Candrakīrti's *Entrance into Centrism* says:

> In order to liberate beings, this identitylessness
> Was taught in two aspects, classified in terms of phenomena and persons.[414]

## From Knowledge to Wisdom

### *The Perfection of Knowledge*

To conclude the discussion of Madhyamaka ground, let us take a closer look at what it is that knows or realizes all these things like "the two realities," "emptiness," "the two identitylessnesses," and "the nature of the mind." As mentioned in the introduction, it is the perfection of knowledge—prajñāpāramitā—that is the primary subject or mental factor that actively develops and experiences all the levels of insight into the nature of all phenomena. As for the scope of the term *prajñā*—knowledge or understanding—in Buddhism, this term does not refer to some kind of passive knowledge or to merely knowing some facts. Rather, it stands for the vast range of actively knowing and investigating the appearances and the true nature of all phenomena from form up to omniscience. It means intelligence in its original sense of being able to know or cognize,[415] which entails the capacity to clearly discriminate. Thus, the definition of "knowledge" in Buddhism is "that which fully and exhaustively discriminates the general and specific characteristics of phenomena."

In other words, prajñā is the basic inquisitiveness and curiosity of our mind, which is very precise and playful at the same time. Usually it is symbolized by a double-bladed, flaming sword. This sword is extremely sharp, and such a thing obviously should be handled with great care. It even may seem somewhat threatening. Prajñā is indeed threatening to our ego and to our cherished belief systems, since it undermines our very notion of reality and the reference points upon which we build our world. Thus, it is what questions who we are and what we perceive. Since this sword cuts both ways, it not only serves to slice up our very solid-looking objective reality, but it also cuts through the subjective experiencer of such a reality. In this way, it is also that which makes us see through our own ego trips and self-inflation. It takes some effort to continuously fool ourselves about ourselves. Prajñā means being found out by ourselves, which first of all requires taking an honest look at the games we play. If we keep inflating ourselves, prajñā is what punctures the balloon of ego and brings us back to where we are.

All of this is especially important on the Buddhist path, since prajñā cuts not only through delusion but also through any tricky attempt by our ego to take credit for doing this. Our ego has no scruples about swallowing spirituality in general or Buddhism in particular and incorporating it into its territory to just serve as a further embellishment of King Me. No, we are not just an ordinary person; now we have become a spiritual person, studying difficult philosophical texts and doing profound meditation practices. Thus, as we proceed along the path, prajñā seems to become increasingly important and must be refined more and more in order to spot and immediately pierce the colorful bubbles of personalized spiritual attainments. This quality of prajñā is symbolized by the flames on the sword: They illuminate our dark corners, put us right under the spotlight, and burn all the seeds of fancy and ignorance. There is a sense of having no escape. We cannot hide from ourselves or pretend to be unaware of what is going on in our mind. Prajñā lights up the entire space of our mind, so where could our mind hide itself? In this way, prajñā is also the direct antidote to the more active tendencies of our ignorance, our not wanting to look too closely at ourselves and our lives.

Sometimes, we think that knowledge means having all the right answers, but prajñā is more like asking all the right questions. Often the question *is* the answer, or much better than any answer. Trying to get all the right answers down may just create more reference points in our mind and thus more rigidity and problems. Also, often one answer produces ten new questions. To let prajñā unfold in a natural way means to give our basic inquisitiveness more space to take a walk and look around on its own with its astute and unbiased freshness. We should not restrict it to merely rearranging or expanding our cocoon of dualistic categories. Iconographically, prajñā is mainly represented by the female deity Prajñāpāramitā and the male deity Mañjuśrī. Prajñāpāramitā has four arms, with her first left hand holding a text, her first right hand raising a flaming sword, and the remaining two being in the gesture of meditation. Together, these represent the three types of prajñā: knowledge through study, cutting through and illuminating delusion, and direct realization of the true nature of all phenomena. These are also called the prajñās through study, reflection, and meditation. Mañjuśrī also holds a wisdom sword in his right hand and usually a lotus flower with a text on it in his left hand. The book stands for knowledge that comes from letters and instructions, while the lotus symbolizes the natural unfolding of our inner seed of prajñā. Instead of the flower and the book, sometimes Mañjuśrī is depicted holding a vase containing the nectar of prajñā. Here the sword indicates the active aspect and the sharpness of prajñā, while the nectar symbolizes its quality of intuitive insight into true reality.

Prajñā may show in knowing and distinguishing ordinary things in the world or in realizing the true nature of the mind by gradually progessing on the Buddhist path. Accordingly, its most basic classification is into mundane knowledge and supramundane knowledge.

Mundane knowledge in general refers to all empirical, scientific, and artistic knowledge that is not specifically related to the Buddhist "science of mind," that is, everything that we may learn in our lives, whether at home, at school, in professional training, or at universities, such as the humanities, the natural sciences, or arts and crafts. Traditionally, it refers to the "four major and five minor common sciences" of Indo-Tibetan culture.[416]

Supramundane knowledge stands for all knowledge, insights, and spiritual realizations in the context of Buddhism as the fifth major science, which is the uncommon inner science of the mind. For the main objective of these teachings is to go beyond the world of cyclic existence. Such knowledge may again be classified as a) lesser supramundane knowledge and b) great supramundane knowledge.

Lesser supramundane knowledge encompasses the knowledge that arises from study, reflection, and meditation in the vehicles of hearers and solitary realizers, such as realizing the four realities of the noble ones and personal identitylessness.

Great supramundane knowledge results from study, reflection, and meditation within the great vehicle of bodhisattvas, such as realizing that all phenomena are unarisen and empty of an inherent nature of their own. As *The Prajñāpāramitā Sūtra in Seven Hundred Lines*[417] says:

> Knowledge is that which realizes that all phenomena are unarisen.

Atīśa's *Lamp for the Path to Enlightenment* states:

> Knowledge is comprehensively explained
> As that which realizes that aggregates,
> Constituents, and sources are unborn
> And empty of a nature of their own.[418]

Thus, among all these types of knowledge, the Centrist teachings primarily deal with the great supramundane knowledge. This knowledge is developed during the three phases of studying, reflecting, and meditating on the profound and vast topics of the great vehicle, so the three types of knowledge that are gained through study, reflection, and meditation are distinguished. Among these three, the first two can only be conceptual in nature, while the latter may be either conceptual or nonconceptual. During the first two of the five paths of the great vehicle—the path of accumulation and the path of junction—the knowledge through meditation is still conceptual, though its conceptuality becomes increasingly refined and subtle. During the meditative equipoises of the paths of seeing and meditation, this knowledge is exclusively nonconceptual, since it directly realizes the nature of all phenomena without any mental reference points. During the phases of subsequent attainment on these paths, however, there are still traces of conceptuality in bodhisattvas. As for the omniscient knowledge of a Buddha on the path of no more learning, it is always nonconceptual and free from reference points, since it is the constant and panoramic awareness of the nature of all phenomena and does not involve any shift between meditative equipoise and subsequent attainment. This knowledge of a Buddha and the knowledge of bodhisattvas during their meditative equipoises are what is called wisdom or the perfection of knowledge in the strict sense. In general, in the *Prajñāpāramitā sūtras,* there are three main ways in which the term "perfection of knowledge" is used. Dignāga's *Summary of Prajñāpāramitā* says:

> The perfection of knowledge is nondual wisdom,
> Which is the Thus-Gone One.
> [Its] texts and the path [bear] its name,
> Since they are associated with this actuality to be accomplished.[419]

The Eighth Karmapa's commentary on *The Ornament of Clear Realization* elaborates:

(1) The definition of the *perfection of knowledge*: Suchness that is never something other and bears the name "wisdom which lacks the duality of apprehender and apprehended." This is [also called] the *natural perfection of knowledge*, which is classified as two:
(a) When suchness is obscured by various formational elements, it is the basic element, the Heart of the Blissfully Gone Ones. [This is called the *causal perfection of knowledge*.]
(b) When this fundamental state itself is free from entanglement—the impregnations of negativity—it is the result, the Dharma Body. [This is called the *resultant perfection of knowledge*.]

(2) The definition of the *scriptural perfection of knowledge*: [All expressions of] the mind that appear as assemblies of names, words, and letters and are suitable to be observed by the disciples' consciousnesses which entail dualistic appearances.

(3) The definition of the *perfection of knowledge of the path*: The perfection of knowledge that arises as the nature of nonconceptual wisdom when settling in meditative equipoise.[420]

### *Wisdom*

As these quotes and Centrist texts in general show, there is a very close connection between knowledge (*prajñā*) and wisdom (*jñāna*). Often, these terms are simply used as synonyms, or it is said that wisdom is nothing but the culmination or perfection of knowledge, prajñāpāramitā. In general, however, knowledge stands more for the analytical and discriminating aspect of superior insight and realization (both conceptual and nonconceptual), while wisdom mainly emphasizes the nonconceptual, immediate, and panoramic aspects of realization. When talking specifically about the wisdom in the meditative equipoise of bodhisattvas and the wisdom of Buddhas, the sūtras and the Centrist texts often use the term "nonconceptual wisdom," which indicates the wisdom that is the direct yogic perception of the nature of phenomena and thus is free from all mental reference points and conceptual projections. One also finds the expression "nondual wisdom," which emphasizes the complete lack of any duality of a perceiving subject (wisdom) that is different from its perceived object (ultimate reality). As noted before, "personally experienced wisdom" means that emptiness or the nature of the mind can be realized only within the individual meditative equipoise of yogic practitioners through the practitioner's own wisdom that constitutes this meditative equipoise, and not through anything else. Thus, here, "personal experience" does not refer to the usual kind of self-awareness in ordinary beings, such as one's own mind experiencing one's own happiness or suffering. Rather, it is the most sublime expression of the principle that mind is able to be aware of itself without the duality of subject and object. This means that the nondual, nonconceptual wisdom in meditative equipoise is aware of its own nature, which is nothing but the lack of any nature. Therefore, it is also called "the awareness of the lack of nature." Candrakīrti says in his *Lucid Words*:

> The ultimate is not known due to something other. It is peace. It is what the noble ones are aware of as that which is to be personally experienced [by them]. . . . This is not consciousness.[421]

> Once stainless nondual wisdom has been manifested . . . through the power of personal realization . . . , one will be released.[422]

His autocommentary on *The Entrance into Centrism* states:

> The ultimate of the Buddhas . . . is ultimate reality by virtue of its very undeceptiveness. Still, all of them have to personally experience it on their own.[423]

The ultimate reality of all phenomena is that they are primordially empty, without nature, and identityless. So ultimately, all phenomena are completely pure and at peace. However, this mere fact does not help anybody who suffers because of not realizing it. For example, in its nature, the gold in gold ore is always completely pure and unaffected by all the dross around it. However, this pure nature of gold does not become manifest and useful for people as long as the elements that cover it are not removed through processing the ore. Likewise, the true nature of the mind of all sentient beings is primordially pure and at peace, but since they take phenomena to be real, they suffer. Consequently, they have to go through the gradual process of realizing and familiarizing themselves with ultimate reality in order to finally experience its benefit of releasing them from suffering. In this way, all the many teachings and methods that the Buddha taught are meant for those who do not realize their true nature. As *The Sūtra of the Ornament of Wisdom Light That Engages the Object of All Buddhas*[424] says:

> The explanations about the connections between causes and conditions
> And the teachings on gradual engagement
> Were spoken as means for the ignorant.
> What gradual training could there be
> In this spontaneously present dharma?

*The Sūtra Requested by Sky Treasure*[425] states:

> As long as we have not fused with the ocean of the expanse of dharmas, there surely are different grounds and paths, but once we have fused with this ocean of the expanse of dharmas, there are not in the slightest any grounds and paths to be traveled.

When one thinks of Centrist reasoning, one might wonder how a conceptual reasoning consciousness could ever give rise to nonconceptual wisdom, since these two types of mind seem so contrary. The classic analogy for this is that if one rubs two sticks against each other, heat is produced that eventually results in fire. The fire burns the two sticks and then dies itself. In the same way, all the way up to the last moment of the path of junction, in our reflection and meditation, we rub the two sticks of the factors to be relinquished and the remedies against each other. This increasingly subtle conceptual activity produces the heat that is an early sign of the actual fire of nonconceptual wisdom on the path of seeing, when the nature of phenomena is directly seen for the first time. When this luminous wisdom blazes forth, both the factors to be relinquished and their remedies melt away. All dullness and all agitation are also outshone. However, once all conceptual firewood is burned, the fire of wisdom does not literally die. Rather, the analogy points out that wisdom is not established as anything separate from the open and luminous nature of the mind and just naturally settles within this nature. As Atīśa says in his *Centrist Pith Instructions*:

> For example, if you rub two sticks [against each other], fire comes forth. Through this condition, the two sticks are burned and become nonexistent. Thereafter, the fire that has burned them also subsides by itself. Likewise, once all specifically characterized and generally characterized phenomena are established as nonexistent [through knowledge], this knowledge itself is without appearance, luminous, and not established as any nature whatsoever. Thus, all flaws, such as dullness and agitation, are eliminated. In this interval, consciousness is without any thought, does not apprehend anything, and has left behind all mindfulness and mental engagement. For as long as neither characteristics nor the enemies and robbers of thoughts arise, consciousness should rest in such a [state].[426]

Thus, although the sticks and the fire are different, when rubbed against each other, the sticks have the capacity to give rise to the fire. Likewise, both our wrong ideas and their remedies appear to be different from nonconceptual wisdom, but when we work on our mistaken notions through Centrist reasoning, there is definitely the chance that this will make wisdom shine forth. Another way to put this is that conceptual thinking—by overheating, so to speak, in the process of reasoned analysis—is potentially self-dissolving. Thus, it has its ordinary quality of being discursive and referential, but it also has a liberating quality of acute sharpness. In a way, it is a matter of how we direct and use its energy. For example, a soft, diffuse light does not illuminate very much, and its glare might even blind us and prevent us from seeing things clearly. However, if this light is concentrated into a laser beam, it is very sharp and penetrating, and we can use it for a lot of purposes, such as cutting hard materials, running sophisticated technical equipment, and heating up things.

When we look at this conceptual reasoning process and how it might turn into the nonconceptual wisdom that realizes its own nature, in terms of the basic experience of our mind, there is neither a gradual process of transformation nor a sudden transmutation of conceptual thinking into direct experience. To progressively negate all our mistaken reference points—to see clearly that none of them exists—is in effect only to work on the direct experience of our mind all the time. For example, we might mistakenly see three dangerous appearances in the twilight, such as a snake, a bear, and a robber. To us, it seems as if we then experience three different kinds of fear and must find out how to get away from these threats. But if we take a closer look, we might first see that the snake is actually a long tree root, and we can recover some of our breath. Next, we dare to investigate the bear and see that it is a big rock with a bearlike shape. We already feel much better. Finally, checking on the robber, we find only an old scarecrow beside the road. In the end, both our false reference points and the misconceptions about them have dissolved and our mind can fully relax, since there is nothing to grasp at and nothing that grasps at something. All three false objects and our subjective experiences of them have dissolved. However, what is left is not just nothing, but throughout this process, there is first the experience of all of this happening in our mind and then the basic experience of this very mind relaxing.

Likewise, in the reasoning process, our subjective mind gradually lets go of holding on to its nonexistent reference points once it acknowledges their nonexistence. The more our mind lets go of its reference points on the object side, the fewer reference points there are on the subject side; that is, there is less and weaker grasping at objects. Clearly, all this is not merely a conceptual operation in which one concept simply cancels out another; the subjective process of letting go is directly experienced in our mind and makes it more relaxed. Once our mind is stripped of all reference points—both objective and subjective—the very experience of a most fundamental relaxation does not dissolve with them. Rather, this is precisely the peaceful experience of the nature of our mind resting at ease within itself, since there are neither any reference points nor something that creates such reference points. Having progressed through the ten grounds of bodhisattvas in this way, the various expressions of nonconceptual dualistic types of consciousness will gradually subside too. Finally, when all fluctuations of mind and mental events have ebbed away, this is called Buddhahood. As Candrakīrti says in his *Entrance into Centrism*:

> The dry firewood of knowable objects having been burned entirely,
> This peace is the Dharma Body of the Victors.
> At this point, there is neither arising nor cessation.
> The cessation of mind is revealed through this Body.[427]

His autocommentary explains:

> In this Body that has the nature of wisdom and [in which] the dry firewood of knowable objects has been burned entirely, there is no arising of knowable objects. Therefore, that which entails such nonarising is the Dharma Body of the Buddhas. Thus, the object of wisdom—true reality—is in no case engaged by the [corresponding] subjects of such [knowable objects], that is, mind and mental events. Therefore, on the seeming level, this is expressed as [true reality] being revealed through this very Body.[428]

The Eighth Karmapa elaborates:

> This "cessation of mind and mental events" does not mean that something that has existed before up through the end of the continuum of the tenth ground [of bodhisattvas] has become nonexistent [now]. The reasons for this are as follows: If it were like that, this would represent the extremes of permanence and extinction. If something [really] existed before, it is impossible that it could become nonexistent later. It is also not justified that what is primordially nonexistent becomes nonexistent later. Therefore, here, it is just the dissolution of all clinging of mind and mental events, or the vanishing of the mistaken appearances of fundamental unawareness, that is conventionally labeled as cessation.[429]

This process does not change or transform the true nature of our mind. Nor is this nature produced from or arising from something else, such as our conceptual reasoning consciousness. Rather, what obscures this fundamental nature—afflictive and cognitive obscurations—has been removed in its entirety. Thus, the primordial unity of expanse and basic awareness can just be clearly as it is. However, strictly speaking, there is nothing to be removed and nothing to be added. The only thing that happens is that mind lets go of its grasping at reference points that never existed in the first place and lets this grasping melt back into its own true nature. This is similar to when powerful waves produce thick foam on the surface of the ocean and thus seem to obscure it. However, we do not have to skim off the foam in order to "uncover" the ocean, since the waves and the foam are parts of the ocean and have the same nature. All we have to "do" is just let the waves and the foam naturally subside into the ocean, which basically means not to interfere with this process by further stirring up the ocean. Likewise, in principle, the Buddhist path simply means letting our grasping—which is part of our mind and has the same nature—settle into its own empty and luminous nature. In practice, there are a variety of methods on different levels of how to let this happen, and the perfection of knowledge through the Centrist approach is one of them. As both *The Ornament of Clear Realization* and *The Sublime Continuum* say:

> There is nothing to be removed from it
> And not the slightest to be added.
> Actual reality is to be seen as it really is—
> Who sees actual reality is released.[430]

## *The Benefit of the Perfection of Knowledge*

The perfection of knowledge or wisdom stands for directly encountering the highest objective of bodhisattvas—ultimate reality—and thus is the main highway to liberation and omniscience. Therefore, to be immersed in such wisdom is explained as the supreme of all practices and realizations. This is why its qualities as well as its profound and far-reaching impact on our minds cannot be overestimated and are repeatedly praised in the scriptures. It is declared that to rest for a single moment within the perfection of knowledge is of far greater merit than—and actually includes—all other perfections, such as generosity. As *The Sūtra of the Meditative Concentration of the Vajra*[431] says:

> If one does not move away from emptiness,
> The six perfections are assembled.

*The Sūtra Requested by Brahmāviśeṣacinti* declares:

> Not reflecting is generosity.
> Not abiding in any difference is ethics.
> Not making any distinctions is patience.
> Not adopting or rejecting anything is vigor.

Not being attached is meditative stability.
Not conceptualizing is knowledge.

Likewise, it is stated that to abide in prajñāpāramitā is far superior to any studies, reflections, or other meditations on the dharma, even if these are performed for many eons. It is also the supreme way of making offerings, taking refuge in the three jewels, generating the mind of enlightenment, and purifying all negativities.

The sūtras and such texts as Maitreya's *Ornament of Clear Realization* describe many signs that indicate increasing familiarity and ease with the perfection of knowledge. To summarize, one is able to see much more clearly in any situation and to deal more carefully with both oneself and others. One mindfully engages in positive actions, and afflictions become weaker. Compassion for sentient beings naturally develops, the dharma is practiced wholeheartedly, and distractions are relinquished. Clinging in general is reduced, particularly the attachment to this life.

There remains the question of how compassion can unfold from the realization of emptiness or from the realization that there is no self. It is the very nature of compassion not to arise on the basis of thinking in terms of ourselves. Rather, it is only to the degree that we gradually let go of concern for ourselves that there is more and more space for compassion to naturally blossom. When all clinging to a personal self and the entire notion of "me and mine" has vanished, all the mental energy that we spent to uphold this illusory reference point is set free. The mental potential does not just disappear, but, having lost its internal mistaken focus of a self, it naturally radiates out to all other beings who are still tied down to their little selves, thus suffering. Once the emptiness of all phenomena and beings is realized, not even a subtle reference point—such as beings who are closer or more distant—is left on which this radiant, unbiased compassion could become stuck or by which it could be inhibited. It is in this way that the realization of identitylessness and emptiness paves the way for all-encompassing and inexhaustible compassion. Then the term "selflessness" can be used in a doubly meaningful way: Being self-less, one cannot but be "selfless," or unselfish, in the best sense of the word.

Technically, there are three types of compassion:

1) the compassion that has all sentient beings as its reference point
2) the compassion that has the dharma (or phenomena) as its reference point
3) nonreferential compassion

The first type corresponds to the compassion of ordinary beings and is not informed by any realization of impermanence or identitylessness. The second is informed by the knowledge of realizing impermanence. This means that, through meditation on the four realities of the noble ones as well as cause and result, the mind turns away from taking things to be lasting and solidly existent. When one sees that other beings suffer because they lack this realization and helplessly cling to things as being permanent, compassion for them arises. The third type unfolds through directly realizing the emptiness or identitylessness of all phenomena. The Eighth Karmapa explains that all three types of compassion equally express themselves in the wish that sentient beings be free from suffering. In terms of their differences, the first compassion is connected to the superimposition that sentient beings or persons exist in some substantial way, thus taking such sentient beings as its reference point. The second is connected to the realization that sentient beings do not exist in a substantial way. However, mere phenomena, such as the five aggregates, are still labeled as sentient beings and taken as the reference point for compassion. The third type springs from the realization that both persons and phenomena are identityless and thus merely labels their very lack of nature as "sentient beings."

Think of a pressure cooker on the stove with the lid on tight, filled with boiling water and highly energetic steam painful to touch. There is no place for this energy to go other than to boil away and dissolve everything inside the cooker. If we try to open the lid slowly, without having read the instruction manual, some steam will hiss out of the cooker and might frighten or burn us, and we will try to tighten the lid again. Once we have read the manual and remove the lid properly, the steam spreads throughout our kitchen and condenses on the windows and walls. If we open the pot outdoors, all the steam naturally spreads into space. As it cools, it may become part of a cloud, moisten the plants, provide water to drink, and so on. In the same way, trapped by the airtight lid of ego-clinging and reification, the natural display of the energy of our mind lacks the quality of spaciousness and just gets uptight and self-destructive. Experiencing a little bit of ordinary compassion may be possible, but it may quickly prove to be too overwhelming or frightening. Having worked with our minds through studying and practicing the instruction manuals of the dharma, the process of "pressure release" for our mental energy becomes more natural, but it still tends to condense on the reference points of those whom we like and burn those whom we do not like. Without such reference points, the moistening warmth of the open and compassionate nature of our mind naturally radiates and intelligently benefits others in many ways.

## *Madhyamaka Path*

Traditionally, the paths in all Buddhist schools or vehicles are presented as threefold—study, reflection, and meditation—or fourfold if we add conduct to the list. The relation between study, reflection, and meditation was highlighted in the introduction, so an example by The Dzogchen Ponlop Rinpoche of how they represent an interconnected process may suffice here. He compares this process to baking chocolate chip cookies. First, we have to read a recipe for such cookies in a cookbook to see what the ingredients are and get an overview of the procedure. This obviously corresponds to the phase of study on the Buddhist path. Next, we make a shopping list and buy all the necessary ingredients. Now we can begin actually preparing the dough, heating up the oven, and so on. Depending on how well we have studied the recipe, we can do this from memory or we might have to consult our book from time to time. Once the cookies are in the oven, we will soon start to smell their appetizing scent. Thus, we arrive at the first direct experience that results from our efforts. At this point, the cookies are no longer just some letters in a book but are about to become delicious food that is a part of our immediate experience. All of this corresponds to the phase of reflection, in which we actively process the things that we have studied and gain some personal experience of them. Finally, the cookies are finished and we can eat them. To relish and assimilate this product means that the actual cookies are directly experienced and become a part of our body. This is the phase of meditation, during which we gradually experience and integrate our studies and reflections into our whole being. This analogy is quite fitting, as the original meaning of the Sanskrit term for meditation—*bhāvanā*—is one of scent fully pervading something like a cloth and actually becoming inseparable from it. In the same way, one might say that we "perfume" our mind stream with liberating insights.

Obviously, the baking process and the resultant quality of the cookies will depend on how well we have followed the recipe. We will be able to enjoy the result of this process—the cookies—only by doing everything properly. Likewise, the efficacy of our reflection depends on how extensively and well we have studied the relevant materials. Consequently, our meditation practice is subject to the certainty that we have gained through systematic reflection. This does not mean that we should exclusively study for many years, then only reflect on all this for even longer, and then finally—if we are still alive—meditate. Rather, Gampopa said that the best way to practice is to do all three steps in an integrated manner: to study a topic, reflect and meditate on it, and then go on to the next topic. Also, Buddhist study should not be approached like a school curriculum in which various topics are studied just so they can be crossed off the list and are never looked at again. Since Buddhist study and practice are meant to change some of our most ingrained habits, they need to be personally worked on and integrated into our whole being. Thus, they are necessarily processes that involve repetition and training until these things become natural and effortless, much as one learns to play an instrument. Processing the same issues again and again enables us to discover new and larger perspectives and understandings each time. This is also the point where conduct comes into play, since conduct in Buddhism basically means taking the insights and experiences that we gained during the more formal phases of studying, reflecting, and meditating and applying them to our daily lives. In summary, such Buddhist rehearsal has the effect of bringing us to increasingly deep levels of experience and realization.

Especially in Centrism, the path also means gradually letting go of both the problems and their respective remedies. As stated earlier, the many volumes of the *Prajñāpāramitā sūtras* and Centrist texts can be epitomized by the following two points: (1) Motivated by the altruistic attitude of the mind of enlightenment for the sake of all beings, bodhisattvas make every effort to attain the omniscience of a Buddha that is accomplished through practicing the six perfections. (2) There are no such things as bodhisattvas, omniscience, Buddhas, beings, the six perfections, or any attainment. To integrate these two aspects in Buddhist practice is called the unity of means and knowledge, or the unity of the seeming and the ultimate mind of enlightenment. The training in the illusionlike means to accomplish the benefit of oneself and others is constantly informed by the knowledge that realizes the empty nature of all phenomena. Thus, motivated by great compassion, the dreamlike accumulations of merit and wisdom that are contained in the perfections are gathered.

The framework for the actual practice on the Centrist path is threefold: preparation, main practice, and conclusion. Every practice starts with bringing to mind our basic motivation for engaging in this path. First, we take refuge in the three jewels: the Buddha, his teachings, and the community of those who practice these teachings. To take refuge in the Buddha does not mean to supplicate some other person for help. Rather, we appreciate the qualities of Buddhahood as the supreme state of liberation and omniscience that is the true nature of our mind and thus strengthen our resolve to accomplish this state ourselves. Taking refuge in the dharma indicates our determination to actually apply the means that enable us to attain Buddhahood. To take refuge in the community of the practitioners of these methods means to open up to our spiritual friends who help us during this journey and to be ready ourselves to help others who travel with us. Next, we affirm our aspiring mind of enlightenment, our wish to perform all our Buddhist practices not just for our own liberation but for the sake of accomplishing perfect Buddhahood for the welfare of all sentient beings. Seen in this way, Buddhahood becomes a sort of by-product of gradually "forgetting" ourselves on the path of a bodhisattva by increasingly focusing on the needs of others. In fact, it is impossible and a contradiction in terms to attain Buddhahood for oneself or by oneself.

All of the main practices are contained in the applied mind of enlightenment, that is, the actual engagement in the six perfections. In general, the first five perfections—generosity up through meditative stability—are considered the means, also called the accumulation of merit. The sixth perfection—knowledge—represents the accumulation of wisdom. However, the crucial point on the Centrist path is to practice wisdom and means as a unity, since this is the only way to attain the great "nonabiding nirvāṇa." Through supreme knowledge, Buddhas and bodhisattvas are not stuck in the extreme of cyclic existence. Through compassion, they are also not just resting in—or limited to—the one-sided nirvanic peace of arhats merely for their own benefit. Thus, through uniting compassion and knowledge, bodhisattvas appear in the world without being in the world. As for such unified practice, it is solely through being inseparably linked with the wisdom of realizing the nature of phenomena—emptiness—that all the perfections become truly supramundane perfections. Only then can they serve as the genuine means for liberation and perfect Buddhahood. Strictly speaking, this is possible only for practitioners on the ten bodhisattva grounds, since they have directly realized the nature of phenomena. However, to some extent, ordinary beings also can—and actually are supposed to—train in the methods to make the perfections supramundane. There are three steps or means to "perfect the perfections":

1) They are enhanced through wisdom.
2) They are expanded through knowledge.
3) They are made limitless through dedication.

Enhancing the perfections through wisdom refers to not fixating on the three spheres, that is, an agent, its object, and the action itself. To take the perfection of generosity as an example, this means that we practice it with the constant awareness that the giver, the recipient, and the act of giving are all illusionlike and empty of a real nature.

The positive impact, or the meritorious power, of the perfections is expanded through knowledge. This is again threefold: First, as for generosity, we practice it not just for the sake of some temporary, limited benefit or relief but—no matter how modest our act of giving may be—always with the supreme motivation that this generosity may be a cause for all beings to attain enlightenment. Second, we do not cling in any way to what we give, which is again based on not taking it to be real in any way. Finally, we do not entertain any hopes or expectations about the personal karmic rewards of our generosity.

Dedication is the third means to perfect the perfections, and it is also the conclusion of every practice. When all positive activities on the path are dedicated for the welfare and enlightenment of all sentient beings, these activities become inexhaustible, just as a drop of water that falls into the ocean does not get lost or exhausted. The supreme way of dedicating does not refer to any dedicator, any beings to whom we dedicate, or any act of dedicating. Since true bodhisattvas perform all their practices exclusively for the sake of all other beings, they have no problem in passing on the benefit of whatever positive actions they commit. For them, dedication is an expression of their all-encompassing activity for others. Moreover, not keeping anything for ourselves directly works on our clinging to "I" and "mine," and by letting go of all our accomplishments, we avoid making them into just another—more sophisticated—hang-up, such as making them a source of pride.

## How Can Madhyamaka Be a Personal Practice?

Before we get into the excruciating intricacies of Centrist reasoning, a short sketch may be useful to convey an idea of how Centrist practice, which includes reasoning, may serve as a practical and transformative path that is very relevant to our personal issues and problems, which often may seem so different from what Centrists address. One of the main problems that arise when we encounter Centrist reasonings is that the classical texts mostly presented them in terms of "how" rather than "why." They may appear as a kind of extremely sophisticated tool kit that we can use to pulverize all kinds of views, if we are so interested, but often there is little background information on why we should ever dive into such complicated argumentations to accomplish this. If any explanations are offered about what the point of this logical overkill may be, they are usually very brief and/or highly technical. Moreover, as for our own worldview, often we do not think we hold any of the views that the Centrists are refuting. Nor do we feel any relation to these ancient people and schools that supposedly maintained such positions many hundreds of years ago in India or Tibet. So why even start to pursue endless chains of complicated reasonings that deal with problems that are not ours and address people whom we do not know?

Now, when we go to a pharmacy, we usually know what our problem is and then select the appropriate medicine for it; we do not consume the entire assortment of drugs. Likewise, we do not go to our physician for help when we have no specific health problem, nor do we want the doctor to put us through every available high-tech diagnostic procedure or prescribe many different pills that we do not need. We definitely prefer to have just our present problem treated. In a similar way, Centrist texts are like well-stocked pharmacies and Centrist masters are like well-equipped physicians, so the issues described equally apply to the treatment of the Madhyamaka type.

First—and this is so self-evident that we usually do not even consider it—we have to decide that we have a problem that needs treatment. If such is the case, we must then identify our individual problem as clearly as possible. There is no point in using any medical or Madhyamaka treatment, if we have no problem or in just applying the treatment to some pseudo-problem. Finally, we have to treat our problem with the specifically appropriate methods. In principle, Centrist texts can help us with all three points, since they keep telling us that we do have a problem, even if we are not aware of it (whether this message rings true for us is of course entirely up to us). The scriptures also clearly identify the basic problem of existence and its ramifications and present a rich variety of remedies. Thus, rather than just plunging into the middle of all kinds of treatments for all kinds of problems, we should be aware of these issues in order to find out which treatment really addresses our own problem.

In general, there are many reasons for engaging in philosophy, but to my knowledge—at least in the West—no philosophers have ever expressed that the fundamental reason for presenting their system is to liberate all sentient beings from their suffering.[432] To some degree, Plato in his final statement in the famous cave dialogue may be an exception. To be sure, I do not intend to present an overview of Western philosophy here, nor do I deny its value. I am just trying to contrast the Madhyamaka approach with the overall approach of classical Western philosophy. If this is too generalized or oversimplified, may the educated philosophers forgive me. Aristotle (384–322 BCE) defined philosophy as the teaching about the first cause and reason. In this sense, philosophy is the search for the initial cause of, or reasons for, what is. It is an attempt to describe or explain the world and our own place in it as coherently as possible and in a way that is assumed to be the way that the world—and what lies beyond it—really is. In this process, such disciplines as logic, ontology, epistemology, metaphysics, and ethics are employed as means to establish one's own worldview and question those of others. On the subjective level, this involves solidifying and reifying one's notions by trying to establish—or just taking for granted—that there is a connection between these notions and something to which they refer. In particular contrast to Buddhism, the issue of a personal self is usually tacitly considered a given (one of the very few exceptions is in the writings of David Hume). As exemplified by Descartes's famous sentence "I think, therefore I am," exactly what this "I" might be is hardly ever questioned. Moreover, as the familiar phrase of "the ivory tower of philosophy" indicates, Western philosophies often remain quite theoretical edifices that offer little practical instruction in how to apply them to our daily problems. Or, as in some modern deconstructive philosophies, we may be left with some kind of "sophisticated" nihilism after having rejected all positivistic philosophical engagement. Some "edifying" philosophers like Heidegger, Wittgenstein, and Dewey seem to have turned away from these tendencies and, as Rorty says, aim "to help their readers, or society as a whole, break free from outworn vocabularies and attitudes, rather than to provide 'grounding' for the intuitions and the customs of the present."[433]

As was stated before, Centrist masters like Nāgārjuna, Candrakīrti, and Śāntideva all clearly agree on their "mission." Their purpose in working with others lies at the heart of what Buddhism is. It is not some theoretical philosophy or metaphysical speculation but a practical system of gradual mind training in order to release sentient beings from suffering. Its intention is to fully realize the true nature of mind, which in itself is beyond the problem of suffering and any of its remedies. Thus, for these masters, their teachings are just tools that they employ out of compassion to help others realize what they realized themselves. Centrists simply do not care about philosophy in the usual sense, or about such things as logic, reasoning, ontology, epistemology, phenomenology, and metaphysics per se. If one of these topics comes into play at some point in their teachings, it is only insofar as it may be suitable to serve the purpose of a provisional device for their liberating activity. As Centrist analysis shows, it is exclusively within the essentially mistaken perspective of deluded beings and their conventional communications that logic, reasoning, and such can be applied as tools to go beyond this framework.

Therefore, the point of engaging in Madhyamaka is not at all to create just another system of philosophy that claims to accurately describe the final picture of the world. We have more than enough ideas about all kinds of things, which, —from the Madhyamaka point of view, is precisely the problem. Rather, it is a matter of letting go of our solidifying notions of the world and not building up even more sophisticated ones. In Madhyamaka, no effort is made to establish any ontology. As was explained earlier, the two realities are not ontological categories, since seeming reality is just the illusion that appears to the mistaken minds of ordinary sentient beings. Ultimate reality is explicitly said to defy any description or accessibility through samsaric mental states and thus also any ontological ascertainment. The two realities are not presented in order to establish an ultimate mode of existence (how reality "really" is) as opposed to a conventional mode of existence (how things seem to be). There is also no attempt to justify or establish anything within seeming reality, such as precisely how it is that karma—cause and effect—works. The thrust of talking about the two realities is soteriological. Seeming reality is identified as the problem, that is, cyclic existence and its cause, which is basic unawareness. Ultimate reality is just the solution to this problem, not a new problem. Thus, to realize ultimate reality does not mean to substitute one thing with another, such as saṃsāra with nirvāṇa. This is very much like when an illness is cured. It is not that the thing "illness" is replaced by the thing "health." Rather, it is just the removal of the causes of the illness that makes its symptoms disappear, and this absence of symptoms is what is called health. So when Centrists address seeming reality, it is only for pedagogical purposes in order to cure samsaric illusion.

In this way, Centrists use their tools quite dispassionately, as if they were merely crutches offered to provide support until the patients—sentient beings—can finally walk alone. Nobody whose broken leg has healed would continue to walk on crutches, and nobody would bother to carry a boat forever once it has reached the other shore of a river. In the same way, those who follow the Centrist approach have no use for their methods once they arrive on the other side of cyclic existence. Instead, the Centrists' rigorous deconstructive analysis of any philosophy or thought system points beyond all of these systems, including Centrism itself. One could say that the Centrist approach has a built-in mechanism of self-destruction, since it not only eliminates other systems but eventually dissolves itself by itself.

In brief, if Madhyamaka were explained as a coherent philosophical, ontological, or logical system, it might appeal much more to our clinging to some neatly organized, all-explanatory picture of the world and our perception of it. We just want to have something that makes good sense, in which all the parts fit together, something on which we can build our belief system. However, any attempt to force Madhyamaka into any system at all must necessarily fail because of the very nature of what Madhyamaka is: the deconstruction of any system and conceptualization whatsoever, including itself. If one were to reintroduce into Madhyamaka any notion of an explanatory or justifying approach, one would simply reestablish the very traps that this specific approach is designed to take apart.

However, Centrists certainly do not go to such great lengths to deconstruct our complex and mistaken mental processes merely to arrive at a big black hole of nothing whatsoever. Nāgārjuna's *Commentary on the Mind of Enlightenment* says:

> The mind is arrayed by latent tendencies.
> Freedom from latent tendencies is bliss.
>
> This blissful mind is peacefulness.
> A peaceful mind will not be ignorant.
> Not to be ignorant is the realization of true reality.
> The realization of true reality is the attainment of liberation.[434]

The contemporary Kagyü meditation master and scholar Khenpo Tsultrim Gyamtso Rinpoche often gives the following example:

> In terms of the sky alone, there is no difference between the sky at night and at day. But in order for rainbows to appear within the sky, there needs to be the quality of light or illumination. If there is just mere empty space with no illuminating quality, rainbows cannot appear. In the same way, blank emptiness cannot give rise to the appearances of saṃsāra and nirvāṇa. Here, space refers to the empty essence of the mind, the light stands for mind's luminous nature, and the rainbows indicate its unimpeded way of manifestation.

If we misunderstand emptiness as mere empty space without awareness, how could this be a liberating realization or even Buddhahood with all its qualities?

Furthermore, it would be very difficult to inspire anybody to embark on a path of hard work for all sentient beings for countless eons just to end up in something like a vacuum. The path to arhathood—to be accomplished within a maximum of seven lifetimes—would certainly be the quicker and better option in that case. Thus, what is stripped away on the path is deluded superficial mental activity, but we are surely not trying to get rid of the nature of our mind. The absence of subject and object, of dualistic clinging, and of any reference point whatsoever does not mean that there is no awareness at all. Pawo Rinpoche comments:

> You might ask, "What kind of result comes from meditating on this?" All aspects of discrimination and observation as such and such are reversed. So one knows that there is no phenomenon whatsoever to be attained through anything, which extinguishes [all] hopes for nirvāṇa. Just like knowing that a dream is a dream, one knows that suffering is not observable through its nature. Thus, there is no fear of cyclic existence. Apart from all phenomena just being mere imputations, they neither abide as any nature whatsoever nor do they abide as anything at all. Just that is what is seen as precisely this empty and luminous expanse of mind. This puts you in the position where you have complete power over everything you could possibly wish for, just as if all phenomena were resting in the palm of your hand.[435]

Practically speaking, Centrism tries to bring the dialogue that we have both with ourselves and others as far as a conceptual or verbal dialogue can possibly go and then has us look for ourselves. The crucial issue here is this: Other than just being intellectual gymnastics, how could this dialogue affect our minds, our subjective experience? From the point of view of personal Buddhist practice, the Centrist approach is not primarily about simply negating all kinds of objects. In terms of mental focus, negating objects is still a somewhat externally oriented conceptual mental activity, even when the object that is negated is one's own mind, that is, the perceiving subject. Negating should also not be understood as a kind of destruction, in the sense that what exists initially is later blown up by emptiness or reasoning. Rather, this approach is an increasingly refined process of just pointing out that none of these objects of negation—our fixed ideas—ever existed at all. Centrism is about facilitating the insight that there is nothing to all that which we assume to exist in the first place.

At the point of having negated everything in this way—even the negation and the negator themselves—we are taught to cautiously shift our focus to the "inside." Of course, strictly speaking, there is no focusing going on at this time and also no reference points of "inside" or "outside." What this means is that our mind directly looks at its own nature in that open space, at the experience of being stripped bare of all clinging and conceptual constructions. What is seen then? Centrists do not give us something to hold on to here—which is their whole point—but as the statements above show, it is certainly not utterly blank nothingness or some kind of coma. It is nothing other than the perfection of knowledge, or prajñāpāramitā. This is called "personally experienced wisdom realizing the nature of phenomena." It is also said to be the "Great Madhyamaka."

In functioning thus as a pointing-out method, Madhyamaka is not really different from the pointing-out instructions in the Mahāmudrā or Dzogchen approach and is indeed very similar to certain Zen methods. Of course, technically speaking, the methods of pointing out might appear rather different in these systems, but what is pointed out is not different in terms of experience. This is amply documented by realized beings in these traditions as well as in such texts as the Eighth Karmapa's *Chariot of the Tagbo Siddhas*, Mipham Rinpoche's *Lamp of Certainty*,[436] and Düdjom Rinpoche's *The Nyingma School of Tibetan Buddhism*. Khenpo Tsultrim Gyamtso Rinpoche commented on verse IX.34 of *The Entrance to the Bodhisattva's Way of Life*:

> At this point, no other aspects except for the genuine object—the nature of phenomena free from discursiveness—appear for the mind. Therefore, also the perceiving subject—the knowledge that realizes emptiness—abides without any observing or apprehending, in a way that is free from discursiveness. Within the natural state of the object (the nature of phenomena free from discursiveness), also the mind that perceives this is nothing but the complete peace of all discursiveness. This situation is then conventionally called "realizing emptiness." "Realizing" is just a conventional term, since here, there is nothing to be realized and nothing that realizes, just like water poured into water. Sometimes one also speaks of emptiness as spaciousness, or openness, because it is free from discursiveness.

On the experience of the expanse of dharmas, he explains:

> The expanse of dharmas in which the aggregates, the sources, and the constituents display is open, spacious, and relaxed. Here, the conventional term "emptiness" is not used. What is described instead is their natural openness and spaciousness, the expanse of dharmadhātu. In order to reverse our clinging to things as being real, we are taught in terms of emptiness. In order to reverse our clinging to things as being empty, we are taught in terms of the expanse of dharmas, the openness, spaciousness, and relaxedness of the dharmadhātu.

Surely, emptiness understood as the free openness of mind's own true space was at least one aspect that Candrakīrti had in mind when he said in his *Entrance into Centrism*:

> Those in whom, even as ordinary beings, upon hearing of emptiness,
> Great joy wells up from within again and again,
> Whose eyes become moistened with tears born from that great joy,
> And whose hairs on the body stand on end—
>
> These persons bear the seed of a perfect Buddha's insight.
> They are the vessels for the teaching on true reality,
> They should be taught ultimate reality,
> And it is they who possess the qualities associated with such.[437]

In terms of our own experience, we can easily compare how we feel when we hear the word "empty" and when we hear "open, spacious, and relaxed." Thus, we have to distinguish between the context of reasoned analysis and looking at our minds in a very direct way. In order to cut through our reference points and superimpositions through reasoning, it is helpful to talk about things being empty of inherent nature, characteristics, or existence. In this context, "empty" refers to a negation, the absence of real existence or properties. As was said, actual ultimate reality is beyond existence and nonexistence or affirmation and negation. We might wonder then why Centrists always talk in negative terms, such as there being no arising and no ceasing. The reason is that we have a much stronger clinging to existence than to nonexistence. And even if we are nihilists and think that nothing exists, there is still the more or less subtle, reifying notion that "nothing exists." Hence, the danger of actually clinging to utter nonexistence is very minor in comparison to the deeply ingrained tendency to take everything to be existent. So it is in order to overcome this strong habit of clinging to existence that Centrists keep pounding us with its opposite, the negation of existence. Once this fundamental grasping at existence is overcome, then all other kinds of clinging to certain attributes of what we assume to exist will collapse naturally, just as it is pointless to ponder the color and shape of the horns of a rabbit or how to best construct a ladder out of them.

However, in the context of practicing meditation on emptiness—when emptiness is fundamentally understood as the richness of the nature of our mind—it is also crucial to not reinforce our habitual poverty mentality when we hear the word "empty." Particularly in experiential terms, it is important to see that when we talk about emptiness, we are surely not talking about it in the negative sense of an empty room or an empty bottle but in the sense of spaciousness, openness, relaxation, and letting go. This means no longer being confined by our own narrow, rigid mental framework. There is another traditional analogy for how to relieve ourselves of fixation and grasping. How can we relieve the pain that is caused by clenching our own fist as hard as possible? Here, leading doctors do not recommend taking painkillers or amputating the hand. We just have to relax our fingers.

In the same way, realizing emptiness has a lot to do with relaxing our clinging mind. It is not merely a matter of following a dry routine of technically negating all the objects of clinging without ever being aware of what this does to the mind that holds on to all these objects. It is crucial to be aware that the actual target of Centrist analysis is not the objects that are refuted but this grasping mind, which—through its clinging to mistaken notions—is the cause of all suffering. However, it is extremely difficult to directly stop it from grasping and make it relax. We cannot simply tell ourselves, "Well, just don't cling." This is why Centrism works at inducing certainty that there are no objects whatsoever that would justify any of our clinging. When we realize that there are no objects for our grasping, we can finally relax and let go of self-inflicted pain.

When Centrists say that everything is like a dream or an illusion, the point is not just to establish the objective side of our experience to be illusory or dreamlike but to see what effect this has on our mind as the subjective experiencer. Again, this is not at all to make an ontological statement about how things exist. Centrists do not really care whether things as such actually exist like illusions or in any other way. However, they are very interested in how we feel about and behave toward illusionlike things as opposed to how we feel about and behave toward solid, really existing phenomena. In his *Treasury of Knowledge*, Jamgön Kongtrul Lodrö Taye says:

> This is like the following example: The realization that it is the nature of space to be accommodating means that space itself has become inseparable from the mental state [that realizes this].[438]

Usually, if we recognize that something is just a dream or an illusion, we do not take it so seriously or fixate on it. It is easier to let go of a bad dream when we recognize that it was just a dream. Being convinced about this makes us relax, which is the aim of Centrist analysis. We learn to relax by becoming convinced that the snake is merely a hose and, apart from our holding on to it, there never was any snake out there, and there is no one in here who could be afraid of it either.

This is also how we evaluate whether our own Centrist analysis has actually become a mind-transforming practice or remains merely intellectual gymnastics. If our mind and the Centrist approach have mixed, we find ourselves more relaxed in encountering the different situations of "real life." If there is more space in the way we experience and react to these situations, we do not immediately look at people and things from our usual narrow, fixed perspectives, which habitually lead to equally rigid patterns of behavior. At the same time, we see that approaching the realization of emptiness does not mean that we become careless, indifferent, or depressed. Rather, such a development widens our perspective and our awareness of people and situations. It enriches our range of possible actions and reactions in the direction of being more mindful, skillful, and compassionate, since we are less caught up in our own fixation and more free to see other people's situations. This can surely be regarded as a first step on the path of realizing emptiness or complete openness. On the other hand, it is a serious error simply to say, "Oh, it's all just an illusion and empty" and not care about anything, especially the suffering of others. This is certainly not the result to be attained through Centrist analysis. So if our genuine interest in other people and our compassion decrease, it is a sure sign that the dharma in general—and Madhyamaka as a personal practice in particular—has not blended with our experience, to say nothing of getting any closer to realizing emptiness.

The process of personally working with Madhyamaka reasoning involves both our wisdom and our ignorance. This can be very interesting and illuminating and at the same time deeply disturbing. It may cause inner resistance to a degree that is hardly expected. On the one hand, when properly applied, the Madhyamaka approach will sharpen and refine our discriminative awareness in a noticeable and broad way, enabling it to function in an increasingly encompassing manner on various levels. This does not refer to just the intellectual realm but also extends into the fields of psychological, emotional, and meditative fine-tuning, which is to say that it is not just a matter of becoming more clever or witty. This process enables us to see more clearly through our fixations and hang-ups in many respects and, as a result, gradually let go of them.

On the other hand, engaging in such analysis exposes our basic and specific ignorance in a very immediate and personal way, which at first might seem to be an unwanted side effect. Sometimes, one's initial reaction to Madhyamaka is to feel stupid or bewildered to the point of utter speechlessness. This shows the deep impact that such an approach may have on our minds. More important, it provides us with otherwise unknown opportunities to have access to the most direct and vivid experiences of the one mental affliction that we usually do not consciously experience: our ignorance or unawareness. We all have plenty of chances to clearly experience all the other afflictions—such as anger, desire, or pride—and are very familiar with them. Although Buddhists always speak of ignorance or basic unawareness as the root of cyclic existence, experientially, we often do not really know what we are talking about here. Of course, we can be aware of our ignorance in the sense of not knowing how to fix our car or where exactly New Guinea is. However, the powerful and profound ignorance that is at the heart of cyclic existence is not just a matter of being ignorant about some facts. It is more the general tendency—on many levels—to be fundamentally unclear about the true nature of one's mind, which leads to becoming caught up in all kinds of beliefs about ourselves and others. Such ignorance contains two aspects: We may be passively ignorant in the sense of not being *able* to look at ourselves and what is going on in our minds, but we may also be actively ignoring things by not *wanting* to look at them and turning away.

One of the characteristics of basic unawareness is that we are literally unaware of our unawareness. Of course, when we think about what unawareness is, it appears obvious that unawareness includes unawareness of itself. However, in terms of our experience, it is precisely because we are unaware of our instinctive and habitual blind spots that we have no idea that we have them; much less do we face them and work on them. So when do we normally get a glimpse of this?

Centrism provides us with the opportunity to gain firsthand insight into how deeply rooted and pervasive our basic unawareness is. Moreover, it lays bare the various intricate layers of this unawareness. Often Centrist reasonings and texts seem overly complex, ramified, and repetitive. However, this is not at all the fault of this system. Centrism is complicated and repetitive only in response to our many layers of complicated concepts, unfounded beliefs, and convoluted trains of thought, most of which are deeply ingrained. Therefore, Centrist texts cannot but go into every little detail we could think of, and even into those that we would not think of. If the targets for Centrist reasoning were just simple issues that are located on the easily accessible surface level of our minds, their discussion could likewise be very simple and straightforward. Obviously, our ability to differentiate and conceptually eliminate what is wrong is not strained when we are only talking about distinguishing tables from chairs. However, we must certainly exercise our discriminative capacity more powerfully when we try to understand subatomic particles and their interactions in quantum physics.

Such discrimination is even more essential when we approach the ultimate nature of phenomena, which is beyond our usual range of cognitions. As was said, this is not an object of any of our present perceptions, such as seeing or hearing, and is also not an object of conceptual mind. So the approach here is basically to refine our initially vague mental image of emptiness into an increasingly vivid notion by gradually eliminating everything that it is not. Emptiness is so subtle and elusive that the whole range of what needs to be negated in order to define it clearly is not immediately apparent, and the process of conceptually refining our understanding naturally requires many details. This conceptual refinement is of course different from the final point of nonconceptual realization of emptiness, but we cannot reach the latter by simply trying to get rid of thoughts. The Centrist approach enables us to strip away mistaken notions by first creating more "correct" ones and then gradually letting go of the correct ones too, including the vivid notion of emptiness itself. We may also compare our thoughts and our intellect to an axe that has to be sharpened before we can use it to cut down a tree obscuring the view from our window. Afterward, we can let go of this axe, but if we throw it away right at the start and just wish for the tree to fall down by itself—or pretend it isn't there at all—we get nowhere. Moreover, the process of refining our insight is not based on mere superficial reflection; it must be deeply and repeatedly cultivated through meditation, that is, the unity of calm abiding and superior insight. There is no question that conceptual mind can be a stepping-stone toward an immediate awareness that simply sees what is, without any conceptual distortion. Thus, we use our intellect in a systematic way that eventually leads to its own exhaustion (which is surely also meant in a literal sense!) and gives way to a different perspective altogether: the natural outlook of the nature of our mind, which is neither tied up in thinking nor caught up in ordinary sense perception.

When we look at the seemingly endless and pointless repetitions of the same reasonings in Centrism, we may also understand them as remedies that poke at our awareness, which tends to fall asleep again and again, since our ingrained tendencies instantly cover up much of what we might have detected about our fixations the first or the second time. Centrists would surely prefer to make all of this much easier, but our discursive mental framework, with its billions of reference points, forces them to relate to at least the main principles of mistakenness therein. Many of our clingings and delusions are unconscious or so subtle that we do not even know we have them. However, they are to a large extent what determines our thinking and our actions. Centrism brings all of our hang-ups to light and at the same time provides the means to face and dissolve them. However, we usually do not want to give in that quickly but desperately try to hold on to our beliefs, however unreasonable they might be. Thus, the reason Centrist texts are often wordy lies mainly in our multiple defense strategies, be they emotional or argumentative. In fact, if just once in a while we could remember to be aware of our unawareness—to look at some of our clinging instead of letting its underground work continue unnoticed—then that alone could remove a tremendous amount of mental dullness. Looking at this unawareness lifts some of the veils that this unawareness casts over the true nature of our mind but also over itself, which means that unawareness itself usually makes sure that we do not want to look at it. And if we are forced to look at it, with unequaled skill it makes us swiftly turn away and escape.

In this process, there is a definite chance for sudden openness, insight, and gap experiences in the midst of reasoning, in the midst of a tornado of whirling thoughts, and in the midst of the dullest states of mind. The crucial point here is again what this analysis does to our minds and how we relate to the experiences it brings up. Do we see more clearly? Do we experience more space? Are we becoming more relaxed?

Another striking feature of Madhyamaka analysis is how much emotional resistance it can produce in us. Normally, we do not really want to get into all these reasonings and deconstructions of concepts, and we find all kinds of wonderful rationales for why this is pointless, counterproductive, too intellectual, and so on. The main reason we do this is that the more active part of our ignorance doesn't want us to look at ourselves. We do not really wish to have our belief systems questioned, probably because we have some feeling that they might not be in such perfect touch with reality as we like them to be. We like our little world as intact and secure as we can possibly make it, or at least pretend so. We actually enjoy our tendency to lump together all kinds of—sometimes contradictory—ideas and beliefs and call that sophisticated. Here, the Madhyamaka approach is actually quite down to earth. Centrists basically say, "Sure, in your mind you can think of and define all kinds of things, but that does not turn any of them into something real. So if you think that certain things really exist, you have to either directly show them to us or come up with some good proof for them. If you cannot do either, then where are these things, other than just in your imagination?"

We do not like other people poking around in our private little thoughts and our treasured ideas about ourselves and the world. Everybody or everything that questions them is immediately registered as a hostile threat to "Planet Ego," and all our defense systems gear up. In this sense, the Madhyamaka system is Public Enemy Number One in Egoland. It does precisely all of this repellent prying into our supposedly private business in a most unnerving and relentless way. It messes up the whole planet—nothing is like before. It even wipes out the defense systems. It does not care about all these signs everywhere that clearly say "off limits—private property—ego-clinging territory." But Madhyamaka just walks straight in and does not go along with our self-cherishing at all. It is as if there is a jumbled storage room in the basement of our mind in which we keep stashing our emotional and conceptual garbage. We try really hard not to look at this mess, let alone clean it up, but Madhyamaka picks up every single piece and holds it under our nose and says, "This thing goes out, and that does too, and all the rest as well. Let's get some space and fresh air in here." It operates with a kind of merciless compassion that does not give up on us, no matter what kind of clever excuses, tricky defenses, or outright escape techniques we might come up with. Somehow it has this tendency to get under our skin and get us at some point, often in unexpected ways. It is like the worst self-unfolding computer virus that sneaks onto our well-protected hard drive of reification and, no matter what we do, wrecks both the software and hardware that run our ego programs, including all firewalls, before it dissolves itself. It affects us even—and maybe most effectively—in the midst of our enormous efforts to ward it off.

It can be overwhelming when we discover this and realize that Madhyamaka analysis and reasoning is not just an intellectual game but can deeply affect us at the basic level of our personal and emotional existence. Suddenly, we may find ourselves not only working with our various ways of clinging to ourselves and our world but also—and maybe even worse—facing our aversion and resistance to the very remedy for that clinging. However, it is important to regard this not as an additional difficulty but as an intrinsic and crucial constituent of the process of applying the Madhyamaka approach as a practice of personal transformation. It is part of the game, so to speak, to acknowledge, look at, and work with our inner resistance to Madhyamaka analysis at the very time we are engaged in it. There are, of course, other topics that we might be more willing to subject to analysis and mindful introspection, but it is very effective to regard whatever comes up in our mind during that process as an immediate and most suitable object to look into. Our direct experience is our mind in action, which displays the whole range of our habitual patterns right there on the spot, so there is plenty of material to work on. We do not have to look very far beyond ourselves, nor for lofty philosophical concepts or at other people, to find proper objects for Madhyamaka analysis. It is meant personally, and if we allow it to be, it gets as personal as anything could get.

When we read Madhyamaka texts, we might think, "I have nothing to do with all these ancient Indian non-Buddhist schools that are the opponents of Centrists. Why should I bother with what these people said and how they were refuted?" Of course, the point is not just to replay ancient debates as if they were famous historical chess games, without being personally concerned with their content. Moreover, it would be an endless enterprise to precisely identify all the opponents in the Madhyamaka texts and their exact views. However, in terms of applying what is said in the Madhyamaka texts, it is of secondary importance who exactly said what—and often this is impossible to ascertain anyway. Rather, it is helpful to take a closer look at the principles reflected in the various positions under debate. When it comes to the fundamental questions of life, human thought in its principal workings is not so different over time and across cultures as we might think. Who knows, at some point some people might bother to write "modern" Madhyamaka texts that address the whole range of Western philosophy, religion, and science, though this would certainly be a monumental task. In the meantime, if we just compare the "ancient" Eastern views with Western ideas, we will find a lot of concepts that are used in Western philosophy, metaphysics, and science too. The old Indian schools will not, of course, use exactly the same words, but if we understand what their terms refer to, we will recognize many of the same things in Western thought, whether the debate revolves around a primal cosmic substance, a creator god, a final cause of the universe, a permanent personal soul, or issues such as universals versus particulars. And even if we do not find our own specific ideas—or anything of modern Western philosophy or science—in Centrist texts, we still can apply Madhyamaka techniques to look into such ideas, once we have understood the principles of these techniques. After all, they are just tools that can be applied to any view or concept. For example, we could approach what these texts present by asking ourselves whether we entertain similar views. Do they provide some guidelines for looking into our own belief systems? Can they stimulate our reflection and understanding? Madhyamaka texts cannot address every detail of any possible view in the past, present, and future and thus provide everything in a predigested manner. Rather, the debates and refutations in these texts are just exemplary models that are to be applied to our individual mental frameworks and views. The parole is "do-it-yourself."

The primary prerequisite for this to work—and it is in fact a significant requirement—is to develop the courage and honesty to really let the Madhyamaka approach illustrated in these texts into our world and our private ideas. Some genuine inquisitiveness and willingness to question our own reference systems is necessary here. This is quite different from keeping our private defense strategies intact while we just go through the motions of some impersonal technical reasonings or merely repeat what we read and hear from others about emptiness. Our ego and our various clingings could not be happier with this latter approach, since it will leave them completely untouched and might even reinforce them. Then, ego rejoices in security and waves smilingly from the far side of any effort we might make. In such a case, our "practice" and our experience or way of life are two different roads that do not meet.

As with any truly transformative process, when taken to heart, this approach can be—and often has to be—quite disillusioning from the standpoint of clinging to our ego and our world. The word "disillusion" usually has quite negative associations. It indicates that we have lost something dear to us, which is, of course, true for our cherished clingings. Actually, however, it refers to something very positive: We see through our illusions and let go of hanging on to them, and thus we realize what is actually there and worthy of being cherished. These different ways of looking at dis-illusionment are reflected in people's various reactions to the Madhyamaka approach. Depending on what it does to their minds, they may be angry and frustrated or utterly thrilled. Following their usual lighthearted way of putting things, Centrists might well epitomize the path by saying, "Buddhism is one disappointment after another, but, fortunately, enlightenment is the last."

As was said earlier, Buddhism in general can be understood as a system of increasingly subtle concepts that counteract relatively coarser concepts. This is especially true of the Madhyamaka teachings. The coarser concepts of reality and true existence are remedied by the more subtle concepts that things are like illusions and dreams and do not really exist. However, these remedial concepts also must be remedied by putting them through all four positions of the typical four-cornered analysis and finally letting go of all of them. So the way Madhyamaka works can be compared to a kind of homeopathic remedy: The disease—mistaken conceptualization—is remedied by this same disease in a more refined form; that is, essentially mistaken conceptions perform the provisonal function of canceling the coarser symptoms of the disease of confused conceptuality. Just as homeopathy allows the body to regain its natural healthy condition through its own balancing power, Madhyamaka assists our mind in finding its way back to its natural, primordial ease by seeing its own fundamental being. And like a homeopathic medicine, the remedy of Madhyamaka dissolves itself in the healing process that it triggers, since it finally has no ground within the resulting healthy state of realizing ultimate reality.

Some may approach reading Madhyamaka as they would a guidebook, and then follow the path it describes. However, it is a very odd guidebook, in that it only tells us where *not* to go. We are instructed to take neither the path of existence, nor the path of nonexistence, nor the path of both, nor the path of neither. Still, the very process of not entering these paths is walking on a path. In more positive terms, this is called the five paths or the ten grounds of bodhisattvas. However, it is up to us to figure out exactly how and where to step. There isn't really any broad highway that stretches out straight ahead of us for miles on which we can just blindly stumble along. This path has more of a sudden, instantaneously emerging quality. There is just a tiny new section appearing each moment, and no trodden path or even any traces when we try to look back at the way we came. As though out of nowhere, each inch of this path reveals itself just in the very immediate and intimate moments when we realize why it is pointless to follow one of the other paths that our guidebook identified as wrong. When we clearly see where not to go to the left, the right, uphill, downhill, and so on, we naturally make our mental steps into just the space in between—or around—all these nonoptions. Yet, even one second before our next step, we actually had not the slightest idea where to go or even whether there was a path at all. Thus, we are led up to the point where we have left behind each of the paths that could have led us astray. At this moment, we realize that we no longer have to watch out for dead ends and misleading routes. Now we just take our nose out of the guidebook for a moment, relax, and look around, and without any warning we happen on this incredible view. We might have completely forgotten about any kind of view while we were busy following this nowhere path. This view comes as completely unexpected, and it is all the more breathtaking, heart-warming, and completely beyond anything we might have imagined. Other than stand and stare, there is nothing left to do—OṂ. We might wonder why our guidebook never said anything about it and want to check—it's GONE. We might want to look at ourselves who walked on the path and arrived now—GONE. We look around and cannot even see the slightest indication of how we got here—GONE BEYOND. But we know for sure now that there is no further path to be searched for or to be avoided either—COMPLETELY GONE BEYOND. Without anybody looking anywhere, the view is astounding and the panorama enjoys itself—BODHI SVĀHĀ.

## Reasoning and Debate in Centrism

In the framework of ground, path, and fruition, Centrist reasoning is usually presented in the context of the ground. However, in terms of the practical application of the Madhyamaka teachings, it seems more appropriate to treat analytical reasoning in the context of the path. For, as was explained earlier in detail, it is not just some abstract logic or theoretical material; it is explicitly meant to be put into practice by being applied to all aspects of our existence.

### *Three Stages of Analysis by Nāgārjuna and Āryadeva*

To give us a slightly broader context for where Centrist reasoning fits in on the path, it is helpful to first take a look at the three phases of Nāgārjuna's and Āryadeva's presentation of the Buddhist teachings. Nāgārjuna spoke of the three turnings of the wheel of dharma as "the wheel that teaches identity," "the wheel that teaches identitylessness," and "the wheel that puts an end to all bases for views." In his *Four Hundred Verses on the Yogic Practice of Bodhisattvas*, Āryadeva says:

> First, one puts an end to what is not meritorious.
> In the middle, one puts an end to identity.
> Later, one puts an end to all views.
> Those who understand this are skilled.[439]

These three wheels of dharma as well as the texts of Nāgārjuna and his followers are often further described in terms of the three stages of no analysis, slight analysis, and thorough analysis. Here, the ground (the aggregates, constituents, and sources), the path (the aspects of conduct and means), and the result (enlightened bodies, enlightened activity, and so on) are described in accordance with the conventions of the worldly seeming, that is, according to what is consensus from the perspective without examination and analysis. Most of what is described in the stage of no analysis exists as worldly seeming reality in such a way that it is already worldly consensus or that it is suitable to serve as such consensus. However, there are also some parts in the presentations of ground, path, and fruition that are adapted to the yogic seeming, such as the ways of appearance during meditative equipoise and subsequent attainment.

Those passages in the texts that negate the object of negation—the two identities—and then present nonarising, emptiness, and ultimate reality are explained from the perspective of slight analysis, that is, for a consciousness based on correct reasoning.

Examples of the final stage, that of thorough analysis, can be found in most of the explicit statements of the *Prajñāpāramitā sūtras.* These say that nothing is established as anything whatsoever—be it as existent or nonexistent, permanent or impermanent, empty or nonempty, and so on—and that nothing is suitable to be apprehended as anything whatsoever. In his *Fundamental Verses,* Nāgārjuna agrees:

> Do not pronounce "empty"
> Nor say "nonempty."
> Do not say both nor neither.
> It is [only] for the sake of imputation that they should be pronounced.[440]

Such passages are explained by relating them to the final stage of thorough or excellent analysis. Here, "analysis" does not mean conceptual analysis but refers to directly seeing the true nature of phenomena as it is. Candrakīrti's *Entrance into the Knowledge of Centrism* says:

> In this natural state of primordial nonarising,
> There is nothing to be negated and nothing to be affirmed.
> Nirvāṇa and nonnirvāṇa
> Are without difference in the natural state of nonarising.
>
> This is not even nonarising as such,
> Because arising things do not exist.
> The seeming does not exist, the ultimate does not exist,
> Buddhas do not exist, sentient beings do not exist,
>
> Views do not exist, something to be meditated on does not exist,
> Conduct does not exist, and results do not exist:
> The actuality of this is what is to be cultivated.
> Let this mind free from thoughts rest in its own peace.
>
> Without identifying something, without being distracted,
> Without characteristics and luminous—thus meditate.[441]

Presented in this way, the Centrist teachings are not at all contradictory to anything the Buddha taught.

The necessity to connect one's dharma practice to the three phases of the Buddha's teaching and the three stages of analysis is argued for as follows. The initial phase of putting an end to what is not meritorious is necessary because, through adopting positive actions and rejecting negative actions without analyzing this process as to its ultimate nature, one first stops what is nonmeritorious and accumulates merit. Thus, the provisional path to favorable rebirth in the higher realms within cyclic existence is accomplished, which serves as the appropriate support for further practice. The second phase of putting an end to identity is necessary because when one brings slight analysis into experience, all mistaken views about personal and phenomenal identities are eliminated. This accomplishes the path to liberation from cyclic existence. The third phase of putting an end to all views is necessary, because when one brings excellent analysis into experience, all reference points of any kind of view will finally dissolve. Thus, the path to omniscience is accomplished.

### *Is Reasoning Reasonable?*

In general, whenever reasoning is used in Buddhism, it is always understood as a means to an end—liberation from suffering—and not as an end in itself. In terms of its practical application, two situations are distinguished. We may employ reasoning as a tool to eliminate our own confusion or to help others dispel their mistaken views. In both cases, our motivation to engage in the process of reasoning and our attitude toward ourselves and others are what determine whether this process just makes us more uptight or serves as a transforming practice that helps us relax our mental grasping. Thus, in Buddhism the motivation to use reasoning should be compassion, which is the heartfelt wish to eliminate suffering for both ourselves and others. When we go through Centrist reasonings for our own sake and do not just analyze outer things or the positions of others in a book but allow the Centrist approach to enter our private territory, it will get very personal. Here, we basically debate with ourselves; in other words, our prajñā communicates with our ignorance and clinging. In this process, having compassion for ourselves means having a very gentle approach when we investigate our belief systems, neuroses, and emotions. We will encounter various degrees of inner resistance depending on the solidity of our clinging to certain fixed ideas or to what seems to make up our personality. If this becomes too overwhelming, we are well advised to take a break, relax, and remember that all of this—including our resistance—is not as real and heavy as it seems. We may also consider that Centrist reasonings can be compared to some temporarily painful surgery that eventually leads to greater well-being. In addition, to look at our resistance too and examine it through Centrist reasoning is an integral and important part of the whole process.

When Centrist reasoning is used in communicating with others, from the perspective of more advanced practitioners who have already gained incontrovertible certainty through these reasonings, debate can only be an expression of their compassion. In other words, for them, discussions with others are only acceptable when they are founded on the motivation to help other people remove their suffering. On the other hand, for people who have not yet gained incontrovertible certainty, their motivation to engage in debate should be twofold: Of course, the basic wish to help others is indispensable, but clearly also the openness to question one's own views and understandings is necessary. It is explicitly said that one should not even start a debate with any other motivation. Thus, reasoning and debate in Centrism are not performed to fulfill a mission, to show off our skill at argumentation, to win a contest and put others down, or to confirm that we are right. When debate is embedded in a genuine mutual wish to sharpen one's understanding in an unbiased way, it is not a contest in which one person wins and the other loses. Rather, in contrast to just reviewing certain topics by oneself, debate is understood as a joint venture of discovering more about the truth by uniting the individual analytic capacities of the two debaters in the investigation of a topic that is of interest to both parties. Consequently, the two parties do not work against each other or fight; they cooperate so that both win in the sense that they mutually enhance their insights. In other words, two eyes of prajñā see better than one.

Needless to say, in order to engage in meaningful debates using Centrist reasonings, one must have gained at least some degree of understanding of these reasonings. There is no point in just reading Madhyamaka books without attempting to practice and understand the reasonings they contain. Otherwise, there is a danger of consequently presenting a wrong view of dharma to others, such as trying to bless the world with one's own version of "the highest Buddhist view that everything is empty." Even if we have the proper motivation and are well versed in the arguments and techniques of debate, we are discouraged from debating with people who are only eager to dispute and not ready to change their minds no matter which arguments they meet (of course, this applies to ourselves too). Also, we definitely should not pour our wisdom—or our lack of it—over someone who does not even want to hear about Buddhism or Centrism. Missionary ambitions are clearly foreign to the Buddhist approach. Furthermore, in both these cases, our efforts would be fruitless and a waste of time. More important, we could create great resistance in other people to the Buddha's teachings, the very means for liberation from suffering. Therefore, it is surely detrimental to use these teachings in a way that makes someone else suffer, such as by forcing them upon a person who shows no interest in them.

Finally, it seems worthwhile to point to the seemingly paradoxical and elusive nature of Centrist reasoning. If properly used, it not only deconstructs what is to be refuted, but at the same time it naturally brings about its own disintegration once its target has been invalidated. Thus, having dissolved both the problem and the remedy, the mind is left at ease, with no dualistic flux stirring in the peaceful, luminous expanse of the unity of wisdom and emptiness. One might wonder, Why not just leave the mind at peace and not disturb it with all this conceptual diffusion? To give a very simplified example, it is a bit like jogging. After we have done our laps and taken a shower, when we sit down at home, we feel relaxed, supple, and at peace. We could, of course, have saved the effort of jogging and just stayed home and relaxed on our couch anyway. However, those who jog know that this is definitely not the same. When we go through the process of making an effort in training the body, our ensuing relaxation has a completely different quality. In the same way, the process of having our mind do its rounds of prajñā training makes a huge difference in the mind's ability to rest in its own true nature. Merely letting it rest naturally is possible too, but this is far from easy. Moreover, just resting the mind is not enough. There also has to be a quality of looking at our mind with fresh sharpness and wakefulness. As Milarepa says:

> Don't be attached to the pool of calm abiding,
> But let the foliage of superior insight burst into open bloom.

This same principle also applies to practicing the various levels of the creation stage (Vajrayāna deity visualization) that generally belong to the category of calm abiding. They are followed by the completion stage, which adds the factor of superior insight. Moreover, such concentrated mental activities as analytical meditation on emptiness or deity visualization may very well provide the chance of a "gap experience" dawning right in their middle. As Jamgön Kongtrul Lodrö Taye sings in his *Song on Having Gained a Mere Fraction of Certainty in the View and Meditation of the Incomparable Tagbo Kagyü, Called The Self-Dawning of the Fundamental State*:

> In the midst of thought I found nonthought.
> Within the freedom from ordinary mental states, wisdom dawned.[442]

As for the benefits of using analytical reasoning in dharma practice, Khenpo Tsultrim Gyamtso Rinpoche says that a great amount of merit can be gathered by doing the standard Tibetan preliminary practices for Mahāmudrā[443] or other Vajrayāna practices. However, only very skillful and well-trained practitioners can accumulate an equal amount of wisdom in this process. On the other hand, through the practice of the progressive stages of meditation on emptiness, large amounts of both merit and wisdom will accrue. This accords with the fact that the practice of the perfection of prajñā includes all forms of meritorious actions. In fact, it was a tradition in India to train in these meditations on emptiness as the preliminary practices for Mahāmudrā and Vajrayāna. Consequently, Khenpo Tsultrim Gyamtso often advises practitioners to follow the approach of using such analytical meditations.

## *Reasons and Negations*

### The Three Modes of a Correct Reason

The standard form of a reasoning consists of three parts: the subject, the predicate, and the reason. For example, in the sentence "Sound is an impermanent phenomenon, because it is produced by causes and conditions," the subject is "sound," the predicate is "an impermanent phenomenon," and the reason is "being produced by causes and conditions." Whether such a reasoning is valid or not mainly depends on the reason. In Buddhist logic, the three criteria to determine a valid reason are called the three modes. The reason in a formal probative argument[444] is a valid means to establish what is to be proven only if the subject, the predicate, and the reason are in correct relationship to each other. The definitions of the three modes are as follows:

1) The *subject property* is a reason that has been determined to be present in all instances of the flawless subject in question in a corresponding formulation.
2) The *positive entailment* is a reason that has been determined to be present only in the homologous set.
3) The *negative entailment* is a reason that has been determined not to be present in a single instance of the heterologous set.

To explain this in a simple way,[445] let's call the subject A, the predicate B, and the reason C. The three modes correspond then to the following diagrams:

subject property

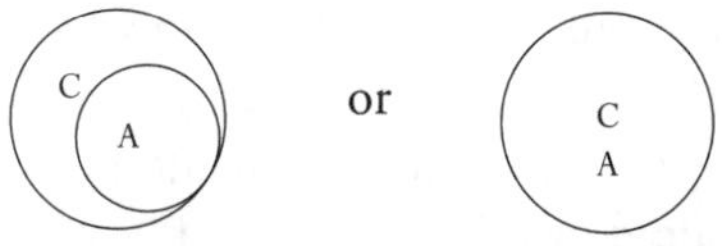


positive entailment

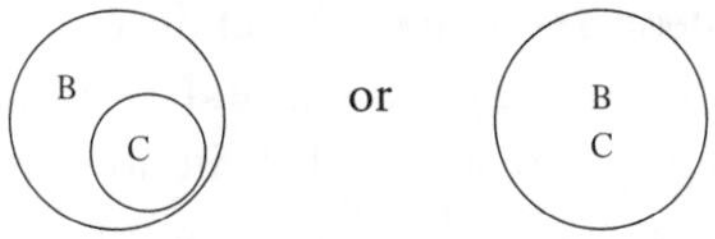


negative entailment

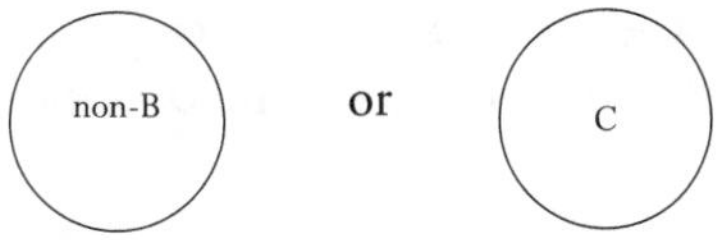

What is the purpose of these three modes? In terms of set theory, if the reason C includes all of the subject A, and the predicate B includes all of the reason C, then automatically the predicate B includes all of the subject A, which is exactly the thesis (A is B) that one wants to prove: If $C \subseteq A$ and $B \subseteq C \Rightarrow B \subseteq A$.

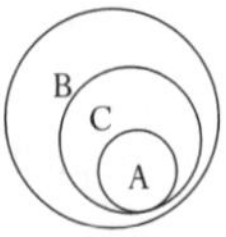


or

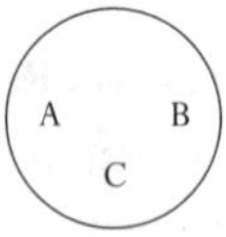


As should be obvious from the diagrams, the subject, the predicate, and the reason refer to sets of phenomena, not just names or abstract features. For example, "sound" means the set of all possible sounds, and "produced by causes and conditions" stands for all phenomena that are so produced. To give an example, we may say, "Sound is an impermanent phenomenon, because it is produced by causes and conditions." Here, the reason "produced by causes and conditions" must include the subject "sound," and the predicate "impermanent phenomenon" must include the reason. In other words, the set of sounds is included in the set of what is produced by causes and conditions, and this latter set is included in—here coextensive with—the set of impermanent phenomena. As a result, the set of sounds is automatically included in the set of impermanent phenomena, which is what is to be proven.

As can be seen from the diagrams, the subject and the reason on the one side and the predicate and the reason on the other side do not necessarily have to be mutually inclusive or coextensive. It is sufficient if the subject is a subset of the reason and the reason is a subset of the predicate, for example, as in "The sound of a flute played by a musician is an impermanent phenomenon, because it is produced by effort." Here, whatever is a sound of a flute played by a musician is necessarily something that is produced by effort, but whatever is produced by effort is not necessarily the sound of a flute played by a musician. Likewise, whatever is produced by effort is necessarily impermanent, but whatever is impermanent is not necessarily produced by effort, such as a tree or a river.

In Buddhist reasoning in general, these three modes can be formulated in two ways. One is called "inference for oneself" and the other "inference for others."[446] The first one serves to allow one to understand by oneself what is to be proven, while the second is employed to assist others in understanding what oneself has already understood. An example of a three-membered inference for oneself is:

> (1) My own five aggregates as the subject are (2) impermanent, (3) because they are produced by causes and conditions.

The same formulated as an inference for others reads:

> (1) Whatever is produced by causes and conditions is (2) impermanent;
> (3) for example, the five aggregates of someone who is dying.
> (4) My own five aggregates too are (5) produced by causes and conditions.

Obviously, the meaning and what is to be proven are the same in both formats. The latter format just adds an example (3) and explicitly states the first mode (4 and 5) and the second mode (1 and 2).[447]

**Types of Reasons**

Regarding the characteristics of the reasons themselves, in Buddhist logic one distinguishes three basic types of reasons:

1) nature reasons
2) result reasons
3) reasons of nonobservation

1) The first is a reason that has the same conventional or relative nature as the predicate. To be sure, here, "nature" does not refer to the ultimate nature of phenomena, emptiness, or the like. It is rather a matter of two sets of things being of the same conventional type or the same category. For example, all vegetables have the nature of being or belonging to the category of plants. Thus, one can say, "Carrots are plants, because they are vegetables." Or, as in the example above, "impermanent phenomena" and "what is produced by causes and conditions" have the same nature in that whatever is the one is necessarily the other. In other words, all impermanent phenomena have the nature of being produced by causes and conditions, and all that is produced by causes and conditions has the nature of being impermanent.

2) Result reasons are reasons that are a result of the predicate and thus prove hidden causal phenomena. For example, when one says, "Behind this hill, there is fire, because there is smoke," smoke is a result of the existence of fire. Thus, from the direct perception of a result (smoke), one can infer the prior existence of its cause (fire).

3) The definition of a correct reason of nonobservation is "a reason with the three modes in the proof of a probandum that is the negation of a phenomenon, or, completeness of the three modes in the negation of that which is to be negated." In general, reasons of nonobservation prove the nonexistence of something

through the fact that this something is not perceptible or observable through any kind of valid cognition. There are two types of reasons of nonobservation:

a) reasons of the nonobservation of something that does not appear[448]
b) reasons of the nonobservation of something that is suitable to appear[449]

a) The definition of a correct reason of the nonobservation of something that does not appear is "a reason with the three modes that negates the conventional expression of 'definite existence' by negating the cognizing subject of something that is not suitable to appear." An example is the reason "because there is no valid cognition that could observe a ghost," which proves that the conventional expression "the definite existence of a ghost" does not apply to the area in front of someone who does not have any propensity to perceive ghosts. In brief, this negation serves to clarify that one cannot claim the general existence of private, delusive appearances such as ghosts for everyone just because they may appear from the perspective of certain people. Otherwise, all things such as hallucinations or appearances in the minds of insane people would have the status of general existence for everyone.

b) The definition of a correct reason of the nonobservation of something suitable to appear is "a reason with the three modes that proves both the fact and the conventional expression of 'nonexistence' by negating the cognizing subject of something suitable to appear." This is the sole type of reason that is employed in the Centrist reasonings that analyze the ultimate nature of phenomena or emptiness. The most straightforward way to put this is to say, for example, "In this room, there is no elephant, because none is observable in it through any kind of valid cognition." Usually, if there is an elephant somewhere, given sufficient light and nothing obscuring it, it is clearly observable to the people present whose sense faculties are intact. Thus, the inverse of this—that is, if an elephant is not observable in this place—means that it does not exist there.

There are many more of these kinds of reasoning that indirectly negate the thing in question. In technical terms, these can be summarized into two:

i) reasons of the nonobservation of something connected[450] (to the predicate of what is to be negated)[451]
ii) reasons of the observation of something contradictory[452] (to the predicate of what is to be negated)

i) Something that is connected to the predicate of what is to be negated can be (1) its conventional nature, (2) any of its results, (3) any of its causes, or (4) a larger category to which it belongs. An example of an unobserved cause is the proof "On this lake, there is no smoke, because fire cannot be observed there." Here, the predicate of what is to be negated is "there *is* smoke." Thus, the fact that the cause (fire) of the phenomenon in question (smoke) cannot be observed at a certain place serves as the reason to negate the existence of this phenomenon (smoke) itself, since smoke is the result that is invariably connected to this cause (fire). In other words, if a certain cause does not exist, its result cannot exist either.

ii) Something that is contradictory to the predicate of what is to be negated may be (1) its nature, (2) its result, or (3) a subset of it. An example of the first is the proof "Right at the location of this blazing fire, there is no coldness, because a blazing fire is observed there." Here, the predicate of that which is to be negated is "there *is* coldness." The opposite of this is that "there is heat, such as a blazing fire." First, the existence of heat somewhere is established through the observation of a blazing fire there. Second, observing a blazing fire and its heat is contradictory to and excludes observing coldness in this very same location. Thus, what is *not* observed there is coldness, which directly negates the existence of coldness. In this way, the observation of fire indirectly serves as the reason to disprove the existence of coldness. Of course, the examples given here consist of mundane trivialities, but when these reasons of nonobservation are applied to such objects of negation as real existence, an intrinsic nature, or the two types of identity, they get right to the heart of the matter of Centrist analysis.

In general, the first two basic types of reasons—nature reasons and result reasons—are called affirming reasons, since they either affirm a common conventional nature of different things or the conventional existence of something. The third type—reasons of nonobservation—is called a negating reason, since it does not affirm anything but merely negates the existence of something.

**Pseudoreasons**

Pseudoreasons are reasons in which one or more of the three modes are not established. There are three main types of such mistaken reasons:

1) nonapplying reasons (reasons that do not apply to the subject as a means of proof)
2) contradictory reasons (reasons that negate their own probandum)
3) uncertain reasons (reasons that create doubt about their own probandum)

1) Nonapplying reasons are of five types:

a) nonapplication for the proponent
b) nonapplication for the opponent

c) nonapplication for both ("Sound is permanent, because it is an object of the eye consciousness.")[453]
d) nonapplication due to its basis being unestablished, that is, the subject in question being nonexistent ("The present king of France has difficulty wearing his crown, because he is bald.")
e) nonapplication because the connection of the subject to the reason is doubtful ("On the middle one of three mountain ridges in front of me, there is a peacock, because I hear the sound of peacock cries.")

2) Contradictory reasons are of four types:

a) contradictory reasons that negate the nature of the predicate ("Sound is permanent, because it is produced.")
b) contradictory reasons that negate the nature of the subject ("Space can hurt, because it is obstructive.")
c) contradictory reasons that negate an attribute of the predicate
d) contradictory reasons that negate an attribute of the subject

3) Uncertain reasons are of three types:

a) uncertain reasons in which the negative entailment is most obviously doubtful ("This man has attachment, because he speaks.")
b) uncertain reasons in which the positive entailment is most obviously doubtful ("This woman is free from attachment, because she does not speak.")
c) uncertain reasons in which both are doubtful ("Living bodies have a self, because they possess a life force.")

**Specific Applications of These Reasons in Buddhism**

The particular topics to which nature reasons, result reasons, and reasons of nonobservation are mainly applied on the Buddhist path are respectively the following:

1) impermanence
2) cause and result
3) the two identitylessnesses and emptiness

1) Nature reasons are mainly employed to prove the impermanence of all conditioned phenomena. To be a conditioned phenomenon means first to be produced by certain causes and conditions. Then, the phenomenon's continuum is sustained by further causes and conditions. Finally, when these specific causes and conditions end at some point, the conditioned phenomenon that was supported

by them must necessarily cease too. Thus, it has the nature of being impermanent, since the definition of being impermanent is to arise, abide, and cease. Reflecting on this coarse aspect of impermanence serves as the primary means to reverse our attachment to the things of this life. Reflecting on the notion of subtle impermanence—the impermanence of all conditioned phenomena changing in every moment—leads us to understand emptiness. It is said that whoever understands arising and ceasing will understand impermanence, and whoever realizes impermanence will realize the unity of dependent origination and emptiness. With respect to dependent origination, Nāgārjuna's *Sixty Stanzas on Reasoning* says:

> Through understanding arising, one understands ceasing.
> Through understanding ceasing, one understands impermanence.
> When one understands how to penetrate impermanence,
> Also this genuine dharma will be realized.[454]

2) Result reasons are used to establish the functioning of cause and result in general. This refers not only to outer or material causes but, more important, to the inner level of causality, which is the operation of karmic causes and results. Karma means that all our physical, verbal, and mental actions or impulses are causes that have effects in the same way any other causes do. In Buddhism, this principle of causality is also employed to establish the continuity of former and later lifetimes. In any case, result reasons infer prior material or mental causes from the observation of certain material or mental conditioned phenomena in the present that are the results of these causes. Basically, Buddhism says that the functioning of cause and effect means both that something cannot come from nothing and that something cannot become nothing. Otherwise, anything could randomly happen at any time or nothing would ever happen. Moreover, without cause and effect, all intentional actions, such as farming to produce the result of a harvest, would be completely unpredictable or pointless.

Therefore, in Buddhism, it is not really a question of just believing or not believing in the law of karma or former and later lifetimes. Rather, if we generally accept the process of cause and effect, we must acknowledge that it does not make sense to arbitrarily exclude some causal phenomena—that is, certain or all of our physical, verbal, and mental actions—from this general principle. This holds true even if we do not see an immediate result of these actions and hope to have avoided their consequences. In fact, we generally do experience the effects of our impulses, emotions, and thoughts, since our physical and verbal actions are constantly driven by them. When we plan a project or do our work, we do not think at all that our mental activities have no results; we take it for granted that our thoughts and imagination will result in visible actions and products. Also, we know very well the strong and possibly devastating effects of certain mental impulses, such as falling in love or declaring war. That it might take a long time for the effect of some action to ripen cannot be a basis for claiming that this action has no effect. Otherwise, it would equally follow that the movements of the original continents on earth are not the causes for the location and shape of the present continents, since the beings at that time did not experience the effect at present, nor do we at present observe these causes.

It would be highly inconsistent to say that some things or experiences have causes while others do not. This would also imply that there are some causes that have results and others that have no results. How could we reasonably define and distinguish between such phenomena? (In addition, for those phenomena that do not have causes, all the above absurd consequences would apply.) Whenever someone discovers the cause of something that was previously considered a random event—as has happened and continues to happen in science—the entire notion of causelessness or randomness is fundamentally questioned. Moreover, how could uncaused phenomena interact with phenomena that do have causes? If they interacted in a purely random way, even phenomena within an established causal continuum would become random phenomena. And if they interacted in a way that is determined by causes, random phenomena would enter the realm of causality. If there were, however, two entirely separate realms of phenomena, they could not interact at all.

As for the classical proof for the existence of past and future lives, we must first realize that if we accept the principle of causality as functioning in an all-encompassing way, then there have to be infinite chains of specific causes and results. For example, a tree that we see now has a beginningless "case history" of causes and conditions, each of which again entails its own causes and conditions. Likewise, according to Buddhism, the present moment of our mind does not come out of nowhere but arises from the immediately preceding moment of this mind. In other words, mind does not depend on anything other than mind as its specific substantial cause.[455] By extending this backward and ahead in time, we naturally arrive at a mental continuum without beginning or end, which manifests as what is called the different lifetimes of cyclic existence. To arbitrarily postulate any starting point or a total extinction of this continuum—such as the beginning or the end of this life—amounts to nothing more than saying that something can come from nothing or something can become nothing. Yet this openly contradicts the notion of cause and result as such in the first place.

Further indications that are adduced for the existence of other lifetimes include facts such as newborn mammals immediately knowing without learning where and how to drink milk from their mothers.[456] Furthermore, what would account for the immense range of differences just among human beings even at birth, such as being born healthy or with a severe disease, being intelligent or dumb, being born rich or in a slum, in a loving family or a violent one? How else could one explain that some people "have success" or get rich almost without any effort and others always "have bad luck" or stay poor even if they work hard? Why is it that some children can play complex pieces of classical music at an early age without training or excel at sports, while others are never able to do nearly as well even with a lot of training? Even conventionally, none of these facts can be sufficiently explained by causes that can be found in this present life, but this usually just leads to subsuming them under rubrics such as "fortune," "fate," or "talent." The most fashionable category these days seems to be that "it's all in the genes." This is not the place to discuss this issue in detail, but if we just consider how little the genetic code of human beings differs from that of chimpanzees and some primitive worms—by just 1 percent and about 30 percent respectively—it is quite amazing to assume that the genes alone can serve as an explanation for all the differences between humans and other beings. To be sure, these differences do not consist of only physical features, but include the entire range of the human mind and its expressions, such as culture, science, philosophy, and religion, not to mention all the mental and behavioral diversity of human beings themselves, who have even less genetic variance from one another.

3) Reasons of nonobservation specifically serve to negate all kinds of imaginary things and mental reference points—such as real outer objects or a self—that are imagined to exist by ordinary worldly persons as well as people who are influenced by certain philosophical systems. Hence, particularly in Centrism, these reasons are not just used to prove the nonexistence of an otherwise existing thing in a certain spot, as in the example of an elephant given earlier. Rather, they are primarily employed to demonstrate the nonexistence of all such hypothetical things that never existed as knowable objects in the first place and thus can neither be directly perceived nor inferred through any means of valid cognition. The general thrust here is that if something that is merely assumed to exist—such as purple rabbits or a real personal self—cannot be observed through any kind of valid cognition, then the only conclusion can be that there is no such thing altogether and that it is just a figment of the imagination.

It is important to distinguish between our concept of, for example, a pink rabbit with wheels and an actual phenomenon that would correspond to this idea. For the mental image of such a pink rabbit has some degree of conventional existence in that it can appear as an object of our thinking mind. Apart from this mere fantasy, though, an actual such animal does not exist and will never appear to us. As was said before, we can think about anything and create all kinds of imaginary things in our conceptual consciousness. However, the mere fact that we can think of or imagine something that does not actually exist does not make it any more real or existent. Thus, what are "refuted" in Centrism are not actually existing, real things or an actual real self. Rather, since we construct all kinds of imaginary notions about such nonexistents (real things and a self), Centrist reasoning only serves to deconstruct our mistaken ideas. For example, the existence of a lasting, independent, and singular personal self within an individual's five aggregates is refuted by observing among them only what is contradictory to such a self. This means that the five aggregates consist only of phenomena that are momentarily impermanent, dependent on various causes and conditions, and do not have an identifiable single core, since all of them can be taken apart infinitely. Thus, all that we can observe among them is dependent, not lasting, and not single. This then excludes the existence of anything in these aggregates that is lasting, independent, and singular, such as this hypothetical self.

Within the specific approach of Centrist reasonings, the two kinds of affirming reasons are used to some extent, but solely with respect to seeming reality and by just employing the conventional notions of others, such as in the context of cause and result. When investigating for ultimate reality—that is, when dealing with emptiness or the two types of identitylessness—Centrists solely employ negating reasons of nonobservation. As was explained at length, in emptiness, there is nothing to be affirmed in terms of either nature or existence nor in terms of nonexistence. Thus, when reasoning is applied in the Centrist search for the ultimate, its only purpose is to eliminate wrong ideas and clinging to real existence. Therefore, affirming reasons—as they are used in accordance with conventional dialectics—are impossible and useless here.

### Negations

Obviously, the conceptual result of negating reasons is a negation. The general definition of a negation is "a phenomenon to be cognized by the cognition that directly cognizes it through excluding its specific object of negation." In Indo-Tibetan logic, there are two kinds of negations:

1) implicative negations and
2) nonimplicative negations.

The definition of an implicative negation is "the implication of another phenomenon as a remainder after the negation of the object of negation by a cognition that directly cognizes the negation itself." Thus, an implicative negation—which may also be called predicative negation—implies or affirms something else as a remainder after having negated certain features with regard to the subject in question. An example would be to say, "Heaven is not impermanent," which implies that it is permanent.[457] The classic example is the statement "Fat Devadatta does not eat during the day." Being fat shows that he does eat, and what is implied as a remainder of the negation of eating during the day is another phenomenon: that he eats during the night.

The definition of a nonimplicative negation is "something that is to be cognized by a cognition that directly cognizes it through merely excluding its specific object of negation." This may also be called "negation of existence," since it means that the existence of something is negated without affirming or implying anything about it instead. Thus, the cognition that directly cognizes a nonimplicative negation cognizes that part of the sentence that represents the mere exclusion—or the mere negation—of its specific object of negation. It does not, however, cognize or imply any other phenomenon, be it directly or indirectly. Examples of this kind of negation are "the nonexistence of heaven," "space,"[458] "emptiness," and "identitylessness." In terms of formulating a nonimplicative negation, it does not matter whether there is a grammatical negative in the formulation that represents the mere exclusion of the specific object of negation (as in "the nonexistence of heaven" or "identitylessness") or whether there is no negative in the actual term (as in "space" or "emptiness"). The point is that, in one way or another, the formulation must indicate the absence of something and not imply anything else in its place.

All Centrist reasonings arrive at nonimplicative negations. There is nothing that is conceptually implied in their analysis of ultimate reality. Therefore, implicative negations are not used in Centrist reasoning for the ultimate. In fact, their use would be counterproductive to the Centrist approach altogether, since they would just supply new reference points by implying something.

In terms of the path, ultimate reality or emptiness has to be realized in two stages: first conceptually and finally within nondual and nonconceptual meditative equipoise. Thus, first one cultivates the particular conceptual consciousness that is based on Centrist reasoning and results from inferential reflection. This is called an "inferential valid cognition." It is the first type of valid cognition to ascertain ultimate reality, and thus it precedes the second and final type of such valid cognition, which is the direct, nonconceptual realization of emptiness from the path of seeing onward.

The cultivation of an inferential valid cognition of emptiness involves again two steps. First, in order to counteract our habitual strong clinging to the real existence of all phenomena, we have to initially cultivate a number of inferential valid cognitions for which various nonimplicative negations clearly appear, such as the nonimplicative negation that "there is no arising, no abiding, and no ceasing" or that "an intrinsic nature of phenomena does not exist." Even on the conceptual level, it is very difficult to immediately gain a correct realization of the actual emptiness that is free from the four extremes and the eight reference points,[459] which means nothing other than the complete lack of reference points. To conceptually arrive at this kind of emptiness is the second stage and at the same time the final result of analytical reasoning.

The negations in both steps are called "nominal ultimate reality," since they more or less accord with actual ultimate reality on the conceptual level. The most subtle conceptual object "freedom from all reference points" is the mental image that appears to an increasingly refined reasoning consciousness and concords with ultimate reality to the highest degree that is possible for conceptual objects. It is the result of prolonged familiarization with the major Centrist reasonings that are all tailored to tackle our clinging to reference points from various angles. Still, no matter how subtle a concept this final step of nominal ultimate reality may be, whether it is "freedom from all reference points" or "no reference point whatsoever, not even the freedom from reference points," it cannot in itself go beyond being a subtle conceptual object.

Thus, to approach the direct realization of actual emptiness in a gradual manner, one first familiarizes oneself with a number of nonimplicative negations that progressively negate each extreme and all reference points. Generally speaking, this is the cultivation of inferential valid cognition as the initial direct remedy for the clinging to real existence. It is a series of conceptual cognitions that progress from eliminating more coarse superimpositions to negating very subtle ones. Finally, the nonimplicative negation of "nothing whatsoever" or "emptiness"—that is, no reference point at all—appears. Here, we have to distinguish clearly between the plain fact of there being no reference point whatsoever and how this fact appears to our conceptual reasoning consciousness. When we reflect on the absence of any reference points, the very appearance of the concept that "there are no reference points whatsoever" is not just nothing at all, but it is an object that appears and thus exists for a conceptual consciousness. As such, it is clearly still a reference point in itself.

Second, once there is familiarity with this conceptual remedy, one needs to go beyond it, which means that this subtle reference point of "no reference point whatsoever" has to be abandoned too at some point. As Nāgārjuna's *Sixty Stanzas on Reasoning* says:

> Those whose minds are not moved,
> Not even by a flicker of a thought about "complete voidness,"
> Have crossed the horrifying ocean of existence
> That is agitated by the snakes of the afflictions.[460]

In other words, negations that merely negate an actual arising, real existence, and such are conceptual and nominal ultimates. These negations are not free from the more subtle reference points of "nonarising," "the lack of real existence," or "the freedom from reference points." The actual direct experience of there being no reference points—including the reference point of there being no reference points—is the actual or nonnominal ultimate.

If one approaches ultimate reality through this twofold process, it is said that it becomes very accessible even for ordinary beings. In this way, it is definitely possible to develop not only the correct conceptual view of nominal ultimate reality but also the immediate experience and direct realization of genuine emptiness or nonnominal ultimate reality. Śāntideva describes this process in three crucial verses:

> Through familiarity with the latent tendencies of emptiness,
> The latent tendencies of entities will be relinquished.
> Through familiarity with utter nonexistence,
> These too will be relinquished later on.
>
> Once this "utter nonexistence"—
> The entity to be determined—cannot be observed,
> How should a nonentity without a basis
> Remain before the mind?
>
> Once neither entities nor nonentities
> Remain before the mind,
> There is no other mental flux [either].
> Therefore, it is utter nonreferential peace.[461]

The commentary of the early Sakya master Sönam Tsemo[462] (1142–1182) explains:

> Proving that the realization of everything as an illusion is the path has three parts:
> 1) Relinquishing clinging to existence
> 2) Relinquishing clinging to nonexistence
> 3) The justification for this
>
> The first refers to "Through familiarity . . ." [lines 32ab above]. When meditating on an object generality[463] of emptiness, through the power of [this] being mutually exclusive with reification, reification is stopped.
>
> The second refers to "Through familiarity with . . ." [lines 32cd]. "These too" refers to [such] positive [conceptual] determinations [of an object generality] of emptiness. They are relinquished later on. If you wonder why, this is through familiarity [with actual emptiness], without there being any negative or positive determinations whatsoever. "So what is the reason for relinquishing the superimposition of a positive determination of emptiness?"

> The justification for this refers to "Once this . . ." [verse 33]. How should nonentities, [such as the negation of entities,] remain before the mind as objects of reasoning? . . . They are without basis, because, through the superimposition that is the negation [of something], the basis [for this negation]—the superimposition of an object of negation—does not exist [anymore]. And if no object of negation is conceived, its negation cannot be conceived [either]. . . . Without a [specific] object of negation being identified, negation would be performed in a [completely] indiscriminate way. Therefore, prior to one's being certain that a [specific] object of negation is negated, [this object] has to be identified, since otherwise there is no focusing on this object of negation as the basis [of its negation]. "How can it be that there is no [such focusing]?" [Such happens] once this "utter nonexistence"—the entity to be determined—cannot be observed.
>
> The way in which supreme knowledge without appearance arises refers to "Once neither . . ." [verse 34]. Once entities do not remain before the mind, this means that they are not established on the path of reasoning. Once nonentities do not remain before the mind, this means that a positive determination of nonexistence is not established as the object of reasoning [either]. Then, the object generalities of existence and nonexistence do not appear and there is [also] no clinging to what is outside. Therefore, this is utter nonreferential peace. It is the arising of supreme knowledge that is without appearance in that there is no focus for superimpositions and the continuum of thoughts has stopped. "However, there may be other superimpositions that represent some mental flux [different from] the object generalities of existence and nonexistence. Therefore, it is not necessarily established that [this knowledge] is without any appearances at all." There is no other mental flux, because there is no [possibility] other than existence and nonexistence.[464]

Thus, it is explained that, after exhausting the power of terms, conceptions, and objects of negation as well as their remedies, the ensuing mental peace is similar to having finally recovered from some serious hardship or struggle.

Centrist treatises set up the positions of others and then analyze them by using a great number of reasonings. However, none of this happens out of hatred of other systems or a mere enjoyment of dispute. Rather, it is done solely from the perspective of others and their benefit, that is, in order to put an end to their intense clinging, bound as they are through the web of their conceptions. As *The Entrance into Centrism* says:

> The analyses in [Nāgārjuna's] treatise were not performed out of attachment to debate.
> [Rather,] true reality has been taught for the sake of complete release.
> It may well be that while explaining true reality
> The scriptures of others become ruined, but there is no fault in this.[465]

Therefore, the whole spectrum of reasoned analysis that is employed in Centrist treatises is nothing but an approach that aims at putting an end to the other party's conceptions that are engaged in superimposition and denial. However, once superimposition and denial have been eliminated, the bare and direct realization of the actual nature of phenomena does not arise through the force of thorough analysis, because this true nature is not an object that can be analyzed or grasped through study, reflection, or conceptual meditation. Thus, *The Entrance into Centrism* says:

> Ordinary beings are bound by conceptions.
> Nonconceptual yogins will find release.
> Hence, the learned state that the result of analysis
> Is that conceptions are at peace.[466]

Here, three things about every nonimplicative negation, no matter how subtle or all-encompassing, should be very clear. First, a negation is by definition exclusively an object of a conceptual consciousness, that is, an inferential valid cognition. It can never be an object of a direct and nonconceptual valid cognition, since the process of negating and its object are of a conceptual nature. Second, since it appears as a conceptual object, in terms of the categories of existents and nonexistents, this negation itself is still considered an existent phenomenon for the conceptual mind. It is the subtle form or way in which "nonexistence" or "the freedom from reference points and extremes" appears to the reasoning consciousness. Therefore, this conceptual object "nonexistence" is not in itself nonexistent, nor is it in itself the actual freedom from all reference points and extremes. Third, one must eventually let go of both this conceptually appearing object—the negation—and the dualistic cognition for which such an object appears, in order for it to give way to the nonconceptual wisdom that directly realizes the actual emptiness free from all reference points.

As Pawo Rinpoche states, a negation is nothing but an imputation by a mind that clings to nonexistence, and an affirmation is just an imputation by a mind that clings to existence. In light of the true nature of phenomena, all clinging—no matter to what—is simply mistaken. Nonimplicative negation is just a technical term whose meaning refers to nothing other than what is normally understood by "nonexistence." Thus, in this context of Centrist reasoning, the meaning of the nonimplicative negation "being nothing whatsoever" refers to the complete nonexistence of reference points. A sūtra states:

> Those who understand this dharma of "being nothing whatsoever"
> Will be without attachment toward all phenomena.

In this way, it is clear that such a nonimplicative negation is just a step toward the direct realization of actual ultimate reality. Otherwise, if ultimate reality itself were nothing but a nonimplicative negation, then it would just be some conceptual kind of nonexistence in the sense of nothing whatsoever. On the other hand, if ultimate reality were an implicative negation or something affirmative, then it would be something actually existent. Obviously, none of these categories applies to the actual or nonnominal ultimate, and there is no third possibility. The Eighth Karmapa denies both the position that ultimate reality is a nonimplicative negation (or even one that is supposed to withstand analysis) and the position that ultimate reality is completely inexpressible. It seems that the first scholar to explicitly identify the ultimate as a nonimplicative negation was Chaba Chökyi Senge.[467] Later, Tsongkhapa and his followers also adopted this position and held that actual emptiness is a nonimplicative negation that withstands analysis. However, if it were possible to arrive at something that withstands analysis, such as the nonimplicative negation "the lack of real existence," this would turn the whole project of Centrism—the demonstration that there is nothing that withstands analysis—upside down. As was explained above, this point is expressed many times in numerous Centrist texts as well as in the *Prajñāpāramitā sūtras*:

> I declare that all phenomena including nirvāṇa—and even if there were any phenomenon more supreme than that—are illusionlike and dreamlike.[468]

The point that there is nothing that can withstand analysis is also the major reason for the detailed presentation of the twenty emptinesses, for each of them serves to eliminate specific and increasingly subtle aspects of holding on to something real. Moreover, since such a nonimplicative negation is supposed to withstand analysis while at the same time being exclusively a conceptual object, there would be no way to ever abandon it in order to directly realize genuine ultimate reality (as described by Śāntideva above). There would not even be a need to abandon this nonimplicative negation and proceed to a direct realization of ultimate reality, since such a negation already *is* the actual ultimate reality.

An exemplary proponent of the view that ultimate reality is absolutely inexpressible was Tsang Nagba Dsöndrü Senge.[469] From this position, it would absurdly follow that—just from the perspective of how Centrists appear to others—those Centrists who, through their skill in means, teach or say anything about true reality would not be Centrists. This would mean that Centrists who negate real existence would not be Centrists. Also, if ultimate reality could not be expressed at all, it would be utterly pointless that the Buddha taught the *Prajñāpāramitā sūtras* and that so many Centrists have composed voluminous texts.

In brief, nonnominal ultimate emptiness—the actual object of the wisdom in the meditative equipoise of noble ones—is beyond either withstanding or not withstanding analysis. In itself, it is inexpressible. On the other hand, the nominal emptiness in the form of a nonimplicative negation that is the object of the worldly valid cognition of a reasoning consciousness[470] definitely cannot withstand analysis. This is also clearly indicated by Śāntideva's third verse above. Nevertheless, there is no problem in Centrists' skillfully using such names as "ultimate reality" or "emptiness" for that which is essentially without name. Thus, since they employ such illustrative designations to point to the ultimately inexpressible true reality, it cannot be said that they are unable to conventionally express it. The Eighth Karmapa emphasizes that this is a very subtle and essential point in the Centrist approach.

### *What Is the Object of Negation in Centrist Reasonings?*

What is refuted through Centrist reasonings? Technically speaking, it is the notion of some real and intrinsic existence or nature of phenomena. This refers to the concept that phenomena exist in an independent way, in and by themselves. If something does not depend on any other factors extrinsic to it—causes, conditions, time, or circumstances—for its existence but stays the same no matter what happens, then it is real in the sense of being unchanging and independent. If some phenomenon really were independently existent in its own right, such independent existence should become even more obvious when it is analyzed. However, in fact, the opposite is the case. The more we look for an inherently existing thing, the less we find it. This unfindable real or independent existence is the direct object of negation that is refuted throughout Centrist texts, whether it applies to the true existence of a personal self or the inherent existence of any other phenomenon. On the other hand, whatever is under the influence of something else and thus originates in interdependence with various conditions is not ultimately real in the above sense but is just something that appears and functions on the level of seeming reality. Thus, from the perspective of their mere appearance and dynamic fluctuation, the entire display of seemingly "outer" objects, "inner" minds that perceive them, and so on is not the target of Centrist refutations. Mere illusionlike appearances as such are not the Centrist objects of negation. As Jñānagarbha's *Distinction between the Two Realities* says:

What has the character of appearance
Is definitely not negated.
It is not appropriate to negate
That which is experienced.

Such aspects as "arising"
Are not what appears.
We negate what is imputed by others,
Such as that [these imputations] are knowable objects in actuality.

Therefore, here it is appropriate
To negate solely such imputations.
Negating what is not an imputation
Is only to harm oneself.[471]

First, it makes no sense to negate what are merely temporary appearances, since there is no way that we could just reason them away. For example, as long as the eyes of someone with blurred vision are not freed from their defects, mistaken visual objects such as floating hairs or double moons will continue to appear for this person. Likewise, the illusionlike appearances of the six consciousnesses will not subside as long as the cognitive obscurations and their latent tendencies that trigger such appearances have not been relinquished, no matter how many reasonings are flung at these appearances.

Nor is there any need to negate mere appearances, because our afflictions and sufferings do not originate from them; they originate from our clinging to them as being real. Just as an illusionist does not cling to the appearance of a handsome young man that was created by her own power, we will not be bound in cyclic existence if we are not attached to its appearances despite their seemingly real existence. On the other hand, just as a naïve audience develops desire for this illusory young man, we cling to the reality of fleeting appearances, and our afflictions increase. If it would work to deliberately negate these mere appearances, then emptiness would be nothing but utter blank nonexistence. Also, if training in meditation on emptiness just meant cultivating a total negation in the sense that nothing exists at all, it would be equivalent to falling into the extreme of extinction or nihilism.

Thus, it is said that mere appearances as such are not what is refuted in Centrism. However, that it is not possible to negate them has to be taken with a grain of salt. Initially, through Centrist reasonings in the context of studying and reflecting, the coarser portion of our clinging that takes these illusionlike mere appearances to be real things is eliminated. This stops the manifest clinging to their real existence. Later, through combining the power of the knowledge gained from studying and reflection with the meditative equipoise that is the unity of calm abiding and superior insight, the undefiled knowledge or "reasoning" that springs from meditation arises. Once even the latent tendencies for real appearances have been eradicated in this way, also the subtle portion of the clinging to reality—which manifests as the appearance of illusionlike mere appearances—becomes pure like space without any reference points. For example, for someone who suffers from blurred vision and mistakenly clings to the appearance of some black dots against the background of a white cup, a skilled physician first clarifies that these dots do not exist by saying, "They only appear because of your disease." By understanding that these dots do not exist, the sick person puts an end to her misconception of there really being such dots in this cup. Nevertheless, since the cause for the plain appearance of these dots has not yet been removed, they still appear. Hence, in order to stop their appearance, the physician has this person take a potent medicine that eliminates blurred vision altogether. Once the disease has been removed, the "dots" are just like space without any reference points.

Therefore, as long as seeming appearances have not been put to an end, it is reasonable to make efforts to eliminate them, such as being heedful with regard to cause and result while meditating on the emptiness of all phenomena. On the other hand, within the meditative equipoise of yogic practitioners who see that all phenomena are free from reference points, there is nothing to be eliminated. However, without these considerations, to say that it is neither possible nor necessary to negate mere appearances through reasoning may become rather absurd. For, if one is not able to negate mere appearances, they would then be ultimate reality, because they are something that withstands analysis and cannot be invalidated through reasoning. It would furthermore follow that worldly people cannot realize true reality, because it is impossible to negate the really existing phenomena of seeming reality. For, if they cannot be negated through reasoning, they also cannot be negated or stopped through the path of meditation. And if they cannot be negated or stopped through either reasoning or the path, there is no other means to put an end to them.

Thus, Centrist reasonings address the basic tendency of mistaking appearances as really existing phenomena and a really existing self, including all the ramifications and implications of such misconceptions. However, when Centrists speak about "real existence," this does not mean that "real existence" is some factor or element that is extrinsic to the phenomena that appear to us. For example, that visible form lacks real existence does not mean that visible form is empty of some real existence that is something other than this visible form itself. As *The Entrance into Centrism* says:

> Since it is its nature,
> [Visible] form is empty of [visible] form.

> Sound, smell, taste, tangible objects,
> And also phenomena are just like that.[472]

Candrakīrti's autocommentary explicitly explains this point:

> Here, one speaks about emptiness [as the fact] that the eyes and so on [are empty] of these very eyes and so on. This makes it completely clear that [this is] the emptiness of a nature, whereas it is not an emptiness of one not existing in an other, [such as] "the eye is empty, since it lacks an inner agent" or "it is empty of the nature of apprehender and apprehended."[473]

In brief, to say that form lacks or is empty of real existence means exactly the same as to say that it lacks a nature or characteristics of its own, that form is empty of form, or, that form is not different from its emptiness. As *The Prajñāpāramitā Sūtra in Hundred Thousand Lines* says:

> Subhūti asked: "How should bodhisattvas train to understand that all phenomena are empty of their own specific characteristics?"
>
> The Blessed One said: "Form should be seen as empty of form, feeling empty of feeling, and so on."
>
> Subhūti asked: "If everything is empty of itself, how does the bodhisattvas' engagement in the perfection of knowledge take place?"
>
> The Blessed One answered: "Such engagement in the perfection of knowledge is non-engagement."[474]

*The Heart Sūtra* states:

> Form is emptiness; emptiness is also form. Emptiness is no other than form, and form is no other than emptiness.

So what exactly is this notion of real existence? On the objective side, it is nothing but a vague idea or mental image. When we think or say "I" or "chair," these are just terms, but at the same time we seem to sense a more or less vague something that floats around in our conceptual mind and to which these terms supposedly correspond.[475] Depending on how much we are influenced by certain views or philosophical systems, these vague conceptual objects may be elaborated into a more or less sophisticated conceptual construct, such as an eternal soul or a real cosmic substance with all its features. However, what is the stuff that these mental images themselves are made of? As long as we do not look too closely at our notions, such as "I" and "chair," they seem to exist and function in a way that feels very natural and real. We might just say, "Of course, I know who I am and what a chair is, and now I will sit down on one." However, as soon as we try to pinpoint—or even analyze—these notions, they become extremely elusive. In fact, the more we look at the ideas that seem to drift through our mind and try to identify them, the less we can find them. This is not because we are not searching properly but simply due to them being the imaginary phantoms that they are.

So we might wonder what good it will do us to refute such phantom ideas. In fact, these figments of our imagination are not the actual problem to be remedied. They are just the objects of negation as they are identified and set up in the formulations of Centrist reasonings. The actual problem that causes us suffering—and the real target of Centrist reasoning—is the subjective side of these imaginations: the fact that we take them to be real, cling to them, and behave as if we and the world around us existed in a way that exactly corresponds to their appearance. Therefore, the way in which Centrist reasonings touch upon our experience is that they indirectly undermine our subjective clinging to the fixed ideas of a real self and real phenomena by directly demonstrating that there is nothing to which these really refer and nothing that corresponds to them. Therefore, it is crucial to see that Centrist reasoning does not mean just shooting at some dead concepts while leaving our direct, living experience of ourselves and others completely untouched. When they are investigated, it becomes clear that our mistaken notions are rootless and baseless. Thus, none of them has ever existed as an object in the first place. However, as long as we take them for granted as real objects, our subjective holding on to them will lead to all the well-known consequences. The only way to let go of them from the side of the experiencer is to realize that there is nothing on the object side that would justify our grasping, just like realizing that a tree in the dark is not a monster.

When we analyze the term "object of negation" in Centrist reasoning, it is obvious that the two types of identity or "real existence" do not exist as actual objects to be negated. They are mere imputations or fictions, since the existence of a permanent, singular, and independent personal identity within the range of all phenomena is impossible. Any other entity that is really established through an intrinsic nature of its own is equally impossible. Since there is thus no actual object of negation on the objective side, there never was or will be anything to be relinquished there. Hence, on the objective side, the object of negation of reasoning is just something that is conceptually imagined by a mistaken cognition, while it does not exist as an object of any unmistaken cognition. For example, from the perspective of a conceptual consciousness that misapprehends a twisted tree in the dark as a monster, a mere imagination of a monster appears. This imagined conceptual object does not itself exist as a monster, nor does it refer to an actual monster out there. However, without our thoughts erroneously setting up this wrong conceptual object of a monster, subjectively, the ensuing mental states of clinging to the existence of this imagined monster and becoming afraid of it would never arise. This is something that is established for everyone in the world by direct experience.

The same relation between conceptual objects and subjects applies to reasoning. On the conventional level, one may set up the proof that "sound is impermanent, because it is produced by causes and conditions." Here, the opposite of what is to be affirmed or proven—"sound is impermanent"—is the object of negation of reasoning, that is, "sound is permanent." This wrong concept "sound is permanent" exists as a phenomenon that is imputed by the corresponding mistaken conceptual consciousness that takes it as its object. However, this concept does not exist as an object of any unmistaken cognition. Therefore, Nāgārjuna said that, on the level of no analysis, all elements of the triad of the object of negation, the means of negation, and the act of negating are presented in mutual dependence. When analyzed, however, there is utter freedom from these three mental reference points. Thus, in the Centrist system, all objects of both negation and affirmation are merely imputedly existent and not substantially existent,[476] nor are they existent in any other real way. If the object of negation of reasoning were not something that is merely imputed, this would contradict the fact that it cannot be found when searched for.

On the subjective side, when it is said that the actual object of negation of the two identitylessnesses is the clinging to these identities, this does not literally mean that this mistaken cognition itself can be negated or annihilated. Rather, when the term "object of negation" is used with regard to the subjective side of our wrong notions, it is just a technical term that indicates that it is nothing but our habitual grasping to reference points that we have to let go. Of course, from the Centrist point of view, this grasping itself is not something real either. However, in a dualistic mind, as long as there is the mistaken notion of a certain object, there will also be the notion of its subject. Only by realizing that the object is illusory can the subject that holds on to it dissolve naturally. On the other hand, if there were any object of negation that is not just an imputation but is established as a really existing entity, we would not be able to negate or relinquish it, no matter how we tried. For it is impossible to negate or eliminate something that actually exists or, for that matter, prove the existence of something that does not exist in the slightest.

Thus, for Buddhist reasoning and meditation to be soteriologically efficient, we must understand that their actual target is not found on the objective level in the form of a real personal or phenomenal identity. Rather, the actual impact of study, reflection, and meditation always lies on the subjective level. This means that we first uncover and then undermine all the largely unconscious and instinctive forms of grasping at the two identities in order to let go of them and enable our mind to rest relaxed in its own natural ease.

In more technical terms, in the context of the knowledge gained through study and reflection, the actual object of negation of reasoning is the instinctive mistaken mode of cognition that, based on our fundamental unawareness, imagines the two kinds of identity (personal and phenomenal) and takes them to be really existent. This very tendency to reify where there is nothing to be reified is also what we have to release in our meditation practice. Thus, it is also the object of negation of the path of yogic valid perception that arises from meditation. In this way, our innate clinging to personal and phenomenal identities is the actual object of negation through both reasoning and the path. *The Entrance into Centrism* says:

> First, we cling to our self, saying "me,"
> Then we develop attachment to things, saying "this is mine."
>
> Through mentally seeing that afflictions and mistakes without exception
> Originate from the views about a real personality
> And realizing that the self is the object of these [views],
> Yogic practitioners negate a self.[477]

Thus, Centrist reasonings primarily work on the experiencing and clinging mind. Consequently, the way to evaluate their effectiveness is to look at what happens to this mind in terms of becoming more flexible and relaxed both during the reasoning process up through gaining incontrovertible certainty and while familiarizing oneself with this certainty in meditation.

## *The Status of Valid Cognition in Centrism*

In general, the Buddhist teachings on valid cognition as systematized by Dignāga and Dharmakīrti assert two types of valid cognition: perceptual valid cognition and inferential valid cognition. These are commonly accepted as undeceiving and reliable means of knowledge. To Centrists, though, just like any other phenomena, they are not exceptions to being empty of a nature of their own. Consequently, all epistemological means and logical techniques are denied the status of true validity or reality. They only serve as illusory remedies for illusory delusions and in fact are not any different in nature from the delusions that they help to overcome. As Atīśa's *Entrance into the Two Realities* clearly says:

> Perceptual and inferential cognition—
> These two are accepted by Buddhists.

Only narrow-minded fools say
That emptiness is realized by these two.

and

Perceptual and inferential cognition are useless.
It is just for the sake of refuting non-Buddhist opponents
That the learned ones have promoted them.

The learned master Bhavya said
That the scriptures are clear about
[The ultimate] being realized neither through
Conceptual nor nonconceptual consciousnesses.[478]

In his *Rebuttal of Objections*, Nāgārjuna invalidates the standard objections to the Centrist approach and elucidates the nature of its dialectic approach. He denies the notion of valid cognition altogether:

If your objects
Are well established through valid cognitions,
Tell us how you establish
These valid cognitions.

If you think they are established through other valid cognitions,
There is an infinite regress.
Then, the first one is not established,
Nor are the middle ones, nor the last.

If these [valid cognitions] are established even without valid cognition,
What you say is ruined.
In that case, there is an inconsistency,
And you ought to provide an argument for this distinction.[479]

His autocommentary on these verses first describes the position of others: "The objects to be validated are established through valid cognitions. Just like these objects to be validated, the validating cognitions themselves are established through other valid cognitions." Nāgārjuna argues that such a process of validating these validating cognitions would never be finished, since each one that is supposed to validate the preceding one in turn needs another one to validate itself. Thus, one would never even get close to validating the actual objects to be validated. On the other hand, someone might think, "These valid cognitions are established even without other valid cognitions, since they establish the objects to be validated."

This statement, however, contradicts and thus ruins the claim that "valid cognitions establish their objects." For there is the internal inconsistency that certain objects would be established through valid cognition, while others—the valid cognitions themselves—would not. To account for such inconsistency, a further argument would have to be provided; that is, there would need to be a reason that only some objects are established through valid cognition. Since nobody is able to come up with such a reason, this latter position is untenable too.[480]

Nāgārjuna further argues that if valid cognition were established as valid cognition through itself alone, it would not be dependent on anything else, not even on its own object to be validated. So, of what would it be a valid cognition? It basically would be a consciousness that is not conscious of anything, which by definition is impossible. On the other hand, if valid cognition is established through its object to be validated, how is this object established in the first place? If it is already established before and without valid cognition, what need is there for any further cognition to validate it? Furthermore, if valid cognition establishes the object to be validated and the object in turn establishes what valid cognition is, then neither of them is really established as such. They are just mutually dependent. One might think that this is just like a child being produced by its father and the father being made into a father through his child. In that case, though, what is produced by what? It is not possible that the same thing is both the cause and the result of something else.

Thus, valid cognitions are neither really established through themselves alone, nor through other valid cognitions, nor through their objects to be validated, nor through mutual production, and also not without any cause at all.[481]

Some opponents try to turn the tables on Nāgārjuna:

> "If a nature of all entities
> Does not exist in any of them,
> Your words are also without nature
> And cannot refute a nature.
>
> However, if these words have a nature,
> Your earlier claim is ruined.
> As there is such inconsistency,
> You should provide an argument for this distinction."

and

> "Arguments are not established,
> Because they are without nature, so where is your argument?
> Once the absence of a reason is established,
> Your point cannot be proven.

> If, however, the rejection of a nature were established
> Even without your having an argument [for this],
> Then it is also established that there is a nature
> Even though we do not have an argument [for it].
>
> However, if arguments exist, it is unjustified
> That entities are without nature.
> Nowhere is there any entity to be found
> That is without nature."[482]

Nāgārjuna's ultimate answer is as follows:

> My words are without nature.
> Therefore, my thesis is not ruined.
> Since there is no inconsistency,
> I do not have to state an argument for a distinction.[483]

Nāgārjuna readily agrees that his words—just like all other things—are also empty, without a nature of their own. Therefore, his own "thesis" that "all entities are without nature" is not ruined, since it is also empty and there are no non-empty—that is, really existing—words to establish it.[484] He never said that his words are not empty while all other things are empty. So there is no difference between theses or words and any other things in that they all lack any intrinsic nature. Therefore, Nāgārjuna does not have to distinguish between empty things on the one hand and "real" words to prove a "true" thesis on the other. However, this categorical answer seems to render Centrism itself completely obsolete, since it eliminates any possible ground for engaging in the process of reasoning altogether. If everything is empty—including the means to come to this conclusion—any use of arguments seems to be utterly pointless, since there is nothing to be affirmed or negated and nothing that could affirm or negate anything.

So is this the final word in Centrism? Ultimately speaking, yes, but in terms of the path, Centrists indeed bother to employ natureless reasonings to take care of our natureless ignorance that otherwise would result in natureless suffering for natureless sentient beings. The only reason they do so is to help us realize that things have no nature. Usually, logic and reasoning are employed to establish and defend certain positions or reference points to which a certain reality is ascribed. However, Centrist reasonings are not refutations in the sense of rejecting an opponent's view and promoting one's own view instead. The Centrists' whole point is to dissolve our already existent reference points and the clinging to them. They definitely do not try to provide new views or reference points to which to cling. This is precisely what they are very careful to avoid.

Thus, their use of logic and reasoning is a critique of reasoning through reasoning itself.

To be consequent in eliminating all views without exception, this same principle must be applied equally to all types of mistakenness and clinging that are entertained by both oneself and others. However, it is not only a matter of being consequent. More important, the main purpose in dissolving all systems and reference points, including one's own, is to bring about liberation from clinging to really existing things, which is what ties beings down in cyclic existence. For how could the deconstruction of all views be helpful in any other way than to eradicate and prevent this same basic mistake of reification that we all constantly make and that causes us to suffer?

If both what is refuted and what refutes are without a nature, this naturally begs the question of how such empty reasonings could be effective in any way. Nāgārjuna answers:

> Just as one magical creation may be annihilated by an[other] magical creation
> And one illusory person by another person
> Produced by an illusionist,
> This negation is the same.[485]

The audience watching a magic show or a movie may experience one illusory being killing another. However, both the being that appears to be the killer and the one that is killed are empty; they are not really existent. Likewise, in the context of seeming reality, it is justified that the empty and illusory words of Nāgārjuna's negations can negate or cancel out an illusory assumed nature of all things, thus arriving at the conclusion that all things are empty. Therefore, Centrists employ reasoning and such as expedient tools in their discourses only inasmuch as these tools have a certain effectiveness as illusory remedies against illusory fixed ideas. In other words, an illusionlike thesis may be deconstructed by an illusionlike refutation, since the latter has some conventional remedial power within the framework of seeming reality that appears due to fundamental ignorance. Śāntideva sets up the question and then addresses this issue:

> "If valid cognition is not valid cognition,
> Isn't what is validated by it delusive?
> In actuality, the emptiness of entities
> Is therefore unjustified."
>
> Without referring to an imputed entity,
> One cannot apprehend the lack of this entity.

Therefore, the lack of a delusive entity
Is clearly delusive [too].

Thus, when one's son dies in a dream,
The conception "He does not exist"
Removes the thought that he does exist,
But it is also delusive.[486]

Here an opponent objects that if there is no valid cognition, there can also be no object that is validated or found by it. Since all Centrist reasonings are supposed to point to emptiness, emptiness—as the outcome of such invalid reasonings—equally cannot be established as valid. Ultimately, Śāntideva and all Centrists simply agree with this, since there is nothing to be found, established, or negated and also nothing to be validated or invalidated. It is precisely this actuality that is called emptiness. As for the term "emptiness" itself, it is part of the means that assist in the realization of this actuality on the seeming level. One reason is that the negation of something has to depend on a preceding notion of the existence of this given something. For example, one cannot speak or think about the nonexistence of a table without having the notion of a table in the first place. Another reason is that communication and conceptual understanding have to rely on conventional notions or terms—which are always imputations—in order to be capable of pointing out what they refer to. For example, if one does not rely on the conventional term or notion of "space," one is not able to understand what it refers to, that is, the absence of things. Thus, without employing the mere imputation of "emptiness" (nominal emptiness), one is not able to apprehend what it points to (nonnominal emptiness): the actual experience that all imputations (including the one of emptiness) do not exist.

Here, Śāntideva's point is that existence and nonexistence can negate each other even if they are both dreamlike. For example, in a dream in which one's child has been born and then dies, there is definitely no difference between the child's birth and its death inasmuch as both are unreal dream appearances. Still, because of the experience in the dream that the child is born, the thought "My child exists" arises. When it then appears to die, the dreamer thinks, "My child has died and does not exist anymore." In the context of such a dream, this latter thought has the capacity to remove the earlier notion that "my child exists." However, since both the existence and the nonexistence of this child are equal in being dream appearances, they are alike in being delusive. Likewise, the lack of a nature applies to both what negates and what is negated.

In order to counteract the clinging to existence, the approach of negating existence with nonexistence is useful despite the temporary danger of clinging to emptiness as being mere nonexistence. Sentient beings wander in cyclic existence because they cling to the reality of delusive things that are mere appearances. Therefore, the understanding that these very appearances are unreal and illusionlike may surely serve as a provisional remedy for their clinging to real things. However, the imputation of the nonexistence of such delusive appearances—"emptiness"—is clearly delusive too. Hence, applying the notion of emptiness is nothing more than engaging in a particular (more subtle) reification, that is, apprehending emptiness, as the remedy for another (coarser) reification: conceiving of things as real. Still, the overall result of this process is an increase in wisdom. Thus, in his *Entrance into Centrism*, Candrakīrti also illustrates it through a positive example:

> Though [the reflection of one's face in a mirror] is not real, it is there for the purpose of beautifying this face.
> Likewise, also here, our arguments are seen
> To have the capacity of cleansing the face of knowledge.
> It is to be understood that what is to be proven is realized even through [arguments] that lack justification.[487]

The Eighth Karmapa comments that the reflection of one's face that appears in a mirror is not real in the sense of actually being one's face. Still, on the level of no analysis, this reflection appears and may serve as a support for beautifying one's face, by shaving or putting on makeup. The same applies in the context of negating the assertions of the world through reasons that are acknowledged by others. It becomes evident to other disputants that Centrist arguments have the capacity of cleansing the stains of ignorance from the face of knowledge. This means that, from the perspective of these people, Centrist invalidations, such as "being empty by nature," possess the power to invalidate what is to be invalidated and to prove what is to be proven. One should understand that what is to be proven is realized even through arguments that are just acknowledged by others, while lacking any justification through the three modes of a reason that are established by their nature.

In his *Rebuttal of Objections*, Nāgārjuna presents a counterargument and then refutes it:

> "If what lacks a nature
> Could stop what lacks a nature,
> Then what lacks a nature would cease
> And a nature become established."
>
> If [you say that only] existents can be negated,
> Is emptiness then not well established?

For you negate the nonexistence
Of a nature of entities.

As for the emptiness that you negate,
If this emptiness is nonexistent,
Does that not ruin your statement
That [only] "existents can be negated?"[488]

His autocommentary says that, in Centrism, what is negated through words that lack a nature is a *nature of entities.* If it were *the lack of a nature of entities* that is negated through words that lack a nature, then entities would indeed become something that has a nature, because what lacks a nature has been negated. Since they thus became something that has a nature, they would not be empty. However, this is not what Nāgārjuna says: He states that entities *are* empty—that is, they lack a nature—and does not claim that they are *non*empty.[489]

Furthermore, what the above counterargument by some opponents implies is that one can only negate something that exists and not something that does not exist—that lacks a nature. However, at the same time, these very people try to negate emptiness, stating that a nature of all entities does not exist. In other words, they say that emptiness does not exist. However, if emptiness—their object of negation—does not exist, then their statement that one can only negate what exists and not what does not exist is wrong. Or, if this statement is correct, since they negate a nonexistent—emptiness—this nonexistent emptiness must then be something existent, because negating a nonexistent results in an existent. And if emptiness exists, this amounts to establishing that a nature of all entities does not exist. At first glance quite impenetrable, these verses just show the stringency with which Nāgārjuna evaporates all possibilities of grasping at a reference point. On top of that, he demonstrates that any attempt at finding a flaw in emptiness is inevitably flung back onto one's own grasping for something really existent, just like a boomerang.

Finally, Nāgārjuna says that, actually, there is neither something to be negated nor any words or persons to negate it, since all things are equally unreal and empty. Thus, in Centrist reasoning, there is never any negation happening. It is only from the perspective of others who cling to the real existence of things that it seems as if these things were negated. Consequently, Centrist reasonings do not annihilate previously existing things; they just elucidate that these things did not really exist in the first place.

I do not negate anything
And there is also nothing to be negated.
Therefore, it is you who slander me
By saying, "You negate."

> To say that the words of a negation
> Work even without existing words
> Makes one understand that words do not exist,
> But it does not serve to eradicate them.[490]

The words "all entities lack a nature" are not the cause that makes things lack a nature. Rather, they serve as a means to help those who do not know that entities lack a nature realize this fact. For example, this is comparable to when someone says, "Devadatta is at home," while Devadatta is in fact not at home. Others who know better might then correct this person by saying, "No, Devadatta is not at home." Obviously, these words do not cause Devadatta to be not at home; all they do is to point to his absence.[491]

Since words, concepts, logic, and reasoning are mere imaginary imputations and do not represent any real world apart from such imputations either, ultimately what is there to be refuted and what to be implied? Words and reasonings neither really exist in themselves nor relate to anything real as their referent objects. Thus, Centrists do not feel obliged to believe in the real existence of the reasonings and methods that they use, nor in their intrinsic power and validity. In terms of the view, Centrists use seeming reality in general and reasoning, words, and concepts in particular in a way that is completely noncommittal.[492] Consequently, in his *Lucid Words*, Candrakīrti says that, unlike some people with sticks and lassos, words do not overpower their speaker. Also, the refutation of something through a nonimplicative negation does not imply its opposite (or anything else, for that matter). So if nothing is implied in a nonimplicative negation and others still insist that it must imply the opposite of what was negated, it is like when a shopkeeper says that there is nothing to be sold and a customer requests, "Then please sell me this nothing." Thus, to negate that things arise from themselves does not imply that they arise from something other, both, or neither, for they simply do not really arise at all. Negations as they are used by Centrists have to be understood in the practical context of removing errors and wrong ideas. They function as "disillusionment" in the most literal sense. Thus, Centrist negations are negations of judgment altogether and not just another judgment. It is as when we say, "I clean up the dirt on the floor." By this statement, we mean nothing but the removal of dirt from the floor. It does not imply that we afterward find a thing called "dirtlessness" on the floor instead.

What is our starting point to evaluate phenomena when using Centrist reasonings in order to realize emptiness? Are phenomena declared to be emptiness because they do not measure up to an ultimate and given true reality? Or do we just examine phenomena from their own side to realize that they are inconsistent, fluctuating, and without a true core, which may open our eyes to discovering their emptiness? From the Centrist point of view, the only way to truly go beyond delusive appearances is to start by taking a closer look at the very appearances of everyday seeming reality that are right in front of our noses, and not to try to compare them with some more or less speculative ultimate reality. Such a comparison must necessarily fail, because any "ultimate reality" that we could conjure up within the limits of our essentially dualistic mental framework could only be just another reference point within this very framework. In other words, there is no way that we could transcend the net of duality by adding another sophisticated knot to it. This is the main reason Centrists are so adamant about not giving us anything to hold on to in terms of ultimate reality. As they keep saying, ultimate reality can only be realized through seeing that seeming phenomena are not what we take them to be. Thus, when we employ Centrist reasoning on the path, we have to proceed from how things seem to be to how they actually are and not the other way around, that is, by trying to look at things from the perspective of some imputed ultimate reality. In other words, the Centrist approach starts with what is right in front of our eyes and not with some ultimate castle in the sky.

As mentioned earlier, this approach necessarily implies that at the end of the process of analysis and deconstruction, our wrong ideas and their remedies must both dissolve naturally, without our having to apply further remedies for the remedies. From the perspective of the ultimate true nature of phenomena, problems and antidotes are both expressions of the fundamental ignorance that obscures this nature. Only when both afflictive and remedial ignorance have subsided is there the possibility of an unobstructed view of what is pointed to through Centrist analysis. Śāntideva explains this by excluding an infinite regress of analysis:

> If what has been analyzed
> Is analyzed through further analysis,
> There is no end to it,
> Because that analysis would be analyzed too.
>
> Once what had to be analyzed has been analyzed,
> The analysis has no basis left.
> Since there is no basis, it does not continue.
> This is expressed as nirvāṇa.[493]

If one Centrist analysis had to be analyzed by another analysis, it would follow that there is no end to analysis, because the analysis of the first analysis would have to be analyzed again by a third one and so on. However, this is not how Centrist reasoning works. Rather, prajñā is the means that analyzes the mistaken ideas that have to be analyzed, and it does so in such a way that gradually they are all addressed. Once these wrong ideas have been thoroughly analyzed by prajñā and are incontrovertibly seen to be mistaken, they dissolve. As soon as they disappear, the purpose of the analysis is fulfilled, and thus the analysis itself will also subside on its own. Therefore, it is nothing more than a specific analysis for a specific purpose. Apart from that, neither mistaken ideas nor their analysis have any special basis or nature. Since there is no purpose left for such analysis, once its specific task has been accomplished, it does not continue after the mistaken idea in question has been put to an end. The analysis stops on its own, just as a fire dies down as soon as the firewood has burned up. Once all clinging in terms of superimposition and denial has come to an end in this way, nothing but the empty and luminous nature of the mind in which there is nothing to be removed or to be added is laid bare as the fundamental state of all phenomena. This is said to be primordial nirvāṇa.

However, if one were to continue with remedial analysis even at the point when its specific target has already dissolved, then the remedy itself would become the problem. For example, once we have overcome an infection through the help of antibiotics, we do not continue to apply this remedy. Not only would it be useless, but it would cause further health problems. In his *Fundamental Verses*, Nāgārjuna explicitly warns against wrong views about emptiness and clinging to them, be it in terms of existence, nonexistence, permanence, or extinction:

> By the flaw of having views about emptiness,
> Those of little understanding are ruined,
> Just as when incorrectly seizing a snake
> Or mistakenly practicing an awareness-mantra.[494]

In his *Lucid Words*, Candrakīrti comments on this:

> If one thinks, "Everything is empty, which means that everything does not exist," this is a wrong view. . . . On the other hand, one may wish not to deny all [phenomena]. Then, however, no matter in which way one may have focused on these entities, how should they become emptiness? Hence, to say that "the meaning of emptiness is not the meaning of lacking a nature"[495] is definitely a rejection of emptiness. Having rejected it in this way, due to the [ensuing] karmic [result] of being deprived of the dharma, one will go to the lower realms.[496]

The most common charge against Centrism and its way of using reasoning was and is the accusation of outright nihilism. In *The Sūtra of the Arrival in Laṅka*, the Buddha himself prophesied that, in the future, those who cling to speaking in terms of existence or nonexistence will deprecate as nihilists those who say that all phenomena lack arising. However, such a charge completely disregards the fact that Centrism as a spiritual path is a comprehensive set of methods with a soteriological purpose. It is clearly intended as a means to attain perfect Buddhahood for the welfare of all sentient beings through the compassionate motivation and practice of a bodhisattva. Obviously, nothing is farther from nihilism. Nāgārjuna's *Commentary on the Mind of Enlightenment* emphasizes not only the ultimate type of the mind of enlightenment but equally the importance of the conventional kind:

> Support [sentient beings] with all things
> And protect them like your own body.
> Make all efforts to avoid
> Lack of affection for sentient beings.[497]

Even when not taking this motivation into account, in terms of the correct view, Centrist masters always make sure to negate the nihilistic position that nothing at all exists. Also, they explicitly and repeatedly explain why the charge of nihilism does not apply to them. This is evident from Candrakīrti's above comment and also from further verses from *The Commentary on the Mind of Enlightenment*:

> To express emptiness as the nature [of entities]
> Is not to say that anything becomes extinguished.
>
> Those who know that entities are empty
> And then rely on karma and its results
> Are more wonderful than wonderful,
> More amazing than amazing.
>
> In this way, through body, speech, and mind,
> They always promote the welfare of sentient beings.
> What they advocate is emptiness,
> But not the contentions of extinction.[498]

In his *Fundamental Verses*, Nāgārjuna presents other Buddhists' attacks against him for denying the Buddha's own teachings on causality, karma, and the four realities of the noble ones:

> "If all of this is empty,
> There is no origination and no cessation.
> Then it follows that the four realities of the noble ones
> Do not exist for you."[499]

He answers by turning the tables on them:

> If you entertain the view
> That entities exist due to their nature,
> Then you view entities
> As lacking causes and conditions.
>
> Then cause and result,
> Agents, actions, and their objects,
> Arising and ceasing,
> As well as any effect are invalidated.
>
> If all of this were nonempty,
> There would be no origination and no cessation.
> It would follow that the four realities of the noble ones
> Do not exist for you.[500]

Thus, it is precisely this notion of real and independently existent things that excludes the existence of any causes that could give rise to such things as well as any results that these things could produce. For, by definition, independently existent phenomena cannot be affected by anything, nor can they themselves affect anything. Thus, it is rather for those people who grasp at a real nature of phenomena that the four realities of the noble ones and the interdependent flow of causality are impossible. Candrakīrti's *Lucid Words* concords:

> Here, it is said, "If you thus present entities as being without nature, this would eliminate all such statements by the Blessed One as 'The ripening of the actions that one has performed will be experienced by oneself.' It would also deny actions and their results. Therefore, you are the chief of nihilists." We are not nihilists. By refuting both the proponents of existence and of nonexistence, we illuminate the path that is without these two [extremes] and leads to the city of nirvāṇa. We also do not say that actions, agents, and results and such do not exist. "So what do you say then?" We say that they are without nature. One might think, "This is fallacious, since actions and agents are not justified with respect to what is without nature." This is not the case either, because it is only among [phenomena] that have a nature that actions are not seen. [In fact,] actions are only seen among what is without nature.[501]

As we have seen, also Śāntideva excludes the notion of utter nonexistence:

Once this "utter nonexistence"—
The entity to be determined—cannot be observed,
How should a nonentity without a basis
Remain before the mind?[502]

Moreover, Centrists do not deny conventionalities, seeming reality, or mere appearances, since the only target of their reasonings is the cause for suffering. As Śāntideva says:

How something is seen, heard, or known
Is not what is negated here.
Rather, the object of refutation
Is the cause for suffering, which is the conception of reality.[503]

Nāgārjuna's *Commentary on the Mind of Enlightenment* states:

Through explaining true reality as it is,
The seeming does not become disrupted.
Unlike the seeming,
True reality is not observable.[504]

*The Rebuttal of Objections* adds:

However, we do not say
That we do not accept conventions.[505]

His autocommentary states that Centrists do not just explain "all entities are empty" without accepting and relying on conventional reality.[506] Candrakīrti's *Lucid Words* agrees:

> Since some people are not skilled in seeming and ultimate reality, by engaging in justifications that end up being unreasonable, they destroy [seeming reality]. Since we are skilled in presenting seeming reality, we stay within worldly positions. In order to eliminate certain worldly positions, we just negate certain justifications that are set up [by our opponents] through other justifications. Like the elders of the world, we only refute those of you who deviate from worldly standards, but not the seeming [itself].[507]
>
> Just like someone who wishes [to drink] water [needs] a container, first one should doubtlessly accept the seeming as it is.[508]

The main reason for needing such a container is that without relying on and using conventional reality, dharma cannot be taught. *The Fundamental Verses* says:

> Without reliance on conventions,
> The ultimate cannot be taught.
> Without realization of the ultimate,
> Nirvāṇa will not be attained.[509]

Nāgārjuna indeed relied on conventions and seeming reality to a great degree in order to teach people, as is amply proven by many of his other texts in which he describes the path of bodhisattvas or gives practical advice to various persons, ranging from ordinary people to kings.[510] The same goes for Śāntideva: chapters one to eight of his *Entrance to the Bodhisattva's Way of Life* are a guidebook for the seeming reality of practitioners of the great vehicle, and his other main text—*The Compendium of Training*—goes into many practical details of applying the teachings.

In his *Jewel Lamp of Centrism*, Bhāvaviveka quotes Āryadeva with the pragmatic advice to avoid nihilism in any case in order to be on the safe side in terms of potential negative karmic results:

> Even if they doubt that there are lifetimes beyond this one,
> Wise people avoid evil actions.
> If there are no [future lifetimes], there is simply nothing,
> But in case there are, give up nihilism![511]

Bhāvaviveka continues by saying that the chain of the appearances of seeming reality is illusionlike. None of it exists for nonconceptual wisdom or the knowledge that realizes ultimate reality. Trying to validate seeming appearances is like asking whether space is broad or narrow, big or small, fragrant or stinking, sweet or sour, soft or rough. Or it is like pondering the shape and color of the horns of a rabbit. As far as true Centrists are concerned, such "things" cannot be experienced, cognized, or validated.[512] Centrists merely point to the fact that all these seeming appearances lack any real existence. So how could they be called nihilists? This is like calling someone a nihilist who points to an empty room and says, "There is no furniture here."

In his *Lucid Words*, Candrakīrti explains that to see emptiness as nonexistence means not to understand Centrism:

> What you apprehend [as emptiness] is not what we state as the meaning of emptiness in this treatise. Since you do not understand the meaning of emptiness, you neither understand emptiness itself nor the

purpose of emptiness. Therefore, through not understanding the actual mode of entities' own nature, you say a lot of unreasonable things that are not related to our explanations. So what is the purpose of emptiness? It is explained in the examination of identity [in *The Fundamental Verses*]:

> Liberation [is attained] through the exhaustion of karma and afflictions.
> Karma and afflictions [come] from conceptions,
> And these [result] from discursiveness.
> Discursiveness is halted through emptiness.[513]

Therefore, emptiness is taught in order to completely pacify all discursiveness without exception. So if the purpose of emptiness is the complete peace of all discursiveness and you just increase the web of discursiveness by thinking that the meaning of emptiness is nonexistence, you do not realize the purpose of emptiness [at all].[514]

Nāgārjuna finishes his *Rebuttal of Objections* by saying:

> For those for whom emptiness is possible,
> Everything is possible.
> For those for whom emptiness is not possible,
> Nothing is possible.
>
> I prostrate to the incomparable Buddha
> Who has perfectly declared
> That emptiness, dependent origination,
> And the middle path are one in meaning.[515]

Equating emptiness, dependent origination, and the middle path refers to the unity of seeming reality and ultimate reality. All seeming phenomena appear as dependent origination through various causes and conditions, while all of them are empty of any real and independent existence. This is nothing other than the middle path of not falling into the extremes of permanence and extinction.

In general, it may be an appropriate and fruitful approach to use epistemology, logic, and reasoning in order to accomplish certain goals in everyday life and the sciences. However, all of this happens only from the perspective of ordinary beings whose worldviews and experiences are distorted by fundamental ignorance about the true nature of phenomena. The Centrist approach is to eventually step out of this playground altogether; it is a completely different ball game, so to speak. This means that the typical four-cornered logical analysis of Centrism is the deliberate stepping-stone to go beyond the square playground drawn by the limitations of dualistic mind. In this way, thoroughgoing negations from many angles lead to the utter collapse of our conceptual efforts to keep our world together. At some point, conceptual grasping becomes literally exhausted and another dimension of seeing the world may open up. To realize emptiness is not only the negation of thought or grasping, but it is the experience of prajñā or nondual wisdom beholding the universe outside of our dualistic playground.

Usually, we like to think of ourselves as critical, modern persons who do not just believe in things unquestioningly. However, when it comes to "the facts of life," experientially, what we really believe in is what we are used to: our sense perceptions, our thoughts, and our feelings. This clearly shows in how we behave toward the world. From this point of view, we actually are very conservative in that we just rely on our limited, dualistic outlook. The only other source of information about the world that we tend to take for granted is modern science. Although we have never seen things such as subatomic particles or complicated biochemical processes, if scientific experts tell us about them, we think they must be true. On the other hand, if the Buddha and other enlightened masters—as the experts in mind science—tell us about karma, past and future lives, buddha realms or emptiness, we are rather skeptical.

Why do we so easily believe in what modern science says but find it so difficult to believe in the much older science of mind? Why do we listen to modern experts and have a hard time listening to the Buddha or Centrists? We usually just follow the habitual tendencies of our minds, which are mainly oriented toward the outside world and hardly ever look inside. Maybe we do not want to grant that the Buddhist experts in mental science know their job as well as modern scientists know theirs. However, we might at least try to muster a bit more openness to consider what they say and not dismiss their findings right away as "unrealistic," "soft evidence," and the like. This alone would loosen up our rigid view of the world and ourselves tremendously. Let's call it "training in openness to the unexpected and unfamiliar."

As for the issues of valid cognition and reasoning, all of them only make sense as long as they are displayed in a framework whose foundation is the notion of really existing things that actually perform functions according to certain accepted principles. In particular, logical rules solely apply for those who buy into such notions. These rules can be considered as structures or laws to organize and focus our thoughts, but in themselves they say nothing about the relation of these thoughts to reality. In addition, various philosophers, scientists, and ordinary people do not even agree on a single set of rules or principles that determine such things as valid cognition or valid reasoning and agree even less on the definition of reality. More important, however, there is no way to establish the validity of knowledge through any criteria that are either intrinsic or extrinsic to this very knowledge itself. As said before, if valid cognition were justified through itself or through other valid cognitions, there is an infinite regress. And if it were justified through something other than valid cognition, how is this other thing validated?

Thus, we have to distinguish clearly between the investigation of objects (whether in everyday life or in science) on the one hand and the scrutiny of the fundamental principles or presuppositions of how we know and what we know on the other. From the Centrist point of view, the first is expedient and the latter is the key to liberation. All empirical knowledge in the world works through these presuppositions of knowing that derive from ignorance about the actual nature of phenomena. It is in this sense that such knowledge as well as the ways in which it cognizes its objects are only a seeming reality.

On the other hand, the critical dialectics of Centrism is not at all a knowledge about seeming reality. Rather, it uncovers and invalidates the very presuppositions of seeming knowledge by getting at their root: our fundamental clinging to reference points. Therefore, the value of the Centrist critique can never lie in its consistency as a system of thought or in any kind of secular utility. Rather, it is geared toward a clear awareness of mind's nature and a spiritual freedom that precisely consists in dropping all these presuppositions and reference points that function as our bondage in cyclic existence. It is a process of unveiling what is primordially unveiled. Thus, it does not at all deny true reality but serves to free it from all the restrictions of our dualistic grasping at reference points.

The crux of Centrism is that it is only possible to get to such freedom by initially employing these very reference points in order to go beyond them. At least to some degree, this approach inevitably involves language and concepts, which by definition cannot go beyond being merely instruments for expressing seeming reality. So the Centrist approach has no choice but to work with language and concepts in order to point to something that is inexpressible through either of them. As Culler puts it:

> [D]econstruction's procedure is called "sawing off the branch on which one is sitting." . . . One can and may continue to sit on a branch while sawing it. There is no physical or moral obstacle, if one is willing to risk the consequences. The question then becomes whether one will succed in sawing it clear through, and where and how one might land. . . . If "sawing off the branch on which one is sitting" seems foolhardy to men of common sense, it is not so for Nietzsche, Freud, Heidegger, and Derrida; for they suspect that if they fall there is no "ground" to hit and that the most clear-sighted act may be a certain reckless saw-

> ing, a calculated dismemberment or deconstruction of the great cathedral-like trees in which Man has taken shelter for millennia.[516]

It should be obvious by now that Centrists belong to the small club of those who are not afraid to hit *no* ground.

The final question here is this: How can we ever validate the Centrist path or true reality if this path includes a denial of valid cognition? The "ultimate test" lies in our own experience. In order to come to a final clarity about whether all of this is "true" in the sense of functioning as a reliable means leading to the realization of ultimate reality and the irreversible liberation from suffering, we have no choice other than to put it into practice and see whether we actually attain Buddhahood through it. Strictly speaking, to gain an incontrovertible experience of being—and staying—free from all suffering and to manifest omniscient wisdom in our own mind stream is the only way to personally verify that the Centrist approach works all the way to the end. As physicians would say, "Whoever heals is right." As is well known, a disease cannot be overcome by just looking at the medicine and pondering the treatment. Obviously, one has to actually swallow the medicine and undergo therapy. Likewise, without actively engaging in Centrist practice on all three levels of study, reflection, and meditation, we will never solve the question of whether it yields the promised result or not. All speculations, theories, and reasonings alone will not do. As in the example of chocolate chip cookies, we will not experience their taste by just studying recipes.

In other words, Centrism does not bother about some universal truth or abstract validity. Rather, true reality or validity always has to be experienced by a mind. If the Centrist approach is helpful for individual beings to end the delusion in their minds, in terms of the individual experiences of these beings, this is all that is needed and all that counts. Even if there might be more sophisticated views or theories, if they fail to remove our suffering, what are they good for? In this way, the Centrist approach is very pragmatic and hinges entirely on personal experience. This also implies that we do not have to wait until perfect Buddhahood to experience any effect of this approach in our lives. When we actively engage in it, Centrism *is* a way of life whose validity is constantly put to the test in our everyday existence. It is not just some spiritual crossword puzzle that is to be solved somewhere up in the clouds. When we apply the Centrist outlook down here on earth, such experiences as every little bit of relaxing our rigid ways of behaving toward the world and ourselves, every little bit of developing more insight into what actually is going on in the situations that we encounter, and every tiny little flower of compassion that starts blossoming in our mind can be seen as a result of being on this path. Thus, there are both immediate and final benefits.

## *Do Centrists Have a Thesis or Position?*

The attitude of Centrists toward valid cognition leads to the much-debated question of whether they have any thesis or position at all. Nāgārjuna's famous statement on this issue in his *Rebuttal of Objections* says:

> If I had any position,
> I thereby would be at fault.
> Since I have no position,
> I am not at fault at all.
>
> If there were anything to be observed
> Through direct perception and the other instances [of valid cognition],
> It would be something to be established or rejected.
> However, since no such thing exists, I cannot be criticized.[517]

His *Sixty Stanzas on Reasoning* agrees:

> Great beings do not have
> Any thesis or dispute.
> And for those who have no thesis,
> How should there be any thesis of others?[518]

Āryadeva's *Four Hundred Verses* declares:

> Against someone who has no thesis
> Of "existence, nonexistence, or [both] existence and nonexistence,"
> It is not possible to level a charge,
> Even if [this is tried] for a long time.[519]

Śāntarakṣita's *Ornament of Centrism* says almost literally the same thing:

> Against someone who does not claim
> "Existence, nonexistence, or [both] existence and nonexistence,"
> It is in no way possible to raise a charge,
> Even if [this is tried] with serious effort.[520]

Candrakīrti's *Lucid Words* quotes the above verses by Nāgārjuna and Āryadeva and adds:

> For Centrists, it is inappropriate to make any autonomous inferences on their own account, because they do not accept any other theses.[521]

and

> because there is no thesis of our own.[522]

Thus, it is often categorically said that Centrists do not have any thesis or claim at all. On the other hand, in his *Fundamental Verses*, Nāgārjuna does not merely negate; he also makes a number of positive statements even about emptiness and the ultimate, such as providing the characteristics of true reality:

> Not known from something other, peaceful,
> Not discursive through discursiveness,
> Without conceptions, and without distinctions:
> These are the characteristics of true reality.[523]

In *The Rebuttal of Objections*, he even speaks about his thesis:

> My words are without nature.
> Therefore, my thesis is not ruined.[524]

Also Śāntideva mentions a thesis:

> Thus, one cannot uphold any faultfinding
> In the thesis of emptiness.[525]

Bhāvaviveka's *Blaze of Reasoning* says:

> As for our thesis, it is the emptiness of nature, because this is the nature of phenomena. Therefore, we are not guilty of caviling.[526]

The explanation for such seeming contradictions is found in Nāgārjuna's *Fundamental Verses*:

> When something is questioned through emptiness,
> Everything that someone may express as a reply
> Does thereby not constitute a reply,
> [For] it would presuppose what is to be proven.
>
> When something is explained through emptiness,
> Everything that someone may express as faultfinding
> Does thereby not constitute any faultfinding,
> [For] it would presuppose what is to be proven.[527]

Any objection to emptiness or the lack of inherent existence of phenomena would be intended to establish that something is not empty, that is, that it has inherent existence. If something is to be proven as inherently existent, it may be assumed to be established in one of two ways. On the one hand, it could be assumed to be inherently existent by itself, that is, to be completely independent of causes and conditions. The problem here is that this presupposes what has to be proven in the first place: inherent self-existence. Alternatively, if this something is claimed to have arisen from something else that is inherently existent, then the inherent existence of this something else would have to be established, which entails the same problem as above and moreover leads to an infinite regress. In the same way, anything that could serve as a reason to establish inherent existence or refute the lack thereof can only be either inherently existent or lack such existence and thus be empty. If it lacks inherent existence in itself, how could it prove something else to be inherently existent? And if it is assumed to inherently exist, this is again just presupposing what has to be proven.

Thus, what is called emptiness refers to just the pointing out that all things lack inherent existence. In the context of explaining or debating this, it may conventionally be called "the thesis of emptiness." However, as was made clear above, neither the means to point this out, nor its result, nor the process as such is really existent. Thus, they all concord with this "thesis" that all things lack inherent existence. Since both the means to point out emptiness and any hypothetical objections lack inherent existence, whatever one may say or think always just points back to this very same actuality that everything lacks an intrinsic nature and that there are no reference points whatsoever. In this way, inevitably, the very attempt to prove or disprove anything in the sense of "that's how it really is" is self-invalidating and self-contradictory. It is just a further entanglement in the web of dualistic thinking instead of a means to step out of it.[528] Candrakīrti's *Entrance into Centrism* says:

> "Does the means to invalidate invalidate what is to be invalidated without encountering it,
> Or does it do so by encountering it?" This flaw that you already mentioned
> Would certainly apply to someone who has a thesis, but we do not have this thesis.
> Hence, it is impossible that this consequence [applies to us].[529]

His autocommentary specifies this: As far as Centrist "theses" in the above sense of lacking real existence are concerned, the means to invalidate does not invalidate what is to be invalidated either by connecting with it or by not connecting with it, because both the means to invalidate and what is to be invalidated are not established by their nature. Therefore, the above question would apply only to someone who has a thesis that involves the inherent existence of both the means to invalidate and what is to be invalidated. However, since Centrists do not have such theses, they do not conceive of this process of invalidation in terms of an encounter or no encounter between the means to invalidate and what is to be invalidated.[530] Thus, it seems that Candrakīrti does not disclaim that Centrists express "theses" in the sense of just pointing out emptiness or making pedagogic statements merely from the perspective of others. In fact, in all Centrist texts, one finds not only absurd consequences or negations of other positions but also numerous statements of a conventionally propositional nature, such as "The nature of cyclic existence is the nature of nirvāṇa" or "Without seeming reality the ultimate cannot be realized." However, what Candrakīrti and all other Centrists definitely deny is that they have any thesis that involves real existence or reference points or any thesis that is to be defended from their own point of view.

The Eighth Karmapa gives the example that the appearance of floating hairs for a person with blurred vision in no way affects the sight of someone without such a visual impairment. Likewise, when Centrists give a conventional, expedient presentation of seeming causes and results on the level of no analysis, how could any critique that is based on causes and results that are regarded as having a nature of their own ever affect the actual lack of such a nature? Therefore, the Eighth Karmapa says, all objections to emptiness by realists are only prompted by their own limited outlook. They cannot help thinking that Centrists definitely must claim the opposite of what they themselves assert. They enter the dispute by assuming that, just like themselves, the Centrists too hold on to things such as theses of their own and others, something to be proven and the means to prove it, something that is to be invalidated and the means to invalidate it. Thus, all attempts by realists to refute Centrists only mean that they did not at all understand the meaning of emptiness in the way that Centrists try to convey it. In this way, realists basically just debate with their own thoughts as opponents.

The crucial point here and in Centrism in general is that inherent existence is simply an incoherent notion altogether that does not withstand analysis. What is called emptiness is just the result of pointing out this fact. In other words, whether one conventionally speaks of "the thesis of emptiness" or says, "I have no thesis," both expressions just announce and highlight the Centrist procedure of demonstrating that all things lack inherent existence—that there are no reference points. Needless to say, such a "thesis of emptiness" is nothing to hold on to either. The Karmapa quotes his guru, the great siddha Sangye Nyenba Rinpoche:

> All you people who assert scriptures and reasonings
> That prove a real identity

> Are very much afraid of the notion that there is no real identity
> And thus perform all kinds of pointless negations and proofs.
>
> Once you do not cling to either of these two theses
> Of a real identity or the lack of a real identity,
> All disputes of negation and proof will subside.
> Then there is no harm even through billions of scriptures and reasonings.[531]

The Second Shamarpa Kachö Wangbo says:

> No matter how excellent a view in a scriptural tradition might be,
> It is mistaken when compared to the actual basic nature.[532]

The same applies to reasoning: No matter how excellent reasonings or theses that are established through valid cognition might be, ultimately, they conflict with the basic nature and thus are just a road to perdition.

Moreover, in terms of Centrists merely pronouncing what conventionally looks like a thesis, one must differentiate between Centrists in different situations. The most fundamental distinction here is twofold:

1) those Centrists who rest in the meditative equipoise of directly seeing the nature of phenomena
2) all other Centrists (those in meditative equipoise who do not directly realize this nature, as well as all those who are in the phase of subsequent attainment).

With regard to those who directly realize emptiness, the question of having a thesis or not simply does not apply, since all mental reference points are completely at peace in such a realization. As for the others, as mentioned earlier, the Eighth Karmapa distinguishes four possibilities in terms of persons who uphold the Centrist view and persons who have realized it. There are the following:

a) people who uphold the Centrist view and in whose continua its realization has not arisen
b) those in whose continua its realization has arisen and who do not uphold the Centrist view
c) those for whom both is the case
d) those for whom neither is the case

It is clear that persons (b) and (d) are not relevant here, since the former do not profess to be Centrists and the latter are not Centrists in any way. This leaves persons (a) and (c) as the ones who may point out to appropriate people in appropriate situations that all things lack a nature of their own, which may be called "the thesis of emptiness." As the First Sangye Nyenba Rinpoche says:

> As for the presentation of the two realities that are set up in dependence,
> We pronounce it merely from the perspective of the worldly consensus of others.
> Now, once you are free from mundane discursiveness,
> All negations and affirmations of existence, nonexistence, being, and not being
> In terms of all characteristics of arising and ceasing
> Through such [criteria] as reality and falsity of dependent phenomena
> Are at peace in the sense that they are not observable.
> In this state, how could there be any view or meditation of our own system?
> Once a philosophical system that is our own system has vanished,
> It is meaningless to refute other systems.
> Therefore, do not even use the label of Madhyamaka.[533]

Karmapa Mikyö Dorje summarizes this issue by saying that, on both the seeming and the ultimate level, Centrists do not have any thesis of their own in the sense of something to defend in debate or something that would represent their own standpoint or the position in which they themselves believe. For, if someone claims something or clings to it, that person is not a Centrist in the first place but inevitably has fallen into some extreme through still having a reference point. Furthermore, even on the conventional or seeming level, Centrists refer to such expressions as "emptiness" or "all phenomena are mere dependent origination" in a way that is free from all reference points and clinging to reference points. Such pronouncements are in no way meant to increase any kind of clinging, since whatever is not free from clinging or even increases it is not suitable as the Centrist path. And if something is not the Centrist path, it is not appropriate as the means to pacify all reference points.

Thus, although Centrists have no thesis or position, from the perspective of others, they still talk about mere names, mere designations, and mere conventions (such as existence, nonexistence, both, and neither; dependent origination; or emptiness). To do so does not contradict having no thesis, since this very way of speaking is the means to make others comprehend the profound actuality that is without any positions or clinging to reference points. For example, people with blurred vision see various delusive appearances and take them to be really existent. In order to put an end to the clinging that these appearances are real, other people with clear vision may say to them, "You surely see such appearances as floating hairs, but none of them exists in the way they appear to you." Clearly, in order for those with clear vision to make such a statement, it is not necessary that floating hairs and such appear to them on the conventional level.

So when Centrists like Nāgārjuna and Śāntideva conventionally speak about "my thesis," "the thesis of emptiness," or a "position,"[534] they do not at all refer to any principle, doctrine, or proposition of their own. Such words are just used as nominal expressions that conform with debate terminology and reasoning as these are agreed upon by others. Thus, such expressions as "the thesis of emptiness" can be understood as a kind of metalanguage that just recalls and epitomizes the whole process of demonstrating that things lack inherent existence. This is similar to when Centrists use the term "nature" in a twofold sense, meaning "an intrinsic and independent nature of entities" as opposed to "the actual or ultimate nature of entities," which is that they have no nature in the first sense.[535] In the same way, "the thesis of emptiness" in the sense of just pointing out that there are no reference points per se excludes any notion of thesis in the usual sense, that of a statement that is based on and expresses one's own reference points. This accords with what Patsab Lotsāwa reportedly said on this issue:

> In the declaration that [Centrists] do not have a position, there is no contradiction, since it [means the following]:They do not have a position that is proven through positive determination, but it is not the case that they do not even have a mere position [in the sense] of negating through negative determination.[536]

As was illustrated by the example of the unblurred vision of one person being unaffected by the blurred vision of someone else, all conventional "theses" such as "positive actions lead to pleasant results and negative actions cause unpleasant results" are made exclusively on the level of no analysis and just from the perspective of others whose wrong ideas are to be dissolved. Thus, they do not affect the vision of those who have realized emptiness, that is, the true nature of all phenomena, including such conventional explanations. As Padma Karpo's *Illumination of Three Centrist Scriptural Systems* says:

> From the perspective of various individual persons, to give various teachings for those who are to be guided through various individual [means], everything may be suitable to be asserted, be it existence, nonexistence, or whatever. From the perspective of a Buddha, there is nothing whatsoever to be asserted. These two [perspectives] are not contradictory.[537]

Lindtner summarizes the whole issue nicely:

> Thus on the *saṃvṛti*-level [the level of the seeming] we find him [Nāgārjuna] engaged either in demonstrating his own standpoint (i.e. *sādhana*), or in refuting that of his opponents (i.e. *dūṣaṇa*). While on this level he willingly complies with the conventional, more or less common-sense, rules of debate current in his days. But sometimes we see him shifting to a hypothetical mode of argument which is quite his own. Now the *svātantrika*, so to speak, becomes a *prāsaṅgika*.
>
> First he hypothetically assumes—*argumenti causa*—that there is such a thing as *svabhāva* (nature/attribute) in order, then, to point out the absurd implications (*prasaṅga*) inherent in this assumption when faced with the stern demands of logic and experience. Here on the *saṃvṛti*-level he has only one thesis to defend, namely that all dharmas are empty of *svabhāva*.
>
> On the *paramārtha*-level, however, he is beyond the ifs and the musts of logic. In his own words, he no longer defends the thesis he took so great pains to defend on the *saṃvṛti*-level: that things lack *svabhāva*. . . .
>
> We may now be tempted to ask whether there is a consistency behind the paradox that Nāgārjuna at the same defends a thesis and also does not defend a thesis.
>
> . . . In both cases he is concerned with one and the same thing, namely lack of *svabhāva*. But a difference remains, it is one of outlook, one might say. On the *saṃvṛti*-level he speaks and argues about lack of *svabhāva* as a truth (an ultimate truth). On the *paramārtha*-level he is still concerned with the same thing (or rather nothing) but here one cannot speak about it. Here it has become reality, as it were.
>
> The distinction (*bheda*) between *truth* and *reality* is solely a question of whether the medium of language is present or not. One can speak the truth, but one cannot possibly speak the reality. At the best one can, as Nāgārjuna points out, "suggest," or "allude" to reality by means of *prajñapti*, or indications.
>
> The final problem, then, is to get "beyond" language—beyond *prapañca* [discursiveness] as Nāgārjuna would say.
>
> There is no theoretical solution to this problem. Theoretical solutions can, at best, offer us truth, not reality. . . .
>
> Of *paramārtha* one cannot speak; it is a matter of belief and personal experience (*aparapratyaya*). Much less can one speak of its relationship to anything, viz. *saṃvṛti*. One must learn to remain satisfied with mere indications—*prajñapti*.[538]

It is important to clearly note that having no thesis or reference point is not just a clever or elusive move in debate. Rather, its main significance lies again in its soteriological effect of liberation from any clinging and the ensuing afflictions. As Nāgārjuna's *Sixty Stanzas on Reasoning* emphasizes:

> By taking any standpoint whatsoever,
> You will be snatched by the cunning snakes of the afflictions.
> Those whose minds have no standpoint
> Will not be caught.
>
> Those whose minds are not moved,
> Not even by a flicker of a thought about "complete voidness,"
> Have crossed the horrifying ocean of existence
> That is agitated by the snakes of the afflictions.[539]

Nevertheless, as for the proper approach of pointing out to others that all things are empty and without reference point, there is some disagreement among Centrists. For example, Bhāvaviveka says that it is inappropriate to not present one's own system and only negate the systems of others, since such a style of disputation amounts to nothing but sophistry and mere deceitful destructiveness. Also, if one's own positions—emptiness, nonarising, and so on—are not established through valid cognition, then one cannot negate the views of others merely by flinging consequences at their positions (such as their claim of inherently arising and existing things). Moreover, one cannot prove the view of one's own system through reasons that are asserted only by others and not by oneself. For these three reasons, certain positions must be asserted that represent one's own system and are established through valid cognition, such as the Centrist arguments and examples that prove nonarising in a conventional context.

Consequentialists answer: It may well be that some people have their own claims and then do not present their own system out of fear of other people's critique or that they negate the systems of others with hostile intentions through merely setting up absurd consequences. In such cases one can rightfully speak of a style of debating that involves hypocrisy and deceit and ends up being mere sophistry and unfair destructiveness. However, we cannot be accused of such, since we neither set up anything in the sense that there exists something to be set up as our own thesis, nor do we negate anything in the sense that there exists something to be negated as the theses of others. If we do not have the slightest thesis of our own that is to be set up, then what is the point of all this toil to search for a means to prove it?

Actually, as explained above, the Centrist approach is not even a negation of something. If one could observe even the minutest existent phenomenon to be negated, it would certainly be appropriate to negate it. However, if one cannot observe anything to be negated, who would want to speak of negation here? As Nāgārjuna says in his *Precious Garland*:

Through destruction or a remedy,
Being existent would become nonexistence.
[However,] since [real] existence is impossible,
How could there be [its] destruction or remedy?[540]

In his *Entrance Gate for the Learned*,[541] Sakya Paṇḍita gives the following example: Just negating while not asserting anything as a kind of deceitful tactic may be compared to not acknowledging that a theft that has been committed. On the other hand, Consequentialist negation and nonassertion is like nonacknowledgment of a theft when no theft has been committed in the first place. Thus, there is a great difference between these two approaches.

Nevertheless, conventionally speaking, from the point of view of delusive appearances, or from the perspective of the subsequent attainment that is informed by preceding meditative equipoise, Centrists not only follow ordinary common consensus but also employ specific Buddhist conventions, such as the two realities, karma, and the stages of the path. For these are the conventional means to transcend the root cause of suffering: the clinging to mere delusive appearances as real. On the other hand, that Consequentialists do not defend such conventions in debate by trying to actually establish or affirm something—not even emptiness—is the expression of the core of their approach, that is, leading others to freedom from reference points and not creating more. Thus, all that Centrists say and teach in their communications with others is always applied as a pedagogic tool that is adapted to the individual perspectives of other people. None of this is apprehended or put forward by Centrists as any system of their own in any way.

In this context, it has to be clearly understood that the above objections by Bhāvaviveka refer only to the situation of communicating emptiness or ultimate reality to others. In actuality, Autonomists such as Bhāvaviveka also aim at nothing but freedom from discursiveness and reference points. Some people say that there is a slight remainder of discursiveness or affirmation in the ultimate view of Autonomists. The Eighth Karmapa argues that this is not the case, because the texts of Autonomists are even clearer than the texts of Candrakīrti in their way of teaching freedom from discursiveness. He quotes Śāntarakṣita's *Ornament of Centrism*:

Because ["nonarising"] concords with the ultimate,
It is called the ultimate.
In actuality, it is the release
From all complexes of discursiveness.

Since arising and so forth do not exist,
Nonarising and so on are impossible.

Since their nature has been negated,
Their verbal terms are impossible.

There is no good formula
To negate nonexistent objects.
[Nonarising and such] depend on conceptions
And thus are seeming, not actual.[542]

and Jñānagarbha's *Distinction between the Two Realities*:

Since the negation of arising and so on
Concords with actuality, we accept it.
Since there is nothing to be negated,
It is clear that, actually, there is no negation.

How should the negation of an imputation's
Own nature not be an imputation?
Hence, seemingly, this is
The meaning of actuality, but not actuality [itself].

In actuality, neither exists.
This is the lack of discursiveness:
Mañjuśrī asked about actuality,
And the son of the Victors remained silent.[543]

Further examples of this stance include Bhāvaviveka's *Summary of the Meaning of Centrism*:

The ultimate is freedom from discursiveness.

Being empty of all discursiveness
Is to be understood
As the nonnominal ultimate.[544]

His *Heart of Centrism* agrees:

Its character is neither existent, nor nonexistent,
Nor [both] existent and nonexistent, nor neither.
Centrists should know true reality
That is free from these four possibilities.[545]

His *Lamp of Knowledge* says:

> This negation "[entities do] not [arise] from themselves" is to be regarded as having the meaning of a non-implicative negation. [This is so], because it is primarily a negation and because [Nāgārjuna's] intention is to thus arrive at nonconceptual wisdom that is endowed with the entirety of knowable objects through negating the web of all conceptions without exception. If it were taken to be an implicative negation, since that is primarily an affirmation, it would teach non-arising by affirming that "phenomena are non-arisen." Hence, it would be distinct from [our] conclusion, since the scriptures say, "If one engages in the non-arising of form, one does not engage in the perfection of knowledge."[546]

and

> Here, the purpose of emptiness is its characteristic of all discursiveness being at utter peace. The characteristic that emptiness is free from all clinging represents the wisdom that observes emptiness. The actuality of emptiness is its characteristic of suchness.[547]

Kamalaśīla's *Establishing That All Phenomena Are without Nature* explains:

> Since this lack of arising is concordant with realizing the ultimate, it is called "the ultimate." Since there is no object of negation, such as arising, that is established, [its] lack [cannot really] be related to this nonexistent object. Therefore, to apprehend the lack of arising and such is nothing but a reference point. . . . Ultimately, true reality cannot be expressed as the lack of arising and such. Therefore, Noble Mañjuśrī asked about true reality and Noble Vimalakīrti said nothing.[548]

And his *Stages of Meditation* says:

> Thus, at the time when yogic practitioners examine through their supreme knowledge and do not observe any nature of entities whatsoever, thoughts about entities do not originate in them. They do not have any thoughts about nonentities either. If there were any entity to be seen, then, by negating [this entity], the thought of "nonentity" would come up. However, when yogic practitioners examine with their eyes of supreme knowledge, they do not observe any entity within the three times. At this point, through negating what [entity] would they entertain a thought of "nonentity"? Likewise, no other thoughts arise

> in them at this time. The reasons for this are as follows: The two [kinds of] thoughts about existents and nonexistents include all [possible] thoughts. Also, since [actually] there is nothing that includes anything, there is also nothing to be included. This is the genuine yoga of nonconceptuality. Since in yogic practitioners dwelling in it all thoughts have vanished, they perfectly relinquish afflictive obscurations and cognitive obscurations.[549]

Thus, Karmapa Mikyö Dorje says that there is actually only one single difference between Autonomists and Consequentialists. In general, it is just on the conventional level that both refute wrong ideas through explaining the words of the Buddha, composing treatises on them, and debating with others. In this conventional context, Consequentialists say that the scriptures and reasonings used to refute wrong views do not even conventionally have the nature of valid cognition or the like and thus lack any real nature that could refute their opposite, which is to say nonvalid cognition. Nevertheless, they simply follow and repeat the verbal consensus on valid cognition that is agreed upon by others. Based on this approach, they negate phenomena that are not even established on the level of correct seeming worldly reality, let alone ultimately. Autonomists agree that, ultimately, the arguments and such that refute wrong ideas do not have a nature that is ultimately established as valid cognition. However, they argue that, when refuting wrong ideas on the conventional level, if one does not conventionally accept that arguments and such are established through valid cognition, the wrong ideas of realists cannot be refuted.

The Karmapa emphasizes that it is merely this difference that led to the distinction between Autonomists and Consequentialists. However, this does not mean that there are any differences in terms of one of these views being more profound or better than the other, since both equally accept the complete freedom from discursiveness and reference points. Moreover, not even the omniscience of a Buddha could see any difference in terms of better or worse between the approaches that they employ in order to put an end to discursiveness and reference points. The Karmapa is very explicit that certain other minor divergences between the approaches of Autonomists and Consequentialists are just of expedient meaning. They in no way justify making a difference in terms of the profundity of their view in terms of the ultimate. In particular, there are no grounds for basing elaborate outlines of two distinct Centrist systems—as they are found in some (mostly later) Tibetan doxographies—on such an assumed difference in profundity.[550]

## *Illusory Lions Killing Illusory Elephants: Empty Reasonings for Liberation*

### Some Essential Points of Centrist Reasoning

The root of all Centrist arguments is the praise to the Buddha that Nāgārjuna proclaims at the very beginning of his *Fundamental Verses on Centrism*:

> I bow down to the perfect Buddha,
> The supreme orator, who taught
> That dependent origination
> Is without ceasing and without arising,
> Without extinction and without permanence,
> Without coming and without going,
> Not different and not one.
> It is the peace in which discursiveness is at complete peace.

Accordingly, there are four root arguments:

1) Outer and inner entities are without ceasing in the end and without abiding in the middle, because they do not arise in the first place.
2) Outer and inner entities are without extinction, because there is no permanence.
3) Outer and inner entities are without coming, because going is not established.
4) Outer and inner entities are not established as different, because there is no entity that is one.

All other Madhyamaka arguments, such as the five great Centrist reasonings, derive from these four basic arguments. It is said that the negation of the eight reference points—arising, ceasing, permanence, extinction, going, coming, oneness, and difference—in the opening verses of *The Fundamental Verses* represents a brief synopsis of both this treatise and Centrist reasoning in general. For the negation of oneness and difference is nothing other than the reasoning of the freedom from unity and multiplicity, while the six other negations of arising and so on primarily depend on the negation of oneness and difference. There are three essential steps in all these reasonings that analyze for the ultimate:

1) One picks a certain phenomenon, such as a book, as one's basis of attribution or analysis.
2) One searches for a nature of this phenomenon that is not self-contradictory.
3) Within this basis of attribution, one looks for something, such as its attributes, that is contradictory to its nature.

Hence, from among all Centrist arguments, the following two are the main reasonings in that they respectively correspond to steps (2) and (3):

a) the reasoning of the freedom from unity and multiplicity in order to analyze a nature
b) the vajra sliver reasoning in order to analyze the attributes

The many other enumerations of arguments that are explained in Centrist texts are merely branches of these two reasonings. In particular, the reasoning of the freedom from unity and multiplicity is the root of all reasonings that negate real existence.

These reasonings are explained in detail below, but to briefly illustrate the above three essential points, we may start, for example, by taking a book as the object of our analysis. When searching for the book's nature, initially, we might think that it really exists and that it is its nature to be a real unity. However, such an assumed nature of being a unity is self-contradictory, since a book can be broken down into infinitely many parts. If we then think that the book must be a real multiplicity, this is also self-contradictory, since we cannot find any real unities in it that could serve as building blocks for a real multiplicity. And since there is no third possibility for the book to really exist, we have to admit that the only nature of this book that is not self-contradictory is that it does not exist either as a real unity or as a real multiplicity. In other words, the book does not really exist altogether. Finally, we look for possible attributes of this book—such as that it really arises—that are contradictory to its nature of lacking real existence. This means that if we were to find some real arising of the book, this would obviously contradict its nature of lacking real existence. However, under analysis, we will find that the book does not really arise from itself, nor from something other, nor from both itself and something other, and also not without any cause. In summary, the book does not really arise at all, which perfectly well accords with its nature of lacking real existence. In this way, the nature of this book (its lack of real existence) and its attribute (its lack of real arising) are found neither to be self-contradictory nor to contradict each other.

Although the actual Centrist reasonings always negate, their point is not to negate away something that really exists, since something really existent cannot be negated anyway. They also do not remove or negate something nonexistent. Since a nonexistent cannot be an object, there is no object to which to refer in the first place. "Negating" just means to demonstrate that things do not exist in the real and solid way that we think they do. Thus, the object of negation of reasoning is not something that does not exist anyway (such as a truly existing nature of things). Technically, the object of negation is merely the mental image that appears for the reifying conceptions of people who mistakenly believe in the existence of what does not exist. Therefore, as far as Centrists are concerned, "real existence" is just something that occurs in a psychological or subjective sense but certainly does not exist in any ontological or objective sense. Consequently, the force of Centrist negation strikes only the realm of our fixed ideas and not something that would appear on any hypothetical level of real or substantial existence. Moreover, as was elaborated above, the words and concepts in Centrist reasonings are as unreal as the words and concepts that they negate. However, from our mental perspective, they still serve their purpose of making us let go of our rigid ideas. Centrist reasonings do not negate mere seeming arising or existence in a categorical way, nor do they take away the possibility of conventionally experiencing both single and many things in our everyday lives. Instead, these reasonings tackle the wrong notions of real arising, real existence, real unity, and real multiplicity.

As for the actual techniques of reasoned analysis, the standard framework of formulating Centrist reasonings is to present dilemmas or even tetralemmas of mutually exclusive and exhaustive possibilities for something, such as existence or arising, which then are refuted one by one. For example, the reasoning of the freedom from unity and multiplicity is presented as a dilemma, that is, really existing things can only exist as a real unity or as a real multiplicity. There is no third possibility, since all existing phenomena are included in these two mutually exclusive and exhaustive categories of existence.

From among the five Centrist reasonings, the three reasonings that negate real arising go even further and investigate four possible ways of arising, such as whether things arise from themselves, from something other, from both, or from neither, which is to say, without any cause. These four possibilities are mutually exclusive and cover all theoretically imaginable ways in which things might arise.[551] Thus, through the refutation of each one of these possibilities, it is shown that things do not really arise at all. The same principle is applied to other issues, such as whether a cause produces a result that is already existent, nonexistent, both, or neither; whether an object exists before, after, or simultaneously with the consciousness that perceives it; and whether some assumed productive potential in a cause is identical to the cause or different from it. On the not so serious side of things, probably the shortest summary of this approach is to say that the classic Madhyamaka statement to which all others can be reduced is "neither nor, nor neither."

Within this framework of analysis, its actual result—elimination of reification—can be achieved either through using formal probative arguments with the three modes of a correct reason (also called "autonomous reasoning") or through drawing unwanted consequences from other people's positions. Somewhat simplified, one could say that autonomous reasoning in this sense refers to any probative argument with the correct three modes that says "how things are" (either conventionally or ultimately). On the other hand, absurd consequences do not have all three—or even none—of the correct modes, whether they include a reason or not. This means that they are just consequences that follow from another position that is already wrong in the first place. Thus, they are logically correct, but their explicit meaning must be false, since it is just an absurd result of a previous false statement.

For example, if someone holds that a vase is permanent, this wrong notion may be dispelled by stating what is correct and giving a proper reason for it, such as "A vase is *not* permanent, because it arises from causes and conditions and thus must disintegrate at some point (such as now when I let it drop)." Here, the three modes are established. Alternatively, one may draw absurd consequences from the position that a vase is permanent, such as saying, "Then it follows that a vase neither arises in the first place nor ceases to exist later." Obviously, in this consequence, the question of the three modes does not apply, since there is no reason. Sometimes the opponent's position is added as the reason to such a consequence, such as by saying, "It follows that a vase does not arise and cease, because—according to your claim—it is permanent." In that case, from the perspective of the opponent, all three modes are established, since a vase is claimed to be permanent and whatever is permanent necessarily does not arise and cease. Therefore, the opponent must accept this unwanted consequence of his or her position. From the perspective of correct worldy conventions, when regarding a vase as an impermanent phenomenon, only the second and third modes are established (which is precisely the correct but, in relation to such an impermanent phenomenon, absurd consequence that whatever is permanent necessarily does not arise and cease). From the perspective of Centrists, ultimately also this is not established, since neither a vase nor something permanent exists and thus cannot be said either to arise and cease or not to. There are also many consequences in which all three modes are not even conventionally established, for example, the consequence "It follows that things do not arise from themselves, since their arising would be pointless and endless" that is drawn from the assertion that things arise from themselves.[552]

All Centrists agree and emphasize that their formulations of negations or absurd consequences in no way imply their reverses or anything else, for that matter. Thus, they are all exclusively nonimplicative negations. For example, to state, "Things do not arise from something other, since then everything could arise from everything"[553] does not imply that things either arise from themselves, from both themselves and others, or without a cause. This is further evidenced by the fact that Centrists explicitly negate all of these possibilities one by one, and there is no fifth possibility.

Another characteristic feature of Centrist reasonings is that they often analyze things in terms of infinitesimal parts and moments in time. For example, in the reasoning of the freedom from unity and multiplicity, one seeks for the final, smallest parts of things that could represent a hypothetical indivisible unity. Most of the arguments and consequences in the context of the three great Centrist reasonings that negate arising are formulated in terms of the individual moments of the process of causality, such as considering the relationship between the last moment of the cause that immediately precedes the first moment of its specific result or whether there exists any simultaneous moment of cause and result during which there is some causal interaction between them.

As for the interaction of this approach of negating mutually exclusive and exhaustive alternatives with the subjective side of our mind that grapples with such reasonings, Centrists just utilize the natural structure of our black-and-white thinking, since this is precisely the way in which dualistic clinging operates. Usually, when we find that something does not exist or is not permanent, we immediately think that it then must be nonexistent or impermanent. On the checkerboard of our dualistic mind that is grounded in really existing things, this may make sense in that the exclusion of one of these possibilities necessarily implies the presence of the other. However, from the perspective of the Centrist view of all appearances' fundamental lack of any real existence, all such possibilities as permanent, impermanent, existent, and nonexistent are just vain attempts by our dualistic fixation to hold on to something within the infinite openness of mind's natural expanse, which cannot be boxed in in any way. In other words, Centrist reasonings beat our fixating mind with its own weapons. When dualistic mind progressively analyzes its own dualistic structure and function, this inevitably leads to its own collapse altogether. When it sees all its reference points dwindle, including itself as that which creates these reference points, it simply goes out of business. Thus, the radical and relentless use of Centrist dilemmas and tetralemmas is a deliberate, systematic, and—in a sense—therapeutic technique to pull each piece of the patchwork of our two-dimensional referential carpet from under our feet and explore the nondimensional, boundless space of mind's true nature.

## Disillusionment with Phenomenal Identity

### The Five Great Madhyamaka Reasonings

In general, various Centrist masters present many different arguments that determine phenomenal identitylessness. In the system of Nāgārjuna and his spiritual heirs, these are mainly "the five great Centrist reasonings":

1) the negation through the analysis of an intrinsic nature: the reasoning of freedom from unity and multiplicity
2) the negation through the analysis of causes: the vajra sliver reasoning[554]
3) the negation through the analysis of results: the reasoning that negates an arising of existents and nonexistents
4) the negation through the analysis of both causes and results: the reasoning that negates arising from the four possibilities

5) the analysis of mere appearances: the reasoning of dependent origination

**Scriptural Sources for the Five Great Reasonings**

As for their scriptural references in the sūtras, the first of these reasonings is, for example, found in *The Sūtra of the Arrival in Laṅka*,[555] the second in *The Rice Seedling Sūtra*,[556] and the fifth in *The Sūtra Requested by the Nāgā King "The Cool One"*[557] as well as in *The Sūtra on Dependent Origination*.[558] The third and fourth reasonings are found in various other sūtras.

In Centrist treatises, the reasoning of the freedom from unity and multiplicity is extensively explained in both Śāntarakṣita's *Ornament of Centrism*[559] and Śrīgupta's (seventh century) *Commentary on Entering True Reality*. It is also used in Nāgārjuna's *Seventy Stanzas on Emptiness*,[560] Āryadeva's *Four Hundred Verses*,[561] and the first volume of Kamalaśīla's *Stages of Meditation*.[562]

The explanation of the vajra sliver reasoning is one of the main themes in Nāgārjuna's *Fundamental Verses* and also forms the major portion of the sixth chapter of Candrakīrti's *Entrance into Centrism*. It is taught in detail in the ninth chapter of Śāntideva's *Entrance to the Bodhisattva's Way of Life*[563] and also presented in Kamalaśīla's *Stages of Meditation*.[564]

As for the negation of the arising of existents and nonexistents, it is taught in the three just-mentioned texts by Nāgārjuna,[565] Candrakīrti,[566] and Śāntideva.[567] It is also mentioned in *The Seventy Stanzas on Emptiness*.[568]

The negation of arising from the four possibilities is found in Jñānagarbha's *Distinction between the Two Realities*[569] and explained in detail in its autocommentary[570] and the subcommentary by Śāntarakṣita[571] as well as in Haribhadra's *Illumination of The Ornament of Clear Realization*.[572] It is also used in Kamalaśīla's *Illumination of Centrism*[573] and his *Establishing that all Phenomena are Without Nature*.[574]

The reasoning of dependent origination is the major theme of Nāgārjuna's *Seventy Stanzas on Emptiness*. It also appears in his *Rebuttal of Objections*,[575] in *Sixty Stanzas on Reasoning*,[576] in several chapters of his *Fundamental Verses*,[577] and in Candrakīrti's *Entrance into Centrism*.[578]

The first known summary of four of these five reasonings (excepting the fourth) is found in Bhāvaviveka's *Summary of the Meaning of Centrism* (lines 14–17). Later, Atīśa gave a more detailed overview of the same four reasonings in his autocommentary on verses 48–52 of *The Lamp for the Path to Enlightenment*.[579] Kamalaśīla explains all five in his *Illumination of Centrism*.[580]

**The Detailed Explanation of the Five Great Reasonings**

Together, these reasonings refute the extremes of existence and nonexistence. Since our clinging to real existence is far stronger than our clinging to nonexistence, the first four reasonings eliminate the imputation that things exist by their own nature. Therefore, they all serve to relinquish the first extreme of existence. The fifth reasoning simultaneously eliminates the extremes of existence and nonexistence. Moreover, it induces certainty about the unity of emptiness and dependent origination.

In what follows, these five reasonings are explained through a three-part reasoning (inference for oneself) and the three modes of a correct reason that were explained above. To reiterate, each such reasoning has a subject, a predicate, and a reason. Its validity is tested by checking the three modes of subject property, positive entailment, and negative entailment.

### I. The analysis of a nature: the reasoning of freedom from unity and multiplicity

#### A. The formulation of the reasoning

All phenomena—such as sprouts—do not really exist, because they lack unity and multiplicity, just as a reflection in a mirror.

#### B. The three modes of the reason

The subject of this reasoning is just mere appearances without examination and analysis. The *subject property* that applies to this subject is as follows: These mere appearances are not a real unity, because they possess many parts. Each of these parts can in turn be broken down into many subparts. Since this process can be infinitely repeated, there is not a single smallest particle that is a really existent and indivisible unity. Without even one real building block, how could you put together many so as to create a really existent thing? Consequently, there can be nothing that is a real multiplicity, because there is no real unity to begin with that could build up such a multiplicity. To be sure, this reasoning does not negate the mere conventionality that one thing has many parts. The point here is that neither the thing in question nor its parts really exist by themselves. Thus, what is denied is not the mere appearance of unity and multiplicity on the level of seeming reality but the existence of any unity or multiplicity that is really established and findable as such.

For example, our body consists of its head, torso, and limbs. The legs can be further broken down into the thighs, knees, calves, ankles, and feet. The feet can be divided into the heel, the toes, and so on. The toes are just an assembly of single knuckles consisting of bone, cartilage, blood vessels, and so forth. Examining the microscopic level of each of these constituents, one arrives at their molecular, atomic, and subatomic structures.

At various points in this process, different Buddhists and non-Buddhists claim that there are smallest (sub)atomic particles that cannot be broken down further. Thus, what is particularly refuted through this reasoning is the existence of such infinitesimal particles, which often are regarded as partless and dimensionless, similar to a mathematical point. In addition, they are said to be the building blocks of all coarse material phenomena. However, if these particles do not have any parts or spatial extensions, they cannot aggregate with others of their kind, since there are no surfaces or sides to contact anything else. Also, even many such dimensionless particles could never add up to some larger phenomenon that is perceptible by our senses, since even a million times zero spatial extension is still zero spatial extension. On the other hand, if these particles could align with others in order to build up larger three-dimensional things, they would have to have at least six sides—front, rear, left, right, top, and bottom—to allow for any form of contact with other particles in order to create a three-dimensional object. This, however, contradicts the claim that these particles are partless and extensionless. Thus, since no indivisible units or smallest possible particles can be found, there are no real multiplicities of phenomena that are built by them.[581]

The *positive entailment* here means that the reason (whatever lacks real unity and multiplicity) may only be found in the homologous set of the predicate (everything that does not really exist). In other words, whatever is neither a real unity nor a real multiplicity must necessarily not really exist. The reverse of this—the *negative entailment*—is that if something really exists,[582] then it must necessarily be either a real unity or a real multiplicity, because unity and multiplicity are mutually exclusive and there is no third possibility. This is the law of the excluded middle that is accepted by all realists.

From among the three doors to liberation, this reasoning teaches the door of emptiness.

#### II. The analysis of causes: the vajra sliver reasoning

The vajra sliver reasoning bears this name because—just as a vajra is indestructible and at the same time capable of destroying everything else—it is able to shatter the huge rock mountain of wrong views that cling to real existence, while being completely unassailable itself. It is explained as it is found in *The Fundamental Verses on Centrism*:

> Not from themselves, not from something other,
> Not from both, and not without a cause—
> At any place and any time,
> All entities lack arising.[583]

Three of these four possibilities of arising are refuted by all Buddhist texts that deal with Centrism or valid cognition in general.[584] These positions are exemplified by the Indian non-Buddhist schools of the Enumerators, who assert that things arise from themselves; the Jainas, who assert that things arise from both themselves and something other; and the Mundanely Minded, who assert that there is no cause. The fourth possibility of things arising from something other—the position of most other Buddhist and non-Buddhist schools—is refuted through Centrist texts alone.

The vajra sliver reasoning analyzes arising by taking the example of a seed (the cause) growing into a sprout (the result) and investigating their exact relationship. For example, we will search for the precise time when the seed is no longer a seed and becomes a sprout instead.

A. The formulation of the reasoning

A sprout is without arising, because it is without arising from itself, from others, from both, and from neither, just like an appearance in a dream.

B. The three modes of the reason

The *positive* and *negative entailment* cannot go beyond these four extremes of arising: Whatever does not arise from itself, from something other, from both, or from neither (that is, without any cause) necessarily does not arise at all. On the other hand, if things were to arise, they necessarily would have to arise either from themselves, from something other, from both, or from neither. There are no other possibilities. This is the case whether one looks at it from the perspective of analyzing for real existence or just in terms of mere arising. It should be clear, however, that this reasoning does not deny the mere appearance of something arising on the bare experiential level, where, because of ignorance, it seems as though things arise.

Here, establishing the *subject property* has four parts, since there are four possibilities of arising to be negated.

1. Establishing the reason that entities do not arise from themselves

The classic example in Centrist texts for people who assert that things arise from themselves are the Enumerators. They claim, "A sprout is merely a manifestation of the sole cosmic cause, which is the permanent primal substance. This really existing primal substance is the sprout's nature. Therefore, this sprout arises from its own nature, which is a permanent entity." By this, they mean that cause and result are one and the same in terms of their nature, substance, and time.

This position, however, leads to absurd consequences. For example, the same thing would be both the phenomenon that is produced and the phenomenon that produces it. This means that the sprout would be identical to both the primal substance and the seed (the latter being just an expression of this primal substance). Furthermore, it would not be justified that the seed from which the sprout has arisen ceases to exist, since this seed is nothing but an expression of the permanent primal substance. Consequently, the seed would either permanently exist or arise all the time. However, if the seed as the cause of the sprout does not cease, then one would not find its result—the sprout—since results can only appear after their causes. In addition, if cause and result—seed and sprout—are the same and if the one arises from the other, the sprout should look exactly the same as the seed. If the seed, however, loses its own nature and turns into something else—a sprout different in color and shape—it cannot have a real and unchangeable nature of its own.

In general, in the context of causality, the result of a specific cause can only be perceived once this cause has ceased. However, if seed and sprout are not different, once the seed ceases, the sprout should also disappear. Or, once the sprout is visible, the seed too should be visible at the same time. Both possibilities contradict the notion of causality altogether. In addition, if things were to arise from themselves, all the distinct things that are agents and the objects upon which these agents act would be one and the same. Thus, that things arise from themselves is neither reasonable on the ultimate level nor accepted on the level of conventional worldly reality.

The Enumerators also say, "In general, only such things that exist already at the time of their causes arise, whereas previously nonexistent things can never arise. For example, sesame oil comes forth from sesame seeds when they are ground, because it already existed before in the seeds. The reason that sesame oil does not appear from grinding sand is that it does not exist in sand." The basic assumption behind this statement is the impossibility of something arising from nothing. Hence, a result cannot arise later without existing at the time of its specific cause. Moreover, there are no other causes apart from its specific cause either that could transform a result that does not exist in the first place into an existent result later. Thus, the Enumerators say, the result must preexist at the time of the cause.

However, if things—that is to say, results—arise from themselves alone, it implicitly follows that they need no other factors for their arising. So why does one have to struggle to grind sesame seeds or farm, since the harvest already exists when the seeds are present? In addition, if the result is the same as its cause, why should the result arise again, since it exists already? In general, if a thing is not yet present, it does not exist as a result. If it is already present, it is pointless for it to arise again. And if the result would still arise even though it exists already, then it would have to arise endlessly. As Buddhapālita's commentary on *Fundamental Verses* I.1 says:

> Entities do not arise from their own intrinsic nature, because their arising would be pointless and because they would arise endlessly. For entities that [already] exist as their own intrinsic nature, there is no need to arise again. If they were to arise despite existing [already], there would be no time when they do not arise; [but] that is also not asserted [by the Enumerators].[585]

The Enumerators may continue, "There are two different phases in the process of arising. If a vase is made out of clay, it is the unmanifest vase in its state of being a lump of clay—the cause—that arises as a manifest vase—the result—later. Of course, we do not think that the vase that is already clearly manifest as the result arises again. Therefore, there is a difference between these two phases of the vase in that it is either clearly manifest or not."

However, if the vase already existed as an entity, it would be utterly pointless for it to arise again. On the other hand, if "it" arose from its state of not being clearly manifest, then it would be nothing other than a nonexistent that newly arises. Here, the Enumerators do not explicitly assert that the clearly manifest result as such does not exist at the time of the cause, but this is what follows from their claim that it becomes clearly manifest only later. In fact, they deny that the result is entirely nonexistent at the time of the cause and that it arises completely anew. However, implicitly, this is exactly what their position boils down to, because by claiming that the result exists as a potential, they just obscure the distinction between the nonexistence of the result at the time of the cause and its later existence. Saying that it is not manifest at the time of the cause amounts to saying that it does not exist. Through talking about "the unmanifest vase in its state of being a lump of clay," the Enumerators simply blend two different things into one, for a lump of clay is clearly not a vase. For one, a lump of clay cannot be said to be a vase, because it does not manifest as a vase. Nor does an "unmanifest vase" make sense, because then it would equally follow that it is an unmanifest cup, an unmanifest statue, or whatever else could be made from that clay. This would lead to the consequence that not only a vase but all these other unmanifest things too should arise from this one lump of clay.

Moreover, if the result existed at the time of the cause, it would have to be observable at this point. However, from that, it would follow that an apple tree can be perceived in an apple seed or milk in the grass eaten by a cow. One of the classic consequences is that an ant should carry around an elephant, the elephant being the karmic result of the existence as an ant to become manifest in one of the ant's future rebirths. In fact, the entirety of all infinite results of a given cause over time should then be observable at the same time in this cause. On the other hand, if the result is not observable at all at the time of the cause, how can it be said to exist?

There is no third alternative of saying that the result is partially existent, although this is precisely what the Enumerators (and many others) try to do by their formulation of an "unmanifest vase." However, even if there were such a partial existence of a vase, what would it look like? Even a partial existence should be observable at the time of the cause, but this is not the case. And if the result were partially existent at the time of the cause, where would the lacking portions of its complete existence come from? In general, it is impossible to identify a distinct point in time at which the result turns from nonexistence into existence. It is also impossible to identify distinct points in time that are related to a gradual increase in the result's existence, such as "Up to here it exists at about 30 percent or 50 percent, and from here onward it exists at 100 percent." Nor does it make any sense that the result would leap from some degree of partial existence to full existence in the next moment. In addition, the most fundamental problem in that respect lies in the Enumerators' own claim that the primal substance as the single and final cosmic cause is not something perceptible in the first place.

In a very general sense, when it is said that all manifestations are potentially present in and as the primal substance and just become manifest at certain times, this would lead to the conclusion that all possible future results exist right from the very beginning. Furthermore, since all causes and results are said to be identical, at any given point in time, all possible results within the past, present, and future of the universe as well as all their causes would have to exist simultaneously.

2. Establishing the reason that entities do not arise from something other (the second part of establishing the subject property of the vajra sliver reasoning)

Our usual idea about causes and results is that things arise from something other than themselves. On the level of worldly seeming reality, both Buddhist and non-Buddhist realists[586] say, "We agree that entities do not arise from themselves, but their arising from something other is established through valid cognition. There are reasons for this. Factually concordant types of consciousness arise from the four conditions,[587] and in general most things arise from causal and dominant conditions. Both causes and results are not just mere mental imputations, but they are established from the object's own side. The fact that they arise withstands analysis. You cannot simply reason them away."

There are many reasonings to negate this position, but they are all contained in two:

a. Arising from something other is impossible.
b. In the context of arising, something other is in itself impossible.

a. Arising from something other is impossible.

Much confusion regarding what is "same" or "other" comes from our very loose and vague use of these notions, such as saying, "other but still similar or same" or "a little bit other" as opposed to "completely other." For example, we may think that, compared to ice, fire is "more other" than water. In the context of Centrist reasoning, the notion of "other" is as strict and literal as can be: Things are either the same or different. Either cause and result are assumed to be identical (as the Enumerators state) or they have to be different, that is, other. There is no third possibility. Thus, being other is not a question of degree: Things are other whether they differ in all or in just one of their many features. Thus, all similar things must necessarily be different from each other, since what is identical is not similar. In other words, the categories of same and different are mutually exclusive and exhaustive.

One of the consequences of this clear delineation is that if things could arise from causes that are other than themselves, it would absurdly follow that anything could arise from anything. For example, deep darkness could originate even from bright light. As *The Entrance into Centrism* says:

> If something were to originate in dependence on something other than it,
> Well, then utter darkness could spring from flames
> And everything could arise from everything,
> Because everything that does not produce [a specific result] is the same in being other [than it].[588]

The reasons for this consequence are as follows: If we consider a wheat seed and a rose seed, they are equal in that they are both something other than a rose sprout, and, in terms of real things, their being other than the rose sprout is something that is established through their own specific natures. Thus, since a wheat seed and a rose seed are equally other than a rose sprout, either both or neither of them should be able to produce the rose sprout.

We usually think that such phenomena as a rose seed and a rose sprout have a close connection, such as sharing some similarities or being in the same continuum, or that the seed as the specific cause has some causal efficacy or potential to produce the sprout as its specific result. On the other hand, we think that there is no such connection between a wheat seed and a rose sprout and even less so between fire and water or light and darkness. However, none of these notions of a relation between certain phenomena that we consider as causes and results solves the issue of arising from something other. They just perpetuate the mere assumption that things arise from something other: Even if causes and results are similar and in the same continuum, or if there were a certain productive potential in some things—the specific causes—and not in others, this does not change the basic fact that causes are still other than their results. Thus, the same consequences as above apply.

Moreover, when analyzed, there is just as much "causal connection" between a rose seed and a rose sprout as between fire and water: none whatsoever. For there is never any time in the process of arising when the cause actually meets the result so that the cause or its productive potential could have any effect on the result. As long as the cause exists, the result is not yet present, and as soon as the result appears, the cause has necessarily ceased. So when would the cause unfold its productive potential? The cause can obviously not unfold it when the cause itself does not exist. If it were an existent cause that displays this productive potential, this would still not make the result appear. It cannot appear during the existence of the cause, since cause and result cannot exist simultaneously. Otherwise, they could not function as cause and result in the first place. In order to speak of causality, the cause has to precede the result.[589] So if the cause must be first and cannot exist simultaneously with the result, there is no connection between cause and result and also no chance for a hypothetical productive potential of the cause to bring about or interact with the result, since they never meet. Therefore, eventually, this position of realists that things arise from something other entails the self-contradictory consequence that a sprout *cannot* arise from a seed, because—according to them—seed and sprout are something other through their respective specific natures.

b. In the context of arising, something other is impossible.

In the context of a result arising from a cause, the notion of "otherness" is altogether inappropriate. The reason for this is that in order to speak of two things as being other, they must exist at the same time. To elaborate, in terms of otherness that is based on really existing and substantial things and does not just refer to a mental image of something that is not present, there have to be two distinct things in the first place that can be contrasted as being "other." These can only be two phenomena that are simultaneously observable as existing in the present, such as the left and the right horn of a cow or two persons in the same room. This then excludes the possibility of cause and result being other, since they are by definition never simultaneous.

Saying it in reverse, nonsimultaneous things cannot be other. Thus, since the result is not present at the time when the cause exists, at the time of the cause, there is just one phenomenon (the cause itself) and not two, that is, no result that could be identified or perceived as other than this cause. The same principle applies to the time when the result exists and the cause has ceased. Consequently, if cause and result were other, they would have to be simultaneous, but this contradicts the process of causality. The simultaneity of cause and result is also refuted through the examination of whether the result that is produced already exists or does not exist at the time of the cause.[590] Thus, *The Lucid Words* says:

> Entities also do not arise from something other, because there is nothing other.[591]

Looking at this issue from the perspective of the reasoning of the freedom from unity and multiplicity, if all things do not really exist and even lack an identifiable nature of their own, what in them should determine one thing to be other than another one? Also, if there is no thing that is really established in itself in any way, how could there be something other whose otherness depends on this first nonexistent thing? As *The Fundamental Verses* says:

> If an entity in itself does not exist,
> An entity other [than it] does not exist either.[592]

The refutation of things arising from something other is likewise accomplished by analyzing the four conditions. They include all possibilities of arising from something that is other than the result. The result, however, is found in none of the four. As *The Fundamental Verses* says:

> Conditions are fourfold:
> Causal, objective,
> Immediate, and dominant.
> There is no fifth condition.
>
> The nature of entities
> Does not exist in conditions and such.[593]

Thus, the nature of a rice sprout does not exist in any of its conditions. It does not exist in its causal conditions (water and manure), nor in its object condition (the harvest), nor in its immediate condition (the last moment of the rice seed), nor in its dominant condition (the person who planted the seed).

*Causal Conditions*

If causal conditions, such as water and manure, intrinsically have functions or productive capacities—such as giving rise to a sprout—they would have to produce sprouts all the time. And if they do not have any such functions or capacities, there could never be any production from them. In this case, however, why would they be presented as conditions for a result at all? Moreover, Nāgārjuna says, the relationship between conditions and their assumed functions cannot be settled:

> Function is not something that entails conditions.
> [Conventionally, however,] there is no function that does not entail conditions.
> [Thus,] what does not entail a function is not a condition,
> And there is none that entails a function.[594]

Further absurd consequences can be drawn when the result and its conditions are placed on a time line. Most people think that water, manure, and such are the conditions of a sprout, since the latter arises in dependence on the former. However, in terms of each moment of the sprout's arising, as long as its respective moments have not arisen and thus are nonexistent, any preceding moments of water and so on cannot be its conditions. And once the sprout's respective moments have arisen, there is no more need for any conditions. Hence, when would they be the conditions of the sprout?

> This is consensus: "Since something arises in dependence on these,
> Therefore, they are its conditions."
> As long as this [something] does not arise,
> How could these not be things that are not its conditions?
>
> For [both] nonexistents and existents,
> Conditions are not reasonable:
> If something does not exist, the conditions of what would they be?
> If something exists [already], what are conditions good for?[595]

In general, upon analysis, any existing or nonexisting phenomenon disintegrates and thus is not established. If no phenomenon can be established, then how could its causes or conditions be established?

> Once phenomena are not established
> As existent, nonexistent, or [both] existent and nonexistent,
> How could one speak of "productive causes"?
> It would be unreasonable, if such applied.[596]

*Object Conditions*

Likewise, the object condition is not established either. In the context of perception, an object is regarded as a condition for the arising of the consciousness that perceives this object. But if they are placed on a time line, we can see that this cannot work. If the object existed before the specific consciousness that is supposedly caused by it, what would this later consciousness perceive? The same applies if the object existed after the consciousness that is its perceiver. And if the object existed simultaneously with it, it could not be the cause of this consciousness.

*Immediate Conditions*

In general Buddhist epistemology, it is consensus that the previous moment of consciousness that has just ceased is the "immediate condition," or the immediately preceding condition of the next moment of consciousness. However, since it has already been refuted that there is anything that arises, something that has ceased cannot be justified. Moreover, since something that has ceased does not exist anymore, it is also not suitable to serve as a condition. Hence, an immediate condition is also not established.

> If phenomena have not arisen,
> Cessation is not justified.
> Therefore, the immediate condition is not reasonable.
> If it has ceased, what would be such a condition?[597]

*Dominant Conditions*

The notion of dominant conditions is mostly used in the process of perception. It refers to the respective sense faculties based on which specific consciousnesses arise, such as the eye consciousness arising on the basis of the eye sense faculty. Since all of the above (and the following) refutations equally apply to dominant conditions, Nāgārjuna does not treat them separately.

Still, Buddhists might argue, "This contradicts the Buddha's teaching. In terms of dependent origination, he said, 'Since this exists, that originates. Since this has arisen, that arises. Due to the condition of basic unawareness, there is formation and so on.'" *The Lucid Words* states:

> These teachings of arising in the sense of dependent origination and so on are not meant in terms of the nature of the object of the uncontaminated wisdom of those who are free from the blurred vision of basic ignorance. "To what do they refer then?" They are meant in terms of the objects of the consciousnesses of those whose eyes of insight are impaired by the blurred vision of basic ignorance.[598]

Hence, a result does not dwell in any of its diverse conditions. Thus, if the result is nonexistent at the time of its causes and conditions, how could such a nonexistent arise as an existent later? If it were to arise despite its nonexistence, then it could arise even from things that are not its causes, or it could arise without any cause at all. As *The Fundamental Verses* says:

> The result does not exist at all
> In any of its diverse conditions or their assembly.
> How could what does not exist in its conditions
> Arise from such conditions?
>
> However, if it does not exist
> And were still to arise from these conditions,
> Why would it not also arise
> From what are not its conditions?[599]

Some people might still argue, "Because the result depends on its conditions, the result is something that has the nature of its conditions." If none of these conditions exists as something that even bears its own nature, how could any of them be the nature of the result? On the other hand, conventionally, there is also no result that does not depend on conditions. Therefore, causes and conditions are nothing but superimpositions.

> You might say, "The result is of the nature of its conditions."
> [However,] conditions do not have a nature of their own.
> What is the result of something that is not an entity in itself?
> How could it be of the nature of [such] conditions?
>
> Therefore, it is not of the nature of its conditions.
> [However,] there is [also] no result with a nature of what are not its conditions.
> Since results do not exist,
> How could nonconditions be conditions?[600]

3. Establishing the reason that entities do not arise from both themselves and others (the third part of establishing the subject property of the vajra sliver reasoning)

Some people, such as the followers of Viṣṇu and the Jainas,[601] say, "That a clay vase arises from itself means that it is made out of clay and still has this nature of clay, thus not being something other than it. That the vase arises from something other means that it arises through the activity of a potter, a potter's wheel, water, and so on. Hence, things do not arise exclusively from themselves nor exclusively from others. Rather they arise from a combination of these two ways of arising."

This third possibility of arising from both is already implicitly refuted through the above negations of things arising from themselves or from something other respectively. Therefore, the negation of the combination of the first two possibilities of arising is usually only touched upon very briefly in Centrist texts. For example, *The Lucid Words* explains:

> Nor do entities arise from both [themselves and others], because this would entail [all] the flaws that were stated for both of these theses and because none of these [disproved possibilities] have the capacity to produce [entities].[602]

Thus, if neither things themselves nor something other than these things have the power to give rise to anything, the combination of two such powerless factors can in no way result in any power that causes things to arise. For example, if a single grain of sand has no power to produce olive oil, many such powerless grains are still equally powerless to produce oil. Or, in mathematical terms, many times zero is still zero.

4. Establishing that entities do not arise without any cause (the fourth part of establishing the subject property of the vajra sliver reasoning)

Most Indian hedonists or materialists claim that things arise without any causes; that is, that they just arise naturally and spontaneously come into being as they are. One of their scriptures says:

> The roundness of peas, the long sharp tips of thorns,
> The colorful patterns of the feathers of a peacock's wings,
> The rising of the sun, and the downhill flow of rivers—
> All these were created by nobody. Their cause is their very nature.

However, this position has completely absurd consequences, such as that things in general would either arise all the time or never arise. Furthermore, it clearly contradicts our everyday perception of results appearing at certain times in dependence on certain things or actions that are their causes, such as a harvest appearing only due to farming. We generally see that results do not occur just by accident or without a cause. If things could indeed appear without any causes, anything nonexistent or impossible could manifest, such as a lotus growing in the sky. A further consequence would be that we could not perceive anything in the world, because there would be no objects that could serve as causes for our perceptions. On the level of common worldly experience, if we see a blue flower, this is due to there being a blue flower to be perceived. If there is no such blue flower, a perception of it does not arise. As *The Lucid Words* says:

> If these beings were empty of being causes, they could not be apprehended,
> Just like the smell and the color of an utpala flower in the sky.[603]

If things arose without causes, no effort would be required to produce or accomplish anything, since things would either arise anyway or not arise even despite such efforts. For example, meals could appear without any ingredients or cooking, or they would not appear at all no matter how diligently we prepared them. In fact, any goal-oriented activity, such as assembling a car, would be completely pointless, since all these activities would never be the causes of a desired result, such as a car that could actually be driven. If we are lucky, though, it might pop up out of nowhere and work anyway. Thus, anything could arise at any time in a completely haphazard way, such as a blazing fire in the depths of the ocean or darkness in the middle of a bright lamp. Or, it would follow that an apple tree could arise not only from an apple seed but also from a rose seed, because—according to the position that things arise without a cause—both seeds are equal in not being the cause for the apple tree. Also, any fruits should be fully ripened all the time or never, because their ripeness does not depend on any other factors, such as chemical processes or time. And since a peacock is not the cause of the colors of its feathers, a crow should also have such beautiful feathers.

One might object, "There is a difference in the case of a flower growing in the sky and such things as a harvest, since the former does not have an existent nature, whereas the latter have." However, even such a difference does not remove the above absurd consequences, since—according to the position that things arise without causes—a result that is assumed to have an existent nature would still be something that arises without a cause and thus is equally subject to the same inconsistencies.

Moreover, the very fact of making any statement or even giving a reason contradicts the original thesis that there are no causes, since making a statement or giving a reason is a cause that makes other persons understand something. If things arise without causes, other persons should understand everything without anybody ever saying anything. Or, nobody would ever understand anything, despite being given the most sophisticated explanations and reasons.

Other hedonists say, "The only kind of valid cognition is direct perception. Thus, only those things that can be directly perceived exist. Their causes are the four great material elements—earth, water, fire, and wind—but not such things as positive or negative actions, whether they happen in this lifetime or in any past or future ones that may be assumed. The same goes for the mind: It is merely something that evolves from the four elements in our body. Just as the mixture of barley and yeast gives rise to the force that inebriates the mind, the ripening of the union of sperm and egg gives rise to the mind."[604]

The first counterargument here is that the elements themselves do not exist. The three preceding possibilities for an arising of things—from themselves, something other, or both—have already been refuted through the corresponding parts of the vajra sliver reasoning. Thus, all phenomena—including the four great elements—do not really arise or exist in the first place. Therefore, the question of whether these elements can be the causes of anything does not apply.

Second, even in the relative world, this position makes no sense. There are a number of inconsistencies and counterarguments, even if the above statements on valid cognition, existence, and the body-mind problem are addressed on the mere conventional level. For example, if only directly perceptible things exist and can serve as causes, it would follow that our own inner organs, such as the heart, do not exist and cannot be the causes for our staying alive, since we never directly perceive them (seeing them in a corpse or on an x-ray can only lead to an inference that we have these organs).

In terms of past and future lives, the hedonists' justification that these do not exist is again that if they existed, they would have to exist in a directly manifest way for our perception. However, since they are not directly perceptible, they are said to be nonexistent. If these people are asked whether their knowledge that such lifetimes are not directly perceptible comes from direct perception or something that is not direct perception, their answer naturally is, "It comes from direct perception." However, then it absurdly follows that the nonexistence of past and future lives as things is something directly perceptible, because they say that the lack of direct perceptibility of these lifetimes is directly perceptible. If this is accepted, it follows that this lack of perceptibility—which is nothing but the nonexistence of things—would nevertheless be an existing thing for the hedonists, since it is directly perceptible, just as existing things are. Then it further follows that also things do not exist, since there is no such thing as the total "lack of things" as a counterpart for things. In other words, "things" cannot be established without "the lack of things" and vice versa. If even this is accepted, it follows that both the elements' existence as things and the nonexistence of past and future lives as things are not justified, because neither things nor the lack of things exist.

At this point, these people might object, "Well, it is very easy to know that something is not directly perceptible, since this is known from the sign or reason that consists in its lack of direct perceptibility." However, from their above position that direct perception is the only kind of valid cognition, it then follows that one is not able to infer the nonexistence of past and future lives, because if the lack of direct perceptibility of these lifetimes is not directly perceived, one is not able to apprehend this lack in any other way at all. If they say, "It is apprehended through inference," this disqualifies their standard statements about inference not being a type of valid cognition, such as, "Since inferring past lives from the sign or reason of varying individual degrees of happiness and suffering in this life is as unjustified as the story of the wolf's footprints,[605] inference is impossible" and "All that exists is limited to the spheres of the five senses." Thus, there is no proof that past and future lifetimes do not exist, while there are many reasons that suggest their existence.[606]

As for the claim that the material elements are the causes of mind, this also cannot be justified. In general, phenomena whose characteristics are contradictory cannot function as the cause and result of each other. For example, fire does not arise from water, and permanent things do not arise from impermanent things. Likewise, on the conventional level, the main characteristics of matter are to have certain shapes and colors, to have extensions in space and time, to obstruct other things, to consist of particles, and to not be conscious. On the other hand, mind has neither shape nor color nor any spatial or durational extension. Mind does not obstruct anything, is not made of particles, and is conscious. Moreover, if the elements in the body were the causes of mind, any changes in these causes would always have to affect the mind as their result in a strictly corresponding way. For example, if the body is healthy or deteriorates, the mind would have to be equally healthy or deteriorating. However, there are numerous counterexamples, such as a very sharp and flexible mind in a frail or handicapped body or a completely deranged mind in a perfectly healthy body. In addition, since outer material things also consist of the four elements, there is no reason that stones and the like should not also exhibit some manifestations of consciousness as well as some other features that are found only in animate bodies, such as respiration, metabolism, movement, and reproduction.[607]

In brief, the appearances of this world do not arise without any causes, because these appearances arise only sometimes. This reason might seem odd at first. However, as was explained above, if things arise without causes, all of them would have to arise all the time or never. Thus, the fact that certain things only arise at certain times and not at others is the most powerful indication that there must be something that accounts for this difference. This "something" is the completeness of all the specific causes and conditions that lead to a certain result. Conversely, if these causes and conditions are incomplete, their specific result does not arise.

To summarize the vajra sliver reasoning, it is clear that there is not the slightest arising through any of the four possibilities described. However, since it is worldly consensus that there is arising, such arising is just presented according to this usual way of thinking. Thus, it is not refuted here that, from the perspective of mere worldly consensus without analysis, it appears as if things arise. Also, the vajra sliver reasoning is definitely not meant to negate the principle of causality altogether. For, when not analyzed, causality clearly performs its function on the level of seeming reality. However, even on this level, people do not claim that results arise from themselves or something other and so on. Rather, they just say that a sprout arises from a seed, but they do not determine whether the seed is identical to or other than the sprout. As *The Entrance into Centrism* says:

> After worldly people have merely implanted a seed,
> They say, "I engendered this child"
> And think, "I planted a tree."
> Therefore, even on the worldly level, there is no arising from
> something other.[608]

Thus, in general, according to Centrists, any attempt to justify everyday experience through something other than just mere conventional consensus must inevitably lead to logical and—more important—spiritual problems. Thus, in its own terms, seeming reality with all its conventional appearances is not to be analyzed, since then one already moves away from this very seeming reality. It functions as such only as long as it is not questioned.

From among the three doors to liberation, the vajra sliver reasoning teaches the door of signlessness.

### III. The analysis of results: the negation of an arising of existents and nonexistents

This reasoning is basically an elaboration of the negation of arising from something other as found in the context of the vajra sliver reasoning.

#### A. The formulation of the reasoning

Mere appearances do not exist by their nature, because neither existents nor nonexistents arise, just like an illusion.

#### B. The three modes of the reason

Here, the *subject property* is that mere appearances do not arise either as existents or as nonexistents. So the question is: "If a sprout arises, does it then arise as something that existed already at the time of the seed, or does it arise as something that did not exist at that time? Can it possibly arise as something that is both existent and nonexistent or as something that is neither?"

As explained above, any phenomenon that exists will not arise, since it has already arisen before. Nonexistents will not arise either, because there is nothing that could arise and because there is no cause whatsoever that could turn a nonexistent into something existent. In addition, if the sprout were to arise as something that already existed at the time of the seed, then it would have arisen either from something other than the seed or without any cause, but obviously not from this seed itself. Moreover, there would be no need for the seed as the sprout's cause, since the latter is already present without having to arise in dependence on this seed. If the sprout has already arisen in dependence on something other than the seed, what would be the point of a seed as yet another cause? And if it had arisen without any cause, the seed would be equally superfluous. On the other hand, if the sprout arose as something that did not exist at the time of the seed, then there would not be the slightest influence or effect that the cause (the seed) could have on such a nonexistent. That the sprout could arise from the combination of both possibilities—existence and nonexistence—is self-contradictory. It is also implicitly refuted through the negations of the first two possibilities, since their inconsistencies just multiply. As for the fourth possibility, there is nothing that is neither existent nor nonexistent, so what would arise?

The *positive entailment* of the reason here is that whatever does not arise either as an existent or as a nonexistent does not exist by its nature, since these two possibilities are mutually exclusive and there is no third. The same reason applies to the *negative entailment*, since anything that is assumed to exist by its nature would necessarily have to arise either as an existent or as a nonexistent.

Exemplary proponents of the first possibility—arising as an existent—include the Enumerators, whose position of the arising of a result that exists already at the time of the cause has been refuted in detail above. The Buddhist school of the Followers of The Great Exposition claims the arising of a result that already exists in the future.[609] This position is refuted as follows: If a thing that has not yet arisen here and now were to exist in some unknown other place at present, it might be reasonable for it to arise here in the future. However, since there is no such place where all future things exist right now, what could arise from this place later? And even if there were such a place with already existing future things, they would have to be perceptible right now. Otherwise, how could one claim that they exist at present? *The Fundamental Verses* says:

> If some nonarisen entity
> Existed somewhere,
> It might arise.
> However, since such does not exist, what would arise?[610]

As for the second possibility—arising as a nonexistent—there are many Buddhists and non-Buddhists who assert the new arising of a result that previously did not exist. However, it is impossible for nonexistents to depend on any causes. Consequently, if something that has not existed before can still arise, it would follow that just about anything can arise, even impossibilities such as a hairy frog.

> If something that lacks arising could arise,
> Just about anything could arise in this way.[611]

From among the doors to complete liberation, this reasoning teaches the door of wishlessness.

**IV. The analysis of both causes and results: the negation of arising from the four possibilities**

A. The formulation of the reasoning

Mere appearances lack arising, because a single result does not arise from a single cause; many results do not arise from a single cause; a single result does not arise from many causes; and many results also do not arise from many causes.

B. The three modes of the reason

As for the *subject property*, when considered just from the perspective of our mistakenness, the following statements are rather unproblematic: "One sprout arises from one seed," "One eye consciousness arises from three conditions," "Many children are born from one mother," and "Many harvests come from many causes, such as seeds, water, and manure." However, from the perspective of reasoning, an arising from any of these four possibilities is impossible, since, briefly put, the reasoning at hand is just an elaboration of the reasoning of the freedom from unity and multiplicity. As was explained above, there is no phenomenon that is a real unity or a real multiplicity in the first place. From this, it naturally follows that there are no real single or multiple causes that could give rise to any single or multiple results.

A more detailed way to look at these four possibilities is found in Jñānagarbha's autocommentary on verse 14 of his *Distinction between the Two Realities*:[612]

1. A single result does not arise from a single cause

For example, if the eye sense faculty only produced the single result that is the next moment of its own continuum, it could not also produce a visual consciousness in this next moment. In that case, everybody would be blind. On the other hand, if the eye sense faculty produced the single result that is a visual consciousness, its own continuum as an eye sense faculty would have to stop at that moment. Naturally, the same goes for the remaining sense faculties as well as for other phenomena, such as a candle flame: Either it produces its own next moment, and thus no visual perception of itself, or it causes a visual consciousness in someone but then becomes extinguished in that very moment.

2. Many results do not arise from a single cause

If a single cause all by itself were to produce a second or more results, cause and result would lack a causal relationship, since the cause would be single while the result would be multiple. In other words, the singularity of the cause does not produce a corresponding singularity of the result. However, if a further factor within or in addition to that single cause is assumed to produce the second result, clearly one is no longer speaking about a single cause.

3. A single result does not arise from many causes

This entails the reverse of the problem in (2), that is, that the multiplicity of the cause does not produce a corresponding multiplicity of the result. Conversely, the absence of multiplicity in the cause would not cause the absence of multiplicity in the result either. For, in this case of a single result arising from many causes, the result lacks multiplicity, while the cause does not. Consequently, neither the multiplicity of the result nor its lack thereof would have a cause, since there is no third category beyond causes and results being either multiple or nonmultiple. Hence, nothing would have a cause. In that case, everything would either exist permanently or not exist at all or would just arise at random.

4. Many results do not arise from many causes

The basic problem of the lack of invariable congruence between cause and result in terms of both being either single or multiple applies here too. Take the example of visual perception: If the cause is multiple (for example, an eye sense faculty, a visual form, and an immediately preceding moment of consciousness), then the result (the single resultant moment of a visual consciousness) should invariably be multiple too, but this is obviously not the case. Likewise, in being a result, a clay vase should be multiple due to the multiplicity of its cause (clay, water, a potter, and a potter's wheel).

As for the *positive entailment* here, it means that whatever does not arise from these four possibilities must necessarily lack arising altogether. The *negative entailment* means that anything that arises must necessarily arise from one of these possibilities.

**V. The analysis of mere appearances: the reasoning of dependent origination**

*The Precious Garland* says:

> Due to the existence of this, that comes to be,
> Just as something short, when there is something long.
> Due to the arising of this, that arises,
> Just as light due to the appearance of a butter lamp.[613]

Accordingly, there are two types of dependence:

A. dependence in terms of dependent imputation, such as being short in dependence on being long
B. dependence in terms of dependent origination, such as the arising of smoke due to the arising of fire

A. Dependence in terms of imputation

1. The formulation of the reasoning

For example, it may be said, "All things are neither really big nor small, because being big and small depend on each other."

2. The three modes of the reason

The *subject property* says that all things depend on each other in terms of being big or small. In other words, anything that is big in comparison to something smaller than itself is at the same time small when compared to some third thing that is even bigger and vice versa. The *positive entailment* means that whatever depends on something else in terms of being big or small is necessarily not really or independently big or small. The *negative entailment* means that if there were something intrinsically big or small, it would have to be independent of everything other in terms of being big or small. The same applies for all other mutually dependent characteristics, such as existent and nonexistent, good and bad, or beautiful and ugly.

B. Dependence in terms of origination

1. The formulation of the reasoning

This reasoning is called "the king of reasonings" through which Centrists demonstrate that phenomena are empty of any true reality, since it eliminates the extremes of both permanence and extinction. Since phenomena originate in dependence on various causes and conditions, on the conventional level of seeming reality, they are not as utterly nonexistent as a long-haired turtle.[614] This eliminates the extreme of extinction. At the same time, phenomena do not exist as permanent things that are established through a nature of their own precisely because they depend on other causes and conditions and thus lack any real and independent nature. As *The Sūtra Requested by the Nāgā King "The Cool One"* says:

> The learned ones realize phenomena that originate in dependence.
> In no way do they rely on views about extremes.

*The Fundamental Verses* states:

> What is dependent origination
> Is explained as emptiness.
> It is a dependent designation
> And in itself the middle path.
>
> Since there is no phenomenon
> That is not dependently originating,
> There is no phenomenon
> That is not empty.[615]

In order to explicitly eliminate the two extremes of permanence and extinction, the reasoning of dependent origination can be formulated in two main ways.

a. To exclude the first extreme, the reasoning may be formulated in a negative way: "Mere appearances do not exist by their nature, because they dependently originate, just like a dream."

b. To eliminate the extreme of extinction and to account for seeming reality, the reasoning may also be stated in an affirmative way: "All phenomena are not nonexistent like the horns of a rabbit, because they dependently originate." Another way to say this would be: "Phenomena are illusionlike, because they dependently originate."

2. The three modes of the reason

At first, the reason "dependently originating" may look like an affirming reason. The *subject property* says that all phenomena necessarily originate in dependence. In terms of its phrasing, this appears to be an affirmative statement. The *positive entailment* is that whatever originates in dependence necessarily does not exist by its nature, is illusionlike, and is also not utterly nonexistent. The *negative entailment* means that if there were anything that existed by its nature, was not illusionlike, or was utterly nonexistent, it would necessarily not originate in dependence. In particular, the explicit words of the reasonings under (B) seem to affirm something about phenomena, that is, their "existence" or "illusionlike being." However, the meaning that is pointed out by the reason "dependently originating" is nothing other than that things are empty of real existence or real arising. Thus, in whatever way this reasoning of dependent origination may be formulated, it never becomes a means to ascertain some really existent things, be they seeming or ultimate, nor does it suggest some really existent kind of dependent origination. Since this is clearly a case of relying not on mere words but on the meaning, the reasoning of dependent origination is a negating reasoning in effect, since "arising from dependently originating conditions" means nothing other than "lack of real arising." Obviously, the word "arising" is used here in two different ways: In the first phrase, it refers to the mere illusionlike display of causes and conditions due to ignorance, from which we gain the wrong impression that things really arise. The second phrase means the denial of any real arising in this illusory display, without denying its mere appearance. As the sūtras say:

> What arises from conditions does not arise.
> It does not have the nature of arising.
> What depends on conditions is explained to be empty.
> Those who understand emptiness are heedful.

Candrakīrti's *Commentary on The Four Hundred Verses* says:

> I do not say that entities do not exist, because I say that they originate in dependence. "So are you a realist then?" I am not, because I am just a proponent of dependent origination. "What sort of nature is it then that you [propound]?" I propound dependent origination. "What is the meaning of dependent origination?" It has the meaning of the lack of a nature and the meaning of nonarising through a nature [of its own]. It has the meaning of the origination of results with a nature similar to that of illusions, mirages, reflections, cities of scent-eaters,[616] magical creations, and dreams. It has the meaning of emptiness and identitylessness.[617]

Thus, this reasoning shows that, just like the two sides of a single coin, dependent origination and emptiness—or appearance and emptiness—are not at all contradictory but an inseparable unity. This means that although dependently originating phenomena lack any ultimately real existence, on the conventional level they are not just completely nonexistent, since—unlike sky-flowers and such—they represent the experiential consensus of our everyday lives. *The Entrance into Centrism* says:

> Just like a vase and such do not exist in true reality
> And at the same time exist as common worldly consensus,
> All entities originate in this very same way.
> Hence, it does not follow that they are the same as the son of a
>   barren woman.
>
> Since both these [causes and results] are illusionlike,
> We are not at fault and the entities of the world do exist [as such].[618]

*The Fundamental Verses* declares:

> Whatever might be used to invalidate emptiness,
> That is, dependent origination,
> Just serves to invalidate
> The entirety of worldly conventions.[619]

If things were not empty of independent and real existence, the interdependent origination of causes and results in the world would be impossible, since nothing could be affected by anything. Thus, none of the appearances and conventions that we constantly deal with would ever come about. However, again, this seeming dependent origination is not something that is presented as part of a Centrist system of its own. All that Centrists say is that, just from the perspective of ordinary worldly experiences, certain appearances seem to appear in dependence on the appearance of certain others, which are called their conditions. Moreover, the presentation of seeming phenomena as dependent origination serves as a proper support to conveniently approach their ultimate reality, which is that causes and results are empty of any nature. All dualistic phenomena (such as cause and result, subject and object, cyclic existence and nirvāṇa, or seeming and ultimate reality) are just set up in mutual dependence, but none of them exists independently through a nature of its own. In this way, the Centrist view is free from the two extremes of permanence and extinction.

The gist of this is as follows: When Centrists present the arising and ceasing of dependently originating causes and results on the level of no analysis, they neither superimpose nor deprecate anything with regard to the seeming worldly reality of mere appearances. Therefore, when Centrists engage in the conventional interactions of adopting certain things and rejecting others, they do not deviate from the ways of seeming reality, since they express things in a way that does not add or remove anything from how people deal with these things in the context of common worldly consensus. While it definitely makes sense to maintain this approach on the level of no analysis, if Centrists were to assert arising and ceasing in terms of dependent origination on the level of analysis, such would only amount to superimposition and deprecation with regard to both realities. Therefore, if Centrists were to approach the ultimate in this way, they would deviate from both realities. From the perspective of analysis, there would be the superimposition of establishing the dependently originating phenomena of seeming reality in some sense, while in fact they are not established. To imagine that these phenomena are somehow established would negate the ultimate freedom from arising and ceasing and thus deprecate ultimate reality.

In a broader sense, the reasoning of mere dependent origination is said to be the king of Centrist reasonings, since it not only dispels the extremes of permanence and extinction but also eradicates all kinds of wrong views. For example, it refutes that things arise without any cause, since this would mean that things do not depend on anything at all, while dependent origination shows the opposite: that things depend on collections of their specific causes and conditions. This reasoning also negates all notions of a permanent, single, and nonconcordant cause, such as a primal substance or a creator god. For, if things arose from a single cause, this would contradict our experience that they in fact depend on vast numbers of conditions. Nor can things depend on a permanent cause, since something permanent is by definition devoid of performing any function or activity, because such already entails a process of change. If things could arise from nonconcordant causes, it would be unreasonable that they have to depend on their own specific causes.

Likewise, the reasoning of dependent origination equally refutes that things arise from themselves, from something other, or from both. In terms of arising from itself, a thing can neither depend on itself nor act upon itself. Furthermore, if a thing is not established in itself, it can be neither something that depends on something else nor something on which something else depends. On the other hand, if a thing were established in itself, it would not have to depend on anything.

As for arising from something other, if things are not established in themselves in the first place, the question of what depends on what as well as the whole notion of "other" is pointless. Even if is assumed that things are established in themselves, this would mean that they do not have to depend on anything other. However, being established by themselves yet still having to depend on something else (such as causes and conditions) is self-contradictory. As for arising from both themselves and something other, obviously, all these flaws would just multiply. *The Entrance into Centrism* summarizes:

> Since entities originate in dependence,
> All these thoughts cannot withstand examination.
> Therefore, this reasoning of dependent origination
> Cuts through the entire web of erroneous views.[620]

**Conclusion**

Each of the five great Centrist reasonings is in itself fully sufficient to produce an understanding that things lack any real or independent existence. However, as was shown for the vajra sliver reasoning and the reasoning of the freedom from unity and multiplicity, they supplement each other in generating incontrovertible certainty and an all-encompassing realization of this lack of real existence. Moreover, in order to approach such a realization, the various reasonings provide a range of different avenues that may be more or less convenient or convincing for individual people with varying capacities, propensities, or particular misconceptions.

In this context of the five great Centrist reasonings, it should be clear that a real and intrinsic nature of things is impossible among knowable objects. Therefore, strictly speaking, from among the three modes of a correct reason, the negative entailment cannot be established here. As was explained, the negative entailment means that the reason may never apply to the heterologous set. In terms of the above five reasonings, the general meaning of the predicate in all of them is "what lacks a real nature." Thus, "what has a real nature" would be the heterologous set. Since it is precisely such a real nature of things that does not exist, it does not make sense to say that the respective reason—such as "being free from unity and multiplicity" or "originating in dependence"—may not apply to a heterologous set (that is, something that has a real nature) that is nonexistent. In other words, the question as to whether something can apply to, entail, or include a nonexistent or not is per se irrelevant.

However, that the third mode cannot be established in no way invalidates the above reasonings. As was explained, there is no doubt that if there were such a thing as a really existing cup, it would necessarily have to be established either as a cup that is a unity or as a cup that is a multiplicity. The same goes for hypothetical, really arising entities. Furthermore, there are many concordant examples for the nonexistence of a real nature—such as illusions, reflections, and dreams—that can be appropriately employed in these reasonings. Finally, what is to be comprehended through the inferential cognitions that are based on such arguments is nothing but the probandum of these arguments—that all things lack a real nature—and never its opposite.

As was explained, there are two types of negating reasons: those that are based on the nonobservation of something connected and those that are based on the observation of something contradictory. The first four Centrist reasonings fall under the first category, and the reason of dependent origination falls under the latter.

In general, there is no disagreement between Autonomists and Consequentialists about either these conventional issues or the essential point of how they understand ultimate reality. Thus, the five great reasonings of Centrism are common to Autonomists and Consequentialists. Both use these arguments to point out phenomenal identitylessness. Their difference is that Consequentialists say that these five reasonings merely follow the conventions of logic as acknowledged by others. On the mere conventional level, Autonomists understand them as autonomous arguments that are acknowledged by both parties.

### Other Reasonings

Apart from the five great Centrist reasonings, there are two further major arguments that are used to determine phenomenal identitylessness.

In the first reasoning, any real existence of the mind as the apprehender is negated through the preceding negation of something apprehended. Thus, through using an appropriate reasoning of one's choice, one starts by refuting the notion of really and independently existent objects. Once no such objects are to be found, there can be no real subject—the apprehending mind—that cognizes them, since the subject has to depend on the existence of its object. If neither subject nor object really exists, all phenomena do not really exist, since phenomena are either subjects or objects. As *The Entrance into Centrism* says:

> In brief, understand this meaning:
> Just as knowable objects do not exist, mind does not exist either.
>
> The Buddhas said, "If there are no knowable objects,
> One easily finds that a knower is excluded."

If knowable objects do not exist, the negation of a knower is established.
Therefore, they first negated knowable objects.[621]

The second reasoning inductively applies the realization of the emptiness of one phenomenon to all phenomena. This is described in Āryadeva's *Four Hundred Verses*:

That which is the observer of one single entity
Is explained to be the observer of everything.
That which is the emptiness of one [entity]
Is the emptiness of everything.[622]

Here, "the observer" refers to the supreme knowledge that realizes emptiness. All things, such as form, appear in different ways, but they are not different in that they do not arise through a real nature of their own. Therefore, if it is understood that one phenomenon does not arise through a nature of its own, then it is also realized that all other phenomena equally do not arise through a nature of their own. This is like every drop of the ocean having the same taste. The experience of the taste of a single drop of ocean water is the same experience as the taste of every drop of the ocean. Likewise, when a single conditioned phenomenon is realized to be empty, the emptiness of all conditioned phenomena is realized, since all phenomena share this basic feature of being conditioned. As *The Sūtra Requested by Sky Treasure* says:

Those who meditate on a single phenomenon and thus understand
That all phenomena are like an illusion and a mirage,
Ungraspable, hollow, false, and not solid,
Will soon proceed to the heart of enlightenment.

*The Sūtra of the King of Meditative Concentration* agrees:

Through one, you will know all.
Through one, you will see all.

It is said that, strictly speaking, the latter reasoning is only suitable for people whose minds are not affected by any Buddhist or non-Buddhist philosophical systems, so that they, from their unquestioning worldly perspective, can directly enter the middle path beyond extremes. Thus, this reasoning is not intended for those who already follow certain philosophical systems. Such people may have determined through their systems that such things as coarse outer objects lack real and independent existence, but it is precisely their adherence to these philosophical systems that prevents them from extending their analysis and realization to other, more subtle things that nevertheless bear this same nature of lacking real existence.

**Unmasking Personal Identity**

In general, all the reasonings that negate phenomenal identity can also be used to negate personal identity and vice versa, since the latter is just a special instance of the former. However, the clinging to a personal identity of our own is singled out to be tackled through additional specific reasonings, since it governs all levels of our thinking and behavior in a very immediate way and is thus directly responsible for the arising of mental afflictions and the ensuing suffering. Moreover, the realization of personal identitylessness that is achieved through these reasonings is the cause for liberation from cyclic existence.

The conceptions of clinging to a personal self focus on the five aggregates that constitute our psychophysical continua. Even if these aggregates themselves are not taken to be our self, any self that is assumed to be something other than the aggregates is always regarded as being related to these aggregates—that is, our immediate personal appearances and experiences—in one way or the other. We think in this way by regarding certain aspects of these aggregates either as being our self or as being connected to or controlled by such a self. Therefore, our grasping at a self constantly engages one or several of the five aggregates. In certain situations, we extend our thoughts of a self even to our friends, relatives, and possessions: If someone else benefits or harms them, we think that this person has helped or harmed us.

Technically speaking, this conceptual object of a "self" that is apprehended through the clinging to the aggregates as being or relating to a self is considered a nonentity;[623] more specifically, it is a term generality[624] that does not correspond to any real object. Obviously, from the perspective of reasonings that analyze for the ultimate, there is no need to talk about the existence of a real personal identity. However, even from the perspective of reasonings that analyze conventional expressions, a real personal identity does not exist.[625] Still, in adaptation to the perspective of worldly consensus without examination and analysis, the Buddha never denied the mere notions of a person or an individual. However, these notions never correspond to any actual object that exists in a substantial way. They are always understood to exist in a purely nominal way in the context of the mere correct seeming. As the sūtras say:

> Just as a collection of [certain] parts
> Is described by the name "chariot,"
> Likewise, in dependence on the aggregates,
> One speaks about "sentient beings" on the seeming level.

The negations of the object of our clinging to a self are usually presented in the framework of the twenty views about a real personality that were explained earlier.[626] In brief, the sūtras describe these twenty views as follows:

- (1–5) the five notions that one of the five aggregates is the self
- (6–10) the five notions that the self possesses one of the aggregates as a companion or retinue
- (11–15) the five notions that one of the aggregates dwells in or is based on the self in such a way that it is supported by the self
- (16–20) the five notions that the self dwells in or is based on one of the aggregates in such a way that this aggregate is its support

That none of these notions applies is expressed in Nāgārjuna's *Letter to a Friend*:

> It is said that form is not the self,
> That the self does not possess form, that the self does not dwell on form,
> And that form does not dwell on the self.
> Please realize that the remaining four aggregates are empty in the same way.[627]

Accordingly, none of the five aggregates is the self, the self does not possess any of the aggregates, nor do they support each other; that is, neither do the aggregates support the self, nor does the self support the aggregates. Thus, refuting these twenty views excludes that there is a self that exists in any relation to the five aggregates. Kamalaśīla's second volume of his *Stages of Meditation* summarizes the negation of such a real person or self:

> [First,] the person is not observed outside of the aggregates, constituents, and sources. The person is also not the nature of the aggregates and such, because the aggregates and such have the nature of being impermanent and multiple and because the person is that which is imputed by others as a permanent and singular entity. A person that is not suitable to be expressed as either the same as or as something other [than the aggregates] is not suitable as an existent entity, because there are no other possibilities of how entities exist.[628]

Thus, the starting point of analyzing whether this self as the hypothetical referent of our clinging to "I" and "me" really exists is the basic question of whether such a self is the same as or different from the aggregates.

The self is not the same as the aggregates, because their respective characteristics do not match. The aggregates are (1) impermanent, (2) a formation of multiple factors, and (3) dependent on others, whereas the self is generally apprehended as something lasting, singular, and independent. In detail, this is as follows:

1) It is established through reasoning that the aggregates are brought about through causes and conditions and are impermanent from moment to moment. On the other hand, it is established through our own experience that we apprehend our self as something lasting, such as when we fancy that we recognize the same self in us that we saw yesterday.
2) The aggregates are clearly a multiplicity; that is, they consist of forms, feelings, and so on, each one in turn having many subdivisions. On the other hand, our experience tells us that we apprehend our self as something singular, such as when we think, "I am an individual, a single person."
3) Analysis shows us that each one of the aggregates is something that arises and ceases in dependence on various causes and conditions. On the other hand, experientially, we apprehend our self as something intrinsic and independent, such as when we focus inwardly and think, "This is me" or "It is only me who decides what I do."

If we then look for a self that is different from our aggregates, we do not find anything either. The reasons for this are as follows:

1) Experientially, our clinging to "I" and "me" does not engage in or relate to anything other than just our aggregates.
2) If there were a self other than our body and mind, it would have to appear to us, because it is impossible for our own self to be a phenomenon that is hidden from ourselves.
3) Something that is free from the characteristics of the aggregates thereby becomes a nonentity, since the aggregates contain only entities, that is, phenomena that perform a function. However, if something is a nonentity, this contradicts its being able to perform a function, such as that the self thinks or is in control of "its" body and mind.

As *The Fundamental Verses* says:

> If the aggregates were the self,
> It would possess arising and ceasing.
> If it were something other than the aggregates,
> It would not possess the characteristics of the aggregates.[629]

Furthermore, things in their entirety are contained in just these five aggregates of form, feeling, discrimination, formation, and consciousness. A self that would be altogether different from these is not observable through any kind of perceptual valid cognition even for a short while. Let alone yogic valid perception, all that the five sense consciousnesses perceive are outer objects such as visible form,[630] while self-awareness by definition is only aware of consciousness itself. Therefore, none of these cognitions can have a self as its object. Furthermore, since neither a nature nor a result of a self that is not contained in the aggregates is observable, there is also no reason that produces a correct inference about such a self. Thus, it cannot be established through inferential valid cognition either.

At this point, one might just say, "This very mental state that thinks, 'This is me' is the subject that validly cognizes the self." However, since this mental state is nothing but a thought whose essential character is clinging, it is not a perceptual valid cognition. Nor is it an inferential valid cognition, because it is a mere assumption that does not rely on any correct arguments. Rather, this thought or impulse is nothing but mere unfounded imagination that emerges under the influence of our beginningless habituation to entertain it. As for the operational mode of this thought, it exactly corresponds to mistaking a rope for a snake. Mistaking the aggregates for a self is just a much more deeply ingrained and solidified habitual mental tendency.

Some people even say that the self exists but that it cannot be determined to be either identical to or different from the aggregates. They also say that it is neither permanent nor impermanent, nor any third possibility.[631] However, such a phenomenon does not exist, since there is nothing that can be observed through any valid cognition as existing either within or outside of the aggregates. Also, it is impossible to observe any existent that is neither permanent nor impermanent nor any third possibility. To postulate such a "self" is nothing but a convoluted way of saying that it simply does not exist at all.

If a self that is established through its own nature is refuted through such an analysis, then what is "mine" is implicitly negated too. This is like the example of the daughter of a barren woman. Since she is not observable in the first place, nothing that would be hers—such as her body or her dress—is observable either. As *The Fundamental Verses* says:

> If there is no self,
> Where should there be what is mine?[632]

The main formal way in which Centrism negates a personal self is *the sevenfold reasoning through the analogy of a chariot.* The analogy of a chariot was taught by the Buddha.[633] Later, Nāgārjuna and his spiritual heirs put it into a systematic format. *The Entrance into Centrism* reads:

It is not asserted that a chariot is something other than its parts.
It is not something that is not other, nor does it possess them.
It does not exist in the parts, nor do the parts exist in it.
It is neither their mere collection nor the shape—thus is the analogy.[634]

The first five points of this analysis were already presented by Nāgārjuna. In addition, Candrakīrti taught the analysis of the collection of the parts and of the shape of the chariot. When one searches for a really existing chariot through these seven points of examination, it neither exists as its parts (such as the wheels) nor as something other than these parts. The collection of the parts and the shape of the chariot are refuted in passing, since one does not find either the collection or the shape as anything other than or above the parts that make up their collection and the particular shape of a chariot. If these seven points are applied in an analogous way to the analysis of a personal self, this self is not found as something other than the aggregates nor as the aggregates themselves. In fact, these two possibilities implicitly cover all seven parts of the analysis, the remaining five being merely their elaborations. For if the self is neither the same as nor different from the aggregates, there is no self at all. Consequently, there is no self to possess or control the aggregates. There is likewise no self that exists in the aggregates, nor can the latter exist in a nonexistent self.[635]

1) The formulation of the reasoning
A personal self does not exist, because it is neither the same as the aggregates nor something other; because it does not possess them; because the self does not exist in the aggregates nor do these aggregates exist in the self; and because it is neither their mere collection nor their shape.

2) The three modes of the reason
The *subject property* means that a hypothetical self does not conform to any of the seven possibilities just mentioned, such as being the same as the aggregates. There is also no other possibility for the existence of such a self. In detail:

a) The self is not something other than the aggregates. As explained above, our experiences and our clinging in relation to a self do not refer to anything outside of the five aggregates or outside of our body and mind. Otherwise, our self would be totally unrelated to our body and mind and at best some nonentity unable to perform any function at all.

b) If the self were the same as the aggregates, there are several possibilities as to how this could be the case. If the self were the same as all the aggregates together, we would have at least five different selves, since there are five aggregates, not to mention their subdivisions. Moreover, since the aggregates momentarily arise and cease, the self would do so too. Thus, we would have a new and different self in every moment. In addition, this would make any memory of actions or experiences impossible, since the self that does or experiences something in a certain moment ceases in the next moment. The new self would have no connection to the old one.

If the self is held to be just one of these aggregates or a certain part of it, which one would it be? As for the aggregate of form, we do not consider outer material things to be our personal self. Experientially, it is also obvious that we do not take just our body to be our self. Moreover, what would then be the difference between me and my corpse? And when we look at all the changes in terms of size, weight, shape, and so on that our body has undergone since we were born, this clearly does not correspond to our sense of a lasting "me." On the other hand, if we think that our mind is our self, we still have four mental aggregates to choose from. In addition, each one of them is itself a collection of many different factors, such as the whole range of all our constantly changing feelings, perceptions, and thoughts. As explained above, nothing in this unceasing and manifold flux corresponds to the features of a lasting, single, and independent self. Certainly, nobody would identify just a single, fleeting emotion, perception, or thought as one's personal self. Also, our minds change tremendously over the span of a lifetime. As babies, we did not even know how to eat and drink properly, and now we might construct spaceships or even read books on Madhyamaka . . . So how does this correspond to our seeming experience of a lasting self? Moreover, such drastic changes of body and mind are not seen merely over the period of a whole life but can happen any moment. For example, consider how "we" feel—or how we experience our self—when we are depressed, lonely, unsuccessful, poor, or ill in contrast to being happy, loved, successful, rich, and healthy.

If the mere continuum of the aggregates is considered to be the self, then the above flaws in terms of it being momentarily impermanent equally apply here, since it is the very nature of a continuum to change moment by moment. Any continuum is not established in itself, since it is just a label that is applied to a series of different moments, such as calling a stream of many drops of water that follow one after the other and are continuously exchanged a "river." If we think that the self is that which holds the moments of our psychophysical continua together, there is nothing that could perform such a function. There is no force or energy that fastens these moments together or underlies them, since all there are in a continuum are these single moments. A hypothetical such force is also not necessary, since any subsequent moment in a continuum arises only in dependence on its previous moment. Since the previous moment has already ceased when the following one arises, they can never be simultaneous. Thus, how could they be joined in any way by anything?

c) The self cannot possess the aggregates, because it has already been refuted that it is the same as or different from the aggregates. So what else could there be to possess them? Moreover, even if the self were all or just one of the aggregates, which would possess which? All aggregates together cannot possess themselves. Nor can the body possess the mind or vice versa, for how should something with form possess something without form or be possessed by it? Also, the mental aggregates cannot possess each other, for they are all formless. In addition, since all aggregates are momentary, which moment exactly could possess which other moments? There is certainly no question of possessing any past or future moments. And as for present moments, how could any one of them influence, control, or possess any other, since not even the smallest indivisible moment can be found?

d) The self neither exists in nor is supported by the aggregates. Otherwise, it would again just be a part of these aggregates or the aggregates would support themselves. Then the same inconsistencies as under (c) would apply. And if the self were something different from the aggregates—a nonentity—how could it exist among them or be supported by them? A nonentity cannot be supported by entities, since there is no possible connection or contact between such mutually exclusive phenomena as entities and nonentities. Moreover, nonentities indicate the absence of entities, so how could an absence, such as the lack of a table, be supported by anything?

e) The aggregates do not exist in the self. If the self were one or all of the aggregates, then the aggregates would have to exist in all or in one of themselves. And if the self were different from the aggregates—if the self were not an entity—how could entities (the aggregates) exist within the absence of entities? Even if the aggregates existed within a self that is the absence of entities (such as space), there could not be the slightest relation or interaction between the aggregates and such a self. The aggregates are also not supported by the self, since the same consequences as under (3) would follow. For if the self were the same as the aggregates, they would have to support themselves; and if it were different, a nonentity would have to support entities.

f) The self is not the mere collection of the aggregates, since it would then still exist even if one's five aggregates were complete but disassembled, for example, when various parts of one's body are cut off and piled up around it. Moreover, if one or several parts of one's aggregates are missing, such as a finger or certain features of one's personality due to Alzheimer's disease, the self would be defective too. In addition, if we just refer to the mere collection of the aggregates as the self and thus give up the notion of a self as something that controls or owns these aggregates, whose aggregates would they then be? Their mere collection does not control or own itself.

g) The self is also not the shape of all the aggregates, since the four mental aggregates do not have any shape and since, experientially, we do not consider the self to be just the shape of our body. Moreover, if this very shape were the self, whose shape would it then be? Also, the shape of each body part cannot be the self, since it then would follow that we have as many selves as we have body parts. In addition, the shapes of the body parts do not change whether the body is a whole or its parts are separated. Thus, if the shapes of the individual parts were the self, it would not make any difference for the self if the body parts were severed from the body.

As for the *positive entailment* of the sevenfold reasoning using the analogy of a chariot, whether we refer to a self or anything else, if something does not exist as any of the above seven possibilities, it cannot exist at all. The *negative entailment* means that if it existed, it would necessarily have to exist as one of these possibilities.[636]

To summarize, from the perspective of mistakenness and without analysis, the self seems to exist just like persons, sentient beings, and so on seem to exist. However, when analyzed, just as a self does not exist, also persons and such do not exist. Likewise, just as cars, tables, forests, and so on exist on the mere conventional level, also the self may be said to exist on this level. Under analysis, just as the self does not exist, all phenomena should be understood to be free from all reference points, such as existence and nonexistence.

### *The Result of Centrist Reasoned Analysis*

Right from the beginning, dependently originating phenomena, persons, and so on are not really established, but non-Buddhists and Buddhist realists still fall into the various extremes of superimposing or denying such phenomena and persons. Therefore, Centrist reasonings serve to put an end to these reifications, be they in terms of existence or nonexistence. Accordingly, everybody in the tradition of Nāgārjuna and his spiritual heirs insists that, in Centrism, it is impossible to attain any realization that bears even the faintest resemblance to entertaining any reference points. The only possible result of properly employed Centrist reasoning is to pass into the peace of nonarising that is free from all reference points. Thus, when phenomena are analyzed with Centrist reasonings, all conceptions of superimposition and denial—such as clinging to identity, identitylessness, existence, nonexistence, arising, ceasing, causes, the lack of causes, and so on—gradually come to an end. This is precisely the purpose of the Centrist approach to reasoning. As *The Entrance into Centrism* says:

> Ordinary beings are bound by conceptions.
> Nonconceptual yogins will find release.
> Hence, the learned state that the result of analysis
> Is that conceptions are at peace.
>
> The analyses in [Nāgārjuna's] treatise were not performed out of attachment to debate.
> [Rather,] he taught true reality for the sake of complete release.

and

> Attachment to one's own view and quarreling about others' views
> Are in themselves nothing but [expressions of reifying] thinking.
> Therefore, setting aside attachment and anger,
> Analysis will swiftly lead to release.[637]

Śāntideva agrees:

> Once neither entities nor nonentities
> Remain before the mind,
> There is no other mental flux [either].
> Therefore, it is utter nonreferential peace.[638]

By relying on extensive Centrist scriptures and reasonings, one starts out with negating all views on existence and nonexistence. Through the discriminating knowledge that arises in this process, one arrives at a conceptual understanding that all phenomena lack an intrinsic nature of their own. Then, based on the meditation of calm abiding in which one rests one-pointedly in this actuality, the increasingly pure meditation of superior insight into the true nature of phenomena is developed. In this way, the accumulations are completed and the mind is purified of both afflictive and cognitive obscurations, which finally leads to attaining the state of perfect Buddhahood. This is why it is said that the supreme cause for attaining liberation and omniscience is the supreme knowledge through study, reflection, and meditation that clearly realizes—in a way in which there is nothing to be realized—that all phenomena are without nature. In other words, the success of the relentless Centrist raid on all objects of reification, including reification and the reifier, is measured by diminishing the clinging to the various layers of fixed ideas that obscure mind's clarity of seeing the nature of things as it is.

## Madhyamaka Meditation

The following exposition is mainly based on Kamalaśīla's three-volume *Stages of Meditation* (the only Indian Centrist text that explains meditation in detail) and on the oral instructions that are transmitted within the Karma Kagyü tradition. As I try to approach Centrist meditation from a number of different angles, some phrases may appear more or less repetitive. However, since this topic is hardly ever treated in great detail, and since meditation is all about repeated familiarization, there seems to be no harm in hearing a few things more than once.

### *Why Is Analytical Meditation Necessary?*

As was explained in detail, the main cause for all our samsaric problems is basic ignorance that expresses itself as our instinctive clinging to a personal self and really existing phenomena. The only means for eliminating this fundamental unawareness is to develop its opposite: an awareness through which we see our mind and phenomena as they really are. In technical terms, this is called discriminating knowledge, which is the seed for the omniscient wisdom of a Buddha. As a sūtra says:

> If you discriminate that phenomena are identityless
> And meditate by discriminating them in this way,
> This is the cause for the result of attaining nirvāṇa.
> Peace will not come about through any other cause.

In general, Buddhism provides a large variety of skillful means to generate insight into the true nature of mind and phenomena, but analytical meditation is the way in which this insight is developed and enhanced in a very systematic and thorough way. This is the first reason analytical meditation is necessary.

Second, when we consider that afflictions and suffering are the negative repercussions of our ignorance and clinging, this may strengthen our wish to tackle them. These repercussions do not only manifest on the private or personal level; but especially in the present time of globalization, it is easy to see how devastating such clinging by even a single person can be for the whole world. For example, take the "innocent" notion of who we are. Ask someone in New York, "Who are you?" and the answer might be, "I am Helen, and I am an American." So far, so good, but the story does not end there. Rather, this notion of being an American involves the feeling of belonging to a certain nation and homeland: "All the land between the East Coast and the West Coast is my country, and all the people who live there are my compatriots." In this way, the sense of "me" and "mine" is extended over large parts of a continent, and the ego reaches out to the borders of the United States, so to speak. It may not even stop there, since patriots love their country and want to protect it. Consequently, they may perceive certain legitimate interests and security concerns across the entire planet. Of course, people in other nations, such as Iraq or Afghanistan, have the same tendencies. Based on this, all nations consider other nations that have the same interests or vision to be their friends, and certain others their enemies. In this way, it is clear that all the attachment and hatred that develop in this process and the many conflicts in the world that result from it are basically rooted in "ego clashes."

Of course, in the midst of such conflicts, be they interpersonal or international, we usually have no idea where things started, and sometimes that even doesn't matter to us anymore. So in this context, we could see analytical meditation as taking a break from our usual behavior patterns and asking ourselves, "Wait a minute, what are we doing here?" Through Centrist analysis, we try to take a closer look at our unquestioned experiences and actions, such as having a self and trying to defend it and its territory. In other words, we take time to sit down and run a thorough check on whether our highly subjective and habitual reactions really make any sense. Do they stand up to the facts and needs within a wider perspective, or is it possible for us to have a much better and more beneficial time with ourselves and one another?

Third, as for removing the root cause for cyclic existence, it is said in all Buddhist schools that just resting the mind in a one-pointed state of calm abiding does not lead to liberation from cyclic existence, let alone Buddhahood. The main reason for this is that whatever meditation we may practice, if it does not work to sever the root of cyclic existence, it will at best calm down our manifest suffering and afflictions. However, it will not eradicate the latent tendencies or mental seeds that make suffering and afflictions arise again when we meet the right conditions at some later point. Most layers of reifying ourselves and other phenomena that provide the fertile ground for such seeds operate at the level of instinct and unconscious impulses. Hence, they can only be brought into awareness and then undermined as we scrutinize our ingrained worldviews and expose them to the light of prajñā through the meditation of superior insight or analytical meditation.

Fourth, in order to properly understand and employ his teachings, the Buddha said, we have to work with the four reliances:

1) Do not rely on persons but on the dharma.
2) As for this dharma, do not rely on the words but on the meaning.
3) As for the meaning, do not rely on the expedient meaning but on the definitive meaning.
4) And as for the definitive meaning, do not rely on ordinary consciousness but on wisdom.

Analytical meditation is the main way to make these distinctions properly, to investigate and cultivate the actual meaning of the dharma, and to provide the ground for the nondual wisdom that directly sees how things are.

Fifth, merely studying and reflecting on all of this is not sufficient. Even if we understand the two types of identitylessness and the emptiness of all phenomena, that alone does not prevent us from continuing to behave as if we had a self and as if things were solidly real. There is definitely a difference between understanding a wall to be empty and being able to walk through this wall. From time without beginning, we have grown thoroughly accustomed to and solidified our belief in a self and really existing phenomena. In fact, this is our most deeply rooted conviction. Since it is so entrenched in us, we cannot expect that a little bit of understanding of emptiness will have the power to overthrow this firm belief immediately. Rather, the only way to replace this mistaken notion is by gradually and thoroughly deconstructing it and cultivating its opposite: the realization of emptiness. Usually, upon first hearing about emptiness and the lack of a self, most of us will say, "No way is this true!" It is only upon a thorough and repeated investigation of the notion of a personal self that we might think, "Okay, I can see that there is no self in my five aggregates, but I do not believe that everything is just empty." For example, who would believe right away that their own bodies, friends, houses, and cars are empty? Thus, we proceed further with our analysis by looking at phenomenal identitylessness. When doing this, we may initially develop doubt that everything is as solidly real as we think it is. Continuing the analysis, we may arrive at the thought "Probably all this is empty." The end of our analysis is reached when we have developed unshakable certainty that all phenomena are empty.

At present, we are extremely well trained in seeing phenomena as nonempty. When engaging in Centrist analysis, we have to retrain in seeing phenomena as emptiness. In other words, over time, we have managed to be completely and effortlessly accustomed to imagining the real existence of a self and phenomena. In Centrist meditation, the point is to grow equally accustomed to the lack of a self and real phenomena, which is possible only through repeated familiarization in meditation. As noted earlier, the Sanskrit term for "meditation" (*bhāvanā*) literally means "to perfume." Thus, meditation is understood as perfuming our mind with emptiness until the scent of emptiness becomes inseparable from the mind's fabric. In the first volume of his *Stages of Meditation*, Kamalaśīla says:

> Thus, through the knowledge [that comes] from reflection, one discriminates true actuality. In order to reveal it, one develops the knowledge [that results] from meditation. *The Jewel Cloud Sūtra*[639] and others teach that this actuality will not be revealed merely through studying and such. It becomes [revealed through] practitioners who make [their

> own] experiences. Without the very clear brilliance of knowledge dawning, the darkness that veils the truth is not dispelled. Practicing meditation many times, knowledge will dawn. . . . In *The Sūtra of the King of Meditative Concentration*, the Blessed One declared:
>
> > This you should understand and strive for: As much as a person examines [something], that much will her mind be molded through the thoughts that dwell on this.[640]

Finally, on the Buddhist path, it is always emphasized that we should gain firsthand experience, direct knowledge, and personal certainty about the way things really are. Just as with our ordinary experiences in life, whatever we ourselves have thoroughly examined and found to be true will be an incontrovertible part of our experience. Then we no longer need to rely on other people or books. Doubts will not arise, nor will our minds be changed by others' questioning our realization. Moreover, when we have an experientially founded understanding of the correct view, we will increasingly be able to evaluate any experiences that might come up in our meditation practice. We can compare them with the correct Centrist view of emptiness and see clearly whether our practice and realization accords with what the Buddha and the great masters describe. In this way, analytical meditation is also very helpful for and informs any other meditation practices, such as deity visualization.

### *Calm Abiding and Superior Insight*

Meditation in Centrism, as in all other Buddhist schools, is divided into two general types: calm abiding and superior insight. One usually begins with calm abiding and then, on the basis of a calm and one-pointed mind, progresses toward superior insight. As proficiency is developed, the two types of meditation are practiced as an inseparable unity. In the middle volume of his *Stages of Meditation*, Kamalaśīla describes this:

> In the beginning, one should practice calm abiding for a while. Once distraction toward outer objects has become calm, one abides in a state of mind that is very supple and delights in being continually and naturally engaged in focusing inward. This is called calm abiding. While focusing on the calm abiding of the [mind], one analyzes this very [mind]. This is superior insight.[641]

The classic metaphor for the necessity of uniting calm abiding and superior insight is a candle flame. When this flame is bright and there is no wind, it is clearly visible and will also illuminate its surroundings. However, if the flame is bright but flickers in the wind, it will neither be seen distinctly itself nor clearly light up anything else. Likewise, if our mind is endowed with both the superior insight that sees true reality and the quality of calm abiding, through which we can one-pointedly direct this insight wherever we please, this mind will see both its own nature and the nature of all phenomena. Once the obscurations are removed, the light of wisdom appears just as sunlight in a cloud-free sky unimpededly illuminates everything.

However, if we have only cultivated undistracted meditative concentration and lack the supreme knowledge that realizes how things actually are, it is impossible to see ultimate reality. On the other hand, if we have the correct view of understanding identitylessness but no meditative concentration in which the mind rests one-pointedly, our mind will be distracted by other objects, not be under control, and thus not be workable. Consequently, it will be impossible for the light of wisdom to shine clearly and realize ultimate reality. Another analogy for the need to combine calm abiding and superior insight as an inseparable unity is a sharp scalpel in the steady hand of an experienced surgeon. If the scalpel is blunt or the surgeon's hand shaky, the operation cannot be performed properly. In the same way, when the mind rests in a state that involves both stillness and a crisp wakefulness or awareness, it is like a steady hand that deftly operates on our objects of investigation with the sharp blade of superior insight.

Since there is a wealth of materials available on the actual training in calm abiding, I will not go into detail here. The essential point of calm abiding in Centrism is to settle the mind within a still yet clear awareness, one-pointedly focused, thus serving as the proper ground for effective engagement in the Centrist analyses of the two types of identitylessness. Any of the numerous techniques to accomplish calm abiding can be used to reach this state. The prerequisites for superior insight are stated in Kamalaśīla's *Stages of Meditation*:

> One may wonder, "What are the prerequisites for superior insight?" [They are] relying on a genuine teacher, making every effort in extensive studies, and appropriate reflection.[642]

These three prerequisites depend on each other. By relying on a teacher who fully masters the Buddha's teachings, one studies the authentic texts and then develops the correct view of emptiness through the two kinds of knowledge that come from studying and reflecting. If the unmistaken view is not developed with certainty, the very basis with which one is to familiarize oneself during the meditation of superior insight is missing. Moreover, in order to develop such a view and make it incontrovertible, it is crucial to rely on the definitive rather than the expedient meaning. Consequently, for the understanding of the profound definitive teachings to dawn, it must necessarily be preceded by knowledge of the difference between these two levels of teaching.

Superior insight in Centrism can be classified as two:

1) a preparatory stage of "discriminating superior insight"[643]
2) the actual main practice of nonconceptual "motionless superior insight," in which there is no duality of meditator and object of meditation

On the basis of a mind that is calm and one-pointed, the two types of identitylessness are analyzed through supreme knowledge. In the second stage, mind is fully aware of and rests right within its own expanse free from all reference points.

All Centrist masters agree that the dawning of nondual wisdom results from the conjoined practice of calm abiding and superior insight, though they may give slightly different methods for developing that unity. For example, according to Bhāvaviveka, cultivating calm abiding is the first step, in which one trains through contemplating such topics as the repulsiveness of the body, loving-kindness, and compassion. Then, superior insight is generated through the power of Centrist reasoning. According to Śāntideva, calm abiding is developed by meditating on the mind of enlightenment, and the supreme knowledge of superior insight is generated through focusing on emptiness. Kamalaśīla recommends training in calm abiding by using an object, such as an image of the Buddha, and then proceeding to superior insight through analysis of the nature of this very object of calm abiding. According to Candrakīrti, both calm abiding and superior insight are to be practiced based on the view that analyzes true reality. All these explanations agree that first calm abiding, then superior insight, and finally their unity are to be practiced in this order, since they are related as causes and results in this way. In general, the main point in all three of these steps is that the mind be one-pointed and undistracted.

When do calm abiding and superior insight become a unity? There are different levels of unity. During the practice of calm abiding and superior insight "with characteristics"—when specific focuses or mental images are used in meditation—the unity occurs when the calmly abiding, thought-free mind that focuses on these mental images and the realization of superior insight that thoroughly discriminates all phenomena based on such images naturally blend into one. In the further stage of practicing calm abiding and superior insight "without characteristics," once both nonconceptual calm abiding and nonconceptual superior insight are attained, they are one in nature and thus said to be a unity. In other words, cultivating the still aspect of our mind means practicing calm abiding, and looking at the nature of both its still and its moving aspects is superior insight. Within the luminous nature of the mind that underlies both its stillness and its movement, these two aspects are an inseparable unity, so calm abiding and superior insight each serve to approach this very unity. Thus, these two meditations' having become a unity means nothing but naturally resting in the nature of the mind and recognizing whatever appears within it as being that nature. In this sense, the perfection of the unity of calm abiding and superior insight is called nonabiding nirvāṇa. As Pawo Rinpoche says, both Nāgārjuna's lineage of profound view and Asaṅga's lineage of vast activity[644] agree on this:

> Both traditions agree that the unity of perfect meditative stability and knowledge is to rest right within profound knowledge's seeing that is without seeing anything and to do so in a way that is without someone who rests and something to be rested in.[645]

Finally, when rising from meditative equipoise, with the awareness that all phenomena are illusionlike, one extensively engages in the accumulation of merit.

### *Analytical Meditation and Resting Meditation*

Another division of meditation is into "the analytical meditation of scholars"[646] and "the resting meditation of mendicants,"[647] or simply analytical meditation and resting meditation.

The analytical meditation of scholars refers to the intellectual examination of all phenomena through reasoning. There are two key terms here: "discriminating knowledge" and "personally experienced wisdom." The first step in this analytical meditation is to cultivate discriminating knowledge. This refers to all the levels of increasingly refined inferential valid cognition that are based on reasoning and developed through studying, reflecting, and meditating. In other words, this is the laser beam of penetrating analysis that scans its various objects once we have one-pointedly focused the diffuse light of our usual discursive thinking. The second term, "personally experienced wisdom," stands for true reality—the unity of wisdom and expanse—directly and nonconceptually realizing itself by itself in a way that is without anything realizing anything.

The way in which ordinary beings engage in analytical meditation during meditative equipoise is mainly through discriminating knowledge and also through a mere likeness of personally experienced wisdom. The latter refers to the most highly refined discriminating knowledge that eventually turns into the actual personally experienced wisdom. In general, ordinary beings are understood to be all those who have not directly realized true reality or emptiness, that is, those who have not yet reached the path of seeing. On the other hand, those who have directly realized emptiness—the noble ones—engage in meditative equipoise through personally experienced wisdom only. So once discriminating knowledge has reached its highest level of refinement at the last moment of the path of junction (illustrated by the well-known example of the two sticks and the fire), the actual personally experienced wisdom springs from it, which marks the beginning of the path of seeing. Thus, through causal discriminating knowledge—which includes resting within the doubt-free certainty that is induced through the analytical power of this knowledge—the fruitional personally experienced wisdom of the unity of awareness and expanse is attained.

This analytical meditation of scholars belongs to the usual gradual approach of the sūtra vehicle. It provides a very firm and clear basis for our practice. Once we have established such a basis, we will no longer make any big mistakes in our meditation. Through gradual study, reflection, and meditation, definite certainty is gained that does not depend on anything or anybody else to tell us how things are. Such unflinching conviction comes solely from our own personal and proper examination of the teachings, which completely eliminates all doubts. At this point, nobody can make us feel that we are wrong. Even the Buddha could not change our mind. This kind of certainty is necessary so that there is not the slightest room for mistakes or doubts to sneak in again. Sometimes, we seem to understand something, but if we do not decide on it in a way that is sufficiently clear and certain enough, then doubts may arise again and destroy our initial understanding, so that no stable progress is possible.

Resting meditation is also called stabilizing meditation. Obviously, it does not refer to just taking a rest and doing nothing but to letting the mind naturally and one-pointedly rest in its own nature with full mindfulness and alertness. "The resting meditation of mendicants in a more narrow sense corresponds to the immediate style of the Vajrayāna. Thus, it is said to be the swifter path that can bring results quite soon. However, at the same time, it is less easy to describe and grasp, since it deals straightaway with the nature of the mind, which cannot be pinpointed as anything whatsoever. Consequently, it may happen that we are not really sure what is going on in our meditation and what we actually have understood. There may be flashes of directly seeing the nature of the mind from time to time, but there is also the danger of not really seeing anything of the kind and just spacing out in some dull, blank state. Contrary to that, the analytical approach is a safeguard against falling into such a state, which is called "the meditation of a fool." Thus, in order to proceed on the correct path, the approach of the resting meditation of mendicants depends very much on the correct initial pointing-out instructions, the continuous qualified guidance, and the blessings of a true guru.

The terms "analytical meditation of scholars" and "resting meditation of mendicants" should not be taken too literally or exclusively. Some people think that the meditation of scholars is purely analytical and that yogic practitioners exclusively practice resting meditation, but this is not at all the case. Rather, such designations are a matter of degree. The scholarly approach to meditation also needs the element of resting or calm abiding in order for the practitioner to stay focused on the object of meditation and to settle in the certainty that has arisen from the preceding analysis. Likewise, yogic practitioners are in need of analytical meditation in order to purify their view of distortions and doubts. If these two are not kept in balance, then any kind of vision of ultimate reality that is attained solely through analytical meditation is a mere intellectual exercise, while the kinds of visions that are achieved through resting meditation alone are just further fleeting and indiscriminate mental experiences among our many others. Therefore, both elements of analysis and resting are indispensable for realizing the essence of meditation, regardless of which approach is personally preferred.

The general scope of analytical meditation encompasses all of the teachings of the Buddha, starting from contemplating impermanence and the preciousness of human existence up through ascertaining the two kinds of identitylessness. Resting meditation includes all types of meditations in which the conclusions achieved through preceding investigation become absorbed by the mind. The freshness of such absorptive resting of the mind is sustained through one-pointed mindfulness and alertness.

Centrist meditation, for the most part, follows the analytical approach. However, once the state of nonconceptual superior insight is attained and blended with nonconceptual calm abiding, the meditating mind finally realizes and rests in its own nature. Hence, also in Centrism, the above two approaches are not in conflict but, properly practiced, enhance each other. When inferential analysis and insight that are informed by Centrist reasonings are combined with directly looking at our mind (during as well as after the analysis), it is actually possible to develop a very stable and alert mind as well as rapidly progress on the path of profound realization.

As for the relation between analytical and resting meditation on the one side and calm abiding and superior insight on the other, calm abiding is not exactly the same as resting meditation, nor is superior insight equivalent to analytical meditation. Rather, analytical and resting meditation each include both calm abiding and superior insight.

The main aspect of resting meditation is the mind's calm abiding, since it primarily means to rest in the nature of the mind. However, this resting itself eventually assumes the quality of superior insight by directly looking at mind's nature. As for analytical meditation, it also includes both calm abiding and superior insight, since any mental investigation—be it conceptual or nonconceptual—needs to be performed on the basis of a calm and one-pointed mind. However, both pairs of meditation have the same final goal. Analytical and resting meditation eventually become a unity, just as calm abiding and superior insight. Ultimately, they have the same destination: the direct realization of the nature of the mind.

Some people think that when one practices calm abiding, there is no need to do any analysis, and when practicing superior insight, one does not need to rest the mind in meditative equipoise. However, during calm abiding, some degree of analysis is definitely required in order to determine whether the mind is still one-pointedly focused, how to deal with thoughts or afflictions that come up, and how to clear away the various obstacles to calm abiding, such as dullness and agitation. Different methods must also be employed to still the mind, and these methods involve scrutiny of the meditative state and its flaws. On the other hand, in superior insight, the emphasis is on developing the clarity of prajñā, but this works all the better the more the mind is resting in a one-pointed and undistracted way.

Other people think that analytical meditation and resting meditation are mutually exclusive, that the mind cannot rest while analyzing nor engage in investigation when resting. They regard analysis as a completely intellectual kind of discrimination and resting meditation as a totally nonconceptual kind of absorption. However, as indicated by the example of a candle flame without wind, the calmer the mind, the more clearly the light of prajñā can illuminate all phenomena. Otherwise, if analytical and resting meditation were mutually exclusive, this would have a number of absurd consequences. For example, it would then be a mistake to use one's discriminative capacity in mastering the various techniques of calm abiding and to eliminate the obstacles that may occur in this process. It would furthermore be impossible for the analyzing mind to eventually settle into a resting state at the end of the analysis. However, many Centrist masters repeatedly and clearly describe that it indeed is the analyzing mind that comes to rest. As Śāntideva's *Entrance to the Bodhisattva's Way of Life* says:

> Once one has analyzed what had to be analyzed,
> The analysis does not have any basis left.
> Since there is no basis, it does not continue.
> This is expressed as nirvāṇa.[648]

Atīśa concurs in his *Centrist Pith Instructions*:

> Once all specifically characterized and generally characterized phenomena are established as nonexistent [through knowledge], this knowledge itself is without appearance, luminous, and not established as any nature whatsoever. Thus, all flaws, such as dullness and agitation, are eliminated. In this interval, consciousness is without any thought, does not apprehend anything, and has left behind all mindfulness and mental engagement. For as long as neither characteristics nor the enemies and robbers of thoughts arise, consciousness should rest in such a [state].[649]

Nāgārjuna's *Commentary on the Mind of Enlightenment* also touches on the same topic:

> So-called entities are conceptions.
> Lack of conceptions is emptiness.
> Wherever conceptions appear,
> How could there be emptiness?[650]

His *Sixty Stanzas on Reasoning* declares:

> Those whose minds are not moved,
> Not even by a flicker of a thought about "complete voidness,"
> Have crossed the horrifying ocean of existence
> That is agitated by the snakes of the afflictions.[651]

Also Kamalaśīla's *Stages of Meditation* repeatedly talks about nonconceptual and unmoving superior insight:

> Once the mind has become stabilized on its focus through calm abiding, if one examines this [mind] through supreme knowledge, the brilliance of perfect wisdom will dawn. At this point, just as darkness is dispelled through bright daylight, obscurations are eliminated. Like one's eyes and light [in producing a visual perception], both [calm abiding and superior insight] are mutually compatible with regard to the emerging of perfect wisdom. It is not that they are incompatible in the way that light and darkness are. The nature of meditative concentration is not darkness. What is it then? Its defining characteristic is a one-pointed mind. [The Buddha] said:
>
> > If one rests in meditative equipoise, one perfectly realizes true actuality just as it is.
>
> Therefore, [calm abiding] is very much in harmony with supreme knowledge and not at all incompatible. Thus, when examining through supreme knowledge that rests in meditative equipoise, the very nonobservation of all phenomena is genuine nonobservation. This characteristic of the state of calm abiding of yogic practitioners means spontaneous presence, since there is nothing else to be seen beyond that. Calmness means that all discursiveness of characteristics, such as existence and nonexistence, is completely at peace.[652]

and

> As for the seeing of genuine true reality, it is the very fact that there is nothing to be seen, when the light of perfect wisdom dawns through the examination of all phenomena with the eye of supreme knowledge. This is also expressed in the sūtras:
>
> > One may wonder, "What is seeing the ultimate?" It means that all phenomena are not seen.
>
> Here, [the Buddha] has talked about "not seeing" by having in mind that there is no such seeing. However, this "not seeing" is not like not seeing when the conditions [for seeing] are incomplete (such as in a blind person and when closing one's eyes) or when one does not mentally engage [in seeing].[653]

Pawo Rinpoche summarizes:

> In brief, the very quintessence of all meditative concentrations of both the sūtras and the tantras of the great vehicle is to see, through supreme knowledge in a way that is without seeing, that no phenomenon whatsoever abides as anything, such as existence or nonexistence, and to undistractedly and nonconceptually rest in this very seeing.[654]

Thus, the question of whether a nonconceptual meditative state concords with the perfect view can be decided by determining whether clear wakefulness, mindfulness, and alertness that are reinforced and sustained by a determinate, immediate awareness of the perfect view are present or absent in the nonconceptual state in question. From this, it is clear that such nonconceptual meditation is not at all like ordinary nonconceptual states such as deep sleep, a faint, or a coma. In the same vein, as these quotations—and many others—amply show, there is not the slightest foundation in Centrist texts for the claims of Tsongkhapa and others that every nonconceptual meditative equipoise that is free from any mode of apprehension[655] is identical to the infamous meditation style of just not thinking anything that is ascribed by Tibetans to the Chinese master Hvashang.

Some people erroneously think that the state of superior insight ceases when resting meditation progresses. Thus, they claim that superior insight is necessarily always linked to the discerning mind. However, in that case, it would be impossible to ever achieve the unity of calm abiding and superior insight. This position also denies the eventual oneness of nonconceptual direct looking and superior insight. Actually, superior insight is not lost when the analyzing prajñā comes to rest after having performed the analysis. Eventually, this very settling of the discriminating aspect of the mind into mind's own spacious and luminous nature is the point of supreme and pure superior insight. Such insight is inseparable from resting in this nature in which there is not the slightest trace of duality, such as subject and object, analyzer and analyzed, or what rests and what it rests in. As Nāgārjuna's *Commentary on the Mind of Enlightenment* says:

> The Thus-Gone Ones do not see a mind
> That involves the aspects of a realizer and what is to be realized.
> Wherever there is a realizer and what is to be realized,
> There is no enlightenment.[656]

What is the difference between analytical meditation and just reflecting? The crucial distinction is that, in analytical meditation, our scrutinizing prajñā operates within a state of mind that is calm and one-pointed, thus bringing the object of analysis very clearly to mind and also being able to stay with it. Moreover, through alternating analysis with nonconceptual resting in the certainty that results from the preceding analysis, this approach taps into much deeper levels of the mind than any pondering on a superficial, intellectual plane. Based on calm abiding, the mind is like a clear mirror or a calm lake in which we can clearly see our own true face—mind's nature—and have a proper look at all its facets and features.

Thus, when beginning to train in calm abiding, one mainly cultivates resting meditation, as, for example, outlined in the nine stages of settling the mind.[657] Still, once calm abiding is achieved, analysis must be applied. To this end, in Buddhism, many general methods of analytical meditation are recommended during the state of calm abiding, such as contemplating the repulsiveness of the body as an antidote to desire, love and compassion as an antidote to hatred, or dependent origination to ignorance. In particular, in Centrism, the main practices of analytical meditation are the investigations of twofold identitylessness as they were described earlier.

### *Working with the Mind in Meditation and Daily Life*

If we lack an understanding of the view of identitylessness or emptiness, any kind of meditation that we do will necessarily miss the point as far as ultimate reality is concerned. Hence, it is important to first establish this view. However, even when endowed with a correct understanding of the view, if we do not meditate by properly resting in such an understanding, our meditation will likewise be out of touch with true reality. Thus, in Centrism, the main part of meditation consists of both the initial analysis of the two types of identitylessness through supreme knowledge and the subsequent resting within the expanse that is free from all mental reference points.

There are two types of training in calm abiding: calm abiding with support and without support, which is mind just resting in its own nature. Supports are again twofold: outer objects (such as a pebble or a Buddha statue) and inner objects. The latter are all kinds of mental images or visualizations, which may correspond to outer objects (such as visualizing a Buddha statue) or not (such as visualizing deities or mantric syllables). All of these are called nonconceptual mental images,[658] since they do not involve any thoughts that analyze for ultimate reality.

When practicing superior insight, we meditate by taking such mental images that, through the power of calm abiding, clearly appear in our mind as the bases for discriminating analysis. Thus, this is not an analysis that is outwardly directed, since the mind only looks inward, at its own images. When such images that arise from meditative concentration are analyzed through superior insight in order to realize true reality, this involves thoughts that examine this true reality. Accordingly, these images are called conceptual mental images.[659] Through the examination of the nature of such images, the nature of all phenomena is realized as it is. This process can be compared to examining the appearance of our face in a mirror. The reflection in the mirror is not our face, but it clearly reveals all the beautiful or ugly features of this face and in this way we can deal with our actual face. Candrakīrti uses this analogy in his *Entrance into Centrism*:

> Although [the reflection of our face in a mirror] is not real, it is there for the purpose of beautifying this face.
> Likewise, also here, our arguments are seen
> To have the capacity of cleansing the face of knowledge.[660]

Especially at the beginning of our practice of analytical meditation, each object must be investigated individually. For if a particular object with certain features has not been clearly identified as the basis for analysis, it is not possible to cut through all the superimpositions with regard to these features. The particular object is then analyzed by means of correct discriminating knowledge and thus is conceptually ascertained to be something that appears while lacking any real nature of its own. While we undistractedly keep the object of meditative concentration in mind, conceptual discrimination is increasingly refined and eventually terminates all by itself, once its equally subtle objects are found to be unfindable. Eventually, this process gives way to the direct and nonconceptual realization that this very object is a mere appearance but has no nature of its own. Thus, by blending the focus of calm abiding and superior insight into one, we train in unifying them.

This process of meditating by focusing on particular objects can be outlined as follows. We start our analytical meditation by taking an outer object, such as a table, as our focus of analysis. In order to realize through discriminating knowledge that this table is empty, the point is simply to focus on the plain mental image of this table and to apply Centrist reasoning to it. Thus, when analyzing the table's nature, we do not consider or focus on its specific characteristics, such as its color, shape, size, or attractiveness. By extending our investigation to other objects of the sense perceptions and so on, we become aware of the emptiness of all the objects that we apprehend, which is like resting in the center of open space. To train in this awareness is called "the yoga of not observing the apprehended,"[661] which means to meditate on everything external as being the unity of appearance and emptiness.

Next, we proceed to the stage of using internal objects of focus, such as our various expressions of consciousness that are the subjects apprehending the above objects. When an instance of apprehending subjective consciousness, such as hatred or desire, arises in our mind stream, we should clearly identify it and then examine it, as if under a magnifying glass, through discriminating knowledge. What is its cause? Where did it come from in the first place? Does it abide on the outside or the inside? Does it have any nature? What is its shape or color? By doing this, we will not find this emotion to be anything whatsoever. Then, we should rest in meditative equipoise in this very actuality of not finding anything. This approach is to be applied not only to any afflictions that may come up in our mind but to the entire range of mental events (such as feelings), to our sense consciousnesses, and to our thoughts. Whether the latter are positive, negative, or just neutral, random thoughts, we should be aware of any thought that arises and use it for our meditation in the way described. This does not mean that we try to rest in meditative equipoise by just observing or focusing on our thoughts, but we train in resting in their very essence, which is emptiness free from reference points. This is "the yoga of not observing the apprehender,"[662] which means meditating on all internal states of mind as being the unity of awareness and emptiness.

After having searched for a real existence of both subject and object, we find neither. In the end, neither the object to be examined (be it external matter or internal mind) nor the examining mind (supreme knowledge) itself is found in any way. In this way, the analysis is self-terminating, just as a fire springs to life when two sticks are rubbed together and then is extinguished once the sticks burn up. At this point, we just rest within this state without any grasping. At this point, even our analyzing mind has vanished into the vast space of the expanse of dharmas free from all reference points. The mind that familiarizes itself with the expanse of dharmas and what it familiarizes with—this very expanse—are not different. Rather, just like water that is poured into water, they are revealed as being one. Naturally, in this state, there is no one resting and nothing that is rested in. *The Stages of Meditation* says:

> When one examines what the mind is, it is realized to be empty. As for the mind that realizes [this], when thoroughly investigating its nature, it is also realized to be empty. Realizing [both of] these in this way, it is said that "the yoga of signlessness"[663] is entered. This teaches that signlessness is entered through this being preceded by discrimination.[664]

In Centrism, all of this is just a conventional description from the perspective of others for the sake of their understanding, given through the supreme knowledge of Buddhas and bodhisattvas who realize the expanse of dharmas. Actually, there is no realizer nor something to be realized here.

During most of our attempts, we will shift between one type of meditation and the other. If our ability to rest evenly decreases due to extensive analytical meditation or if we become distracted, then resting meditation should be emphasized in order to restore the still aspect of the mind. On the other hand, if we err on the side of too much resting meditation, we will lose interest in the analysis and become dull. We should then return to analytical meditation. Especially for beginners, it is necessary and very helpful to alternate analytical and resting meditation. If we do not alternate analyzing and resting in our practice of superior insight, it will deteriorate and at best become just calm abiding. However, the goal is always to approach the unity of calm abiding and superior insight, since true meditation and realization blossom only when these two have blended into one. When the unity of calm abiding and superior insight is experienced, we should just settle in and gently sustain this effortless equanimity without interfering with it in any way. As long as the mind stays in this natural state of resting insight, there is no need to go back to any conceptual analysis, since this state is the supreme kind of nonconceptual superior insight. It is the living experience of certainty about emptiness acquired through the preceding conceptual analysis.

This process can also be understood in terms of the three types of awareness: awareness of something other, self-awareness, and awareness of the lack of a nature. In the context of analytical and resting meditation, the first awareness corresponds to the stage of analytical meditation. During analysis, our awareness deals with objects that, conventionally speaking, are different from the analyzing awareness itself, such as outer objects, conceptual images, and investigations of these images. The second type of awareness—self-awareness—corresponds to the resting meditation of ordinary beings, since there is neither focusing on outer objects nor any conceptual analysis going on. Rather, at this point, the emphasis is on the mind directly experiencing itself as being without concepts but pervaded by and inseparable from the taste of some new insight. The third type of awareness—the awareness of the lack of a nature—is the actual perfect experience of the unity of calm abiding and superior insight that directly and nonconceptually realizes and at the same time rests in emptiness, the true nature of phenomena.

An analogy for these three stages is the process of making a sweet drink. The first step is to pulverize the big, hard sugar chunks of our rigid worldviews through the grinder of conceptual analysis. The resultant fine sugar powder of certainty looks nice and delicate, but it is not of much use if it does not become mixed with the water of our mind. Thus, the second stage is to let this fine sugar dissolve in the water of our mind stream and become one with it. Since the powder is so fine, it blends into the water much more quickly and easily than a big chunk of sugar would. The third stage is the direct experience of relishing the single taste of sweet water in which sugar and water have become completely inseparable.

In brief, calm abiding and superior insight are most effective when practiced equally as described. This is clearly expressed in many meditation manuals, such as *The Stages of Meditation*:

> Through the cultivation of superior insight, supreme knowledge becomes very prominent. Since calm abiding is weaker at this time, like an oil lamp that is placed in the wind, the mind may waver. Therefore, true reality is not clearly seen. Calm abiding should be cultivated at this point. Then, if calm abiding becomes excessive, supreme knowledge should again be cultivated. When a balance of these two is attained, as long as body and mind do not ache, one should dwell [in that balanced state] without interfering [with it]. When the body and so on starts to ache, as long as this interval lasts, the whole world should be regarded as being like an illusion, a mirage, a dream, a [reflection of] the moon [in] water, and an optical illusion. . . . Furthermore, great compassion and the mind of enlightenment [for the sake of those who do not realize true reality] should be brought forth. Then, take a rest. [After a while,] in the same way [as before], one should once more enter the meditative concentration in which all phenomena do not appear. When the mind becomes fatigued again, take a rest in the same way [as described]. This is the path of the unification of calm abiding and superior insight, which is to [alternately] focus on conceptual and nonconceptual images.[665]

When we rise from formal meditation sessions, our practice does not simply stop. Rather, during the periods between these sessions, we try to bring what we have realized or attained in meditation into our daily lives as much as possible. This is why these phases are called subsequent attainment. In this phase, we do not reject anything that appears from the perspective of our everyday level of consciousness, while, from the perspective of wisdom, we do not make any of these appearances into a reference point. Within this state, we gather as much of the accumulation of merit as we are able to. In this way, the accumulation of merit is conjoined with the supreme knowledge that is free from the reference points of the three spheres (agent, object, and action).

In particular, in between our sessions, we train in the thirty-seven dharmas that concord with enlightenment.[666] The enumeration of these thirty-seven factors in the great vehicle is the same as in the tradition of the hearers, but the focus is vaster and more profound. This may be illustrated through the first set of these thirty-seven, the fourfold application of mindfulness[667] on the lesser path of accumulation. The hearers use this practice as a method for exploring the pervasiveness of suffering, impermanence, and the lack of a personal self. The great vehicle goes further and has us regard our body, our feelings, our mind, and all phenomena as being without any nature in order to cultivate an understanding that they are nonconceptual in essence. This is the profound aspect of these practices. In addition, we cultivate the recognition of our body as being like an illusion, our feelings as being like a dream, our mind as being like luminous space, and all phenomena as being like fleeting clouds. This represents the vast aspect of such fourfold mindfulness. In this way, we enhance our realization of the inseparability of appearance and emptiness. As we do so, all differences between meditative equipoise and subsequent attainment gradually vanish. When these two phases have become inseparable, the realization of true reality is unchanging in all situations, which is nothing other than Buddhahood.

### *How to Practice a Session of Analytical Meditation*

A session of Buddhist analytical meditation starts with taking refuge in the three jewels and generating the mind of enlightenment. There follows a brief period of calm abiding to create the proper ground for engaging in the actual analysis. Then, within this state of calm abiding, we clearly bring to mind the particular object to be analyzed. This could be the first thing that comes to mind; however, especially when involved in training in the progressive stages of meditation on emptiness as outlined below, we should choose an object that suits our individual level in terms of our investigation of either personal or phenomenal identitylessness. As a guideline for our analysis, we mainly apply the reasonings and considerations described in the preceding discussions of twofold identitylessness and Centrist reasoning (such as the five great Centrist reasonings and the sevenfold reasoning using the analogy of a chariot).

As a preparatory step for beginners, it is fine to read through these reasonings one at a time, to recite them , and thus clearly bring them to mind. The idea is not just to echo such reasonings as if turning a prayer wheel or reciting a mantra but—once we are more familiar with them—to be a little bit more creative in our analytical approach. Our creativity and inspiration to engage in analysis will certainly not bloom if we regard analytical meditation as dry mental gymnastics or the repetition of sterile formulas. Rather, Centrist analytical meditation is meant to provide the ground for experimenting with our basic curiosity and openness to investigate ourselves and the world around us. Thus, it is often quite helpful to consider what we actually want to know about this world and ourselves—what our real questions of immediate personal concern are—and then to apply Centrist principles of investigation, rather than to just follow the beaten path of standardized reasonings against standardized opponents as found in Centrist texts. For example, we may feel overworked and depressed, have an identity crisis, quarrel with our partner, see someone as our enemy, or be very happy and newly in love, or self-indulgent, or proud—all these states can be scrutinized for their solidity and reality. This includes coming up with our own reasons, examples, and questions. Furthermore, instead of trying to prove emptiness or identitylessness, we may as well take the opposite route, looking for reasons that things really exist and then checking out whether these reasons withstand analysis.

Whichever approach we choose, it is important to pick a distinct object (such as our head or a chair), clearly bring it to mind, and then stay with it as our object of analysis until some degree of certainty as to its features—or the lack thereof—is achieved. This means that there is no point in just thinking in a general way, "All phenomena are empty," or "Everything is beyond unity and multiplicity," without really having a clear picture of any particular phenomenon, let alone all phenomena. Nor is it helpful to jump from one object to the next every few minutes without having gone any deeper. Especially in the beginning, it is very important to restrict our analysis to a rather limited portion of a given object or topic and to try to gain some certainty about it. This is accomplished through looking into it as thoroughly as possible. For example, if we feel that our head is not our self, we should not just leave it at this feeling but try to come up with as many reasons as we can find that explain why it is not the self, or to find the absurd consequences if indeed it were the self.

The next step is to go beyond conceptual analysis in order to gain incontrovertible, experiential certainty. Conceptual analysis (whether we use Centrist reasonings or another approach) will serve only to enhance our conceptual or intellectual certainty. Such analysis is important as a start, but it is not sufficient to affect the deeper levels of our latent tendencies of reification. Hence, we must proceed to absorb whatever degree of conceptual certainty we may have attained by resting in this certainty in a nonconceptual way that is free from reference points. Through this method, we familiarize our minds with the insights that we have gained through the preceding analysis. For example, once we have attained certainty that our head is not our self, we should stop analyzing but maintain one-pointed mindfulness and alertness and just let this certainty sink in deeply. If we feel that we have not gained any understanding or insight at all, we just practice calm abiding for a while and then resume the analysis until some insight dawns. Especially at the beginning, such insights do not have to be great, profound insights into emptiness or what holds the world together. Rather, we may and should use any level of new understanding about our specific object of analysis.

When we rest the mind in this way and thus absorb our newly developed convictions, the analyzing facet of our mind naturally settles into mind's nature, just as a wave rolls back into the ocean or the space within a cup becomes one with the infinity of all space once the cup is broken. In this way, discriminating knowledge is also nothing but the unity of awareness and the expanse of dharmas, in which no traces of analyzing subject and analyzed object can be found. In this way, we allow for and cultivate a very lucid nonconceptual certainty on the level of immediate experience that gradually can become an intrinsic and natural part of our way of seeing the world and acting in it. In other words, this is the way to change our instinctive habits and to bring the understanding we have from our head into our heart.

What is the reason for alternating between analyzing and resting? In brief, each approach performs a different but mutually enhancing function. Analyzing means seeing through our useless grasping, while resting provides the space to adapt to this seeing. Through analytical meditation, we relinquish our many-layered conscious and unconscious reifying tendencies of holding on to a self and to things as really existent. The remedy for these tendencies is the irreversible certainty that there are neither real things nor a self. These two mental states—reification, which is to be relinquished, and certainty about emptiness as its remedy—are mutually exclusive and cannot exist in our mind at the same time, just as it is impossible to experience love and hatred simultaneously. Therefore, to whatever degree reification becomes gradually undermined through analysis, to that same degree certainty about emptiness increases.

Finally, even if we do not enhance such understanding through further explicit analysis, experiential certainty arises naturally through the power of having repeatedly cultivated it during the phases of analytical and resting meditation. At this point, other than just resting in this very state of the lucid presence of such certainty, there is no need to actively or deliberately redevelop it over again, since we have already accomplished this certainty through prior analysis. For example, when we have determined through close examination that a hose with a zigzag pattern is not a snake, this very certainty stops us from apprehending the hose as a snake. To continue to analyze the hose at this point and to keep telling ourselves, "It is not a snake" would seem pointless and foolish. However, we might need to take a minute to let that knowledge sink in and see the consequences of there being no snake in the hose. Then, once we have gained irreversible certainty that there is no snake and this conviction has become a natural part of our experience, the thought of such a hose being a snake will never cross our mind again. We might even laugh at our own previous confusion the next time we happen to see a hose with zigzag pattern.

Thus, it is important not to do just a bit of analysis and then drop it, totally forgetting about any insights (however limited they may be) that we have gained through this analysis and shifting into mere calm abiding. In other words, analysis and calm abiding should not be alternated in a completely unrelated or arbitrary way. Rather, there should be some sense that the insights gained through analysis are being carried over into the phase of resting meditation. To facilitate bringing the analysis into the resting phase, it is helpful to briefly summarize the insight from our analysis in one sentence before engaging in the actual resting meditation. Beginners may want to briefly recall whatever insight has been obtained a few times during the resting meditation and then let it sink in again. After resting the mind in this way for a while, or when the mind starts to get dull, we resume our analysis of the same object. We do not have to start our analysis anew but can just continue from where we stopped before the resting meditation. Depending on how complete our analysis has been, we may also shift to another object at this point.

If in this process we get distracted and lose our focus on the object of analysis, we may initially try to gently bring our mind back to the object and continue investigating it. If, however, our analysis becomes discursive and the mind runs all over the place, or if we become too tired and thus cannot focus anymore, we should not push or strain. Strained analytical meditation deteriorates into mere ordinary thinking, in which one train of thought just follows after the other without leading anywhere. As long as there is precision, clarity, and mindfulness during the investigation, it is analytical meditation, but if these features are lacking, it is neither analysis nor meditation. Hence, when we become aware that our analysis loses these qualities, then it is definitely better to shift into a period of calm abiding. If that does not help either, we should simply take a break. Just sit and relax, without trying to do any meditation at all for a while. After a while, we can resume the analysis where we left off while still in a state of clear focus. Another possibility at that point is to end the session altogether by dedicating all the positivity that arose from our meditation and come back for another session later. In between sessions, as described earlier, we engage in the illusionlike accumulation of merit while pursuing our everyday activities.

It is generally much better to meditate repeatedly for short periods with good concentration and wakefulness than to ineffectively prolong a state of distraction or mental fatigue and misconstrue this as meditation. The latter will eventually make us fed up with meditation. Thus, it is said that the best way to meditate is to start out by welcoming meditation like a dear old friend and to stop meditating while we are still good friends. If we end our session while still focused and awake, we will look forward to coming back to that state, but if we always stop our session when we feel dull, distracted, or weary, this will not inspire us to return to our practice. It will only create bad habits for our meditation.

As a simple example to illustrate the process of analysis, let's use meditating on impermanence. After identifying an object to be analyzed for its impermanence, pick one of the many reasons that things are impermanent, such as that they are produced by causes and conditions. This argument looks at the process of objects arising through specific causes, their continuum being temporarily sustained through certain conditions, and their consequent ceasing once these conditions are no longer present. Assume the object chosen is an apple. Examine in a way that is as concrete and detailed as possible how this reason for impermanence applies to the individual causes and conditions of this apple, such as an apple tree, water, earth, sunshine, minerals, and so on. Trace back the origins of these factors themselves and find out how each one of them influences the arising, staying, and ceasing of this apple. When you feel convinced that this reason for impermanence applies to the apple, do not continue the analysis further. Initially, you may have gained only a somewhat more vivid and comprehensive picture of the many constantly changing factors that are involved in the appearance of such a fruit. Then, just let your mind rest one-pointedly in this certainty—or this wider picture of the apple's presence—and absorb it for a while without reflecting on its impermanence or anything else. This provides the initial opportunity for such an understanding to sink in to the deeper levels of your mind and thus create a much more powerful mental habit than just saying a few times, "This apple is impermanent." After a while, resume your analysis—continuing with either the same reason or another one—and thus repeat this shift from analytical to resting meditation and back several times. To conclude, it is recommended that you end the session with a brief period of calm abiding and then make the dedication. In later sessions, you can successively apply the same or other reasons to many other objects, be they various outer things unrelated to yourself, personal possessions, friends, relatives, or your own body and mind.

Obviously, this process of alternating analytical meditation and resting meditation has to be repeated many times in order to truly affect our strong tendencies to see things as really existent, lasting, and unchanging. The purpose of all this could be said to be "reprogramming our mental habitual patterns. Such is effected by gradually replacing concepts that are not in accord with basic reality—and thus produce suffering—with stronger tendencies of progressively refined concepts, finally leading to a direct experience of reality that relinquishes suffering. As the contemporary Kagyü master Khenpo Tsultrim Gyamtso Rinpoche says, Buddhism is a system of increasingly subtle concepts that counteract relatively coarser concepts. However, this should certainly not be misunderstood to mean that we try to brainwash ourselves or make something up in our analytical meditation. It is not that we "make" things empty through our concepts or analyses. Being empty is just their nature, whether we analyze them or not. Through the analytical approach, we proceed toward realizing for ourselves how things really are. If we do not apply essential Buddhist notions to the deeply ingrained habitual tendencies of our belief systems and only work with them on a superficial intellectual level, the teachings will be merely words without a deeper impact on our experiential world. As it is said, mind and dharma will not blend into one. This is especially important with such key Buddhist topics as emptiness, personal identitylessness, and phenomenal identitylessness, since it is precisely the instinctive assumption of a personal self and really existent phenomena that governs our experience and actions. To address these topics and make them personally relevant to our life cannot be accomplished without some degree of personal investigation, which entails honestly looking into our own view of the world and being willing to revise it.

Atīśa's *Centrist Pith Instructions, Called The Open Jewel Casket* highlights the essential points of the entire process:

> One may wonder, "From where did all of this come in the first place, and to where does it depart now?" Once examined in this way, [one sees that] it neither comes from anywhere nor departs to anywhere. All inner and outer phenomena are just like that. Therefore, everything is the illusory magical display of one's own mind. It is appearing yet delusive, and delusive while appearing. Thus, all of it is contained in the body, and the [body] is again contained in the mind. As for the mind, it has no color and no shape. It is natural luminosity that is primordially unborn. The very knowledge that discriminates this is also luminosity. In this interval, consciousness is nothing whatsoever, does not abide as anything, is not established as anything, and has not arisen as any aspect, and all discursiveness without exception is completely at peace. This meditative concentration of space-vajra that is without appearance and in which the entire dust of characteristics has vanished is like the very center of the sky that is lit up by the autumn sun. In it, dwell as long as possible.[668]

## *The Progressive Stages of Meditation on Emptiness*

The systematic, gradual succession of meditations that deal with personal and phenomenal identitylessness is often called the progressive stages of meditation on emptiness.[669] These stages are briefly outlined in the sūtras and further explained in Centrist texts such as Nāgārjuna's *Commentary on the Mind of Enlightenment* and his *Stages of Meditation*,[670] Bhāvaviveka's *Jewel Lamp of Centrism*, Jñānagarbha's *Path of Yoga Meditation*, Kamalaśīla's *Stages of Meditation* and *Entrance into Yoga Meditation*, Atīśa's two *Centrist Pith Instructions*, Jñānakīrti's *Instructions on the Stages of Meditation of the Vehicle of Perfections* and *Entrance into True Reality*,[671] and Vimalamitra's *Topics of Gradualist Meditation*.[672] From among these, Kamalaśīla's three-volume *Stages of Meditation* gives by far the most detailed instructions. This text also calls the meditative progression "the stages of prajñā meditation."

To illustrate this gradual progression, Nāgārjuna begins his *Commentary on the Mind of Enlightenment*[673] by saying that bodhisattvas, after having generated the aspiring mind of enlightenment, should generate the ultimate mind of enlightenment through the power of meditation. Thus, he commits to explaining the meditation on this mind of enlightenment that destroys cyclic existence. The actual progression of this meditation starts with analyzing for the lack of a real personal identity. The reason to start with negating personal identity is that it represents the object of a coarser level of clinging to real existence than the clinging to a real identity of all phenomena. Accordingly, Nāgārjuna first shows that there is no personal self within the five aggregates, the twelve sources, and the eighteen constituents.

Next, Nāgārjuna turns to phenomenal identitylessness. He negates the possibility of infinitesimal material particles—as asserted by various non-Buddhist schools as well as the Buddhist Followers of the Great Exposition and the Sūtra Followers—by showing that such particles can be broken up infinitely without any remaining indivisible core ever being found. As a consequence, Nāgārjuna states that whatever appears and is experienced is nothing but an appearance in one's own mind and that there are thus no outer material objects that are established as something other than or independent of mind. His text says:

> As the entities of apprehender and apprehended,
> The appearances of consciousness
> Do not exist as outer objects
> That are different from consciousness.
>
> Therefore, in the sense of having the nature of entities,
> In any case, outer objects do not exist.
> It is these distinct appearances of consciousness
> That appear as the aspect of form.
>
> Just as people with dull minds
> See illusions, mirages,
> And the cities of scent-eaters,
> So do form and such appear.[674]

Nāgārjuna further emphasizes that the reason the Buddha taught the aggregates, sources, and constituents was solely to negate a personal self and not to establish what is contained within these aggregates and so on as really existing entities. The text continues:

> The teachings on the aggregates, constituents, and so on
> Are for the purpose of stopping the clinging to a self.
> By settling in mere mind,
> The greatly blessed ones let go of these too.[675]

In the above four verses, Nāgārjuna clearly presents the intermediate step of realizing that all appearances occur solely within one's own mind as the expressions of this mind. However, just like all other Centrists, he does not stop at that point but—as the following verses and all his other texts show—negates the real existence of the mind as well. Candrakīrti's *Entrance into Centrism* also mentions this step as a help for those who do not immediately see that, just as all other appearances, the mind as their experiencer is empty too:

> The Buddhas said, "If there are no knowable objects,
> One easily finds that a knower is excluded."
> If knowable objects do not exist, the negation of a knower is established.
> Therefore, they first negated knowable objects.[676]

Thus, in terms of the view, Centrists make sure to refute all philosophical systems that assert any kind of truly established mind. At the same time, in the context of the progression of an individual's personal meditation and realization of emptiness on the path, the intermediate step of seeing that, just as in a dream, all appearances are nothing but mental images is considered crucial, for it eliminates the clinging to a solid and really existing material world that "leads a life of its own" apart from our perceiving mind. According to Centrists, the main reason the Buddha taught the three realms to be "mere mind" was in order to refute any kind of creator or agent that creates the world. Rather, everything in cyclic existence appears as the result of the karmic actions that originate and are experienced within the minds of individual sentient beings. Another reason for the expedient teachings on mere mind is to temporarily calm people's fear of the complete emptiness of all phenomena without any reference point to hold on to. As Nāgārjuna says:

> The teaching of the Sage that
> "All of these are mere mind"

> Is for the sake of removing the fear of naïve beings
> And not [meant] in terms of true reality.[677]

The third step in Nāgārjuna's analysis is that mind itself is also unarisen, without nature, and empty. He describes what this emptiness means and why the example of space is used to illustrate it.

> It is without characteristics and unarisen,
> Not existent, and free from the ways of speech.
> Space, the mind of enlightenment,
> And enlightenment have the characteristic of not being two.[678]

In his *Exposition of The Commentary on the Mind of Enlightenment*, the Fourth Shamarpa Chökyi Tragba[679] (1453–1524) explains this emptiness of mind. He starts by quoting the Indian master Smṛti's commentary on Nāgārjuna's text:

> Our own mind is primordially unarisen.
> It has the nature of emptiness.

and continues:

> This meaning of Madhyamaka in our own [Buddhist] system—as it is expressed in the lines [of Nāgārjuna's verse 46]—is extensively taught. [Madhyamaka or emptiness] means being without characteristics that define true reality. It [means] to be unarisen, since it is neither existent nor nonexistent. It is neither something existent that has already arisen nor something nonexistent that is not suitable to arise. It is free from being demonstrable through words and expressions by the [various] ways of speech. This [emptiness] has the characteristic that space as its suitable example, nonconceptual wisdom (the mind of enlightenment), and enlightenment that clearly realizes all phenomena in an unmistaken way are not two [that is, not different]. The meaning of this is as follows: Conventionally, space exists, but ultimately it is unobservable. Likewise, enlightenment exists on the seeming level, but ultimately it does not exist. Also the nonconceptual mind of enlightenment can be expressed in conventional terms, but it is without nature when analyzed. Therefore, the characteristics of these [three] are not different.[680]

Fourth, Nāgārjuna presents the defining characteristics of the proper meditation on emptiness and identifies three ways of misunderstanding emptiness.

> The emptiness that is called "nonarising,"
> "Emptiness," and "identitylessness"
> Is what inferior beings meditate on.
> It is not the meditation on the [actual emptiness].
>
> What has the characteristic of the stream
> Of positive and negative thoughts being cut off
> The Buddhas taught to be emptiness.
> The other [emptinesses] they did not declare to be emptiness.
>
> To abide without observing the mind
> Is the characteristic of space.
> Their meditation on emptiness
> Is declared to be space meditation.[681]

Chökyi Tragba comments:

> One may wonder, "Is there a difference between being skilled and being unskilled in the way of meditating on emptiness?" [These verses] teach that there is a difference. [The three emptinesses as misunderstood by inferior beings] are the [kind of] emptiness that [merely] represents the lack of reality. They are called [1] "nonarising" of all phenomena, these being like sky-flowers,
>
> > [2] "Emptiness" that is a nonimplicative negation,
> > And [3] "identitylessness" even on the conventional level.[682]
>
> Inferior beings are those of weak insight, which is to say those without much study or beginners who have not trained in knowledge. The emptiness in the sense of extinction on which they meditate in these [three] ways is not the meditation on this [actual] emptiness of true reality. . . .
>
> Positivity means to abandon killing and such. Negativity means to engage in the karma of putting [others] down and so on. Or, positivity [can refer to] sharp knowledge that analyzes conceptuality, while negativity is its opposite, ignorance. [However, all] such thoughts are [just various forms of] clinging to characteristics in terms of the factors to be relinquished and their remedies. Only [the meditation on emptiness] that is characterized by the stream of [these thoughts] being cut off is what the Buddhas taught to be the supreme nonconceptual meditation on emptiness. They did not declare that [to meditate on] the

> other [emptinesses listed above] is the meditation on emptiness and identitylessness.
>
> Therefore, to abide within the state that is without observing any conceptual characteristics with regard to nonconceptual wisdom (the ultimate mind of enlightenment) refers to the characteristic of space that was explained above. Hence, the proper meditation of yogic practitioners on emptiness is declared to be the meditation that is nonconceptual like space. . . . This meditation that is praised by noble Nāgārjuna in such a way is proclaimed by some earlier and later Tibetans to be the meditation of the Chinese Hvashang. However, in this treatise, [Nāgārjuna] takes it to be the style of the great bodhisattvas.[683]

To summarize this quote, meditation on emptiness is mistaken when emptiness is misunderstood as (1) absolute nonexistence (such as the nonexistence of a sky-flower), (2) a mere nonimplicative negation, or (3) total identitylessness or utter nonexistence of things even on the conventional level.

Fifth, Nāgārjuna states that both cyclic existence (ignorance) and liberation (realization of true reality) occur within and depend on our mind. Thus, the meditation and realization of emptiness is not spacelike in the sense of a blank nothingness, but it is an open, nonreferential state of mind that is at the same time profoundly peaceful and blissful.

> The seeming comes from afflictions and karma.
> Karma originates from the mind.
> The mind is constituted by latent tendencies.
> Freedom from latent tendencies is bliss.
>
> This blissful mind is peacefulness.
> A peaceful mind will not be ignorant.
> Not to be ignorant is the realization of true reality.
> The realization of true reality is the attainment of liberation.[684]

Kamalaśīla's *Stages of Meditation* presents the exact same progression of meditation on emptiness but in a much more detailed way. The meditation likewise starts with personal identitylessness and then proceeds to phenomenal identitylessness. As a sūtra source for these stages of meditation, Kamalaśīla quotes three crucial verses from *The Sūtra of the Arrival in Laṅka* for a brief overview and then explains them in detail:

> By relying on mere mind,
> One does not imagine outer objects.

By resting in the observed object of suchness,
One should go beyond mere mind too.

Going beyond mere mind,
One must even go beyond the nonappearance [of apprehender and apprehended].
The yogic practitioner who rests in nonappearance
Sees the great vehicle.

This spontaneously present, peaceful resting
Is completely purified through aspiration prayers.
Genuine identityless wisdom
Sees by way of nonappearance.[685]

The meaning of this is as follows: First, yogic practitioners should analyze phenomena with form that are imputed by others as outer objects, such as visible forms. "Is it that these are something other than consciousness, or is it consciousness itself that appears in this way? Is this just like in a dream?" Thus, they investigate infinitesimal particles external to consciousness. When these infinitesimal particles are examined as to their parts, yogic practitioners do not see such [outer] objects. Since they do not see them, they reflect, "All of these are mere mind, while outer objects do not exist." Thus, it has been said above:

By relying on mere mind,
One does not imagine outer objects.

This refers to relinquishing conceptions about phenomena that have form. For when one analyzes what [first seems to] possess the characteristic of being suitable to be observed, it is not observable. After one has investigated phenomena that have form, those that have no form should be investigated. Here, "mere mind" means that when there is nothing apprehended, an apprehender is not reasonable [either], because an apprehender depends on something apprehended. Therefore, the conclusion is that mind is devoid of something apprehended and an apprehender and is just without this pair [or nondual in this sense]. This is the characteristic of nonduality [on this level]. By resting in the observed object of suchness, you should go beyond mere mind too. Go far beyond [any] aspect of an apprehender and thus rest in the nonappearance of this pair [of apprehender and apprehended], that is, in consciousness without these two. Thus, having gone beyond

> mere mind, go beyond even this consciousness without the appearance of this pair. Since it is not justified that entities arise from themselves or something other, apprehender and apprehended are nothing but delusive. Since such a [consciousness without apprehender and apprehended] does not exist apart from these two, it is also not real. Having examined [in this way], also abandon reification with respect to such a consciousness without this pair. This means that you should solely rest in the wisdom that is without [even] the appearance of nondual wisdom. In other words, rest in the realization that all phenomena are without nature. Through [your] resting in this [realization], supreme true actuality and thereby nonconceptual meditative concentration are entered.
>
> At the point when yogic practitioners rest within the wisdom that is without the appearance of nondual wisdom, they dwell on the path of seeing. Therefore, they see the great vehicle. Seeing genuine true reality is called the great vehicle. As for the seeing of genuine true reality, it is the very fact that there is nothing to be seen, when the light of perfect wisdom dawns through the examination of all phenomena with the eye of supreme knowledge. This is also expressed in the sūtras:
>
>> One may wonder, "What is seeing the ultimate?" It means that all phenomena are not seen.
>
> Here, [the Buddha] talked about "not seeing" by having in mind that there is no such seeing [of any phenomenon]. However, this "not seeing" is not like not seeing when the conditions [for seeing] are incomplete (such as in a blind person and when closing one's eyes) or when one does not mentally engage [in seeing]. . . . It is through this sequence of meditation that one should meditate on the true reality [of all phenomena].[686]

These successive stages of Centrist meditation on emptiness represent the basic structure of Kamalaśīla's entire text. The major portions of his work consist of detailed elaborations on the various aspects of the above progression. Atīśa's *Centrist Pith Instructions* agrees on the same outline:

> Entities are of two kinds: those that possess form and those that are without form. Those that possess form are collections of infinitesimal particles. When these are analyzed and broken up in terms of their directional parts, not even their minutest [part] remains and they are

> without any shape. Since they are just like space, they are not established. Or, they are free from unity and multiplicity. Thus, they are without color and utterly without appearance.
>
> What is without form is the mind. As for that [mind], the past mind has [already] ceased and perished. The future mind has not [yet] arisen or originated. As for the present mind, it is also difficult to examine: It has no color and is without any shape. Since it is just like space, it is not established. Or, when analyzed and scrutinized with the weapon of reasoning, it is free from unity and multiplicity. In other words, it is unarisen. Or, [it may be said that] it is natural luminosity and so on. Therefore, one realizes that it is not established.
>
> At the point when these two [what possesses form and what is without form] definitely do not exist and are not established as [having] any nature whatsoever, the very knowledge that discriminates them is not established either. . . . once all specifically characterized and generally characterized phenomena are established as nonexistent [through knowledge], this knowledge itself is without appearance, luminous, and not established as [having] any nature whatsoever. . . . For as long as neither characteristics nor the enemies and robbers of thoughts arise, consciousness should rest in such a [state]. When wishing to rise [from the meditation], slowly open the cross-legged position and stand up. Then, in an illusionlike frame of mind, perform as much positivity with body, speech, and mind as possible.[687]

These stages of meditation on emptiness by Nāgārjuna, Kamalaśīla, and Atīśa are presented here in detail to clearly put forth the standard outline of the Centrist approach to such meditation. In addition, the way in which these masters unfold this progression shows a clear continuity in what is known as the progressive stages of meditation on emptiness as they are explained in the Kagyü lineage.

The Kagyü version of such meditation on emptiness, as presented by Khenpo Tsultrim Gyamtso Rinpoche, names the above stages after certain Buddhist philosophical systems as they are presented in Tibetan Buddhism. His book *Progressive Stages of Meditation on Emptiness* lists the following five stages:

1) the hearers[688]
2) Cittamātra
3) Svātantrika
4) Prāsaṅgika
5) Shentong-Madhyamaka

These correspond respectively to meditating on
1) personal identitylessness
2) mere mind without the duality of an internal subject and external objects
3) emptiness as a spacelike nonimplicative negation
4) emptiness as utter freedom from discursiveness
5) emptiness and luminosity inseparable

As the book says at the outset, these stages are given the names of these schools, but in terms of actually practicing such analytical meditations, the point is not to ascertain these schools' precise positions nor to look for the exact historical and philosophical correspondences between these five stages and the views of the schools whose names they bear. The presentation of these stages is meant to be understood as a pedagogical model for the progression of the personal insights of a practitioner who meditates on emptiness. This is, for example, evident from many Autonomist texts in general and the quotes from *The Stages of Meditation* above, in which the Autonomists themselves say that the notion of emptiness as a mere nonimplicative negation has to be left behind. Moreover, Autonomists also emphasize the freedom from discursiveness and its inseparability from luminosity.[689]

So the crucial point here—and this cannot be overemphasized—is that the focus of this progressive meditation is not at all on what various people or schools say or think but on the development of experience and realization in the minds of individuals who are actually engaging in such meditation. Thus, these stages represent a succession from a coarse understanding to increasingly subtle and refined insights that culminate in the direct seeing of emptiness or true reality. Except for a few especially gifted persons, most people cannot immediately grasp—let alone fully realize—the more subtle aspects of the teachings on emptiness. Rather, they have to take a gradual approach by starting with the most fundamental issues and then proceeding to the subtle points, just as physicians do not start their careers by performing open-heart surgery but first study the anatomical and physiological basics. All the details of the very subtle states of mind during the more advanced stages of meditation on emptiness are not likely to be understood if we have not gone through the basic levels of this process. In other words, in order to be able to tackle our subtle mental obscurations and to see the true nature of our mind, we have to start with its coarser obscurations. Otherwise, we would not even be aware that we have these subtle obscurations, just as a person whose entire body is in severe pain due to cancer is not aware of a minor twinge that is caused by a little scratch on the back.

This progressive approach can also be compared to a treasure hunt. If we are told about a treasure somewhere under a finger-shaped rock in a remote place, we first have to get a large-scale map that shows us how to get to the area where this treasure lies. Then we need a small-scale map of that area. Eventually, having arrived in the area in question, we have to find this particular fingerlike rock with our own eyes, dig up the treasure with our own hands, and enjoy its beauty with our own senses. In the same way, we are gradually guided toward the realization of emptiness, but in the end the true nature of our mind can be seen by nothing but this mind itself.

Since a number of books provide detailed instructions on how to proceed through these progressive stages of meditation, I will offer just a few practical remarks here.[690] The above five stages as they are outlined in all the texts mentioned simply sketch the gradual dwindling of all our reference points in terms of personal and phenomenal kinds of real identity. This is just another way of saying that emptiness is initially understood on increasingly subtle, conceptual levels and finally directly realized.

The first step—the meditation on personal identitylessness, or looking for a self in relation to our five aggregates—can basically have two approaches. First, we may compare all the various parts of our five aggregates with what we spontaneously or experientially feel our self to be. We simply ask ourselves questions such as: Is my body my self? Is my head my self? Do I think that my mind is my self? Are my emotions my self? Are they controlled by my self? If so, how? For many of these questions, our spontaneous answer will be no. For example, during analysis, we do not feel that our self is limited to only our body or any of its parts. This simply is not our experience of "me." However, when it comes to mind, emotions, and so on, the answer might not be that straightforward. When not sure, we should analyze further. We could ask: If our mind is our self, how exactly is that so? Is it our entire mind or just parts of it? Does this correspond to our experience of "me" in all situations?[691] By going deeper with our analysis, sooner or later we will inevitably hit the crucial question that actually should have been posed at the beginning of our search: What exactly is my self?

This leads us to the second, more systematic and thorough approach of investigation. In general, to compare two things, we must know what each of them is. We cannot really compare the five aggregates with our self if we do not know what this self is. So the next step is to try to define or describe our self. This process in itself is already very illuminating in terms of whether the self exists or not, since—apart from a definite "feeling" that we have a self—most people have a very hard time coming up with an exact description of what it might be. Paradoxically, one of the major reasons we are convinced that we have a self is that we don't actually know what it is or what it looks like. Since our sense of having a self is so vague, it is open to almost any kind of projection or identification. In fact, we constantly shift the objects on which we build this idea of a self. Sometimes we relate it more to our body, sometimes more to our thoughts, sometimes to our emotions, sometimes to our career, and so on. We tend to say such things as "I am sick," "My head hurts," "I am a doctor," "I quit being a doctor," "I think," "There are too many thoughts in my mind," "I am sad," or "My depression has worsened." All of these statements expose a variety of different ways of assuming and relating to an underlying self, yet we usually do not see the contradictions. Therefore, it is easy to take the existence of some underlying true "I" somewhere in our five aggregates for granted and to constantly refer to it

As was said earlier, in Buddhism in general, a personal self is described as something that is single, lasting, and independent or in control. These are very general features that for most people apply to their sense of self. Usually, we think that we have a single self and not multiple selves; that this self has a lasting quality and does not constantly change; and that we are—more or less at least—in control of or independent in what we think and do. However, when doing the actual analysis here, it is very important to try to come up with our own description or definition that applies to our personal sense of self and corresponds to our actual experience of "me." Otherwise, we are just comparing our five aggregates with some vague general notion of self that has little to do with how we experience our own self in everyday life. Once we have found such a description—even if it is not completely satisfying—we should then see whether something can be found in our five aggregates that matches this identification of our self. To do this in a systematic way, we can use the sevenfold reasoning of a chariot that was explained earlier.

We may compare this analysis to searching a house for a lost car key. First, we have to know what this key looks like—otherwise, what are we looking for? We are not looking for just any key. We also have to know how many rooms the house has and where they are, including the basement and the attic. Then we can systematically go through each room, open all the closets and drawers, look under the beds, and so on. Once we are sure that this key is not in one room, we go on to the next. Finally, when we have not found it any place, we have to conclude that there is no such key in the house. As we probably all know, when searching for something, we sometimes remain unsure and think, "It must be here somewhere." Then we go back and repeat our search even more thoroughly. This may happen several times before we finally have no doubt that there is no key, since we have turned the whole house upside down. In a similar way, when we look for our self, we have to know what we are looking for, and we must clearly identify the places in which we are looking for it, that is, our five aggregates. If we do not search in every corner of them, or if we still have doubts as to whether there is something that corresponds to our individual notion of a self, we have to repeat our analysis until we are absolutely sure that there is no such self in our aggregates. If we still think there must be some self, we can go back and repeat the same search with an alternative description of what this self might be. In this way, we have to go through this process again and again until we never again experience the slightest doubt that there is no personal self of any kind. This then is the realization of personal identitylessness.

The discussion up to this point has concerned the first step of the progressive stages of meditation on emptiness, the stage of the hearers who investigate the lack of a personal self. Now, from the second step (Cittamātra) onward, we deal only with phenomenal identitylessness. This second step of "mere mind" basically says that all our experiences, whatever they and their objects may look like, do not occur anywhere other than within our mind. In other words, both the apprehending subject and the apprehended object are of a mental nature. The analysis here involves two parts:

1) Through analysis, the existence of outer objects as anything other than mental experiences is negated.
2) The meditator rests in nondual experience without subject and object.

The first step—negating outer objects—is approached from three sides:

1) breaking them down into infinitely smaller pieces
2) analyzing the object and our perception of it on a causal time line
3) seeing the subjectivity of every appearance and experience

The issue of whether there are any really existing outer objects can be analyzed through an approach very similar to that of modern physics: by breaking up these objects into smaller and smaller parts without finding any indivisible core. If there are no identifiable external objects, we must conclude that what we experience as outer objects is nothing but a projection in our mind, just as in a dream, in which we also seem to experience outer objects while clearly there are none.

Second, the analysis focuses on whether there is any causal relation between objects and our perception of them. We consider that, in terms of our personal perception, we can only speak about the existence of an object once we perceive it. As long as we do not perceive it, we have no way of directly knowing whether there is such an object. Thus, it is obvious that what we call an object and the subjective consciousness that is aware of this object occur simultaneously. However, if there were outer objects that exist external to our mind and serve as the causes for our perception of them, they would have to exist before the perceptions that are their results. For, causes must precede their results in time and must also cease before the arising of these results. But if these outer objects existed before our perception of them, what would we perceive, since they are already gone at the time of this perception? This is the background for one of the two major reasonings that are used in this context of denying outer objects, which is called "the invariable co-observation"[692] of appearances and mind.

The third approach focuses on the subjectivity of perception. If we consider what exactly we know of objects, then we see that every perception is only a subjective experience in our mind as the perceiver. If we touch or smell a rose, "its softness" or "its fragrance" is nothing but our mental experience of softness or fragrance. This accords well with what modern science says: that there is no other or "objective" softness and fragrance apart from what we subjectively experience. It is this fact that is expressed by the second major reasoning concerning the nonexistence of outer objects, which is called "invariable sameness of appearances and mind as the nature of mere lucidity."[693] It says that there are no objects outside of the mind, because all our perceptions and what they perceive are alike in that they are nothing but immaterial clear appearances in our mind. In other words, objects are not different from the cognizing consciousness because of the very fact of being cognized. The reason is that consciousness—lucid awareness that neither consists of particles nor has spatial extension—can only cognize what has the same nature as consciousness, but not some material objects that have an altogether different nature (that is, lacking cognizance, consisting of particles, and possessing spatial dimensions). Consequently, objects in a dream and in the waking state are not fundamentally different. Both seem to perform their functions in their respective contexts, but in actual fact, none of them is really existent as something separate from our experience. This is not to deny that the objects of our perceptions appear to us as if they existed externally. However, apart from the fact that it subjectively appears this way, there is no evidence that there really are external objects in any way other than what appears as such objects in the mind. The relatively greater stability and regularity of daytime appearances in comparison to, for example, appearances in a dream, is said to be experienced only because of comparatively more stable and regular patterns of habitual tendencies for such appearances in our minds.

In the second part of the stage of "mere mind," the meditator rests in the nondual experience of the lack of subject and object. If there are no really existent objects, neither is there a really existent corresponding subject that perceives them. However, since our mind is not just nothing but is full of experiences, clarity, and movement, the meditation and realization of this step is said to be resting in bare mental experience without the duality of subject and object.

The third step in the progressive stages of meditation on emptiness is named after the Autonomists and refers to emptiness as a spacelike nonimplicative negation. Even if we realize that there are neither really existent outer objects nor subjects to perceive them, there is still the subtle clinging to the reality of our mere mental experience free from perceiver and perceived. Therefore, through the five great Centrist reasonings and such, we proceed to the stage of seeing that this lucid momentary experience too is empty of an intrinsic nature. Thus, starting with our self, we find neither any material objects nor mental subjects nor a bare experience free from duality. This nonfinding of all phenomena, or the absence of an inherent real nature of all phenomena—a nonimplicative negation—is then the object of our meditation in the third stage.

The fourth step in the progressive stages of meditation on emptiness is called the stage of Consequentialists and presents emptiness as utter freedom from discursiveness. As was explained, any nonimplicative negation is still a conceptual object and thus a reference point. So even the nonimplicative negation of emptiness in the sense of the mere absence of a real nature, nonarising, and such (as in the third step) is still a subtle reference point. In order for our mind to be able to fully relax within the space of the expanse of dharmas free from center or edge, it has to let go of even its most subtle grasping at any reference point including the freedom from reference points. This is the space of the actual freedom from all discursiveness that we allow for during the fourth step.

The fifth step in the progressive stages of meditation on emptiness is named after Shentong-Madhyamaka and presents emptiness as inseparable from mind's luminosity. Since the very freedom from discursiveness and reference points described in the last step is not just some blank space or mere absence (which would be the extreme of extinction or nihilism), it is also described as luminosity, or the unity of wisdom and expanse. Hence, in terms of the actual nature of mind, the fifth stage is not really an additional or higher stage above the freedom from discursiveness. As Sakya Paṇḍita says in his *Distinction of the Three Vows*, the very attempt to go higher or beyond the freedom from all reference points would just mean to fall out of nonreferentiality by inevitably creating a reference point again.[694] Thus, the fourth and fifth stages indicate the two aspects of the nature of our mind, which is the undifferentiable unity of the freedom from discursiveness and luminosity. *Moonbeams of Mahāmudrā* also highlights the eventual experiential unity of the last two steps:

> There are many ways in which mind is similar to space, but here this refers to the following: When one analyzes through discriminating knowledge, finally, also the very [process of] discrimination subsides, upon which [the mind] becomes pure as [a state of] nonconceptuality, just as seeing ceases through looking at space. As Tilopa says:
>
> > For example, through looking at space, seeing will cease.
> > Likewise, when mind is looking at mind,
> > The collection of thoughts ceases and unsurpassable enlightenment is attained . . .[695]
>
> First, one analyzes [the mind] through discriminating knowledge. It is explained that, through this, the very [process of] discrimation itself

> subsides, upon which nonconceptual wisdom dawns. You may then wonder whether there is some difference between mind and space. Yes, there is, since space is not a cognition that personally experiences itself. When mind is realized, this in itself is explained to be personally experienced wisdom.[696]

In summary, we could outline the progression of our experiences and realizations while meditating on emptiness in this way as follows. We start with the meditation and realization of personal identitylessness. Then, in terms of phenomenal identitylessness, we proceed from the coarse notion of real outer objects via the more subtle notions of mere nondual mental experience and emptiness as a nonimplicative negation all the way up—or rather back—to just letting our mind be in its natural state of nonreferential freedom, unconditionally aware of its own radiant display.

### *Mental Nonengagement in Meditation*

One of the main issues in the well-known debate at Samye, where the Indian master Kamalaśīla is said to have defeated his Chinese opponent Hvashang Mahāyāna, was whether meditation on the ultimate is to be understood as just letting the mind settle in a state that is completely without any thought or focus or whether analysis and some focus are required. This is related to the question of whether progress on the path is gradual or instantaneous. Since that time, the designation "Hvashang meditation" has become Tibetan shorthand for an exclusive cultivation of a thought-free mental state as representing the realization of the ultimate. It goes along with a complete rejection of the aspect of means, such as the accumulation of merit and proper ethical conduct. It was after this debate that Kamalaśīla wrote his *Stages of Meditation* in order to clarify such issues by establishing the gradualist approach and describing in detail how to train in meditation on emptiness. Despite the different accounts of what the view of the Chinese master Hvashang really was and what exactly happened during the debate at Samye, all of its issues continued to be major points of controversy between the different schools of Tibetan Buddhism.[697]

One of the key terms in the context of how to properly cultivate meditation on emptiness is what is called "mental nonengagement." Pawo Rinpoche summarizes the correct understanding of mental nonengagement:

> Its meaning is to rest one-pointedly on the focal object [of meditation], without being distracted by other thoughts. If this [one-pointed resting] were stopped, all meditative concentrations would stop. Therefore, in general, "mental nonengagement" has the meaning of not

> mentally engaging in any object other than the very focus of the [respective] meditative concentration. In particular, when focusing on the ultimate, [mental nonengagement] has the meaning of letting [the mind] be without even apprehending this "ultimate." However, this should not be understood as being similar to having fallen asleep.[698]

Since this term is also frequently used in the Mahāmudrā and Dzogchen teachings, other schools mistakenly equate the correct notion of mental nonengagement with the stereotypic Hvashang meditation and thus deprecate the meditation styles of these two systems as being just some mindless state of spacing out.

More important, though, the notion of mental nonengagement, or mental disengagement, is intimately connected to the relationship between analytical and resting meditation as discussed above. Ultimately, mental nonengagement indicates nothing but the subjective side of what is called freedom from discursiveness. In other words, the only way in which the mind can truly engage in this "object" that is the absence of any object or reference point is precisely by not engaging in any object, that is, not creating any reference points. The absence of reference points can only be realized by a nonreferential mind, since this is the only perceptual mode that exactly corresponds to it. That this is not an invention by later schools or a mistaken approach to meditation is clearly demonstrated by numerous passages in the sūtras. For example, *The Sūtra Requested by Ocean of Intelligent Insight*[699] states:

> Do not mentally engage in phenomena.
> Completely abandon doing anything further.
> Realize all phenomena
> As equality in true reality.
>
> What is taught is the application of mindfulness
> Without mindfulness or something to be mentally engaged.

*The Prajñāpāramitā Sūtra in Eight Thousand Lines* agrees:

> This meditation on the perfection of knowledge means not meditating on any phenomenon.[700]

Atīśa's autocommentary on *The Lamp for the Path to Enlightenment* quotes Nāgārjuna:

> Not imagined by imagination,
> Mind completely nonabiding,

> No mindfulness, no mental engagement,
> To nonreferentiality I prostrate.[701]

Similar quotes from Indian Centrist texts were presented in the discussion of analytical meditation and resting meditation.

It is noteworthy in this context that Kamalaśīla as the generally accepted winner of the Samye debate addresses the issue of mental nonengagement in great detail in his *Stages of Meditation* and—more briefly—in his commentary on *The Dhāraṇī of Entering Nonconceptuality*.[702] He underlines the distinction between mental nonengagement and the absence of mental engagement. The first is understood as the fundamental noninvolvement in dualistic appearances while sustaining fresh wakefulness, once discriminating knowledge has determined that there are no dualistic phenomena whatsoever. This can also be understood as mental disengagement in the sense of not interfering with the nature of the mind as it is. On the other hand, absence of mental engagement describes the mere absence of any mental activity, such as in a faint, deep sleep, or mental stupor, which does not lead to any realization or liberation at all. Thus, Kamalaśīla emphasizes that the first is a crucial factor in meditation, while the latter is obviously to be avoided.

This might shed a different light on the debate of Samye and how it was used polemically against systems such as Mahāmudrā and Dzogchen. Especially, the claim that mental nonengagement is equivalent to Hvashang meditation is seen to be completely absurd, since even Kamalaśīla, the very master who is accepted by all Tibetan schools as the one who defeated Hvashang, greatly advocates mental nonengagement. Otherwise, it would absurdly follow that Kamalaśīla himself was a proponent of Hvashang's infamous style of meditation and that he had refuted his own view in debate. And on what grounds would he later have written an extensive treatise that justifies this very view in detail? Thus, at least in terms of meditation practice proper, the issue in the Samye debate seems to have been more one of mental nonengagement versus absence of mental engagement altogether, rather than one of analysis and accumulation of merit versus mere trancelike meditation. In detail, in the first volume of his *Stages of Meditation*, Kamalaśīla quotes *The Dhāraṇī of Entering Nonconceptuality*[703] and explains:

> Through mental nonengagement, the characteristics of form and so on are relinquished.

> What [the Buddha] had in mind when he said this was that [in meditation] one does not mentally engage in what is not observable once it has been examined through knowledge. However, this does not refer to a mere absence of mental engagement. As exemplified by such

> [mental states] as the meditative absorption without discrimination, the beginningless clinging to forms and such is not relinquished through merely relinquishing mental engagement in it. Without having relinquished doubts, one is not able to relinquish the mental engagement in clinging to previously observed forms and such, just as it is not possible to eliminate the heat [of a fire] without eliminating the fire. Thus, it is not possible to expel these conceptions about forms and such from the mind as if removing a thorn from it with one's hands, because the seeds of doubt must be relinquished.
>
> As for these seeds of doubt, when yogic practitioners examine [forms and such] through their eye of supreme knowledge and in the light that springs forth from their meditative concentration, previously observed objects such as forms that [seemed to] have the characteristic of being suitable to be observed are no longer observed. Therefore, they are relinquished just like the notion that a rope is a snake, and not in any other way. At this point, freed from the seeds of doubt, one is able to relinquish mental engagement in the characteristics of forms and such, but not in any other way. Otherwise, if the light of the meditative concentration of yogic practitioners does not shine and if they are not looking with their eye of supreme knowledge, they do not remove their doubts about the existence of forms and such. This is just like a person in a dark [house] who has doubts about whether there are vases and such in this house. . . . [On the other hand,] when such [examination] has been performed, just as uprooted trees do not grow in the earth again, the mind that wrongly conceptualizes will not arise again, since it has no more root.[704]

Kamalaśīla continues in the third volume of his text:

> Thus, to say, "Nothing whatsoever is to be thought" means to abandon the supreme knowledge that has the characteristic of perfectly discriminating actual reality. Since perfect discrimination is the root of perfect wisdom, its root is cut by abandoning this [discriminating knowledge]. Hence, supramundane supreme knowledge is abandoned and without this, omniscience will also be rejected. . . .
>
> Without perfect discrimination, through which means should yogic practitioners rest the mind within the state of nonconceptuality, when this mind is habituated to entities such as forms and clings to them since beginningless time? Someone might say, "They engage [in this

state] through the absence of attention[705] and the absence of mental engagement with regard to all phenomena." This is not appropriate. Without perfect discrimination, all experienced phenomena cannot be rendered into something that is not mentally engaged in or to which no attention is paid. People [may try to] meditate by thinking, "I shall not pay attention to these [phenomena] and not mentally engage [in them]" and thus [attempt to] meditate without paying attention or mentally engaging them. At that point, [however, it is precisely] through this [approach] that one will have paid a lot of attention to them and will have very much mentally engaged in them.

If the mere nonexistence of attention and mental engagement is taken to be "nonattention" and "mental nonengagement," it is to be analyzed in what way these two [attention and mental engagement] are nonexistent. [Some utter] nonexistence is not suitable as a cause [for anything], so how could [plain] signlessness and [mere] nonexistence of mental engagement become the state of nonconceptuality? If just this [nonexistence of attention and mental engagement] were sufficient to be [true] nonconceptuality, this state of nonconceptuality could be entered even through fainting, since it is [a state] without attention and mental engagement. Without perfect discrimination, there are no other means in any other way to bring about nonattention and mental nonengagement. And if there is [nothing but] nonattention and mental nonengagement, without perfect discrimination, how could one engage in the lack of nature of all phenomena? Of course, the only way that phenomena actually are is that they are empty of nature. However, without discrimination and [just] through the [lack of attention and mental engagement], one will not realize this emptiness. Without the realization of emptiness, the obscurations will not be relinquished. Otherwise, everybody would always be self-liberated. . . .

Also, as long as yogic practitioners who evenly rest in meditative concentration have a mental consciousness, this [consciousness] must undoubtedly refer to something, [since] the consciousness of ordinary sentient beings does not abruptly become nonreferential. If they had no [such referential consciousness at all], how would they realize that phenomena are without nature? . . . Therefore, the arising of nonattention and mental nonengagement with regard to the genuine dharma should be regarded as something that is preceded by perfect discrimination. Why? Because it is through perfect discrimination that one is able to bring about nonattention and mental nonengagement,

> and not in any other way. Thus, when yogic practitioners have examined through perfect supreme knowledge, ultimately they do not see any arisen phenomena whatsoever within the three times. At this point, how should they be attentive to and mentally engage in [anything]? Ultimately, since the three times do not exist, how can they be attentive to and mentally engage in the absence of experiencing them? Therefore, since all discursiveness is completely at peace, this is entering nonconceptual wisdom. Having entered it, [yogic practitioners] realize emptiness. Through the realization of [emptiness], the entire web of bad views is relinquished. . . .
>
> Thus, whenever one hears such words as "inconceivable" [in the Buddha's teachings], they [are meant to] teach that phenomena are just the object of personal experience in order to put an end to the pride of those who think that true reality [can be] realized through merely studying and reflecting on it as being such and such. [Such words] should also be understood as negating improper reflection. However, they are not [taught as] a negation of perfect discrimination. Otherwise, as explained before, they would contradict a vast number of scriptures and reasonings. Moreover, what one must familiarize oneself with through the supreme knowledge that arises from meditation is nothing else but the very realization [that has been attained] through the [preceding] supreme knowledge that arises from studying and reflection, just as a horse runs on its familiar ground.[706]

As was explained above, what is to be relinquished in meditation (reification or clinging to real existence) and its remedy (discriminating knowledge) are mutually exclusive and cannot exist simultaneously. Therefore, the more reification is weakened through Centrist analysis, the more vividly the certainty about emptiness is experienced. Finally, such certainty does not need to be further enhanced through explicit analysis, since it has become a natural part of our mind through the power of having repeatedly nurtured it during the phases of resting meditation. At this point, other than just resting with unwavering awareness right within this very lucid presence of immediate certainty, there is no need to deliberately bring it to mind again and again.

For example, as children, many of us believed in the real existence of Santa Claus here on earth, but at some point we started to develop doubts. We investigated further, questioned our parents and friends, and finally discovered that the Santa Claus whom we saw at home every year was our uncle or even our father. Once we became absolutely sure there was no Santa Claus, we did not need to analyze this fact any further or keep repeating to ourselves, "There is no Santa

Claus, there is no Santa Claus." Even if other people claimed the opposite, there was no way we would change our minds. The existence of Santa Claus is simply no longer an issue, since we have developed irreversible and natural certainty that he does not exist, which leaves no room for any doubts. Thus, even when we tell our own children the same story later, in our own mind, the thought of a real Santa Claus never appears again.

Contrary to the above presentation of mental nonengagement and nonconceptual meditation, Tsongkhapa holds that apprehending a mental image[707] of emptiness is necessary, liberating, and not to be relinquished or negated. Thus, according to him, while sustaining the actual main phase of meditative equipoise, one must constantly bring clearly to mind the mode of apprehending emptiness as a nonimplicative negation.[708] In other words, the meditator is supposed to create a powerful awareness that apprehends phenomena's emptiness of inherent existence as the antidote to the clinging to their inherent existence. Tsongkhapa claims that all meditations of superior insight that do not involve this mode of apprehension are flawed.[709]

However, since this approach necessarily involves conceptualizing the lack of inherent existence or a real nature, it is not at all different from clinging to such an emptiness—a nonimplicative negation—in a more or less subtle way. A mental image always entails some degree of apprehension or clinging. So, although the existence of real identities is negated, the conceptual grasping at identitylessness or emptiness still persists. Hence, this approach is limited to and cannot go beyond cultivating an intellectually fabricated emptiness. In fact, the more powerful the apprehension of such an emptiness is, the more intense one's grasping and clinging to a reference point becomes, rather than letting go of all reference points and—as *The Dhāraṇī of Entering Nonconceptuality* and Kamalaśīla put it—entering the expanse of nonconceptuality. Thus, from the perspective of the ultimate expanse of emptiness, to claim that the conceptual object of the nominal ultimate—the absence of real existence by the negation of real existence—is the actual ultimate is nothing but a case of confusing the finger that points to the moon with the moon itself.

As shown before, there are countless passages in the sūtras and Centrist texts that explicitly reject an approach that insists on the ongoing cultivation of this mode of apprehending emptiness as a nonimplicative negation. For example, *The Sūtra Requested by Kāśyapa* says:

> Kāśyapa, as emptiness means to emerge from all views, I declare that those who have views about this very emptiness are incurable.

Nāgārjuna's *Sixty Stanzas on Reasoning* states:

Those whose minds are not moved,
Not even by a flicker of a thought about "complete voidness,"
Have crossed the horrifying ocean of existence
That is agitated by the snakes of the afflictions.[710]

His *Commentary on the Mind of Enlightenment* says:

So-called entities are conceptions.
Lack of conceptions is emptiness.
Wherever conceptions appear,
How could there be emptiness?

The emptiness that is called "nonarising,"
"Emptiness," and "identitylessness"
Is what inferior beings meditate on.
It is not the meditation on the [actual emptiness].

What has the characteristic of the stream
Of positive and negative thoughts being cut off
The Buddhas taught to be emptiness.
The other [emptinesses] they did not declare to be emptiness.[711]

Candrakīrti's *Entrance into Centrism* says:

Ordinary beings are bound by conceptions.
Nonconceptual yogins will find release.
Hence, the learned state that the result of analysis
Is that conceptions are at peace.[712]

In his *Entrance into the Two Realities*, Atīśa agrees:

In the very profound sūtras,
It is said that nonseeing is to see this.
Here, there is no seeing and no seer,
No beginning and no end, just peace.

Entities and nonentities are left behind.
It is nonconceptual and nonreferential.[713]

This applies in particular to the direct and nonconceptual realization of the expanse of dharmas on the paths of seeing and meditation. At this point, noble beings no longer meditate through conceptual analysis, since they have already directly realized the true nature of phenomena free from dualistic appearances such as analysis and the object of analysis. Once there is such an immediate and direct vision of ultimate reality that permeates one's whole being, there is absolutely no need to apply any investigation to ascertain a knowable object—emptiness as a nonimplicative negation—in an indirect way through inferential valid cognition based on reasoning. Tsongkhapa explicitly asserts that emptiness is a nonimplicative negation, so by definition, it can only be the object of a conceptual consciousness, since perceptual valid cognitions cannot have nonimplicative negations as their objects. Thus, if what is to be cultivated in meditative equipoise even by bodhisattvas on the path of seeing and the path of meditation is emptiness as a nonimplicative negation, the consciousness that cognizes this negation can only be an inferential valid cognition. However, this would categorically exclude any possibility of a nonconceptual yogic valid perception of emptiness. In addition, since—according to Tsongkhapa—such a nonimplicative negation already is the actual ultimate reality, there would be no need to abandon it and proceed to a direct realization.

According to the teachings of the Buddha and the Indian commentaries, however, such direct seeing of emptiness is precisely what happens in meditative equipoise from the path of seeing onward upon the self-termination of conceptual analysis once its objects are seen through, just as in the familiar example of a fire dying down without firewood. Therefore, when the special irreversible certainty that is the actual freedom from all discursiveness and reference points is directly realized and experienced, without any reference points, what object would be left for any analysis or any mode of apprehending anything? In the same vein, to apprehend emptiness as a nonimplicative negation in meditative equipoise moreover contradicts the standard Gelugpa position that the meditative equipoise of noble ones is completely without appearance. For if there are no appearances, there can be neither an object of analysis nor the subjective aspect of a mind that analyzes or apprehends anything.

On the other hand, if there is any analytical mode of apprehension during meditative equipoise, this still represents the reference point of a more or less subtle clinging to or an apprehension of characteristics. Therefore, just like the coarser apprehension of real existence, this very apprehension of a characteristic—be it emptiness, nonarising, a nonimplicative negation, or anything else—will also obscure the direct seeing of true reality as it actually is. In other words, within the meditative equipoise of noble ones that by definition is free from all dualistic appearances (that is, the nonconceptual and personally experienced wisdom that realizes the unity of appearance and emptiness), even supreme discriminating knowledge itself has dissolved. Unlike such a direct vision through nonconceptual wisdom, discrimination or analysis cannot be without some object or reference point that it discriminates. In terms of the example of sugar dissolving in water, trying to maintain a powerful awareness of emptiness as a nonimplicative negation in meditative equipoise is like trying to hold on to the fine particles of sugar in the water in order to prevent them from fully dissolving.

In his *Chariot of the Tagbo Siddhas*, the Eighth Karmapa comments on the way in which the supreme knowledge that realizes the two realities enters the ultimate meditative absorption of cessation:

> The rays of the insight that has arisen from analysis dispel the darkness of the obstacles to seeing true reality and thus allow the light of true reality to clearly shine. . . . Ultimately, there is no entering into the meditative absorption of cessation. However, when engaging in [this process on the level of] worldly conventional reality, through its power, the meditative absorption of cessation free from discursiveness is entered. Now, when [this insight] enters the meditative absorption of the cessation of [ordinary] mind and mental events, does it rest in this meditative absorption by eliminating the superimpositions of [such] mind and mental events, or does it rest in it without eliminating these superimpositions? In the first case, in terms of negative determination, the valid cognition of the supreme knowledge that arises from meditation would eliminate the superimpositions of mind and mental events. In terms of positive determination, it would directly appear for this cognition that these objects—mind and mental events—are unarisen, which would be realized through personally experienced wisdom. Therefore, [this scenario] amounts to there being both a cognition and its object even within this meditative equipoise of cessation, that is, within emptiness, the nature of phenomena. In this case, entering the meditative absorption of cessation would be nothing but a name.
>
> As for the second case, some people might be concerned, "If the valid cognition of the supreme knowledge that arises from meditation does not eliminate superimpositions, the meditative equipoise of [resting in] true reality—this meditative absorption of cessation—would not be unmistaken." [In fact,] the valid cognition of the supreme knowledge that arises from meditation indeed eliminates the superimpositions that are discordant with this meditative absorption of cessation. However, when it eliminates [these superimpositions], in terms of positive determination, no direct appearance of mind and mental events not being established as anything whatsoever (such as them being unarisen) is brought about within such a cognition. The reason is that, once the valid cognition of the supreme knowledge that arises from meditation

> has eliminated all referential extremes of mind and mental events, it is absorbed in what is determined—the way in which mind and mental events are unarisen—in such a way that it is not absorbed in existence, nonexistence, entity, nonentity, appearance, or nonappearance at all. When resting in this meditative equipoise of true reality in such a way of not resting in meditative equipoise, there is no objective appearance and no subjective cognition that exist as one or different.[714]

The Eighth Karmapa also discusses the emptiness of nirvāṇa:

> From the perspective of both analysis and the seeing of noble ones, mere dependent origination and also the completely releasing liberation that is based on it are inexpressible as something other than perfect nirvāṇa. Hence, neither something to be attained, nor the means to attain it, nor any attainment are established. However, at this point, it is also not said that "these do not exist." Nor are they expressed as being both existent and nonexistent or being neither. Thus, without thinking or apprehending anything and without any effort, one evenly rests in just this uncontrived and relaxed great ease in which there is nothing to do. Then, no matter what inner and outer appearances of the six collections [of consciousness] and their objects (the bearers of the nature [of phenomena]) emerge, through discriminating supreme knowledge and mindfulness, all of them are realized as their true nature, the natural state of emptiness. Just like snowflakes falling [and melting] on a hot stone, one looks straight at appearance-emptiness, sound-emptiness, and awareness-emptiness and is directly released.[715]

In brief, as long as the direct vision of ultimate reality has not dawned in the mind, one definitely has to rely on the gradual refinement of discriminating knowledge that entails more or less subtle modes of apprehension. However, once the nature of mind is directly realized, all analyses and modes of apprehension naturally subside on their own, just as there is no longer a need to ponder elaborate descriptions of the taste of an unknown Chinese dish on the menu once it finally is in your mouth. Therefore, in terms of the different phases of the path, it is definitely inappropriate to insist on either the exclusive use of analytical meditation or the exclusive cultivation of resting meditation during the entire path. Rather, the distinction should concern the appropriate timing of analytical meditation with its various modes of apprehension and resting meditation.

## Madhyamaka Conduct

In Buddhism, "conduct" generally means carrying the insights and experiences from the more formal phases of studying, reflecting, and meditating into our daily lives. When we as ordinary beings look at our minds, there often is quite a gap between the experiences on our meditation cushion and those in "real life." In meditation, our mind may be lighter, more at ease, more transparent, and more compassionate than usual. In contrast, we may experience our everyday lives as much more real, solid, constricted, and painful, and we may have difficulties in always being loving and compassionate toward ourselves and others. We might have glimpses of things as dreamlike and of genuine compassion or blessings, but none of these are very stable or lasting. Rather, such experiences depend very much on various outer and inner conditions, both favorable and unfavorable.

When we compare our own experience to the descriptions of how bodhisattvas on the ten grounds see the world, there is a big difference. From the first ground onward, in between their formal sessions of meditation, bodhisattvas actually experience everything as illusionlike in a very immediate manner, without having to remind themselves that this is how things are. Finally, it is said that in a Buddha's mind there is no experiential difference or separation at all between "being in meditation" and "doing other things." In more technical terms, the two phases of meditative equipoise and subsequent attainment have blended into one taste, which is the constant awareness of the true nature of phenomena in whatever is experienced or done. As the *Prajñāpāramitā sūtras* say:

> The mind does not entertain any such fancies as "I rest in meditative equipoise" or "I rise [from it]." If you wonder why, this is because the nature of phenomena is fully understood.

The single factor that accounts for these differences is the wisdom that realizes emptiness. One's experiences and reactions outside of formal meditation are determined by the degree to which one is able to uninterruptedly sustain the basic ground of nonreferential ultimate reality in every moment. In other words, the more prajñā's direct realization of emptiness becomes an integral part of one's everyday experience, the less there is a gap between the two. In this way, conduct is nothing other than continuing, sustaining, and enhancing our meditation after having left our meditation cushions. Hence, in terms of having realized emptiness, conduct means "being free from the three spheres"—that is, any notion of agent, object, and action—in all activities.

Meditation and conduct are thus mutually beneficial. Not only does our meditation inform and support our conduct, but the training in eliminating our deeply ingrained habits also supports and enhances our insights in meditation. Proper conduct is also helpful, because without enriching and moistening our minds through accumulating huge quantities of positive mental imprints and cultivating compassion, there is no way for our minds to turn into the fertile ground that is necessary for cultivating the realization of emptiness. In the end, meditation and conduct become inseparable once the direct realization of the nature of our minds and all phenomena is continuously present throughout day and night. This is what is called Buddhahood.

This intimate relation between prajñā and conduct, or the means, is also expressed in the first verse of the ninth chapter of *The Entrance to the Bodhisattva's Way of Life*:

> All of these branches [of the first five perfections]
> Were taught by the Sage for the sake of knowledge.
> Therefore, those who wish for suffering
> To subside should develop knowledge.

Thus, knowledge or wisdom always pervades all other practices of a bodhisattva, and these in turn support and further the realization of emptiness. In fact, Śāntideva's entire text is nothing but a practice manual on how to link the realization of ultimate reality to all the aspects of skillful compassionate conduct. Precisely this is "the bodhisattva's way of life," which is nothing other than the unity of knowledge and means.

Since Buddhist studies and practices are designed to influence our most ingrained habitual tendencies, they generally represent processes that naturally require repeated efforts and skillful training until their transformative power becomes directly and continually manifest in the way in which we experience our world. Just as we need training when learning to play a musical instrument, conduct is the continuous rehearsal of our lessons in meditation. Thus, after having trained in the safe surroundings of the calm pool of our meditation, we can dare to jump into the big waves of the ocean of daily life and maybe even surf them.

Especially in Centrism, conduct involves the notion of gradually going beyond both our problems and their remedies. As a bodhisattva, one develops the aspiring mind of enlightenment by taking the vow to liberate all sentient beings from suffering. Motivated by this altruistic attitude, conduct is the expression of practically applying this vow by continuously working with the six perfections until one attains the omniscience, infinite compassion, and power of a Buddha, which continually and effortlessly accomplish the welfare of all beings. At the same time, conduct equally entails familiarization with the fact that there are no such things as bodhisattvas, sentient beings, the two obscurations, the six perfections as their remedies, the relinquishment of stains, or the attainment of qualities. In terms of bodhicitta, to infuse altruistic conduct with the realization of its illusionlike nature is called "the unity of the seeming and the ultimate mind of enlightenment." Thus, motivated by great compassion for those who do not realize this, one gathers the dreamlike accumulations of merit and wisdom. As the *Prajñāpāramitā sūtras* say:

> Understanding the five aggregates as illusionlike,
> Not taking illusions and the aggregates to be different,
> Being free from all kinds of notions, and being engaged in utter peace,
> This is the conduct of the supreme perfection of knowledge.

The unity of realization and activity is wonderfully summarized by Padmasambhava:

> Our view is as high as the sky
> And our conduct is as fine as barley flour.

Milarepa puts it as follows:

> Regard this life as a dream and an illusion,
> And cultivate compassion for those who do not realize this.

Thus, the realization of emptiness in no way undermines the compassionate efforts of bodhisattvas to liberate all beings, nor does it turn these efforts into absurdities. Rather, it opens up a wider perspective in each situation and helps bodhisattvas see clearly what actions are most beneficial. The realization of emptiness enhances their mindfulness and compassion and enables them to care about every detail of mental, verbal, and physical actions in the realm of seeming reality. At the same time, seeing the dreamlike quality of all of this turns the conduct of a bodhisattva into a graceful dance of comforting those who do not see this quality and thus teaching them how to dance too. The melodious sound of emptiness is the perfect tune to accompany the elegant and supple steps that compassion takes. This dance may assume limitless expressions, such as a bodhisattva attending a sick person, reciting prayers, or even debating with others by using Centrist reasonings.

## *Madhyamaka Fruition*

Ultimately speaking, of course, perfect Buddhahood as the fruition of the Centrist path is inexpressible. Thus, many Centrist texts say that a Buddha does not have wisdom and that the three enlightened bodies do not exist. However, in typical Centrist discourse, this does not imply the absolute and total nonexistence of wisdom or the enlightened bodies, just as the negation of arising does not mean that nonarising is established or asserted. Any thinking in dualistic categories, such as existence or nonexistence, is considered by Centrists to be just an expression of a reifying mind. Since the very aim of Centrism is to eliminate all reification and fixation, one also needs to let go of the notion that wisdom or Buddhahood is established as something existent in any way. Nor is it some inert thing or utter nothingness after everything has become annihilated. As the nature of all phenomena is completely free from all reference points, so also is the nature of wisdom when analyzed. Since even ordinary things do not fit into any categories, such as existent and nonexistent, how could these categories ever apply to the very result of eliminating all these dualistic notions?

Similarly, the phrase "Buddhas do not have wisdom" points to the transcendence of subject and object. The wisdom of the vajralike meditative concentration at the very end of the tenth bodhisattva ground naturally settles within the expanse of dharmas. Within the nature of phenomena, there is no difference between subject and object, but ignorant beings superimpose subjects and objects onto the expanse of dharmas and cling to them. Once all clinging is exhausted, this expanse, which is primordially without the duality of subject and object, is realized as it is.

Saying what Buddhahood is and what it is not are two ways of saying the same thing. The exhaustion of all clinging and reference points is called "perfect relinquishment," that is, relinquishment of both afflictive and cognitive obscurations together with all their latent tendencies. The undifferentiable unity of nonreferential expanse and nondual wisdom is called "perfect realization." However, since the very exhaustion of clinging and reference points reveals the expanse of dharmas, relinquishment and realization are simply two different ways of expressing the same state, which is perfect Buddhahood. Thus, when the aspect of the twofold purity of the "enlightened" expanse of dharmas—its primordial purity and its purity in the sense that all adventitious stains have been relinquished—is emphasized, it is also called Essence Body. When one refers to this expanse of dharmas in terms of the aspect of wisdom or realization, it is usually called Dharma Body. Another way of expressing the meaning of "Buddha" refers to awakening from the dull sleep of ignorance into the bright daylight of the expanse of omniscient wisdom.

Thus, in this expanse of Buddahood whose nature it is to be without subject and object, there is no wisdom as the realizing subject of any object to be realized. On the other hand, if Buddhas had no omniscient wisdom at all, it would follow that their relinquishment of cognitive obscurations in order to directly realize all knowable objects would be pointless. It would be useless to relinquish all cognitive obscurations, because this would not bring about such omniscient wisdom. Also, if there were no wisdom, all mundane and supramundane qualities that are based on it would not exist either. However, the *Prajñāpāramitā sūtras* say again and again that all qualities of the other five perfections and so on do not come about without the perfection of knowledge or wisdom. The Eighth Karmapa suggests that, on the mere conventional level, there is no contradiction in saying, "An illusionlike knowable object that lacks a nature is known or realized by an illusionlike knowing that lacks a nature," since, conventionally, it is taught that "to see what is not to be seen is to see the truth." This is just as undeniable in terms of mere worldly convention as describing the reflection of my face in a mirror as "seeing my face in the mirror." In actual fact, however, since Centrists simply make no statement about whether wisdom exists or does not exist, they do not even say, "In our own system, we do not say anything about whether wisdom exists or does not exist."

Thus, any presentations of "buddhology" in Centrist texts are meant as conventional descriptions that in themselves point to nonreferential openness-awareness. The three enlightened bodies, the four or five wisdoms, nonreferential compassion, and enlightened activity certainly do function and interact with sentient beings, but they cannot be solidified or pinned down in any way.

Conventionally speaking, wisdom and Buddhahood may be expressed in either a negative or an affirmative way. They may be described through the *via negationis*, in terms of what they are not or what they are free from. Or, sometimes even in the *Prajñāpāramitā sūtras*, they are described through the *via eminentiae*, in terms of very rich presentations of a Buddha's omniscient wisdom and the various bodies of enlightenment with their infinite marvelous qualities and enlightened activities. In general, Centrists usually follow the first approach, while such texts as Maitreya's *Ornament of Clear Realization* and his *Sublime Continuum* often take the latter. However, in the end, both approaches share the desired effect of "blowing your mind": transcending all conceptual limitations regarding Buddhahood.

Candrakīrti's *Entrance into Centrism*, in basing its explanations on Nāgārjuna's work, mainly employs the negative approach. However, by also relying on *The Sūtra of the Ten Grounds*,[716] Candrakīrti describes omniscient wisdom as being free from all reference points and at the same time possessing all Buddha qualities, such as the ten powers.

> Just as space is without divisions through the divisions created by vessels,
> In true reality, there are no divisions that are created by entities.
> Therefore, by perfectly realizing them to be of equal taste,
> You, excellent Knower, realize [all] knowable objects in a single moment.
>
> The profound [quality] is emptiness.

The other qualities are vast.
Through the knowledge of the ways of profundity and vastness,
These qualities will be swiftly obtained.[717]

Candrakīrti's text elaborates on the three enlightened bodies of a Buddha and their qualities, especially the ten powers.[718] His *Autocommentary* supports this explanation by extensively quoting from various sūtras that describe these qualities in very rich and colorful detail. Pawo Rinpoche explains the example of space in the first verse above:

> All phenomena always abide as the true reality, that is, the expanse of dharmas that is unconditioned like space. This is similar to the lack of a difference between the space within a vase and the space outside of it, even if this vase has not been broken. When the vase is broken, the undifferentiable unity of the space within it and outside of it becomes revealed as this undifferentiable unity. The nature of the mind that primordially abides as the expanse of dharmas is similar to the space within the vase. Just as in the case of the undifferentiable unity of the space within this vase and outside of it when the vase is broken, once all vaselike thoughts and mental currents completely subside, [the nature of the mind] is revealed to be no different from the expanse of dharmas. Just as nobody can identify the size of space, nobody can imagine the nature of the Thus-Gone Ones. Just as space provides room for all things, [Buddhahood] serves as the support for all sentient beings. Just as space may appear in any size that corresponds to [every phenomenon], from a trichiliocosm down to the [empty] husk of a mustard seed, [Buddhahood] appears as [manifold] enlightened bodies for all those that are to be trained. Just as one is not able to label all these [kinds of] space as being one or different, all the bodies of the Buddhas cannot be designated as being one or different either. . . . [As for this undifferentiable unity,] there is no difference whether someone has become enlightened or not. Conventionally though, not realizing this [undifferentiable unity] is labeled "the phase of cyclic existence," while its realization, just as it is, [is called] "the attainment of Buddhahood." At this point, however, there is neither a conditioned nor an unconditioned substance or entity that is attained, nor [is there] anybody or anything that is the attainer [of anything]. Therefore, [the Buddha] said that the mere exhaustion of mistakenness is liberation.[719]

Elsewhere, Pawo Rinpoche mentions that Atīśa explains the final view of Śāntideva as being the undifferentiable unity of expanse and wisdom.

An analogy for the exhaustion of mistakenness is when the disease of blurred vision has been removed, and there are no more appearances of floating hairs and such. Likewise, for a Buddha, all causes for mistakenness have been completely relinquished, so from the perspective of a Buddha's wisdom, the phenomena of seeming reality no longer appear. Just as not seeing any floating hairs is said to be correct seeing, not seeing any reference points whatsoever is expressed as "seeing the basic nature of these phenomena." Another example of seeing by not seeing is a person who wonders whether it is possible to paint space. Through not "seeing"—that is, not finding—any possibility of applying paint to space, this person "sees" in the sense of understanding that one is not able to paint space. In consequence, one may wonder whether Buddhas see the five aggregates and such or not. Since there is no mental flux, such as arising or ceasing, in a Buddha, from a Buddha's own perspective, there is no flux in terms of seeing and not seeing or in terms of wisdom arising and ceasing. From the perspective of others, however, it appears as if a Buddha has the omniscient wisdom of the ten powers and such that sees all phenomena, because this wisdom undeceivingly occurs as the mere dependently originated result of having fully gathered the accumulation of wisdom.

Unlike our physical body, which can only be trained up to a certain limit—such as jumping no higher than eight feet or lifting no more than eight hundred pounds—Buddhism says that there is no limit in training the mind, since it is not bound by any physical dimensions. The Buddhas have accumulated the two infinite accumulations of merit and wisdom through infinite skillful means and knowledge for many eons in order to benefit infinite sentient beings. So in terms of the law of causality, it is only justified that this infinity of causes bring about the infinite results of a Buddha's wisdoms and enlightened activities for the welfare of infinite sentient beings as long as cyclic existence exists.

Some people say that, on the level of a Buddha, there exists a momentarily arising and ceasing chain of awareness and illusionlike mistaken appearances. However, this is not justified. First, since all phenomena are free from all such extremes as arising and ceasing, a Buddha's wisdom is no exception. If a Buddha's wisdom, though free from reference points, involved arising and ceasing, then it would entail reference points. It makes no sense that a Buddha's wisdom should have realized that all phenomena lack arising but not realize that it itself lacks arising too. Furthermore, it would follow from the above position that worldly beings who are ensnared by the web of reference points, such as arising and ceasing, also see true reality. In addition, it would not be suitable for the noble ones to teach such beings that all phenomena lack arising. And since mistaken appearances only appear due to basic unawareness, there would also be basic unawareness on the level of a Buddha, because false objects appear to them, just as it is the case for a dream-consciousness. Some people claim, "The Buddhas have such appearances, but since they do not cling to them as being real, they are not mistaken." However, then it would absurdly follow that the consciousnesses of people with blurred vision who see floating hairs and double moons are also not mistaken, as long as they do not cling to these hairs and moons as being really existent.

Another position regarding what enlightened beings see is the argument of "pure vision," which is found in such statements as "Since ignorance is the cause for impure appearances, such as stones and earth, they do not appear to Buddhas. On the other hand, completely pure appearances, such as mandalas, emerge within the natural unceasing display of wisdom. Since Buddhas have such pure appearances, they are not mistaken." However, also these pure appearances are not established as pure by their own nature, because they originate from prior positive actions, such as making aspiration prayers and purifying Buddha-fields. Thus, they are nothing but dependent origination. Therefore, it is not contradictory that the seeming does not appear for the Buddhas' own perspective yet they still perform activities for the welfare of others, such as knowing the range of all phenomena and turning the wheel of dharma. The reason is that such activities are the result of having perfectly engaged in their causes—the dependent origination of the accumulation of merit—during their prior times as bodhisattvas on the various paths.

In brief, there is no way to identify the wisdom of a Buddha through any discussions in terms of existence or nonexistence. Rather, since it is the ultimate nature of all phenomena to be completely free from reference points, ultimately, any kind of mind must be free from reference points too. In particular, in order to be able to realize this freedom from reference points, the wisdom of a Buddha as the subject to realize this must necessarily be free from all clinging to reference points with regard to true reality, including the latent tendencies for such clinging. Therefore, Buddhahood means to rest in the undifferentiable unity of wisdom and the expanse of dharmas that is free from being one and different, subject and object, and so on. In this unity, all phenomena, such as samsaric flaws and nirvanic qualities, are just equality. That this is what constitutes Buddhahood was said by Buddha Śākyamuni, his regent Maitreya, Nāgārjuna and his spiritual heirs, as well as many others time and again. Here, Centrists say that from the perspective of worldly mistakenness without analysis, just as all phenomena of seeming reality exist, the wisdom of a Buddha also exists. When analyzed, from the perspective of Buddhahood, just as the wisdom experience of a Buddha is free from all reference points of existence and nonexistence, likewise all phenomena are free from such reference points.

As for the enlightened bodies of a Buddha, *The Entrance into Centrism* states:

> The dry firewood of knowable objects having been totally incinerated,
> This peace is the Dharma Body of the Victors.

> At this point, there is neither arising nor ceasing.
> The cessation of mind is revealed through this Body.[720]

Candrakīrti's autocommentary explains:

> In this Body that has the nature of wisdom and [in which] the dry firewood of knowable objects has been totally burned away, there is no arising of knowable objects. Therefore, that which entails such nonarising is the Dharma Body of the Buddhas. Thus, the object of wisdom—true reality—is in no case engaged by the [corresponding] subjects of such [knowable objects], that is, mind and mental events. Hence, on the seeming level, this is expressed as [true reality] being revealed through this very Body.[721]

When the verse speaks about "the cessation of mind," this does not mean that some mind that still really existed at the end of the tenth bodhisattva ground becomes nonexistent when Buddhahood is attained. It is impossible for something that really existed before to become nonexistent later. Likewise, what never existed in the first place cannot later become nonexistent either. Thus, the expression "cessation of mind" is just a conventional label for the dissolution of the entirety of clinging in terms of mind and mental events or for the vanishing of all mistaken appearances of basic unawareness.

Pawo Rinpoche comments that, through training on all the paths of familiarizing with the fact that the entire collection of the firewood of knowable objects lacks a nature, this firewood has become free from the dampness of reification. At the end of the tenth bodhisattva ground, the completely dried-out remainder of this firewood is instantly consumed by the momentary blazing wisdom of the vajralike meditative concentration. Once there is no firewood left, the fire itself then subsides too. This example should not be misunderstood to mean that the Dharma Body is just utter nonexistence, because the firewood that is burned by firelike wisdom consists of precisely these reifications of existence and nonexistence. When wisdom has consumed all there is to consume, it just naturally settles within the primordial expanse. In this way, the expanse of dharmas is revealed in its primordial uncontrived state. This is what is called "attaining the Dharma Body" and "the perfection of one's own welfare." This very Dharma Body then appears to various disciples as the manifold manifestations of the two Form Bodies: the Body of Complete Enjoyment and the Emanation Body. Through such appearances, it teaches the dharma and helps the disciples realize true reality, or the Dharma Body. In this way, the Form Bodies constitute "the perfection of the welfare of others."

The relationship between these three enlightened bodies is often illustrated by comparing the Dharma Body to the sun in the sky, the Body of Complete

Enjoyment to the reflection of the sun in a lake, and the Emanation Body to this reflection's reflection in a mirror. Just as both reflections depend on the sun in the sky and may serve to make us see this sun, the two Form Bodies depend on and point back to the Dharma Body. The Dharma Body—freedom from reference points—is what Buddhas themselves experience or see through their personally experienced wisdom. The reference points of the Form Bodies with all their qualities and activities are seen by different disciples in dependence on the various degrees of purification of their lakelike or mirrorlike minds. The disciples also hear the words of these Form Bodies and practice the dharma that comes from the minds of these Form Bodies as an object of their own minds when they study, reflect, and meditate on it. However, all of this is not possible with regard to the Dharma Body. Even when the Buddhas themselves see this Dharma Body, they only see it in a manner of nonseeing. Thus, other beings are definitely not able to observe it in any way that involves a seer and something seen.

It is said that the Body of Complete Enjoyment appears only in the oceanlike mirror of the stainless wisdom attained by bodhisattvas on the tenth ground who are free from reference points. This appearance of the Body of Complete Enjoyment possesses the five certainties:

1) Its abode is certain as being only the sphere of Akaniṣṭha.[722]
2) Its nature is certain in that it is adorned with the major and minor marks of a Buddha.
3) Its retinue is certain in that it consists only of bodhisattvas on the ten grounds.
4) Its time is certain, meaning that it appears in an unceasing way.
5) Its certain enjoyment is solely the teachings of the great vehicle.

As for the Emanation Body, there are three main types:

1) Supreme Emanation Bodies show as fully enlightened Buddhas (such as Buddha Śākyamuni) with all their major and minor marks and perform the twelve deeds of such Buddhas.
2) Artistic Emanation Bodies can, for example, manifest as a masterful lute player among the celestial musicians to teach them in this way, or as great scientists, physicians, and artists who benefit many beings.
3) Incarnated Emanation Bodies can appear in all kinds of animate and inanimate forms, such as various gods, animals, and even bridges or trees appearing in order to help certain sentient beings.

The appearance of the two Form Bodies with their enlightened activities depends on the coming together of three conditions:

1) the blessings or the potency of the Dharma Body
2) a Buddha's former aspiration prayers
3) the appropriate karmic and mental dispositions of individual disciples

If the Form Bodies and their enlightened activities could operate due to the potency of the Dharma Body alone, all sentient beings would effortlessly meet Buddhas and attain liberation, since the Dharma Body is omnipresent and all-pervading. This is not to say that the Form Bodies and enlightened activity are merely an appearance from the perspective of ordinary sentient beings, since the mental perspective of ordinary beings is essentially deceiving in that they mistakenly perceive and conceive what is actually not there. So if the Form Bodies were just appearances in the mistaken minds of sentient beings, and if these sentient beings could become enlightened in dependence on such appearances, it would absurdly follow that we all have been enlightened for a long time, since we all have engaged in mistaken appearances since beginningless time. Nor are the Form Bodies and their enlightened activities solely an outcome of the impetus of a Buddha's former aspiration prayers alone. Such aspiration prayers are made for the sake of all sentient beings, so if only these prayers were needed, all sentient beings would be liberated without any efforts of their own.

The completion of former aspiration prayers and the two accumulations of merit and wisdom are the causes for the ongoing impetus of enlightened activity. Once enlightened wisdom displays its activity, it manifests in a spontaneous and unceasing way that is completely effortless and nonconceptual. Thus, a bodhisattva's progression on the path that eventually results in such Buddha activity within the expanse of nonreferentiality can be compared to the flight of a rocket. Initially, it requires a lot of energy to lift off the ground, but the higher the rocket ascends, the easier and faster its motion becomes and the less energy it needs. Finally, once it glides in the vacuum of outer space, it moves on forever without needing any further energy, just through the power of the fuel that has already been spent.

In brief, a "Buddha" is not a person in the sense of a collection of matter and consciousness. Buddha Śākyamuni himself said that if one thinks that his physical appearance and speech are the Buddha, one could not be more mistaken. The appearances of a Buddha's Form Bodies are neither a part of the aggregate of form nor a part of any of the mental aggregates, since Buddhahood transcends the five aggregates and is completely beyond both cyclic existence and nirvāṇa. However, this does not mean that, conventionally, the Form Bodies are not Buddhas, since what they say is the Buddhadharma, which when practiced accordingly by sentient beings leads to their enlightenment. Nor are the Form Bodies the same as the bodies of ordinary sentient beings; they are the bodies of Buddhas, and this is also how they appear to various disciples. Thus, Buddhahood is beyond form but still displays all kinds of form. It is without sound but nevertheless possesses the perfect melodious speech with sixty excellent qualities. It is not a part of the three realms of cyclic existence, but it never moves away from them either. It is not an object of the minds of sentient beings, but it appears in the form of limitless illusionlike manifestations that individually guide these beings. That it is without middle and end goes even beyond the example of space, since it is at the same time the sole foundation for the true benefit and happiness of all beings.

Therefore, when the enlightened bodies of a Buddha are presented in terms of the two realities, their characteristics are described solely in dependence on the minds of certain disciples. In the context of the two realities, it is said that the Dharma Body and the Essence Body are nothing but freedom from reference points without any arising and ceasing, while the Body of Complete Enjoyment and the Emanation Body involve reference points, such as arising and ceasing. However, from the perspective of a Buddha, there is not the slightest difference between these four enlightened bodies, such as that certain ones among them represent ultimate reality and others belong to seeming reality, or that only some represent Buddhahood while others do not. *The Ornament of Sūtras* says:

> Buddhahood is all phenomena,
> But it is no phenomenon whatsoever.

and

> With regard to the stainless expanse of dharmas,
> This explanation of the profound characteristics,
> The state, and the activity of the Buddhas
> Is nothing but sketching a colorful painting onto the sky.[723]

# 3

## *The Distinction between Autonomists and Consequentialists*

The Autonomist-Consequentialist distinction first appeared in Tibetan writings. In India, some rather late and quite loose distinctions within Centrism were made, but none was labeled Autonomism or Consequentialism, nor did the content of these Indian distinctions match this later Tibetan one. This is not to say that the basis for the Autonomist-Consequentialist distinction cannot be traced back to Indian Centrist texts, but there were certainly no subschools with such names. The best way to understand this distinction is in terms of methodology, as different approaches to understanding and communicating the same emptiness.

### *Classifications of Centrism in India and Tibet*

Despite certain disagreements on some issues between individual Centrist masters in India (such as Buddhapālita, Bhāvaviveka, and Candrakīrti), for many centuries there appeared no divisions into Centrist subschools.[724] Before the time of Bhāvaviveka, no controversy among Centrists is recorded at all. Bhāvaviveka's own *Jewel Lamp of Centrism* talks about two levels within Centrist practice as a whole, but these are equally taught by all Centrists and thus not meant as a distinction between two schools or views.

> Having thus taught the coarse yoga, now, the subtle yoga is to be taught: . . . In just the way that all phenomena occur as appearances of mere illusory mind, in that way mere illusory mind is beyond the three times, without color and shape, naturally luminous, and without appearance. Therefore, it is to be understood that all phenomena are illusory mind. Thus, to speak about seeming reality in the way of the hearers is the "outer, coarse Centrism." That this [seeming reality] abides as one's own mere mind is the "subtle, inner Centrism."[725]

In the eighth century, Śāntarakṣita's own commentary on his *Ornament of*

*Centrism* distinguishes two ways of Centrists analyzing the causally efficient entities of seeming reality:

1) those like himself who consider these entities as having the nature of mere mind[726] and
2) those who accept them as outer objects and thus interpret the teaching on "mere mind" as merely negating an agent and an experiencer.

As an example of the latter approach, he quotes Bhāvaviveka's *Heart of Centrism* V.28cd.[727]

Kamalaśīla's subcommentary on Śāntarakṣita's text glosses this difference as "the two Centrist paths that analyze this [issue] to be analyzed" and explicitly confirms Bhāvaviveka's text as representing the latter "path."[728] On the other hand, in his *Commentary on The Synopsis of True Reality,*[729] he speaks of undifferentiated Centrists, while dividing the Yogācāra school into Aspectarians and Non-Aspectarians.

As for the various Indian commentaries on Śāntideva's *Entrance to the Bodhisattva's Way of Life* (ranging from the late tenth to the early thirteenth century) that are preserved in the *Tengyur,* both when referring to Śāntideva's words and in general, all of them only speak about "Centrists," never mentioning any subdivisions. This is especially noteworthy in light of the fact that Śāntideva is considered a Consequentialist by many Tibetan teachers (as mentioned earlier, the Eighth Karmapa sees him as a "Centrist of the model texts").[730]

One of Atīśa's teachers, Ratnākaraśānti (early eleventh century), in his *Presentation of the Three Vehicles,*[731] classifies Centrists as follows:

1) Centrists who regard the seeming as an aspect of consciousness
2) Centrists who regard the seeming as mere latent tendencies

Atīśa's main Centrist teacher Bodhibhadra (c. 1000), in his *Explanation of The Compendium of the Heart of Wisdom,* also mentions a difference between Centrists as to how they present seeming reality:

1) those like Bhāvaviveka who do not evaluate appearances
2) those like Śāntarakṣita who say that appearing entities are not as they seem but that it is solely internal consciousness that appears as various things[732]

The position of Atīśa (982–1054) himself is rather complex. His *Centrist Pith Instructions* identifies the Centrist texts by Nāgārjuna, Āryadeva, Mātṛceṭa,[733] Kambala,[734] and Candrakīrti as the unrivaled model texts for all Centrist scriptures. Other masters in his list of Centrists include Bhāvaviveka, Buddhapālita, Devaśarman,[735] Avalokitavrata, Śāntarakṣita, and Kamalaśīla.[736] In his *Entrance into the Two Realities*, he says that the ones who have fully understood emptiness are Nāgārjuna and Candrakīrti.[737] On the other hand, he uses the distinction of the correct and false seeming and defines the correct seeming in precisely the same way as Jñānagarbha and Śāntarakṣita, who at a later point came to be called Autonomists.[738] Also in contrast to Nāgārjuna and Candrakīrti, Atīśa in his autocommentary on *The Lamp for the Path to Enlightenment* explicitly recommends the provisional use of valid cognition (particularly inference) as presented by Dharmakīrti and Dharmottara when meditating on the ultimate as it is transmitted in Nāgārjuna's pith instructions.[739] The same text identifies Āryadeva, Candrakīrti, Bhāvaviveka, Śāntideva, and Atīśa's own teacher Bodhibhadra as the true authorities of Centrism who follow Nāgārjuna.[740] Later, he repeats this list as representing those who have unmistakenly realized true reality (the essence of the meaning of the perfection of knowledge) and adds Aśvaghoṣa and Candragomī[741] to it.[742]

In his *Precious Garland of True Reality*,[743] Maitrīpa (1012–1097) presents the following classification of Centrism:

1) Proponents of Illusionlike Nonduality[744] and
2) Proponents of the Complete Nonabiding of all Phenomena

Through a quotation from Bhāvaviveka's texts, Maitrīpa aligns him with the first approach, while it remains unclear who represents the second.[745] The same distinction is made in Candrahari's *Jewel Garland*[746] and alluded to in Aśvaghoṣa's *Stages of Meditation on the Ultimate Mind of Enlightenment*.[747] Both reject the approach of establishing illusions in any way.

*The Treasury of Knowledge*[748] reports that the eleventh-century Kashmiri master Lakṣmīkara in his *Commentary on The Five Stages*[749] explains a threefold classification:

1) the Centrism of Sūtras[750]
2) the Centrism of Yoga Practice[751]
3) the Centrism of the Mother of the Victors (the perfection of knowledge)

Sahajavajra (eleventh/twelfth century), in his *Commentary on The Ten Verses on True Reality*,[752] speaks about Aspectarian Centrists[753] (such as Śāntarakṣita) and Non-Aspectarian Centrists[754] (such as Kambala) as those Centrists who do not teach the definitive meaning of true reality, which is presented by Centrists such as Nāgārjuna, Āryadeva, and Candrakīrti.

This shows that even in late Indian Buddhism there was no clear or mutually exclusive distinction of subschools in Indian Centrism and that the works of all the above masters were evidently studied side by side. The main distinction, if any, seems to have been between those who conventionally accept outer objects as a part of seeming reality (either explicitly or by following common worldly consensus) and those who interpret seeming reality in a way similar to the Yogācāras. Unlike the Autonomist-Consequentialist distinction, this would place Bhāvaviveka and Candrakīrti on the same side. On the subject of a distinction within Centrism, Candrakīrti is conspicuously never even mentioned. Atiśa seems to have held him in high regard but does not distinguish his view from Bhāvaviveka's.

In Tibet, it was the great translator Yeshe De[755] (early ninth century) in his *Differences of the Views*[756] who first used the terms "Centrism of Sūtras" and "Centrism of Yoga Practice," with Bhāvaviveka belonging to the former and Śāntarakṣita to the latter. Other texts from this early period also mention one or both of these names.[757] In one of the Tibetan manuscripts from Dunhuang, a distinction is made between "outer Centrism"[758] and "inner Yoga-Centrism."[759] The great Sanskrit-Tibetan Dictionary *Mahāvyutpatti*,[760] compiled in the ninth century by a number of Indian paṇḍitas and Tibetan translators, has no subdivisions of its entry "Centrists."

In three of his texts, the eleventh-century Nyingma master Rongzom Paṇḍita Chökyi Sangbo[761] refers to the Centrism of Sūtras and the Centrism of Yoga Practice.[762] Among these, *The Memorandum on the Views* says:

> The two types of Centrism are dissimilar as to the mode of being of the seeming. As for which one [of them] is greater in terms of scripture and reasoning in this respect, it seems that, according to the general ways of sūtras and tantras, the general ways of reasoning, and the texts of the Centrist preceptors Nāgārjuna and Āryadeva as the masters who composed the [Centrist] model texts, the texts of the Centrists of Yoga Practice are of greater significance.[763]

Once, Rongzom Paṇḍita also mentions the distinction between those who assert everything as illusionlike and those who assert nonabiding. He nowhere speaks of the Autonomist-Consequentialist distinction.

Rog Bande Sherab Ö[764] distinguishes "factional Centrism" after the model texts by Nāgārjuna and Āryadeva into the Centrism of Sūtras (Jñānagarbha), the Centrism of Yoga Practice (Śāntarakṣita), and the texts of Centrism in general (Kamalaśīla).

Gampopa (1079–1153) classified Centrism as illusionlike nonduality and complete nonabiding.[765] He subdivided the latter into "complete nonabiding of unity"[766] and "complete nonabiding of severed continuity."[767]

Whether this latter classification matches with the Autonomist-Consequentialist distinction and whether it differentiates the view of Centrists on ultimate reality was a subject of some discussion in Tibet. Ngog Lotsāwa rejected the latter point, and Tsongkhapa stated that this rejection is good. *The Treasury of Knowledge* portrays the Proponents of Illusionlike Nonduality (such as Kamalaśīla) as saying that the compound of appearance and emptiness is ultimate reality. The Proponents of Complete Nonabiding (such as Buddhapālita) say that ultimate reality is what is positively determined through the negative determination that consists in excluding all discursiveness with regard to appearances. Another way to put this is that all phenomena are merely designated through names, symbols, and conventions but do not abide in any such ways as they are designated. Padma Karpo's *Illumination of Three Centrist Scriptural Systems* explains the difference between these two types of Centrists and presents Autonomists and Consequentialists as subdivisions of the Proponents of the complete Nonabiding of all Phenomena:

> Those who speak about [everything] being illusionlike assert that all outer and inner phenomena are illusionlike, both from the point of view of cutting through discursiveness and from the point of view of nonconceptual resting in meditative equipoise. Even when Buddhahood has dawned, also nondual wisdom or the three enlightened bodies are illusionlike. This is the case, because it is said in [the sūtras of] the Mother of the Victors:
>
> > All phenomena, nirvāṇa, and even a hypothetical phenomenon that is much superior to this are illusionlike and dreamlike.[768]
>
> The system of the nonabiding Centrists does not itself have anything that is to be positively determined or proven but puts an end to the claims of others. It is twofold: Autonomists are those who negate the claims of others by relying on reasonings that cut through discursiveness and stem from the three modes being established by valid cognition. Consequentialists do not accept that the three modes are established by valid cognition and negate the wrong ideas of others by stating the claims of these [others] as reasons.[769]

The first one to introduce the terms "Autonomists" and "Consequentialists" is said to be Patsab Lotsāwa in the eleventh century, but none of his texts is preserved.[770] So the earliest available Tibetan source for the explicit distinction between Autonomists and Consequentialists seems to be the commentary on the ninth chapter of *The Entrance to the Bodhisattva's Way of Life*[771] by Sönam Dsemo (1142–1182), the second supreme head of the Sakya school.

The Eighth Karmapa refers to Majaba[772] and other logicians as considering degrees of superiority and inferiority in terms of the knowledge that results from studying, reflecting, and meditating as the means to establish Madhyamaka as well as whether there is something to be evaluated with regard to the content that is to be established. Based on such considerations, they speak about two kinds of Centrists: those who, in the context of Centrism, establish referents[773] and those who establish conventions.[774] The Centrists who establish referents are not the superior Centrists, while those Centrists who do not establish referents, but establish mere conventions in order to put an end to wrong ideas, are the superior Centrists. As for the knowledge that realizes Madhyamaka or emptiness as that which is to be established through these two ways of determining, Majaba and others delineate a difference as to this knowledge being inferential valid cognition and it being the valid cognition that is a reasoning consciousness. Due to these differences, they say that these two systems are inferior and superior respectively.

Majaba Jangchub Dsöndrü's commentary on *The Fundamental Verses* uses the term "Centrists who propound autonomous [reasoning]."[775]

The third head of the Sakyapas, Tragba Gyaltsen[776] (1147–1216), gives a fivefold classification of Centrists with regard to seeming reality:

1) followers of common worldly consensus
2) those who accord with the way of the Followers of the Great Exposition
3) illusionists
4) followers of the sūtras
5) yoga practitioners[777]

Other early Tibetan writers such as Sakya Paṇḍita (1182–1251), Butön Rinchen Drub (1290–1364), Longchen Rabjampa (1308–1363), Barawa Gyaltsen Balsang[778] (1310–1391), and Rendawa[779] (1349–1412) employed one or more of the above classifications.

Specifically, Butön in his *History of Buddhism*[780] uses a threefold classification:

1) the Centrism of Sūtras (Bhāvaviveka)
2) the Centrism of Yoga Practice (Jñānagarbha, Śrīgupta, Śāntarakṣita, Kamalaśīla, and Haribhadra)
3) the Centrism following common worldly consensus (Buddhapālita, Candrakīrti)

He explicitly gives "Consequentialist Centrists" as another name for the Centrists following common worldly consensus but does not even mention the term "Autonomists." Butön is moreover reported to have said that, after the debate of Samye, Centrism branched into three lineages, with Kamalaśīla establishing a third lineage (the Centrism of Yoga Practice) as distinct from the lineages of Bhāvaviveka and Candrakīrti.[781] Elsewhere Butön says that the distinction between Autonomists and Consequentialists is a conceptual construct by Tibetans that is not found in India. The two do not differ with regard to ultimate reality but just employ varying approaches to explain the scriptures.[782]

Longchen Rabjampa, in three of his seven *Treasure* texts, discusses the distinction between Autonomists and Consequentialists, explicitly affirming the latter as the supreme system in the sūtra vehicle.[783]

The fourteenth-century Kadampa master Üba Losal[784] also employs the above threefold classification but puts Jñānagarbha together with Candrakīrti into the category of Centrists who follow common worldly consensus.[785] Distinct from this classification, he also uses the Autonomist-Consequentialist division, with Jñānagarbha as an Autonomist.

The most prolific writer of Tibetan history, Bodong Paṇchen Choglay Namgyal[786] (1376–1451), divides Centrists into two branches:

1) those who follow reasoning
2) those who follow common worldly consensus (Nāgārjuna, Āryadeva, Candrakīrti, and Śāntideva)

The first branch has four subdivisions:

1) those who accord with the Followers of the Great Exposition, such as Ārya-vimuktisena
2) those who accord with the Sūtra Followers, such as Bhāvaviveka
3) those who accord with the Yogācāras, such as Śāntarakṣita, Kamalaśīla, and Haribhadra
4) those who accord with and follow common worldly consensus, such as Jñānagarbha

Neither of the two still available works of the important historian Gö Lotsāwa (1392–1481)—his *Commentary on The Sublime Continuum* and *The Blue Annals*—refers to any subschools of Centrism.[787] The chapter in *The Blue Annals* on the spreading of the Centrist teachings in Tibet does not even mention Buddhapālita or Bhāvaviveka. In the context of the lineage of Ngog Lotsāwa, Gö Lotsāwa just remarks that Chaba Chökyi Senge wrote many refutations of the works of Candrakīrti, while Tsang Nagba Dsöndrü Senge "followed the method of Candrakīrti" and Majaba Jangchub Dsöndrü "preferred the system of Jayānanda."[788] The exposition of the basic texts by Candrakīrti in Tibet is explained to have originated with Patsab Lotsāwa and his followers.[789]

Karmapa Mikyö Dorje defines and uses the distinction between Autonomists and Consequentialists in a rather narrow sense. He equates the former with "those who establish illusions through reasoning." (This is discussed further below.)

In all of these distinctions by early authors, it is to be noted, none of them presented the Centrists of Sūtras and the Centrists of Yoga Practice as subdivisions of the Autonomists. The first scriptural evidence for classifying these two as subschools of the Autonomists is found in a Bon text on philosophical systems[790] from the early fourteenth century. Like Butön, the text equates the Centrists following common worldly consensus with the Consequentialists. Since this is a Bon text, one would naturally assume that also the subclassification of Autonomists was taken from Buddhist precursors, but we do not have any such evidence in earlier Buddhist texts. In presently available Buddhist works, this subclassification implicitly starts to show in Tsongkhapa's *Elucidation of the Intention*[791] (his commentary on *The Entrance into Centrism*) and the writings of his student Kedrub Geleg Balsang[792] (1385–1438). It is explicitly stated by Sera Jetsün Chökyi Gyaltsen (1469–1546) and nearly all subsequent Gelugpa masters. Later, the terminology of "Autonomist Centrists who follow the Sūtras"[793] and "Autonomist Centrists of Yoga Practice"[794] became more or less universally accepted by all four schools of Tibetan Buddhism.

One should be aware, however, that these terms combine two classification schemes on two different levels: The one (Sūtra versus Yogācāra) is a distinction as to how seeming reality is presented, while the other (Autonomists versus Consequentialists) pertains to the approach to Centrist reasoning. Also, as can be seen above, initially these two classifications were absolutely limited to these two respective levels (seeming reality and reasoning) and clearly kept apart, whereas later they were turned into names for actual Centrist subschools, which included more or less extensive elaborations on additional differences on a number of other levels too.

This account shows clearly that for centuries there was no universal agreement, in either India or Tibet, as to whether or how to classify Indian Centrist masters. In India, it was a long time before there were any indications of Centrism becoming divided into two branches, and even then it was a rather loose division. In Tibet, the most common early distinction seems to have been into the Centrists of Sūtras and the Centrists of Yoga Practice. More elaborate distinctions, including the one into Autonomists and Consequentialists, clearly only developed later and coexisted or were combined with the earlier ones. Among these, evidently, the Autonomist-Consequentialist division was not regarded as *the* main distinction by any author before Tsongkhapa.

In India, the Autonomist approach in terms of reasoning was far more common among later Centrists. Most major masters after Bhāvaviveka actively employed it, and nobody but Candrakīrti and Jayānanda objected to it. Thus, there is no evidence at all that the Consequentialist approach was generally considered any better than the Autonomist one. In fact, the texts of those Centrists who later came to be labeled Autonomists enjoyed widespread high esteem. In particular, Candrakīrti's critique of Bhāvaviveka is never even mentioned in any other Indian Centrist texts. He is hardly ever quoted in any of them,[795] and there is only a single known commentary on his works by Jayānanda as late as the eleventh century.[796] Thus, Candrakīrti's criticism, which only became considered a devastating attack on Autonomism many centuries later by Tibetan and Western interpreters, simply went largely unnoticed in India. Rather, everything indicates that Candrakīrti's place in Indian Buddhism was rather limited. He was definitely not the towering figure in Centrism that he later became in Tibet, but basically just one Centrist master among many others (to be sure, this is not to deny that he was an outstanding scholar and highly realized being). In brief, there is no evidence at all that Candrakīrti's approach ever dominated the Indian Centrist scene. One can speak even less about a distinct school of Consequentialists; the only two Indian masters ever to explicitly favor the use of consequences over autonomous reasoning were Candrakīrti himself and—much later—Jayānanda.[797]

## *Refutation of Mistaken Assumptions about Autonomists and Consequentialists*

In his *Chariot of the Tagbo Siddhas*, the Eighth Karmapa portrays a number of common Tibetan claims—"well known as the wind"—as to the distinction between Autonomists and Consequentialists:[798]

1) Autonomists accept (a) the perceptual and inferential valid cognitions of ordinary people[799] as correct valid cognitions. (b) They accept them as being valid cognitions that operate through the power of (real) entities. (c) On the basis of this acceptance, such valid cognitions are not just seen as the assertions of others but are established through the experiences in the Autonomists' own continua. By relying on these accepted valid cognitions, they affirmatively prove emptiness and negate its opposites.

2) Phrased in terms of the Autonomists' acceptance of these three features of valid cognition (a–c) as the basis for negation and proof, the Consequentialists in general (a) do not accept any valid cognition as the basis for negation and proof with regard to emptiness, nonarising, and such. (b) Even if they accept such valid cognition, they do not accept any valid cognition that operates through the power of entities. (c) And even if they accept a valid cognition that operates through the power of entities, they do not have any autonomous valid cognition. Even in this

case, any valid cognition as the basis for negation and proof with regard to the meaning of emptiness is solely based on what is acknowledged by others.

3) Autonomists debate in accordance with the presentation of correct and seeming negations and proofs in the system of Dignāga and Dharmakīrti, while Consequentialists do not debate in accordance with their presentation. For if they debated in accordance with negations and proofs used in a system of proponents of real entities, they would also incur the flaw of being such realists. Instead, Consequentialists have their special presentation of negations and proofs that the proponents of real entities do not have. This presentation consists of five elements:

(a) inference acknowledged by others, (b) consequences that expose contradictions, (c) analogous applicability of the opponent's reason, (d) nonapplication of the means of proof due to presupposing the probandum,[800] and (e) not having an autonomous position.[801] The first four are said to be like weapons to vanquish the theses of others and the fifth to be like armor to protect one's own thesis. On this, the writings of Patsab Lotsāwa's disciple Shang Tangsagba are quoted:

> Consequences that expose contradictions and analogous applicability of the opponent's reason are the reasonings that, like Viṣṇu's spear, invalidate the theses of others. Nonapplication of the means of proof due to presupposing the probandum is the armorlike reasoning to protect one's own thesis by giving the lack of a thesis of one's own the name of "a thesis of one's own." Inference acknowledged by others is the refereelike reasoning that makes the two opponents be in unison.

The Karmapa analyzes each of these statements as presented here below.

1a) As for the perceptual and inferential valid cognitions of ordinary people, Autonomist masters give presentations of valid cognitions that are presumed to be ordinary people's own valid cognitions from the perspective of just these ordinary people themselves. However, Autonomists do not accept that such valid cognitions are correct valid cognitions in the Centrist system. As Bhāvaviveka's *Blaze of Reasoning* makes clear:

> The Blessed One taught the two realities by giving presentations of the nature and characteristics of phenomena on the seeming level while saying that ultimately they lack a nature:

> Kauśika, all phenomena are empty of nature. That all phenomena are empty of nature means that entities do not exist. That entities do not exist is the perfection of knowledge.

In accord with many such statements, if even entities as such do not exist, forget about any nature of theirs. Therefore, there is no invalidation [of the lack of nature] through our accepting [entities such as the five aggregates that were expediently taught by the Buddha]. There is also no invalidation through perception. Since objects are false and the sense faculties foolish, seeing has no [epistemic] power. Like the appearance of floating hairs, bees, and flies to someone with blurred vision, or an echo and so on, perception too is just obvious self-indulgence. . . . There is also no invalidation through common consensus, since [the eyes of] the world are covered by the membrane of ignorance. Consequently, in the situation of analyzing for the ultimate, since [the world] does not realize the [ultimate], there is no invalidation through [the world's] common consensus, just as [experts in] examining precious gems [are not affected by] the examinations of blind people.[802]

Kamalaśīla's *Illumination of True Reality* says:

> Since falsities that are like dreams and such
> Are undeceiving in terms of the desired purpose,
> Conventionally, it should be said
> That there is valid cognition for worldly entities.
>
> But how could this be ultimate?
> It is nothing but a name and [thus] not to be removed.
> Among what occurs for ordinary people,
> Who could possibly remove [anything, so why] this?[803]

If, in actuality, there is no perceptual valid cognition, there is also no inferential valid cognition, since all valid cognitions primarily depend on whether there is an establishment through perception. In particular, Autonomists declare that the minds and mental events of ordinary people that are regarded as valid cognitions by common consensus entail conceptuality (which is the cause for bondage) but are definitely not actual valid cognitions. As Jñānagarbha's *Distinction between the Two Realities* says:

> Minds and mental events in the three realms
> Are conceptuality that involves the aspect of superimposition.

> [The Buddha] expressed them in just the way
> In which he saw them as the very cause for bondage.[804]

In brief, Autonomists validate ordinary people's cognitions only insofar as their appearance for these very people is concerned, but not by regarding such validation as a part of the Centrist system, let alone validating any kind of ultimate existence.

1b) As for the Autonomists' acceptance of a valid cognition that operates through the power of entities, it is a great flaw not to precisely discriminate the distinctive features of such acceptance. "Valid cognition that operates through the power of entities" is usually explained as follows. The aspect that an entity performs a function means that it performs a function through the power of the very nature of this intrinsically real entity without being dependent on anything else. The performance of a function in this sense is also intrinsically real, and an intrinsically real valid cognition in this sense is said to be a valid cognition that operates through the power of entities. This characterizes the acceptance of this kind of valid cognition as found in Dharmakīrti's *Commentary on Valid Cognition.* His valid cognition through the power of entities that negates both the apprehending and apprehended aspects of consciousness reads as follows:

> Once the entities [of apprehender and apprehended] are analyzed by this,
> In true reality, they do not exist as entities,
> Because they do not have a nature
> Of unity or multiplicity.
>
> "In whatever ways referents are reflected upon,
> In just these ways they are free [from being such referents]."
> What the learned thus declare
> Results from the power of entities.[805]

As Centrists, Autonomists do not accept any real existence of entities. So if the above intrinsically real entities and valid cognitions that operate through the power of these entities were accepted by Autonomists,[806] all their efforts in studying, reflecting, and meditating would be pointless. So would their activities of explaining, debating, and composing texts to the effect of showing that all phenomena are empty of a nature of their own and not established as intrinsically real.

1c) It is not justified to say that Autonomists establish emptiness as their own experience and that they express this experience solely through the above valid cognitions that are part of their own system,[807] while not expressing it in any other way. Not only Consequentialists but also Autonomists express the experience of profound emptiness in their own minds as the "nonrealization of the profound actuality of emptiness" and say that this profound actuality is beyond being an object of cognition. As Bhāvaviveka's *Heart of Centrism* declares:

> Once the mind turns away from
> Conceptuality and the lack of conceptuality,
> Since the mind is without object then,
> It is the very peace in which discursiveness is at utter peace.[808]

*The Distinction between the Two Realities* says:

> Since there is nothing to be negated,
> It is clear that actually there is no negation.
>
> How should the negation of an imputation's
> Own nature not be an imputation?
> Hence, seemingly, this is
> The meaning of actuality, but not actuality [itself].
>
> In actuality, neither exists.
> This is the lack of discursiveness:
> Mañjuśrī asked about actuality,
> And the son of the Victors remained silent.[809]

Śāntarakṣita's *Ornament of Centrism* states:

> Since arising and so forth do not exist,
> Nonarising and so on are impossible.[810]

Therefore, it is clear that Autonomists accept emptiness as being free from speech, thought, and expression. If they did not accept it in this way, who in their right mind could call them Centrists?[811]

2a) The claim that Consequentialists generally do not even provisionally accept any valid cognition as the basis for negation and proof from the perspective of the disciples, and that they therefore do not express any such valid cognition, is not justified. In his *Lucid Words*, Candrakīrti defeats all Buddhist and non-Buddhist opponents by accepting the presentation of all four types of valid cognition that function as the basis for negation and proof (perception, inference, verbal testimony, and analogy)[812] and by commenting on them in detail.

2b) Specifically, Candrakīrti does not assert that any phenomena are established in the sense of operating through the power of real entities on either of the two levels of reality. However, when he engages in negation and proof, in accordance with the common consensus in the world and learned treatises that all entities perform their functions through their own intrinsic power, he expresses things in a way that follows what is acknowledged by others. It is only in this way that he extensively refutes others by means of valid cognition that operates through the power of entities. For example, take the consequence that it is pointless for something to repeatedly arise from itself when it already exists. For people with unquestioning worldly minds, this consequence works precisely and only through their assumption of the power of real entities. In order for the Enumerators to understand such a consequence of their own position, Candrakīrti formulates it in the above way and thus refutes that anything arises from itself. In this way, there are infinite such pronouncements by Consequentialists for the sake of invalidating all other such reasonings brought up by their opponents based on the latter's assumption of real entities with a power of their own.

2c) As a heartfelt position of their own, Consequentialists certainly never accept any probandum or means of proof that is grounded in any kind of real entity. However, from the perspective of others to be trained and in adaptation to what is acknowledged by others, in their very own words, both Buddhapālita and Candrakīrti extensively formulate the triad of subject, predicate, and reason in terms of an autonomous probandum and means of proof. For example, in the thirteenth chapter of his *Lucid Words*, Candrakīrti formulates an autonomous probative argument:

> Since they do not have a nature as they [seem], all conditioned phenomena are delusive, because they have the property of being deceiving, just like the water of a mirage. Whatever is real is not something that has the property of being deceiving, for example, nirvāṇa.[813]

So how is this formulated as an autonomous probative argument? Taking "all conditioned phenomena" as the subject, "are delusive" is the predicate of what is to be proven, and "because they are deceiving" represents the subject property. "Since they do not have a nature as they [seem]" shows that the reason of being deceiving applies to the subject in question. "The water of a mirage" is the example for the positive entailment of the predicate by the reason. "Whatever is real is not something that has the property of being deceiving" refers to the negative entailment (that is, the total absence of the reason in the opposite of the predicate), and "for example, nirvāṇa" illustrates this negative entailment.

Furthermore, from the perspective of others, Consequentialists *do* formulate the autonomous three modes of a reason. If they did not formulate them, even Consequentialists would not be able to generate in others an inference acknowledged by these others. The first chapter of *The Lucid Words* states what inferential cognition is:

> The consciousness that has a hidden object and arises from a reason that is unmistaken with regard to the probandum is inference.[814]

Here, the word "reason" refers to the subject property, and to say that it "is unmistaken with regard to the probandum" is the acceptance of the positive and negative entailment.

One might object, "These are not the autonomous three modes but the three modes that are acknowledged by others. Thus, through stating them in a way of accepting them as acknowledged by others, Consequentialists are able to generate inferential valid cognition in disciples." For a reasoning to be an autonomous reasoning, the Eighth Karmapa says, it does not matter whether others accept such three modes or not. When a debater generates an inferential cognition in another debater in such a way that the first debater himself or herself pronounces the three modes, then these three modes are autonomously or independently pronounced as such by the first debater and not in dependence on others.[815] Therefore, for Centrists, there are no three modes that are established through the Centrists' own system in the sense of an actual opinion of their own. However, when Centrists refute others in such a way that they themselves pronounce what is acknowledged by others as valid cognition with the three modes, it is obvious that they merely formulate something that has the three modes and is pronounced in this autonomous or independent way.

The gist of this is that we can distinguish between a mere nominal system of one's own in discourse and the general lack of an actual Centrist system of its own:

First, Centrists may be said to employ a rhetorical system of their own in the sense of what is explicitly expressed by the very words of Centrist debaters who verbalize what is suitable to be common consensus—that is, the subject property and so on in reasonings to invalidate others that appear in the minds of these Centrists themselves—whether this is already acknowledged by other debaters or not.

At the same time, Centrists lack any presentation of a Centrist system of their own that reflects their actual opinion on things. This is because any opinion of their own that they may express in the above ways as to a subject property and so on is not at all established on either of the two levels of reality through any valid cognition that is part of a Centrist system of their own.

A "system of their own" as expressed in the first way is voiced by Centrists as a mere nominal pronouncement of "a system of their own." It is not a system of their own with a certain meaning as its object to be expressed. If it were, there would be the flaw that Centrists have a system of their own, while it is the whole point of Centrism to eliminate any system building. At the same time, any attempt to refute the verbal statements of their opponents without at least voicing some nominal or rhetorical pronouncement of the three modes and such as "a system that is autonomously pronounced by Centrist debaters themselves" is only absurd. In other words, without saying anything, any possibility of even starting to debate with others is out of question. However, through their own mouths, Centrists *do* pronounce subject properties and so on, as found in the consequence "It follows that the arising of a vase is pointless, because it exists already" that is directed at those who assert that things arise from themselves. When Centrists pronounce this, it is indubitable that this is their system to put an end to the wrong ideas of others in the context of debate. Therefore, it is not true that Consequentialists themselves never voice the three modes as they are acknowledged by others as their own pronouncement for the sake of refuting the wrong ideas of others in debate. Otherwise, when Consequentialists and realists debate, that which makes the Consequentialist responses would have to be some inanimate sound.[816] This is the absurd consequence of the claim that Consequentialists are beyond any system of voicing their own pronouncements, for this means that the only possible activity of responding in a debate would have to be through pronouncements that are not brought about by any effort of beings.

Thus, in the context of debate, there are two kinds of "own system":

- an own system in the sense of explicit words being voiced as the debater's own pronouncement
- an own system in the sense of declaring some actual opinion of one's own to be a distinct philosophical system by way of this very system.

Taking it for granted that Consequentialists do not assert the second kind of system, through verbally pronouncing the first kind of "own system," they voice autonomously made pronouncements. Voiced in this way, this does not amount to presenting an autonomous own system. Thus, it is definitely suitable for Consequentialists to personally voice their own three modes.

In brief, even for Consequentialists, there is no problem with employing probative arguments per se or because they entail the three modes. This kind of reasoning is only inadmissible for Centrists if some sort of underlying ontology, epistemological grounding, or thesis in such reasoning is assumed as being established as part of one's own system.[817]

Conversely, the use of consequences in general is not a problem for Autonomists (not even for Bhvaviveka), as their texts amply show. In his *Commentary on*

*The Ornament of Centrism*, Kamalaśīla even says that the exclusive use of consequences in certain contexts is fine:

> As for [notions that refer to] some intrinsic nature of entities, are not common consensus, and are [just] imputed by others (such as space [as an entity that performs a function]), [they can be disproved] by adducing consequences alone. As for some intrinsic nature of [entities] that is common consensus, there is no flaw [in negating it] in both ways [through consequences and probative arguments], since others accept that all entities are [included] in the two sets of permanent and impermanent phenomena.[818]

The above passages show clearly that the way in which the distinction between Autonomists and Consequentialists is drawn hinges on what exactly is understood by "autonomous," be it in terms of reasoning or a thesis. Obviously, there is quite a variety in different masters' views, ranging from the Gelugpa "ontological extreme" of autonomous reasoning (entailing the three modes that are grounded in specifically characterized phenomena established through conventional valid cognition even for oneself) to the more "pragmatic extreme" that autonomous reasoning more or less means any probative argument with the three modes that is pronounced by merely following common logical consensus.

Another common claim is: "When Consequentialists engage in negation and proof, they must solely pronounce arguments as expressed by others, whereas they may not pronounce any reasonings of their own." This cannot categorically be said to be the position of Consequentialists, since Candrakīrti explains the following: Consequentialists may find themselves in situations in which they are not able to refute others through the obviously defective and insufficient arguments of these others (if these arguments were correct, Consequentialists would not attack them in the first place). In such cases, they must defeat the inconsistencies of others by employing justified reasonings that properly address these inconsistencies, and they must do so by formulating these reasonings in just the way that they appear in the minds of the Centrists themselves. Otherwise, if Centrists simply hoped that defective arguments would invalidate others and then voiced such arguments themselves, they would just be affected by the same flaws as their opponents. In other words, it is impossible to defeat defective arguments with these very arguments or other defective ones. Rather, it has to be clearly demonstrated that and how such arguments are defective, which is possible only through other, correct arguments that are not part of the opponents' flawed repertory. As the ninth chapter of Candrakīrti's commentary on Āryadeva's *Four Hundred Verses* says:

> Here, the opponents impute infinitesimal particles of earth, water, fire, and wind that do not possess arising and ceasing. Since they do not have any cause, just like a sky-flower, they do not have any existence. To establish these nonexistents as being impermanent through establishing their arising by [first] superimposing existence onto them is not reasonable, because an actual object that is a result is not established for oneself, and it is extremely absurd to accept something established for others as [one's own] argument. Since the opponents must be refuted by their accepting that entities are unreasonable [altogether], it is also not reasonable to accept something permanent as an actual object that is a result. Hence, [in such a case,] it is not reasonable to infer something from the position of others or to expose [its internal] contradictions, because [these two options] are solely expressed through something that is established for both [parties]. In any case, [some people] hold, "Since it is impossible to invalidate [the positions of others] by way of something that is established for both [realists and Centrists], invalidation comes about through an inference by what is established for oneself [only]." [However,] this just amounts to lack of skill in demonstrating the meaning. Those who are skilled do not demonstrate, through something difficult, a meaning that is easily demonstrated.[819]

The Karmapa explains the meaning of this passage. The Differentiators claim that the atoms of the four elements are unarisen and permanent. To answer this by saying, "They are arisen, because they are causes" and thus trying to prove their impermanence by way of establishing their arising is not reasonable. Since the atoms of the four elements that are imputed by others are not suitable as really existing entities in the first place, it is explained here that the subject in question is not established at all.[820] Based on the subject being unestablished, it is not established for the Centrists themselves that it is a cause that could have an actual result. Therefore, this cannot serve as an argument. If Centrists accepted something that is established for others as an argument despite its not being established for themselves, this would be very absurd. If one thinks that Centrists intend to counteract the systems of opponents through temporarily accepting something that is only established for others, one has to see that, generally, accepting something that is unreasonable and in this way wishing to put an end to the mistakenness of others is in itself very unreasonable. Some say, "As for expressing an invalidation of others, one needs something that is acknowledged through common consensus for both, since one is not able to generate a completely pure valid cognition in the continua of others through a statement that utterly lacks any certainty for oneself. It is necessary to generate definitive certainty about the meaning of such an invalidation in the opponents and thus to eliminate their wrong ideas precisely through this certainty." However, this just describes the kind of defective arguments that are acknowledged by others. Since there are many situations in which one, from the perspective of others, is not able to put an end to their wrong ideas through such defective arguments, it makes no sense to apply them in these situations. This is an essential point.

There are other times when it is not reasonable to use such defective arguments. For example, when Centrists themselves defend the Buddhist philosophical system and in this process refute non-Buddhists by verbally employing something that corresponds to what other, inferior Buddhist proponents say, they would denigrate what is established for Buddhists if they were to take the reasonings of non-Buddhists as valid cognition. Another example of this is the context of Centrists debating with Buddhist realists. Here, for those realists, there is no valid cognition acknowledged by others, let alone any autonomous valid cognition, that can prove really existing phenomena (such as the five aggregates). Hence, in all these cases, it is not reasonable for Centrists to accept any kind of valid cognition acknowledged by others. This is also explained in the sixteenth chapter of Candrakīrti's commentary on Āryadeva's *Four Hundred Verses*:

> Those who state the reasonableness of emptiness do not accept any arguments that are common consensus in other scriptural traditions, because they wish to demonstrate precisely the unreasonableness of these very scriptural traditions of others. Whenever debaters have a concordant view, both accept it as having a certain [identical] meaning. It is through this [acceptance] that it is suitable as valid cognition [for them], since logicians solely embrace meanings or philosophical systems that possess justification.[821]

When proponent and opponent debate about the suchness of all phenomena, through reasoning, they must both engage solely in such objects for which no invalidation through valid cognition is visible. But if they just speak out of clinging to the real existence of their own respective theses that they accept as valid cognition acknowledged by either themselves or others, there is neither victory nor defeat. Thus, whatever being engaged in the suchness of all things may be, it is definitely not the understanding of such debaters.

3) It is also claimed that "Consequentialists never debate in accordance with negation and proof in the system of Dignāga and Dharmakīrti" and that "Consequentialists accept the five uncommon features of negation and proof, such as consequences that expose contradictions." These two claims contradict each other perfectly. To repeat, the five features are:

a) inference acknowledged by others
b) consequences that expose contradictions
c) analogous applicability of the opponent's reason
d) nonapplication of the means of proof due to presupposing the probandum
e) not having an autonomous position

3a) From among these five, inference acknowledged by others is found in the system of Dignāga and Dharmakīrti, because it is the implicit proof by a consequence[822] that is able to generate an inference in the opponent. For example, Dharmakīrti says, "Whatever is connected to a multiplicity, is necessarily not a unity. Just as in the case of juniper in relation to different containers, you accept that also the generality "cattle" (which you consider to be a unity) is connected with a multiplicity of its own instances."[823]

3b) Consequences that expose contradictions are explained in the system of Dignāga and Dharmakīrti as the correct consequences that refute the theses of others.[824]

3c–d) The analogous applicability of the opponent's reason and the nonapplication of the means of proof due to presupposing the probandum are explained by Dignāga and Dharmakīrti as the answers in response to an opponent's seeming invalidation.[825] The two features (c) and (d) respectively demonstrate that the entailment and the reason are not established.

Thus, the claim that "the Consequentialist way of negation and proof is other than the system of Dignāga and Dharmakīrti" is unfounded.

With regard to the purpose of the four ways of reasoning (a–d above) in Consequentialism, *The Treasury of Knowledge* quotes Śākya Chogden's explanation:

> Through (b) consequences that expose contradictions, one counters the reasons that others accept with their unwanted consequences. Through (c) the analogous applicability of the [opponent's] reason, one produces certainty about the entailment of these consequences for the mental perspective of the other party through examples. Through (d) [the nonapplication of] the means of proof due to presupposing the probandum, one demonstrates that others are not able to iron out such a counter with [unwanted] consequences. Through these three consequences (b–d), one proves the subject property and the entailment, which are acknowledged by others, for the mental perspective of the opposing party. Following that, through (a) arguments acknowledged by others, an inferential valid cognition is generated within the perspective of others.[826]

To illustrate how Consequentialists may use these four kinds of reasoning, their application to negating the four possibilities of arising shall be demonstrated.

First, the Enumerators accept that things (A) *arise from themselves.* They say: "Only such things that exist already at the time of their causes arise, whereas previously nonexistent things never arise. For example, sesame oil comes forth from sesame seeds, because it already existed in them. The reason it does not come forth from sand is that it does not exist in sand."

In order to negate this, the above four reasonings ([a] through [d]) are used as follows:

(b) The consequence that exposes contradictions says: "For things as the subject, it follows that their arising is meaningless, because they are already present at the time of their causes."

The opponents might say, "The reason does not entail the predicate."[827] Now, (c) the opponent's reason is applied in an analogous manner: "Then it follows that the arising of things is endless, because —according to your objection— they can still arise, although they are already present."

They might continue, "There are two phases in the process of arising that are not the same. It is the vase in its state of being a lump of clay that arises, but the vase that is already clearly manifest does not, of course, arise again. Therefore, there is a difference between these two states of the vase in that it is either clearly manifest or not." The answer to this is (d) the nonapplication of this means of proof due to presupposing its initial probandum: "According to your initial position, the vase that is not clearly manifest in its state of being a lump of clay is also existent. "[828]

Finally, there follows (a) the inference acknowledged by others: "Therefore, inner and outer things as the subject do not arise from themselves, because—according to you—they exist already."

Second, there are many Buddhists and non-Buddhists who accept (B) *arising from something other,* such as that a sprout arises from a seed or a consciousness from its object.

(b) The consequence that exposes contradictions says: "From this it follows that seed and sprout are not something other through their respective natures, because the sprout arises from the seed."

If the opponents say, " The reason does not entail the predicate," (c) the opponent's reason is applied in an analogous manner: "Then it follows that deep darkness can originate even from bright flames, because—according to your objection—something can arise from a cause that is something other than its result through their respective natures."

They may object, "But there is a difference as to whether the capacity to make the result arise exists in the cause or not." There follows (d) the nonapplication of this means of proof due to presupposing its probandum: "Your objection presupposes your initial probandum that the sprout arises from something other, because—even if this capacity to give rise to the result exists in the cause—this does not change anything in cause and result still being something other."

Finally, we come to (a) the inference acknowledged by others: "Therefore, a sprout does not arise from a seed, because—according to you—seed and sprout are something other through their respective natures."

Third, the Jainas assert that things (C) *arise both from themselves and from something other.* They say, "That a clay vase arises from itself means that it arises from the nature of clay. That it arises from something other means that it arises due to a potter, water, and so on." The negation of this position does not go through the above four steps. Rather, it is already implicitly refuted through the above negations of things arising from themselves (A) or from something other (B), since it is nothing but the sum of the fallacies of possibilities (A) and (B).

Finally, others assert that the world and its beings (D) *arise without a cause.*

(b) The consequence that exposes contradictions says, "It follows that this world as the subject is not directly perceptible, because it does not have a cause."

If the opponents say, " The reason does not entail the predicate," (c) the opponent's reason is applied in an analogous manner: "Then it follows that even a flower in the sky can be perceived, because—according to your objection—it is something that can be perceived, although it does not have a cause."

They may argue, "In these two cases, there is a difference as to whether a given phenomenon has a nature or not." There follows (d) the nonapplication of this means of proof due to presupposing its probandum: "This presupposes your initial probandum, because the result—even if it has a nature—is still something without a cause."

Finally, (a) the inference acknowledged by others states, "Therefore, this world as the subject is not something that arises without a cause, because it arises sometimes."[829]

(3e) The fifth feature above—the claim that Consequentialists, in their own system, do not have a position—is not suitable as a distinctive feature of the Consequentialists' own system, because Consequentialists are free from saying, thinking, and expressing things like "This is our own system." Consequently, they do not mentally or verbally conceptualize, "We do not have a position."

In his *Commentary on The Ten Verses on True Reality*, Sahajavajra says that since there is no valid cognition, it is difficult to find entities that are to be proven or serve as means of proof. All of them are just seeming, not ultimate. Nevertheless, when engaging in negation and proof, Centrists do not just play around as they please but present valid cognitions according to the system of Dharmakīrti, the foremost among Buddhist logicians. Otherwise, one is not able to defeat what is unreasonable or to confirm what is reasonable. To merely follow this system does not mean that valid cognitions or their objects become established by their nature on either level of the two realities. Rather, it is like temporarily giving extensive presentations of outer referents for certain expedient purposes, while subsequently entirely uprooting any notions of such referents through progressively superior reasonings.[830]

The Eighth Karmapa also mentions certain Tibetan doxographies that distinguish Autonomists and Consequentialists on the basis that Autonomists assert the distinction between the correct and the false seeming, while Consequentialists do not.[831] Some people also say that this distinction exists as part of the Consequentialists' own system too, and some that it does not even conventionally exist in the latter's system.

However, all of these positions are unfounded. The Autonomists' own system too does not make the slightest difference in terms of being correct or false between appearances at daytime and appearances in a dream or between two dream appearances. Like Consequentialists, Autonomists also make this distinction not as part of their own system but only in accordance with common worldly consensus. This is expressed by Bhāvaviveka in his *Lamp of Knowledge*:

> All phenomena are equal to nirvāṇa. However, in order to realize the ultimate, many accumulations [of merit must be] gathered. Therefore, in accordance with this [purpose] and because it is [considered to be] the case in worldly conventions, [it may be said that] outer and inner entities are something correct in common worldly consensus. [However,] it is known that, actually, they are not correct. It [only] refers to the conventional level when it is said that "everything may be correct or false." The same is expressed by the Blessed One:
>
> > Whatever is known as existent in the world, that I too declare as existent. Whatever is known as nonexistent in the world, that I too declare as nonexistent.[832]

Jñānagarbha's *Distinction between the Two Realities* says:

> Although [phenomena] are similar in appearance,
> Since they are able to perform functions or not,
> They are correct or false.
> In this way, the division of the seeming is made.

> We even assert nonexistents to be effective,
> Just in accordance with the way they are imputed.
> [Buddhas] do not see existents as effective
> In any way whatsoever.[833]

His autocommentary explains:

> They are deceiving or undeceiving with regard to performing the function that corresponds to the way they appear. Having ascertained this, worldly people cognize water and such as correct and mirages and such as false. Actually, however, both are completely alike in their nature in that they lack any nature. . . . To be deceiving or undeceiving with regard to performing a function is just how this is according to common consensus, because such [being deceiving or undeceiving] lacks any nature too.[834]

Śāntarakṣita's subcommentary elaborates:

> One might wonder, "If distinct phenomena that are correct and false exist, then entities do not lack a nature." The answer to this is "Actually, both are completely alike." "How are they alike?" In that they lack any nature.[835]

If it were not that correct and false seeming phenomena equally lack any nature, how could it be justified that Autonomists, by using many examples for delusive things (such as illusions and dreams), prove that all phenomena are without nature? If all seeming phenomena did not equally lack a nature, such examples and the meaning to which they refer (the lack of nature) would be completely dissimilar. Furthermore, Autonomists explain again and again that all illusionlike phenomena of the seeming lack any really or ultimately established nature. As Kamalaśīla's *Stages of Meditation* says:

> Although what has causes is ultimately delusive, it simply arises, just like an illusion, a reflection, or an echo. On the level of the seeming, illusions and such dependently originate, but since they do not withstand examination, ultimately they are not existent entities.[836]

Hence, it makes no sense to claim the possibility of conventionally establishing this illusionlike seeming through conventionally valid reasoning, since both what is to be proven and the means to prove it lack any nature. So what should be proved through what?

Some people argue, "But Autonomists assert that seeming reality is established from the conventional perspective through conventional valid cognition, because they assert that the horses and elephants that are conjured up by an illusionist are established from the perspective of the visual consciousness that is affected by the illusionist's tricks through this visual consciousness itself. So why would they not assert that seeming reality is actually established in their own system?" Autonomists do not assert this, since there is no entailment in the above argument. In his *Lucid Words*, Candrakīrti has pointed out that if Autonomists were to say something like this, they would say something in which there is not only no entailment but entailment to the contrary. In other words, it is unreasonable to say, "Illusionlike seeming reality is both the means of proof and what is to be proven conventionally through conventional valid cognition, that is, correct reasoning." For it is said at the same time that all illusionlike phenomena do not have a nature that is actually or ultimately or really established. In his critique of Bhāvaviveka, Candrakīrti shows that in all the inferences in which Bhāvaviveka states reasons or subjects that are treated as real entities established through conventional valid cognition, it is precisely on Bhāvaviveka's own account that such reasons and subjects are neither established for himself (ultimately) nor established for his realist opponents (as mere seeming entities). Since his reasons are thus not reasons that are acknowledged as commonly appearing to both debaters, what is to be proven—profound true reality—and all means of proof collapse.[837]

One might think, "Since Autonomists state that 'ultimately or actually, all phenomena are not established,' why would they have to say that phenomena are not established conventionally?" Consequentialists say that this qualm does not make sense. If phenomena do not have any reality actually or ultimately (which is an all-inclusive qualifier), then they are not established through valid cognition conventionally either, just like the appearance of floating hairs for those with blurred vision.

The Karmapa says that it is due to Candrakīrti's extensive refutation of this feature of conventionally valid establishment in the Autonomist system that it seems that Centrists divided into the two great traditions of "Autonomists" and "Consequentialists." Therefore, he holds that the main difference between Autonomists and Consequentialists comes down to nothing but this. Based on this assertion by Autonomists, some Autonomist masters asserted that certain conventional phenomena (such as the ground consciousness) conventionally exist as something validly established through conventional valid cognition, while others asserted that they do not exist. Candrakīrti's refutation is then directed only against those who assert such existence.

In summary, the way that Autonomists assert the correct and false seeming is not different from the Consequentialist way of asserting these, because both types of seeming reality equally exist as mere unexamined appearances, and both equally do not exist once they are analyzed. This is clearly expressed by both Autonomists and Consequentialists. Of course, such masters as Nāgārjuna and Candrakīrti are well known for this stance of no analysis with regard to the seeming. It is, however, quite common among Centrists who are usually considered Autonomists too. For example, in his autocommentary on verse 21 of *The Distinction between the Two Realities*, Jñānagarbha says:

> The seeming is just as it appears. In this, there is nothing to be analyzed as it was explained [above with Centrist reasoning] . . . . We do not analyze this, but stop any performance of analysis . . . . Once the seeming just as it appears is analyzed, one arrives at something different. Therefore, only invalidation will come about.[838]

Also Śāntarakṣita's *Ornament of Centrism* includes "being unexamined" among the criteria of what is the seeming:

> What satisfies only when unexamined,
> Has the features of arising and ceasing,
> And is able to perform functions
> Is realized as being the seeming.[839]

Śrīgupta's *Commentary on Entering True Reality*[840] agrees, and Bhāvaviveka's *Jewel Lamp of Centrism* uses nearly the same words:

> Just like the aggregation of a banana tree,
> What has the characteristic of satisfying only when unexamined
> Arises from causes and performs functions.
> This is the seeming of ordinary people.[841]

The exact same point is made in *The Entrance into the Two Realities* by Atīśa, who is usually considered a Consequentialist:

> The seeming is asserted as twofold:
> The false one and the correct one.
> The first is twofold: [appearances of floating] hairs and [double] moons
> As well as the conceptions of inferior philosophical systems.
>
> These arising and ceasing phenomena,
> Only satisfying when they are not examined
> And being able to perform functions,
> Are asserted as the correct seeming.[842]

In brief, all Centrists agree that the seeming can only refer to mere appearances, as long as these appearances are not questioned. On this basis then, some Centrists (such as those just quoted) provide some seeming characteristics of these unexamined, seeming appearances, while others (such as Nāgārjuna and Candrakīrti) refrain from doing so. Thus, the distinction between Autonomists and Consequentialists by Tsongkhapa and many others that the former analyze and establish seeming reality conventionally, while the latter do not, does not apply. Neither the issue of no analysis nor the feature of whether seeming characteristics of the seeming are provided can serve as hard-and-fast criteria to distinguish Autonomists and Consequentialists. The inherent problem with trying to analyze and establish conventional seeming reality through reasoning and such is that this very process starts to shake the unquestioned ground of what we experience as seeming reality. In other words, whenever we try to establish the existence of seeming reality, we are already departing from or destroying it. If the analysis is carried through to its end, it naturally leads to not finding anything, which is to say, freedom from reference points. And if not, we get stuck somewhere in between mere unquestioned appearances and ultimate reality, thus creating a third "reality." This is why so many Centrists refrain from analyzing or even establishing seeming reality.

In the epilogue of his autocommentary on *The Entrance into Centrism*, Candrakīrti refers to the mistaken positions of those who say that what the Followers of the Great Exposition or the Sūtra Followers take to be the ultimate is respectively presented as the seeming by Centrists.[843] The Eighth Karmapa's commentary identifies those who make such statements as Autonomists.[844] What the two lower schools referred to assert as the ultimate are partless, infinitesimal particles and moments in time. However, the Karmapa says, it is simply impossible for Centrists to accept these as seeming reality. If anything, the imputations by these two schools represent just the false seeming as described by Autonomists. Therefore, not even worldly people assert them as part of their seeming reality that is the basis for the ordinary transactions of adopting certain things and rejecting others. Thus, what bigger mistake could Centrists make than accepting such things? This consideration likewise negates the two claims that "the Centrists who follow common worldly consensus agree in their presentation of the seeming with the Followers of the Great Exposition" and that "there are no Centrists at all who accord in their way of presenting the seeming with the Followers of the Great Exposition."

As for the Centrists of Yoga Practice, such as Śāntarakṣita, the Karmapa says, since they were not around at the time of Candrakīrti, he did not directly refute them. However, one should understand that, implicitly, their presentations of seeming reality are refuted both through the above consideration and Candrakīrti's section on negating the "Mere Mentalists." In this way, when compared to the Consequentialists, also the system of the Centrists of Yoga Practice is not the fully perfect system of Centrism. To sum up, in terms of their different ways of presenting the conventional seeming, one may speak of four kinds of Centrists: the three who adapt their presentation of the seeming to the three Buddhist philosophical systems just mentioned[845] and those who follow common worldly consensus.

## *The Actual Distinction between Autonomists and Consequentialists*

After having refuted the above mistaken opinions, Mikyö Dorje proceeds to present his own view on the distinction between Autonomists and Consequentialists. He states that there is no difference between the explanations of Autonomists and Consequentialists with regard to the expanse of dharmas or profound emptiness (the ultimate object to be observed). They also agree that the operational mode of the wisdom mind (the subject) that realizes this object is the mental peace of being free from all discursiveness. This should be evident from the great number of quotations from both Autonomist and Consequentialist texts that have been provided so far.[846] Thus, a few verses from Bhāvaviveka's *Heart of Centrism* shall suffice here:

> No conception, no consciousness,
> Nothing to be imputed, without example,
> Without characteristics and without appearance,
> Without thoughts and without letters—
> There is no seeing of something to be realized
> By the observing mind. Through this, it is seen.[847]

Autonomists and Consequentialists concur in that the Dharma Body refers to this wisdom not stirring from the great pacific ocean of the ultimate, nonabiding nirvāṇa, in which all the ripples of the operational flux of knowable objects and a knower are at rest due to complete freedom from any discursiveness of object and subject. This is what the disciples call Buddha or the Thus-Gone One, but actually it is completely beyond any object connected to terms or symbols.

> Since something to be realized
> By cognition about existence or nonexistence has been negated,
> The nonconceptual insight of the learned
> Arises in the way of no-arising.[848]

It is explained that Buddhahood is not only without conceptions but it even lacks the discursiveness of any flux of nonconceptual wisdom.

> Since all aspects of knowable objects are not established,
> There will not even arise
> A mental state that does not conceive anything.
> Those who know it say that this is unequaled, true reality.
>
> Since this is realized, the actual Buddhas
> Are those who lack any arising of cognition,
> Because [their minds] became awakened from conceptuality
> And unfolded through nonconceptuality.[849]

Nevertheless, when investigating for true reality by relying on the presentations of seeming reality with all its vast discursiveness, there are certain differences between Autonomists and Consequentialists as to their ways of conventionally presenting seeming phenomena. On this conventional level, Autonomists say, "Since all these experiencers perform functions (such as perception) with regard to all these phenomena, they are conventionally established as entities." In this way, they exhibit not only the innate kind of reifying clinging to entities but also the one through imputation. Still, this is very different from the realists' understanding of ultimately real entities that perform ultimately real functions. Both Autonomists and Consequentialists agree that any performing of functions that operates through the power of ultimately real entities as well as any valid cognitions through which such functioning is established do not exist in any of the two realities, because ultimately real entities that perform functions do not exist within the scope of knowable objects.

Still, when Autonomists present seeming reality, they say no more or less than that the seeming phenomena that perform functions operating through the power of illusionlike entities, as well as the illusionlike valid cognitions through which these phenomena are established, exist as such illusionlike phenomena. All presentations of any kind of seeming entities are given from the point of view that these entities are able to perform functions and bear certain characteristics. One can only talk about such entities in relation to certain causes and conditions that in turn perform functions and bear characteristics only through the power of still other entities that serve as the factors for presenting the former causes and conditions. Thus, as shown by the quotations of various Autonomists in the last section, they describe three main criteria for seeming entities that represent the correct seeming:

a) performing a function that corresponds to the way they appear

b) arising from causes and conditions
c) being satisfying only when not examined[850]

In contrast, the false seeming is something that appears but cannot perform a function that corresponds to the way that it appears, such as a mirage, a hologram, or the notion of permanent sound.

The intention behind this presentation is to eliminate the poison of clinging to inner and outer entities by accepting dependent origination and valid cognition that operate through the power of seeming, illusionlike entities. Because of such descriptions, in India Autonomists were called "the Centrists who establish illusion through reasoning."

However, even if it were just on the seeming level that such illusionlike phenomena were to operate through the power of seeming entities and were established through valid cognition, they would have to exist as such entities in an undeceiving way. If they really and undeceivingly existed as such entities, all seeming, conditioned phenomena would not be delusive. Therefore, it is internally inconsistent to accept phenomena that operate through the power of illusionlike entities as being established through valid cognition, because if an illusory horse were established through valid cognition that operated through the power of entities, this illusory horse would not be an illusion but a horse that was an autonomous entity. Hence, when adhering by means of valid cognition to the point that all phenomena are real merely in the manner of illusions, it is obvious that this involves a slight remainder of apprehending discursive characteristics. As Aśvaghoṣa's *Stages of Meditation on the Ultimate Mind of Enlightenment* says:

> Thus, [illusory appearances] satisfy when unexamined.
> Through examining mere illusions, one is deceived.
> The mind is an expression of illusion,
> And enlightenment is like an illusion too.
>
> Hence, once verbal expression has been relinquished,
> It is free from discursiveness, not seen by Mañjuśrī.
> Illusory [phenomena] are not mere illusions:
> If they were, they would not be established as such [phenomena].
>
> If they were established, it would follow
> That [such] illusory phenomena are [taught] in the scriptural systems of others too.
> Therefore, the illusory nature [of phenomena],
> Just like an illusion, is inexpressible as being "this."

and

Through specifications such as emptiness,
Limitless examples such as being illusionlike,
And the methodical approaches of various vehicles,
The nonabiding middle is illustrated.

Despite being illustrated, it cannot be illustrated.
There is nothing to be removed from it.
Even emptiness is empty of being empty.
In this, there are neither Buddhas nor sentient beings.[851]

Candrahari's *Jewel Garland* agrees:

If illusionlike phenomenal existence
And illusory wisdom Buddhas
Were illusions that are established through reasoning,
It would follow that they are not illusory but true.

If you say, "The unchanging is established as illusion,"
What is established through reasoning becomes untrue.[852]

One may wonder here, "Would it then not be the case that actual, true reality is not realized by relying on the dharma system of the Autonomists?" This is not the case. Although they do not entirely fulfill the intention of the Buddha and Nāgārjuna, they eventually do realize the actuality of emptiness (as what is to be proven) with regard to all subjects in question by way of reasons such as the freedom from unity and multiplicity. Thus, the difference between Autonomists and Consequentialists lies in the assertion as to whether such means of proof are or are not established as mere conventionalities. However, in the Autonomist system too, the mental states that adhere to probandum and means of proof being conventionally established are later naturally put to an end through the force of extensively and thoroughly becoming familiar with the Centrist view.

In brief, the essential difference between Autonomists and Consequentialists is as follows. In terms of a Consequentialist system of their own, there is no presentation of anything to be proven or any means of proof. Nevertheless, they pronounce negation and proof in accordance with the world for the sake of eliminating the imputations of others. In the Autonomists' own system, in terms of ultimate reality, there is also nothing to be proved nor any means of proof. However, in terms of seeming reality, through the justified presentations of what is to be proved and the means of proof as the technique to investigate for true reality, Autonomists pronounce particular negations and proofs that eliminate the imputations of others.

When Consequentialists engage in negation and proof, from the perspective of their opponents and as mere pronouncements that follow the common consensus of others, as they see fit, they may formulate consequences that either impel or do not impel an autonomous reasoning,[853] probative arguments with regard to the meanings of such consequences, or inferential statements by proving each of the three modes individually. At times, they also state positions and then prove the modes of these. However, by doing so, they do not become Autonomists, since they do not accept any of these utterances as real or established through valid cognition on any level of reality. Nevertheless—or rather, precisely because of this—it is completely fine for them to formulate any statement whatsoever that serves the purpose of dispersing the wrong ideas of others. From the Consequentialists' own perspective, all negations and proofs are as fleeting as a mirage dissolving in space. In verbally pronouncing such negations and proofs, they just follow others' wishes to dispel their own misconceptions. Unlike iron hooks used to direct elephants, such negations and proofs are not means to lead others somewhere against their wishes.

In this context, the claim "All that Consequentialists do is to draw absurd consequences from the position of others" overlooks the fact that, when explaining Nāgārjuna's *Fundamental Verses* in his *Lucid Words*, even a Consequentialist like Candrakīrti several times formulates the classical Indian five-membered probative argument (containing a position, a reason, an example, an application, and a conclusion)[854] as it is used by non-Buddhist logicians as well as Autonomists like Bhāvaviveka. Candrakīrti also provides an explanation of Buddhapālita's consequences with regard to the Enumerators' claim of things arising from themselves in affirmative terms:

> We do not see any purpose for something that exists to arise again, and we also see that it would do so endlessly. You [Enumerators] neither assert that something arisen arises again nor assert that it does so endlessly. Therefore, your argument lacks justification, and you contradict what you yourselves accept.[855]

Needless to say, when Candrakīrti employs such formulations, he always does so without any underlying ontological or real epistemological foundation. In general, all Consequentialist pronouncements in debate are exclusively made for the purpose of invalidating the mistaken ideas of others about true reality. To achieve this purpose, Consequentialists sometimes just employ absurd consequences and at other times describe things the way things are. The Consequentialists' approach of not claiming anything themselves and merely invalidating the positions of others is not a case of mere caviling or sophistry, since their intention is very different. As for people who have wrong ideas about true reality and consequently suffer, their minds are stuck in holding on to their own positions and reference points. It is from their perspective and for their benefit that all their positions are eliminated through justified reasonings that they themselves acknowledge. In this way, Consequentialist reasoning helps them to come to a point where they can give up all reference points and directly realize true reality on their own.

Moreover, Consequentialists are not the only ones who make statements that some of their presentations are expedient and just made from the perspective of others, while they themselves do not assert such. Dharmakīrti has repeatedly employed the same approach. For example, his *Commentary on Valid Cognition* says:

> This meaning of a term and a common locus,
> Although they do not exist,
> Are expressed according to common consensus.
> In entities, they do not exist.
>
> The presentations of properties and what bears these properties,
> Of what is different and what is not different, however they are,
> [Are given] without examining actual true reality,
> Just as they are common worldly consensus.
>
> It is on this basis alone
> That all proofs and what is to be proven are presented.
> For the sake of introducing [others] to ultimate reality,
> They were made by the learned.[856]

The same applies to Śāntarakṣita and Kamalaśīla, who many times explicitly say that certain reasonings they employ (which have all the formal elements of an autonomous inference) are only given by way of provisionally applying certain subjects, predicates, and reasons in such inferences, without any of these representing their own position. Such reasonings are employed on various levels of what McClintock calls "sliding scales of analysis." She presents a very clear example from Śāntarakṣita's *Synopsis of True Reality* and its commentary by Kamalaśīla[857] for this approach, which is the argument that "infinitesimal particles are not beyond the sense faculties, that is, they are perceptible, because they are the objects of the sense faculties." Here, Kamalaśīla explicitly states that he and Śāntarakṣita do not accept either the subject (infinitesimal particles) or the predicate (being perceptible) or the reason (being objects of the sense faculties), not even conventionally at respectively higher levels of their analysis.[858]

Some people might wonder here, "If Consequentialists give extensive presentations of the seeming while seeming phenomena are not established through seeming valid cognition even on this seeming level, does this not mean that seeming karmic causes and results, bondage and liberation, and so on never existed on the seeming level?" The answer is no, because Consequentialists pronounce these things according to the presentations of the seeming from the perspective of no analysis as these were provided by the genuine beings who strive for higher realms, liberation, and Buddhahood. It might be said that without karmic causes and results of the seeming level being established, no presentations of such seeming karmic causes and results are appropriate. However, there is no contradiction in this because, from the perspective of mental mistakenness, there indubitably appear many conventions for various approaches of doing certain things in certain ways and not in others, and these are undeceivingly experienced and common consensus in the world, although none of them is really established. As Buddhapālita comments:

> It is because of worldly conventions that [Nāgārjuna says]:
>
> > Everything is true or untrue,
> > Both true and untrue . . .[859]

Consider two children who read a comic book. One of them might say, "The guy with the long snout and hanging ears is Donald Duck, and the fellow with the yellow beak and white feathers is Goofy." The other may reply, "No, you are wrong. The one with the long snout and hanging ears is Goofy, and the other one is Donald Duck." To settle their dispute, they might ask their elder sister to tell them who is right and who is wrong. Knowing very well that both Goofy and Donald Duck do not exist and are just pictures in a comic book, she still answers in accordance with the common conventions of the world of comic books. Therefore, on this level, she cannot be accused of telling lies. Likewise, although the Buddha directly saw that the nature of all phenomena is emptiness, by considering worldly conventions, he declared some things to be true and others to be untrue:

> Whatever is asserted as existent in the world, that I assert as existent too. Whatever is asserted as nonexistent in the world, that I assert as nonexistent too.

The First Sangye Nyenba Rinpoche says:

> Although there is no establishment of seeming karmic causes and results through seeming valid cognition even on the seeming level, it

> is fine to present their existence as conventions in dependence on the perspective of the consciousnesses of those for whom they appear as if they existed as such causes and results. However, through just such a degree of imputed existence, seeming karmic causes and results do not qualify as something that actually exists on either level of the two realities. For, if they did, the discursive extreme of existence would not be a discursive extreme.[860]

Then, the Eighth Karmapa presents his own understanding of how the split between Autonomists and Consequentialists originated. Based on Nāgārjuna's refutation of things arising from themselves, Bhāvaviveka disagreed with Buddhapālita as to whether, on the seeming level, there is a need to establish for both the proponent and the opponent a seeming subject of debate through seeming valid cognition. In his defense of Buddhapālita, Candrakīrti explained that when Centrists debate with realists, not only is there no need for a common subject of debate that is established for both through valid cognition, but such a common basis for negation and proof is by definition impossible to establish for both Centrists and realists. Centrists, through valid cognition acknowledged by others, negate that there is any reality in a given phenomenon, whereas realists, through autonomous valid cognition, cling to this phenomenon as being real and try to affirm it.

So, if the very nature of any basis for negation and proof, such as a subject in question, is negated, how then can a subject of debate be presented? Obviously, it cannot be anything on the seeming level that either falsely appears (such as a mirage) or is falsely imputed (such as a real self). Rather, what is taken as such a subject in question are the mere appearances, such as a sprout, that appear due to fundamental ignorance and are accepted by the world as ultimate reality. For Centrists, these do not exist as actual knowable objects on any level of the two realities, but they generally describe them as "the correct seeming." This is the subject in question that appears from the cognitive perspective of the natural, unquestioning mental states experienced by everybody from shepherds to learned scholars. In this way, such a subject of debate is adapted to the perceptions and the thinking that are acknowledged by other debaters. Centrists only adopt such appearances as the subject in question for the sake of negating any status of reality that is mistakenly ascribed to it by other people. For Centrists, there is no other subject in question that would be established through seeming valid cognition as a part of their own system. Hence, no such thing can be taken by them as a proper subject of negation and proof in debate. Since the same goes for the predicate and the reason, none of the three modes of a correct reason can be established through their own system either. Consequently, there is nothing to be proven in any way through any kind of valid cognition of their own system.

In this way, any charges of incurring the flaw of the subject of debate being not established[861] are rendered pointless as well.

Of course, this does not mean that Centrists are not able to refute wrong ideas about really existing phenomena and real causality. Their approach here can be compared to the one of Buddhist realists. In their own systems, Buddhist realists do not assert that imputations such as the Enumerators' primal substance are knowable objects. Nevertheless, they take these mere imputations that are just acknowledged by others as the subject in question and then employ probative arguments for the sake of refuting the wrong ideas of others that such imputations exist as actual knowable objects.

The Eighth Karmapa quotes from Śāntarakṣita's autocommentary on *The Ornament of Centrism*:

> If one accepts that all phenomena are without nature, the subject property and so on are not established for oneself. Is it not therefore the case that the conventions of inference and something to be inferred are not established? So how does the one who makes the inference ascertain something? If no reason that proves that "all phenomena are without nature" is pronounced, this [statement] is not established, since there is no reason [for it]. Therefore, the desired purpose [of showing that all phenomena are empty] is not accomplished. However, if [a reason that actually proves this] is pronounced, this reason exists. In that case, again, it is not established that all phenomena are without nature.[862] Therefore, the desired purpose is not accomplished either. So, things look pretty bad here. Thus, [I say:]
>
> By setting aside the particular subjects
> That are the products of scriptures,
> It is to those entities that are common consensus
> For [everybody] from children and women to scholars
>
> That these entities of proof and what is to be proven
> Will be correctly applied without exception.
> Otherwise, with what words could answers
> About an unestablished basis and such be given?
>
> I do not negate
> Entities in their ordinary state of appearing.
> In this way, there is no disorder in presenting
> Proofs and what is to be proven.

> In fact, we engage in all conventions of inference and something to be inferred by casting aside the different subjects in question that are the products of mutually discordant philosophical systems. Rather, [our engagement] is based on those subjects in question, such as sound, that lie on the side of the ordinary appearances to the visual, auditory, and other consciousnesses of [everybody] from children and women to scholars.[863] Otherwise, the basis of the reasons of all those who wish to prove [the existence of] fire [through the perception] of smoke, or the impermanence [of something through its] being existent, would not be established, because the natures of subjects to be proven such as [the Nyāya-Vaiśeṣika notions of] wholes or properties of space are not established...
>
> One may wonder what need there is for these [terminologies] that are the common consensus of scholars, if the above conventions of proof and what is to be proven are also accepted by [everybody] else. This approach is only to express the flaws in the theses of others without considering any thesis of one's own. I too definitely do not eliminate the ordinary entities that appear for the eye consciousness and so on. However, if analyzed through knowledge and wisdom, just as in the trunk of a banana tree, not even a tiny core appears [in such entities]. Hence, I do not assert them ultimately. In this way, through not negating what appears, I engage without clinging in the conventions of proof and what is to be proven. For this reason, there is no invalidation whatsoever of the statement that all phenomena are without nature. As it is said:
>
> By not depending on ill clinging,
> Conventions are nicely established.
> By being learned in conventions,
> One is not ignorant about the meaning of the treatises.[864]

Jñānagarbha's *Distinction between the Two Realities* and his autocommentary also agree with this. He says that, apart from the aspect of simple, immediate appearances in the minds of both debaters, there is nothing on whose status the proponents of different traditions agree. Thus, those who take these plain appearances as the subject have to accept that it is only through employing reasons and such of this very same level of mere appearance that they can reflect on whether this very subject actually exists or not.[865]

In brief, the later Autonomist masters say that there are no theses or their properties and so on that are commonly established for both debaters. Therefore, within the context of debate, they take things such as apples and books that appear for the unquestioning consciousnesses of both debaters. The Consequentialists say that any autonomously established thesis or its properties and so on that are commonly established for both debaters are impossible. Therefore, within the perspective of debate, Centrist debaters adapt to their opponents by just verbally following the pronouncements of those theses and their properties that are voiced by these opponents. Except for Autonomists and Consequentialists using slightly different words here, the Karmapa says, the meaning of their statements is the same.

This means that, having made it sufficiently clear that mere appearances have no reality, Centrists can still go on to discuss these appearances, in the same way in which non-Centrists can talk about all the aspects of what appears for them. In this way, believe it or not, the Centrist approach is in fact very much down to earth, for how could we ever pretend to meaningfully discuss all kinds of metaphysical speculations if we have not even properly analyzed the status of what is right before our eyes? Thus, any philosophical analysis must start with what directly appears to us and then enter the reasoning process from there.

Is there any way to say then that these appearances are similar for Centrists and their opponents? Take an adult and a small child who watch the same movie on TV and then discuss what they see, the former being fully aware that nothing that appears in the movie is real and the latter lacking such awareness. (Of course, we may have experienced that it is sometimes exactly the other way around . . .) Still, if the adult wishes to explain to the child that none of what appears on the screen is real, there is no way to do so except by referring to these very appearances.

Other than for Buddhas or bodhisattvas in the meditative equipoise of directly realizing emptiness, dualistic appearances arise for all beings, whether they are Centrists or not. When not resting in such meditative equipoise, even bodhisattvas on the ten grounds have remainders of such appearances, although they immediately recognize them as the illusions that they are. The difference lies in the degree of their habitual tendencies to reify (or their complete lack of such tendencies). All ordinary beings are subject to the same type of fundamental ignorance about the nature of phenomena and thus experience illusory appearances. Thus, a mere intellectual ascertainment of all these appearances being empty is a necessary step but in itself is not a sufficient antidote to fully eradicate the deeply rooted ignorance that causes dualistic appearances to arise. In brief, dualistic appearances do not simply cease when emptiness is conceptually understood through reasoning.

When Centrists engage in debate with others, depending on the opponent, they may choose to talk on a lower level of analysis by seemingly assuming some grosser type of reality, be it external material objects or the level of mere mental experience. They may do so in order to eliminate an opponent's wrong views by starting with the most coarse notions, such as permanence, and then showing that all things are momentary and impermanent. Obviously, there are not too many people in the world with whom one can successfully talk right away about all phenomena in heaven and on earth being empty of any reality whatsoever. However, during the whole process of employing such provisional levels of analysis that may include what looks like autonomous reasoning to others, for Centrists it is never a question that all of these are merely skillful, expedient means to address people individually on the levels of understanding that they can manage, but these means are applied without ever reifying the techniques or the resultant understanding.

After all, exactly what appears to different people, in what way, and whether we see the same or not is not the point. Obviously, when the child in front of the TV analyzes and realizes the unreality of what appears on the screen, she does so solely on the basis of what appears to her own mind. Likewise, in Centrist analysis, the point is not to scrutinize the appearances of others but to focus on what appears for oneself and then analyze it as to its reality. What is to be tackled through this analytical process is solely one's own ignorance and delusion, which produces one's own experiences and the ensuing mental afflictions. What makes us suffer is our own reifying experience of our own appearances due to our own ignorance, not others' experience of what appears to them due to their ignorance. Consequently, if we wish to stop being ignorant, we must go through our own analysis based on our own appearances. All that others can do is to assist us in this job by providing the analytic tools (Centrists are happy to do so), but the actual understanding can only come about in our own minds through our efforts in applying these tools.

In brief, the Karmapa says, with regard to the manner of what is to be proven and the means of proof in terms of emptiness, the intentions of Autonomist and Consequentialist masters are not different, as they are all great bodhisattvas who have directly seen the actual nature of phenomena and wish to introduce all sentient beings to nothing but this nature. The only distinction lies in their slightly differing approaches as to how the correct view of the ultimate is generated in the mind stream and accordingly communicated to others. Just as skilled physicians eliminate various diseases by prescribing different sweet and sour medicines, all Centrists eradicate various kinds of reification through different ways of teaching the dharma to those who entertain specific reifications. Therefore, who could be concerned about these masters having discordant intentions just because of their limitless, specific ways of teaching the dharma? As Jigden Sumgön says:

> All assemblies of noble ones—the Buddhas, bodhisattvas, vīras, ḍākiṇīs, dharma protectors, and guardians in the ten directions and three times—are of one mind with regard to the profound expanse of dharmas free from discursiveness. Also, all the teachings that teach this and express the inexpressible are of one melody and one voice.

Finally, the Karmapa emphasizes that the Autonomist and Consequentialist approaches are both soteriologically efficient; that is, they are suitable foundations for attaining liberation from cyclic existence and a Buddha's omniscience.

Autonomists say that if phenomena are analyzed through reasoning that analyzes for the ultimate, there is nothing to be found at all, be it a basis for emptiness or any properties of which this basis is empty, the fact of being empty or not being empty, the nature of phenomena, or the bearers of this nature. Hence, all phenomena are the utterly peaceful absence of all discursiveness and characteristics. However, these appearances of mind and objects in their illusionlike nature cannot be negated through reasoning that analyzes conventions. Thus, by conventionally taking these appearances as the bases of emptiness, Autonomists assert that ultimately they are empty of all properties that may be imputed by Buddhist and non-Buddhist realists. They assert that all phenomena are empty of a nature of their own and that, from the perspective of perfect study, reflection, and meditation, or from the perspective of the meditative equipoise of the noble ones of the great vehicle, all discursiveness and characteristics are at utter peace. Therefore, this is greatly superior to any kind of emptiness asserted by realists and is definitely suitable to serve as the foundation for the path to liberation and as the remedy for the two obscurations.

However, if the Autonomist position is taken to mean that, conventionally, the appearances of mind and objects appear for the meditative equipoise of the noble ones of the great vehicle, then either these appearances would become the ultimate and something that withstands analysis or this meditative equipoise would be mistaken. On the other hand, if it were said that these appearances do not appear in this way, there would be the flaw of this meditative equipoise denying phenomena on the conventional level, since phenomena that conventionally are not empty are made into emptiness. In this case, the teachings on the definitive meaning (emptiness), the supreme knowledge of perfect study, reflection, and meditation, as well as the wisdom of a Buddha would all become causes that destroy entities on the conventional level. To think like this is thus not suitable and also contradicts what is accepted by Autonomists.

As was said earlier, according to Consequentialists, emptiness does not mean that phenomena are really existent before being analyzed and then are made empty through reasoned analysis, just as a vase being smashed with a hammer. In the same way, phenomena are not non-empty as long as the wisdom of noble ones has not dawned and then become empty once it has. Emptiness does also not signify that something first exists and subsequently becomes non-existent (such as a flame having died down), nor is emptiness total non-existence (like a flower in the sky). Consequentialists do not just contrive some conceptual emptiness, such as pretending phenomena to be empty when in fact they are not. Also, emptiness does not mean that phenomena are empty of an object of negation that is something other than these very phenomena, such as a vase being empty of water. All of these notions are not the actual emptiness as understood in Centrism, since they do not mean being empty of an intrinsic nature and thus are just various kinds of mentally contrived emptiness, emptiness in the sense of extinction, or limited emptiness. Therefore, none of these mistaken notions of emptiness is suitable to serve as the proper basis for the path to liberation or as the remedy for the two obscurations.

What then is suitable? All phenomena are primordially not established as any reference point for discursiveness, be it the four extremes of existence, nonexistence, and so on; the eight extremes of arising, ceasing, and so on; or the fourteen extremes of permanence and impermanence,[866] being empty or not empty, or real or delusive. Just this is conventionally labeled as "emptiness," "true reality," "suchness," and so on. It is suitable to serve as the foundation for the path to liberation and as the remedy for the two obscurations, since afflictive and cognitive obscurations originate from the reifying clinging to real entities. Once yogic practitioners realize that all phenomena are primordially free from all discursiveness, the entirety of reifying clinging to real entities is put to an end.

Therefore, conventionally, the remedy for all obscurations is to rest in meditative equipoise within this emptiness of all phenomena being empty of a nature of their own, which is the natural, true way of being of all knowable objects. This is the sun that outshines the darkness of mistaken views and the cure that eliminates the poison of reification. It is the quintessence of the Buddha's teaching and the supreme cause for gaining mastery over the five inexhaustible spheres of adornment of all Blissfully Gone Ones (enlightened body, speech, mind, qualities, and activity). Therefore, the Karmapa says, those who wish for liberation and omniscience from the depths of their hearts should engage in it through study, reflection, and meditation.

## *How the Distinction between Autonomists and Consequentialists by Later Tibetans Is a Novelty*

After his own description of the distinction between Autonomists and Consequentialists, the Eighth Karmapa presents the novel position of Tsongkhapa on this distinction by reporting the gist of what the foremost representatives of Tsongkhapa's system say. The statements of his two main students, Kedrub Geleg Balsang (1385–1438) and Gyaltsab Darma Rinchen[867] (1364–1432), are in accord with Tsongkhapa's own explanations in both his *Great Stages of the Path* and his *Essence of Good Explanations on the Expedient and the Definitive Meaning.*

Kedrub Je explains that for Consequentialists, even conventionally, there is no valid cognition that evaluates a subject to be evaluated as established through its own specific characteristics. From this perspective, a subject that is established through valid cognition as common to proponent and opponent is impossible. Nevertheless, they generate in others the realization of the lack of reality merely through inferences acknowledged by others and consequences. These are arguments that are formulated on the basis of two factors. First, in general, a subject is established through valid cognition for both proponent and opponent. Second, the establishment of subject, subject property, and so on through valid cognition is accepted in the system of the opponent. Autonomists identify what is unmistakenly found about something to be evaluated that is established through its own specific characteristics from the perspective of the object's own way of being.[868] It is in this sense that, based on a subject of debate that is established as appearing in common for the systems of both the proponent (the Autonomist) and the opponent, they formulate reasons to prove the predicate of the probandum about which the proponent wishes to make an inference. This is the meaning of an autonomous reason.[869] On what is ascribed here to the Autonomists, McClintock comments:

> This stipulation recalls the general principle of Indian Buddhist debate logic that the three characteristics of the evidence (*trirūpahetu*) in an inference-for-others (*parārthānumāna*) must be acknowledged by both parties to the debate. But on mKhas grub's reading, there is also the *added* requirement that the subject and other elements in the inference must be "established as appearing similarly." What is noteworthy is the insistence that even the *means* (i.e., the *tshad ma*) by which the elements of the inference come to be established for the parties in the debate must be established as appearing similarly. In other words, for mKhas grub it is central to the definition of an autonomous inference that the two parties *understand exactly the same thing in exactly the same way* when they assert that the subject and the evidence and so on are established by a *tshad ma*.[870]

Gyaltsab Je says that the system of the Autonomists is to engage in negation and proof based on what is established as appearing in common for both proponent and opponent by investigating the meaning of what is conventionally labeled as subject, predicate, and reason. The system of the Consequentialists is to engage in negation and proof based on subject, predicate, and reason being established through conventional valid cognition as appearing in common for both proponent and opponent, although there is nothing that is established through valid cognition when investigating for the meaning of what is labeled as subject, predicate, and reason.[871]

The Karmapa refutes these claims by initially entering into the style of formal debate. He says that, on both levels of reality, the great Consequentialist masters never asserted that subject, reason, and predicate are established through any kind of valid cognition for two reasons: First, they are neither established through the valid cognition of the reasoning consciousness that evaluates the ultimate nor through the valid cognition of the wisdom in the meditative equipoise of noble ones. Second, Consequentialists say that a valid cognition that evaluates conventions is not established as valid cognition on both levels of reality. The first reason applies because if what Kedrub Je and Gyaltsab Je say is established were established through such a reasoning consciousness or the wisdom in the meditative equipoise of noble ones, then subject, reason, and predicate would be ultimate reality. This latter reason entails the predicate, since this is what Kedrub and Gyaltsab themselves accept.[872] There is also no way for them to just accept this consequence.

The second reason also applies, because Consequentialists declare that they do not assert other-dependent, worldly, seeming phenomenal entities, such as subject, predicate, and reason, but speak of them from the perspective of the world. However, not only ultimately but even on the seeming level, they do not accept any claim that these seeming entities are established through conventional valid cognition as something that performs a function. As Candrakīrti's *Entrance into Centrism* says:

> It is not in the way of you asserting other-dependent entities
> That I accept the seeming.
> For the sake of the result, despite their nonexistence,
> By referring to the perspective of the world, I say, "They exist."
>
> [The seeming] does not exist for arhats
> Who have entered peace by relinquishing the aggregates.
> If it did not exist for the world in just the same way,
> I would not say, "It exists" in dependence on the world.
>
> If you are not invalidated by the world,
> Just keep negating this [seeming reality] that depends on the world.
> You should debate with the world about this,
> And later I will rely upon the one who prevails.[873]

Furthermore, Consequentialists do not say that there is a valid cognition that establishes subject, predicate, and reason as something that appears in common for Centrists and realists. Quite to the contrary, Candrakīrti's autocommentary on *The Entrance into Centrism* states:

> All these entities that are like reflections have neither any specific characteristics nor any general characteristics. So what perceptual or inferential cognition would there be [for them]? There is only one immediate perception, which is omniscient wisdom.[874]

His *Lucid Words* agrees:

> If there were any so-called certainty for us, it would have to arise from either valid cognition or from something that is not valid cognition. However, [such certainty] does not exist. How is that? If there were any [real] uncertainty, there would also be some certainty that depends on and serves as the remedy for this [uncertainty]. However, when uncertainty does not exist for us, how could there be any certainty as its opposite, since it does not depend on any other counterpart? This is just like [discussing] the short and the long horn of a donkey. Once there is no certainty in this way, for the sake of proving what should we come up with any valid cognitions? What would be their number, their characteristics, and their objects? Would they arise from themselves, from others, from both, or without a cause? We do not lose a word on all of this.[875]

In particular, on either level of the two realities, this master nowhere asserts that the entities of subject, predicate, and reason (that are established through a reasoning consciousness or some conventional valid cognition in dependence on the two realities) exist as being established in common with the world. Rather, he says:

> Nowhere did the Buddhas teach that "entities exist."[876]

It may be objected, "The Consequentialists' investigation for true reality means to eliminate the wrong ideas of the world based on pronouncements that are acknowledged by others in the world. Therefore, in just the way that subject, predicate, and reason (which are established through worldly conventional valid cognition) are established by the world, Consequentialists also must accept these as being established as something that appears in common to both parties." Anticipating such wrong objections, Candrakīrti already gave an answer in the sense that such a necessity to accept worldly valid cognition does not follow. In the context of investigating for true reality, all negations and proofs to ascertain true reality are not established through any autonomous or independent valid cognition, be it worldly or supramundane. At the same time, through the mere dependent origination of reasonable and unreasonable thoughts of the two debaters, the correct meaning is made clear through the elimination of conceptions that do not accord with the dharma. As *The Entrance into Centrism* says:

> If worldly [seeing] represented valid cognition,
> The world itself would see true reality,
> So what need is there for other noble ones, and what is the point of the path of the noble ones?
> It is not suitable for [the minds of] fools to be valid cognition.
>
> Since worldly [seeing] in no way is valid cognition,
> In the context of [analyzing] true reality, there is no invalidation through the world.[877]

What is seen by a mistaken consciousness cannot invalidate what is seen by an unmistaken consciousness, just as someone with no knowledge about jewelry cannot invalidate the knowledge of an experienced jeweler.

In particular, the same people claim, "When investigating for suchness free from discursiveness, one must definitely identify a subject, a predicate, and a reason on the worldly seeming level that serve as the basis for this investigation and are established through conventional valid cognition." Such is just a claim that does not consider the meaning of Candrakīrti's statement that all entities are not established through their nature. Moreover, it simply ignores Candrakīrti's explicit proclamation that, in the context of investigating for true reality, the bases for this investigation (subjects, predicates, and reasons) on the worldly seeming level are not to be analyzed as to whether they are established through conventional valid cognition. Rather, the valid cognition of a reasoning consciousness that investigates for true reality does not find that subject, predicate, and reason on the worldly seeming level are established through conventional valid cognition as anything other than true reality itself. It is precisely this fact of *not* finding something established through conventional valid cognition that invalidates the claim that such could be found. As *The Entrance into Centrism* states:

> If these [worldly] entities are analyzed,
> Apart from just being what bears the nature of true reality,
> They are not found to abide on the hither side.
> Therefore, worldly conventional reality should not be analyzed.[878]

His *Lucid Words* makes the same point:

> Hence, it is in this way that the understanding of things in the world is presented through the four [kinds of] valid cognition. These are

established in mutual dependence: When there are valid cognitions, there are referents to be evaluated, and when there are referents to be evaluated, there are valid cognitions. However, neither valid cognitions nor what is to be evaluated are established through their natures. Hence, let there be only the worldly just as it is seen.[879]

Actually, in the context of investigating for true reality, let alone establishing anything through conventional valid cognition, even when one engages in conventional negations in dependence on certain opponents through reasonings that analyze for true reality, there is an essential practical point. While investigating for true reality, it is crucial not to mentally engage in any negations and proofs with regard to the ultimate, and thus rest the mind free from all discursiveness of negation and proof. As *The Entrance into the Supreme Knowledge of Centrism* declares:

Both negation and proof are simply to be stopped.
Actually, there is no negation and proof at all.
When one has made oneself familiar with this mode,
True excellence will be attained.[880]

It is only from the perspective of worldly people who speak about perceptual and inferential valid cognition as it is acknowledged by these people themselves that Candrakīrti pronounces such valid cognitions. He just follows what these people say without examining it and then employs it as a basis for negation and proof in the investigation for true reality. However, even if worldly seeming subjects, predicates, and reasons were established through conventional valid cognition as things that appear in common to both proponent and opponent, his same text states that he would never use any such subjects, predicates, and reasons that are established in this way:

You might say, "This contradicts perception and such."
It does not: I do not negate
[Appearances] that [only] satisfy when unexamined.
Since they are just established as mere conventions,
They are not a position or a reason.[881]

One may want to ask Candrakīrti, "If no valid cognition to establish certainty is presented in your own system, how do you ascertain that all things are without arising from themselves and so on?" He answers in *The Lucid Words*:

Such pronouncements of certainty exist [only] for worldly people by way of justifications that are established for themselves, but not for the noble ones. "So do the noble ones not have any justifications?" Who can say whether they have or not? The ultimate of the noble ones is a matter of utter silence. Therefore, how should there be any discursiveness where there is neither justification nor nonjustification?[882]

A further question might then be, "However, if the noble ones, in this context of investigating for true reality, do not establish this profound reality through reasonings that are established through conventional valid cognition, by what means do they make others realize it?"

The noble ones do not pronounce justifications through worldly conventions. However, they [provisionally] accept the justifications that are common consensus for the world alone only in order to induce realization in others. It is precisely through this that they make worldly people realize [true reality].[883]

The Karmapa concludes his argument by saying that Tsongkhapa and his followers either did not gain certainty about all these extensive explanations by Candrakīrti or they even went so far as to claim that these are not Candrakīrti's words. In this vein, Tillemans's judgment on Tsongkhapa's own position on these issues can only be repeated:

It does seem that there is an overly baroque transformation of Prāsaṅgika thought largely due to the extreme reluctance on Tsong kha pa's part to take some of Candrakīrti's claims at their radical face value, and especially due to his own attempt to harmonize Prāsaṅgika philosophy with that of the logicians. In particular, in making Prāsaṅgikas adopt a *logician's* positions on things being established by pramāṇas, Tsong kha pa introduces into Candrakīrti's philosophy a kind of lingering deference to objective facts which I think a simpler and more literal reading of Candrakīrti just does not bear out. *It is ironic that Tsong kha pa, who more than anyone brought out differences between Svātantrika and Prāsaṅgika, read Candrakīrti as being de facto an adherent of Buddhist logic.*[884]

In line with the Karmapa, Huntington sees Candrakīrti being misrepresented in an even more general sense:

And so—in what amounts to a deeply ironic twist of fate—Candrakīrti was posthumously awarded highest honors from an orthodox scholarly tradition that could sustain its authority only by refusing to take seriously what he had himself insisted upon: Nāgārjuna is not in the business of providing rational arguments designed to substantiate, prove, establish, or make certain anything.[885]

As for the Autonomists, Tsongkhapa and his followers claim, "Autonomists conventionally accept that phenomena such as subject, predicate, and reason are established through their own specific characteristics from the perspective of the object's own way of being. They also accept that their being established in this way is what is found through unmistaken valid cognition." In his *Essence of Good Explanations*, Tsongkhapa specifies what he sees as the main support for his claim of Autonomists conventionally accepting that entities are established through their own specific characteristics (which is taken over by his followers). There, he quotes the following very problematic passage from Bhāvaviveka's *Lamp of Knowledge*:

> If you say here that "the imaginary nature, which is mental and verbal speech about what is called form, does not exist," this is a denial of [certain] entities, because it denies mental and verbal speech.[886]

At the same time, Tsongkhapa says:

> With regard to conventional existents, terms such as their "nature" and their "specific characteristics" are often also employed in Consequentialist texts, while terms such as "not being established through a nature of their own," "not arisen by nature," and "not being substantially established" abound in Bhāvaviveka's scriptures too. Therefore, they seem difficult to distinguish. Nevertheless, this [above] explanation [by Bhāvaviveka] on the meaning of the existence or the lack of a nature in terms of characteristics that is taught in *[The Sūtra] That Unravels the Intention* is the clearest source for [the fact] that this master conventionally asserts that entities are established through their own specific characteristics.[887]

To be sure, the above passage in *The Lamp of Knowledge* is found in the overall context of explaining *Fundamental Verses* XXV.24:

> Peace is the utter peace of all observed objects
> And the utter peace of discursiveness.
> At no time did the Buddha teach
> Any dharma to anybody.

What Tsongkhapa quotes is just a consequence drawn by Bhāvaviveka from what he reports as the position of a hypothetical Yogācāra opponent in terms of the three natures. This opponent says that it is due to the imaginary nature's lack of nature in terms of specific characteristics that one speaks about its nonexistence in the sense of lacking a nature. Bhāvaviveka's consequence in this quote then identifies the imaginary nature with verbal and mental speech, that is, thoughts. This in itself is already questionable, since the usual Yogācāra description of the imaginary nature does not refer to thought and speech themselves (which would belong to the other-dependent nature) but to the imaginary *objects* of thoughts and speech. But leaving that aside, Tsongkhapa claims that Bhāvaviveka's assertion of entities being established through their own specific characteristics is due to his rejection of the Yogācāra claim of the nonexistence of the imaginary nature in this consequence. By this, Tsongkhapa in effect says that Bhāvaviveka has committed himself to the opposite of what he rejects here, that is, to the imaginary nature existing *with* its own specific characteristics. However, Bhāvaviveka's rejection in itself does not imply anything about his own position, let alone the particular position that entities are conventionally established through their specific characteristics. In fact, he presents it as one of his main principles that none of his denials of the positions of opponents imply that he has to assert the opposite (or anything else). For, in both his *Lamp of Knowledge* and *The Blaze of Reasoning*, he repeatedly insists that his negations are nonimplicative negations.[888]

Moreover, just a little bit further down from the passage in Bhāvaviveka's *Lamp of Knowledge* that Tsongkhapa quotes, this very text explicitly says:

> Those who wish to demonstrate that imaginary referents (*don*) do *not* exist should assert the justified Centrist way stated by master [Nāgārjuna].[889]

Considering these points and Tsongkhapa's own admission that Consequentialist and Autonomist texts are difficult to distinguish, while he nevertheless is not shy in providing such an out-of-context quote as the clearest evidence for his own claim that Autonomists assert entities as being established through their own specific characteristics, one cannot escape the conclusion that there is simply no evidence for this claim at all.[890]

This is not just a minor or isolated point, but the crucial stepping-stone for Tsongkhapa's whole reinterpretation of Centrism and the Autonomist-Consequentialist distinction. For Tsongkhapa and his followers take precisely this nonevidence for entities being established through their own specific characteristics as the basis for spinning off the elaborations of most of their essential points in Centrism as well as their supposed consequences. It is consistently on the basis of this notion of "phenomena that are conventionally established through their own specific characteristics" that they explain the nature of autonomous arguments, the Autonomists' distinction between the correct and false seeming, the assumed ontological and epistemological differences between Autonomists and Consequentialists, Autonomists' failure to comprehend and negate the full range of the Consequentialists' object of negation, their differing views on emptiness, and the resulting superiority of the latter over the former.[891] As Tillemans says:

> Tsong kha pa gives virtually no other *arguments* worthy of the name to prove that the Indian authors themselves had the positions on customary truth that he attributes to them, although he does consecrate an enormous amount of energy to elaborating what these positions are and what consequences they entail. This is in a way very typical Tsong kha pa: as is the case for his doctrine of "recognizing the object to be refuted" (*dgag bya ngos 'dzin*), he seems to have elaborated many of his most fertile and sweeping philosophical ideas and interpretative schemes on the basis of the slimmest, and sometimes even misconstrued, Indian textual evidence.[892]

Even Hopkins emphasizes "how thin, even how flimsy the evidence is," but he takes this very fact as the basis for praising Tsongkhapa's interpretive skills. Instead of acknowledging that Tsongkhapa makes a lot out of nothing, Hopkins just follows Tsongkhapa in insisting that there indeed *is* subtle evidence for a difference in the view of emptiness between Autonomists and Consequentialists:

> More bluntly, one might say that the evidence for a difference in the view of emptiness between Candrakīrti and Bhāvaviveka is so thin that even great Indian scholars did not notice it. [893]

Through this, Hopkins even seems to support Tsongkhapa's own modest claim that there was only a single person in India—Candrakīrti—and a single person in Tibet—himself—who actually realized the true meaning of Centrism, implying that all other great masters in India and Tibet were too dull to get the supreme view in Buddhism. Quite absurdly, this would then apply even to the Buddha himself as well as Nāgārjuna, the acknowledged founder of Centrism. Pawo Rinpoche answers this claim with a question:

> However, if [it really were the case that] the teaching of the Blessed One Śākyamuni had liberated only one single human being in India and one single human being in Tibet, then what kind of enlightened activity of the Blessed One [for the welfare of all sentient beings] is this supposed to be?[894]

One more example of Tsongkhapa's approach here is the statement in his *Essence of Good Explanations* that Autonomists and Consequentialists differ in their views on emptiness. First, he acknowledges that Avalokitavrata, Śāntarakṣita, and Kamalaśīla do not state any difference in terms of identitylessness between Bhāvaviveka's and their own systems on the one hand and those of Buddhapālita and Candrakīrti on the other. Then, Tsongkhapa continues by introducing a certain passage from Candrakīrti's autocommentary on the epilogue in his *Entrance into Centrism.* He says:

> Candrakīrti asserts [here] that, since Buddhapālita has commented on the intention of noble [Nāgārjuna] just as it is, there is no difference between this [comment by Buddhapālita] and his own way of presenting the ultimate and the seeming. He explains that his own system diverges from the comments by other Centrists.[895]

However, Candrakīrti never mentions or quotes Buddhapālita in his entire autocommentary (neither in the passage Tsongkhapa explicitly quotes nor anywhere else), let alone makes the assertion about Buddhapālita that Tsongkhapa claims he does.[896] The passage in question in Candrakīrti's text reads:

> Except in [Nāgārjuna's][897] Centrist treatise, this dharma called "emptiness" is not expressed in an unmistaken way in other treatises. Likewise, the approach [Tib. lugs] that is found here and which I explained together with answers to objections by certain [other] approaches, in its conformity to the dharma of emptiness, does not exist in other treatises. I request the learned to gain certainty about this. Therefore, it should be understood that the statement by some people, "It is just what the system of the Sūtra Followers propounds as the ultimate that is asserted as the seeming by Centrists" is made only because of not really understanding the true purport of the subject of [Nāgārjuna's] Centrist treatise. Also, those who think, "What is propounded by the Followers of the Great Exposition as the ultimate is [propounded] as the seeming by Centrists" simply do not fully understand the true purport of the subject of [Nāgārjuna's] Centrist treatise, since it is not appropriate that the supramundane dharma conforms to mundane dharmas. Thus, the learned should gain certainty that this approach [here] is uncommon.[898]

Thus, Candrakīrti does not speak about a difference with regard to the actual view or even the realization of emptiness (that is, ultimate reality) among Centrists. First, he only says in a general way that, just as Nāgārjuna's unmistaken presentation of emptiness, his own approach (since it accords with Nāgārjuna's teaching on emptiness) likewise does not exist in any other treatises. (As in the case of Nāgārjuna, he does not specify these treatises, but most commentators gloss them as being the texts by other followers of Nāgārjuna.) Second, what Candrakīrti means by "his own approach" becomes clear through two points: (1) The two specific differences with other Centrists that he explicitly mentions in this passage both address—in his eyes—mistaken ways in which some Centrists present seeming reality. (2) In the next passage, he further glosses the supramundane dharma as "dependent origination." He has someone ask whether earlier commentators such as Vasubandhu, Dignāga, and Dharmapāla have rejected the meaning of the supramundane dharma of dependent origination as it is unmistakenly taught by Nāgārjuna and affirms that such is the case.[899] Hence, for Candrakīrti, the difference between him and other Centrists—as well as other Buddhist masters—obviously lies in whether seeming reality is presented as nothing but mere dependent origination (as Nāgārjuna clearly does) or as something reified, be it material particles or a really existing consciousness. The point is that, in the latter case, the inseparable unity of dependent origination and emptiness—seeming and ultimate reality—is missed.

Having been thoroughly trained in the Gelugpa tradition himself, Dreyfus concludes with regard to this issue:

> It is difficult to follow Tsong kha pa in his suggestion that the Svātantrika and Prāsaṅgika views of emptiness differ substantively. Tsong kha pa's analysis is extremely sharp but suffers from a real gap in credibility, which is well exposed by his critics when they argue that it is hard to believe that Candrakīrti, who was a relatively obscure figure until the tenth or eleventh century, is to be considered the main interpreter of Nāgārjuna, whereas the great Indian Mādhyamikas such as Bhāvaviveka and Śāntarakṣita, who are counted as Svātantrika by most Tibetan scholars, are dismissed as having only a partial understanding of Madhyamaka. This conclusion is unlikely, and Tsong kha pa's discussion does not seem to meet the high burden of proof it would require.[900]

Disagreeing with Tsongkhapa and his followers, the Eighth Karmapa and many others make it clear not only that Bhāvaviveka, who initiated the Autonomist system, nowhere explicitly asserts entities as being conventionally established through their own specific characteristics (a point even Tsongkhapa concedes) but that such is not even implied in his writings. The Karmapa adduces a number of passages from Bhāvaviveka's texts to support this. First, he says, if the Autonomists really claimed that the entities of the seeming level exist as specifically characterized phenomena, then how are the following statements in Bhāvaviveka's *Blaze of Reasoning* to be explained?

> [The aggregates and such] exist merely as imputed entities on the seeming level. As the Blissfully Gone One said:
>
> > The three realms are just mere imputations.
> > They do not exist as having the nature of entities.
> > It is those with bad conceptions who think
> > That imputations are actual entities.
>
> Likewise:
>
> > Form is like a ball of foam.
> > Feelings resemble bubbles.
> > Discrimination is like a mirage.
> > Formations are equal to a banana tree.
> > Consciousness is like an illusion.
> > Thus spoke the one who sees true reality.[901]

The same text in fact explicitly denies that entities are established through specific characteristics:

> Some say, "Entities definitely have a nature, because they have characteristics. Nonexistents, such as the child of barren woman, do not have characteristics." This statement is not established. As I say:
>
> I do not assert that entities have a nature
> Because of having characteristics.[902]

Moreover, if Autonomists accepted something that is established as a specifically characterized phenomenon, they would contradict themselves. Therefore, they do not accept this.

> Hence, the meaning of the reason is not established.
> It is even of opposite meaning.
>
> How is that? It has been taught earlier that entities are without nature. Hence, the meaning of the opponents' reason "because they have characteristics" is not established for Centrists, because all phenomena are without characteristics. [Consequently,] the meaning of this reason is even the opposite, since the meaning of the reason "because it is seen

> that they have characteristics" is the opposite [of a reason] in order to establish [entities] that are without nature, such as earth.[903]

If entities were established through their own characteristics, one would have to assert that, for example, solidity as the specific characteristic of earth is autonomously established through the actual way of being of earth as the object in question. However, this is also refuted by Bhāvaviveka:

> It is not suitable that the characteristic of earth
> Is characterized as solidity through earth itself,
> Since it is a cause for the body consciousness,
> Just as it is not suitable [to be characterized] as such through fire.
>
> This is the refutation that [characteristics and the basis to which they pertain] are one. It is not suitable that the characteristic of earth is characterized as solidity through earth itself, since [solidity] is [just] a cause for the arising of a body consciousness. This is just as unsuitable as, for example, the characteristic of fire being characterized as solidity through fire itself. . . . For example, how can you see that [someone in a monastery] is a disciple in dependence on a vase [to refill offering bowls], or a teacher in dependence on disciples? It is through carrying this vase that [someone] is characterized as a disciple, whereas it is by guiding disciples that [someone else] is characterized as a teacher [but neither of them is so characterized through themselves].[904]

Despite certain claims to the contrary, according to Bhāvaviveka, characteristics and the basis to which they apply are not different either:

> The characteristics of an ox are not asserted
> By the ox itself as a hump, a dewlap, and so on,
> Since they are imputed by a particular cognition,
> Just as the characteristics of a donkey.
>
> This is the refutation that [characteristics and the basis to which they apply] are different, . . . just as one is not able to characterize the characteristics of a donkey through an ox.[905]

Then follows the summary of refuting the existence of something that is found as a specifically characterized entity through unmistaken valid cognition by negating that any characteristic and the basis to which it pertains are neither the same nor different:

> So if they were one, how could anything be the characteristic,
> Since it does not characterize itself?
> If they are other, how could anything be the characteristic,
> Since one thing does not characterize something other?[906]

The same is expressed in Bhāvaviveka's *Lamp of Knowledge*:

> The nature of entities
> Does not exist in conditions and such.
>
> "Entities" are eyes and so on. "The nature" is their specific character.[907] "Conditions" are sperm and egg and so on. . . . Since this [nature] does not exist, whose conditions would these conditions be?[908]

Thus, there is abundant and easily understandable evidence in Bhāvaviveka's works that seeming entities are not established through their nature, their specific character, or their specific characteristics, nor are they established as existent through other conditions. Considering this evidence, the Karmapa wonders what result is expected by putting so much effort into repeatedly claiming that "Autonomists assert some specifically characterized entity that is conventionally established through the object's own way of being," although such an entity is nowhere to be found in their texts.

In the same vein, Gorampa's *Elimination of Bad Views* says:

> If Autonomists were to accept autonomous reasonings, since they must prove phenomena that are established through their own specific characteristics, . . . it would absurdly follow that Autonomists prove a phenomenon that is established through its own specific characteristics when they prove the position that consists in the negation of arising from the four extremes.[909]

The Karmapa does not quote Bhāvaviveka's *Jewel Lamp of Centrism*, but that text says again and again that all outer and inner entities are delusive and illusionlike. From causes and conditions that are mere imputations arise results that are mere imputations. On seeming reality, we read:

> "Seeming" refers to entities, such as form, just as they appear. These are "real" inasmuch as they represent valid cognition from the perspective of ordinary people and unmistaken worldly conventions.[910]

Thus, it is made clear that "validity" refers only to the mistaken perspective of ordinary worldly people. It is only in this context then that Bhāvaviveka's text *does* talk about specific characteristics, but exclusively in terms of mere appearances from this mistaken perspective as long as these are not analyzed:

> How is seeming reality?
> Seeming reality means to know
> The general and specific characteristics
> Of all phenomena to be known.
>
> When this seeming just as it appears
> Is examined through reasoning, nothing is found.
> The fact of not finding is the ultimate.
> Therefore, the seeming has to be understood [first].[911]

Thus, from the context, it is obvious that there are no entities that are established by way of their "specific characteristics," especially not through any valid cognition that is other or better than what ordinary beings perceive as valid. In a way, it is quite ironic that the only passage in Bhāvaviveka's writings that at least mentions the term "specific characteristics" (though not at all in Tsongkhapa's sense) is denied by Tsongkhapa and his followers as being authored by Bhāvaviveka, since they regard *The Jewel Lamp of Centrism* as the work of a later author by the same name.[912]

Also the Autonomist Śāntarakṣita, in the context of analyzing for true reality, negates the general category of mere entities that are able to perform functions. By doing so, he demonstrates the implicit negation of any instance of this category of entities, be it a generally characterized or a specifically characterized entity. This negation includes any entity of a valid cognition as the means to establish other entities. As his own *Commentary on The Ornament of Centrism* says:

> I did nothing but speak about all these [entities that are able to perform functions] in a pretentious way. However, when those with realization analyze what is free from all ability to perform a function, there is no such function whatsoever, because the ability to perform a function is a conceptual object. Otherwise:
>
> What is the point, if what is not able to perform a function
> Is examined by those who assert that it [is able to]?
> What is the benefit for lustful people to examine
> Whether a neuter has a nice body or not?
>
> Therefore, the learned say that "performing a function" is the defining

> characteristic of an entity. It is with regard to such [mere] appearing aspects of entities that personal and phenomenal identitylessness are taught and their opposite—any superimposed nature—is negated, since the result that is called "the welfare of persons" depends on exactly this to come forth. As for anything else, there is neither proof nor negation, since [all of] this is just something that is to be left as it is. Thus, do not think, "It has not been taught that all objects that are entities are identityless and so on."[913]

The Karmapa adds that there are many further statements in other Autonomist texts that the seeming does not exist as something real that is established through its own specific characteristics on the seeming level.

In her thorough analysis, McClintock clearly brings out the difference between Kedrub Je's understanding of autonomous reasoning and Śāntarakṣita's and Kamalaśīla's approach. She says:

> Śāntarakṣita and Kamalaśīla have a different understanding of autonomous inference, one that dispenses with the metalogical requirement that all elements in the inference be established as appearing similarly (*mthun snang du grub pa*) as mKhas grub understands this requirement. . . .
>
> mKhas grub's argument depends, in part, on the idea that the subject in an autonomous inference must be established as appearing commonly for both parties in the debate. And here, as in the commentaries, we find Śāntarakṣita and Kamalaśīla insisting that their Madhyamaka arguments are not open to the charge of subject failure precisely because the subject of the arguments appears in the awareness of both parties to the debate. But there is an important distinction between the two formulations of what it means to appear commonly, for mKhas grub rje specifically requires that the subject be established as appearing commonly according to the *philosophical systems* (*lugs*) of both the proponent and the opponent, while Śāntarakṣita emphasizes that inferences should be formulated "having *precluded* the various subjects that are produced through mutually incompatible philosophical systems." . . . Entities that have been qualified in ways that arise through philosophical theorizing . . . are purposefully and emphatically excluded from being the subject of a debate.[914]

McClintock calls the levels of Sūtra Followers, Yogācāras, and Centrists as they are used in the texts by Śāntarakṣita and Kamalaśīla "sliding scales of analysis." In their flexible approach, these Autonomist masters use different reasons when faced with different opponents, thus only provisionally employing certain subjects, predicates, and reasons on the respectively lower levels of analysis, which become gradually negated on the higher levels. This very approach is also clearly described by Mipham Rinpoche in his commentary on *The Ornament of Centrism*, where he explains the five special points of this text.[915] In this model of "sliding scales of analysis," just like the two preceding scales of Sūtra Followers and Yogācāras, also the scale of Centrist analysis clearly still belongs to the level of *conventional* analysis. As the Eighth Karmapa, Mipham Rinpoche, and McClintock point out, it is on this level that Autonomists deny any conventional existence (let alone ultimate existence) of real entities, be these material or mental, with specific characteristics or without. Thus, it seems that Kedrub Je failed to properly evaluate this system of different levels of analysis by these Autonomist masters. Tillemans comments:

> One of the most extraordinary ideas in Tsong kha pa and the dGe lugs pa tradition is that Svātantrika philosophers not only accept that customary things are established intrinsically, from their own side, etc., but in so doing end up in a very subtle way being *like* realists, i.e., "advocates of real entities" (*dngos smra ba*), and hence essentially in the same camp as all lower Buddhist schools and perhaps even non-Buddhists. Of course, Tsong kha pa is not saying that Svātantrikas *are* themselves *dngos smra ba*. Nonetheless, the *rapprochement* is very clear. . . . As we see in the quote from Tsong kha pa . . . the realist (*dngos smra ba*) and Svātantrika supposedly do not differ so much in their ontology, i.e., *what* they accept as existing, but instead on the level of truth to which this ontology is assigned . . . And in key contexts concerning the Svātantrika-Prāsaṅgika debates, the Svātantrika *are* regularly grouped together with the lower Buddhist schools under the designation *rang rgyud pa man chad* ("[thinkers] from Svātantrika on down"), these all being contrasted with the Prāsaṅgika. Odd as it may seem to us, Tsong kha pa and his followers, in effect, divided all Buddhist philosophy into two significant camps: realists and Svātantrikas on the one hand and Prāsaṅgikas on the other.[916]

In light of all this, one wonders whether Tsongkhapa still considers Autonomists to be Centrists. In his *Essence of Good Explanations*, he has someone ask this question and answers:

> These learned ones are also Centrists, since they negate the philosophical systems of really existent phenomena through many reason-

> ings and accept [phenomena] to be not really existent. This is not in contradiction to [Candrakīrti's] statement that it is not suitable for Centrists to employ autonomous [reasoning], just as it is not suitable for fully ordained monks[917] with vows to act contrary to these vows, but the mere [fact of] acting contrary to them does not necessarily mean that they are not fully ordained monks.[918]

If this example refers to monks actually breaking their vows in a repeated and intentional way, what kind of monks are they supposed to be? If the example means only committing minor infractions of the vows that can be restored, the differences between Autonomists and Consequentialists cannot be as numerous and substantial as Tsongkhapa usually claims them to be. It is noteworthy that here he focuses solely on their difference in methodology. After having emphasized their many ontological and epistemological differences at length (such as a different view on emptiness), he does not mention any of them here and downplays the single methodological difference of using autonomous reasoning as not withstanding the Autonomists' ranking as Centrists. Considered together, this is like saying, "I have shown you all the many big differences between a rubber duck and an actual duck, but the mere fact that the former makes sounds that are not typical of ducks does not mean that it is not a duck." Thus, Tsongkhapa does not really address the issue that the substantial differences he ascribes to Autonomists and Consequentialists seriously call into question the Autonomists' identity as Centrists.

To sum up, the Karmapa says that for Consequentialists there are no positions or arguments to be formulated with regard to any phenomena in the sense of entities that are established through valid cognition by either naïve beings or noble ones on any level of the two realities. Therefore, the Consequentialist system is free from taking up any thesis whatsoever. Nevertheless, many people stubbornly keep saying, "Since you Consequentialists do not take up any position, it follows that you say you have no position" and then proclaim, "In that case, this becomes your position." There is an answer to this. Since Consequentialists realize that no phenomenon or entity is established through valid cognition, anything to be expressed about such phenomena by terms or concepts is meaningless. Nevertheless, for the sake of eliminating the superimpositions and denials in terms of existence and nonexistence of others, Consequentialists wish to pronounce something by terms and concepts from the perspective of these others in order to invalidate their wrong views. In fact, it is solely for this reason that they pronounce anything at all. However, even during this whole process, they never think, "We do not take up any position." Thus, while not entertaining even the faintest mental flux, how could it possibly follow that they voice their not having a position as a position?

Some people might object, "For Consequentialists, there is nothing to be presented as a system of their own that is established through valid cognition. Hence, it must follow that there are also no absurd consequences for them that invalidate the positions of others, since they do not have any thought of wishing to pronounce these consequences. On the other hand, if they have such thoughts of wishing to pronounce consequences, there must equally arise in them the mental state of wishing to pronounce the positions that are the opposites of these consequences. And if such a mental state arises, there is no way not to take up by terms and concepts the positions that are the opposites of these consequences." This is not the case, since Consequentialists indeed have the wish to pronounce something for the sake of eliminating the wrong ideas of others. However, if there is no case of them taking up a position that is an expression of any wrong ideas of their own, what is wrong with that? When Consequentialists pronounce arguments or examples, this can be compared to a physician with clear vision operating on the eyes of someone with cataracts. The physician wishes to use a surgical scalpel to open up the patient's eyes, which are covered by turbidities, and in fact does open them. However, the physician, who has clear vision, does not need to have the wish to open her own eyes in this way.

Still, some people insist that the very fact of not having a position represents a position. In this case, the Karmapa says, why should they then not equally conclude that a nonimplicative negation itself is an implicative negation, or hope that the very fact of no rain falling is the falling of rain?

## *The Origin of the Controversy between Autonomists and Consequentialists*

The starting point for what came to be called the Autonomist-Consequentialist distinction was in fact rather limited. It is to be found in Bhāvaviveka's critique of Buddhapālita's way of commenting on Nāgārjuna's *Fundamental Verses* I.1:

> Not from themselves, not from something other,
> Not from both, and not without a cause—
> At any place and any time,
> All entities lack arising.

Subsequently, Candrakīrti defended Buddhapālita and rebutted Bhāvaviveka. It was only later in Tibet that especially Candrakīrti's statements were commented on and elaborated on very extensively.

### Showing That Buddhapālita Has No Flaw

#### Buddhapālita's Position

Buddhapālita's commentary on Nāgārjuna's verse starts with negating the first possibility of arising:

> Entities do not arise from their own intrinsic nature, because their arising would be pointless and because they would arise endlessly. For entities that [already] exist as their own intrinsic nature, there is no need to arise again. If they were to arise despite existing [already], there would be no time when they do not arise; [but] that is also not asserted [by the Enumerators].[919]

Buddhapālita briefly continues in a similar style to negate the remaining three possibilities. He says that entities do not arise from something other, because then everything could arise from everything. They do not arise from both themselves and others, since this possibility just combines the flaws of the two previous ones. They also do not arise without any cause, because, again, everything could arise from everything and all undertakings would be pointless.

The Karmapa's *Chariot of the Tagbo Siddhas* adds what is found in the texts of early Tibetan Centrists on the meaning of Buddhapālita's negation of the first possibility of arising. Whether Buddhapālita's phrase "entities do not arise from themselves" is formulated as an autonomous reasoning or as a consequence, in any case, it is a correct position to invalidate others. However, it is not a correct position in the sense of t something to be presented as the Centrists' own system. From the Enumerators' assertion that entities arise from themselves, it simply follows that such arising is pointless and endless, because these entities exist already, just like a clearly manifest vase. But the Enumerators cannot accept this consequence, since it is based on precisely what they seek to maintain. In an analysis of the above quote from Buddhapālita's text in terms of this consequence, the word "their" in his reason clause above ("because *their* arising would be pointless and because they would arise endlessly") should be taken as the example (a clearly manifest vase), the reason (already existing), and the predicate (such arising is pointless and endless), while the repeated occurrence of the word "because" in this reason clause is *not* the reason in Buddhapālita's consequence. The passage that starts with "For entities that already exist as their own intrinsic nature" is the detailed explanation of this. Simply put, it means, "Entities do not arise from themselves, because they already exist as their own intrinsic nature, just as the clearly manifest vase in front of us." Bhāvaviveka, however, has misunderstood this structure of Buddhapālita's statement.[920]

**Bhāvaviveka's Critique**

Bhāvaviveka's *Lamp of Knowledge* (his own commentary on Nāgārjuna's text) first presents his own probative argument to negate that entities arise from themselves:

> It is certain that, ultimately, the inner sources do not arise from themselves, because they exist [already]—just like an existent consciousness.[921]

This is the same basic argument as is implied in Buddhapālita's consequence, yet Bhāvaviveka goes on to criticize Buddhapālita's way of negating that entities arise from themselves:

> This [refutation by Buddhapālita] is inappropriate, (1) because he does not state a reason and an example, (2) because he fails to eliminate the [possible] flaws adduced by others [against him], and (3) because it is a [consequential] statement that affords an opportunity [for objections by an opponent].[922] The [third reason] means that, through reversal of the meaning stated [in Buddhapālita's consequence], a probandum and a reason with reversed meanings would appear. Thus, entities would arise from something other, because their arising would be fruitful and because their arising would come to an end. [However, this] would contradict [Buddhapālita's own] position.[923]

In an analogous way, Bhāvaviveka criticizes the arguments of Buddhapālita with regard to the possibilities of arising from something other and without any cause (he offers no comment on the latter's negation of arising from both).[924]

The Eighth Karmapa elaborates on Bhāvaviveka's criticism by asking whether, there being no arising of entities from themselves, Buddhapālita's formulation of "it being pointless" and so on is an autonomous probative argument or the construction of a consequence.

If it is meant as an autonomous probative argument, it is highly inappropriate as such because (1) it does not state the standard branches of a proof. These are the reason (as the subject property) that entities do not arise from themselves ("because they exist already") and an example that illustrates that the reason entails the predicate (such as Bhāvaviveka's own example "just like an existent consciousness"). (2) Buddhapālita's formulation is furthermore inappropriate because it fails to eliminate the possible flaws that may be adduced by others against him. These are the following two flaws with regard to the position and the reason. The Enumerators may say, "If you Buddhists mean to prove the position that 'something that exists as bearing the intrinsic nature of its result does not arise,' you just prove what is already established for us, since we too do not assert that existing results arise. And if you understand your reason to mean, 'because the arising of something that exists as bearing the intrinsic nature of its cause is pointless,' it amounts to a reason that proves the opposite of what you want to prove, since it is precisely what we say, which is that all that arises exists as its cause."

(3) If Buddhapālita's formulation is meant as a consequence, through the reversal of the meaning stated, a probandum and a reason with reversed meanings would appear. This means that such a consequence would imply that entities arise from something other, because their arising is fruitful and comes to an end. Thus, since Centrists do not set forth these three positions, such a consequence would contradict their position.

The writings of early Tibetan Centrists comment that it is Bhāvaviveka's and others' fancy to say, "Since a negation must necessarily imply its opposite, if arising from itself is reversed, there is no way not to accept arising from something other instead. This fact that a consequence implies its opposite is present in all philosophical systems." A good response to this criticism was given by the great Consequentialist master Mahāsumati, when he arrived in Tibet and was asked by Tibetan teachers, "Is the Centrist philosophical system good in itself?" He answered, "A philosophical system is called a view, and all views are precisely what is to be relinquished. Therefore, when Centrists do not assert that a consequence implies its opposite, they merely do not accept what pervades all foolish philosophical systems like an infectious disease. Thus, it seems that calling just this approach 'a good philosophical system' means giving it a bad name."

In the systems of those who, like Bhāvaviveka, accept an implicit proof by a consequence, such consequences would impel an autonomous argument as to the reversed meaning.[925] However, as for Buddhapālita's and others' pronouncement of invalidating consequences, since it is not connected with any wish to state the reversed meaning of such consequences, they cannot be reversed, no matter how hard one tries. This can be compared to a weapon that is hurled at a person, flies through space, and hits this person. Even if the person reverses the weapon and tries to hurl it back at space to hit it, the person will not be able to hit space. Thus, Bhāvaviveka's refutation of Buddhapālita was made without understanding the intention of the latter, who first simply considered, "It is implied in the Enumerators' position that entities do not arise from themselves, because this would be pointless and endless." However, once he had hurled the unwanted consequences as formulated in these two reasons at the Enumerators, Buddhapālita continued to invalidate the position of the Enumerators by formulating further absurd consequences using their other claims as reasons.

## Candrakīrti's Defense of Buddhapālita and Rebuttal of Bhāvaviveka's Critique

The first chapter of Candrakīrti's *Lucid Words* presents most of Buddhapālita's arguments above as well as all of Bhāvaviveka's critique of them. Candrakīrti's detailed rebuttal of Bhāvaviveka's position, however, focuses on what the latter explains concerning the first possibility of arising. This rebuttal, Candrakīrti says later, equally applies to what Bhāvaviveka explains concerning the remaining possibilities. The sections that follow here are based on Candrakīrti's text together with the Eighth Karmapa's commentary.[926]

*1) There is no flaw in not stating an example and a reason, since Centrists do not pronounce autonomous reasonings that are established through valid cognition as their own system.*[927]

Candrakīrti declares that Bhāvaviveka's entire critique of Buddhapālita is unfounded. He starts with the former's accusation (1) that the latter "does not state a reason and an example." He says that the Centrists' own system does not state a reason and an example that are established through valid cognition but that this is not a fault. He explains why by saying that the system of Centrists means to be free from all discursiveness—including valid cognition—on both levels of reality. This does not prevent Centrists from stating reasons and examples that are acknowledged by others, as will be explained further below. However, in the case of the Enumerators who assert that entities arise from themselves, it is possible to put an end to their wrong ideas by just confronting them with the internal contradictions of their position.[928]

"Arising from itself" means that the cause itself exists as bearing the same nature as the result and that it is this same cause that arises. To say that "entities arise from themselves, because they arise from being existent as themselves" is contradictory to the reason entailing the predicate, since something already existent is supposed to arise, which is pointless. And if what already exists were nevertheless to arise in this way, one should see its endless arising. These consequences cannot be accepted by the Enumerators, since they do not assert that something that has arisen is what arises again, nor that it keeps arising endlessly. Therefore, their position is both without justification and self-contradictory.

Thus, the Enumerators are challenged by just these consequences that demonstrate the internal contradictions of their system and have the same effect of negating arising from itself as the autonomous arguments and examples of someone who chooses the Autonomist approach. The crucial question here is whether the Enumerators, upon being confronted with the contradictions between what they want to prove in their philosophical system and the means to prove it, accept their self-contradictions. After all, the direct function of absurd consequences is to make one realize internal contradictions, while their implicit function is to make one drop a philosophical system that involves such self-contradictions.[929] However, if some opponents are so shamelessly stubborn as not to withdraw from their positions once they are confronted with the contradictions in those positions, they will also not withdraw from them even if provided with further autonomous arguments and examples that are established through valid cognition in one's own system. As Candrakīrti says, Centrists do not debate with the insane. Thus, by putting forth inferences that are established through one's own system, Bhāvaviveka just displays his fondness for such inferences even when they are out of place.

*2) Since Centrists do not formulate consequences that impel an autonomous argument of reversed meaning, there is no contradiction to what they accept.*[930]

For Centrists, it is inappropriate to make any autonomous inferences on their own account, because they do not accept any other theses either. In other words, Centrists do not posit any unmistaken consciousness that realizes something to be inferred that is established through some valid cognition in their own system. For they also do not accept any other thesis different from such unmistakenness, that is, something established as mistaken through some valid cognition in their own system. Centrists do not find anything that they feel could be presented as an inference that is thoroughly grounded in their own system. Rather, instead of seeing a need to present some—anyway nonexistent—thoroughly established inferences of the systems of others merely in order to find something that they could present as an established inference, Centrists always say that presenting such is categorically to be avoided. As Āryadeva's *Four Hundred Verses* explains:

> Against someone who has no thesis
> Of "existence, nonexistence, or [both] existence and nonexistence,"
> It is not possible to level a charge,
> Even if [such is tried] for a long time.[931]

Nāgārjuna's *Rebuttal of Objections* says:

> If I had any position,
> I thereby would be at fault.
> Since I have no position,
> I am not at fault at all.
>
> If there were anything to be observed
> Through direct perception and the other instances [of valid cognition],

It would be something to be established or rejected.
However, since no such thing exists, I cannot be criticized.[932]

In other words, if Centrists had any position of the nature of an existing or nonexistent entity being established through valid cognition on either level of the two realities in their own system, they would thereby incur the two faults of (1) not formulating a reason and an example and (2) failing to eliminate the possible flaws that may be adduced by others against them. However, for Centrists, the ultimate means freedom from all discursiveness and the seeming means mere appearances that are presented in contingency. Apart from this, on any level of the two realities, they do not have any position that is established through valid cognition in their own system as such and such. Therefore they are not at fault in not formulating a reason and an example for entities not arising from themselves. If, through the four kinds of valid cognition, there were any phenomenal entity to be observed as being established, there would be something to be established or rejected in their own system. However, since no such thing exists, Centrists cannot be criticized for incurring the above flaws.

*3) Since Centrists do not state reasons and such that are established through valid cognition as their own system, there is no need for them to eliminate possible flaws with regard to a position and a reason that are solely stated from the perspective of a proponent who has such positions and reasons.*[933]

As Centrists simply do not state any autonomous inferences, how could they have an autonomous thesis like Bhāvaviveka's that says, "The inner sources do not arise from themselves"? Against such a thesis, the Enumerators could well retort, "What does your thesis mean? Does 'from themselves' mean 'from the intrinsic nature of the result' or 'from the intrinsic nature of the cause'? If it means 'from the intrinsic nature of the result,' you just prove what is already established for us, since we too do not assert that existing results arise. If it means 'from the intrinsic nature of the cause,' it amounts to a reason that proves the opposite of what you want to prove, since we say that all that arises exists as the intrinsic nature of the cause." Centrists do not have to eliminate such flaws, because their pronouncement "Arising from itself does not exist" is merely meant as an invalidation of the assertion, "Arising from itself exists" as being something that is established through valid cognition in someone else's system. However, Centrists do not put forward a "nonexistence of arising from itself" that is in any way established through valid cognition in their own system.

Also, how could Centrists have the reason "because they exist already" (as stated by Bhāvaviveka) as something that is established through valid cognition in their own system? This would only involve the above flaws of proving what is already established or proving the opposite and thus commit them to struggle in order to eliminate these two flaws. But if they do not have any such theses or reasons, why would they have to eliminate any of their fallacies? If there is no harvest, there is no need to protect it from hailstorms. In brief, since Centrists are not susceptible to the above flaws alleged by others, Buddhapālita did not need to specify any answers to such flaws.

*4) Despite not making any assertions of their own, Centrists possess reasons, examples, and so on for the sake of invalidating the positions of others.*[934]

Someone like Bhāvaviveka might think, "According to the Consequentialists, since there is no thesis, reason, or example that is established through valid cognition in their own system, they do not state autonomous inferences. Therefore, they neither establish the content of the thesis that consists in the negation of arising from itself nor eliminate the position of others through an inference that is established through valid cognition for both parties in the debate. However, taking into account the need to explicitly express the contradictions within the positions of others that come about through their own inferences, it is precisely from the perspective of the opponents themselves that there must be a thesis as well as a reason and an example (for the logical entailment) that are free from possible flaws. However, Buddhapālita did not express such a reason and example that are established in his own system and did also not eliminate the flaws of the position. Hence, he incurs both the flaw of not providing a reason and an example capable of negating arising from itself and the flaw of not eliminating the above fallacies as under point (3) above that an Enumerator may bring up against his thesis of 'entities not arising from themselves.'"

Candrakīrti's reply is that none of these flaws applies to Buddhapālita. In debate, those (such as the Enumerators) who hold a position (such as arising from itself) out of the wish to generate a certainty in others that is just like their own certainty[935] must demonstrate to the other party the justification on the grounds of which the content of this position is understood. Therefore, it is the procedure of people who have philosophical systems that the proof of the content of a position (such as arising from itself) which is accepted by a certain person should be advanced by just this person. This means that, as the next step after the Centrists' statement of consequences, it is the Enumerators' task to eliminate the flaw in their own position that is exposed by the Centrists (who do not assert that something already existent arises). This flaw is expressed in the entailment of the predicate by the reason in the Centrists' absurd consequence, "It follows that entities do not arise from themselves, because they exist already" (which uses a reason and an example acknowledged by others). In other words, it is not the Centrists' job to provide some probative arguments—be they autonomous or just acknowledged by others—but the opponents' job to address the faults in their own position. However, when the Enumerators try to do so, it becomes all the more obvious that they do not have any valid reasons to eliminate the flaw exposed by Centrists and thereby prove that entities arise from themselves. None of the reasons that the Enumerators might adduce to eliminate their fault are valid reasons for Centrists. Nor are any of their other reasonings, such as "Entities arise from themselves, because they cannot arise from nothing. Hence, existents must arise from existents, as in the case of sesame oil existing in and coming forth from sesame seeds, while not existing in and coming forth from sand." Rather, since they have no reason or example for their own position that entities arise from themselves, the arguments that they advance to prove its content all come down to being nothing but this very position.[936] Since the Enumerators claim a thesis that is devoid of any justification either by sheer conventional, worldly standards or through logical reasoning, their reasoning is just self-deceiving. Consequently, their reasoning cannot generate any certainty in other persons that entities arise from themselves.

If Centrists thus do not put forward "their own" reasonings, how is the assertion of the Enumerators invalidated? Candrakīrti says that the clearest invalidation of their position is precisely the fact that they are not able to prove its content. So what would be the need here to point out its invalidation through an inference of the Centrists' own system?

Someone like Bhāvaviveka might still object: "Still, the fault of the Enumerators contradicting themselves through their own inferences must undoubtedly be expressed by Consequentialists like Buddhapālita." Although Consequentialists do not state reasons and examples that are established through valid cognition as their own system, it is not the case that they, from the perspective of others, do not pronounce reasons and examples that are acknowledged by others, nor do they fail to eliminate the flaw of proving what is already established for the opponent. In fact, Candrakīrti says, this is just what Buddhapālita did. What the latter had in mind was the following statement:

(1) "Entities do not arise from themselves, because they already exist as their own intrinsic nature, just as the clearly manifest vase that sits in front of us."

Based on this, he then made the well-known explicit statement in his commentary that was quoted above:

(2) (a) "Entities do not arise from their own intrinsic nature, because their arising would be pointless and because they would arise endlessly. (b) For entities that [already] exist as their own intrinsic nature, there is no need to arise

again. (c) If they were to arise despite [already] existing, there would be no time when they do not arise, [but] that is also not asserted."

So how does statement (2) teach the reason and the example of reasoning (1) that he had in mind? Candrakīrti takes the word "their" in the reason clause in (2a) to indicate the reason "they already exist as their own intrinsic nature" in (1). In fact, (2b) is Buddhapālita's commentary on his brief statement (2a). Also, (2b) implicitly indicates the concordant example (a clearly manifest vase) that is acknowledged by the Enumerators and possesses the properties of both what is to be proven (entities do not arise from themselves) and the means of proof (already existing as their own intrinsic nature). "Already existing as their own intrinsic nature" in (2b) identifies the reason. "Because their arising would be pointless" in (2a) identifies the predicate of what is to be proven (not arising from themselves) by drawing an unwanted consequence (that it is pointless for existents to arise again) from the opponent's claim to be negated (arising from themselves).

Take the following example of a classical Indian five-membered probative argument:

> [1, thesis] Sound is an impermanent phenomenon [2, reason] because what is produced is impermanent. It is seen that what is produced is impermanent, [3, example] just as in the case of a vase. Likewise, [4, application] sound is produced. [5, conclusion] Therefore, because of being produced, sound is an impermanent phenomenon.

In the same way, Buddhapālita too provides a probative argument:

> [1, thesis] Entities like vases and so on do not arise from their own intrinsic nature [2, reason] because it would be pointless for something already existing as its own intrinsic nature to arise again. It is seen that what already exists as its own intrinsic nature does not depend on its repeated arising from itself, [3, example] just as in the case of a manifest vase and so on. [4, application] Likewise, you Enumerators assume that something like a vase exists as its own intrinsic nature even in its previous state as a lump of clay. [5, conclusion] Then, for something that exists as its own intrinsic nature even at that time, there is no arising.[937]

In this way, the reason "already existing as its own intrinsic nature" is revealed in the above application (4). This reason is unmistaken with regard to negating that entities (re)arise from themselves. Through this reason (which is accepted by the Enumerators themselves), it is pointed out that the Enumerators contradict themselves through their own inferences. Therefore, how can Bhāvaviveka say, "This refutation by Buddhapālita is inappropriate, because he does not state a reason and an example"?

Thus, not only is it not the case that Buddhapālita did not state a reason and an example, but he also did not fail to eliminate the two possible flaws that may be adduced by the Enumerators. These two flaws are, first, that the reason is contradictory to what it is supposed to prove and, second, proving a position that is already established for the opponent. The first flaw is eliminated because the Enumerators do not assert that a vase, present in front of them and having the nature of being clearly manifest, manifests again. Hence, such a manifest vase is established as the proper example that concords with Buddhapālita's reason (in that it already exists) and his predicate (in that it does not arise again from itself). The second flaw is eliminated because what is to be proven here by Buddhapālita is specified as the negation of the arising of a *potential* vase whose nature—according to the Enumerators—it is to be unmanifest and to have the causal potential of producing a manifest vase. The negation of the arising of a potential vase is not what is already established for the Enumerators. Instead, they only accept the nonarising of an already manifest vase, but they assume that a potential vase *does* arise into a manifest vase.

Furthermore, the subject in Buddhapālita's unpacked probative argument is formulated as "entities like vases and so on." Since the words "and so on" include all entities that are asserted as arising, the reason does not contain the flaw of being uncertain by way of not covering all other entities besides vases.

In brief, this reason that negates that entities arise from themselves does not fall under any of the three categories of pseudoreasons (nonapplying, contradictory, or uncertain).[938]

Candrakīrti continues by providing an alternative probative argument to the same effect of negating that entities arise from themselves. This argument follows from the Enumerators' own description of the elements of reality. From among their set of twenty-five such elements, "the person,"[939] or "spirit," is said to exist in and by itself, that is, independently of the primal substance.[940] The remaining twenty-four elements are either this primal substance itself or just its various manifestations. Thus, the probative argument reads:

> The objects different from the person that the Enumerators claim to be arising from themselves (that is, from the primal substance as their intrinsic nature) do not arise from themselves, because they already exist as their own intrinsic nature, just like the person.

Not too surprisingly, a hypothetical Bhāvaviveka might wonder at this point, "Considering that Buddhapālita's original consequence does not state any of what you have said, how did you get to your analysis?" Candrakīrti answers that Buddhapālita's above statements are full of (implied) meaning (in that they rely on the actual meaning instead of mere words). They are of few words but great import. Therefore, their words contain the above-mentioned content and thus lead to these detailed statements about it. When explained, the original words yield the nature of this content. Hence, nothing of what was explained above should be regarded as not indicated by Buddhapālita.

*5) A reversed meaning of consequences is not related to the Centrists but only to others, such as the Enumerators.*[941]

Next, Candrakīrti addresses the third flaw that Bhāvaviveka ascribes to Buddhapālita (that the latter's consequence affords the opportunity for objections by the opponent). This means that the reversed meaning of his consequence becomes revealed, which shows in the appearance of a probandum and a reason with reversed meanings. Thus, according to Bhāvaviveka, Buddhapālita's consequence that "entities do not arise from themselves, because their arising would be pointless and because they would arise endlessly" implies that entities arise from something other, because their arising is fruitful and comes to an end. All of this, he says, is contradictory to Buddhapālita's own position.

Candrakīrti says that the reversed meaning of consequences is related only to the opponents (in this case the Enumerators), never to Centrists, because they do not have any position of their own (such as any of the four possibilities of arising). This includes not having any reasons to prove a position or any of the three modes of a reason that are established through any kind of valid cognition in their own system. So how should there be any contradiction to any philosophical system of their own? In fact, the whole spectrum of the many flaws of self-contradiction that come about for the opponent through the reversal of consequences is just what Centrists wish for. So how then could master Buddhapālita as a follower of the unmistaken system of master Nāgārjuna have made a statement that affords the opportunity for objections by opponents?

It might be said, "Since it is Centrists who pronounce these consequences, the flaws related to their reversal must be theirs too." According to Candrakīrti, if Centrists (who speak of the lack of nature of all phenomena) adduce a consequence for realists (who claim that all phenomena have a nature), how could there follow for the former a reversed meaning of the consequences that they stated, since they do not at all pronounce them out of the wish to imply their reverse? Words do not overpower their speaker, unlike people with sticks and lassos who could force someone to do or say certain things. Rather, inasmuch as words have the capacity to demonstrate a certain meaning, they conform to what the speaker wants to say. When Centrists adduce consequences that expose the opponents' internal contradictions, these consequences solely have the effect of negating the opponents' position. Hence, there is no reversed meaning of these consequences for the Centrists who pronounce them.[942]

*6) Nāgārjuna also invalidates the positions of others by mainly employing consequences.*[943]

Candrakīrti continues by giving examples from *The Fundamental Verses* to show that Nāgārjuna also eliminates the theses of others mostly by means of adducing consequences.

> Prior to the characteristics of space,
> Space does not exist in the slightest.
> If it did [exist] prior to its characteristics,
> It would follow that it is without its characteristics.
>
> If there were form apart from the cause of form,
> It would follow that form is without a cause.
> However, nowhere is there any object
> That is without a cause.
>
> Nirvāṇa is not an entity,
> [For] it would follow that it has the characteristics of aging and dying.
> There is no entity
> Without aging and dying.[944]

Nāgārjuna occasionally also negates the positions of others through an alternative method. For the sake of invalidating the theses of his opponents, he takes the meaning of a consequence unwanted for them as the probandum and then states how this probandum includes their own thesis.

> The Blessed One has said
> That any deceptive phenomenon is delusive.
> All conditioned phenomena are deceptive phenomena.
> Therefore, they are delusive.[945]

Candrakīrti's *Lucid Words* comments:

> As for deceptive phenomena, they are what appears as beguiling and mistaken, just like a circling firebrand. Through not being of a nature of their own, all conditioned phenomena are delusive, because they

are deceptive phenomena, just like the water of a mirage. What is real is an undeceptive phenomenon, such as nirvāṇa. Hence, due to the reasonings and quotations that were demonstrated, it is established that entities lack a nature, since [also] the *Prajñāpāramitā sūtras* say:

> All phenomena are empty, which is due to their mode of being of lacking a nature.[946]

The Karmapa adds that certain Tibetans say, "Consequentialists formulate consequences that negate the assertion that phenomena have a nature and make statements that establish such a negation. However, they never formulate probative arguments that establish the lack of nature [itself], because, if they did, Consequentialists would become Autonomists." Since there are many other instances such as the above in the words of Nāgārjuna and Candrakīrti, he says, these Tibetans should think well about the meaning of these words before making such unfounded and suspect statements of their own.

As for the absence of formal probative arguments and the use of consequences, Bhāvaviveka's own commentary says that the words of Nāgārjuna imply many probative arguments.[947] So Candrakīrti asks him why he does not consider Buddhapālita's consequences in the same way. It is Bhāvaviveka's own style of commenting on Nāgārjuna that implies the answer that Candrakīrti makes him give: "It is the approach of commentators to extensively formulate probative arguments." However, Candrakīrti retorts, this is particularly untrue in the case of Nāgārjuna, since the latter did not formulate probative arguments when he commented on his own *Rebuttal of Objections*.[948]

All of this is closely linked to the question of what kind of negation—implicative or nonimplicative—Centrists use. As was explained earlier, all Centrists agree that the negations that they formulate when analyzing for the ultimate are exclusively nonimplicative negations. This is explicitly stated several times in the commentaries on *The Fundamental Verses* by both Bhāvaviveka[949] and Candrakīrti,[950] even with specific reference to the negation of entities arising from themselves. This fact alone should already suffice to show that Bhāvaviveka's third flaw ascribed to Buddhapālita is unjustified. For Buddhapālita's consequences are clearly nonimplicative negations, which is underlined by the fact that he—just like Nāgārjuna—exhaustively negates all four possibilities of arising. Moreover, when commenting on Nāgārjuna's own consequences in *The Fundamental Verses*, Bhāvaviveka explicitly regards them as negating one alternative without implying any other or committing Nāgārjuna to their reversed meaning.[951] But when he turns to Buddhapālita's consequences, as we have seen, he takes the exact opposite stance. That Bhāvaviveka so obviously changes his way of evaluating consequences, depending on whether they were put forward by Nāgārjuna or

Buddhapālita, is hard to interpret as anything other than Bhāvaviveka simply treating Buddhapālita unfairly here.

As a final remark on this critique that Bhāvaviveka addressed to Buddhapālita, it should be noted that it was entirely focused on methodological questions in Centrism rather than on any issue of its content.[952]

### Showing That Bhāvaviveka Incurs Flaws That Contradict His Own Assertions

#### Stating Bhāvaviveka's Own Approach[953]

Candrakīrti says that Bhāvaviveka, simply out of the wish to exhibit his own great expertise in the treatises of reasoning, formulates autonomous probative arguments despite accepting the Centrist view. This approach becomes the ground for incurring a great many fallacies. Recall that when commenting on entities not arising from themselves, Bhāvaviveka had stated the following probative argument:

> It is certain that, ultimately, the inner sources do not arise from themselves, because they exist [already]—just as an existent consciousness.

#### Exposing the Many Fallacies in This Approach[954]

1) The fallacies in the qualification "ultimately"

To start, Candrakīrti asks whether the qualification "ultimately" in the above reasoning is meant to apply to the predicate or the subject.

a) The three fallacies if "ultimately" applies to the predicate

First, Bhāvaviveka might say: "I affixed this qualification because the Centrists' acceptance of arising on the worldly seeming level is not what is to be negated. Moreover, if it were negated, its negation would be invalidated through what Centrists accept, that is, arising on the level of seeming reality." Candrakīrti says that this is unfounded, because Centrists may talk about mere conventional arising, but any arising *from itself* is never accepted by Centrists even on the seeming level. He quotes from *The Rice Seedling Sūtra*, *The Sūtra of Vast Display*,[955] and *The Fundamental Verses*[956] in order to show that both the Buddha and Nāgārjuna refuted arising from itself in general without the specification "ultimately."

Second, it might be argued, "The qualification 'ultimately' is affixed in relation to the system of the Enumerators because they assert that, ultimately, entities arise from themselves." This is also unfounded, because the Enumerators' presentation is not accepted by the Centrists even on the level of seeming reality. Candrakīrti says that since the non-Buddhists deviate from correctly seeing both levels of reality, it is all the better the more one refutes them in both these respects.

The third and last try might be: "Ordinary worldly people say that things arise from themselves. Since this is not negated, the qualification 'ultimately' is used."[957] It is not correct that ordinary people think or speak in terms of things arising from themselves. All they understand and say is that "results arise from causes," without engaging in any analyses such as whether these results arise from themselves or from something other. This is also the way in which Nāgārjuna has presented this. When worldly seeming conventions are used, the seeming is not examined (such as analyzing from which level of reality things arise).

In brief, the qualification "ultimately" is meaningless in all these respects.

b) The fallacy if "ultimately" applies to the subject

If Bhāvaviveka made this qualification out of the wish to negate the arising of ultimately existing subjects (such as the inner sources) on the level of seeming reality, then he ends up with either the fallacy called "a thesis with an unestablished basis" as the subject or the fallacy called "a reason with an unestablished basis," because he himself as a Centrist does not accept these inner sources ultimately.

It may be objected, "The first of these fallacies does not apply, since the inner sources, such as the eyes, exist on the seeming level." However, if "ultimately" is not taken as qualifying the subject in question either, then what does it qualify? "Since it is negated that seeming phenomena, such as the eyes, arise ultimately, 'ultimately' qualifies the negation of arising." In that case, Bhāvaviveka should have said, "Ultimately, there is no arising of *seeming* phenomena, such as the eyes," but no such thing was stated. And even if the subject had been stated as "seeming phenomena, such as the eyes," it is still not suitable, because realist opponents such as the Enumerators claim that the eyes and so on are substantially (that is, ultimately) existent and not that they are imputedly (that is, seemingly) existent. Therefore, the fallacy called "a thesis with an unestablished basis from the perspective of the opponent" is incurred.

In brief, if "ultimately existing eyes and such" are taken as the subject, it is not established for the Centrist. If "seemingly existing eyes and such" are taken, the subject is not established for any realist opponent. In either case, the fallacy of a thesis with an unestablished basis is incurred.

2) There is no commonly appearing subject for Centrists and realists

As a consequence of the above fallacies, someone like Bhāvaviveka might then decide to simply drop all qualifications such as "ultimately" or "seemingly" and just take some unqualified subject (such as eyes in general) that is common to both parties. For him, in the inference that "sound is an impermanent phenomenon," mere generalities of sound and impermanent phenomena, but not particulars, are to be taken as the subject and the predicate. If particulars were taken, there would be no conventions in terms of inference and what is to be inferred in a debate between followers of different philosophical systems.

To demonstrate this for the subject "sound," if Buddhists take "sound that derives from the four great elements" as the subject, it would not be established for non-Buddhists such as the Differentiators.[958] And if the latter's notion of "sound that is a quality of space" is taken, the subject would not be established for Buddhists. Likewise, when people like the Differentiators or the Followers of the Great Exposition[959] hold the position that "sound is an impermanent phenomenon" and use "sound that is produced" as the subject, it cannot be established for the Analyzers, but if they use "sound that is manifest"[960] (as opposed to unmanifest), it cannot be established for themselves.

As for the predicate, if the impermanence of sound is associated with a kind of perishing that needs an extra cause apart from sound, it would not be established for Buddhists (who say that sound does not need additional causes for its perishing). If sound's being impermanent is taken to be its uncaused perishing, it would not be established for opponents such as the Differentiators.

Not surprisingly, Candrakīrti answers that taking a mere general subject as was just explained is unfounded too. In the context of an inference when the negation of arising is asserted as the probandum, Bhāvaviveka himself accepts the failure, through a mere mistaken mind, to find any entity (such as mere eyes) that exists as the subject of this inference, since mistakenness and unmistakenness are different. This means that the objects of a mistaken, conventional mind that evaluates the seeming (eyes and such) and the objects of the mind of a noble one that evaluates the ultimate (freedom from discursiveness) are different. Hence, in the context of a mistaken mind that takes as existent what does not exist—just as floating hairs are by those with blurred vision—how could even the slightest really existent thing be observed? Conversely, from the perspective of an unmistaken mind that does not superimpose anything unreal—just as floating hairs are not perceived by those without blurred vision—how could even the slightest seemingly existing thing, such as eyes, be observed? Needless to say, ultimately existing eyes and such are also not suitable to be taken as the subject, since they are not established conventionally, nor through a reasoning consciousness, nor through the wisdom of the noble ones. Therefore, Nāgārjuna's *Rebuttal of Objections* says:

> If there were anything to be observed
> Through direct perception and the other instances [of valid cognition],
> It would be something to be established or rejected.
> However, since no such thing exists, I cannot be criticized.[961]

Since mistaken and unmistaken minds and their objects are different, in general, there exists nothing mistaken from the perspective of an unmistaken reasoning consciousness that analyzes true reality. So how could there be any seeming eyes and such (as instances of what is mistaken) that serve as the subject in question? Consequently, neither the fallacy of a thesis with an unestablished basis nor the fallacy of a reason with an unestablished basis are removed by the unjustified suggestion to use commonly appearing generalities as the subject in question.

Despite all of these lucid words by Candrakīrti, the Karmapa adds that Tsongkhapa and his heirs—who moreover see themselves as Candrakīrti's main followers—still proclaim that "conventionally, entities that perform functions are established through conventional valid cognition for Consequentialists." They also say that "in the Consequentialist system, the subject, such as a sprout, that is taken as the basis for reasonings such as the freedom from unity and multiplicity, is real inasmuch as such a sprout's own performing of a function is established through conventional valid cognition. Therefore, this sprout is not the really existent entity that is the object of negation by the valid cognition of a reasoning consciousness. Rather, the object of negation that is to be negated by such a reasoning consciousness is 'real existence.' This is the profound and secret ear-whispered pith instruction." Conversely, they claim that others with wrong views and little merit, in particular the great early Consequentialists of Tibet, deprecate the Consequentialists' presentation of seeming reality.[962] However, the Karmapa says, these people are just like young fledgling owls whose eyes cannot bear the radiant, bright sunlight of Candrakīrti.

Moreover, the above example of a debate between two realists about general, unqualified sound is not comparable to a debate between Centrists and realists. In the example, a generality of sound and a generality of being impermanent (neither of which is asserted as being qualified in any way through particular philosophical systems) are indeed established as what appears in common to the minds of the two realist debaters. However, when Centrists who speak of emptiness debate with realists who speak about nonemptiness, the former do not accept even on the level of the seeming that generalities of eyes and such are established in common, let alone being established ultimately. Thus, there is no commonly appearing subject for the Centrist Bhāvaviveka and realists (ultimately existing eyes and such are not established for the former, while seemingly existing eyes are not established for the latter). Hence, the above way of exposing the fallacy of a thesis with an unestablished basis applies equally to exposing the fallacy that the basis of the reason "because they exist already" in Bhāvaviveka's original probative argument is unestablished.

In summary, the Karmapa says, what Bhāvaviveka takes as the basis of debate are seeming eyes as something merely seeming by way of seeming valid cognition.

According to Candrakīrti, this is contradictory to both valid cognition and what is accepted by all Centrists including Bhāvaviveka himself. If the seeming existed as entities that perform functions on the seeming level, this contradicts every Centrist's acceptance that all phenomena (that is, all entities that perform a function) are empty of their own respective natures. On the other hand, if it is asserted that there is an entity that is not established as a particular instance of either of the two realities while being established as its mere generality, then such an entity is excluded from the set of knowable objects through the perceptual valid cognitions and the common consensus of all ordinary beings and noble ones as well as through the detailed scriptural authority of the Buddha's words. This represents the essential dividing line between Autonomists and Consequentialists.

**Relating This Critique to What Bhāvaviveka Himself Accepts**[963]

What was explained in this way—that the subject and the reason are not established on either level of the two realities and do not appear in common to both parties—is in fact accepted by Bhāvaviveka himself. In his *Lamp of Knowledge*, a Buddhist opponent (a hearer) states the following probative argument:

> There definitely are causes that produce the inner sources, because the Thus-Gone One said so. What the Thus-Gone teaches in a certain way is just so, for example, [his statement that] "nirvāṇa is peace."

In this probative argument, Bhāvaviveka exposes the following fallacy:

> What do you assert is the meaning of the reason here? Do you mean "because the Thus-Gone One said so in terms of the seeming" or "because he said so in terms of the ultimate"? If it refers to the seeming, the meaning of the reason is not established for yourself [because you claim that the Buddha asserts the inner sources ultimately]. However, if it refers to the ultimate [consider *The Fundamental Verses*]:
>
> > When no phenomenon that is existent,
> > Nonexistent, or [both] existent and nonexistent is produced . . .[964]
>
> This refers to the elimination of any conditions that produce a result that has the nature of being either existent, nonexistent, or both existent and nonexistent. Therefore [the verse continues]:
>
> > This being so, how is it feasible
> > For a cause to be a producer?

> The meaning of this statement [by Nāgārjuna] is that what [ultimately exists] is definitely not a cause that produces something. Hence, since ultimately something produced and a producer are not established, your reason is either not established in meaning [when referring to the ultimate] or contradictory in meaning [when referring to the seeming].[965]

Through this examination in terms of the two realities, Bhāvaviveka has exposed the fallacy of the reason being neither established for the hearers themselves nor for Centrists like him.

The gist of this is as follows. For the assumed existence of causes for the inner sources, the hearers give as a reason only "because the Thus-Gone One said so." However, according to Bhāvaviveka, in terms of either of the two realities, there is nothing to be stated as a reason that says only that much (that is, a reason that is unqualified in terms of referring to the seeming or the ultimate level). Likewise, Candrakīrti says that Bhāvaviveka tries to state a subject that is only "the inner sources" and a reason that is only "because they exist already." However, again, in terms of either of the two realities, there is nothing to be stated as such an unqualified subject or reason. Consequently, it is highly self-contradictory for Bhāvaviveka to state such subjects and reasons, saying that a seeming subject and a reason that are established through seeming valid cognition on the seeming level exist as something that appears in common for both parties. Just as Bhāvaviveka himself tells the hearers that the scriptures in which the Buddha spoke of the existence of the inner sources are not commonly established for him and them, Candrakīrti denies Bhāvaviveka's claim that his subject and reason exist as something commonly established for both him and his realist opponents.

How then is it to be understood that Consequentialists themselves pronounce subjects such as "the inner sources" and reasons such as "because they exist already" as parts of their statements from the perspective of the Enumerators, doing so for the sake of relinquishing the latter's superimpositions and denials with regard to true reality? Do Centrists pronounce such subjects and reasons by taking them as generalities without differentiating them in terms of the two realities or as particulars by differentiating them in this way? The answer is not too hard to guess. Of course, Consequentialists do not pronounce subjects and reasons in either of these ways, because they pronounce the parts of their statements by strictly following the dance steps in the unquestioned choreography of debate as it is acknowledged by others. The Karmapa compares this to the following example. When a human person meets a person that is just a magical creation and when the human person, through acting in certain ways, makes the magically created person cut off her own head with her own weapon, then the head of this magically created person was obviously not cut off by any weapon of the human person at all, much less was such a weapon a general weapon that is not differentiated in terms of the two realities or a particular weapon that is so differentiated.

Candrakīrti continues that, since Bhāvaviveka himself has accepted the nonestablishment of the reason through his critique of the hearers' above probative argument, the same fallacy applies to all of Bhāvaviveka's own probative arguments as well. In all inferences in which he states reasons or subjects that are treated as real entities, it is precisely on his own account that such reasons and subjects are neither established for himself (ultimately) nor for his realist opponents (as mere seeming entities). Since his reasons are thus not reasons that are established as commonly appearing to both debaters, what is to be proven—profound true reality—and all means of proof collapse.

Take the following examples of probative arguments in Bhāvaviveka's *Lamp of Knowledge*:

> Ultimately, the inner sources do not arise from their conditions that are other [than them] because of being other, just as a vase.
>
> The producers of the inner sources such as the eyes—which others intend to express as ultimately [existent]—are ascertained as not being conditions because of being other [than the inner sources], just as yarn.[966]

In these probative arguments, the reason "being other" and so on are (ultimately) not established for Bhāvaviveka himself.

In another case, an opponent says:

> Inner entities [that is, the sources such as the eyes] are definitely arisen, because specific conventional expressions for the [persons] whose [appearance] involves the objects [visual form and so on] of these [sources] are used [such as "people sit" or "they go"].

Wanting to expose the nonestablishment of the above reason stated by the opponent, Bhāvaviveka says:

> [If your reason refers to the level of seeming reality, it is not established for yourself as a realist.] If, ultimately, arising, going, and so on were established as existent for a yogin in meditative equipoise who, through the eye of supreme knowledge, sees the real nature of entities just as it is, then the [above] reason—"because specific conventional expressions for the [persons] whose [appearance] involves the objects [visual form and so on] of these [sources] are used [such as 'people sit'

> or 'they go']"—is unestablished in meaning, because going is likewise negated through precisely the negation of arising [in *The Fundamental Verses* that precedes it].[967]

On account of just this analytical approach, the same is to be applied to Bhāvaviveka's own probative arguments:

> Ultimately, what is not yet gone over is not being gone over [right now] because of being a [not-gone-over] path, just like the path already gone over.[968]

Here, the reason "being a [not-gone-over] path" is ultimately not established for Bhāvaviveka himself.

The same applies to the following probative arguments in Bhāvaviveka's *Lamp of Knowledge*:

> Ultimately, an eye that is operative [as the medium of a visual consciousness] does not see forms because of being an eye sense faculty, just like an inoperative [eye sense faculty when asleep].[969]

and his *Heart of Centrism*:

> The eye does not see form, because it derives from the elements, just as its own form.[970]
>
> Earth is not hard in nature, because it is an element, just as wind.[971]

Also, in Bhāvaviveka's original probative argument, the reason is uncertain:

> It is certain that, ultimately, the inner sources do not arise from themselves, because they exist [already]—just as an existent consciousness.

The reason is uncertain because the entailment of the predicate by the reason is dubitable for his opponents, the Enumerators. For they might wonder, "Is it that the inner sources do not arise from themselves because they exist already, just as consciousness exists, or is it that they do arise from themselves, just like vases and such?"

Bhāvaviveka might say, "Although it is not explicitly stated as the probandum that vases and such do not arise from themselves, they are equally—that is, implicitly—established as not arising from themselves, because they exist already. Hence, there is no uncertainty of the reason." However, this is not so, because

Bhāvaviveka stated only the inner sources as the subject, but not any outer sources, such as vases.

In brief, all these fallacies are not incurred by Bhāvaviveka merely because he employs such reasonings (we saw that Nāgārjuna and Candrakīrti do as well), but because he takes them to be probative arguments whose elements (the subject and so on) as well as the relationships between these elements (the three modes) are established as appearing similarly to both parties.

### Showing That Candrakīrti Incurs No Flaws of Internal Contradiction[972]

Bhāvaviveka and others might object here, "The very fallacies that Candrakīrti ascribes to Bhāvaviveka's inferences equally apply to his own inferences. These equally must obtain the fallacies of an unestablished basis and an unestablished reason and so on. Thus, what represents a fallacy for both Candrakīrti and Bhāvaviveka should not be used as an objection against just one of them, which means that all these fallacies adduced against Bhāvaviveka are unfounded."

Candrakīrti answers that these flaws of the subject and the reason not being commonly established through valid cognition apply only to those who employ autonomous inferences in which the subject property and the entailment are commonly established through valid cognition, but not to Consequentialists like himself. If Consequentialists do not formulate inferences that are established through valid cognition in their own system, they would not even in their dreams formulate any autonomous inferences that are established through valid cognition in common with anybody else's system, since the inferences of Consequentialists have the effect of merely negating the positions of others. This means that these inferences are invalidating consequences that cut through all kinds of superimpositions and denials in the minds of others, while the minds of true Centrists, when pronouncing such statements, remain throughout free from all discursiveness of wishing to express anything that is to be understood or causes understanding.

How then do Consequentialists pronounce such inferences that are consequences to invalidate the positions of others? For example, some people, such as the hearers, think that the eye sees what is other than itself, even though it does not see itself. They can be refuted through inferences that are acknowledged by themselves. For, on the one hand, they assert that the eye has the property of not seeing itself (thus accepting the subject property in the Consequentialists' consequence to come). On the other hand (as for the eye being able to see at all), they still accept its necessary concomitance with the property of seeing something other, such as the color blue. However, based on their own examples such as a vase, they at the same time accept the necessary concomitance that something cannot see something else without seeing itself (thus accepting the entailment of the predicate by the reason in the Consequentialists' consequence to come). Hence, by formulating the three modes as accepted in this way, Candrakīrti's consequence to invalidate the positions of these opponents runs as follows:

> Wherever there is no seeing of itself, there is no seeing of something other, just as in the case of a vase. For the eye, there is no seeing of itself. Therefore, there is no seeing of something other for it either.[973]

Therefore, the eye's seeing of something other (such as the color blue), which is in fact contradictory to not seeing itself, is contradicted by an inference in which the subject property and the entailment are acknowledged by the opponents themselves. In this way, the wrong ideas of the opponents are eliminated through the use of an inference that is established for these very opponents. Since it is only such a negation of a thesis of others that is pointed out through inferences pronounced by Consequentialists, how could their position be affected by the fallacies mentioned above, so that they would incur the same flaws?

Bhāvaviveka and others may question this, asking, "Is there any invalidation through inference even by way of an inference that is acknowledged by only one of the two parties in debate?" There is, but only through a reason that is acknowledged by the very person whose position is invalidated, not through a reason that is acknowledged by the other debater, because such is seen as being practiced in the world. In the world, sometimes victory or defeat comes about through the words of a referee whom both parties take to be authoritative, and sometimes it comes about only through one's own words. However, neither victory nor defeat comes about through the words of the other party alone. This means that if we speak the truth without any contradictions, then such a statement neither turns into defeat through someone else saying that it is wrong nor becomes true (or even more true) by another approving of it. Likewise, if our own words are wrong, we just defeat ourselves. It is not that our words or thoughts are made wrong by another person. In general, we are convinced by what is established for ourselves and not merely by the fact that certain reasons are established for others. In other words, other people may help us through their words to see for ourselves that we are wrong, but the actual understanding of this can only happen in our own minds through our own insights.

Others might still object, "This is how it is in the world, but not in the situation of stating logical reasonings." For example, Vasubandhu says:

> Since [in debate] one has the desire to refute what is acknowledged by others, an[other's] inference cannot be invalidated through the force of what is acknowledged by others.[974]

Dignāga's *Gate to Reasoning* considers:

> That which states what is certain for both [parties] may serve as either proof or invalidation, but not a statement that is acknowledged by [only] one of the two or about which there is doubt.[975]

In other words, these two say that victory and defeat come about through a debate in which both parties accept the three modes, whereas this does not happen if one debater accepts the modes and the other does not. However, just as it is in the world, so it is also for logicians, because in the treatises on reasoning, nothing but worldly conventions are relevant for the decisions as to what is suitable or not. Hence, by following the world's conventions as to what is suitable and what is not, also the above people should accept the aforesaid procedure with regard to inference: that it is sufficient for consequences and such to be established for others, even if they are not established for those who pronounce them.

In the same vein, Buddhist invalidation of non-Buddhist positions through scripture is generally not accomplished by way of scriptures that are acknowledged by both parties, since non-Buddhist scriptures are obviously not acknowledged by both Buddhists and non-Buddhists. Rather, the invalidation of the assertions of non-Buddhists is accomplished by means of their own scriptures that are acknowledged only by themselves (that is, by exposing their internal contradictions). Likewise, when Centrists and Buddhist realists debate, those Buddhist scriptures in which entities are described as being established are regarded by Centrists as being of expedient meaning and by realists as being of definitive meaning. Therefore, they are not equally acknowledged by both. Nevertheless, it is not the case that Centrists, in the context of refuting certain features of the assertions of Buddhist realists, do not put forward such Buddhist scriptures (in which entities are described as being established) as an invalidation for these realists.

In the case of inference for oneself (for example, in analytical meditation), it is obvious that what is acknowledged by oneself naturally prevails in all cases and not what is acknowledged by both oneself and someone else. For example, when a person infers the existence of fire behind a hill, it is because this person herself sees the related smoke and then makes the connection to the fire. This person's realization of the existence of fire because of seeing smoke is not at all affected by the fact that a blind person in her company cannot see the smoke and thus does not realize the existence of fire.

In summary, in contrast to the approach of Bhāvaviveka and others, it is unnecessary to state defining characteristics in terms of rational logic as to the modes of a reason being commonly established. For, although the Buddhas themselves do not cling to such notions as purity and impurity or truth and untruth, they assist the beings who are to be trained and ignorant about true reality with justifications of purity and impurity or truth and untruth just as these are acknowledged by those attached beings themselves. Likewise, the noble ones are completely free from any words, thoughts, and expressions of existence, nonexistence, both, or neither with respect to arising from the four extremes. Nevertheless, for the sake of opponents who conceive of any kind of arising in terms of the four extremes, they negate such arising by relying on the functions of valid cognition as these are established through the opponents' own valid cognition. As Āryadeva's *Four Hundred Verses* states:

> Just as barbarians cannot understand
> Through any other language [than their own],
> So the world cannot understand
> Except through the worldly.[976]

Perhaps a more inviting way of saying this is that ordinary language and conventions serve as the receptacles for the nectar of wisdom.

Finally, Candrakīrti ends this little excursion in the first chapter of his *Lucid Words* by exclaiming, "Enough of all this ancillary discursiveness now!"

To conclude, it should be noted that Candrakīrti's entire critique of Bhāvaviveka solely pertains to the understanding and the use of reasoning in Centrism. Candrakīrti clearly considers Bhāvaviveka a Centrist and does not question his understanding of the contents of Centrism per se. This is also highlighted in the colophon of *The Lucid Words*:

> In order to delight those who have great intelligence, I taught [here] by putting together the good explanations by Bhāvaviveka upon [his] having seen the commentary composed by Buddhapālita (the former [commentary] thus coming about via the latter) as well as what I found through thorough discrimination myself.[977]

Thus, unlike what Tsongkhapa and others superimpose, Candrakīrti does not attack Bhāvaviveka for his insufficient realization of emptiness, his too-narrow object of negation, his assertion of conventional phenomena existing by virtue of their own specific characteristics, or the like, but just for his approach to reasoning in order to make others too realize the selfsame emptiness.

The following briefly shows how Tsongkhapa reinterpreted Candrakīrti's critique outlined above. In general, Tsongkhapa and his followers vehemently deny that Centrists have no thesis, that they do not have their own system, and that nothing is established through valid cognition, despite the fact that Candrakīrti—

whom they claim to strictly follow—explicitly and repeatedly said so. Tsongkhapa reinterprets autonomous reasoning in general as an inference that presupposes the acceptance of phenomena being (conventionally or ultimately) established through their own specific characteristics by valid cognition. In particular, Bhāvaviveka is taken as an Autonomist who conventionally employs precisely this kind of autonomous reasoning. In contrast to Candrakīrti then, Tsongkhapa criticizes Bhāvaviveka not for his use of autonomous reasoning per se—he rather sees it as legitimate within his assumed Autonomist ontology—but more for the latter's ontology of specifically characterized phenomena. However, as was made clear in detail above, Tsongkhapa grounds his critique entirely on his own baseless definition of an Autonomist ontology of specifically characterized phenomena that does not exist in Autonomist texts. It is solely Tsongkhapa and not Candrakīrti who brings up the Autonomists' supposed acceptance of phenomena as being conventionally established through their own specific characteristics. In other words, Tsongkhapa criticizes Bhāvaviveka for positions that Tsongkhapa himself has superimposed on him.[978]

Yoshimizu gives a very clear outline of how Tsongkhapa has made substantial shifts from Candrakīrti's original critique of Bhāvaviveka.[979] Having objected to the kind of autonomous reasoning that is based on specifically characterized phenomena, Tsongkhapa goes a step further and, in his own version of Consequentialism, sanctions the use of inferential proof (in addition to just formulating absurd consequences) as well as the two kinds of valid cognition proposed by Dignāga and Dharmakīrti (perception and inference). Thus, he claims that Candrakīrti only rejected the kind of autonomous reasoning that involves phenomena established through their own specific characteristics. We have seen, however, that Candrakīrti rejects the use of autonomous reasoning, because Centrists do not have any thesis of their own.

Tsonkhapa's first major shift is to take Bhāvaviveka not only as the proponent of the inferential proof of nonarising but also as the opponent to be refuted by the Consequentialists. In this way, it is the Consequentialist who becomes the proponent of an inferential statement instead of the Autonomist Bhāvaviveka, who is regarded as "someone who states that a nature exists" (Tib. rang bzhin yod par smra ba). In this context, Tsongkhapa also modifies Candrakīrti's explanations of what it means for the subject in question to be established as something that appears in common for both opponent and proponent by taking this to be the similarity of the valid cognition that establishes the elements of an inference. In brief, there are two criteria for Candrakīrti as to the common establishment of the subject in question:

A) The main criterion is the ontological issue of whether this subject exists in an ultimate or a conventional sense.

B) The objects of unmistaken (Tib. phyin ci ma log pa) cognition belong to the ultimate, and the objects of mistaken (Tib. phyin ci log pa) cognition belong to the seeming.

Tsongkhapa differs:

A) The main criterion is the ontological question of whether the subject exists as being established through its own specific characteristics.
B) The object of nonerroneous (Tib. ma 'khrul pa) valid cognition is what is established through its own specific characteristics (ultimately or conventionally), and the object of an erroneous (Tib. 'khrul pa) cognition is what is not so established.

Thus, Tsongkhapa has substituted his own criterion for common establishment based on the appearance of real specific characteristics for the criterion of Candrakīrti, which is based on the distinction between what is ultimate and what is seeming. This is also reflected in his shift from Candrakīrti's terms "mistaken/unmistaken" by tacitly equating them with "erroneous/nonerroneous."[980] Tsongkhapa's second major shift concerns why Consequentialists do not propound autonomous inferences. Candrakīrti's idea of autonomous inference as indicated in his *Lucid Words* is as follows:

1) Autonomous inference is a proof based on a thesis or position of one's own, as opposed to a reasoning employed solely in order to negate any thesis of others.
2) Or, it is a proof based on what is established for oneself, that is, based on a subject in question and its properties that are established for the proponent independently of others. This contrasts with a reasoning based on a subject and its properties that are established solely for others.

Accordingly, by giving two reasons, Candrakīrti explains why Centrists do not propound autonomous inferences:

1) Centrists do not have any thesis or position of their own, nor do they have any valid cognition to prove such a thesis.
2) There is nothing to be established for Centrists themselves through valid cognition.[981]

In contrast, as listed by Yoshimizu, Tsongkhapa's theory of Autonomists employing autonomous reasoning on the basis of phenomena established through their own specific characteristics can be summarized as follows:

a) Autonomists conventionally accept phenomena established through their own specific characteristics.
b) Therefore, they accept unmistaken valid cognitions that establish such phenomena via their specific characteristics.
c) Therefore, they share with their realist opponents not only a common appearance of valid cognition but also of the subject, reason, and example in their inferential statements.
d) Therefore, they can properly make use of autonomous inferences.

Correspondingly, Tsongkhapa's reasons for explaining the Consequentialists' rejection of autonomous reasoning are the following:

a) Consequentialists do not even conventionally accept phenomena established through their own specific characteristics.
b) Therefore, they do not accept any unmistaken valid cognitions that establish such phenomena.
c) Therefore, they share with their realist opponents (including the Autonomists) neither a common appearance of valid cognitions nor of subject, reason, and example in their inferential statements.
d) Therefore, they do not propound an autonomous inference.

Thus, through ontological and epistemological modifications that are all based on his initial claim that Autonomists conventionally assert phenomena established through their own specific characteristics, Tsongkhapa outrightly denies Candrakīrti's answer (1) and significantly revises answer (2) to the question above as to why Consequentialists do not propound autonomous inferences.
To sum up, Tsongkhapa's main points in his reinterpretation of Candrakīrti's critique of autonomous inference are as follows:

1) Autonomous inference is a proof in which its elements are established through their own specific characteristics by valid cognition either ultimately or conventionally for the proponents themselves.
2) Common establishment means that these elements of an inference are commonly established through their own specific characteristics by valid cognition for both proponent and opponent.
3) Autonomists, such as Bhāvaviveka, can properly propound such autonomous inferences to their realist opponents precisely because they conventionally accept phenomena established through their own specific characteristics and thus fulfill the condition for common establishment as in (B) above.
4) In his *Lucid Words*, Candrakīrti criticizes Bhāvaviveka not only as the propo-

nent of an inferential statement but also as one of the realist opponents to be refuted by Consequentialists.

5) Candrakīrti criticizes autonomous inference, because he neither ultimately nor conventionally accepts phenomena as being established through their own specific characteristics, but not because he thinks that Centrists have no thesis of their own.

With all of these reinterpretations, however, Candrakīrti's arguments against Bhāvaviveka and the radical critique of valid cognition and probative reasoning lose their point. According to Candrakīrti, the main reason that Bhāvaviveka's autonomous inferences are wrong is that each of their subjects is neither ultimately existent nor established for Bhāvaviveka himself (since, as a Centrist, he must deny any intrinsic, real existence) nor as something on the mere seeming level for his realist opponents.

## *Do Hearers and Solitary Realizers Realize Emptiness?*

As mentioned earlier, apart from the purely methodological issues in terms of reasoning, Bhāvaviveka on the one side and Buddhapālita and Candrakīrti on the other also disagreed on a more substantial issue. This revolves around two related questions: (1) whether emptiness is taught in the sūtras of the hearers and (2) whether they and the solitary realizers realize both kinds of identitylessness (personal and phenomenal).

### *Buddhapālita's Position*

This controversy is based on the commentaries of these masters on Nāgārjuna's *Fundamental Verses* VII.34:

> Like a dream, like an illusion,
> And like a city of scent-eaters,
> Thus, arising, abiding,
> And also ceasing are said to be.

Buddhapālita does not explicitly address the above two questions but comments that examples such as an illusion, an echo, a reflection, a mirage, a dream, a ball of foam, a bubble, and a banana tree in general illustrate the identitylessness of all conditioned phenomena (thus also alluding to *Saṃyutta Nikāya* III.141-2 quoted just below). He says that "All phenomena are identityless" and that "identitylessness" (*nairātmya*) refers to the lack of nature (*niḥsvabhāva*), because the term "identity" (*ātman*) is a word for "nature" (*svabhāva*).[982]

**Bhāvaviveka's Position**

Bhāvaviveka denies that emptiness is taught in the sūtras of the hearers as well as that hearers and solitary realizers realize both kinds of identitylessness.

As for the first question, when commenting on the above verse by Nāgārjuna in his *Lamp of Knowledge*,[983] Bhāvaviveka makes a distinction as to whether the examples for identitylessness appear in the sūtras of the lesser or the great vehicle. He says that the Buddha gave the following verse as a remedy for only the afflictive obscurations, because a nature of a self and what is mine does not exist, although it seems to.

> Form is like a ball of foam.
> Feelings resemble bubbles.
> Discrimination is like a mirage.
> Formations are equal to a banana tree.
> Consciousness is like an illusion.
> Thus spoke the one who sees true reality.[984]

On the other hand, in the great vehicle, conditioned phenomena are constituted by their lack of nature, although they appear as if they had a nature. Therefore, such statements as in the concluding verse from *The Diamond Cutter Sūtra* are given as a remedy for both the afflictive and the cognitive obscurations:

> Like stars, blurred vision, lamps,
> Illusions, dew, bubbles,
> Dreams, lightning, and clouds,
> Thus, conditioned phenomena are to be viewed.

In general, the five aggregates (in the first quote) and conditioned phenomena (in the second) are equivalent, so for Bhāvaviveka the difference obviously lies not in these statements themselves but rather in whom they address. He criticizes Buddhapālita's comment that all these examples refer to phenomenal identitylessness by saying that "identitylessness" in the vehicle of the hearers specifically refers to "personal identitylessness." Hence, the term cannot demonstrate phenomenal identitylessness. If it could, it would be pointless to take up another (that is, the great) vehicle.[985]

As for the second question, when commenting on *Fundamental Verses* XVIII.4–5,[986] Bhāvaviveka says that the liberation of hearers and solitary realizers means only the removal of the afflictive obscurations through realizing personal identitylessness. Bodhisattvas relinquish both obscurations and realize both types of identitylessness, thus achieving Buddhahood.

The relation of the two obscurations to the realization of the two kinds of identitylessness is addressed in more detail in Bhāvaviveka's *Blaze of Reasoning*.[987] He says that afflictive obscurations are twofold: those that have the nature of binding and those that are latent tendencies. Cognitive obscurations only have the nature of binding. From among these, hearers and solitary realizers relinquish merely the binding afflictive obscurations, but not their latent tendencies or the cognitive obscurations. Therefore, it cannot be said that arhats pass into nirvāṇa, since they still have obscurations, just like stream-enterers.[988] Ignorance is of two types: afflicted and unafflicted. The first shows in being attached to and proud of one's self and so on, whereas the latter has the nature of latent tendencies. From among these two, arhats fully relinquish afflicted ignorance, since they realize personal identitylessness. They still have unafflicted ignorance, which does not, however, obscure their mere liberation from cyclic existence. Thus, despite the presence of such unafflicted ignorance, it is said that "they attained the knowledge of termination and nonarising."[989] As for the latent tendencies of the afflictions, unafflicted ignorance, and the cognitive obscurations, all these can only be relinquished through meditation on emptiness on the special path of the great vehicle.

**Kamalaśīla's Position**

Kamalaśīla's *Stages of Meditation* quotes *The Sūtra of the Ten Grounds*:

> O son of good family, this is the true nature of phenomena. No matter whether the Thus-Gone Ones appear or not, this expanse of dharmas just abides. Thus, all phenomena are emptiness, and all phenomena are unobservable. This is not just a characterization limited to the Thus-Gone Ones, but all hearers and solitary realizers too attain this nonconceptual nature of phenomena.[990]

and *The Sūtra of the King of Meditative Concentration*:

> To discern phenomenal identitylessness
> And meditate on what has been discerned
> Is the cause that results in the attainment of nirvāṇa.
> Other causes will not bring about [this] peace.[991]

Kamalaśīla identifies the root or cause of the afflictions as the mistaken reification of phenomena that actually are unarisen and unceasing (that is, the clinging to real entities despite there being none). He supports this by several quotes from *The Sūtra That Teaches Seeming and Ultimate Reality*.[992] His *Commentary on The Ornament of Centrism* agrees that all afflictions are solely triggered by this mistaken reification, which shows in wrongly focusing on what lacks a nature. Thus, such mistakenness can only be relinquished through its opposite, the realization of the lack of nature.[993] *The Stages of Meditation* adds that it is only when mistaken reification has been eliminated that both afflictive and cognitive obscurations are fully relinquished. Thus, on the path of hearers and solitary realizers, the two obscurations are not properly relinquished, since the entirety of such mistakenness is not eliminated.[994] Despite Kamalaśīla's quote from *The Sūtra of the Ten Grounds* above (and in contrast to Candrakīrti), he seems to conclude that hearers and solitary realizers do not realize phenomenal identitylessness and thus are not really liberated, since he next adduces *The Sūtra of the Arrival in Laṅka* saying that the hearers' liberation is limited in this way:

> Others, by seeing that all phenomena depend on causes, come to a certain realization that they consider "nirvāṇa." However, since they do not see phenomenal identitylessness, Mahāmati, they do not possess liberation. Mahāmati, those who have the disposition for the clear realization of the vehicle of hearers develop a mental state of being released within nonrelease.

Thus, since there is no liberation through other paths, the Buddha has said that there is only a single vehicle. The paths of hearers and so on are comparable to one child protecting another and are only taught with the intention of introducing them into the great vehicle. Hence, by meditating that the mere aggregates exist but without a self existing in them, the hearers engage in personal identitylessness. Meditation on phenomenal identitylessness starts with the level of meditating that all appearances are mere mind and culminates in realizing that mind too is identityless.[995] Similar to Bhāvaviveka, Kamalaśīla understands personal identitylessness as the aggregates being without a self and "mine." Phenomenal identitylessness means that these very aggregates are illusionlike.[996]

**Candrakīrti's Position**

Bhāvaviveka's denial that the sūtras of the lesser vehicle teach emptiness and that hearers and solitary realizers realize both kinds of identitylessness hinges on three main points: the different meanings of "identity" and "identitylessness" in the sūtras of the lesser and the great vehicle, the way of distinguishing the two obscurations, and what distinguishes the great vehicle from the lesser. Candrakīrti criticizes him on all three points.

First, unlike Bhāvaviveka, Candrakīrti does not distinguish between personal identitylessness and phenomenal identitylessness in terms of subtlety. Rather, he understands identitylessness in the general sense of the absence of an intrinsic nature in any given referent, be it the person or any other phenomenon. As his commentary on Āryadeva's *Four Hundred Verses* says:

> "Identity" refers to a nature or essence of entities that does not depend on anything other. The nonexistence of this is identitylessness. Through classifying it in terms of phenomena and persons, it is understood as twofold: "phenomenal identitylessness" and "personal identitylessness."[997]

All that Candrakīrti says in his *Lucid Words* (commenting on *Fundamental Verses* XVIII.4–5) is that Bhāvaviveka has not understood that hearers and solitary realizers possess the realization of emptiness. As a support, he quotes *The Prajñāpāramitā Sūtra in Eight Thousand Lines*, which says that also those who want to train in the grounds of hearers and solitary realizers should train in the perfection of knowledge by listening, reading, and meditating.[998] Candrakīrti concludes by saying that Bhāvaviveka obviously does not follow Nāgārjuna in this point and refers to his own detailed treatment of the issue in his autocommentary on *The Entrance into Centrism*.[999] *The Entrance into Centrism* itself says:

> Even those [bodhisattvas] who abide on the first [ground through their] view of the perfect mind of enlightenment
> Prevail over [hearers] born from the speech of the Sage and solitary realizers
> Through the force of their merit and will increase [it further].
> On [the ground] "Gone Afar," also their insight will be superior.[1000]

By following Candrakīrti's commentary, the Eighth Karmapa elaborates on the issues at hand.[1001] Bodhisattvas on the first ground surpass hearers and solitary realizers through their development of the mind of enlightenment on the level of the seeming (that is, all the merit they have accumulated out of the wish to attain Buddhahood for the sake of all beings). Bodhisattvas on the seventh ground are superior in terms of both this and their realization of the ultimate mind of enlightenment (insight into emptiness). They do not even cling to any characteristics, let alone to any real existence of things, be it in terms of the scriptures or the expanse of dharmas itself. This process of becoming superior in all respects is usually illustrated by a classic example from the sūtras (such as in *The Sūtra of the Ten Grounds* and *The Liberating Life Example of Maitreya*). A newborn prince is already superior to all the king's ministers inasmuch as he is born into a royal family. However, in terms of his own mental power while still a child, he is not. Finally, when he has grown up and received the best possible education, he surpasses the king's ministers in all respects. Likewise, once bodhisattvas have truly generated the mind of enlightenment, they are superior to hearers and solitary realizers in terms of their motivation but not their mental power. On the seventh ground, by their great insight, they surpass hearers and solitary realizers in all respects.

Candrakīrti says that this passage in the sūtras shows that hearers and solitary realizers possess the realization of phenomenal identitylessness. He supports this by adducing (1) three reasonings and (2) seven further quotations.[1002]

1) The three reasonings are stated in the form of absurd consequences that follow if hearers and solitary realizers did not posses such realization.

a) It follows that hearers and solitary realizers as the subject can be outshone in terms of mental power even by bodhisattvas on the first ground, because hearers and solitary realizers do not realize that entities are without nature, just like worldly people free from attachment.[1003] The reason is accepted and its entailment of the predicate is established. But if this consequence is accepted, it contradicts the quote from *The Sūtra of the Ten Grounds.*

b) It follows that hearers and solitary realizers as the subject have not relinquished all afflictions of the three realms, because, by mistakenly focusing on form and such as being really established by their own nature, their thus mistaken minds become afflicted, just like worldly people free from attachment.

c) It follows that hearers and solitary realizers who cling to the aggregates as entities that are impermanent, without a self, and so on as the subject do not even realize personal identitylessness, because they possess the view of focusing on the aggregates, which is the cause for imputing a self. For example, if the clinging to the reality of the individual parts of a chariot is not put to an end, the clinging to the reality of the chariot that is composed of these parts is not put to an end either.

In this consequence, the subject property is accepted. The entailment of the predicate by the reason is established as follows: Through viewing the aggregates as substances that are impermanent, suffering, without a self, and so on, one is unable to eradicate either the clinging to a self with regard to such aggregates or the afflictions (such as desire and hatred) that result from such clinging, since the cause of self-clinging and afflictions—the reifying clinging to entities—has not been undermined at all. Whether the aggregates are regarded as substantial entities that are impermanent or permanent, with or without a self, all such views are equal in being mistaken with regard to emptiness as the true nature of phenomena. Hence, they cannot serve as remedies for reification, just as aversion to ugly objects cannot fundamentally eradicate the attachment that holds objects to be beautiful. *The Fundamental Verses* says:

If clinging to what is impermanent
As being permanent is wrong,
How could clinging to emptiness
As being impermanent not be wrong?[1004]

This is the meaning of the teaching that, without realizing precisely the equality of all phenomena, nirvāṇa is not attained through a comparatively limited realization of the four realities of the noble ones. As *The Large Prajñāpāramitā Sūtra* says:

> One will not completely pass into nirvāṇa through understanding suffering and also not through suffering [itself]. One will not completely pass into nirvāṇa through understanding the origin of suffering and also not through the origin of suffering [itself]. One will not completely pass into nirvāṇa through understanding cessation and also not through cessation [itself]. One will not completely pass into nirvāṇa through understanding the path and also not through the path [itself]. I teach that such equality of these four realities of the noble ones is complete purity: equality is suchness.

Some people think, "Through regarding the aggregates as impermanent and so on, the clinging to a self that is permanent, single, and independent is put to an end. Therefore, all afflictions will be relinquished." This is not the case. Through merely realizing that there is no permanent, single, and independent self that is something other than the aggregates, neither the clinging to a self whose cause lies in its imputation onto these aggregates themselves nor the resulting afflictions can be put to an end. The notion of a permanent, single, and independent self is not the basis that serves as the object of the innate clinging to "me." Moreover, it can be seen that even those who do not have any clinging to such a notion of a self still possess the clinging to "me" and afflictions. This is expressed in *The Entrance into Centrism*:

The yogins of your [tradition]who see the lack of a self [that is permanent and so on]
Do not realize the true reality of form and so on.
Since desire and such operate by focusing on form,
They will still arise, because the nature of the [aggregates] is not realized.

When you realize the lack of a self, you relinquish a permanent self,
Which is not asserted as the basis for the [innate] clinging to "me."

Therefore, it is amazing to say that the [innate] views about a self
Are eradicated through understanding the lack of a [permanent] self.

That while seeing a snake that lives in a hole in the wall of your house
Your concerns [could be] eliminated [by saying], "There is no elephant here,"
And thus also your fear of the snake be relinquished,
Oh, my, this is nothing but a laugh for others.[1005]

In other words, the clinging to (a) the imputed notion of a permanent, single, and independent self is gross and obvious like an elephant. However, it is just a coarser, additional layer on the more deeply ingrained and "sneaky," snakelike innate clinging to (b) the notion of "me" (which is the root of afflictions and suffering). The latter is in turn based on the underlying clinging that all phenomena (such as the five aggregates) are really or inherently existent, which thus provides the reference point for all levels of clinging to a personal self. This is why removing the clinging to (a) does not affect the clinging to (b). Therefore, it is indispensable to tackle the clinging to real existence in order to fundamentally eradicate the clinging to a personal self.[1006]

2) The seven quotations are the following.

a) Nāgārjuna's *Precious Garland* teaches that cyclic existence functions or comes to an end in dependence on whether there is reification of the five aggregates.

As long as the clinging to the aggregates exists,
For that long there is also [the clinging to] "me."
Through this identification with "me,"
Again, there is karma and thus, again, rebirth.

With three paths[1007] without beginning, middle, or end
Serving as its mutual causes,
This round of cyclic existence spins
Like the round of a circling firebrand.

Since this [round] is neither obtained as oneself,
Nor others, nor both, nor in the three times,
The clinging to "me" is exhausted,
And thus karma and birth too.[1008]

b) The same text explains why nirvāṇa is not attained without the realization that entities such as the aggregates are without nature:

Just as eyes, through being mistaken,
Apprehend a circling firebrand,
So the sense faculties
Apprehend the present objects.

Sense faculties and their referents
Are regarded as having the natures of the five elements.
Since each of the elements does not exist as a referent,
In actual fact, these [faculties and their objects] do not exist as referents.

If each of the elements were distinct,
[The possibility of] a fire without firewood would follow.
If they were a conglomerate, they would be without [distinct]
characteristics.
It is certain that the same applies to [all] remaining [things too].

Since the elements thus do not exist as referents
In these two ways, there are no referents composed [of them].
Since there are no referents composed [of them],
In actual fact, also form does not exist as a referent.

Likewise, as for consciousness, feelings, discrimination,
And formations, an identity of their own
Exists neither in all of them nor in them individually.
Therefore, in actual fact, they do not exist as referents.

Just as we pride ourselves with actual pleasure
When we have overcome some suffering,
So we identify with suffering
When it so happens that our pleasure is destroyed.

Since they are without nature,
The craving to find happiness
And the craving to be separated from suffering are relinquished.
Hence, those who see in this way are released.

You may wonder, "What is it that sees?"
Conventionally, it is expressed as "mind."

Without mental events, there is no mind.
Since they do not exist as referents, they are not regarded as existent.

Knowing thus that, in actuality just as it is,
Beings do not exist as referents,
Just as a fire [not existing] without its causes,
Lacking propensities for and appropriation of [rebirth], one passes
into nirvāṇa.[1009]

One might think that this passage was taught in terms of bodhisattvas attaining the nonabiding nirvāṇa of Buddhas. However, the quote up to here does not speak about bodhisattvas. In clear contrast, they are only mentioned in the next verse:

Also bodhisattvas, upon seeing in this way,
Definitely wish for enlightenment.
It is solely through their compassion
That they connect with cyclic existence until enlightenment.[1010]

Thus, it is hearers and solitary realizers who, upon realizing that entities are without nature, manifest the nirvāṇa of extinction described above, whereas bodhisattvas, despite realizing the same, do not pass into this kind of nirvāṇa.

The above reasonings and quotations show not only that hearers and solitary realizers indeed realize emptiness—the lack of an intrinsic nature in all phenomena—but that such realization is indispensable even for "mere" liberation from rebirth in cyclic existence, since it is impossible to realize personal identitylessness without realizing phenomenal identitylessness. This is also stated in Candrakīrti's commentary on Nāgārjuna's *Sixty Stanzas on Reasoning*:

> The relinquishment of the afflictions will not happen for those who assert that it is suitable to relinquish the afflictions despite observing a nature of form and so on.[1011]

This means that the clinging to reality or real existence is the kind of ignorance that serves as the root of cyclic existence and that there is no such clinging in the continua of noble ones. Thus, it is the flawless, unique position of the Consequentialists that the clinging to reality is necessarily an afflictive obscuration. Furthermore, *The Entrance into Centrism* says:

Since ignorance obscures its true nature, this is the seeming.
The Sage has declared that seeming reality

Is what is fabricated and appears as real through this [ignorance].
Thus, fabricated entities are the seeming.[1012]

The Karmapa says that this verse shows that a mental state that apprehends seeming reality is necessarily an afflictive obscuration, since it is through basic ignorance (the root of cyclic existence) that the appearances of seeming reality are displayed. Seeming reality appears for ordinary beings in whom this ignorance has not subsided, but it does not appear for the noble ones in whom it has subsided. What the latter see during subsequent attainment is called the "mere seeming." That delusive phenomena (this "mere seeming") still appear for hearers, solitary realizers, and bodhisattvas who have relinquished afflicted ignorance and see them as similar to the existence of reflections in a mirror is a natural occurrence on their paths. However, such appearances have no reality for them, since they do not take them to be real. Therefore, in the sense of appearing as seeming *reality*, mere appearances are only deceiving for ordinary beings. For the noble ones, they are *mere* seeming and illusionlike fictions that dependently originate. This "mere seeming" appears to them only while they are not in meditative equipoise (that is, when they experience objects that entail appearance), because—unlike ordinary beings—they are only affected by the type of ignorance that is unafflicted (the ignorance that constitutes the cognitive obscurations). During their meditative equipoise—when they experience the object that is the very lack of appearance—not even the "mere seeming" appears.

As shown above, Nāgārjuna and his spiritual heirs say that without realizing the lack of reality of the five aggregates—the phenomena that are the bases for imputing a personal self—one cannot realize the nonexistence of such a personal self. Consequently, they say that the conceptions of real existence constitute the type of ignorance that is an afflictive obscuration. If these conceptions were not the afflicted type of ignorance, the twelve links of dependent origination would not originate from it. *The Seventy Stanzas on Emptiness* says:

These conceptions about the actual existence
Of entities that depend on causes and conditions
Are ignorance, the Teacher said.
From them, the twelve links originate.[1013]

Such clinging to reality is presented as an afflictive obscuration, since it mainly obscures liberation from cyclic existence and is not present in the continua of noble ones who are liberated from it. The cognitive obscurations that are still present in them consist of the latent tendencies of the clinging to reality plus the clinging to the fact that the aggregates *lack* any reality and are illusionlike, since all of these mainly obscure omniscience.[1014]

From this follows a further unique statement of the Consequentialists: that seeming phenomena do not appear for Buddhas under any circumstances, because the entire flux of mind and mental events has completely subsided. Not seeing any reference points is expressed as seeing their actual nature. As far as ordinary beings and other noble ones—arhats and bodhisattvas—are concerned, it is in terms of whether they are affected by afflicted or unafflicted ignorance that the Buddha spoke about seeming reality and the mere seeming, respectively. What ordinary beings see as reality plain and simple is seen as something false—a mere seeming—by the noble ones when not in meditative equipoise. The nature of this mere seeming—that is, emptiness (seen from the perspective of these noble ones in meditative equipoise)—is the ultimate. Buddhas do not mistake this undeceiving ultimate for anything else, but ordinary beings observe it as just the deceiving phenomena of seeming reality. Since the causes (afflicted and unafflicted ignorance) have ceased in Buddhas, their respective results (seeming reality and the mere seeming) have subsided too.

c) In particular, for the sake of the hearers relinquishing the afflictive obscurations, it is also taught in the sūtras of the hearers that everything conditioned is without nature. The quote through which Candrakīrti illustrates this is *Saṃyutta Nikāya* III.141–2, also cited above by Bhāvaviveka.

d–e) In this way, hearers and solitary realizers are taught impermanence through the fact that entities perish and thus become terminated. At the same time, through negating that these impermanent entities are ultimately impermanent, the emptiness of them not being established as entities is taught. Instructed in this way, those who are fortunate enough to gain direct realization of this emptiness as hearers and solitary realizers experientially go beyond their specific philosophical systems and pass into nirvāṇa by realizing that everything conditioned is without nature. Those who are not able to gain such direct realization are taught that everything conditioned is impermanent, while nirvāṇa is not. Thus, it is asserted that only the latter are the hearers who propound reifying philosophical systems that are based on clinging to real entities. In order to seek for the real nirvāṇa in terms of their own path, they seriously engage in the accumulations of ethics, studying, and meditative stability. As *The Precious Garland* says:

> "Nonarising" as taught in the great vehicle
> And "termination" as in other [sūtras] are emptiness.
> In actual fact, termination and nonarising are the same.
> Hence, bear with [the great vehicle as the Buddha's word].[1015]

*The Fundamental Verses* states:

Through his knowledge of entities and nonentities,
In The Instruction for Kātyāyana,
The Victor has refuted
Both [their] existence and nonexistence.[1016]

One might think, "Then hearers and solitary realizers would relinquish the cognitive obscurations, since they realize phenomenal identitylessness." This is not the case, since then it would equally follow that all obscurations are relinquished on the path of seeing of the great vehicle. Hearers and solitary realizers do not familiarize themselves with phenomenal identitylessness for countless eons for the sake of relinquishing the cognitive obscurations, because they already attain their specific result of mere liberation from cyclic existence by having practiced for a few lifetimes.

To this, some say, "Then the cognitive obscurations that are relinquished by bodhisattvas on the sixth ground and below would equally be relinquished by those arhats of hearers and solitary realizers who abide for countless eons in meditative absorption in the expanse without remainder. The reason is that the latter in this way gain familiarity with phenomenal identitylessness for many countless eons and that bodhisattvas on the sixth ground and below are not able to outshine these arhats through their own mental power."

There are two answers to this reasoning: one in terms of content and the other in terms of format. First, arhats without remainder and bodhisattvas are not comparable in this respect. Arhats without remainder familiarize themselves with phenomenal identitylessness through abiding in the meditative absorption of cessation that is characterized by phenomenal identitylessness, but they do not familiarize themselves with phenomenal identitylessness for the sake of relinquishing the cognitive obscurations. Even if they did so, due to their duller faculties, unlike bodhisattvas, they would not be able to relinquish the cognitive obscurations.

The second answer in terms of the above reasoning's format is that the entailment of the predicate by the reason is not certain, because from such entailment it would follow that bodhisattvas on the seventh ground and below relinquish the entirety of the afflicted mind and the afflictions. The reason for this is that, according to the above opponents, hearers and solitary realizers have relinquished the entirety of the afflicted mind and the afflictions immediately upon becoming arhats while not at all having realized phenomenal identitylessness and not even having meditated for a long time on personal identitylessness either, whereas bodhisattvas have familiarized themselves with both types of identitylessness for many eons.

f) Some might further object, "Then the teachings of the great vehicle become pointless, since also the vehicles of hearers and solitary realizers teach phenomenal identitylessness, which means that there is no difference between the dharma approaches of the great and lesser vehicles." One cannot say that there is no difference, because it is not the case that the great vehicle does not teach anything but phenomenal identitylessness. Rather, it teaches the grounds, the perfections, and the great aspiration prayers of bodhisattvas; the four immeasurables; the dedications for great enlightenment; the two accumulations; and that the Buddhas teach the dharma by residing on a single atom while at the same time being surrounded by a retinue equal in number to all atoms that exist in the universe. Thus, in the great vehicle, there are these and infinitely many other ways in which the inconceivable nature of phenomena is presented in relation to all phenomena within the two realities. As *The Precious Garland* says:

> In the vehicle of the hearers,
> The aspiration prayers, the conduct, and the dedications
> Of bodhisattvas are not explained.
> So how could one become a bodhisattva through it?
>
> In the sūtras [of the hearers], [the Buddha] did not discuss
> The topics concerned with the conduct of bodhisattvas,
> But he discussed them in the great vehicle.
> Therefore, the learned should accept it [as Buddha's word].[1017]

g) Some people might argue now, "It is not justified to say that the perfections and so on are not taught in the vehicles of the hearers and solitary realizers, because they have generosity and so on there, which—according to what is said here—is seized by the supreme knowledge that realizes phenomenal identitylessness." This is not the case, since hearers and solitary realizers do not have generosity and such that possess the six kinds of genuineness (such as dedications deliberately made for the welfare of all sentient beings), the four dharmas, the four or eight qualities, or the twelve kinds of genuineness.[1018] "But is it not the case that being seized by the realization of phenomenal identitylessness represents the criterion that makes generosity and so on the perfection of generosity and so on?" In general, the criterion for presenting generosity and so on as the perfections is explained as follows: Presupposing the generation of the mind of enlightenment as its basis, if generosity does not lead to going beyond this world, it is mere generosity, but if it does so, it is the perfection of generosity.

The gist of this is as follows: The actions of the body, speech, and mind of noble hearers and solitary realizers that are seized by the realization of both kinds of identitylessness do not become the perfections and the grounds of bodhisattvas. Hearers and solitary realizers strive only for liberation from cyclic existence; they do not train and engage in the perfections and grounds of bodhisattvas for the sake of knowing the infinity of knowable objects for the welfare of others. Moreover, in the vehicles of hearers and solitary realizers, phenomenal identitylessness is not taught extensively but only in a very concise form. If phenomenal identitylessness were not taught in at least a concise form, hearers and solitary realizers would not become liberated from cyclic existence by becoming arhats. At the same time, even if phenomenal identitylessness were taught extensively, it is not something that they strive for. As *The Praise to the Supramundane* states:

> Without realizing signlessness,
> You said, there is no liberation.
> Therefore, you taught it
> Fully in the great vehicle.[1019]

As for the meaning of phenomenal identitylessness being concise or extensive, some Tibetans say that this refers to the conciseness or extensiveness of the nature of phenomenal identitylessness (as that which is to be proven) or to the conciseness or extensiveness of reasonings (as the means to prove it). However, neither of these is justified, because phenomenal identitylessness is not established by a nature of its own in the first place. In it, neither conciseness nor extensiveness can be observed. Rather, it is as follows: What bears characteristics is called a phenomenon. The understanding that a phenomenon is free from characteristics in the sense that it is empty of them is expressed as phenomenal identitylessness. This is absolutely equal for all three kinds of noble ones (hearers, solitary realizers, and bodhisattvas). Even for bodhisattvas, there is nothing to be realized that is a more extensive phenomenal identitylessness superior to that.

Regarding the reasonings (the means of proof), if phenomenal identitylessness is established through the concise means of proof stated in the lesser vehicle, there is no need for extensive means of proof in the great vehicle, since the latter would just prove what is already established in the lesser vehicle. On the other hand, if phenomenal identitylessness is not established through the concise means of proof in the lesser vehicle, it would be appropriate to teach phenomenal identitylessness through very extensive means of proof even to hearers and solitary realizers.

Thus, the meaning of concise versus extensive phenomenal identitylessness is as follows: It is presented as concise or extensive in terms of whether certain persons reveal or do not reveal that the nature of phenomena—the nature of being identityless—is related to every seeming bearer of this nature in the sense of support and supported. From among the entirety of phenomena that bear this nature, hearers and solitary realizers realize the following to be not established through a nature of their own: the aggregates, sources, and constituents that make up their own continua and are conditioned by karma and afflictions, as well as the phenomena of the uncontaminated reality of the path. This is all they are interested in for the sake of attaining personal liberation. However, they are not concerned about and thus do not reveal the nature of phenomena in its relation to all remaining knowable objects pertaining to themselves and all other beings. These knowable objects include the cause that is not conditioned by the karma and afflictions contained in one's own continuum (the Heart of the Blissfully Gone Ones); the inconceivable true nature of the seeming way of appearance that depends on this cause (such as noble bodhisattvas, through their activities of accumulation and purification, emanating Buddhas equal in number to all atoms in the universe on a single atom and then withdrawing them); and the results of such practices (such as the Dharma Body and the wisdom of the expanse of dharmas).

Hearers and solitary realizers do not reveal the nature of phenomena in its relation to all knowable objects without exception, because they are not interested in and thus do not strive for omniscience with regard to all knowable objects. In particular, the nature of phenomena in relation to the Dharma Body and the wisdom of the expanse of dharmas as specific bearers of this nature is realized only by those who possess the Dharma Body of a Buddha. It is not realized by any hearers, solitary realizers, or bodhisattvas, since the Dharma Body and its wisdom are not the spheres of any minds in which the latent tendencies of the three obscurations have not been completely cleansed. This is expressed not only by Candrakīrti but also by Bhāvaviveka's *Heart of Centrism*:

> This Dharma Body of the Buddhas
> That is endowed with countless accumulations of merit
> And knows infinite knowable objects
> Is the peace in which discursiveness is at peace.
>
> It is not seen by fleshly eyes,
> Nor is it seen by divine eyes.
> It is difficult to see for any consciousness
> That is conceptual or nonconceptual.
>
> It is neither the object of the higher realms nor [the object] of
> those with negative deeds,
> Neither [the object] of those without afflictions nor [the object]
> of those with [afflictions].
> Just as the sun is not an object of the blind,
> It is not the sphere of dialecticians.[1020]

As for those hearers and solitary realizers who have gone beyond philosophical systems and thus have attained true realization, from the point of view of having no clinging to the reality of cessation being substantially established, they are portrayed as having realized phenomenal identitylessness. On the other hand, it is also said that possessing the realization of the reality of cessation being unconditioned does not amount to having meditated on phenomenal identitylessness in all its extensiveness. Still, in a general sense, these two statements may well be considered equivalent. The point is that, despite such hearers and solitary realizers realizing identitylessness in a concise way, that is, to the limited extent covered by the lack of reality of conditioned phenomena, they do not extensively and fully realize that unconditioned phenomena as well are free from all discursiveness and reference points. Thus, from the point of view of phenomenal identitylessness as what is to be proven, the realizations of the above hearers and solitary realizers do not amount to the extensive realization of phenomenal identitylessness. In terms of mere identitylessness and the mere lack of reality as what is to be proven, they indeed have realized a mere negation (of identity and reality) that in itself is free from being concise or extensive. However, as for certain instances of phenomena from among the four realities (as the phenomena that are the bases for what is to be proven), while not (actively) apprehending them as having an identity, they also do not realize their identitylessness. Therefore, they do not fully realize extensive phenomenal identitylessness.

Another common example for this is that when you drink a sip of ocean water at the Florida coast, you know how "the ocean" tastes, since its taste is the same everywhere. However, despite knowing this, you do not know all the places in the world where you could possibly taste the ocean (such as the beaches of the Bahamas or the depths of the Pacific), nor have you tasted the ocean in all these places.

Some people might think, "Then it follows that hearers and solitary realizers do not realize phenomenal identitylessness, because they do not realize it in terms of certain instances of phenomena." But then it should equally follow that one's own visual consciousness does not cognize blue, because it does not cognize all blues that exist among knowable objects. "But it would follow that hearers and solitary realizers belong to the great vehicle, since they are Centrists in whose continua the realization of the two kinds of identitylessness has arisen." Even if certain people may be Centrists, they do not have to be Centrists who propound the philosophical system of Centrism. And even if they do, vehicles and philosophical systems are different categories. So how could this follow?

In other words, hearers and solitary realizers definitely see the mere conditionality of dependent origination, but they do not have the fully complete cultivation of phenomenal identitylessness, because they do not emphasize the knowledge of all knowable objects and the welfare of all sentient beings. In a comparatively short time, through meditating on the phenomenal identitylessness of the aggregates, sources, and constituents of their own continua, they merely relinquish the afflictions of engaging in the three realms of cyclic existence. Thus, they possess complete cultivation of personal identitylessness.

Bodhisattvas gather the accumulation of wisdom for the welfare of all sentient beings for countless eons. They do so through realizing phenomenal identitylessness (the ultimate mind of enlightenment that actually makes them attain Buddhahood) and its being connected as one in taste to the infinite dharmas of the seeming mind of enlightenment (the secondary causes for attaining Buddhahood). Thus, their accumulation of wisdom becomes equal in extent to the infinite number of all these bearers of the nature of phenomena. Through this, they attain the profound and vast Dharma Body of a Buddha. Hearers and solitary realizers cultivate phenomenal identitylessness in a way in which the two types of the mind of enlightenment are dissociated; that is, their realization of phenomenal identitylessness is not unified with the vast dharmas of noble bodhisattvas that cause the latter to attain completely perfect Buddhahood. Therefore, hearers and solitary realizers attain their final direct realization of phenomenal identitylessness by entering the expanse of complete release. However, through this way of cultivating phenomenal identitylessness, not even a tiny bit of the qualities of the Dharma Body appears for them.

## *Conclusion*

### The Summary of the Distinction between Autonomists and Consequentialists

Referring to the oral instructions of the Eighth Karmapa, Pawo Rinpoche summarizes the basic difference between Autonomists and Consequentialists as follows:

> "A sprout as the subject is without arising, because it is free from arising from any of the four extremes, just as a frog's long hair."
>
> Here, master Bhavya states [this as] the main argument, and then he formulates four autonomous reasons as the means to prove the subject property. The venerable and fearless Candrakīrti presents this by labeling the mere refutation of arising from the four extremes a "position." He teaches the invalidation of the opposite [positions] of this [refutation] through consequences that expose contradictions and through the analogous applicability of the [opponents'] reason [to something that contradicts their position]. However, he does not formulate a main argument, nor does he assert arguments that establish the subject property through valid cognition. It is merely on the grounds of this

> [difference] that one refers to Autonomists and Consequentialists.[1021]

Apart from this main point, he lists some further ancillary differences in terms of ground, path, and fruition:

> In the context of the ground, there is the difference that [Autonomists] present the seeming in accordance with proponents of philosophical systems [such as the Sūtra Followers or the Yogācāras] and that [Consequentialists] present it in accordance with common worldly consensus.[1022] When presenting the ultimate, [Autonomists] accept objects (that is, seeming [phenomena]), that bear the nature of phenomena, while [Consequentialists] do not accept such. [Another difference is] that [Autonomists] accept valid cognition that is undeceiving with respect to objects (that is, conventional reality), and [Consequentialists] do not accept such.
>
> In the context of the path, [Autonomists] settle in meditative equipoise within spacelike emptiness of appearance and [Consequentialists] settle in meditative equipoise within illusionlike emptiness of reality.
>
> In the context of the result, they differ in that [Autonomists state that] the aspects of the seeming emerge within the self-appearances of the wisdom that knows the extent [of phenomena],[1023] while such is not the case [for Consequentialists].[1024] They also have a different [opinion] as to whether discursiveness is ended gradually or all at once.
>
> For those with sharp faculties who take the instantaneous approach, the Consequentialist [approach] is better, and for those with weaker faculties who take the gradual approach, the Autonomist [approach] is better. Some [aspects] of the seeming [reality] of yogins have to be accepted by both Autonomists and Consequentialists after analysis through reasoning, such as the four seals of the view that are a sign of the Buddha's speech and the aspect of emptiness of reality free from discursiveness. It is not that these [aspects] are presented as the seeming from the point of view of having been analyzed [and found] through reasoning. Rather, they are presented as the seeming from the point of view of [still] apprehending characteristics in what is analyzed.[1025]

### The Five Main Points of Consequentialism

*The Treasury of Knowledge* summarizes Consequentialism in five main points,[1026] which accord with the presentation by the Eighth Karmapa:

1) *All phenomena are only nominally existent.* Let alone from the perspective of reasoning, all presentations in terms of conventional valid cognition or nonvalid cognition and of anything that could be established by such valid cognition are rejected even on the conventional level. All phenomena are just mental imputations through language, thinking, and means of expression; that is, they exist only nominally. Thus, it is explained that horses and oxen in a dream and in the waking state are completely equal in terms of being real or false. This includes the rejection of autonomous reasoning in the sense that the subject and the three modes are established through valid cognition as commonly appearing to both parties.

2) *Conditioned phenomena are necessarily false and deceiving.* Not only do they not withstand analysis through reasoning, but there is not even a trace of something that is established from the perspective of reasoning. Consequently, there is no common locus between conditioned phenomena and what is established through valid cognition. If thoroughly analyzed, even nirvāṇa (or any hypothetical phenomenon that may be superior to it) definitely does not exist as something that is established from its own side. Nevertheless, from the perspective of slight analysis, it is explained that solely nirvāṇa is undeceiving.

3) *The clinging to reality is an afflictive obscuration.* The root of cyclic existence is the clinging to real existence. If it is not eliminated, liberation from the clinging to a self and the ensuing afflictions is impossible. Therefore, the afflictive obscurations consist of the clinging to reality and all afflictions together with their accompanying mental factors that are produced through this clinging. The cognitive obscurations are described briefly as the clinging to characteristics and in detail as "the one hundred eight conceptions about the apprehended and the apprehender." Thus, Consequentialists do not assert any common locus between clinging to reality and cognitive obscurations. As explained earlier, this also establishes that the realization of phenomenal identitylessness is indispensable for the liberation of hearers and solitary realizers.

4) *The wisdom on the paths of seeing of the three vehicles is equal.* In fact, the paths of seeing in the three vehicles neither have several moments[1027] nor are they distinct in terms of their insights. Rather, *The Entrance into Centrism* states that the single wisdom that sees the single nature of phenomena is identical in the nominal three vehicles:

> Also this insight that is the subject of true reality is not disparate.
> Hence, you taught that the dissimilar vehicles for beings are not distinct.[1028]

The autocommentary says that there are different ways of seeing through studying, reflecting, and meditating on true reality, but true reality as such is without divisions and change. Hence, also the wisdom as the subject that realizes true reality is of a single nature. If the nature of this wisdom were multiple, it would not realize true reality, because it would not realize its nature just as it is. Since true reality is single, the wisdom that realizes it cannot be disparate. Hence, there is only a single vehicle and not three vehicles. As a sūtra says:

> Kāśyapa, when all phenomena are realized to be equality, this is nirvāṇa. It is just a single one and not two or three.[1029]

5) *The appearing of Buddhas is a mere appearance for others.* Just like a wish-fulfilling jewel or a garuda reliquary, the Form Bodies and enlightened activities of Buddhas are free from thoughts, without the need for any mental impulse of an intention upon which to act. Rather, they are nothing but the free display of appearances for other beings which comes about under the influence of former aspiration prayers by the Buddhas and the good karma of particular beings to be trained. From a Buddha's own perspective, however, all appearances of consciousness and objects of consciousness have completely vanished.

**Concluding Remarks**

As was amply shown, the Autonomist-Consequentialist controversy arose not from a disagreement on emptiness or ultimate reality but from different opinions on how to communicate the realization of it to others. A brief look at the particular context in the general history of Indian thought from which this methodological disagreement appeared may be helpful.

Bhāvaviveka lived in the middle of a long period of great fertility and evolution in Indian philosophy as a whole. His training was not only Buddhist; he had an encyclopedic knowledge of all branches of traditional Sanskrit learning, including the common fields of education (such as grammar and poetry) and all non-Buddhist philosophical systems. In order to defend Centrism against both Buddhist and non-Buddhist schools (which had evolved greatly since the time of Nāgārjuna), he seems to have seen it as his task to extensively study and refute the manifold tenets of his opponents on their own grounds through the means of commonly accepted probative arguments. At that time in India, the common rules of debate required that in order to uphold one's position, one had to prove it by arguments that contain reasons and examples. In addition, one was expected to refute, by the same approach, the counterpositions and eventual objections of one's opponents. One's position could not contradict immediate perception, one's own words, or commonly acknowledged consensus. Also, the reasons for defending one's position could not be unrelated to the subject, contradictory, uncertain, or otherwise lacking validity. So Bhāvaviveka seems to have emphasized probative arguments with all their requirements in order to comply with the contemporary standards of debate and reasoning. In combination with his extensive discussions of Buddhist and non-Buddhist schools, this may be seen as an effort to ground Centrism within a common logico-epistemological framework mutually acknowledged by Centrists and their realist opponents. In other words, he attempted to "dress up" Centrism in a way that he thought would make it a more relevant player in accordance with the rules on the large stage of general philosophical inquiry of his time. That this approach obviously was quite successful is evidenced by the fact that the vast majority of later Centrists in India more or less followed it.

Clearly, one of the few who did not follow Bhāvaviveka in this was Candrakīrti. The main thrust of his critique of Bhāvaviveka seems to be that the latter, by his use of probative arguments, compromises too much of Nāgārjuna's radical message that leaves not a single one of our belief systems and reference points—not even Buddhahood and nirvāṇa—unassailed. In other words, Bhāvaviveka reintroduces a plethora of old and new reference points rather than focusing on the main goal of Centrism, which is the elimination of all reference points altogether. For Candrakīrti, Bhāvaviveka definitely stepped over the demarcation line of the pedagogically unavoidable use of discursiveness and reference points that is necessary for guiding others to utter freedom from such discursiveness. In a way, for Candrakīrti (and certainly for Nāgārjuna too), Bhāvaviveka tried to lock up the wild bird of emptiness in the cage of conventional reference points, such as formal arguments. A bird may touch the earth once in a while, but its actual nature is to roam in the sky without restrictions and independent of the earth. Thus, if one is to experience the free flight of a bird, it does not help to make it sit still by trapping it in a cage and then counting its feathers.

On the other hand, leaving aside ontological or epistemological commitments, it can be said that all Centrists are both Autonomists and Consequentialists in that they use both approaches to reasoning, though certain masters prefer the one over the other. In other words, it is a matter of choice whether faultfinding or probative arguments are employed to point to emptiness, but the fundamental objective—making others realize the nature of phenomena—is exactly the same for all Centrists. Thus, the difference lies in the way the ultimate is communicated. As implied by the Eighth Karmapa, the more radical style of Consequentialists may involve difficulties for some people in that it "shoots too high to soon," since, right from the start, it does not provide anything to hold on to and just cuts through any ground one may try to stand on. The Autonomist approach is in many ways more down to earth in the sense of at least initially being more grounded in and allowing for our ordinary thinking. It may thus be considered by some people to provide a more convenient framework for peeling away the many layers of our belief systems in a more gradual and moderate manner.

From all that has been said on the Autonomist-Consequentialist distinction, it should be clear that there are many other—quite different—dividing lines that could be drawn between individual Centrist masters. In particular, the evident differences may be considered between Bhāvaviveka (who extensively attacked the Yogācāra system) on the one hand and Śāntarakṣita and Kamalaśīla (who adopted this system in many respects) on the other, with Jñānagarbha somewhere in between. Apart from their having a similar approach to reasoning, it is far from clear why they should all belong to a particular Centrist subschool called Autonomists with a common set of fixed doctrines. When looking at their own works (and not only at later classification schemes), many other subsequent Indian Centrists, such as Haribhadra, Abhayakāragupta, Bodhibhadra, Ratnākaraśānti, and Atiśa also defy any easy classification. The same goes for many early Tibetan Centrists. Of the vast and intricate web of doxographical distinctions over the centuries, Ruegg says:

> The fact that texts (and masters) that differ significantly in their doctrines have sometimes been assigned by authors of doxographical and philosophical works to a single division or category, such as the Svātantrika or Prāsaṅgika branches of the Madhyamaka, appears to indicate that such taxonomies current in Tibet . . . have often to do with lines of magisterial transmission and pupillary succession . . . rather than with immutable and altogether discrete philosophical positions and with standardized and uniform school doctrines. Still, as templates . . . these categorizations and taxonomies might be thought to have their uses for descriptive, interpretative or heuristic purposes in historical and philosophical discussion and analysis.
>
> With respect to both the Indian and the earlier Tibetan Madhyamaka authors they can, however, hardly be expected to provide a comprehensive and definitive frame or norm for analyzing and classifying the totality of the doctrines and philosophemes that have been subsumed by doxographers under a given taxonomic category; nor can it be supposed that the elaborate nomenclature for doctrinal divisions and subdivisions used in the doxographical taxonomies would always have been familiar to these masters themselves.[1030]

In particular, as for Candrakīrti's *Entrance into Centrism*, given the lack of substantial differences between Autonomists and Consequentialists, the all but dominant position of Candrakīrti in India, the almost complete lack of Indian commentaries on his works, and, in contrast, the wealth of literature by other Indian Centrists (be they Autonomists or others), one may wonder why—from about the fourteenth or fifteenth century onward—this one of all texts became the single Centrist work to serve as the absolutely predominant basis for Centrist studies at Tibetan monastic colleges. The issue is certainly rather complex, but there seem to be two main reasons. One was the intense propagation of Candrakīrti's works by Tsongkhapa and the predominant Gelugpa school, proclaiming them as the only correct explanation of Centrism, superior in particular to all Autonomists. The other reason has more to do with the structure and contents of *The Entrance into Centrism.* Unlike most other Centrist texts, it not only explains the classical Centrist topics by giving explanations on the meaning of *The Fundamental Verses* but combines them with an outline of the path and its fruition as described in *The Sūtra of the Ten Grounds.* Thus, Candrakīrti's text does not merely discuss the Centrist view; it also describes the nature and the qualities of the ten causal grounds of bodhisattvas as well as the resultant level of Buddhahood with its enlightened bodies and wisdom.

As a final consideration of all these distinctions that may seem clear and obvious at first glance, it seems that the more we look into their details and try to identify what exactly it is that separates the various Autonomist and Consequentialist masters, the more this process in itself becomes a perfect example of the Centrist principle that there is nothing to be found under analysis. Given this result of not finding anything, the obvious question is, why should we even bother investigating all these different views and their negations? It is precisely for this result of not finding anything. To the extent that we work our way through various distinctions, they become the means to sharpen our wisdom and let go of all reference points in order to approach the actual experience of what they are all talking about. As Khenpo Tsultrim Gyamtso's *Magical Key* says:

> The manifold divisions of vehicles in this way
> Are means to put an end to discursiveness.
> Thus, once actual equality free from discursiveness is realized,
> The analysis of views is completed.
>
> Although the progressive stages of views differ,
> In the basic original nature, there is no difference.
> The apprehension of differences is the flaw of thinking mind,
> Eventually merging into the Great Seal's nature free from
> consciousness.[1031]

# 4

## *Is There Such a Thing as Shentong-Madhyamaka?*

Most people think that, in terms of its Madhyamaka alignment, the Kagyü school is a monolithic bloc of staunch supporters of Shentong-Madhyamaka ("other-empty Madhyamaka"). However, as should be clear by now, there are quite a number of masters in this school who do not follow what is known as Shentong. Even Milarepa sometimes adopts a typical Rangtong ("self-empty") approach in his enlightened songs.[1032] Still, the reader may be wondering why a book on Madhyamaka in the Kagyü lineage has thus far barely mentioned the term "Shentong," much less presented the system it refers to. The answer is simple and may be shocking to some: There is no Shentong-Madhyamaka nor any need to make one up. The subdivision of Madhyamaka into "self-empty" and "other-empty" is obsolete.

Before I am excommunicated from the Kagyü lineage for making this statement, let me say that I am just going by what the Eighth Karmapa and Pawo Rinpoche say in *The Chariot of the Tagbo Siddhas* and *The Commentary on The Entrance to the Bodhisattva's Way of Life*. I also want to make it clear from the outset that the reason for such a statement is not at all to deprecate the contents or the value of the teachings that came to bear the name Shentong in Tibet. Rather, the reason is quite the contrary, since what is called Shentong is nothing other than the Yogācāra[1033] (Yoga Practice) system of Maitreya, Asaṅga, and Vasubandhu, also called "the lineage of vast activity."[1034] Just like Centrism, in its rich entirety, this system is a distinct, well-established, and—at least in India—unequivocally renowned system of presenting the teachings of the Buddha. It can stand very well on its own and has no need to be included under Centrism or even to be promoted as the better brand of Centrism. It is all the more inappropriate to wrongly subsume it—as many Tibetan doxographies do—under the questionable category of "Mere Mentalism"[1035] and thus regard it as inferior to Centrism. It would definitely contribute to the appreciation of this Yogācāra system for what it is if it were called neither Mere Mentalism nor Shentong but simply "the Yogācāra System of Maitreya/Asaṅga" or "the lineage of vast activity." The following presentation will provide sufficient evidence for this by highlighting some essential points of Yogācāra in the original texts, consulting the main Kagyü sources on both Centrism and Yogācāra, and comparing the relationship between these two systems.[1036]

As for the question of whether there is a Shentong-Madhyamaka, both the Eighth Karmapa and Pawo Rinpoche give a very clear answer: "No!" They not only refute any realistic interpretation of what the word *shentong* might refer to, such as the notion of a permanent, intrinsically existing Buddha nature;[1037] they simply consider this term a misnomer altogether. At the same time, the two systems of Nāgārjuna—the lineage of profound view—and Asaṅga—the lineage of vast activity (to which the term "Shentong" usually refers) are clearly distinguished. When questioned, The Dzogchen Ponlop Rinpoche confirmed that it is indeed better to make a distinction in terms of the lineages of profound view and vast conduct than between some lineages of "Rangtong" and "Shentong," since the former two are the clear lineages of transmission that can be traced back to India. Pawo Rinpoche explicitly explains that the final intention of these two systems is identical, while the Eighth Karmapa in his *Chariot of the Tagbo Siddhas* does so implicitly.[1038] Moreover, Pawo Rinpoche emphasizes that what Tibetans call "Mind Only" or "Mere Mentalism" is not the lineage of vast activity.[1039]

In his *Chariot* commentary, the Eighth Karmapa says that, in general, there is no difference between Buddha Śākyamuni and Maitreya in that they are both Buddhas. However, the sole teacher of this realm of Buddha activity who appears as the Supreme Emanation Body of a perfect Buddha is Buddha Śākyamuni, and there is no dispute that he prophesied Nāgārjuna and Asaṅga as the founders of Centrism and Yogācāra. Thus, whoever is a Centrist in the setting of the teachings of this realm must definitely be in accord with the Centrism of Nāgārjuna and his spiritual heirs. Imputations of different kinds of Centrism (such as one specific to Maitreya) that do not correspond to Nāgārjuna's system are rejected by the Eighth Karmapa. He says that if there were a Centrism of Maitreya, then it would be equally fine to present innumerable forms of Centrism, such as the eight kinds of Centrism that were asserted by the eight close bodhisattva sons of the Buddha and the thousand different kinds of Centrism that are asserted by the thousand Buddhas of this fortunate eon. Some people might object that if this newly named Centrism of Maitreya does not fulfill the function of actual Centrism, then the Centrism of Nāgārjuna also would not fulfill this function, because both system founders are equal in being noble bodhisattvas. However, by using the same kind of argument, it would then also follow that the vehicles of the hearers and solitary realizers that were taught by the Buddha are the great vehicle, because they are equal in being vehicles and being spoken by the Buddha.

The Karmapa corrects another misunderstanding regarding what is called "self-emptiness" and "other-emptiness." He says that some Tibetans assert the absence of a nature of their own in phenomena as being the meaning of "self-emptiness" and the absence of other phenomena as being the meaning of "other-emptiness." This is not justified, because such an explanation or terminology does not exist in the topics of the sūtras on emptiness. Nor is it found anywhere in the treatises of the two system founders Nāgārjuna and Asaṅga, whose authority in this matter rests at least in part on the fact that they were prophesied by the Buddha as the ones to comment on the intentions of the topics of these very sūtras in terms of Centrism and Yogācāra respectively.

In particular, the Eighth Karmapa takes issue with the position of Dölpopa Sherab Gyaltsen, which he reports as follows: "On the level of seeming reality, phenomena are empty of a nature of their own. Therefore, they are self-empty. In ultimate reality, the supreme other consciousness that is not empty of its own nature—the permanent entity of the Heart of the Blissfully Gone Ones—is empty of all other seeming phenomena. This is explained as 'other-empty.' The Centrists who propound other-emptiness are the Great Centrists, and the Centrists who propound self-emptiness turn the Centrist view into something like poison."

The Karmapa regards such an explanation as a deprecation of the meaning of Prajñāpāramitā for several reasons. To start with, if one claims an ultimate phenomenon that is really established and not empty of its own nature, this contradicts the Buddha's determination of the definitive meaning, which is that all phenomena are emptiness. In particular, this explanation is also contradictory to all commentaries on the intention of this definitive meaning that were given by Centrists, including Āryavimuktisena and Haribhadra, the two main Indian commentators on the hidden meaning of the *Prajñāpāramitā sūtras.* With regard to "the emptiness of other-entity,"[1040] the sūtras clearly negate this "other-emptiness" by saying, "Since it lacks any solid abiding and ceasing, it is empty of itself." Following this, Āryavimuktisena, Ratnākaraśānti, and others say, "Since it is an emptiness that is not produced by others, it is the emptiness of other-entity" and "Since it is the entity that is not produced by others, it is the other-entity." Thus, they take solely the emptiness that is natural emptiness (and not any nonempty entity) as the basis of being empty of something other. On the other hand, in the scriptures, there never appear any reifying explanations in the sense that, by taking the supreme and permanent other-entity—the Heart of the Blissfully Gone Ones—as the basis for emptiness, this Heart is empty of all other seeming phenomena and that this is the meaning of other-emptiness.

Before Dölpopa, the Karmapa says, nobody in India or Tibet had ever stated that there are these two systems of "self-emptiness" and "other-emptiness" within the philosophical system of Centrism. If one follows Centrism, it is impossible to assert an ultimate phenomenon that is really established and to say at the same time that the seeming is without reality in that it is empty in the sense of self-emptiness. If one were to propound something like this, one would just be a realist. It is obvious that one cannot be a realist and at the same time speak about the center free from all reference points.

In his commentary on *The Ornament of Clear Realization*, the Eighth Karmapa identifies the correct referent of using the term "other-empty" in an expedient, functional way (if one wants to use this term, that is). However, he emphasizes that the nature of phenomena is neither self-empty nor other-empty anyway, let alone really existent:

> The name "other-empty" is applied to emptiness [in the sense] that the other features within this basis [emptiness] are empty of their own respective natures. Therefore, the other-empty's own nature does not become nonempty. The reason for this is that the name "other-empty" is [only] applied to the compound meaning that this basis [ emptiness] is empty of such and such [and not to this basis being other-empty in itself].[1041] However, it is not asserted that this basis—the nature of phenomena—is empty of its own nature. [Likewise, as was just said,] this [basis itself] is not other-empty either. Therefore, if it is not other-empty, forget about it being self-empty [since these two are just mutually dependent]. . .
>
> This basis—the nature of phenomena—is neither other-empty nor self-empty, because [let alone being other-empty or self-empty,] it is not even suitable as a mere emptiness that is not specified as being empty or not empty of itself or something other. The reason for this is that it has the essential character of being the utter peace of all discursiveness regarding being empty and not being empty. Thus, from the perspective of the [actual] freedom from discursiveness, no characteristics whatsoever of being empty of itself or something other transpire within the basis that is the nature of phenomena.[1042]

In brief, "other-empty" in this sense, as a mere matter of conventional parlance, means the following. By definition, emptiness can in no way be identified or reified. It is the very freedom from all reference points, not still another reference point. So, it is nothing but this emptiness that is empty of everything "other," such as reifications, discursiveness, reference points, and so on.

As for wisdom, it cannot be an ultimate entity either. In his *Chariot*, the Karmapa adds that some proponents of other-emptiness assert that it is not consciousness that is ultimately existent, but wisdom, and that this is the crucial difference between Mere Mentalism and the Centrism of other-emptiness. However, he says, this is just an attempt to sell Mere Mentalism as Centrism. For as long as a really established cognition in the sense of a momentary, mere mental experience that is clear and aware is asserted, it does not matter whether this is called consciousness or wisdom.

Therefore, Mikyö Dorje says that he does not at all direct his mind to any of the various presentations of Centrism, Yogācāra, or any other system by those people who say that Centrism has this twofold division into the Centrism of self-emptiness and the Centrism of other-emptiness. Among such people, some claim that the view of the Centrism of self-emptiness is higher and others the opposite. Rather, the Karmapa says that he prefers to present the philosophical systems of Centrism and Yogācāra and so on from their own sides and in their own right through correct reasons.[1043]

Pawo Rinpoche presents the contradiction inherent in the claim of some people who say that the Centrism explained in the second turning of the wheel of dharma represents the teaching on self-emptiness and that the Centrism explained in the final turning of the wheel of dharma is the teaching on other-emptiness, which represents the ultimate view. Since the perfection of knowledge has already been explained in the second turning, these people implicitly accept that the final turning is not the perfection of knowledge; and since its teachings are not included in any of the other perfections either, they would consequently not even belong to the great vehicle. These people might then object that the teachings of the final turning belong to the category of meditative stability, the fifth perfection. However, according to this position, the direct fruition of meditative stability—the perfection of supreme knowledge—is self-emptiness. Therefore, to say that the third turning belongs to the category of meditative stability contradicts their claim that this turning is the ultimate view—that is, other-emptiness—since its fruition is self-emptiness.

Then, Pawo Rinpoche takes on the position of "some Tibetan scholars who are as well-known as the sun and the moon."[1044] They say, "One must definitely accept a middle between the two extremes. This is the great ultimate that is empty of other. It is a permanent, unchanging, and solid entity that is empty of adventitious stains and not empty of all Buddha qualities, such as the ten powers. This is the great kingdom of wisdom."

Pawo Rinpoche refutes this view by pointing to the intentions behind different presentations of emptiness. Although there surely are many explanations that the nature of phenomena is permanent and lasting and such, these explanations are given with particular issues in mind. For example, the descriptions of the infinite positive qualities of Buddhas are provided in order to eliminate clinging to a certain kind of limited emptiness, that is, taking the ultimate to be utter nonexistence. Such explanations may also be given for those pure disciples who are already released from believing in extremes, such as permanence and extinction. Obviously, these disciples would no longer set up any reference points in terms of superimposition and denial, no matter how they are taught the nature of phenomena. They are like people who are cured of a disease and have regained their full strength. Such people may relish all kinds of tasty and nourishing dishes. However, the dietary situation of those people who suffer from the nasty illness of being inflated by entertaining reference points is a different story. They are definitely in need of curing this disease through the purging medicine of emptiness. As for a middle and extremes, these are only established in mutual dependence. Thus, if the extremes have been refuted, their middle cannot be established either, because a middle without extremes is impossible. If there is a middle, there are also extremes, because as long as there is clinging to a middle, the clinging to extremes operates too, just as even an infinitesimal particle entails at least a left side, a right side, and a middle. Its middle part can again be divided into a middle, left, and right, and so on. As *The Sūtra of the Meditative Concentration of the Direct Presence of All Present Buddhas* states, both middle and extremes are seeming and not ultimate:

> Not observing, not conceptualizing, and not establishing the two extremes, not mentally engaging, and not being occupied with them is what is taught in a nominal way and through the worldly seeming. Therefore, it is called "the middle way." However, ultimately, neither extremes nor middle can be observed here.

The sūtra continues by saying that followers of the great vehicle should also not cling to wisdom:

> A bodhisattva mahāsattva should wish for wisdom but not cling to wisdom.

Nāgārjuna's *Fundamental Verses* says that as long as one entertains reference points, such as existence, nonexistence, or a middle in between, Buddhahood is out of reach.

> The four possibilities of permanent, impermanent, and so on,
> Where should they be in this peace?
> The four possibilities of finite, infinite, and so on,
> Where should they be in this peace?
>
> Those who entertain discursiveness with regard to the Buddha,
> Who is beyond discursiveness and inexhaustible,
> As a consequence of being affected by all this discursiveness,
> They will not see the Thus-Gone One.[1045]

In the same vein, Pawo Rinpoche ridicules some people's claim of resting in a nonconceptual way within the state of both knowing that the adventitious stains do not exist and knowing that the ultimate exists. He says that it is truly amazing to rest in a nonconceptual way within a state in which there is clinging to the nonexistence of stains and clinging to the existence of the ultimate.

Also, there is no separate "kingdom of wisdom" or "kingdom of consciousness."

> What is the nature of the Thus-Gone One
> Is the nature of beings.
> The Thus-Gone One is without nature
> And all beings are without nature.[1046]

If there were a single, ultimately existing nature of all phenomena, it would follow that these phenomena could not have different characteristics. Moreover, if an ultimate emptiness were definitely established, this emptiness would not be the means to vanquish reification but rather something to be vanquished itself.

Some people claim, "The other-empty ultimate is an existent beyond existence and nonexistence." However, in a way, this is just a play on words. For what would be wrong then in claiming a nonexistent that is beyond existence and nonexistence? And how would one then refute the claim of a nonexistent that is even beyond such an existent beyond existence and nonexistence? As is obvious from this, there would moreover follow an infinite regress, starting with an existent beyond an existent beyond existence and nonexistence. Therefore, Pawo Rinpoche says, it is problematic to introduce conventions, such as other-emptiness, that are not known in the Buddha's teachings and proclaim them to be the heart of his teachings.

Then there are those who talk in a one-sided way in terms of Mere Mentalism and say that the other-dependent nature empty of the imaginary nature is the perfect nature. This is just something that is set up by their own minds, without an understanding of the true intention of the lineage of vast activity. For, following *The Sūtra That Unravels the Intention*, the lineage of vast activity explains that the imaginary nature is like being affected by the disease of blurred vision; the other-dependent nature is like the manifestations that appear due to blurred vision; and the perfect nature is like the natural object of clear vision upon being cured. This means that once the disease of blurred vision has been cured, the appearance of floating hairs vanishes. Likewise, when the fundamental disease of the most subtle level of the imaginary nature—mind's nature or the expanse of dharmas being blurred by the dualistic split into subject and object—is eradicated, then the seeming appearances of the other-dependent nature will vanish. At that point, the more coarse levels of the imaginary nature—which come about through focusing on the appearances of the other-dependent nature and labeling them—automatically do not remain either. What remains is the perfect nature, the expanse of dharmas as it is, seen by the unimpeded, natural vision of personally experienced wisdom.[1047]

Furthermore, notions such as existence and nonexistence belong to the imaginary nature. So, if one claims the ultimate existence of the perfect nature, one in fact claims that the perfect nature is the imaginary nature. This was prophesied by the Buddha in *The Sūtra of the Arrival in Laṅka*:

> In the future, those who cling to non-Buddhist thinking will conceptualize that the wisdom of the noble ones exists as an object of personal experience and as having the nature of an entity. . . . How could such notions operate in the noble ones? If such [notions] were entertained, they would be nothing but the clinging to an identity.

Then, Pawo Rinpoche quotes a seemingly contrasting passage from *The Sūtra of the Great Nirvāṇa*:[1048]

> Before, in Varaṇasi, I taught impermanence, suffering, emptiness, and identitylessness to those of medium vigor. Now that I turn the wheel of dharma here in Kuśinagara, I teach completely pure permanence, purity, bliss, and identity.

He explains that the Buddha taught on the Dharma Body by emphasizing that it is endowed with the four qualities of permanence, purity, bliss, and identity in order to counteract mainly the clinging to the extreme of deprecation, such as regarding the Dharma Body as impermanent. In this context, permanence means that the completely pure nature of phenomena will never change into something impure. However, this is not a teaching on any kind of reified permanent substance. This sūtra furthermore says that Buddhahood can be attained if there is mind, just as butter can appear if there is milk. Therefore, all sentient beings are said to have Buddha nature. However, in dependence on the capabilities of various disciples, identity may be explained as identitylessness and identitylessness as identity. Just as blind people do not see visible forms, sentient beings do not see their own nature that is like a powerful vajra. Although yogurt does not exist in milk as long it is milk, yogurt may come forth from milk. It is from this point of view that one says, "Yogurt exists in milk." Likewise, the teaching that Buddha nature exists in sentient beings is given in the same way. As *The Sūtra Requested by Brahmā* says:

> O Blessed One, those who seek for nirvāṇa as an entity do not go beyond cyclic existence. Why? O Blessed One, "nirvāṇa" is utter peace

> of all characteristics, the cessation of all mental flux. O Blessed One, foolish persons who seek nirvāṇa as an entity, while taking ordination in the well-spoken vinaya of the dharma, fall into the views of the forders. O Blessed One, those who seek nirvāṇa within all phenomena that are fully in the state of nirvāṇa, [just like extracting] sesame oil from sesame seeds or butter from milk, I declare to be vain forders.[1049]

It is important, when looking at the teachings of the Buddha, to be aware that the meanings of certain terms can change according to different contexts. For example, "causes" can have two meanings: causes for the arising of something and causes for something to become clearly manifest. Here, it is taught that the "actual cause" for sentient beings to have Buddha nature is sentient beings' own mind, while the conditional causes are the six perfections, such as generosity. In other contexts, it is also explained that confidence, the four immeasurables, or the ten bodhisattva grounds and such are Buddha nature. Thus, it is taught again and again that all phenomena are undetermined and subject to conditions.

The same goes for the term "nonexistence," since there are six ways in which it may be used. It can mean total nonexistence, temporary nonexistence, nonexistence due to insignificant quantity, nonexistence because of not being experienced, nonexistence due to the adoption of bad dharmas, and nonexistence because of the lack of a counterpart to depend on.

"Not being seen" can have eight meanings: not being seen due to being too distant, not being seen due to being too close (such as one's eyelashes), not being seen due to ceasing, not being seen due to the seer being upset, not being seen because of being too subtle, not being seen due to being obscured, not being seen due to a lack of quantity (such as a sesame seed in a heap of rice), and not being seen due to similarity (such as a lentil in a heap of peas).

All of these specifications are used in many places in various ways, but it is clearly said that, in terms of the actual heart of the matter, they are not to be imagined as anything whatsoever. Thus, no matter whether it is existence, nonexistence, permanence, impermanence, or anything else that one doggedly sticks to, such clinging always deprecates the ultimate. As *The Sūtra of the Great Nirvāṇa* declares:

> O son of good family, one might say, "Definitely, Buddha nature exists in all sentient beings," or one might say, "Definitely, Buddha nature does not exist." No matter what you say, it is a deprecation of the Buddha, the dharma, and the spiritual community. O son of good family, therefore, I have taught in the sūtras that there are two types of people who deprecate the Buddha, the dharma, and the spiritual community: those who have no trust and a mind full of aversion, and those who have trust but do not understand the meaning.

Such sūtras as the *Aṅgulimālīyasūtra, The Great Drum Sūtra,* and others say that the Heart of the Thus-Gone Ones and Buddhahood are permanent, lasting, and changeless. However, this is in order to eliminate the clinging that the ultimate is utter nonexistence. As the Buddha says:

> O Mañjuśrī, in the world, there are two types of persons who destroy the genuine dharma: those who have strong views about emptiness and those who propound a self. These two destroy the genuine dharma and turn the genuine dharma upside down.

Furthermore, it is generally asserted that the liberation of hearers and solitary realizers is the discontinuation of the five aggregates, just like the dying of a flame, and that the welfare of others cannot be promoted through the nirvāṇa without remainder. On the other hand, it is said that complete Buddhahood is adorned with all positive qualities and entails the feature of continuous and all-encompassing welfare for others. It is just in order to highlight this difference that the liberation of hearers and solitary realizers is presented as being a nonentity and without a self or form, while the liberation of the great vehicle is taught as an entity, a self, and something that has form. However, this is not a teaching that the liberation of the great vehicle is something material. Rather, it shows that an emptiness that is merely utter and complete nonexistence cannot possibly be the emptiness of Centrists. Those who still have clinging to such nonexistence cannot realize emptiness. *The Fundamental Verses* says:

> By the flaw of having views about emptiness,
> Those of little understanding are ruined,
> Just as when incorrectly seizing a snake
> Or mistakenly practicing an awareness-mantra.[1050]

Karmapa Mikyö Dorje explains that the teachings on Buddha nature being a self, permanent, substantial, really existent, indestructible, and so on are of expedient meaning.[1051] The same is clearly expressed by Candrakīrti in his *Lucid Words* by extensively quoting that *The Sūtra of the Arrival in Laṅka* itself takes Buddha nature as an expedient meaning.[1052] The reason such teachings are of expedient meaning is that they entail the following:

1) a basis of intention
2) a specific purpose
3) the invalidation of their explicit statements through reasoning

1) As for the basis of intention, the Karmapa says that, in India, there obviously

have been various positions on this topic among Yogācāras and Centrists. Based on the meaning of what is said in such texts as *The Sūtra of Richly Adorned* and *The Sūtra of the Arrival in Laṅka*, different Yogācāras make a number of assertions: Buddha nature is the ground consciousness; it is the seeds of purified phenomena within the ground consciousness; it is the entity of the perfect nature in the sense of the other-dependent nature being empty of the imaginary nature; or it is the stainless ninth consciousness.[1053] On the other hand, Centrists say that from the perspective of analysis or the seeing of the noble ones, all reference points, such as existence and nonexistence, have completely vanished. It is in this way that the suchness of Buddhas and ordinary sentient beings is equality in the sense of natural, complete purity. However, from the mundane perspective of no analysis, when the presentation of cyclic existence and nirvāṇa is taught, it is done by bearing in mind that the disposition to accomplish Buddhahood exists in the continua of sentient beings and that the Body of Perfect Buddhahood radiates from this disposition in accordance with the disciples to be guided. As *The Sublime Continuum* says:

> Since the Body of Perfect Buddhahood radiates,
> Since suchness is undifferentiable,
> And since the disposition exists,
> All beings are always endowed with the Buddha-Heart.[1054]

2) As for the specific purpose of teaching Buddha nature as permanent and so on, it is necessary to present it in this way for the sake of gradually guiding certain disciples who still entertain various levels of reification. As Nāgārjuna's *Precious Garland* says:

> Just as grammarians introduce you [to grammar]
> By reading the fundamentals of the alphabet,
> The Buddha teaches his disciples
> The dharma to the degree they can bear.[1055]

Āryadeva's *Four Hundred Verses* agrees:

> First, one should explain
> Whatever is pleasant to specific people.
> There is no way that someone who is repelled
> Can be a suitable receptacle for the genuine dharma.[1056]

In particular, *The Sublime Continuum* says:

Why did the Victors teach here
That the Buddha-Heart exists in all sentient beings?

They taught this in order to eliminate
The five faults in those in whom they exist.
These are faintheartedness, denigrating inferior sentient beings,
Clinging to what is not the actual, denying the actual dharma, and excessive attachment to oneself.[1057]

3) In the literal sense of being taught as permanent and such in the sūtras, this Buddha nature is not established even conventionally, let alone ultimately, since the Buddha himself refuted all of this. In addition, such sūtras as *The Sūtra of the Great Nirvāṇa*[1058] say again and again that the qualities of the major and minor marks of a Buddha do not exist in any sentient being. The same sūtra, *The Sūtra of the Lion's Roar of Queen Śrīmālā*,[1059] as well as *The Sublime Continuum* together with its commentary by Asaṅga and other texts repeatedly state that such permanence, self, bliss, and complete purity do not exist in the impure phase of sentient beings. For example, *The Sublime Continuum* explicitly says:

Since Buddha wisdom is present in [all] kinds of sentient beings,
Since its stainlessness is by nature without duality,
And since the Buddha disposition is metaphorically referred[1060] to [by the name of] its fruition,
All sentient beings are said to possess the Buddha-Heart.[1061]

Moreover, if the Buddha-Heart were asserted as a self and an uncreated entity, all Buddhist refutations of the notions of a self as entertained by non-Buddhists would be pointless. In some sūtras, such as *The Sūtra of the Arrival in Laṅka*, the Buddha even taught that our ordinary mind, the ground consciousness, is the Buddha-Heart:

Mahāmati, what is positive and negative is as follows: It is [nothing but] the eight consciousnesses. What are these eight? [First,] the Heart of the Thus-Gone Ones is proclaimed as "the ground consciousness."[1062]

Thus, since this Buddha-Heart itself is taught to be of expedient meaning in this sūtra, the ground consciousness also is taught as an expedient meaning. Likewise, through this passage from *The Sūtra of the Arrival in Laṅka*, all scriptural passages that teach about the cut-off disposition; the absolutely definite dispositions of hearers, solitary realizers, and bodhisattvas; the certainty of three vehicles in the final sense; other-emptiness; and self-awareness are shown to be of expedient meaning.

## The Yogācāra System in General

The Tibetan tradition divides the great vehicle into the lineage of profound view and the lineage of vast activity. The former refers to the Madhyamaka system as transmitted by Mañjuśrī to Nāgārjuna, and the latter is the Yogācāra system as presented by Maitreya, Asaṅga, and Vasubandhu. Since the overall tradition that is generally called Yogācāra contains a number of different philosophical streams that may even overlap among various masters, it is impossible to determine *the* single philosophical system of this school, and even a rough outline is certainly beyond the scope of this book.[1063] What follows is a brief sketch of the school, its history, and some of its positions.

In general, the masters of the Yogācāra tradition saw their system as a continuation of all the preceding developments in Buddhism (be it in terms of Abhidharma or Centrism) and not as a radical departure from them or even as a distinct new school per se.[1064] They tried to retain what was useful in other traditions of Buddhism, but in a way that was not ignorant of Centrist warnings against reifications of any kind.[1065] Thus, Yogācāra writings incorporate virtually everything that previous Buddhist schools developed, including intricate abhidharmic systems, detailed explications of the many stages on the different paths of the three vehicles, subtle descriptions of the processes in meditation, explorations of mind and its manifestations on the levels of both ignorance and enlightenment, as well as commentaries on major sūtras, such as the *Prajñāpāramitā sūtras*[1066] and those related to the third turning of the wheel of dharma.[1067] In addition, such masters as Dignāga and Dharmakīrti developed an extensive system of epistemology and reasoning.

Specifically, Asaṅga's hermeneutic framework of the three natures is not at all put forward to contradict the *Prajñāpāramitā sūtras* and Nāgārjuna. Rather, it interprets emptiness within this framework. This is also expressed in Atīśa's autocommentary on *The Lamp for the Path to Enlightenment*:

> The learned in the world say the following: Noble Asaṅga's specific way of explaining the teachings speaks about the meaning of prajñāpāramitā as mere cognizance. At present, this is also what my gurus Suvarṇadvīpa and Ratnākaraśānti think.[1068]

Asaṅga's approach may be seen as a contextualizing comment on the sūtras and as a supplement to Nāgārjuna's view. Because of Nāgārjuna's radical deconstructive analysis of all phenomena, including the Buddhist teachings, in Asaṅga's time even many Buddhists misconceived emptiness in a nihilistic way. Thus, Asaṅga attempted to redress such tendencies and to give a somewhat more positive explanation of emptiness. In addition, in contrast to the Centrists' reserve in talking about the specifics of seeming reality and the Buddhist path of purifying the deluded mind, Asaṅga elaborated on the details of this deluded mind and its gradual purification on the path into the undeluded wisdom that sees ultimate reality. Thus, he investigated not only the true meaning of the scriptures but also what experientially happens in the minds of those who study and practice this meaning.

As will be shown, there is a danger of misinterpreting Yogācāra by focusing only on its commonly associated key notions such as "mere mind," "mere cognizance," the three natures, the ground consciousness, and the eight consciousnesses. As was just said, Yogācāra texts deal with many other topics as well, and ignoring them tends to cause the above notions to be misunderstood because they are taken out of their respective contexts. It is only when taken out of context that Yogācāra texts may seem to introduce novelties or even to be removed from the rest of the Buddhist tradition. Moreover, the key notions of the Yogācāras were not invented by them but clearly appear in various sūtras.[1069]

The central point in the Yogācāra tradition is that everything that we experience or know, affirm or deny, always happens in our minds. Our impression that things, such as matter, exist externally to mind can only occur within this very mind. Thus, the term *cittamātra* (mere mind) refers to all of this being our mere subjective experience. Even the realization that ultimately there is no mind cannot but happen within the mind. As *The Sūtra of the Arrival in Laṅka* formulates:

> Mere mind is in the mind, and no-mind is mind-sprung too.[1070]

Despite reports to the contrary, the vast majority of Yogācāra masters were not led by this fact to the conclusion that this consciousness itself is *ultimately* real or even the *only* reality. Rather, such terms as "mere mind" and "mere cognizance" indicate that both a distinct experiencer and what is experienced are mere projections of our dualistic mind, which thus gets caught in its own web. As Sutton puts it:

> This, indeed, represents the most important epistemic thesis of the Yogācāra philosophy, namely that every statement about the world is a *metaphorical* statement, a mere representation of it (Vijñapti-mātra) which tells us more about our own mind, our own tainted perceptions, reasoning, and memory of past experiences and habits (*vāsanās*),

> than about the external Reality as such (Tathatā). Thus, the statement "Mind-only" (Citta-mātra) is not a prima facie description of the world and its essence, but a characterization of all ultimate reality statements *about* the world and their unavoidable limitations.[1071]

Thus, to realize that it is our own mind that projects our subjective world is a step toward liberation from this intricate web. Despite what other people may claim, it is more than evident from the Yogācāra texts themselves that the term "mere mind" and its equivalents mean neither that the mind alone exists nor that it really exists. Clearly, in the Yogācāra system, the dualistic, projecting mind is the problem and not the solution.[1072] Very similar to Centrism, this system thus focuses on overcoming our fundamental cognitive problem (here called "mere cognizance" or "mere mind") with regard to true reality, which is the basic concern of all Buddhist soteriology. Whatever the Buddhist system, the process of overcoming our own basic ignorance cannot but take place within our own mind. As the name Yogācāra ("practicing meditation") indicates, this school is concerned first and foremost with the mind (its nature, development, and functions on both the deluded and enlightened planes), since it regards the mind as being both the main actor and the stage in the process of meditation. Thus, the path of Yogācāra is explicitly described in terms of a gradual progression from mistaken and thus impure states of mind to the unmistaken, pure wisdom that realizes true reality.

In the Yogācāra system's own terminology, the meditator proceeds from "mere mind" to "the nonduality of apprehender and apprehended" and finally to "nonconceptual wisdom," which is the experiential or "subjective" pole of ultimate reality and inseparable from its "objective" pole, which is the expanse of dharmas. In Centrism, this experiential side of the path is mostly not explicitly stated, but it is implied as the realization that takes place in the mind when Centrist reasonings are used within the framework of the two realities to eliminate this mind's mistaken reference points. In Western terms, one could say that Centrism addresses the issue of overcoming our basic ignorance and clinging through a fundamental critique of any realistic epistemology or ontology by way of dialectic reasoning. On the other hand, Yogācāra describes the same process from a more psychological and introspective point of view by mainly using terminology, such as the three natures, that is derived from meditative states and insights.

Lindtner summarizes the differing approaches of Centrism and Yogācāra to the same end:

> Granting that the common ultimate goal of Mahāyāna (i.e., Madhyamaka as well as Yogācāra) is to achieve *nirvikalpasamādhi* [nonconceptual meditative concentration], or *advayajñāna* [non-dual wisdom] etc., the decisive and fundamental point of dissension remains. How

> can the illusion of the world best be accounted for — in terms of *satyadvaya* [the two realities], or in terms of *svabhāvatraya* [the three natures]? This . . . is, in all its ramification, what the debate between Madhyamaka and Yogācāra is all about.[1073]

Asaṅga is usually regarded as the founder of the Yogācāra system. Significantly, it is said that he felt he did not understand the *Prajñāpāramitā sūtras* well enough and thus supplicated Maitreya, who then taught him "the five dharma works of Maitreya," starting with *The Ornament of Clear Realization*, which is the commentary on the hidden meaning of the *Prajñāpāramitā sūtras.*[1074] Later, Asaṅga is said to have converted his half-brother Vasubandhu to the teachings of the great vehicle, upon which the latter also first focused on studying and commenting on the *Prajñāpāramitā sūtras.* (It was only subsequently that he composed his "typical" Yogācāra works.) That these are not just ephemeral, historical features of the origin of the Yogācāra school is reflected in the fact that this school is—not exclusively, but very clearly—grounded in the *Prajñāpāramitā sūtras.* After Vasubandhu, different currents of thought and interpretation developed within the Yogācāra school.[1075]

Thus, as a very rough outline, one may distinguish three main streams:

1) the distinct system of Maitreya, Asaṅga, and Vasubandhu (the lineage of vast activity)
2) a later, in parts more "idealistic" Yogācāra, as exemplified by Dharmapāla[1076]
3) an epistemologically oriented tradition, headed by Dignāga and Dharmakīrti[1077]

## *The System of the Lineage of Vast Activity*

The objective of this section is to provide evidence for three major points:

1) The lineage of vast activity is not some kind of idealism.
2) It is not what Tibetans call Mere Mentalism.
3) Its final intention is the same as that of Centrism.

As for the scriptural sources of the lineage of vast activity, in his commentary on *The Ornament of Clear Realization*, the Eighth Karmapa lists "the twenty dharma texts that are connected to Maitreya."[1078] With respect to the five main texts—the dharma works of Maitreya himself—in Tibet there is just about every possible interpretation in terms of which of them belong to Mere Mentalism, Autonomism, Consequentialism, Yogācāra, or the Centrism of other-emptiness.

What is clear is that, in terms of their contents, these five texts cover the entire range of the Buddha's teachings. The Eighth Karmapa reports the position of his main teacher, the First Sangye Nyenba Rinpoche:

> All these five dharma works by Maitreya are established as commentaries on the intentions of the entirety of the words of the Buddha in the causal and fruitional great vehicle. The reasons are as follows: As for the middle three treatises, it is not the case that they do not teach the way of dharma of Centrism in an ancillary way. However, their explicit teaching is the distinct system of Yogācāra.[1079] The first dharma work of Maitreya is a common treatise of Centrism and Yogācāra. The last dharma work of Maitreya is a common treatise of sūtra and tantra.[1080]

In terms of the practical application of these teachings, *The Treasury of Knowledge* says that, in terms of the two types of disciples (common and uncommon ones), the first three texts stand for cutting through reference points by way of hearing and reflecting, while the last two are the way to explain complete certainty about the ultimate through meditation.

As for the transmission of these five dharma works by Maitreya, *The Treasury of Knowledge* states that their general philosophical system was explained in detail through many excellent teaching traditions, such as those of Dignāga and Sthiramati. The uncommon philosophical system of these texts was sustained in such a way that the most supreme disciples transmitted it orally. This meant that the first three texts of Maitreya were widely taught in India, while *The Distinction between Phenomena and Their Nature* and *The Sublime Continuum* were not commonly available and are only rarely mentioned in other—mostly late—Indian treatises. After these latter two texts were eventually lost, the mahāsiddha Maitrīpa rediscovered them inside an old stupa and received direct instructions from Maitreya. He then passed on all five works to Paṇḍita Ānandakīrti and others. The latter transmitted them to the great Kashmiri Paṇḍita Sajjana in the eleventh century.

From Sajjana, two main lines of transmission into Tibet started.[1081] First, the two translators Zu Gaway Dorje (eleventh century)[1082] and Dsen Kawoche[1083] (born 1021) studied with this master and translated Maitreya's works.[1084] The translation and transmission of *The Sublime Continuum* and the other texts of Maitreya (particularly *The Dharmadharmatāvibhāga*) through these two translators is called "the meditative tradition of the dharma works of Maitreya." The other line of transmission and translation of these texts by Ngog Lotsāwa—who also studied with Sajjana and Dsen Kawoche—is called "the tradition of hearing and reflection."[1085]

In Tibet, the two translators Zu and Dsen orally passed on the first transmission. Among many others, Dsen taught it to Changrawa,[1086] and the latter to Tarma Dsöndrü[1087] of Chog Dodebu,[1088] who composed an extensive commentary on *The Ornament of Sūtras.* Then, the great eleventh-century siddha Yumowa Mikyö Dorje[1089] and others brought parts of this system into a written form for the first time.[1090] Apparently, Dölpopa Sherab Gyaltsen was the first to use the terms "other-empty" and "self-empty" and widely propagated this system.[1091] So what had been known in Tibet by such names as "the meditative tradition of the dharma works of Maitreya," "False Aspectarian Centrism,"[1092] and "profound luminous Centrism"[1093] was from then on increasingly referred to as "the system of other-emptiness" and eventually as "other-empty Centrism." There were many other masters who greatly elucidated the uncommon essential points of this system, such as the Third Karmapa Rangjung Dorje, Śākya Chogden[1094] (1428–1507), Tāranātha[1095] (1575–1635), the Seventh Karmapa Chötra Gyamtso, the Bhutanese Panchen Śākya Rinchen, Katog Rigdzin Tsewang Norbu[1096] (1698–1755), the Eighth Situpa Chökyi Jungnay (1699–1774), Jamyang Khyentse Wangpo[1097] (1820–1892), and Jamgön Kongtrul Lodrö Taye. Mipham Rinpoche (1846–1912) himself claimed to be a Consequentialist, but he also wrote on other-emptiness, which led to a number of different opinions as to his position.[1098] Prominent recent masters of this tradition include Kalu Rinpoche (1905–1989), Düdjom Rinpoche (1904–1987), and Dilgo Khyentse Rinpoche (1910–1991).

The tradition of other-emptiness is far from a monolithic doctrine. For example, there are great differences between Dölpopa and most of the later proponents, who also have varying views on certain aspects of the teachings.[1099] A major distinction within the system of other-emptiness is into "the other-emptiness of luminosity"[1100] and "the other-emptiness of the expanse."[1101] The first one means that the wisdom of Buddha nature is empty of adventitious stains (the "other") and that this wisdom itself is not empty but really existent as the ultimate nature of luminosity. Thus, the luminous nature of mind and its innate Buddha qualities are emphasized. Typical proponents are Dölpopa and his followers. "The other-emptiness of the expanse" means that Buddha nature's wisdom itself is free from reference points. For example, such is presented by the Eighth Karmapa in his commentary on *The Ornament of Clear Realization* and also in the writings of the Sixth Shamarpa Chökyi Wangchug. The most common version of other-emptiness that is widely taught nowadays in the Kagyü school is the one by Jamgön Kongtrul Lodrö Taye, which is largely based on Tāranātha's presentation and more oriented toward "the other-emptiness of luminosity."[1102]

## *A Brief Presentation of the Main Points of the Lineage of Vast Activity*

The following presentation of the major points of the lineage of vast activity relies mainly on the texts by Maitreya, Asaṅga (in particular his *Synopsis of the*

*Great Vehicle*), and Vasubandhu.[1103] The methodological basis for looking at any philosophical or religious text is well expressed by Schmithausen:

> I presuppose that the texts I make use of are to be taken seriously, in the sense that one has to accept that they mean what they say, and that what they mean is reasonable within its own terms.[1104]

Having attempted to follow this approach with regard to Centrist texts, I believe that the works of Yogācāra in general and the lineage of vast activity in particular are to be treated in the same way, without looking at them through the eyes of Centrism or any other system extrinsic to them. *The Distinction between the Middle and Extremes* says:

> False imagination[1105] exists.
> Duality does not exist in it.
> Emptiness exists within it,
> And it also exists within this [emptiness].
>
> Neither empty nor nonempty—
> In this way, everything is explained.
> Because of existence, because of nonexistence, and because of existence,
> This is the middle way.[1106]

To explain this from the point of view of cutting through reference points, it is said that, on the level of seeming reality, consciousness that appears as various appearances—that is, mere false imagination—exists. Since the apprehending part and the apprehended part that appear within this false imagination are merely mentally imputed, they are not even existent on the conventional level. Thus, seeming reality is free from the two extremes:

1) It is free from the extreme of nonexistence and the extreme of extinction through accepting the mere nominal existence of false imagination on the seeming level.
2) It is free from the extreme of permanence and the extreme of existence through lying beyond all mutually dependent and imputed phenomena, such as an apprehending and an apprehended aspect.

As for emptiness free from reference points, it ultimately exists within consciousness—that is, within false imagination—as the mode of the true nature of this false imagination. When emptiness is thus said to exist, it cannot be overstressed that this means that it exists as the ultimate *mode* of being of all phenomena and not itself as any reified entity. For Yogācāras, existence and nonexistence are not ontological assertions but rather phenomenological descriptions of what is experienced in the mind. Thus, in the phase of ordinary beings with stains, dualistic consciousness (that which bears the nature of emptiness) exists within the nature of phenomena as adventitious stains that are separable. "Adventitious" means that these stains do not really exist and are the factors to be relinquished. Thus, ultimate reality is also free from the two extremes:

1) It is beyond the extremes of nonexistence and extinction, because emptiness is ultimately established as undeceiving.
2) It is beyond the extremes of existence and permanence, since all phenomena that consist of the duality of apprehender and apprehended—such as false imagination—do not really exist.

So, the seeming—apprehender and apprehended—is merely something that emerges as an appearance of mistakenness. Apart from this mere appearance, there is nothing that is established through a nature of its own. Therefore, the seeming is empty of a nature of its own. In terms of the dichotomy of self and others, it is obviously also empty of what is other than itself, since something that is established as the nature of something other than itself is not possible among knowable objects. Therefore, the seeming is empty in all aspects—self and other—and thus not something nonempty. On the other hand, emptiness can be said to be established from the very beginning through its own nature—the lack of nature—which is always unchanging. It is solely in this way, nominally speaking, that it can be said to be not empty of its own nature and always existent. Furthermore, it is empty of everything other, that is, the adventitious stains.

The three natures—the imaginary, the other-dependent, and the perfect nature[1107]—are described in *The Sūtra That Unravels the Intention*:

> Guṇākara, what is the imaginary characteristic of phenomena? It is what is presented as names and symbols in terms of a nature or the particulars of phenomena in order to subsequently designate conventional terms in accordance with [this]. Guṇākara, what is the other-dependent characteristic of phenomena? It is just the dependent origination of phenomena. This is as follows: "Since this exists, this originates. Since this has arisen, that arises. Through the condition of unawareness, formations [arise] . . . " up to "Thus, nothing but this great mass of suffering will happen." Guṇākara, what is the perfect characteristic of phenomena? It is the suchness of phenomena.[1108]

The other-dependent nature is the mere consciousness of false imagination that appears as the entities of apprehender and apprehended, because these are appearances under the influence of something other, the latent tendencies of unawareness. It appears as the outer world with its various beings and objects; as one's own body; as the sense consciousnesses that perceive these objects and the conceptual consciousness that thinks about them; as the clinging to a personal self and real phenomena; and as the mental events, such as feelings, that accompany all these consciousnesses. Thus, false imagination bifurcates experience into seemingly real subjects that apprehend seemingly real objects. This split into subject and object—the imaginary nature—does not exist even on the seeming level, but the mind that brings about this split exists and functions on this level.

The imaginary nature is the entire range of what is superimposed by conceptions as a self and really existent phenomena onto the various apprehended aspects within the other-dependent nature. In other words, what appears as one's own body and mind forms the bases for imputing a personal self. All that appears as other beings, outer objects, and the consciousnesses that relate to them provides the bases for imputing really existent phenomena. This imaginary nature exists only conventionally as a nominal object for the consciousnesses of ordinary sentient beings. It is in no way substantially established, since it does not withstand analysis. In detail, it consists of the following:

- the aspects that appear as conceptual objects, such as the mental image of a form
- the connections of names and referents (the notion that a name is the corresponding referent and the mistaking of a referent for the corresponding name)
- all that is apprehended through mental superimposition, such as outer, inner, middle, end, big, small, good, bad, direction, time, and so on
- all nonentities, such as space

The perfect nature is emptiness in the sense that what appears as other-dependent, false imagination is primordially never established as the imaginary nature. This emptiness is the sphere of nonconceptual wisdom, and its nature is phenomenal identitylessness. *The Sūtra That Unravels the Intention* says:

> Lack of nature, phenomenal identitylessness, suchness, and the observed object for purification, these are the perfect characteristic.[1109]

Why is this emptiness called "the perfect nature"? It is perfect because it never changes into something else, is the supreme among all dharmas, and is the observed object to be focused on during the process of purifying the mind from adventitious stains. Due to its quality of never changing into something else, it is also named suchness. Since it is unmistaken, it is called the true end. As it is the utter peace of all discursiveness, it is signlessness. Because it is the sphere of ultimate wisdom, it is the ultimate. Through realizing it, the dharmas of the noble ones are attained. Thus, it is the expanse of dharmas.

Just like the limitless expanse of space, the nature of the expanse of dharmas is of one taste. Therefore, ultimately, there are no divisions in it. However, conventionally, the perfect nature may be presented as twofold:

1) the emptiness of nonentities
2) the emptiness of the nature of nonentities

The first is the emptiness in the sense that the other-dependent nature is devoid of any personal and phenomenal identities. This has the nature of a nonimplicative negation. The second is the emptiness in the sense that this very other-dependent nature is not established as the nature of these two types of identity. This has the nature of an implicative negation and refers to the actual nature of other-dependent cognition, or what is called "mind's natural luminosity."[1110] Another classification of this nature into two is as follows:

1) the unchanging perfect nature[1111] (suchness)
2) the unmistaken perfect nature[1112] (the wisdom that realizes this suchness)

It can also be presented as these two:

1) the path of purification
2) the observed object of this path

1) The path of purification is again divided into two:
   a) cause
   b) result

a) The cause of the path of purification is the naturally abiding disposition. It is constituted by the uncontaminated seeds in the ground consciousness that are primordially present by the very nature of phenomena. These seeds are the latent tendencies of listening[1113] to the genuine dharma, the natural outflow[1114] of the expanse of dharma. The latent tendencies of listening are the seeds that spring from listening to and understanding the meaning of the Buddhadharma and thus serve as the cause for the Dharma Body. However, since they abide in the mind stream from the very beginning through the nature of phenomena, they are merely revived through listening; they are not newly created. Asaṅga's *Synopsis of the Great Vehicle* says:

> The [supramundane wisdom] originates from the natural outflow of

the completely pure expanse of dharmas, that is, the latent tendencies of listening that comprise all seeds.

One may say, "What are these latent tendencies of listening? Are they the very entity of the ground consciousness or are they not? If they were the very entity of the ground consciousness, how should they be suitable as the seeds of its remedy? And if they are not its entity, then what is the matrix of these seeds of latent tendencies of listening?" The matrix that is entered by these latent tendencies of listening in dependence on the enlightenment of Buddhas is the consciousness of complete ripening. [The latent tendencies of listening] enter it in a way of staying together with it like milk and water. They are not the ground consciousness, because they are the very seeds of its remedy. . .

The small, medium, and great latent tendencies of listening are to be regarded as seeds of the Dharma Body. Since they are the remedy for the ground consciousness, they are not of the nature of the ground consciousness. [In the sense of being a remedy,] they are something mundane, but since they are the natural outflow of the supramundane, the utterly completely pure expanse of dharmas, they are the seeds of supramundane mind. Although supramundane mind did not originate, they are the remedy for entanglement through being afflicted, the remedy for migration in the unpleasant realms, and the remedy that makes all wrongdoing vanish. They are what is in complete concordance with meeting Buddhas and bodhisattvas.

Although [these latent tendencies in the minds of] beginner bodhisattvas are mundane, they should be regarded as constituted by the Dharma Body and [those of] the hearers and solitary realizers as constituted by the Body of Complete Release.[1115] These [latent tendencies] are not the ground consciousness but are constituted by the Dharma Body and the Body of Complete Release. To the extent that they gradually shine forth in a small, medium, and great way, to that same extent also the consciousness of complete ripening wanes and changes state too. If it has changed state in all aspects, the consciousness of complete ripening becomes devoid of seeds and is also relinquished in all aspects.

One might wonder, "How is it that the ground consciousness, which abides together with what is not the ground consciousness like water and milk, can wane in all aspects?" This is like geese[1116] drinking milk from

> water. It is similar to the change of state when, being free from mundane desire, the latent tendencies of what is not meditative equipoise wane, while the latent tendencies of meditative equipoise increase.[1117]

Thus, Asaṅga's explanation implies that the mere actuality of the nature of phenomena, suchness or emptiness, is not the naturally abiding disposition. Rather, the naturally abiding disposition is what realizes this actuality: It is these latent tendencies of listening, the aspect of supreme knowledge that realizes the nature of phenomena (not, however, as a distinct thing different from itself). The reason given is that the latent tendencies of listening render the sets of the six inner sources[1118] of individual sentient beings distinct from each other. Thus, the naturally abiding disposition is what is called "the distinct feature of the six sources."[1119] This means that, through the latent tendencies of listening that serve as the cause for the path of the great vehicle, the six inner sources that exist within the continuum of that person who has revived these latent tendencies are made distinct from the inner sources of those sentient beings who have not revived such tendencies. These tendencies are the indicator that the person who is endowed with them has the disposition of the great vehicle. The same goes for the latent tendencies of listening that serve as the causes for the paths of hearers and solitary realizers respectively.

Why are the latent tendencies of listening included in the perfect nature? As the above quote from *The Synopsis of the Great Vehicle* shows, they are neither the imaginary nor the other-dependent nature, since they constitute the remedy for affliction and so on.

b) The results in terms of the path of purification are the actual paths that are an outcome of the latent tendencies of listening, that is, the paths of the three vehicles, such as the thirty-seven dharmas concordant with enlightenment and the six perfections.

2) The observed object of these paths—the genuine dharma—is also included in the perfect nature. It is not the imaginary nature, since the genuine dharma is the cause for purification. It is also not the other-dependent nature, since this dharma does not originate from the seeds of affliction. Rather, the dharma is the result that is the natural outflow of having realized the completely pure expanse of dharmas.

In brief, the other-dependent nature is like the basic materials from which an illusionist creates an illusion. The imaginary nature is like the various mistaken appearances of illusory animals that may appear to the audience due to these materials, although there clearly are no such animals in the materials. The perfect nature is like the space that pervades all of this. It is not a superimposition like the imaginary nature; in other words, it is not a superimposition in the sense that nonexistents are taken to exist or that existents are taken not to exist. Nor does the perfect nature originate from other-dependent conditions, which are the seeds of the latent tendencies for affliction.[1120] However, the perfect nature cannot be said to be either identical to or different from the other-dependent nature. Therefore, in its nature, the perfect nature is inseparable from the other-dependent nature and is merely mentally imputed as something different, because the perfect nature is the nature of phenomena and the other-dependent nature is what bears this nature.

As for the division into seeming reality and ultimate reality, the imaginary and the other-dependent natures are only seemingly established, since they are the mistaken mind and the appearances due to this mistakenness. The perfect nature is ultimately established, since it is real as the object of the ultimate supramundane wisdom.

The seeming may be classified as threefold:

1) The imaginary nature is the imaginary seeming.
2) The other-dependent nature is the seeming in terms of consciousness.
3) The terms that express the perfect nature are the seeming in terms of expression.

The ultimate is also threefold:

1) Suchness is the ultimate object.
2) Nirvāṇa is the ultimate attainment.
3) The path is the ultimate practice.

As *The Distinction between the Middle and Extremes* says:

> What is imaginary, consciousness,
> And also expressions are coarse.

and

> Object, attainment, and practice
> Are asserted as the three aspects of the ultimate.[1121]

The imaginary and the other-dependent natures are equal in three respects: They do not really exist, are appearances of mistakenness, and are something seeming and false. Nevertheless, it is necessary to classify them separately through their characteristics. The imaginary does not even exist on the level of the seeming, while the other-dependent exists on the level of the seeming. The perfect does not exist on the level of the seeming, but it exists as the ultimate nature.

Furthermore, the imaginary nature is called "the lack of nature in terms of characteristics"; the other-dependent nature is "the lack of nature in terms of arising"; and the perfect nature is "the ultimate lack of nature." Vasubandhu's *Thirty Verses* says:

> Based on the three kinds of lack of nature
> Of the three kinds of nature,
> It is taught that all phenomena
> Are without nature.[1122]

The imaginary nature is like mistakenly apprehending the visual appearances that are caused by blurred vision to be floating hairs and such. Since this is nothing but names and superimpositions, it does not exist at all. Therefore, the imaginary nature is "the lack of nature in terms of characteristics."

The other-dependent nature consists of dependently originating appearances, like the plain visual appearances seen by someone with blurred vision. These appear in an illusionlike manner but are without any nature of their own and do not really arise. Therefore, the other-dependent nature is "the lack of nature in terms of arising."

The ultimate lack of nature of the perfect nature has two aspects. First, although there is no personal identity, the perfect nature is what functions as the remedy for the notion of a personal identity. Just as an illusory ship to cross an illusory ocean, it serves as the means to cross the ocean of cyclic existence to the other shore of nirvāṇa. This remedial aspect is actually contained within the other-dependent nature, but it is the cause for realizing the ultimate. Therefore, it is included in the category of "the ultimate lack of nature." The second aspect of the perfect nature is the one from which enlightenment is attained through actively engaging in it. This aspect is undifferentiable from phenomenal identitylessness. Like space, it is omnipresent and not established as anything whatsoever. It can be compared to the free space that is the natural object of unimpaired vision when the eye defect of blurred vision has been cured and one realizes that what appeared as floating hairs never actually existed anywhere. This aspect is "the ultimate lack of nature" per se.

The above is how the three natures and the threefold lack of nature are taught in the sixth and seventh chapter of *The Sūtra That Unravels the Intention.* There, the Buddha also says:

> Having this threefold lack of nature in mind—the lack of nature in terms of characteristics, the lack of nature in terms of arising, and the ultimate lack of nature—I have taught, "All phenomena lack a nature."[1123]

On the seeming level, the imaginary is nominally existent and the other-dependent is substantially existent. The perfect nature does not exist in any of these two ways, but it exists in a way of being without reference points. Thus, the imaginary is also called "the emptiness of the nonexistent," the other-dependent "the emptiness of the existent," and the perfect "the ultimate emptiness." As Maitreya says in his *Ornament of the Sūtras*:

> If one knows the emptiness of the nonexistent,
> Likewise the emptiness of the existent,
> And also natural emptiness,
> Then this is expressed as "knowing emptiness."[1124]

Therefore, it is asserted in this system that all knowable objects are pervaded by emptiness and the lack of nature. One may wonder, "If the perfect nature exists as something really and ultimately established, does it then exist as something that arises, abides, and ceases; as something that comes and goes, changes, or disappears; as something in space and time; as a unity or a multiplicity?" None of these is the case. The kinds of existents just mentioned necessarily do not really exist and are just seeming appearances. The perfect nature, however, is not connected with any seeming phenomena whatsoever. It is without arising, abiding, and ceasing and also without coming and going. It is neither a unity nor a multiplicity, neither a cause nor a result. The triad of definition, definiendum, and illustrating example is irrelevant to it. It is free from all reference points, such as space and time. Because of all this, it is said to be naturally permanent. Likewise, it is partless, because it cannot be divided into different pieces. It is omnipresent and all-encompassing, because it is the true nature of all phenomena.

**The Lineage of Vast Activity Is Not the Same as "Mere Mentalism"**

Since Tibetan texts so often mention—more or less pejoratively—those called Mere Mentalists or Proponents of Cognizance, we should investigate their purported assertions and positions. Karmapa Mikyö Dorje briefly identifies them as those within the general Yogācāra tradition who interpret the framework of the three natures in a realistic sense. They are portrayed as asserting that consciousness is really and ultimately existent, referring to the other-dependent nature in general and the ground consciousness in particular.[1125] Mere Mentalists are also said to describe the perfect nature as the really existent other-dependent nature being empty of the imaginary nature. Based on the passage in various sūtras that "the whole universe which consists of the three worlds is mere mind," another major position that is often ascribed to them is that only mind is real and that everything in the universe is nothing other than mind and created by it.[1126] However, as will be shown immediately below, these positions attributed to the Mere

Mentalists cannot be ascribed to the lineage of vast activity, since none of them is found in the texts of this lineage and most of them are explicitly rejected.

The lineage of vast activity denies any real or ultimate existence of "mere mind" or "mere cognizance." For example, Asaṅga's *Synopsis of Ascertainment* refutes both "Śramanas and Brahmans who claim some substantially existing mere mind" by using reasoning and scripture.[1127] Vasubandhu's *Commentary on The Distinction between the Middle and Extremes* says:

> Based on the observation of mere cognizance, the nonobservation of [outer] referents arises. Based on the nonobservation of referents, also the nonobservation of mere cognizance arises. Thus, one engages in the characteristic of the nonexistence of both apprehender and apprehended. Therefore, observation is established as the nature of nonobservation, because if there is no referent to be observed, an observation [of it] it is not suitable. Thus, one should understand observation and nonobservation as being equal.[1128]

Sthiramati's subcommentary on this text elaborates:

> Thus, in its nature, observation is nonobservation. . . . [This means that] there is no difference between the nonobservation of referents and the observation as mere cognizance in that [both] do not exist. Thus, they are to be understood as equal. . . . [The latter] is just called "observation," since an unreal object appears [for it]. However, since there is no [actual] referent, nothing is observed by this ["observation"]. Therefore, ultimately, its nature is nonobservation. . . . Hence, it is said that it does not exist as the nature of observation. In such observation, neither is the nature of observation to be eliminated, nor is the nature of nonobservation to be established. They are the same in that they are undifferentiable. . . . "So why is [mere] cognition called 'observation' then?" In its nature, it is nonobservation, but [it is designated] in this way, since an unreal object appears [for it], as this is the convention in the world and the treatises.[1129]

Maitreya's *Ornament of Sūtras* says:

> The mind is aware that nothing other than mind exists.
> Then, it is realized that mind does not exist either.
> The intelligent ones are aware that both do not exist
> And abide in the expanse of dharmas in which these are absent.[1130]

Even *The Sūtra of the Arrival in Laṅka*, which is so often considered one of the classic sūtras of Mere Mentalism in the above sense, declares:

> Through reliance on mere mind,
> One does not imagine outer objects.
> By resting in the observed object of suchness,
> One should go beyond mere mind too.
>
> Going beyond mere mind,
> One must even go beyond the nonappearance [of apprehender and apprehended].
> The yogic practitioner who rests in nonappearance
> Sees the great vehicle.
>
> This spontaneously present, peaceful resting
> Is completely purified through aspiration prayers.
> Genuine identityless wisdom
> Sees by way of nonappearance.[1131]

The same is clearly stated again and again in other texts of this tradition too, such as Maitreya's *Distinction between Phenomena and Their Nature*:

> Through [outer referents] being observed in this way, they are observed as mere cognizance.
> Due to observing [them] as mere cognizance,
> Referents are not observed,
> And through not observing referents,
> Mere cognizance is not observed [either].
> Through not observing this [mere cognizance],
> One enters into the observation of both being without difference.
> This nonobservation of a difference between these two
> Is nonconceptual wisdom.
> It is without object and without observing,
> Since it is characterized
> By nonobservation of all characteristics.[1132]

Vasubandhu's *Instruction on the Three Natures* agrees:

> Through the observation of [objects] being merely mind,
> A referent to be known is not observed.

> Through not observing a referent to be known,
> Mind cannot be observed [either].
> Through not observing both,
> The expanse of dharmas is observed.[1133]

His *Thirty Verses* says:

> When consciousness itself
> Does not observe any observed object,
> It rests in the actuality of mere consciousness,[1134]
> Since there is no apprehender without something apprehended.
>
> Being no-mind and nonreferential,
> It is supramundane wisdom.
> This is the complete change of state
> And the relinquishment of the twofold impregnations of negativity.
>
> It is the undefiled expanse
> That is inconceivable, positive, and constant.
> It is the blissful Body of Release
> And the Dharma Body of the Great Sage.[1135]

In the gradual process of realizing true reality, the expedient purpose of the step of describing objects as being "merely mind" or "merely cognition" is to prevent the total denial of seeming reality in which subject and object appear. To start by presenting just the unqualified nonexistence of mind (the perceiving subject) courts the danger of falling into a nihilistic extreme by failing to account for the mere appearance of the interaction between mind and its objects. Such is stated in Sthiramati's *Subcommentary on The Distinction between the Middle and Extremes*:

> "[If neither objects nor mind exist,] then why is the nonexistence of mere cognizance not presented right from the start?" The apprehender depends on the apprehended. Consequently, if [it is established that] there is no object to be observed [by the apprehender], one may easily realize [the nonexistence of the apprehender too], since something that has the nature of being [its] observed object has been eliminated. Otherwise, existence would be altogether denied due to the lack of mutual dependence of apprehender and apprehended.[1136]

This does not differ from what Candrakīrti's *Entrance into Centrism* says:

The Buddhas said, "If there are no knowable objects,
One easily finds that a knower is excluded."
If knowable objects do not exist, the negation of a knower is established.
Therefore, they first negated knowable objects.[1137]

The lineage of vast activity clearly postulates that the actual liberating purpose of "mere mind" lies in going beyond it, that is, transcending duality by pointing beyond this very mind and entering the middle path of emptiness or suchness. In this, *The Sūtra of the Arrival in Laṅka* is followed:

The [Buddhas] do not see mere mind.
Since there is nothing to be seen [by it], it does not arise.
This middle path is what is taught
By me as well as by others.

Arising and nonarising
As well as entities and nonentities are emptiness.
The lack of nature of [all] entities
Is not to be conceived in terms of such pairs.

Through the realization that what is seen is of one's own mind,
Clinging to duality is abandoned.
Abandoning means fully understanding
And not destroying mind's imagining activity.

Through the full understanding that what is seen is of one's own mind,
Mind's imagining activity ceases to operate.
Since mind's imagining activity ceases to operate,
Suchness has become free from mind.[1138]

From all of these sources, it should be very clear that such Yogācāra terms as "mere mind," "mere cognizance," and "mere consciousness" are used in describing a meditative progression or as provisional antidotes for clinging to external referents.[1139] However, these notions are in no way ontologically or metaphysically reified. Rather, once their purpose is fulfilled—that is, realizing that both apprehender and apprehended do not really exist—they are put out of commission. The notion of "mere mind" in Yogācāra is as self-negating as the notion of emptiness in Centrism. Just as in the case of emptiness, to reify or cling to the antidote only turns it into poison. This is most clearly expressed by the Chinese Yogācāra Hsüan Tsang in his *Ch'eng wei-shih lun*:

> Since *citta* and *caittas*[1140] depend on other things to arise (*paratantra*), they are like a magician's trick, not truly substantial ('real') entities. But so as to oppose false attachments to the view that external to *citta* and *caittas* there are perceptual-objects (ching, *viśaya*) [composed of] real, substantial entities, we say that the only existent is consciousness. But if you become attached to the view that *vijñāpti-mātra* is something truly real and existent, that's the same as being attached to external perceptual-objects, i.e., it becomes just another dharma-attachment [and definitely not liberating].[1141]

The same point can be found in Centrist texts. For example, Nāgārjuna's *Sixty Stanzas on Reasoning* says:

> What is stated as the four great elements and such
> Is contained in consciousness.
> Since such [consciousness] is left behind through wisdom,
> Is it not falsely conceived?[1142]

His *Commentary on the Mind of Enlightenment* agrees:

> As the entities of apprehender and apprehended,
> The appearances of consciousness
> Do not exist as outer objects
> That are different from consciousness.
>
> Therefore, in the sense of having the nature of entities,
> In all cases, outer objects do not exist.
> It is these distinct appearances of consciousness
> That appear as the aspects of forms.
>
> The aggregates, constituents, and so on were taught
> In order to counteract the clinging to a self.
> By abiding in [the view of] mere mind,
> Those with good fortune relinquish them too.[1143]

And Kamalaśīla's *Stages of Meditation* states:

> Outer form does not exist.
> It is one's own mind that appears [as something] outside.[1144]

Furthermore, the lineage of vast activity does not claim that the world is *created* by mind. There is no such statement in any Yogācāra texts. What they do say, though, is that we mistake our mentally projected constructions for some real or external world.

To summarize, ultimate reality in Yogācāra is clearly not some real mind or "mere mind." Vasubandhu's verses above explicitly say that it is "no-mind (*acitta*)," meaning free from dualistic, reifying mind. Instead, Yogācāra often explains the characteristics of the ultimate in a way that is as non-affirming as Centrist descriptions. Asaṅga's *Commentary on The Sūtra That Unravels the Intention* says:

> Here, the Buddha teaches the five characteristics of the ultimate. The five characteristics of the ultimate are the characteristic of being inexpressible, the characteristic of being nondual, the characteristic of being completely beyond the sphere of dialectic, the characteristic of being completely beyond difference and nondifference, and the characteristic of being of one taste in everything.[1145]

*The Ornament of Sūtras* gives the following five pairs of characteristics of the ultimate:

> Neither existent nor non-existent, neither same nor other,
> Neither arising nor ceasing, neither increasing nor decreasing,
> Not purified and yet purified again—
> These are the characteristics of the ultimate.[1146]

The lineage of vast activity also does not assert that the ground consciousness is inherently or ultimately existent. Rather, it must be eliminated in order for one to attain enlightenment. As *The Sūtra That Unravels the Intention* says:

> Viśālamati, bodhisattvas . . . do not see an appropriating consciousness. . . . They do not see a fundamental ground, nor do they see a ground consciousness.[1147]

and

> The appropriating consciousness is profound and subtle.
> All seeds flow [toward it] like the stream of a river.
> It is inappropriate to conceive of it as a self.
> I did not teach it to naïve beings.[1148]

Asaṅga's commentary elaborates on this verse:

> The [ground consciousness] is difficult to understand, since it is not [taught] on the lower levels of the teachings, since it abides as bearing the characteristics of the seeds of the [six] operative consciousnesses, and since it does not abide through having any characteristics of its own.[1149]

This means that the ground consciousness is nothing but the sum of its seeds[1150] and that there is no other underlying, permanent substratum or entity of a ground consciousness apart from the seeds that constitute it. Since the seeming continua of these seeds are impermanent, the ground consciousness is merely a seeming, impermanent continuum too. It also does not actively create anything. Thus, it is not at all like the Hindu ātman or a creator. Rather, *The Synopsis of the Great Vehicle* says:

> The ground consciousness is like an illusion, a mirage, a dream, or [the appearances of] blurred vision.[1151]

As quoted above, the same text also explains that the ground consciousness is remedied by the latent tendencies of listening. Thus, Vasubandhu's *Thirty Verses* states:

> In arhathood, it becomes annulled.[1152]

The ninth chapter ("the grounds without mind")[1153] of Asaṅga's *Grounds of Yoga Practice* says:

> In terms of the presentation of the ultimate, the ground without mind is the expanse of the nirvāṇa without remainder. Why? Because the ground consciousness ceases in it.[1154]

The text says that this applies to arhats, bodhisattvas who will not revert, and Buddhas alike and elaborates in several places on the details of the relinquishment of the ground consciousness. Similar statements are also found in the *Nivṛtti* portion of Asaṅga's *Synopsis of Ascertainment*[1155] and his *Synopsis of the Great Vehicle*.[1156]

The final realization of true reality as explained by the lineage of vast activity is the nonreferential, nondualistic wisdom that realizes and is inseparable from the expanse of dharmas free from both afflictive and cognitive obscurations. This is the Dharma Body of a fully enlightened Buddha. As in Centrism, this wisdom is typically described by Yogācāras by merely excluding what it is not. *The Distinction between Phenomena and Their Nature* says that nonconceptual wisdom is characterized by the exclusion of five aspects.[1157] First, as was explained before about the correct notion of mental nonengagement, nonconceptual wisdom is not just the mere absence of mental engagement. Rather, in the direct seeing of the true nature of phenomena, all reference points have vanished for this wisdom. Thus, since there is no reference point for it to engage in anymore, any mental engagement in reference points naturally subsides. This does not mean, however, that this wisdom lacks wakefulness and one-pointed, sharp mindfulness. It is also not without knowing, since it directly realizes the nature of phenomena. Second, it is not just a state of being beyond coarse and subtle conceptual analysis, since this likewise applies to the upper three meditative concentrations of the form realm. Third, nonconceptual wisdom is not the mere subsiding of all thoughts, for otherwise deep sleep, fainting, being completely drunk, or the meditative absorption of cessation would also qualify as such wisdom. Fourth, it is not something that is by its very nature without thoughts, such as matter. Fifth, it is also not the state of trying not to think anything, since this is just another subtle thought or grasping in itself. *The Ornament of Sūtras* says:

> Just as the heat in [a piece of] iron
> And blurred vision in the eyes vanish,
> The mind and wisdom of a Buddha
> Are not expressed as existent or nonexistent.[1158]

*The Sūtra That Unravels the Intention* says:

> "O Blessed One, through which perfection do bodhisattvas apprehend the lack of nature of phenomena?" "Avalokiteśvara, they apprehend it through the perfection of knowledge." "O Blessed One, if they apprehend the lack of nature through the perfection of knowledge, why do they not also apprehend that [phenomena] have a nature?" "Avalokiteśvara, I definitely do not say that a nature apprehends the lack of nature. However, without teaching through letters, one is not able to teach the lack of nature, that which is without letters, or what is to be personally experienced. Therefore, I declare that '[the perfection of knowledge] apprehends the lack of nature.'"[1159]

As for the Dharma Body, the tenth chapter of *The Synopsis of the Great Vehicle* makes it very clear that this Dharma Body is not something outside of emptiness. Specifically, it says that it is free from the duality of existence and nonexistence (X.3). Asvabhāva's (450–530) *Explanation of The Synopsis of the Great Vehicle* elaborates:

> [The phrase] "[The Dharma Body] is characterized by the nonduality of existence and nonexistence" [means that] it does not have the characteristic of existence, since all phenomena have the essential character of the nonexistence of entities. Nor does it have the characteristic of nonexistence, because its nature is emptiness.[1160]

In an insertion into his Chinese translation of Vasubandhu's commentary, Paramārtha emphasizes here that all the enlightened bodies of a Buddha must be interpreted through the understanding of emptiness.[1161] In both *The Sublime Continuum*[1162] and *The Ornament of Sūtras*,[1163] the Dharma Body is said to be spacelike and is equated with the completely pure expanse of dharmas as well as the naturally luminous nature of the mind.

*The Synopsis of the Great Vehicle* compares the ways of understanding the three natures:

> "In this teaching that is the very extensive teaching of the great vehicle of the Buddhas, the Blessed Ones, how should the imaginary nature be understood?" It should be understood through the teachings on the synonyms of nonexistents.
>
> "How should the other-dependent nature be understood?" It should be understood to be like an illusion, a mirage, an optical illusion, a reflection, an echo, [the reflection of] the moon in water, and a magical creation.
>
> "How should the perfect nature be understood?" It should be understood through the teachings on the four kinds of completely pure dharmas. As for these four kinds of completely pure dharmas, (1) natural complete purity means suchness, emptiness, the true end, signlessness, and the ultimate. Also the expanse of dharmas is just this. (2) Unstained complete purity refers to [the state of] this very [natural purity] not having any obscurations. (3) The complete purity of the path to attain this [unstained purity] consists of all the dharmas concordant with enlightenment, the perfections, and so on. (4) The completely pure object in order to generate this [path] is the teaching of the genuine dharma of the great vehicle. In this way, since this [dharma] is the cause for complete purity, it is not the imaginary [nature]. Since

> it is the natural outflow of the pure expanse of dharmas, it is not the other-dependent [nature either]. All completely pure dharmas are included in these four kinds [of purity].[1164]

The text elaborates further on the unreal nature of the other-dependent nature. However, this lack of reality does not prevent the mere appearance and functioning of various seeming manifestations for deluded and undeluded minds:

> Why is the other-dependent nature taught in such a way as being like an illusion and so on? In order to eliminate the mistaken doubts of others about the other-dependent nature. . . . In order to eliminate the doubts of those others who think, "How can nonexistents become objects?" it is [taught] to be like an illusion. In order to eliminate the doubts of those who think, "How can mind and mental events arise without [outer] referents?" it is [taught] to be like a mirage. In order to eliminate the doubts of those who think, "How can likes and dislikes be experienced if there are no referents?" it is [taught] to be like a dream. In order to eliminate the doubts of those who think, "If there are no referents, how can the desired and undesired results of positive and negative actions be accomplished?" it is [taught] to be like a reflection. In order to eliminate the doubts of those who think, "How can various consciousnesses arise if there are no referents?" it is [taught to be] like an optical illusion. In order to eliminate the doubts of those who think, "How can various conventional expressions come about if there are no referents?" it is [taught] to be like an echo. In order to eliminate the doubts of those who think, "If there are no referents, how can the sphere of the meditative concentration that apprehends true actuality come about?" it is [taught] to be like [a reflection of] the moon in water. In order to eliminate the doubts of those who think, "If there are no referents, how can unerring bodhisattvas be reborn as they wish in order to accomplish their activity for sentient beings?" it is [taught] to be like a magical creation.[1165]

and

> How should one engage in [appearances as being mere cognizance]? . . . One engages in this just like in the case of a rope appearing as a snake in a dark house. Since a snake does not exist, [to see it] in the rope is mistaken. Those who realize [that the rope] is its referent have turned away from the cognition of [seeing] a snake where there is none and dwell in the cognition of [apprehending] a rope. [However,] when regarded in a subtle way, such is also mistaken, since [a

> rope] consists of [nothing but] the characteristics of color, smell, taste, and what can be touched. [Thus,] based on the cognition of [seeing color] and so on, the cognition of [apprehending] a rope has to be discarded too. Likewise, based on the cognition of [seeing] the perfect nature, . . . also the cognition of mere cognizance is to be dissolved. . . . Through engaging in mere cognizance, one engages in the other-dependent nature.
>
> How does one engage in the perfect nature? One engages in it by dissolving the notion of mere cognizance too. . . . Therefore, there is not even an appearance of [phenomena] as mere cognizance. When bodhisattvas . . . dwell in the expanse of dharmas in an immediate way, what is observed and what observes are equal in these bodhisattvas. In consequence, what springs forth [in them] is equal, nonconceptual wisdom. In this way, such bodhisattvas engage in the perfect nature.[1166]

From the point of view that Yogācāra presentations are based on the view that everything is experienced only in our mind, the three natures can be summarized in yet another way. The imaginary nature stands for our habitual way of misperceiving the other-dependent nature. We insist that dependently originating mere appearances in the mind are real and distinct subjective and objective entities, such as inner consciousness and external objects. However, even if such dualistic appearances have no ground, they still appear and are experienced. The perfect nature refers to perceiving the unity of dependently originating mere appearances and emptiness. This means realizing that any imaginary subject-object duality and all superimpositions of personal and phenomenal identities never existed in other-dependent appearances. In other words, this is the realization of the unity of form and emptiness.

Thus, the three natures are not three different ontological "things." It is not that by subtracting one (the imaginary nature) from the other (the other-dependent nature), one arrives at the third (the perfect nature). Rather, Yogācāra talks about the other-dependent nature as the experiential ground for a dynamic process of disillusioning and refining our perception, with the imaginary nature and the perfect nature being the "extremes" of mistaken and pure perception respectively. Thus, the other-dependent nature stands for the continuity of experience, which is impure when imagined as the imaginary nature and pure or perfected when this imaginary nature has been seen through. Since the realization of the perfect nature is still an experience and not something abstract or just nothing, it is said that the other-dependent nature in its pure aspect is the perfect nature. In this way, "other-dependent nature" is just a term for the compound meaning of the imaginary nature and the perfect nature, which points to the underlying experiential continuity of a mind stream that becomes increasingly aware of its own true nature.

In summary, in the lineage of vast activity, there is clearly no trace of reifying any of the three natures. Again, this just follows what *The Sūtra of the Arrival in Laṅka* says:

> When scrutinized with insight,
> Neither the imaginary, nor the dependent,
> Nor the perfect [nature] exists.
> So how could insight conceive of an entity?[1167]

In his explanation of the four purities that comprise the perfect nature (natural complete purity, unstained complete purity, the complete purity of the path, and the completely pure object), Vasubandhu adds that the first two purities are the unchanging perfect nature, while the last two are the unmistaken perfect nature.[1168] Both his and Asvabhāva's commentary identify natural complete purity with Buddha nature.[1169] As for the genuine dharma as the completely pure object, Vasubandhu elaborates on why the teachings of the great vehicle are completely pure and are therefore included in the perfect nature:

> Thus, whatever dharma arises from the imaginary arises from afflicted causes. Whatever [dharma] arises as the other-dependent is not true. However, since it is the natural outflow of the pure expanse of dharmas, [the completely pure object] is neither of these, is not untrue, and arises from the perfect [nature] itself.[1170]

When the genuine dharma becomes an object of a conceptual consciousness or is verbally expressed during the initial stages of the path, it is imaginary. Since the inner subject of such processes is false imagination—that is, the other-dependent nature in its unawareness of the ultimate—the dharma also becomes entangled with and thus blurred by the other-dependent nature. Finally, on the level of nondual, nonconceptual wisdom that directly realizes the expanse of dharmas (the actual, complete purity of the path), there is no more separation or difference between subject and object. This is the culmination of the path as the passage from engagement in the dharma to its clear manifestation as the nature of one's entire being: enlightenment. Surely, the immediate experience of the expanse of dharmas itself is beyond thought and expression, but its natural expression or outflow for the benefit of others is the genuine dharma as it is compassionately communicated by those who have this experience. This represents the passage from enlightenment to communicating the dharma to others, which is clearly expressed in *The Prajñāpāramitā Sūtra in Eight Thousand Lines*:

> When the dharma taught by the Thus-Gone One is taught, the disciples reveal and seize the nature of phenomena. While [being in the state of] having revealed and seized the nature of phenomena, whatever they explain, whatever they teach, whatever they relate, whatever they express, whatever they clarify, and whatever they perfectly illuminate, all of this is not in contradiction to the nature of phenomena. Venerable Śāriputra, when the nature of phenomena is explained by the children of good family in this way, it is not in contradiction to the nature of phenomena. It is the natural outflow of the dharma taught by the Thus-Gone One.[1171]

Inasmuch as such genuine dharma itself is the natural expression of the expanse of dharmas, it is not subject to change. It is only the experiential, inner subjectivity of the practitioner engaging in this dharma that may be fully aware of the ultimate source of this natural expression or not. The former experience is then called "nondual, nonconceptual wisdom," while the latter is other-dependent consciousness.

In Yogācāra, everything is contained within the expanse of dharmas, or natural complete purity. Although the Yogācāra system is expressed within the framework of the three natures, the ground consciousness, and such, it is important to keep in mind that this entire edifice is grounded in and built from within the perspective of direct insight into the expanse of dharmas. The dharma as well as the ensuing path of engaging in it stem from this natural ground, and when this ground is directly realized, then both this dharma and the path merge back into the expanse of dharmas. As *The Ornament of Sūtras* says:

> It is said that enlightenment is attained
> By those nonconceptual bodhisattvas
> Who regard all that has been explained
> As mere conception.[1172]

This also points to the relationship between the four purities. The latent tendencies of listening as the outflow of "one's own" expanse of dharmas (natural purity) are the remedy for the ground consciousness (the ground of delusion) in the same mind stream. On the path, it is not that consciousness is an indiscriminate blend of both illusion and truth. Rather, within the naturally pure, fundamental space of the expanse of dharmas, the purity of the path manifests from engaging in the completely pure object, that is, the genuine dharma as the natural expression of others' realization of the expanse of dharmas. This path results in a radical change of state[1173] of one's inner subjectivity; that is, dualistic consciousness unaware of the expanse of dharmas is revealed as nondual wisdom and expanse inseparable. This is nothing other than unstained complete purity. Vasubandhu's commentary on *The Synopsis of the Great Vehicle* says:

> Unstained complete purity means that the very same suchness [natural complete purity] becomes Buddhahood. This is characterized as pure suchness in that it is free from the stains of afflictive and cognitive obscurations.[1174]

As for the statement that the perfect nature is the other-dependent nature empty of the imaginary nature (which is said to be the position of the Mere Mentalists), it is also found in the texts of the lineage of vast activity. However, according to *The Synopsis of the Great Vehicle*, its meaning is to be understood as follows: The aspect of affliction refers to the existence of the imaginary nature in the other-dependent nature. The aspect of complete purity refers to the existence of the perfect nature in the other-dependent nature. Thus, the other-dependent nature itself is involved in both of these aspects. This is what the Buddha had in mind when he taught the three natures. The analogy for this meaning is gold ore, which may also be said to involve three aspects: stone, gold, and gold ore as their compound. Before being processed in an oven, gold ore looks like ordinary stone, although it actually is gold. In itself, it is just the compound of stone and gold. After having been processed in a furnace, only the gold is visible and not the stone. Likewise, as long as ordinary consciousness has not been touched by the fire of nonconceptual wisdom, this consciousness appears as the nature of false imagination, but not as the true reality, which is the perfect nature. Once ordinary consciousness has been touched by the fire of nonconceptual wisdom, this consciousness appears as the perfect nature and no longer as the nature of false imagination. Thus, the consciousness that is false imagination—the other-dependent nature—is involved in both aspects, just as gold ore contains both stone and the gold that exists within it.[1175]

Thus, the other-dependent nature may be considered under two aspects. In its first aspect, it is contaminated by false imagination, with the result that a world of dualistic appearances is constructed. Appearances are imputed to possess an intrinsic nature of their own, though they do not exist in this way from the ultimate point of view. This is why the other-dependent nature in its imaginary aspect is called the basis for the appearance of all entities. Since we are trapped by such imagination into a false view of things that leads to suffering, the other-dependent nature is said to pertain to suffering. The second aspect of the other-dependent nature is its being uncontaminated by the above processes and being identical to the perfect nature. This is said to be the aspect pertaining to purity. In other words, if there is absolutely nothing, not even some illusory, impure, and dualistic mind at the beginning of the path to liberation, then there cannot be any purified, nondual mind as the result of this path. Thus, the mere fact of emptiness or the expanse of dharmas alone is not enough for enlightenment; there has to be an experience of it.

One of the crucial reasons to propose the other-dependent nature is to account for the continuity of a mind stream from impure to pure experiences. In the lineage of vast activity, it is only in this sense that the other-dependent nature being empty of the imaginary nature is said to be the perfect nature. These are also referred to as the pure and the impure other-dependent nature. *The Synopsis of the Great Vehicle* says:

> In one sense, the other-dependent nature is other-dependent; in another sense, it is imaginary; and in yet another sense, it is perfect. In what sense is the other-dependent nature called "other-dependent"? It is other-dependent in that it originates from the seeds of other-dependent latent tendencies. In what sense is it called "imaginary"? Because it is both the cause of [false] imagination and what is imagined by it. In what sense is it called "perfect"? Because it does not at all exist in the way it is imagined.[1176]

and

> Thus, in terms of its imaginary aspect, this very other-dependent nature is saṃsāra. In terms of its perfect aspect, it is nirvāṇa.[1177]

Such statements may also be seen as justifications for the relationship between the three natures as it is usually described by the proponents of other-emptiness: that the perfect nature is empty of both the imaginary and the other-dependent natures. Vasubandhu's *Bṛhaṭṭīkā* (his major commentary on the *Prajñāpāramitā sūtras*) likewise interprets the three natures in this sense. In any case, due to the dual status of the other-dependent nature (pure and impure) at different stages of the path, whether it is said that the perfect nature is the other-dependent nature empty of the imaginary nature or that the perfect nature is empty of both the imaginary and the other-dependent natures, the meaning is the same.

As for the notion of Buddha nature, there is no reifying interpretation of it in any of the texts of the lineage of vast activity. The teachings on Buddha nature are not meant as a philosophical or even ontological alternative to emptiness. Buddha nature or the luminous nature of the mind is not seen as a monistic absolute beside which all other phenomena have an illusionlike status. Rather, it is the undeluded state of mind in which its self-delusion has fully and irreversibly ceased to operate. The main example that is used for it is space. However, in order to clarify that the insubstantial expanse of the mind is not like mere inert, outer space but that it is the luminous, natural unity of wisdom and expanse, the teachings on Buddha nature also give many examples for the luminous aspect of mind's nature and its boundless, inseparable qualities.[1178] Asaṅga's commentary on *The Sublime Continuum*'s most famous two verses explains:

> Those whose minds stray from emptiness are those bodhisattvas who have newly entered the [great] vehicle. They deviate from the principle of what emptiness means in terms of the Heart of the Thus-Gone Ones. [Among them,] there are those who assert the door to liberation that is emptiness due to the destruction of [real] entities, saying, "The subsequent extinction and destruction of an existing phenomenon is perfect nirvāṇa." Or, there are also those who rely on emptiness by mentally focusing on emptiness [as some real entity], saying, "In a way that is distinct from form and so on, what is called 'emptiness' exists as some entity which is to be realized and meditated on." So, how is the principle of what emptiness means in terms of the Heart of the Thus-Gone Ones expressed here?
>
> There is nothing to be removed from it
> And not the slightest to be added.
> Actual reality is to be seen as it really is—
> Who sees actual reality is released.
>
> The basic element is empty of what is adventitious,
> Which has the characteristic of being separable.
> It is not empty of the unsurpassable dharmas,
> Which have the characteristic of being inseparable.[1179]
>
> What is elucidated by this? There is nothing to be removed from this basic element of the Thus-Gone Ones that is naturally completely pure, since the emptiness of [all] expressions of afflicted phenomena (the adventitious stains) is its nature. Nor is the slightest to be added to it, since the expressions of purified phenomena (the fact of inseparable dharmas) are its nature. Hence, it is said [in *The Sūtra of the Lion's Roar of Queen Śrīmālā*] that the Heart of the Thus-Gone Ones is empty of all the cocoons of afflictions, which are separable [from it] and realized as being relinquished. It is not empty of the inconceivable Buddhadharmas, which are inseparable [from it], realized as not being relinquished, and greater in number than the sands of the river Gaṅgā. Thus, one clearly sees that when something does not exist somewhere, the [latter] is empty of that [former]. In accordance with reality, one understands that what remains there always exists.[1180] These two verses

> unmistakenly elucidate the defining characteristic of emptiness, since it [thus] is free from the extremes of superimposition and denial. Here, those whose minds stray away and are distracted from this principle of emptiness, do not rest [in it] in meditative concentration, and are not one-pointed [with regard to it] are therefore called "those whose minds stray from emptiness." Without the wisdom of ultimate emptiness, it is impossible to realize and reveal the nonconceptual expanse.[1181]

Thus, what remains after the adventitious stains are realized to be non-existent is clearly not some reified entity, but the naturally pure expanse of dharmas free from reference points, just as it is.

Immediately after the above verses, *The Sublime Continuum* explains the reason for teaching Buddha nature, even though it is impossible for anyone but a Buddha to directly realize it:

> Having taught in certain places that, just like clouds, dreams, and illusions,
> All knowable objects are empty in all aspects,
> Why did the Victors teach here
> That the Buddha-Heart exists in all sentient beings?
>
> They taught this in order to eliminate
> The five flaws in those in whom they exist.
> These are faintheartedness, denigrating inferior sentient beings,
> Clinging to what is not the actual, denying the actual dharma, and excessive attachment to oneself.[1182]

Accordingly, Karmapa Mikyö Dorje in his *Lamp That Excellently Distinguishes the Tradition of the Proponents of Other-Emptiness*[1183] states that the existence of Buddha nature is taught in order to awaken all sentient beings' disposition for Buddhahood and to relinquish the five flaws. Some scholars say that the teachings on the existence of Buddha nature in all sentient beings have to be interpreted as merely an expedient meaning, since they—according to the above verses—only serve to eliminate these five flaws. The Karmapa counters this argument in good Consequentialist manner by drawing absurd consequences from it. He says that if these teachings were only of expedient meaning, there would be no need to give up these five flaws. This means that there would be no flaw in looking down on inferior beings, because beings do not really have Buddha nature. Consequently, there is no reason to believe that such beings have Buddha nature's enlightened qualities. There would also be no flaw in denying the possibility of enlightenment, since the nonexistence of Buddha nature means the nonexistence of the Dharma Body. When rejecting enlightenment, one would not fall into the extreme of false denial, since Buddha nature as its very ground never existed. Rather, one would express just the true way things are. Thus, it would also be fine to be fainthearted and lack confidence in ever attaining enlightenment, since Buddha nature does not indeed exist in one's own mind stream. Hence, to have self-confidence in it being one's true nature would be an attitude that does not at all correspond to the facts.

The Karmapa does not explicitly mention this, but following his same line of argument for the remaining two flaws, people would be fully entitled to be proud and self-satisfied when achieving any new qualities. Since there would be nothing behind the delusions and obscurations that manifest as cyclic existence, it would be justified to take these deluded states as the only reality. Consequently, any attempt at practicing the Buddhist path would be pointless. Moreover, if the teachings on Buddha nature are understood as an expedient meaning, that is, as mere skillful means to address some specific flaws, it would follow that all other teachings of the Buddha as well, including those on emptiness, are of expedient meaning, since it is common to all teachings of the Buddha that they were given for specific purposes and as remedies for specific problems. Thus, there would be nothing of definitive meaning in the Buddha's teachings.

The above absurd consequences by the Karmapa in no way imply that he affirms any reified existence of Buddha nature. This is very clearly described in his commentary on *The Ornament of Clear Realization*:

> In this context, in order to know exactly what the mode of the supreme vehicle is, one must know what is the true reality, the nature of phenomena. In the mantra vehicle, this is explained as being the principal of the divisions of all dispositions, the lord of the circle of the ultimate mandala, and the remaining, irremovable continuum of all aspects of ground, path, and fruition in which the three poisons are relinquished and whose own nature is not impermanent. This actual mode of being is declared as "the Heart of the Thus-Gone Ones" by venerable Maitreya. His intention was that this Heart is the Dharma Body endowed with twofold purity and that, by labeling a part with the name of the whole, sentient beings have one dimension, that is, "natural purity," of the Buddha-Heart endowed with twofold purity. In this way, he spoke of "sentient beings who have the disposition of the Buddhas." . . .
>
> In his *Autocommentary on The Profound Inner Reality*,[1184] [the Third Karmapa Rangjung Dorje] . . . explains that those who possess impure mental impulses are sentient beings and thereby elucidates that the

> expanse of dharmas does not exist in such sentient beings. He presents these very sentient beings as *being* the adventitious stains, that is, what is produced by false imagination which deviates from the expanse of dharmas. By giving the pure mind names such as "ordinary mind," "original protector," and "original Buddha," he says that exactly this [mind] is what involves the mode of being inseparable from the Buddha qualities.[1185] This kind of [pure mind] is also the [Buddha-]Heart that actually fulfills this function.
>
> At this point one might ask, "What does this pure mind refer to?" It is "the luminous nature of the mind." The meaning of "luminous" is that the [deluded] mind that has deviated [from its nature] is [nevertheless] naturally pure. It is said that such a naturally pure Heart exists in sentient beings, [but] that is also not meant literally. Rather, by taking the naturally luminous Heart as the basis, [the fact] that impure sentient beings exist in *it* as that which is to be purified is stated [as] "Buddha exists in sentient beings." Yet, it is likewise [only] under the influence of other-dependent mistakenness that sentient beings exist as what is to be purified, whereas, according to the definitive meaning, the adventitious stains which are to be purified do not exist right from the start.[1186]

Thus, the teachings on Buddha nature do not mean that there is some nucleus of Buddhahood enclosed in sentient beings behind the obscuring adventitious stains. Rather, our whole existence as sentient beings is in itself the sum of adventitious stains that float like clouds in the infinite, bright sky of Buddha nature, the luminous, open expanse of our mind that has no limits or boundaries. Once these clouds dissolve from the warm rays of the sun of wisdom shining in this space, nothing within sentient beings has been freed or developed, but there is just this radiant expanse without any reference points of cloudlike sentient beings or cloud-free Buddhas.

In brief, not only is there no statement in the texts of Maitreya, Asaṅga, and Vasubandhu that mind, the ground consciousness, any of the three natures, or even Buddha nature is really or ultimately existent, but this is precisely what is explicitly and repeatedly denied. This is also expressed in *The Sūtra of the Arrival in Laṅka*:

> Having thoroughly meditated on all phenomena being free from mind, mental cognition, consciousness, the five dharmas, and the [three] natures, Mahāmati, a bodhisattva mahāsattva is skilled in phenomenal identitylessness.[1187]

Most modern scholars who do not base their writings and research on Gelugpa presentations alone also agree that the essential purport of the system of Maitreya, Asaṅga, and Vasubandhu is not at all idealistic and that there is no claim of a really existing mind or other such entities. In fact, in much the same way as the Centrists, Yogācāras like Asaṅga and Vasubandhu introduce and employ expedient concepts, such as "mere mind," only for the sake of dissolving previous ones. Once these concepts on different levels have fulfilled their purpose of redressing specific misconceptions, they are replaced by more subtle ones, which are similarly removed later in the gradual process of letting go of all reference points.

The outcome of the above presentation is that the refutations in the Centrist texts of Mere Mentalism in general and of a really existing self-awareness or ground consciousness and so on in particular cannot be directed against the system of these masters. I have gone to some length here to provide evidence for this for two main reasons. First, it is quite an important point that Centrism and the lineage of vast activity are not mutually exclusive. Second is the need to redress the common but mistaken conflation of the lineage of vast activity with what Tibetans call Mere Mentalism, which invariably leads to its rejection.

**Who Were the Mere Mentalists?**

The question whether any actual Indian proponents of what Tibetans call "Mere Mentalism" ever existed and who these might have been is difficult to answer. Any conclusive evaluation must depend on a precise comparison of the relevant Indian sources that are still available with what is understood by the later Tibetan category "Mere Mentalism," but such a process has hardly started yet. Moreover, the term and scope of "Mere Mentalism" is understood in various ways in different Tibetan doxographies, often with no clear distinction as to what the names Yogācāra, Proponents of Cognizance, and Mere Mentalists refer to (sometimes they are taken as equivalents and at other times not).

Both Tāranātha's *History of Buddhism in India*[1188] and *The Treasury of Knowledge*[1189] speak about the first five hundred masters of the great vehicle, such as Avitarka, *Vigatāradvaja, Divyākaragupta, Rāhulamitra, *Jñānatala, and *Saṅgatala (all c. first century CE). Tāranātha calls them and their followers "Yogācāra Mere Mentalists"[1190] and *The Treasury of Knowledge* says that they are known as "Proponents of Cognizance." In the same context, both texts also mention two contemporaries of these teachers, the brothers Udbhaṭasiddhisvāmin and Śaṃkarapati. *The Treasury of Knowledge* reports that subsequent masters have composed many treatises that elucidate the scriptural system of Yogācāra. Among these, Nanda, *Paramasena, and *Saṃyaksatya are mentioned by name and said to be "the early Yogācāras." Except for three devotional praises by Udbhaṭasiddhisvāmin and Śaṃkarapati in the *Tengyur*, no works of any of these masters have survived, so it is impossible to determine their views. Later, *The Treasury of Knowledge* explicitly clarifies that Maitreya, Asaṅga, and Vasubandhu are not "Mere Mentalists" and identifies the above five hundred masters, some of their followers, and also some later (unidentified) Proponents of Cognizance as the teachers of the system of "Mere Mentalism."[1191] Among later Indian Yogācāra masters, the main one who may be said to exhibit some more "idealistic" and realistic tendencies in his works—such as claiming a really existent other-dependent nature—was Dharmapāla (530-561). He also carried this flavor over to terms that were not interpreted in this way by, for example, Vasubandhu and Sthiramati.[1192]

In Indian Centrist texts, there is only limited information about individual Yogācāra opponents and their specific positions. There is no scriptural evidence for any conflicts between Yogācāras and Centrists before the time of Bhāvaviveka. To the contrary, as mentioned above, Asaṅga and others even wrote commentaries on Nāgārjuna's *Fundamental Verses.*

Bhāvaviveka's critique of Yogācāra starts in *The Lamp of Knowledge,* his commentary on *The Fundamental Verses.* In the first chapter of this text, he criticizes Guṇamati's commentary on *The Fundamental Verses.* In the twenty-fifth chapter, he attacks the view of the three natures, especially that the other-dependent nature is really existent (a position held by Guṇamati and Dharmapāla).[1193] Here, he quotes seven verses from Maitreya's *Distinction between the Middle and Extremes* and once from Asaṅga's commentary on *The Fundamental Verses.* At some point, he seems to refer to Sthiramati too. The same topic is also briefly treated in the fourth chapter of his later *Jewel Lamp of Centrism,* which mainly elaborates on refuting both Real Aspectarians and False Aspectarians. In this context, he quotes from Vasubandhu's *Twenty Verses.* He also attacks the notion of self-awareness and what he perceives as inconsistencies in Dignāga's *Compendium of Valid Cognition.*

The Yogācāra reaction to Bhāvaviveka's *Lamp of Knowledge* came from his contemporaries, primarily Guṇamati's student Sthiramati (in his commentary on Nāgārjuna's *Fundamental Verses*) and Dharmapāla (in the tenth chapter of his commentary on Āryadeva's *Four Hundred Verses on the Yogic Practice of Bodhisattvas*).[1194] Bhāvaviveka's detailed response to these two Yogācāras is found in his *Heart of Centrism* and its autocommentary *Blaze of Reasoning* (fifth chapter).[1195] In these texts, he attacks realistic notions of the three natures, self-awareness, the ground consciousness, and some of the arguments for the nonexistence of external objects.[1196] Once, he also polemically mentions that "other masters of the great vehicle, such as Asaṅga and Vasubandhu" claim to be the only ones who teach how to engage well in the nectar of true reality, while Centrists fail to do so.[1197] However, the only clearly identifiable Yogācāra who actually claimed this was Dharmapāla in his above commentary, while there is no scriptural evidence that Asaṅga or Vasubandhu ever denigrated Centrism in any way. In summary, among all Centrists, Bhāvaviveka is the one who provides the most detailed critique of reified versions of Yogācāra.[1198] At the same time, his general indebtedness to Dignāga in the field of epistemology is complete and evident.

Tāranātha reports that after Bhāvaviveka passed away, some of his disciples came to debate with the disciples of Sthiramati, objecting to the latter's commentary on Nāgārjuna's *Fundamental Verses.* He says, "The followers of the doctrine of naturelessness claim that in this debate the disciples of Bhavya were victorious. But this debate should be viewed as similar to that between Candragomī and Candrakīrti."[1199]

As for Candrakīrti, his *Lucid Words* refers to some passages of Dignāga's texts and once to Vasubandhu. However, these references are found in the context of Candrakīrti's criticism of the fundamentals of their epistemology, which often rest on the realistic system and terminology of the Sūtra Followers.[1200] To be fair, unlike non-Buddhist logicians, Dignāga does not really claim that valid cognition or its objects are ultimately real entities. He only assumes an ontology for the purpose of outlining the valid means of knowledge as the tools to investigate the ultimate nature of phenomena, but he does not enter this investigation himself. Thus, similar to Nāgārjuna, Candrakīrti's main point seems to be that no system of valid cognition can be established, whether it is founded on an ontology or not.

In his *Entrance into Centrism,* Candrakīrti's general critique of a ground consciousness, self-awareness, the other-dependent nature, and specifically characterized phenomena may be seen as addressing such masters as Dharmapāla and Dignāga. As for the refutation of an effective potential[1201] that is said to trigger subsequent cognitions, this is a concept that is mainly found in texts of the Sūtra Followers, but only rarely in works of Yogācāra writers, an exception being Dignāga's *Ālambanaparīkṣā.*[1202] In his autocommentary on *The Entrance into Centrism,* Candrakīrti identifies such masters as Vasubandhu, Dignāga, and Dharmapāla as having rejected the meaning of dependent origination as taught by Nāgārjuna.[1203] Candrakīrti never mentions Maitreya, Asaṅga, or his own contemporary Dharmakīrti by name, nor does he quote them. A number of sources report that Candrakīrti had an ongoing debate with Candragomī, who upheld the view of Maitreya/Asaṅga, for seven years, without either one of them being able to win (Candrakīrti is said to have been supported by Mañjuśrī and Candragomī by Avalokiteśvara).[1204]

Jñānagarbha's *Distinction between the Two Realities* says that even great charioteers are ignorant about the two realities, let alone others.[1205] Śāntarakṣita's subcommentary identifies these as Dharmapāla and his followers.[1206] This subcommentary also says that the positions refuted in Jñānagarbha's autocommentary on verse 15 are those of Devendrabuddhi[1207] and Dharmapāla. Śāntarakṣita also refutes the statement by Sthiramati that it is not suitable for the seeming not to have any basis.[1208] After Śāntarakṣita, there seems to be no more mention of

Dharmapāla by name in Centrist texts. However, despite their synthesis of Yogācāra and Centrism, all Yogācāra-Mādhyamikas, such as Jñānagarbha, Śāntarakṣita, Kamalaśīla, and Haribhadra, unanimously refute the notion of a really existent consciousness or self-awareness in both the versions of the Real Aspectarians and the False Aspectarians, without, however, mentioning specific persons.[1209] They also attack Dharmakīrti's presentations of causality (one cause producing many results, many causes producing one result, and many causes producing many results). At the same time, on the conventional level, they strongly rely on his principles of epistemology and reasoning.[1210]

Other later Centrists, such as Śāntideva and his commentators, for the most part seem quite unspecific about Yogācāra opponents and mainly refute a really existent consciousness and self-awareness.[1211]

In summary, prior to Bhāvaviveka, the Yogācāras sought to assimilate rather than to oppose Centrism. A particularly striking example of this is Kambala's (early sixth century) *Garland of Light*,[1212] which displays a most remarkable early synthesis of Yogācāra and Madhyamaka. After Bhāvaviveka's critique, however, though never rejecting Nāgārjuna and Āryadeva, on certain points the later Yogācāras seemed to be at odds with the later Centrists,[1213] mainly accusing each other of reification or nihilism respectively. However, what often happened in these controversies was the general problem of one philosophical system attacking the other with its own terminology and systemic framework and not on the grounds of the terminology and the context of that other system. In particular, Bhāvaviveka's interpretation of Yogācāra is a perfect example of an extremely literal reading without considering the meaning in terms of the Yogācāra system's own grounds, instead exclusively treating it on Centrist grounds. Thus, when abstracted from the obvious polemical elements and out-of-context misinterpretations of what the opponents actually meant by certain terms, not much is left in terms of fundamental differences between the later Centrists and Yogācāras,[1214] which basically boil down to two issues: (1) whether there is an ultimately real mind (no matter whether this is called other-dependent nature, self-awareness, ground consciousness, or nondual wisdom) and (2) whether any epistemology is possible at all.

Thus, except for a few exceptions mainly in Bhāvaviveka's texts, the actual Yogācāra opponents in Centrist texts obviously did not come from the early Yogācāra of Maitreya, Asaṅga, and Vasubandhu (stream 1) but from the later developments in the Yogācāra tradition. The main opponent was clearly Dharmapāla, followed by Sthiramati (stream 2), Dignāga, and Dharmakīrti (stream 3). They were accused either of claiming a really existent other-dependent nature and self-awareness or of setting realistic foundations of epistemology and causality.

Contrary to rather common Tibetan and Western claims that there were great rivalries between the two schools of the great vehicle, apart from the specific issues mentioned above, there is no evidence that they considered their systems as such to be mutually exclusive. Also, when compared to the attention that other Buddhist and especially non-Buddhist opponents of Centrists receive throughout the latter's texts, it is obvious that the Yogācāras were not at all the main opponents of the Centrists. Moreover, it cannot be overemphasized that most of these disputes between Centrists and Yogācāras represent differences in terms of contexts of meaning rather than content per se. As Keenan rightly states:

> Indeed, in the history of Mahāyāna thinking, the most crucial arguments occur not over issues within a shared context of meaning, but precisely over shifts in that context itself.[1215]

In other words, in their own ways, both systems basically attempt to follow the Buddha in addressing the same fundamental problem of clinging to reference points or extremes. They just tackle this issue from different angles, with different terminologies and methods. As Harris says:

> Nāgārjuna and Asaṅga . . . have set themselves the common task of rendering traditional Buddhist doctrine in such a way that it can be used to tackle particular problems. Furthermore it is pointless categorizing them as nihilists or idealists or anything else of the kind. They should be seen as expositors, adapting traditional doctrine to meet the needs of particular tasks while at the same time leaving the body of the doctrine fundamentally unchanged and unquestioned.[1216]

As stated above, the Eighth Karmapa also emphasizes that these two systems have to be treated on their own terms. Śākya Chogden agrees:

> Therefore, through the scriptures and reasonings of one of these [systems], one is not able to negate the other.[1217]

### *The Centrist Interpretation of the Teachings on Mere Mind*

All Centrists agree that the sources in the sūtras that speak about "mere mind" should not be understood as saying that mind alone is existent or any more real than everything else. Rather, such statements are an expedient teaching within the progressive stages of eliminating all reference points. The Centrists ground their understanding on passages such as this one in *The Sūtra of the Arrival in Laṅka*:

Just as a physician prescribes [various] medicines
To each individual suffering patient,
The Buddha also advocates [the teaching of]
Mere mind to sentient beings.[1218]

Jñānagarbha's autocommentary on verse 32 of his *Distinction between the Two Realities* says:

This compassionate being,
Seeing those who are fettered by their conceptions,
Has taught bondage and liberation
Through such specifications as mere mind.

The Blessed One, . . . in accordance with their thinking, has eliminated all reifications without exception through progressively teaching the aggregates, constituents, and sources; mere mind; and the identitylessness of all phenomena.[1219]

According to Nāgārjuna, specific reasons for the teachings on "mere mind" are to reverse the clinging to the five aggregates as being real entities and to temporarily calm some people's fear of the complete emptiness of all phenomena without any reference point. His *Commentary on the Mind of Enlightenment* says:

The teachings on the aggregates, constituents, and so on
Are for the purpose of stopping the clinging to a self.
By settling in mere mind,
The greatly blessed ones let go of these too.

The teaching of the Sage that
"All of these are mere mind"
Is for the sake of removing the fear of naïve beings
And not [meant] in terms of true reality.[1220]

Sahajavajra's *Commentary on The Ten Verses on True Reality* agrees in very similar terms.[1221]

Both Bhāvaviveka and Candrakīrti explain that the intention of the teachings on mere mind is to conventionally eliminate the notion of an agent, creator, or experiencer other than the mind. Bhāvaviveka's *Heart of Centrism* says:

What is taught in the sūtras about mere mind
Is in order to negate an agent and an experiencer.[1222]

He elaborates on this in his *Lamp of Knowledge*[1223] and *Blaze of Reasoning*,[1224] where he quotes *The Sūtra of the Ten Grounds*:

> O children of the Victors, thus all these three realms are mere mind. They are brought about by the mind and written by the mind, whereas there is no agent or experiencer other than the mind.

Specifically, Bhāvaviveka links this statement to repudiating any entity different from consciousness, such as a self or a soul, as being the one that commits karmic actions and experiences their results. He says that this does not mean to establish the nonexistence of external objects.

Candrakīrti starts his explanation on the meaning of mere mind in a similar way. In his *Entrance into Centrism* VI.84, he clarifies the passage in *The Sūtra of the Ten Grounds* that bodhisattvas on the sixth ground realize all three realms to be mere mind. This was taught in order to realize that the three realms are not created by a permanent self or a creator, since these bodhisattvas realize that, on the seeming level, the active cause for cyclic existence is merely mind. Candrakīrti further quotes from that sūtra in his autocommentary:

> [These bodhisattvas] properly examine dependent origination in its progressive order. They think, "It is in such a way that this bare heap of suffering becomes established, without someone who creates the tree of suffering or experiences it." They reflect in this way, "Through clinging to a creator, karmas exist, but wherever there is no creator, ultimately, neither can karma be observed." They further think, "Thus, these three realms are mere mind. All these twelve links of existence that were taught by the Thus-Gone One in multiple aspects depend on a single mind."[1225]

He continues by saying that *The Sūtra of the Arrival in Laṅka* has to be understood in the same way:

> Persons, continua, aggregates,
> Likewise conditions and particles,
> The primal substance, Īśvara, and an agent
> Are to be thought of as mere mind.[1226]

Verses VI.87–91 of *The Entrance into Centrism* state that the teachings on mere mind are meant to indicate the primary role of mind in the world on the seeming level, but not to establish that it is the only entity that ultimately exists nor to negate the existence of material form and such. On the mere conventional level, Candrakīrti makes no distinction between form and mind being equally existent. However, unlike mind, material form does not act as the agent or creator of karmic actions. So without the mind, conventionally, there would be no karma and thus no beings in their various situations of life in different realms. All of this does not mean, of course, that Candrakīrti *asserts* the existence of material forms. As he emphasizes so often, to negate one statement (to negate that mere mind means to deny the existence of material form) does not mean to assert its opposite. All he says is that the teachings on mere mind have a different intention from establishing mind's sole existence or denying material form. He furthermore explicitly states that the five aggregates do not appear for the wisdom that realizes true reality. In brief, verse VI.92 says:

> If form does not exist, do not cling to the existence of mind;
> And if mind exists, do not cling to the nonexistence of form.
> The Buddha, in the sūtras of supreme knowledge,
> Has equally rejected both, while teaching them in the Abhidharma.

Whether on the level of no analysis or with analysis, it is never justified that mind exists whereas form does not exist. Under analysis, when form has been found not to exist, mind cannot exist either, because the two are established in mutual dependence. Without analysis, according to common worldly consensus, both are equally said to exist.

In verse VI.94, Candrakīrti adds that the teachings that the mind appears as all kinds of outer objects should be understood as an expedient denial of outer forms intended for those who are overly attached to material forms. He concludes this topic as follows:

> The Buddhas said, "If there are no knowable objects,
> One easily finds that a knower is excluded."
> If knowable objects do not exist, the negation of a knower is established.
> Therefore, they first negated knowable objects.[1227]

In his autocommentary, he accepts the step of first negating knowable objects and then the knower as a help for those who do not immediately see that, just as all other appearances, the mind as their experiencer is empty too:

> The blessed Buddhas introduce the disciples into the lack of nature in a gradual way. Those who have practiced merit will easily enter into the nature of phenomena. Consequently, [the Buddhas] first talked about generosity and such, since these are the means to enter into the nature

> of phenomena. Likewise, since the negation of knowable objects is a means to realize identitylessness, the Blessed Ones have initially only spoken about the negation of knowable objects, because those who understand the identitylessness of knowable objects will easily enter into the identitylessness of the knower. [From among] those who understand the lack of nature of knowable objects, [some] will realize the lack of nature of the knower all by themselves at some point, while [others] will do so at some other point through a little supplementary instruction. Therefore, the negation of knowable objects was taught first.[1228]

Jñānagarbha's autocommentary on verse 30 of his *Distinction between the Two Realities* explicitly says that one is not able to deny the appearance of mere mind:

> Therefore, it is appropriate here
> To negate only such imputations.
> Denying what is not imputed
> Will only invalidate oneself.
>
> Not only can nobody deny the appearance of mere consciousness whose nature is other-dependent and not affected by the flaw of conceptions of a body with form and so on, but those who make any such [denial] only invalidate themselves by perception and such.[1229]

As mentioned above, he also regards the teachings on mere mind as an integral part of the Buddha's progressive instructions:

> The Blessed One, . . . in accordance with their thinking, has eliminated all reifications without exception through progressively teaching the aggregates, constituents, and sources; mere mind; and the identitylessness of all phenomena.[1230]

Later Centrists who synthesize Yogācāra and Madhyamaka, such as Śāntarakṣita, Kamalaśīla, and Haribhadra, present this gradual approach as the core of this synthesis. As *The Ornament of Centrism* says:

> Based on mere mind,
> One should understand that outer entities do not exist.
> Based on such a mode of being,
> That [mind] too must be understood as being completely identityless.[1231]

Kamalaśīla's *Illumination of Centrism* explains:

> Thus, those who cannot understand all at once that all phenomena lack a nature, for the time being, gradually engage in the lack of nature of outer objects on the basis of [them being] mere mind. Therefore, [*The Sūtra of the Arrival in Laṅka* X.154ab] says:
>
> > Apprehender and apprehended cease
> > In those who look with reasoning.
>
> > Following this, by gradually examining the nature of that mind, they understand that also the [mind] is without identity and thus engage in the profound way of being.[1232]

A similar approach is found in Haribhadra's *Illumination of The Ornament of Clear Realization*.[1233]

In brief, it appears that most Centrists clearly distinguish between accepting a nonreifying notion of mere mind as a step in the more practical context of the progressive stages of meditation on emptiness and refuting any reifying interpretation of mind in the more theoretical context of philosophical analysis.

## *The Treatment of Yogācāra and the Rangtong-Shentong Controversy in Tibet*

### Common Tibetan Systems of Classifying Yogācāra

The later Tibetan tradition in particular deals with the Indian Yogācāra tradition in a somewhat peculiar manner. Most Tibetan schools seem to distinguish between the first and third streams of Yogācāra, that is, the systems of Maitreya/Asaṅga (stream 1) and Dignāga and Dharmakīrti (stream 3). However, sometimes the third stream is placed outside of the Yogācāra system by relating it to the system of the Sūtra Followers. In addition, later Yogācāras, such as Dharmapāla (stream 2), are either conflated with the first stream or distinguished from it as Mere Mentalists. In the latter case, the first stream is then called Shentong-Madhyamaka.

Thus, two main ways of dealing with the various streams within Yogācāra can be distinguished.

In the first case, particularly in the Gelugpa school, often streams 1 and 2 are categorically referred to as Mere Mentalism or Mind Only. Stream 3 is regarded as the basis for both of the Gelugpa doxographical categories of "the Sūtra Followers Following Reasoning" and "the Mere Mentalists Following Reasoning."

Usually, the system of epistemology and reasoning of stream 3 is treated separately from the doxographic presentations of Yogācāra as the distinct curricular topic of valid cognition, which is understood as being based on the system of the Sūtra Followers. Tsongkhapa's version of Centrism attempts to incorporate this system into Candrakīrti's Consequentialism. By following Tsongkhapa and looking for certain key terms—such as the three natures and the ground consciousness—in the scriptures, the Gelugpa school also subsumes certain sūtras, all texts of Vasubandhu, and all but two texts of Maitreya/Asaṅga under the label of Mere Mentalism. Nevertheless, in an attempt to claim the generally esteemed bodhisattva Asaṅga for the distinct interpretation of Consequentialism in the Gelugpa school, it is asserted that, in his final view, Asaṅga is a Consequentialist Centrist. This leads to classifying *The Sublime Continuum* as a Consequentialist text and—except for *The Ornament of Clear Realization*[1234]—all other texts of Maitreya and Asaṅga as Mere Mentalism. In terms of doxography, all that is labeled Mere Mentalism is considered inferior to Centrism, and the existence of a Shentong-Madhyamaka is categorically denied in terms of both terminology and content. Rather, it is said that "Shentong" is nothing but "False Aspectarian Mere Mentalism."[1235]

The other common Tibetan classification scheme is to label streams 2 and 3 as Mere Mentalism and place them doxographically below Centrism, which is then called "the system of self-emptiness" (*rangtong*). The system of Maitreya, Asaṅga, and Vasubandhu is labeled "the Centrism of other-emptiness" (*shentong*) and categorized under Centrism. This approach is usually taken by the followers of Shentong-Madhyamaka, such as Jamgön Kongtrul Lodrö Taye. Often then, this latter form of "Centrism" is considered to be superior to the former. In this approach too, the system of epistemology and reasoning of stream 3 is usually treated separately as the distinct topic of valid cognition.

To reiterate, no such divisions existed in India. Some Tibetans, such as Mikyö Dorje and Pawo Rinpoche, refused to follow either of these later doxographical approaches. Rather, they insisted on treating the lineage of profound view and the lineage of vast activity on their own grounds and did not simply equate the latter with Mere Mentalism. In this, they agreed with other Tibetan masters, such as Śākya Chogden and Mipham Rinpoche, as well as with many modern scholars.

## The Development of the Rangtong-Shentong Controversy

Why did the divisions into Mere Mentalism, self-empty, and other-empty originate and become so widespread in Tibet? Throughout Tibetan dharma history (particularly after the fourteenth century), to a greater or lesser extent, there was a tendency to neglect the Yogācāra tradition as a whole and treat it mainly through its refutations in Centrist texts. This tendency started at the outset of the spread of dharma in Tibet, since, in terms of the sūtra view, all the major Indian masters, such as Śāntarakṣita, Kamalaśīla, and Atīśa, who were involved in bringing the Buddha's teaching to Tibet were Centrists. Although the first two masters incorporated some Yogācāra elements in their Yogācāra-Madhyamaka synthesis, the transmission of the entire lineage of vast activity was clearly secondary. A clearly traceable stream was the transmission from Sajjana to Dsen Kawoche and Zu Gaway Dorje, which was, however, more or less limited to the five texts by Maitreya/Asaṅga. Except for Vasubandhu's *Treasury of Abhidharma* (which is not a Yogācāra work anyway) and—to a lesser degree—Asaṅga's *Compendium of Abhidharma*, the other works of these two masters, let alone of other Yogācāras (such as Sthiramati or Dharmapāla), were usually not studied much in Tibet.

The neglect of Yogācāra is also reflected in the traditional curriculum of the five major topics of sūtra studies as it developed in Tibetan monastic colleges: Vinaya, Abhidharma, Pramāṇa (Tib. tshad ma; valid cognition), Prajñāpāramitā, and Madhyamaka. In the traditional aproaches of presenting this curriculum, the Yogācāra system or the lineage of vast activity is hardly represented, if at all. Abhidharma is studied solely through Vasubandhu's *Treasury of Abhidharma* (which treats the systems of the Followers of the Great Exposition and the Sūtra Followers). Pramāṇa is based on the epistemological texts of Dignāga and Dharmakīrti as being mainly an expression of the system of the Sūtra Followers, without much reference, if any, to the Yogācāra system. The hidden meaning of paths and grounds in the *Prajñāpāramitā sūtras* is studied through Maitreya's *Ornament of Clear Realization*, but this text is commonly considered to present the view of Yogācāra-Svātantrika-Madhyamaka. Finally, Madhyamaka, which mainly treats emptiness as the explicit meaning of the *Prajñāpāramitā sūtras*, is usually studied solely through a Consequentialist text, Candrakīrti's *Entrance into Centrism.*[1236]

This core curriculum is supplemented by systematic studies of the four Buddhist philosophical systems according to Tibetan categorization. It is here that the two classification schemes outlined above are treated in detail. These doxographical classifications, in particular the issue of how Mere Mentalism is treated and whether a Shentong-Madhyamaka is accepted, inform and shape the studies of the core curriculum to a high degree.

Dölpopa was one of the first Tibetans to vehemently deny that the lineage of vast activity is Mere Mentalism. He often called these two streams "ultimate Cittamātra" and "seeming Cittamātra" respectively. He greatly stressed the unity of the lineages of profound view and vast activity and disclaimed that the latter is inferior to Centrism. Instead, he asserted that Indian masters such as Nāgārjuna, Asaṅga, Vasubandhu, and Dignāga all belong to the tradition that he called "Great Madhyamaka." Dölpopa also elaborated on the correct understanding of the framework of the three natures, largely following Vasubandhu's Prajñāpāramitā commentary *Bṛhaṭṭīkā.* Consequently, he criticized the position that all scriptures in which the three natures appear are just Mere Mentalism. As for the distinction between "self-empty" and "other-empty," Dölpopa said that seeming reality is self-empty, while ultimate reality—Buddha nature or the nature of mind—is other-empty, that is, empty of adventitious stains but not empty of Buddha qualities. It is moreover asserted to be the genuine self, which is permanent and pure.[1237]

As Stearns puts it, for many of Dölpopa's contemporaries as well as later masters, his entire system including the novel use of terminology came as a "hermeneutical shock."[1238] It was first severely criticized during Dölpopa's time by parts of the Sakya school. Later, Tsongkhapa rejected Dölpopa in all aspects, and this rejection persisted throughout the Gelugpa school. The critiques by the Eighth Karmapa and Pawo Rinpoche were explained at the beginning of the chapter.

Following the unfortunate but common pattern throughout Tibetan history of mingling politics, religious patronage, and monastic rivalries, the gradual growth of the Gelugpa school's spiritual influence was coupled with an increase in its political power. This culminated in the Fifth Dalai Lama's installation as the supreme ruler of all Tibet and the Tibetan government being run exclusively by Gelugpa authorities. Eventually, as a consequence of the total rejection of the view of Dölpopa's school of Jonang by Tsongkhapa and his followers and the ascendance of the Gelugpa school to a kind of state church, all texts by Dölpopa and other Jonangpas were forbidden and their printing blocks sealed and locked away. Gradually, all Jonangpa monasteries (as well as a considerable number of Nyingma and Kagyü monasteries) were converted into Gelugpa monasteries, the last one being Tāranātha's monastery in 1650. From 1685 onward, the Jonangpa lineage was completely suppressed as an independent school in western and central Tibet, although its teachings were still practiced in secrecy. The only openly Jonang establishment at that time was the monastery of Dzamthang and its affiliates in a remote area of Amdo in eastern Tibet.

The ensuing revival of the Jonangpa system, however, came about through a number of prominent masters of the Kagyü and Nyingma lineages in eastern Tibet. It started with Katog Rigdzin Tsewang Norbu (1698–1755) and his student, the Eighth Situpa Chökyi Jungnay (1699–1774), who promoted and further developed these teachings. Apart from the mere doctrinal differences between the predominant Gelugpa school on the one side and the Sakya, Nyingma, and Kagyü schools on the other, as a result of the conflicts described above, the Rangtong-Shentong controversy definitely came to assume a political dimension too. The Shentong view increasingly served as a kind of common "corporate identity" for those schools that were opposed—both doctrinally and politically—to the Gelugpas, whose institutional identity naturally lies in the unique system of Tsongkhapa. The sense of a common doctrinal ground was also one of the underlying forces of the nineteenth-century nonsectarian Rime movement in eastern

Tibet, which included many Sakya, Nyingma, and Kagyü masters.

Moreover, since Centrism was universally accepted in Tibet as the highest philosophical system on the sūtra level, it was clear that any claim to the superiority of a certain view could be made only from within this system. Therefore, for many who rejected Tsongkhapa's interpretation of Centrism, it seemed mandatory not only to counterbalance his interpretation but in addition to promote the lineage of vast activity by referring to it as "Shentong-Madhyamaka" or "Great Madhyamaka." Usually, the latter was then claimed as the superior type of Centrism, while "Mere Mentalism" was declared to be inferior to Centrism in general.

Of course, such a Shentong-Madhyamaka or even Great Madhyamaka superior to Candrakīrti's and Tsongkhapa's Madhyamaka—which is then called "Rangtong" in an often pejorative sense—is fiercely opposed by the Gelugpa school. It is completely rejected as a continuation of Dölpopa's censored views, which are even denied to be Buddhist and instead equated with Hindu views on a really existent, permanent ātman. Another response is to categorize the teachings of Shentong-Madhyamaka as Mere Mentalism (usually of the False Aspectarian brand). In both cases, it is merely seen as a convenient target for Centrist refutations.

Thus, over the centuries, there were many polemics from both sides. A natural part of this process was the attempt to claim the most prominent figures of Indian and Tibetan Buddhism for one's own side in this controversy. For example, the followers of Shentong-Madhyamaka claim not only Maitreya, Asaṅga, and Vasubandhu as their roots, but also many masters such as Nāgārjuna (through his *Collection of Praises*), all the mahāsiddhas (such as Saraha and Maitrīpa), Longchen Rabjam, Karmapa Mikyö Dorje, and Mipham Rinpoche.[1239] Conversely, the Gelugpas hold that Maitreya and Asaṅga are Consequentialists in their final view and usually even claim Rendawa and Sakya Paṇḍita as being in accord with Tsongkhapa's interpretation of Centrism, which is clearly not the case.[1240]

This controversy was one of the ways in which strong rival group identities developed in the four Tibetan schools. Often, this even led to severe criticism of their members from within these schools, if they seemed to deviate from the official party line. Examples can be found in a certain opposition even within the Kagyü school to the Eighth Karmapa's interpretation of Centrism with its rejection of a Shentong-Madhyamaka. Conversely, Śākya Chogden received fierce criticisms from others in the Sakya school for his sympathies for the other-empty approach and his attempts to show the final unity of Nāgārjuna's and Asaṅga's systems. In the Gelugpa school, Gendün Chöpel became persona non grata for refuting Tsongkhapa's interpretation of Centrism.

I think one of the big opportunities in the spread of Buddhism to the West is that Western students of Buddhism, especially in its Tibetan form, now have the chance to take a fresh look at the original Indian and Tibetan sources and to reevaluate the various Indo-Tibetan controversies without immediately getting caught up in centuries-long entrenchments of sectarian polemics. Fortunately, some signs of such a development are to be found.

**What If the Buddha and Nāgārjuna Were Mere Mentalists?**

As has been shown, to categorically label the lineage of vast activity "Mere Mentalism" with the typical assumed reifications and to regard it as inferior to Centrism is in outright contradiction to the Indian sources. Thus, a few words seem appropriate with regard to the treatment of this lineage by Tsongkhapa and his followers.

By and large, in the Gelugpa school, the views of Yogācāras in general and the masters of the lineage of vast activity in particular are only consulted for the sake of studying epistemology and logic through the system of Dignāga and Dharmakīrti as well as for describing some aspects of conventional reality. The views of these masters on ultimate reality are either studied only to be refuted or not studied at all. If there seem to be inconsistencies, the overall context is often not considered, but statements are taken in a limited and literal way. Not only with regard to the Yogācāra school but in general, the monastic colleges almost exclusively use the digests of their own textbooks, largely based on the views of Tsongkhapa and his followers, and hardly ever consult the original Indian sources. Asaṅga is traditionally venerated as one of the two supreme system founders in the great vehicle along with Nāgārjuna, but this is merely lip service. In reality, he is either refuted, downgraded, or silenced. In the same vein, Tsongkhapa's early work *Ocean of Good Explanations*,[1241] in which he explains the ground consciousness and the afflicted mind according to Asaṅga, is consequently considered by Gelugpa authorities not to represent Tsongkhapas's "mature view."

The standard Gelugpa claim that certain texts are Mere Mentalism and thus only of expedient meaning is put forward on the grounds that certain key terms, such as the three natures, mere mind, or the ground consciousness, appear in these texts. However, this approach does not properly consider how such terms are explained in the Yogācāra system itself and what they mean in a variety of contexts. Consequently, not only the works of Maitreya, Asaṅga, and Vasubandhu but also certain sūtras and even the entire third turning of the wheel of dharma by the Buddha are classified as teaching Mere Mentalism. This resembles the approach of a child who is asked to describe an elephant concealed behind a high wall and tries to do so by peeping through a small hole in the wall. Seeing only the end of the elephant's tail, the child exclaims, "An elephant looks like a paintbrush!"

Such a "hermeneutic approach" leads to a considerable number of exegetical convolutions, inconsistencies, and absurd consequences. If Maitreya and Asaṅga are deemed Mere Mentalists simply because the terms of the three natures and such appear in their texts, it follows that the Buddha himself was a Mere Mentalist, since he teaches mere mind, the three natures, and so on in many sūtras. It also follows that even some of the *Prajñāpāramitā sūtras*—which according to the Gelugpa classification are of definitive meaning—are only Mere Mentalism and thus of expedient meaning, since the three natures are taught in them. Similarly *The Sūtra on the Ten Grounds* must then be a text of Mere Mentalism, since it—just like *The Sūtra of the Arrival in Laṅka*—says, "These three realms are merely mind." However, since this text is one of the two universally acknowledged foundations (along with *The Fundamental Verses*) of Candrakīrti's *Entrance into Centrism*, what light does that throw on Candrakīrti's text itself? If one is only looking for certain key terms, many tantras too may well be regarded as teaching Mere Mentalism. For the same reason, all texts by Centrists such as Śāntarakṣita and Kamalaśīla would belong to that category, as would certain texts by Nāgārjuna . For example, his *Twenty Verses on the Great Vehicle* says, "All of this is mere mind."[1242] *The Praise to the Inconceivable* uses the terminology of the three natures.[1243] *The Praise to the Expanse of Dharmas* employs the typical Yogācāra term "complete change of state"[1244] and even says that Buddha nature is not affected by the teachings on emptiness.[1245]

If the same narrow approach to determine the content of scriptures merely on the basis of certain key words is equally applied to the *Prajñāpāramitā sūtras* and Centrist texts with their relentless negations, it is very easy—as many people did and still do—to wrongly categorize them as plain nihilism, especially when they are not read in their own context (such as their frequent warnings against nihilism and the careful explanations of what "the lack of nature" means).

Out of context, at certain points, Centrist texts seem to assert the fourth extreme of neither existent nor nonexistent that is typically negated. For example, Nāgārjuna's *Fundamental Verses* says:

> Therefore, it is suitable that nirvāṇa
> Is neither an entity nor a nonentity.[1246]

Now consider the following verses:

> Just as phenomena are not existent
> And just as they appear in various ways,
> Thus they are neither phenomena nor the nonexistence of phenomena.
> [The Buddha] taught them as the actuality of nonduality.
>
> From certain single perspectives,
> He taught them as either "nonexistent" or "existent."

From both perspectives,
He expressed them as "neither existent nor nonexistent."

Since they do not exist as they appear,
He talked about their "nonexistence."
Since they appear in such ways,
He spoke about their "existence."

Since they do not have any intrinsic character,
Since they do not abide as their own entities,
And since they do not exist as they are apprehended,
He presented them as the lack of nature.

As each [of the following] is the basis for the next,
Their lack of nature establishes them
As being without arising, without ceasing,
Primordial peace, and natural nirvāṇa.

Where do you think these verses come from? As they stand, there is no reason to assume that they were not written by a Centrist master such as Nāgārjuna, Candrakīrti, or Śāntideva. Sorry, wrong guess. They come from Asaṅga's *Synopsis of the Great Vehicle.*[1247] Thus, if certain texts are claimed to be Mere Mentalism just because they contain a certain terminology, this example—among many others— shows that it is very easy to equally claim that all texts that use Centrist style or terminology, such as "the lack of nature" or "being without arising," are Centrist texts too. Further examples include many sūtras of the lesser vehicle (such as the *Kaccāyanagottasutta*), Maitreya's *Distinction between the Middle and Extremes,* and Sthiramati's commentary on Vasubandhu's *Thirty Verses,* which may all be considered Centrist texts, because they use terms such as "the middle," "the middle path," and "emptiness" and also describe the elimination of various sets of extremes.

The Gelugpa claim that Asaṅga in his final view is a Consequentialist—which is based only on *The Sublime Continuum* of all texts—is completely unfounded. First of all, as generally accepted, *The Sublime Continuum* is by Maitreya and not by Asaṅga. Everybody who reads this text cannot but notice the completely different approach in terms of both style and content in comparison to anything written by Consequentialists such as Candrakīrti. Likewise, Asaṅga's *Exposition of The Sublime Continuum* does not exhibit any trace of Consequentialism. Thus, the claim that Asaṅga is a Consequentialist is based solely on a complete reinterpretation of the straightforward verses of *The Sublime Continuum* in typical Gelugpa commentaries, which tortuously force these verses into the framework of their own version of Consequentialism, thus interpreting Buddha nature as simply being emptiness in the sense of a nonimplicative negation.[1248]

Moreover, if—according to this claim—Buddha nature refers to nothing other than the emptiness that is a nonimplicative negation, why would the Buddha have bothered to elaborate on merely this emptiness through abundant words in many sūtras of the third turning of the wheel of dharma, when he had already taught the emptiness of all phenomena at length in the *Prajñāpāramitā sūtras* of the second turning? If—as per the Gelugpas—the third turning only teaches Mere Mentalism, then it is definitely contradictory that this very turning teaches the emptiness as found in the *Prajñāpāramitā sūtras* (that is, also Buddha nature being nothing but a nonimplicative negation), which they themselves consider the definitive meaning. But if the third turning indeed teaches this emptiness, then it must be of definitive meaning too. Furthermore, if Buddha nature is nothing but emptiness in the sense of a nonimplicative negation, how should such a negation alone serve as the potential or basis for Buddhahood with all its qualities and enlightened activity? And since such an emptiness is present in all phenomena in an equal way, why couldn't stones and books become enlightened too?

If, based on *The Sublime Continuum*, Asaṅga were a Consequentialist, then Maitreya as its actual author must certainly be one too. However, at the same time, the Gelugpas claim that Maitreya's *Ornament of Clear Realization* represents the view of the Yogācāra-Svātantrika-Madhyamaka. They also say that the remaining texts of Maitreya and Asaṅga are the foundation of Mere Mentalism. Even for the Gelugpas themselves, there is no case of any other master in Buddhism being claimed as featuring in three different schools. It does not make much sense to regard Asaṅga as not just one of the followers of Mere Mentalism but as its very founder and still to say that he actually is a Consequentialist, on the basis of a single text that is not even his. Do we know of any other Consequentialist who founded a non-Consequentialist, even non-Madhyamaka school?

Why not equally say then that Nāgārjuna's final view is Shentong-Madhyamaka (based on his *Praise to the Expanse of Dharmas*), while he is also the founder of the inferior, provisional Rangtong-Madhyamaka based on his other texts, such as *The Fundamental Verses*? In fact, *The Praise to the Expanse of Dharmas* provides a much better basis for someone wanting to interpret it as Shentong-Madhyamaka than *The Sublime Continuum* does for regarding it as a Consequentialist text. In the same vein, one could very well claim that Tsongkhapa's final view was Mahāmudrā, since the Gelugpa tradition itself reports him as having given restricted talks on Mahāmudrā as well as having said to his early teacher Rendawa that he had uncommon guiding instructions based on the Mahāmudrā explanations of the Great Madhyamaka, but it was not yet time to propagate it widely.[1249]

Instead, one may say, he just outwardly founded the new lineage of his own particular version of Consequentialism and propagated it widely.

Actually, if Maitreya and Asaṅga were indeed Consequentialists and thus Centrists, then this would in effect serve to support the proponents of other-emptiness who regard the lineage of Maitreya and Asaṅga as Centrism.

As for Maitreya's *Ornament of Clear Realization*, even today, the whole curriculum of the hidden meaning of grounds and paths in the *Prajñāpāramitā sūtras* in Tibetan monastic colleges is based solely on this text. As for categorizing this text, either one accepts it as a Yogācāra text, which means that the study of the hidden meaning of the *Prajñāpāramitā sūtras* is based on a work of the Yogācāra system (or even Mere Mentalism)—a position that is, of course, completely unacceptable to the Gelugpas—or, as they prefer, one considers this work a Centrist text of the "Yogācāra-Svātantrika" branch. The latter then leads to the wonderfully simple and elegant exegetical situation that Maitreya—an actual Consequentialist who nevertheless mainly teaches Mere Mentalism—also composed an Autonomist text. Even more amazing, he did so many centuries before any division between Autonomists and Consequentialists occurred, let alone one between so-called Yogācāra-Svātantrika and Sautrāntika-Svātantrika.

There are further inconsistencies in this Gelugpa position. Like all other Tibetan schools, the Gelugpas accept *The Ornament of Clear Realization* as the final authority on the hidden meaning of the *Prajñāpāramitā sūtras*, that is, the progressive stages of a bodhisattva's supreme knowledge realizing emptiness. At the same time, however, they say that it represents the Autonomist view. From this, it absurdly follows that the hidden meaning of the *Prajñāpāramitā sūtras* is Autonomism. Moreover, the explicit meaning of the *Prajñāpāramitā sūtras*—emptiness—is said to be taught in Centrism, which is divided into Autonomism and Consequentialism. Among these, Consequentialism is regarded as providing the supreme presentation of emptiness. The Consequentialists themselves do not give a presentation of the hidden meaning of the *Prajñāpāramitā sūtras* different from the—allegedly—Autonomist explanation in *The Ornament of Clear Realization*. Therefore, it absurdly follows that the supreme knowledge that realizes emptiness corresponds to Autonomism and thus does not concord with what it realizes, which is emptiness as understood in Consequentialism, since in the Gelugpa presentation Autonomism and Consequentialism have many essential differences. For example, Autonomism is claimed to still entail some remainder of discursiveness and reference points, while Consequentialism is utter freedom from these. From this, it absurdly follows that the supreme knowledge that realizes freedom from discursiveness and reference points itself entails discursiveness and reference points. Gelugpas also claim that emptiness is only partially understood and realized in Autonomism, since the object of negation—real existence—is not fully negated. Thus, it follows that the supreme knowledge that is described in detail in the Autonomist *Ornament of Clear Realization* is not the final remedy for the object of negation and thus does not fully realize emptiness.

Traditionally, there is no dispute in Tibetan Buddhism that Nāgārjuna and Asaṅga as the founders of the two great philosophical systems of the great vehicle are "the two most supreme ones" in Indian Buddhism. However, if Asaṅga really were a Consequentialist, then both founders of these two systems would be Centrists, the one being only disguised as a Mere Mentalist. So why continue to talk about two founders of two distinct systems? And how could Asaṅga be one of the two "supreme ones" side by side with Nāgārjuna, if the Gelugpas consider all his own works to be "Mere Mentalism" and thus inferior to Centrism? According to their understanding of supremacy, it would make much more sense to put Candrakīrti or even Bhāvaviveka in Asaṅga's place. At the same time, according to several of the Buddha's prophecies in the sūtras and tantras, all Tibetan schools hold that Nāgārjuna and Asaṅga were bodhisattvas on the first and third bodhisattva grounds respectively. Maitreya is even regarded as the highest of all bodhisattvas who dwell on the tenth ground, being Buddha Śākyamuni's regent and the coming fifth Buddha to manifest on earth in this present eon. To dwell on lower or higher bodhisattva grounds is not just a matter of ranking among the "top ten" of bodhisattva celebrities, but the Buddhist teachings contain detailed descriptions of the exponential increase in wisdom and positive qualities while progressing through these grounds. In particular, the full capacity to teach the dharma in a completely perfect way to any kind of audience is only accomplished on the ninth ground. Within such a framework, it could very well be argued then that it makes much better sense to regard the texts by Asaṅga and the coming Buddha Maitreya as being more authoritative in explaining the final purport of Buddha Śākyamuni's teachings than the works of Nāgārjuna.

### Why All the Fuss?

In an attempt to step outside of the well-established defense lines in the Rangtong-Shentong controversy, some fresh air might be provided by looking at the notions of self-emptiness and other-emptiness from a number of different perspectives.

For example, the Eighth Karmapa, Mipham Rinpoche, and other masters turn the tables on their Gelugpa opponents by saying that the term "other-emptiness" is equally applicable to how the followers of Tsongkhapa understand emptiness, since they claim that, for example, form is not empty of form but form is empty of real existence (Tib. bden grub). This means that form is not empty of itself but of something other, that is, real existence. However, the proponents of other-emptiness see a big difference between this kind of other-emptiness and its correct understanding as presented in the Shentong school. The latter is said to be the actual "other-emptiness of the nature of phenomena,"[1250] while Tsongkhapa's understanding of emptiness is called the limited "other-emptiness of what bears the nature of phenomena."[1251] This one is identified as "the emptiness of one not existing in an other," which is regarded by all Tibetan schools as a mistaken emptiness that is to be rejected. As the second chapter of *The Sūtra of the Arrival in Laṅka* says:

> This emptiness of one [not existing in] an other, Mahāmati, is very inferior, and you should abandon it.[1252]

Perhaps a surprising aspect of the Rangtong-Shentong controversy is that it can be easily demonstrated that emptiness, Buddha nature, and ultimate reality are both self-empty and other-empty. In fact, the same applies to all phenomena in general. On the one hand, all phenomena are extensively shown to be empty of themselves (a table is empty of being a table). On the other hand, even conventionally, all phenomena are empty of something other, since there is no phenomenon that exists as something other than itself. Obviously, both ultimately and conventionally, a table is empty of everything that is other than this table, such as a chair. In this way, self-empty and other-empty are not at all contradictory or mutually exclusive. This stance does not contradict the Centrist teachings, since it is precisely what Nāgārjuna declares in his *Seventy Stanzas on Emptiness*:

> The eye is empty of an intrinsic identity of its own.
> It is also empty of any other identity.
> [Visible] form is empty in the same way,
> And also the remaining sources are alike.[1253]

In light of this, it is very hard to claim Nāgārjuna as an exclusive proponent of either self-emptiness or other-emptiness.

A related issue is that ultimately all phenomena lack a really existent, intrinsic nature of their own, but at the same time, on the level of mere appearances, individual phenomena can be clearly distinguished from others. This is expressed in *The Sūtra of the Arrival in Laṅka*:

> Mahāmati, the learned should understand the meaning of my statement, "All phenomena are identityless." Mahāmati, identityless entities are identitylessness. Just like a horse and an ox [are distinct], all phenomena exist as their own entity, but not as an other entity. It is thus, Mahāmati, the entity of an ox is not of the nature of a horse, and the entity of a horse is not of the nature of an ox. [It is in this way that] they exist and are not nonexistent. These two are not nonexistent in terms

of their specific characteristics. Rather, these two do exist in terms of their specific characteristics. Likewise, Mahāmati, all phenomena are not nonexistent in terms of their specific characteristics, but do exist [in this respect]. Thus, naïve, ordinary sentient beings understand them as identityless by conceptually apprehending them, but not in a nonconceptual way. In the same way, all phenomena should be understood as emptiness, lacking arising, and lacking a nature.[1254]

As for Buddha nature, there is no Indian text that describes it as either being self-empty or other-empty. It is only said that Buddha nature is both empty of adventitious stains—that is, distinguishable from them—and not empty of its qualities—that is, indistinguishable from them. *The Sublime Continuum* declares:

The basic element is empty of what is adventitious,
Which has the characteristic of being separable.
It is not empty of the unsurpassable dharmas,
Which have the characteristic of being inseparable.[1255]

This is nothing extraordinary either. In a way, it is like saying that a book is empty of, or separable from, the dust that covers it. On the other hand, as long as one refers to a book at all, it is not empty of, or inseparable from, its pages and letters. Yet this does not necessarily imply that the book or its components are reified as ultimately identifiable entities. The same goes for Buddha nature, the Dharma Body, or nonconceptual wisdom. As *The Sūtra of the Arrival in Laṅka* says:

In the future, those who cling to non-Buddhist thinking will conceive of the wisdom of the noble ones as existing as an object of personal experience and as having the nature of an entity. . . . How could such notions operate in the noble ones? If such [notions] were entertained, they would be nothing but the clinging to an identity.

and

Mahāmati, if various kinds of illusions are regarded as something other respectively, they are discriminated as [distinct] other appearances by naïve beings, but not by the noble ones.[1256]

The last quote points to a very important factor as to why the terms "self-emptiness" and "other-emptiness" do not have to be contradictory. As Ruegg says:

> [O]ne could assume an incompatibility, at one and the same level of reference, between two philosophical propositions, both of which cannot be true in accordance with the principle of contradiction. Alternatively, one might perhaps suppose a complementarity — perhaps even an incommensurability — between two doctrines that relate to different levels of reference or discourse, and which are accordingly not mutually exclusive or contradictory.[1257]

In fact, this is precisely one of the major points in Dölpopa's original presentation of self-emptiness and other-emptiness that was often overlooked by later proponents of other-emptiness as well as their opponents. Despite the claims of his opponents, Dölpopa's use of this distinction is epistemological in nature and not ontological or reifying. In his main work, *A Mountain Dharma, The Ocean of Definitive Meaning,*[1258] he himself makes a clear distinction between a "philosophical system" (Skt. siddhānta, Tib. grub mtha') based on certain explanations and arguments and a "point of view" in the sense of an outlook (Skt. darśana, Tib. lta ba). For him, the latter is understood in the broad sense of including what is directly experienced in meditative equipoise. This is what he calls "Great Madhyamaka" and "other-emptiness," the outlook of noble beings who see how things really are. As such, it is clearly contrasted with Madhyamaka as a mere philosophical system. Thus, on these two levels, the entire perspective of mind and, consequently, the way of discourse are quite different.

For whatever reasons, many later proponents of other-emptiness and their opponents do not follow this epistemological distinction and often speak of both self-emptiness and other-emptiness as philosophical systems. Dölpopa himself never spoke about proponents of self-emptiness as opposed to proponents of other-emptiness. Rather, he sees self-emptiness as a philosophical system that he accepts himself as far as it goes, which is to say, by definition not applying to the level of direct meditative insight. Thus, a major part of the later controversy is due to the confusion as to whether the Rangtong-Shentong contrast pertains to the level of philosophical systems or the level of the direct insight in meditative equipoise. For Dölpopa, it clearly was the contrast between a philosophical system on the one hand and a direct vision of true reality on the other.

To sum up, it seems that the Rangtong-Shentong issue is only a problem if self-empty and other-empty are regarded as mutually exclusive on the same level of realization and discourse.

In the end, the whole controversy is highly dualistic in itself, since what is talked about—emptiness or ultimate reality—is in fact neither self-empty nor other-empty anyway. As the Eighth Karmapa Mikyö Dorje's commentary on *The Ornament of Clear Realization* says:

> This basis—the nature of phenomena—is neither other-empty nor self-empty, because it is not even suitable as a mere emptiness that is not specified as being empty or not empty of itself or something other. The reason for this is that it has the essential character of being the utter peace of all discursiveness of being empty and not being empty. Thus, from the perspective of the [actual] freedom from discursiveness, no characteristics whatsoever of being empty of itself or something other transpire within the basis that is the nature of phenomena.[1259]

As for doxographical classifications in general, they may be helpful to gain an overview of the overwhelming amount and diversity of scriptural output of Indian and Tibetan masters. They may also be beneficially employed to refine one's own understanding against the background of ascending levels of analysis as presented in such classifications of hierarchic tenets. However, there is the danger in all broad categorizations, such as the classification of Buddhist teachings as self-empty or other-empty, that they obscure or prevent attempts to look seriously at the more subtle aspects of the issues at hand. In particular, to categorize certain masters as proponents of self-emptiness or other-emptiness may obstruct our view on the often individual and specific presentations of these masters. Moreover, such categorizations do not take into account that many masters comment on scriptures from different systems, such as Yogācāra and Madhyamaka, in quite different ways that accord with the backgrounds of these systems. Also, since the teaching styles of individual masters are usually adapted to the capacities and needs of individual disciples, they may teach very different things in different situations. After all, the teachings of the Buddha are always meant to be put into practice in order to remove mental afflictions and suffering, and not primarily as a philosophical system to be established in one way or another. Usually, in Buddhism, philosophical considerations come in response to practical and soteriological issues. In this sense, the question of the actual or ultimate view of a certain master is moot. The most obvious example is the Buddha himself, who gave an extremely wide range of teachings to many different beings in many different situations. Obviously, he cannot be categorized as being a proponent of Madhyamaka, Yogācāra, self-emptiness, other-emptiness, or anything else. As Kapstein rightly says:

> I would suggest, therefore, that . . . doxographic labels such as gzhan stong pa and rang stong pa are best avoided, except of course where they are used within the tradition itself. Our primary task must be to document and interpret precise concepts and arguments, and in many cases the recourse to overly broad characterizations seems only to muddy the waters.[1260]

Huntington agrees:

> In working to develop a critical intellectual history of early Indian Mahāyāna, then, the focus of our attention must shift from "tenets" and "schools" . . . to individual authors and their own original words.[1261]

As for the soteriological efficacy of the Buddhist teachings, no matter which labels may be attached to them, what counts in the end is whether their practical application leads to freedom from ignorance, afflictions, and suffering. As Maitreya's *Sublime Continuum* says, this is the criterion for genuine dharma, no matter who teaches it.

> The words that are endowed with welfare, are connected to the dharma,
> Relinquish the afflictions of the three realms,
> And teach the benefit of peace
> Are the words of the Great Seer.[1262] Their opposite is something else.
>
> Whatever is explained by someone with an undistracted mind,
> Inspired solely by the teachings of the Victor,
> And in accordance with the path of attaining liberation
> Is to be placed on your head just like the words of the Great Seer.[1263]

## *The Single Final Intention of the Two Philosophical Systems of the Great Vehicle*

*The Treasury of Knowledge* confirms the universal acceptance in the great vehicle that the two great system founders Nāgārjuna and Asaṅga were prophesied by the Buddha and that both dwell on the levels of noble bodhisattvas. In the sky of the Sage's teaching, they resemble the sun and the moon, and there are no other ornaments more supreme than these two great scriptural traditions. In their intention, there is no difference in terms of superior or inferior. Therefore, to realize the ways of the individual scriptural systems of these two system founders without intermingling them is to realize that their final intention constitutes a single meaning. Should this appear differently to some people, the reason lies only in their own limited understanding. By slavishly echoing minor texts of ordinary paṇḍitas who are like the dim light of stars and planets, such people only ripen trifling results. By following such an approach, they merely cultivate more discursiveness in terms of negations and proofs through many fictitious scriptures and reasonings. This only develops and fortifies biased clinging.

The supreme systems of the two chariots do not contradict each other. Therefore, it is appropriate to engage in all their essential points of hearing, reflection, and meditation in an absolutely equal way. Through assimilating them in this way, one goes beyond minor results, is released from the many flaws of superimposition and denial, and becomes endowed with the stainless eye of insight that correctly views all sūtras and tantras. Thus, without the views of sūtras and tantras being affected by any flaws of contradiction, the unmistaken intention of the Buddha that is free from the mental imputations of ordinary sentient beings will be realized. *The Treasury of Knowledge* quotes Śākya Chogden:

> To explain the intention of Nāgārjuna, the way of explanation of the self-empty [system] is the supreme. To comment on the intention of venerable Maitreya, the other-empty system is very profound. Therefore, through the scriptures and reasonings of one of these [systems], the other cannot be negated. Otherwise, [if one wanted to do so,] one would have to strongly support the scriptures and reasonings of honorable Asaṅga, because he was prophesied as the person to attain the state of a noble one and differentiate [between the expedient and] the definitive meaning. In this way, he is the foremost system founder of the great vehicle. [Furthermore,] although Candrakīrti resolved that the way of explanation of honorable Asaṅga is not the intention of noble Nāgārjuna, he did not state that honorable Asaṅga had not realized the meaning of Centrism.[1264]

Pawo Rinpoche comments that, in Tibet, the intention of the lineage of profound view is usually explained as self-emptiness, that is, as a nonimplicative negation in which nothing whatsoever exists as a remainder after analysis through reasoning. The intention of the lineage of vast activity is explained as the other-empty ultimate that exists as a permanent and lasting remainder after such analysis. By clinging to one of these views as being the true meaning, the respective other one is then presented as a view of either permanence or extinction. However, these one-sided options, such as existence, nonexistence, permanence, and extinction, are neither the ultimate of the lineage of profound view nor the ultimate of the lineage of vast activity. As *The Fundamental Verses* says:

> To say "existence" is the clinging to permanence.
> To say "nonexistence" is the view of extinction.
> Therefore, the learned should not dwell
> In either existence or nonexistence.[1265]

The lineage of vast activity explains that both existence and nonexistence are just imaginary; they are completely nonexistent, just like a sky-flower. Asaṅga's *Synopsis of the Great Vehicle* lists ten conceptual distractions[1266] as the divisions of the imaginary nature. The first two among these are the conceptions about nonexistence and the conceptions about existence. Maitreya's *Distinction between the Middle and Extremes* states:

> Neither empty nor nonempty—
> In this way, everything is explained.[1267]

In general, Pawo Rinpoche says, the intentions of these two systems of the great vehicle are one and the same. The reasons for this are as follows: As shown above, the seeming in the explanation of the two realities in the lineage of profound view is simply classified as twofold in the lineage of vast activity. All superimpositions, such as names, are called the imaginary nature, and the delusive appearances of dependent origination are designated as the other-dependent nature. The ultimate is referred to as the perfect nature. However, both systems teach that the actual ultimate is the utter peace of all discursiveness.[1268]

Through the example of floating hairs that do not exist by their nature and are not even real at the time when they appear for those with blurred vision, both lineages teach that the seeming is illusionlike. They agree that, just as space is not established as anything and yet is omnipresent, the ultimate cannot be pinpointed as anything whatsoever, and yet it is not the case that it does not pervade all phenomena. It is the nature of being beyond speech, thought, and expression. Therefore, in the lineage of profound view, the elimination of the clinging to the extremes of superimposition and denial is given the name "realizing the true reality." The lineage of vast activity says that once the appearances of floating hairs vanish through the removal of blurred vision, space is seen just as it is. Likewise, the vanishing of the appearances of the other-dependent nature through the removal of even the most subtle levels of the imaginary nature is referred to by the conventional expression of "seeing the perfect nature." Therefore, in the end, there is not even a slight difference between the presentations of these two lineages.

Furthermore, since knower and what is known are just mutually dependent concepts, ultimately, neither is established. Thus, what is referred to by such conventional expressions as "liberation," "nirvāṇa," "seeing what is true," or "residing in the expanse of dharmas" is nothing but the state of having let go of mistakenly setting up reference points in terms of superimposition and denial. *The Ornament of Sūtras* says:

> Therefore, liberation is only the exhaustion of mistakenness.

Here, in terms of the ultimate mode of being,
There is no difference between peace and arising.[1269]

*The Distinction between the Middle and Extremes* agrees:

As for false imagination, . . .
Once it is exhausted, this is asserted as liberation.[1270]

*The Fundamental Verses* states:

Where there is no production of nirvāṇa,
There is no elimination of cyclic existence either.
So what is cyclic existence,
And which nirvāṇa do you consider?

When thinking in terms of self and mine
With regard to the external and the internal is exhausted,
The perpetuating [aggregates] will cease.
Since they cease, birth is exhausted [too].

Liberation [is attained] through the exhaustion of karma and afflictions.
Karma and afflictions [come] from conceptions,
And these [result] from discursiveness.
Discursiveness is halted through emptiness.[1271]

Just as in Centrism, the lineage of vast activity simply regards an extreme as any rigid assertion about the true nature of phenomena. This is well elucidated in Vasubandhu's commentary on the list of twenty-eight extremes in *The Distinction between the Middle and Extremes* V.23–26.[1272] Like the Centrists, he uses the well-known passage from *The Kāśyapa Chapter Sūtra* as the source for "the practice of the middle path of eliminating all extremes."[1273] A few of his comments may suffice:

The middle path for completely relinquishing the [extremes of identity and identitylessness] is that which is the middle between both identity and identitylessness, that is, nonconceptuality as such. . . .

The middle path for completely relinquishing the [extremes of mind being real or not] is that in which there is no mind (citta), no intention, no mental cognition, and no consciousness. . . .

> The middle path for completely relinquishing the [extremes of apprehender and apprehended] is [referred to in] the extensive passage about "awareness and unawareness not existing as two" [in *The Kāśyapa Chapter Sūtra*], because awareness, unawareness, and such do not exist as any entities of apprehender and apprehended. . . .
>
> The middle path for completely relinquishing the [extremes of entities and nonentities] is the extensive passage [in this sūtra] that says, "The person is not empty, because it is destroyed, but the person is empty just through emptiness. The former extreme is empty and the latter extreme is empty."
>
> Conceptions of something to be pacified are an extreme. Conceptions of something that pacifies are also an extreme, because one fears emptiness through thinking about something to be relinquished and something that relinquishes it. In order to completely relinquish these two extremes of conceptions, the example of space [is given].[1274]

In addition, Vasubandhu comments on verse 1.2 of the same text:

> As for "This is the middle path," it means that everything is neither absolutely empty nor absolutely nonempty. In this way, such is in accordance with what appears in the *Prajñāpāramitā sūtras* and others:
>
>> All this is neither empty nor nonempty.[1275]

This shows that, fundamentally, Maitreya's and Vasubandhu's view of the middle is not different from the Centrist understanding, since both wish to rid mind of all kinds of fixed views and reference points that prevent recognition of the true nature of phenomena and thus lead to suffering. Just as for Centrists, according to Vasubandhu, the realization of emptiness is a state in which all discursiveness and reference points are absent.

Thus, whether this is based on practicing the system of Yogācāra or Centrism, once mind lets go of all reference points (in the phase of putting an end to all bases for views), the two systems of the great vehicle are clearly revealed to have the same intention. Initially, Centrism focuses mainly on negating all theorization in terms of thinking, language, and reasoning, while Yogācāra affirms and emphasizes subjective experience. In other words, Centrists strip mind of all reference points and do not talk much about the experiencer of this process. Yogācāras too strive to eliminate the imaginary constructs of mind, but they focus more on the knowing of this process and the underlying primordial purity of mind. Nevertheless, both agree in their warnings against reducing our experiences to a theory of experience. They simply use somewhat different methods for undoing such "reductionism," which constricts mind's natural awareness. Eventually, for both, unmediated and uncontrived experience of true reality is primary. Thus, Pawo Rinpoche says, both Nāgārjuna's and Asaṅga's traditions agree that the unity of perfect meditative stability and knowledge is to rest right within the seeing through profound knowledge that is without seeing anything and to do so in a way that is without someone who rests and something to be rested in.

Both traditions agree on the nonaffirming characteristics of the ultimate. Asaṅga's *Commentary on The Sūtra That Unravels the Intention* states:

> Here, the Buddha teaches the five characteristics of the ultimate. The five characteristics of the ultimate are the characteristic of being inexpressible, the characteristic of being nondual, the characteristic of being completely beyond the sphere of dialectic, the characteristic of being completely beyond difference and nondifference, and the characteristic of being of one taste in everything.[1276]

*The Ornament of Sūtras* says:

> Neither existent nor non-existent, neither thus nor otherwise,
> Neither arising nor ceasing, neither increasing nor decreasing,
> Not purified and yet purified again—
> These are the characteristics of the ultimate.[1277]

*The Sublime Continuum* speaks about the dharma as the realization of the ultimate:

> Neither nonexistent nor existent, neither [both] existent and nonexistent nor something other than existent and nonexistent:
> It cannot be conceived as any of these, is free from verbalization, and is to be personally realized and peaceful.[1278]

The same text says about Buddhahood:

> It is not an object of speech, constituted by the ultimate,
> Not the domain of reasoning, beyond example,
> Unsurpassable, neither included in [samsaric] existence nor [nirvanic] peace.
> For all these reasons, the sphere of the Victors is inconceivable even for the noble ones.[1279]

This corresponds well with Nāgārjuna's characteristics of true reality in his *Fundamental Verses*:

> Not known from something other, peaceful,
> Not discursive through discursiveness,
> Without conceptions, and without distinctions:
> These are the characteristics of true reality.[1280]

On the reverse side, more affirmative descriptions of ultimate reality are not necessarily limited to the texts of the lineage of vast activity. Nāgārjuna's *Praise to the Expanse of Dharmas* states:

> Imagine that a [metal] garment that has been purified through fire
> Becomes contaminated by various kinds of stains later.
> When it is put into a fire [again],
> Its stains are burned, but the garment is not.
>
> Likewise, luminous mind
> Has the stains of desire and so forth.
> The fire of wisdom burns its stains,
> But not luminous true reality.
>
> All the many sūtras spoken by the Victor
> That teach emptiness
> Make the afflictions subside,
> But they do not weaken the basic element.[1281]

The eleventh chapter of *The Entrance into Centrism* explains the final result of enlightenment with all its qualities, such as the ten powers, in detail. In brief:

> What is profound is emptiness.
> The other qualities are vast.
> Through the knowledge of the mode of profundity and vastness,
> These qualities will be obtained.[1282]

In the same vein, as mentioned before, the Eighth Karmapa's introduction to *The Chariot of the Tagbo Siddhas* says that, implicitly, Maitrīpa's system of Centrism also teaches the profound actuality of both sūtras and tantras, which is Buddha nature, the ordinary and extraordinary ultimate Heart of the Blissfully Gone Ones.[1283]

All nonsectarian Shentong masters, such as the Seventh Karmapa Chötra

Gyamtso, Śākya Chogden, and Jamgön Kongtrul Lodrö Taye, agree that the systems of Nāgārjuna and Asaṅga do not exclude each other and are in fact complementary. The Seventh Karmapa states in his *Ocean of Texts on Reasoning* that their systems are identical in their ultimate essential point, because Nāgārjuna mainly determines the nature of phenomena from the side of outer objects, while Asaṅga does the same mainly from the side of the inner subject, the mind. He says:

> Therefore, the great Yogācāra Centrists who follow noble Asaṅga and his brother mainly teach the wisdom that realizes self-aware, self-luminous mind by ascertaining that the dualistic appearances of apprehender and apprehended that obscure true reality are not established in the way they [appear].
>
> Noble Nāgārjuna and his spiritual heirs mainly teach that the nature of luminous mind abides as emptiness by thoroughly analyzing the clinging to real [existence] and its objects that obscure true reality through the great [Centrist] arguments. In this way, they ascertain that [this clinging and its objects] are without nature.
>
> Both systems do not differ in teaching the final true reality, since this very nature of luminous mind primordially is emptiness, and this emptiness primordially abides as the essential character of luminosity.[1284]

When speaking of the unity of these systems by means of the terminology of self-emptiness and other-emptiness, the above masters emphasize that a proper understanding of the approach of self-emptiness is in fact indispensable for a correct, nonreifying understanding of other-emptiness. When properly combined, the approaches of self-emptiness and other-emptiness eliminate the more subtle levels of the extremes of existence and nonexistence respectively. Moreover, the Centrist—specifically the Consequentialist—approach is not merely a skillful means to cut through discursiveness and reference points on the seeming level, but it is definitely a means to point beyond this level to the ultimate that is inexpressible and inconceivable. Thus, in terms of what is to be finally realized, there is no contradiction to the approach of other-emptiness that agrees that the ultimate is inexpressible, inconceivable, and nondualistic, while its indications of ultimate reality mainly serve to highlight the experiential character of mind realizing its own ultimate nature. In other words, the positive description of a nonconceptual experience of ultimate reality in the teachings on other-emptiness only starts to speak to us from within the "noble silence" of the complete freedom from all discursiveness (as illustrated in the *Vimalakīrtisūtra*) that is arrived at through the teachings on self-emptiness.

In brief, Centrists focus more on the objective side and dissolve all reference points within the mind, including mind itself. In this way, they attempt to let us awaken into an uncontrived experience of the ultimate nature of this very mind without any seeming obscurations or reference points. Yogācāra focuses more on the subjective side—mind itself—and describes both its impure and pure aspects. The journey from the impure appearance to the pure nature of the mind leads through the provisional and seeming stages of "mere mind" and the nonduality of apprehender and apprehended to nonconceptual wisdom as the experiential dimension of ultimate reality.

Considering the example of blurred vision that is used by both systems, when the eye disease has been removed and the appearances of floating hairs have disappeared, what is seen is the clear sky. This aspect of clearly seeing the open sky as it is corresponds to the final view of suchness (the perfect nature) of the lineage of vast activity. The suchness as explained by the lineage of profound view through this example is the very freedom from the appearances of floating hairs. Thus, the only difference is that the lineage of profound view emphasizes more the aspect of freedom from delusion, while the lineage of vast activity emphasizes more what is seen within this freedom. In other words, the latter tells more about the experiential side of reaching the state of being free from all clinging and reference points.

As a slightly more frivolous example of different approaches to the same end, imagine three people sitting in a park and happily munching on the latest candy bar on the market. Some other people may come by and ask, "How does it taste?" The first of the three munchers may just stay silent and keep munching. The second states, "It is beyond words." The third raves, "It's the most wonderful taste in my whole life, fabulous, amazing!" Curious, some of the onlookers sit down in front of the first muncher, waiting for the direct candy bar transmission. This group consists of those of both the sharpest and the dullest faculties. The more analytically minded, fond of cryptic riddles, may further question the second muncher, "Can't you delineate it with some hints?" Those with a more emotional and imaginative mind probably request of the third muncher, "We need to hear everything about this wonderful taste." The second muncher may reply, "It's not like Snickers, not Mars, not M&M . . ." Naturally, the third utters all the most poetic and rich imagery about this new taste.

So, who is right? Is anybody describing the taste more correctly than the others? In terms of the actual experience of that taste, whatever is said or not said, whatever is heard or not heard, and whatever is conceptualized on the basis of all that, is wrong anyway, since none of it *is* the actual experience of this taste. At the same time, there is no problem in any of the three munchers' approaches precisely because this taste is inexpressible, so it does not matter whether they just stay silent or describe it in one way or the other. The only reason they can go on describing it endlessly is that it is indescribable. However, there is more to these three approaches, since each one can be seen as an attempt to communicate the way in which other people eventually come to know how the new candy bar tastes. The people of highest capacities in front of the silent muncher get it after a while and leave, while those of dullest wits keep waiting for "it" to happen. The analytical questioners give up at some point during "not this, not that" and leave too. The people in the third group also leave once their mouths water enough. Where did they all go? Those who got the point will meet at the grocery store around the corner and have their munch-in. In different ways, they all realized that the only way to know how this candy bar tastes is to get one of their own, put it in their mouths, and chew. Only those who kept waiting for the effortless and spontaneous taste transmission and eventually dispersed after their "guru" has left them (to finally *buy* them the new bar) are not to be found munching at the store.[1285]

Clearly, the Buddha used all three approaches to communicate that we can experience the taste of mental freedom only by making our own steps on the path that leads there. This can be seen in the wide range of styles in his instructions, such as sometimes answering by remaining silent (as Vimalakīrti does), teaching the nonreferential *Prajñāpāramitā sūtras*, and teaching the sūtras that richly describe the qualities of Buddha nature, pure Buddha realms, and enlightenment. The varying approaches of Nāgārjuna, Asaṅga, and other masters may be regarded in the same way.

As for the details of pointing out the actual path that leads to mental freedom, the two lineages of profound view and vast conduct employ different styles of guidance, but they arrive at the same destination. Both Asaṅga and Nāgārjuna know the wonderful castle in the middle of town that we all wish to see. Explaining the route to get there, Nāgārjuna would only say such things as, "If you follow this road, you will get to a dead end. If you follow that avenue, you will face a lot of one-way streets and just go in circles. This way, you will end up on the highway out of town. Here, there is a major construction site and you'll get completely lost." In this way, he excludes all the wrong ways, false exits, and blocked roads. What remains unsaid is the right way to arrive at our sightseeing place.

Asaṅga's approach seems to be more straightforward, since he just tells us where to go: "Start on highway 1, take exit 24, go to the left up to this rotary, follow the signs that say 'Center,' and you will arrive at this magnificent castle with beautiful gardens and lakes." This seems easier, but once we hop into our car, we might become confused about the right exit and which rotary is the one we are supposed to take, because there is heavy traffic and we get lost. Then, Nāgārjuna's precise instructions on where not to go and why come into play. We can clearly identify the wrong roads and say, "No, that's not it, we have to go further." On the other hand, once we are on our way, just knowing all the roads on the town map that are not to be taken does not always immediately give us a clear idea where we should actually go. So knowing that there must be a certain rotary coming up soon is also helpful.

This approach of using the description of which roads and turns we have to take while identifying the ones to avoid is precisely how we usually try to find our way. Thus, the most effective path is to combine the approaches of the lineage of profound view and vast conduct. Nāgārjuna's style might have the occasional drawback of losing sight of the final destination by dealing exclusively with side-tracks. However, it also has the bonus of the surprise effect when we actually arrive at this breathtaking castle. With Asaṅga's style, there is hardly any chance that we will forget about the castle, since it is so abundantly described, but we might also sometimes get stuck in these descriptions and daydream about the castle instead of actually proceeding toward it. Śākya Chogden summarizes the need for both approaches as follows:

> If there were not these texts of Asaṅga's position—
> The dharma system of the fundamental ground and the presentation
> of the three emptinesses—
> Through what could the basis of purification and the means for
> purification
> As well as the presentation of outer, inner, and other in the texts
> of the great mode of being[1286] be explained?
>
> If there were not the way in which nondual wisdom is empty
> of nature
> That is differentiated by the texts of Consequentialists
> and Autonomists,
> What would relinquish our clinging to profound luminous
> wisdom's reality
> And our conceptions of being attached to magnificent deities?[1287]

I would like to conclude this chapter with a famous verse that is found in a number of texts of both the lineage of profound view and the lineage of vast activity:

> There is nothing to be removed from it
> And not the slightest to be added.
> Actual reality is to be seen as it really is—
> Who sees actual reality is released.[1288]

Gampopa's *Jewel Ornament of Liberation*[1289] says that this verse originally stems from *The Sūtra Requested by Sky Treasure.*[1290] It is one of the most essential verses in both *The Sublime Continuum* (I.154) and *The Ornament of Clear Realization* (V.21) by Maitreya. It is also found as the last verse (7) of Nāgārjuna's *Verses on the Heart of Dependent Origination*[1291] and is quoted in his autocommentary on *The Praise to the Three Enlightened Bodies.*[1292] Also Pawo Rinpoche echoes this verse:

> Once clinging in terms of superimposition and denial has come to an end in such a way, just this empty and luminous nature of phenomena in which there is nothing to be removed or to be added is the fundamental state of phenomena. This is expressed as primordial nirvāṇa as such.[1293]

# 5

# *The Distinction between Expedient and Definitive Meaning*

## *The Three Turnings of the Wheel of Dharma*

THE TIBETAN TRADITION in general accepts the division of the Buddha's teachings into the three turnings of the wheel of dharma.[1294] In different sūtras and treatises, these three turnings are referred to by different names.

In *The Sūtra That Unravels the Intention*, they are given the following names:

1) the first wheel that is turned through teaching the four realities of the noble ones
2) the second wheel that is turned in the form of speaking about emptiness
3) the third wheel that is endowed with the excellent distinction (between expedient and definitive meaning)[1295]

*The Sūtra Requested by King Dhāraṇīśvara*[1296] matches them with the example of the gradually refined cleansing of a precious stone and refers to the third wheel as "the wheel of irreversibility." It also calls the three turnings by the following names:

1) the mode of the four realities
2) the mode of emptiness
3) the mode of the Heart of the Thus-Gone Ones

Maitreya's *Sublime Continuum of the Great Vehicle* refers to three similar phases of progressively guiding sentient beings:

1) making samsaric beings enter the path to peace of hearers and solitary realizers
2) bringing hearers and solitary realizers to maturation in the great vehicle
3) on the eighth bodhisattva ground, granting them the prophecy of their supreme enlightenment[1297]

Nāgārjuna speaks of the three wheels:

1) the wheel that teaches identity
2) the wheel that teaches identitylessness
3) the wheel that puts an end to all bases for views

This corresponds to the three stages of analysis in Āryadeva's *Four Hundred Verses*:

> First, what is not meritorious is ended.
> In the middle, identity is ended.
> Later, all views are ended.
> Those who understand this are skilled.[1298]

In the initial phase of putting an end to what is not meritorious, through adopting positive actions and rejecting negative actions without analyzing such conduct as to its ultimate nature, one first exhausts what is not meritorious and accumulates merit instead. In the second phase of putting an end to identity, through applying slight analysis, one eliminates all mistaken views about personal and phenomenal identities. During the third phase of putting an end to all views through becoming fully immersed in excellent analysis, all reference points of any kind of view will finally dissolve. As Pawo Rinpoche says:

> [Actually,] in the Centrist system itself, the stage of no analysis through reasoning refers to the cycle [of teachings] that first puts an end to what is not meritorious, that is, the vehicle that [leads to] the higher realms. The intermediate phase of putting an end to identity means [using] Centrist reasonings to counteract [all types of] clinging in Buddhist and non-Buddhist philosophical systems. The phase of putting an end to all bases for views refers to the final complete elimination of [any] clinging to true reality. Hence, there is no need for anybody to reduce these [phases] or add anything to them. By relating all these three [stages of no analysis, slight analysis, and intense analysis] solely to the intermediate phase of putting an end to identity, clinging to the nonexistence of the dross [of mental obscurations] and clinging to the existence of the pure essence [of the mind] are developed. [Moreover,] one [mistakenly] considers merely not giving an answer as the ultimate actuality.[1299]

The Third Karmapa Rangjung Dorje says:

> In general terms, Noble [Nāgārjuna]'s "wheel that puts an end to all bases for views" and Venerable [Maitreya]'s "wheel of prophecy" come

down to the same essential point. This essential point is that whatever is the final wheel is necessarily the wheel that teaches freedom from discursiveness. [However,] there are some particular distinct features through which they are not the same. In the former [wheel], nothing but mere freedom from discursiveness is taught, while the latter explains the distinctive feature that the wisdom free from discursiveness is to be experienced by the wisdom through which it is personally encountered. One might wonder, "Is it then the case that Nāgārjuna and his spiritual heirs do not assert the wisdom that is free from discursiveness?" No, this is not the case, since they explicitly teach it in such [works] as *The Collection of Praises* and *The Four Hundred Verses on the Yogic Practice of Bodhisattvas.*[1300]

**Expedient Meaning and Definitive Meaning Defined**

Mikyö Dorje, Pawo Rinpoche, and Padma Karpo agree that the distinction between expedient and definitive meaning is itself only made on the level of the expedient meaning. In terms of the actual definitive meaning, the Buddha never taught anything whatsoever. As a sūtra says:

> Śāntamati, between the night that the Thus-Gone One became a fully perfect Buddha in unsurpassable, utterly perfect enlightenment and the night that he will pass into complete nirvāṇa, the Thus-Gone One did not speak so much as a single syllable, nor will he speak any.

*The Fundamental Verses* agrees:

> At no time did the Buddha teach
> Any dharma to anybody.[1301]

From the perspective of various disciples, however, it seems that the Buddha taught in many different ways according to their capacities and needs. When classifying his teachings as the three turnings of the wheel of dharma, which are of expedient meaning and which are of definitive meaning? Different sūtras and treatises make varying distinctions. *The Sūtra That Unravels the Intention* says:

> Initially, at the site of the antelope grove of Ṛiṣivadana near Vārāṇasi, the Blessed One taught the four realities of the noble ones to those who had correctly entered the vehicle of the hearers. Thus, he turned the wonderful and marvelous wheel of dharma. . . . This turning of the wheel of dharma by the Blessed One is surpassable, and there is a possibility [for refutation]. It is of expedient meaning and a basis for debate.

> Then, starting with the lack of a nature of phenomena, he [taught] that they lack arising and lack ceasing, that they are primordial peace and by nature perfect nirvāṇa. Thus, for those who had correctly entered the great vehicle, in the form of speaking about emptiness, he turned the very wonderful and marvelous second wheel of dharma. This turning of the wheel of dharma by the Blessed One is [also] surpassable, and there is a possibility [for refutation]. It is of expedient meaning and a basis for debate.
>
> [Finally,] starting with the lack of a nature of phenomena, he [taught] that they lack arising and lack ceasing, that they are primordial peace and by nature perfect nirvāṇa. Thus, for those who had correctly entered all vehicles, he turned the exceedingly wonderful and marvelous third wheel of dharma that is endowed with excellent and thorough distinction. This turning of the wheel of dharma by the Blessed One is unsurpassable, and there is no chance [for refutation]. It is of definitive meaning and not a basis for debate.[1302]

*The Sūtra Requested by King Dhāraṇīśvara* describes the process of cleansing an encrusted jewel in three stages with increasingly refined chemical solutions and cloths. This analogy serves to illustrate the progressively advanced teachings of the Buddha:

> Likewise, the Thus-Gone One knows the potentials of very impure sentient beings, and through his words [that cause] revulsion, such as impermanence, suffering, identitylessness, and impurity, he produces weariness in those sentient beings who like cyclic existence. Thus, he introduces them to the noble dharma of the vinaya. [However,] the Thus-Gone One does not confine himself to this amount of effort. Thereafter, through speaking on emptiness, signlessness, and wishlessness, he makes them realize the way of being of the Thus-Gone Ones. [However,] the Thus-Gone One does not confine himself to this amount of effort either. Through speaking on the wheel of irreversibility and by speaking on the complete purity of the three spheres, he makes sentient beings with their causal [potentials] of various natures engage in the object of the Thus-Gone Ones.[1303]

Both *The Sūtra of the Teaching of Akṣayamati*[1304] and *The Sūtra of the King Of Meditative Concentration* make a general distinction between expedient and definitive meaning, but do not relate this to an evaluation of the three turnings of the wheel of dharma. In its explanation of the inexhaustible four reliances, *The Sūtra of the Teaching of Akṣayamati* states:

> One may wonder, "What are sūtras of expedient meaning?" The sūtras that teach seeming reality are of expedient meaning. "What are sūtras of definitive meaning?" The sūtras that are taught in order to reveal ultimate reality are of definitive meaning. The sūtras in which manifold words and letters are used are of expedient meaning. The sūtras that speak about the profound that is difficult to see and difficult to realize are of definitive meaning. The sūtras that use a variety of terms and phrasings in a manner as if there were an owner where there is no owner, such as self, sentient being, soul, [life-]sustainer, individual, person, Manu-born,[1305] son of Manu,[1306] agent, or experiencer are of expedient meaning. The sūtras that teach emptiness, signlessness, wishlessness, nonapplication, nonorigination, nonarising, nonentity, no self, no sentient beings, no soul, no person, no owner up through the doors to complete liberation are of definitive meaning. Thus, rely on the sūtra collection of definitive meaning, but do not rely on the sūtra collection of expedient meaning.[1307]

In explaining the meaning of this passage in his *Chariot of the Tagbo Siddhas*,[1308] the Eighth Karmapa says that the sūtras' explicit meaning that can be invalidated through reasoning is of expedient meaning. For in order to initially introduce disciples to the path and to mature their mental continua, these scriptures primarily teach seeming reality through various words and letters that are adapted to the minds and inclinations of individual persons. Thus, the explicit words of such teachings can be invalidated through reasoning, but they are nevertheless pronounced as means to guide various disciples gradually. On the other hand, the sūtras' explicit meaning that cannot be invalidated through reasoning is of definitive meaning. Through the profound actuality that is difficult to see and primordially void, these texts teach ultimate reality in accordance with the wisdom of the noble ones in order that the disciples engage in the fruition and that their mental continua become liberated. These texts are a cause for the attainment of liberation, since they cannot be invalidated through reasoning and produce the realization of this profound actuality while being taught.

All in all, *The Sūtra of the Teaching of Akṣayamati* lists eight criteria that distinguish expedient and definitive meaning:

1) The expedient meaning assists entry onto the path, while the definitive meaning guides disciples to engage in the fruition.

2) The expedient meaning deals with the seeming, while the definitive meaning deals with the ultimate.
3) The expedient meaning teaches about afflicted phenomena, and the definitive meaning teaches about purified phenomena.
4) The expedient meaning teaches how to engage in proper actions, and the definitive meaning shows how karma and afflictions become exhausted.
5) The expedient meaning causes weariness with cyclic existence, while the definitive meaning demonstrates that cyclic existence and nirvāṇa are undifferentiable.
6) The expedient meaning teaches a variety of terms and definitions, whereas the definitive meaning teaches the profound, true reality that is difficult to see and realize.
7) The expedient meaning gives detailed explanations in accordance with worldly conduct, while the definitive meaning focuses on concise and pithy instructions for cultivating meditative concentration.
8) The expedient meaning teaches about sentient beings, persons, a self, and so on, while the definitive meaning teaches about the three doors to complete liberation, nonapplication, nonorigination, nonarising, nonentity, identitylessness, and such.

*The Sūtra of the King Of Meditative Concentration* says:

> According to how the Blissfully-Gone One explained emptiness,
> One understands the specific feature of the sūtra collection of definitive meaning.
> All those dharmas in which sentient beings, persons, and individuals are taught
> Are understood to be of expedient meaning.[1309]

Thus, this sūtra distinguishes between expedient and definitive meaning in a way that accords with the eighth of the above points in *The Sūtra of the Teaching of Akṣayamati.* Nāgārjuna's *Praise to the Inconceivable* obviously follows these sūtras:

> It is the nectar of the teachings of the Buddhas,
> Called "the gift of the dharma,"
> That is declared to be the definitive meaning.
> This is only the emptiness of phenomena.
>
> The instructions on arising, ceasing, and such,
> As well as on sentient beings, souls, and so on,
> Have been taught by you, O Protector,
> To be of expedient meaning and in terms of the seeming.[1310]

Avalokitavrata in his *Commentary on The Lamp of Knowledge* also complies with the distinction made by these sūtras.[1311]

Candrakīrti's *Lucid Words* says that Nāgārjuna's *Fundamental Verses* were composed in order to demonstrate the distinction between sūtras of expedient and definitive meaning. Here, the teachings on arising and such in terms of dependent origination are not given with respect to the nature of the object of the uncontaminated wisdom of those who are free from the blurred vision of ignorance. Rather, they are given with respect to the objects of the consciousnesses of those whose eyes of insight are impaired by such blurred vision. With respect to seeing true reality, Candrakīrti quotes the Buddha:

> Oh fully ordained monks, this is ultimate reality. It is as follows: Nirvāṇa has the property of being undeceiving, whereas all formations have the property of being delusive and deceiving.

Through not understanding the true intention of the Buddha's teaching in this way, some people may entertain doubts as to which teachings pertain to actual true reality and which have a certain intention. Also, due to weak intelligence, certain people may understand teachings of expedient meaning as being of definitive meaning. Hence, Nāgārjuna wrote his text for the sake of eliminating the doubts and wrong ideas of these two kinds of disciples. These statements are then followed by the above two quotations from *The Sūtra of the King Of Meditative Concentration* and *The Sūtra of the Teaching of Akṣayamati.*[1312]

Candrakīrti's *Entrance into Centrism* takes the same approach:

> Once you have understood the account of the scriptures in this way,
> Understand that the sūtras that are not true reality and have a meaning
> to be explained
> Are taught as the expedient meaning. Having realized this, they are
> for guidance.
> Those that bear the meaning of emptiness are of definitive meaning.[1313]

His autocommentary explains that this distinction between the expedient and the definitive meanings is based on the above-cited two sūtras: *The Sūtra of the Teaching of Akṣayamati* and *The Sūtra of the King of Meditative Concentration.*[1314] The only extant Indian commentary on *The Entrance into Centrism,* by Jayānanda, follows this distinction and elaborates on it.[1315] Karmapa Mikyö Dorje comments on Candrakīrti's above verse by saying that those sūtras which do not explicitly elucidate the true reality of dependent origination free from the eight extremes such as arising[1316] and which have an explicit meaning that is to be explained further (such as arising, ceasing, or an intrinsic reality) are taught as the expedient meaning for the sake of guiding individual disciples in approaching the profound ultimate actuality. On the other hand, those sūtras that bear the meaning of explicitly teaching dependent origination free from the eight extremes as emptiness are of definitive meaning. For, unlike the expedient meaning, the definitive meaning can by definition not serve to guide disciples toward anything other than what it says in itself.

**Relating the Three Turnings of the Wheel of Dharma to the Two Levels of Meaning**

There are different presentations as to which of the three turnings of the wheel of dharma are of expedient meaning and which are of definitive meaning. Everybody in the great vehicle seems to agree that the first turning is of expedient meaning. The dispute concerns the status of the second and third turnings.

*The Treasury of Knowledge*[1317] says the following: By quoting *The Sūtra That Unravels the Intention*, Asaṅga's *Synopsis of Ascertainment* explains that the third turning is the final definitive meaning.[1318] Vasubandhu agrees with this position.[1319] However, both Asaṅga and Vasubandhu never say that the second turning of the wheel of dharma is of expedient meaning.[1320] As for Nāgārjuna and Āryadeva, both take the threefold process of cleansing in *The Sūtra Requested by King Dhāraṇīśvara* to be of definitive meaning. Candrakīrti only makes a general distinction between sūtras of expedient and definitive meaning based on *The Sūtra of the Teaching of Akṣayamati.* However, nowhere does he give a presentation of the three turnings of the wheel of dharma, let alone relate his distinction of expedient and definitive meaning to these three turnings. It seems that Tibetan teachers did a lot of chattering about discriminating between the second and third turnings in terms of expedient versus definitive meaning and supreme versus inferior without having properly examined this situation. In terms of the eight criteria in *The Sūtra of the Teaching of Akṣayamati* that distinguish the expedient from the definitive meaning, the first seven are equal in putting both the second and third turnings in the category of the definitive meaning. As for the eighth criterion—identitylessness—Candrakīrti presented merely being empty of the two kinds of identity as the definitive meaning. Asaṅga, Vasubandhu, and their followers determine that the meaning of identitylessness refers to the nonexistence of any kind of identity as imagined by naïve beings, and they contrast this with what the Buddha taught about Buddha nature and how the latter is not to be mistaken for a self or any kind of identity. Thus, they say that the second and third turnings are equally of definitive meaning. The difference is that the second turning is the definitive meaning that cuts through temporary reference points, while the third turning is the definitive meaning that teaches the final basic nature.[1321]

As indicated by this, the issue of how expedient and definitive meaning are related to the second and third turnings turned into a major controversy in Tibet. Those who assert that the second turning is of definitive meaning and the third of expedient meaning are mainly found in the Gelugpa school. In this school, it is often said that "only the second turning of the wheel of dharma is the final definitive meaning, since Candrakīrti has explained it this way." However, this is not justified for two main reasons. First, as was explained earlier, Candrakīrti only distinguished between sūtras of expedient and definitive meaning according to *The Sūtra of the Teaching of Akṣayamati*, without relating this distinction to the three turnings. All he said was that sūtras of definitive meaning are those that teach emptiness, the lack of arising, and so on. Second, even when taking this criterion and applying it to the three turnings, one can find numerous passages in the sūtras of the third turning that teach emptiness equally clearly. Moreover, there are even some passages in the sūtras of the first turning that teach the meaning of emptiness, such as the negation of the four extremes of existence, nonexistence, and so on in the *Kaccayānagottasutta*.[1322] Therefore, Candrakīrti's distinction between the two levels of meaning cannot be used to support the claim that only the second turning is of definitive meaning. In addition, if only the second turning were of definitive meaning and the other two of expedient meaning, one might ask how much sense it makes for the Buddha to have taught first the expedient meaning, then the definitive meaning, and finally again nothing but the expedient meaning.

There is a further mistaken view, which says, "In the texts of the lineage of profound view, expressions such as 'all phenomena lack arising' are explained as something to be taken literally. In the scriptures of the lineage of vast activity, based on the fact that the Buddha used such expressions with the threefold lack of nature in mind, they are explained as something that is not to be taken literally." However, in the lineage of profound view, ultimately, expressions such as "all phenomena lack arising" are also not to be taken literally because arising and nonarising are mutually dependent. If there really is arising, its lack cannot be established. If there is no arising, a lack of arising that depends on arising in the first place cannot be established either. Thus, no matter in which turning they appear, expressions such as "all phenomena lack arising" are only taught for beginners in order to remove their clinging to arising and ceasing and so on. Hence, these statements were made with an intention behind them.

Others claim that only the third turning is of definitive meaning. Some of them say, "*The Sūtra That Unravels the Intention* declares that the sūtras that teach that all phenomena are without nature are of expedient meaning. It says that those sūtras are of definitive meaning that teach that the imaginary nature does not exist, while the other-dependent nature and the perfect nature exist. So what about this statement?" Mere Mentalists take it literally, thus claiming that the sūtras of the second turning, such as the *Prajñāpāramitā sūtras*, which teach that all phenomena are without nature, are of expedient meaning. The sūtras of the final turning, such as *The Sūtra That Unravels the Intention*, are held to be of definitive meaning, since they distinctly teach which among the three natures exist and which do not.

The Eighth Karmapa rejects all such positions. First, he makes it clear that explicit teachings, such as "all phenomena are devoid of nature," are of definitive meaning. They are definitive because they cannot be invalidated through reasoning, whereas all attempts to invalidate them, such as presuming arising from any of the four extremes, have already been refuted and will continue to be refuted. Furthermore, the real existence of the other-dependent nature and the perfect nature can also be invalidated through reasoning. The existence of a substantially established other-dependent nature has been refuted, for example, in *The Entrance into Centrism.*[1323] And, if such an other-dependent nature does not exist, then a real nature of phenomena (the perfect nature) that lacks a bearer of this nature (the other-dependent nature) is impossible.

The Eighth Karmapa then presents the Centrist opinion on this issue, which is that such texts as *The Sūtra That Unravels the Intention* also teach exclusively in accordance with what Centrists say. For them, all classifications of existence and nonexistence with regard to the three natures in these sūtras are of expedient meaning, and their meaning is not to be taken literally. The definitive meaning is that all three natures lack a nature. For example, this sūtra makes numerous such statements as:

> Subhūti, why is this? Ultimate suchness, or phenomenal identitylessness, is not something that has originated from causes. It is not conditioned, nor [is it] that which is not the ultimate. There is no need to search for an ultimate other than that ultimate.[1324]

The sūtra teaches that all three natures refer to nothing but the lack of a nature:

> That which is the perfect characteristic of phenomena is called "the ultimate lack of nature." Paramārthasamudgata, why is this? That which is phenomenal identitylessness is called "their lack of nature." This is the ultimate. Since the ultimate is characterized by being the lack of nature of all phenomena, it is called "the ultimate lack of nature." Paramārthasamudgata, for example, you should regard the lack of a nature in terms of characteristics as being like a sky-flower. For example, Paramārthasamudgata, you should view the lack of a nature in terms of arising as being like an illusion that has been conjured up. The ultimate lack of nature should be regarded as being one with this. For example, Paramārthasamudgata, [space] is characterized

> by being the mere lack of a nature of forms within space and by being omnipresent. Likewise, you should regard the ultimate lack of nature as that which is characterized by being phenomenal identitylessness and omnipresent.[1325]

As for the Centrists themselves, Kamalaśīla in his *Illumination of Centrism* quotes the above sūtra and also interprets it as referring to the lack of nature as understood by Centrists.[1326] Furthermore, Nāgārjuna's *Commentary on the Mind of Enlightenment* says:

> As for the imaginary, the other-dependent,
> And the perfect [natures],
> Their nature is the single character of emptiness.
> They are imputations onto mind.[1327]

The explanations by the lineage of vast activity say exactly the same in regard to the lack of nature. For example, *The Ornament of Sūtras* declares:

> If one knows the emptiness of the nonexistent,
> Likewise the emptiness of the existent,
> And also natural emptiness,
> Then this is expressed as "knowing emptiness."[1328]

Vasubandhu's *Thirty Verses* agrees:

> Based on the three kinds of lack of nature
> Of the three kinds of nature,
> It is taught that all phenomena
> Are without nature.[1329]

Moreover, in his *Commentary on The Sūtra That Unravels the Intention*, Asaṅga says in the context of the sūtra's seventh chapter that the threefold lack of nature is taught as a remedy for four wrong ideas about the meaning of what is taught through the lack of nature. For example, it is a misconception to think that the lack of nature is mere nonexistence or to believe that what is without nature cannot arise even as a mere appearance on the seeming level.[1330] On the passage in the sūtra's eighth chapter that talks about the characteristics of emptiness, such as the imaginary characteristic, the other-dependent characteristic, and the perfect characteristic, he comments that these are taught in order to eliminate the fear of emptiness.[1331]

Since sūtras such as *The Sūtra That Unravels the Intention* teach this definitive meaning, they do not teach according to the assertions of Mere Mentalism. Therefore, they cannot be established as sūtras that teach Mere Mentalism or Mind Only. In fact, all the individual assertions of realists (such as Mere Mentalists) that contradict both realities do not constitute the meaning as it is explained in the Buddha's teachings. If they did, all his teachings would be self-contradictory and could be invalidated through reasoning. This would contradict the fact that the Buddha speaks about the dharma with the complete self-confidence that nothing of what he says can be refuted by anyone.[1332] If these teachings really conveyed what Mere Mentalists propose, this would also mean that the Buddha is not omniscient and just teaches others without having resolved the meaning for himself. Furthermore, it would contradict the fact that all his teachings have different letters but conform to one meaning. As *The Sūtra of the King of Meditative Concentration* says:

> The sūtras that I taught
> In many thousands of worldly realms
> Have different letters but one meaning.

Thus, to take the teachings of expedient meaning to be of definitive meaning is to be mistaken about what the Buddha explains. As *The Ornament of Sūtras* states:

> If one understands [just] the literal meaning,
> One becomes arrogant and one's mind deteriorates.
> Through rejecting the excellent teachings,
> One will be pulverized and obscured by anger toward the dharma.[1333]

According to Karmapa Mikyö Dorje, the gist of this is that the second turning of the wheel of dharma is of definitive meaning and that, in the third turning, there are both expedient and definitive meanings. The definitive meaning in the third turning can be found in the teaching that all phenomena are without nature. Its expedient meaning is comprised by the teachings that talk about the other-dependent nature, self-awareness, a ground consciousness, a self, nonempty permanence, the cut-off disposition, the absolutely definite dispositions for the three vehicles, the ultimate existence of three distinct vehicles, and so on, since their explicit and literal words do not hold in actuality.

In his *Cutting Through Doubts about the Threefold Progression of the Wheels of Dharma*,[1334] Padma Karpo objects to those people who "take the *Prajñāpāramitā sūtras* as the basis for identifying them as the second turning as it is described in *The Sūtra That Unravels the Intention*, while taking *The Sūtra That Unravels the Intention* and others as the basis for the third turning." On the basis of this mistaken matching, he says, the proponents of self-emptiness hold the second turning to be of definitive meaning and the third to be of expedient meaning, while the proponents of other-emptiness give the reverse interpretation of these two turnings. According to Padma Karpo, this error comes from a more fundamental wrong assumption, that each turning must be based on a distinct set of scriptures. For him, both the second and third turnings are primarily based on the *Prajñāpāramitā sūtras.* He also shows that *The Sūtra That Unravels the Intention* teaches both Yogācāra and Centrism and thus cannot be established as a sūtra that teaches only Mere Mentalism.

Some people might still wonder, "*The Sūtra That Unravels the Intention* declares that the second turning is of expedient meaning, while the third is of definitive meaning. So what about this?" The Eighth Karmapa says that this is merely taught from the perspective of certain disciples. However, since this distinction between expedient and definitive meaning is not the final distinction of the Buddha's intended meaning, there is no invalidation of the above explanation, as will be explained immediately below.

All three turnings of the wheel of dharma were generally taught to a range of various disciples who all had their individual dispositions for distinct paths and vehicles. Thus, depending on the capacities of these disciples, there are more coarse and more subtle teachings. In the first turning, the four realities of noble ones were taught; in the second, the lack of nature; and in the third, the three natures and such. With regard to these three turnings, those who believe in really existing things regard expedient meanings as definitive meanings. Hence, they affirm the teachings of definitive meaning to be of expedient meaning and comment accordingly on the Buddha's intention. On the other hand, those who do not have the reference point of really existing things do not take the expedient meaning to be the definitive meaning. Rather, by seeing the definitive meaning as what it is (nothing but the definitive meaning), they comment on the Buddha's intention in this way.

However, one should be equally aware that, within the entirety of the Buddha's teachings of expedient and definitive meaning in his three progressive cycles of dharma, there is not a single one that does not serve as a skillful means for certain of the disciples of the three vehicles to attain the higher realms and liberation. The only reason teachings of expedient meaning are given is that, due to the different capacities of disciples, it is not possible to teach the definitive meaning to everyone immediately. As *The Sūtra of the Treasury of the Thus-Gone One* makes clear:

> Kāśyapa, it is as follows: Some people may suffer from the unfounded worry that [they have swallowed some] poison. They say, "I drank poison! I drank poison!" and beat their breasts and lament. For their sake, a person who is skilled in medical treatments will act in such a way as

> to remove this unreal poison [by, for example, administering an emetic], thereby overcoming the [person's] belief that stems from suspecting [the ingestion of] poison. As a consequence, they are relieved from their torments. . . . Likewise, Kāśyapa, for naïve beings who are beset by afflictions, I teach the dharma in an untrue manner.[1335]

Nāgārjuna's *Precious Garland* says:

> In terms of true reality as it is,
> Neither identity nor identitylessness obtains.
> Thus, both the views of identity and identitylessness
> Have been dispelled by the Great Sage.
>
> Just as grammarians introduce you [to grammar]
> By reading the fundamentals of the alphabet,
> The Buddha teaches his disciples
> The dharma to the degree they can bear.
>
> To some, he teaches the dharma
> In order to eliminate negative actions,
> And to some, in order that merit is accomplished.
> To some, [he teaches] based on duality,
>
> To some, not based on duality,
> And to some, the profound that is frightening to the anxious,
> Emptiness with a heart of compassion
> That accomplishes enlightenment.
>
> Through seeing this, the learned should let go
> Of anger toward the great vehicle.
> In order to accomplish perfect enlightenment,
> They should have utmost and deepest confidence.[1336]

His *Fundamental Verses* declares:

> They made the designation "identity"
> And also taught "identitylessness,"
> [But] the Buddhas taught as well
> That "there is no such thing as identity or identitylessness."[1337]

Āryadeva's *Four Hundred Verses* states:

> [The Buddha] spoke about "existence, nonexistence,
> [Both] existence and nonexistence, as well as neither of these two."
> But in dependence on the [specific] diseases [to be treated],
> Does not everything become what we call medicine?[1338]

Given this wide perspective, all the teachings of the Buddha can be established as the supreme cause for liberation, since all sūtras of expedient meaning are imbued with the definitive meaning. *The Sūtra That Unravels the Intention* explains this through four examples:

> Blessed One, for example, all medicinal powders and elixirs are supplemented with dried ginger. Likewise, starting with the lack of nature of phenomena, their lack of arising, their lack of ceasing, that they are primordial peace and by nature perfect nirvāṇa, the Blessed One supplements all sūtras of expedient meaning with this definitive meaning.
>
> Blessed One, for example, the background of a painting, be it blue, yellow, red, or white, is uniform throughout the entire picture and also highlights what is painted [on it]. Likewise, this teaching of the definitive meaning by the Blessed One, ranging from the lack of nature of phenomena up through them being by nature perfect nirvāṇa, is uniform in all sūtras of expedient meaning and also highlights these expedient meanings.
>
> Blessed One, for example, when one adds clarified butter to all kinds of dishes, such as cooked grain and cooked meat, they become very pleasing. Likewise, when this teaching of the definitive meaning by the Blessed One, ranging from the lack of nature of phenomena up through them being by nature perfect nirvāṇa, is added to all sūtras of expedient meaning, it is pleasing, indeed supremely pleasing.
>
> Blessed One, for example, space is uniform in everything and does not obstruct any activities. Likewise, this teaching of the definitive meaning by the Blessed One, ranging from the lack of nature of phenomena up through them being by nature perfect nirvāṇa, is uniform in all sūtras of expedient meaning and does not obstruct any activities in the vehicle of hearers, the vehicle of solitary realizers, or the great vehicle.[1339]

*The Sūtra of the King of Meditative Concentration* says:

If one reflects about a single entity,
One will meditate on all of them.
The many dharmas of all the Buddhas,
However many are taught,
Consist in the identitylessness of all phenomena.
If those people who are learned in the meaning
Train in this very point,
The qualities of the Buddhas will not be difficult to find.[1340]

Some people think that expedient meanings are false and deceiving and thus should not be relied upon. Also, some Buddhists say, "We are practitioners of Madhyamaka" or "We just follow the Vajrayāna," and deprecate the rest of the Buddha's teachings. Clearly, all such attitudes are completely mistaken. In general, the Buddha never said anything false or deceiving. Moreover, since all expedient meanings are pervaded by the definitive meaning, they are the methods of becoming introduced to the definitive meaning and realizing it. This is the same as when it is said that seeming reality is the means and ultimate reality is the outcome of this means. Thus, all the turnings of the wheel of dharma serve as means to cut through the entirety of reference points with regard to the way things appear and teach their true way of being. Consequently, Nāgārjuna and others have said that all approaches of the dharma that were taught by the Buddha have the same intention. As his *Commentary on the Mind of Enlightenment* states:

The teachings of the protector of the world
Follow the intentions and capacities of sentient beings.
These [teachings] also differ in many aspects
In terms of the many means in the world.

They may differ in terms of profundity and vastness
Or, in some cases, in both of these characteristics.
Although they are taught differently,
They are not different in terms of emptiness and nonduality.[1341]

Asaṅga declared that those who assert that one group of sūtras is contradicted by another are rejecting the genuine dharma. In his *Sublime Continuum*, Maitreya warns against bringing disorder to the sūtras as they were presented by the Buddha himself:

> There is no one in this world more learned than the Victor.
> Unlike anybody else, through his omniscience, he knows [everything] without exception as well as true reality just as it is.
> Hence, one should not cause disorder in the sūtra collection as presented by the Seer himself.
> Since this destroys the approach of the Sage, it causes harm to the genuine dharma too.[1342]

Jamgön Kongtrul Lodrö Taye's commentary *The Unassailable Lion's Roar* explains that one should not cause disorder in the sūtra collection as it is presented by the Victor himself as the expedient and definitive meaning by self-fabricated statements such as referring to the expedient meaning as the definitive meaning and the definitive meaning as the expedient, thus explaining it incorrectly. Since this destroys the Buddha's own approach of the dharma, it brings harm to the genuine dharma too, constituting the serious flaw of rejecting the dharma.[1343]

The Seventh Karmapa Chötra Gyamtso says:

> [All] the teachings of the Victor without exception were spoken by him as nothing but the definitive meaning. Under the influence of the disciples' various ways of understanding [these teachings], they were understood as the expedient meaning and such. Therefore, the presentation of expedient and definitive [meaning] is [only made] in dependence on the disciples. However, from the perspective of the dharma itself, all of it is nothing but the definitive meaning.[1344]

In his *History of the Dharma,* Pawo Rinpoche states:

> [The Eighth Karmapa always] taught according to the propensities of the disciples and not by just clinging to a single [meaning]. For it is possible that what is just an expedient meaning for some disciples may be the definitive meaning for some others and that what is taught as the expedient meaning in some contexts may be the definitive meaning in other contexts. On the one hand, all dharma [teachings] can be said to be solely of expedient meaning, since they express the inexpressible. On the other hand, since the words of the Buddha are never deceiving and [always] represent the definitive meaning with regard to those disciples [whom they personally address], all of them can [equally] be said to be of definitive meaning. Nevertheless, [these two perspectives] are [obviously] not contradictory.[1345]

**The Meaning of the Three Natures**

What then is the meaning of the imaginary nature, the other-dependent nature, and the perfect nature that are taught in so many sūtras? The Eighth Karmapa presents the Centrist view on this as follows: For example, in dependence on a coiled rope, a snake is only an imputation, because what is imagined as a snake does not exist in this coiled rope. With regard to an actual snake, this notion of a snake is perfectly established, because—conventionally and in terms of dependent origination—a snake is established as a snake, and the conventional term that is used for it is imagined accordingly. Likewise, a real nature of things is imagined in dependence on the unreal bearers of this nature that are conditioned, dependently originating, and other-dependent, while it actually does not exist in them.[1346] If it indeed existed, any ultimate real nature could not be something fabricated and imputed but would have to exist as some unfabricated and inherent nature. However, fabricated, conditioned phenomena cannot have an unfabricated, unconditioned nature of their own. This is just the same as when worldly beings who do not question things say that the nature of gold exists in something that has the unfabricated nature of gold, such as a refined piece of gold. They would not claim that a piece of brass fabricated to resemble gold actually has the nature of gold. Centrists say that this notion of a real nature just demonstrates valid cognition as acknowledged by others, since *The Fundamental Verses* states:

> Natures are unfabricated
> And not dependent on anything else.[1347]

In brief, whatever has a real and intrinsic nature cannot possibly be produced by something else, and what is produced by causes and conditions cannot really exist. Therefore, the other-dependent nature does not exist as a real thing, since it is produced in the manner of dependent origination, just like a reflection in a mirror. Still, some Proponents of Cognizance imagine that both the perfect nature, or emptiness, and the other-dependent nature, which is the nature of cognition, exist in the other-dependent nature itself. However, these two do not exist as the nature of the other-dependent nature in the way that these people imagine it, since such real existence is impossible. This means that, when analyzed, unfabricated emptiness (the perfect nature) is not established. Nevertheless, without analysis, this nature is established as the sphere of the Buddha's wisdom that sees the ultimate that is neither conditioned by other-dependent origination nor imagined by conceptions. A really established nature of cognition in the sense of a really existent other-dependent nature is extensively refuted in Centrist texts, since it cannot be established on any level, neither with analysis nor without analysis.

In this sense, one's mind not moving away from true reality is expressed as

"Buddhahood." If the other-dependent nature were real, one should be able to observe certain characteristics or reference points in the sense of a real entity that is the other-dependent nature. However, true reality whose sole nature is the emptiness of all phenomena from form up through omniscience is precisely revealed through not observing any characteristics or reference points whatsoever. As usual, the Eighth Karmapa does not tire of emphasizing that, from the Centrist perspective, all presentations such as "realizing true reality" are merely given in accordance with the common consensus of others without analysis. It is only in such a didactic context that this is said to be the nature of phenomena, which means lacking any nature in the sense of a real entity. Thus, in produced phenomena, such as the other-dependent nature, a real nature is not observable. This is why the wisdom of Buddhas does not see phenomena as being or having any nature at all, which is the way that true reality is realized.

The Karmapa says that this presentation is justified on the worldly level without analysis, since it does not contradict common worldly consensus. On the other hand, the presentation of the three natures and a real nature of things by the Proponents of Cognizance is unjustified on both the ultimate level and the conventional level without analysis, because such a really established nature is contradictory even to worldly valid cognition. Centrists, when analyzing, do not express emptiness, or ultimate reality, as an unconditioned nature. If they were to express it in this way, their extensive refutations of the existence of any nature within either of the two realities would be meaningless. Furthermore, how could the very nonexistence of a nature turn into any kind of nature? For Centrists, nothing could be more foolish to proclaim than that. It would be like saying that the nonexistence of the horns of a rabbit is the horns of a rabbit.

Therefore, when the three natures are presented without analysis, seeming dependent origination is the other-dependent nature, because it is common, conventional consensus that it originates in dependence on causes and conditions. As for both material things and cognitions that are assumed to constitute real entities, a true way of being, or a nature, they all represent the imaginary nature, because they are superimposed in such ways onto seeming, dependently originating phenomena. Emptiness—ultimate reality—is the perfect nature. This just follows the common consensus of presentations in mutual dependence: If what is fabricated and conditioned is presented as the seeming, then what is unfabricated and unconditioned has to be presented as the ultimate. This is the explanation of the intention of the sūtras in a way that is merely not contradicting the conformity of the worldly consensus of others.

On the other hand, the Proponents of Cognizance say that mistaken imagination or mere cognizance is the other-dependent nature, that apprehender and apprehended are the imaginary nature, and that the other-dependent nature empty of the imaginary is the perfect nature. However, this is not justified, because it contradicts the assertion of three natures. Even conventionally, through valid cognition, one cannot observe any imaginary or perfect nature that is suitable to appear and is other than the mere illusion of the dependently originating and other-dependent phenomena of the seeming level that are common consensus in the world. Moreover, to present the existence of an unchanging perfect nature in these other-dependent phenomena is nothing but an instance of the imaginary nature. For an unchanging perfect nature is only justified in what is not fabricated by causes and conditions, whereas the assumed existence of such a perfect nature in other-dependent phenomena that are in fact fabricated by causes and conditions is just something imaginary.

Then what meaning is intended by the statement in the sūtras that the imaginary nature does not exist, while the other-dependent nature exists? Without analyzing the notions of existence and nonexistence, one can say that the other-dependent nature exists as illusionlike dependent origination, because this is what conventionally exists as mere appearances that satisfy as long as they are left unquestioned. As for the imaginary notions and things that are superimposed by various Buddhist and non-Buddhist philosophical systems and do not accord with normal, common worldly consensus, they do not exist, because they are merely imputed as something real by these systems, yet they are not even conventionally established.

The Proponents of Cognizance also say, "The other-dependent nature is substantially established and the imaginary nature exists conventionally, although it does not exist ultimately." This is not justified either. A substantially established other-dependent nature is refuted in many Centrist texts, for example, in *The Entrance into Centrism.*[1348] Moreover, the apprehender and the apprehended that are asserted as the imaginary nature do not exist as something other than the nature of the other-dependent nature, since the other-dependent nature is just what is commonly known as conventionally existent dependent origination that entails fabricated and conditioned functions. But the imaginary idea of the Proponents of Cognizance that the imaginary nature has any sense of an unfabricated nature of certain characteristics of its own is not even conventionally established.

Sūtras such as *The Sūtra That Unravels the Intention* declare that the imaginary nature is the lack of a nature in terms of characteristics, the other-dependent nature is the lack of a nature in terms of arising, and the perfect nature is the ultimate lack of a nature.[1349] According to the Karmapa, Centrists say that the meaning of this specific statement is very much justified in the sense in which the proponents of the three natures themselves express it. For, just like the horns of a rabbit, the imaginary nature is not even conventionally established through valid cognition. Just like an illusion, the other-dependent nature lacks any arising through its own makeup but depends on specific causes and conditions. As for the perfect nature, since it even conventionally constitutes the nature that is emptiness, it is the lack of nature per se. Since this lack of nature is in fact undeceiving, it is also established as the ultimate.[1350] In this vein, Jayānanda's *Commentary on the Entrance into Centrism* says:

> "[Thus,] the intention of the sūtras is to be explained [by an understanding of the presentation of the three natures: the imaginary, the other-dependent, and the perfect nature]."[1351] [This means that] the expedient and the definitive meanings of the sūtras are to be explained as follows: The sūtras taught in dependence on the meaning of the imaginary and the other-dependent [nature] are of expedient meaning, and those taught in dependence on the meaning of the perfect [nature] are of definitive meaning.[1352]

Again, all of this is presented merely on the level of seeming reality without analysis. When analyzed, the ultimate is devoid of being either deceiving or undeceiving, so there is plenty of room to speculate as to how it could ever be ultimately established as undeceiving. Moreover, according to the Proponents of Cognizance, it could not even be the case that the other-dependent nature is the lack of a nature in terms of arising, because they claim arising on the ultimate level.

Karmapa Mikyö Dorje says that, in the context of compassionately and skillfully taking care of individual disciples, even the Buddha taught some expedient meanings as if they were true reality. Since Centrists just follow this approach, by having another basis of intention in mind and for the sake of certain purposes, in many of their texts, they also talk about such topics as knowable objects in terms of the five bases, the three natures, and the eight consciousnesses. For example, in his *Commentary on the Mind of Enlightenment*, Nāgārjuna talks about the ground consciousness and latent tendencies:

> Likewise, the ground consciousness
> Is not real but appears as if it were real.
> When it moves to and fro,
> It retains the [three] existences.[1353]
>
> The seeming originates from karma and afflictions.
> Karma originates from the mind.
> The mind accrues through latent tendencies.
> If one is free from latent tendencies, one is happy.[1354]

He further says that there are no outer objects and that it is mind that appears as such objects:

Thus, in no way whatsoever is there an outer referent
In the form of a [real] entity.
This consciousness that appears in particular ways
Appears as the aspect of form.[1355]

He speaks favorably of working with the notion of "mere mind" as a step in the process of realizing emptiness:

The teachings on the aggregates, constituents, and so on
Are for the purpose of stopping the clinging to a self.
By settling in mere mind,
The greatly blessed ones let go of these too.[1356]

In his *Praise to the Inconceivable*, he quotes the Buddha as saying that all phenomena are "mere conception":[1357]

Therefore, you have shown that all phenomena
Are "mere conception."
You proclaimed that this conception
By which emptiness is conceived does not exist.[1358]

He does not even avoid referring to the three natures. For example, the same text explicitly equates dependent origination and the other-dependent nature:

The seeming is origination from causes and conditions
And the other-dependent.
This has been proclaimed as the other-dependent,
But the ultimate is unfabricated.[1359]

His *Praise to the Vajra of Mind* identifies mind as the basis of both cyclic existence and nirvāṇa:

To obtain mind is enlightenment.
The mind is the five [kinds of] beings.
The characteristics of both pleasure and suffering
Do not exist in the slightest apart from the mind.[1360]

In brief, what Centrists refute is any notion of real or absolute existence or an intrinsic nature that is attributed to any phenomenon, whether it is material form, ordinary consciousness, omniscient wisdom, Buddhahood, the Dharma Body, or Buddha nature. Centrists make no difference in this respect between refuting the positions of Buddhists and non-Buddhists. They do not even hesitate to apply such a critique to anything that is—correctly or incorrectly—understood as "Centrism." Thus, if the teachings on the three natures are explained so as to even slightly suggest real existence, be it on the seeming or the ultimate level, be it by the Proponents of Cognizance, so-called Mere Mentalists, or Shentong-Mādhyamikas, Centrists will speak up against this. However, when the presentation of the three natures is understood as the Karmapa explained it above, it is not something that has to be discarded by Centrists but comes down to the same essential point of ultimate nonreferentiality that is explained in the Centrist teachings.

**Are There Three Vehicles or Only One?**

Centrists say that, ultimately, there is only a single vehicle, which is the vehicle of becoming a perfect Buddha. This is the definitive meaning. All teachings that there are three distinct vehicles—those of the hearers, the solitary realizers, and the great vehicle of bodhisattvas—are of expedient meaning.[1361] A sūtra says:

> Kāśyapa, when all phenomena are realized to be equality, this is nirvāṇa. It is a single one and not two or three.

Nāgārjuna's *Praise to the Incomparable* states:

> Since the expanse of dharmas is without distinctions,
> There are no distinctions of the vehicles of the Lord.
> That you spoke of three vehicles
> Was in terms of introducing sentient beings [to the teachings].[1362]

Candrakīrti's *Entrance into Centrism* agrees:

> Here, other than knowing true reality, there is no endeavor that eliminates all stains.
> The true reality of phenomena does not depend on any distinctions in terms of manifestation.
> Also this insight that is the subject of true reality is not disparate.
> Hence, you taught that the dissimilar vehicles for beings are not distinct.[1363]

Thus, the object to be realized—true reality—is without distinctions. So if the path that is to serve as the means to realize true reality does not realize this fact, it is ineffective in eliminating all stains. When true reality is realized, there is no distinction in this realization either. Hence, ultimately, there is only a single Buddhist path and its fruition, although there is no doubt about the temporary existence of three vehicles for different disciples.

All who assert that a single vehicle is the definitive meaning agree that, eventually, hearers and solitary realizers become enlightened in the great vehicle. As mentioned earlier, some assert that hearers and solitary realizers realize only personal identitylessness, not phenomenal identitylessness. Thus, they assert that, temporarily, there definitely are three vehicles. Nevertheless, in order to attain Buddhahood, everybody must eventually enter the path of the great vehicle. Others assert that hearers and solitary realizers realize phenomenal identitylessness too. They say that since there are no distinctions in the wisdom that realizes true reality, this true reality must also be the object of the wisdom of hearers and solitary realizers. In other words, the very process of eliminating all stains through such wisdom constitutes just a single vehicle, which is the vehicle of becoming a Buddha. When this single process is expressed as three vehicles, this is a statement of expedient meaning. Other than realizing true reality in an unmistaken way, there is no remedy for relinquishing afflictive and cognitive obscurations. Therefore, it is said here that, in general, hearers and solitary realizers also realize true reality, both personal and phenomenal identitylessness. However, due to various capacities and means, there are surely differences as to how swiftly different beings proceed on the path.

Some people might wonder, "Does this not contradict the explanation that the paths of hearers and solitary realizers even represent obstacles for attaining enlightenment?" Persons of lesser capacity are not able to attain enlightenment without having gone through the paths of the lower vehicles as preliminaries. Nevertheless, via these paths of hearers and solitary realizers, they eventually attain unsurpassable Buddhahood. It is due to their lesser capacities and the incompleteness of particular skillful means that they first have to enter the paths of the lower vehicles. In general, since it is possible to eliminate all stains through becoming increasingly familiar with ultimate true reality, these lower vehicles also are parts of the single vehicle of becoming a Buddha. However, as for persons of the sharpest faculties who naturally aspire to what is profound and vast, if they were to go through the paths of the lower vehicles first, it would take them an unnecessarily long time to attain complete Buddhahood. Thus, it is only for such persons of the sharpest faculties and in this sense that the paths of the lower vehicles are explained as obstacles for attaining enlightenment.

The classic example of how the lower vehicles are to be understood from the Buddha's point of view is described by Candrakīrti:

> Due to the existence of the impurities that produce flaws in beings,
> The world cannot [directly] approach the Buddha's profound sphere.

O Blissfully Gone One, since you possess supreme knowledge,
compassion, and the means,
And since you promised, "I shall liberate sentient beings,"

Therefore, just as a skillful [captain] creates a delightful city
That allays the fatigue of his crew en route to an island of jewels,
So you joined the minds of the disciples to this vehicle, the way of
[achieving] peace,
And separately taught those who have [thus] purified their minds with
regard to voidness.[1364]

From the point of view of the single path to perfect Buddhahood, the vehicles of hearers and solitary realizers are for those who cannot make the whole journey in one stretch so that they may temporarily rest in these vehicles' result of a peaceful nirvāṇa for oneself. At a certain point, however, they are awakened from this blissful state by the Buddhas with a multitude of light rays and called upon to continue their journey to Buddhahood. Hence, Centrists say that the arhats of hearers and solitary realizers do not possess the final nirvāṇa that fully qualifies as such. For, according to those Centrists who assert that arhats realize phenomenal identitylessness, these arhats still have not relinquished the cognitive obscurations. According to those who assert that these arhats do not realize phenomenal identitylessness, they have implicitly realized natural enlightenment or nirvāṇa, but this realization is limited, since they have not fully perfected their familiarization with natural nirvāṇa. Thus, they have not yet relinquished the entirety of the two obscurations together with their latent tendencies. It is from the point of view of both of these assertions that *The Sūtra Requested by Crown Jewel* states:

> Without familiarization with the emptiness endowed with the supreme of all aspects, such qualities as omniscience will not be accomplished. If these are not accomplished, there is no nirvāṇa that fully qualifies as such.

*The Sūtra of the Lion's Roar of Queen Śrīmālā* says that arhats have not relinquished all obscurations because they still have latent tendencies of basic unawareness. *The Sūtra of the White Lotus of Genuine Dharma*, *The Sūtra of the Arrival in Laṅka*, and the *Prajñāpāramitā sūtras* all declare that hearers and solitary realizers conventionally take rebirth again and do not possess the final nirvāṇa. *The Sublime Continuum* says:

> Therefore, without the attainment of Buddhahood,
> Nirvāṇa is not attained,
> Just as one is not able to watch the sun
> Separated from its light and rays.[1365]

In summary, the vehicles of hearers and solitary realizers are valid, though limited, steps along the broad highway of the one vehicle that leads to Buddhahood.

# 6

## *An Outline of Some Major Differences between Mikyö Dorje's and Tsongkhapa's Interpretations of Centrism*

WHY DID GREAT INDIAN and especially Tibetan masters have so many intense disputes on a number of controversial topics? There are a number of possible reasons: worldly motives of a sociopolitical nature, such as competition among scholars, monasteries, and entire schools for reputation, sponsors, and large entourages; struggles for political power; or the wish to provide a distinct group identity for one's own school or subschool. However, we should not lose sight of the internal spiritual reasons for these controversies, such as aiming at establishing the proper view that does not allow for ethical misconduct, or—as Cabezón puts it—what "in our postmodern age, is becoming increasingly difficult for us to recognize: the search for what is true"[1366] and what that means for our lives.

In the light of a genuine "search for truth," the controversies between great masters may be seen as always entailing certain intentions and purposes to further spiritual progress. Thus, when great masters like Tsongkhapa and the Eighth Karmapa debated, they did so based on great compassion in order to assist others in their own quest for liberation. It needs to be emphasized that, in such a context, all arguments in terms of different interpretations or refutations of certain views are in no way meant as fights leaving a winner and a loser. From their own perspective, whatever great masters may say and however it may sound to others, they conduct their expositions and debates with an attitude of mutual appreciation[1367] and concern for the benefit of others. Düdjom Rinpoche's *Nyingma School of Tibetan Buddhism* lists many famous masters in both India and Tibet (including Tsongkhapa and Mikyö Dorje) who came to be criticized by other people and concludes:

> If all the doctrines refuted by learned and accomplished Tibetans were false, no authentic doctrine would be found. . . .
>
> For all these arguments there was certainly a basic intention and special need; . . . If the doctrines, which were well expounded by such

> great persons as these, who were praised in the indestructible prophecies of the Buddha himself . . . , and which explicitly abide in what is meaningful, are impure, it would seem that most Tibetans ought to be excommunicated from the teaching of the Conqueror![1368]

All great masters have their own good reasons to express inexpressible true reality in various ways for the sake of various people in different situations. From the perspective of other people following their controversies, the fact that such masters bring up difficult or controversial issues on various levels of the Buddhist teachings provides helpful opportunities for others to think these issues over and, by comparing various takes on them, analyze them on their own, thus eventually reaching their own decisions.

In the end, we cannot but rely on our own intelligence and wisdom to figure things out; just blindly following one of the many views presented by different masters and schools will not help. Once Khenpo Tsultrim Gyamtso Rinpoche was debating with some advanced Kagyü students from the Tibetan Institute for Higher Learning in Sarnath, India. They kept asking very eagerly what the "official" Kagyü position on various issues is. Rinpoche replied every time that it is of no importance what the commonly acknowledged stance in a certain camp is; we have to investigate and find out for ourselves what we personally think is correct. If we look at the controversies between great masters or schools in this way, they can be helpful as models to gauge and refine our personal insights. They may be compared to lights that signal to the left and right of a dangerous passage in the ocean to make us aware of rocks, shallow places, and so on.The task to steer the ship, however, lies with ourselves. The following considerations are thus not to be seen as personal attacks but as means to sharpen our own wisdom.

In the presentation of Tibetan Buddhism in the West so far, there is an abundance of extensive volumes on the Centrist system of Tsongkhapa and his followers, so there is no need to go into the details of their positions here. In this chapter, I will not compare each point in Tsongkhapa's system with what the Eighth Karmapa said on them, nor will I attempt anything like an all-inclusive refutation of Tsongkhapa. Instead I will briefly address some of the most crucial issues raised in the Karmapa's remarks on Tsongkhapa's system.

When looking at Tsongkhapa's innovative interpretation of Centrism, it seems that he had two main issues in mind. First, he often expressed his concerns about widespread ethical misbehavior in Tibet due to all kinds of wrong views concerning the Buddhist teachings, especially on the status of seeming reality. Second, for him, the entire teaching of the Buddha must be presented as a completely coherent system in which everything makes sense from beginning to end and in which the lower views are incorporated in the higher ones. In particular, in terms of Centrism, these issues are reflected in Tsongkhapa's opposition to what he saw as a nihilistic reading of Consequentialism, to what he deemed the legacy of the stereotyped Hvashang view in some Tibetan interpretations of Centrism, and to the Shentong view. At the same time, he made a great effort to validate seeming reality, in particular the law of karmic cause and effect.[1369] However, Tsongkhapa was definitely not alone in his concern about the serious lack of proper ethics due to wrong views at that time, this issue being addressed by others too, among them the Eighth Karmapa[1370] and Pawo Rinpoche.[1371]

In contrast to Tsongkhapa, for the Karmapa the foremost issue in Centrism is not one of ultimate versus conventional but of ultimate versus pedagogic. He focuses on the soteriological efficacy of the Centrist view rather than its philosophical coherence on the level of seeming reality. Thus, his refutations of certain interpretations by other Tibetan masters are not primarily a matter of streamlining his own position or exposing others' philosophical and technical inconsistencies (though he does not hesitate to do the latter when he sees fit). Rather, his essential criterion for the correct Centrist view is whether such a view is appropriate to serve as the basis for the spiritual path to attain liberation from cyclic existence and Buddhahood. Needless to mention, in a view and a path that indeed are the means to achieve such results, proper ethical conduct is indispensable.

All critics of Tsongkhapa, including the Eighth Karmapa, agree that many features of his version of Centrism are novelties that are not found in any Indian sources and see this as a major flaw. However, the main problem is not that Tsongkhapa said something new that was not said before in a tradition that is cast in stone and not to be touched. In Buddhism, there always were—and still are—people who said something that was not said in this way before, one of the best examples being Nāgārjuna himself. To a certain extent, over the centuries, some things must be rephrased in order to adapt them to different times and circumstances, be it in order to introduce the Buddha's teaching in a different sociocultural context or to break up various structures of dogmatic traditionalism. Düdjom Rinpoche says:

> [W]hen the greater vehicle was expounded by master Nāgārjuna, the pious attendants invented negative prophecies about lord Nāgārjuna and, having inserted them in the scriptures, proclaimed that [the sūtras of] the greater vehicle were not the transmitted precepts [of the Buddha]. When the sublime Asaṅga commented upon the final transmitted precepts in accord with the intention of the great regent [Maitreya], he and his followers were expelled from the greater vehicle. . . .
>
> In Tibet as well, when the venerable Daö Zhönu [Gampopa] taught that the abiding nature of reality, as it is explained in the sūtras, is the Great Seal, [his critics] maintained that this was not at all the teaching of the Buddha, saying it was "Takpo's fanciful doctrine." The all-

> knowing Rangjung Dorje [Karmapa III] and Chödrak Gyamtso [Karmapa VII] expounded [the teaching] in accord with the intention of the final transmitted precepts, but later Mikyö Dorje [Karmapa VIII] and others did not adhere to their view. When master Tölpopa declared that the ultimate truth was permanent and stable, the Tibetans considered him to be merely a Sāṃkhya extremist. After the venerable Tsongkhapa had explained relative appearance to be logically verifiable later scholars assaulted him with HŪṂ! and PHAṬ! [i.e. showered him with derision]. The great paṇḍita Zilungpa [Śākya Chokden] had to be ejected from the Sakyapa ranks for explaining that the *Analysis of the Three Vows*[1372] was of provisional meaning. Moreover, the all-knowing Great Fifth, having studied and meditated upon the authentic teachings impartially, was very nearly excluded from the Gedenpa [i.e. Gelukpa] order. . . .
>
> As long as we have not acquired the pure eye of the doctrine, whereby the truth about doctrines and individuals is seen, it is an unbearably terrible deed to analyse things through exaggeration and depreciation, saying this is perverse, this is impure, and that artificial.[1373]

As the examples of these accomplished masters show, the mere fact of something being a novelty or being opposed by an existent tradition is not the problem per se.[1374] Rather, the point here is whether what is said accords with and serves to accomplish the Buddha's fundamental concern of liberation from cyclic existence and attaining Buddhood. It should be kept in mind that, for Karmapa Mikyö Dorje, this is what lies at the heart of each specific critique he may advance against others. On this basis, his objections in *The Chariot of the Tagbo Siddhas* are not at all limited to Tsongkhapa and his followers. Rather, he addresses the whole range of Tibetan views on Centrism in his time, including Dölpopa, Śākya Chogden, Bodong Paṇchen, and others. In his text, the Karmapa identifies two main types of misunderstanding emptiness:[1375]

1) misconceiving emptiness as utter nonexistence
2) misconceiving emptiness as a real entity

The first is again twofold. There are those groups in Buddhism who deny the scriptures of the great vehicle by saying that the Buddha's teaching cannot be on emptiness, since this means a view of extinction and total nonexistence. The second group is identified as certain adherents of the Dzogchen teachings who take emptiness to mean nonexistence and thus overly deprecate all phenomena. None of these two will attain liberation.

To misconstrue emptiness as some real entity can also happen in two ways.

Tsongkhapa and his followers claim that emptiness is an existent and thus the actual nature of entities, which are its supports. Most other Tibetans in this category, such as Dölpopa and Śākya Chogden, say that only emptiness (which is really established) exists, whereas, ultimately, all other phenomena of the seeming level do not exist. Both of these views are mistaken with regard to the path to liberation. In *The Sūtra Requested by Kāśyapa*, the Buddha himself warned against any views about emptiness:

> Kāśyapa, those who conceptualize emptiness by focusing on it as emptiness I explain as those who fall away from this teaching. Kāśyapa, those who have views about the person that are as big as Mount Meru are better off than those who proudly entertain views about emptiness. Why is this? Kāśyapa, as emptiness means to emerge from all views, I declare that those who have views about this very emptiness are incurable.

*The Sūtra of the Arrival in Laṅka* agrees:

> Mahāmati, having this in mind, I explained that "even the views about a self that are as big as Mount Meru are better than any views about emptiness entertained by those who pride themselves on it being existence or nonexistence." Mahāmati, those who pride themselves on it being nonexistence are ruined, and those whose thinking falls into specific and general characteristics . . . are ruined too.[1376]

**Tsongkhapa's Unique Features of Consequentialism**

To compare Tsongkhapa's and the Karmapa's views on Centrism, we may start with three lists by Tsongkhapa that sum up the unique features of Consequentialism. The first are "the eight unique features of Consequentialism" (A) in his *Elucidation of the Intention*:

> This unique [Consequentialist] system has many [features of a] pure philosophical system not shared by other commentators. To state the main ones:
> 1–2) a unique way of refuting [even conventionally] a ground consciousness and self-awareness that are different in nature from the six collections of consciousness
> 3) not accepting that the view of true reality is generated in the continuum of an opponent through autonomous probative arguments
> 4) the necessity to accept outer objects just like accepting consciousness
> 5) that hearers and solitary realizers possess the realization that entities lack a nature
> 6) presenting the clinging to phenomenal identity as an affliction

7) disintegratedness being a functional entity[1377]
8) a unique way of presenting the three times because of (7)[1378]

This list differs somewhat from "the eight difficult points of *The Fundamental Verses*" (B) that are found at the very beginning of Gyaltsab Je's *Notes on the Eight Great Difficult Points,*[1379] a record of oral teachings given by Tsongkhapa. Here, A7 and A8 are replaced by two other points:

B7) not even conventionally accepting specifically characterized phenomena (Tib. rang mtshan)
B8) the mode of a Buddha knowing the extent of the phenomenal world (Tib. ji snyed mkhyen pa).[1380]

In *The Essence of Good Explanations*, there is a further list of seven "unique features of Consequentialism" (C).[1381] The last four points of this list, in due order, correspond to points A1, A2, A4, and A3, while its first three points differ:

C1) the unique way of Consequentialists identifying and negating the specific object of negation (Tib. dgag bya), that is, a nature established by its own specific characteristics (Tib. rang gi mtshan nyid kyis grub pa'i rang bzhin)
C2) both personal and phenomenal identitylessness are taught in the sūtras of hearers
C3) the unique way of Consequentialists realizing identitylessness and distinguishing between coarse and subtle forms of clinging to identity

When all the distinct points from lists A, B, and C are added up, the total is thirteen. What is generally denied by Tsongkhapa's critics is his claim that Consequentialists have a unique philosophical system of their own. In particular, from the three lists, points A7, A8, B8, C1, and C3 are rejected by everybody outside the Gelugpa tradition.

As for list A, Tsongkhapa's first critic, Rongtön Sheja Künrig, mainly rejected the points pertaining to the distinction between Autonomists and Consequentialists and whether Centrists have a thesis. His two students Gorampa and Śākya Chogden, as well as Dagtsang Lotsāwa, went into great detail in their refutations of all the points above. Dagtsang Lotsāwa lists eighteen major internal contradictions in Tsongkhapa's system.[1382] Gorampa categorically rejects all eight points on list A, giving his own sixteen points instead. He denies points A5–A7 in particular, pointing to the fact that A7 corresponds to a notion specific to the non-Buddhist Differentiators, while he affirms that Consequentialists conventionally accept a ground consciousness and self-awareness. He also says that the difference between Autonomists and Consequentialists lies mainly in their ways of formulating reasonings for proving the ultimate.[1383] *The Treasury of Knowledge* quotes Śākya Chogden as declaring that, except for the purely nominal statement that the noble ones of hearers and solitary realizers realize phenomenal identitylessness, the other seven points represent a philosophical system that Consequentialists would not even dream of. He adds that, in particular, the refutation of a ground consciousness and self-awareness even on the conventional level has no value for understanding ultimate reality, or emptiness. So to present such refutations as unique features of Consequentialists is quite an overstatement[1384] (I think the same can be said for points A7 and A8 as well). Mipham Rinpoche definitely disagrees with points A1–A2 and A5–A8. He seems to agree with A3 but is not really outspoken on A4 and B7–B8.[1385] Padma Karpo and Pawo Rinpoche largely accord with Karmapa Mikyö Dorje.

As for list C, from among the three points that are different from the other two lists, C1 and C3 are equivocally denied by all of Tsongkhapa's critics, while C2 is included in their respective treatments of A5.

As was made clear so often, there is no question that Karmapa Mikyö Dorje denies that Consequentialists have any philosophical system of their own, let alone unique distinctive features of such a system. However, his explanations so far also clearly show that, when the points in Tsongkhapa's above lists are understood as mere pedagogic and expedient conventionalities to counteract wrong views from the perspective of others, contrary to what one might expect, the Karmapa in fact agrees with more of these points (seven) than he denies (six).

In detail, the Karmapa agrees that Consequentialists refute a ground consciousness (A1), self-awareness (A2), and specifically characterized phenomena even conventionally (B7), since these notions are not common worldly consensus but imputations by certain philosophical systems.

As for the existence of external objects (A4), the Karmapa does not accept this as an assertion within a Consequentialist system of its own. However, as explained above, he follows verse VI.92 of *The Entrance into Centrism*:

> If form does not exist, do not cling to the existence of mind;
> And if mind exists, do not cling to the nonexistence of form.
> The Buddha, in the sūtras of supreme knowledge,
> Has equally rejected both, while teaching them in the Abhidharma.

Thus, whether on the level of no analysis or with analysis, it is not appropriate that mind exists while form does not. Under analysis, when outer objects such as form have been found not to exist, mind cannot exist either, because the two are mutually dependent. Without analysis, by just following common worldly consensus, both are equally said to exist.

Mikyö Dorje's explanations on phenomenal identitylessness being taught in the sūtras of the hearers (C2), hearers and solitary realizers realizing phenomenal identitylessness (A5), and the related classification of clinging to real existence or phenomenal identity as an afflictive obscuration (A6) are to be found in detail earlier.[1386]

The Karmapa rejects points A3, A7, A8, B8, C1, and C3. From among these, the refutations of A3 and B8 have been explained in detail above. Point A8 is obviously considered a secondary issue and only addressed in passing when negating A7. Points A7, C1, and C3 are refuted in great detail throughout the Karmapa's commentary and are briefly addressed in the following.

These latter points are connected with a number of other features in Tsongkhapa's system, such as seeming reality being established through conventional valid cognition; the special identification of the object of negation; differences between Autonomists and Consequentialists as to this object of negation and their realization of emptiness; emptiness being an existent and a nonimplicative negation; ordinary persons being able to realize the ultimate; the Autonomist distinction of the seeming into correct and false being allegedly based on phenomena as being established through their own specific characteristics; the notion of a personal self that is established through valid cognition and serves as the support for the continuity of karmic actions and their results; and the incorporation of the epistemological system of Dignāga and Dharmakīrti into Consequentialism.

Further peculiarities of Tsongkhapa's version of Centrism include his different interpretation of the two realities, the approach to the analytical meditation on emptiness, the redefinition of autonomous reasoning along with its rejection by Consequentialists, and that even Consequentialists have a thesis and a system of their own. These have been dealt with above.

### Establishment through Conventional Valid Cognition

According to Tsongkhapa and subsequent Gelugpa scholars, the task of Consequentialists lies not only in refuting false notions that obscure the nature of ultimate reality but also in validating all phenomena of cyclic existence and nirvāṇa. Otherwise, Consequentialists would fall into the extreme of nihilism. Moreover, without conventionally existing phenomena, their real nature—emptiness—would also not exist. However, since emptiness is firmly asserted as an existent by Tsongkhapa, that which bears the nature of this existent emptiness must also somehow exist. This leads to the assertion that conventional phenomena are "established by conventional valid cognition" that certifies their causal efficiency, especially in terms of karmic actions and their results. Clearly, this approach is based on introducing into Consequentialism the logico-epistemological methods of Dignāga and Dharmakīrti, who establish the ultimate existence of phenomena by using the same criterion.

Generally speaking, if a given philosophical system differentiates the two levels of seeming and ultimate reality, then in whatever way it does so, once it speaks about seeming, relative, or deceiving phenomena, it must also accept this to mean that such phenomena are precisely something that is not established. Otherwise, why differentiate between two such levels of reality in the first place? Tsongkhapa claims the opposite when he says that even Consequentialists accept seeming reality as being established through conventional valid cognition. However, either phenomena are established as something or they are not. If seeming phenomena are analyzed by reasoning that investigates for the ultimate and are seen to be not really or ultimately established, this means that they are not established on either level of reality. If something cannot be found on the level of true insight into the nature of phenomena, how can it be found on the level of delusion? This is expressed in *The Entrance into Centrism*:

> Likewise, although all entities are empty,
> They arise from what is empty.
> Since they lack a nature in both realities,
> They are neither permanent nor extinct.[1387]

So what is gained by putting so much effort into establishing illusory appearances only to find out through analyzing for the ultimate that they are not established anyway? By doing so, one is left with purely nominal entities, like the Hindu notion of an ātman, and just engages in more reifications rather than working on recognizing illusions for what they are.

As shown above, the importance of not analyzing seeming appearances is repeatedly expressed by all kinds of Centrists, particularly Candrakīrti. After all, the whole point of Centrism is to show that illusory seeming appearances lack any kind of ontological status in order to put an end to our clinging to them. The Karmapa says that the floating hairs that appear to people with blurred vision do not even conventionally exist for those with normal vision. However, in order to put an end to the former's clinging to the real existence of floating hairs, the latter may say, "These floating hairs may appear to you, but they are without any nature." In the same way, when the seeming is analyzed, it is seen to be completely free from all discursiveness and reference points. It does not even conventionally appear for the meditative equipoise of noble ones. Still, exclusively from the perspective of others, the noble ones, by not rejecting the mere conventionalities of phenomena from form up through omniscience, expediently refer to the seeming by pointing out its lack of nature. The reason they do so is precisely that this is the means to put an end to all clinging to any kind of real existence that is imputed by both worldly people and philosophers onto these mere appearances as they display from the perspective of mistaken minds. Thus, there is no falling into any of the extremes of existence, nonexistence, extinction, or permanence. From the perspective of others, what appears for ordinary beings as seeming reality is addressed but not reified. However, from their own perspective, what should be established by those who analyze for the actual nature of things or noble ones in meditative equipoise, if they do not find any reference points in the first place?

Moreover, with phenomena being established on the seeming level but not at all ultimately, the two realities are very far apart, in fact contradictory. So how can there ever be the unity of the two realities that is supposed to be the very essence of the Centrist view? Thus, the Eighth Karmapa, Pawo Rinpoche, and Padma Karpo insist that neither of the two realities can be established by itself, not even conventionally, and they emphasize their essential unity.

There is a further inconsistency here. On the one hand, Autonomists are (falsely) accused of asserting that the phenomena of correct seeming reality are established through their own specific characteristics, while Consequentialists are said to vehemently reject this assertion together with the distinction of the correct and false seeming. On the other hand, the very similar notion of seeming reality being established through conventional valid cognition is introduced into Consequentialism (to which it is completely alien). The question is how the phenomena of seeming reality can be validly established as conventionally existent, if they are not so established through some specific characteristics of their own that allow for distinguishing them from other such validly established phenomena.

A further problem lies in the Gelugpa identification of the seeming as being equivalent to the two kinds of obscurations, which in turn are identified as the object of negation of the path. So if the seeming, obscurations, and the object of negation are equivalent, what could possibly be established as valid in obscurations and that which is to be negated as the root of cyclic existence? What sense does it make to validly establish obscurations and what is to be relinquished? If obscurations and the object of negation could be validly established, why and how should they be obscurations and be negated? In fact, if they are validly established, they are something that withstands analysis and thus cannot be negated or relinquished. After all, the nature of obscurations and what is to be relinquished is precisely their lack of being established as anything, and liberation means nothing but realizing this lack. So trying to establish obscurations and what is to be eliminated on the path just means working against this realization.[1388]

**The Object of Negation**

In general, Tsongkhapa makes a distinction between "existence" ( conventional existence) and "real existence" or "being really established" (Tib. bden grub). On this basis, he emphasizes the correct identification of the object of negation in Centrism and further differentiates between "the object of negation of reasoning" and "the object of negation of the path." He says that the object of negation of reasoning in all Centrist texts is an object's "real existence" in the sense of it being established through its own nature, that is, its own way of being, be it a really existent person or a phenomenon. This "real existence" is not a knowable object; it is a nonexistent. However, all knowable objects, which "exist" as being established through conventional valid cognition, are neither the objects of negation through reasoning nor invalidated through the valid cognition of a reasoning consciousness, because otherwise one would fall into a great extreme of extinction. The object of negation of the path is the ignorance that clings to such real existence (in other words, the two obscurations). This ignorance is a knowable object, which is to say, an existent.

In his texts, Tsongkhapa deals mainly with the object of negation of reasoning. He emphasizes that, for example, a book (the basis of negation) is not empty of this book (a nature of its own), but that a book is empty of real existence or of being really established (the object of negation). Thus, the basis of negation and the object to be negated in it are different. This, Tsongkhapa says, is the actual meaning of "phenomena being empty of themselves" that is taught in both sūtras and Centrist texts. In other words, phenomena that are established through conventional valid cognition are not empty of a nature of their own but of something else. This, however, flies in the face of what Candrakīrti (whom Tsongkhapa claims as his chief authority) says in his *Lucid Words*:

> One may wish to not deny all [phenomena]. Then, however, no matter in which way one may have focused on these entities, how should they become emptiness? Hence, to say that "the meaning of emptiness is not the meaning of lacking a nature" is definitely a rejection of emptiness. Having rejected it in this way, due to the [ensuing] karmic [result] of being deprived of the dharma, one will go to the lower realms.[1389]

In search of scriptural authority in Indian Centrist texts for this presentation, Tsongkhapa runs into a further problem, because the topic of identifying an object of negation (let alone differentiating it in terms of reasoning and the path, or Autonomists and Consequentialists) was never even an issue in these texts. Therefore, Tsongkhapa cannot (and does not) quote any texts by Nāgārjuna, Āryadeva, Buddhapālita, or Candrakīrti. What does he do? His *Elucidation of the Intention* offers another one of his highly inventive solutions by quoting Śāntideva:

> As for this determination of phenomena lacking reality, if one does not properly know how the mode of being really established is and what the mode of clinging to reality is, one certainly misses the view

of true reality. As *The Entrance to the Bodhisattva's Way of Life* says:

> Without referring to an imputed entity,
> One cannot apprehend the lack of this entity.[1390]

> Through this, [Śāntideva] says that if the imputed entity, that is, the generality of the object of negation, does not properly appear to the mind, the nonexistence of this object of negation cannot be properly apprehended. Hence, if the aspects of [both] real existence (which is what is nonexistent) and the object of negation of which something is empty do not appear to the mind just as they are, it is impossible to ascertain the nature of the lack of reality and emptiness.[1391]

This is yet another case of Tsongkhapa taking a quotation totally out of context and reinterpreting it in the light of his own agenda, here his own ideas about the object of negation. The lines he quotes from Śāntideva's text have nothing to do with identifying the object of negation as Tsongkhapa understands it and what he claims Śāntideva as intending to say here. Rather, Śāntideva's point in this verse and its context is that the negation of an imputed entity is as unreal as that very entity. The imputation of the nonexistence of an entity must refer to a preceding imputation of that entity itself. Since both of these imputations—an entity and its negation—are thus mutually dependent, the next two lines of this verse say that they are equally delusive, which is illustrated in the following verse by the illusory death of one's child in a dream. This is also what all Indian commentaries explain.[1392]

To address Tsongkhapa's identification of the object of negation, the Karmapa first asks whether, according to Tsongkhapa's system, a vase is empty of its own nature. Tsongkhapa cannot say that it is not empty of its own nature, because he asserts that his way of explaining Centrism is the Centrism that propounds the lack of nature. So, if the vase is empty of its own nature, is its own nature then the entity that has the defining characteristics of having a round belly and a flat bottom and of performing the function of carrying water, or is it its real existence that is established through its own way of being? It is impossible that the vase's own nature is the latter, since (as Tsongkhapa agrees) such does not exist among knowable objects. However, if the vase's own nature is the former, it follows that Tsongkhapa is not at all someone who propounds the Centrism that says that all phenomena lack a nature of real entities for two reasons: As accepted, the vase's own nature is the entity that has the defining characteristics of having a round belly and a flat bottom and of performing the function of carrying water, and (as he claims above) this entity is not empty of the nature of this entity (but of real existence).

Moreover, the Buddha has identified the definitive meaning many times as solely that a vase is empty of a vase, while a vase being empty of something other does not qualify as the vase's emptiness. For example, in the collection of sūtras in *The Jewel Mound*, it is said:

> Form is not empty through the emptiness of form, but this very form is emptiness.

If a vase is not empty of its own nature, it becomes established. If that is accepted, the vase is something found under analysis through reasoning. If that is also accepted, such a vase must be either one of its infinitesimal particles or their collection. As for the latter possibility, if even the followers of lower Buddhist philosophical systems do not accept that the coarse object of a vase can withstand analysis through reasoning, how could any Centrist accept this? It is also not suitable that one of its infinitesimal particles is the vase, because such a particle can never be established as a coarse object.

If a table is different from its real existence, in terms of affecting the clinging to this table, what does it do to the table itself if one negates some hypothetical "real existence" that is different from the table and is even said to be nonexistent? This leaves the table fully intact and in fact makes it an ultimate reality, because it is still found after the reasoned analysis for the ultimate[1393] (that is, the negation of real existence that is to be negated and other than the table). Therefore, to first set up some phantom notion of "real existence" different from the "table that is established through valid cognition" and then to negate this construct does nothing to stop one from taking this very table to be a real table and continuing to reify it as such. To be sure here, it is fine to say that a table is empty of real existence if that is understood as equivalent in meaning to a table being empty of itself. The problem appears only if the table's real existence is taken to be something other than this very table.

This is what Tsongkhapa's critics call a "hornlike object of negation": If you first fix a horn on the head of a rabbit and then remove it again, the rabbit might wonder what you are doing, but your whole maneuver affects neither the rabbit's existence nor your taking the rabbit for a rabbit. This is precisely why it is said that such an approach to the object of negation is not suitable for relinquishing the reifying clinging to persons and phenomena and thus does not lead to liberation from cyclic existence. Through negating the hornlike object of negation called "real existence" with regard to a table, we will neither relinquish the clinging to the reality of this table nor realize its ultimate nature. Even great masters from the Gelugpa tradition, such as Janggya Rölpay Dorje[1394] (1717–1786), Dendar Lharamba[1395] (born 1759), and of course Gendün Chöpel, were not unaware of this problem. As Janggya Rölpay Dorje says in his *Song on the View, Called Recognizing the Mother*:

Nowadays, some of our great luminaries
Cling to terms such as solid, real existence.
Hence, by firmly setting up quivering appearances in their own place,
They are seen to search for something hornlike to be negated.

In the face of the Mother free from obscurations,
There is not a word on these fluctuating, quivering [appearances] being existent.
If they keep explaining lots and lots without hitting negation's essential point,
I am afraid this old mother will run away from them.[1396]

In other words, our clinging to personal and phenomenal identities does not concern some abstract, nonexistent notion of "real existence" but what appears right in front of our eyes, which is what we then reify as tables, books, or persons. "Real existence" never appears for any kind of consciousness, since it is not a knowable object. Also, to identify and negate such an extrinsic, abstract notion as the Centrist object of negation openly contradicts both the sūtras and the Indian Centrist treatises. As *The Prajñāpāramitā Sūtra in Hundred Thousand Lines* says:

> Subhūti asked: "How should bodhisattvas train to understand that all phenomena are empty of their own specific characteristics?"
>
> The Blessed One said: "Form should be seen as empty of form, feeling empty of feeling, and so on."
>
> Subhūti asked: "If everything is empty of itself, how does the bodhisattvas' engagement in the perfection of knowledge take place?"
>
> The Blessed One answered: "Such engagement in the perfection of knowledge is non-engagement."[1397]

Candrakīrti explicitly clarifies in his autocommentary on *The Entrance into Centrism*:

> Here, one speaks about emptiness [as the fact] that the eyes and so on [are empty] of these very eyes and so on. This makes it completely clear that [this is] the emptiness of a nature, whereas it is not an emptiness of one not existing in an other, [such as] "the eye is empty, since

> it lacks an inner agent" or "it is empty of the nature of apprehender and apprehended."[1398]

What is said here is that the eye and such are empty of themselves—that is, they lack a nature in the sense of being empty of a nature of their own—and that this is their nature. That the eye is empty of a nature of its own does not mean that the eye is empty of a nature that is something other than this very eye itself.

To the contrary, Tsongkhapa says above that phenomena, such as a table, are not empty of themselves or their own nature but empty of an other object of negation (real existence) and that this qualifies as phenomena being empty of their own nature. However, from this, it absurdly follows that the emptiness of a table being empty of the horns of a rabbit is the emptiness of this table being empty of its own nature. The reason is as follows: Despite a table not being empty of a table, the emptiness of the table being empty of the object of negation that is real existence is said to be the emptiness of this table being empty of its own nature. At the same time, this object of negation and the horns of a rabbit are equal in not existing among knowable objects. If this is accepted, then precisely because of such acceptance, it follows both that the horns of a rabbit are the nature of the table and that the table's emptiness of the horns of a rabbit is the actual true nature of the table.

The main reason for Tsongkhapa's vehement refusal to say that the eye is empty of itself lies in his unique take on avoiding the two extremes, which is his concern that seeming reality becomes extinct or invalidated if a phenomenon is empty of that very phenomenon. So he claims to avoid the extreme of extinction through the appearance of conventionally valid phenomena and the extreme of permanence through positing these phenomena as being empty of real existence. This is his interpretation of the fundamental Centrist statement that "all phenomena are neither existent nor nonexistent." For Tsongkhapa, this means that phenomena are not nonexistent conventionally and not existent ultimately. However, almost all of his critics take this statement to mean that it is the nature of all phenomena to be primordially and utterly free from any reference points in terms of existence or nonexistence.

On the level of no analysis, the Karmapa says, when Centrists speak with people who do not like to talk in a manner consistent with the principle of dependent origination, for the purpose of removing such people's fear of this principle and on the level of the expedient meaning, Centrists speak about existence and nonexistence. When they speak with people who like to talk in a manner consistent with dependent origination, Centrists speak about the utter freedom from all discursiveness in terms of existence and nonexistence. At the time when Centrists analyze, since nothing is established as anything whatsoever, they do not conceive of or express anything whatsoever. This is comparable to when a mirage appears as water: Concerning this "water" and its emptiness, one cannot provide any factually concordant, conventional expressions of the existence or nonexistence of the water's emptiness in this "water." Therefore, all claims of qualifying form as being established through conventional valid cognition, not being empty of its own nature, and not being the object of negation of reasoning are in contradiction with what the Buddha taught many times. As the *Prajñāpāramitā sūtras* say:

> In the perfection of knowledge, no [notions] such as "form is permanent" or "form is impermanent" are observable. If even a form as such is not observable, how could this be the case for [its] being permanent or impermanent? The same holds for [all phenomena] up through omniscience.

*The Sūtra of the Great Nirvāṇa* states:

> O son of good family, all phenomena are empty of nature. Why? Because all phenomena are not observable as a nature.

*The Sūtra of the Meeting of Father and Son* reads:

> Blessed One, ignorance does not exist through ignorance. Why? Ignorance is free of any nature. Any phenomenon that does not have a nature does not exist as an entity. What does not exist as an entity is not established. What is not established neither arises nor ceases. What neither arises nor ceases cannot be labeled as "something in the past." It is not something in the future, nor can it be called "what occurs in the present." What is unjustified [as existing] in the three times has neither name, nor defining characteristics, nor signs, nor can it be designated. . . . Ignorance is ultimately not observable. A phenomenon that is ultimately not observable cannot be designated. It cannot be designated even conventionally. It cannot be expressed. Blessed One, what is merely nominal is not actual.

The Karmapa clearly says that both the object of negation of reasoning and the object of negation of the path are nothing but the innate clinging to an intrinsic nature or identity of persons and phenomena. This is explained clearly and in detail in *The Entrance into Centrism* and its autocommentary. However, he says, despite this fact, Tsongkhapa and others still search for an object of negation somewhere else. They are like a thief on the run who sees a hiding place in the forest on the mountain on the far side of a valley and still keeps searching for materials to cover himself on the lawn on the hither side. Likewise, who would want to engage in such painful conventional analyses that are fruitless toils and completely unnecessary for those who strive for liberation from cyclic existence?

In other words, Tsongkhapa's identification of the object of negation (real existence) as something other than the basis of negation (a table) is just what Candrakīrti's *Entrance into Centrism* rejects:

> That while seeing a snake that lives in a hole in the wall of your house
> Your concerns [could be] eliminated [by saying], "There is no elephant here,"
> And thus also your fear of the snake be relinquished,
> Oh, my, this is nothing but a laugh for others.[1399]

Of course, neither personal nor phenomenal identity has any possible existence as an actual object that is to be negated. However—and this cannot be said too often—the actual target in the context of negating the two identities is the clinging to these identities on the subject side. In other words, the object of negation in the sense of what has to be stopped is a mistaken cognition, a wrong conception that apprehends something nonexistent as existent. Since there is no actual object of negation on the objective side, there is nothing to be relinquished there. So "negating an identity" is just another expression for the process of letting go of our subjective clinging to what appears to us as being existent in and as itself. With the realization that an object has no nature of its own, the subject that holds on to this object dissolves naturally.

**Tsongkhapa as Shentongpa and Realist**

Maybe the worst critique of Tsongkhapa's view on the relation between the basis of negation and the object of negation is that the Karmapa identifies it as being nothing but a type of "other-emptiness" (*shentong*), the view that the Gelugpas themselves so vehemently reject. Clearly, in their view, a book (the basis of negation) is not empty of itself but of something other, that is, real existence (the object of negation), while this book itself is left untouched as a remainder after the analysis. This means moreover that the book itself as the basis of being empty of something other is not empty. For if a phenomenon is empty of something other than itself, how should that phenomenon itself become emptiness through that? If such were the case, then, based on the twenty emptinesses, the Buddha would only have to explain the notion of other-emptiness and not explain self-emptiness, because this very other-emptiness has the meaning of self-emptiness.

In the same vein, the Karmapa identifies this as the limited "emptiness of one not existing in an other," which is regarded by all Tibetan schools as one of the grossest misconceptions of emptiness that is to be rejected. As *The Sūtra of the Arrival in Laṅka* says:

> This emptiness of one [not existing in] an other, Mahāmati, is very inferior, and you should abandon it.[1400]

Consequently, for the Karmapa, Tsongkhapa's understanding of emptiness based on his object of negation even puts him into the camp of realists. He shows how, in the other Buddhist philosophical systems below Centrism (according to Tibetan doxography), specific objects of negation are progressively negated, while a certain unnegated remainder is left in all of them.

For those Buddhists who assert that there is a real person, the bases of emptiness are all phenomena, that is, the five aggregates and this person. These are then said to be empty of the extremes of permanence (such as a permanent, single, and independent self as imputed by non-Buddhists) and extinction (the nonexistence of karma, causes and results, or former and later lifetimes).

For those Followers of the Great Exposition who do not accept a real person, the bases of emptiness are all conditioned and unconditioned phenomena in the three times (the five aggregates, eighteen constituents, and twelve sources). These are empty of the extremes of permanence and extinction, such as a person that is imputed by those who assert a real person. However, all knowable objects that are empty of these extremes exist by their nature.

For the Sūtra Followers, the present aggregates, constituents, and sources as the bases of emptiness are empty of the extremes of permanence and extinction, the self as imputed by non-Buddhists and those Buddhists who assert a real person, and also of the imputations of the Followers of the Great Exposition (such as substantially established past and future phenomena). However, the partless, infinitesimal particles of matter and the partless, infinitesimal moments of consciousness are said to be real.

For "the Real Aspectarian Mere Mentalists," the basis of emptiness is the present moment of awareness including the aspect of its object. This is empty of all kinds of personal and phenomenal identities that are imputed by non-Buddhists and hearers. However, the other-dependent nature and the nondual, self-luminous self-awareness that are empty of all the above are asserted to be not empty of the perfect nature.

For "the False Aspectarian Mere Mentalists," the basis of emptiness is the other-dependent mere experience of luminosity and awareness. This is empty of all kinds of identities as imputed by non-Buddhists and hearers and also of all stains of the aspects imputed by the Real Aspectarians. However, both the substantially established, other-dependent mere cognizance that is empty of all the above and the perfect nature (the true reality of nonduality) are asserted to be ultimately existent as mere cognizance and as being neither the same nor different from each other.

Tsongkhapa holds that entities established through conventional valid cognition (the bases of negation) are empty of the entity that is the object of negation of reasoning. However, he asserts that emptiness itself exists as being established in these bases of negation.

Thus, the Karmapa says, with regard to all of the above kinds of emptiness as understood by these realists, the respective imputed phenomena about which they speak are empty of a nature of their own, but the respective bases of emptiness are all asserted to be real. Also, the emptiness of these bearers of emptiness is said to exist in a way of neither being one in entity with its bearers nor being expressible as exactly the same as them or something other. Hence, both the nature of phenomena and the bearers of this nature are not empty of a nature of their own, while they are empty of an object of negation that is something other. Hence, just like the kinds of emptiness of non-Buddhists, the above types of emptiness represent only limited and nominal types of emptiness. They are not the actual emptiness that is suitable as the foundation for the path to liberation. For, if both the nature of phenomena and its bearers really exist, it is not appropriate to eradicate the mental states that apprehend them as real. And if these reifications are not eradicated, the seeds of afflictive and cognitive obscurations cannot be eliminated.

By placing Tsongkhapa in the category of realists with a soteriologically insufficient understanding of emptiness, the Karmapa implies that Tsongkhapa's system does not qualify as Madhyamaka in this crucial respect, which is after all nothing less than the very pith of Centrism. Taking into account the various additional points in Tsongkhapa's system that Mikyö Dorje and other Tibetan masters reject, it is natural that a number of these masters would raise serious doubts as to whether the Gelugpa version of Madhyamaka is still to be considered Centrism, let alone Consequentialism.

In general, the Karmapa says, any meditation or conduct based on the notion of an isolated nature of phenomena that is not connected to anything that bears this nature is not appropriate as either the foundation for the path to liberation or the remedy for obscurations. For any meditation or conduct based on a nature of phenomena that is unrelated to these phenomena cannot relinquish the two obscurations of clinging to the reality of these very phenomena as the seeming bearers of this nature. In terms of such a disconnected nature of phenomena, it does not matter whether it is said to be a nonentity that is a nonimplicative negation (as held by Tsongkhapa) or a permanent ultimate entity (as maintained by Dölpopa and others). Both are equally soteriologically ineffective. *The Sūtra of the Great Nirvāṇa* says:

> Since bodhisattvas, the great beings, are endowed with five things, they see the nature of phenomena that is empty and peaceful right from the beginning. O son of good family, if monastics or brahmans see the nature of all phenomena as not being empty, they are neither monastics nor brahmans, do not attain the perfection of knowledge, do not pass into nirvāṇa, and do not directly see Buddhas and bodhisattvas. You should understand that they are the retinue of māra. O son of good family, all phenomena are naturally empty. Through meditating on their being empty, bodhisattvas see that all phenomena are empty.

In contrast to all the above misconceptions of emptiness, according to Mikyö Dorje, Autonomists and Consequentialists understand emptiness in a way that is soteriologially effective.

Autonomists say that, if investigated through reasoning that analyzes for the ultimate, there is nothing to be found at all, be it a basis of emptiness or properties of which this basis is empty, the fact of being empty or not being empty, the nature of phenomena, or the bearers of this nature. By conventionally taking mere illusionlike appearances as the bases of emptiness, Autonomists say that, ultimately, these appearances are empty of all properties that may be imputed by Buddhist and non-Buddhist realists. They assert that all phenomena are empty of a nature of their own. From the perspective of correct reasoning and the meditative equipoise of the noble ones of the great vehicle, all discursiveness and characteristics are at utter peace. Hence, the Autonomists' understanding of emptiness is greatly superior to any of the realist notions of emptiness above and is definitely suitable as the foundation for liberation and the remedy for both kinds of obscurations.

Consequentialists say that all phenomena are primordially not established as any reference points for discursiveness, be it the four extremes, the eight extremes, being empty or not empty, real or delusive. It is just nonreferentiality that is conventionally labeled "emptiness," "true reality," and so on. This is suitable as the foundation for liberation and the remedy for the two obscurations, since both afflictive and cognitive obscurations originate from the reification of entities. Once yogic practitioners realize that all phenomena are primordially free from all discursiveness, the entirety of reifying clinging to real entities is put to an end.[1401]

In summary, in terms of its soteriological efficacy, the Eighth Karmapa considers Tsongkhapa's presentation of the object of negation and emptiness to be a form of realism outside of Centrism and, in terms of doxographical ranking, to be located between Mere Mentalists and Autonomists.

**Do Autonomists and Consequentialists Have a Different Object of Negation?**

Tsongkhapa explains in detail how Autonomists and Consequentialists differ in the subtlety of their objects of negation and thus have a different realization of emptiness. According to the Gelugpa system, the object of negation in general is specified by six notions. These are considered to be more or less equivalent, but—as Tauscher (1995) pointed out—are divided into two groups. The first group of three consists of the following:

1) being really established or really existent (Tib. bden par grub pa)
2) being ultimately established (Tib. don dam par grub pa)
3) being truly established (Tib. yang dag par grub pa)

These three terms refer to any kind of absolute existential status of phenomena and imply their complete independence of causes and conditions. The second group of three contains the following:

4) being established through its own nature or from its own side (Tib. rang gi ngo bos or rang ngos nas grub pa)
5) being established through its own specific characteristics (Tib. rang gi mtshan nyid kyis grub pa)
6) being established through its nature (Tib. rang bzhin gyis grub pa)[1402]

These latter three terms refer to the epistemological status of phenomena as objects in their relation to the subjects that cognize them. In particular, (4) and (6) indicate an intrinsic mode of existence of objects independent of their cognitions.

It is said then that Consequentialists understand all six notions to be their object of negation, whereas Autonomists take only the first three. Hence, this difference is again just a consequence of Tsongkhapa's well-known claim that Autonomists conventionally assert appearances as being established through their own specific characteristics.[1403] From the Gelugpa Consequentialist point of view, this entails a certain degree of existence in an absolute sense and thus constitutes the subtle difference in the object of negation between Autonomists and Consequentialists, that is, (1) being really existent versus (6) being established by its nature. This difference is said to entail a further distinction between coarse and subtle forms of personal and phenomenal identity in Centrism, which may be briefly outlined as follows:

| | Coarse self | Subtle self | Coarse ph. identity | Subtle ph. identity |
|---|---|---|---|---|
| Autonomists Following the Sūtras | a permanent, independent, single person | a self-sufficient[1404] person | — | really existent phenomena |
| Autonomists of Yoga Practice | a permanent, independent, single person | a self-sufficient person | object and subject as different entities | really existent phenomena |
| Consequentialists | a self-sufficient person | a person established through its nature | — | phenomena established through their nature[1405] |

The question here is exactly how Tsongkhapa's special object of negation of Consequentialists, as opposed to the one negated by Autonomists, can be identified. From among the four extremes of existence, nonexistence, both, and neither in Centrist reasonings, does the Consequentialists' special object of negation correspond to the first extreme of existence? If that is affirmed, any understanding of emptiness that results from the negation of just this one extreme must be only partial, since the remaining three extremes, particularly that of nonexistence, are not negated. Does that mean that emptiness is either nonexistent, both existent and nonexistent, or something that is neither? In any case, statistically speaking, 75 percent of the possible extremes have not been negated, so how could this be called freedom from extremes? On the other hand, if this special object of negation is not the first extreme of existence, which of the others would it be? None of them looks like a promising candidate. And what could a fifth extreme beyond the usual four extremes be? Moreover, a fifth extreme would blow up the entire Centrist approach to reasoning in terms of mutually exclusive and exhaustive possibilities to be negated. If Centrist negations cannot be limited to the four extremes, one inevitably ends up in an infinite regress, since if there is a fifth extreme, one can easily find a sixth, and so on.[1406]

So if the Consequentialist object of negation and the resulting realization are indeed superior to what Autonomists negate and realize, this would either mean the elimination of a further extreme or reference point or, since Autonomists equally and thoroughly negate all four extremes and cultivate the freedom from all reference points, it would mean that Consequentialists revert from this freedom from all reference points to again having a reference point. What more than all reference points can one possibly eliminate? And what more is emptiness? As Sakya Paṇḍita says, "The very attempt to go higher or beyond the freedom from all reference points would just mean falling out of nonreferentiality by inevitably creating a reference point again."

Once Autonomists realize the freedom from all extremes, there is no point in making a distinction between them and Consequentialists in terms of the latter's object of negation being more subtle and their realization of emptiness being superior. Either Autonomists reject the four extremes and thus realize the freedom from reference points or they do not and consequently should not be counted as Centrists, for this is precisely what Centrism is about. If Autonomists indeed had an object of negation that is not as all-inclusive as that of Consequentialists, it can only mean that they do not reject all four extremes and thus do not become Buddhas. So why would they still be counted as Centrists? In other words, such an assumed fundamental inferiority of Autonomists makes the Autonomist-Consequentialist distinction as a subdivision of a single school more than questionable. And if they do not belong to the same school due to substantial differences, then doxographically one should speak of five rather than four Buddhist philosophical systems. This, however, contradicts the Gelugpas' own doxographical scheme.

Similar problems apply to the notion of a special Consequentialist object of negation with regard to a personal self as outlined above. For this means that all followers of other Buddhist philosophical systems do not actually realize personal identitylessness. Consequently, all lower vehicles and philosophical systems except Consequentialism are teachings that are inefficient for relinquishing the clinging to a personal self, which means that it was pointless for the Buddha to teach them. This leads to the further conclusion that hearers and solitary realizers do not even attain liberation from cyclic existence, let alone realize phenomenal identitylessness. Moreover, it is self-contradictory to accept, on the one hand, that the wisdom that realizes the sixteen aspects of the four realities of the noble ones is yogic valid perception (that is, the unmediated cognitive mode of realizing identitylessness) and, on the other hand, that this wisdom (which is the only direct mode of realizing personal identitylessness that is explained in the scriptures of hearers and solitary realizers) is not able to uproot the innate clinging to personal identity.

According to Tsongkhapa, the Consequentialist system also asserts a personal self that is apprehended by the innate clinging to a self (and is said to be different from the personal self that is the object of negation of reasoning). This first kind of self is not to be negated but serves as the support for karmic actions and their result. However, if such a personal self existed, then the wisdom that realizes identitylessness would not engage the actual nature of its object, while the mode of apprehension of the innate clinging to identity would be unmistaken.

Moreover, Tsongkhapa thus contradicts his own claim to be a Centrist propounding that all phenomena are identityless.

Tsongkhapa's emphasis on the distinction between "existence" on the one hand and "real existence" or "being established by its nature" on the other also entails a practical problem on the path, since he himself says that this distinction is so subtle that it cannot be grasped by ordinary beings but only by noble ones from the path of seeing onward. In other words, only at this point is it possible to differentiate between the basis of negation and the object of negation. If the basis of everyone's progress on the path is a distinction that is said to be noticeable only to highly advanced practitioners, then for a long time (that is, during all of the paths of accumulation and junction, which are usually said to take at least one infinite eon), the vast majority of practitioners can have no chance to practice this correctly. And if they cannot practice properly, how should they ever get to this resultant, advanced stage where they are finally supposed to be able to see what they should have been practicing all along? What should a beginner think of an instruction that says, "It is absolutely crucial for you to clearly make this distinction to properly progress on the path, but there is no way you will get it"? This sounds like the well-known statement, "You have no chance, but use it." Moreover, Tsongkhapa's statement that ordinary beings cannot grasp this subtle but all-decisive distinction evidently contradicts his other claim that ordinary beings *can* realize actual emptiness.

Also, by focusing on the fictitious construct of real existence rather than on Centrism being about eradicating our very sense of any reference points of existence, nonexistence, and so on, Centrist reasonings and negations almost inevitably turn into mere intellectual exercises of negating something "out there" that is totally unrelated to our subjective experience of instinctively taking things to be real and thus developing attachment and aversion.[1407]

**Does Emptiness Exist?**

Tsongkhapa and his followers insist that emptiness is an existent and a nonimplicative negation. As explained above, they maintain that it is "real existence" as the object of negation that must be refuted, but that the mere nonimplicative negation that is the nonfinding of that putative object through reasoned analysis is the fully qualified, actual ultimate. They further claim that the apprehension of that emptiness, even a conceptual one by a correct reasoning consciousness of an ordinary being, is a realization of the ultimate. Hence, such an apprehension is not an object of negation, whereas the apprehension of reality or real existence is.

All of this is definitely alien to Centrism. First, we have to remember how existents and nonimplicative negations are understood. Also in the Gelugpa tradition, an existent is usually defined as "what is established or observable through valid cognition." Valid cognitions are two: perception and inferential valid cognition. This means that an existent cannot but be observed through either of these two. As for a nonimplicative negation, it was explained earlier that it is defined—by Gelugpas as well—as an object of a conceptual consciousness. Thus, it can never be an object of any kind of nonconceptual perception (which is, however, exactly what the Gelugpa tradition claims it to be in the case of emptiness as a nonimplicative negation).

To start with, claiming that emptiness is an existent openly contradicts what Nāgārjuna and other Centrists say:

> To say "existence" is the clinging to permanence.
> To say "nonexistence" is the view of extinction.
> Therefore, the learned should not dwell
> In either existence or nonexistence.[1408]

If emptiness were an existent—something observable through valid cognition—it would follow that it cannot be realized at all, since Atīśa and many other Centrists say that emptiness cannot be realized through valid cognition. As his *Entrance into the Two Realities* drastically clarifies:

> Perceptual and inferential cognition—
> These two are accepted by Buddhists.
> Only narrow-minded fools say
> That emptiness is realized by these two.
>
> Perceptual and inferential cognition are useless.
> It is just for the sake of refuting non-Buddhist opponents
> That the learned ones have promoted them.
>
> The learned master Bhavya said
> That the scriptures are clear about
> [The ultimate] being realized neither through
> Conceptual nor nonconceptual consciousnesses.[1409]

*The Entrance to the Bodhisattva's Way of Life* agrees:

> The ultimate is not the sphere of cognition.
> It is said that cognition is the seeming.[1410]

Since all valid cognitions are classified as subcategories of cognition, the ultimate is not an object of any valid cognition and thus cannot be an existent.

Given that Centrists like Nāgārjuna and Candrakīrti explicitly reject the notion of valid cognition, except on the level of mere worldly conventions, how could emptiness as the ultimate reality be established or observed by something that is itself not established as anything other than a seeming convention? If something that is a mere worldly convention is sufficient to realize emptiness, what is the need for the supramundane insight of the noble ones? Also, if emptiness were realized by valid cognition that is a mere worldly convention, it could only be established as some worldly convention too. Thus, it is not the ultimate, but just seeming reality.

The above verses also contradict Tsongkhapa's claim that even ordinary beings could realize the fully qualified ultimate reality through a correct reasoning consciousness. But even if they could, what would be the point of going through the paths of seeing and meditation or the ten grounds of bodhisattvas? If ordinary beings indeed realize the actual ultimate, it follows that they are Buddhas or at least bodhisattvas on the path of seeing. In fact, any realization of the ultimate by ordinary beings as a nonimplicative negation for a correct reasoning consciousness can only refer to nominal ultimate reality, which still belongs to seeming reality. However, Tsongkhapa insists that this realization of ordinary beings is a realization of actual ultimate reality, just in a conceptual way. But if actual ultimate reality is indeed realized by a conceptual consciousness, it follows that the ultimate itself is a conceptual object, which in turn rules out that it can be the object of the nonconceptual wisdom in the meditative equipoise of noble ones. This leads to the paradox that ordinary beings realize ultimate reality, while the noble ones, such as Buddhas and bodhisattvas, do not. In other words, the conceptual realization of emptiness by ordinary beings would be the perfect seeing, and its realization by noble ones the false seeing. This is not only absurd but also the reverse of what Candrakīrti's *Entrance into Centrism* says:

> It is through the perfect and the false seeing of all entities
> That the entities that are thus found bear two natures.
> The object of perfect seeing is true reality
> And false seeing is seeming reality.[1411]

Another complication here is that, following Dignāga and Dharmakīrti, all Buddhist systems agree that conceptuality and direct (nonconceptual) perception are mutually exclusive. In uniquely stark contrast to the otherwise strictly followed epistemology of Dignāga and Dharmakīrti, the Gelugpa Consequentialist system does *not* consider conceptuality and direct perception as mutually exclusive, thus blurring the clear-cut and strict distinction by these masters between the two types of valid cognition. It is held that, following an initial moment of an ordinary being's inferential cognition of emptiness, all subsequent valid cognitions[1412] in that same cognitional sequence are *direct* valid perceptions of emptiness despite being conceptual. Unlike the initial inferential cognition, they do not depend on a reason but on the power of that inference. It gets even better: Such *conceptual* subsequent cognitions are explicitly said to be *mistaken* consciousnesses affected by ignorance, because only Buddhas and noble bodhisattvas in meditative equipoise are not affected by the latent tendencies of ignorance. But at the same time, these conceptual cognitions are held to be *direct* valid cognitions that realize actual emptiness. Isn't it good news for all ordinary beings that a *conceptual* and *mistaken* consciousness can be a *direct* and *valid* cognition of emptiness? Never mind the minor detail that if emptiness can be realized by a mistaken consciousness, it cannot by definition be the true, unmistaken nature of phenomena.

Furthermore, if emptiness were an existent, then it would just be one of the four extremes negated in all Centrist reasonings. Since emptiness is again and again said to be the very freedom from all four extremes, how could it be one of them? This is like saying that the lack of all color is blue. It also follows that the Buddha, Nāgārjuna, and all other Centrists did not realize emptiness, because they realized and taught emptiness as the freedom from all extremes of existence, nonexistence, and so on. In other words, if emptiness were an existent, it could not be realized by the nonreferential wisdom of the noble ones, since such wisdom does not observe either existence or nonexistence. If emptiness were an existent and a nonimplicative negation, then, even if it were realized, how would one ever attain the freedom from all reference points, since being existent and being a nonimplicative negation are nothing but reference points? Moreover, it follows that all Centrists who teach and realize the freedom from all extremes and reference points would not be Centrists, since emptiness is an existent and a nonimplicative negation, which is a reference point for a conceptual consciousness.

In an attempt to tackle this problem, Tsongkhapa differentiates between "being ultimate" (Tib. don dam yin pa) and "ultimately existing" (Tib. don dam du yod pa). Emptiness is said to be ultimate but not to ultimately exist. However, from this it only follows that emptiness must solely exist on the conventional or seeming level, since it is said to be existent but not ultimately existent, and there is no third possibility.

There is no doubt in any Centrist text that the fully qualified, actual ultimate is solely realized in the meditative equipoise of noble ones. Candrakīrti defines the seeming as the object of false seeing. Therefore, unlike the actual emptiness that is directly perceived by the yogic valid perception of noble ones, an emptiness in the sense of a nonimplicative negation (which by definition can only be ascertained through inferential valid cognition) belongs only to seeming reality and is thus just deceptively true. To claim that a conceptual object—the absence of real existence through the negation of real existence—is the fully qualified ultimate is simply to confuse the pointing finger with the moon to which it points. Since a nonimplicative negation cannot appear to any kind of nonconceptual perception, not even to a mistaken one, how should it ever appear for the wisdom minds of noble ones or a Buddha in whom even the most subtle discursiveness has subsided? On the other hand, if such a nonimplicative negation would appear to the yogic valid perception of noble ones, it would inevitably follow that this perception is a conceptual consciousness, which by definition it is not. And if emptiness as a nonimplicative negation does not appear to such yogic perception, it simply follows that the noble ones do not realize emptiness.

When Tsongkhapa and his followers attempt to sustain their claim of emptiness as a nonimplicative negation being the object of even the nonconceptual wisdom in meditative equipoise, by insisting that yogic direct perception directly cognizes such a nonimplicative negation, they again blur the distinction between the two types of valid cognition (inferential/conceptual and perceptual/nonconceptual valid cognition). However, in the same way as these two categories of valid cognition that are meant to be mutually exclusive then come to overlap, the nature of this nonimplicative negation as an object of both inferential and perceptual valid cognition is also dual and thus highly unclear. It would be the only phenomenon ever to be an object of both a conceptual and a nonconceptual consciousness, but what should that be? Is it a functional entity, a nonentity, both, or neither? It cannot be an entity, because functional entities by definition cannot be cognized by conceptual consciousnesses. Moreover, entities are parts of seeming reality, and emptiness as a nonimplicative negation is supposed to be the ultimate. For the same reason, it cannot be a nonentity either. A hypothetical something that is both an entity and a nonentity is by definition not an existent, since existents are exhaustively divided into entities and nonentities, whereas emptiness as a nonimplicative negation is held to be an existent. The same problem applies to a hypothetical something that is neither an entity nor a nonentity.

The difference between the conceptual cultivation of a negation and direct seeing may be illustrated by an example. When people with blurred vision consult a doctor, they might be told, "There is no doubt that you see all these things like floating hairs, but none of them really exists." By keeping this in mind, the patients may eventually cease to be confused and upset by these appearances. However, merely cultivating this notion of the actual nonexistence of what they see does not eliminate the appearances themselves. Once the patients become cured and thus see unobscured, open space without floating hairs, they obviously do not see "the nonimplicative negation of the real existence of floating hairs." Technically speaking, one may say that they see space "qualified" by the absence of floating hairs, but in terms of immediate experience, they just see "what is as it is," since it is no longer obscured by anything.

Furthermore, since also Tsongkhapa and his followers say that the meditative equipoise of noble ones is without appearance, how could a nonimplicative negation be perceived in such a meditative equipoise, if it does not even appear for it? And if something does not appear in the meditative equipoise of noble ones, how can it be said to exist as ultimate reality? What does not appear in their meditative equipoise could only be either their "mere seeming," the seeming reality of ordinary beings, or the false seeming (such as a hallucination). In general, what can be said to exist without even appearing or being cognized? So if ultimate reality—emptiness as a nonimplicative negation—cannot appear to the wisdom in the meditative equipoise of noble ones, what is it then that is realized in such a supramundane meditative state? And how could the ultimate ever be realized, if not through this wisdom?

In general, every negation must depend on the rejection of an affirmation or proposition, which means that emptiness as a nonimplicative negation is not only conceptual but also dependent on something else. In fact, the very existence of a negation can only make sense in opposition to an affirmation. Hence, it is a mutually dependent phenomenon caught in the dichotomies of being and not being, thus belonging to the realm of seeming reality. How could such a dichotomous conceptual fabrication be the ultimate nature of all phenomena? In addition, as a seeming, dependent phenomenon that is an object of a conceptual consciousness, every nonimplicative negation in itself cannot withstand analysis. This means that if emptiness were a nonimplicative negation, then it would not be findable under analysis for the ultimate. Hence, even for Gelugpas it cannot be ultimate reality, since their standard definition of ultimate reality is "what is found from the perspective of the final reasoning consciousness."

If emptiness were an existent and a nonimplicative negation, it would not be emptiness, because every existent is just a *bearer* of emptiness as the nature of all phenomena and is not this nature itself. Moreover, this contradicts the emptiness of emptiness, since it follows that the emptiness of emptiness is an existent and a nonimplicative negation too, but not emptiness as the freedom from all extremes. So what is the difference between the emptiness of emptiness as a nonimplicative negation and the emptiness of a table as a nonimplicative negation? In other words, the emptiness of emptiness must then be the nonimplicative negation of a nonimplicative negation. But what is that supposed to be? A negation of a negation resulting in an affirmation? Since emptiness is said to be an existent, whatever the emptiness of emptiness as a nonimplicative negation of this existent might be then, it would definitely not be an existent. Thus, it follows that emptiness and its own emptiness would be different. By extrapolating this, such an emptiness of emptiness can only lead to an infinite regress.

According to Tsongkhapa, only the apprehension of real existence (as the object of negation) is to be discarded, but the apprehension of emptiness as a nonimplicative negation is explicitly to be sustained. From this, it follows that the teachings and any meditation on the emptiness of emptiness (as the nonimplicative negation of this nonimplicative negation) are superfluous, since the first emptiness and its apprehension are not to be given up. Moreover, this contradicts numerous Centrist statements about actually *not* sustaining any mode of apprehension or reference points, which includes letting go of negations too. As Śāntideva's famous verses say:

> Through familiarity with the latent tendencies of emptiness,
> The latent tendencies of entities will be relinquished.
> Through familiarity with "utter nonexistence,"
> These too will be relinquished later on.
>
> Once neither entities nor nonentities
> Remain before the mind,
> There is no other mental flux [either].
> Therefore, it is utter nonreferential peace.[1413]

As mentioned above, Tsongkhapa says that emptiness can only exist as the nature of a given phenomenon X. This means that without X, there is no emptiness of X. In effect, emptiness thus depends on the existence of a conventionally established phenomenon X. In other words, emptiness itself is a dependently originated phenomenon. From this, it follows that emptiness is not ultimate reality but belongs to seeming reality. Phenomenon X is said to be empty precisely because it exists in dependence on something else. That is why it is part of seeming reality. If emptiness also exists only in dependence on something else, it must be a part of seeming reality too. One may well adduce the unity of dependent origination and emptiness here, but the point is that if emptiness *itself* exists—or worse, originates—in dependence, it cannot be the ultimate. And if it still were the ultimate, then everything that depends on something else would be the ultimate.

In the same vein, if emptiness—a nonimplicative negation and thus a nonentity—is an existent that exists in entities such as form, does it so exist as something mutually exclusive or as something connected to these entities? If it is supposed to exist as something mutually exclusive to them, it obviously cannot exist in them at all. And if it existed as something connected to them, it would have to exist either through being connected causally or in terms of identity, but, by definition, neither of these connections is possible for nonentities.[1414] In fact, any connection between entities and nonentities is by definition impossible, just like space is neither identically nor causally connected to the matter within space. To be really picky, if emptiness is an existent and a nonimplicative negation, does it then imply its own existence or not? If it does, it is not a nonimplicative negation; and if it does not, it does not exist.

In his *Great Stages of the Path*, Tsongkhapa says:

> When the existence of a nature is negatively determined, no doubt the lack of a nature must be positively determined.[1415]

Since the lack of a nature is understood as equivalent to emptiness, this means that emptiness is to be positively determined, which clearly contradicts the claim that emptiness is a nonimplicative negation.

In terms of the result of realizing emptiness as a nonimplicative negation, since the state of Buddhahood is nothing but the complete revelation of emptiness, it must also be a nonimplicative negation. But how could the mere absence of real or inherent existence be Buddhahood? Apart from being absurd, how could such a fruition appeal to anybody or make anybody take up a path that leads to that sort of attainment? Why should any bodhisattva-to-be be inspired to strive for attaining a mere negation or extinction that is even less of an attainment than arhathood? And how does a mere negation or absence of real existence account for all the infinite qualities and activities of a Buddha? Moreover, since Tsongkhapa claims that the wisdom that realizes emptiness is impermanent and belongs to seeming reality, how can something impermanent that only operates in seeming reality realize something permanent[1416] and ultimate? If emptiness is a nonimplicative negation and thus by definition permanent, it follows that Nāgārjuna and others were wrong in making statements such as:

> The four possibilities of permanent, impermanent, and so on,
> Where should they be in this peace?[1417]

At this point, this should be too obvious to mention, but it is one of the standard objections to the refutation of emptiness being an existent and a nonimplicative negation to answer that emptiness must then be a nonexistent or an implicative negation. Clearly, none of the above consequences or negations of emptiness being existent and a nonimplicative negation implies any such thing, since—unlike emptiness—they in fact *are* nonimplicative negations. Otherwise, they would just lead to other inconsistencies that are the inverse of the problems demonstrated. Moreover, it was explained over and over that dichotomous—or any other—categories simply do not apply to emptiness.

It must be likewise clear that none of this means to deny or downplay the important role in Centrism of negation in general and of nonimplicative negation in particular. However, it can only be repeated that all reasonings and negations work solely on the level of seeming reality. At best, as nonimplicative negations, they can refer to the nominal ultimate but never to the actual ultimate free from all discursiveness and reference points, such as existence, nonexistence, affirmation, and negation.

**Can an Absence Perform a Function?**

Tsongkhapa says that Consequentialists refute all kinds of supports for the continuity between karmic actions and their results that are asserted by other non-Buddhists and Buddhists, such as a self, "attainment,"[1418] a ground consciousness, or mind. He is, however, concerned about the possible problem of Consequentialism being left with no basis for a connection between karmic causes and effects at all and thus no basis for proper conduct, with the result of falling into the extreme of extinction or nihilism. Hence, Tsongkhapa claims that one of the unique features of Candrakīrti's system is that disintegratedness as a functional entity serves as the support to connect past actions and their results. For scriptural support, he refers to two quotes from the sixth chapter of *The Sūtra of the Ten Grounds* in Candrakīrti's *Lucid Words*:

> Dying has two functions: It makes formations disintegrate and brings forth the cause for ignorance not being interrupted.
>
> [D]eath [comes about] through the condition of birth.

He also refers to a line from *The Fundamental Verses*:

> Entities and nonentities are conditioned.[1419]

The contexts of these quotes in Candrakīrti's text are as follows:

> As for something disintegrating, in terms of its own nature, it is an entity, but since its nature is that a phenomenon (such as form) comes to an end, it is a nonentity. Furthermore, it is said, "Dying has two functions: It makes formations disintegrate and brings forth the cause for ignorance not being interrupted." So, based on this passage, how should something disintegrating not be something that has a cause?[1420]

Nāgārjuna's entire verse reads:

> How could nirvāṇa be
> Both an entity and a nonentity?
> Nirvāṇa is unconditioned.
> Entities and nonentities are conditioned.

Candrakīrti comments:

> Entities are conditioned, since they originate from the gathering of their own causes and conditions. Nonentities are also conditioned, since they come about in dependence on entities and because it is said that "death [comes about] through the condition of birth." Therefore, if nirvāṇa had the nature of both an entity and a nonentity, it would be conditioned. But if it were conditioned, [this is contradictory to the fact] that it is not asserted as something conditioned [here by Nāgārjuna]. Therefore, it is not suitable to be either an entity or a nonentity.[1421]

First, it is to be noted that none of these passages speaks about the state of *having disintegrated* but about *something disintegrating* (or dying).[1422] Candrakīrti says that, from different perspectives, something disintegrating (not the state of something having already disintegrated) can be regarded as either an entity or a nonentity. He states that something disintegrating (or dying) is not uncaused, but he does not state that the state of having disintegrated itself causes something else. As for the statement that "Dying brings forth the cause for ignorance not being interrupted," this just points to the continuation of the twelve links of dependent origination, with the link of ignorance following that of dying. Also, the phrase "Death [comes about] through the condition of birth" refers to this continuity of the twelve links. Obviously, this does not mean that dying (or having died) itself causes ignorance.[1423] Candrakīrti's text also quotes a long passage from *The Rice Seedling Sūtra* that glosses this expression and explains the nature of all the twelve links of dependent origination:

> The aggregates . . . becoming disintegrated is called "Aging and dying [come] from birth." Thus, these twelve links of dependent origination . . . are neither permanent nor impermanent, neither conditioned nor unconditioned, . . . not phenomena that become extinguished, not phenomena that disintegrate, not phenomena that cease. Their uninterrupted operation since beginningless time flows like the stream of a river . . . [1424]

When Nāgārjuna's verse speaks about both entities and nonentities as being conditioned, he means that the former dependently arise and the latter are imputed in dependence on entities. In this way, both entities and nonentities stand in contradistinction to nirvāṇa, which is unconditioned in both of these ways. If Tsongkhapa's claim were correct that the state of having disintegrated is a functional entity, then Nāgārjuna would contradict himself by saying that nirvāṇa is unconditioned. For nirvāṇa is the state of the afflictions or obscurations having disintegrated. Therefore, it should be a functional entity and thus by definition conditioned. This, however, would entail nirvāṇa's own disintegration at some point, resulting in one's falling back into cyclic existence. Another question is what would be caused by the functional entity that is this state of the obscurations having disintegrated. If the disintegratedness of actions can cause the results of these actions, why should the disintegratedness of obscurations not cause the results of these obscurations?

In brief, neither Nāgārjuna nor Candrakīrti says anywhere that the state of having disintegrated is an entity or that this state itself causes something else. Thus, Tsongkhapa's critics all agree that the above quotes are taken out of context and unrelated to what he tries to establish through them. Moreover, there are many passages in the texts of Nāgārjuna, Buddhapālita, and Candrakīrti that clearly speak to the contrary. For example, Nāgārjuna's *Fundamental Verses* says:

> If remaining until the time of ripening,
> Actions would be permanent.
> If they cease, having ceased,
> How would their results arise?
>
> Why do actions not arise?
> Because they lack a nature.
> Since they are unarisen,
> They do not go to waste.[1425]

Buddhapālita comments on the latter verse:

> Hence, not understanding the meaning of true reality, people make a lot of different, insubstantial statements by clinging to the mere words of "not going to waste" as being a functional entity. Thus, actions decidedly lack a nature. Because they lack a nature, they are unarisen. And since they are unarisen, they do not go to waste. This is how they definitely should be regarded.[1426]

Candrakīrti's autocommentary on *The Entrance into Centrism* says:

> Conditioned phenomena originate from coming together.
> They do not originate from being separated.
> Conditioned phenomena originate from gathering.
> They do not originate from nongathering.[1427]

and

> In the light of karmic actions not arising through their own intrinsic nature, they do not cease, and it is also not impossible that [their] results originate due to [them] *not* having disintegrated. Hence, since actions do *not* disintegrate, the connection between actions and their results is very much justified.[1428]

The Karmapa clarifies that if it really were one of Candrakīrti's unique points that disintegratedness is a functional entity, his last paragraph should have read:

> it is also not impossible that [their] results originate due to [their] *having* disintegrated. Hence, since actions *do* disintegrate, *due to disintegratedness*, the connection between actions and their results is very much justified.

Moreover, since both Nāgārjuna and Candrakīrti emphasize again and again that all phenomena are without arising and ceasing, how could their having ceased or disintegrated exist, let alone perform a function? As Nāgārjuna says:

> If the arising
> Of all phenomena is unjustified,
> Then the ceasing
> Of all phenomena is not justified [either].
>
> Since arising, abiding, and disintegrating
> Are not established, there are no conditioned phenomena.
> Since conditioned phenomena are not established,
> How could unconditioned phenomena be established?[1429]

It is highly absurd that disintegratedness is an entity that can perform a function, since this is simply the nonexistence of whatever entity has disintegrated. If an entity has disintegrated, how can its absence also be an entity? Otherwise, everything that is mutually exclusive would not be so, and the lack of rain would be rain. Also, if the disintegratedness—that is, the absence of an action—is an entity that can perform a function, then it follows that its opposite—this action as long as it exists—is a nonentity that cannot perform a function. Thus, all Buddhist texts' classifications of entities and the lack of entities (or nonentities) would be wrong. However, with this one peculiar exception of disintegratedness as a functional entity, Tsongkhapa and his followers are very clear that an entity (defined as what performs a function) is mutually exclusive with the lack of entity (what cannot perform a function). So only something that has *not* disintegrated and is thus not absent, such as gas in the tank of a car, can be an existent functional entity. If what is an existent functional entity—the gas—has disintegrated (become nonexistent), we are only left with the very lack of that entity: no gas in the tank. And what function would the nonexistence of gas perform? That the car no longer functions is a clear sign that the nonexistence of gas is the absence of functioning. It might be said that the lack of gas performs the function of making us angry. However, this is not the case, because what makes us angry is rather the mental state of our unfulfilled desire to drive somewhere. Otherwise, if it were the nonexistence of gas as such that had the function of producing anger, then everybody would be angry wherever there is no gas and never be angry wherever there is gas. Also, if disintegratedness were an existent entity, everything would be permanent, because there would never be a case of the simple nonexistence of some prior existent that is the exact reverse of its existence.

Some might say that darkness comes from the extinction of light, so the light's extinction must be a causal, functional entity. From this it absurdly follows that light is the indirect cause for darkness, since without light there would be no extinction of light and thus no darkness. A further consequence is that in all places where there never has been any light, such as in an unopened nutshell, there can be no darkness, since there was no light to be extinguished in the first place. If extinction of light is said to refer to just nonexistent light, then a skyflower must have withered and become extinct, since it is nonexistent. Likewise, if one's old car has disintegrated in the crusher, one is forced to walk. Hence, it follows that people who have never had a car in the first place never need to walk, since their cars never disintegrated.

The notion of disintegratedness as a functional entity is clearly not common worldly consensus either. Ordinary people talk about disintegration only in terms of coarse changes in the continua of entities, such as when a house collapses or an apple has completely decayed and disintegrated, but they do not analyze the disintegration of entities in terms of their mode of momentary, subtle impermanence. Also, when notions such as self-awareness and a ground consciousness are rejected even conventionally because of merely being imputations by Buddhist philosophical systems, there is no ground for replacing these with yet another such imputation as being a part of conventional reality, especially when it is a notion held by non-Buddhist philosophical systems such as the Differentiators. After all supports for karmic continuity imputed by others have extensively been refuted, to reintroduce such a support that is moreover claimed to be a functional entity established by valid cognition is only a sign of reification *not* having disintegrated.

In brief, all presentations such as happiness and suffering arising as the results of positive and negative actions and cyclic existence being the result of karma and afflictions are given without analysis from the perspective of worldly beings. It may be analyzed whether these results arise from the functional entity that is the cause's disintegratedness or from the functional entity that is its not having disintegrated, but such analysis is still a presentation of causes and results on the level of seeming reality. However, to say, "When analyzed through reasoning, with regard to causes and results on the level of seeming reality, such and such is established through the valid cognition of reasoning as something that withstands analysis" means nothing and only entertains the superimpositions and denials of realists.

As for Centrists, once they have analyzed, they do not actively put forward any seeming reality, since actively putting forward something like this means incurring the formidable fallacy of having to claim that some phenomena withstand analysis. In particular, when analyzed, a result arises from neither disintegrated nor undisintegrated causes. If the result arose after the cause has disintegrated, it would follow that everything can arise from everything. If the result arose while the cause has not disintegrated, the result would not depend on causes and conditions. If it is presumed that a result arises after the cause has already disintegrated, such a result would just be an extinct entity, since the continuity between cause and result has been interrupted. If it is presumed that a result arises while the cause has not disintegrated, all entities would be simultaneously permanent. In summary, something that has already disintegrated is not suitable as a cause, and something lasting that has not disintegrated yet is not suitable as a cause either. In fact, what represents the unsurpassable tradition of Centrists is this very lack of being weighed down by any discursiveness of attempting to even conventionally set something up in terms of the connection between cause and result or their support.

The Karmapa adduces many other refutations of disintegratedness as a functional entity through both reasoning and scripture (including Nāgārjuna, Bhāvaviveka, Śāntarakṣita, and Sakya Paṇḍita). However, I refrain from further elaboration out of the concern that this could perform the function of causing the last patient readers to disintegrate too.

Tsongkhapa's view on dependent origination in Centrism goes in the same direction in the sense that he says that it must be established. He asserts that it is the unique feature of Centrists to give a presentation of arising and ceasing in terms of dependent origination as their own system that is justified through reasoning, because to properly establish illusionlike arising and ceasing without real existence serves to avoid the extreme of extinction. However, the expression "illusionlike arising and ceasing without real existence" that is used by Centrists refers to passages that prove that, from the perspectives of analysis and the perception of noble ones, arising and ceasing in terms of dependent origination are free from arising and ceasing, just like the merely seeming arising and ceasing of an illusion. Centrists would never even dream of considering such an expression to prove any established existence of arising and ceasing.

For this reason, the Centrist approach of presenting mere conditionality without analysis is in clear opposition to any reifications of asserting arising from the four extremes. Hence, the Centrist way of presenting the two realities is highly superior to any such approach by realists, since it expresses the knowable objects of all persons from ordinary beings to Buddhas in a way that does not contradict common worldly consensus. As was said before, to abstain from reifying things such as karma, cause and effect, ethics, and the means to achieve liberation in no way makes these things lack their justification or functioning. To the contrary, it is precisely the fact of their emptiness—their lack of solid and independent existence—that allows for the unimpeded and dynamic flow of the dependent origination of conditioned phenomena. As Nāgārjuna says:

> For those for whom emptiness is possible,
> Everything is possible.
> For those for whom emptiness is not possible,
> Nothing is possible.

and

> If all of this were not empty,
> Nothing would originate and disintegrate,
> And it would follow that, for you,
> The four realities of the noble ones do not exist.[1431]

**Autonomist Elements in Gelugpa Consequentialism**

Many Tibetan and Western scholars have observed that it is quite paradoxical for Tsongkhapa and his followers to emphasize such a sharp distinction between Autonomists and Consequentialists, and to posit the superiority of the latter over the former, while at the same time using many elements typical of Autonomists in their version of Consequentialism. Consequently, there were voices wondering whether Tsongkhapa's presentation can be called Consequentialism at all. Most of the Autonomist features in Tsongkhapa's system are the result of his emphasizing the validity of seeming reality and thus introducing into Consequentialism the notion of "establishment through conventional valid cognition."

To start with, Tsongkhapa is even more persistent than Bhāvaviveka in using qualifiers such as "ultimately," "actually," "inherently," and "by its nature" in order to emphasize that phenomena do not arise or exist ultimately but validly arise and exist on the level of seeming reality. He uses such qualifiers both when commenting on Indian Centrist texts and in his own works, and thus he needs to add words to almost every sentence in Indian Centrist texts, most of which do not employ such qualifications, and even reject them. Despite Candrakīrti's outspokenness on the subject of rejecting such qualifiers, Tsongkhapa obviously feels obliged to introduce them even into Candrakīrti's own system. The main reason for this is Tsongkhapa's sharp distinction between the two realities and his insistence on the validity of seeming reality, which is also more an Autonomist than a Consequentialist feature.

In his use of the logico-epistemological system of Dignāga and Dharmakīrti, Tsongkhapa definitely follows the main and most controversial innovation by the Autonomist Bhāvaviveka, who was the first to introduce that system into Centrism. In many respects, in his version of Consequentialism, Tsongkhapa even employs it in a far more extensive way than Indian Autonomists, notwithstanding the fact that Candrakīrti repeatedly rejected that system in detail.

Tsongkhapa criticizes the alleged assertion of Autonomists that phenomena are conventionally established through their own specific characteristics. At the same time, he elaborates on the phenomena of seeming reality in Consequentialism being established through conventional valid cognition. For him, such valid cognition is entirely based on the epistemological system of Dignāga and Dharmakīrti, which in turn revolves around specifically characterized and generally characterized phenomena as the two objects of the two types of valid cognition. For example, he literally accords with Autonomists such as Jñānagarbha, Śāntarakṣita and Kamalaśīla when he says in his *Great Stages of the Path*:

> Entities that are able to perform a function are not negated on the conventional level.[1432]

In particular, Tsongkhapa criticizes autonomous reasoning on the basis of specifically characterized phenomena established through conventional valid cognition, but at the same time he claims that Consequentialists engage in negation and proof based on subjects, predicates, and reasons that are established through conventional valid cognition as appearing in common for both proponents and opponents. However, such establishment through valid cognition as well as something appearing in common for Centrists and their realist opponents is denied in detail by Candrakīrti.

It is generally known that Tsongkhapa follows Chaba Chökyi Senge in many features of the latter's epistemology. In addition, Tauscher has pointed to further striking similarities between the two concerning a number of important topics in terms of the ontological position in Centrism.[1433] Such topics include the basis of distinguishing the two realities, their relation, identifying the object of negation, and emptiness or ultimate reality being a knowable object and a nonimplicative negation.[1434]

Finally, Tsongkhapa's Consequentialist system also makes use of the distinction between nominal and nonnominal ultimate reality, a feature that was clearly developed in Indian texts unanimously regarded as Autonomist.

**Being Discursive about Nondiscursiveness**

When considering the development of Centrism over the centuries, one cannot help noticing a progressive increase of elaboration, if not discursiveness (*prapañca*), in the texts of later masters. Comparing Nāgārjuna's very simple and straightforward message of the freedom from all discursiveness (*niṣprapañca*) and how it was formulated in later Indian Centrist texts or even Tibetan presentations, it seems that *niṣprapañca* has often been replaced by *prapañca*. Nāgārjuna and Āryadeva demonstrated the utter incoherence of our ordinary notions and experiences, leaving nothing whatsoever unassailed and intact among these conventional entities. Bhāvaviveka started to reintroduce many such conventionalities into Centrism. He was criticized for this by Candrakīrti, who obviously tried to get back to the Centrist basics, that "Nāgārjuna is not in the business of providing rational arguments designed to substantiate, prove, establish, or make certain anything." Not without irony though, despite his radical stance, Candrakīrti's "getting back to the roots" went through a lot of *prapañca* too. This trend toward extensive explanations, refutations, and rebuttals of objections reached its culmination in the writings of many Tibetan masters, particularly Tsongkhapa and his followers. In the maze of usually highly technical and verbose exegeses of Centrism, very often the healthy shock effect of the original Centrist writings gets lost and one starts to wonder what all of this actually was about to begin with. So how much *prapañca* do we need to reach *niṣprapañca*?

There are a number of scholars—both Western and Tibetan—who praise especially the writings of Tsongkhapa for their logical simplicity, their philosophical elegance, and their exegetical ingenuity. Be that as it may, such criteria are purely technical or pertain to the building of a philosophical system. As was said before, Buddhism in general and Centrism in particular is not meant as a philosophical edifice but as a set of tools for experientially attaining an irreversible state of freedom from suffering for both oneself and others. From the point of view of the Buddha, Nāgārjuna, and Candrakīrti, it is not at all the point to be eloquent and erect an impressive monument of brilliant ideas and concepts. If anything, this is the complete antithesis (if there is such a thing) of what Buddhism and Centrism are about and just turns the whole project of striving for the freedom from reference points upside down. Particularly in Centrism, we are not talking about philosophical elegance, systemic coherence, or the need to make perfect sense on the level of conceptual conventions, but about the liberation of our mind, which is a different ball game altogether. Setting up some philosophy is simply not the same as striving for all beings' freedom from suffering.[1435]

As Napper says, Tsongkhapa "insisted that the whole system should fit together, that it should make sense. For him, there are no paradoxes."[1436] However, such notions are purely related to system building, which may or may not make sense on some level. In contrast, what Nāgārjuna and Candrakīrti demonstrated so extensively is precisely that nothing makes sense when it is analyzed, not even such ordinary, everyday things as going. In this sense, the fact that nothing really makes sense is called saṃsāra. Experientially, as long as nobody analyzes ordinary appearances, they just appear and function. From this perspective, the question of whether they make sense or not does not even arise. This is merely a matter of questioning what appears to us and trying to make sense of it. Nirvāṇa then does not mean the grand idea that suddenly everything makes sense or that one realizes the true meaning of life. From the perspective of attaining *niṣprapañca,* it just means letting go of trying to make sense of all these things that cannot make sense. Thus, the decisive criterion for any presentation of the heart of Centrism is not whether it makes good sense (which does not, of course, mean that, conventionally, it should *not* make sense) but whether what is presented serves as a means for ending ignorance and afflictions and thus leading to Buddhahood.

All that Nāgārjuna and Candrakīrti ever point to is the dissolution of the web of our many reference points; they are far from seeking to introduce new ones. On the one hand, Tsongkhapa seems to follow them by rejecting certain notions of other philosophical systems, such as a real self, a ground consciousness, and self-awareness, even on the conventional level. On the other hand, he introduces a whole new set of reifying concepts, such as "establishment through conventional valid cognition," "identification and subdivisons of the object of negation," "disintegratedness as a functional entity," and "emptiness as an existent and nonimplicative negation." In terms of *niṣprapañca,* all of this places him light-years away from Nāgārjuna and Candrakīrti, whom he claims to follow so closely. Even worse, the Karmapa says, none of these new concepts is in any way helpful for remedying the afflictions or leading to liberation; they just add to the gigantic web of reifying *prapañca* that we keep spinning.

And even in terms of simply formulating a philosophical system, Siderits puts the crux of the Centrist view as follows:

> Thus the Madhyamaka position would appear to be that it is not sufficient to attach to one's theory of knowledge the proviso that it is formulated entirely at the level of conventional truth; if one's theory purports to be more than a provisional description of conventional epistemic practices, if there is about it any pretense at systematicity, rigor, and theoretical elegance, it will inevitably come up against the fact that no metaphysical theory can be fully adequate to the nature of the world.[1437]

This is precisely the problem Tsongkhapa and his followers run into, especially since they commit themselves to a large number of fixed points that are regarded as definite and incontestable. Thus, Tsongkhapa's own history as a writer and the subsequent philosophical history of Gelugpa exegesis consist to a large degree of elaborating on these points, attempting to remove any inconsistencies, making additional and ever more intricate distinctions and classifications, and defending these increasingly monumental constructions against any criticism, be it within different Gelugpa colleges or by other schools.[1438] From the perspective of Centrism, this is an infinite process without any hope of final success. In a way, it wonderfully illustrates the basic problem as identified by Centrists: If you start to set up even one reference point, you will inevitably have to create more and more of them, spinning yourself into a big cocoon. It is the nature of reference points that each one implies further ones and that all of them need to be constantly patched up in order to somehow stick together in a more or less coherent way.

In brief, if Centrism is explained as a consistent philosophical, ontological, or logical system, that may appeal to our wish for some well-organized, all-explanatory picture of the world and how we perceive it. Usually, we just want to have something that makes good sense, something on which we can build our belief systems or, in the case of Centrism, a belief system for why and how we should not have any belief system. However, all attempts to force Centrism into any kind of system at all must necessarily fail due to the very nature of what Centrism is: the radical deconstruction of any system and conceptualization whatsoever, including itself. Reintroducing into Centrism any notions of justification, validity, or making sense (with more subtle ones being more tricky here than gross ones) precisely reestablishes and fortifies the very traps that the Centrist approach wants us to let go of altogether. To this, Centrists could be tempted to say, "Talking heads, stop making sense!"

It is precisely this soteriological issue of untrapping ourselves that lies at the heart of the Eighth Karmapa's critique, and not primarily whether there are any philosophical or logical inconsistencies. Like Nāgārjuna and Candrakīrti, he genuinely distances himself from engaging in inflationary *prapañca*, especially when such is not conducive to attaining *niṣprapañca*. Instead, he never tires of pointing to *niṣprapañca*, both explicitly and by every so often cutting through treasured beliefs and reference points, both Buddhist and non-Buddhist. Of course, as the Karmapa's explanations amply show, this in no way means to completely shun *prapañca* by falling into the other extremes of merely not saying and thinking anything at all or simply remaining stupid. Rather, only certain kinds and certain amounts of *prapañca* (determined solely by their soteriological relevance) are employed in an expedient way in order to gradually sharpen our wisdom, but they are meant to be immediately dropped once their purpose is accomplished.

Another way to put this is that, for the Karmapa, the issue is not whether one manages to find out the single right view as opposed to all wrong views, but whether there is clinging to any view at all, whether it is "right" or "wrong." For better or worse, this is sometimes called "the view of no view." Seen from the perspective of analysis for the ultimate and the meditative equipoise of noble ones, all views are neither right nor wrong but are simply different types of clinging to various reference points. As the famous Sakya pith instruction called "freedom from fourfold clinging"[1439] says:

> If you cling to this life, you are not a dharma practitioner.
> If you cling to cyclic existence, it is not renunciation.
> If you cling to your own welfare, it is not the mind of enlightenment.
> If there is clinging, it is not the view.

Since Centrism is about the experience of freedom from all reference points, any reference points, whether they are called "views," "right," "wrong," "freedom from reference points," or "the view of no view," are eventually to be dropped. From the point of "view" of the nonreferential expanse of ultimate reality, apprehending, viewing, preferring, or even insisting on anything is nothing but self-imposed bondage within mind's open and spacious nature.

All of this is intimately connected with the Karmapa's emphasis on actually putting the Centrist approach into practice and making it a living experience. In fact, all Centrist texts and reasonings are utterly pointless when not personally employed as tools to work with one's own mind. If the remedy is not used for its only purpose—removing individual reifications and the ensuing suffering—it will inevitably turn into the very problem that it is meant to overcome. Instead of leading to *niṣprapañca*, it will just be another set of—at best—more sophisticated *prapañca* or simply a waste of time. At worst, it may even be misused to build up intellectual pride and further wrong views. Moreover, the significance of many topics in Buddhism and Centrism as well as certain ways to phrase them become clear only when applied to one's own experience.

As with any other tool, whether Centrism is soteriologically effective or just another headache depends solely on the user. Even the best tool is worth nothing if it is not put into action. For example, if we want to cut down a tree with an axe, it is helpful and necessary to sharpen the axe as well as to receive some instructions on how to handle it properly, but at some point we simply have to cut the tree. It does not make the job any easier to figure out who made the axe, of which alloy it consists, the exact angle at which the axe will hit the tree, how it will come out of the wood again, and at what speed the tree will fall. That such speculations are even more out of place in the context of eliminating suffering is dramatically illustrated by the Buddha in a famous example:

> This is as if a man is hit by an arrow thickly smeared with poison. His friends will call a physician, but [the wounded person] says: "I will not

> pull out this arrow until I know the name and the family of the archer, whether he is tall or short, has black, brown, or golden skin, where he lives, how bow and string are made, what the constituents of the arrow are, and the feathers of which bird are attached to it." This man, Māluṅkyaputta, would die before knowing all that.[1440]

The preeminence of the experiential and pragmatic ground from which all Buddhist teachings grow is also highlighted by D. T. Suzuki:

> We must keep one thing always before our minds, . . . which is, that Buddhist thought is always the outcome of Buddhist life; that is, its logic, or psychology, or metaphysics cannot be understood adequately unless we realize that facts of Buddhist experience are at its basis and, therefore, that pure logic is not the key to the understanding of Buddhist philosophy.[1441]

On the one hand, using precise philosophical categories and analyses in scriptures such as the Centrist ones, whose primary aim is to provide the means for the transcendence of dualistic thinking altogether, in order to give way to unmediated direct insight into the nature of all phenomena is like attempting to apply a mathematical formula in order to capture the experience of being completely absorbed in a wonderful piece of music or watching a breathtaking sunset. So, "pure logic" is surely not the ultimate key to understanding Buddhist texts and views, and we should not expect to find the ultimately correct conceptual presentation of facts and experiences on the Buddhist path that by definition lie outside the realm of conceptual mind anyway. Even on the mundane plane, what would be *the* finally correct presentation of the taste of chocolate? And even if there were such a thing, what would its relevance be for the actual experience of tasting chocolate? After all that has been said here, it should be clear that I do not hold a brief for some kind of "mysticism" or even "irrationalism." At the same time, we must accept that "pure experience" per se does not lead to an understanding of treatises that are grounded in a rational format to speak about something that is beyond the confines of language and reason. In the realm of the actual experience that such texts point to, reason and language have lost all meaning and the work of the scholar has reached its end. Still, in exploring the rational dimension of our minds—without which Centrist texts could never be written or read by us—such texts may well serve as the means to encounter in this very mind the experience behind (or in the very middle of) all the words and reasonings.

The Buddha himself always emphasized that trust is good but knowing is better. He explicitly put his teachings out in the open to be tested and not simply believed or accepted out of blind faith or polite respect for his sheer authority. Thus, if we really want to know whether and how these teachings work as techniques for mental transformation, we must find out for ourselves in the only suitable lab we have—our own mind. Let me conclude here with the Buddha's own words from the *Kālāmasutta*:[1442]

> Do not believe in anything simply because you have heard it. Do not believe in traditions because they have been handed down for many generations. Do not believe in anything because it is spoken and rumored by many. Do not believe in anything simply because it is found written in your religious books. Do not believe in anything merely on the authority of your teachers and elders. But after observation and analysis, when you find that anything agrees with reason and is conducive to the good and benefit of one and all, then accept it and live up to it.

# PART TWO

## *The* Bodhicaryāvatāra *and Pawo Tsugla Trengwa*

# 7

## *Some Remarks on the* Bodhicaryāvatāra *and Pawo Rinpoche's Commentary*

### A Brief Account of Śāntideva's Life

The bodhisattva later known as Śāntideva was born in a small kingdom in Saurāṣṭra in India as the first son of King Kalyāṇavarman and was named Śāntivarman.[1443] From an early age, he had visions of Mañjuśrī in his dreams. As the young crown prince grew up, the day approached when he was to ascend the throne. The night before his coronation, Śāntideva had a dream in which he saw the throne of the kingdom already occupied by Mañjuśrī, who said to him, "This is my throne and I am your spiritual friend. It is very inappropriate to sit on the same throne as me." He also dreamed of Āryatārā in the guise of his own mother, who poured hot water over his head. When the young prince asked her why she did so, she replied, "A kingdom is just like the boiling waters of hell, and I am blessing you with this water." Śāntideva regarded these visions as clear indications that he should not take over his kingdom, and thus, before the break of dawn, he ran away. After twenty-one days of walking, tired and thirsty, he happened upon a beautiful spring at the edge of a forest. As he was about to have a sip, a beautiful young lady suddenly appeared. She told him not to drink this water—which turned out to be poisonous—and offered him some much more delicious water to quench his thirst. She then escorted him to her teacher Mañjuśrīvajrasiddhi, who was meditating nearby, and Śāntideva stayed to study with this master for a long time. Needless to say, the young lady was none other than Tārā, and the teacher was Mañjuśrī.

After about twelve years, Śāntideva's teacher said that he should go to the eastern part of India, so he went and lived among the attendants of King Pañcamasiṃha. Because of Śāntideva's skill in all arts and crafts as well as his intelligence, the king requested him to become one of his ministers, and he accepted for the time being. During that period, Śāntideva had a strong and beneficial spiritual influence in the kingdom, which made the other ministers jealous. They said to the king, "This man is very deceitful. Even his sword is not a real one; it is just made of wood." (In fact, this sword, which Śāntideva always carried, was the symbol of his teacher Mañjuśrī.) Upon hearing this, the king asked all the ministers to show him their swords. When Śāntideva's turn came, he said, "O Lord, it is not good for you to view my sword, it will harm you." Of course, the king only became more suspicious and insisted on seeing the sword. Śāntideva answered, "If you really want to see it, please cover your right eye and look at it only with your left." When Śāntideva drew his sword out of its sheath, the shine was so powerfully dazzling that the king's left eye went blind for a while. Quickly Śāntideva put the sword back, and everybody realized that he was not just an ordinary person but a great siddha. The king and his ministers requested him to stay on, but he refused and advised the king to rule the country in accordance with the dharma and to establish twenty centers for Buddhist learning.

Having given this advice, he left the kingdom and journeyed toward the central part of India. When he arrived at the great Buddhist university of Nālandā, he was ordained by the preceptor Jayadeva and received the name Śāntideva. After his ordination, he lived among all the other great masters and mahāpaṇḍitas at Nālandā. Inwardly, he continuously received teachings from Mañjuśrī and, in his cell, wrote two scriptures known as *The Compendium of Training* and *The Compendium of Sūtras.*[1444] In his outer appearance, however, Śāntideva was just sleeping day and night. The only time his fellow monks would see him was at meals, when he would eat a huge amount of rice. After a while, everybody became quite upset about him. They said, "He is just wasting the offerings of food and drink that people make to the monastery out of devotion. Monastics are supposed to engage in study, reflection, and meditation, but he is doing none of these."

So the paṇḍitas discussed the matter and decided to expel him from Nālandā. They came up with a scheme to have the monks take turns reciting the scriptures. They thought this would make Śāntideva leave on his own, since he would have nothing to say. When his turn came to recite something, at first he refused to do it. Upon being repeatedly pressed, he eventually agreed and asked the monks to set up a seat for him. At this, some of them became a little suspicious, but nevertheless they built a throne and assembled with the intention to humiliate Śāntideva. He came, sat on the throne, and asked them, "What do you want me to teach, something that has already been taught or something that has never been taught before?" Eager to make fun of him, they cried, "Recite something new!" So Śāntideva recited the entire *Bodhicaryāvatāra* as spontaneous verse. It soon became clear to this audience of great scholars that his teaching was something extraordinary, and they started to memorize it. Eventually, Śāntideva came to verse IX.34:

> Once neither entities nor nonentities
> Remain before the mind,
> There is no other mental flux [either].
> Therefore, it is utter nonreferential peace.

At this point, he rose up into the sky, and soon his body disappeared completely, but his voice continued to be heard until the end of the last chapter. After his voice had stopped, the paṇḍitas compared what they had memorized and found that among them they had three versions. The Kashmiri scholars had memorized more than a thousand verses but had missed the verses of homage in the beginning. Of course, nobody had been paying attention at the beginning, since everybody thought that Śāntideva had no clue about anything. The scholars from eastern India had only seven hundred verses, again missing the homage and also the second and ninth chapters. The version of the scholars from central India was missing the homage and the tenth chapter on dedication. So they discussed the matter and finally decided to send three scholars to see Śāntideva and ask for his advice.

Tāranātha's account says that Śāntideva was staying in a place called Kaliṅga in Triliṅga, while other historical reports say that he lived in Śrī Dakṣiṇa in south India. When the three scholars found Śāntideva, they supplicated him to return to Nālandā, but he refused. They then asked, "So how should we study *The Compendium of Training* and *The Compendium of Sūtras* that you mentioned in the *Bodhicaryāvatāra*? Where are these three texts?" Śāntideva replied, "The first two texts are written on birch bark, and you can find them on the windowsill of my cell at Nālandā. As for the *Bodhicaryāvatāra*, the version of the scholars from central India is the correct one."[1445]

At that time, Śāntideva was living with five hundred other monks in a great Buddhist monastery located in a nearby forest full of deer and other animals These creatures were very tame and used to come to the humans in the monastery. However, many of the deer that Śāntideva's fellow monastics saw going into his room never came out again. They also noticed that the number of wild animals in the forest kept decreasing. So some monks started to peep through his window, and they saw Śāntideva eating the flesh of these animals. Especially for a monk, this was considered a really bad thing to do in India. However, when the monks accused him of doing this, Śāntideva instantly revived all the animals, and they came out of his room stronger and healthier than before. As usual, he was asked to stay and, as usual, he refused.

This time, though, Śāntideva did not just leave the monastery but left monasticism altogether. He became a wandering yogin practicing Vajrayāna in many unconventional ways. Thus, he acted just like other great siddhas, such as Nāropa and Maitrīpa, who had also been mahāpaṇḍitas at Nālandā and also left. Śāntideva went to southern India and engaged in contests of debate and magic with non-Buddhist scholars and yogins. He performed many supernatural activities for the benefit of others, such as miraculously providing food or stopping a war. Thus, he became one of the well-known mahāsiddhas of this time in India.

### *The Entrance to the Bodhisattva's Way of Life* and Its Ninth Chapter

As can be seen, *The Entrance to the Bodhisattva's Way of Life* was not created as a scholarly work but as a *dohā*, a spontaneous yogic song of realization. All mahāsiddhas, such as Saraha, Tilopa, and Nāropa, sang many such songs, and Milarepa's *Hundred Thousand Songs* are very well known by most Buddhists. In a similar way, Śāntideva delivered his text as extemporaneous verses in superb Sanskrit poetry. However, it is more than just a masterpiece of Sanskrit literature. More important for the Buddhist practitioner is that, because of the way this text originated, it also carries the blessing of the supreme realization of a great bodhisattva and mahāsiddha. At the same time, in terms of its content, Śāntideva's text describes the entire path of a bodhisattva in a lucid style that is very practice oriented and often sounds like personal advice. For these two reasons, this text is said to represent the lineage of practice and blessing.[1446] Thus, it is highly accessible even for ordinary beings who wish to follow the path of a bodhisattva and at the same time masterfully spreads both of the two great wings of this path: the knowledge of cultivating the profound view of emptiness and the compassionate means of vast skillful activities. Therefore, the text is said to represent the lineage of the unity of view and activity,[1447] starting with the cultivation of the mind of enlightenment as the root of all practices of the great vehicle and then presenting detailed instructions on all six perfections, from generosity up through supreme knowledge. For all these reasons, at all times, Buddhist scholars and practitioners alike consider Śāntideva's text to be very special, and it has enjoyed great popularity to the present day.

In this vein, its ninth chapter on the perfection of prajñā has to be seen as an organic and integral part of the whole text and not as standing in sharp contrast to the other chapters that seem so much more accessible and down-to-earth. Despite Śāntideva's rising into the sky while reciting the ninth chapter, it is not something far out. Just like the rest of *The Entrance to the Bodhisattva's Way of Life*, it is meant to be practiced, not just read or studied. People going through this text from the beginning are often quite shocked upon encountering the acuity and dissecting quality of the ninth chapter. It seems to annihilate the entire beautiful edifice of the path of compassion that Śāntideva so eloquently built throughout the first eight chapters. To put it bluntly, many feel that they plunge from "love and light" right into "brainy hairsplitting." However, after all that has been said about the project of Centrism, it should be clear that this is not at all what the ninth chapter is about. Rather, as the chapter's title says, it is about perfecting the most profound insight into the true nature of all phenomena. Moreover, Śāntideva uses reasoning in other chapters of his text too, particularly in the sixth on patience. Obviously, for him, intellect and compassion—or insight and means—are not mutually exclusive, nor do they obstruct each other. Rather, the whole text is an expression of the inseparable unity of wisdom and compassion. It is precisely through cultivating this unity that one practices the way of life of a bodhisattva. Thus, the other chapters of *The Entrance to the Bodhisattva's Way of Life* are in fact included in the ninth and support it, while the spirit of this chapter pervades them all. This is expressed by verse IX.1:

> All of these branches
> Were taught by the Sage for the sake of knowledge.
> Therefore, those who wish for suffering
> To subside should develop knowledge.

As for Śāntideva's view, Pawo Rinpoche quotes Atīśa as saying that his ultimate view is the undifferentiable unity of wisdom and the expanse of dharmas. His approach in the chapter on prajñā is aimed at opening our minds into wakeful spaciousness by relentlessly undermining all clinging to reference points. By mainly just formulating absurd consequences that follow from the positions of others, he clearly follows the style of a Consequentialist. In a way, Śāntideva surveys the whole range of Centrist opponents and arguments from the time of Nāgārjuna to the eighth century. For example, Nāgārjuna mainly challenged the realism of the Buddhist systematizers of the Abhidharma. Āryadeva concentrated on the ātman of the Enumerators and the theories of the Logicians and the Analyzers. Later, Candrakīrti launched his attack on Mere Mentalism and Bhāvaviveka's way of reasoning. Śāntideva addresses both Buddhist and non-Buddhist opponents but focuses on the systems of the Enumerators, Logicians, and Analyzers as well as on the notion of a creator god in the form of the Hindu deity Īśvara.

## Śāntideva's Presentation of the Two Realities

In verse IX.2 of his *Entrance to the Bodhisattva's Way of Life*, Śāntideva describes the two realities as follows:

> The seeming and the ultimate—
> These are asserted as the two realities.
> The ultimate is not the sphere of cognition.
> It is said that cognition is the seeming.

Here, "cognition" translates the Sanskrit term *buddhi* (Tib. blo), which has a wide range of meanings. In its most general sense, it refers to the basic cognitive capacity or intelligence of the mind, be it in sense perception or conceptual thinking. More specifically—as outlined in detail in the teachings on valid cognition—this term is applied to all facets of the entire spectrum of consciousness, be they conceptual or nonconceptual, ordinary or yogic. Both in this verse and in general, the usual translation of this term as "intellect" or "conception" suggests only the conceptual aspect of the mind.[1448] However, in the next verse, Śāntideva clearly refers to the entire way in which the world is seen:

> Thus, two kinds of world are seen:
> The one of yogins and the one of common people.[1449]

Almost all commentaries explicitly state that the term "cognition" refers not only to conceptual thinking but to all consciousnesses that entail the duality of subject and object; that is, it also applies to nonconceptual cognitions, such as sense perception. Pawo Rinpoche says:

> Thus, the native nature of all phenomena was not, is not, and cannot become the sphere of the consciousnesses of any ordinary beings, noble ones, learners, or nonlearners whatsoever, be they conceptual or nonconceptual [consciousnesses], perceptions, or inferential cognitions.[1450]

*The Sūtra of Richly Adorned* agrees:

> [The ultimate] is free from cognition and knowable objects.
> Measure and faculties have been relinquished.
> It is not the object of minds and consciousnesses.
> This is the object of those who are released.[1451]

Atīśa's *Entrance into the Two Realities* declares:

> The learned master Bhavya said
> That the scriptures are clear about
> [The ultimate] being realized neither through
> Conceptual nor nonconceptual consciousnesses.[1452]

Moreover, if it were just the intellect and its objects that constitute seeming reality, then sense perceptions and other nonconceptual consciousnesses would not be included in such a seeming reality. Either they would then have to be a third category of reality altogether or, if the definite number of only two realities is retained, sense perceptions and so on would have to be ultimate reality and thus the perceivers of the ultimate. As *The Sūtra of the King of Meditative Concentration* says:

> Neither the eye, the ear, nor the nose is valid cognition,
> Nor is the tongue, the body, or mental cognition valid cognition.

> If these sense faculties were valid cognition,
> Whom would the path of noble ones do any good?[1453]

Prajñākaramati's commentary on *The Entrance to the Bodhisattva's Way of Life* quotes *The Sūtra of Engaging in the Two Realities*:[1454]

> Devaputra, if ultimate reality were ultimately the sphere of body, speech, and mind, it would not fall into the category of "ultimate reality." It would be nothing but just seeming reality. However, Devaputra, ultimate reality is beyond all conventions. Actually, it is unarisen and unceasing, free from any object of expression or means of expression, free from knowable object and knower. It even transcends being an object of the omniscient wisdom that is endowed with the supreme of all aspects. This is ultimate reality.[1455]

As illustrated by such passages, the majority of sūtras and all Indian commentaries on Śāntideva's text support the reading of the above verse on the two realities as it was explained. Thus, no type of dualistic consciousness can perceive ultimate reality. Rather, it is often said that ultimate reality is seen by "personally experienced wisdom." There are two major objections that can be raised here:

1) In general, in Buddhism, the terms "cognition" and "consciousness" are equivalent. Thus, if the ultimate is not the sphere of cognition, this contradicts the explanation that the ultimate is the sphere of personally experienced wisdom. Thus, this verse cannot be taken literally.
2) It follows that the ultimate is not a knowable object, because the definition of knowable object is "that which is suitable to be taken as an object of a cognition."[1456]

The first objection does not apply to Śāntideva's verse, as this verse is surely not to be understood as negating that the personally experienced wisdom of the noble ones sees the nature of phenomena just as it is. When all mistaken clinging has completely vanished, the nondual unity of expanse and awareness in the mental continua of noble ones is without any conceptual entanglement. It is like a still pond when the wind has subsided: free from waves. In this unity of expanse and awareness, there are no reference points of subject and object. However, following this meditative equipoise, the consciousness during the phase of subsequent attainment applies the conventional terms "what is realized" and "what realizes" to expanse and awareness respectively. The expression "personally experienced wisdom realizes the ultimate" is used solely in this way. On the other hand, in meditative equipoise, there are not even the most subtle characteristics of cognition, such as realizing or not realizing. So how should any perceptual mode of self-awareness or a perceptual mode that is not self-awareness remain there? With this in mind, the reason Śāntideva did not assert personally experienced wisdom and such in this context was to reverse our clinging to characteristics with regard to the ultimate. Had he asserted personally experienced wisdom and such, it would be difficult to relinquish the Mere Mentalists' clinging to the existence of self-awareness. Moreover, from the perspective of debate, such an assertion would have amounted to a claim—such as "This is the self-awareness that we call the ultimate"—that could be attacked through reasoning. Also, one does not get any closer to the nature of phenomena merely by thinking, "The ultimate is the object of personally experienced wisdom." On the other hand, the elimination of all characteristics of reference points does not become an obstacle to approaching the nature of phenomena via cultivating and refining a conceptual mental image of the ultimate during the paths of accumulation and junction.

The second objection also does not apply. To state the definition of knowable object as "that which is suitable to be taken as an object of a cognition" is only taught in texts for beginners[1457] as a step in order to unfold their intelligence. However, these texts also give the definition of consciousness as "the cognition that is clear and aware of objects." Thus, not only in terms of definition but also in the actual process of perception, consciousness and the object that it cognizes mutually depend on each other. Thus, one can never ascertain one of them without the other. In general, knowing consciousnesses and knowable objects are only imagined by the ignorance of ordinary beings. Actually, there are no such entities. When the Buddha used such labels, he did so only provisionally for certain purposes, such as to communicate his teachings about ultimate reality.

So then is the ultimate a knowable object or not? For beginners, the following is taught: Through knowing the seeming, one just cognizes worldly conventional terms and events, but this has no greater significance. Through knowing the ultimate, one goes beyond cyclic existence. Therefore, the only correct object to be known is the ultimate. However, again, this is said only for a specific purpose, which is to introduce beginners to the nominal ultimate. For those who are already intensely trained in the path and then conceptualize the ultimate as a thing with characteristics, it is taught that the ultimate is not even a mere knowable object, since knower and knowable object are just conventions on the level of seeming reality. This is said in order to remove all mental reference points that cling to the ultimate in terms of subject and object. If these are not removed, they function as subtle obstacles to "actually" perceiving the ultimate as it is. The direct cognition of the ultimate only engages in the nature of phenomena just as it is, when there are no more remainders of knower, knowable object, true seeing, false seeing, and so on in such a cognition.

In brief, existence, nonexistence, and so on are nothing but what is grasped at by the mind through certain modes of apprehension. No matter how cognitions apprehend the nature of phenomena, this is not how it actually is. When analyzed, in principle, there is no phenomenon whatsoever that could be apprehended by cognition. Still, due to mistaken habituations, we imagine that we apprehend and seize "something," although it is unreal. Thus, some intrinsic "existence" or "nonexistence" that is more than just an imaginary notion apprehended by certain cognitions is impossible. As *The Sūtra That Unravels the Intention* says:

> Conditioned phenomena are neither conditioned nor unconditioned. As for unconditioned phenomena, they are also neither unconditioned nor conditioned. O son of good family, "conditioned phenomena" are words that are imputed by the Teacher. Words that are imputed by the Teacher originate from imagination and are expressed as conventional terms. What is expressed as the conventional terms of various imaginations is not at all established.[1458]

How does mind apprehend existence and nonexistence? To take an example, neither the horns of a cow nor the horns of a rabbit are real in the sense of intrinsically existing or intrinsically nonexisting. Still, when we see these two things that stand out from the head of a cow, we ascribe certain characteristics to them; we say, "These are horns" and "There are horns on the head of this cow." When we see a rabbit later, we do not see on its head the things we saw on the cow's head. Therefore, we ascribe the feature of nonexistence to the mere fact of not seeing here and now what we saw somewhere else before and say, "There are no horns on the head of a rabbit." So the common consensus that the horns of a cow exist while the horns of a rabbit do not exist comes from common conventional expressions. If there is no cognition that apprehends the existence of horns on a cow in the first place, there will also be no cognition that apprehends the nonexistence of horns on a rabbit. Thus, we may apprehend what we imagine as existence or nonexistence, but none of this is real as some kind of intrinsic existence or nonexistence apart from what appears to our mind. We may see a movie in which a cow and a rabbit appear, or we may dream of them, but once the movie stops or we wake up, we gain certainty that both the existence of the cow's horns and the nonexistence of the rabbit's horns were equally unreal. Even while watching such a movie or a dream, there is not the slightest difference between the existence of cow horns and the nonexistence of rabbit horns, or between the one being real and the other delusive. If even the very bases—cow and rabbit—to which we attribute certain features do not really exist in any way other than being mere appearances, what is there to say about any real specific features, such as the existence or nonexistence of horns, that we attribute to these bases?

In this way, all our mental operations of imputing existence, nonexistence, entities, nonentities, being real or delusive, and so on are compared to tying knots into space. When these dissolve, there is nothing else that binds us. Thus, what is conventionally called "seeing true reality" or "seeing the ultimate" is just like the subsiding of our grasping at a mirage as being water. At this point, neither do we see something that did not exist before nor does anything that existed before cease. It is not that the water of the mirage dried up, nor that the nonexistence of water is added. However, as long as our apprehension of this water has not dissolved, we tire ourselves out trying to get there to drink it. As soon as we become "dis-illusioned" from this fantasy of water, we know that such efforts are pointless, and we relax.

Again, the essential point here is to let go of our grasping that constantly superimposes or denies something with regard to the display of mere appearances. It is not a matter of annihilating or eradicating the appearance of things and producing some spacelike nothingness instead. As Śāntideva says:

> How something is seen, heard, or known
> Is not what is negated here.
> Rather, the object of refutation
> Is the cause for suffering, which is the conception of reality.[1459]

When our clinging to a mirage as being water stops, this obviously does not depend on whether or not the mere visual aspect of some shape and color that looks like water appears to us. Likewise, we now entertain ordinary worldly types of consciousness that take whatever appears to be real in just the way that it appears. On the Buddhist path, we might furthermore try to make these appearances nonexistent through the remedy of a misunderstood and contrived emptiness. Thus, we might cling to the ultimate as being like an extinguished flame or like the empty space that is left after an old house has collapsed. Once both of these mistaken cognitions—clinging to real existence or some kind of nonexistence—have subsided, in terms of the plain appearance of illusionlike phenomena when their specific causes have come together versus their nonappearance when their causes are incomplete, there is no difference between the time when superimposition and denial were still operating and the time when these have vanished. However, there is a difference as to whether the nature of these appearances is realized or not. Therefore, from the point of such realization onward, one is not under the sway of either appearances or the lack thereof, much like someone who, while dreaming, recognizes this dream as a dream and just enjoys its appearances. This is what it means to abide within cyclic existence without being affected by its flaws, just like a lotus grows in muddy water without being stained by it.

Since such realization is undeceiving, it is called "seeing what is true." As it is the opposite of worldly seeing, it may also be called "not seeing anything." Since it is the opposite of reification, it is expressed as "seeing emptiness." It is also referred to as "being released from empty and nonempty," because neither something empty nor something nonempty is observed. Since emptiness is nothing but a name, it is also described as "not seeing emptiness." Because it is the source of all positive qualities, it is designated as "seeing the emptiness endowed with the supreme of all aspects." It is called "seeing identitylessness," for it is the opposite of clinging to personal and phenomenal identities. Since it is the opposite of both clinging to a self and clinging to the lack of a self, it is said to be "seeing the genuine self." As any notion of a mind has vanished, it is labeled as "mind having vanished." It is also referred to as "realizing or seeing one's own mind," because the primordial basic nature of one's own mind is realized in just the primordial way it is. When "not seeing anything" is explained as "seeing what is true," this is to be understood just like our immediate certainty that we see space when we do not see anything. As the Buddha said:

> Beings constantly use the words, "I see space."
> You should examine the point of how you see space.
> Those who see in this way see all phenomena.
> I am not able to explain seeing through another example.

## The Indian Commentaries on the Bodhicaryāvatāra

Tibetan sources say that there existed more than one hundred Indian commentaries on *The Entrance to the Bodhisattva's Way of Life*, but only a few of them have survived. The only one that is preserved in Sanskrit is Prajñākaramati's *Commentary on the Difficult Points*. All others exist only in Tibetan translations.[1460] In due order, volume 100 of the *Tengyur* lists the following ten texts as commentaries on *The Entrance to the Bodhisattva's Way of Life*:

Prajñākaramati (ca. 950–1000). *Commentary on the Difficult Points of The Entrance to the Bodhisattva's Way of Life.* (Bodhicaryāvatārapañjikā. Byang chub kyi spyod pa la 'jug pa'i dka' 'grel). Commentary on chapters 1–9. P5273, pp. 1.1.7–113.1.5.

Anonymous (possibly Dānaśīla). *Commentary on the Difficult Points in the Exposition of The Entrance to the Bodhisattva's Way of Life.* (Bodhisattvacaryāvatāravivṛttipañjikā. Byang chub sems dpa'i spyod pa la 'jug pa'i rnam par bshad pa'i dka' 'grel). P5274, pp. 113.1.5–141.3.5.

Kalyāṇadeva (11th c.?). *The Excellent Composition of The Entrance to the Bodhisattva's Way of Life.* (Bodhisattvacaryāvatārasaṃskāra. Byang chub sems dpa'i sypod pa la 'jug pa'i legs par sbyar ba). P5275, pp. 143.1.1–186.4.7.

Kṛṣṇapāda (10th/11th c.). *The Ascertainment of the Points in The Entrance to the Bodhisattva's Way of Life That Are Difficult to Understand.* (Bodhisattvacaryāvatāraduravabodhanirṇayanāmagranthā. Byang chub sems dpa'i spyod pa la 'jug pa'i rtogs par dka' ba'i gnas gtan la dbab pa). P5276, pp. 186.4.7–189.2.4.

Vairocanarakṣita (11th c.). *Commentary on the Difficult Points of The Entrance to the Bodhisattva's Way of Life.* (Bodhisattvacaryāvatārapañjikā. Byang chub sems dpa'i spyod pa la 'jug pa'i dka' 'grel). P5277, pp. 189.2.5–218.5.7.

Anonymous. *Commentary on the Difficult Points of the Knowledge Chapter.* (Prajñāparicchedapañjikā. Shes rab le'u'i dka' 'grel). Commentary on chapter 9 only. P5278, pp. 218.5.7–228.2.5.

Anonymous. *Exposition of The Entrance to the Bodhisattva's Way of Life.* (Bodhisattvacaryāvatāravivṛtti. Byang chub sems dpa'i spyod pa la 'jug pa'i rnam par bshad pa). Commentary on chapters 9 and 10. P5279, pp. 228.2.5–233.4.2.[1461]

Dharmapāla[1462] (ca. 1000). *A Summary of The Entrance to the Bodhisattva's Way of Life in Thirty-six Points.* (Bodhisattvacaryāvatāraṣattriṃśātapiṇḍārtha. Byang chub sems dpa'i spyod pa la 'jug pa'i don sum cu rtsa drug bsdus pa). P5280, pp. 233.4.2–235.2.5.

Dharmapāla. *A Summary of The Entrance to the Bodhisattva's Way of Life.* (Bodhisattvacaryāvatārapiṇḍārtha. Byang chub sems dpa'i spyod pa la 'jug pa'i don bsdus pa). P5281, pp. 235.2.5–235.5.8.

Vibhūticandra (12th/13th c.). *Commentary on the Intention of The Entrance to the Bodhisattva's Way of Life, Called The Illumination of the Distinctive Features.* (Bodhicaryāvatāratātparyapañjikāviśeṣadyotanīnāma. Byang chub kyi spyod pa la 'jug pa'i dgongs pa'i 'grel pa khyad par gsal byed ces bya ba). P5282, pp. 235.5.8–281.3.4.[1463]

Considering the fact that P5279 is just a part of P5274 and that the two works of Dharmapāla are only brief outlines of Śāntideva's text, this leaves us with seven actual commentaries on *The Entrance to the Bodhisattva's Way of Life* (P5278 is on the ninth chapter only). From among these, Prajñākaramati's extensive work is regarded as the most important commentary.[1464]

## Selected Tibetan Commentaries

As for Tibetan commentaries on *The Entrance to the Bodhisattva's Way of Life*, a huge number have been written throughout many centuries. Apart from Pawo Tsugla Trengwa's commentary, I have consulted the following ones:

*A Commentary on The Entrance to the Bodhisattva's Way of Life* (Byang chub sems dpa'i spyod pa la 'jug pa'i 'grel pa), the earliest extant Tibetan commentary by Sönam Tsemo (1142–1182), the second head of the Sakya school.[1465]

*The Ocean of Good Explanations* (Byang chub sems dpa'i spyod pa la 'jug pa'i 'grel pa legs bshad rgya mtsho) by the Sakya master Ngülchu Togme[1466] (1295–1369), a widely used commentary.

*A Stepping-Stone for the Children of the Victors* (Byang chub sems dpa'i spyod pa la 'jug pa'i rnam bshad rgyal sras 'jug ngogs) by Gyaltsab Darma Rinchen (1364–1462), one of the two main disciples of Tsongkhapa.

*The Lamp for the Middle Path* (Spyod 'jug 'bru 'grel dbu ma'i lam gyi sgron ma) by the Drugpa Kagyü master Padma Karpo (1527–1596).

*An Easily Understandable Explanation of the Words and the Meaning of the Chapter on Knowlege, The Ketaka Jewel* (Shes rab le'u'i tshig don go sla bar bshad pa nor bu ke ta ka) by the Nyingma master Ju Mipham Gyamtso[1467] (1846–1912).

*The Drops of Nectar That Are the Excellent Words of Guru Mañjughoṣa* (Byang chub sems dpa'i spyod pa la 'jug pa'i 'grel pa 'jam dbyangs bla ma'i zhal lung bdud rtsi'i thig pa) by Mipham Rinpoche's disciple Khenpo Künzang Pelden[1468] (ca. 1870–1940), which preserves many of the famous oral instructions on Śāntideva's text by Dza Patrul Rinpoche Orgyen Jigme Chökyi Wangbo[1469] (1808–1887).

## Introduction to Pawo Tsugla Trengwa's *Commentary on The Entrance to the Bodhisattva's Way of Life*

In the Karma Kagyü school, Pawo Rinpoche's commentary on *The Entrance to the Bodhisattva's Way of Life* is considered both the standard commentary on this text and—together with the Eighth Karmapa's *Chariot of the Tagbo Siddhas*—the standard presentation of Madhyamaka, especially in its Consequentialist approach. Since the Second Pawo Rinpoche was a disciple of the Eighth Karmapa, his commentary preserves many of the Centrist pith instructions of Karmapa Mikyö Dorje.

Of all the commentaries on Śāntideva's text, it is by far the most voluminous (975 folios). However, not only its length distinguishes it from other Tibetan commentaries. First, in terms of its scriptural sources, there is an unparalleled abundance of at times extensive quotes from the sūtras to support the main points of the commentary. It is the only commentary that gives synopses of the relevant passages from the major Indian commentaries for each topic of the text.[1470] In addition, it quotes a number of the earliest Tibetan commentaries, such as those written by the Sakya master Sabsang Mati Panchen Jamyang Lodrö[1471] (1294–1376) and the Kadampa master Tsonaba Chenbo Sherab Sangbo[1472] (fourteenth century).

In terms of its approach and contents, Pawo Rinpoche's commentary generally follows the Consequentialist brand of Madhyamaka. Usually, Centrist texts instruct us in relinquishing all reference points but hardly mention what it might be like when the mind actually *is* free from all reference points. Having followed the thorough Centrist dissolution of reference points, unlike most other such texts, Pawo Rinpoche's commentary also offers us a few glimpses of the experience of a mind free from reference points. Thus, having made sure that there is no ground to stand on through the typical Consequentialist approach of relentlessly pulverizing our ordinary world, he does not shy away from describing the resultant groundlessness in somewhat more positive, experiential terms. In this way, he addresses the question of what happens when Centrist reasoning has been successful in emptying our mind of its mistaken constructions and grasping. Of course, by its very nature, the experiential ultimate result of the Centrist path is beyond imagination. However, it is clearly not a mere negation or blank nothingness. Rather, when both the objects of refutation and their remedy—reasoning—dissolve, they do so within the empty and luminous expanse of our mind. From the perspective of this expanse, all analyses and their objects, including the mind that performs all these analyses, are still somewhat externally oriented and essentially dualistic. Finally, mind turns its looking "inside" toward the center of its own open space that is completely without direction or duality. In the words of Pawo Rinpoche:

> Apart from all phenomena just being mere imputations, they neither abide as any nature whatsoever, nor do they abide as anything at all. Just this is what is seen as the very expanse of mind that is empty and luminous. This puts you in a position where you have complete power over everything you could possibly wish for, just as if all phenomena were resting in the palm of your hand. Thus, . . . compassion for the assembly of sentient beings who do not realize this in the same way wells up unbearably. . . . To the same extent that great compassion

> increases, also this very [realization] that, primordially, nothing can be observed . . . grows and increases. This is the ultimate seeing which is like the orb of the sun. When it becomes stable and increases in such a way, great compassion—which is like the light rays of the sun—will grow even more than before. [Beings with such realization] do not behold sentient beings, but great compassion still flowers in them. They do not behold themselves either, but they still lend their support to all sentient beings. They do not behold anything to be attained whatsoever, but they still establish beings in great enlightenment. Just as there is no place whatsoever to go to beyond space, they do not behold anybody who would go somewhere beyond, but they still display [the activity of] liberating sentient beings from cyclic existence.[1473]

and

> Once clinging in terms of superimposition and denial has come to an end in such a way, just this empty and luminous nature of phenomena in which there is nothing to be removed or to be added is the fundamental state of phenomena. This is expressed as primordial nirvāṇa as such.[1474]

In addition to being a commentary on *The Entrance to the Bodhisattva's Way of Life*, Pawo Rinpoche's text provides several long accounts on such topics as Madhyamaka in general, the distinction between Autonomists and Consequentialists, prajñā, emptiness, the two realities, and the nature and qualities of Buddhahood. It decribes the four major Buddhist philosophical systems and how the great vehicle represents the words of the Buddha. In addressing the issue of so-called Shentong-Madhyamaka, he also elaborates on the lineage of vast activity and shows that it is not the same as Mere Mentalism.

As for the structure of Pawo Rinpoche's specific commentary on the ninth chapter of *The Entrance to the Bodhisattva's Way of Life*, its brief outline is presented through five main points:

1) Teaching the benefit of prajñā, or knowledge (verse 1)
2) Identifying the nature and scope of this knowledge (2–55)
   - Showing that everything that is contained in the two realities is emptiness (2–29)
   - Demonstrating that realizing emptiness constitutes the path of bodhisattvas (30–55)
3) Outlining the actual way to meditate on emptiness (56–110)
   - Meditating on personal identitylessness (56–77)
   - Meditating on phenomenal identitylessness (78–110)

4) Refuting reification (111–150)
   - Showing that there are no means to prove the notion of real existence (111–115)
   - Teaching the means to invalidate this notion (116–150)
5) The result of having meditated on emptiness (151–167)
   - Transcending cyclic existence through not being carried away by afflictions (151–155)
   - Not falling into the one-sided peace of nirvāṇa through compassion (156–165)
   - Protecting all sentient beings (166–167)

# 8

# *The Ninth Chapter of Pawo Rinpoche's Commentary on* The Entrance to the Bodhisattva's Way of Life

## Exposition of *The Entrance to the Bodhisattva's Way of Life*

## The Essence of the Immeasurable, Profound, and Vast Ocean of the Dharma of the Great Vehicle

## The Ninth Chapter on Knowledge

Completely free from conceptions and concepts,
Not an object of cognition, suchness,
To her, this perfection of knowledge,
I prostrate in the manner of such realization.

Even the arising of doubt about her
Is able to tear existence into shreds.
I shall comment on the chapter on knowledge
That elucidates inconceivable true reality.

Through such efforts in perfect meditative stability [as explained in the eighth chapter], one manifests [the various types of] knowledge up to the knowledge of termination and nonarising. Therefore, the explanation of the perfection of knowledge follows right after [the explanation of] meditative stability.

Here, Vibhūticandra says:

Without meditative stability, knowledge does not originate.
If calm abiding does not exist, this also does not exist.[1475]

On this first [verse] that establishes the connection [with the preceding chapter], Kalyāṇadeva [comments]:

> Since from settling in meditative equipoise a cognition of true reality will arise . . .[1476]

*The Great Commentary on the Difficult Points* reads:

> Because the perfection of knowledge that has the name superior insight is taught . . .[1477]

*The Small Commentary on the Difficult Points of the Knowledge Chapter Only* says:

> Superior insight is taught after the explanation of meditative stability that has the defining characteristic of representing the assembly of the causes for the accumulation of merit, such as generosity, as well as the cause for the accumulation of wisdom, which is calm abiding. In order to [teach] it . . .[1478]

In this way, the connection [with the preceding chapters] is established.

You might raise this objection: "It is stated, 'Without superior insight, there is also no calm abiding.' But if superior insight is the topic of this chapter, then, since meditative stability must arise from superior insight, the order of the previous and this [ninth] chapter [in Śāntideva's text] must be reversed. Or, otherwise, the mistake of mutually dependent conceptions[1479] would follow, because superior insight does not arise without relying on calm abiding, and calm abiding too does not arise without relying on superior insight."

In those of sharpest faculties, superior insight that fully qualifies as such arises first, and, through their settling one-pointedly in this with meditative equipoise, the purpose [of calm abiding] is fulfilled too. In those of weaker faculties, [642][1480] calm abiding arises through settling [the mind] while focusing on merely partial superior insight. Through this, the knowledge that ensues from meditation—superior insight—increases further. On the basis of that, in turn, stable calm abiding comes about in the way that a bird flaps its [two] wings. In this way, unified calm [abiding] and superior [insight] of the respective ground become very stable. Thus, one proceeds on the path of partial concordance with definite distinction.[1481]

Then, the knowledge of one single moment sees the nature of phenomena. This is the arising of the path of seeing, that is, [the arising] of superior insight that fully qualifies as such. On the path of meditation, this very [insight] becomes more and more stable in the form of unified calm [abiding] and superior [insight]. Consequently, at the end of the seventh ground, superior insight with pure observation in [meditative] equipoise and subsequent [attainment] arises.

Since this becomes [even] more stable, all meditative concentrations are perfected. At the end of the continuum of the tenth ground, one-pointed meditative concentration and the knowledge that knows extinction and nonarising—the knowledge that knows the means for the extinction of contaminations—are inseparable. This is the vajralike meditative concentration that vanquishes all stains so that they never arise [again]. This is true and perfect enlightenment of all phenomena through the knowledge of one single moment. It is the unwaning achievement of the inseparability of ultimate calm abiding—not rising from the great cessation—and ultimate superior insight—the knowledge of the suchness and the extent [of phenomena].

Therefore, both calm [abiding] and superior [insight] have limitless subdivisions on each [ground], starting from a beginner with very weak faculties up through the ground of a Buddha. When specified in terms of [different] sentient beings, the development of calm [abiding] and superior [insight] in individual persons is something that should be guided by spiritual friends according to the constitutions and faculties of these [individuals]. However, nobody is able to write down all the possible ways of doing so.

This means that these [calm abiding and insight] are just taught in a very general manner in terms of the main issues. Therefore, the meditative concentration that focuses on approximately concordant superior insight is called meditative stability. That which is generated through this, that is, [643] the actual knowledge that sees true reality, [is called] superior insight. Thus, they are taught in the manner of cause and effect.

The actual text has five parts:

1) The benefit of knowledge
2) The identification of knowledge
3) The way to meditate on emptiness
4) The refutation of reification
5) The result of meditating on emptiness

## 1. The Benefit of Knowledge

> **All of these branches**
> **Were taught by the Sage for the sake of knowledge.**
> **Therefore, those who wish for suffering**
> **To subside should develop knowledge.** [1][1482]

**All of these** five **branches**, such as generosity, **were taught by the Sage**, the Blessed One, solely **for the sake of** developing the main body or result, **knowledge**. This is the case because the result—the accumulation of wisdom (knowledge)—arises from the cause—the accumulation of merit, which is the five [perfections], such as generosity. *The Mother* [*Sūtras*][1483] say:

> Without the accumulation of merit being gathered, the perfection of knowledge will not even come to one's ears.

**Therefore, those who wish for** all **suffering**—their own and others'—**to subside should** not be content with just five [perfections], such as generosity, but should make further serious efforts to solely **develop knowledge.** You might disagree and say, "This contradicts the explanation that one needs knowledge before [one develops] the five [perfections], such as generosity:

> As for generosity, knowledge is that which precedes generosity.
> Ethics, patience, vigor, and meditative stability are just like that."

This refers to the five [perfections], such as plain generosity, which are like [people] who are born blind. If they are led by a guide—knowledge—they will also become [true] perfections. Therefore, this teaches that they need knowledge in order to be presentable as [true] perfections. But since knowledge also does not arise without the accumulation of merit, the plain five [perfections], such as generosity, are implied here. As it is said in *The Precious Garland*: [644]

> Due to small merit, about this dharma
> Not even the slightest doubt arises.
> Even the arising of doubt about this
> Will tear existence into shreds.[1484]

## 2. The Identification of Knowledge

This has two parts:

1) The proof that the objects to be known—the two realities—are emptiness
2) The proof that the knowledge of this is the path

## 2.1. The Proof That the Objects to Be Known—the Two Realities—Are Emptiness

This has four parts:

1) The classification of the two realities
2) Their definitions
3) Establishing the [two realities]
4) Removing objections to that

### 2.1.1. The Classification of the Two Realities

> **The seeming and the ultimate—**
> **These are asserted as the two realities.** [2ab]

The nature of these [two realities] has already been taught extensively in the general topics of the fourth chapter. Still, a brief summary is given here:

That which is to be understood are **the seeming** reality **and the ultimate** reality: **These** temporary knowable objects are definitely accepted **as the two realities** by the great being Śāntideva himself when he says "**asserted.**"

In this context, [the etymology of "seeming" (literally "all-deceptive") is as follows:] "All" is a plural and has the meaning of [all phenomena] that appear in various forms. "Deceptive" has the meaning of delusive: This means that since [appearances] are not real in the way that they appear, they are nothing but mere vanities, nullities, and insignificances.

You might wonder, "Why then is the seeming presented as a reality?" This is [done] provisionally for the sake of conventions in order to guide the world. It is presented as a provisional reality, because worldly people cling to [appearances] as being real in just the way that they appear, and also because causes and results appear to perform their functions unmistakenly from the perspective of provisional reasoning. It is not a stable reality, [however,] because it does not withstand analysis and because it does not appear as an object of the meditative equipoise of the noble ones.

[The etymology of "ultimate" (literally "supreme object") is as follows:] It is called "object" because one engages in the fundamental nature in dependence on the seeming, and because it is what is to be strived for. It is "supreme" because it is essential for those who wish for liberation and undeceiving with respect to the result, which is Buddhahood. Thus, it is a term for [such] a common locus.

Through this [etymology], [645] the assertion [of others] that "ultimately real" is a term for a basis of attribution and an attribute is also eliminated.

This [ultimate reality] is what abides as the actual nature of all phenomena. It is the object of the profound meditative equipoise of noble ones. Therefore, it is presented as a stable reality in dependence on the seeming. [However,] it is not [such a stable reality] independently through its nature, because the Buddhas themselves behold neither real nor delusive phenomena.

(The word "and" [in line 2a] is both a term that differentiates "the seeming and the ultimate which is other than that" and a collective term [indicating that] "both of these are equal insofar as they are just realities.")

### 2.1.2. Their Definitions

> **The ultimate is not the sphere of cognition.**
> **It is said that cognition is the seeming. [2cd]**

You might say, "However, in this dichotomy of the two realities, what is ultimate reality and what is seeming reality?"

[The first one] is that for which it does not matter whether Buddhas have arrived or not; it is what could not be contrived even by the Buddha. He taught:

> Even I did not behold it, do not behold it, and will not behold it.

Thus, the native nature of all phenomena was not, is not, and cannot become the sphere of the consciousnesses of any ordinary beings, noble ones, learners, or nonlearners whatsoever, be they conceptual or nonconceptual [consciousnesses], perceptions, or inferential cognitions. For this expanse of dharmas just as it is, the conventional term "ultimate reality" is used.

You might object, "What do you mean? If it is not an object of any consciousness whatsoever, one is not even able to focus on it. Therefore, how can it at the same time be presented as the ultimate?" In general, in all this labeling with conventional terms, it is not the case that the direct observer of a given phenomenon is doing the labeling. [For example,] when one labels [something] with the conventional term "blue utpala,"[1485] the observer of that is a [visual] sense consciousness. But this [consciousness itself] does not conceive of the attribute that is the name "utpala" or the attribute "blue color," [646] because it is nothing but mere direct and nonconceptual experiencing.

That which labels with conventional terms is a subsequent apprehending conception of this [direct experience]. This [involves] the presumption that the preceding nonconceptual sense consciousness—the [actual] experiencer—is the apprehending conception itself. By apprehending the object—the mere utpala [flower]—as something else, the [subsequent conception] conceives of it as name and color while presuming, "I see this." [This] is like a carpenter who presumes, "I have made this" with respect to a clay pot that was made by a potter.

Also, when one thoroughly analyzes a continuum on the seeming level, [one finds that] the utpala at the time when it is seen and the utpala at the time when it is [conceptually] apprehended are different entities. Furthermore, the sense consciousness that experiences it and the apprehending conception are different entities [as well]. They are just like a stream of water. If perception does not conceive of the object and conception does not experience it, which consciousness focuses on what kind of utpala? [This is the point here,] because, if one analyzes, this is nothing but seeing utter mistakenness.

For example, when one [mentally] analyzes the Brahmā world, [such an investigation] is nothing but an analysis through imagining [this world within] one's own cognition that thinks, "The Brahmā world is something like this." [Thus,] this [cognition] possesses the aspect of an object generality in the form of the Brahmā world. However, through that, the Brahmā world does not come here, and neither does the analyst go to the Brahmā world. Hence, this [type of analysis] mistakes the analysis of one's own mind through one's own mind for [an actual analysis when one directly faces the Brahmā world and thus may say,] "I analyze the Brahmā world." Consequently, [even] focusing on the ultimate is also nothing but this kind of [mistakenness]. Therefore, **the ultimate is** definitely **not the sphere of cognition.**

You might say, "However, since the seeming is also nothing different, it is not the sphere of cognition." [Ultimately,] this is very true indeed. Therefore, it is definitely stated that all phenomena have one single reality and that just this that is called "real" or "delusive" is not observed. Nevertheless, in order for naïve beings to be able to leave their fear behind, the provisional presentation of subject and object [647] is [given as] something that leaves the status quo of mere common worldly consensus as it is. Thus, naïve beings are guided by using the conventional term "seeming reality."

You might wonder, "Why is the ultimate not the sphere of cognition?" Because **it is** asserted **that cognition,** or consciousness, **is the** very **seeming** and it is impossible for the seeming to take the ultimate as its object.

[You continue,] "Through what is it certain that the ultimate is not an object of cognition?" This is certain through the reasoning of the inconceivable nature of phenomena. When the great noble ones settle in meditative equipoise within the expanse of dharmas, then this becomes all the more subtle and inconceivable the more they settle [within it]. This is so for the following reasons: That very something that is settled in meditative equipoise and the one who settles it will subside, while one is not able to realize a limit of the expanse of dharmas. Even the Thus-Gone Ones do not state any extent of the expanse of dharmas.

Thus, it is seen that the expanse of dharmas is not an object of speech, reflection, or expression. It is for just this [type of seeing] that the conventional terms "penetrating the nature of phenomena" and "beholding ultimate reality" are used. The conventional term "personally experienced wisdom" is then used for the very knowledge that does not observe the characteristics of discursiveness in terms of subject and object. Thus, the nature of phenomena is not seen through apprehending a subject and an object. Rather, if one knows that subject and object are not observable, one engages in the nature of phenomena. Therefore, [the expression] "personally experienced wisdom realizes the nature of phenomena" is a conventional term that is used based on something else. However, in no way does this abide in the mode of subject, object, something to be realized, and a realizer in the way that these are imputed by cognition. Subject, object, something to be realized, and a realizer are merely entities that are based on superimposition; they are never entities that exist in this way through a nature of their own.

### 2.1.3. Establishing the Two Realities

> **Thus, two kinds of world are seen:**
> **The one of yogins and the one of common people.** [648]
> **Here, the world of common people**
> **Is invalidated by the world of yogins.** [3]
>
> **Also the yogins, due to differences in insight,**
> **Are overruled by successively superior ones** [4ab]

You might object, "Of course, the seeing of ordinary beings is not ultimate. Nevertheless, since the ultimate is the direct object of the noble ones, it is reasonable that the vision of the noble ones is ultimate." In order to teach the answer to that, [the text says]: **Thus,** in the **world, two kinds of** the seeming **are seen: the** seeing **of common** worldly **people and the** seeing **of yogins** who have entered the [Buddhist] path.

Here, common worldly people are of two [kinds]: average individuals who are not engaged in philosophical systems and non-Buddhists who are engaged in philosophical systems. As for yogins, there are many types, classified by the proponents of the four [Buddhist] philosophical systems, the five paths, and the ten grounds on [the paths of] seeing and meditation.

For [all of] them, [it is true] that the seeing of the respective former ones is invalidated by the reasonings of the respective following ones. This is the case for the following reasons: The assertions of individuals who are not engaged in philosophical systems are invalidated by the reasonings of those non-Buddhists who are engaged in philosophical systems, that is, those non-Buddhists who are trained in linguistics and valid cognition and who regard the others as just like cattle. [On the other hand,] the [Buddhist] seers take people who cling to assertions as their objects of compassion.

**Here, common people** may be engaged in philosophical systems or not, but they all cling to the five aggregates as being clean, an identity, blissful, and permanent. **Their world is invalidated by the world of** the Buddhist **yogins** who are the Followers of the Great Exposition, that is, through their reasonings of the seeming level that demonstrate that [the aggregates] are unclean, identityless, suffering, and impermanent.

**Also,** as for **the yogins** themselves, **due to** the great **differences in** higher or lower **insight** that exist [among them]—such as having purified their continua or not, or being of sharp or weak faculties—the assertions of the respectively inferior ones are **overruled by** the reasonings of **successively superior ones.** [649] [As a consequence, the former] are not able to give answers that are concordant with the dharma.

The assertion of the Followers of the Great Exposition that object and consciousness [actually] meet is invalidated by the Sūtra Followers' reasoning that negates the lack of an aspect. The assertion of both the Followers of the Great Exposition and the Sūtra Followers that specifically characterized referents and consciousnesses are substantially established is invalidated by the Mere Mentalists' reasoning that refutes outer objects. The assertion of the Mere Mentalists that mind is real is invalidated by the Centrists' [reasonings of] "freedom from unity and multiplicity" and "the negation of arising from the four possibilities."

Surely the emptiness of the Centrists is not deliberately hit by invalidations through reasoning. Nevertheless, during the phase of engagement through devoted interest with [its stages of] heat, peak, patience, and supreme [phemomenon] and during direct engagement in this [emptiness] on the ten grounds, the presumptions that any previous seeing [of emptiness] was perfect become just like games of little children when the respectively following [kinds of seeing] are attained. Even the manner in which someone on the tenth ground beholds [emptiness] does not remain on the ground of a Buddha. Therefore, [emptiness] is not an object of the cognitions of hearers, solitary realizers, and bodhisattvas. Due to the complete change of state of the five aggregates, the Thus-Gone Ones do not have any flux of discriminations. Hence, [emptiness] is also not an object of [something like the] cognition of Buddhas, because they do not have [such a thing as] cognition.

You might say, "It is an object of the knowledge [of a Buddha]." Since true, perfect enlightenment of all phenomena in every way has been found, no other object that is something to be known is left over. Furthermore, since such a knowledge without something to be known is untenable, ultimately, Buddhas do not have anything called "knowing" or "not knowing" at all.

### 2.1.4. Removing Objections

This has two parts:

1) The brief introduction
2) The detailed explanation

### 2.1.4.1. The Brief Introduction

> **Through examples that are asserted by both,**
> **While not analyzing what serves the result.** [4cd]

**In the way that worldly people see things,**
**They conceive them as facts**
**But not as illusionlike.**
**Herein lies the dispute between yogins and worldly people.** [5]

[650] You might argue, "However, if all cognitions were mistaken, consciousnesses that apprehend form and such would be completely nonexistent, since mistakenness is something nonexistent itself. If this were the case, it would be impossible for forms, sounds, and such to appear."

Forms, sounds, and such as well as the cognitions that apprehend them are not entities that appear due to the fact that they exist. Rather, they are solely entities that appear through the delusive appearance of dependently originating collections and do not [really] exist. This is the case because one is able to illustrate it **through examples,** such as illusions and dreams, **that are** unanimously **asserted** as entities that appear while not existing **by both** common people and yogins, or proponents and opponents.

Again, you might say, "If all cognitions were mistaken, then even the five perfections, such as the mental state of generosity, would not be the path." They represent the cause—the accumulation of merit—from which **the result**—the accumulation of wisdom—arises. Since Buddhahood is attained due to these [two accumulations], for the time being, **while not analyzing** whether they are real, delusive, existent, or nonexistent, one engages in them by means of the mere correct seeming, **which serves** to attain this state [of Buddhahood]. Thus, there is no mistake here.

In brief, **worldly people**—whether they are engaged in philosophical systems or not—think, "**Things,** such as forms, are real **in** just this **way that** we **see** them." Thus, **these** [people] **conceive** mere appearances and experiences **as facts, but** do **not** understand **them** as entities that do not withstand analysis nor **as illusionlike** [phenomena] that appear but are without nature. **Here, in** this explanation that [things] are illusionlike, **the dispute between yogins and worldly people** has its start. As [the sūtras] state:

> Sentient beings like abodes and wish for objects.
> To abide in grasping and be foolishly ignorant without any skill is like darkness.
> The dharma to be attained is without abiding and without grasping.
> Therefore, dispute happens in the worlds.

and

> The world disputes with me, but I [651] do not dispute with the world.

### 2.1.4.2. The Detailed Explanation

This has eight parts:
(Teaching the six [points] that remove objections about the seeming)

1) Removing contradictions to valid cognition
2) Removing contradictions to scripture
3) Removing the consequence that no merit would come about by offering to the Buddha
4) Removing the consequence that sentient beings would not be reborn after death
5) Removing the consequence that no negativity would occur from killing
6) Removing the consequence that even the Buddha would circle again [in cyclic existence]

([Teaching] the two [points] that remove objections about the ultimate)

7) Removing the consequence that an illusion would not exist even on the seeming level
8) Removing the consequence that there would be no support for talking [about cyclic existence]

### 2.1.4.2.1. Removing Contradictions to Valid Cognition

> **Also perceptions of forms and such**
> **Are based on common consensus and not on valid cognition.**
> **This is delusive, just as the common consensus**
> **That something unclean is clean and so on.** [6]

You might think, "Forms, sounds, and such factually exist, because they are directly experienced." **Also perceptions of** seeing **forms and such are** nothing but the arising of cognitions that [perceive] these [objects], which is [in itself entirely] **based on** mere **common** worldly **consensus.** This means that such [perception] is [just something that comes from our] habituation through clinging to successive chains [of events] **and not** something that is established through **valid cognition.** This is like the following: Because of one's habituation to latent tendencies of apprehending water, clinging to water arises even when one sees an illusory river. Also *The Sūtra of the King of Meditative Concentration* says:

> Neither the eye, the ear, nor the nose is valid cognition,
> Nor is the tongue, the body, or mental cognition valid cognition.
> If these sense faculties were valid cognition,
> Whom would the path of noble ones do any good?[1486]

In *The Great Commentary*, one finds the following quotation [from Nāgārjuna's *Praise to the Inconceivable*]:

> If just this that the sense faculties observe
> Were true reality,
> Naïve beings would be aware of true reality.
> So what would be the point of realizing true reality then?[1487]

Therefore, one grasps at something that [merely] appears while it does not exist [and takes it] to be something that is directly [652] seen. **This is just as the common consensus that** an **unclean thing**—such as the body, which is the source of feces and urine—**is clean.** The term "**and so on**" includes [other cases of common consensus, for example, the notion that] an impermanent thing like water that flows downward is a permanent water stream. Such is of an unreal and **delusive** nature.

### 2.1.4.2.2. Removing Contradictions to Scriptsure

> **For the sake of introducing worldly people,**
> **The protector taught in terms of entities.**
> **In actuality, these are not momentary phenomena.**
> **You might object, "On the seeming level, they are incompatible."** [7]
>
> **There is no flaw in that they are the seeming of yogins.**
> **When compared to worldly people, this refers to seeing true reality.**
> **Otherwise, the ascertainment**
> **That women are impure would be invalidated by the world.** [8]

The Followers of the Great Exposition and the Sūtra Followers in our own [Buddhist] faction might say, "If forms and such were not existing, that would contradict the Buddha's statement that conditioned phenomena are momentary." **For the sake of introducing worldly people** to true reality, **the protector** merely **taught in terms of entities** in order to counteract coarse conceptions of reality:

> All conditioned phenomena are momentary. You should not rely on them.

However, this is not a statement that [phenomena] are established as something momentary. For example, it is like when one says, "This is illusory water." This points out that [what appears] is illusory, yet it does not point out that [this appearance] is established as water. *The Sixty Stanzas on Reasoning* says:

It was for a purpose
That the Victors spoke of "I" and "mine."
Likewise, they talked about aggregates, sources,
And elements for a purpose.[1488]

Therefore, **these** [entities] are not [phenomena] to which one could cling as being momentary phenomena **in actuality**, because, if analyzed, they **are not** established as **momentary phenomena** either.

**You might object**, "However, if momentary phenomena are not the ultimate, it is even more **incompatible** to present **them on the seeming level**, since the seeming is just how [things] appear for the world, and momentary phenomena are not what appears for the world. Thus, it follows that either they are not included in the two realities [653] or they are a third reality." Although momentary phenomena are not the seeming of worldly people, **they are the seeming of yogins**. Thus, **there is no flaw**.

You might say, "This contradicts the Buddha's statement that seeing momentary phenomena is seeing reality." It is not contradictory, because it is stated that, **when compared to** the seeming of **worldly people, this refers to seeing** the **true reality** of these [phenomena].

You might say, "It is unjustified to present the seeming of yogins." Yet it is justified, because if it were not presented [as the seeming of yogins], **the ascertainment** and vision **that women are impure** and [nothing but] skeletons—which is what yogins [see] who are familiar with [the meditation on the body's] repulsiveness—would have to be presented as the seeming of worldly people. However, in this case, the [yogic understanding] **would be invalidated** by common worldly consensus, that is, **by the world** that apprehends bathed women as pure and beautiful.[1489]

### 2.1.4.2.3. Removing the Consequence That No Merit Would Come About by Offering to the Buddha

**Merit in relation to illusionlike Victors**
**Is just the same as in the case of real entities.**[1490] [9ab]

You might say, "However, it follows then that offering to the Buddhas would not constitute any merit, because the Buddhas are like an illusion." Illusionlike **merit** is obtained **in relation to** making offerings to **illusionlike Victors.** This **is just the same as in the case** when you proponents of [outer] referents assert that through offering to Buddhas who are real **entities**, one obtains some merit that is a real entity.

### 2.1.4.2.4. Removing the Consequence That Sentient Beings Would Not Be Reborn after Death

> **You might wonder, "If sentient beings are illusionlike,**
> **How can they be reborn after death?"** [9cd]
>
> **For as long as the conditions are assembled,**
> **For that long even an illusion will manifest.**
> **How should sentient beings be really existent**
> **Merely because their continua last for a longer time?** [10]

**You might wonder, "If sentient beings are** also something **illusionlike, how can they be reborn after death?"** There is no mistake: **For as long** [654] **as the conditions** for an illusion—[such as certain] mantras and performances[1491]—**are assembled, for that long even an illusion will manifest.** Likewise, for as long as the causes and conditions—such as basic unawareness—are assembled, for that long illusionlike sentient beings will manifest.

You might think, "Since an illusion is something adventitious, it is unreal. But since sentient beings have come [a long way] from beginningless [time], they are real." **How should sentient beings be really existent** in any way **merely because** they appear **for a longer time?** [They are not any more real,] for whether dreams and illusions appear for such [a long time] as eighty thousand eons or just for one single moment, their duration does not make a difference in terms of their being real or delusive.

### 2.1.4.2.5. Removing the Consequence That No Negativity Would Occur from Killing

> **When illusory beings and such are killed,**
> **There is no negativity, because they do not have minds.**
> **Merit and negativity originate**
> **With those who possess the illusion of a mind.** [11]
>
> **Since mantras and such do not have the potential,**
> **They do not manifest illusory minds.**
> **Having manifested from manifold conditions,**
> **Illusions are manifold too.** [12]
>
> **Nowhere is there a single condition**
> **That has the potential for everything.** [13ab]

You might say, "However, then it follows that there would be no negativity even if one has killed sentient beings, because sentient beings are something illusionlike and there is no negativity in having killed an illusory individual." There is no mistake: **When illusory beings and such**—that is, mechanical beings or magical creations—**are killed, there is** certainly **no negativity**, even when [it looks as if] they have been killed, **because they do not have minds.** However, it is not like that with sentient beings, because they are illusory beings **who possess illusory minds.** Therefore, **merit and negativity originate** from benefiting and harming **those who possess the illusion of a mind.**

You might wonder, "However, what is the reason that illusory minds do not originate in illusory beings?" **Since mantras and such** that are [used] for [creating] illusions [655] do have the potential to produce illusory shapes of horses, elephants, and such, but **do not have the potential** to produce illusory minds, **they do not manifest illusory minds** in these [illusions].

You might disagree, "If they have the potential to magically create illusory human beings, they should also have the potential to magically create minds." **Having manifested from manifold** distinct **conditions**, accordingly, **illusions are manifold** and distinct **too.** This is just like the conditions that produce horses and elephants, which do not, however, [produce] a palace and such; or, the conditions that produce a palace, which do not, however, [produce] horses and elephants. Therefore, **nowhere** and at no time **is there** such **a single condition that has the potential for** producing **everything.**

### 2.1.4.2.6. Removing the Consequence That Even the Buddha Would Circle Again in Cyclic Existence

> **"If those who have ultimately passed beyond it**
> **Still circle in cyclic existence on the seeming level,** [13cd]
>
> **Then even Buddhas would circle in it.**
> **Therefore, what is the point of bodhisattva conduct?"**
> **If the continuum of its conditions is not interrupted,**
> **Even an illusion will not cease.** [14]
>
> **However, if the continuum of conditions is interrupted,**
> **It will not manifest even on the seeming level.** [15ab]

You might say, "However, if the obscurations were nonexistent by their nature, one would always have been enlightened [already]. If this were the case, cyclic existence would not be possible." We answer: It is not contradictory that what has primordially been pure still appears as cyclic existence on the seeming level under the influence of not realizing it as just this [purity].

Then the proponents of [outer] referents might say, "**If** it is not contradictory that **those who have ultimately passsed beyond cyclic existence still** appear to **circle in it on the seeming level, then** one **would** have to **circle in** cyclic existence again **even** after **Buddha**hood [is attained], since [your] very reasoning equally applies [to this case too]. **Therefore, what is the point of bodhisattva conduct?**"

Here we say: There is no difference between Buddhas and sentient beings in terms of being pure by nature. However, on the seeming level, there is a difference as to whether they circle in cyclic existence or not. This is the case because in Buddhas the continuum of conditions for cyclic existence—such as basic unawareness, craving, and grasping—has been [permanently] interrupted, whereas in sentient beings [656] the continuum of these [conditions] has not been interrupted. Therefore, this is the same as [with illusions]: **If the continuum of its conditions is not interrupted, even an illusion will not cease. However, if the continuum of conditions** for an illusion **is interrupted,** the illusion **will not manifest even on the seeming level.**

### 2.1.4.2.7. Removing the Consequence That an Illusion Would Not Exist Even on the Seeming Level

> **"When even mistakenness does not exist,**
> **What would observe the illusion?" [15cd]**

[657] These two lines present the objection that it follows that an illusion is not observed unless mistakenness exists.[1492]

The Proponents of Cognizance argue, "Although it is certainly true that outer objects are without nature, this explanation of illusions and such by you Centrists as examples that are held in common by both debaters does not apply to yourselves: **When** you claim that **even mistakenness does not exist, what would observe the** very **illusion?** That is, where should the illusion exist, if mistakenness does not exist?"

> **When, according to you, the illusion itself does not exist,**
> **What is observed? [16ab]**

These two lines express the equal applicability of this [reasoning].

We answer you Mere Mentalists: **When, according to you,** even **the illusion itself does not exist, what** example of an illusion **is observed,** since you yourselves assert that outer objects do not exist? Thus, the entailment [of your objection in lines 15cd] [658] applies equally [to your own position].[1493]

> **You might say, "It is an aspect of mind itself,**
> **Even though there is something other in terms of its own**
> **state."** [16cd]

These two lines present the assertion of the Real Aspectarians.[1494]

The Real Aspectarians **might say,** "Illusions and such do not exist as outer objects. However, **there is something other in terms of the** plain **own state** of these examples, such as illusions, that is, an aspect that appears as this [illusion]. **It is an aspect** that is [only] real as that for which [the illusion] appears, that is, **mind itself.**"

> **Once mind itself is the illusion,**
> **Then what is seen by what?**
> **The protector of the world has declared,**
> **"Mind does not see mind."** [17]

> **Just as the blade of a sword**
> **Cannot cut itself, so it is with the mind.** [18ab]

These one and a half verses refute self-awareness in general.

If outer objects do not exist, it is contradictory that aspects of outer objects exist. It is certainly the case that this is just as unreasonable as the difference between the nonexistence of the horns of a rabbit and the existence of their aspect. [Moreover,] the mind itself too entails dependence, does not withstand analysis, and is like an illusion, because it was declared that [everything] from form up through omniscience is [that way], and if there existed a phenomenon superior to nirvāṇa, then this [phenomenon] as well would be illusionlike. Therefore, **once** even **mind itself is illusion**like, **then what** object to be seen **is seen by what** seer? [There is no such object,] because there is nothing to be seen other than mind, and mind does not see itself.

This is also established through reasoning, because it is contradictory that a given thing is itself [both] object and agent, and because something to be seen and a seer do not meet in the same place simultaneously when those who are involved in yoga internally examine their own minds. This becomes more profound and subtle in direct proportion to the extent to which it is examined, until finally the very discursiveness of something to be seen and something that sees subsides. This is like when one [tries to] gauge the proportions of the width and the circumference of [the flame of] a butter lamp with a thread, during which the thread itself is burned. Thus, this leaves one unable to determine the size [of the flame].

This is established through scripture too, because **the protector of the world has declared** in *The Sūtra Requested by Crown Jewel*:

**Mind does not see mind.**[1495]

He stated that, **just as the blade of a sword cannot cut itself, so it is** also **with the** single **mind** that [cannot] simultaneously be the triad of the object to be seen, the seer, and the seeing. This is so because he said in *[The Sūtra of ] the Arrival in Laṅka*:

Just as a sword and its own blade [659]
Or just as a finger and its own tip
Do not cut or touch [themselves],
Likewise, mind does not see mind.[1496]

**If it were just like a lamp**
**That perfectly illuminates its own entity,** [18cd]

**The lamp is nothing to be illuminated,**
**Because it is not obscured by darkness.**
**"Just like the blue of something like a crystal**
**And blueness that does not depend on something other,** [19]

**Some things are seen to depend on others**
**And some to be independent."**
**What is not blue**
**Cannot make itself blue by itself.** [20]

**You might say, "A lamp is said to illuminate**
**Once this is known by a consciousness."**
**Upon being known by what do you state**
**That cognition is illuminating?** [21]

**Once this is not seen by anything,**
**"Illuminating" and "not illuminating"**
**Are like the looks of a barren woman's daughter—**
**Even if described, they are meaningless.** [22]

These four and a half verses refute the assertion of self-illumination.

The Proponents of Cognizance might answer to the [above], "**Just like a lamp** is self-illuminating, since itself **perfectly illuminates its entity** of [being a] lamp, the mind too is self-illuminating." [The refutation of] this is explained as follows: This is an example that does not apply. "Illuminating" means that some form is illuminated by having ended darkness. This is presented as the conventional expression that a lamp illuminates [something]. But **the lamp** itself does **not** need **to be illuminated, because** the lamp **is not obscured by darkness.** *The Fundamental Verses on Centrism* says:

In a lamp and wherever
It stands, there is no darkness.
How does a lamp light up [things]?
It is something that lights up by eliminating darkness.[1497]

Furthermore, if a lamp were self-illuminating, one would have to assert that it lights up other things too. If that were the case, then darkness would obscure both itself and others:

If a lamp did light up
Itself and other things,
Then there is no doubt that also darkness
Would obscure itself and other things.[1498]

The Proponents of Cognizance might answer, "There is no mistake: **Something like a** translucent **crystal** is not blue, but it appears to be **blue** through the condition of blue silk being close [to it]. This is [a case of an] illumination that depends on other conditions. **And** [on the other hand, there is] the **blueness** of such things as an utpala [flower] **that does not depend on some other** conditions but is naturally blue. **Just like** this, **some** phenomena **are seen to depend on other** conditions, **and some** [are seen] **to be independent** just as they are by their very nature. Therefore, consciousness does not depend on other conditions but is self-illuminating by its very nature."

The refutation of this is [threefold]:

[Natural] blue is not a concordant example for self-awareness, [660] because, first, the blue of an utpala has certainly not primordially existed as blue by its very nature. Rather, it has been produced as blue through other causes and conditions, such as the translucence of the elements. However, self-awareness has not been produced as something self-illuminating by causes and conditions. Furthermore, awareness depends on something that it is aware of and something that is aware, while illumination depends on the phase of nonillumination. Therefore, once there are [such] counterparts to depend on, self-illuminating self-awareness is not established due to the mistake of mutually dependent conceptions.[1499] And if there are no counterparts to depend on, it would be even less established than if there were.

[Second, the example of the crystal is also not concordant] because of the following: A crystal may certainly appear blue through such conditions as silk or a colored glass vessel [next to it]. However, this is nothing but seeing the color of the silk or the colored glass vessel in an unobscured way because of the translucence of the crystal, whereas the crystal [itself] did not become blue.

[Third, this example is furthermore not concordant] because, even through these conditions, **what is not blue**—the crystal—cannot be made into a **blue** crystal and the crystal **cannot make itself** blue **by itself** either.

All of this is certainly true, but we still ask, upon being known by whom it is stated that **the lamp illuminates? You might say,** "Such **is said once this** [illumination] **is known by a consciousness.**" However, **upon being known by what do you state that cognition is illuminating?** You will affirm, "This is [known] by self-awareness." [However, in this case, your reason, which is self-awareness,] which [should] prove [the probandum], is equivalent to the probandum, so prove self-awareness itself![1500]

> **"If self-awareness did not exist,**
> **How would consciousness be recollected?"**
> **Recollection comes from the connection with other experiences,**
> **Just as with the rat's poison.** [23]
>
> **You might say, "Since it sees through its association with**
> **other conditions,**
> **Self-awareness is self-illuminating."**
> **Through applying the eye lotion of accomplishment,**
> **You see the vase and not the eye lotion itself.** [24]

These two verses refute [the attempt to] prove self-awareness.

The Proponents of Cognizance might ask, "**If self-awareness did not exist, how would** a previously experienced **consciousness be recollected** later?" The Centrists say: Such recollection is not due to the existence of self-awareness. At the given time, the arising of a **recollection** that focuses on a previous situation **comes from the** influencing **connection with experiencing other** causes and conditions.[1501] However, this is nothing but mistaking a present experience for a previous situation. However, this [recollection] is not the previous situation itself, because that has already ceased. It is never and nowhere possible that something that has ceased could arise again.

Therefore, [661] this is **just as with** the [following story]: Once upon a time, a snake proudly said [to a rat], "I seize people with powerful poison and make them afraid by doing that, but nobody is afraid of someone like you." To that, the rat answered, "It is not your poison [that makes them afraid] but just their thoughts. If you do not believe me, I will show you." They both sat beside the road. When a man came by, the rat bit his foot without him noticing it, while the snake showed itself to him. This made the man [cry out], "I have been stricken by the poison of a snake." He fainted and writhed on the ground. Another man came by, and the snake bit him without the man seeing it, while the rat pretended to be the one who had bitten him. Then the man said, "Why would anyone be afraid after being bitten by a rat?" (The [corresponding] thought "Nothing really went wrong at all" is also well known to many people practicing meditative stability.)

When such a recollection has arisen that involves the concern that one has been poisoned, great harm is produced through the notion that the bite of the rat is the [deadly] poison[ous bite] of the snake. On the other hand, when one has the notion that the attack by the snake is [just] **the rat's** [mildly] **poison**[ous bite], there is no harm.[1502] This fits well with the following statement:

> For example, through one's anxious assumptions,
> One will faint, although the poison is gone and did not enter inside.

Here, Kalyāṇadeva has explained the meaning of this example in the following way:

> This is connected to the question "How will the poison of the rat be recollected?" When in the summertime rats become poisonous and one realizes that they are around, then right after one has been seized by the fangs of a snake, one may not see the snake but sees the harmful changes [caused by its poison] in one's body. Therefore, while there is no poison of a rat, a [seeming] recollection that one has been seized by the poison of that [rat] certainly does happen, whereas the poison of the snake is definitely something other than that. While there are only the wounds or other discomforts, but no consciousness of a rat's poison, still [such] a recollection [arises]. Similar to this, what is expressed as the very absence of self-awareness [662] constitutes the origination of a recollection of consciousness.[1503]

**You** Proponents of Cognizance **might say, "Through its association with other conditions**, such as meditative concentration, **self-illuminating self-awareness is** existent, **since it** [then] **sees** its own knowledge of the minds of others and recollections of previous situations of oneself and others." Though one may know the minds of others and such, through this one does not see [one's] own mind. The reason is that [this is similar to the following example:] just through seeing forms, the eye does not see the eye itself. It is like this: **Through applying** such things as a concoction of **the eye lotion of accomplishment**—administering warmth, smoke, and blazing light to the eyes—**you see** and obtain **the** excellent [treasure] **vase**, jewels, and such that exist far away below the earth and so forth. However, you do **not** see **the eye lotion itself** that was administered to the eye or the eye itself.[1504]

You might continue, "The very consciousness that recollects previous situations and such is self-illuminating, because it has arisen as something that has the nature to be illuminated through the condition of meditative concentration." However, then it follows that also the [treasure] vase would be an eye with the eye lotion, because it has arisen as something that has the nature to be illuminated through the condition of the eye. Therefore, [all of] the following are superimpositions: the object of awareness itself, what is aware of it (consciousness), and the way of being aware (apprehension in an illuminating way). Rather, this very consciousness does not exist as something that would rise as all three of these simultaneously.

> **How something is seen, heard, or known**
> **Is not what is negated here.**
> **Rather, the object of refutation**
> **Is the cause for suffering, which is the conception of reality.** [25]

This one verse teaches that the object of negation is solely the clinging to reality.

It might be said, "However, when self-awareness does not exist, then awareness of something other is not justified either. Therefore, all experiences of consciousness and all experiences of forms, sounds, and such would not be justified." The knowledges of **how** they are experienced—such as seeing forms and hearing sounds—are **not what is negated here** in this context of analyzing true reality.[1505] **Rather, the object of refutation is** solely **the cause for** the **suffering** of cyclic existence, **which is the** clinging to the **reality** of such [phenomena] as the consciousnesses that see and hear. [663]

This corresponds to what the Mere Mentalists do when they negate the outer objects [that] the proponents of outer objects [assert]: They do not prove that, as by deaf and blind people, forms are not seen and sounds are not heard, but they solely negate the grasping at forms and sounds as real. Also here, the mere experience of illuminating consciousness is not negated, but the grasping that this is established as the experience of illumination is negated. Therefore, we cannot be rebutted with such [an objection as the one above]. However, if we state the reverse [of your objection] to you Proponents of Cognizance by saying, "When awareness of something other does not exist, then self-awareness would not exist either," then you lack an answer.

**If an illusion is not something other than mind**
**And is not conceived as not something other either,**
**Then, if it is an entity, how could it not be something other?**
**If you say, "It is not something other," [mind] would not exist as an entity. [26]**

**"An illusion is not real, but it can still be seen."**
**Well, likewise is the mind that sees. [27ab]**

These one and a half verses are the refutation of the assertion of the Non-Aspectarians.[1506]

Furthermore, the Non-Aspectarians state, "It is certainly the case that these mistakes apply to those who assert that the aspect [of mind that appears as an object] is real. However, there is no mistake [in our position], since we assert that also this aspect is delusive like an illusion and that it cannot be expressed as being the mind itself or something other either."

The rebuttal of that is as follows: You assert that **an illusion is not something other than mind and** assert that it **is not something other** than that—that is, it is not the same—**either.** So **if** you assert that it cannot be expressed as [mind] itself nor as something other, what is left [that would justify] to rebut us by [adducing lines 15cd] "When even mistakenness does not exist . . ." because you yourselves have accepted [then] that an illusion does not exist.

They might say, "We did not accept this, but since it was accepted by others [in this verse], we will [accept] it here." Then you should also accept that all phenomena are without nature, because others accept this.

Well, **then, if** you assert that an illusion **is an entity, how could it not be something other** than mind? In fact, it must be something other than mind. You might say, "Why?" [It is something other] because an illusion depends on being magically created by an illusionist with [certain] substance mantras, whereas consciousness does not depend on an illusionist. **If you** assert, "An illusion **is not something other** than mind," then, since these two are not different, mind **would not exist as an entity,** [664] because illusions [too] do not exist as entities.

Wanting to remove this objection to their [position], they might try, "**An illusion is not real, but** it is the common consensus of the world that **it is still** just something that **can be seen.**" Well, that is fine, but you should know that also **the mind that sees** [it] **is** not real as anything—such as self-awareness—and that it is merely in terms of common consensus that it is the seer.

### 2.1.4.2.8. Removing the Consequence That There Would Be No Support [for Talking about Cyclic Existence]

> **You might say, "Cyclic existence entails an entity as its support.**
> **Otherwise, it would be just like space." [27cd]**

These two lines present the objection.

**You** Proponents of Cognizance **might say,** "This **cyclic existence** certainly is a nonentity, because outer objects do not exist. However, it still appears, since it **entails** being **supported** by **an entity,** which is self-awareness. **Otherwise,** if this were not the case, **it would be** something without appearance, **just like space.**"

> **Even if a nonentity is supported by an entity,**
> **How could it become active?**
> **Your mind would be isolated**
> **And completely solitary. [28]**
>
> **If the mind is free from apprehended objects,**
> **Everyone is a Thus-Gone One.**
> **In this case, what qualities are gained**
> **By conceptualizing it as "merely mind"? [29]**

These two verses refute that [objection].

**Even if a nonentity is supported by an entity, how could it become active?** It is like the horns of a rabbit. No matter what they might be supported by, they will not be able to pierce [anything]. If you accept that, Proponents of Cognizance, it **would** follow that **your mind is isolated** from cyclic existence and a **completely solitary** ultimate [entity], that is, nirvāṇa. And if you accept that, there would be no need to accept an ultimate self-awareness for the sake of its being a support for cyclic existence.

Therefore, **if the mind is free from** all observed or **apprehended objects** to which it clings, it will be seen that **every** phenomenon **is** not different from the very nature of the **Thus-Gone Ones.** Also, just what is seen will be realized in the manner of nonseeing. [665] You might agree, "It certainly is like this." **In this case, what** purpose does it have that you emphatically **conceptualize it as "merely mind"** and furthermore as "self-awareness"? It is as purposeless as gauging the size of space through clinging to it, although one has [already] understood that space has no limit.

## [Synopsis of Other Commentaries]

With respect to these [verses up to now, master Dharmapāla] from Suvarṇadvipa has taught that the whole chapter on knowledge is summarized in the following three and a half verses that can be found in both of his [summaries of *The Entrance to the Bodhisattva's Way of Life*, entitled] *A Summary in Thirty-Six Points* and *A Summary in Eleven Points.*[1507]

> Thus, all of these
> Were stated by the Sage for the sake of knowledge.
> Therefore, those who wish for nirvāṇa
> And bliss should develop knowledge.
>
> The ultimate and the seeming
> Are asserted as the two realities.
> The ultimate is not the sphere of cognition.
> Cognition and terms are the seeming.
>
> So the world is seen in the two fashions
> Of yogins and common people.
> Here, through the world of yogins,
> The world of common people is refuted.
>
> Through the differences of respectively superior ones,
> Yogins are refuted too.

*The Great Commentary on the Difficult Points* ascertains the nature of knowledge:

> Thus, the very nonexistence of a nature is the fundamental state of entities. It does not abide through the nature of the ultimate. Just that is expressed as the supreme and especially noble purpose of individuals. [However,] one should not firmly cling to this either. Otherwise, there is not the slightest difference between firmly clinging to entities and firmly clinging to emptiness, because both [types of clinging] are obscurations that have the character of an imputation. There is not even the slightest self-nature [that is established] through the nature of an imputation in the sense of nonexistence, nor is "nonentity" the reverse of "entity," because a reverse is without nature.
>
> Therefore, there is not the slightest nature of "real entity" [666] that could be called "nonentity." Through stating "entity" and "nonentity"

in this order, they are [both] taught to be nonexistent. Thus, neither is there something that has the character of both being mixed, nor is there any nature of the negation of both. Since this very conception of [real] entities is the cause of all conceptions, by negating the one [conception of entities], all these [other conceptions] are eliminated through a single negation. Therefore, something existent, something nonexistent, something that is both existent and nonexistent, and also something that has the character of neither—none of these should be conceived of as an object of clinging even in the slightest way.[1508]

[In this context, the commentary] presents [several] quotes:

As the *Prajñāpāramitā* [*Sūtras*] say:

Venerable Śāriputra, here the correct understanding of "form is empty" by a son or a daughter of the noble family of those who belong to the vehicle of bodhisattvas but are not skillful in means is [just a type of] clinging.[1509]

This is to be applied to [everything] up through [the category of] phenomena.

[*The Praise to the Supramundane*] says:

In order to relinquish all imagination,
You taught the nectar of emptiness.
However, those who cling to it
Are also blamed by you.[1510]

[Bhāvaviveka's *Heart of Centrism* states]:

Its character is neither existent, nor nonexistent,
Nor [both] existent and nonexistent, nor neither.
Centrists should know true reality
That is free from these four possibilities.[1511]

As for the presentation of the two realities, [*The Great Commentary*] says:

Here, seeming reality is the nature of worldly unmistakenness. In terms of ultimate reality, reality is what is undeceiving. True reality is the [reality] of the noble ones. This is the difference. . . . All these entities perfectly arise through bearing two natures: the seeming and the ultimate. The first [nature] is the clinging of those whose eyes are obscured by the blurred vision of basic unawareness. These ordinary beings who [see] that which bears the character of falsity [cling to the fact] that precisely their delusive seeing of objects is the correct seeing. The other [nature] is [667] the object of those who are endowed with the eyes of perfect knowledge [that result] from the elimination of the membrane of basic unawareness with the ophthalmological scalpel of complete distinction. This is [the object] of the perfect knowledge of the noble ones who are aware of true reality. Thus, it is presented as the [actual] nature.[1512]

Thus, [this commentary] explains the seeing of naïve beings as the seeming and the seeing of the noble ones as the ultimate. [It continues:]

> You might say, "That may well be the case. However, since the seeming is displayed through basic unawareness, it is of the nature of a false superimposition. Hence, if it disintegrates hundreds of times due to thorough analysis, how could it be a reality?" You are absolutely right. However, it is [only] due to the clinging of worldly people that such is expressed as "seeming reality." It is just worldly people who assert a "seeming reality." In compliance with this, [whenever] the Blessed One spoke about the "seeming reality," he did so by setting aside true reality. This is why master [Nāgārjuna] in his treatise [called *The Fundamental Verses on Centrism*] said:
>
> > Worldly seeming reality . . . [1513]
>
> Actually, there is just a single [reality], which is ultimate reality. Thus, there is not even the slightest fallacy [here]. The Blessed One said:
>
> > Oh fully ordained monks, this ultimate reality is single. It is as follows: Nirvāṇa has the property of being undeceiving, whereas all formations have the property of being delusive and deceiving.[1514]

As for the way in which [ultimate reality] is not the sphere of cognition, [*The Great Commentary*] says:

> The gist of this is: "Cognition" refers to all consciousnesses. Since [ultimate reality] is beyond the objects of all consciousnesses, it is not [their] sphere; that is, it is not an object [at all]. No aspect whatsoever

> of all these cognitions is able to take this [ultimate reality] as its object. So how could they show its nature as it is? Thus, it is the nature of complete release from all discursiveness, suchness, the true reality that is ultimate reality. Therefore, it is not seen by conceptions in any fashion whatsoever, [668] because it is free from all distinctive features.[1515]

Thus, it is explained that [ultimate reality] is primarily not an object of conception.

Furthermore, as for [verse 6,] "Also perceptions of forms and such are based on common consensus and not on valid cognition," [*The Great Commentary*] says:

> These words were spoken by people who dedicatedly work on refutations for the perspective of the seeing of those with blurred vision. Although they have expressed these statements in such a way, [actually] there are no negations or proofs that have been carried out. . . . Thus, the ultimate is not an object of expression. However, it is taught in correspondence with the seeing by using imputations in a way [that is informed] through seeing ultimate true reality. On the other hand, through relinquishing all conventional terms without exception, one is not able to speak about the nature of entities. As it is said [in *The Sūtra of the King of Meditative Concentration*]:
>
> As for the dharmas without letters,
> What listener and what teacher would there be?
> The meaning[1516] that is listened to and taught is superimposed.
> Therefore, it is without letters.
>
> Thus, by relying on these two conventional realities, the ultimate is taught. To realize the teaching about the ultimate is to reveal the ultimate, because this very [teaching] is the means for the [realization of the ultimate].[1517]

[*The Great Commentary*] quotes *The Sūtra of Engaging in the Two Realities*:

> Devaputra, if ultimate reality ultimately were the sphere of body, speech, and mind,[1518] it would not fall into the category of "ultimate reality." It would be nothing but just seeming reality.
>
> Because of precisely this, [the ultimate] is not an object of conceptions. Entity and nonentity, self-entity and other-entity, real and

> unreal, permanence and annihilation, permanence and impermanence, happiness and suffering, clean and unclean, identity and identitylessness, empty and not empty, one and many, arising and ceasing—all such distinctive features are not possible as the true reality, because they are seeming phenomena.[1519]

I see these detailed elucidations [from *The Great Commentary*] as objects for paying my respects.

As for the poison of the rat and so on [in line 23d], *The Great Commentary* says:

> It is like the poison of the rat that strikes the body instantaneously and becomes active later due to the condition of thunder.[1520] [669] Therefore, one is not aware of a self-aware consciousness in even the slightest way. [Nāgārjuna's *Commentary on the Mind of Enlightenment* says:]
>
> > A mind with the aspects of what is to be realized and what realizes
> > Is not seen by the Thus-Gone Ones.
> > In whomever there is realization and realizer,
> > There is no mind of enlightenment.[1521]
>
> Thus, because all conceptions have vanished in this way, release from every obscuration arises.[1522]

[In] Vibhūticandra's [commentary,] the following statement [about line 2c] appears:

> The ultimate is not even the sphere of omniscient wisdom. The vajralike meditative concentration that focuses on the ultimate that is [both] naturally [pure] and pure of adventitious stains is Buddhahood. In it, not even a fraction of an aspect exists.[1523]

However, the vajralike meditative concentration is not Buddhahood, because it is what vanquishes the obscurations of the continuum of the tenth ground, and [only the state] thereafter is presented as Buddhahood. This [vajralike meditative concentration] is also not the phase in which all phenomena are presented as the nature of Buddhahood.

Furthermore, [concerning the example of the illusionist,] he says:

> The people [in the audience] see nothing but the manner in which these magically created elephants and so on [appear], whereas the magician sees [them] as just wood and such.[1524]

[However, this explanation] is not appropriate, because if a magician were to see [his magical creations] as [just] wood, the [opponent's] answer in the [later] debate [in lines 30cd]

> Attachment for an illusory woman
> Might arise even in her very creator

would become meaningless.

About killing illusory human beings [in lines 11ab], he says:

> The actual part of taking life does not occur, because [illusory human beings] do not have any life. [However,] the negativity of beating them, which leads to [this killing], does happen.[1525]

[This phrase] is not nice, because it is a joke that there should be no negativity through killing whereas there is negativity through beating. Some might still argue, "This is due to the wish to beat." Well, then why should the wish to kill not produce negativity?

Therefore, if one kills [illusory beings] with the knowledge that an illusion is an illusion, since there is no motivation in terms of the wish to kill that really qualifies as such [a wish to kill], there is no negativity. However, if one beats or kills [illusory beings] while clinging to autonomous continua [of theirs], although there certainly is no beating or killing of anybody at all, still, through the intention of killing and the intention of beating, one produces negativities that come from hatred. [670] This is the case because it is equal to the statement that one produces negativity if one awakes while one is killing [someone] in a dream and then rejoices [in this killing]. Therefore, the implication in [verse 11] "When illusory beings and such are killed . . . " is that one knows that these are illusions.

Concerning [lines 23cd] "Recollection comes from . . . ," [Vibhūticandra] states:

> [The example of] the rat here [refers] to applying [remedial] arsenic [to the rat bite]: The poison of the rat that has spread previously throughout the body through the wound of the bite will become active later at the time when thunder resounds. Thus, [the poison] was not active at the time of the bite but became active at another time. Likewise, consciousness is not experienced at the time of experiencing the object but is recollected at some other time.[1526]

With respect to [verse 25] " How something is seen, heard, or known . . . ," he says:

> I ask you, "Are you saying that seeing and hearing do not exist ultimately, or are you saying that they do not exist on the seeming level?" If the first is the case, I accept, because everything seeming does not exist within this [ultimate]. If the latter is the case, it is not established: [This here] is not a negation of what is seen, heard, and known. Rather, just leave these [as they are] without analyzing them—they are not ultimate. As it is said:
>
> > The Sage did not state
> > That seeing, hearing, and such are real or delusive.
> > Because one side has an opposite side,
> > These two do not exist ultimately.[1527]

With respect to [verse 26], "If an illusion is not something other than mind, . . ." he asks:

> Is an illusion something other than mind, not something other, both, or neither—which of these four possibilities is it?[1528]

He then [answers in the following vein]: [An illusion] is not something other than mind, because [the Mere Mentalists themselves] assert that it is established as mere mind. If it were something other, the illusion would be nonexistent, because they assert that there are no phenomena apart from mind. It is not both, since that is [internally] contradictory. So they might say, "It is neither." [However,] if one [possibility out of the two dichotomous possibilities of] being something other or not being something other does not apply, then one cannot reject the other [possibility either, because there is no third option in a dichotomy]. Therefore, it is impossible that [an illusion] is this fourth possibility [of being neither].

On [lines 27cd–29ab] "You might say, 'Cyclic existence . . . ,'" he comments as follows:

> If cyclic existence were mind, it follows that it would be what is purified, since the mind is naturally luminous. If it were not mind, your own philosophical system collapses, since you then accept an entity that is not mind. If cyclic existence were a nonentity, it would not perform a function. Or, [671] since it then would be without nature, you would enter the philosophical system of Centrists. . . . If you say that mind alone is the ultimate, you must assert that it is free from apprehended and apprehender. If this is the case, it follows that all sentient beings are Buddhas.[1529]

*The Small Commentary on the Difficult Points*[1530] comments:

> [As for lines 2cd:] Not to be the sphere of cognition is the expression for being free from all defining characteristics. The reason for this is: If there were any defining characteristics, they would necessarily be the sphere of the mental state of omniscience. [However, omniscience does not see any defining characteristics.]
>
> A knower of entities and nonentities
> Is not even seen by the All-Knowing One.
> What kind of entity
> Would be analyzed by the view of utter peace?
>
> Therefore, the definition of the ultimate is freedom from all [kinds of] nature, because it is expressed as the very nonexistence of defining characteristics. For example, it is like [saying], "Is the very freedom from qualities not the quality of [phenomena]?" To say "all objects of cognition" is regarded as stating the definition of seeming reality.
>
> [Line 3b:] "Yogins" start with those who are stream-enterers and so on, and include solitary realizers, bodhisattvas on the ten grounds, and Buddhas. "Common people" are the followers of Kapila, Akṣapāda,[1531] and so forth.
>
> [Lines 7–8ab:] You might object, "This contradicts the statement that momentariness and identitylessness are the ultimate." [They are taught] "for the sake of introducing worldly people . . ." You might ask, "Do you not accept that those who are called yogins see true reality? How could momentariness and such that they see be the seeming? Then it follows that they do not see true reality." When compared to the world, they see true reality. Those who are superior to ordinary people belong to the ranks of yogins.
>
> [Lines 13cd–15ab:] You might say, "It follows that it is possible that even the Buddha circles [in cyclic existence], because natural purity and the existence of adventitious stains are not contradictory, just as this is the case in the impure phase [of sentient beings]." In terms of natural purity, there is no difference between Buddhas and sentient beings. However, on the seeming level, they are distinguished by having the causes for cyclic existence or not.

[Lines 23cd:] Though one did not feel any sign that the poison of the rat had entered the body, due to seeing its results, one remembers, "The poison of the rat has entered me." [672] Likewise, though one does not experience consciousness itself, through seeing the object connected to it, one will remember, "A consciousness has arisen in me."

[Verse 24:] You might wonder, "If one knows the mind of a distant individual, why should one not be aware of one's own mind, which is so close? If one sees a distant needle, why should one not see a vase close by?" If one sees the treasure vase through putting the eye lotion onto [one's eyes], why does one not see the eye lotion itself?

[Lines 27cd–28ab:] This is like [the fact that] one cannot prove that the horns of a rabbit pierce [something] through being supported by a vase.

[Lines 28cd–29:] Since [mind in] cyclic existence were then free from the counterpart of the seeming, ultimate nirvāṇa would be singular. If this were the case, it follows that one would attain liberation without effort. If it were like this, despite your claim of self-awareness as the support for cyclic existence, [self-awareness] would not be able to create cyclic existence. Hence, it would be without purpose to claim ultimate self-awareness.

*The Small Commentary on the Difficult Points of the Knowledge Chapter* states:

The poison of the rat has entered [the body] at one time, but its potency awakens at another time. Likewise, self-awareness does not exist even in the slightest.[1532]

*The Synopsis of Good Explanations*[1533] points out [knowledge]:

In terms of the support, [there are] two sufferings: physical and mental [sufferings]. In terms of nature, [there are] three: the suffering of suffering, [the suffering of] change, and the suffering of conditioned existence. In terms of time, [there are] three: the suffering of the visible phenomena [of this life], [the suffering] in the next [life], and suffering in the long term. Having thus identified the factor to be relinquished—suffering—one eliminates the harms of this life and lower migrations through the knowledge that knows action and result.

> The suffering of conditioned existence is relinquished through the knowledge that realizes the ultimate for the following reason: Contaminated actions arise from afflictions, and these arise from reification. As the opposite [of reification], the knowledge that realizes the lack of a nature vanquishes [reification] at the root.

It quotes [Nāgārjuna's] *Sixty Stanzas on Reasoning*:

> If there is the claim of entities,
> The sources of desire and hatred—
> Improper bad views—are grasped
> And dispute will arise from this.
>
> By taking any standpoint whatsoever,
> You will be snatched by the cunning snakes of the afflictions.
> Those whose minds have no standpoint [673]
> Will not be caught.[1534]

[and continues:]

> At the time of preparation, one analyzes with reasonings—such as the freedom from unity and multiplicity—and ascertains emptiness through the knowledge of discriminating examination. At the time of meditative equipoise, through a mental state that does not see any object whatsoever, one cultivates a meditative stability that does not conceptualize [emptiness] as anything at all. Having risen from this [meditative equipoise], through being mindful of the lack of nature of appearances, one knows them to be dreamlike. Through this, one should be without attachment or aversion toward the eight [worldly] dharmas.
>
> You might say, "It follows that the ultimate is not an object of meditation, because its nature is not established." Ultimately, this is accepted. However, on the seeming level, the entailment is not established.[1535] As a nonimplicative negation, the ultimate serves as the remedy for reification. As an implicative negation, it functions as the remedy for discursiveness. Hence, these [two] are not contradictory in the sense of [one of them] not being an object of meditation. [Experiencing] the death of a child in a dream is a wrong consciousness, but it still serves as a remedy for the superimposition of apprehending the existence of this child. Likewise, the illusionlike seeming is a wrong

consciousness, but it still serves as a remedy for some factors to be relinquished. Thus, it is reasonable to meditate [on this seeming]. The result is as follows: Provisionally, one relinquishes one's own afflictions, and, out of compassion, one seizes a completely pure [form of] cyclic existence for the welfare of others. Finally, through being familiar with the lack of a nature, one attains the Dharma Body in which all mistakenness has become extinguished. Through the impetus of compassion and aspiration prayers, one attains the Form Bodies for the welfare of others.

[As for line 2c:] The ultimate is a knowable object in terms of negative determination. However, it is not a knowable object in terms of positive determination.

Here, [lines 4ab] "Also the yogins, due to differences in insight, . . ." teach the four grounds of yoga: [the yogas of] the two identitylessnesses, of the nonexistence of discursiveness, and of signlessness; or the three grounds of yoga: the yogas of identitylessness, of nonentity, and of no mental engagement; or the two grounds of yoga: the yoga that focus on existence or nonexistence and the nonreferential yoga. [674]

### 2.2. The Proof That the Knowledge of This [Emptiness] Is the Path

This has three parts:

1) The proof that seeing [entities] as illusions is the path
2) The proof that seeing [entities] as emptiness is the path
3) The summary of the function of both of these [types of seeing]

### 2.2.1. The Proof That Seeing [Entities] as Illusions Is the Path

This has six parts:

1) Removing objections
2) Teaching that the remedy for reification is emptiness
3) Attaining one's own welfare—the Dharma Body—through being free from apprehending extremes
4) The way in which the Form Bodies effortlessly originate from this
5) The way in which enlightened activity is uninterrupted through the impetus of aspiration prayers
6) Obtaining merit through worshipping despite the fact that [the Buddha] does not possess a mind

### 2.2.1.1. Removing Objections

> **"Even if you understand the similarity to illusions,**
> **How should afflictions cease?**
> **Attachment for an illusory woman**
> **Might arise even in her very creator."** [30]
>
> **Her creator did not relinquish the afflictions'**
> **Latent tendencies toward knowable objects.**
> **Thus, when he sees her,**
> **His latent tendencies of emptiness are very weak.** [31]

The Proponents of Cognizance might say, "**Even if you** Centrists **understand** that all phenomena are **similar to illusions, how should afflictions cease?** [They do not,] because **attachment for an illusory woman might arise even in her very creator,** the illusionist." All that **her creator**—the illusionist—did was to practice mantras [that are used] for [producing] illusions. However, he **did not** suppress **the afflictions toward knowable objects** nor **relinquish** [their] **latent tendencies. Thus, when he sees the** illusory woman, **his latent tendencies of emptiness are very weak.** Therefore, he cannot help it that attachment arises [in him].

### 2.2.1.2. Teaching That the Remedy for Reification Is Emptiness

> **Through familiarity with the latent tendencies of emptiness,**
> **The latent tendencies of entities will be relinquished.**
> **Through familiarity with "utter nonexistence,"**
> **These too will be relinquished later on.** [32]
>
> **Once this "utter nonexistence"—**
> **The entity to be determined—cannot be observed,**
> **How should a nonentity without a basis**
> **Remain before the mind?** [33]

[675] One should cultivate the discriminating notion that all phenomena are illusionlike. Once one is familiar with this [notion], [phenomena] will not even be observed as mere illusions [but] will be seen as empty aspects. **Through familiarity with the latent tendencies of emptiness, the latent tendencies of entities**—which apprehend all such varieties as the same and different—**will be relinquished.** All phenomena will be seen as nothing at all. You might wonder, "Is this very 'utter nonexistence' the ultimate?" Also this ["utter nonexistence"] is just some kind of discriminating notion, [a step in] a remedial sequence. However, it is not the per-

fect nature [itself], because it does not even abide as this very "utter nonexistence." Venerable Nāgārjuna [said] in his *Praise to the Supramundane*:

> In order to relinquish all imagination,
> You taught the nectar of emptiness.
> However, those who cling to it
> Are also blamed by you.[1536]

Nevertheless, this laxative of seeing nothing at all is applied as the remedy for the disease of apprehending discursiveness [that exists] in sentient beings who are in trouble merely because of this discursiveness. **Utter nonexistence**, such as attaining something or not attaining it, being bound or being released, seeing or not seeing, means seeing [emptiness] as the aspect that is the extinction of all discursiveness. **Through** becoming increasingly accustomed to and **familiar with** exactly this [notion of utter nonexistence], **this** cognition that apprehends utter nonexistence **will be relinquished later on too.**

Through one's seeing all phenomena as illusionlike, the reification that is entailed in the conception of reality is reversed. Then, even **this "utter** and complete **nonexistence"**—the very nonexistence that is **the entity to be determined** [here]—**cannot be observed. Once** [such is the case,] all phenomena do not exist as any entities or nonentities whatsoever, and there is freedom from all flux of discriminating notions, such as [notions] about a basis and something based on it. However, **how should** even this firewoodlike entity—a mere **nonentity without a basis—remain before the** immaculate knowledge of true reality that is [676] a **mind** similar to the conflagration at the end of time? Once the firewood is consumed, the fire also subsides on its own. Likewise, also this very mind of immaculate knowledge subsides in such a way within the expanse of true reality that is always at peace in that it is the very nature of primordial nonarising and nonceasing.

### 2.2.1.3. Attaining the Dharma Body through Being Free from Apprehending Extremes

> **Once neither entities nor nonentities**
> **Remain before the mind,**
> **There is no other mental flux [either].**
> **Therefore, it is utter nonreferential peace.** [34]

[793][1537] On the respective grounds [of bodhisattvas], one has generated the aspiring mind [that is directed] toward enlightenment and has truly trained in the nature of the engaging mind of enlightenment, that is, the perfections. Through this, one arrives at the final culmination of supreme familiarity with the ultimate

mind of enlightenment: emptiness and great compassion as one taste. This has the [quality of] nonabiding abiding in any phenomenon whatsoever and is the actuality in which there is nothing with which to be familiarized as anything by anybody in any way. Thus, **once** the knowledge that lasts for one single moment sees true reality in the manner of nonseeing, **neither entities nor nonentities remain before the** perfect **mind** of immaculate knowledge.

Here, one should understand the distinctive feature that the phrase "neither [entities] nor [nonentities]" is not [just] a dual[1538] but serves as a plural: Exemplified by entities and nonentities, anything that is observed as a phenomenon—such as cyclic existence and nirvāṇa, conditioned and unconditioned, empty and nonempty, permanent and impermanent, real and delusive, seeming and ultimate—[does not remain before immaculate knowledge]. Through having revealed the very [actuality] that these phenomena do not abide by their nature in any form whatsoever, one has reached the final culmination of the supreme [actuality] that no phenomenon has been seen, is seen, or will be seen.

For example, by their nature, there are certainly no floating hairs in space whatsoever, be they long or short, very thin, tangled or untangled, and so on. However, from the perspective of someone with blurred vision, floating hairs appear in various forms. Once the blurred vision is completely healed by treating it with medicine and mantras, any observation of such floating hairs has completely subsided too, no matter whether [these floating hairs] had been observed [before] as tangled (which illustrates samsaric phenomena), untangled (which illustrates nirvanic phenomena), long (the seeming), tiny (the ultimate), or even very thin (the expanse of dharmas) [794]. Then, there is no conditioned mental flux of such [aspects] as the enlightenment that is attained, the one who attains it (the bodhisattva), the place where it is attained (Akaniṣṭha and such), or the manner in which it is attained (the gradual progression of becoming enlightened), nor is there any **mental flux** of some **other** [aspects] than these. **There is not** even enlightenment itself as something observable. Through **not** even **referring** to whether there is something to be observed or not, one is not able to label the expanse of dharmas just as it is as being one or different. Thus, in any case and in every way, all entities are just **utter peace** in exactly the way they primordially have been at peace. Even all the perfect Buddhas themselves do not mention, think, or express the very nature of this. Nevertheless, for the sake of indicating just this for those who are to be trained, [the Buddha] taught:

> Through knowledge that lasts one single moment, in the place Richly Adorned Akaniṣṭha which encompasses the entirety of the expanse of dharmas, I became enlightened as the Ultimate Body that is my own welfare. [This happened] in a manner of there being no phenomena whatsoever to become truly and perfectly enlightened.

### 2.2.1.4. The Way in Which the Form Bodies Effortlessly Originate from This

> **Just as a wish-fulfilling jewel and a wish-fulfilling tree**
> **Fully satisfy [all] desires,**
> **Likewise, appearances of the Victors are seen**
> **Because of their aspiration prayers and those to be trained.** [35]

There is no question that at that point [of utter mental peace] all observed objects, such as oneself and others, completely vanish and that the motions of discrimination entirely discontinue. This [mental peace] is not something without discrimination, nor does it possess any motivational aspects at all. Still, it is stated:

> Because they delight in all endeavors . . .

Accordingly, since beginningless [time] before this [state], [bodhisattvas] did not have even an atom of considering their own welfare. Rather, the benefit of others was simply all they had in mind. [At last,] supreme familiarity with this has reached its final culmination, and inconceivable aspiration prayers are accomplished. Therefore, when discursiveness is at peace like space, the welfare of all sentient beings will be simultaneously and uninterruptedly accomplished without any effort through the impetus of aspiration prayers and enlightened compassion.

**Just as a wish-fulfilling jewel** [795] grants those who pray [to it] all needs and wishes without thinking **and** [just as] all that one wishes—such as garments, jewelry, food, and drink—comes forth from **a wish-fulfilling tree,** ready to be picked, **likewise, because of their aspiration prayers**, the enlightened activity [of Buddhas] will interact with the assembly of **those to be trained.** For the pure ones to be trained, it appears as the Body of Perfect Enjoyment that is like a wish-fulfilling jewel. Through this, the oceanlike needs and wishes in terms of the dharma are granted. For those who are [only] slightly pure, it appears as a supreme Emanation Body that is like a wish-granting tree. Through this, the beginners are given the vehicle of higher states that is like food and drink; the common ones to be trained [are given] the vehicle of definite excellence[1539] that is like garments; and the special ones to be trained [are given] the dharma of the great vehicle that is like the best of jewelry. It promotes great welfare through appearing in all possible and impossible forms for those who are not yet ripened, starting with such [appearances] as bodhisattvas, hearers, solitary realizers, and Brahmā up to such [appearances] as ships and bridges. Thus, for those to be trained, the very Dharma Body that does not abide anywhere happens to be **seen** as the **appearances** of the Form Bodies **of the Victors.**

### 2.2.1.5. The Way in Which Enlightened Activity Is Uninterrupted through the Impetus of Aspiration Prayers

**For example, when a worshipper of Garuda**
**Has built a pillar and passed away,**
**It still neutralizes poisons and such**
**Even when he has been long dead. [36]**

**Likewise, through following enlightening conduct,**
**The pillar of the Victor is built too.**
**It continues to promote all welfare**
**Even after the bodhisattva has passed beyond. [37]**

**For example,** an individual who has practiced the awareness-mantra of **Garuda** may have built a **pillar** out of jewels on the shore of the ocean and formed an effigy of Garuda on its top.[1540] After he **has built** this [pillar] through such a mantra, its constructor **passes away** some time later. **Even when he has been dead** for a very **long** time, such as many millions of years, there is no difference in the state of this pillar [compared to] the time before [when he was alive]: When one sees or touches it, **it still neutralizes** visible poisons, consumptive poisons, ingestive **poisons**, or [poisons that work through] contact and [pacifies] the torments through nāga diseases **and such.**

**Likewise, through following enlightening conduct, the pillar of the Victor is built too** by the bodhisattva. [796] The continuum of mind and mental events that served as the basis to ascribe the name **bodhisattva** terminates completely upon the realization of true reality through the vajralike meditative concentration. Thus, [the bodhisattva] **has passed beyond** the locations of cyclic existence and nirvāṇa. Through such enlightenment in the expanse of dharmas, there is no observation of oneself and others. However, **even after** [enlightenment], enlightened activity takes place and **continues to promote** the **welfare** of **all** sentient beings without exception in a nonconceptual way.

### 2.2.1.6. Obtaining Merit through Worshipping Despite the Fact That [the Buddha] Does Not Possess a Mind

**"Worshipping someone without a mind—**
**How could that have any result?"**
**The reason is that being alive and having passed into nirvāṇa**
**Are explained to be exactly the same. [38]**

**No matter whether on the seeming or the actual level,**
**According to the scriptures, this has a result,**
**Just as worshipping a real Buddha**
**Will yield a result.** [39]

[Buddhist] realists might say, "However, if the perfect Buddha does not have a mind, **how could worshipping someone without a mind** be a positive action that **has any result?" The reason is that** worshipping a Buddha who **is alive**, such as by [offering] a midday meal, **and** worshipping relic pills from the physical remains of someone who **has passed into nirvāṇa are explained to be exactly the same** inasmuch as they do not differ in merit. This is the case because *The Flower Mound Dhāraṇī*[1541] says:

> One should know that the merit of someone who sees the Buddha and then worships him with confidence and [the merit] of someone who worships a reliquary of relic pills of the Thus-Gone One are equal.

> Those who worship someone alive
> Or the physical remains of somebody who has passed into nirvāṇa
> With attitudes of equal confidence
> Will receive equal merit through such worship.

*[The Sūtra of] the Scriptural Collection of Bodhisattvas*[1542] says:

> Those who worship someone alive
> And those who worship a relic pill of somebody who has passed into nirvāṇa
> That has the mere size of a mustard seed
> Are equal in attitude as well as result.

The same is also stated in *The Basis of Scriptural Medicine of the Vinaya.*[1543]

You might ask, "Is it on the seeming or the ultimate level that a result comes about through worshipping an illusionlike Buddha?" The answer is: For the time being, it does not **matter whether** this refers to **the seeming** [level] **or the** true, [797] **actual level,** because **the scriptures** of both the greater and the inferior vehicle state that meritorious actions **have** abundant **results.** This is something one should trust in. Here, for the time being, the two realities do not need to be analyzed, because even our Teacher himself said such without analyzing the two realities. As *The Precious Garland* says:

> Other than the Victor, who could have a valid cognition
> Of this actuality that is superior?[1544]

*The Sublime Continuum* says:

> You wonder why? In this world, there is no one who is more skilled than the Victor . . .
> Therefore, do not mess up what represents the sūtra collection that was presented by the Seer himself.[1545]

One can also see the following alternative formulation of this answer: Worshipping someone who does not have a mind results in benefit too. This is like the benefit of worshipping reliquaries and volumes of texts. Through worshipping illusionlike Buddhas, the merit [from this] arises as a mere illusion. This is **just as** the assertion by you realists that worshipping **a real Buddha will yield** the manifestation of **a** real **result.**

### [Synopsis of Other Commentaries]

As for these [verses], Kalyāṇadeva explains:

> Emptiness is the wisdom of true reality. The seeds of this are the latent tendencies [of emptiness]. To cultivate it means to develop complete familiarity with cultivation. This relinquishes and eliminates the latent tendencies of entities, which are the seeds of the conceptions of form and such. [Lines 32cd] "Through familiarity with . . ." refer to nonentities. . . .
>
> Having explained the nirvāṇa with remainder in this way, [verse 33] "Once . . ." [is taught] in order to teach the [nirvāṇa] without remainder.
>
> [Verse 37:] After the Body of the Victor is accomplished, the bodhisattva who has a mind has passed away. Still, through the twofold force of aspiration prayers and those to be trained, the welfare of all sentient beings [798] will be brought about. Thus, this is not a total nirvāṇa like in the case of the hearers. . . .
>
> [Verses 38–39:] Before it was explained that merit arises from a mind that is equal to an illusion, and [now] it is said, "Although the [bodhisattva] is not here now, . . ." [However,] this case is special. Here, it

> is established through scriptural valid cognition that the result of merit is equivalent. Therefore, whether this applies to the seeming or to the ultimate level, [making offerings to a Buddha who has passed away] yields results in a similar way as when one makes offerings to a Buddha who is alive.[1546]

Vibhūticandra explains:

> [As for lines 32cd:] You might maintain, "There is nothing wrong in apprehending emptiness." Through familiarity with [the notion] that "entities or [even] emptiness does not exist at all," later the latent tendencies of emptiness also are relinquished, because the means are like a boat [to be left behind upon reaching the other shore].
>
> [Verse 34:] As for the lack of an ultimately existing entity, not even [this] lack of entity exists. Therefore, these two [entity and nonentity] do not appear from the perspective of [this] mental state. Since a third alternative that would be neither an entity nor a nonentity does not exist either, there is no observed object and no support. Like a fire whose firewood has been exhausted, the mind has then passed into nirvāṇa.
>
> [Verse 37:] The Body of the Victor that is endowed with the major and minor marks will appear. You might wonder, "From what [does it appear]?" It does so from the fully ripened roots of virtue of those to be trained and the aspiration prayers of the Blessed One . . .
>
> [Verse 38:] It is like this: A physician who eliminates poison and has attained the potency of mantra, through that mantra, prepares plants, such as trees [as antidotes to poison]. When he dies, he thinks, "Even if I am not here [anymore], may all poisons still be eliminated through this [remedy]." Then, even if a long time has elapsed [since his death], [the remedy] still eliminates the negative influences of poison, spirits, and so on . . .
>
> [Verse 39:] Here, reasoning is not necessary. The result [of worshipping Buddhas who have passed away] can be found in the scriptures.

One has to assert this as the seeming of the Centrists and your ultimate.[1547]

*The Small Commentary on the Difficult Points* comments:

> You might wonder, "Is the conception that [everything] is illusion not relinquished?" It surely is. [799] [This is indicated by lines 32cd] "Through familiarity with 'utter nonexistence,' . . ."
>
> Even the very apprehension of nonexistence is relinquished, [which is shown by verse 33] "Once this 'utter nonexistence' . . ." You might ask, "What is nonexistence?" The answer is, "It is a vase." If a vase is not established through mundane seeing, also [its] negation, which depends on this, is not established. Hence, this very nonexistence too is not observed. You might think, "However, what is seen by the knowledge of a Buddha that is the final seeing of true reality?" Since ultimately no consciousness whatsoever engages [an object], there is no arising of a consciousness that sees this [ultimate nature]. This is taught by [verse 34:] "Once neither entities nor nonentities . . ." Just as the nonobservation of all aspects of form is expressed as "seeing space," likewise, all that is done here is to express the very nonobservation of all aspects of signs as "the expanse of signlessness." *The Sublime Continuum* says:
>
> > The assertion is that all exertion is at peace
> > And the reason [for this] is mind's nonconceptuality.[1548]
>
> Thus, through knowledge that lasts one single moment, the suchness of all phenomena has become truly and perfectly enlightened. After that, when the path of complete release has become manifest, the continuous engagement of mirrorlike wisdom is the Body of Enjoyment. Due to this, various emanations that accord with the individual intentions [of sentient beings] engage in all the worlds. This is the attainment of the Emanation Body.
>
> This mirrorlike [wisdom] is the dominant cause for the appearance of the Form Bodies, or the cause for form. . . . Emanations are the Form Bodies that have the definining characteristic of appearing as form, because they are seen as form in the world.

There appears no explanation in *The Small Commentary on the Difficult Points* for [verse 39] "No matter whether on the seeming or the actual level . . ." However, *The Small Commentary on the Difficult Points of the Knowledge Chapter Only* explains:

> If Buddhahoood itself and the results of generosity and such are [established] through the scriptures, then [800] no matter whether these are seeming or ultimate, there is no problem—what is the difference?[1549]

The [master] from Sabsang[1550] supplements the following words:

> This is adequate for both the seeming—the Form Bodies—and the ultimate, the Dharma Body. . . . The pillar that was accomplished by the Brahman Śaṅku before . . .

Some notes on *The Entrance to the Bodhisattva's Way of Life* that were transmitted through the Great Lord [Atīśa] say:

> In former times, in the area where the Brahman called Śrī Śaṅku lived, everybody was afflicted by nāga diseases. So he went to look for a mantra that would bring the nāgas under control. [On his way,] he saw a black woman who had laid down a small child [next to a field]. While she was weeding, the small child cried, and the woman strewed white mustard seeds upon it. This caused a black snake to come forth and lick the [child], which made it appear to be dead. When [the woman] had finished weeding, she strewed another substance [upon the child]. This caused a white snake to come forth, which licked [the child] and thus revived it. [The Brahman] then requested the awareness mantra from the [woman]. When she made him drink eight one-ounce [cups] of milk from a black bitch, he drank seven and then poured off the [last cup that was still] full. Thus, he won mastery over seven nagas, but he did not win unlimited mastery over the eighth one. Therefore, a child told [him], "When poisonous ulcers on the shoulders appear, scoop some foam from the ocean and drink it." In this way, the Brahman pacified many diseases. [However,] later on he did not obtain [enough] foam from the ocean for all the limitless inflictions. So he carried a corpse [from] a house to a garuda pillar and leaned it against [the pillar], thus reviving it. For a long time he benefited the people and made aspiration prayers that this pillar would be able to neutralize all poisons.

[This pillar] appears [today] in the same way as when the Brahman Śaṅku was alive. In general, since it is certain that there is a clear source for this example, it is appropriate to search for this [pillar].[1551]

### 2.2.2. The Proof That Seeing [Entities] as Emptiness Is the Path

This has two parts:
1) The proof through scripture
2) The proof through reasoning

### 2.2.2.1. The Proof through Scripture

This has three parts:
1) Presenting the objection
2) The brief answer in the scriptures
3) The proof that the great vehicle is Buddha's speech

### 2.2.2.1.1. Presenting the Objection

> [801] **"You will be released through seeing the realities,**
> **But what is the point of seeing emptiness?"** [40ab]

[803] A proponent of the philosophical system of the hearers might say, **"You will be released** from cyclic existence **through seeing** the four **realities** in sixteen aspects,[1552] **but what is the point of seeing emptiness?"**

### 2.2.2.1.2. The Brief Answer in the Scriptures

> **The reason is that the scriptures declare**
> **That there is no enlightenment without this path.** [40cd]

**The reason is that the scriptures** of our very Teacher **declare that there is no** attainment of **enlightenment without this path** of seeing emptiness, because this is extensively stated in such texts as *The Mother of the Victors*:[1553]

> Those with the discriminating notion of "entities" lack the meditation that is [characteristic of] the perfection of knowledge. They lack it starting from all the gates of meditative concentration and dhāraṇi, the powers, the fearlessnesses, and the individual perfect awarenesses up through the meditation on the unique qualities of a Buddha.

*The Sūtra of Entering Equality*[1554] says:

> O Mañjuśrī, through mentally engaging in emptiness, this attainment

of all three [types of] enlightenment is the case and there is the chance for it. For those with the discriminating notion of "entities," this attainment of the three [types of] enlightenment is not the case and there is no chance for it.

The path of all the past and future Victors and of those who live in the ten directions [at present]
Is this perfection. [Everything] else is not [their path].

It is not possible that the noble ones of the hearers reject the great vehicle [804], for the following reason: It is stated that it is not the case and that there is no chance that any arhat who hears this great vehicle will not have true confidence. Through this, it can be illustrated that [there is a tendency in this] direction [of the great vehicle] all the way down even to stream-enterers. Also among those who have attained any of the twenty discriminating notions[1555] and who dedicatedly work on meditative stability, there are generally few who reject the great vehicle, because there is a majority of those who are dedicated to examining the status of their own continua.

However, once one has attained the actual state of the fourth meditative stability and then attains the meditative absorption without discrimination in which discriminations and feelings have ceased, one might [still] cling to the idea that "I have attained arhathood." This is called "[an arhat] with the manifest pride of being an arhat." It is possible that one rejects the great vehicle through this [pride] for the following [two] reasons: Such is explained in *The Jewel Casket Sūtra.* In general, seers who possess the five supernatural knowledges can see five hundred former lifetimes with the [kind of] supernatural knowledge that remembers former states, [but] they do not see beyond this [time span]. Therefore, wrong philosophical systems of a fixed number of former and laterlives—such as [thinking], "Beyond that [time] I do not exist"—have originated.

Thus, it is mainly hearers fond of dialectic who cling to any mere words from the three scriptural collections[1556] and become arrogant through presuming that this [clinging] is the self-confidence of awareness and release.[1557] They are well known and self-appointed as paṇḍitas and such. While not understanding the inconceivable dharma of the Buddha, they presume to apprehend and grasp the scope of the unlimited space of dharma with their own understanding that is like the wingspan of a bee. They say that everything that is not in accordance with this is not dharma and angrily denounce and reject it.

This is the case because [of the following:] We find reports of this kind—such as in *The Great Cloud* [*Sūtra*][1558] and *The Great Drum* [*Sūtra*]—about [people] who were self-appointed hearers and rejected the great vehicle in India's central provinces as well as in its east, west, and so forth. These [reports] include prophecies that they will all descend into countless bad migrations through their obscurations of rejecting the dharma. [805]

Also here in the land of Tibet, it seems that there were limitless people who negated the "view that eliminates the four extremes" by calling its [propounders pejoratively] "those who [have the view of] neither existence nor nonexistence";[1559] who dismissed the "meditation that is free from cognition and without mental engagement"[1560] by saying, "This is the tradition of the Chinese Hvashang"; who held that the "teaching about the nature of conception being the true nature of phenomena"[1561] and the "teaching that there is nothing to be adopted or rejected"[1562] and so forth are limitless perverted dharmas. They presumed that [they themselves] are the suns of speech.[1563] Even today, their followers greatly enhance their talking in the style of mangy horses,[1564] which rejects the dharma, and thus open the gates [that lead] beneath the earth.

### 2.2.2.1.3. The Proof That the Great Vehicle Is Buddha's Speech

> **If the great vehicle is not established,**
> **How are your scriptures established?**
> **"Because they are established for both [of us]."**
> **[However,] they were not established for you at first. [41]**
>
> **You should apply the conditions that made you believe in them**
> **In the same way to the great vehicle too. [42ab]**

These six lines express the equal applicability [of the reason].

Thus, those who have such a bad fate and are like evil spirits say, "A great vehicle does not exist for the following reasons: (a) Those in the direct retinue of our Teacher, such as Śāriputra, did not hear it. (b) If they had heard it, it would be reasonable that it would have come to us hearers, but that did not happen. (c) It was stated that something is Buddha's speech if it is contained in the sūtra collection, appears in the vinaya, and does not contradict the true nature of phenomena. However, the great vehicle is not something like this, because it is not contained in our sūtra collection and so on."

Here, we ask in return: **If it is not established** that **the great vehicle** is the Buddha's speech, **how** is it **established** that the **scriptures** of **you** hearers—the three scriptural collections—**are established?** They might say, "[They are established,] **because they are** well known and **established for both** of us." So do you believe that they are the Buddha's speech since beginningless time, or did you come to know them as the Buddha's speech later by virtue of spiritual friends?

The **first** alternative does not apply, because it was **not established for you** that the [scriptures of the hearers] are the Buddha's speech when you were a newborn child that was not grown up yet and when you were a lay person who was not engaged in any philosophical system and thus was ignorant even about the conventional term "Buddha's speech."

If there are certain **conditions,** such as spiritual friends, [806] **that made you believe in the** Teacher being the Buddha, his teaching being the genuine dharma, and the guides being the spiritual community, **you should equally apply** these [conditions] **to the great vehicle too.** [This is just the same case,] because the belief in the inconceivable Dharma Body and the Form [Bodies], the limitless scriptural collections of the great vehicle, and the marvelous spiritual community of bodhisattvas arises from the conditions that are the spiritual friends of the great vehicle and the profound and vast scriptural collections.

It is also not the case that great hearers, such as Śāriputra, did not hear the [great vehicle], because their names are mentioned in the introductions to great sūtras of the great vehicle and [because] they and the great bodhisattvas ascertained the dharma through questions and answers. That imperfect hearers who are not vessels for the great vehicle did not hear and experience it does not serve as a correct reason to prove that the great vehicle does not exist. One might as well say, "It is not possible that bees extract honey from a lotus, because if the lotus had honey, the insects and frogs that continuously hang on to the roots of the lotus must have tasted it, but they do not taste it." What would be the difference [between this and your statement above]?

> **The discourses that are included in the sūtra collection**
> **You assert as the words of the Buddha.**
> **Does this not simply amount to asserting**
> **That most of the great vehicle is equal to your sūtras? [49]**[1565]

This verse proves that [the great vehicle] is included in the sūtra collection and so on.

**You** certainly **assert the discourses that are** the words that are **included in the sūtra collection**, appear in the vinaya, and do not contradict the true nature of phenomena **as the words of the Buddha.** However, then [it follows that] all three scriptural collections of the hearers are not the Buddha's speech either, because they are not included in the sūtra collection of the great vehicle, do not appear in its vinaya, and contradict the true nature of phenomena.

**If** you think, "There is no such mistake, because they are included in just the hearers' sūtra collection and so on," well, then, since also the dharma of the great vehicle is included in the great vehicle's sūtra collection and so on, why should one not be able to prove [through this] that [the great vehicle] is the Buddha's speech? Consequently, **most of the great vehicle** too **is equal to your sūtras.** Why **do** you **not simply assert that** [the great vehicle] is the Buddha's speech that was spoken at certain occasions?

Here, the [Tibetan] translation [of line 49c] as "Does this not . . . ?" [reads] like a [plain] interrogative phrase and is [807] not a very effective translation. [The phrase,] "Why do you not simply assert . . ." [used in the preceding paragraph] is explained to mean that "even you [hearers] who do not assert [the existence of the great vehicle] would still have to accept it."

> **If the entirety were flawed**
> **On the basis of a single aspect that is determined as unsuitable,**[1566]
> **Why would not the entirety be the Buddha's word**
> **On the basis of a single corresponding sūtra?** [50]

This verse shows that if one were able to negate [that the great vehicle is the Buddha's speech] through a [flawed] mode of negative [entailment], one is [equally] able to prove this through the [corresponding] mode of positive [entailment].

You might argue, "Our sūtras teach impermanence and such, whereas the great vehicle teaches emptiness. Thus, it is not Buddha's speech." **If** one **were** able to prove **on the basis of a single aspect that is determined as unsuitable**—or on the basis of a single divergent reason—that **the entire** scriptural tradition is **flawed,** [your above objection] could be formulated as the following probative argument: "The sūtras of the great vehicle as the subject are not Buddha's speech, because, unlike the sūtras of the hearers, they do not teach impermanence." In this [sentence] also the reason certainly does not apply. However, for the time being, the equal applicability of the reverse [formulation of the reason and the predicate] is used in a way that is analogous [to your sentence]: "Well, then the sūtras of the great vehicle as the subject are Buddha's speech, because, just like the sūtras of the hearers, they teach the four realities and the thirty-seven factors for enlightenment." So **why would** one **not** also be able to prove that **the entirety** [of the great vehicle] is **the Buddha's word on the basis of** such **a single** reasoning **that** [one aspect of its sūtras] **corresponds** to your **sūtras?**[1567]

> **Mahākāśyapa and others did not fathom**
> **The depth of these discourses,**
> **So who would regard them as unacceptable**
> **Just because you do not understand them?** [51][1568]

These four lines teach that not realizing [something] oneself cannot serve as an argument to negate that others [realize it].

Thus, **these discourses** of the great vehicle possess the meanings of limitless aspects of intentions[1569] and flexible intentions.[1570] Even **Mahākāśyapa**, Śāriputra,[1571] **and others did not fathom** their **depth** for the following reasons: When Śāriputra was asked about all the profound points, he had a hard time answering, since he had reached the end of his self-confidence. Then [his questioner said,] "What, did the Thus-Gone One not prophesy you as the most excellent one among those who possess knowledge?" [Śāriputra] answered, "He taught that I am the most excellent one among those who possess knowledge in terms of the hearers who are endowed with one-sided knowledge. However, he did not [say this] in terms of the bodhisattvas who are endowed with inconceivable knowledge." [Furthermore,] it has been taught that the young lady Excellent Moon,[1572] the woman [called] "Renowned to Be without Change and Stain," [808] and others have outshone great hearers with their self-confidence.

Why **would** anybody **regard the** great vehicle **as** an **unacceptable** [source of] valid cognition **just because** of the reason that **you** dialecticians with your one-sided knowledge **do not understand these** [teachings] that possess such inconceivable meanings? If one were able to prove that something is not correct because someone does not understand it, then that would apply in the same way to the inferior vehicle too, because an ox does not realize it.

> **If something were true just because two different parties assert it,**
> **Then also the Vedas and such would be true.** [42cd]
>
> **If you say, "Because the great vehicle is disputed,"**
> **You should abandon your scriptures,**
> **Because these scriptures are disputed by the forders,**
> **As are certain of their parts between you and others.** [43]

These six lines [802] teach that one is not able to establish any kind of reason through [the power of] entities, neither through the reason that something is asserted by both [parties] nor [through the reason] that it is disputed.

[808] Furthermore, also your [previous] answer [in line 41c], "You wonder why? These are established for both [of us]" is uncertain as to the mode of positive concomitance. **If something were true just because two** disputing parties—oneself and someone **different**—provisionally **assert** that **it** is established, **then also the** four **Vedas and such would be** something to be accepted as **true**, because they are provisionally accepted by both Buddhists and non-Buddhists. **If you say,** "This is not the same, **because the great vehicle is disputed** as to whether it

is the Buddha's speech or not," it would follow that **you should** also **abandon your scriptures** of the inferior vehicle. This is **because the scriptures** of the inferior vehicle **are** also **disputed by the** non-Buddhist **forders,** such as when they say, "Alas, what the Erudites[1573] say is like the footprints of a wolf."[1574] There **are** also disputes about **certain of the parts** of these Buddhist scriptures **between your** own faction [within the lesser vehicle]—the Proponents of the Existence of All Bases[1575]—**and others**, that is, all [remaining] of the eighteen sects, such as the Venerated Ones.[1576]

## [Synopsis of Other Commentaries]

The learned one of *The Great Commentary*[1577] and Vibhūticandra explain:

> Since these verses [49–51, beginning,] "The discourses that . . . ," are unrelated [to Śāntideva's text], they do not represent the words of this master .[1578]

Kalyāṇadeva and Dānaśrī explain:

> It is stated that [these verses 49–51] are not considered to be related [to this text], since it is a text that emphasizes practice.[1579]

Such explanations certainly do exist. However, personally, I think that these [verses] do not entail any mistake whatsoever of being unrelated [to this text] for the following reasons: The meaning of the great vehicle is inconceivable. [809] Thus, [Śāntideva] gives an answer [here] by establishing the great vehicle's own texts as a [source of] valid cognition [by saying], "How should you fathom something whose depths Mahākāśyapa and others were not able to fathom before?" If this [verse 51] did not represent the words of master [Śāntideva], [what remains of this whole] *śloka*[1580] would be very little, because then line [51e] "This would apply in the same way to the inferior vehicle too"[1581] would be empty of something that is expressed [by it].

Such [considerations] certainly do apply. However, in this Land of Tibet, it is not that the great vehicle is negated by people who claim to be hearers. Rather, the profound essential points of the great vehicle are negated only people who claim to be followers of the great vehicle. In this newly founded great tradition of rejecting the dharma in such a way, they exclaim, "We distinguish between dharma and nondharma." This seems to be a great abyss for those who wish for liberation.

With respect to these [verses], Kalyāṇadeva explains:

> [Line 41d] "[However,] they were not established for you at first" means: Without the great vehicle, one would not become enlightened, and without this [enlightenment], your scriptures are also not established.[1582]

*The Small Commentary on the Difficult Points* formulates the thesis of the opponent [in lines 40ab] as follows:

> One will be released through seeing what is real—the nature that actually exists—but not through seeing that nothing whatsoever is established.

*The Small Commentary on the Difficult Points of the Knowledge Chapter* supplements the following words:

> As for [the words] "for both [of us]" [in line 41c]: The [scriptures of the hearers] are established for both the opponent and the proponent. [Line 41d] "[However,] they were not established for you at first" means that the [scriptures of the hearers] were not established [for you hearers] before you accepted them.[1583]

The [master] from Sabsang appears to give the following explanation:

> You might say, "The inferior vehicle is the Buddha's speech, since both the persons of the great vehicle and those of the inferior vehicle assert it as the Buddha's speech. However, the great vehicle is not the Buddha's speech, because we hearers do not assert it as the Buddha's speech." However, then also the inferior vehicle would not have been established as the Buddha's speech during the time when, first, nobody else believed in it. [810]

The Blessed One Maitreya proves in *The Ornament of Sūtras*[1584] that the great vehicle is the Buddha's speech. [Here,] the way in which he does so shall be given as an ancillary explanation.

Those who reject the dharma are those who have inferior faculties by nature and are controlled by negative friends:

> They aspire to what is inferior, and their constitutions are also very much inferior.
> They are completely surrounded by inferior friends.

> If to this dharma that excellently explains what is profound and vast
> They do not aspire, it is established [as supreme].[1585]

The way they reject [the great vehicle] is by saying, "Since there were a great many who attained arhathood by means of the vehicle of the hearers, the demons[1586] taught the great vehicle in which one must stay in cyclic existence for the welfare of others until cyclic existence is emptied. Therefore, everybody entered this [vehicle] and those who attain arhathood have become less. Thus, it has been taught as an obstacle to liberation."

Some also say, "This great vehicle was concocted by dialecticians in order to mock the teachings. [This is the case] because the texts of those dialecticians who are the Mundanely Minded teach that nothing at all exists, and this [great vehicle] also teaches that—from form up through omniscience—nothing exists. [Moreover,] the definition of the Buddha's speech is: 'That which serves as the remedy for cyclic existence and teaches the unmistaken view.' However, this [great vehicle] does not function as a remedy for cyclic existence, because it teaches that one has to remain in cyclic existence for a long time. [Also,] its view is mistaken, because it teaches nonexistence. Therefore, it is not the Buddha's speech."

Here, [Maitreya] invalidates wrong conceptions through a sevenfold reasoning:

> [The great vehicle is Buddha's word,] for [the following] reasons:
> There was no prophecy before; it originated simultaneously;
> It is not an object; it is established;
> If it exists, it exists, and if it did not exist, [the inferior vehicle] would not exist either;
> It is a remedy; its terms are different.[1587]

1) It was not concocted by demons, because if this were the case, it would have been reasonable that the Buddha Kāśyapa,[1588] just as in his prophecies in relation to the dreams of [King] Krikri,[1589] had prophesied, "The so-called great vehicle that was created by demons [811] will originate." But he did not teach this.

Some people think, "He did not prophesy this, since he did not know about it, or considered it to be of little purpose, or did not see it because it happened at some future time." This is not reasonable because of the following: [The Buddha] has direct vision of all knowable objects. Since there is nothing higher and superior to the teaching of the Buddha, it is not suitable for him to be indifferent about the great essential points in it. [The Buddha] does not have obscurations of wisdom with respect to the past and the future.

The Buddhas [have] direct vision,
They also protect the teachings,
And their wisdom is unobscured in terms of time too.
Therefore, it does not make sense that [the Buddha] was indifferent.[1590]

2) Furthermore, [in general,] if something is an obstacle, then the obstructing phenomenon must happen after the prior occurence of the phenomenon that is obstructed. In contrast, the great vehicle and the inferior vehicle occured together at the same time. Thus, how could one set them up as something that obstructs and something that is obstructed? This [teaching of the inferior vehicle] was given in order to avoid frightening the followers of the inferior vehicle and in order to guide them. Correctly speaking, in this teaching [of the great vehicle], the inferior vehicle is nothing but the first discourse for the group of five [disciples].[1591] However, the great vehicle [itself] is limitless, [which is] also [illustrated by] the dharma collections that were taught before the first wheel [of dharma on earth], such as the teaching of "the one hundred eight gates that illuminate the dharma" that [the Buddha gave] when he was about to move from Tuṣita[1592] and the proclamation of *The Sūtra of Vast Arrays of Buddhas*[1593] when he became enlightened [in Akaniṣṭha].

3) [The great vehicle] was not concocted by dialecticians for the following reason: Since their dialectic depends on naïve beings and does not have any essence, it is something uncertain, does not encompass perfect actuality, and teaches the seeming.

Dialectic is dependent and uncertain,
Not encompassing, seeming, and involves weariness.
It is asserted that it depends on naïve beings.
Therefore, this [great vehicle] is not their object.[1594]

Such profound and vast points [812] like these [in the great vehicle] are not the sphere of dialecticians.

4) Some people claim, "Though [the great vehicle] is not an object of other dialecticians, the seer Kapila and others have become omniscient. Thus, it was created by so-called special Buddhist dialecticians." Or, some say, "It was taught by a Buddha other than the Blessed One." However, then the great vehicle is established as Buddha's speech. This is just the same as the Buddha speech of Buddha Kāśyapa and the Buddha speech of Buddha Śākyamuni being equal in that [both] are Buddhas' speech. Not only is this definitely the case, but moreover, it is explained even in the sūtras of the inferior vehicle that a second teacher [who is

a Buddha] does not manifest in the single sphere [of one Buddha's activity]. In consequence, these people claim something that is contradictory to the sūtras, because they claim the Buddha speech of Buddha Kapila and [thus] that a Buddha other than our teacher has manifested in this sphere here during the present time [of our teacher].

5) Again, does a great vehicle exist or does it not exist? If it exists, it is reasonable that it is solely this [great vehicle under consideration], because if another [great vehicle] than this one existed, it should be suitable to appear, whereas, in fact, another [great vehicle] is not observable. If [the great vehicle] did not exist, the means for attaining Buddhahood would not exist [either]. If this were the case, also the inferior vehicle would not be Buddha's speech, since Buddhahood is not possible [given this absence of means for attaining it].

Some might say, "This very vehicle of the hearers is the great vehicle." This vehicle of the hearers is not the great vehicle—which is the means to accomplish Buddhahood—for the following reasons: (a) The ten perfections are not complete [in the vehicle of the hearers]. (b) It contradicts the path of great enlightenment, since it accomplishes only the minor welfare of oneself. (c) It is not the means for perfection, maturation, and purification.[1595]

> [It is] incomplete, contradictory,
> And not the means. Since it does not teach the like,
> This vehicle of the hearers
> Is not called the "dharma of the great vehicle."[1596]

Thus, this vehicle of the hearers and solitary realizers is inferior in its intention, which means that it intends the limited welfare of oneself. That it is inferior in its teaching [813] means that it teaches nothing but solely the means for liberation from cyclic existence. It is inferior in its training; that is, it is not conjoined with special means and knowledge. That it is inferior in its reliances means that it relies only on small accumulations and personal identitylessness. It is also [inferior] in terms of time, since [its practitioners] wish for a quick limited nirvāṇa, because they are not able to don the armor [of vigor] for the time of inconceivable eons. Since it is contradictory [to the great vehicle in these ways], it is called the "inferior vehicle."

> In intention, teaching,
> Training, reliance,
> And time it is contradictory. What is inferior because of these [factors]
> Is just something inferior.[1597]

6) Furthermore, [the great vehicle] is qualified by the three seals that indicate Buddha's speech, for the following reasons: (a) It applies to its own sūtra collection, since it teaches the inconceivable actuality. (b) It appears in its own vinaya, since it vanquishes the afflictions, including their latent tendencies. (c) It is not contradictory to the profound and vast nature of phenomena. Hence, it is perfect Buddha speech.

> Because it applies to its very own [sūtras]
> And also appears in its own vinaya,
> Because it is profound, and because it is vast,
> There is no contradiction to the nature of phenomena.[1598]

[The great vehicle] is the supreme of remedies because it releases numberless sentient beings from cyclic existence, to say nothing of vanquishing one's own cyclic existence. This is the case because it teaches the vast dharmas—seeming reality, the accumulation of merit, and the Form Bodies—in order to completely mature [beings] as well as the nonconceptual profound dharmas—ultimate reality, the accumulation of wisdom, and the Dharma Body. Thus, this [teaching] is the unsurpassable great means.

> Because it is vast, because it is profound,
> And because it is completely maturing and nonconceptual,
> Both [dharmas] are taught in this one here.
> This is the unsurpassable means.[1599]

7) Also, such [expressions] as "nonexistence" are to be taught through words of implications and flexible implications as such terms that differ [from their superficial meanings]. Certainly, [814] these are not to be taken literally. It is explained that they were stated in the texts of profound view in order to eliminate superimposition and denial and that they were stated in the texts of vast conduct with the implication of the threefold lack of a nature. However, they are not to be clung to as exclusively this.

> [The great vehicle is the Buddha's word,] because there are no others than this [and because] it is very profound and concomitant.
> It entails teaching the whole variety and teaching continuously through a multitude.
> Its meaning is not just literal and the implications of the Conqueror are very profound.
> If the learned ones examine properly, they will not be frightened by this dharma.[1600]

Therefore, if one listens to and hears the collection of the great vehicle with its profound and vast meanings, proper mental engagement in its meaning that is approximately concordant with meditative concentration will arise. From this, special knowledge of having attained certainty about perfect actuality will arise.

> Here, proper mental engagement that relies on hearing originates first.
> From proper mental engagement comes wisdom that has perfect actuality as its object.
> From this the dharma is obtained, and, due to its presence, intelligent insight arises vividly.[1601]

Therefore, the causes that make one reject the dharma originate from inferior intelligence, little confidence, great haughtiness due to pride about [having] some little knowledge and so on, clinging to solely the sūtra collection with expedient meaning, craving for gain and honor, and relying on friends or tutors who delight in rejecting the dharma. *The Sublime Continuum* says:

> Because they are of inferior intelligence, because they lack the aspiration for the bright [qualities], because they rely on improper pride,
> Because they have the character of being obscured through missing the genuine dharma, because they grasp at the expedient meaning as being the definitive, true reality,
> Because they yearn for gain, because they are under the sway of [wrong] views, because they rely on those who criticize the dharma,
> Because they fend off the holders of dharma, and because they have inferior aspirations, they reject the dharma of the arhats.[1602] [815]

Except for rejecting the dharma, there is no action whatsoever to be afraid of. Here, even such actions as the five deeds without interval[1603] cannot be adduced as [counter-]examples, because these deeds without interval will certainly be shattered by [the power of one's] regret. In contrast, [usually,] one does not regret having rejected the dharma and, on top of this, [even] regards [such rejection] as something superior. [*The Sublime Continuum* states:]

> Learned beings should not be as deeply afraid of fire, the poison of venomous snakes, executioners, or lightning
> As they should be of falling away from the profound dharma.
> Fire, snakes, enemies, and thunderbolts may only end your life,
> But the beings in [the hell of] utmost torture will not be very afraid of them.

> Some persons may have relied on evil friends again and again and thus committed the heinous actions
> Of heeding a bad intention toward a Buddha, killing their parents or an arhat, or splitting the highest community.
> If they sincerely reflect on the nature of phenomena, they will be swiftly released from these [actions],
> But where should there be liberation for someone whose mind hates the dharma?[1604]

In brief, those who speak with strong clinging do not transcend rejecting the dharma. *The Sūtra That Is a Synopsis of the Entirety of Complete Pulverization*[1605] says:

> Undefeatable One,[1606] for those who remain in the discriminating notion of sentient beings and the discriminating notion of phenomena, there are actions to actually be committed. However, for those who are nonreferential, there are none.
>
> Mañjuśrī, if some have the discriminating notion "good" and some have the discriminating notion "bad" toward the Buddha's speech that is proclaimed by the Thus-Gone Ones, they reject the dharma.
>
> To say, "This is reasonable" and "This is unreasonable" means rejecting the dharma. To state, "This was declared for the sake of bodhisattvas" and "This was declared for the sake of hearers" is to reject the dharma. To say, "This is a training for bodhisattvas" and "This is not [such] a training" means rejecting the dharma.

[816] It is stated that also [the following factors] are included in rejecting the dharma: all attributions of mistakes (such as with respect to the conduct of proponents of the dharma, their words, the meaning [of these], whether these are contradictory or repetitive), all doubts, and all discriminating notions of rejecting or adopting with respect to the Buddha's speech. [A sūtra] reports:

> During [the time of] the teachings that are renowned to come from the previous Thus-Gone One "Radiating Immaculate Light," the present Buddha Amitāyus was a fully ordained monk called "Entirely Pure Conduct." He adopted sixty thousand sūtras of complete pulverization and one hundred million sūtra collections. Then he tamed an infinite number of individuals within the three vehicles through teaching in accordance with their aspirations. The Thus-Gone One himself[1607] was

> a fully ordained monk called "Dharma." He adopted one thousand sūtras of complete pulverization, attained the fourth meditative stability, and became endowed with the [twelve] qualities of training.[1608] Then he taught that anything other than just emptiness is not the Buddha's speech and deprecated the previous dharma. Through this, he was born in the hells for seventy eons and forgot the mind of enlightenment for sixty eons. After that, although the Thus-Gone One "Completely Hidden Jewel Light" had caused him to generate the mind [of enlightenment], he became an animal for ninety thousand lifetimes and a poor human being for sixty thousand [lifetimes]. However, in all of these [rebirths,] he was [born] without a tongue.

It is further stated that, even if someone who rejects the dharma will become enlightened, demons will appear, degenerated times will happen, and many obstacles to the teaching will too.

*The Sūtra That Teaches the Nonorigination of All Phenomena*[1609] explains:

> During the teaching of the previous Buddha "King Truly Noble Like the Highest Mountain," there was the Thus-Gone One "Unshakable Fully Ordained Monk with Completely Pure Conduct" together with his retinue. He was not watching the sense faculties, consciousnesses, or observed objects; that is, he was endowed with conduct that is skillful in means. Our Teacher [Buddha Śākyamuni] himself was a fully ordained monk called "Intelligent Insight of Conduct." He had attained the five supernatural knowledges, was endowed with ethics and skilled in the vinaya, had qualities of purification, liked seclusion, and had a retinue that was just like him. [817] He disparaged the former [Thus-Gone One by saying], "He has corrupted ethics," and deprecated his dharma too. Thus, after his transition from this lifetime, he experienced unbearable sufferings in the lower realms and such, just like the aforementioned one.

Even Mañjuśrī reported the following [in a sūtra]:

> In the Buddha-field "Great Illumination" of the former Thus-Gone One "Lion's Roar, King of Drum Sound," the present Buddha "Immaculate Abundant Splendor Who Outshines Sun and Moon" was an upholder of the dharma called "Utterly Joyous Senses." He was endowed with the conduct of means of someone who does not think about something to be adopted or to be discarded. He taught those

with sharp faculties who wish for just the expression of the initial phrases [with the words], "All phenomena have the nature of desire. They have the nature of hatred and dullness. They are unobscured. Also all conduct has the same defining characteristic." Thus, he placed them in [the state of] endurance.[1610]

At that time, I (Mañjuśrī) was [also] an upholder of the dharma called "Intelligent Insight of the Victors." I had attained the meditative [stabilities of the form] and the form[less realms], was endowed with the qualities of purification, and proclaimed the flaws of worldly hustle and bustle as well as the praises of solitary seclusion. One day I enjoyed my alms in the home of a lay man who was a disciple of the above upholder of the dharma and taught the dharma to the lay man's son who had attained endurance. When I deprecated the dharma and this person by saying, "This former upholder of the dharma taught wrongly," the lay man's son said, "Venerable One, how do You understand desire?" "I understand it as completely afflicted." "Well, then, is desire inside or is it outside? Desire is neither inside nor is it outside. In this way, desire is neither inside nor outside. Thus, it is also not in any of the cardinal and directional points. If this is the case, it is unarisen: So what from among afflicted phenomena or purified phenomena could exist in what is unarisen?" Having heard this, I (this fully ordained monk) got irritated and angry, went off without even taking my alms with me, [818] and accused the above upholder of the dharma in the middle of the spiritual community. Then the above upholder of the dharma said amid the spiritual community:

It was declared that desire is nirvāṇa.
Hatred and dullness are just like this.
Enlightenment is their very abode.
A Buddha's enlightenment is inconceivable.

Those who completely impute desire
And do so with hatred and dullness too,
For them, a Buddha's enlightenment is as far away
As the sky from the earth.

The duo of enlightenment and desire do not exist as two.
Engaging in them is the same; they are endowed with equality.
For naïve beings who are frightened by the dharma of these,

Buddha enlightenment is far away.

Desire does not arise and does not cease.
Mind does not become afflicted.
Those whose minds are attached to observed identities
Are thrown into the lower realms through desire.

and

For those who become mad through being bloated with ethics
And who remain entirely in referential views,
There is no enlightenment nor any Buddha qualities.

and

Those who see the conditioned and the unconditioned
Will not move somewhere other than within samsaric phenomena.
Those who realize the basic element [as] equality
Will swiftly become supremely enlightened beings.

If someone never sees any
Of the Buddha's qualities nor the Buddha's speech,
That one is untainted by all phenomena,
Vanquishes the demons, and will also truly awaken into
enlightenment.

and

The Buddhadharmas equal space . . .

This dharma of the genuine king of dharma is unmoving,
Without being, without characteristics, and in the same way
Empty of nature. Not hearing this dharma,
Naïve beings fall into the great abyss. [819]

Through such teachings, thirty-two thousand gods attained endurance of the unarisen dharma, and eighty thousand fully ordained monks attained arhathood. After I (the fully ordained monk "Intelligent Insight of the Victors") had died, I experienced limitless lower realms and even as a human being I [only] earned disgrace. For many hundred thousand eons I did not hear the name Victor; for seventy-six thousand lifetimes I fell away from ordination; and for many thousand lifetimes my faculties were weak. Nevertheless, because of having heard these verses, my actions became purified and I attained this kind of endurance [that was taught above] wherever I was born. Thus, I became Mañjuśrī, the supreme of the bodhisattvas who propound emptiness.

After [Mañjuśrī] had reported this, the Blessed One declared, "Since entities are like that, it does not matter whether one enters the vehicle of bodhisattvas or enters the vehicle of hearers. If someone does not have such obscurations of painful toil and no such sufferings, such a being will not reject the genuine dharma, will not disparage the genuine dharma, and will not be angry toward any dharma whatsoever."

*The Sūtra That Is a Synopsis of the Entirety of Complete Pulverization* says:

> Mañjuśrī, I do not call clinging "bodhisattva conduct." I do not call attachment to a home "completely pure livelihood." I do not say that those who teach duality are released from being destitute of dharma. I do not say that those who teach one single nature are released from the lower realms. I do not say, "Those who delight in talking are entirely pure." Mañjuśrī, I teach the gates of dharma which are as numerous as the grains of sand in the river Gaṅgā in a way that is nonreferential.
>
> Likewise, there are so many ways that this is taught, starting from the gates of discriminating notions that involve observed objects, emptiness, and sentient beings, followed by signlessness, nonconceptuality, and [820] wishlessness, the person and the nonexistence of the person, existence and nonexistence, the conditioned and the unconditioned, expediency and the nonexistence of expediency, secrecy and the nonexistence of secrecy, cyclic existence and nirvāṇa, the mundane and the supramundane, desire, hatred, and dullness, up to and including the gate of relinquishment. Mañjuśrī, if all of these were the way of being of the perfection of knowledge through [just] the way of being of impermanence, then you would only know a single tiny fraction of a fraction of the [perfection of knowledge] and thus deprecate the Thus-Gone One.
>
> If people who have rejected the dharma confess this three times every twenty-four hours for seven years, they are purified. If [such persons] are close to attaining endurance, they will [attain it] in ten eons.
>
> It is stated that you will regress [in your spiritual development] if you talk about this dharma without having trained in it first. You should

speak about it through abiding in the four equalities: the equality of sentient beings, the equality of phenomena, [the equality of] enlightenment, and [the equality of] insight. Otherwise, you will regress.

*The Ornament* [*of Sūtras*] states:

If [anger] is inappropriate even toward inappropriate forms,
There is no need to mention [the anger] toward the dharma that one doubts.
Therefore, it is excellent to rest in equanimity—this has no flaw.[1611]

In this land of Tibet, those who know a little bit of the dialectic approach and such are very haughty. It seems that they grasp at the scope of all phenomena and decide, "There are no explanations [of the dharma] except for [those in] all the sūtras and tantras." The one who loudly proclaims such things as, "Except for Candrakīrti in India and me in Tibet, there is no one who understands the Centrist view" is set up by them as the supreme one among the learned.[1612] Nevertheless, such [assertions] are just points to be examined for a while, but I certainly have my doubts about taking them as my refuge.

Therefore, [*The Sūtra of*] *the Arrival in Lanka* [821] says:

O Mahāmati, what is called "having studied a lot" means being skilled in the meaning but does not mean being skilled in the terms. Being skilled in the meaning refers to such words that are not blended with any of the words of the ford-builders[1613]Thus, what will never make either yourself or others fall, O Mahāmati, is to keep in mind a lot of studies that pertain to the meaning.[1614]

The peel of a sugar cane plant does not have any core at all,
[But] what is delightful dwells inside it.
Human beings who eat the peel
Are not able to find the delicious taste of sugar cane.
Here, what resembles the peel are the words,
And what resembles the taste is reflecting about the meaning.[1615]

Thus, it is taught that words and letters are very insignificant.

However, if [it really were the case that] the teaching of the Blessed One Śākyamuni had liberated only one single human being in India and one single human being in Tibet, then what kind of enlightened activity of the Blessed One [for the welfare of all sentient beings] is this supposed to be?

In this way, it is difficult to aspire to and have trust in this topic of the inconceivable great vehicle. Hence, it is explained in every sūtra of the great vehicle, such as the perfection of knowledge, that [even] mere conviction and rejoicing in the dharma of the great vehicle is of greater benefit than generosity and making offerings:

> Merely not rejecting this sūtra and having confidence in it is of greater benefit than providing all the necessary supplies for numerous Buddhas for many eons.

Therefore, *The Sublime Continuum* says:

> Those with intelligent insight who are filled with devotion for this object of the Victors
> Are vessels for the assembly of the Buddha qualities.
> Through truly taking delight in the assembly of inconceivable qualities,
> They outshine the merits of all sentient beings.
>
> Some who strive for enlightenment may constantly offer golden [Buddha-]fields bedecked with jewels
> That are equal in number to the particles of [all] Buddha-fields to the dharma kings every day.
> Others [822] may hear just one word of this [dharma] and, upon hearing it, their hearts will overflow with devotion.
> These persons will obtain merits far greater than the virtues that spring from such generosity.
>
> Some with intelligent insight who wish for unsurpassable enlightenment
> May observe immaculate ethics with body, speech, and mind through great effort for many eons.
> Others may just hear one word of this and, upon hearing it, their hearts will overflow with devotion.
> These persons will obtain merits far greater than the virtues that spring from such ethics.
>
> Some may complete right here the meditative stabilities that extinguish the blaze of all afflictions within the three realms of existence—
> The meditative states of the gods and Brahmā—and thus cultivate them as the means for perfect immutable enlightenment.
> Others may hear just one word of this and, upon hearing it, their hearts will overflow with devotion.

> These persons will obtain merits far greater than the virtues that spring from such meditative stabilities.[1616]

To say nothing of other virtues, [this is even true for] all virtues such as the following: Some people with the inspiration of the special engaging mind [of enlightenment] may perform generosity toward as many Buddhas as there are grains of sand in the river Gaṅgā every day for eons, such as offering them special things like golden Buddha-fields bedecked with jewels whose number equals the particles of Buddha-fields. Others may observe pure ethics for the sake of unsurpassable enlightenment for many eons. Some may cultivate meditation up to the fourth meditative stability as well as the aspiring and engaging mind of enlightenment for a long time. However, if you hear just a few words that are dressed in any one of the seven vajra points, then this virtue outshines all these former virtues. This is the case because the sūtras state that for each and every one of these [virtues above] you will obtain far greater merits [through the vajra points] than through them.

This is also established through reasoning because of the following: Through generosity, one obtains nothing but mere wealth. Through ethics, nothing but a body in the higher states [is gained]. [823] Through meditation, one achieves nothing but the relinquishment of the afflictive obscurations, but this does not function as the direct remedy for all obscurations. On the other hand, the knowledge that sees true reality relinquishes the two obscurations together with the latent tendencies at their root. The sole cause for the arising of such knowledge is hearing such profound specifications of the dharma [of knowledge].

> You wonder why? Generosity accomplishes wealth,
> Ethics higher states, and meditation relinquishes afflictions.
> Knowledge relinquishes all afflictive and cognitive [obscurations].
> Therefore, it is the most sublime and its cause is hearing this.[1617]

This is the way in which the Blessed One Maitreya has established the [great vehicle] through both scripture and reasoning.

Thus, it is difficult to aspire to this dharma of the great vehicle with inferior intelligent insight. If one has rejected it, one has to experience grave [results of] complete maturation for a while. However, precisely the mere hearing [of the dharma of the great vehicle] is what puts an end to the [cyclic] existence of such a sentient being later. Hence, the benefit of hearing it is immeasurable. *The Sūtra That Teaches Bodhisattva Conduct*[1618] states:

> Three years after the boy [called] Precious Gift had been born, he attained endurance at the time when our Teacher first developed the mind of enlightenment in the past. After three hundred thousand eons

had passed, [Precious Gift] taught that all phenomena are nothing to be adopted or rejected. At that point, Mañjuśrī asked him, "If your dharma teaching is of this kind, which words do you use to teach it to beginner bodhisattvas?"

He said, "[I start with] such [statements] as, 'Do not reject desire, do not dispel hatred, do not eliminate dullness, do not ascend above a real personality.' Then I say, 'Do not engage mentally in the Buddha, do not think about the dharma, do not make offerings to the spiritual community, do not take up the trainings, do not strive for utter peace of existence, do not cross the river.' With these kinds of instructions, beginner bodhisattvas [824] should be counseled and taught. You might wonder why [I say this]. The reason is that the nature of all phenomena is just abiding. Naïve beings specify them as arising and ceasing phenomena. [However,] this expanse of dharmas is characterized by nonconceptuality. Such realization of the nature of these phenomena is enlightenment. You should understand this by thinking, 'If someone is instructed in the aforesaid manner and is not afraid, is not frightened and will not be frightened, e ma, this is a bodhisattva who does not revert. This [bodhisattva] has the karmic disposition for the ground of irreversibility.' Thus, through these instructions, one should develop delight again and again."

At that point, eight fully ordained monks [whose minds] were referential did not feel devotion for such [teachings] and went away from the retinue. They died upon vomiting fresh blood and were reborn in the howling hell. Mañjuśrī said, "Alas, now look at all this harm that your dharma specification has inflicted on these fully ordained monks!"

The Blessed One pronounced, "Mañjuśrī, do not talk like this. If they had not heard this dharma, they would not even be reborn in any pleasant realms for one million eons, let alone become enligthened. It is precisely through hearing this dharma with their qualms that they become liberated from hell this very day and are reborn as gods in Tuṣita. They will please ten billion Buddhas for sixty-eight eons and live as miraculously born wheel-rulers[1619] throughout this time. Thereafter, they will become Buddhas who are [all] called Immaculate Light." During this prophecy, the sons of the gods arrived and said, "Blessed One, we rejoice in this specification of the dharma." They became nonreturners in this very moment.

*The Sūtra of the Abiding of Mañjuśrī*[1620] says:

> It is without analysis, [825] without discursiveness, utter peace. There is no claim of any statements such as "It exists," "It does not exist," "It both exists and does not exist," or "It does neither exist nor not exist." Once these are not claimed, this is nonreferentiality. Since this is freedom from all discursiveness, there is no mind and [there is] freedom from mind. It is called "abiding in the dharma of practicing positivity in the manner of nonabiding."
>
> Through this teaching, four hundred fully ordained monks became arhats. Another one hundred [fully ordained monks] were deeply disturbed and stayed behind. They fell into the howling hell.

[This sūtra] gives the following prophecy:

> If they had not heard this dharma, they definitely would have fallen into this hell [realm anyway], but through hearing this dharma, they come into contact with the sufferings of this hell only for a single moment and are instantly reborn as gods in Tuṣita. [Later,] they will attain arhathood as the first followers of [the coming Buddha] Maitreya.

Also *The Dharmamudrā Sūtra*[1621] states:

> [The Buddha] spoke, "Neither going beyond the phenomena of ordinary beings nor attaining uncontaminated phenomena—this is the ordination in the excellently spoken dharma of the vinaya and the supramundane completion of the vows. With this [kind of ordination and vows] it is appropriate to partake of [offerings] that are given out of confidence, whereas everything else is perverted ordination." Then Śāriputra and Subhūti ascertained the meaning of this, through which seven hundred fully ordained monks became arhats. One hundred got up [and left] because of not feeling devotion for this [teaching]. Five rejected it and stayed behind. Through [having heard] it, they fell into the hells but were instantly liberated [from them].

There are also many other [quotations] like these.

Thus, I can only pray: You self-appointed learned ones, please do not delimit the scope of the dharma, and do not reject some dharmas just because they may not be in accordance with some fraction of your own texts or just because they may not be in accordance with some fraction of the phraseology of naïve masters or their textbooks.

In this way, the establishment [of the great vehicle] through scripture [826] has been explained extensively by including supplementary remarks.

### 2.2.2.2. The Proof through Reasoning

**The root of the teaching is full monkhood,**
**And this full monkhood is ill established.**
**A nirvāṇa of those whose minds are referential**
**Is ill established too.** [44]

This [verse] teaches that one does not attain [the state of] the ultimate fully ordained monk and nirvāṇa if one does not realize emptiness.

[826] If one does not rely on the great vehicle, one does not obtain the teaching of the Buddha completely. The reason for this is: It is certainly the case that **the root of the teaching is full monkhood, and this full monkhood is** very **ill established.**

You might think, "What are you talking about? [It is said,] 'There are five [types of] fully ordained monks [that are described] in the vinaya: the fully ordained monk who just bears this name, the pretending fully ordained monk, the fully ordained monk who just seeks [alms], and the fully ordained monk who has vanquished the afflictions. [The fifth] is the one who has fully entered the order.[1622] [This is accomplished] through the fourfold act of requesting[1623] [that is performed] in this dharma [tradition]. [Here,] the intention is that he is the one who is to be called "fully ordained monk."' Thus, it is stated that the very one who receives the vows through the ritual of fourfold [activity], such as requesting, is the fully ordained monk. Therefore, [full monkhood] is well established."

Such an [explanation] is nothing but an approach to temporarily take care of naïve beings. This is the case because the [actual] intention [here] is that the perfect fully ordained monk is the ultimate fully ordained monk. This is the [monk] who has vanquished the afflictions, and the only one who has completely vanquished the afflictions is the Buddha.

Hence, **a nirvāṇa of those whose minds are referential is ill established too** for the following reasons. Many sūtras—such as *The Sūtra of the White Lotus of Genuine Dharma*—explain this in an extensive way:

> All the hearers did not pass into nirvāṇa.
> By engaging in enlightening conduct,
> All these hearers will become Buddhas.[1624]

The vehicle is just one, there are no two.
I taught two vehicles for the sake of [some needing to] take a rest.
Therefore, you fully ordained monks,
I do not pass into nirvāṇa today for just that much.
For the sake of omniscient wisdom,
You should generate extensive and genuine vigor.[1625]

Noble Śāriputra spoke [in this sūtra]:

Before, I was attached to views,
A wandering mendicant[1626] honored by the forders.
Then, the Protector knew my thoughts
And spoke about nirvāṇa in order that I be freed from views.

Having been freed from all that is a view, [827]
I attained the dharma of emptiness.
Therefore, I think, "I passed into nirvāṇa."
Yet this is not what is called "nirvāṇa."

When one has become a Buddha, the principal of sentient beings,
Honored by gods, humans, harmbringers, and evil ghosts,
And possesses the body with the thirty-two marks,
Then this is complete nirvāṇa.[1627]

The Blessed One Maitreya['s *Sublime Continuum*] explains:

Thus, without the attainment of Buddhahood,
Nirvāṇa is not attained,
Just as one is not able to watch the sun
Separated from its light and rays.[1628]

[The Buddha] has declared that one does not transcend being referential if one does not realize emptiness and that there is no way that someone who is referential could attain endurance.[1629] As he said this, how could it be possible that someone attains enlightenment who has not even attained endurance?

**If liberation came from relinquishment of the afflictions,**
**It should happen immediately after this.**
**However, one sees the efficacy of actions**

**Even in those who lack afflictions. [45]**

**You might argue, "Here it has been determined**
**That they do not have any craving that appropriates."**
**Why should they not also have unafflicted craving,**
**Just as they have basic ignorance? [46]**

**Craving comes from the condition of feelings,**
**And they do have feelings. [47ab]**

These two and a half verses teach that even arhats are not released from karma.

You might say, "Even without the realization of emptiness, **if** one is **liberated** from **the afflictions**, this in itself is enlightenment." Then it **would** follow that the [state that is attained] **immediately after this** liberation from the afflictions is perfect **relinquishment.** However, you cannot assert this, because it is explained that many results that are induced by former actions [exist] **even in those who** are asserted to be arhats of the inferior vehicle and **lack** manifest **afflictions.** [This can be seen from] such cases as Maudgalyāyana's limbs being smashed by wandering ascetics, Udāyin being beheaded by a robber chief, Little Kubja [dying from] eating mud soup at the end of being ill for seven days, and Upasena being caught by poisonous snakes.

[Also the effects of] latent tendencies of afflictions are explained here, such as in the case of the arhat Kapītanaḥ who destroyed the reliquary of [a person called] Thursday out of his latent tendencies of hatred. There were also some [arhats] who yelled, "Ain't they gorgeous!" at women and got all excited while guffawing with laughter. Or, we have such [reports] as the one about the two sons of Ānanda's sister [828] who were fooling around with their miraculous powers after they had attained novitiate and arhathood at the age of seven: On their way to fetch water, they would send the pot ahead in space while they followed behind. Furthermore, there was Gavāmpati, who, due to his latent tendencies of affection, cried out, "Brother Pūrṇa!"[1630] Thus, **one sees** that they possess **the** latent tendencies **of actions.**

**You might argue,** "This is certainly true. However, **here, it has been determined that they do not have any craving that appropriates** further existences." Agreed, those who are asserted to be hearer arhats surely do not have afflicted ignorance. However, since they do have unafflicted ignorance, their wisdom cannot engage in all knowable objects. Hence, they do not have this afflicted craving, but **why should they not have unafflicted craving, just as** they have unafflicted **basic ignorance?** [They indeed have unafflicted craving], because one sees them looking for food, taking medicine, and so on. You might think, "Well, then, that follows for the Buddha too." It does not: The purpose of such [beings] as the Buddha going for alms was already taught earlier.

Furthermore, [arhats of] the hearers and solitary realizers possess craving, because **craving** originates **from the condition of feelings, and they do have feelings.** You might say, "However, then it follows that coming into existence and being reborn must exist for them too, since craving leads to grasping, and [grasping] is followed by coming into existence." They do not have any grasping or birth that are induced by manifest actions and afflictions. However, they do have [the kind of] grasping and birth that is the transformation in the form of inconceivable death and transition that is based on imprints through subtle latent tendencies. This is the ground of latent tendencies of basic unawareness.

Therefore, *The Sūtra of* [*the Lion's Roar of Queen*] *Śrīmālā* and others declare that [arhats] do not attain the perfection of ultimate purity—the relinquishment of the ground of latent tendencies of basic unawareness—nor the [perfection] of ultimate permanence—the relinquishment of inconceivable death and transition. [829]

> **Referential minds**
> **Become stuck here and there.** [47cd]
>
> **Without emptiness, a fettered mind**
> **Will arise again,**
> **Just as in the case of the meditative absorption without discrimination.** [48a–c]

These five lines teach that the stream of births will not be interrupted if one does not realize emptiness.

Of course, there are cases of **minds** that **refer** to some objects and thus **become stuck** somewhere, that is, in some meditative concentrations, for many eons. However, such is not essential at all. **Without** the realization of true **emptiness, a mind** that is **fettered** [in this way] at one time **will arise again** due to other conditions [at a later time], **just as in the case of the meditative absorption** of someone **without discrimination.** One's mind stream is interrupted [in this meditative absorption] for [long periods], such as eighty-four thousand great eons, but one awakens again [from it] and is reborn in another place in cyclic existence.

### 2.2.3. The Summary of the Function of Both of These [Types of Seeing]

> **Thus, you should meditate on emptiness.** [48d]

**For the sake of those who are burdened with suffering due to ignorance,**
**One is released from the extremes of attachment and fear**
**And will manage to remain in cyclic existence.**
**This is the result of emptiness. [52]**

These five lines explain the result of having meditated on emptiness.

**Thus,** no one at all is observable who is a meditator (a self or a person) and nothing whatsoever is visible that is to be meditated upon (any such aspect as conditioned or unconditioned, permanent or impermanent, real or delusive). Hence, no discrimination whatsoever is adopted or discarded, and nothing is observed in any way of meditating whatsoever. Even the apprehension of observation or nonobservation does not exist before immaculate knowledge. In consequence, no one abides at any point in anything whatsoever, and also this is not seen as an aspect of anything. This [nonseeing] means seeing perfect actuality and knowing that there is nobody who meditates on anything in any way whatsoever. Thus, not being stirred from just this is called "to meditate on emptiness." A sūtra says:

> Through this, once mind and observed object are perfectly and most directly not seen, this is seeing what is perfect.

*The Sūtra of the King of Meditative Concentration* says:

> One finds that phenomena are unfindable,
> But also in [this] finding there is no finding.
> Those who know phenomena in this way
> Will realize ultimate enlightenment.
>
> Space is explained to be ungraspable.
> You do not find anything to grasp in it.
> The nature of phenomena is precisely this—
> Ungraspable, just as space.
>
> In this way, the dharma is taught: [830]
> There is nothing whatsoever in it to be seen.
> Inconceivable is this dharma
> Of those who do not see this dharma.

*The Sūtra of [the Meditative Concentration of] the Collection of All Merits*[1631] says:

> If these phenomena are unobservable,

The unskilled ones who observe [them]
Do not release themselves from suffering
And their sufferings will increase.

You might ask, "What does it mean to see phenomena just as they are?" This is what it is: just nonseeing.

These and other [quotations] explain this extensively.

To abide in this emptiness is supreme love, the supreme of all perfections, [supreme] complete upholding of the genuine dharma, and supreme pure ethics. *The Sūtra [Requested by the King of the Kinnaras, Called] "Tree,"*[1632] says:

"Sound of Music" [asked]:

"How come you embrace beings with love,
When you have realized identitylessness?
Identitylessness and love,
How could they be the same?"

The emanated bodhisattvas who dwelled on lotus flowers on the tips of light rays answered:

Those who fully know emptiness
Have internalized identitylessness.
Those who know that beings are empty
Are supreme in their love.

*The [Sūtra Requested by] Sky Treasure* applies this to all six [perfections], such as:

Not apprehending any phenomenon is supreme giving.

*The Sūtra of the King of Meditative Concentration* says:

Those who delight in peaceful emptiness
Are those who have grasped this dharma of the Victor.
Those who have grasped this meditative concentration
Have taken ordination in my teaching
And are the fully ordained monks with complete vows who perform the activities of restoration and purification.[1633]

This is also explained in many other places in the oceanlike collection of sūtras.

Therefore, in a manner of not meditating on anything at all, **you should meditate on** precisely just this perfect actuality that is beyond all observation.

You might ask, "What kind of result comes from meditating on this?" [831] All aspects of discrimination and observation as such and such are reversed. Thus, one knows that there is no phenomenon whatsoever to be attained through anything. This extinguishes [all] hopes for nirvāṇa. Just like knowing that a dream is a dream, one knows that suffering is not observable through its nature. Hence, there is no fear of cyclic existence. Apart from all phenomena just being mere imputations, they neither abide as any nature whatsoever nor do they abide as anything at all. Just this is what is seen as the very expanse of mind that is empty and luminous. This puts you in a position where you have complete power over everything you could possibly wish for, just as if all phenomena were resting in the palm of your hand.

Thus, by gaining power over and becoming very skilled in the dependent origination of the collections of causes for the entirety of cyclic existence and nirvāṇa, compassion for the assembly of sentient beings who do not realize this in the same way wells up unbearably. [However,] at this point, there is nothing to be observed as either oneself or sentient beings. To the same extent that great compassion increases, also this very [realization] that, primordially, nothing can be observed as sentient beings, what is not sentient beings, suffering, happiness, and so on grows and increases. This is the ultimate seeing that is like the orb of the sun. When it becomes stable and increases in such a way, great compassion—which is like the light rays of the sun—will grow even more than before. [Beings with such realization] do not behold sentient beings, but great compassion still flowers in them. They do not behold themselves either, but they still lend their support to all sentient beings. They do not behold anything to be attained whatsoever, but they still establish beings in great enlightenment. Just as there is no place whatsoever to go to beyond space, they do not behold anybody who would go somewhere beyond, but they still display [the activity of] liberating sentient beings from cyclic existence.

Thus, who would be able to realize the way of conduct of those who possess demeanors that [seem to be] contradictory to the world? Therefore, [832] what is the point of draining ourselves—who are just flies buzzing around—by [trying to] gauge the scope of these skylike bodhisattvas with our wingspan? Consequently, we should sincerely devote ourselves to being respectful [to them], rejoicing [in their actions] with nothing but respect, praising their qualities, and aspiring that we too will be like them.

Hence, just as skillful physicians exert themselves for the sake of the diseased, one makes one-pointed efforts **for the sake of those who are ignorant** since beginningless time because of various [ways of] having reference points. [Ignorant beings] only exert themselves for the causes of **suffering** and then angrily look at the results [of this]. They **burden** themselves **with** their own sufferings by plunging into a swamp that they stirred up themselves, and then they have no clue what to do. Just as [people outside the swamp] know that this swamp in which these naïve beings are drowning is shallow and small, one fully comprehends the nature of cyclic existence through knowing true reality. Thus, **one is released from** both **the extremes of attachment** to **and fear** of swamplike cyclic existence. Through knowing that oneself moreover has the ability to pull sentient beings out [of this swamp], one **will manage to remain in cyclic existence** for the sake of others as long as space exists. **This is the** direct **result of** having meditated on **emptiness.** The Blessed One Maitreya says [in *The Sublime Continuum*]:

> With supreme knowledge, they cut through craving for identity without exception.
> Because they cherish sentient beings, they possess loving kindness and do not attain peace.
> In this way, through relying on insight and loving kindness, the means for enlightenment,
> The noble ones dwell neither in the seeming nor nirvāṇa.[1634]

and [in *The Ornament of Clear Realization*]:

> Not abiding in existence through knowledge,
> Not abiding in peace through compassion . . .[1635]

> **Thus, one cannot uphold any faultfinding**
> **In the thesis of emptiness.**
> **Therefore, you should meditate on emptiness**
> **Without entertaining any doubts.** [53]

This verse instructs one to relinquish doubts.

To wish for a harvest—the result—but to reject farming—its cause—is something that is ridiculed in the world even by cattle herders. **Thus,** in the same way, the ones who wish for enlightenment—the result—**cannot uphold any faultfinding in** or any denial of **the thesis of emptiness**—its cause. [833] **Therefore,** by not relying on the talk of evil friends and **without entertaining any doubts, you should meditate** solely **on** this **emptiness**, the basic nature of entities which is the nature of all phenomena.

> [803] **Emptiness is the remedy for the darkness**

**Of afflictive and cognitive obscurations.**
**So how could those who wish for omniscience**
**Not swiftly meditate on it? [54]**

**Granted, things that produce suffering**
**Will give rise to fear.**
**However, emptiness is what relieves suffering,**
**So why should it provoke any fear? [55]**

These [two] verses teach that it is very reasonable to meditate on [emptiness].

You might think, "What are you talking about? [In lines 52cd,] you proclaim:

> And will manage to remain in cyclic existence.
> This is the result of emptiness.

If this is the case, then this is something through which one does not attain liberation from cyclic existence."

In general, solely through one's understanding cyclic existence and nirvāṇa as emptiness, the chains of both existence and peace will uncoil by themselves. There is no question that precisely this is a liberation that cannot be rivaled even by one hundred thousand liberations of hearers and solitary realizers. However, one still abides in cyclic existence for the sake of others through compassion, just as a skilled physician does not abandon the assembly of the diseased. [Such abiding] is nothing other than [abiding] like a lotus that is unstained by mud. Hence, [a person who abides] in such a way is not called "someone in cyclic existence," just as a physician is not called a "sick person."

This much is certainly true, but, moreover, only **emptiness is the** direct **remedy for the** thick inner **darkness** that obscures true reality, that is, the collection **of afflictive and cognitive obscurations.** Because one has engaged in emptiness through devoted interest on [the paths of] accumulation and junction, emptiness—which is, like space, without any difference—is realized on the path of seeing in a manner of being omnipresent. Through the power of eliminating adventitious stains on the paths of meditation, every aspect of the qualities intrinsic to emptiness is revealed. [This is] as if one were to fathom the extents and special features of every [instance of] space exactly as they are, starting from the space of the limitless realms of sentient beings down to the [space] that is enclosed by the fibrils of the split tip of a hair. Finally, it is as if one were to simultaneously and fully comprehend in one single moment the entirety of the element of space that is included in the three times and is beyond unity and multiplicity. Likewise, in one single moment, one simultaneously and fully comprehends the entirety of the expanse of dharmas (or emptiness) exactly as it is. It is beyond unity and multiplicity and has always been intrinsic to all Buddhas, bodhisattvas, hearers, solitary realizers, and sentient beings; to all the five aggregates; the eighteen constituents; the twelve sources; and to all the factors to be relinquished [834] or to be attained. In dependence on the worldly seeming level, [this final realization is described by] saying, "Perfect Buddhahood is attained."

Thus, it does not matter whether this pertains to **those who wish for swift** attainment of **omniscience** or to bodhisattvas who adopt the subjugating conduct[1636] of great desire and wish to remain in cyclic existence for the sake of others for as long as space exists. Since the cause for attaining such a [goal] is solely the knowledge of emptiness, **how could they not meditate on** emptiness? Rather, it is [truly] appropriate to meditate on this very [emptiness].

You might venture, "Since we did not train in emptiness, we are afraid of it." **Granted**, in worldly contexts, it is adequate that **things that produce suffering will give rise to fear. However,** in such worldly contexts, it is [likewise] stated as inadequate to be afraid of something that is beneficial, just as one is afraid of a disease but not of medicine and a physician. **So** if this **emptiness** is like the supreme physician, since it **is what relieves** the entire disease of reification and the **suffering** [that is connected with it], **why should it provoke any fear?** Rather, this [emptiness] is doubtlessly something to put your confidence in.

### [Synopsis of Other Commentaries]

As for [verse 44], Kalyāṇadeva says:

> Just this one who serves as a basis that contains the root of the vows of a fully ordained monk is the fully ordained monk. However, this very [monk] is ill established, since there is dispute [about him] with the forders.[1637]

Thus, he puts forth the speculation that there is an equal application of the entailment by[the reason in lines 43cd:] "As are certain of their parts [disputed] between you and others." [He continues with verses 44–47:]

> As long as there is clinging to the aggregates by those who are referential, for that long the pride of clinging to an I is generated and there are actions and births. Thus, nirvāṇa is ill [established] too. You might object, "It is not ill [established], because the afflictions are relinquished by seeing reality." Therefore, [verse 45] "If liberation came from . . ." is [taught]. . . . Someone else [835] might say, "Here, afflicted and neutral craving as well as negativities of the desire realm are used in terms of the origination of further existences. If possessing joyous

desire means possessing afflictions, why were [lines 45cd] 'However, one sees the efficacy of actions . . .' spoken?" The implication [of this] is as follows: It is asserted that dullness is afflicted too, since it is the great seed for afflictions. Its latent tendencies exist also in this referential mind of unafflicted ignorance that entails basic unawareness. Likewise, unafflicted latent tendencies exist also in unafflicted craving: These are feelings. . . . [Feelings themselves] are not afflicted, but if they meet with cooperative causes, they produce something afflicted. This is what is taught by the term "also" [in line 46c]. Therefore, [lines 46cd–47ab] "Why should they not . . ." are stated. You might say, "Causes are not something that definitely produces results." Therefore, [lines 47cd] "Referential minds . . ." are given.[1638]

These are the passages that appear [in Kalyāṇadeva's commentary]. However, this answer [to the question about lines 45cd] that he gives—that "dullness is an affliction"—is a basis for analysis. The reason for this is that [his answer] is affected by the [above] qualm [of the opponent] that it is not reasonable [for Śāntideva] to say, "However, one sees the efficacy of actions . . ."

Vibhūticandra comments:

> The one who has extinguished the afflictions is the fully ordained monk. This is not accomplished if emptiness is not realized. [This meaning] is established by [verse 45] "If liberation came from . . ."
>
> [Line 44b] "And this full monkhood is ill established" and the two lines [44cd] "A nirvāṇa of those whose minds are referential . . ." teach again that nirvāṇa is difficult for those who mentally engage in discursiveness.[1639]

He removes objections:

> You might wonder, "However, if suffering does not actually exist, what is the point of remaining in cyclic existence?" The reason is that, on the seeming level, sentient beings are observed.[1640]

In *The Small Commentary on the Difficult Points*, the following appears:

> [As for verse 44:] Among the five [kinds of] fully ordained monks, the fully ordained monk who has vanquished the afflictions is the one to be identified here [836]. If emptiness does not exist, it follows that the fully ordained monk of the nirvāṇa with remainder does not exist

> [either]. Those who have vanquished the afflictions are the roots of the teaching for the following reasons: (a) The assembly of arhats collects, upholds, and protects the teaching. (b) It is explained that they remain even now in different countries, such as Kashmir, for the sake of upholding and protecting the teaching. (c) If someone asks, "How is it that having vanquished the afflictions is unjustified without emptiness?" the reason is that the [afflictions] arise again, since their seeds have not been relinquished. Or [you might say], "Having vanquished the afflictions is justified, but nirvāṇa without remainder is not justified." [The answer is in lines 44cd] "A nirvāṇa of those whose minds are referential . . ." [You might continue,] "However, once the aggregates that were induced in the past are extinguished, this is nirvāṇa, since [there are] no [aggregates] that could be reborn." In order to anticipate such a qualm, [verse 46 says,] "You might argue, 'Here, it has been determined . . .'" [Arhats] do not possess any striving for such aggregates that involve clinging to an I. However, they do possess craving that strives for the aggregates [as such], because they possess striving for food. It is taught that such [craving] exists [in them], since its causes are complete. [This is found in verse 47] "Craving comes from . . ." It is explained in such [scriptures] as *The Sublime Continuum* and *The Sūtra [of the Lion's Roar of Queen] Śrīmālā* that inconceivable death and transition exist [for these arhats].

The following phrases [indicate that the opponents] are forced to accept that these passages above do apply to the inferior vehicle's [own] texts:

> You yourself assert that those who have vanquished the afflictions are the supreme fully ordained monks, because it is the arhats who perform the actual main activities of the teaching.

Following this, there appears what seems to be a further rebuttal by using the great vehicle's own texts as [a source of] valid cognition:

> If you do not realize emptiness, you are not able to relinquish the afflictions. Hence, there is no nirvāṇa or arhathood in the inferior vehicle.

In *The Small Commentary on the Difficult Points of the Knowledge Chapter Only*, both [versions] appear as supplementary words: Full monkhood is ill established for the reason that there is dispute about it and that it is hard to vanquish the afflictions.[1641]

### 3. The Way to Meditate on Emptiness

This has two parts:

1) Personal identitylessness
2) Phenomenal identitylessness

### 3.1. Personal Identitylessness

This has five parts: [837]

1) Teaching that a [personal] identity in general is not established
2) The particular refutation of the Enumerators' assertion
3) The refutation of the Logicians
4) Teaching that karma is not contradictory to identitylessness
5) The ancillary refutation of the Analyzers and of the [specific kind of] person [that is asserted by] the followers of Vātsīputra in our own faction

### 3.1.1. Teaching That a [Personal] Identity in General Is Not Established

**If there were something called "I,"**
**It might be afraid of things here and there.**
**However, since there is no "I" at all,**
**Who is it who could be afraid?** [56]

This first verse teaches that there is no self that is the one who is afraid.

[839] It has been taught [in verse 55] that emptiness is not something to be afraid of:

> However, emptiness is what relieves suffering,
> So why should it provoke any fear?

This is definitely the case. On the other hand, **if there were something called "I"** that is the one who is afraid, it would of course be reasonable that **it might be afraid of things here and there** that one can be afraid of. **However, since there is no "I" at all**—not even a tiny one—it is not reasonable to be afraid. So first, [840] examine the one **who could be afraid.**

**I am not the teeth, hair, or nails,**
**Nor bones or blood.**
**I am neither nasal mucus nor phlegm,**
**Nor lymph or pus.** [57]

**I am not marrow nor sweat,**
**Nor am I fat, entrails,**
**Or any of the other inner organs.**
**I am also not excrement or urine.** [58]

**I am not flesh or sinew,**
**Nor am I the body's warmth, its respiration,**
**Or its orifices.**
**I am not the six consciousnesses in any way either.** [59]

[The first eleven lines of] these verses teach that the body is not the self, and the last line teaches that the mind is not the self either.

You might state, "The body is the self." There is no body other than the collection of its parts. However, the parts are not the self, nor is there any self within them. Thus, **I am not teeth, hair, or nails**, as these are [just] bones and hairs. It is not reasonable that **I am** such [things] as **bones** or body hairs. Likewise, **I am not blood** and blood is not me either. **I am neither nasal mucus nor phlegm, nor lymph or pus.** This is the case because these [substances] are filthy and it is not reasonable that the self is something filthy, nor is it reasonable that something filthy is the self.

**I am not marrow nor sweat**, as these two [substances] are nothing but the water element [in] the interior [of the body]. **I am not fat, entrails, or any of the other inner organs**, because they are nothing but flesh. **I am also not excrement or urine**, because these two [substances] are the waste products of food and drink. **I am not flesh or sinew**, nor bones, blood vessels, nerves, or tendons. The reasons are as follows: [Everybody can] see that flesh and so forth that are scattered on a charnel ground are not the self, nor are they what belong to this self at all. Furthermore, one [can]not see a difference between the [flesh and such on a charnel ground] and the flesh and so forth of this [living] body. [Thus,] these [nine lines of verse] teach that the [inner] earth element and water element are not the self.

In the same way, **I am not the body's warmth** (the fire element) or **respiration**[1642] (the factor of the breath that involves inhalation, exhalation, and pause). These are just like fire in a stove and the wind that kindles it, which are not the self. **Nor** am I **its** various other inner **orifices**, such as the ones in the nose. They are just like outer windows, which are not the self.

Now you might continue, "Granted, the body is surely not the self, but the mind is the self." **I am not** these **six consciousnesses** that engage in objects, such as the eye [consciousness], **in any way either.** The reasons are as follows: These [consciousnesses] arise in dependence on objects, such as form, [841] whereas it is not reasonable that the self depends on conditions. Also, they are referred to as "mine" by such discriminating notions as "my eye consciousness." If they were the self, it would be contradictory [to say] that they are mine, because this is as impossible as something being both me and my horse. There is also no mind that is other than the six collections [of consciousness], because consciousness is just one single collection of consciousness and it is just this [single collection of consciousness] that is presented as sixfold due to [its apprehension of six kinds of] objects.

Then you might try, "The ground consciousness is the self." [However,] this is taught nowhere other than in the context of the great vehicle. [For example, *The Sūtra That Unravels the Intention* says]:

> The appropriating consciousness is profound and subtle.
> All seeds flow into it like a river.
> It is not appropriate to conceive of it as a self.
> Hence, I did not teach it to naïve beings.[1643]

Even when one [tries to] present the ground consciousness [as the self], this is not the self either, because it is also referred to by the discriminating notion "mine." In general, [the Buddha] proclaimed the ground [consciousness] with an intention, which was to reverse the view of causelessness. However, the [ground consciousness] is not something that exists by its nature for the following reasons: It is not present on the Buddha ground. [The Buddha's] main teaching is the dharma wheel in which, on the final level, the ground [consciousness] does not exist. There, he said:

> Those who assert the ground [consciousness] do not assert the dharma.

If there were a self other than body and mind, it would be reasonable that it appears to oneself, because it is impossible for it to be a phenomenon that is hidden from oneself. [However,] such [a self] does not appear. Thus, whether it is on the seeming level or the ultimate level, and whether it is under analysis or [just] conventionally, a self is never possible.

### 3.1.2. The Particular Refutation of the Enumerators' Assertion

The Enumerators state the following: The self is [mere] consciousness. [The self's] own nature is [called] "the individual"[1644] which is endowed with this [mere consciousness]. Due to [the individual's] desire, the equilibrium of the triad of "motility," "darkness," and "lightness"[1645]—that is, the permanent "nature"[1646]— becomes imbalanced. This is what is called universal flux[1647] [or "manifestation"], which involves arising and ceasing. [842] [In this process, first,] "the great one," or "cognition,"[1648] [splits off] from its [original] unity with this permanent ["nature"].

From ["cognition" manifests] "identification,"[1649] and thence the five "essential elements,"[1650] such as the one of sound. These become shifted toward "cognition," which is like a two-sided mirror. Thus, they appear for and are experienced by the self like reflections [in a mirror]. Apprehending [these objects] through "cognition" is what is sensed by "the individual." Hence, the self is something that permanently has the nature of consciousness, such as [the consciousness] of sound.[1651]

The refutation of this is as follows:

> **If [the self] were the consciousness of sound,**
> **It would perceive sound all the time.**
> **Excuse me—without a knowable object, what is it aware of?**
> **So why do you even speak about "consciousness"? [60]**
>
> **You might venture, "It is consciousness without something knowable."**
> **Then it would follow that even a piece of wood is consciousness.**
> **It is definite that there is no consciousness**
> **Without a knowable object being close by. [61]**

These two verses refute permanent perception of sound.

**If**, according to you, [this permanent self] **were the consciousness of sound,** then it follows that sound resounds uninterruptedly, since this consciousness **would perceive sound all the time**. Therefore, the sound of conch shells and the sound of lutes **would** be uninterrupted and [would occur] independent of any effort, such as blowing these conch shells or playing the lutes. You might say, "Sometimes sound does not occur, since the object sound is not close by." **Excuse me—if there is no knowable object**, since sound is not close by, **what is** this consciousness **aware of** at this time? **So** tell us—**why do you even speak about "consciousness** of sound"?

**You might venture, "It is consciousness** of sound even when it is **without the knowable** object sound." **Then it would follow that even a piece of wood is consciousness**, because [consciousness] does not need to be conscious of an object. **It is definite that there is no** arising of **consciousness without a knowable object being close by**. Therefore, do not prattle about a consciousness that perceives sound even when there is no sound.

> **You might continue, "Exactly this is what is conscious of form."**
> **Then why would it not also hear at that time?**
> **You might say, "Because no sound is close by."**
> **In that case, there is also no consciousness of it. [62]**

> **How is it that something whose nature it is to perceive sound**
> **Could perceive form? [63ab]**

These one and a half verses refute that this [very consciousness of sound] perceives form.

**You might continue, "Exactly this** permanent cognition [that perceives sound] **is what is conscious of form** when an object is close by, even when it is not conscious of sound." **Then why would it not also hear** sound **at that time?** [It should do so,] because it is permanent as the consciousness of sound. Furthermore, the following [consequence] will fall on you: You would have to hear the sound of a conch shell when you see a white conch shell, because a white conch shell is the support for the sound of this conch shell and [because, according to you,] this permanent consciousness sees the form of the conch shell close by, while at the same time there is no difference between the sound of this conch shell and the form of this conch shell in that the [first of these two] objects is close by and [the other] is far away. **You might say,** "There is no sound, **because no** object **sound is close by." In that case, there is also no consciousness of this** sound. If there is no horn of a rabbit, [843] where should there be a consciousness of it? This is just the same. If you agree here [by saying], "This is how it is," then [your] thesis of a permanent consciousness of sound has just collapsed.

So, again we have to ask you: How should this work? **How is it that** this consciousness **whose nature it is to perceive sound could perceive form?** You might say, "This is just like a single person who may be presented as a son in dependence on [his] father and as a father in dependence on [his] son."

> **One single person may be conceived as both father and son,**
> **But this is not how it really is. [63cd]**
>
> **Thus, lightness, motility, and darkness**
> **Are neither father nor son.**
> **One does not see their nature**
> **In connection with the perception of sound. [64]**

These one and a half verses refute the example of dependence that is given [by the opponent].

**One single person may** sometimes **be conceived as father and** sometimes as **son.** These are [just] conceptions in dependence [on other persons], **but** his [being a father or a son] **is not how it really is,** since [such a person] is neither father nor son when not considered in dependence [on his child or parents respectively]. **Thus, lightness** (pleasure), **motility** (suffering), **and darkness** (dullness) that you assert **are neither father nor son**, because they do not depend on anything whatsoever.[1652] You might disagree, "They depend on manifestations." However, at the time of not being dependent [on these manifestations], nobody **sees the nature** of motility, darkness, and lightness **in connection with the perception of sound.**[1653]

> **"Just like an actor, this same entity assumes different forms."**
> **However, then it is something impermanent.**
> **You might continue, "The same entity has different natures."**
> **Such a singularity is something unprecedented indeed. [65]**
>
> **You might say, "Its different forms are not real."**
> **Then just describe its own form!**
> **Your answer is, "It is just consciousness."**
> **In that case, it would follow that all beings are one. [66]**
>
> **Also, the cognizant and the incognizant would be one,**
> **Because both are equal in just being existent.**
> **Now, when the particulars are mistaken,**
> **What would be their common ground? [67]**

These verses refute that [the self] is real as something permanent and single.

You might say now, "**Just like an actor** takes on different forms—such as Arjuna or Bhīma[1654]—in every moment, **this same** consciousness **assumes** different aspects in **different forms.**" **However, then** it is certain that **this** consciousness **is something impermanent**, because it changes moment by moment. **You might continue,** "The actor takes on various **different natures**, but the actor **is the same.** Likewise, though it assumes different aspects, this self that entails a permanent consciousness that perceives sound is just a single one. Hence, there is no mistake." Well, we can only rebuke you: If [the self] is supposed to be both the **singularity** of a self that entails this permanent consciousness that perceives sound and at the same time changes into all kinds of things—such as perception of form and perception of smell—then **such a** [self] **is something unprecedented** in the world and impossible **indeed.**

Furthermore, if the self is permanent as the consciousness of the essential element sound, it has to be permanent as the consciousness of all five essential elements, such as the essential element form. [844] If that is the case, all five [essential elements], such as form, would have to be perceived permanently, even if there are no objects or sense faculties.[1655] And if this is so, what [kind of] job should the self of blind and deaf people or the self at the time of sleeping and fainting be doing?

**You might say,** "Since the permanent single self is **not real** as these **different forms**, they do not contradict its being permanent and single." Well, **then, just describe** what the self's **own form** is! **Your answer is, "It is just** mere **consciousness." In that case, it would follow that all beings are one,** because they are not different in being this one self that is mere consciousness. It **would also** follow that **the cognizant** individual **and the incognizant** primal substance[1656] **are one, because** they are this one self. Then you might agree, "We accept that the nature and the individual are the same, since **both are equal in just being existent.**" **Now, when the** specific **particulars** that were presented by you—the individual who has a mind and the nature that does not have a mind—**are mistaken, what would be the ground** or the basis of attribution that these two distinct features—with mind and without mind—have in **common** or in which they are included as being one? There is no basis whatsoever of these two that is other than these two. They are also not one and the same, because these two are not mutually included in each other.

**[Synopsis of Other Commentaries]**

With respect to these verses, Kalyāṇadeva states the opponents' theses and refutes them:

> The assertions by Vātsaḥ and others that a so-called self, soul, or person exists are invalidated. The Enumerators label consciousness as the "self." . . .[1657]

He refutes [objections]:

> You might say, "Since sound and so on does not always remain in a certain place, it is not heard all the time." Therefore, [lines 60cd] are given, "Excuse me—if there is no knowable object, what is it aware of? Why do you then say 'consciousness'?"[1658]

He comments further:

> [Verses 62–63ab:] If perception of form and perception of sound were one, [845] to label the sense faculties as five would also be meaningless.
>
> [Verses 63cd–64:] If the nature is a permanent singularity, it is not justified that, gradually—just as a son comes from a father—the "individual" arises from the "nature," "cognition" from the [nature], "identification" from [cognition], the "essential elements" from [iden-

tification], and so forth. . . . You might object, "Although it is a singularity, it is suitable to be labeled as many [things], just as a single being may be called both father and son." Since [its constituents], such as lightness, are taught as something single, they are [just] labeled as mere "manifestations." However, this "universal flux" is not something that has arisen from the [constituents]. Hence, truly, lightness and so on are neither father nor son.

[Verses 65–67:] You might say, "Just like an actor, this very consciousness of sound is what appears [now] as the consciousness of form." If this were the case, just like the actor, this consciousness would be impermanent. You might argue, "It is this very [consciousness] that [just] has another nature." This very same [consciousness of sound] does not exist up to this present point, because this very same [earlier consciousness of sound] is mutually contradictory to the other [consciousness of form that exists now]. Thus, it is refuted that [these two] are one. Then you might agree, "Granted, it is wrong that it is [the same consciousness] that [just] has another nature. It does not exist in this way." If this is the case, then state how the very nature or entity of this self is. "It is just consciousness." Then this entails the mistake that it would follow that all beings are one; that is, beings who are released or not released [from cyclic existence] would be completely identical. Furthermore, it follows that the individual who has a mind and the nature that does not have a mind are one and the same. [Here, you] Enumerators say, "We accept that the individual and the nature are the same, since they are equal and identical in being existent." The Centrists answer with [lines 67cd], "Now, when . . ." This means that there is no particular difference between the individual and the nature in that they have mind or not and that they are both free from progressive or nonprogressive activity. Hence, if, just like the horns of a rabbit, [846] they are utterly nonexistent, then what is their condition of likeness? There is none at all. Therefore, they are also not the same. These [verses] also eliminate [the notion of] generalities, such as cause, [that are something separate from their instances] and [the notion of] sharing the same status.[1659]

[As for verse 56,] Vibhūticandra gives a quotation:

When one analyzes this so-called self, there is nothing but words or conceptions. At this point, who is it who has fear?

> Now, a self will not come forth anymore.
> Also "mine" will now not show up again.
> Naïve beings are afraid of it.
> In the learned ones, fear is exhausted.[1660]

He comments further on [verses 65–67]:

> The example of the actor is not justified, because it does not accord with the probandum to abandon [this actor's] first mode of being and then to seize another mode of [his] being. If you state that the actor is the very same but is still of a different nature, then such a singularity is something unprecedented indeed. Since something other is different from the very same, [this example] is extremely contradictory. You might argue, "[There] is the very consciousness and perceptions of form and such. [The latter] are [its] second modes of being. The modes of being of perceptions of form and such depend on objects like the color of a crystal. Hence, they are not real." So what is the mode of being of their nature? "It is just consciousness." All right, you have asserted that the two different consciousnesses that are the perception of sound and the perception of form are one. According to [this assertion], it follows that all beings are one, because they do not differ with respect to consciousness. Moreover, if you discard distinctions and take [things] to be one due to just some arbitrary [common] mode of being, then mind (the phenomenon that is the "individual") and what is not mind (such phenomena as the "nature") would not be different, because both are equal in being existent. [Here,] you might agree, "I accept." [However,] at this point when particular entities are wrong, what would be their common ground? If there are many different similar entities, they are taken to be one through their similarity. However, such do not exist [here].[1661]

[As for line 57d,] *The Small Commentary on the Knowledge Chapter* explains:

> Lymph [847] is the rotten liquid that comes from scratching when one itches. Fat is a rotten liquid that remains inside.[1662]

This is not the case: Lymph is the very transparent fluid that arises from flesh and blood. Fat is the condensed grease of the body. It is such things as blood that turn into pus when they rot.

[Then, this commentary] supplements some words for [line 65d], "Such a singularity is something unprecedented indeed" to the effect that it is contradictory for the self to be both single and of another nature. Therefore, it is indeed something amazing that is unprecedented.[1663]

There follow some supplementary words [for verses 66–67]:

> If the nature of the self were consciousness, it would follow that all beings are one, since there would be no difference [in them] as far as mere consciousness is concerned. Also, it would follow that mind and what has no mind—the "individual" and the "nature"—are the same. Why? They are equal in "just being existent," that is, in merely having a state of being, because they are not different [in this respect]. Furthermore, if the distinctions that consist of the perception of form and such are mistakenly stated, since they are not real, then there would be no common ground [for them]. The reason is that, if there are no distinctions—as in the similarity of an ox and a gavayaḥ[1664]—to be identified, then there is no [common ground of such distinctions either]. [It would moreover follow that] multicolored and pale yellow [oxen] do not possess a difference, because they are the very objects that are expressed by the term "ox."[1665]

*The Great Commentary* [on lines 63cd–64ab and 67cd] is paraphrased here according to its meaning:

> Someone may be presented as father and son in mutual dependence, but when he is [considered] independently, he is neither father nor son. The Enumerators themselves assert that the equilibrium of the three constituents is the permanent "primal substance" which is not fluctuating and that their disequilibrium turns into the impermanent "universal flux." However, this is just a presentation in dependence on temporary "manifestation," whereas ultimately it comes down to the assertion that there is no difference between earlier and later and that the "nature" is [just] a single one.[1666]
>
> You might say, "The particulars of consciousness—the 'manifestations' of the five 'essential elements' (such as the perception of form)—appear in a mistaken way. Therefore, they do not exist." What then is their common ground in terms of being mere consciousness? [There is none,] because they are not established.[1667] [848]

In brief, Kalyāṇadeva asserts that this phrase [in line 67b], "Because both are equal in just being existent" represents the answer of the Enumerators who say, "The nature and the individual are one, because they are equal in being existent." The other [commentator]s assert that [this phrase] refers to our own [Centrist] statement, "It follows that 'the individual' and 'the nature' are one, because they are equal in being existent."

### 3.1.3. The Refutation of the Logicians

> **Something incognizant is also not the self**
> **For the very reason that it has no mind, just like a garment and such.**
> **However, if it is consciousness, because it possesses mind,**
> **It follows that its incognizance is invalidated. [68]**
>
> **You might think, "In fact, the self is unchanged."**
> **In what way then should mind have affected it?**
> **Thus, if it is incognizant and free from activity,**
> **This amounts to referring to space as the self. [69]**

The first verse refutes a self without mind, and the following verse refutes the assertion that such a self is unchanging.

You Logicians say, "If one claims the self to be something that has mind, these mistakes [above] certainly do apply, but we claim that it is something without mind." **Something incognizant is also not the self for the very reason that it has no mind,** for example, **just like a garment** or cloth **and such.** You might venture, "Granted, the self is without mind, but since it meets with a distinct quality, called consciousness, it becomes cognizant." **However, if it is** the case that the self turns into **consciousness, because it possesses mind, it follows that** your former claim of **its incognizance is invalidated.** Since you asserted before that it does not possess mind and asserted later that it does so, this is also contradictory to your assertion that the self is permanent.

**You might think, "In fact,** this permanent **self is unchanged."** With **what** [kind of] means for the arising of consciousness **should** this feature of consciousness or **mind have affected**—or ever affect—**the self?** [This is impossible,] because something permanent is incapable [of functioning] as any kind of agent or object whatsoever.[1668] **Thus, if** you label something **incognizant and free from** agent and object as the self, **this amounts to** labeling **space as the self.** Hence, from now on, take space as your self!

### 3.1.4. Teaching That Karma Is Not Contradictory to Identitylessness

> **You might say, "If there is no self,**
> **The connection between actions and their results is not possible.**

**As actions disappear, once they have been committed,**
**Who would experience their results?"** [70]

This verse formulates the objection.

Thus, it is taught that neither an innate nor an imaginary self exists. At this point, **you** followers of Kāṇāda[1669] and others **might say, "If there is no self,** it follows that **the connection between actions and their results is not possible. As** there is no self that is an agent and the **actions** themselves **disappear, once they have been committed** and completed, [849] **who would experience their results** later? In whom would their results mature?"

**Since it is established for both of us**
**That action and result have different bases**
**And that a self does not have any function in this,**
**Is your objection here not quite pointless?** [71]

This verse teaches that the positions of both disputants are equal in that there is no self as an agent.

You asserted a permanent self that does not act, and now also we Buddhists assert that there is no self. Hence, **both our** parties accept the following: The **action**—that is, [committing] some deed (the time of the cause)—**and** its completion (the time of the **result**) **have different bases** or supports, and they entail an earlier and a later time. At both of these times, **a self does not have any function** at all. **Since** we equally [accept] this, and, in consequence, **your objection here** just works against yourself, is it **not quite pointless?**

**One never sees it happen**
**That the provider of a cause is the recipient of its result.**
**It is just in dependence on a single continuum**
**That a so-called agent and experiencer are taught.** [72]

This verse teaches that it is impossible for a cause and [its] result to be simultaneous.

Based on just a single phenomenon, **one never sees it happen** in the world **that the provider of a cause is** simultaneously **the recipient of its result.** This is just like the following example: As long as a lotus seed has not perished, it is impossible that its sprout nevertheless would grow, or that its flower would open without the sprout having ceased, or that its fruit would ripen while the flower leaves do not wither.

You might argue, "Your own teacher has stated that the agent of actions experiences the result." He **taught** the following: There is no self in a river at all, and its earlier [moments] are different from its later ones. However, it is presented as one due to being a stream. Likewise, there is no [personal] self at all. [Rather,] **it is just in dependence on a single** mental **continuum that** [its] earlier [moments] are **called "agent"** at the time of committing an action **and** [its] later [moments are called] **"experiencer"** at the time of experiencing the result. Thus, there is no self that is an agent, and it has been refuted that [such a self] is this very mind that represents the agent. However, just through the mere continuum of this [mind], you will certainly experience what has completely ripened [in it] without anything becoming lost.

### 3.1.5. The Ancillary Refutation of the Analyzers and of the [Specific Kind of] Person [That Is Asserted by] the Followers of Vātsīputra in Our Own Faction

> **The past and the future mind**
> **Are not the self, because they do not exist.**
> **You might say, "Well, then the just-arisen mind is the self,"**
> **But when it has ceased, there is no self anymore.** [73]

The first half of this verse teaches that the past and the future [mind] are not the self, while the second half [teaches] that the present [mind] is not the self [either].

At this point, you Analyzers and others say, "Just this mind stream is the self." This is also not the case: The mind is something that entails the aspect of a stream. **The past and the future mind are not the self, because that** which is past does not exist after it has ceased (just as yesterday's offering lamp) and because that which is in the future does **not exist** now, since it did not arise yet (just as tomorrow's rainbow does not exist now). [850] **You might say, "Well, then the mind** that has **just arisen** and not yet ceased **is the self," but** even this [present mind] is something that entails extremely infinitesimal fractions of the three times. If you analyze precisely, you are not able to observe what is present. Even if you consider it roughly, **when** you grasp [at the present moment of mind] as the self, what you have grasped at **has** already **ceased** [in the next moment]. Hence, in this way, **there is no**thing in the present [moment of mind] that is a **self.**

> **For example, there is nothing**
> **If you take the trunk of a banana tree apart.**
> **Likewise, if you search for it with thorough analysis,**
> **The self is not really true either.** [74]

This verse teaches that the self is unfindable.

Here, the followers of Vātsīputra in our own faction say, "The self cannot be expressed as anything at all that would be the same as or other than the aggregates." This is not the case either: **For example, you** may cut up **the trunk of a banana tree**, slice it into pieces, and also **take** each one of these [pieces] completely **apart**. Then you might wonder, "Now, in which of these [parts] is the trunk of the banana tree?" **If** [you look closely], you will see that apart from these parts **there is nothing** whatsoever that is a trunk that possesses the parts. You see furthermore that also each one of these parts is not the trunk. Thus, your clinging to the trunk of a banana tree has become completely reversed. **Likewise, if you search with thorough analysis** through reasoning in all the inner and outer aggregates, you will see that this very **self** that is inexpressible as the same as or something other [than these aggregates] **is not really true either.** Rather, you will not see any so-called self whatsoever.

> **You might object, "If there are no sentient beings,**
> **For whom should you have compassion?"**
> **It is for those who are conceived through the ignorance**
> **That we embrace for the sake of the result.** [75]
>
> **"Without sentient beings, whose is the result?"**
> **This is true, but we still strive on the level of ignorance.**
> **For the sake of completely pacifying suffering,**
> **You should not spurn this ignorance in terms of the result.** [76]
>
> **Self-centeredness—the cause for suffering—**
> **Increases through the ignorant belief in a self.**
> **You might say, "You cannot put an end to this,"**
> **But it is better to meditate on identitylessness.** [77]

These three verses remove the objection that compassion is not justified if there are no sentient beings.

**You might object,** "Thus, since self, sentient being, and person are synonymous terms, if there is no self, this would lead to the claim that there are also no sentient beings. **If there are no sentient beings** either, then at that point, who **should** cultivate **compassion for whom?** This is contradictory to the explanation that compassion is the main object of meditation for you followers of the great vehicle." In general, in the context of not analyzing with knowledge, this is merely a position that is **embraced** out of compassion for the welfare of others, that is, **for the sake of the result** that is the attainment of perfect Buddhahood.

However, when one analyzes, one understands that any kind of self, sentient being, and suffering are not even established as mere things in a dream. At this point, [851] loving-kindness for those who do not realize this will increase a hundred times. Since they [do not have] such [realization], they are completely ignorant due to this pile of stupidity that consists of views about themselves, others, and suffering.[1670] Sentient beings are **those who** superimpose and **are** superimposed as something real—such as self and others— **through** this **ignorance.**

You might continue, "**Without sentient beings** who are the objects of one's intent, for **whose** sake **is** the attainment of Buddhahood, **the result** that is intended for them?" **This is true, but we still strive** to promote the welfare of these [sentient beings], starting with those **on the level of ignorance** who do not understand this in such a way.[1671] You might argue, "Even if you wish to attain Buddhahood for the sake of others, this is ignorance about the result." When you consider the final ultimate level, there is no question that this is the case. However, **for the sake of completely pacifying** the **suffering** of all sentient beings, for the time being, **you should not spurn this ignorance about the result**, even though you know that it is ignorance. This is comparable to physicians who definitely rely on certain types of poison as remedies for [certain] diseases. "Anyway, you might deliberately not relinquish this ignorance about the result, but what then?" Just as [its] fragrance [dissipates] when a flower fades away, at the time of awakening from the sleep of basic unawareness, [also this ignorance] will naturally become pure.

You might argue, "However, just as you do not reverse the ignorance about the result as a temporary support on the path, it is equally fine to rely on the clinging to a self." [All kinds of water] are equal in that they are water, but [only water] that possesses the eight qualities[1672] is used [for drinking], whereas poisonous water or water from rocks is not used in this way. Likewise, though they are equal in that they are ignorance, one does not rely on the clinging to a self in the same way as one does on the ignorance about the result, because **self-centeredness**[1673]—the entity that is **the cause for** all **suffering—increases** due to this **ignorant belief in a self.** Thus, **you** should **put an end to this** clinging to a self by all means. **You might say,** "So what should we do?" You should **meditate on** only this **identitylessness** of all phenomena and the utter peace of discursiveness. This **is** the **best** and most excellent activity.

## [Synopsis of Other Commentaries]

Kalyāṇadeva [describes a further objection]: [852]

> You might say, "We assert that the assembly of body, mind, and mental events is the self."[1674]

He refutes this with the example of the banana tree and briefly quotes [Nāgārjuna's] *Precious Garland*.[1675]

With respect to [lines 72cd] "It is just in dependence on a single continuum . . . ," Vibhūticandra says:

> You wonder why? The very continuum
> In which the latent tendencies of actions are placed
> Is that in which the result matures,
> Just as red [color] in cotton wool.
>
> One may repeatedly apply some [red] dye to a seed of cotton wool. Then, whatever grows out of this [seed]—from the sprout up through the fruit—will be red only. Likewise, [action and result] are different, but the mind stream that has performed an action is exactly the one in which the result matures. Therefore, qualms do not occur here.[1676]

He teaches the example of the trunk of a banana tree in his "summarized explanation [of this section]."[1677]

As for [lines 76cd] "For the sake of completely pacifying suffering, . . ." he says:

> Ignorance is [both] the cause for engaging in existence and the cause for putting an end to existence.[1678]

This teaches that the causes for putting an end [to cyclic existence], such as compassion, are not negated, while the cause for engaging [in cyclic existence]—clinging to an identity—is negated. Someone might say, "There is no certainty that cyclic existence is put to an end through [realizing] identitylessness." There is [such certainty]:

> Since the seeds of views about an identity have been relinquished,
> This is an irreversible state.

[Kalyāṇadeva] gives a quote from *The Sūtra of the Secrets of the Thus-Gone Ones*:[1679]

> Śāntimati, it is like this: Through cutting the root of a tree, all the branches and leaves will become dry. Likewise, through the views about a real personality being completely at peace, all afflictions will be at peace.[1680]

### 3.2. Phenomenal Identitylessness

One meditates on phenomenal identitylessness through the four applications of mindfulness.

This has two parts:
1) The general topic
2) The meaning of the text

### 3.2.1. The General Topic

I will explain the application of mindfulness.
Its object of observation is fourfold: body, feelings, mind, and
phenomena.
Its nature is the knowledge that understands these.
Its aids are the accompanying factors mindfulness and alertness.

The way to meditate is to meditate that the body is impure,
That feelings are suffering, that the mind is impermanent, [853]
And that all phenomena are identityless.

The results: Reversing the clinging to the body's purity
Is nonattachment, the understanding of the reality of suffering.
Comprehending all feelings as pain
Reverses craving and relinquishes the origin [of suffering].

Through seeing that the mind is momentary,
One understands that there is no person and meditates on the path.
Through seeing that all phenomena are identityless,
One is free from dullness and attains cessation.

In order to attain one's own release,
By focusing on the body and so on that are contained in one's own
continuum,
One meditates and apprehends them thus.
These are the applications of mindfulness of the limited vehicle.

Since one wishes for enlightenment for the welfare of others,
One meditates by focusing on the bodies and so forth
Of [all beings in] the three times whose [number] equals space.
At the same time, one does not observe these as impurity,

Suffering, impermanence, or even mere identitylessness.
This is the great path of the Victors' children.
Hence, through fourteen aspects,
The applications of mindfulness of the great vehicle are most eminent.

The higher abhidharma says:

> The applications of mindfulness should be understood in terms of (1) observed object, (2) nature, (3) aids, (4) meditation, and (5) result of meditation.[1681]

1) Beings in cyclic existence cling to the body as the support for the self, to feelings as that which is experienced by the self, to the mind as that which is grasped as the self, and to phenomena as the causes for bondage or release of the self. Since cyclic existence is produced through the intense clinging to these four, this set of four—body, feelings, mind, and phenomena—constitute the objects to focus on.

2) The nature [of the applications of mindfulness] is the knowledge that understands the nature of body, feelings, mind, and phenomena. To understand that the body is impure is the nature of the application of mindfulness of the body, because this is the knowledge that understands how its nature in dependence on the seeming level is. [The same applies for] the remaining [three]. *The Treasury [of Abhidharma]* says:

> Application of mindfulness [854] is knowledge: . . .[1682]

3) As for the aids, this knowledge is embraced by mindfulness and alertness. Through this, it is not forgotten and is associated with its congruent factors, which are the five omnipresent mental events that arise simultaneously with it, because the application [of mindfulness] is not accomplished if these [factors] are not present. What one is "mindful" of is precisely this knowledge. "Intense" means not distant, that is, not interrupted by something else. "Application" means that the mind is fused with this mindfulness; it remains within the stream of mindfulness through alertness. Therefore, this is called "intense application of mindfulness."

4) The way to meditate

a) One's own body and those of others are collections of impure phenomena. Through the intense mindfulness of the body, one understands that this is actually the case. In particular, from among the twenty notions [to come], here one meditates on the [first] ten: the notions of (1) a dead person, (2) a repulsive corpse, (3) a putrid blue corpse, (4) a putrid black corpse, (5) a swollen corpse, (6) a maggot-ridden corpse, (7) a mangled corpse, (8) a putrid red corpse, (9) a scattered corpse, and (10) dry bones.

b) The intense mindfulness of feelings is the remedy for attachment to pleasant feelings, aversion to suffering, and dullness toward neutral ones. In the sūtras, it is repeatedly said:

> Everything contaminated is suffering.

and

> Thus, whatever you might feel, this is suffering.

Accordingly, one meditates by understanding [feelings] in such a way. Here, the suffering of suffering refers to everything that is evident as manifest suffering. The suffering of change is the entirety of those feelings to which one clings as being pleasant. The suffering of conditioned existence refers to any situation that this mere body that one has taken on and [its] mere mind or consciousness experience from [one's birth] onward. This suffering of conditioned existence is like living with a feeling of indifference when one's [latent] disease of stomach cancer has not yet matured. The suffering of change is like the delicious flavor when one eats boiled rice mixed with poison. The suffering of suffering [855] is like the experience of feeling ill when the poison [in the rice] has become active or like the arising of an ulcer on top of [this] stomach cancer. In brief, [here] one should meditate on the following six notions: (11) the notion that impermanent phenomena are suffering, (12) the notion that food is an adverse factor, (13) the notion of disliking the whole world, (14) the notion of [its] defects, (15) the notion of relinquishing [it], and (16) the notion of being free from desire [for it].

c) The intense mindfulness of mind is the remedy for clinging to mind as something permanent and single. [The Buddha] said:

> Everything conditioned is impermanent.

Accordingly, forms—clouds, steam, smoke, flames, and so on—do not remain as such and such [forms] even for a moment. Also [phenomena] such as water streams and the movements of the wind do not remain for even one moment beyond the specific [moment of] time [when they occur]. Their previous [moments] are not the following ones, and these again do not remain as their following ones. When one examines mind with examples such as these, the mind—

this mere stream of consciousness that experiences—does not remain for even a moment. Its previous [moment] is not the following one, and there is nothing in between the previous and the following moment. Hence, it does not last even for just a moment and cannot be labeled as something single or multiple. [The intense mindfulness of mind] is what makes one understand this. Thus, [here] one should cultivate (17) the notion that everything conditioned is impermanent.

d) The intense mindfulness of phenomena is the remedy for clinging to the phenomena constituent[1683] or the phenomena source[1684]—which is superimposed as the object of the sixth consciousness (the mental [consciousness])—as being such and such [phenomena]. One contemplates dependent origination in progressive order and reverse order. Additionally, in the great vehicle, one analyzes these [phenomena] with reasons and arguments, such as the freedom from unity and multiplicity, and the refutation of arising from the four possibilities. Through this, one understands that bondage and release are not observable in any phenomenon whatsoever. Thus, [here] one meditates on (18) the notion of cessation and on (19) the notion of discriminatingly examining emptiness.

5) The result

[The result is] (20) the understanding that the fourfold mistakenness of clinging to these four—the body and so on—as something pure, pleasant, permanent, and an identity functions as the cause for acquiring bad places of birth. Hence, one is not attached to a body and does not wish for a body. [856] This is the understanding of [the reality of] suffering. Through understanding feelings as suffering, one is free from craving. This means to relinquish the origin [of suffering]. Through seeing that the basis to which one clings—the mind—is impermanent, the clinging to "me" is reversed. Thus, one is free from the fear of nirvāṇa, from the concern that the self becomes extinct. Hence, one gradually manifests cessation. Through being aware that all phenomena are not different, that is, spacelike emptiness and illusionlike dependent origination, one is free from ignorance. This means to engage in the reality of the path.

By going beyond these four—contaminated body, feelings, mind, and phenomena—one attains mastery over uncontaminated body, feelings, mind, and phenomena. [*The Distinction between the*] *Middle and Extremes* says:

> Because of impregnations of negativity, because of craving's cause,
> Because of the basis, and because of nonignorance,
> One engages in the four realities.
> Through this, one cultivates the applications of mindfulness.[1685]

The applications of mindfulness of the inferior vehicle are as follows: With a mind that strives for peace for one's own sake, one meditates by focusing on just the five aggregates that are seized by oneself and on just those other beings who dwell in places that are suitable to appear [to oneself]. These [objects] are then apprehended as impure and so on.

The applications of mindfulness of the great vehicle are as follows: Through being embraced by the mind of enlightenment, one meditates by focusing on the entire spectrum of the aggregates and so on in the three times that pervade space. This [leads to] the reversal of apprehending them as pure, pleasant, permanent, and an identity. At the same time, one [mentally] engages in emptiness, that is, that they are not observable as impure and such either. *The Ornament* [*of Sūtras*] states:

> The applications of mindfulness of those with insight
> Are without comparison
> Through fourteen aspects of meditation.
> Hence, these render them more eminent than others.[1686]

Accordingly, they are more eminent through the following fourteen [aspects]:

1) The support, which is the knowledge that arises from the profound and vast dharmas of the great vehicle
2) The remedy, which is the knowledge that eliminates the extremes of both superimposition and denial
3) Engagement of oneself and others in the four realities of the great vehicle
4) Focusing on inconceivable dharmas [857]
5) Mental engagement that everything is like space
6) Attainment of nonabiding in existence or peace
7) Concordance with the perfections
8) Ensuing engagement according to the inclinations of those to be trained
9) Complete understanding that the body is like an illusion, that feelings are like dreams, that mind is like space, and that phenomena occur adventitiously like clouds
10) Attainment of births as one pleases, in which one is without afflictions despite assuming supreme bodies, like those of Śakra or a wheel-ruler, and experiencing the supreme among feelings
11) Outshining the great meditations of others even through one's minor meditations, since one has sharp faculties and is skilled in means
12) [Everything] being one taste as the supremacy of genuine enlightenment
13) Endowment with inexhaustible meditations even after the attainment of nirvāṇa

14) Accomplishment of the ten grounds and the result of buddhahood

[As *The Ornament of Sūtras* says]:

They are other due to support, remedy,
Likewise ensuing engagement,
Focus, mental engagement,
More eminent meditation through attainment,

Concordance, ensuing engagement,
Complete understanding, birth,
Greatness, supremacy,
Meditation, and perfect accomplishment.[1687]

### 3.2.2. The Meaning of the Text

This section has four parts, which are the four applications of mindfulness:

### 3.2.2.1. The Application of Mindfulness of the Body

This has two parts:
1) The individual body parts are not the body.
2) The refutation of something that possesses the body parts.

### 3.2.2.1.1. The Individual Body Parts Are Not the Body

**The body is neither feet nor shanks,**
**Nor is it the thighs or the waist.**
**The abdomen and the back are not the body,**
**And neither are the chest or arms. [78]**

**Hands and sides are not the body,**
**Nor are armpits or inner organs.**
**Also head and neck are not the body.**
**So if it is none of these, what is this body? [79]**

The [first] seven[1688] lines [teach] that none of the various distinct parts is the body, and the last [line] teaches that the body [858] is a superimposition.

If you call this assembly of various body parts "body" and cling to it as such [a body], it is reasonable to examine this for a while: [859] What is it that you name "body"? **The body is neither feet nor shanks, nor is it the thighs or the waist. The abdomen and the back are not the body, and neither are the chest or arms. Hands and sides are not the body, nor are armpits or inner organs.** In the same way, **also head and neck,** and all individual parts other than these, **are not the body. So if** it appears that you have gained certainty that **it is none of these** [parts], **what is this** so-called **body?** It is nothing but a mere name, just a superimposition.

### 3.2.2.1.2. The Refutation of Something That Possesses the Body Parts

> **If this body were present**
> **In all of them as their exact match,**
> **Then the parts would of course dwell in the parts,**
> **But where would itself stay? [80]**
>
> **If the entire body**
> **Were present in the hands and such,**
> **There would be as many bodies**
> **As there are hands and so forth. [81]**
>
> **If the body does not exist inside nor outside,**
> **How could the body be in the hands and such?**
> **It also does not exist separate from the hands and so forth,**
> **So how could it possibly be found? [82]**

These three verses refute that the body abides in [any of] all [its] parts.

Here, the Differentiators and others say, "These are [just] the parts of the body, but the actual body that possesses these parts abides in such a way that it encompasses all [its] parts." Also, some later Tibetans say, "The six [kinds of] parts (such as nectar, pus, and blood) abide within that which possesses these parts (a bowl full of that which is wet and moistening)."[1689]

Our objection[1690] to this is: **If this** very **body were present in all** its parts **as their exact match, then the** individual **parts**—like the eyes—**would dwell in** just these individual **parts.**[1691] If you state such a superimposition, it is **of course** nothing but an imputation, **but** then we ask: **Where would** the body **itself stay** among these parts?

**If** you assert that this body—that is, **the entire body** with all its parts—**were to dwell in** each of **the hands and so on, there would be as many bodies** in number **as there are hands and so forth,** such as the body that dwells in the hands and the body that dwells in the feet. Hence, there would be many bodies. [Moreover,] there would be the following consequences: The body that dwells in the hands [would entail] two bodies, one in the right and one in the left [hand].

Each of these [two bodies] in turn would have three [more] bodies that are related to its major joints, five bodies in the fingers, and fifteen bodies in the knuckles and so on, until finally there would be as many bodies as there are infinitesimal particles [in the body]. Thus, you are not able to assert [such a position] for the following reasons: If it were like this, [860] it would follow that each and every [body] part is the body. Therefore, your claim of an encompassing body that possesses its parts collapses. Furthermore, it is a most amazing feat indeed that a single individual should have a number of bodies [that equals the number] of infinitesimal particles [in the body].

Therefore, **if** you see that, when analyzed, **not** even an atom of **the** so-called **body exists** anywhere **outside**, as an appearance of matter, **nor inside**, as an appearance of consciousness, **how could** you say, "**The body** is **in the hands and such**"? Even if you were to grind the hands and the like to dust, you would not find a body in them. You might assert then that there is a body that is not these [body] parts. [However,] in this case, the body would not be harmed even if you dissect it all the way down to its life force, because the body is something other than these [body parts]. Hence, each part—**the hands and so forth**—is not the body, and **the** body **also does not exist separate from** these parts, **so how could** the body **possibly be found?** In this way, [the body] is understood to be a mere name.

**Thus, the body does not exist, but one perceives a body**
**In the hands and so on due to ignorance,**
**Just as one may perceive a human being in some pile**
**Because of its specific configuration.** [83]

**As long as the conditions are assembled,**
**This figure**[1692] **looks like a person.**
**Likewise, as long as such is the case for the hands and so forth,**
**One will see a body there.** [84]

These two verses teach that [the perception of] a body is comparable to apprehending a pile of stones as a human being.

**Thus,** no matter whether it is something that possesses its parts or something else, **the** so-called **body does not exist** at all, **but one perceives a body in the** assembly of **hands and so on.** This happens **due to** a dull mind's **ignorance.** It is **just like** the following [example]: When one looks at a human being and some pile of stones from afar, they look similar in that they are just some dark shape [in the distance. Thus, it is merely] **because of its specific configuration** that **perceiving some pile** leads to the thought, "**A human being** appears."

You might say, "[Your example] is nothing but mistaking a pile of stones for a human being for just a moment, whereas the perception of hands and the like as a body occurs over a long time. Thus, they are dissimilar." **As long as the** causes and **conditions** for it **are assembled,** it may happen that **this figure looks like a person. Likewise, as long as such** [an assembly of] causes and conditions **is the case for the hands and so forth,** this **will** give rise to a cognition that **sees a body there.** Hence, there is no difference.

> **In the same way, what would a foot be,**
> **Since it is just a collection of toes?**
> **As these are collections of knuckles,**
> **The knuckles can likewise be divided into their parts.** [85]
>
> **Consequently, the parts too can be broken down into particles,**
> **And the particles may be divided into their directional parts.**
> **Since these directional divisions lack any parts,**
> **They are like space. Therefore, not even particles exist.** [86]

These two verses teach that, when analyzed, the body parts and their subparts also are not established.

Not only is the apprehension of the body as a unit reversed in this way, but also its parts are not established under analysis. **In the same way, what would a foot be, since it is just a collection of toes? As these** [toes] **are collections of knuckles, the knuckles** [861] **can likewise be divided into their parts. Consequently, the parts too can be broken down into particles, and the particles may be divided into their directional parts. Since these directional divisions lack any parts, they are like space. Therefore, not even particles exist** as something that can be observed.

> **So which person who analyzes**
> **Would take delight in dreamlike forms?**
> **Once thus the body does not exist,**
> **What is a man and what is a woman?** [87]

This verse teaches that, consequently, forms are dreamlike.

**So which person who analyzes would take delight in dreamlike forms? Once thus the body does not exist, what is a man and what is a woman?** The meaning of this is as follows: Men and women are nothing but [labels] that are set up due to differences in the sexual organs, and [such labels] come from the clinging that the sexual organs are [parts of] the body. When one understands that the body itself is not observable, where should its distinct features remain as a residue?

## [Synopsis of Other Commentaries]

Here, Kalyāṇadeva explains the following and other speculations:

> [The variant of line 84b] "the body looks like a person" in some editions should be explained in another way: As long as the collection of conditions of mental dullness exists, the body looks like a person, although a person has never existed in it. Likewise, as long as the collection of conditions for the hands and so on exists, the ignorance that they are the body arises.[1693]

*The Small Commentary*[1694] mentions the same speculation by extending it further:

> Just as some pile is mistaken for a person, [our range of mistakenness] starts with mistaking the hands and so on for the body and extends to [such cases as] mistakenly [apprehending] grass due to [a collection of] particles.

Then there appears the following:

> This śloka [84] "As long as the conditions are assembled . . ." was inserted later.

### 3.2.2.2. The Application of Mindfulness of Feelings

This has four parts:

1) Feelings as such are not established.
2) There is no cause for feelings.
3) There is no object that is felt.
4) There is no apprehender of feelings.

#### 3.2.2.2.1. Feelings as Such Are Not Established

> **If suffering actually exists,**
> **Why does it not oppress those who are cheerful?**
> **If delicacies and such are pleasure,**
> **Why do those troubled with sorrow and the like not delight in them? [88]**

This verse teaches that suffering does not ultimately exist.

[863] Feelings are of six [types], such as feelings due to the condition of eye contact [with form]. When summarized, they are included in the triad of pleasure, suffering, and neutral [feelings].[1695] Thus, **if** it is certain that the temporary feeling of **suffering** is real as and **actually exists** as suffering, **why does it not oppress the** feelings of **cheerfulness** and pleasure? [In fact, it should do so,] because this very suffering exists even at the time of a feeling of pleasure, since it is real as the feeling of suffering as such. **If pleasure** exists ultimately, **why does** relishing delicious tastes **and such not delight** and please even those who are in the state of being **troubled with sorrow**, suffering, **and the like?** [It should delight them,] because pleasure is ultimately real and their minds are involved with this [pleasure, when they relish food and so on].

> **You might say, "It is not experienced,**
> **Because it is overridden by something stronger."**
> **How could something be a feeling**
> **That does not have the nature of an experience? [89]**

This verse refutes the assertion that [suffering] is overridden by pleasure.

**You might say,** "There is no question that the feeling of suffering exists. However, suffering **is not experienced** in a situation in which pleasure is experienced, **because it is overridden by** pleasure that is **stronger."** Such suffering **that has the nature of** being overriden by **an experience** of pleasure [864] is **not** suffering anyway: If suffering designates something that is felt and experienced, **how could something be a feeling** that is not experienced by anybody?

> **You might say, "Isn't it that suffering exists in a subtle form,**
> **Once its gross form is removed?"**
> **If the [feeling] other than that is mere joy,**
> **Any subtlety must still pertain to this. [90]**[1696]
>
> **If suffering does not arise**
> **Due to the arising of its adverse condition,**
> **This can only mean**
> **That feelings are just imaginations of our conceptions. [91]**

These two verses refute the existence of subtle suffering.

**You might say, "Suffering exists in a subtle form.** Therefore, its continuum is not interrupted." However, **isn't it that** this experience and existence of subtle suffering **removes** even the **gross form** of pleasure [that exists] at this same time? [In fact, it should,] because it is not possible that subtle suffering and gross pleasure are experienced simultaneously by a single consciousness.

You might argue, "Since **this** subtle suffering arises at **some** time that is **other than the** [time of] gross pleasure, there is no mistake." **Any subtlety** of suffering **must still pertain to this** gross pleasure in that it is **its adverse condition. Due to this**, it is impossible that pleasure **arises** while suffering exists. Rather, it would follow that it is never possible for pleasure to arise, since suffering ultimately exists. You might say, "**Suffering does not arise** as something permanent by nature; it merely originates from an assembly of causes and conditions." **If** this is the case, **this can only mean that** this [suffering] appears in different situations merely due to an assembly of delusive causes and conditions. Thus, **our conceptions** of pleasurable, painful, and neutral **feelings** and our apprehension of them as actualities **are** nothing but **just** mistaken **imaginations.**[1697]

> **For this reason, you should cultivate**
> **This analysis as the remedy for such.**
> **Meditative stability that springs from the field of examination**
> **Is the food of yogins. [92]**

This verse teaches that feelings are without nature.

**For this reason, you should cultivate this analysis** of feelings' own nature **as the remedy for such** clinging that [takes] feelings, such as pleasure, to be real. This is the sprout of **meditative stability that** grows **from the** fertile **field of** proper **examination.** It is weighed down with the fruits of knowledge and is freed from the husks of discursiveness. It **is the** most genuine **food** to sustain the well-being of **yogins** who engage in authentic knowledge.

### 3.2.2.2.2. There Is No Cause for Feelings

> **If there is a distance between the senses and their objects,**
> **Where would they meet?**
> **If there is no distance between them, they are a single unit.**
> **So what would meet what? [93]**

> **Infinitesimal particles do not interpenetrate infinitesimal particles,**
> **As they lack free space and are uniform.**
> **Without interpenetration, there is no intermingling,**
> **And without intermingling, there is no contact. [94]**

> **So how could you possibly say**
> **That partless entities come into contact?**
> **Should you ever bump into a meeting of partless entities,**
> **Please be so kind as to introduce us to it.** [95]

These three verses refute that sense faculties and their referents come into contact.

In this context, the Followers of the Great Exposition school of our own [Buddhist] faction say, "When the senses meet with their objects, this is contact. From this, feelings arise ultimately." [865] We ask: How is it, do [these feelings] arise in such a way that there is something in between the senses and their objects, or do they arise without something in between? **If** they arise so that **there is a distance between the sense** consciousnesses **and their objects** in the sense that [these two] are separated by an aspect or anything else, **where would the** senses and their objects **meet?** [They would not meet at all,] because they are separated by something else in between. **If**, however, you assert that **there is no distance between the** senses and their objects, then upon meeting, **the** two would be mingled as **a single unit**, because they are not separated by anything else in between. Hence, in terms of senses and their objects, **what would meet what?** When analyzed, [the notion of] meeting collapses.

You might argue, "It is not the coarse entities that meet. Rather, the infinitesimal particles meet." **Infinitesimal particles do not interpenetrate** these very **infinitesimal particles**, because it is you hearers who assert the nature of these infinitesimal particles as follows: **They lack** any **free space** or volume **and** they **are uniform**, that is, partless units. Hence, just like water in water, **without** one [particle] **interpenetrating** into the other, **there is no intermingling, and without intermingling, there is no contact** in the sense of touching [each other] everywhere.[1698]

**So how could you possibly say that entities** that are **partless** in time and space **come into contact?** Therefore, **should you ever bump into** such a common locus of entities that are **partless** in terms of time and space [on the one hand] and [entities] that [can] **meet** [on the other hand], **please be so kind as to introduce us to it** and bless us with your amazing discovery.

> **It is absolutely illogical**
> **To have any contact with nonphysical consciousness.**
> **The same goes for a collection, since it is a nonentity,**
> **Which was already analyzed earlier.** [96]

This verse teaches that it is not justified to come into contact with consciousness.

In a general way, [conventionally speaking,] physical phenomena do surely come into contact, but **it is absolutely illogical** [for a physical thing] **to** mutually **have any contact with nonphysical consciousness.** You might venture, "[Our] presentation that they come into contact with consciousness is based on the collection [of senses, objects, and consciousnesses]." **The same goes for a collection, since,** when analyzed, **it is a nonentity, which was already analyzed earlier** with the examples of a rosary, an army, and such.[1699]

**If thus there is no contact,**
**Where would feelings come from?**
**So what is the purpose of tiring yourself out?**
**And who would be afflicted by what? [97]**

**When there is nobody who feels**
**And no feeling either,**
**Then, seeing this situation,**
**Why, O craving, do you not burst asunder? [98]**

These two verses teach that consequently there is no contact, and thus feelings do not come into being.

**If thus there is no** mutual **contact** between the senses and their objects, **where would feelings** that [depend] on this [contact] **come from?** This is like smoke without fire. You might go on, "[Their] cause may not be seen, but there still are mere feelings." [866] **So what is the purpose of tiring yourself out** in such a way by asserting that there is a result even if there is no cause? What are your tiring efforts good for?[1700]

Thus, **when there is nobody who feels and no feeling either, then, seeing this situation, why, O craving, do you not burst asunder?** [You should do so,] because craving comes from feelings and [usually] the result subsides, once the cause has ceased.

### 3.2.2.2.3. There Is No Object That Is Felt

**Even what you see and touch**
**Is by its nature dreamlike or illusionlike. [99ab]**

Furthermore, if there were any objects to be felt, feelings would of course depend on them. However, **even** these objects that appear as **what you see and** what you **touch**[1701] manifest [just] **by** their **nature** of being **like** something that is seen and touched in a **dream or** something that is seen and touched in an **illusion**, because they do not in the slightest exist as something else.

### 3.2.2.2.4. There Is No Apprehender of Feelings

> **A feeling is not seen by the mind,**
> **Since it arises simultaneously with it.** [99cd]
>
> **Something earlier may be remembered**
> **By what arises later, but not experienced.** [100ab]

These four lines refute an apprehender of feelings in the three times.

Furthermore, feelings do not actually exist, because the mind does not experience them for the following reasons: When **a** moment of feeling **arises simultaneously with** a moment of mind, the mind is not seen by the feeling, and the **feeling is not seen by the mind.** This means that [any interaction between] an agent and an object is contradictory to [their] simultaneity.[1702] As for **some earlier** feeling, it **may be remembered by** a mind **that arises later, but** it is **not experienced** by this following [moment of] mind, because it has already ceased. For example, this is like mentally engaging today in yesterday's cold sensation. If the mind were [to arise] earlier and the feeling later, the same mistake would apply.

> **It does not experience itself,**
> **Nor is it experienced by something other.** [100cd]
>
> **There is no experiencer of feelings at all.**
> **Therefore, in true reality, there are no feelings.** [101ab]

These four lines teach that there is no experiencer of feelings.

A feeling **does not experience itself,** because this is comparable to the eye not seeing itself.[1703] **Nor is** this feeling **experienced by something other** than the feeling itself, just as form does not experience sound. Once one has analyzed in this way, from the perspective of stainless knowledge, **there is** nothing that is felt, **no experiencer** who **feels**, and no way in which feelings are felt **at all. Therefore, feelings** are [just] appearances through superimposition from the perspective of mistakenness without analysis. When analyzed, however, they **are not true reality.**

> **So what in this collection without any identity**
> **Could be harmed by them?** [101cd]

These two lines summarize the meaning of the topic in a general way.

**So what** benefit or **harm could these** superimposed feelings do **in this** mental and physical **collection without any** phenomenal or personal **identity** that is a mere illusion? [867] This is just like illusory space not being harmed by illusory fire or water.

This is the perfect meditation of the application of mindfulness of feelings. [As *The Sūtra Requested by Crown Jewel*] says:

> Mañjuśrī, those who do not observe these very feelings are the ones who intensely apply their mindfulness to feelings by inspecting feelings.

## [Synopsis of Other Commentaries]

Kalyāṇadeva says:

> [As for verse 92,] conceptual meditative stability [that analyzes true reality] is the food without contamination. It has the defining characteristic of realizing true reality. The one in whom it exists is a yogin, because studying gives rise to reflection, [reflection] to meditation, and [meditation] to the wisdom of true reality. Just as the killing of an illusory elephant by an illusory lion is not [happening] in actuality, the analysis of true reality vanquishes wrong conceptions while, actually, [both] do not exist.[1704]
>
> These [lines 98d–99b that start] " Why, O craving, do you not burst asunder?" refute also the followers of Kaṇāda[1705] and others. They say, "There are two types of substance, what is seen and what is touched. The consciousnesses that originate from the meeting of the senses and their referents are perceptions." Through this way of analyzing, [one sees that] there is neither substance nor meeting. In other words, one may see or touch such entities as a vase that look like substance (such as form), but none [of them] exists. The term "even" [in line 99a] refers to the acceptance of [such entities] on the seeming level. Ultimately, however, there is nothing to be seen or touched whatsoever.[1706]

Vibhūticandra comments:

> Feelings are just imaginations. . . . The very pleasure of one [being] is the suffering of another. Something that one has heard before might have given rise to suffering, [but] if one sees it at some other time, it

may give rise to pleasure. Therefore, feelings and their causes are nothing but imputations. [There is] also the following explanation:

> Snakes make the peacock feel happy.
> Poison is pleasure for those familiar with extracting the essence.[1707]
> Thorns that hurt you [868]
> Are a special treat in the mouth of a camel.[1708]

*The Small Commentary* presents [lines 90a–c] as the statement of others:

> You might argue, "Since [suffering] exists [here] in a subtle way, it exists as the very feeling [of suffering]. [However,] since [its] gross [aspect] may be dispelled [by gross pleasure], it is also not contradictory to [say] that [suffering] does not remove pleasure. Furthermore, it does not follow that this [subtle suffering] goes beyond the definition of feeling, because it is experienced. In this way, it is merely something other than that [gross pleasure]. The subtle suffering [at the time of gross pleasure] is something other than great pleasure; it has the character of subtle pleasure that is empty of supreme pleasure." [Thus, lines 90a–c would read as follows:]
>
> You might say, "Isn't it that suffering exists in a subtle form,
> Once its gross form is removed?
> It is merely something other."

[This commentary says that lines 90d–91d] "Any subtlety must still pertain to this . . . " teach the refutation [of this statement].

### 3.2.2.3. The Application of Mindfulness of Mind

This has two parts:
1) Mind is not established.
2) Objects are not established.

### 3.2.2.3.1. Mind Is Not Established

> **Mind does not dwell in the senses**
> **Nor in form and such, nor in between.**
> **The mind is also not found inside nor outside,**
> **Nor anywhere else. [102]**

**What exists neither in the body nor elsewhere,**
**Neither intermingled nor separate,**
**That is just nothing.**
**Therefore, sentient beings are by nature completely liberated.** [103]

The first six lines teach that mind does not withstand analysis, and the last two lines teach that it is pure from the very start.

You might think, "Feelings exist, because the experiencer of feelings—the mind—exists." Cognizance or **mind does not dwell in the senses,** [869] **nor in** objects, **such as form, nor** does it dwell **in between** these two. Hence, what does not dwell anywhere at all is not something that exists by its very nature. So who [or what] is the mind? If you examine this question, **the mind is also not found inside** (as a sense faculty), **nor** is the mind an **outside** object, **nor** is it **anywhere else** than inside or outside as a mind that is something different [from sense faculties and objects].

Thus, if nobody sees the one who is the mind, what is it now that is labeled "mind"? You might think, "If mental cognition itself is a sense faculty, how could it be that it does not dwell in the sense faculties?" In general, it is of course the case that such [terms] as "mental sense faculty"[1709] and "mental conception"[1710] [are used] with reference to "mental cognition" as their basis of attribution. During [mental cognition]'s [initial] phase of [manifesting as] nonconceptual perception, it is presented as "the [mental] sense faculty," while its ensuing operation [as] apprehending conceptions is presented as "mental conception." However, even in such cases it is not adequate to say, "The basis of attribution (mental cognition) dwells in the attribute (the mental sense faculty)." This is just as inadequate as saying, "The body dwells in the hand." If you assert that mental cognition itself is the mental sense faculty, how could it be adequate that something dwells in itself? That something dwells in something [can only] refer to phenomena that are different, but how could you present [such a notion of] dwelling with respect to [phenomena] that are not different?

Thus, **that** mental cognition **which exists neither in the body nor anywhere** other than the body, **neither intermingled** with the body **nor** in a way that it could be seen **separately** from the body, **is not** seen as **anything** at all that has a nature of its own. **Therefore,** right from the start, the minds of **sentient beings are by nature completely liberated** and unaffected by discursiveness.

### 3.2.2.3.2. Objects Are Not Established

**If consciousness came before the knowable object,**
**Based on what would it arise?**

**If it were together with the knowable object,**
**Based on what would it arise? [104]**

**If it came after the knowable object,**
**From what would consciousness arise then? [105ab]**

Here, the mistakes of [consciousness existing] earlier than, simultaneously with, or later than its knowable object are each taught by two lines.

You might think, "Consciousness actually exists, because [its] objects—knowable objects—exist by their nature." However, then we should ask: What comes first, consciousness or knowable object? You might say, "Consciousness is first." **If** it were the case that **consciousness came before the knowable object, based on what would** this consciousness **arise?** [In fact, it does not arise,] because it cannot have any other object than its [specific] knowable object, and this knowable object has not arisen yet. **If** you **were** to say, "**It** occurs [870] **together with the knowable object** at the same time," **based on what would** this consciousness **arise?** [It does not arise,] because it cannot evaluate [any object], since simultaneity contradicts any [interaction between] agent and object.[1711] **If it came after the knowable object, from what would consciousness arise then?**

Thus, arising, abiding, and ceasing of all phenomena as well as subject, object, and so forth are nothing but imputations through clinging to the stream of mistakenness that is our habituation to latent tendencies. However, these [phenomena] do not exist from the perspective of correct consciousness.

## [Synopsis of Other Commentaries]

In general, as for [lines 102cd] "The mind is also not found inside . . . ," most commentaries supplement the following words: "It also does not dwell on the inside . . ." [However,] if this were [the meaning of these lines], they would [just] repeat [lines 102ab]—that [the mind] does not dwell in the senses [and so on]—and the effect of the term "also" in [the phrase] "also not found inside" would fall away.[1712] Hence, one should not comment [on these lines] in such a way.

According [to these verses above], mind is pure from the very start. To see this is the application of mindfulness of mind. *The Sūtra [Requested by] Crown Jewel* says:

> When you search for the mind everywhere, you do not really see the mind on the inside, nor on the outside, nor on both [sides], nor in the aggregates, the sources, or the constituents either.

and

> Mañjuśrī, if someone understands the mind as a mere name, this is someone who intensely applies the mindfulness in which mind inspects mind.

[As for lines 104–105ab,] Kalyāṇadeva says:

> Since knowable objects, such as form, are momentary, they do not have parts [that could be apprehended by a later moment of mind], because they perish and are gone instantaneously. Even if they had parts, an earlier moment of mind [that could perceive them now] does not exist, because [an earlier moment] is a nonentity [now]. Consciousness and knowable object do exist simultaneously, just like the beams of a scale, but none is the cause for the other. Therefore, actually, both of them do not exist.[1713]

[As for line 105b,] *The Small Commentary on the Knowledge Chapter* says:

> From what would consciousness arise anyway, since it is unborn in the first place?[1714]

### 3.2.2.4. The Application of Mindfulness of Phenomena

This has three parts:

1) Teaching that all phenomena are without arising
2) Dispelling consequences of extreme absurdity
3) Dispelling the consequence of infinite regress [871]

#### 3.2.2.4.1. Teaching That All Phenomena Are without Arising

> **Thus, you cannot come to the conclusion**
> **That any phenomenon arises.** [105cd]

Once you have ended your clinging to body, feelings, and mind in this way, there is no other phenomenon than these left. Therefore, you fully grasp that all phenomena are without nature. **Thus,** you understand that **you cannot come to the conclusion that any phenomenon arises.** Hence, you turn away from apprehending any arising [of phenomena altogether] and, consequently, do not observe [their] abiding or ceasing either. Through this, you fully grasp that they are primordially free from discursiveness.

### 3.2.2.4.2. Dispelling Consequences of Extreme Absurdity

> **"In this case, the seeming does not exist,**
> **So where would this leave the two realities?**
> **If it came through another seeming,**
> **Where would there be liberated beings?"** [106]
>
> **They are just conceptions in the minds of others,**
> **But they do not exist in terms of their own seeming.**
> **Later, when this has been verified, it exists.**
> **If it has not, the seeming does not exist at all.** [107]

The first verse states the objections, and the second provides the answer.

At this point, the Proponents of Cognizance and the realists might say, "**In this case** of everything being without arising, **the seeming does not exist. So where would this** position that the seeming does not exist [872] **leave the two realities?** This contradicts your earlier presentation of the two realities. [Furthermore,] the seeming is not put forward from the perspective that the seeming has a nature of its own. Rather, it is posited on the basis of another reason, that is, in terms of interdependence. This is comparable to when one conceives of a mirage as water. [This concept] is not something that is brought up by the mirage [itself]. Rather, it is set up **through another seeming** [phenomenon], which is the cognition that conceives of it." **If** they were to argue like this, [someone else might answer,] "However, **where would there be liberated beings?** [Beings could not pass into nirvāṇa at all] for the following reasons: If the seeming does not exist, then there are no sentient beings [either]. Or it is possible that even someone who has already become a Buddha is presented by others as someone with basic unawareness."

[Here, in verse 106, Śāntideva] has anticipated some of his opponents' qualms in the form of the above objection and answer and has set up this ostensible dispute. He then [continues with verse 107] in order to provide an answer to this [discussion]:

> **They are just conceptions in the minds of others,**
> **But they do not exist in terms of their own seeming.**

**Such** presentations that someone has become a Buddha or not **are just** imputations that [come] from the **conceptions of others' minds.** It is **not** that these presentations of having become a Buddha or not are made, because such a **seeming** [event of becoming a Buddha] is seen from the perspective of a Buddha**'s own** nature. The reason for this is: [A Buddha] sees that, right from the start, all phenomena are nothing whatsoever by their very nature and has completely eliminated [all] discriminations, such as real or delusive.

In general, it is suitable that seeming dependent origination appears within emptiness, just like clouds in the sky or waves on the ocean, while one is not able to label the ocean and its waves as one or different. Once the ultimate Dharma Body has been revealed, the seeming Form Bodies spring forth without effort among what appears for others. In this way, it is not contradictory that the seeming does not exist by its very nature, while a great variety of appearances present themselves as this seeming, just as it is not contradictory that the form of the moon [which is reflected] in the water is not a real [moon] and yet appears.

> **Later, when this has been verified, it exists.**
> **If it has not, the seeming does not exist at all.**

**Later, when** you **gain certainty about this** way [of how things are] and realize it, you will fully grasp that ultimate nonarising does not contradict the illusionlike existence of the seeming. [873] **If** the ultimate were **not** nonarising, then—despite your assertion to the contrary—you would have to accept that **the seeming does not exist at all**, because [Nāgārjuna] states [in his *Fundamental Verses on Centrism*]:

> For those to whom emptiness makes sense,
> Everything makes sense.
> For those to whom emptiness does not make sense,
> Nothing at all makes sense.[1715]

and

> If all of this were not empty,
> Nothing would originate and disintegrate,
> And it would follow that, for you,
> The four realities of the noble ones do not exist.[1716]

### 3.2.2.4.3. Dispelling the Consequence of Infinite Regress

> **"Both conceiver and what is conceived**
> **Are mutually dependent."**
> **All analysis is expressed**
> **On the basis of its accord with common consensus.** [108]

The first two lines state the objection, and the second two lines give the answer.

You might say, "In dependence on a consciousness that is the **conceiver**, one assigns a knowable object **that is conceived.** Likewise, one assigns consciousness in dependence on what is conceived. When one does so, **both** consciousness and knowable objects **are** [just] **mutually dependent** conceptions. Therefore, one will never be able to analyze [anything]."

If one analyzes [consciousness and knowable objects] in such a way, they are [indeed] mutually dependent thoughts. Therefore, they are both not established, and [just] this is their ultimate state. Temporarily, however, in this context of presenting the seeming, one does not analyze these phenomena—such as form—about which there is common consensus between both debaters. It is from such a perspective then that **all analysis is expressed on the basis of** this mere **accord with** [such] **common consensus.** The reason for [such analysis] is that it is necessary to put an end to the wrong ideas of others. However, also the analysis itself is not something that is real as such [an analysis] by its very nature.

> **If what has been analyzed**
> **Is analyzed through further analysis,**
> **There is no end to it,**
> **Because that analysis would be analyzed too.** [109]
>
> **Once what had to be analyzed has been analyzed,**
> **The analysis has no basis left.**
> **Since there is no basis, it does not continue.**
> **This is expressed as nirvāṇa.** [110]

The first two lines state the opponents' answer [to the above] and the remaining lines eliminate their qualms.

You might argue, "However, this analysis too must be analyzed by another analysis." In this case, it would definitely follow that **if what has been analyzed is analyzed through further analysis, there is no end to it, because that** [further] **analysis would be analyzed too.** However, it is not like this: Knowledge is the means that analyzes **what had to be analyzed**—the wrong ideas of the opponents—in a way that it [addresses] all [of these wrong ideas], however many they may be. **Once** the wrong ideas of the opponents **have been analyzed** with [this knowledge], they are put to an end. As soon as they have come to an end, the purpose of the analysis is accomplished, and therefore, also the analysis itself will subside on its own. Thus, it is nothing more than an analysis for this specific purpose. However, **the analysis** in itself **has no** particular **basis** or nature. [874] **Since there is no basis** or purpose **left, this** very analysis **does not continue** after wrong ideas have been put to an end, just as a fire goes out on its own as soon as the firewood is burned up. As *The Sūtra of* [*the Prophecy of the Young Lady*] *Excellent Moon*[1717] says:

> "O young lady, who gave you this self-confidence of yours?" "The Elder himself imparted it [to me], because this self-confidence of mine would not have arisen if the Elder had not questioned [me]."

Once clinging in terms of superimposition and denial has come to an end in such a way, just this empty and luminous nature of phenomena in which there is nothing to be removed or added is the fundamental state of phenomena. **This is expressed as** primordial **nirvāṇa** as such. Thus, since no conditioned or unconditioned phenomena whatsoever are observed [at this point], there is no ground for apprehending them as something positive or negative either. This is the perfect application of mindfulness of phenomena. [As *The Sūtra Requested by Crown Jewel*] says:

> Mañjuśrī, if someone does not observe positive or negative phenomena, then this is someone who intensely applies the mindfulness of phenomena that inspects phenomena.

**[Synopsis of Other Commentaries]**

As for [verse 106], Kalyāṇadeva formulates some quite speculative objections:

> If one definitely examines the explanation that—on the seeming level of this—cognitions exist by nature, then they also do not exist, since self-awareness is not established. Therefore, actually, both realities do not exist. Or, if the seeming becomes the seeming through some other causes or due to something later, it is established as something separate. Therefore, sentient beings could not pass into nirvāṇa. Since the seeming is labeled as something other, where would there be a nirvāṇa for sentient beings? In some [other] editions [of Śāntideva's text], [line 106d] reads, "Hence, there is no nirvāṇa." To this [phrase, we say]: However, if it is established that [nirvāṇa] is another seeming, it is taken as another one. Hence, sentient beings would not pass into nirvāṇa.

[He continues with the answer:]

> "Conceptions in the minds of others" [in line 107a refers to] "of others" or "others." This refers to the seeming, which is the conception that a mind exists as the continuum of another one or as a later mode of being. When [the text] says "mind" [here], this is distinguished from the "conceiver"[1718] of the Grammarians. What is labeled "mind" in other theses [875] is not what is to be identified here, because this

discussion essentially concerns itself with practice [and not philosophical theories]. To say "conception" [here] indicates that this mind is mere delusion. Therefore, [line 107b] says, "not in terms of their own . . ." You might wonder, "So who are these others?" This is [indicated] by [line 107b] "they do not exist in terms of their own seeming." That which does not exist as one's own seeming [in the first place] is subsequently ascertained through analysis as nothing but nonexistent. Before this [analysis], there was this aspect of an unquestioned, satisfying presence [of things]. As [*The Sixty Stanzas on Reasoning*] says:

> In the beginning, those who search for true reality
> Should be told that everything exists.
> Later, when they have realized actuality
> And lack attachment, they are free.[1719]

If [things really] existed before they were examined, one would not be able to eliminate them even through later examination.[1720]

Thus, it appears that, explicitly, [Kalyāṇadeva] proves that the seeming is simply nonexistent by its nature. [Actually,] however, he seems to explain the following: The mere, simple presence of the objects of clinging when they are not examined is not contradictory to their nonexistence when they are analyzed.

Vibhūticandra sets up the following objections:

"If all phenomena are unarisen and unceasing, the seeming does not exist. Thus, conventionality is not established. Since ultimate reality is then the one and only reality that is established, the two realities, merit, and such would not exist. If such a seeming that is assigned by the cognitions of the continua of others were to exist, then ultimate reality would not be the only one. However, if this seeming is assigned by the conceptual cognitions of others, where should there be a nirvāṇa for sentient beings? Since emptiness too is taken as an object by conceptions, it would then be the seeming. [Furthermore,] through the realization of the ultimate, all discursiveness is no longer observed. Therefore, which sentient beings would pass into nirvāṇa? And if they were to proceed toward nirvāṇa, it would then be through mental observation. Also, since nirvāṇa is expressed by seeming cognitions, it too would be the seeming."

[Verse 107] "They are . . ." is the answer [to this]. Since nirvāṇa is taken as an object of the cognitions of people who explain [about it] and are different from those who have passed into nirvāṇa, it is [just] these conceptions of theirs. Therefore, it is not reasonable that nirvāṇa is the seeming; it is just nirvāṇa. [876] Why? It does not exist based on one's own seeming, because all one's own conceptions have ceased in it. You might wonder, "How then should it [exist] due to the seeming of others?" This is stated in [lines 107cd] "Later, when this has been verified . . ." The conceptions of others appear to yogins through dependent origination: "If this exists, that originates." Since [yogins] verify the conceptions of others during the aftermath of the actual part of their main meditative concentration, for the yogins, the seeming exists. The vajralike meditative concentration is the Dharma Body of the Buddhas, which is the nonobservation of any phenomenon. From this [manifests] the Body of Complete Enjoyment, the six supernatural knowledges, and omniscience. This is the mirrorlike wisdom, because all entities appear in the mirror of wisdom inasfar as it is suitable for past, future, present, distant, or close phenomena to show [in it].

You might ask, "However, since the past and the future do not exist, how could they appear?" The following is stated: Distance in time is just like distance in space, because the wheel of the six kinds [of beings] has neither beginning nor end. Since the amazing Buddhas are the sources of merit and knowledge, they see what is distant in space and by nature. Likewise, why should they not see what is distant in time, such as the past? Since the same reasoning applies in both [cases], they see the wheel of the six kinds [of beings] that is free from a beginning, an end, and something in between. Thus, it is established that beings have no beginning and that the Teacher is omniscient. This explanation does not deal with the following question: "Since the [beginning and end of] cyclic existence are not known, if it is without beginning and end, how is omniscience established?" Rather, [it says that] the wheel of the six kinds [of beings] has neither beginning nor end and is still directly seen. Therefore, [it is said]:

> For the omniscient ones,
> Beings without exception appear like the present.
> In dependence on the view of ordinary people,
> Threefold distance is explained.[1721]

As for the Body of Complete Enjoyment, due to the influence of those to be trained and [previous] aspiration prayers, it also [entails] the Emanation Body, the wisdom of equality [877], and so forth. There-

> fore, there is no contradiction between the ultimate nonexistence of arising and such and their seeming existence. You might ask, "Granted, yogins know the conceptions of others through their supernatural knowledge that knows the minds of others, but how should they know imputed things?" To this we say: Since these two—conceptual cognitions and the knowable objects that are imputed by these—entail interdependence, [yogins] know the objects of conceptions too. You might argue, "However, what is the basis of analyzing the seeming then? It is not the seeming, since this has been refuted. It is not the ultimate [either], since it is impossible to analyze it." We say: In order to make people understand, here [all worldly analysis] is expressed in dependence on entities and analyses as these are common consensus in the world.[1722]

Thus, he explains the meaning of the two lines [107ab] "They are . . ." as follows: At the time when latent tendencies are vanquished by the vajralike meditative concentration, the seeming does not exist from the point of view of a nature of its own. [Line 107c] "Later, when this has been verified, it exists" means that mirrorlike wisdom knows the seeming. [Then he says above:] "You might ask, '[Yogins] know the conceptions [of others], but how should they know the objects?'" It seems that he explains [verse 108] "Both conceiver and . . ." as the answer [to this question]. However, there appear no supplementary words for [line 107d] "If it has not, the seeming does not exist at all."

*The Small Commentary* says:

> "If you analyze in this way, even the seeming would be nonexistent. So where would this leave the two realities? This is contradictory to what you claimed [before]. However, seeming mistaken consciousness exists from the perspective of others who are mistaken. Hence, if you analyze just this, it does not exist, but this does not mean that it does not exist on the seeming level." This qualm is anticipated by [line 106c] "If it came through another seeming . . ."
>
> The invalidation of this is as follows: [Line 106d] "Where would there be liberated beings?" indicates the [second] thesis of the opponent, which means, "Since even Buddhas may appear as someone with basic unawareness for the thinking of others who are mistaken, on the seeming level, they would circle [in cyclic existence] just like any other sentient being." [Then, line 107a] "They are just conceptions in the minds of others" [878] refers to the fact that Buddhas, ignorance, and so on are merely made up by the conceptions of others. [Line 107b] "But

> they do not exist in terms of their own seeming" means that it does not follow that Buddhas [have] basic unawareness on the seeming level, since this is not what the Buddhas themselves experience. You might ask, "Well, then how do the ignorance and suffering of sentient beings exist on the seeming level?" [The answer lies in line 107c,] "Later, when this has been verified, it exists": The results—ignorance and suffering—exist only if they exist subsequently to some [moments of] mind that preceded them. [Line 107d] "If it has not, the seeming does not exist at all" means: If the cause exists, [resultant ignorance and suffering] exist. However, if one's own continuum does not experience [its own] causes and results independently of the conceptions of others, [these causes and results] are nonexistent even on the seeming level, just like the horns of a rabbit.

This comment on [verse 107] means the following: No matter how something is mentally labeled by others, if it is not experienced by oneself, then it does not exist [for oneself] even on the seeming level. On the other hand, if it is experienced by oneself, it is presented as something that exists on the seeming level.

*The Small Commentary on the Knowledge Chapter Only* comments:

> [Verse 106] "In this case . . ." anticipates the qualms of others who might say, "The seeming is imputed by other seeming [phenomena]: The conception of a mirage as water is an imputation by other seeming cognitions for which [something] appears as water. Likewise, even a Buddha who has passed into nirvāṇa is observed by the consciousnesses of others, such as bodhisattvas. Hence, ultimately, even a Buddha would not have passed into nirvāṇa."
>
> Here, master [Śāntideva] gives [line 107a] "They are . . . ." This thought, "I see the consciousness of a Buddha" is one's very own conception for which something other appears in such and such a way. Merely because something comes to someone else's mind, it does not become existent on the seeming level. You might continue, "Buddhas themselves experience their own consciousnesses, which are their own seeming. Therefore, these exist on the seeming level." [879] That this is not the case [is shown in line 107b] "But they do not exist in terms of their own seeming." If you assert [the existence of] this seeming in Buddhas, then they have seeming consciousnesses. Therefore, they would not have attained precisely this ultimate consciousness [which is the very makeup of Buddhahood].

> You might wonder, "How does the seeming abide then?" [The meaning of lines 107cd] "Later, when . . ." is expressed as follows: "That which is ascertained [to be] subsequent to [its] cause is what undoubtedly originates [from it]. Then, this is its result and the other [phenomenon] is the cause." If there is such a conventional defining characteristic of this mere conditionality, then [one can say that] the seeming exists. However, if there is no such [characteristic], the seeming does not exist. You might still wonder, "If consciousnesses and knowable objects are not exactly such [consciousnesses and knowable objects], then what about the conventional expression, 'This is a conception and that is what is conceived'?" The [answer] is stated in [lines 108ab:] "Both conceiver and . . . ." This conventional expression of "mutual dependence" is something imputed.[1723]

These comments appear to have the following meaning: Since Buddhas have no seeming consciousness, there is no experience of themselves by themselves. If all phenomena are without arising, the seeming does not exist. Hence, where are the two realities? One labels the seeming as existent, if it is ascertained that a subsequent result arises from a cause that preceded it. One also labels, "If there is no arising of this [result], the seeming does not exist." Actually, consciousnesses and knowable objects do not exist. However, in dependence on conceptions and what is conceived, they are expressed in accord with common worldly consensus.

The [master] from Sabsang says:

> You might say, "If all phenomena are without arising, the seeming does not exist. Hence, where are the two realities? If the seeming were an imputation by the mistaken cognitions of others, then sentient beings would by their very nature not pass into nirvāṇa." This seeming is nothing but the conceptions of the minds of others, that is, of those in cyclic existence. Therefore, when analyzed, it does not exist. Nirvāṇa's own nature is not this that appears as the seeming. Rather, [880] it abides as the unchanging ultimate. When there is the certainty and understanding that results are what subsequently originate from causes, then causes and results that are real as mere appearances exist. Hence, the presentation of the two realities is justified. When the above is not the case—that is, once these mere appearances have ceased—the seeming does not exist. However, nirvāṇa—the single reality—is established. Therefore, there is no mistake [in presenting the two realities].

This certainly looks like an expression of being greatly habituated to mental states that cling to the real [existence of] the ultimate. However, his answer to this objection, "It follows that the two realities are not justified, because the seeming does not exist," is to accept its reason on the ultimate level. At the same time, he himself claims this entailment that "it follows that the two realities are justified, because one reality is justified." Thus, it seems to me that he provides a feast of laughter for others.

### 4. The Refutation of Reification

This has two parts:

1) Teaching that there are no means to prove [real] entities
2) Teaching the means to invalidate this [notion of entities]

### 4.1. Teaching That There Are No Means to Prove [Real] Entities

> **Those for whom these two are real**
> **Have a very hard time with it.** [111ab]

These two lines give a brief introduction.

[881] [There are] the systems of the realists **for whom these two**, the analyzer and the object of analysis, **are real** by their very entities. However, **they have a very hard time with** this pair of a real analyzer and a real object of analysis. Hence, nobody can establish them, because the analyzer and the object of analysis mutually depend on each other, and neither exists independently.

> **If objects are established by virtue of consciousness,**
> **What support for the existence of consciousness do you have?** [111cd]
>
> **"Well, consciousness is established by virtue of knowable objects."**
> **So what support is there for the existence of knowable objects?**
> **"They exist by virtue of each other."**
> **Then neither of these two exists.** [112]

These six lines teach that consciousness and knowable objects are not established.

**If** you proponents of [outer] referents say, "Outer **objects**, such as form, **are established by virtue of consciousness,**" please tell us first **what support** or justification **for the existence of consciousness you have.** You might answer, **"Well,** the subject—**consciousness—is established by virtue of** the existence of its objects, that is, **knowable objects." So what** argument **is there** to **support the**

**existence of** its **knowable objects?** You will say, "Since knowable objects are established by virtue of consciousness, and consciousness is established by virtue of knowable objects, **they exist by virtue of** being dependent on **each other.**" Good enough—**then neither of these two exists** independently, because knowable objects do not exist independently of consciousness, and consciousness does not exist independently of knowable objects.

> **If there is no father without a son,**
> **Where would a son come from?**
> **If there is no son, there is no father.**
> **Likewise, these two do not exist.** [113]

This verse explains the example for such [dependent existence].

For example, one speaks about a son in dependence on him having been engendered by a father and about a father in dependence on having engendered a son. Therefore, **without a son** who has been engendered by him, **there is no father.** Likewise, **if** there is no father, **where would his son come from? There is no** way to speak of someone as a **father if there is no son** who has been engendered by him. Hence, **like** [consciousness and knowable objects], **these two**—father and son—**do not exist** when they are [regarded] independently.

> **"A sprout arises from a seed,**
> **And this points to the seed.**
> **So why should the existence of a knowable object not be verified**
> **Through the consciousness that arises from it?"** [114]
>
> **The existence of the seed is verified**
> **Through consciousness, which is something other than the sprout.**
> **What should realize the existence of this consciousness**
> **That verifies a knowable object?** [115]

These two verses teach that this is not comparable to the example of seed and sprout.

They might argue, "**A sprout arises from a seed, and this points to** [the existence of] **the seed. So why should the existence of a knowable object not** also **be verified through the consciousness that arises from** this knowable object?"

This is a nonconcordant example: **The existence of the seed is verified through consciousness, which is something other than** and different from **the sprout.** [882] The consciousness that arises from a knowable object **verifies,**

"There is **a knowable object.**" **What** reason **should** prompt any consciousness other than **this** [first] **consciousness** to **realize** its **existence?** [There is no such other consciousness,] because one cannot observe any consciousness other than this consciousness that has arisen from knowable objects, that is, any other consciousness that realizes [this first one].[1724]

### [Synopsis of Other Commentaries]

Kalyāṇadeva expounds these [verses above] as the detailed explanation of [lines 108ab]:

> Both conceiver and what is conceived
> Are mutually dependent.[1725]

[Furthermore, as for lines 115cd,] the following appears [in his commentary]:

> Why should the existence of consciousness itself be realized, since self-awareness does not exist?[1726]

Some other [commentators still] relate these [verses] to the application of mindfulness of phenomena.

### 4.2. Teaching the Means to Invalidate This [Notion of Entities]

This has two parts:
1) The general topic
2) The meaning of the text

### 4.2.1. The General Topic

In general, in the context of Centrism, [there are] five great reasons that eliminate discursiveness.

1) The reason of dependence, or dependent origination

[This can be formulated] in terms of a negation: "These mere appearances as the subject do not exist by their nature, because they are something dependent, just like an illusion."

[It can] also [be stated as] an affirming argument: "These [appearances] as the subject are also not nonexistent like the horns of a rabbit, because they are something dependent." This latter [formulation] is for the sake of presenting the seeming.

There are two types of dependence:

a) dependence in the sense of dependent arising, such as the arising of light due to the arising of a butter lamp

b) dependence in the sense of dependent imputation, such as short in dependence on long

*The Precious Garland* says:

> Due to the existence of this, that comes to be,
> For example, just as something short when there is something long.
> Due to the arising of this, that arises,
> Just as light due to the appearance of a butter lamp.[1727]

In this text [*The Entrance to the Bodhisattva's Way of Life,* this reasoning] is not deliberately taught, because one understands it implicitly from the teaching that all phenomena are illusionlike.

Apart from this [reasoning, there are] four other negating arguments:

2) The analysis of a nature: the freedom from unity and multiplicity

"A sprout as the subject is not actually [883] established, because it is not established either as a unity or as a multiplicity." In the present [text], [this reasoning] is included in [the section on] the application of mindfulness and others.

3) The analysis of the way of arising—the refutation of arising from the four possibilities[1728]—will be implicitly understood from the refutation of arising.[1729]

Therefore, the [remaining] two [reasonings]—the analysis of the cause (the vajra sliver [argument]) and the analysis of the result (the argument that refutes an arising of existents and nonexistents) —will be explicitly explained here.

4) The vajra sliver argument[1730]

Just like a vajra, [this argument] is unobstructed with respect to anything whatsoever. Therefore, it is called "vajra slivers." It is to be explained as it is found in *The Fundamental Verses on Centrism*:

> Not from themselves, not from something other,
> Not from both, and not without a cause—
> At any place and any time,
> All entities lack arising.[1731]

Thus, the positions of the Hedonists[1732] who assert that there is no cause, the Enumerators who assert that [entities] arise from themselves, and the Nudes[1733] who assert that [entities] arise from both are refuted by all texts of Centrism and valid cognition. The assertion that [entities] arise from something other, which is the position of our [other] three [Buddhist] factions—the Mere Mentalists and the [two schools] below them—is eliminated through Centrist texts [alone].

The oral pith instructions on Centrism by my mentor, the Omniscient Victor,[1734] say:

> "A sprout as the subject is without arising, because it is free from arising from any of the four extremes, just as a frog's long hair."

> Here, master Bhavya states [this as] the main argument and then formulates four autonomous reasons as the means to prove the subject property. The venerable and fearless Candrakīrti presents this by labeling the mere refutation of arising from the four extremes a "position." He teaches the invalidation of the opposite [positions] of this [refutation] through consequences that reveal contradictions and through the analogous applicability of the [opponents'] reason [to something that contradicts their position]. However, he does not formulate a main argument, nor does he assert arguments that establish the subject property through valid cognition. It is merely on the grounds of this [difference] that one refers to Autonomists and Consequentialists. However, it is not that [884] there were any differences in terms of better or worse in the views of these two. The reasons for this are: Both accept the freedom from discursiveness in which all complexes of discursiveness have been ended without exception. Not even the Omniscient Ones would see a difference in terms of better or worse between the ways in which these two put an end to discursiveness.

> One might wonder, "How can this be? There is a slight remainder of discursiveness left in the view of the Autonomists." This is not the case, because the texts of Autonomists are much clearer in their way of teaching freedom from discursiveness than the texts of venerable Candrakīrti. *The Ornament of Centrism* says:

> Because ["nonarising"] concords with the ultimate,
> This is called "the ultimate."
> In actuality, it is the release
> From all complexes of discursiveness.

Since arising and so forth do not exist,
Nonarising and so on are impossible.
Since their nature has been negated,
Their verbal terms are impossible.

There is no good formulation
To negate nonexistent objects.
[Nonarising and such] depend on conceptions
And thus are seeming, not actual.[1735]

*[The Distinction between] the Two Realities* agrees:

Since the negation of arising and so on
Concords with actuality, we accept it.
Since there is nothing to be negated,
It is clear that, actually, there is no negation.

How should the negation of an imputation's
Own nature not be an imputation?
Hence, seemingly, this is
The meaning of actuality, but not actuality [itself].

In actuality, both do not exist.
This is the lack of discursiveness:
Mañjuśrī asked about actuality
And the son of the Victors remained silent.[1736]

This is extensively taught in other [texts] too. The school of Yoga Practice explains this as the wisdom that is empty of the duality of apprehender and apprehended and free from discursiveness. From the perspective of this wisdom itself, it is definitely free from discursiveness, but, in general, a [certain] remainder of discursiveness is left. Therefore, this is not all-encompassing freedom from discursiveness.

Thus, the differences between Autonomists and Consequentialists [in terms of ground, path, and fruition] are as follows: In the context of the ground, there is the difference that [Autonomists] present the seeming in accordance with proponents of philosophical systems [such as the Sūtra Followers or the Yogācāras] and that [Consequentialists] present it in accordance with common worldly consensus.[1737] When presenting the ultimate, [Autonomists] accept objects (that is, seeming

> [phenomena]) that bear the nature of phenomena, while [Consequentialists] do not accept this. [885] [Another difference is] that [Autonomists] accept valid cognition that is undeceiving with respect to objects (that is, conventional reality), and [Consequentialists] do not accept it.
>
> In the context of the path, [Autonomists] settle in meditative equipoise within spacelike emptiness of appearance, and [Consequentialists] settle in meditative equipoise within illusionlike emptiness of reality.
>
> In the context of the result, they differ in that [Autonomists state that] the aspects of the seeming emerge within the self-appearances of the wisdom that knows the extent, while such is not the case [for Consequentialists]. They also have a different [opinion] as to whether discursiveness is ended gradually or all at once.
>
> For those with sharp faculties who take the instantaneous approach, the Consequentialist [approach] is better, and for those with weaker faculties who take the gradual approach, the Autonomist [approach] is better. Some [aspects] of the seeming [reality] of yogins have to be accepted by both Autonomists and Consequentialists after analysis through reasoning, such as the four seals of the view that are a sign of the Buddha's speech and the aspect of emptiness of reality free from discursiveness. It is not that these [aspects] are presented as the seeming from the point of view of having been analyzed [and found] through reasoning. Rather, they are presented as the seeming from the point of view of [still] apprehending characteristics in what is analyzed.

[Now follows the actual explanation of the vajra sliver reasoning:

a) The refutation of the first extreme: arising from itself]

There is no arising [of an entity] from itself for the following reasons: If it is not yet present, it does not exist, which makes it unsuitable as a cause. If it is already present, it would be pointless that something that is already present arises again. Moreover, it would follow then that it arises forever without reaching an end. In his *Lucid Words*, [Candrakīrti] quotes Buddhapālita's commentary [on Nāgārjuna's *Fundamental Verses*]:

> There is no arising of entities from themselves, because their arising would be pointless and because it would be completely absurd. There

> is no need for entities that [already] exist as their own identity to arise again. Why is that? If they were to arise although they [already] exist, there would be no time when they do not arise.[1738]

[In his *Lamp of Knowledge*], master Bhāvaviveka formulates this as an autonomous reason:

> It is certain that, ultimately, there is no arising of the inner sources from themselves, because they [already] exist, for example, like an existent consciousness.[1739]

Master Candrakīrti objects to this:

> Why do you introduce this distinction "ultimately" here? [886] You might answer, "My reasons are: To accept arising on the seeming worldly level is not what is to be negated. Moreover, even if [this arising] were negated, it follows that [such a negation] would [still] be invalidated through what [the world] accepts." This is not reasonable, because an arising from itself is not accepted even on the seeming level. . . . You might argue, "This distinction is made in dependence on the systems of others." This is also not reasonable, because their presentations are not accepted even on the seeming level. Even worldly people do not think that [entities] arise from themselves. Worldly people [simply] do not engage in such analyses as whether [things arise] from themselves or others. All they think is that "results originate from causes." Also master [Nāgārjuna] presented this in such a way. Therefore, it is certain that "this distinction is meaningless in all aspects."
>
> Furthermore, if you wanted to refute arising on the seeming level and thus set up this distinction, then the flaw of a subject that is an unestablished base or the mistake of an argument that is an unestablished base falls upon yourself, because, ultimately, you yourself do not claim the sources, such as the eyes. . . . You might say, "Because we refute that the seeming, such as the eyes, arises ultimately, to say 'ultimately' indicates a special case of refuting arising." Well, if this were your concern, you should say, "Seeming [entities], such as the eyes, are ultimately without arising . . ." [However,] you did not teach such a phrase.[1740]

If one were to insert "ultimately" in order to refute an arising on the seeming level that is claimed by worldly people or the Enumerators, [this is pointless, since] they do not present the two realities but merely assert that "[entities] simply arise." This was all that the venerable master Nāgārjuna has refuted. Thus, this is not a refutation by differentiating the two realities. Since worldly people do not claim that [entities] arise from themselves, [887] there is no purpose in inserting "ultimately." [Furthermore,] if this were done in order to refute arising on the seeming level, since master Bhāvaviveka himself does not assert that, ultimately, the sources, such as the eyes, exist, then to set up "exist" as the reason [in his autonomous reasoning above] would be a nonapplying argument. If [this insertion of "ultimately"] were made for the sake of understanding that the eyes and so on are the seeming, there is the mistake of not arriving at this meaning, since [in order to do so] one would have to say, "Seeming [entities], such as the eyes, are ultimately without arising . . ."

By refuting [Bhāvaviveka in this way, Candrakīrti] asserts that there is never any arising from the four extremes, whether it is in worldly and non-Buddhist contexts of no analysis in terms of the two realities or whether it is in the Buddhist context of presenting the two realities. However, then [there are] those later Tibetans who presume to be Consequentialist Centrists and who are in the tight grip of dense referential views. They proclaim, "When one sets up Centrist reasons, there is the flaw of denying the seeming, if one does not insert 'ultimately,' 'actually,' or 'when analyzed.'" [There are] also those who talk about the three phases of no analysis, slight analysis, and intense analysis [in this context]. From what Candrakīrti [said above], it is very clear that [such people] are not followers of this master.

Thus, also the following explanation is nothing but [an attempt to] make some pale yellow metal look like the finest gold from the river Jambu: "Without analysis, I accept [entities] in accordance with common worldly consensus. Under slight analysis, I accept such [positions] as the following: Cyclic existence does not exist and, when distinguishing the pure essence[1741] [of wisdom mind] from the dross[1742] [of ordinary consciousness], the dross is necessarily that which does not exist.[1743] At the point of intense analysis, if you ask me what the ultimate is, I do not say anything at all."

[Actually,] in the Centrist system itself, the phase of no analysis through reasoning refers to the cycle [of teachings] that first puts an end to what is not meritorious, which is the vehicle that [leads to] the higher realms. The intermediate phase of putting an end to identity means to counteract [all types of] clinging of Buddhist and non-Buddhist philosophical systems with Centrist reasonings. The phase of putting an end to all bases for views refers to the final complete elimination of [any] clinging to true reality. Hence, there is no need for anybody to reduce these [phases] or add anything to them. [888] Once one relates all these three [phases of no analysis, slight analysis, and intense analysis] solely to the intermediate phase of putting an end to identity, one develops clinging to the nonexistence of the dross and clinging to the existence of the pure essence. [Moreover,] one considers merely not giving an answer as the ultimate actuality. For those who understand the meaning of Centrism, this [mistaken presentation] certainly provides a good chance for a laugh. However, for some ignorant people who wish for liberation, it still serves as an issue that makes them tremble with awe.

Therefore, it is explained that when Mañjuśrī asked Vimalakīrti about the perfect actuality, the genuine answer [in this case] was to not give an answer. However, when one naïve being does not give an answer to the question of another one, how could these two cases ever be comparable? Please understand the difference between a bodhisattva in his last existence who dwells under the bodhi tree and Devadatta who is sitting under a nimba tree. If you think, "These are comparable," then just ask an ox about the ultimate and you will get the final answer that you wish for [from this ox].

b) The refutation of the second extreme [that is, arising from something other]:

[Candrakīrti's *Lucid Words* quotes Buddhapālita on this]:

> Master Buddhapālita says:
>
> > Things are without arising from something other, because [otherwise] it would follow that everything arises from everything.[1744]

Venerable Candrakīrti himself says:

> Things also do not arise from something other, because there is nothing other.[1745]

In *The Entrance [into Centrism]*, he states:

> If something were to originate in dependence on something other than it,
> Well, then utter darkness would spring from flames
> And everything would arise from everything. Why?
> [Also] everything that does not produce [this] is the same in being other.[1746]

Furthermore, if [entities] were to arise from causes and conditions, [as *The Fundamental Verses* says, there] are only four conditions:

> Conditions are fourfold: Causal,
> Observed, immediate,

And dominant.
There is no fifth condition.[1747]

For example, the nature of a rice sprout does not exist in any of [its conditions:] neither in its causal condition (water and manure), nor in its observed condition (the harvest), not in its immediate condition [889] (the last moment of the seed), and also not in its dominant condition (the person who plants [the seed]):

The nature of entities
Does not exist in conditions and such.[1748]

When one analyzes this with [the reasoning of] the freedom from unity and multiplicity, then if an [entity] in itself is not established, where should there be something other that depends [for its otherness] on this [first entity]?

If an entity in itself does not exist,
An entity other [than it] does not exist either.[1749]

If conditions (such as water and manure) have functions (such as producing a sprout), they would have to produce sprouts all the time. If they do not have any functions, there would never be any function. However, if they do not have any functions, why are they presented as conditions?

Function is not something that entails conditions.
[Conventionally, however,] there is no function that does not entail conditions.
What does not entail a function is not a condition.[1750]

You might say, "However, since [the sprout] arises in dependence on these, they are its conditions." As long as it does not arise, they are not its conditions, and once it has arisen, its conditions are not needed [anymore]. Hence, when would they be its conditions?

This is consensus: "Since it arises in dependence on these,
Therefore, they are its conditions."
As long as it does not arise,
How could these not be things that are not its conditions?

For [both] nonexistents and existents,
Conditions are not suitable:
If something does not exist, whose conditions would they be?

If something exists [already], what are conditions good for?[1751]

Hence, once one examines any existing or nonexisting phenomenon, it disintegrates and is thus not established. In this situation, how could [its] causes be established?

Once phenomena are not established
As existent, nonexistent, or [both] existent and nonexistent,
How could you speak of "causes that accomplish [them]"?
Once such is the case, this is not reasonable.[1752]

Likewise, the observed condition is not established either:

An existent phenomenon [that is a consciousness] reveals
Nothing but the nonexistence of [its] observed object.
If a phenomenon [itself] is not observable,
Where would [its] observed object exist?[1753]

It is surely a consensus that the previous moment that has just ceased is the immediate condition. However, since there is nothing that arises, something that has ceased is not justified. Moreover, since something that has ceased is not existent [anymore], it is also not suitable as a condition. Hence, the immediate condition is also not established:

If phenomena have not arisen,
Cessation [890] would not be justified.
Therefore, the immediate [condition] is not reasonable.
If it has ceased, what would be such a condition?[1754]

You might argue, "The Blessed One stated, 'Since this exists, that originates. Since this has arisen, that arises. Due to the condition of basic unawareness, [there] is formation.' Is this not [what he said]?" *The Lucid Words* states:

These teachings of arising in the sense of dependent origination and so on are not [meant] in terms of the nature of the object of uncontaminated wisdom of those who are free from the blurred vision of basic unawareness. "Well, [in terms of] what are they [meant] then?" They are [meant] in terms of the object of consciousness of those whose eyes of intelligent insight are impaired by the blurred vision of basic unawareness. It is in terms of seeing precisely this that the Blessed One has made statements such as:

> Oh fully ordained monks, this ultimate reality is single. It is as follows: Nirvāṇa has the property of being undeceiving, whereas all formations have the property of being delusive and deceiving.[1755]

[The text then] continues with many further quotations to prove this.

Hence, a result does not dwell in any of its diverse conditions. Thus, if it is a nonexistent [at the time of its conditions], how could this nonexistent arise [as an existent later]? If it were to arise despite its nonexistence, it would arise even from [entities] that are not its causes. [*The Fundamental Verses on Centrism* says:]

> If, for whatever reason, there is no existence
> Of things that do not exist by their nature,
> It is not justified to say,
> "Since this exists, that originates."
>
> The result does not exist at all
> In any of its diverse conditions or their assembly.
> What does not exist in its conditions,
> How should that arise from such conditions?
>
> However, if it does not exist
> And were still to arise from these conditions,
> Why would it not also arise
> From [entities] that are not its conditions?[1756]

You might say, "Because the result depends on its conditions, the result is something that has the nature of its conditions." If even these very conditions do not exist as [something that bears] its own nature, how should they exist as the nature of the result? [On the other hand,] there is also no result that does not depend on conditions. Therefore, causes and conditions are nothing but superimpositions.

> You might say, "The result is of the nature of its conditions."
> [However,] conditions do not have a nature of their own. [891]
> What is the result of something that is not an entity in itself?
> How could it be of the nature of [such] conditions?
>
> Therefore, it is not of the nature of [its] conditions.
> [However,] there is [also] no result with the nature of what are not its conditions.

> Since results do not exist,
> How should nonconditions be conditions?[1757]

c–d) The [refutation of] the remaining two extremes: [arising from both or arising without a cause]

*The Lucid Words* explains:

> Things also do not arise from both [themselves and others], because this would entail [all] the flaws that were stated for both of these theses and because each one of these [extremes] does not have the capacity to produce [entities].
>
> > If suffering were produced by each one of them,
> > It would be produced by both.[1758]

This will be explained [below].

[Entities] also do not arise without a cause. This would entail the following and other mistakes that will be explained below:

> If there were no causes, results
> And causes would not be justified either.[1759]

Other flaws would follow as well:

> If these beings were empty of causes, they could not be apprehended,
> Just like the smell and the color of an utpala flower in the sky.[1760]

5) The analysis of the result: the argument that refutes arising of existents and nonexistents[1761]

[The basic reasoning] is formulated as follows: These mere appearances as the subject do not exist by their nature, because neither existents nor nonexistents arise, just like an illusion.

a) Those who assert the arising of a result that [already] exists in the cause now are the Enumerators.
b) The people who assert the arising of [a result] that [already] exists in the future belong to the Great Exposition School in our own [Buddhist] faction.[1762]
c) Those who assert the new arising of [a result] that did not exist before are some other followers of our own faction.

a) If the sprout existed in the seed right now, it would follow that it is pointless for it to arise again. [The Enumerators] would say, "Its nature is established [already now]. However, it exists in such a way that it arises as something clearly manifest [later]." From the point of view of its nature, it would then be pointless for it to arise again, and from the point of view of its clear manifestation, it would be a nonexistent that arises.

b) Also something that [already] exists in the future does not arise for the following reason: If an entity that has not [yet] arisen [here] existed in some unknown [other] place right now, it would be reasonable that it might arise [here] in the future. However, since there is no such [entity], what is it that could arise? [*The Fundamental Verses on Centrism* says:]

> If some nonarisen entity
> Existed somewhere,
> It might arise.
> However, if it does not exist, what would arise?[1763]

c) If something that has not existed before were to arise, [892] it would follow that even the horns of a rabbit could arise. [Moreover,] it would follow that just about anything could arise. The reason for these [consequences] is that [a nonexistent] does not depend on any cause [at all].

> If something nonarisen could arise,
> Just about anything could arise in this way.[1764]

Thus, when we analyze with these [five] great reasonings, all our clinging to causes, the lack of causes, arising, ceasing and so on—that is, all conceptions of superimposition and denial—subside, which is [precisely] the purpose of this [approach]. *The Entrance [into Centrism]* says:

> Ordinary beings are bound by conceptions.
> Nonconceptual yogins will find release.
> Hence, the learned state that the result of analysis
> Is that conceptions are at peace.[1765]

### 4.2.2. The Meaning of the Text

This has two parts:

1) The analysis of the cause: the vajra slivers

2) The analysis of the result: the refutation of an arising of existents and nonexistents

### 4.2.2.1. The Analysis of the Cause: The Vajra Slivers

This has five parts:

1) The refutation of arising without a cause
2) The four refutations of arising from something other
3) The three refutations of arising from itself
4) Teaching that the cognition that negates the existence of objects is a valid cognition
5) Stating the meaning that is ascertained through valid cognition

### 4.2.2.1.1. The Refutation of Arising without a Cause

> **Temporarily, worldly perception**
> **Sees all kinds of causes.** [116ab]

These two lines teach that causes are directly seen by the world.

Some Mundanely Minded assert that there are no causes at all. They say, "The cause of things is their very nature, because they originate through their own nature. [As our scriptures say]:

> The roundness of peas, the long sharp tips of thorns,
> The colorful patterns of the feathers of a peacock's wings,
> The rising of the sun, and the downhill flow of rivers—
> All these were created by nobody. Their cause is their very nature.

To this we say: **Temporarily,** it is neither the case that there are no causes [893] nor that [entities] are [just as they are] by their very nature, because **perception sees all kinds of causes** in the **world**, such as a seed being the cause of a sprout.

> **The distinct parts of a lotus, such as its stalk,**
> **Are produced by distinct causes.** [116cd]

These two lines teach that there are various causes for [a flower's] stalk, its petals, and so on.

There are different causes for each individual color on the multicolored feathers of a peacock's wings. Likewise, **the distinct parts of a lotus, such as its stalk,** its leaves, its anthers, its pistils, and its various colors, **are produced by distinct** individual **causes.** In a single seed, these causal aspects are present in an inseparable way. They are the objects of the vision of those who are not obscured with respect to the whole range of what bears the nature of phenomena, but naïve beings do not understand this.

> **You might ask, "What created the variety of causes?"**
> **It comes from the variety of preceding causes.**
> **"Why are causes able to produce results?"**
> **This is due to the force of the preceding causes.** [117]

This verse teaches that these [causes] arise from previous causes.

**You might ask, "What created this variety of causes?** If there is no creator, they are established as nonexistent." Later [causes] become gradually established **from the variety of causes** in their respective **preceding** moments. You might continue, **"Why are causes able to produce results?" This is due to the force of the preceding** beginningless **causes**, through dependent origination in which one [cause] sequentially leads to another one. Furthermore, it is an immediate contradiction to assert that there is no cause and at the same time to formulate an argument for this. The reason is that an argument is the cause that makes one understand [something], and if this [cause] exists, then also the existence of other causes is etablished.

### 4.2.2.1.2. The Refutation of Arising from Some Other Cause

This has four parts:

1) Teaching that Īśvara[1766] is not established
2) Teaching that his results are impossible
3) Teaching that it is contradictory for him to be a creator
4) The refutation of infinitesimal particles

### 4.2.2.1.2.1. Teaching That Īśvara Is Not Established

> **If Īśvara is the cause of the world,**
> **Just tell us who Īśvara is.**
> **If you say, "He is the elements," that is surely fine,**
> **But then why all this fuss over a mere name?** [118]
>
> **Moreover, the earth and such are multiple,**
> **Impermanent, inactive, not divine,**

> **Something trampled upon, and impure.**
> **Therefore, they are not Īśvara.** [119]

[894] These two verses teach that the four elements are not Īśvara.

You Differentiators and others say, "There is the god called Īśvara who is pure, vast, worthy of veneration, permanent, single, and an omnipresent creator. He is the one who has absolute power over everything. [As the scriptures say]:

> He who is subtle, singular, the source . . .

and

> It is said that Īśvara functions as the cause
> For everything else that entails conditions.
> What has no mind is not capable
> Of assembling its results by itself."

Here we ask: [895]

> **If Īśvara is the cause of the world,**
> **Just tell us who Īśvara is.**

**If you say,** "We assert that **the** great **elements** are Īśvara," **that is surely fine, but** we too assert that the elements are causes, so **why** should we create **all this fuss** by debating **over mere** different **names**, such as "elements" or "Īśvara"? We will not debate [about mere terminology].

**Moreover,** [what you say] contradicts your own system for the following reasons: The elements—**earth and such—are multiple,** while you assert that Īśvara is singular. Earth and such are **impermanent,** but you assert that Īśvara is permanent. Earth and so on are [mentally] **inactive** and thus have no mind, while your position is that Īśvara has an [active] mind.[1767] Earth and so forth are **not divine and something** that your feet **trample upon**. However, you claim that Īśvara is divine and worthy of veneration. Earth and such are necessarily **impure**, but you assert that Īśvara is pure. **Therefore,** in your own system, the elements **are not Īśvara.**

> **Īśvara is not space, because it is inactive.**
> **He is not the self, because this has already been refuted earlier.**
> **If he is inconceivable, his state as a creator is inconceivable too,**
> **So what can you say about it?** [120]

This verse teaches that space or something inconceivable is not Īśvara [either].

You might continue, "Īśvara is space." **Īśvara is not space, because** Īśvara is active, while space **is inactive.** Then you might try, "The self is Īśvara." A **self,** which is never possible, **is not** Īśvara, **because this** self **has already been refuted earlier.** Your last shot might be, "Īśvara is inconceivable." **If** the **state** of Īśvara **as an inconceivable creator is inconceivable,** you are not able to **say** something **about it. So what is the point of** calling him Īśvara?

### 4.2.2.1.2.2. Teaching That His Results Are Impossible

> **And what could he want to create?** [121a]

This line teaches that there is nothing that could be created by him.

Thus, since Īśvara is not established, **what could** be the phenomena other [than him] that **he wants to create?**

> **If it were a self, isn't that eternal?**
> **[Likewise,] the nature of earth and such, Īśvara,** [121bc]

These two lines refute the assertion that the self is Īśvara.

You might say, "Since everything is emanated by the self, the **self** is Īśvara." **If** you assert that Īśvara is this singular and eternal [self], it follows either that he creates all things, **such as earth,** simultaneously and all the time, or it follows that he never creates them. **Isn't it** that you assert **Īśvara**'s **nature** as **eternal?**[1768]

> **And consciousness arising from knowable objects are all without beginning.** [121d]

> **Suffering and happiness come from actions.**
> **So please tell us what he has created.** [122ab]

These three lines teach that [results] are produced by actions.

Hence, **consciousness** and **knowable objects arise from** being dependent on each other. **Beginningless** [896] **suffering and happiness** arise **from** one's own **actions. So please tell us what** this Īśvara who is nothing but a mere name **has created.**

#### 4.2.2.1.2.3. Teaching That It Is Contradictory for Him to Be a Creator

> **If the cause does not have a beginning,**
> **Where should there be a beginning of its result? [122cd]**
>
> **Why does he not create all the time,**
> **Since he does not depend on anything other?**
> **There is nothing that was not created by him,**
> **So on what should this [creation] of his depend? [123]**
>
> **If it were dependent [on other factors], their coming together**
> **Would be the cause, but again Īśvara would not.**
> **Once these have come together, he could not but create,**
> **And without them, he could not but not create. [124]**

These lines teach that collections [of various causes and conditions] are the [actual] cause [of the world].

Furthermore, **if the cause**—Īśvara—**does not have** a point where it **begins, where should there be a beginning of** the **result** that originates from it? If you assert such a [permanent cause], it follows that newly originated results are impossible.[1769]

If Īśvara is the creator of everything, **why does he not create all the time**, also doing such things as fetching water and making fire? If he did so, of course, [everything] would be created by Īśvara, but what would be the point in others, [such as] servants, taking care [of these things too]? Some [permanent] creating [that is performed] by Īśvara alone would surely **not depend on any other** causes. However, the [whole] world can directly see that these phenomena do depend on other causes: If you want fire, you need firewood, but what help is Īśvara in this? **There is nothing that was not created by** Īśvara, **so on what** other causes and conditions **should this** [creation] **of his**, such as clay pots and butter lamps, **depend?** Thus, it is not reasonable that [such an exclusive creating activity] could depend [on anything].

On the other hand, however, we can see that a clay pot is not created by Īśvara but by a potter, and that a [burning] butter lamp does not arise from Īśvara but originates from fat, a wick, a small bowl, and fire. Therefore, **if it** [his creation] **were dependent on** such causes and conditions, **their coming together would be the cause, but again Īśvara would not. Once** causes and conditions **have come together,** Īśvara **could not but create,** even if **he** wished not to create. **And without them** coming together, **he could not but not create**, even if he wished to create.

**If Īśvara were to create without desiring to,**
**It would follow that he is under the sway of something else.**
**If he creates because he so desires, he would depend on his desire.**
**So what has become of your Īśvara then? [125]**

This verse teaches that Īśvara does not have absolute power.

Again, we ask: How is it, does Īśvara create without desiring to, or does he create out of desiring to? **If Īśvara were to create without** himself **desiring to, it would follow that he is** someone **under the sway of something else**, because, just like a servant, he would have to create despite not wishing to. **If** you say, **"He creates because he so desires," he would** be someone who is under the sway of his own desire, because he **depends on his desire** and follows it. **So** in both cases, **what has become of your** absolutely powerful **Īśvara then**, since [your idea] that he has absolute power is ruined?[1770]

### 4.2.2.1.2.4. The Refutation of Infinitesimal Particles

**Those who propound permanent infinitesimal particles**
**Have already been disproved earlier. [126ab]**

Thus, the Differentiators [897] and others [who claim the existence of Īśvara] have been refuted. Now, there is also no justification [for the claim of] **those** other people, such as the Analyzers, **who propound** that the entire animate and inanimate world arises from **permanent**ly existing **infinitesimal particles** that have no parts. Infinitesimal partless particles are not established, because [Vasubandhu's] *Twenty Verses* says that partlessness is not established:

If six [particles] join it simultaneously,
This infinitesimal particle would have six parts.
If all six together are partless,
Then also their aggregation would be just an infinitesimal particle.[1771]

[Furthermore,] infinitesimal particles are not established for the following reason: If you take some [particles] that are golden, then a mountain that consists of them must also be golden. Likewise, if they are permanent, it would follow that the things that consist of them—such as Mount Meru or houses—are permanent too. Hence, also those systems **have already been disproved earlier** by such [lines as 86cd]:

Since these directional divisions lack any parts,
They are like space. Therefore, not even particles exist.

## [Synopsis of Other Commentaries]

Here, Kalyāṇadeva explains:

> [Earth and such are not Īśvara] for the following reason: You assert that he is single, permanent, endowed with excellent intelligence, and divine. Therefore, even such things as a liṅgam are pure and not to be stepped upon. You might assert that Īśvara is space. However, this is also not Īśvara, since it is free from activity and deliberate engagement. Also a self that has the character of venerating sun or moon and such is not Īśvara, because it has been refuted by [verses 57–59]:
>
> > I am not teeth, hair, or nails . . .
>
> You might end up saying, "Īśvara is inconceivable." Since his creating activity also is inconceivable, what can you say? How could something inconceivable be an object of expression? And even if we assume this, what things could he wish to bring forth or produce? If he wishes to bring forth a so-called self, this [self] is not like [inconceivable] Īśvara, since you say that it is permanent and stable.[1772]

Vibhūticandra states the thesis of the opponents [about Īśvara] as follows:

> The Logicians and others say, "There is this Blessed One, who is skilled in creating various beings. His power never declines. He is the beginning, eternal, omniscient, [898] and almighty. He is the cause of the world and creates bodies, realms, mountains, oceans, and such. He is the cause of abiding and ceasing, the Great Almighty."[1773]

### 4.2.2.1.3. The Refutation of Arising from Itself

This has three parts:

1) The refutation of the primal substance of the Enumerators
2) Dispelling the assertion that pleasure and such are permanent
3) The refutation of the assertion that the result abides in the cause

### 4.2.2.1.3.1. The Refutation of the Primal Substance of the Enumerators

> **The Enumerators assert that the primal substance**

**Is the permanent cause of the world. [126cd]**

**The equilibrium of the constituents**
**"Lightness," "motility," and "darkness"**
**Is called "primal substance."**
**Universal flux is explained through their disequilibrium. [127]**

These one and a half verses state the thesis of the opponent.

[899] **The** non-Buddhist **Enumerators assert that the primal substance is the permanent cause of the** animate and inanimate **world. The equilibrium of the** three **constituents "lightness," "motility," and "darkness" is called "primal substance."** They assert that it has five attributes: It is permanent, material, not appearing, and single, and it is the nature [of everything] but not [any of that nature's] manifestations. They further claim that it is only a cause but not a result. The so-called **universal flux is explained through** the three constituents being in the phase of **their disequilibrium.** The [other] twenty-four [factors of their system are the following]:[1774]

2) the self [or individual], which has five attributes: it is aware, permanent, single, and contained in the continuum of individuals, and it is the experiencer but not an agent or a creator

The [remaining] twenty-three [factors of universal flux] gradually originate from the primal substance:

3) the "great one" or "cognition," which is like a crystal mirror with two sides[1775]

4) from this comes "identification," which evolves into—the eleven faculties:

5–9) the five [sense faculties], such as the eye sense faculty and the ear sense faculty

10–14) the five operative faculties, such as speech

15) the faculty that is both operative and mental, that is, mental cognition [900], and

—the five essential elements:

16–20) the essential elements, such as sound, which in turn evolve into

21–25) the five [coarser] elements, such as space

[The Enumerators] assert that, from among these, the eleven faculties and the five elements are only causes. They say, "Since the manifestations of both the self and [outer] objects appear simultaneously within [the two-sided mirror of] cognition, the individual experiences objects. When the individual realizes that these are created by the primal substance, the primal substance becomes ashamed and does not create these manifestations [anymore]. Thus, the self becomes separated from the primal substance and is released." The objections to this are as follows:

> **Since three natures in a single entity**
> **Are not possible, it does not exist.**
> **Likewise, the constituents do not exist,**
> **Because each of them has three aspects too.** [128]

This verse refutes the constituents.

That **three natures** exist **in a single** primal substance is **not possible,** because it then follows that the primal substance is not single but triple. You might argue, "It exists as a triad, but this is not contradictory to being one." However, then it follows that it is also not contradictory for a vase and a cloth to exist as two but still to be one. **Since** [this is impossible,] a primal substance that is their equilibrium **does not exist. Likewise, the** three **constituents** themselves—motility, darkness, and lightness—**do not exist,** because if they existed, they should be suitable to appear, but they cannot be observed anywhere. [Furthermore,] there follows an infinite regress, **because** you yourselves assert that **each of them too has three aspects**, such as the motility of motility and so forth.

> **If these constituents do not exist,**
> **The existence of sound and such becomes extremely far-fetched.** [129ab]

These two lines refute sound and such that are produced by the [constituents].

**If** thus **these** very **constituents do not exist, the existence of** the essential elements, **such** as **sound**, and the [coarser] elements—which are [all] produced by the primal substance that entails these [three constituents]—**becomes extremely far-fetched.** This is just like the case of the son of a barren woman: If he does not exist, then his youth or old age do not exist either.

> **Moreover, pleasure and such are impossible**
> **In something without mind, such as cloth.** [129cd]

**You might think, "Entities have the nature of their causes."**
**However, did we not analyze entities already?**
**Anyway, your cause is pleasure and such,**
**But cloth and the like do not come from this.** [130]

**If it were that pleasure and such come from cloth and so forth,**
**Once these do not exist, pleasure and the like do not exist either.**
[131ab]

These eight lines fling the extremely absurd consequence [at the opponent] that earth and so on have pleasure and such.

**Moreover,** it is not reasonable that all twenty-three factors of universal flux possess the three constituents, **such** as **pleasure**, because an experience of these feelings—pleasure (lightness), suffering (motility), and dullness (darkness)—**is impossible in something without mind, such as** earth.[1776] ([Here,] the word "moreover" implies the following: "It is not only the case that the three constituents themselves do not exist, [but it is moreover impossible that there is pleasure and such in something without mind.]")

**You might think, "Entities have the nature of their causes,** which are [the three constituents,] pleasure and so on. Hence, pleasure and such [can in turn] arise from earth and the like." **However, did we not** refute these very entities **already** before by analyzing them from their infinitesimal particles all the way up to collections? We surely did. [901] **Anyway,** you Enumerators with **your** system may well assert that the **cause is pleasure and such,** but [the truth is that] **cloth and so on do not come from this** [kind of cause], because nobody has [ever] seen that cloth arises from pleasure.

**If** your philosophical system **were** to say **that pleasure and such** arise **from cloth and so forth,** [conventionally speaking,] this would be appropriate. The reason for this is that **once these** garments made of cloth and such **do not exist,** the **pleasure** of warmth **and the like** [that would come from them] **do not exist either.**[1777] [However,] in this case, none of these [things], such as cloth and pleasure, would ever be established, because the cause for such things as pleasure is cloth and so forth, and the cause for such things as cloth is pleasure and so on.[1778]

**4.2.2.1.3.2. Dispelling the Assertion That Pleasure and Such Are Permanent**

**Also, pleasure and so forth are never seen**
**To have any permanence.** [131cd]

**If there is clearly manifest pleasure and such,**
**Why would such an experience not be perceived?** [132ab]

These four lines teach that pleasure and such do not permanently exist, because they are not experienced [all the time].

Furthermore, the primal substance and its constituents cannot be permanent, because their results—**pleasure and so forth—are** also **never seen to have any permanence.** You might say, "Pleasure and such do exist permanently. All we are saying is that they are just not [permanently] experienced."[1779] **If there is** some **clearly manifest** particular or distinct **pleasure and such, why would such an experience not be perceived?** [It must be perceived] for the following reason: If consciousness is that which experiences and yet does not experience [such pleasure], this would contradict [its role] as that which experiences.

**"That same [experience] becomes subtle."**
**How could the same be gross and subtle?** [132cd]

These two lines teach that it is not reasonable [to distinguish between] gross and subtle with regard to something permanent.

You might continue, "Since **that same** experience **becomes subtle,** it is not perceived." **How could** it **be** possible to present **the same** single [and permanent phenomenon]—that is, pleasure and such—as both **gross and subtle?**

**If it becomes subtle only upon ceasing to be gross,**
**Being gross or subtle means nothing but impermanence.**
**So why do you not likewise accept**
**The impermanence of all phenomena?** [133]

**If the grossness of pleasure is not something other than it,**
**It is clearly evident that pleasure is impermanent.** [134ab]

These six lines teach that pleasure and such are impermanent.

**If** pleasure and such **become subtle only upon ceasing to be gross** from one moment to the next, it is definite that the various [states of] **being gross or subtle mean nothing but impermanence.** In this case, [the notion of] permanent constituents collapses. **So** if you see that pleasure and such are impermanent, **why do you not likewise accept the impermanence of all phenomena?** It is certain that they are impermanent. **If** you assert that **the grossness** and subtlety **of pleasure** and such are **not something other than it,** you will directly understand by yourself **that**

**pleasure** and suffering are **impermanent**, because they arise from conditions, [appear] in an intermittent way, and serve as mutually exclusive conditions.[1780]

### 4.2.2.1.3.3. The Refutation of the Assertion That the Result Abides in the Cause

> **You assert, "Something that does not exist**
> **Cannot arise because of its nonexistence."** [134cd][1781]
>
> **You may not wish for a nonexistent to arise as something manifest,**
> **But this is exactly what it comes down to.** [135ab]

These four lines teach that the [Enumerators] implicitly claim that [entities] arise from themselves.

**You assert,** "When one analyzes in this way, granted, it is true that the primal substance is not a cause. However, [all entities] are their own causes. There is no question that entities arise from themselves, **because something that does not exist cannot arise** and also [because] **of the nonexistence** of any other cause [for their arising]." [902] You do not [really] see that [entities] arise from themselves, but you just speculate and say, "One needs to accept that they arise from themselves." According to this [position], **you may not wish for** [entities] **to arise** even when the collection of [their] causes does **not exist as something manifest, but what it comes down to is** that you have to accept **exactly this.**[1782]

> **If the result were present in the cause,**
> **To eat food would amount to eating excrement.** [135cd]
>
> **And for the price that you pay for cotton cloth**
> **You should rather buy cotton seeds and wear them.** [136ab]

These four lines state extremely absurd consequences [that follow] if cause and result are simultaneous.

This [above conclusion] is definitely what you get, but **if** you still **were** to assert that **the result is present in the cause,** then **to eat food**, such as cooked rice, **would amount to eating excrement**, or feces, because the result—feces—is present in its cause, the food. **And for the price that you pay for cotton cloth you should rather buy** pealike **cotton seeds and wear them** as your garments, because the results—cotton wool and cotton cloth—are present in the cause—these very cotton seeds.

**You might argue, "Worldly people do not see this because of ignorance."**
**However, this is the very position of the knowers of this reality.** [136cd]

**Anyway, even worldly people have knowledge about this,**
**So why should they not see it?**
**"Worldly people do not have valid cognition."**
**Then their perceptions of manifest things would not be true either.** [137]

These six lines refute the answers to [the above consequences].

**You might argue,** "The result definitely does exist in the cause, but **worldly people do not see this because of ignorance.**" **However,** then [at least] you yourselves who presume to be **the knowers of this reality** should buy cotton seeds for the amount of money that you pay for cotton and wear just these seeds as your garments, thus substantiating your **very position** of before. This is the way in which [you should be consequent]. **Anyway,** [even] if you [claim] to be those who know that the result (cotton cloth) exists in its cause (cotton seeds), **even worldly people have** some **knowledge about this,** that is, that the result (cotton cloth) is accomplished based on its cause (cotton wool). **So why would** worldly people **not** also **see that** cotton cloth exists in cotton seeds? [In fact,] they would have to see this [too].[1783] You might think, "That worldly people do not see this is not a mistake [in our position], as **worldly people do not have valid cognition.**" However, **then** [all] **their perceptions of manifest things**, such as arising, **would not be true either.** [Unfortunately, however, such perceptions accord with your own. Consequently], just like such worldly [mistaken perceptions], [your] imputations—such as a self or the primal substance—are also not true.

### 4.2.2.1.4. Teaching That the Cognition That Negates the Existence of Objects Is a Valid Cognition

**"If valid cognition is not valid cognition,**
**Isn't what is validated by it delusive?**
**In true reality, the emptiness of entities**
**Is therefore unjustified."** [138][1784]

[903] This verse states the objection.

The opponents might say, "**If** you assert in your Centrist system that even all **valid cognition**—which is the means of evaluation—**is not valid cognition, isn't** a phenomenon **that is validated by it delusive** too? If one analyzes **in** accord with

**true** Centrist analysis, emptiness is not established, and, in consequence, meditation on **emptiness is unjustified** as well."

> **Without referring to an imputed entity,**
> **One cannot apprehend the lack of this entity.**
> **Therefore, the lack of a delusive entity**
> **Is clearly delusive [too]. [139]**

This verse teaches that [everything] is mere delusion.

**Without referring to**—that is, without relying on—**a** mere **imputed entity, one** is also **not** able to **apprehend** or present **the lack of this entity**, which is emptiness. The reason is that if one does not rely on the conventional term [or notion of] space, one is not able to present space as [referring to] the lack of any entities.[1785] **Therefore,** since sentient beings cling to the reality of **delusive entities** that are mere appearances, they plunge into cyclic existence. If one understands that these very [appearances] are unreal and illusionlike, this [understanding] surely serves as the remedy for the [clinging to reality]. However, emptiness—which is this imputation in the sense of **the lack of** such **delusive** [appearances] that appear as **entities—is clearly delusive** too. In the same way as an illusory lion kills an illusory elephant, this is [nothing more than] engaging in the [particular] reification of understanding emptiness as the remedy for the reification that conceives of real [entities].

> **Thus, when one's son dies in a dream,**
> **The conception "He does not exist"**
> **Removes the thought that he does exist,**
> **But it is also delusive. [140]**

This verse teaches that the [cultivation of emptiness] is the remedy for reification.

**Thus,** if one experiences **in a dream** that **one's son** has been born and then **dies,** inasmuch as this is a dream, there is definitely no difference between the [son]'s birth and his death. Still, due to one's seeing [in the dream] that he has been born, there arises the mental state that conceives, "My son exists." When there is the appearance that he has died, there emerges **the conception** "My son has died and now **he does not exist,**" [904] which **removes the thought** that fancies, "My son **does exist.**" However, since both—the existence and the nonexistence of this son **too**—are equal in being a dream, they are alike in being **delusive.**

#### 4.2.2.1.5. Stating the Meaning That is Ascertained through Valid Cognition

> **Hence, through having been analyzed in this way,**
> **Nothing exists without a cause,**
> **Nor is anything contained**
> **In its individual or combined conditions.** [141]
>
> **Neither does anything come from something other,**
> **Nor does it abide, nor does it go.** [142ab]

These six lines teach that causes are not established when one analyzes them.

**Thus, through having been analyzed in this way, no** phenomenon **exists** in a way that it arises **without a cause. Nor is any** result **contained in its individual** causes **or in a combination** of many of them. **Neither does anything come from some other** causes, **nor do** results **abide** in their causes, **nor do** causes cease or **go** after they have produced their results.

> **So what is the difference between illusions**
> **And what is taken to be real by ignorant people?** [142cd]

These two lines teach that everything is illusionlike.

**What is the difference between illusions and** all that **is taken to be real** and apprehended as [real] **by ignorant people?** In fact, one has to understand it as being like an illusion. Therefore, the *Mother* [*Sūtras*] teach that [everything] from form up to nirvāṇa [is illusionlike] and that any hypothetical phenomenon superior to it would be illusionlike too.

#### [Synopsis of Other Commentaries]

As for these [verses], in the section that refutes the Enumerators, Kalyāṇadeva [first] states their assertion:

> "Pleasure and such are the nature or entity of the cause. Since things, such as garments, have the nature of this cause, they are this cause. Since its results are garments and so on, pleasure and such exist in these. If they did not exist [in them], pleasure and such would not arise from them."[1786]

He teaches that this is refuted by [line 130b] "However, did we not analyze entities already?" Then he states the consequence that pleasure and such would have to exist all the time if they were permanent. [He continues:]

> Again, you might say, "When this permanent [pleasure] is clearly manifest, it appears as pleasure. However, when its full potential is not clearly manifest, it does not appear." This is refuted by [lines 132ab] "If there is clearly manifest pleasure and such . . ." . . . You might argue, "The phases of being gross and subtle are different, but since there is no difference in the basis of these phases—pleasure and such—there is no mistake." The objection to this is [found in lines 133ab] "If it becomes subtle only upon ceasing to be gross . . ." You might think, "The basis of these phases is permanent." This is refuted by lines [134ab] "If the grossness of pleasure is not something other than it . . ."[1787]

As for [line 137d] "Then their perceptions of manifest things would not be true either," he says:

> This demonstrates that the existence of sound and such is perceived as something manifest. [Here,] the term "either" teaches that what exists in inferences and scriptures would not be true either.[1788]

He explains that [verse 143] "What is created by illusion . . ." also belongs to this section. [905]

*The Small Commentary on the Knowledge Chapter* says:

> When stating these [lines 132ab] "If there is clearly manifest pleasure and such, . . ." master [Śāntideva] had in mind that it is the position of the Enumerators to express the assembly of the result with the term "clear manifestation."[1789]

[In *The Small Commentary* the objection in verse 138] that emptiness is unjustified receives the following answer:

> We do not say, "Emptiness is the negation of both entity and nonentity." The reason for this is that, ultimately, the negation of these is not capable of making concrete phenomena in the three times into [phenomena that have] the nature of a negation. You might ask, "So what is [emptiness] then?" It is that which is superimposed as the nature [of all phenomena], because a purpose entails something that serves this purpose.[1790]

[*The Small Commentary's*] concluding summary [of this section] explains that "without a cause," "individual," "combined," and "coming from something other" [in verses 141–142] are, in due order, a synopsis of the refutations of the following [opponents]: those who say that there are no causes, the followers of Īśvara, other opponents, and those who say that [entities] shift in time.[1791] Then it adduces the passages in [verses 143–144] "What is created by illusions . . ." as the proof for this [statement].[1792]

### 4.2.2.2. The Analysis of the Result: The Refutation of an Arising of Existents and Nonexistents

This has two parts:

1) The nature of the reason
2) The meaning that is ascertained through valid cognition

#### 4.2.2.2.1. The Nature of the Reason

**What is created by illusion**
**And what is created by causes—**
**Examine where each has come from**
**And also where they go. [143]**

[906] This verse teaches that, just like an illusion, [things] are without coming, going, and abiding.

There is not the slightest difference between the appearance of an illusion **that is created by** mantras and such that [produce] an **illusion and** this mere appearance as things **that is created by causes** and conditions that are presumed to be fully qualified causes. **Examine** both of them [to see] **where each has come from, where they go, and also** how they abide right now, and you will find neither of these two.

**How could there be any reality**
**In artificial entities that are equal to reflections**
**And only seen in conjunction with something other**
**But not in its absence? [144]**

This verse teaches that, just like reflections, [things] are not real.

Thus, just as in the case of a reflection [that appears] in conjunction with a mirror and a form, [things] are **seen in conjunction with some other** causes and conditions, **but not in** the **absence** of such conjunction with causes and conditions.

**Artificially** created **entities,** like an elephant [played] by an actor, and what is **equal to reflections** in a mirror do not withstand analysis. When not examined, they are just a plain, satisfying presence. **How could there be any reality in** them?[1793]

**What use is a cause**
**For a thing that already exists?**
**And what use is a cause,**
**If it does not exist?** [145]

**Even billions of causes**
**Cannot alter the lack of an entity.** [146ab]

These one and a half verses teach that there are no existents or nonexistents whatsoever that need causes.[1794]

**How could such a state turn into an entity?**
**And what else could turn into this entity?** [146cd]

**If an entity is impossible during the lack of this entity,**
**When should this turn into an entity?**
**For while an entity does not arise,**
**The lack of this entity will not disappear.** [147]

**Without the lack of this entity having disappeared,**
**The opportunity for an entity does not arise.**
**Also, an entity does not turn into the lack of this entity,**
**Because it would follow that it has a dual nature.** [148]

These two and a half verses refute that the lack of an entity turns into an entity and that an entity turns into the lack of an entity.

You might say, "The state of the lack of an entity [907] turns into an entity later." **How could** it **be** that **such a state** of the lack of an entity turns into **an entity** later? In just the same way, a lotus in the sky does not turn into an utpala [flower] in the water later. You might try, "It is not this [lack of an entity itself] that turns [into an entity], but some other state that turns into an entity." **And what else could** be a state that turns **into an entity?** [There is no] such [state], because [a state of being] neither an entity nor the lack of this entity is impossible.

Hence, whether it is an entity or the lack of this entity, some state of [both of] these, or something other than these, none of them turns into an entity. **If an entity is impossible during the lack of this entity, when should** any **entity** arise from this prior [state of the lack of this entity]? If the mere horns of a rabbit are impossible, where in the world should there arise the horns of a white rabbit that are as clear as crystal? In relation to a single basis, as long as **an entity does not arise, the lack of this entity will not disappear. Without the lack of this entity having disappeared, the opportunity for an entity does not arise** within this [lack of this entity]. Hence, **also** any former existent **entity does not turn into the lack of this entity** later. [Here,] the term "also" [implies that] a former nonexistent also does not turn into a later existent, **because it would follow** [in both cases] **that** a single entity **has the dual nature** of being both existent and nonexistent at the same time.

### 4.2.2.2.2. The Meaning That Is Ascertained through Valid Cognition

> **Thus, never is there any cessation**
> **Nor are there any entities either.**
> **Therefore, this whole universe**
> **Is unborn and without cessation.** [149]

This verse teaches that all phenomena are without arising and ceasing.

**Thus,** since there is no arising, **there is never any cessation** or abiding either. Since there is no arising and no cessation, **there are no** conditioned entities **either.** The term "either" [implies that] their counterparts—unconditioned phenomena, or nonentities—do not exist and that something other than these does not exist either. **Therefore, this whole universe is unborn and without cessation.**

> **Rather, the migrations of beings are dreamlike.**
> **On analysis, they are just like banana trees.**
> **In substance, there is no difference**
> **Between those who are released and those who are not.** [150]

This verse teaches that cyclic existence and nirvāṇa cannot be observed.

Hence, just **like** water and a dry place in a **dream**, cyclic existence and **being released** [from it] too are nothing but imputations, that is, mere remedial conceptions. All phenomena are always just beyond cognition, ineffable, inconceivable, inexpressible, [908], and completely pure by their very nature right from the start.

### [Synopsis of Other Commentaries]

In Kalyāṇadeva's [commentary], the following phrase [on line 150b] appears:

> Just as one does not find a core, if one examines a banana tree by dissecting it and breaking it into parts, . . .[1795]

However, [this line] is an explanation that a banana tree has no core, since it is [found to be] hollow inside when dissected. On the other hand, the mere [fact of] not finding a core by breaking something into its parts is the same for other trees as well. Thus, it is said:

> That "a banana tree has no core"
> Is taken as an example in the world, but . . .

This eliminates the need for identifying a banana tree [as a special example of a tree that has no core].

*The Small Commentary on the Knowledge Chapter* explains:

> Having refuted arising in this way, [verse 149] "Thus, . . ." refutes perishing.[1796]

### 5. The Result of Meditating on Emptiness

This has three parts:

The twofold qualities that are one's own welfare

1) Transcending existence through not being carried away by afflictions
2) Not falling into [the state of one-sided] peace through the arising of compassion for those who lack realization

The qualities that are the welfare of others

3) Protecting all sentient beings

### 5.1. Transcending Existence through Not Being Carried Away by Afflictions

> **When phenomena are empty in this way,**
> **What is there to gain and what to lose?**
> **Who can be honored**
> **Or despised by whom? [151]**

**Where do happiness and suffering come from?**
**What is there to like, and what is there to dislike?** [152ab]

These one and a half verses teach that one is not swayed by the eight dharmas of desire.

[910] Through having familiarized oneself with the sproutlike seeming mind of enlightenment, the ultimate mind of enlightenment—which is like a [cereal plant's] ear—will arise. The remedy that removes all diseases of reification at their root is the profound heart of the dharma of all Buddhas, which is the perfection of knowledge, the ultimate mind of enlightenment, the complete peace of all discursiveness, true reality. When one has become familiar with it **in this way**, just this nature of all phenomena that is completely pure right from the start and not an object of speech, reflection, knowledge, or expression will be seen in such a way. At that point, all these phenomena that are mere sights and sounds are fully realized as naturally **empty phenomena** that are just like appearances in a dream. Hence, with respect to these phenomena that are just reflections, [all] mental states of wishing or not wishing for them, hope and fear, and adopting and rejecting will naturally perish:

**What is there to gain and what to lose?**
**Who can be honored**
**Or despised by whom?**

**Where do happiness and suffering come from?**
**What is there to like, and what is there to dislike?**

Thus, attachment and aversion in terms of the eight [worldly] dharmas will perish as a matter of course. [911] There is no question that the learned ones do not give any considerations to the objects that naïve beings cling to, but these [objects] as such do not represent some [intrinsic positive] qualities for these [beings themselves] either. The reason for this is: It seems that, even [among] those beings who are equal in that they are engrossed in all the bondage in the world, grown-ups do not give any importance at all to those things that small children cling to, such as castles made of sand or horses and elephants made of clay.

**What is craving and for what is this craving,**
**When investigated in its nature?** [152cd]

**If you analyze, what is this world of living beings**
**And who is it who will die in it?** [153ab]

These four lines teach that [emptiness] is the direct antidote to the cause of cyclic existence, which is the craving for the three realms.

**If you investigate** what is to be evaluated through knowledge that examines in a discriminating way and rest with personally experienced wisdom in meditative equipoise **in** the actual **nature,** which craver **is craving for what** object **and** for what reason? You will see all phenomena in exactly the same way as when deer in a dream crave for a mirage in this dream. **If you analyze** properly in this manner, at the time of not having realized this before, the entirety of these worldly appearances appeared as if they were so real and **alive,** but from the perspective of this stainless knowledge, **what is it, and who is it who will** seemingly **die** or has died **in it?** This utterly hollow delusion will collapse instantaneously. It does not perform any function whatsoever.

> **What will come to be, and what has been?**
> **Also, what are relatives, and who is whose friend?** [153cd]
>
> **May persons like myself fully grasp**
> **That everything is just like space.** [154ab]

These four lines teach that everything is seen as spacelike.

At this point, **what** is the future that **will come to be, and what** are these past phenomena that are apprehended as what **has been? Also, what** or who **are** beloved **relatives and friends?** The term "also" [here implies] enemies, or those whom we label as not our loved ones. **Every** phenomenon **is** by its very nature right from the start **just like space.** It has no being, it is inconceivable, and its extension or size cannot be observed. It is not visible at any time, nor is it not visible at any [point]. The [next two lines] contain the advice that [Śāntideva] gave here: "**May I**—the bodhisattva—and also those intelligent **persons** whose karmic dispositions are **like my** own **fully grasp**, perfectly comprehend, completely assimilate, and take seriously **that** this is the way it is."

### 5.2. Not Falling into [the State of One-Sided] Peace through the Arising of Compassion for Those Who Lack Realization

> **Beings become enraged and elated**
> **Through the causes for quarrels and celebrations.** [154cd]
>
> **They grieve and toil, they despair,**
> **And they mutilate and slay each other.**

**Through all this and further evil deeds, they lead miserable lives,
Always longing for their own happiness. [155]**

These one and a half verses teach compassion and loving-kindness for those who commit negative deeds.

You might say, "However, since the cause of cyclic existence is craving, and craving is reversed through meditating on emptiness, one becomes an arhat of the hearers or solitary realizers [through such meditation]. In that case, this contradicts the explanation that [becoming] a hearer or solitary realizer represents an abyss for the followers of the great vehicle." [912]

Since cyclic existence together with its fundamental basis is fully comprehended [through meditation on emptiness] in this way, there is no question that nirvāṇa has arrived in the palm of your hand. However, this is not in the slightest considered as anything such as an infinitesimal particle. You see it as nothing but the nirvāṇa of all phenomena right from the start, as enlightenment by its very nature. Hence, you are just like a person who, when arriving at the foot of the seven golden mountains, does not treasure a piece of brass as if it were gold. This is definitely the way it is. Still, for those sentient beings who do not realize this, what wells up [in you] in an unbearable way is solely great compassion. However, even at this point, nothing in the slightest is observed as sentient beings or suffering. It is just this that leads to the increase of nothing but unrestrained great compassion. It is hard for us naïve beings even to hear about this, let alone to have trust in and be convinced of such a great mode of being of bodhisattvas. This is their outstanding and amazing miraculous display, such as fire blazing from the upper part [of the body] while water gushes from [its] lower part,[1797] which cannot be matched by billions of [other] outstanding miraculous displays.

There is no question that this is the way it is. Still, when we look at the situation of these [beings] who, like crazy old women, are tainted by their flaws no matter what they do, compassion for each other may appear in an unbearable manner even in us childlike beings. If [this can dawn in us even now], why should it not [be possible to continue in this way]? [This means that] we [can] become familiar with love and compassion for limitless eons and relinquish every aspect of considering our own happiness. We assume the entirety of enlightened body, speech, mind, qualities, and activities solely for the sake of sentient beings. The countless streaming rivers of our great compassion flow naturally in an effortless and nonconceptual way. [Their flux] is uninterrupted, shows no fluctuations, and has left behind the banks of permanence and extinction. They sparkle in a translucent way due to their gems of infinite uncontaminated qualities and represent the sole support for all beings. So why should their waves not surge high [for these beings]?

Since these assemblies of our [former and present] parents **long for their own happiness**, there is not a single one [among them] who does not commit **evil deeds.** Since they wish to be unrivaled, they kill others. **Through this cause,** [913] they are born in the reviving hells for many lifetimes. Thus, they experience killing **each other** tens of thousands of times each day. And even when they become liberated from these [states], wherever they are reborn, their lives will be short, they will have many diseases, and they will experience themselves now being **slain** by others. Since they continue to engage in actions that accord with their causes, they [still] take delight in [killing] and are inclined to kill. Hence, it is difficult to turn away from this. Through the completely ripened results of these [actions], they circle again in the hells and so on, just like a continuously moving waterwheel. Thus, there is no time when they would become liberated from suffering.

Wanting to be wealthy, they rob and steal the possessions of others and thus take what was not given to them. This determines the completely ripened result of being tormented by the sufferings in innumerable states of hell beings and hungry ghosts. Furthermore, wherever they are reborn after this, they will again be poor and destitute. All that will happen [to them] is that their [few] things will be of no benefit to them and go to waste in useless ways, such as falling prey to robbers and thieves, or be ruined by fire or water. Under the sway of their latent tendencies, wherever they are reborn, they will still be inclined to take what was not given, and it will be hard to turn away from this. Then, they will [again] experience the completely ripened results of this and so forth. Thus, they will uninterruptedly circle [in cyclic existence].

You should understand that the same applies to all seven [negative actions of body and speech] that are to be relinquished. [Imagine that] you were to sell the entirety of your food, clothes, and possessions of this life from today onward, buy [for them] a charmed potion that is poisonous to touch, and apply it to your own body. In just the same way, [to commit these negative actions] means only to sell the entirety of your happiness in hundreds of thousands, millions, and billions of countless future lifetimes just for the sake of a few tiny scraps of seeming happiness in this life.

Likewise, [such people] do not worry about all their parents in each one of these lives who experience excruciating sufferings in limitless ways for a long time. However, in this single lifetime [right now], they take as their kinfolk [some of these beings], who are just [like] guests gathered in a hotel for one day. When a single one of them dies, **they** roll back and forth on the ground in **grief.** They do not exert themselves in generosity—the cause for wealth—but rather engage in meaningless business and so forth. Through this, they **toil** only to tire themselves out completely. **They** strive merely for the sake of food and clothing and **lead miserable lives.** Therefore, [Śāntideva says:]

**Beings become enraged and elated**
**Through the causes for quarrels and celebrations.**
**They grieve and toil, they despair,**
**And they mutilate and slay each other.**
**Through all this and further evil deeds, they lead miserable lives,**
**Always longing for their own happiness.**

So who would not feel compassion and loving-kindness for them?

**Upon dying, they fall into the long and unbearable sufferings**
**Of dreadful existences again and again.**
**Then, they surface in pleasant migrations**
**And indulge in their pleasures again and again.**[1798] [156]

This verse teaches compassion and loving-kindness for those in higher states of existence.

It is stated that through making a single prostration to a reliquary that contains relic pills, one obtains a thousand times as many [rebirths as] a wheel-ruler as there are sand grains in the area that one has covered with one's body [while prostrating] all the way down to the golden ground.[1799] Accordingly, each tiny little positive action bears the capacity that [beings] obtain many hundreds of thousands of divine and human bodies. If these positive actions are not wasted, [beings] obtain a corresponding number of divine and human bodies. In these [bodies] **they** are able to **indulge in** infinite great riches, such as kingdoms, and to live for many hundreds of thousands of human years and so forth. This certainly happens to them, but if they do not produce some further special positive actions, the positive actions that previously had propelled [them into such states] just become exhausted. Thereafter, **they** will circle **in dreadful existences** and experience **unbearable sufferings** again:

**Upon dying, they fall into the long and unbearable sufferings**
**Of dreadful existences again and again.**
**Then, they surface in pleasant migrations**
**And indulge in their pleasures again and again.**

**Many are the abysses in existence,**
**And all you find there is true reality's lack.**
**Existence entails mutual opposition,**

**And what you do not find in it is true reality.** [157]

**It contains oceans of suffering**
**That are horrible, unending, and beyond compare.** [158ab]

These one and a half verses teach that the entirety of cyclic existence is suffering.

Hence, this cyclic existence is nothing but a place on which you cannot rely at all, [a place] that is frightening from top to bottom, dreadful, and terrifying. **Many are** these kinds of **abysses in existence, and** in any state that you are born in, you just fall down and become separated [from true reality]. So **all you find there is the lack** of a core, that is, **true reality.** No matter where you are born, **it entails** that you are under the control of only these **mutually contradictory** mental states of attachment to happiness and aversion to suffering. Therefore, out of your wish for happiness, you will only strive to accomplish suffering. However, even in mere dreams, **what you do not find in** this **existence is** any engagement in **true reality** by which you understand that the nature of happiness and suffering is not real.

Hence, in a dream, there is no happiness, suffering, or experiencer whatsoever. However, as long as you do not realize this, from the perspective of mistakenness, it seems as if all kinds of things are experienced. Likewise, wherever you are born, it seems that you experience **oceans of suffering** in it **that are horrible, unending, and beyond compare.** [915] This is just like the suffering of being separated from a friend who is an illusion.

**Thus, there is little strength here,**
**And life is short too.** [158cd]

**Also, with activities for staying alive and healthy,**
**In hunger, fatigue, and exhaustion,**
**In sleep, misfortunes,**
**And the fruitless company of fools,** [159]

**Life passes quickly and in vain,**
**With hardly any chance for investigation.** [160ab]

These eight lines teach that such analysis [as described above] is hard to find even when one is born as a human being.

Even for those in the higher states of pleasant migrations, **there is little strength** in their remedies [for suffering], **and** their **lives** are **short.** As long as they are alive **here,** they are tormented by diseases. Even if they are in good **health,** they become exhausted through various worries and deprivations. **In the company of fools,** they drag along, helplessly forced by others. Since they suffer in all these various ways, **life** becomes exhausted **in vain, with hardly** ever **any chance for** such an **investigation** of the genuine dharma:

> **Thus, there is little strength here,**
> **And life is short too.**
> **Also, with activities for staying alive and healthy,**
> **In hunger, fatigue, and exhaustion,**
> **In sleep, misfortunes,**
> **And the fruitless company of fools,**
> **Life passes quickly and in vain,**
> **With hardly any chance for investigation.**

> **Where could beings find a way here**
> **To turn away from their habitual distraction?** [160cd]

> **Here, demons combine all their efforts**
> **To cast them into the dreadful lower realms.**
> **As wrong paths are plentiful here,**
> **It is hard to overcome doubts.** [161]

These one and a half verses teach that even when [such analysis] has been found, it is hard to put an end to the actions of demons.

Even though it is possible for [beings] to find the entrance to the dharma at some point, they are habituated to nothing but distraction since limitless lifetimes. Therefore, it is difficult for them **to turn their** minds **away from distraction.** Moreover, they are under the sway of the demon of the aggregates (attachment to the aggregates) and the demon of the afflictions (the afflicted mind). Hence, they are propelled **into the dreadful lower realms.** Also, the demon of the divine son—which appears from dependent origination due to basic unawareness—assumes the guise of spiritual friends and displays a great variety of different guises, such as the guise of the dharma, the great vehicle, Centrism, and the secret mantra. This creates obstacles for higher states and liberation. Since fake **paths are** more than **plentiful here,** the places on the path to go astray are plentiful [too], and **it is hard** for beings **to** believe in perfect actuality. Since those who are inclined to [take] paths that go astray are plentiful as well, those who accomplish the path are very few:

**Where could beings find a way here**
**To turn away from their habitual distraction?**
**Here, demons combine all their efforts**
**To cast them into the dreadful lower realms.**
**As wrong paths are plentiful here,**
**It is hard to overcome doubts.**

**It is not easy to obtain this chance again.**
**The presence of Buddhas is very hard to find,**
**And it is difficult to ward off the flood of afflictions.**
**Alas, suffering is an endless stream! [162]**

**Oh dear, it is more than appropriate to feel deep concern**
**For those who are thus immersed in the torrents of suffering**
**And do not see their wretched state**
**Even though they are in such great misery. [163]**

**Just as some [fool] would take a [cool] bath again and again**
**And thereafter go to a fire every time,**
**They think of their distressing situation**
**As being sheer happiness. [164]**

**Those who lead their lives like this**
**As if aging and dying were not meant for them**
**Just approach their being put to death**
**As the first of many horrific tortures to come. [165]**

These four verses teach that such sentient beings are the objects of our deep-felt compassion.

Since the time has come now at which you have **obtained** a human body and met with the dharma, [916] this is like finding a jewel in the middle of sweepings. If you do not make any effort in this [situation], **it is not easy to** accomplish it [again] later, which means that you will then have to roam around in cyclic existence without end:

**It is not easy to obtain this chance again.**
**The presence of Buddhas is very hard to find**
**And it is difficult to ward off the flood of afflictions.**
**Alas, suffering is an endless stream!**

**Thus,** [beings] are tormented by nothing but **distressing situations** since beginningless time without any interruption for even one moment. Still, on top of not becoming weary [of this], they are [even] concerned about not obtaining [more] suffering. Being just like moths who kill themselves in a fire, **they** nevertheless **think of** [this situation] **as being sheer happiness. They** are even proud [of this] and cling to [the idea] that it is just fine to remain in this lifetime forever without **dying.** However, **first,** their wealth is destroyed by dwindling away. [Then,] their youth is destroyed by **aging**; their health is destroyed by sickness; their companionship is destroyed by separation; and their life is destroyed by death. After having gradually **been put to death** through these [circumstances], they will have to experience further **horrific tortures.** Not being able to bear [all this, Śāntideva] considers them: "If I can just [help them], any means is fine!" Thus, he speaks these words of utmost compassion:

**Oh dear, it is more than appropriate to feel deep concern**
**For those who are thus immersed in the torrents of suffering**
**And do not see their wretched state**
**Even though they are in such great misery.**

**Just as some [fool] would take a [cool] bath again and again**
**And thereafter would go to a fire every time,**
**They think of their distressing situation**
**As being sheer happiness.**

**Those who lead their lives like this**
**As if aging and dying were not meant for them**
**Just approach their being put to death**
**As the first of many horrific tortures to come.**

### 5.3. Protecting All Sentient Beings

**When will the time come that I pacify**
**The torments of suffering's scorching fires**
**With my offerings of happiness**[1800]
**That stream forth from the clouds of merit? [166]**

This verse teaches that one will [eventually] become the support for the benefit and welfare of sentient beings.

The elephant [named] "Son of the Protector of the Earth"[1801] enters a lake without hesitation, since he has an overview of its size. Likewise, stainless knowledge has penetrated the flaws of cyclic existence. Hence, one has no fear and has complete control over all phenomena. However, [one's mind] is still governed by compassion, so that one is able to vanquish sentient beings' basic unawareness and such through knowing that these are adventitious and not their actual mode of being. Since the basic element of sentient beings is pure right from the start, they abide in the very nature of enlightenment. This makes one [917] see that they are all destined to become enlightened and that there is no difficulty in eliminating this adventitious basic unawareness. Through [seeing] this, one generates the unlimited mind [of enlightenment] and dons its inconceivable armor for the welfare of [all sentient beings], who are like people who suffer because of not knowing that a [magical] illusion is an illusion. [To generate the mind of enlightenment and don its armor in this way] is the very nature of phenomena. Therefore, [Śāntideva] says:

**When will the time come that I pacify**
**The torments of suffering's scorching fires**
**With my offerings of happiness**
**That stream forth from the clouds of merit?**

[Thus,] through the whole range of provisions that please and benefit all sentient beings, one eliminates their suffering and satisfies them in every temporary and ultimate aspect.

**As a result of [my] careful gathering of the accumulation of merit**
**By means of the seeming and in a nonreferential manner,**
**When will I teach emptiness**
**To those who have referential views?**[1802] [167]

This verse teaches that one establishes all beings in [the state of] enlightenment through turning the wheel of dharma.

Without moving away from stainless knowledge—that is, **the accumulation** of wisdom—one fully accomplishes the means, which are the five perfections. Through this, one manifests unsurpassable enlightenment. Then, one turns the wheel of dharma of profound **emptiness**, which is the perfection of knowledge that eradicates referentiality and [all] views about characteristics at the root. [One teaches it] **to these** sentient beings **who** suffer solely because they are clinging, [apprehend] characteristics, and are **referential.** They are just like people who sink into a swamp through their own movements or silkworms who tie themselves up with their own saliva. Through [turning the wheel of dharma], one puts them into the state of revealing the Dharma Body in their own continua.

[Thus, Śāntideva] generates the aspiring mind [of enlightenment] by saying, "May the time come **when I will** be like this."

In this way, through knowledge, one does not remain in existence, and, through compassion, one does not remain in [one's own] peace. This is the complete perfection and full completion of the great vehicle. [Thus, the last verse] teaches, all in one, what is to be meditated upon (emptiness and compassion), the benefit of having meditated, and the function of this.

## [Synopsis of Other Commentaries]

If [line 166c] is read as "with my offerings of happiness," it refers to "being just like when all one's necessities stream forth from the clouds during [the eon of] perfection,[1803] since 'offerings' has the meaning of all necessary provisions." [Alternatively,] many editions [of Śāntideva's text] say, [918] "with the rains of my own happiness." Accordingly, this should be explained as being "like rains that stream forth from the clouds."[1804]

As for the [preceding verses], Kalyāṇadeva says:

> In order to teach that the eight worldly dharmas, such as gain, and everything such as craving are delusive, we have [verses 151–152ab:] "When phenomena are empty . . ." . . . Since these worldly dharmas originate from craving, [lines 152cd] "What is craving . . ." are given.[1805]

He supplements some words in the sense that living and dying are not established when analyzed:

> You might say, "We need craving so that we do not die and so on." This is answered in [lines 153ab] "If you analyze . . ."[1806]

His further comments are just some supplementary words:

> Someone might say, "One craves for bodies that will come to be." This is referred to in [line 153bc] "and who is it . . . ." Someone might say, "There is craving in the wish to meet with relatives and friends." This is addressed in [line 153d] "Also, what are relatives, . . . ." . . . Actually, all of these are unborn. Therefore, they are nonentities, just like space. Since [Śāntideva] composed this text for those who are of equal status with himself, he says in [lines 154ab], "May persons like myself fully grasp . . ."
>
> You might say, "There is a mind that is happy and suffers." [Lines

> 154cd–157ab] "Beings become enraged . . ." address this. . . . Thus, these [experiences] are taught to be illusionlike. . . . There are also mutual oppositions in this [cyclic existence]: One lives with such [sensations] as heat and cold and also with mutual disharmony between different sentient beings.
>
> "Not craving" [refers to lines 157cd]: As long as craving is not gone, this [cyclic existence] which is not true reality will not disappear [either].
>
> "The clouds of merit" [in line 166d] are the collection of merit. . . . "Gathering" [in line 167a means] brought together.[1807]

Vibhūticandra says:

> [As for verses 151–152:] If one clings to what is delusive through not knowing true reality, it is oneself who creates one's own suffering. Through the path that was explained in this way, [one understands the following:] In terms of all this which is without a nature, from where should anything be obtained and to whom should whose [things] be lost?
>
> [Verse 153:] If you analyze, what is this living world, since it does not exist? Who is it who will die here? What has happened, and what will come to be, since the past and so on entail [mutual] dependence?
>
> [Lines 154ab:] That everything is like space is what appears for the yogi's wisdom that originated from the final special familiarity with actual reality. In the same way, also other persons like myself should seize true reality without doubt.
>
> [Lines 154cd–155ab:] Naïve beings are deeply upset through the causes for quarrels and become elated through the causes for delight. [919]
>
> [Verse 157:] In this existence, such [things] as form and so on—which are not true reality—confuse [beings]. They then happen to be in mutual opposition for the sake of these [things], because they do not realize true reality free from the four extremes.
>
> [Lines 161cd:] Since wrong paths—such as those of the Mundanely Minded and Analyzers—are plentiful, it is hard to overcome doubts.[1808]

As for "being put to death" [in line 165c], he quotes *The Sūtra of the Instructions for the King,*[1809] [which says] that one is reduced to dust from the four [main] directions through the four mountains of sickness, aging, death, and decline. He [further] explains that the first of the last two verses relates to higher states [within cyclic existence] and that the latter relates to definite excellence.[1810]

*The Small Commentary* says:

> [Verses 151–154ab] "When phenomena are empty . . ." teach that there is no difference between qualities and flaws. Then, [verses 154cd–157ab] "Beings become enraged . . ." teach the ignorant behavior of naïve beings who are blinded by basic unawareness.
>
> You might say, "However, why do you not assert perfect consciousness itself as the cause through which the suffering of cyclic existence arises?" [The answer is given in lines 157cd] "Existence entails . . ." To be hurt by extremely unbearable feelings is the great hardship of mutual opposition within cyclic existence. Where such [great hardship] exists, it is absolutely certain that this kind of perfect consciousness is not justified as the cause for existence. [These two lines] "Existence entails . . ." make it clear that [such a consciousness] simply does not exist in this very [cyclic existence].
>
> [As for verse 159:] This is [spoken] because of such activities as hoping to be alive, hoping to be healthy, relying on others, and so forth.
>
> "Wrong paths" [in line 161c refers to] falling into wrong views.
>
> [Verse 165] "Those who lead their lives . . ." teaches that there is no point in saying more [about this], as all of these [activities] are expressions of basic unawareness.

[This commentary] explains that [verse 167] has a twofold meaning:

> Having accomplished the accumulation of merit through not referring to the three spheres [of agent, object, and action], when will I teach others? Or, having accomplished the two accumulations through not referring to the three [spheres], when will I teach emptiness to those who are referential?

Some Tibetans [say] that the activity for attaining knowledge is [twofold]: the way of meditating on emptiness by oneself and the way of meditating on compassion for others. They explain that the first [pertains to verses 151–154ab] "When phenomena are empty . . ." and that the second [is contained in verses 154cd–167] "Beings become enraged . . ." [However, this explanation] seems to [provide] an outline that is not so nice, [920] because compassion too must be meditated upon by oneself. Therefore, it is better if this is explained as "meditating on the basic nature, which is emptiness, and meditating on compassion for those who do not realize this."

**This was the elucidation of the ninth chapter on the Perfection of Knowledge from *The Entrance to the Bodhisattva's Way of Life.***

# APPENDIX I:

## *A Short Biography of the Second Pawo Rinpoche Tsugla Trengwa*[1811]

According to the Tibetan calender, Pawo Tsugla Trengwa was born in the male Wood Mouse year of the eighth sixty-year cycle (1504) in the hill area of Uru Nyethang[1812] in the family line of Nyag Jñānakumāra.[1813] His father was Lama Tar[1814] and his mother Lamnye Drölma.[1815] He was born with eyes wide open and caused no pain for his mother. Soon after, his first words were, "May I be able to benefit all kinds of beings!" At the age of five, he was recognized as the reincarnation of the first Pawo Rinpoche Chöwang Lhündrub[1816] (1440–1503) by Genyen Chalung[1817] and enthroned at the great monastery of Trowo Lung in Lhotra.[1818] There he went through the basic monastic training with the realized Lama Gendün Gyamtso.[1819]

When he was nine years old, he took lay and novice vows from the Fourth Shamarpa Chökyi Tragba (1453–1524) and received the ordination name Mipham Chökyi Gyalpo.[1820] He studied many teachings of the secret mantrayāna from both the old and the new transmissions with several masters, such as the Fourth Shamarpa, Paṇḍita Ngawang Tragba,[1821] Tagbo Paṇḍita Chögyal Tenpay Gyaltsen,[1822] and Ü Nyön Heruka Kunga Sangbo.[1823] From the latter, he also received Mahāmudrā instructions. In particular, from the age of nine until he was twenty-eight, he relied on the great Karma Trinlayba and studied numerous teachings with him. At seventeen, he went to the great dharma seat of Legshay Ling[1824] and mastered the great texts of sūtra and tantra, such as the four great instructions,[1825] through study and debate among many scholars. After reaching his twenty-third year, he took full ordination as a monk from the great translator of Shalu, Chökyong Pal Sangbo.[1826] Then, he went to Trowo Lung and stayed in a meditation retreat for three years.

At the age of twenty-nine, he went to Kongbo[1827] and met the Eighth Karmapa Mikyö Dorje at Zingbo Bumpa Gang.[1828] Pawo Rinpoche offered the Karmapa his own monastery, his retinue, and all his possessions. From then on, he received the majority of his instructions in the sūtras, tantras, and common sciences from the Eighth Karmapa and reached the peak of erudition and knowledge through an unusual combination of untiring vigor and supreme analytic skills. Therefore, the Eighth Karmapa gave him the name Pal Tsugla Trengwa.[1829]

Starting at the age of thirty-seven, he accomplished three years and nine fortnights of retreat practice in Tsari at the "small ravine of Naynang,"[1830] the secret cave of the Ḍākiṇi with the four-cornered bow,[1831] the secret cave of Karö,[1832] and Padmasambhava's Garuda Fortress of White Lake.[1833] When he brought into his experience what he had studied before, this was not restricted to a mere conceptual understanding, but he realized the dharma as the actual remedy for taming the afflictions in his own mind stream and as the root for the benefit and happiness of all beings. Thus, he attained supreme siddhi.

When the Eighth Karmapa passed away, Pawo Rinpoche offered a reliquary shrine and enthroned the Fifth Shamarpa Göncho Yenla as his regent. In 1544, he started to compose his *History of the Dharma, a Feast for the Learned* and completed it in 1564 after twenty years of detailed and difficult research. This work on the general history of India and Tibet and the various dharma lineages is based on a wealth of ancient and rare source materials and displays a high level of research methodology that was quite unusual for its time. Hence, it provides extensive and detailed information that is not found in other historical works in Tibet. Even to the present day, modern historians value it as a very comprehensive and reliable sourcebook. The commentary on *The Entrance to the Bodhisattva's Way of Life* was written in 1565, the year before Pawo Rinpoche's passing.

During the time when the Fifth Shamarpa and the Fourth Gyaltsab Tragba Töndrub[1834] (1550–1617) traveled to Kham in order to escort the young Ninth Karmapa Wangchug Dorje to his main seat at Tsurpu, Pawo Rinpoche served as the regent for both them and the Karmapa. He journeyed on foot through most of central and southern Tibet and gave teachings, reading transmissions, and empowerments as he saw fit. He also restored Milarepa's tower and erected many statues in various temples. Upon the return of the Ninth Karmapa with Shamarpa and Gyaltsab Rinpoche, it was Pawo Rinpoche who enthroned him at Tsurpu. Later, he also bestowed novice vows on both the Karmapa and Gyaltsab Rinpoche. Every day, he imparted the oceanlike profound teachings of the Kagyü lineage to these bearers of the black and red hats as well as to those who came from all over Tibet to study.

From all the offerings that Pawo Rinpoche received, he kept only a minimal amount for food and clothing, giving the rest away to support the monastic community and to produce representations of the three jewels, such as stupas, texts, statues, and paintings. He did not strive for position or fame in this life. When he composed texts, he wrote down everything in precise concordance with the particular teaching, without distorted explanations or lofty, self-aggrandizing remarks. Thus, he authored only excellent expositions that delight people with honest minds. In such a way, he spent his whole life retaining, protecting, and furthering the teachings of the practice lineage. He performed the three activities of the learned (explaining the dharma to others, debating, and composing texts) and did research in the history and sciences of Tibet. At the age of sixty-two, at the dawn of the sixteenth day of the tenth month in the male Fire Tiger year of the ninth sixty-year cycle (1566), his mind passed into the expanse of dharmas and he temporarily withdrew his display of a physical body.

Pawo Rinpoche's many disciples included the Ninth Karmapa Wangchug Dorje, the Fifth Shamarpa Göncho Yenla, as well as the Third and Fourth Gyaltsab tulkus, Tragba Paljor[1835] (1519–1549) and Tragba Töndrub.

Besides his *History of the Dharma* and the commentary on the *Bodhicaryāvatāra*, he wrote many other treatises, such as his famous *Great Exposition of Vajravarahī*;[1836] *A Treatise on Astrology, Called The Precious Treasury*;[1837] *An Exposition of the Four Tantras of Medical Science*;[1838] and *Some Notes on Medical Treatment, Called The Concise Essence.*[1839]

# APPENDIX II:

## *Non-Buddhist Indian Schools*

In general, the philosophical systems in India can be classified in various ways, such as the "orthodox" schools that accept the Vedas as supreme scriptural authority versus the "heterodox" schools that reject them, or the schools that hold a view of permanence versus the schools that hold a view of nihilism. (In the description below, I follow the former distinction.) Some of the non-Buddhist Indian schools—the systems of the early Vedas and the Epics, the Vedānta, the Yoga, and the bhākti traditions—are not addressed below, since they are not mentioned either in the *Bodhicaryāvatāra* or in Pawo Rinpoche's commentary. Thus, the following is only a brief outline of those non-Buddhist philosophical systems that are relevant in Śāntideva's text. It is not meant as a comprehensive exposition of the positions of these schools.[1840]

### Orthodox Schools That Adhere to the Vedas

**Mīmāṃsaka** (Tib. dpyod pa pa), "Analyzers." The main text of this school is Jaimini's *Mīmāṃsasūtra* (about 200 CE), though the system of thought itself is much older. Originally, the Mīmāṃsakas were not at all concerned with philosophy but with systematizing and harmonizing the extensive ritual precepts in the Vedas, which were considered an eternal, unauthored, and unmistaken revelation. Thus, *mīmāṃsa* refers to the analysis of the principles that determine the interpretation of these sacred texts. In the course of the development of other philosophical systems, there appeared the need for justifying the ultimate authenticity of the Vedas through rational investigation. However, except for the acknowledgment of a supernatural sphere of being and the Vedas as that which enables one to gain knowledge about it, the philosophical theory that evolved out of this need for vindication is pure empiricism. In being of a realistic and pluralistic outlook, it largely follows the Nyāya-Vaiśeṣika system and contains only minor elements that are related to the philosophic passages of the Vedas (these features are close to the Vedānta). The Analyzers' main arguments for the unmistakenness and self-existence of the Vedas are that knowledge is self-valid and that these texts are an expression of omnipresent eternal sound.[1841] Similar to the Enumerators, they understand the relation between cause and result as being one of identity in difference.[1842] The description of the self and how it becomes liberated is very similar to what the Nyāya-Vaiśeṣikas say. However, unlike the other orthodox schools that mainly rely on the cultivation of meditation and wisdom in order to achieve liberation of the self, the Mīmāṃsakas strongly emphasize that such liberation can only come about through the strict application of the rituals and proper ways of conduct that are prescribed in the Vedas.

**Naiyāyika** (Tib. rigs pa can pa), "Logicians." The school originated with Gautama (a.k.a. Akṣapāda), the author of the *Nyāyasūtra* (its oldest commentary is Pakṣilasvāmī Vātsyāyana's *Nyāyabhāṣya*, fifth century CE). The Logicians blended the old Indian natural philosphy with an extensive system of logic and dialectics. Many of their views, such as on the self, Īśvara, and causation, accord with those of the Differentiators, and eventually the two merged to form the Nyāya-Vaiśeṣika school. However, the Differentiators treat the existence of things from the ontological point of view, while the Logicians are more concerned about epistemology, that is, how things are known or validated. They present sixteen categories that constitute the world, the main ones being valid cognition or means of knowledge[1843] (perception, inference, verbal testimony, and analogy)[1844] and what is to be evaluated[1845] by these means (which includes all seven categories of the Differentiators).

**Sāṃkhya** (Tib. grangs can pa), "Enumerators." The school claims that its origins go back to the Vedic mythical sage Kapila, to whom the composition of the *Sāṃkhyasūtra* is ascribed.[1846] The classical scripture is the *Sāṃkhyakārikā* by Īśvarakṛṣna (fifth century CE) Its followers are called Enumerators because they enumerate twenty-five factors that make up the universe. The original distinction that this system makes is between (1) *prakṛti*[1847]—the infinite, single, and unconscious primal substance—and (2) *puruṣa*[1848] (person, self, or ātman), which is infinite consciousness. The primal substance is permanent, partless, all-pervading, yet imperceptible. It is described as the primordial undifferentiated equilibrium of the three "constituents":[1849] motility, darkness, and lightness.[1850] *Rajas* (literally, passion) stands for whatever is active and energetic, *tamas* for what is coarse and heavy, and *sattva* for everything that is fine and light. When related to what is experienced by the puruṣa, in due order, they correspond to suffering, dullness, and pleasure or to hatred, ignorance, and desire respectively. However, since the puruṣa itself is not derived from the primal substance, it lacks these three qualities. Each sentient being has a puruṣa, which is permanent but is not an agent for anything. It is pure sentience, the experiencer of pleasure, pain, and all manifestations of the prakṛti. It is said to be neither a cause nor a result, neither the primal substance itself nor one of its manifestations. In other words, it independently exists in and by itself.

Except for the puruṣa, all other manifold appearances of the world manifest out of the primal matter and are nothing but various expressions or perturbations of this single nature (thus, the implication that things arise from themselves). These expressions are called "universal flux"[1851] or "manifestations"[1852] and are regarded as illusory. In this process of gradual evolution of the world's complexity, first, (3) cognition, or "the great one,"[1853] splits off from its original unity with this permanent "nature." This cognition (which in itself is matter) is like a two-sided mirror, in which outside objects and the person on the inside meet like reflections. Thus, the puruṣa can experience the manifestations only through this cognition, which renders the senses cognizant and apprehends the objects that these perceive. These in turn are then known by the person and trigger his or her experiences of pleasure or pain. Cognition produces (4) identification,[1854] which stands for the basic mistaken tendency of the puruṣa to identify itself with the manifestations of the prakṛti, become entangled in them, and thus suffer. From this principle, the remaining twenty-one manifestations evolve. These are (5–9) the five "essential elements,"[1855] such as sound; (10–20) the eleven faculties; and (21–25) the five elements. The eleven "faculties" consist of (10–14) the five sense faculties, (15–19) the five physical faculties (speech, arms, legs, anus, genitalia), and (20) the mental faculty, or thinking.

According to the Enumerators, cyclic existence comes from the puruṣa's desire to enjoy objects, which perturbs the natural equilibrium of the primal substance and leads to all the various forms in which this manifests as objects. When one diminishes one's desire through cultivating the meditative concentrations of the form realm and the formless realm, one develops the divine eye. When this eye looks at the prakṛti, the individual realizes that the objects are nothing but illusory expressions of the primal substance. It is said that when the primal substance has been spotted in this way, it becomes embarrassed and all its manifestations merge back into it. Liberation is attained when these manifestations have ceased and the puruṣa remains alone.

This system was also adopted by Patañjali and his followers as the main philosophical foundation of the classic school of Yoga. In contrast to the nontheistic Sāṃkhyas, however, the followers of Patañjali assert the existence of Īśvara and that the manifestation of the phenomenal world depends on his intent.

**Vaiśeṣika** (Tib. bye brag pa), "Differentiators." The origins of the school reach back many centuries BCE. Its founder is considered to be Kaṇāda, who wrote the *Vaiśeṣikasūtra*. The school's system is a natural philosophy in the sense of a pluralistic realism. Its name indicates the view that diversity and not unity is at the heart of the universe. As elaborated in Praśastapāda's *Padārthadharmasaṃgraha* (sixth century CE, the main commentary on the *Vaiśeṣikasūtra*), the classic Vaiśeṣika system presents knowable objects in six categories: substance, quality, action, generality, particular, and inherence (later, a seventh—negation—was added). The first category is classified as ninefold: self, time, mental cognition, direction, space, earth, water, fire, and wind. All of these nine are considered to be ultimately existent. As for causation, it is maintained that the result inheres in the material cause. The self is described as unconscious and permanent. It exists in an all-pervading manner, since its qualities can be experienced. In its obscured state in saṃsāra, it has nine temporary qualities, the main one being consciousness. It is only through its possible association with consciousness that the self apprehends pleasure and suffering as its own experiences (pleasure and suffering are also considered material derivatives of the primal matter) . Through studying the scriptures, reflecting on them, and meditating on the true nature of the self, the self is able to rid itself of its nine specific qualities. In such a liberation, it not only transcends the world but even ceases to be the subject of any experience, even of itself. In addition, the school speaks of Īśvara as a permanent and omniscient creator-god who is also the author of the Vedas. However, unlike the Vedānta, his existence is established through inference and not through revelation.

**Vyākaraṇa** (Tib. brda sprod pa), "Grammarians." They are sometimes counted as a separate school of thought. However, they were not really propagating a full-fledged philosophical system. As their name indicates, the Grammarians were mainly concerned with linguistics and philosophy of language. The famous grammarian Bhartṛhari (about 460–520 CE) said that words are the fundamental ground of all things. Based on this view, it was especially the Grammarians' theories on the actual referents of words, on the connection between generalities and their instances, and on the related epistemological issues that influenced many of the other schools of thought.

## Heterodox Schools That Reject the Vedas

**Ājīvika** (Tib. kun tu 'tsho ba), "those who follow special rules with regard to livelihood." At the time of the Buddha, this school of wandering mendicants was led by Maskarī Gośālīputra, one of the six great non-Buddhist teachers of his time (he died in 501 BCE). First, he was a companion of Vardhamāna before the latter became the founder of Jainism. After they separated, Gośālīputra joined the Ājīvikas and eventually became their supreme head. The main doctrine of this school is a strict determinism. All beings are merely subject to their fixed destinies that make them experience various kinds of happiness and suffering. There is no room for karma and its results or salvific activity. For many eons, all beings—whether they are learned or fools—have to go through an individually set number of rebirths in the six realms of cyclic existence before they finally attain liberation. The more theoretical considerations in the teachings of Gośālīputra belong to the same philosophical stream as Jainism.

**Jaina** (Tib. rgyal ba pa), "Followers of the Victor." Its founder was Vardhamāna (born 557 BCE), called Nirgrantho Jñātaputra. He is better known as Mahāvīra ("Great Hero") and Jina ("Victor"), a name indicating someone who is victorious over the passions and has obtained mastery over the soul. In terms of his teachings, he is considered the last in a long row of gurus, called Tīrthakaras. In Buddhist texts, Jainists are often called Nirgrantha (literally "Those Free from Bondage," also interpreted as "The Nudes"). Originally, this name referred to the followers of Pārśva (eighth century BCE), in whose very ascetic tradition Jina grew up and which he continued, finally—like his parents—fasting to death (485 BCE). Within Jainism, the yogic practitioners who are wandering ascetics, smearing their bodies with ashes and walking about completely naked, are called Digambaras ("Sky-Clad Ones"). All other followers are named Śvetāmbaras ("White-Clad Ones"). The scriptural canon of Jainism—which includes the teachings of Mahāvīra—is vast but only transmitted by the latter group. Jainism stands somewhat between Buddhism and the Vedic schools. On the one hand, it rejects the authority of the Vedas and does not assert a supreme god. On the other hand, it believes in permanent souls[1856] and permanent matter. An infinite number of individual souls exist even in the smallest atoms of matter, which also explains the strict emphasis on complete nonviolence (Skt. ahiṃsā). The soul is the experiencer and agent. In itself, it is perfect as infinite intelligence, bliss, and power. However, the karma of physical, verbal, and mental activities—which is regarded as very subtle matter—infiltrates the soul and "weighs it down" to its union with a physical body in the gross material world of saṃsāra, which obscures its intrinsic qualities. Through various means, mainly meditative absorptions and ascetic practices, the soul may eventually be completely liberated from karma. At this point, it ascends to the highest point of space in the universe, where it then dwells in eternal bliss.

**Lokāyata** (Tib. 'jig rten rgyang 'phen pa), "MundanelyMinded;" also known as Nāstika (Tib. med pa pa, Nihilists) or Cārvākas (Tib. tshu rol mdzes pa pa, Hedonists/Materialists). Some say that the latter name comes from one of the main proponents of this school. It may also derive from *cāruvāka*, meaning "sweet-talker," since the Lokāyatas so eloquently advocate the mere concern with the pleasures of this life. The origins of this school are not clear, but it certainly was one of the oldest in India. None of its scriptures, however, have survived. It propounds a kind of materialistic hedonism that denies the existence of an eternal soul (ātman), causes and results that are not directly visible, as well as former and later lives. The body is said to be composed of the four elements, and mind to be just an epiphenomenon of matter. The only kind of valid cognition is sense perception, while inference is denied altogether. Its followers deny any consequences of one's actions. For them, there is no harm in killing or stealing and no merit in any spiritual practice either (thus their rejection of the Vedas). Consequently, they deny all moral values and emphasize enjoyment of the pleasures of this life. It is no wonder that such views were always closely connected to political philosophy—which was systematically developed in ancient India very early—and were strongly supported by the more ruthless rulers. In an attempt to base its teachings on scriptural authority, the school claims that its origins lie with Bṛhaspati, the accomplished guru of the gods and mythological founder of the philosophy of state. He is said to have composed the *Bṛhaspatisūtra* that was later propagated on earth by Vālmīki. Prominent materialists at the time of Buddha Śākyamuni were Pūraṇa Kāśyapa, Ajita Keśakambala, and Kakuda Kātyāyana.

# APPENDIX III:

## *Tibetan Text of the Ninth Chapter of the* Bodhicaryāvatāra

༡ །།ཡན་ལག་འདི་དག་ཐམས་ཅད་ནི། །ཐུབ་པས་ཤེས་རབ་དོན་དུ་གསུངས།
དེ་ཡི་ཕྱིར་ན་སྡུག་བསྔལ་དག །ཞི་བར་འདོད་པས་ཤེས་རབ་བསྐྱེད།

༢ །ཀུན་རྫོབ་དང་ནི་དོན་དམ་སྟེ། །འདི་ནི་བདེན་པ་གཉིས་སུ་འདོད།
།དོན་དམ་བློ་ཡི་སྤྱོད་ཡུལ་མིན། །བློ་ནི་ཀུན་རྫོབ་ཡིན་པར་བརྗོད།

༣ །དེ་ལ་འཇིག་རྟེན་རྣམ་གཉིས་མཐོང་། །རྣལ་འབྱོར་པ་དང་ཕལ་པའོ།
།དེ་ལ་འཇིག་རྟེན་ཕལ་པ་ནི། །རྣལ་འབྱོར་འཇིག་རྟེན་གྱིས་གནོད་ཅིང་།

༤ །རྣལ་འབྱོར་པ་ཡང་བློ་ཁྱད་ཀྱིས། །གོང་མ་གོང་མ་རྣམས་ཀྱིས་གནོད།
།གཉི་ག་ཡང་ནི་འདོད་པའི་དཔེས། །འབྲས་བུའི་དོན་དུ་མ་དཔྱད་ཕྱིར།

༥ །འཇིག་རྟེན་པ་ཡིས་དངོས་མཐོང་ཞིང་། །ཡང་དག་ཉིད་དུའང་རྟོག་བྱེད་ཀྱི།
།སྒྱུ་མ་ལྟ་བུར་མིན་པས་འདིར། །རྣལ་འབྱོར་པ་དང་འཇིག་རྟེན་རྩོད།

༦ །གཟུགས་སོགས་མངོན་སུམ་ཉིད་ཀྱང་ནི། །གྲགས་པས་ཡིན་གྱི་ཚད་མས་མིན།
།དེ་ནི་མི་གཙང་ལ་སོགས་ལ། །གཙང་སོགས་གྲགས་པ་བཞིན་དུ་བརྫུན།

༧ །འཇིག་རྟེན་གཞུག་པའི་དོན་དུ་ནི། །མགོན་པོས་དངོས་བསྟན་དེ་ཉིད་དུ།
།དེ་དག་སྐད་ཅིག་མ་ཉིད་མིན། །ཀུན་རྫོབ་ཏུ་ཡང་འགལ་ཞེ་ན།

༨ །རྣལ་འབྱོར་ཀུན་རྫོབ་ཉེས་མེད་དེ། །འཇིག་རྟེན་ལ་ལྟོས་དེ་ཉིད་མཐོང་།
།གཞན་དུ་བུད་མེད་མི་གཙང་བར། །ངེས་རྟོག་འཇིག་རྟེན་གྱིས་གནོད་འགྱུར།

༩ །སྒྱུ་འདྲའི་རྒྱལ་ལས་བསོད་ནམས་ནི། །ཇི་ལྟར་དངོས་ཡོད་ལ་ཇི་བཞིན།
།གལ་ཏེ་སེམས་ཅན་སྒྱུ་འདྲ་ན། །ཤི་ནས་ཇི་ལྟར་སྐྱེ་ཞེ་ན།

༡༠ །ཇི་སྲིད་རྐྱེན་རྣམས་འཚོགས་གྱུར་པ། །དེ་སྲིད་སྒྱུ་མའང་འབྱུང་བར་འགྱུར།
།རྒྱུན་རིང་ཙམ་གྱིས་ཇི་ལྟར་ན། །སེམས་ཅན་བདེན་པར་ཡོད་པ་ཡིན།

༡༡ །སྒྱུ་མའི་སྐྱེས་བུ་བསད་སོགས་ལ། །སེམས་མེད་ཕྱིར་ན་སྡིག་མེད་དེ།
།སྒྱུ་མའི་སེམས་དང་ལྡན་པ་ལ། །བསོད་ནམས་དང་ནི་སྡིག་པ་འབྱུང་།

༡༢ །སྔགས་སོགས་རྣམས་ལ་ནུས་མེད་ཕྱིར། །སྒྱུ་མའི་སེམས་ནི་འབྱུང་བ་མེད།
།སྣ་ཚོགས་རྐྱེན་ལས་བྱུང་བ་ཡི། །སྒྱུ་མ་དེ་ཡང་སྣ་ཚོགས་ཉིད།

༡༣ །རྐྱེན་གཅིག་གིས་ནི་ཀུན་ནུས་པ། །གང་ན་ཡང་ནི་ཡོད་མ་ཡིན།
།གལ་ཏེ་དོན་དམ་མྱ་ངན་འདས། །འཁོར་བ་ཀུན་རྫོབ་དེ་ལྟ་ན།

༡༤ །སངས་རྒྱས་ཀྱང་ནི་འཁོར་འགྱུར་བས། །བྱང་ཆུབ་སྤྱོད་པས་ཅི་ཞིག་བྱ།
།རྐྱེན་རྣམས་རྒྱུན་ནི་མ་ཆད་ན། །སྒྱུ་མའང་ལྡོག་པར་མི་འགྱུར་གྱི།

༡༥ །རྐྱེན་རྣམས་རྒྱུན་ནི་ཆད་པས་ན། །ཀུན་རྫོབ་ཏུ་ཡང་མི་འབྱུང་ངོ་།
།གང་ཚེ་འཁྲུལ་པའང་ཡོད་མིན་ན། །སྒྱུ་མ་གང་གིས་དམིགས་པར་འགྱུར།

༡༦ །གང་ཚེ་ཁྱོད་ལ་སྒྱུ་མ་ཉིད། །མེད་ནའང་དེ་ཚེ་ཅི་ཞིག་དམིགས།
།གལ་ཏེ་དེ་ཉིད་དུ་གཞན་ཡོད། །རྣམ་པ་དེ་ནི་སེམས་ཉིད་ཡིན།

༡༧ །གང་ཚེ་སེམས་ཉིད་སྒྱུ་མ་ན། །དེ་ཚེ་གང་ཞིག་གང་གིས་མཐོང་།
།འཇིག་རྟེན་གྱི་ནི་མགོན་པོས་ཀྱང་། །སེམས་ཀྱིས་སེམས་མི་མཐོང་ཞེས་གསུངས།

༡༨ །རལ་གྲི་སོ་ནི་རང་ལ་རང་། །ཇི་ལྟར་མི་གཅོད་དེ་བཞིན་ཡིད།
།ཇི་ལྟར་མར་མེ་རང་གི་དངོས། །ཡང་དག་གསལ་བར་བྱེད་བཞིན་ན།

༡༩ །མར་མེ་གསལ་བར་བྱ་མིན་ཏེ། །གང་ཕྱིར་མུན་གྱིས་བསྒྲིབས་པ་མེད།
།ཤེལ་བཞིན་སྔོན་པོ་སྔོ་ཉིད་ལ། །གཞན་ལ་ལྟོས་པ་ཡོད་མ་ཡིན།

༢༠ །དེ་བཞིན་འགའ་ཞིག་གཞན་ལ་ནི། །ལྟོས་དང་ལྟོས་མེད་པ་ཡང་མཐོང་།
།སྟོ་ཉིད་མིན་ལ་སྟོན་པར་དེ། །བདག་གིས་བདག་ཉིད་བྱས་པ་མེད།

༢༡ །མར་མེ་གསལ་བར་བྱེད་དོ་ཞེས། །ཤེས་པས་ཤེས་ཏེ་རྗོད་བྱེད་ན།
།བློ་ནི་གསལ་བ་ཉིད་ཡིན་ཞེས། །གང་གིས་ཤེས་ནས་དེ་སྐད་བརྗོད།

༢༢ །གང་ཚེ་འགས་ཀྱང་མཐོང་མིན་ན། །གསལ་བའམ་ནི་མི་གསལ་བ།
།མོ་གཤམ་བུ་མོའི་འགྱིང་བག་བཞིན། །དེ་ནི་བརྗོད་ཀྱང་དོན་མེད་དོ།

༢༣ །གལ་ཏེ་རང་རིག་ཡོད་མིན་ན། །རྣམ་ཤེས་དྲན་པར་ཇི་ལྟར་འགྱུར།
།གཞན་མྱོང་བ་ན་འབྲེལ་བ་ལས། །དྲན་འགྱུར་བྱི་བའི་དུག་བཞིན་ནོ།

༢༤ །རྐྱེན་གཞན་དག་དང་ལྡན་པ་ནི། །མཐོང་ཕྱིར་རང་ཉིད་རང་གསལ་ན།
།གྲུབ་པའི་མིག་སྨན་སྦྱོར་བ་ལས། །བུམ་མཐོང་མིག་སྨན་ཉིད་འགྱུར་མིན།

༢༥ །ཇི་ལྟར་མཐོང་ཐོས་ཤེས་པ་དག །འདིར་ནི་དགག་པར་བྱ་མིན་ཏེ།
།འདིར་ནི་སྡུག་བསྔལ་རྒྱུར་གྱུར་པ། །བདེན་པར་རྟོག་པ་བཟློག་བྱ་ཡིན།

༢༦ །སེམས་ལས་སྒྱུ་མ་གཞན་མིན་ཞིང་། །གཞན་མིན་པར་ཡང་མི་རྟག་ན།
།དངོས་ན་ཇི་ལྟར་དེ་གཞན་མིན། །གཞན་མིན་ཞེ་ན་དངོས་པོར་མེད།

༢༧ །ཇི་ལྟར་སྒྱུ་མ་བདེན་མིན་ཡང་། །བལྟ་བྱ་དེ་བཞིན་ལྟ་བྱེད་ཡིད།
།གལ་ཏེ་འཁོར་བ་དངོས་རྟེན་ཅན། །དེ་ནི་གཞན་དུ་མཁའ་འདྲར་འགྱུར།

༢༨ །དངོས་མེད་དངོས་ལ་བརྟེན་པས་ན། །བྱེད་དང་ལྡན་པར་ཇི་ལྟར་འགྱུར།
།ཁྱོད་ཀྱི་སེམས་ནི་གྲོགས་མེད་པ། །གཅིག་པུ་ཉིད་དུ་འགྱུར་བ་ཡིན།

༢༩ །གང་ཚེ་སེམས་ནི་གཟུང་བྲལ་བ། །དེ་ཚེ་ཐམས་ཅད་དེ་བཞིན་གཤེགས།
།དེ་ལྟ་ན་ཡང་སེམས་ཙམ་དུ། །བརྟགས་ལ་ཡོན་ཏན་ཅི་ཞིག་ཡོད།

༣༠ །སྒྱུ་མ་ལྟ་བུར་ཤེས་ན་ཡང་། །ཇི་ལྟར་ཉོན་མོངས་ལྡོག་འགྱུར་ཏེ།
།གང་ཚེ་སྒྱུ་མའི་བུད་མེད་ལ། །དེ་བྱེད་ཉིད་ཀྱང་ཆགས་སྐྱེ་འགྱུར།

༣༡ །དེ་བྱེད་པ་ནི་ཤེས་བྱ་ལ། །ཉོན་མོངས་བག་ཆགས་མ་སྤངས་པ།
།དེས་ན་དེ་མཐོང་བ་ན་དེ། །སྟོང་ཉིད་བག་ཆགས་ཉམ་ཆུང་ཉིད།

༣༢ །སྟོང་ཉིད་བག་ཆགས་གོམས་པས་ནི། །དངོས་པོའི་བག་ཆགས་སྤོང་འགྱུར་ཞིང་།
།ཅི་ཡང་མེད་ཅེས་གོམས་པས་ནི། །དེ་ཡང་ཕྱི་ནས་སྤོང་བར་འགྱུར།

༣༣ །གང་ཚེ་གང་ཞིག་མེད་དོ་ཞེས། །བརྟག་བྱའི་དངོས་པོ་མི་དམིགས་པ།
།དེ་ཚེ་དངོས་མེད་རྟེན་བྲལ་བ། །བློ་ཡི་མདུན་ན་ཇི་ལྟར་གནས།

༣༤ །གང་ཚེ་དངོས་དང་དངོས་མེད་དག །བློ་ཡི་མདུན་ན་མི་གནས་པ།
།དེ་ཚེ་རྣམ་པ་གཞན་མེད་པས། །དམིགས་པ་མེད་པར་རབ་ཏུ་ཞི།

༣༥ །ཡིད་བཞིན་ནོར་བུ་དཔག་བསམ་ཤིང་། །ཇི་ལྟར་རེ་བ་ཡོངས་སྐོང་བ།
།དེ་བཞིན་གདུལ་བྱ་སྨོན་ལམ་གྱི། །དབང་གིས་རྒྱལ་པོའི་སྐུར་སྣང་ངོ་།

༣༦ །དཔེར་ན་ནམ་མཁའ་ལྡིང་གི་ནི། །མཆོད་སྡོང་བསྒྲུབས་ནས་འདས་གྱུར་པ།
།དེ་འདས་ཡུན་རིང་ལོན་ཡང་དེ། །དུག་ལ་སོགས་པ་ཞི་བྱེད་བཞིན།

༣༧ །བྱང་ཆུབ་སྤྱོད་པའི་རྗེས་མཐུན་པས། །རྒྱལ་བའི་མཆོད་སྡོང་བསྒྲུབ་པ་ཡང་།
།བྱང་ཆུབ་སེམས་དཔའ་མྱ་ངན་ལས། །འདས་ཀྱང་དོན་རྣམས་ཐམས་ཅད་མཛད།

༣༨ །སེམས་མེད་པ་ལ་མཆོད་བྱས་པས། །ཇི་ལྟར་འབྲས་བུར་ལྡན་པར་འགྱུར།
།གང་ཕྱིར་བཞུགས་པའམ་མྱ་ངན་འདས། །མཚུངས་པ་ཉིད་དུ་བཤད་ཕྱིར་རོ།

༣༩ །ཀུན་རྫོབ་བམ་ནི་དེ་ཉིད་དུའང་། །རུང་སྟེ་དེར་འབྲས་ལུང་ལས་ཡིན།
།དཔེར་ན་བདེན་པའི་སངས་རྒྱས་ལ། །ཇི་ལྟར་འབྲས་བུར་བཅས་པ་བཞིན།

༤༠ །བདེན་པ་མཐོང་བས་གྲོལ་འགྱུར་གྱི། །སྟོང་ཉིད་མཐོང་བས་ཅི་ཞིག་བྱ།
།གང་ཕྱིར་ལུང་ལས་ལམ་འདི་ནི། །མེད་པར་བྱང་ཆུབ་མེད་པར་གསུངས།

༤༡ །གལ་ཏེ་ཐེག་ཆེན་མ་གྲུབ་ན། །ཁྱོད་ཀྱི་ལུང་ནི་ཇི་ལྟར་གྲུབ།
།གང་ཕྱིར་གཉིས་ཀ་ལ་འདི་གྲུབ། །དང་པོ་ཁྱོད་ལ་འདི་མ་གྲུབ།

༤༢ །རྒྱུན་གང་གིས་ནི་དེར་ཡིད་ཆེས། །དེ་ནི་ཐེག་ཆེན་ལ་ཡང་མཚུངས།
།གཞན་གཉིས་འདོད་པས་བདེན་ན་ནི། །རིག་བྱེད་སོགས་ཀྱང་བདེན་པར་འགྱུར།

༤༣ །ཐེག་ཆེན་རྩོད་བཅས་ཕྱིར་ཞེ་ན། །ལུང་ལ་མུ་སྟེགས་པ་རྣམས་དང་།
།ལུང་གཞན་ལ་ཡང་རང་གཞན་དག །རྩོད་བཅས་ཡིན་ཕྱིར་དོར་བར་འགྱུར།

༤༤ །བསྟན་རྩ་དགེ་སློང་ཉིད་ཡིན་ན། །དགེ་སློང་ཉིད་ཀྱང་དཀའ་བར་གནས།
།སེམས་ནི་དམིགས་དང་བཅས་རྣམས་ཀྱི། །མྱ་ངན་འདས་པའང་དཀའ་བར་གནས།

༤༥ །ཉོན་མོངས་སྤངས་པས་གྲོལ་ན་དེའི། །དེ་མ་ཐག་ཏུ་དེར་འགྱུར་རོ།
།ཉོན་མོངས་མེད་ཀྱང་དེ་དག་ལ། །ལས་ཀྱི་ནུས་པ་མཐོང་བ་ཡིན།

༤༦ །རེ་ཞིག་ཉེར་ལེན་སྲེད་པ་ནི། །མེད་ཅེས་ངེས་པ་ཉིད་ཅེ་ན།
།སྲེད་དེ་ཉོན་མོངས་ཅན་མིན་ཡང་། །ཀུན་རྨོངས་བཞིན་དུ་ཅི་སྟེ་མེད།

༤༧ །ཚོར་བའི་རྒྱུན་གྱིས་སྲིད་པ་ཡིན། །ཚོར་བ་དེ་དག་ལ་ཡང་ཡོད།
།དམིགས་པ་དང་ནི་བཅས་པའི་སེམས། །འགའ་ཞིག་ལ་ནི་གནས་པར་འགྱུར།

༤༨ །སྟོང་ཉིད་དང་ནི་བྲལ་བའི་སེམས། །འགགས་པ་སླར་ཡང་སྐྱེ་འགྱུར་ཏེ།
།འདུ་ཤེས་མེད་པའི་སྙོམས་འཇུག་བཞིན། །དེས་ན་སྟོང་ཉིད་བསྒོམ་པར་བྱ།

༤༩ །ངག་གང་མདོ་སྡེ་ལ་འཇུག་དེ། །གལ་ཏེ་སངས་རྒྱས་གསུངས་འདོད་ན།
།ཐེག་ཆེན་ཕལ་ཆེར་ཁྱེད་ཅག་གི །མདོ་དང་མཚུངས་འདོད་མིན་ནམ་ཅི།

༥༠ །གལ་ཏེ་མ་གཏོགས་གཅིག་གིས་ནི། །ཐམས་ཅད་སྐྱོན་དང་བཅས་འགྱུར་ན།
།མདོ་མཚུངས་གཅིག་གིས་ཐམས་ཅད་ནི། །རྒྱལ་བས་གསུངས་པ་ཅིས་མ་ཡིན།

༥༡ །ངག་གང་འོད་སྲུངས་ཆེན་པོ་ལ། །སོགས་པས་གཏིང་དཔོགས་མ་གྱུར་པ།
།དེ་ནི་ཁྱོད་ཀྱིས་མ་རྟོགས་པས། །གཟུང་བྱ་མིན་པར་སུ་ཞིག་བྱེད།

༥༢ །རྨོངས་པས་སྡུག་བསྔལ་ཅན་དོན་དུ། །ཆགས་དང་འཇིགས་མཐའ་ལས་གྲོལ་བ།
།འཁོར་བར་གནས་པ་གྲུབ་འགྱུར་བ། །འདི་ནི་སྟོང་ཉིད་འབྲས་བུ་ཡིན།

༥༣ །དེ་ལྟར་སྟོང་པ་ཉིད་ཕྱོགས་ལ། །སྐྱོན་འབྱིན་པ་ནི་འཐད་མ་ཡིན།
།དེས་ན་ཐེ་ཚོམ་མི་ཟ་བར། །སྟོང་པ་ཉིད་ནི་བསྒོམ་པར་བྱ།

༥༤ །ཉོན་མོངས་ཤེས་བྱའི་སྒྲིབ་པ་ཡི། །མུན་པའི་གཉེན་པོ་སྟོང་པ་ཉིད།
།མྱུར་དུ་ཐམས་ཅད་མཁྱེན་འདོད་པས། །དེ་ནི་ཇི་ལྟར་སྒོམ་མི་བྱེད།

༥༥ །དངོས་གང་སྡུག་བསྔལ་སྐྱེད་བྱེད་པ། །དེ་ལས་སྐྲག་པ་སྐྱེ་འགྱུར་ན།
།སྟོང་ཉིད་སྡུག་བསྔལ་ཞི་བྱེད་པ། །དེ་ལ་འཇིགས་པ་ཇི་ལྟར་སྐྱེ།

༥༦ །གལ་ཏེ་བདག་འགའ་ཡོད་ན་ནི། །ཅི་ཡང་རུང་ལས་འཇིགས་འགྱུར་ན།
།བདག་ཉིད་འགའ་ཡང་ཡོད་མིན་པས། །འཇིགས་པར་འགྱུར་བ་སུ་ཞིག་ཡིན།

༥༧ །སོ་དང་སྐྲ་སེན་བདག་མ་ཡིན། །བདག་ནི་རུས་པ་ཁྲག་མ་ཡིན།
།སྣབས་མིན་བད་ཀན་མ་ཡིན་ཏེ། །ཆུ་སེར་དང་ནི་རྣག་ཀྱང་མིན།

༥༨ །བདག་ནི་ཞག་དང་རྡུལ་མིན་ཏེ། །གློ་མཆིན་དག་ཀྱང་བདག་མ་ཡིན།
།ནང་ཁྲོལ་གཞན་ཡང་བདག་མིན་ཏེ། །བདག་ནི་ཕྱི་ས་གཅིན་མ་ཡིན།

༥༩ །ཤ་དང་པགས་པ་བདག་མིན་ཏེ། །དྲོད་དང་རླུང་ཡང་བདག་མ་ཡིན།
།བུ་ག་བདག་མིན་རྣམ་ཀུན་ཏུ། །རྣམ་ཤེས་དྲུག་ཀྱང་བདག་མ་ཡིན།

༦༠ །གལ་ཏེ་སྒྲ་ཡི་ཤེས་རྟག་ན། །ཐམས་ཅད་ཚེ་ན་སྒྲ་འཛིན་འགྱུར།
།ཤེས་བྱ་མེད་ན་ཅི་ཞིག་རིག །གང་གིས་ཤེས་པ་ཞེས་བརྗོད་བྱེད།

༦༡ །གལ་ཏེ་ཤེས་མེད་ཤེས་ཡིན་ན། །ཤིང་ཡང་ཤེས་པར་ཐལ་བར་འགྱུར།
།དེས་ན་ཤེས་བྱ་ཉེར་གནས་པ། །མེད་པར་ཤེས་པ་མེད་ཅེས་ངེས།

༦༢ །དེ་ཉིད་ཀྱིས་ནི་གཟུགས་ཤེས་ན། །དེ་ཚེ་ཐོས་པའང་ཅི་སྟེ་མིན།
།གལ་ཏེ་སྒྲ་མི་ཉེ་ཕྱིར་ན། །དེས་ན་དེ་ཡི་ཤེས་པའང་མེད།

༦༣ །སྒྲ་འཛིན་རང་བཞིན་གང་ཡིན་པ། །དེ་གཟུགས་འཛིན་པར་ཇི་ལྟར་འགྱུར།
།གཅིག་ནི་ཕ་དང་བུ་ཉིད་དུ། །བརྟགས་ཡིན་ཡང་དག་ཉིད་མིན་ཏེ།

༦༤ །འདི་ལྟར་སྙིང་སྟོབས་རྟུལ་དང་ནི། །མུན་པ་བུ་མིན་ཕ་ཡང་མིན།
།དེ་ནི་སྒྲ་འཛིན་དང་ལྡན་པའི། །རང་བཞིན་དུ་ནི་མཐོང་མ་ཡིན།

༦༥ །གར་མཁན་ལྟ་བུར་ཚུལ་གཞན་གྱིས། །དེ་ཉིད་མཐོང་ན་དེ་རྟག་མིན།
།གལ་ཏེ་ཚུལ་གཞན་དེ་ཉིད་ན། །གཅིག་ཉིད་དེ་ནི་སྔོན་མེད་གཅིག

༦༦ །གལ་ཏེ་ཚུལ་གཞན་བདེན་མིན་ན། །དེ་ཡི་རང་གི་རང་བཞིན་སྨྲོས།
།ཤེས་ཉིད་ཅེ་ན་དེ་ལྟ་ན། །སྐྱེས་ཀུན་གཅིག་ཏུ་ཐལ་བར་འགྱུར།

༦༧ །སེམས་པ་སེམས་མེད་དེ་དག་ཀྱང་། །གཅིག་འགྱུར་གང་ཕྱིར་ཡོད་ཉིད་མཚུངས།
།གང་ཚེ་བྱེ་བྲག་ཕྱིན་ཅི་ལོག །དེ་ཚེ་འདྲ་བའི་རྟེན་གང་ཡིན།

༦༨ །སེམས་མེད་པ་ཡང་བདག་མིན་ཏེ། །སེམས་མེད་ཉིད་ཕྱིར་བུམ་སོགས་བཞིན།
།འོན་ཏེ་སེམས་དང་ལྡན་པའི་ཕྱིར། །ཤེས་ན་མི་ཤེས་འཇིག་པར་ཐལ།

༦༩ །ཇི་སྟེ་བདག་ལ་འགྱུར་མེད་ན། །སེམས་པས་དེ་ལ་ཅི་ཞིག་བྱས།
།དེ་ལྟར་ཤེས་མེད་བྱ་བྲལ་བ། །ནམ་མཁའ་བདག་ཏུ་བྱས་པར་འགྱུར།

༧༠ །གལ་ཏེ་བདག་ནི་ཡོད་མིན་ན། །ལས་འབྲས་འབྲེལ་པ་རིགས་མིན་ཏེ།
།ལས་བྱས་ནས་ནི་ཞིག་པས་ན། །སུ་ཡིས་ལས་སུ་འགྱུར་ཞེ་ན།

༧༡ །བྱ་བ་འབྲས་གཞི་ཐ་དད་དང་། །དེ་བདག་བྱེད་པ་མེད་པར་ཡང་།
།ཡུ་བུ་གཉི་ག་ལ་གྲུབ་པས། །འདིར་བརྩད་དོན་མེད་མ་ཡིན་ནམ།

༧༢ །རྒྱུ་ལྡན་འབྲས་བུ་དང་བཅས་ཞེས། །མཐོང་བ་འདི་ནི་སྲིད་མ་ཡིན།
།རྒྱུད་གཅིག་ལ་ནི་བརྟེན་ནས་སུ། །བྱེད་པོ་སྤྱོད་པོ་ཞེས་བྱར་བསྟན།

༧༣ །འདས་དང་མ་འོངས་པ་ཡི་སེམས། །བདག་མིན་དེ་ནི་མེད་པའི་ཕྱིར།
།འོན་ཏེ་སྐྱེས་སེམས་བདག་ཡིན་ན། །དེ་ཞིག་ན་ཡང་བདག་མེད་དོ།

༧༤ །དཔེར་ན་ཆུ་ཤིང་སྡོང་པོ་དག །ཆ་ཤས་ཕྱེ་ན་འགའ་མེད་པ།
།དེ་བཞིན་རྣམ་པར་དཔྱད་པ་ཡིས། །བཙལ་ན་བདག་ཀྱང་ཡང་དག་མིན།

༧༥ །གལ་ཏེ་སེམས་ཅན་ཡོད་མིན་ན། །སུ་ལ་སྙིང་རྗེ་བྱ་ཞེ་ན།
།འབྲས་བུའི་དོན་དུ་ཁས་བླངས་པའི། །རྨོངས་པས་བརྟགས་པ་གང་ཡིན་པའོ།

༧༦ །སེམས་ཅན་མེད་འབྲས་སུ་ཡི་ཡིན། །བདེན་ཏེ་འོན་ཀྱང་རྨོངས་ལས་འདོད།
།སྡུག་བསྔལ་ཉེ་བར་ཞི་དོན་དུ། །འབྲས་བུའི་རྨོངས་པ་བཟློག་མི་བྱ།

༧༧ །སྡུག་བསྔལ་རྒྱུ་ཡི་ང་རྒྱལ་ནི། །བདག་ཏུ་རྨོངས་པས་འཕེལ་བར་འགྱུར།
།དེ་ལས་ཀྱང་བཟློག་མེད་ཅེ་ན། །བདག་མེད་བསྒོམ་པ་མཆོག་ཡིན་ནོ།

༧༨ །ལུས་ནི་རྐང་པ་བྱིན་པ་མིན། །བརླ་དང་རྐེད་པའང་ལུས་མ་ཡིན།
།ལྟོ་དང་རྒྱབ་ཀྱང་ལུས་མིན་ཏེ། །བྲང་དང་དཔུང་པའང་ལུས་མ་ཡིན།

༧༩ །རྩིབ་ལོགས་ལག་པའང་ལུས་མིན་ཏེ། །མཆན་ཁུང་ཕྲག་པའང་ལུས་མ་ཡིན།
།ནང་ཁྲོལ་རྣམས་ཀྱང་དེ་མིན་ལ། །མགོ་དང་མགྲིན་པའང་ལུས་མིན་ན།
།འདི་ལ་ལུས་ནི་གང་ཞིག་ཡིན།

༨༠ །གལ་ཏེ་ལུས་འདི་ཐམས་ཅད་ལ། །ཕྱོགས་རེ་ཡིས་ནི་གནས་གྱུར་ན།
།ཆ་རྣམས་ཆ་ལ་གནས་གྱུར་མོད། །དེ་རང་ཉིད་ནི་གང་ལ་གནས།

༨༡ །གལ་ཏེ་བདག་ཉིད་ཀུན་གྱི་ལུས། །ལག་སོགས་རྣམས་ལ་གནས་ན་ནི།
།ལག་སོགས་དེ་དག་ཇི་སྙེད་པ། །དེ་སྙེད་ཀྱི་ནི་ལུས་སུ་འགྱུར།

༨༢ །ཕྱི་དང་ནང་ན་ལུས་མེད་ན། །ཇི་ལྟར་ལག་སོགས་ལ་ལུས་ཡོད།
།ལག་སོགས་རྣམས་ལས་གཞན་མེད་ན། །དེ་ནི་ཇི་ལྟར་ཡོད་པ་ཡིན།

༨༣ །དེས་ན་ལུས་མེད་ལ་སོགས་ལ། །རྨོངས་པ་ཡིས་ནི་ལུས་བློར་འགྱུར།
།དབྱིབས་སུ་བཀོད་པའི་ཁྱད་པར་གྱིས། །ཐོ་ཡོར་ལ་ནི་མི་བློ་བཞིན།

༨༤ །ཇི་སྲིད་རྐྱེན་ཚོགས་དེ་སྲིད་དུ། །ལུས་ནི་སྐྱེས་བུ་ལྟར་སྣང་བ།
།དེ་བཞིན་ཇི་སྲིད་ལག་སོགས་ལ། །དེ་ཡོད་དེ་སྲིད་དེ་ལུས་སྣང་།

༨༥ །དེ་བཞིན་སོར་མོའི་ཚོགས་ཡིན་ཕྱིར། །ལག་པའང་གང་ཞིག་ཡིན་པར་འགྱུར།
།དེ་ཡང་ཚིགས་ཀྱི་ཚོགས་ཡིན་ཕྱིར། །ཚིགས་ཀྱང་རང་གི་ཆ་ཕྱེ་བས།

༨༦ །ཆ་ཡང་རྡུལ་དུ་ཕྱེ་བས་ཏེ། །རྡུལ་དེའང་ཕྱོགས་ཆའི་དབྱེ་བ་ཡིས།
།ཕྱོགས་དབྱེའཞག་ཆ་ཤས་དང་བྲལ་ཕྱིར། །མཁའ་བཞིན་དེས་ན་རྡུལ་ཡང་མེད།

༨༧ །དེ་ལྟར་རྨི་ལམ་ལྟ་བུ་ཡི། །གཟུགས་ལ་དཔྱོད་ལྡན་སུ་ཞིག་ཆགས།
།གང་ཚེ་དེ་ལྟར་ལུས་མེད་པ། །དེ་ཚེ་སྐྱེས་གང་བུད་མེད་གང་།

༨༨ །སྡུག་བསྔལ་དེ་ཉིད་དུ་ཡོད་ན། །ཅི་སྟེ་རབ་དགའ་ལ་མི་གནོད།
།བདེ་ན་མྱ་ངན་གདུང་སོགས་ལ། །ཞིམ་སོགས་ཅི་སྟེ་དགའ་མི་བྱེད།

༨༩ །སྟོབས་དང་ལྡན་པས་ཟིལ་མནན་ཕྱིར། །གལ་ཏེ་དེ་མྱོང་མ་ཡིན་ན།
།གང་ཞིག་ཉམས་མྱོང་བདག་ཉིད་མིན། །དེ་ནི་ཚོར་བ་ཇི་ལྟར་ཡིན།

༩༠ །སྡུག་བསྔལ་ཕྲ་མོ་ཉིད་དུ་ཡོད། །འདི་ཡི་རགས་པ་བསལ་མིན་ནམ།
།དེ་ནི་དེ་ལས་གཞན་དགའ་ཙམ། །ཞེ་ན་ཕྲ་ཉིད་དེ་ཡང་དེའི།

༩༡ །གལ་ཏེ་འགལ་རྐྱེན་སྐྱེས་པས་ན། །སྡུག་བསྔལ་སྐྱེས་པ་མིན་ན་ནི།
།ཚོར་བར་རྟོག་པ་མངོན་ཞེན་ཉིད། །ཡིན་ཞེས་བྱ་བར་གྲུབ་མིན་ནམ།

༩༢ །དེ་ཉིད་ཕྱིར་ན་འདི་ཡི་ནི། །གཉེན་པོ་རྣམ་དཔྱོད་འདི་བསྒོམ་སྟེ།
།རྣམ་བརྟགས་ཞིང་ལས་བྱུང་བ་ཡི། །བསམ་གཏན་རྣལ་འབྱོར་པ་ཡི་ཟས།

༩༣ །གལ་ཏེ་དབང་དོན་བར་བཅས་ན། །དེ་དག་གང་དུ་ཕྲད་པར་འགྱུར།
།བར་མེད་ན་ཡང་གཅིག་ཉིད་དེ། །གང་ཞིག་གང་དང་ཕྲད་པར་འགྱུར།

༩༤ །རྡུལ་ཕྲན་རྡུལ་ཕྲན་ལ་འཇུག་མེད། །དེ་ནི་སྐབས་མེད་མཉམ་པ་ཡིན།
།མ་ཞུགས་པ་ལ་འདྲེ་མེད་ཅིང་། །མ་འདྲེས་པ་ལ་ཕྲད་པ་མེད།

༩༥ །ཆ་མེད་པ་ལའང་ཕྲད་པ་ཞེས། །བྱ་བ་ཇི་ལྟར་འཐད་པར་འགྱུར།
།ཕྲད་པ་དང་ནི་ཆ་མེད་པར། །གལ་ཏེ་མཐོང་ན་བསྟན་པར་གྱིས།

༩༦ །རྣམ་ཤེས་ལུས་མེད་པ་ལ་ནི། །ཕྲད་པ་འཐད་པ་མ་ཡིན་ཉིད།
།ཚོགས་པའང་དངོས་པོ་མེད་ཕྱིར་ཏེ། །སྔར་ནི་ཇི་ལྟར་རྣམ་དཔྱད་བཞིན།

༩༧ །དེ་ལྟར་རིག་པ་ཡོད་མིན་ན། །ཚོར་བ་གང་ལས་འབྱུང་བར་འགྱུར།
།ངལ་འདི་ཅི་ཡི་དོན་དུ་ཡིན། །གང་གིས་གང་ལ་གནོད་པར་འགྱུར།

༩༨ །གང་ཚེ་ཚོར་པོ་འགའ་མེད་ཅིང་། །ཚོར་བའང་ཡོད་པ་མ་ཡིན་པ།
།དེ་ཚེ་གནས་སྐབས་འདི་མཐོང་ནས། །སྲེད་པ་ཅི་ཕྱིར་ལྡོག་མི་འགྱུར།

༩༩ །མཐོང་བའམ་ནི་རེག་པ་ཡང་། །རྨི་ལམ་སྒྱུ་འདྲའི་བདག་ཉིད་ཀྱིས།
།སེམས་དང་ལྷན་ཅིག་སྐྱེས་པའི་ཕྱིར། །ཚོར་བ་དེ་ཡིས་མཐོང་མ་ཡིན།

༡༠༠ །སྔར་དང་ཕྱི་མར་སྐྱེས་པས་ཀྱང་། །དྲན་པར་འགྱུར་གྱི་མྱོང་མ་ཡིན།
།རང་གིས་བདག་ཉིད་མྱོང་མིན་ལ། །གཞན་དག་གིས་ཀྱང་མྱོང་མ་ཡིན།

༡༠༡ །ཚོར་པོ་འགའ་ཡང་ཡོད་མིན་ཏེ། །དེས་ན་ཚོར་བ་དེ་ཉིད་མིན།
།དེ་ལྟར་བདག་མེད་ཚོགས་འདི་ལ། །འདི་ཡིས་ཅི་སྟེ་གནོད་པར་བྱ།

༡༠༢ །ཡིད་ནི་དབང་རྣམས་ལ་མི་གནས། །གཟུགས་སོགས་ལ་མིན་བར་ནའང་མིན།
།ནང་ཡང་སེམས་མིན་ཕྱི་མིན་ཞིང་། །གཞན་དུ་ཡང་ནི་རྙེད་མ་ཡིན།

༡༠༣ །གང་ཞིག་ལུས་མིན་གཞན་དུ་མིན། །འདྲེས་མིན་ལོགས་སུའང་འགར་མེད་པ།
།དེ་ནི་ཅུང་ཟད་མིན་དེའི་ཕྱིར། །སེམས་ཅན་རང་བཞིན་མྱ་ངན་འདས།

༡༠༤ །ཤེས་བྱ་ལས་སྔར་ཤེས་ཡོད་ན། །དེ་ནི་ཅི་ལ་དམིགས་ནས་སྐྱེ།
།ཤེས་དང་ཤེས་བྱ་ལྷན་ཅིག་ན། །དེ་ནི་ཅི་ལ་དམིགས་ནས་སྐྱེ།

༡༠༥ །འོན་ཏེ་ཤེས་བྱའི་ཕྱིས་ཡོད་ན། །དེ་ཚེ་ཤེས་པ་གང་ལས་སྐྱེ།
།དེ་ལྟར་ཆོས་རྣམས་ཐམས་ཅད་ཀྱི། །སྐྱེ་བ་རྟོགས་པར་འགྱུར་མ་ཡིན།

༡༠༦ །གལ་ཏེ་དེ་ལྟར་ཀུན་རྫོབ་མེད། །དེ་ལ་བདེན་གཉིས་ག་ལ་ཡོད།
།དེ་ཡང་ཀུན་རྫོབ་གཞན་གྱིས་ན། །སེམས་ཅན་མྱ་ངན་ག་ལ་འདའ།

༡༠༧ །འདི་ནི་གཞན་སེམས་རྣམ་རྟོག་སྟེ། །དེ་ནི་རང་གི་ཀུན་རྫོབ་མིན།
།ཕྱིས་དེ་ངེས་ན་དེ་ཡོད་དེ། །མིན་ན་ཀུན་རྫོབ་མེད་པ་ཉིད།

༡༠༨ །རྟོག་དང་བརྟག་པར་བྱ་བ་དང་། །གཉིས་པོ་ཕན་ཚུན་བརྟེན་པ་ཡིན།
།ཇི་ལྟར་གྲགས་པ་ལ་བརྟེན་ནས། །རྣམ་པར་དཔྱད་པ་ཐམས་ཅད་བརྗོད།

༡༠༩ །གང་ཚེ་རྣམ་པར་དཔྱད་པ་ཡི། །རྣམ་དཔྱོད་ཀྱིས་ནི་དཔྱོད་བྱེད་ན།
།དེ་ཚེ་རྣམ་དཔྱོད་དེ་ཡང་ནི། །རྣམ་དཔྱོད་ཕྱིར་ན་ཐུག་པ་མེད།

༡༡༠ །དཔྱད་བྱ་རྣམ་པར་དཔྱད་བྱས་ན། །རྣམ་དཔྱོད་ལ་ནི་རྟེན་ཡོད་མིན།
།རྟེན་མེད་ཕྱིར་ན་མི་སྐྱེ་སྟེ། །དེ་ཡང་མྱ་ངན་འདས་པར་བརྗོད།

༡༡༡ །གང་གི་ལྟར་ན་འདི་གཉིས་བདེན། །དེ་ཉིད་ཤིན་ཏུ་དཀའ་བར་གནས།
།གལ་ཏེ་ཤེས་དབང་ལས་དོན་གྲུབ། །ཤེས་ཡོད་ཉིད་ལ་རྟེན་ཅི་ཡོད།

༡༡༢ །འོན་ཏེ་ཤེས་བྱ་ལས་ཤེས་གྲུབ། །ཤེས་བྱ་ཡོད་ལ་རྟེན་ཅི་ཡོད།
།དེ་སྟེ་ཕན་ཚུན་དབང་གིས་ཡོད། །གཉི་ག་ཡང་ནི་མེད་པར་འགྱུར།

༡༡༣ །གལ་ཏེ་བུ་མེད་ཕ་མིན་ན། །བུ་ཉིད་གང་ལས་བྱུང་བ་ཡིན།
།བུ་མེད་པར་ནི་ཕ་མེད་པ། །དེ་བཞིན་དེ་གཉིས་མེད་པ་ཉིད།

༡༡༤ །མྱུ་གུ་ས་བོན་ལས་སྐྱེ་ཞིང་། །ས་བོན་དེ་ཉིད་ཀྱིས་རྟོགས་བཞིན།
།ཤེས་བྱ་ལས་སྐྱེས་ཤེས་པ་ཡིས། །དེ་ཡོད་པ་ནི་ཅིས་མི་རྟོགས།

༡༡༥ །མྱུ་གུ་ལས་གཞན་ཤེས་པ་ཡིས། །ས་བོན་ཡོད་ཅེས་རྟོགས་འགྱུར་ན།
།གང་ཕྱིར་ཤེས་བྱ་དེ་རྟོགས་པ། །ཤེས་པ་ཡོད་ཉིད་གང་ལས་རྟོགས།

༡༡༦ །རེ་ཞིག་འཇིག་རྟེན་མངོན་སུམ་གྱིས། །རྒྱུ་རྣམས་ཐམས་ཅད་མཐོང་བ་ཡིན།
།པདྨའི་སྡོང་བུ་སོགས་དབྱེ་ནི། །རྒྱུ་ཡི་དབྱེ་བས་བསྐྱེད་པ་ཡིན།

༡༡༧ །རྒྱུ་དབྱེ་གང་གིས་བྱས་ཞེ་ན། །སྔར་གྱི་རྒྱུ་དབྱེ་ཉིད་ལས་སོ།
།ཅི་ཕྱིར་རྒྱུ་ཡིས་འབྲས་སྐྱེད་ནུས། །སྔར་གྱི་རྒྱུ་ཡི་མཐུ་ཉིད་ལས།

༡༡༨ །དབང་ཕྱུག་འགྲོ་བའི་རྒྱུ་ཡིན་ན། །རེ་ཞིག་དབང་ཕྱུག་གང་ཡིན་སྨྲོས།
།འབྱུང་རྣམས་ཞེ་ན་དེ་ལྟ་མོད། །མིང་ཙམ་ལ་ཡང་ཅི་ཞིག་ངལ།

༡༡༩ །འོན་ཀྱང་ས་སོགས་དུ་མ་དང་། །མི་རྟག་གཡོ་མེད་ལྷ་མིན་ཞིང་།
།འགོམ་བྱ་ཉིད་དང་མི་གཙང་བས། །དེ་ནི་དབང་ཕྱུག་ཉིད་མ་ཡིན།

༡༢༠ །དབང་ཕྱུག་མཁའ་མིན་གཡོ་མེད་ཕྱིར། །བདག་མིན་སྔར་ནི་བཀག་ཟིན་ཕྱིར།
།བསམ་མིན་པ་ཡི་བྱེད་པོ་ཡང་། །བསམ་མིན་བརྗོད་པས་ཅི་ཞིག་བྱ།

༡༢༡ །དེས་བསྐྱེད་འདོད་པའང་གང་ཞིག་ཡིན། །བདག་ནི་དེ་དང་ས་སོགས་དང་།
།དབང་ཕྱུག་ངོ་བོའང་རྟག་མིན་ནམ། །ཤེས་པ་ཤེས་བྱ་ལས་སྐྱེ་དང་།

༡༢༢ །ཐོག་མེད་བདེ་སྡུག་ལས་ལས་ཡིན། །དེ་ཡིས་གང་ཞིག་བསྐྱེད་པ་སྨྲོས།
།རྒྱུ་ལ་ཐོག་མ་ཡོད་མིན་ན། །འབྲས་བུའི་ཐོག་མ་ག་ལ་ཡོད།

༡༢༣ །རྟག་ཏུ་ཅི་ཕྱིར་བྱེད་མིན་ཏེ། །དེ་ནི་གཞན་ལ་ལྟོས་པ་མིན།
།དེས་བྱས་མིན་གཞན་ཡོད་མིན་ན། །དེས་འདི་གང་ལ་ལྟོས་པར་འགྱུར།

༡༢༤ །གལ་ཏེ་ལྟོས་ན་ཚོགས་པ་ཉིད། །རྒྱུ་ཡིན་འགྱུར་གྱི་དབང་ཕྱུག་མིན།
།ཚོགས་ན་མི་སྐྱེ་དབང་མེད་ཅིང་། །དེ་མེད་པར་ནི་སྐྱེ་དབང་མེད།

༡༢༥ །གལ་ཏེ་དབང་ཕྱུག་མི་འདོད་བཞིན། །བྱེད་ན་གཞན་གྱི་དབང་དུ་ཐལ།
།འདོད་ནའང་འདོད་ལ་རག་ལས་འགྱུར། །བྱེད་ནའང་དབང་ཕྱུག་ག་ལ་ཡིན།

༡༢༦ །གང་དག་རྡུལ་ཕྲན་རྟག་སྨྲ་བ། །དེ་དག་ཀྱང་ནི་སྔར་བཟློག་ཟིན།
།གཙོ་བོ་རྟག་པ་འགྲོ་བ་ཡི། །རྒྱུ་ཡིན་པར་ནི་གྲངས་ཅན་འདོད།

༡༢༧ །སྙིང་སྟོབས་རྡུལ་དང་མུན་པ་ཞེས། །བྱ་བའི་ཡོན་ཏན་མཉམ་གནས་ནི།
།གཙོ་བོ་ཞེས་བྱར་རབ་བརྗོད་དེ། །མི་མཉམ་འགྲོ་བ་ཡིན་པར་བརྗོད།

༡༢༨ །གཅིག་ལ་རང་བཞིན་གསུམ་ཉིད་ནི། །རིགས་མིན་དེས་ན་དེ་ཡོད་མིན།
།དེ་བཞིན་ཡོན་ཏན་ཡོད་མིན་ཏེ། །དེ་ཡང་སོ་སོར་རྣམ་གསུམ་ཕྱིར།

༡༢༩ །ཡོན་ཏན་མེད་ན་སྒྲ་སོགས་ཀྱང་། །ཡོད་ཉིད་ཤིན་ཏུ་རྒྱང་རིང་འགྱུར།
།སེམས་མེད་གོས་ལ་སོགས་པ་ལ། །བདེ་སོགས་ཡོད་པ་སྲིད་པའང་མིན།

༡༣༠ །དངོས་རྣམས་དེ་རྒྱུའི་རང་བཞིན་ན། །དངོས་པོ་རྣམ་དཔྱད་མ་ཟིན་ནམ།
།ཁྱོད་ཀྱི་རྒྱུ་ཡང་བདེ་སོགས་ཉིད། །དེ་ལས་སྣམ་སོགས་འབྱུང་བའང་མེད།

༡༣༡ །སྣམ་སོགས་ལས་ནི་བདེ་སོགས་ཡིན། །དེ་མེད་ཕྱིར་ན་བདེ་སོགས་མེད།
།བདེ་སོགས་རྟག་པ་ཉིད་དུ་ཡང་། །ནམ་ཡང་དམིགས་པ་ཡོད་མ་ཡིན།

༡༣༢ །བདེ་སོགས་གསལ་བ་ཡོད་ཉིད་ན། །མྱོང་བ་ཅི་ཕྱིར་འཛིན་མ་ཡིན།
།དེ་ཉིད་ཕྲ་མོར་གྱུར་ན་དེ། །རགས་དང་ཕྲ་བའང་ཇི་ལྟར་ཡིན།

༡༣༣ །རགས་པ་དོར་ནས་ཕྲ་གྱུར་པས། །ཕྲ་རགས་དེ་དག་མི་རྟག་ཉིད།
།དེ་བཞིན་དངོས་པོ་ཐམས་ཅད་ནི། །མི་རྟག་ཉིད་དུ་ཅིས་མི་འདོད།

༡༣༤ །རགས་པ་བདེ་ལས་གཞན་མིན་ན། །བདེ་བ་གསལ་བ་མི་རྟག་ཉིད།
།གལ་ཏེ་མེད་པ་འགའ་ཡང་ནི། །སྐྱེ་མིན་མེད་ཕྱིར་ཞེས་འདོད་ན།

༡༣༥ །གསལ་བ་མེད་པ་སྐྱེ་བར་ནི། །ཁྱོད་མི་འདོད་ཀྱང་གནས་པ་ཉིད།
།གལ་ཏེ་རྒྱུ་ལ་འབྲས་གནས་ན། །ཟན་ཟ་མི་གཙང་ཟ་བར་འགྱུར།

༡༣༦ །རས་ཀྱི་རིན་གྱིས་རས་བལ་གྱི། །ས་བོན་ཉོས་ལ་བགོ་བར་གྱིས།
།འཇིག་རྟེན་རྨོངས་པས་མ་མཐོང་ན། །དེ་ཉིད་ཤེས་ཀྱིས་བཞག་དེ་ཉིད།

༡༣༧ །ཤེས་དེ་འཇིག་རྟེན་ལ་ཡང་ནི། །ཡོད་པས་ཅི་སྟེ་མཐོང་མ་ཡིན།
།འཇིག་རྟེན་ཚད་མ་ཉིད་མིན་ན། །གསལ་བ་མཐོང་བའང་བདེན་མ་ཡིན།

༡༣༨ །གལ་ཏེ་ཚད་མ་ཚད་མིན་ན། །དེས་གཞལ་བརྫུན་པར་མི་འགྱུར་རམ།
།དེ་ཉིད་དུ་ན་སྟོང་པ་ཉིད། །སྒོམ་པ་དེ་ཕྱིར་མི་འཐད་འགྱུར།

༡༣༩ །བརྟགས་པའི་དངོས་ལ་མ་རེག་པར། །དེ་ཡི་དངོས་མེད་འཛིན་མ་ཡིན།
།དེ་ཕྱིར་བརྫུན་པའི་དངོས་གང་ཡིན། །དེ་ཡི་དངོས་མེད་གསལ་བར་བརྫུན།

༡༤༠ །དེས་ན་རྨི་ལམ་བུ་ཤི་ལ། །དེ་མེད་སྙམ་པའི་རྣམ་རྟོག་ནི།
།དེ་ཡོད་རྣམ་པར་རྟོག་པ་ཡི། །གེགས་ཡིན་དེ་ཡང་བརྫུན་པ་ཡིན།

༡༤༡ །དེ་བས་དེ་ལྟར་རྣམ་དཔྱད་པས། །འགའ་ཡང་རྒྱུ་མེད་ཡོད་མ་ཡིན།
།སོ་སོ་བའམ་འདུས་པ་ཡི། །རྐྱེན་རྣམས་ལ་ཡང་གནས་མ་ཡིན།

༡༤༢ །གཞན་ནས་འོངས་པའང་མ་ཡིན་ལ། །གནས་པ་མ་ཡིན་འགྲོ་མ་ཡིན།
།རྨོངས་པས་བདེན་པར་གང་བྱས་འདི། །སྒྱུ་མ་ལས་ནི་ཁྱད་ཅི་ཡོད།

༡༤༣ །སྒྱུ་མས་སྤྲུལ་པ་གང་ཡིན་དང་། །རྒྱུ་རྣམས་ཀྱིས་ནི་གང་སྤྲུལ་པ།
།དེ་ནི་གང་ནས་འོངས་གྱུར་ཅིང་། །གང་དུ་འགྲོ་བའང་བརྟག་པར་གྱིས།

༡༤༤ །གང་ཞིག་གང་ནི་ཉེ་བ་ཡིས། །མཐོང་གྱུར་དེ་མེད་ན་མིན་པ།
།བཅོས་བུ་གཟུགས་བརྙན་དང་མཚུངས་པ། །དེ་ལ་བདེན་ཉིད་ཇི་ལྟར་ཡོད།

༡༤༥ །དངོས་པོ་ཡོད་པར་གྱུར་པ་ལ། །རྒྱུ་ཡིས་དགོས་པ་ཅི་ཞིག་ཡོད།
།འོན་ཏེ་དེ་ནི་མེད་ན་ཡང་། །རྒྱུ་ཡིས་དགོས་པ་ཅི་ཞིག་ཡོད།

༡༤༦ །བྱེ་བ་བརྒྱ་ཕྲག་རྒྱུ་ཡིས་ཀྱང་། །དངོས་པོ་མེད་པ་བསྒྱུར་དུ་མེད།
།གནས་སྐབས་དེ་དངོས་ཇི་ལྟར་ཡིན། །དངོས་འགྱུར་གཞན་ཡང་གང་ཞིག་ཡིན།

༡༤༧ །མེད་ཚེ་དངོས་ཡོད་སྲིད་མིན་ན། །དངོས་པོ་ཡོད་པར་ནམ་ཞིག་འགྱུར།
།དངོས་པོ་སྐྱེས་པར་མ་གྱུར་པར། །དངོས་མེད་དེ་ནི་འབྲལ་མི་འགྱུར།

༡༤༨ །དངོས་མེད་དང་ནི་མ་བྲལ་ན། །དངོས་པོ་ཡོད་པའི་སྐབས་མི་སྲིད།
།དངོས་པོའང་མེད་པར་འགྱུར་མིན་ཏེ། །རང་བཞིན་གཉིས་སུ་ཐལ་འགྱུར་ཕྱིར།

༡༤༩ །དེ་ལྟར་འགག་པ་ཡོད་མིན་ཞིང་། །དངོས་པོའང་ཡོད་མིན་དེ་ཡི་ཕྱིར།
།འགྲོ་བ་འདི་དག་ཐམས་ཅད་ནི། །རྟག་ཏུ་མ་སྐྱེས་མ་འགགས་ཉིད།

༡༥༠ །འགྲོ་བ་རྨི་ལམ་ལྟ་བུ་སྟེ། །རྣམ་པར་དཔྱད་ན་ཆུ་ཤིང་འདྲ།
།མྱ་ངན་འདས་དང་མ་འདས་པའང་། །དེ་ཉིད་དུ་ན་ཁྱད་པར་མེད།

༡༥༡ །དེ་ལྟར་སྟོང་པའི་དངོས་རྣམས་ལ། །ཐོབ་པ་ཅི་ཡོད་ཤོར་ཅི་ཡོད།
།གང་གིས་རིམ་གྲོ་བྱས་པའམ། །ཡོངས་སུ་བརྙས་པའང་ཅི་ཞིག་ཡོད།

༡༥༢ །བདེ་བའང་སྡུག་བསྔལ་གང་ལས་ཡིན། །མི་དགར་ཅི་ཡོད་དགར་ཅི་ཡོད།
།དེ་ཉིད་དུ་ནི་བཙལ་བྱས་ན། །གང་ཞིག་སྲེད་ཅིང་གང་ལ་སྲེད།

༡༥༣ །དཔྱད་ན་གསོན་པོའི་འཇིག་རྟེན་འདི། །གང་ཞིག་འདིར་ནི་འཆི་འགྱུར་ཏེ།
།འབྱུང་འགྱུར་གང་ཡིན་བྱུང་གྱུར་གང་། །གཉེན་དང་བཤེས་ཀྱང་གང་ཞིག་ཡིན།

༡༥༤ །ཐམས་ཅད་ནམ་མཁའ་འདྲ་བར་ནི། །བདག་འདྲས་ཡོངས་སུ་གཟུང་བར་གྱིས།
།བདག་ཉིད་བདེ་བར་འདོད་རྣམས་ནི། །འཐབ་དང་སྤྲོ་བའི་རྒྱུ་དག་གིས།

༡༥༥ །རབ་ཏུ་འཁྲུག་དང་དགའ་བར་བྱེད། །མྱ་ངན་འབད་རྩོལ་རྩོད་པ་དང་།
།ཕན་ཚུན་གཅོད་དང་འབིགས་པ་དང་། །སྡིག་དག་གིས་ནི་ཚེགས་ཆེན་འཚོ།

༡༥༦ །བདེ་འགྲོར་ཡང་དང་ཡང་འོངས་ཏེ། །བདེ་བ་མང་པོ་སྤྱད་སྤྱད་ནས།
།ཤི་ནས་ངན་སོང་སྡུག་བསྔལ་ནི། །ཡུན་རིང་མི་བཟད་རྣམས་སུ་ལྷུང་།

༡༥༧ །སྲིད་པ་ན་ནི་གཡང་ས་མང་། །དེར་ནི་དེ་ཉིད་མིན་འདི་འདྲ།
།དེར་ཡང་ཕན་ཚུན་འགལ་བས་ན། །སྲིད་ན་དེ་ཉིད་འདི་འདྲ་མེད།

༡༥༨ །དེ་ཡང་དཔེ་མེད་མི་བཟད་པའི། །སྡུག་བསྔལ་རྒྱ་མཚོ་མཐའ་ལས་འདས།
།དེར་ནི་དེ་ལྟར་སྟོབས་ཆུང་ཞིང་། །དེར་ནི་ཚེ་ཡང་ཐུང་བ་ཉིད།

༡༥༩ །དེར་ཡང་གསོན་དང་ནད་མེད་ཀྱི། །བྱེད་དང་བཀྲེས་ནའི་ངལ་བ་དང་།
།གཉིད་དང་འཚེ་དང་དེ་བཞིན་དུ། །བྱིས་དང་འགྲོགས་པ་དོན་མེད་ཀྱིས།

༡༦༠ །ཚེ་ནི་དོན་མེད་མྱུར་འདའ་ཡི། །རྣམ་དཔྱོད་ཤིན་ཏུ་རྙེད་པར་དཀའ།
།དེར་ཡང་རྣམ་གཡེང་གོམས་པ་ནི། །བཟློག་པའི་ཐབས་ནི་ག་ལ་ཡོད།

༡༦༡ །དེར་ཡང་ངན་སོང་ཆེན་པོར་ནི། །ལྷུང་ཕྱིར་བདུད་ནི་བརྩོན་པར་བྱེད།
།དེར་ནི་ལོག་པའི་ལམ་མང་ཞིང་། །ཐེ་ཚོམ་ལས་ཀྱང་བརྒལ་དཀའ་སྟེ།

༡༦༢ །སླར་ཡང་དལ་བ་རྙེད་དཀའ་ཞིང་། །སངས་རྒྱས་འབྱུང་རྙེད་ཤིན་ཏུ་དཀའ།
།ཉོན་མོངས་ཆུ་བོ་སྤང་དཀའ་སྟེ། །ཨེ་མ་སྡུག་བསྔལ་བརྒྱུད་པར་གྱུར།

༡༦༣ །དེ་ལྟར་ཤིན་ཏུ་སྡུག་བསྔལ་ཡང་། །རང་སྡུག་མི་མཐོང་གང་ཡིན་པ།
།སྡུག་བསྔལ་ཆུ་བོར་གནས་འདི་དག །ཀྱི་ཧུད་མྱ་ངན་བྱ་བར་འོས།

༡༦༤ །དཔེར་ན་འགའ་ཞིག་ཡང་ཡང་ཁྲུས། །བྱས་ཏེ་ཡང་ཡང་མེར་འཇུག་པ།
།དེ་ལྟར་ཤིན་ཏུ་སྡུག་བསྔལ་བར། །གནས་ཀྱང་བདག་ཉིད་བདེར་རློམ་བཞིན།

༡༦༥ །དེ་ལྟར་རྒ་དང་འཆི་མེད་པ། །བཞིན་དུ་སྤྱོད་པས་གནས་རྣམས་ལ།
།དང་པོ་ཉིད་དུ་སད་བྱས་ནས། །ངན་སོང་ལྟུང་བ་མི་བཟད་འོང་།

༡༦༦ །དེ་ལྟར་སྡུག་བསྔལ་མེས་གདུངས་ལ། །བསོད་ནམས་སྤྲིན་ལས་ལེགས་འཁྲུངས་པའི།
།རང་གི་བདེ་བའི་ཚོགས་ཆར་གྱིས། །ཞི་བྱེད་པར་བདག་ནམ་ཞིག་འགྱུར།

༡༦༧ །ནམ་ཞིག་དམིགས་པ་མེད་ཚུལ་དུ། །གུས་པས་བསོད་ནམས་ཚོགས་བསགས་ཏེ།
།དམིགས་པས་ཕུང་བར་འགྱུར་རྣམས་ལ། །སྟོང་པ་ཉིད་ནི་སྟོན་པར་འགྱུར།

།བྱང་ཆུབ་སེམས་དཔའི་སྤྱོད་པ་ལ་འཇུག་པ་ལས། །ཤེས་རབ་ཀྱི་ཕ་རོལ་ཏུ་ཕྱིན་པའི་ལེའུ་སྟེ་དགུ་པའོ།།
(computer-generated edition input by *Nitartha International Document Input Center, Kathmandu, Nepal*)

# GLOSSARY

## *English–Sanskrit–Tibetan*

| English | Sanskrit | Tibetan |
| --- | --- | --- |
| absence of mental engagement | manasikārābhāva | yid la byed pa med pa |
| acknowledged as commonly appearing to both | ubhayasiddhatva | gnyis ka la mthun snang du grub pa |
| adventitious stain | āgantukamala | glo bur gyi dri ma |
| afflicted ignorance | kliṣṭāvidyā | nyon mongs can gyi ma rig pa |
| afflicted phenomenon | saṃkleśa | kun nas nyon mongs pa |
| affliction | kleśa | nyon mongs |
| afflictive obscuration | kleṣāvaraṇa | nyon mongs pa'i sgrib pa |
| aggregate | skandha | phung po |
| alertness | saṃprajanya | shes bzhin |
| analogous applicability of the opponent's reason | *tulyahetu | rgyu mtshan mtshungs pa'i mgo snyoms |
| analogy | upamāṇa | dpe nyer 'jal |
| analytical meditation | — | dpyad sgom |
| Analyzer | Mīmāṃsaka | dpyod pa pa |
| Aspectarian | sākāravādin | rnam bcas pa |
| Autonomist | *svātantrika | rang rgyud pa |
| autonomous | svatantra | rang rgyud |
| awareness | vidyā | rig pa |
| awareness of something other | *anyavedana | gzhan rig |
| awareness of the lack of nature | *niḥsvabhāvavedana | rang bzhin med par rig pa |
| basic element | dhātu | khams |
| basis of emptiness | — | stong gzhi |
| basis of negation | — | dgag gzhi |
| Blissfully Gone One | sugata | bde bzhin gshegs pa |
| Body of Complete Enjoyment | saṃbhogakāya | longs spyod rdzogs pa'i sku |
| calm abiding | śamatha | zhi gnas |
| causal condition | hetupratyaya | rgyu rkyen |

| | | |
|---|---|---|
| Centrism | madhyamaka | dbu ma |
| Centrist | mādhyamika | dbu ma pa |
| clinging | abhiniveśa, graha(na) | mngon zhen, 'dzin pa |
| clinging to reality/real existence | *satyagrahaṇa | bden 'dzin |
| cognition | buddhi | blo |
| cognitive obscuration | jñeyāvaraṇa | shes bya'i sgrib pa |
| common worldly consensus | lokaprasiddha | 'jig rten gyi grags pa |
| complete change of state | āśrayaparivṛtti | gnas yongs su gyur pa |
| completion stage | saṃpannakrama | rdzogs rim |
| conception | kalpanā, vikalpa | rtog pa, rnam rtog |
| conditioned (phenomenon) | saṃskṛta | 'dus byas |
| consciousness | (vi)jñāna | (rnam par) shes pa |
| consequence that exposes contradictions | *virodhacodanāprasaṅga | 'gal ba brjod pa'i thal 'gyur |
| Consequentialist | *prāsaṅgika | thal 'gyur pa |
| constituent | dhātu | khams |
| contradictory reason | viruddhahetu | 'gal ba'i gtan tshigs |
| contraposition of a consequence | prasaṅgaviparyaya | thal 'gyur blzog pa |
| convention(al) | vyavahāra | tha snyad |
| creation stage | utpattikrama | bskyed rim |
| definitive meaning | nītārtha | nges don |
| denial | apavāda | skur 'debs |
| dependent origination | pratītyasamutpāda | rten cing 'brel bar 'byung ba |
| Dharma Body | dharmakāya | chos kyi sku |
| Differentiator | Vaiśeṣika | bye brag pa |
| discriminating knowledge | pratisaṃkhyāprajñā | so sor rtog pa'i shes rab |
| discursiveness | prapañca | spros pa |
| dominant condition | adhipatipratyaya | bdag rkyen |
| Emanation Body | nirmāṇakāya | sprul sku |
| emptiness endowed with the supreme of all aspects | sarvākāravaropetāśūnyatā | rnam kun mchog ldan gyi stong pa nyid |
| emptiness in the sense of extinction | — | chad pa'i stong pa nyid |
| emptiness of analyzing all aspects | sarvākāravicāraśūnyatā | rnam kun rnam dpyad kyi stong pa nyid |
| emptiness of one not existing in an other | itaretaraśūnyatā | gcig gis gcig stong pa nyid |
| entailment | vyāpti | khyab pa |
| entity | bhāva/vastu | dngos po |
| Enumerator | Sāṃkhya | grangs can pa |

| | | |
|---|---|---|
| Essence Body | svabhāvakāya | ngo bo nyid kyi sku |
| established through conventional valid cognition | — | tha snyad tshad grub |
| established through its own, specific characteristics | lakṣaṇasiddha | rang gi mtshan nyid kyis grub pa |
| expanse of dharmas | dharmadhātu | chos kyi dbyings |
| expedient meaning | neyārtha | drang don |
| False Aspectarian | alīkākāravādin | rnam brdzun pa |
| false imagination | abhūtaparikalpa | yang dag ma yin kun rtog |
| five-membered probative argument | pañcāvayavavākya | ngag yan lag lnga ldan |
| Follower of the Great Exposition | vaibhāṣika | bye brag smra ba |
| order | tīrthika | mu stegs pa |
| Form Body | rūpakāya | gzugs kyi sku |
| four realities of the noble ones | caturāryasatya | 'phags pa'i bden pa bzhi |
| four reliances | catvāri pratisaraṇāni | rton pa bzhi |
| fourfold application of mindfulness | catuḥ smṛtyupasthāna | dran pa nye bar bzhag pa bzhi |
| freedom from discursiveness | niṣprapañca | spros bral |
| generally characterized (phenomenon) | sāmānyalakṣaṇa | spyi mtshan |
| Grammarian | vyākaraṇa | brda sprod pa |
| Great Perfection | mahāsandhi | rdzogs pa chen po |
| Great Seal | mahāmudrā | phyag rgya chen po |
| ground consciousness | ālayavijñāna | kun gzhi'i rnam shes |
| hearer | śrāvaka | nyan thos |
| Heart of the Blissfully Gone Ones | sugatagarbha | bde gshegs snying po |
| heterologous set | vipakṣa | mi mthun phyogs |
| homologous set | sapakṣa | mthun phyogs |
| identity | ātman | bdag |
| identitylessness | nairātmya | bdag med |
| imaginary (nature) | parikalpita (svabhāva) | kun brtags (kyi rang bzhin) |
| immediate condition | samanantarapratyaya | de ma thag rkyen |
| implicative negation | paryudāsapratiṣedha | ma yin dgag |
| imputedly existent | prajñaptisat | btags yod |
| inference acknowledged by others | *paraprasiddhānumāna | gzhan grags kyi rjes dpag |
| inference for oneself | svārthānumāna | rang don rjes dpag |
| inference for others | parārthānumāna | gzhan don rjes dpag |
| inferential valid cognition | anumāṇapramāṇa | rjes dpag tshad ma |
| infinitesimal particle | paramāṇu | rdul phra rab, rdul phran |

| | | |
|---|---|---|
| innate | sahaja | lhan skyes |
| intention | abhisaṃdhi, abhiprāya | dgongs pa |
| isolate | vyatireka | ldog pa |
| knowable object | jñeya | shes bya |
| (supreme) knowledge | prajñā | shes rab |
| knowledge of termination and nonarising | kṣayānutpattijñāna | zad dang mi skye shes pa |
| latent tendency | vāsanā | bag chags |
| limited emptiness | prādeśikaśūnyatā | nyi tshe ba'i stong pa nyid |
| lineage of profound view | — | zab mo lta rgyud |
| lineage of vast activity | — | rgya chen spyod rgyud |
| Logician | naiyāyika | rigs pa can pa |
| meditative absorption without discrimination | asaṃjñisamāpatti 'jug | 'du shes med pa'i snyoms |
| meditative equipoise | samāhita | mnyam bzhag |
| mental consciousness | manovijñāna | yid kyi rnam shes |
| mental nonengagement | amanasikāra | yid la mi byed pa |
| mentally contrived emptiness | — | blos byas kyi stong pa nyid |
| mere cognizance | vijñaptimātra | rnam rig tsam |
| Mere Mentalist | — | sems tsam pa |
| mere mind (Mere Mentalism) | cittamātra | sems tsam |
| mind of enlightenment | bodhicitta | byang chub kyi sems |
| mindfulness | smṛti | dran pa |
| mode of apprehension | — | 'dzin stangs |
| Mundanely Minded | lokāyata | 'jig rten rgyang 'phen pa |
| naturally abiding disposition | prakṛtisthagotra | rang bzhin gnas rigs |
| nature | svabhāva | rang bzhin/ngo bo nyid |
| nature of phenomena | dharmatā | chos nyid |
| nature reason | svabhāvahetu | rang bzhin gyi gtan tshigs |
| negative determination | viccheda | rnam bcad |
| negative entailment | vyatirekavyāpti | ldog khyab |
| nirvāṇa with remainder | sāvaśeṣanirvāṇa | lhag bcas myang 'das |
| nirvāṇa without remainder | nirupadhiśeṣanirvāṇa | lhag med myang 'das |
| nominal ultimate | paryāyaparamārtha | rnam grangs pa'i don dam |
| nonabiding nirvāṇa | apratiṣṭitanirvāṇa | mi gnas pa'i mya ngan las 'das pa |
| nonapplication of the means of proof due to presupposing the probandum | *sādhyasādhana-samāsiddha | sgrub byed bsgrub bya dang mtshungs pa'i ma grub pa |
| nonapplying reason | asiddhahetu | ma grub pa'i gtan tshigs |

| | | |
|---|---|---|
| Non-Aspectarian | nirākāravādin | rnam med pa |
| nonconceptual wisdom | nirvikalpajñāna | rnam par mi rtog pa'i ye shes |
| nondual wisdom | advayajñāna | gnyis med ye shes |
| nonentity | abhāva/avastu | dngos med |
| nonimplicative negation | prasajyapratiṣedha | med dgag |
| nonnominal ultimate | aparyāyaparamārtha | rnam grangs ma yin pa'i don dam |
| nonobservation | anupalabdhi, anupalambha | mi dmigs pa |
| nonreferential | anupalambha, anālambana | mi dmigs pa, dmigs med |
| object condition | ālambanapratyaya | dmigs rkyen |
| object generality | arthasāmānya | don spyi |
| object of negation | pratiṣedhya | dgag bya |
| object of negation through reasoning | — | rigs pa'i dgag bya |
| object of negation through the path | — | lam gyi dgag bya |
| other-dependent (nature) | paratantra(svabhāva) | gzhan dbang (gi rang bzhin) |
| other-empty | — | gzhan stong |
| perceptual valid cognition | pratyakṣapramāṇa | mngon sum tshad ma |
| perfect (nature) | pariniṣpanna(svabhāva) | yongs grub (kyi rang bzhin) |
| perfection | pāramitā | pha rol tu phyin pa |
| personal identitylessness | pudgalanairātmya | gang zag gi bdag med |
| personally experienced (wisdom) | pratyātmavedanīya(jñāna) (svapratyātmāryajñāna) | so so rang rig (pa'i ye shes) |
| phenomenal identitylessness | dharmanairātmya | chos kyi bdag med |
| philosophical system | siddhānta | grub mtha' |
| position | pratijñā | dam bca' |
| positive determination | pariccheda | yongs gcod |
| positive entailment | anvayavyāpti | rjes khyab |
| predicate of what is to be negated | pratiṣedhyadharma | dgag bya'i chos |
| predicate of what is to be proven | sādhyadharma | bsgrub bya'i chos |
| probandum | sādhya | bsgrub bya |
| probative argument | prayoga(vākya) | sbyor ba('i ngag) |
| Proponent of Cognizance | vijñaptivādin | rnam rig smra ba |
| Proponent of Illusionlike Nonduality | māyopamādvayavādin | sgyu ma lta bu gnyis med smra ba/sgyu ma rigs grub smra ba |
| proponent of (outer) referents | arthavādin | don smra ba |

| | | |
|---|---|---|
| Proponent of the Complete Nonabiding of all Phenomena | sarvadharmāpra-tiṣṭhānavādin | chos thams cad rab tu mi gnas par smra ba |
| Proponent of the Lack of Nature | niḥsvabhāvavādin | ngo bo nyid med par smra ba |
| purified phenomenon | vyavadāna | rnam par byang ba |
| Real Aspectarian | satyākāravādin | rnam bden pa |
| realist | vastusatpadārthavādin | dngos po (yod pa)r smra ba |
| reality | satya | bden pa |
| reason of nonobservation | anupalabdhihetu | mi dmigs pa'i rtags |
| reason with an unestablished basis | āśrayāsiddho hetu | gzhi ma grub pa'i gtan tshigs |
| reasoning of dependent origination | pratītyasamutpādanyāya | rten 'brel gyi rigs pa |
| reasoning of the freedom from unity and multiplicity | ekānekaviyogahetu | gcig du bral gyi gtan tshigs |
| reasoning that negates arising from the four possibilities | catuṣkoṭyutpāda-pratiṣedhahetu | mu bzhi skye 'gog gi gtan tshigs |
| reasoning that negates arising of existents and nonexistents | *sadasadutpāda-pratiṣedhahetu | yod med skye 'gog gi gtan tshigs |
| reference point | prapañca | spros pa |
| reification | bhāvagrāha | dngos 'dzin |
| resting meditation | — | 'jog sgom |
| result reason | kāryahetu | 'bras bu'i gtan tshigs |
| reversed meaning of a consequence | prasaṅgaviparītārtha | thal 'gyur bzlog pa'i don |
| seeming (reality) | saṃvṛti(satya) | kun rdzob (bden pa) |
| self-aware(ness) | svasaṃvedana, svasaṃvitti | rang rig |
| self-empty | — | rang stong |
| solitary realizer | pratyekabuddha | rang rgyal, rang sangs rgyas |
| source | āyatana | skye mched |
| specifically characterized (phenomenon) | svalakṣaṇa | rang mtshan |
| sphere | gocara | spyod yul |
| subject (of debate) | dharmin | chos can |
| subject property | pakṣadharmatā/-tva | phyogs chos |
| subsequent attainment | pṛṣṭhalabdha | rjes thob |
| substantially existent | dravyasat | rdzas yod |
| superimposition | samāropa | sgro 'dogs |
| superior insight | vipaśyanā | lhag mthong |
| Sūtra Follower | sautrāntika | mdo sde pa |
| system founder | — | shing rta srol 'byed |

| | | |
|---|---|---|
| term generality | śabdasāmānya | sgra spyi |
| tetralemma | catuṣkoṭi | mu bzhi |
| thesis | pakṣa | phyogs |
| thesis with an unestablished basis | asiddhādhāraḥ pakṣa | gzhi ma grub pa'i phyogs |
| thirty-seven dharmas that concord with enlightenment | saptatriṃśadbodhi-pakṣadharma | byang chub phyogs chos gsum bcu so bdun |
| three modes | trairūpya, trirūpa | tshul gsum |
| three natures | trisvabhāva | ngo bo nyid/rang bzhin gsum |
| three spheres | trimaṇḍala | 'khor gsum |
| Thus-Gone One | tathāgata | de bzhin gshegs pa |
| true reality | tattva | de (kho na) nyid |
| ultimate reality | paramārthasatya | don dam bden pa |
| unafflicted ignorance | akliṣṭāvidyā | nyon mongs can ma yin pa'i ma rig pa |
| uncertain reason | anaikāntikahetu | ma nges pa'i gtan tshigs |
| unconditioned (phenomenon) | asaṃskṛta | 'dus ma byas |
| unestablished subject | āśrayāsiddha | (chos can) gzhi ma grub pa |
| unity | yuganaddha | zung 'jug |
| vajra sliver reasoning | vajrakaṇahetu | rdo rje gzegs ma'i gtan tshigs |
| vajralike meditative concentration | vajropamasamādhi | rdo rje lta bu'i ting nge 'dzin |
| valid cognition | pramāṇa | tshad ma |
| valid cognition that operates through the power of (real) entities | vastubalapravṛttānumāna | dngos po stobs zhugs kyi tshad ma |
| verbal testimony | śabda | sgra |
| views about a real personality | satkāyadṛṣṭi | 'jig tshogs la lta ba |
| what is to be negated | pratiṣedhya | dgag bya |
| what is to be proven | sādhya | bsgrub bya |
| wisdom | jñāna | ye shes |
| Yoga Practice (Yoga Practitioner) | yogācāra | rnal 'byor spyod pa |
| yogic valid perception | yogipratyakṣapramāṇa | rnal 'byor mngon sum tsha ma |

# GLOSSARY

## *Tibetan–Sanskrit–English*

| Tibetan | Sanskrit | English |
|---|---|---|
| kun brtags (kyi rang bzhin) | parikalpita(svabhāva) | imaginary (nature) |
| kun nas nyon mongs pa | saṃkleśa | afflicted phenomenon |
| kun rdzob (bden pa) | saṃvṛti(satya) | seeming (reality) |
| kun gzhi'i rnam shes | ālayavijñāna | ground consciousness |
| skur 'debs | apavāda | denial |
| skye mched | āyatana | source |
| bskyed rim | utpattikrama | creation stage |
| khams | dhātu | constituent, basic element |
| khyab pa | vyāpti | entailment |
| 'khor gsum | trimaṇḍala | three spheres |
| gang zag gi bdag med | pudgalanairātmya | personal identitylessness |
| grangs can pa | Sāṃkhya | Enumerator |
| grub mtha' | siddhānta | philosophical system |
| glo bur gyi dri ma | āgantukamala | adventitious stains |
| dgag bya | pratiṣedhya | object of negation, what is to be negated |
| dgag bya'i chos | pratiṣedhyadharma | predicate of what is to be negated |
| dgag gzhi | — | basis of negation |
| dgongs pa | abhisaṃdhi, abhiprāya | intention |
| 'gal ba brjod pa'i thal 'gyur | *virodhacodanāprasaṅga | consequence that exposes contradictions |
| 'gal ba'i gtan tshigs | viruddhahetu | contradictory reason |
| rgya chen spyod rgyud | — | lineage of vast activity |
| rgyu rkyen | hetupratyaya | causal condition |
| sgyu ma lta bu gnyis med smra ba/sgyu ma rigs grub smra ba | māyopamādvayavādin | Proponent of Illusionlike Nonduality |
| rgyu mtshan mtshungs pa'i mgo snyoms | *tulyahetu | analogous applicability of the opponent's reason |
| sgra | śabda | verbal testimony |

| | | |
|---|---|---|
| sgra spyi | śabdasāmānya | term generality |
| sgrub byed bsgrub bya dang mtshungs pa'i ma grub pa | *sādhyasādhana-samāsiddha | nonapplication of the means of proof due to presupposing the probandum |
| sgro 'dogs | samāropa | superimposition |
| bsgrub bya | sādhya | probandum, what is to be proven |
| bsgrub bya'i chos | sādhyadharma | predicate of what is to be proven |
| ngag yan lag lnga ldan | pañcāvayavavākya | five-membered probative argument |
| nges don | nītārtha | definitive meaning |
| ngo bo nyid | svabhāva | nature |
| ngo bo nyid kyi sku | svabhāvakāya | Essence Body |
| ngo bo nyid med par smra ba | niḥsvabhāvavādin | Proponent of the Lack of Nature |
| dngos po | bhāva/vastu | entity |
| dngos po stobs zhugs kyi tshad ma | vastubalapravṛttānumāna | valid cognition that operates through the power of (real) entities |
| dngos po (yod pa)r smra ba | vastusatpadārthavādin | realist |
| dngos med | abhāva/avastu | nonentity |
| dngos 'dzin | bhāvagrāha | reification |
| mngon zhen | abhiniveśa | clinging |
| mngon sum tshad ma | pratyakṣapramāṇa | perceptual valid cognition |
| gcig gis gcig stong pa nyid | itaretaraśūnyatā | emptiness of one not existing in an other |
| gcig du bral gyi gtan tshigs | ekānekaviyogahetu | reasoning of the freedom from unity and multiplicity |
| chad pa'i stong pa nyid | — | emptiness in the sense of extinction |
| chos kyi sku | dharmakāya | Dharma Body |
| chos kyi bdag med | dharmanairātmya | phenomenal identitylessness |
| chos kyi dbyings | dharmadhātu | expanse of dharmas |
| chos can | dharmin | subject (of debate) |
| chos nyid | dharmatā | nature of phenomena |
| chos thams cad rab tu mi gnas par smra ba | sarvadharmā-pratiṣṭhānavādin | Proponent of the Complete Nonabiding of all Phenomena |
| 'jig rten gyi grags pa | lokaprasiddha | common worldly consensus |
| 'jig rten rgyang 'phen pa | lokāyata | Mundanely Minded |

| | | |
|---|---|---|
| 'jig tshogs la lta ba | satkāyadṛṣṭi | views about a real personality |
| 'jog sgom | — | resting meditation |
| rjes khyab | anvayavyāpti | positive entailment |
| rjes thob | pṛṣṭhalabdha | subsequent attainment |
| rjes dpag tshad ma | anumāṇapramāṇa | inferential valid cognition |
| nyan thos | śrāvaka | hearer |
| nyi tshe ba'i stong pa nyid | prādeśikaśūnyatā | limited emptiness |
| nyon mongs | kleśa | affliction |
| nyon mongs can gyi ma rig pa | kliṣṭāvidyā | afflicted ignorance |
| nyon mongs can ma yin pa'i ma rig pa | akliṣṭāvidyā | unafflicted ignorance |
| nyon mongs pa'i sgrib pa | kleṣāvaraṇa | afflictive obscuration |
| gnyis ka la mthun snang du grub pa | ubhayasiddhatva | acknowledged as commonly appearing to both |
| gnyis med ye shes | advayajñāna | nondual wisdom |
| mnyam bzhag | samāhita | meditative equipoise |
| btags yod | prajñaptisat | imputedly existent |
| rten cing 'brel bar 'byung ba | pratītyasamutpāda | dependent origination |
| rten 'brel gyi rigs pa | pratītyasamutpādanyāya | reasoning of dependent origination |
| rtog pa | kalpanā | conception |
| rton pa bzhi | catvāri pratisaraṇāni | four reliances |
| stong gzhi | — | basis of emptiness |
| tha snyad | vyavahāra | convention(al) |
| tha snyad tshad grub | — | established through conventional valid cognition |
| thal 'gyur pa | *prāsaṅgika | Consequentialist |
| thal 'gyur blzog pa | prasaṅgaviparyaya | contraposition of a consequence |
| thal 'gyur bzlog pa'i don | prasaṅgaviparītārtha | reversed meaning of a consequence |
| mthun phyogs | sapakṣa | homologous set |
| dam bca' | pratijñā | position |
| de (kho na) nyid | tattva | true reality |
| de ma thag rkyen | samanantarapratyaya | immediate condition |
| de bzhin gshegs pa | tathāgata | Thus-Gone One |
| don dam bden pa | paramārthasatya | ultimate reality |
| don spyi | arthasāmānya | object generality |

| | | |
|---|---|---|
| don smra ba | arthavādin | proponent of (outer) referents |
| drang don | neyārtha | expedient meaning |
| dran pa | smṛti | mindfulness |
| dran pa nye bar bzhag pa bzhi | catuḥ smṛtyupasthāna | fourfold application of mindfulness |
| bdag | ātman | identity |
| bdag rkyen | adhipatipratyaya | dominant condition |
| bdag med | nairātmya | identitylessness |
| bde bzhin gshegs pa | sugata | Blissfully Gone One |
| bde gshegs snying po | sugatagarbha | Heart of the Blissfully Gone Ones |
| bden pa | satya | reality |
| bden 'dzin | *satyagrahaṇa | clinging to reality/ real existence |
| mdo sde pa | sautrāntika | Sūtra Follower |
| 'du shes med pa'i snyoms 'jug | asaṃjñisamāpatti | meditative absorption without discrimination |
| 'dus byas | saṃskṛta | conditioned (phenomenon) |
| 'dus ma byas | asaṃskṛta | unconditioned (phenomenon) |
| rdul phra rab | paramāṇu | infinitesimal particle |
| rdo rje lta bu'i ting nge 'dzin | vajropamasamādhi | vajralike meditative concentration |
| rdo rje gzegs ma'i gtan tshigs | vajrakaṇahetu | vajra sliver reasoning |
| ldog khyab | vyatirekavyāpti | negative entailment |
| ldog pa | vyatireka | isolate |
| brda sprod pa | vyākaraṇa | Grammarian |
| gnas yongs su gyur pa | āśrayaparivṛtti | complete change of state |
| rnam kun mchog ldan gyi stong pa nyid | sarvākāravaropetāśūnyatā | emptiness endowed with the supreme of all aspects |
| rnam kun rnam dpyad kyi stong pa nyid | sarvākāravicāraśūnyatā | emptiness of analyzing all aspects |
| rnam grangs pa'i don dam | paryāyaparamārtha | nominal ultimate |
| rnam grangs ma yin pa'i don dam | aparyāyaparamārtha | nonnominal ultimate |
| rnam bcad | viccheda | negative determination |
| rnam bcas pa | sākāravādin | Aspectarian |
| rnam rtog | vikalpa | conception |
| rnam bden pa | satyākāravādin | Real Aspectarian |
| rnam par byang ba | vyavadāna | purified phenomenon |

| | | |
|---|---|---|
| rnam par mi rtog pa'i ye shes | nirvikalpajñāna | nonconceptual wisdom |
| rnam par shes pa | vijñāna | consciousness |
| rnam med pa | nirākāravādin | Non-Aspectarian |
| rnam brdzun pa | alīkākāravādin | False Aspectarian |
| rnam rig smra ba | vijñaptivādin | Proponent of Cognizance |
| rnam rig tsam | vijñaptimātra | mere cognizance |
| rnal 'byor mngon sum tshad ma | yogipratyakṣapramāṇa | yogic valid perception |
| rnal 'byor spyod pa | yogācāra | Yoga Practice (Practitioner) |
| dpe nyer 'jal | upamāṇa | analogy |
| dpyad sgom | — | analytical meditation |
| dpyod pa pa | Mīmāṃsaka | Analyzer |
| spyi mtshan | sāmānyalakṣaṇa | generally characterized (phenomenon) |
| spyod yul | gocara | sphere |
| sprul sku | nirmāṇakāya | Emanation Body |
| spros pa | prapañca | discursiveness, reference point |
| spros bral | niṣprapañca | freedom from discursiveness/reference points |
| pha rol tu phyin pa | pāramitā | perfection |
| phung po | skandha | aggregates |
| phyag rgya chen po | mahāmudrā | Great Seal |
| phyogs | pakṣa | thesis |
| phyogs chos | pakṣadharmatā/-tva | subject property |
| 'phags pa'i bden pa bzhi | caturāryasatya | four realities of the noble ones |
| bag chags | vāsanā | latent tendency |
| byang chub kyi sems | bodhicitta | mind of enlightenment |
| byang chub phyogs chos sum cu so bdun | saptatriṃśadbodhipakṣadharma | thirty-seven dharmas that concord with enlightenment |
| bye brag pa | Vaiśeṣika | Differentiator |
| bye brag smra ba | vaibhāṣika | Follower of the Great Exposition |
| blo | buddhi | cognition |
| blos byas kyi stong pa nyid | — | mentally contrived emptiness |
| dbu ma | madhyamaka | Centrism |
| dbu ma pa | mādhyamika | Centrist |
| 'bras bu'i gtan tshigs | kāryahetu | result reason |

| | | |
|---|---|---|
| sbyor ba('i ngag) | prayoga(vākya) | probative argument |
| ma grub pa'i gtan tshigs | asiddhahetu | nonapplying reason |
| ma nges pa'i gtan tshigs | anaikāntikahetu | uncertain reason |
| ma yin dgag | paryudāsapratiṣedha | implicative negation |
| mi mthun phyogs | vipakṣa | heterologous set |
| mi gnas pa'i mya ngan las 'das pa | apratiṣṭitanirvāṇa | nonabiding nirvāṇa |
| mi dmigs pa | anupalabdhi, anupalambha | nonobservation, nonreferential |
| mi dmigs pa'i rtags | anupalabdhihetu | reason of nonobservation |
| mu stegs pa | tīrthika | forder |
| mu bzhi | catuṣkoṭi | tetralemma |
| mu bzhi skye 'gog gi gtan tshigs | catuṣkoṭyutpāda-pratiṣedhahetu | reasoning that negates arising from the four possibilities |
| med dgag | prasajyapratiṣedha | nonimplicative negation |
| dmigs rkyen | ālambanapratyaya | object condition |
| dmigs med | anupalambha, anupalabdhi | nonreferential, nonobservation |
| tshad ma | pramāṇa | valid cognition |
| tshul gsum | trairūpya, trirūpa | three modes |
| 'dzin stangs | — | mode of apprehension |
| 'dzin pa | graha(na) | apprehending, clinging |
| rdzas yod | dravyasat | substantially existent |
| rdzogs pa chen po | mahāsandhi | Great Perfection |
| rdzogs rim | saṃpannakrama | completion stage |
| zhi gnas | śamatha | calm abiding |
| gzhan grags kyi rjes dpag | *paraprasiddhānumāna | inference acknowledged by others |
| gzhan stong | — | other-empty |
| gzhan don rjes dpag | parārthānumāna | inference for others |
| gzhan dbang (gi rang bzhin) | paratantra(svabhāva) | other-dependent (nature) |
| gzhan rig | *anyavedana | awareness of something other |
| gzhi ma grub pa | āśrayāsiddha | unestablished subject |
| gzhi ma grub pa'i gtan tshigs | āśrayāsiddho hetu | reason with an unestablished basis |
| gzhi ma grub pa'i phyogs | asiddhādhāraḥ pakṣa | thesis with an unestablished basis |
| zad dang mi skye shes pa | kṣayānutpattijñāna | knowledge of termination and nonarising |
| zab mo lta rgyud | — | lineage of profound view |

| | | |
|---|---|---|
| zung 'jug | yuganaddha | unity |
| gzugs kyi sku | rūpakāya | Form Body |
| yang dag ma yin kun rtog | abhūtaparikalpa | false imagination |
| yid kyi rnam shes | manovijñāna | mental consciousness |
| yid la byed pa med pa | manasikārābhāva | absence of mental engagement |
| yid la mi byed pa | amanasikāra | mental nonengagement |
| ye shes | jñāna | wisdom |
| yongs grub (kyi rang bzhin) | pariniṣpanna(svabhāva) | perfect (nature) |
| yongs gcod | pariccheda | positive determination |
| yod med skye 'gog gi gtan tshigs | *sadasadutpāda-pratiṣedhahetu | reasoning that negates arising of existents and nonexistents |
| rang gi mtshan nyid kyis grub pa | lakṣaṇasiddha | established through its own, specific characteristics |
| rang rgyud | svatantra | autonomous |
| rang rgyud pa | *svātantrika | Autonomist |
| rang stong | — | self-empty |
| rang don rjes dpag | svārthānumāna | inference for oneself |
| rang mtshan | svalakṣaṇa | specifically characterized (phenomenon) |
| rang bzhin | svabhāva | nature |
| rang bzhin gyi gtan tshigs | svabhāvahetu | nature reason |
| rang bzhin gnas rigs | prakṛtisthagotra | naturally abiding disposition |
| rang bzhin med par rig pa | *niḥsvabhāvavedana | awareness of the lack of nature |
| rang bzhin gsum | trisvabhāva | three natures |
| rang rig | svasaṃvedana, svasaṃvitti | self-aware(ness) |
| rang sangs rgyas | pratyekabuddha | solitary realizer |
| rig pa | vidyā | awareness |
| rigs pa can pa | naiyāyika | Logician |
| rigs pa'i dgag bya | — | object of negation through reasoning |
| lam gyi dgag bya | — | object of negation through the path |
| longs spyod rdzogs pa'i sku | saṃbhogakāya | Body of Complete Enjoyment |
| shing rta srol 'byed | — | system founder |
| shes bya | jñeya | knowable object |
| shes bya'i sgrib pa | jñeyāvaraṇa | cognitive obscuration |

| | | |
|---|---|---|
| shes bzhin | saṃprajanya | alertness |
| shes rab | prajñā | (supreme) knowledge |
| sems tsam | cittamātra | mere mind (Mere Mentalism) |
| sems tsam pa | — | Mere Mentalist |
| so so rang rig (pa'i ye shes) | pratyātmavedanīya(jñāna) (svapratyātmāryajñāna) | personally experienced (wisdom) |
| so sor rtog pa'i shes rab | pratisaṃkhyāprajñā | discriminating knowledge |
| lhag bcas myang 'das | sāvaśeṣanirvāṇa | nirvāṇa with remainder |
| lhag mthong | vipaśyanā | superior insight |
| lhag med myang 'das | nirupadhiśeṣanirvāṇa | nirvāṇa without remainder |
| lhan skyes | sahaja | innate |

# *Bibliography*

## Abbreviations

| | |
|---|---|
| ACIP | Electronic files of the Asian Classics Input Project (www.acip.org) |
| AS | Asiatische Studien |
| IHQ | Indian Historical Quarterly |
| IIJ | Indo-Iranian Journal |
| JIABS | Journal of the International Association for Buddhist Studies |
| JIBS | Journal of Indian and Buddhist Studies (Indogaku Bukkyōgakku Kenkyū) |
| JIP | Journal of Indian Philosophy |
| LTWA | Library of Tibetan Works and Archives |
| P | Tibetan Tripitaka, Peking Edition. Tokyo-Kyoto: Suzuki Research Foundation, 1956 |
| PEW | Philosophy East and West |
| T | A Complete Catalogue of the Tibetan Buddhist Canons. Tohoku Imperial University, 1934 |
| Taisho | Taisho shinshu dai zokyo (The Chinese Buddhist Canon). Ed. J. Takakusu, K. Watanabe, et al. Tokyo: Taisho Issaikyo Kankokai, 1924-1932 |
| TJ | The Tibet Journal |
| WZKS | Wiener Zeitschrift für die Kunde Südasiens |

## Canonical Works[1857]


Anonymous. (possibly Dānaśīla). *Commentary on the Difficult Points in the Exposition of The Entrance to the Bodhisattva's Way of Life.* (Bodhisattvacaryāvatāravivṛttipañjikā. Byang chub sems dpa'i spyod pa la 'jug pa'i rnam par bshad pa'i dka' 'grel). P5274. ACIP TD3873.

——. *Commentary on the Difficult Points of the Knowledge Chapter.* (Prajñāparicchedapañjikā. Shes rab le'u'i dka' 'grel). Commentary on chapter 9. P5278. ACIP TD3876.

——. *Exposition of (the Difficult Points of the Knowledge and Dedication Chapters of) The Entrance to the Bodhisattva's Way of Life.* (P: Bodhisattvacaryāvatāravivṛtti. Byang chub sems dpa'i spyod pa la 'jug pa'i rnam par bshad pa. T: Bodhisattvacaryāvatāraprajñāparicchedaparinṇamapañjikā. Byang chub sems dpa'i spyod pa la 'jug pa'i shes rab le'u dang bsngo ba'i dka' 'grel). Extract from P5274 on chapters 9 and 10. P5279. ACIP TD3877.

Āryadeva. *The Compendium of the Heart of Wisdom.* (Jñānasarasamucchaya. Ye shes snying po kun las btus pa). P5251. ACIP TD3851.

——. *Four Hundred Verses on the Yogic Practice of Bodhisattvas.* (Bodhisattvayogacarācatuḥśataka. Byang chub sems dpa'i rnal 'byor spyod pa bzhi brgya pa). Sanskrit edition by K. Lang (1986). P5246. ACIP TD3846.

Asaṅga. *Commentary on The Sūtra That Unravels the Intention.* (Āryasaṃdhinirmocanabhāṣya. 'Phags pa dgongs pa nges par 'grel pa'i rnam bshad). P5481.

——. *The Compendium of Abhidharma.* (Abhidharmasamucchaya. Mngon pa kun btus). P5550.

——. *Exposition of The Sublime Continuum.* (Ratnagotravibhāgavyākhyā or Mahāyānottaratantraśāstravyākhyā. Theg pa chen po'i rgyud bla ma'i bstan bcos rnam par bshad pa). Sanskrit ed. by E. H. Johnston. Patna: Bihar Research Society, 1950. P5526.

——. *The Grounds of Yoga Practice.* (Yogācārabhūmi. Rnal 'byor spyod pa'i sa). P5536–8. ACIP TD4035.

——. *The Synopsis of Ascertainment.* (Viniścayasaṃgrahaṇī. Gtan la dbab pa bsdu ba). P5539. ACIP TD4038-1

——. *The Synopsis of the Great Vehicle.* (Mahāyānasaṃgraha. Theg chen bsdus pa). P5549.

Asvabhāva. *Explanation of The Synopsis of the Great Vehicle.* (Mahāyānasaṃgrahopanibandhana. Theg chen bsdus pa'i bshad sbyar). P5552.

Aśvaghoṣa. *The Stages of Meditation on the Ultimate Mind of Enlightenment.* (Paramārthabodhicittabhāvanākrama. Don dam byang sems sgom pa'i rim pa). P5308/5341.

Atīśa. *Centrist Pith Instructions.* (Madhyamakopadeśa. Dbu ma'i man ngag). P5324/5381.

——. *The Centrist Pith Instructions Called The Open Jewel Casket.* (Ratnakaraṇḍodghātanāmamadhyamakopadeśa. Dbu ma'i man ngag rin po che'i za ma tog kha phye ba). P5325.

——. *Commentary on the Difficult Points of The Lamp for the Path to Enlightenment.* (Bodhipathapradīpapañjikā. Byang chub lam gyi sgron ma'i dka' 'grel). P5344. ACIP TD3948.

——. *The Entrance into the Two Realities.* (Satyadvayāvatāra. Bden pa gnyis la 'jug pa). P5298. ACIP TD3902.

——. *The Lamp for the Path to Enlightenment.* (Bodhipathapradīpa. Byang chub lam gyi sgron ma). P5343/5378. ACIP TD3947.

Avalokitavrata. *Commentary on The Lamp of Knowledge.* (Prajñāpradīpaṭīkā. Shes rab sgron ma'i 'grel pa). P5259. ACIP TD3859.

Bhāvaviveka. *The Blaze of Reasoning.* (Madhyamakahṛdayakārikāvṛttitarkajvālā. Dbu ma'i snying po'i 'grel pa rtog ge 'bar ba). P5256. ACIP TD3856.

——. *The Heart of Centrism.* (Madhyamakahṛdayakārikā. Dbu ma'i snying po'i tshig le'ur byas pa). P5255. ACIP TD3855.

——. *The Jewel Lamp of Centrism.* (Madhyamakaratnapradīpa. Dbu ma rin po che'i sgron ma). P5254. ACIP TD3854.

——. *The Lamp of Knowledge.* (Prajñāpradīpamūlamadhyamakavṛtti. Dbu ma'i rtsa ba'i 'grel pa shes rab sgron ma). Sanskrit edition of chapters I–II by M. Walleser. Bibliotheca Indica, New Series, No. 1396. Calcutta, 1914. P5253. ACIP TD3853.

——. *The Summary of the Meaning of Centrism.* (Madhyamakārthasaṃgraha. Dbu ma'i don bsdus pa). P5258. ACIP TD3857.

Bodhibhadra. *Explanation of The Compendium of the Heart of Wisdom.* (Jñānasārasamucchayanibandhana. Ye shes snying po kun las btus pa'i bshad sbyar). P5252. ACIP TD3852.

Buddhapālita. *Buddhapālita.* (Buddhapālitamūlamadhyamakavṛtti. Dbu ma rtsa ba'i 'grel pa Buddhapālita). Sanskrit edition of chapters I–XII by M. Walleser. Bibliotheca Buddhica XVI. St. Petersburg, 1913-14. P5242. ACIP TD3842.

Candrahari. *Jewel Garland.* (Ratnamālā. Rin po che'i phreng ba). P5297. ACIP TD3901.

Candrakīrti. *Commentary on The Entrance into Centrism.* (Madhyamakāvatārabhāṣya. Dbu ma la 'jug pa'i bshad pa). P5263. ACIP TD3862.

——. *Commentary on The Four Hundred Verses on the Yogic Practice of Bodhisattvas.* (Bodhisattvayogacaryācatuḥśatakaṭīkā. Byang chub sems dpa'i rnal 'byor spyod pa bzhi brgya pa'i rgya cher 'grel pa). P5266. ACIP TD3865.

——. *Commentary on The Seventy Stanzas on Emptiness.* (Śūnyatāsaptativṛtti. Stong nyid bdun cu pa'i 'grel pa). P5268. ACIP TD3867.

——. *Commentary on The Sixty Stanzas on Reasoning.* (Yuktiṣaṣṭikāvṛtti. Rigs pa drug cu pa'i 'grel pa). P5265. ACIP TD3864.

——. *The Entrance into Centrism.* (Madhyamakāvatāra. Dbu ma la 'jug pa). Sanskrit edition with *Madhyamakāvatārabhāṣya* by L. de La Vallée Poussin. Bibliotheca Buddhica IX. St. Petersburg, 1907–12. P5261/5262. ACIP TD3861.

——. *The Entrance into the Supreme Knowledge of Centrism.* (Madhyamakaprajñāvatāra. Dbu ma shes rab la 'jug pa). P5264. ACIP TD3863.

——. *The Lucid Words.* (Mūlamadhyamakavṛttiprasannapadā. Dbu ma'i rtsa ba'i 'grel pa tshig gsal ba) Sanskrit edition with Nāgārjuna's *Mūlamadhyamakakārikā* by L. de La Vallée Poussin. Bibliotheca Buddhica IV. St. Petersburg, 1903–13. (Corrections publ. by J. W. de Jong, IIJ 20, 1978, pp. 25–59, 217–52). P5260. ACIP TD3860.

Dharmakīrti. *Commentary on Valid Cognition.* (Pramāṇavārttika. Tshad ma rnam 'grel). P5709. ACIP TD4210.

——. *The Drop of Reasoning.* (Nyāyabindu. Rigs pa'i thig pa). P5711. ACIP TD4212.

Dharmapāla. *A Summary of The Entrance to the Bodhisattva's Way of Life.* (Bodhisattvacaryāvatārapiṇḍārtha. Byang chub sems dpa'i spyod pa la 'jug pa'i don bsdus pa). P5281. ACIP TD3879.

——. *A Summary of The Entrance to the Bodhisattva's Way of Life in Thirty-Six Points.* (Bodhisattvacaryāvatāraṣattriṃśātapiṇḍārtha. Byang chub sems dpa'i spyod pa la 'jug pa'i don sum cu rtsa drug bsdus pa). P5280. ACIP TD3878.

Dignāga. *The Compendium of Valid Cognition.* (Pramāṇasamucchaya. Tshad ma kun btus). P5700. ACIP TD4203.

——. *A Summary of Prajñāpāramitā.* (Prajñāpāramitārthasaṃgraha. Sher phyin bsdus pa/brgyad stong don bsdu). Also called *Prajñāpāramitāpiṇḍārtha.* P5870. ACIP TD3809.

Haribhadra. *The Illumination of The Ornament of Clear Realization.* (Abhisamayālaṃkārālokā. Mngon par rtogs pa'i rgyan gyi snang ba). Sanskrit edition by Unrai Wogihara. Fasc. 1–7. Tokyo: The Tokyo Bunko, 1932–35. P5192.

Jayānanda. *Subcommentary on The Entrance into Centrism.* (Madhyamakāvatāraṭīkā. Dbu ma la 'jug pa'i 'grel bshad). P5271. ACIP TD3870.

Jñānagarbha. *Commentary on The Distinction between the Two Realities.* (Satyadvayavibhāgavṛtti. Bden pa gnyis rnam par 'byed pa'i 'grel pa) [not in P]. T3882. ACIP TD3882.

——. *The Distinction between the Two Realities.* (Satyadvayavibhāga. Bden gnyis rnam 'byed) [not in P]. T3881. ACIP TD3881.

——. *The Path of Yoga Meditation.* (Yogabhāvanāmārga. Rnal 'byor sgom pa'i lam). P5305/5452. ACIP TD3909.

Jñānakīrti. *The Entrance into True Reality.* (Tattvāvatāra. De kho na nyid la 'jug pa). P4532.

——. *Instructions on the Stages of Meditation of the Vehicle of Perfections.* (Pāramitāyānabhāvanākramanirdeśa. Pha rol tu phyin pa'i theg pa'i sgom pa'i rim pa'i man ngag). P5317.

Kalyāṇadeva. *The Excellent Composition of The Entrance to the Bodhisattva's Way of Life.* (Bodhisattvacaryāvatārasaṃskāra. Byang chub sems dpa'i spyod pa la 'jug pa'i legs par sbyar ba). P5275. ACIP TD3874.

Kamalaśīla. *Commentary on The Dhāraṇī of Entering Nonconceptuality.* (Avikalpapraveśadhāraṇīṭīkā. Rnam par mi rtog pa la 'jug pa'i gzungs kyi rgya cher 'grel pa). P5501.

——. *Commentary on the Difficult Points of The Ornament of Centrism.* (Madhyamakālaṃkārapañjikā. Dbu ma rgyan gyi dka' 'grel). P5286. ACIP TD3886.

——. *Commentary on The Synopsis of True Reality.* (Tattvasaṃgrahapañjikā. De kho na nyid bsdus pa'i dka' 'grel). P5765.

——. *The Entrance into Yoga Meditation.* (Bhāvanāyogāvatāra/Yogabhāvanāvatāra. Rnal 'byor sgom pa la 'jug pa). P5313/5451. ACIP TD3918.

——. *Establishing That All Phenomena Are without Nature.* (Sarvadharmāsvabhāvasiddhi. Chos thams cad rang bzhin med par grub pa). P5289. ACIP TD3889.

——. *Illumination of Centrism.* (Madhyamakāloka. Dbu ma snang ba). P5287. ACIP TD3887.

——. *Illumination of True Reality.* (Tattvāloka. De kho na nyid snang ba). P5288. ACIP TD3888.

——. *The Stages of Meditation.* (Bhāvanākrama. Sgom pa'i rim pa). Sanskrit edition of First *Bhāvanākrama* by G. Tucci. *Minor Buddhist Texts.* Part II. Serie Orientale Roma IX/2. 1958 (Delhi: Motilal Banarsidass, reprint 1986, pp. 497–539). Third *Bhāvanākrama* by G. Tucci. *Minor Buddhist Texts.* Part III. Serie Orientale Roma XLIII. 1971. P5310-5312. ACIP TD3915–3917

Kambala. *A Garland of Light.* (Ālokamālā. Snang ba'i phreng ba). P5866. ACIP TD3895.

Kṛṣṇapāda. *The Ascertainment of the Points in The Entrance to the Bodhisattva's Way of Life That Are Difficult to Understand.* (Bodhisattvacaryāvatāraduravabodhanirṇayanāmagranthā. Byang chub sems dpa'i spyod pa la 'jug pa'i rtogs par dka' ba'i gnas gtan la dbab pa). P5276. ACIP TD3875A.

Maitreya. *The Distinction between Phenomena and Their Nature.* (Dharmadharmatāvibhāga. Chos dang chos nyid rnam par 'byed pa). P5523/5524.

——. *The Distinction between the Middle and Extremes.* (Madhyāntavibhāga. Dbus dang mtha' rnam par 'byed pa). P5522.

——. *The Ornament of Clear Realization.* (Abhisamayālaṃkāra. Mngon rtogs rgyan). P5148. ACIP TD3786.

——. *The Ornament of Sūtras.* (Mahāyānasūtrālaṃkāra. Theg pa chen po'i mdo sde rgyan). P5521.

——. *The Sublime Continuum.* (Ratnagotravibhāgamahāyānottaratantraśāstra. Theg pa chen po'i rgyud bla ma) Sanskrit edition by Edward H. Johnston. Patna, India: The Bihar Research Society, 1950 (includes the *Ratnagotravibhāgavyākhyā*). P5525. ACIP TD4024.

Maitrīpa (Advayavajra). *Ten Verses on True Reality.* (Tattvadaśaka. De kho na nyid bcu pa). P3080.

——. *The Precious Garland of True Reality* (Tattvaratnāvalī. De kho na nyid kyi rin chen phreng ba). P3085.

Nāgārjuna. *The Commentary on the Mind of Enlightenment.* (Bodhicittavivaraṇa. Byang chub sems kyi 'grel pa). P5470.

——. *Commentary on The Rebuttal of Objections.* (Vigrahavyāvartanīvṛtti. Rtsod pa bzlog pa'i 'grel pa). P5228. ACIP TD 3832.

——. *The Compendium of Sūtras.* (Sūtrasamucchaya. Mdo kun las btus pa). P5330. ACIP TD 3934.

——. *The Fundamental Verses on Centrism.* (Prajñānāmamūlamadhyamakakārikā. Dbu ma rtsa ba'i tshig le'ur byas pa shes rab ces bya ba). P5224. ACIP TD3824.

——. *The Heart of Dependent Origination.* (Pratītyasamutpādahṛdayakārikā. Rten cing 'brel bar 'byung ba'i snying po'i tshig le'ur byas pa). P5236.

——. *Letter to a Friend.* (Suhṛllekha. Bshes pa'i springs yig). P5682.

——. *The Praise to the Expanse of Dharmas.* (Dharmadhātustotra. Chos dbyings bstod pa). P2010.

——. *The Praise to the Incomparable.* (Niraupamyastava. Dpe med par bstod pa). P2011.

——. *The Praise to the Inconceivable.* (Acintyastava. Bsam gyis mi khyab par bstod pa). P2019.

——. *The Praise to the Supramundane.* (Lokātītastava. 'Jig rten las 'das pa'i bstod pa). P2012.

——. *The Praise to the Vajra of Mind.* (Cittavajrastava. Sems kyi rdo rje bstod pa). P2013.

——. *The Precious Garland.* (Rājaparikathāratnāvalī. Rgyal po la gtam bya ba rin po che'i phreng ba). P5658.

——. *The Rebuttal of Objections.* (Vigrahavyāvartanīkārikā. Rtsod pa bzlog pa'i thsig le'ur byas pa). Sanskrit edition by E. H. Johnston and A. Kunst in Bhattacharya (1978). P5224. ACIP TD3828.

——. *The Seventy Stanzas on Emptiness.* (Śūnyatāsaptati. Stong nyid bdun cu pa). P5227. ACIP TD3827.

——. *The Sixty Stanzas on Reasoning.* (Yuktiṣaṣṭīkā. Rigs pa drug cu pa). P5225. ACIP TD3825.

——. *The Stages of Meditation.* (Bhāvanākrama. Sgom pa'i rim pa). P5304.

——. *Twenty Verses on the Great Vehicle.* (Mahāyānaviṃśika. Theg pa chen po nyi shu pa). P5465. ACIP TD3833.

Prajñākaramati. *Commentary on the Difficult Points of The Entrance to the Bodhisattva's Way of Life.* (Bodhicaryāvatārapañjikā. Byang chub kyi spyod pa la 'jug pa'i dka' 'grel). Commentary on chapters 1–9. Sanskrit edition: L. de La Vallée Poussin. Calcutta: Bibliotheca Indica, 1902–14. P5273. ACIP TD3872.

Rāhulabhadra. *Praise to the Perfection of Knowledge.* (Prajñāpāramitāstotra. Sher phyin la bstod pa. P2018; attributed to Nāgārjuna). Sanskrit version found at the beginning of the Suvikrāntavikrāmiparipṛcchāprajñāpāramitāsūtra (ed. R. Hikata), the Aṣṭasāhasrikā, and the Pañcaviṃśatisāhasrikāprajñāpāramitāsūtra (ed. N. Dutt).

Ratnākaraśānti. *A Presentation of the Three Vehicles.* (Triyānavyavasthāna. Theg pa gsum gyi rnam bzhag). P4535.

Sahajavajra. *Commentary on The Ten Verses on True Reality.* (Tattvadaśakaṭīkā. De kho na nyid bcu pa'i grel pa). P3099.

*Saṃyutta Nikāya.* Ed. Leon Feer. London: Pali Text Society, 1884–1904.

Śāntarakṣita. *Commentary on the Difficult Points of The Distinction between the Two Realities.* (Satyadvayavibhāgapañjikā. Bden pa gnyis rnam par 'byed pa'i dka' 'grel). P5283. ACIP TD3883.

——. *Commentary on The Ornament of Centrism.* (Madhyamakālaṃkāravṛtti. Dbu ma rgyan gyi 'grel pa). P5285. ACIP TD3885.

——. *The Ornament of Centrism.* (Madhyamakālaṃkāra. Dbu ma rgyan). P5284. ACIP TD3884.

——. *The Synopsis of True Reality.* (Tattvasaṃgraha. De kho na nyid bsdus pa). P5764.

Śāntideva. *The Compendium of Training.* (Śikṣāsamucchayakārikā. Bslab pa kun las btus pa'i tshig le'ur byas pa). P5336.

——. *The Entrance to the Bodhisattva's Way of Life.* (Bodhisattvacaryāvatāra. Byang chub sems dpa'i spyod pa la 'jug pa) Sanskrit editions: L. de La Vallée Poussin with Prajñākaramati's Bodhicaryāvatārapañjikā. Calcutta: Bibliotheca Indica, 1902–14. P. L. Vaidya. Buddhist Sanskrit Texts No. 12. Darbhanga, 1960. Vidhushekhara Bhattacharya (Bibliotheca Indica 280). Kolkata: Asiatic Society Calcutta, 1960. P5272. ACIP TD3871.

Śrīgupta. *Commentary on Entering True Reality.* (Tattvāvatāravṛtti. De nyid la 'jug pa'i 'grel pa). P5292. ACIP TD3892.

Sthiramati. *Subcommentary on The Distinction between the Middle and Extremes.* (Madhyāntavibhāgaṭīkā. Dbus mtha' rnam 'byed kyi 'grel bshad). P5534.

Vairocanarakṣita. *Commentary on the Difficult Points of The Entrance to the Bodhisattva's Way of Life.* (Bodhisattvacaryāvatārapañjikā. Byang chub sems dpa'i spyod pa la 'jug pa'i dka' 'grel). P5277. ACIP TD3875B.

Vasubandhu. *Commentary on The Distinction between Phenomena and Their Nature.* (Dharmadharmatāvibhāgabhāṣya. Chos dang chos nyid rnam 'byed kyi 'grel pa). P5529. ACIP TD4028.

——. *Commentary on The Distinction between the Middle and Extremes.* (Madhyāntavibhāgabhāṣya. Dbus mtha' rnam 'byed kyi 'grel pa). P5528. ACIP TD4027.

——. *Commentary on The Synopsis of the Great Vehicle.* (Mahāyānasaṃgrahabhāṣya. Theg bsdus kyi 'grel pa). P5551.

——. *Instruction on the Three Natures.* (Trisvabhāvanirdeśa. Rang bzhin gsum nges par bstan pa). P5559.

——. *The Thirty Verses.* (Triṃśikākārikā. Sum cu pa). P5556.

——. *The Treasury of Abhidharma.* (Abhidharmakoṣa. Mngon pa mdzod). P5590. ACIP TD4089.

——. *The Twenty Verses.* (Viṃśatikākārikā. Nyi shu pa). P5557.

Vibhūticandra. *Commentary on the Intention of The Entrance to the Bodhisattva's Way of Life, Called The Illumination of the Distinctive Features.* (Bodhicaryāvatāratātparyapañjikāviśeṣadyotanīnāma. Byang chub kyi spyod pa la 'jug pa'i dgongs pa'i 'grel pa khyad par gsal byed ces bya ba). P5282. ACIP TD3880.

## Tibetan Works

Bdud 'joms 'jigs bral ye shes rdo rje. 1991. *The Nyingma School of Tibetan Buddhism.* 2 vols. Trans. Gyurme Dorje and M. Kapstein. Boston: Wisdom Publications.

Bsod nams rtse mo. 1994. *Byang chub sems dpa'i spyod pa la 'jug pa'i 'grel pa.* In *Sa skya gong ma rim byon gyi gsung 'bum phyogs gcig tu bsgrigs pa legs bshad gser gyi bang mdzod,* vol. 4, pp. 1052–1179. Kansu, China: Kan su'u mi rigs dpe skrun khang.

Btsun pa chos legs. 2000. *Four Unknown Works of the Bo-dong-pa School.* Lumbini, Nepal: Lumbini International Research Institute.

Bu ston rin chen grub. 1931. *History of Buddhism.* Trans. E. Obermiller. Heidelberg: Otto Harrassowitz.

——. 1971. *Byang chub sems dpa'i spyod pa la 'jug pa'i 'grel pa byang chub kyi sems gsal bar byed pa zla ba'i 'od zer.* In *Collected Works of Bu ston.* Ed. Lokesh Chandra, vol. 19, pp. 181–602. New Delhi: International Academy of Indian Culture.

Chos kyi grags pa (Shamarpa IV). 2001. *Exposition of The Commentary on the Mind of Enlightenment* (Byang chub sems 'grel gyi rnam par bshad pa tshig don gsal ba). In *Gsung gi bdud rtsi nor bu'i phreng ba ri mo'i srad bur rgyun gcig tu byas pa ngo mtshar gyi glegs bam yid bzhin gyi za ma tog chen po* (a collection of texts of the Kagyü lineage), vol. 1, pp. 62–123. Dharamsala, India: 'Gro phan gtsug lag dpe skrun khang.

Chos grags rgya mtsho (Karmapa VII). 1985. *The Ocean of Texts on Reasoning* (Tshad ma legs par bshad pa thams cad kyi chu bo yongs su 'du ba rigs pa'i gzhung lugs kyi rgya mtsho). Sikkim, India: Karma Thupten Chophel, Rumtek.

Chos kyi 'byung gnas (Situpa VIII) and 'Be lo Tshe dbang kun khyab. 1972. *Liberating Life Stories of the Karma Kamtshang Lineage, Called Moon Crystal Jewel* (Sgrub brgyud karma kaṃ tshang brgyud pa rin po che'i rnam par thar pa rab 'byams nor bu zla ba chu shel gyi phreng ba). 2 vols. New Delhi: Gyaltsan and Kesang Legshay.

Dar ma rin chen (rGyal tshab rje). 1980. *Dbu ma'i rtsa ba'i dka' gnas chen po brgyad kyi brjed byang.* In *The Collected Works (gsuṅ 'bum) of rGyal-tshab Rje Dar-ma-Rin-chen,* vol. 1, pp. 312–43. New Delhi: Ngag dbang dge legs bde mo.

——. 2001. *Byang chub sems dpa'i spyod pa la 'jug pa'i rnam bshad rgyal sras 'jug ngogs.* New Delhi: Bod gzhung shes rig dpar khang.

Dbang phyug rdo rje (Karmapa IX). n.d. *Dbu ma dvags grub shing bde bar 'dren byed skal bzang dga' ston.* n.p.

*Dbu ma gzhan stong skor bstan bcos phyogs bsdus deb dang po.* 1990. Sikkim, India: Karma Shri Nalanda Institute, Rumtek.

Dge 'dun chos 'phel. 1989. *Dbu ma'i zab gnad snying por dril ba'i legs bshad klu sgrub dgongs rgyan.* In *Mkhas dbang dge 'dun chos 'phel gyi gsung rtsom phyogs sgrig.* Chengdu, China: Si khron mi rigs dpe skrun khang.

Dngul chu thogs med bzang po dpal. 1979. *Theg pa chen po mdo sde rgyan gyi 'grel pa rin po che'i phreng ba.* Bir, India: Dzongsar Institute Library.

——. 1988. *Byang chub sems dpa'i spyod pa la 'jug pa'i 'grel pa legs bshad rgya mtsho.* Sarnath, India: Sakya Students Union, Central Institute of Higher Tibetan Studies.

Dol po pa Shes rab rgyal mtshan. 1988. *Ri chos nges don rgya mtsho.* Beijing: Mi rigs dpe skrun khang.

Dpa' bo gtsug lag phreng ba. 1986. *History of the Dharma, a Feast for the Learned* (Dam pa'i chos kyi 'khor lo bsgyur ba rnams kyi byung ba gsal bar byed pa mkhas pa'i dga' ston). 2 vols. Beijing: Mi rigs dpe skrun khang.

——. n.d. *The Essence of the Immeasurable, Profound and Vast Ocean of the Dharma of the Great Vehicle.* (Byang chub sems dpa'i spyod pa la 'jug pa'i rnam bshad theg chen chos kyi rgya mtsho zab rgyas mtha' yas pa'i snying po). Rouffignac, France: Nehsang Samten Chöling.

Dvags po bkra shis rnam rgyal. n.d. *Moonbeams of Mahāmudrā* (Nges don phyag rgya chen po'i sgom rim gsal bar byed pa'i legs bshad zla ba'i 'od zer). N.p.

Go rams pa bsod nams seng ge. 1968–69. *Dbu ma la 'jug pa'i dkyus kyi sa bcad dang zhung so so'i dka' gnas la dpyad pa lta ba ngan sel.* In *Sa skya pa'i bka' 'bum,* vol. 13. Ed. Bsod nams rgya mtsho. Tokyo: The Tokyo Bunko.

'Gos lo tsā ba gzhon nu dpal. 1984. *Deb ther sngon po.* 2 vols. Chengdu, China: Si khron mi rigs dpe skrun khang.

——. 1996. *The Blue Annals.* Trans. G. N. Roerich. Delhi: Motilal Banarsidass.

——. 2003. *A Commentary on The Sublime Continuum* (Theg pa chen po'i rgyud bla ma'i bstan bcos kyi 'grel bshad de kho na nyid rab tu gsal ba'i me long). Ed. Klaus-Dieter Mathes. Nepal Research Centre Publications 24. Stuttgart: Franz Steiner Verlag.

'Ju mi pham rgya mtsho. 1979. *The Ketaka Jewel* (Shes rab le'u'i tshig don go sla bar bshad pa nor bu ke ta ka). Gangtok, India: Shes rab rgyal mtshan bla ma.

——. c. 1990. *Collected Works* (Gsung 'bum). Kathmandu: Dilgo Khyentse.

Ko zhul grags pa 'byung gnas dang rgyal ba blo bzang mkhas grub. 1992. *Gangs can mkhas grub rim byon ming mdzod.* Kansu, China: Kan su'u mi rigs dpe skrun khang.

Kong sprul blo gros mtha' yas. 1970. *A Commentary on The Profound Innner Reality, Called Illuminating The Profound Reality* (Rnal 'byor bla na med pa'i rgyud sde rgya mtsho'i snying po bsdus pa zab mo nang don nyung ngu'i tshig gis rnam par 'grol ba zab don snang byed). Sikkim, India: Rumtek.

——. 1982. *The Treasury of Knowledge* (Theg pa'i sgo kun las btus pa gsung rab rin po che'i mdzod bslab pa gsum legs par ston pa'i bstan bcos shes bya kun khyab; includes its autocommentary Shes bya kun la khyab pa'i gzhung lugs nyung ngu'i tshig gis rnam par 'grol ba legs bshad yongs 'du shes bya mhta' yas pa'i rgya mtsho; abbr. Shes bya kun khyab mdzod). 3 vols. Beijing: Mi rigs dpe skrun khang.

——. n.d. *A Commentary on The Sublime Continuum, Called The Unassailable Lion's Roar* (Theg pa chen po rgyud bla ma'i bstan bcos snying po'i don mngon sum lam gyi bshad srol dang sbyar ba'i rnam par 'grel ba phyir mi ldog pa seng ge nga ro). Sikkim, India: Rumtek.

Kun bzang dpal ldan. 1994. *The Nectar Drops That Are the Excellent Words of Guru Mañjughoṣa* (Byang chub sems dpa'i spyod pa la 'jug pa'i 'grel pa 'jam dbyangs bla ma'i zhal lung bdud rtsi'i thig pa). Beijing: Mi rigs dpe skrun khang.

Khro ru mkhan po tshe rnam. 1989. *Dpal mnyam med mar pa bka' brgyud kyi grub pa'i mtha' rnam par nges par byed pa mdor bsdus su brjod pa dvags brgyud grub pa'i me long.* Beijing: Mi rigs dpe skrun khang.

Mi bskyod rdo rje (Karmapa VIII). 1990. *The Lamp That Excellently Distinguishes the Tradition of the Proponents of Other-Emptiness* (Dbu ma gzhan stong smra ba'i srol legs par phye ba'i sgron me). In *Dbu ma gzhan stong skor bstan bcos phyogs bsdus deb dang po.* Sikkim, India: Karma Shri Nalanda Institute, Rumtek.

——. 1996. *The Chariot of the Tagbo Siddhas* (Dbu ma la 'jug pa'i rnam bshad dpal ldan dus gsum mkhyen pa'i zhal lung dvags brgyud grub pa'i shing rta). Seattle: Nitartha *international* Publications.

——. n.d. *The Noble One Resting at Ease* (Shes rab kyi pha rol tu phyin pa'i lung chos mtha' dag gi bdud rtsi'i snying por gyur pa gang la ldan pa'i gzhi rje btsun mchog tu dgyes par ngal gso'i yongs 'dus brtol gyi ljon pa rgyas pa). Sikkim, India: Karma Shri Nalanda Institute, Rumtek. (The part of this text that is the direct commentary on *The Ornament of Clear Realization* including some of the related, general topics is translated in Brunnhölzl 2001.)

Mi nyag dgon po. 1999. *Gangs can mkhas dbang rim byon gyi rnam thar mdor bsdus bdud rtsi'i thigs phreng.* Krung go'i bod kyi shes rig dpe skrun khang.

Ngag dbang yon tan bzang po. 2000. *Jo nang chos 'byung dang rje jo nang chen po'i ring lugs.* Beijing: Mi rigs dpe skrun khang.

Padma dkar po. 1973. *Chos 'khor rim pa gsum gyi dogs gcod.* In *Collected Works of Kun-mKhyen Padma dkar po.* Darjeeling.

——. 1982. *Spyod 'jug 'bru 'grel dbu ma'i lam gyi sgron ma.* Sarnath, India: Kargyud Relief and Protection Committee, Central Institute of Higher Buddhist Studies.

——. n.d. *An Illumination of Three Centrist Scriptural Systems* (Dbu ma'i gzhung gsum gsal byed nges don grub pa'i shing rta. In *Dbu ma yang dag par brjod pa dang dbu ma'i gzhung gsum gsal byed sher phyin lung la 'jug pa'i sgo*). Sarnath, India: Kargyud Relief and Protection Committee, Central Institute of Higher Buddhist Studies.

Padmavajra, rdzogs chen mkhan chen. 2001. *Dbu ma'i gtan tshigs lnga'i bsdus 'grel dī paṃ ka ra'i zhal lung.* In *Rdzogs chen mkhan chen padma badzra'i gsung thor bu.* Chengdu, China: Si khron mi rigs dpe skrun khang.

Rang byung rdo rje (Karmapa III). n.d. *Autocommentary on The Profound Inner Reality* (Zab mo nang gi don gsal bar byed pa'i 'grel pa). Sikkim, India: Rumtek.

Red mda' ba gzhon nu blo gros. 1993. *Dbu ma la 'jug pa'i rnam bshad de kho na nyid gsal ba'i sgron ma.* Sarnath, India: Sakyapa Students' Union, Central Institute of Higher Buddhist Studies.

Rma bya ba byang chub brtson 'grus. 1975. *Dbu ma rtsa ba shes rab kyi 'grel pa 'thad pa'i rgyan.* Sikkim, India: Rumtek.

Rong ston shes bya kun rig. n.d. *Dbu ma la 'jug pa'i rnam bshad nges don rnam nges.* In *Two Controversial Madhyamaka Treatises.* Thimpu, Bhutan.

Rong zom chos kyi paṇḍita. n.d. *Grub mtha' so so'i bden gnyis kyi 'jog tshul.* In *Rong zom bka' 'bum,* vol. Ā, pp. 161a–165b. Rdzogs chen Monastery, India: Rdzogs Chen Śrī Siṃha Chos Grva.

Sa bzang ma ti pan chen 'jam dbyangs blo gros. 1975. *Byang chub sems dpa'i spyod pa la 'jug pa'i rnam bshad gzhung don rab gsal snang ba.* Delhi: Tashi Dorje.

Sgam po pa. 1975. *Gsung 'bum.* Delhi: Khasdub Gyatsho Shashin.

——. 1990. *The Jewel Ornament of Liberation* (Thar pa rin po che'i rgyan). Chengdu, China: Si khron mi rigs dpe skrun khang.

Śākya mchog ldan. 1975. *Theg pa chen po dbu ma rnam par nges pa'i mdzod lung dang rigs pa'i rgya mtsho.* In *The Complete Works (gsuṅ 'bum) of gSer-mdog Paṇ-chen Śākya-mchog-ldan,* vol. 14. Ed. Kunzang Tobgey. Thimpu, Bhutan.

——. 1992. *Dbu ma la 'jug pa'i rnam par bshad pa nges don gnad kyi ṭīka.* In *Dbu ma la 'jug pa rtsa ba dang 'grel pa.* Chengdu, China: Si khron mi rigs dpe skrun khang.

——. 2000. *Three Texts on Madhyamaka.* Trans. Iaroslav Komarovski. Dharamsala, India: LTWA.

Stag tshang lo tsā ba shes rab rin chen. 1976. *Grub mtha' kun shes nas mtha' bral grub pa zhes bya ba'i bstan bcos dang rnam par bshad pa legs par bshad kyi rgya mtsho.* Thimpu: publ. by Kun-bzang sTob-rgyal. Also in *Grub mtha' kun shes kyi rtsa 'grel.* Beijing: Mi rigs dpe skrun khang, 1999.

Tāranātha. 1980. *History of Buddhism in India.* Trans. Lama Chimpa and Alaka Chattopadhyaya. Calcutta: Bagchi.

Tsong kha pa blo bzang grags pa. 1973. *The Elucidation of the Intention* (Dbu ma la 'jug pa'i rgya cher bshad pa dgongs pa rab gsal). Sarnath, India: Pleasure of Elegant Sayings Press. Also P6143.

——. 1975–79. *The Great Stages of the Path* (Skyes bu gsum gyi nyams su blang ba'i rim pa thams cad tshang bar ston pa'i byang chub lam gyi rim pa; abbr. Lam rim chen mo). In *Collected Works.* dGe ldan gsung rab mi nyams rgyun 'phel series 79-105, vols. 19 and 20. Delhi. Also P6001.

——. 1990–1991. *The Essence of Good Explanations* (Drang ba dang nges pa'i don rnam par phye ba'i bstan bcos legs bshad snying po). Ed. Palden Drakpa and Damdul Namgyal. Mundgod, India: Drepung Loseling Library Society. Also in *Collected Works.* dGe ldan gsung rab mi nyams rgyun 'phel series 79-105, vol. pha: 478–714. Delhi: 1975–79. Also P6142.

Vimalamitra. *The Topics of Gradualist Meditation* (*Kramaprāveśikabhāvanāpada. Rim gyis 'jug pa'i sgom don). P5334.

## Modern Works


Ames, William L. 1986a. "Buddhapālita's Exposition of the Madhyamaka." *JIP* 14: 313–48.

——. 1986b. "Bhāvaviveka's Prajñāpradīpa: Six Chapters." Ph.D. diss., University of Washington.

Anacker, Stefan. 1986. *Seven Works of Vasubandhu.* Delhi: Motilal Banarsidass.

Āryadeva and Gyel-tsap. 1994. *Yogic Deeds of Bodhisattvas.* Trans. Ruth Sonam. Ithaca, N.Y.: Snow Lion Publications.

Batchelor, Stephen, trans. 1979. *A Guide to the Bodhisattva's Way of Life.* Dharamsala, India: LTWA.

Bhattacharya, Kamaleswar. 1978. *The Dialectical Method of Nāgārjuna (Vigrahavyāvartanī).* Delhi: Motilal Banarsidass.

Broido, Michael. 1985. "Padma Karpo on the Two Satyas." *JIABS* 8: 7–59.

——. 1988. "Veridical and Delusive Cognition: Tsongkhapa on the Two *Satyas.*" *JIP* 16: 29–63.

——. 1989. "The Jo-nang-pas on Madhyamaka: A Sketch." *TJ* 14, no. 1: 86–91.

Brunnhölzl, Karl, trans., ed., and ann. 2001. *A Commentary on the Perfection of Knowledge: The Noble One Resting at Ease.* Sackville, New Brunswick, Canada: Nitartha Institute.

——. 2002a. *The Presentation of Grounds, Paths, and Results in the Causal Vehicle of Characteristics in The Treasury of Knowledge* (Shes bya kun khyab mdzod, ch. 9.1 and 10.1). Sackville, New Brunswick, Canada: Nitartha Institute.

——. 2002b. *The Presentation of Madhyamaka in The Treasury of Knowledge* (Shes bya kun khyab mdzod, Selected passages from ch. 6.3, 7.2, and 7.3). Sackville, New Brunswick, Canada: Nitartha Institute.

Buescher, John. 1975. "Mādhyamika Reasoning." Master's thesis, University of Virginia.

Bugault, G. 1983. "Logic and Dialectics in the Mādhyamikakārikās." *JIP* 11, no. 1: 7–76.

Cabezón, José I. 1992. *A Dose of Emptiness.* Albany: State University of New York Press.

Chandrakirti. 2002. *Introduction to the Middle Way.* Trans. Padmakara Translation Group. Boston: Shambhala Publications.

Conze, Edward. 1960. *The Prajñāpāramitā Literature.* 's Gravenhage, Netherlands: Mouton.

Cozort, Daniel. 1998. *Unique Tenets of the Middle Way Consequence School.* Ithaca, N.Y.: Snow Lion Publications.

Crosby, Kate, and Andrew Skilton, trans. 1995. *Śāntideva. The Bodhicaryāvatāra.* Oxford: Oxford University Press.

Culler, J. 1982. *On Deconstruction.* Ithaca, N.Y.: Cornell University Press.

Dalai Lama, H. H. 1988. *Transcendent Wisdom.* Trans. B. Alan Wallace. Ithaca, N.Y.: Snow Lion Publications.

——. 1994. *A Flash of Lightning in the Dark of Night.* Boston: Shambhala Publications.

——. 1997. *The Gelug/Kagyü Tradition of Mahamudra.* Ithaca, N.Y.: Snow Lion Publications.

Dargyay, Lobsang. 1990. "What Is Non-Existent and What Is Remanent in *Śūnyatā*." *JIP* 18: 81–91.

Davidson, Ronald M. 1985. "Buddhist Systems of Transformation: Asraya-parivrtti/-paravrtti among the Yogacara." Ph.D. diss., University of California.

de Jong, Jan Willem. 1972a. "The Problem of the Absolute in the Madhyamaka School." *JIP* 2: 1–6.

——. 1972b. "Emptiness." *JIP* 2: 7–15.

——. 1975. "La Légende de Śāntideva." *IIJ* 16: 161–82.

Della Santina, P. 1986a. *Madhyamaka Schools in India: A Study of the Madhyamaka Philosophy and of the Division of the System into the Prāsaṅgika and Svātantrika Schools.* Delhi: Motilal Banarsidass.

——. 1986b. "The Madhyamaka and Modern Western Philosophy." *PEW* 36, no. 1: 40–54.

——. 1987. "The Madhyamaka Philosophy." *JIP* 15: 173–85.

Dietz, Siglinde. 1999. "Śāntideva's Bodhisattvacaryāvatāra, Das Weiterwirken des Werkes dargestellt anhand der Überlieferungsgeschichte des Textes und seiner Kommentare." In *Buddhismus und Gegenwart,* Bd. III, pp. 25–41. Hamburg: Universität Hamburg.

Douglas, Nik, and Meryl White. 1976. *Karmapa: The Black Hat Lama of Tibet.* London: Luzac.

Dragonetti, Carmen. 1979. "Some Notes on the Pratītyasamutpādahṛdayakārikā and the Pratītyasamutpādahṛdayavyākhyāna Attributed to Nāgārjuna." *Buddhist Studies* 6: 70–73.

Dreyfus, Georges B. J. 1997. *Recognizing Reality.* Albany: State University of New York Press.

——, and Sara L. McClintock, eds. 2003. *The Svātantrika-Prāsaṅgika Distinction.* Boston: Wisdom Publications.

Dzogchen Ponlop, Rinpoche. 1998–2001. *Commentary on "The Chariot of the Dakpo Kagyü Siddhas."* Transcripts of oral teachings at Nitartha Institute, Gampo Abbey and Mt. Allison University, Canada. 4 vols. Halifax: Nitartha Institute.

——. 2000–2001. *A Commentary on the Ninth Chapter of the Bodhicaryavatara on Supreme Knowledge.* Transcripts of oral teachings at Nitartha Institute, Kamalashila Institut Langenfeld. 2 vols. Hamburg: Nitartha Institut.

Ebbartson, Peter R. 1980. "The Two Truths in Buddhist Thought with Special Reference to the Mādhyamika System." Ph.D. diss., University of Oxford.

Eckel, Malcolm D. 1978. "Bhāvaviveka and the Early Mādhyamika Theories of Language." *PEW* 28, no. 3: 323–37.

——. 1985. "Bhāvaviveka's Critique of Yogācāra Philosophy in Chapter XXV of the *Prajñāpradīpa.*" In *Indiske Studier V,* ed. Christian Lindtner, pp. 24–75. Copenhagen: Akademisk Forlag.

——. 1987. *Jñānagarbha's Commentary on the Distinction between the Two Truths.* Albany: State University of New York Press.

Fenner, Peter. 1991. *The Ontology of the Middle Way.* Boston: Kluwer Academic Publishers.

——. 1995. *Reasoning into Reality.* Boston: Wisdom Publications.

Frauwallner, Erich. 1956. *Geschichte der indischen Philosophie.* 2 vols. Salzburg: Otto Müller Verlag.

——. 1994. *Die Philosophie des Buddhismus.* Berlin: Akademie Verlag.

Garfield, Jay L. 1995. *The Fundamental Wisdom of the Middle Way.* New York and Oxford: Oxford University Press.

Gómez, L. O. 1976. "Proto-Mādhyamika in the Pāli Canon." *PEW* 26: 137-165

Griffiths, Paul J., et al. 1989. *The Realm of Awakening.* Oxford: Oxford University Press.

Guenther, Herbert. 1973. "Saṃvṛti and Paramārtha in Yogācāra according to Tibetan Sources." In *The Problem of Two Truths in Buddhism and Vedānta,* ed. M. Sprung, pp. 89–97. Dordrecht and Boston: Reidel,

Gyamtso, Khenpo Tsultrim. 1988. *Progressive Stages of Meditation on Emptiness.* Trans. Shenpen Hookham. Oxford: Longchen Foundation.

——. 1992. *A Presentation of the Two Truths in the Three Yānas and the Mahāyāna Philosophical Traditions.* Halifax: Nālandā Translation Committee.

——. 1994. *Stufenweise Meditationsfolge über Leerheit.* Trans. Jane Friedewald. Wachendorf: Kagyü Dharma Verlag.

——. 1995. *Talks and Songs on the Progressive Stages of Meditation on Emptiness.* Trans. Susanne Schefczyk. Kathmandu: Marpa Translation Committee.

——. 2003. *The Sun of Wisdom.* Trans. Ari Goldfield. Boston: Shambhala Publications.

Hakamaya, Noriaki. 1980. "The Realm of Enlightenment in *Vijñaptimātratā*: The Formulation of the 'Four Kinds of Pure Dharmas.'" *JIABS* 3: 22–41.

Harris, Ian Charles. 1991. *The Continuity of Madhyamaka and Yogācāra in Indian Mahāyāna Buddhism.* Leiden, Netherlands: E. J. Brill.

Hirabayashi, Jay, and Shotaro Iida. 1977. "Another Look at the Mādhyamika versus Yogācāra Controversy Concerning Existence and Non-Existence." In *Prajñāpāramitā and Related Systems.* Ed. L. Lancaster. Berkeley: University of California Press.

Hiriyanna, M. 1973. *Outlines of Indian Philosophy.* Bombay: George Allen & Unwin.

Hookham, Shenpen. 1991. *The Buddha Within.* Albany: State University of New York Press.

Hopkins, Jeffrey. 1983. *Meditation on Emptiness.* Boston: Wisdom Publications.

——. 1989. "A Tibetan Delineation of Different Views of Emptiness in the Indian Middle Way School." *TJ* 14, no. 1: 10–43.

——. 1992. "A Tibetan Contribution on the Question of Mind-Only in the Early Yogic Practice School." *JIP* 20: 275–343.

——. 1996. "The Tibetan Genre of Doxography: Structuring a Worldview." In *Tibetan Literature.* Ed. J. Cabezón and R. Jackson. Ithaca, N.Y.: Snow Lion Publications.

Huntington, C. W., Jr. 1983. "The System of the Two Truths in the Prasannapadā and the Madhyamakāvatāra: A Study in Madhyamaka Soteriology." *JIP* 11, no. 1: 77–107.

——. 1986. "The Akutobhayā and Early Indian Madhyamaka." Ph.D. diss., University of Washington.

——. 1989. *The Emptiness of Emptiness.* Honolulu: University of Hawaii Press.

——. 1995. "A Lost Text of Early Indian Madhyamaka." *AS* 49, no. 4: 693-767

Ichigo, Masamichi. 1989. "The Madhyamakālaṃkāra." In *Studies in the Literature of the Great Vehicle.* Ed. L. Gómez and J. Silk. Ann Arbor: University of Michigan Press.

Ichimura, Shohei. 1981. "A Study on the Mādhyamika Method of Refutation and Its Influence on Buddhist Logic." *JIABS* 4, no. 1: 87–95.

——. 1982. "A New Approach to the Intra-Mādhyamika Confrontation over the Svātantrika and Prāsaṅgika Methods of Refutation." *JIABS* 5, no. 2: 41–52.

Iida, Shotaro. 1973. "The Nature of Saṃvṛti and the Relation of Paramārtha to It in Svātantrika-Mādhyamika." In *The Problem of Two Truths in Buddhism and Vedānta,* ed. M. Sprung, pp. 64–77. Dordrecht and Boston: Reidel.

Inada, Kenneth K. 1970. *Nāgārjuna: A Translation of His Mūlamadhyamakakārikā with an Introductory Essay.* Tokyo: Hokuseido Press.

Iwata, Hakashi. 1993. *Prasaṅga und Prasaṅgaviparyaya bei Dharmakīrti und seinen Kommentatoren.* Wien: Arbeitskreis für Tibetische und Buddhistische Studien Universität Wien.

Jackson, David P. 1985. "Madhyamaka Studies among the Early Sa-skya-pas." *TJ* 10, no. 2: 20–34.

——. 1990. "Sa skya Paṇḍita the 'Polemicist': Ancient Debates and Modern Interpretations." *JIABS* 13, no. 2: 17–116.

——. 1994. *Enlightenment by a Single Means.* Wien: Verlag der Österreichischen Akademie der Wissenschaften.

Jackson, Roger. 1993. *Is Enlightenment Possible?* Ithaca, N.Y.: Snow Lion Publications.

——. 2001. "The dGe ldan-bKa' brgyud Tradition of Mahāmudrā. *How Much dGe ldan? How Much bKa' brgyud?*" In *Changing Minds: Contributions to the Study of Buddhism and Tibet in Honor of Jeffrey Hopkins,* ed. Guy Newland, pp. 155–91. Ithaca, N.Y.: Snow Lion Publications.

Jinpa, Thubten. 1998. "Delineating Reason's Scope for Negation. Tsongkhapa's Contribution to Madhyamaka's Dialectical Method." *JIP* 26: 275-308

——. 1999. "Tsongkhapa's Qualms about Early Tibetan Interpretations of Madhyamaka Philosophy." *TJ* 24, no. 2: 3–28.

——. 2000. "The Question of Development in Tsongkhapa's Madhyamaka Philosophy." *AS* 54, no. 1: 5-44

Kajiyama, Yuichi. 1957. "Bhāvaviveka and the Prāsaṅgika School." *The Nava-Nalanda-Mahavihara Research Publication.* Vol. 1. 1, pp. 289–331. Ed. S. Mookerjee. London: Collins.

Kaplan, Stephen. 1990. "A Holographic Alternative to a Traditional Yogācāra Simile: An Analysis of Vasubandhu's Trisvabhāva Doctrine." *The Eastern Buddhist* 23: 56–78.

Kapstein, Matthew T. 1988. "Mipham's Theory of Interpretation." In *Buddhist Hermeneutics,* ed. D. S. Lopez, pp. 149–74. Honolulu: University of Hawaii Press.

——. 2000. "We Are All Gzhan stong pas." *Journal of Buddhist Ethics* 7: 105–25.

——. 2001. "Abhayākaragupta on the Two Truths." In *Reason's Traces.* Ed. M. Kapstein. Boston: Wisdom Publications.

Karma Thinley. 1980. *The History of the Sixteen Karmapas of Tibet.* Boulder, Colo.: Prajñā Press.

Karmay, Samten Gyaltsen. 1988. *The Great Perfection (rDzogs chen). A Philosophical and Meditative Teaching in Tibetan Buddhism.* Leiden, Netherlands: E. J. Brill.

Kawamura, Leslie. 2000. "The Middle Path according to the *Kāśyapaparivarta-sūtra.*" In *Wisdom, Compassion and the Search for Understanding,* ed. J. Silk, pp. 221–32. Honolulu: University of Hawaii Press.

Keenan, John P. 1989. "Asaṅga's Understanding of Mādhyamika." *JIABS* 12: 93–107.

——. 1997. *Dharmapāla's Yogācāra Critique of Bhāvaviveka's Mādhyamika Explanation of Emptiness.* Studies in Asian Thought and Religion, vol. 20. Lampeter, U.K.: Edwin Mellen Press.

King, Richard. 1994. "Early Yogācāra and its Relationship with the Madhyamaka School." PEW 44 (4): 659-683

Kuijp, Leonard W. J. van der. 1983. *Contributions to the Development of Tibetan Buddhist Epistemology. From the Eleventh to the Thirteenth Century.* Alt- und Neu-Indische Studien 26. Wiesbaden: Franz Steiner Verlag.

Lang, Karen. 1986. *Āryadeva's Catuḥśataka.* Copenhagen: Akademisk Forlag.

——. 1990. "Spa-tshab Nyi-ma-grags and the Introduction of Prāsaṅgika Madhyamaka into Tibet." In *Reflections on Tibetan Culture,* ed. L. Epstein and R. Sherburne, pp. 127–41. Lampeter, U.K.: Edwin Mellen Press.

Lindtner, Christian. 1981a."Atiśa's Introduction to the Two Truths, and Its Sources." *JIP* 9: 161–214.

——. 1981b. *To Buddhistiske Laerdigte. Nāgārjuna: "Brev til en ven" (Suhṛlekka). Śāntadeva: "Om en Bodhisattvas livsform" (Bodhisattvacaryāvatāra).* Indiske Studier I. Copenhagen: Akademisk Forlag.

——. 1981c. "Buddhapālita on Emptiness." *IIJ* 23: 187–217.

——. 1982a. *Nāgārjuniana.* Indiske Studier IV. Copenhagen: Akademisk Forlag.

——. 1982b."On the Authenticity of Madhyamakaratnapradīpa." *WZKS* 26: 172–84.

——. 1983. "Nāgārjuna's Vyavahārasiddhi." In *Contributions on Tibetan and Buddhist Religion and Philosophy. Proceedings of the Csoma de Körös Symposium held at Velm-Vienna, Austria, 13.-19. September 1981,* ed. E. Steinkellner and H. Tauscher, pp. 147–59. Wiener Studien zur Tibetologie und Buddhismuskunde, Heft 11. Wien: Arbeitskreis für Tibetische und Buddhistische Studien Universität Wien.

——. 1986a. "Bhavya's Critique of Yogācāra in the Madhyamakaratnapradīpa, Chapter IV." In *Buddhist Logic and Epistemology,* ed. B. K. Matilal and R. D. Evans. Dordrecht, Netherlands: Reidel.

——. 1986b. "Materials for the Study of Bhavya." In *Kalyāṇamitrārāgaṇam,* ed. E. Kahrs, pp. 179–202. Oxford: Norwegian University Press.

——. 1992. "The Laṅkāvatārasūtra in Early Indian Madhyamaka Literature." *AS* 46, no. 1: 244-279

——. 1997. "*Cittamātra* in Indian Mahāyāna until Kamalaśīla." *WZKS* 41: 159–206.

——. ed. 2001. *Madhyamakahṛdayam of Bhavya.* Chennai: Theosophical Publishing House.

Lipman, Kennard. 1979. "A Study of Śāntarakṣita's Madhyamakālaṃkāra." Ph.D. diss., University of Saskatchewan.

——. 1982. "Cittamātra and Its Madhyamaka Critique." *PEW* 32: 295–308.

Lopez, Donald S. Jr. 1987. *A Study of Svātantrika.* Ithaca, N.Y.: Snow Lion Publications.

——. 1988b. *The Heart Sūtra Explained.* Albany: State University of New York Press.

——. 1988c. "Do Śrāvakas Understand Emptiness?" *JIP* 16: 65–105.

——. 1996a. *Elaborations on Emptiness.* Princeton, N.J.: Princeton University Press.

——. 1996b. "Polemical Literature (dGag lan)." In *Tibetan Literature,* ed. J. Cabezón and R. Jackson. Ithaca, N.Y.: Snow Lion Publications.

——. 2001. "Painting the Target: On the Identification of the Object of Negation (dgag bya)." In *Changing Minds: Contributions to the Study of Buddhism and Tibet in Honor of Jeffrey Hopkins,* ed. Guy Newland, pp. 63–81. Ithaca, N.Y.: Snow Lion Publications.

——, ed. 1988a. *Buddhist Hermeneutics.* Honolulu: University of Hawaii Press.

Lusthaus, Dan. 2002. *Buddhist Phenomenology. A Philosophical Investigation of Yogācāra Buddhism and the* Ch'eng Wei-shih lun. London: Routledge and Curzon.

Mathes, Klaus-Dieter. 1996. *Unterscheidung der Gegebenheiten von ihrem wahren Wesen (Dharmadharmatāvibhāga).* Swisttal-Odendorf, Germany: Indica et Tibetica Verlag.

——. 1998. "Vordergründige und höchste Wahrheit im *gZhan stong*-Madhyamaka." *Annäherung an das Fremde.* XXVI. Deutscher Orientalistentag vom 25. bis 29.9. in Leipzig, ed. H. Preissler and H. Stein. *Zeitschrift der Deutschen Morgenländischen Gesellschaft* 11: 457–68.

——. 2000. "Tāranātha's Presentation of *trisvabhāva* in the *gŻan stoṅ sñiṅ po.*" *JIABS* 23: 195–223.

——. 2002. "'Gos Lo tsâ ba gZhon nu dpal's Extensive Commentary on and Study of the *Ratnagotravibhāgavyākhyā.*" In *Religion and Secular Culture in Tibet.* Tibetan Studies II. Proceedings of the International Association of Tibetan Studies 2000, vol. 2/2, ed. H. Blezer with the assistance of A. Zadoks, pp. 79–96. Brill's Tibetan Studies Library. Leiden, Netherlands: E. J. Brill.

Matics, Marion L., trans. 1970. *Entering the Path of Enlightenment.* New York: Macmillan.

Matilal, Bimal K. 1971. *Epistemology, Logic and Grammar in Indian Philosophical Analysis.* The Hague and Paris: Mouton.

——. 1992. "Is *Prasaṅga* a Form of Deconstruction?" *JIP* 20: 345–62.

Matilal, Bimal K., and R. D. Evans, ed. 1986. *Buddhist Logic and Epistemology: Studies in the Buddhist Analysis of Inference and Language.* Dordrecht: Reidel, 1986

McEvilley, Thomas. 1981. "Early Greek Philosophy and Mādhyamika." *PEW* 31, no. 2: 141–64.

Mimaki, K. 1983. "The Blo gsal grub mtha' and the Madhyamaka Classification in Tibetan Grub mtha' Literature." In *Contributions on Tibetan and Buddhist Religion and Philosophy. Proceedings of the Csoma de Körös Symposium held at Velm-Vienna, Austria, 13.–19. September 1981,* ed. E. Steinkellner and H. Tauscher, pp. 161–67. Wiener Studien zur

Tibetologie und Buddhismuskunde, Heft 11. Wien: Arbeitskreis für Tibetische und Buddhistische Studien Universität Wien.

Moriyama, Seitetsu. 1984. "Kamalaśīla's and Haribhadra's Refutation of the Satyākāra and Ālīkākāra-vādins of the Yogācāra School." *JIBS* 33, no. 1: 389–93.

——. 1991. "The Later Mādhyamika and Dharmakīrti." In *Studies in the Buddhist Epistemological Tradition. Proceedings of the Second International Dharmakīrti Conference, Vienna, June 11–16, 1989*, ed. E. Steinkellner. Wien: Verlag der Österreichischen Akademie der Wissenschaften.

Murti, T. R. V. 1955. *The Central Philosophy of Buddhism: A Study of the Madhyamaka System.* London: George Allen & Unwin.

Nagao, Gadjin M. 1978. "'What Remains' in Śūnyatā: A Yogācāra Interpretation of Emptiness." In *Mahāyāna Buddhist Meditation: Theory and Practice*, ed. by Minoru Kiyota, pp. 66-82. Honolulu: University of Hawai'i Press.

——. 1989. *The Foundational Standpoint of Mādhyamika Philosophy.* Trans. J. P. Keenan. Albany: State University of New York Press.

——. 1991. *Mādhyamika and Yogācāra. A Study of Mahāyāna Philosophy.* Trans. L. Kawamura. Albany: State University of New York Press.

Nagasawa, Jitsudo. 1962. "Kamalaśīla's Theory of the Yogācāra." *JIBS* 10, no. 1: 364–71.

Napper, Elizabeth. 1989. *Dependent Arising and Emptiness.* Boston: Wisdom Publications.

Nayak, G. C. 2001. *Mādhyamika Śūnyatā: A Reappraisal.* New Delhi: Indian Council of Philosophical Research.

Newland, Guy. 1992. *The Two Truths.* Ithaca, N.Y.: Snow Lion Publications.

——. 1999. *Appearance and Reality. The Two Truths in the Four Buddhist Tenet Systems.* Ithaca, N.Y.: Snow Lion Publications.

——. 2001. "Ask a Farmer: Ultimate Analysis and Conventional Existence in Tsong kha pa's *Lam rim chen mo.*" In *Changing Minds: Contributions to the Study of Buddhism and Tibet in Honor of Jeffrey Hopkins*, ed Guy Newland, pp. 49–62. Ithaca, N.Y.: Snow Lion Publications.

Ng, Yu-Kwan. 1987. "The Arguments of Nāgārjuna in the Light of Modern Logic." *JIP* 15: 363–84.

Obermiller, Eugene. 1933. "A Study of the Twenty Aspects of Śūnyatā (Based on Haribhadra's *Abhisamayālaṃkarāloka* and the *Pañcaviṃśatisāhasrika*)." *IHQ* 9: 170–87.

——. 1934. "The Term *Śūnyatā* and Its Different Interpretations." *Journal of the Greater Indian Society* 1: 105–17.

Oetke, Claus. 1991. "Remarks on the Interpretation of Nāgārjuna's Philosophy." *JIP* 19: 315–23.

Olson, Robert F. 1974. "Candrakīrti's Critique of Vijñānavāda." *PEW* 24, no. 1: 405–11.

Pandeya, R. C. and M. 1996. *Nāgārjuna's Philosophy of No-Identity. With Philosophical Translations of the* Madhyamaka-Kārikā, Śūnyatā-Saptati and Vigrahavyāvartanī. Delhi: Eastern Book Linkers.

Pelden, Künzang, and Minyak Künzang Sönam. 1993. *Wisdom: Two Buddhist Commentaries.* Trans. Padmakara Translation Group. Saint-Leon-sur-Vezere, France: Editions Padmakara.

Perdue, Daniel. 1993. *Debate in Tibetan Buddhism.* Ithaca, N.Y.: Snow Lion Publications.

Pettit, J. W. 1999. *Mipham's Beacon of Certainty.* Boston: Wisdom Publications.

Pezzali, A. 1968. *Śāntideva, mystique bouddhiste des VIIe et VIIIe siècles.* Firenze: Vallecchi.

Powers, John. 1992. *Two Commentaries on the Samdhinirmocana-Sutra by Asanga and Jnanagarbha.* Lampeter, U.K.: Edwin Mellen Press.

——, trans. 1994. *Wisdom of Buddha, The Saṃdhinirmocana Mahāyāna Sūtra.* Berkeley: Dharma Publishing.

Robinson, Richard H. 1976. *Early Mādhyamika in India and China.* Delhi: Motilal Banarsidass.

Rorty, R. 1979. *Philosophy and the Mirror of Nature.* Princeton, N.J.: Princeton University Press.

Ruegg, David Seyfort. 1963. "The Jo naṅ pas: A School of Buddhist Ontologists according to the *Grub mtha' śel gyi me loṅ.*" *Journal of American Oriental Society* 83: 73–91.

——. 1969. *La théorie du tathāgatagarbha et du gotra.* Paris: Publications de l'École Française d'Extrême-Orient.

——. 1971. "On the Knowability and Expressibility of Absolute Reality in Buddhism." *JIBS* 20, no. 1: 489–95.

——. 1977. "The Uses of the Four Positions in the Catuṣkoṭi and the Problem of the Description of Reality in Mahāyāna Buddhism." *JIP* 5, no. 1: 1–71.

——. 1981. *The Literature of the Madhyamaka School of Philosophy in India.* Wiesbaden: Otto Harrassowitz.

——. 1983. "On the Thesis and Assertion in the Mādhyamika/dBu Ma." In *Contributions on Tibetan and Buddhist Religion and Philosophy. Proceedings of the Csoma de Körös Symposium held at Velm-Vienna, Austria, 13–19 September 1981,* ed. E. Steinkellner and H. Tauscher, pp. 205–41. Wiener Studien zur Tibetologie und Buddhismuskunde, Heft 11. Wien: Arbeitskreis für Tibetische und Buddhistische Studien Universität Wien.

——. 1984. "Towards a Chronology of the Madhyamaka School." In *Indological and Buddhist Studies,* 2nd ed, ed. L. A. Hercus et al. Delhi: Sri Satguru Publications.

——. 1986. "Does the Mādhyamika Have a Thesis and a Philosophical Position?" In *Buddhist Logic and Epistemology: Studies in the Buddhist Analysis of Inference and Language,* ed. Bimal K. Matilal and R. D. Evans, pp. 229–37. Dordrecht: Reidel.

——. 1988. "A Kar ma bka' brgyud Work on the Lineages and Traditions of the Indo-Tibetan dbu ma (Madhyamika)." In *Orientalia Iosephi Tucci Memoriae Dicata,* ed. Gnoli and L. Lanciotti, pp. 1249–80. Rome: Istituto Italiano per il Medio ed Estremo Oriente.

——. 1991. "On Pramāṇa Theory in Tsoṅ kha pa's Madhyamaka Philosophy." In *Studies in the Buddhist Epistemological Tradition. Proceedings of the Second International Dharmakīrti Conference, Vienna, June 11–16, 1989,* ed. E. Steinkellner, pp. 281–330. Wien: Verlag der Österreichischen Akademie der Wissenschaften.

——. 1995. "Some Reflections on the Place of Philosophy in the Study of Buddhism." *JIABS* 18: 145–81.

——. 2000. *Three Studies on the History of Indian and Tibetan Madhyamaka Philosophy. Studies in Indian and Tibetan Madhyamaka Thought, Part 1.* Wiener Studien zur Tibetologie und Buddhismuskunde, Heft 50. Wien: Arbeitskreis für Tibetische und Buddhistische Studien Universität Wien.

——. 2002. *Two Prolegomena to Madhyamaka Philosophy. Candrakīrti's Prasannapadā Madhyamaka-vṛttiḥ on Madhyamakakārikā I.1 and Tsoṅ kha pa blo bzang grags pa/rgyal tshab dar ma rin chen's dka' gnad/gnas brgyad kyi zin bris. Studies in Indian and Tibetan Madhyamaka Thought, Part 2.* Wiener Studien zur Tibetologie und Buddhismuskunde, Heft 54. Wien: Arbeitskreis für Tibetische und Buddhistische Studien Universität Wien.

Saito, Akira. 1993. *A Study of Akṣayamati(=Śāntideva)'s* Bodhisattvacaryāvatāra *as Found in the Tibetan Manuscripts from Tun-huang.* A Report of the Grant-in-Aid for Scientific Research (C). Mie, Japan.

——. 1994. "On the Difference between the Earlier and the Current Versions of Śāntideva's *Bodhi(sattva)caryāvatāra,* with special reference to Chap. 9 (/8) entitled: 'Perfection of Wisdom (prajñāpāramitā).'" Research paper presented at Ninth World Sanskrit Conference, 9–15 January 1994, Melbourne, Australia.

——. 1997. "Bu ston on the *sPyod 'jug* (*Bodhisattvacaryāvatāra*)." *Proceedings of the 7th Seminar of the International Association of Tibetan Studies, Graz 1995,* ed. Ernst Steinkellner, pp. 79-85. Wien: Verlag der Österreichischen Akademie der Wissenschaften.

——. 1998. "Bhāvaviveka and the *Madhya(anta)vibhāga/-bhāṣya.*" *JIBS* 46, no. 2: 1038–32.

Śāntideva. 1997. *The Way of the Bodhisattva.* Trans. Padmakara Translation Group. Boston: Shambhala Publications.

Sato, M. 1983. "Die Madhyamaka-Philosophie der Sa skya pa-Schule - Red mda' ba gzhon nu blo gros -." In *Contributions on Tibetan and Buddhist Religion and Philosophy. Proceedings of the Csoma de Körös Symposium held at Velm-Vienna, Austria, 13-19 September 1981,* ed. E. Steinkellner and H. Tauscher, pp. 243–57. Wiener Studien zur Tibetologie und Buddhismuskunde, Heft 11. Wien: Arbeitskreis für Tibetische und Buddhistische Studien Universität Wien.

Schmithausen, Lambert. 1967. "Sautrāntika-Voraussetzungen in Viṃśatikā und Triṃśikā." *WZKS* 11: 109–36.

——. 1969a. "Zur Literaturgeschichte der älteren Yogācāra-Schule." *Zeitschrift der Deutschen Morgenländischen Gesellschaft,* Supplementa I: 811–23.

——. 1969b. *Der Nirvāṇa-Abschnitt in der Viniścayasaṃgrahaṇī der Yogācārabhūmiḥ.* Österreichische Akademie der Wissenschaften, Philosophisch-historische Klasse, Sitzungsberichte, 264. Band, 2. Abhandlung. Wien: Hermann Böhlaus Nachf.

——. 1971. "Philologische Bemerkungen zum Ratnagotravibhāga." *WZKS* 15: 123–77.

——. 1973. "Zu D. Seyfort Rueggs Buch 'La Théorie du Tathāgatagarbha et du Gotra' (Besprechungsaufsatz)." *WZKS* 22: 123–60.

——. 1981. "On Some Aspects of Descriptions of Theories of 'Liberating Insight' and 'Enlightenment.'" In *Studien zum Jainismus und Buddhismus: Gedenkschrift für L. Alsdorf,* ed. K. Bruhn and A. Wezler. Wiesbaden: Franz Steiner Verlag.

——. 1987. *Ālayavijñāna: On the Origin and the Early Development of a Central Concept of Yogācāra Philosophy.* 2 vols. Tokyo: International Buddhist Institute for Buddhist Studies.

——. 1999. "Nichtselbst, Leerheit und altruistische Ethik im Bodhisattvacaryāvatāra." In *Buddhismus und Gegenwart,* Bd. III, pp. 129–44. Hamburg: Universität Hamburg.

——. 2000. "On Three *Yogācārabhūmi* Passages Mentioning the Three *Svabhāvas* or *Lakṣaṇas*." In *Wisdom, Compassion and the Search for Understanding,* ed. J. Silk, pp. 245–63. Honolulu: University of Hawaii Press.

Schumann, Hans Wolfgang. 1982. *Der historische Buddha.* Köln: Eugen Diederichs Verlag.

Sharma, Parmananda. 1990. *Śāntideva's Bodhicaryāvatāra, Original Sanskrit Text with English Translation and Exposition based on Prajñākaramati's Pañjikā.* 2 vols. New Delhi: Aditya Prakashan.

Shastri, Haraprasad, ed. 1927. *Advayavajrasaṃgraha.* Gaekwad's Oriental Series, XL. Baroda, India.

Siderits, Mark. 1980. "The Madhyamaka Critique of Epistemology I." *JIP* 8: 307–36.

——. 1981. "The Madhyamaka Critique of Epistemology II." *JIP* 9: 121–60.

——. 1988. "Nāgārjuna as Anti-Realist." *JIP* 16: 311–25.

Smith, E. Gene. 2001. *Among Tibetan Texts: History and Literature of the Himalayan Plateau.* Boston: Wisdom Publications.

Sparham, Gareth. 1993. *Ocean of Eloquence.* Albany: State University of New York Press.

——. 2001. "Demons on the Mother: *Objection to the Perfect Wisdom Sūtras in Tibet.*" In *Changing Minds: Contributions to the Study of Buddhism and Tibet in Honor of Jeffrey Hopkins,* ed. Guy Newland, pp. 193-214. Ithaca, NY: Snow Lion Publications.

Sprung, Mervyn. 1973. "The Mādhyamika Doctrine of Two Realities as a Metaphysics." In *The Problem of Two Truths in Buddhism and Vedānta,* ed. M. Sprung, pp. 40–53. Dordrecht and Boston: Reidel.

——. 1979. *Lucid Exposition of the Middle Way.* Boulder, Colo.: Prajñā Press.

Stearns, Cyrus. 1995. "Dol-po-pa Shes-rab rgyal-mtshan and the Genesis of the *gzhan stong* Position in Tibet." *AS* 49, no. 4: 829–52.

——. 1999. *The Buddha from Dolpo.* Albany: State University of New York Press.

Streng, Frederick J. 1967. *Emptiness: A Study in Religious Meaning.* Nashville: Abingdon Press.

Sutton, Florin Giripescu. 1991. *Existence and Enlightenment in the* Laṅkāvatāra-sūtra*: A Study in the Ontology and Epistemology of the Yogācāra-School of Mahāyāna-Buddhism.* Albany: State University of New York Press.

Sweet, Michael J. 1977. "Śāntideva and the Madhyamika: The Prajñāpāramitā-Pariccheda of the Bodhicaryāvatāra." Ph.D. diss., University of Wisconsin.

——. 1979. "*Bodhicaryāvatāra* 9:2 as a Focus for Tibetan Interpretations of the Two Truths in the Prāsangikā Mādhyamika." *JIABS* 2, no. 2: 79–89.

Tauscher, Helmut. 1992. "Controversies in Tibetan Madhyamaka Exegesis: sTag tshaṅ Lotsāba's Critique of Tsoṅ kha pa's Assertion of Validly Established Phenomena." *AS* 46, no. 1: 411-436

——. 1995. *Die Lehre von den zwei Wirklichkeiten in Tsoṅ kha pas Madhyamaka-Werken.* Wiener Studien zur Tibetologie und Buddhismuskunde, Heft 36. Wien: Arbeitskreis für Tibetische und Buddhistische Studien Universität Wien.

——. 1999a. "Phya pa chos kyi seng ge's Opinion on Prasaṅga in his *Dbu ma'i shar gsum gyi stong thun*." In *Dharmakīrti's Thought and Its Impact on Indian and Tibetan Philosophy. Proceedings of the Third International Dharmakīrti Conference, Hiroshima, 4–6 November 1997*, ed. S. Katsura. Wien: Verlag der Österreichischen Akademie der Wissenschaften.

——. 1999b. "Die zwei Wahrheiten." In *Buddhismus und Gegenwart*, Bd. III, pp. 93–110. Hamburg: Universität Hamburg.

Thabkhay, Yeshe. 1992. "The Four Assertions: Interpretations of Difficult Points in Prasangika Madhyamika." *TJ* 17, no. 1: 3–35.

Thrangu Rinpoche. 1997. *The Open Door to Emptiness*. Trans. Shakya Dorje. Vancouver: Karma Thekchen Chöling.

Thurman, Robert A. F. 1979. "Tsong-kha-pa on Analytical Meditation." *TJ* 4, no. 4: 3–16.

——. 1989. *The Speech of Gold*. Delhi: Motilal Banarsidass.

——, trans. 1997. *The Holy Teaching of Vimalakīrti*. University Park: Pennsylvania State University Press.

Tillemans, Tom. 1982. "'The Neither One Nor Many' Argument for *Śūnyatā* and Its Tibetan Interpretations: Background Information and Source Materials." *Études des Lettres*, University of Lausanne, no. 3, July-September, pp. 103–28.

——. 1984. "Two Tibetan Texts on the 'Neither One Nor Many' Argument for Śūnyatā." *JIP* 12: 357–88.

——. 1990. *Materials for the Study of Āryadeva, Dharmapāla, and Candrakīrti*. 2 vols. Wiener Studien zur Tibetologie und Buddhismuskunde, Heft 36. Wien: Arbeitskreis für Tibetische und Buddhistische Studien Universität Wien.

——. 1992. "Tsong kha pa *et al.* on the Bhāvaviveka-Candrakīrti Debate." In *Proceedings of the Fifth Seminar of the International Association of Buddhist Studies, Narita 1989*, ed. S. Ihara and Z. Yamaguchi, pp. 315–26. Narita, Japan: Naritasan Shinshoji.

——. 1999. *Scripture, Logic, Language*. Boston: Wisdom Publications.

Tillemans, Tom, and Toru Tomabechi. 1995. "Le *Dbu ma'i byuṅ tshul* de Śākya mchog ldan." *AS* 49, no. 4: 891-918

Tola, Fernando, and Carmen Dragonetti. 1983. "The Trisvabhāvakārikā of Vasubandhu." *JIP* 11: 225–66.

——. 1985. "Nāgārjuna's Catustava." *JIP* 13: 1–54.

Tsonawa, Lobsang N., trans. 1985. *Indian Buddhist Pandits*. Dharamsala, India: LTWA.

Tuxen, Poul. 1911. *Yoga. En oversigt over den systematiske Yogafilosofi på grundlag af kilderne*. Copenhagen: H. Hagerups Boghandel.

——. 1936. *Indledende Bemærkninger til buddhistisk Relativisme*. Copenhagen: H. Hagerups Boghandel.

Ueda, Yoshifumi. 1967. "Two Main Streams of Thought in Yogācāra Philosophy." *PEW* 17: 155–65.

Viévard, Ludovic. 2002. *Vacuité (Śūnyatā) et Compassion (Karuṇā) dans le Bouddhisme Madhyamaka*. Serie in-8, Fascicule 70. Paris: Collège de France, Publications de l'Institut de Civilisation Indienne.

Wallace, B. Alan. 1996. *Choosing Reality: A Buddhist View of Physics and the Mind.* Ithaca, N.Y.: Snow Lion Publications.

Wallace, Vesna, and B. Alan Wallace, trans. 1997. *A Guide to the Bodhisattva Way of Life.* Ithaca, N.Y.: Snow Lion Publications.

Walser, Joseph. 1998. "On the Formal Arguments of the Akutobhayā." *JIP* 26: 189-232

Weber-Brosamer, B., and M. D. Back. 1997. *Die Philosophie der Leere. Nāgārjunas Mūlamadhyamaka-Kārikās. Übersetzung des buddhistischen Basistexts mit kommentierenden Einführungen.* Wiesbaden: Otto Harrassowitz.

Williams, Paul. 1980. "Some Aspects of Language and Construction in the Madhyamaka." *JIP* 8: 1–45.

——. 1982. "Silence and Truth: Some Aspects of the Madhyamaka Philosophy in Tibet." *TJ* 7, no. 1–2: 67–80.

——. 1983a. "A Note on Some Aspects of Mi bskyod rdo rje's Critique of Dge lugs pa Madhyamaka." *JIP* 11: 125–45.

——. 1983b. "On Rang Rig." In *Contributions on Tibetan and Buddhist Religion and Philosophy. Proceedings of the Csoma de Körös Symposium held at Velm-Vienna, Austria, 13-19 September 1981,* ed. E. Steinkellner and H. Tauscher, pp. 321–32. Wiener Studien zur Tibetologie und Buddhismuskunde, Heft 11. Wien: Arbeitskreis für Tibetische und Buddhistische Studien Universität Wien.

——. 1985. "rMa bya pa Byang chub brtson 'grus on Madhyamaka Method." *JIP* 13: 205–25.

——. 1989. "Introduction: Some Random Reflections on the Study of Tibetan Madhyamaka." *TJ* 14, no. 1: 1–9.

——. 1991. "On the Interpretation of Madhyamaka Thought. Review of *The Emptiness of Emptiness* by C. W. Huntington." *JIP* 19: 191–218.

——. 1998a. *Altruism and Reality: Studies in the Philosophy of the Bodhicaryāvatāra.* Surrey, U. K.: Curzon Press.

——. 1998b. *The Reflexive Nature of Awareness.* Surrey, U. K.: Curzon Press.

Willis, Janice D. 1979. *On Knowing Reality: The* Tattvārtha *Chapter of Asaṅga's* Bodhisattvabhūmi. New York: Columbia University Press.

Yoshimizu, Chizuko. 1993. "The Madhyamaka Theories Regarded as False by the dGe lugs pas." *WZKS* 37: 201–27.

Yotsuya, Kodo. 1998. *The Critique of Svatantra Reasoning by Candrakīrti and Tsong-kha-pa.* Tibetan and Indo-Tibetan Studies 8. Stuttgart: Franz Steiner Verlag.

Zimmermann, Michael. 2002. *A Buddha Within: The Tathāgatagarbhasūtra. The Earliest Exposition of the Buddha Nature Teaching in India.* Bibliotheca Philologica et Philosophica Buddhica VI. Tokyo: International Research Institute for Advanced Buddhology, Soka University.

# *Endnotes*

1 From among the two available Sanskrit manuscripts of the text, the longer one (edited by de La Vallée Poussin and Vaidya) is titled *Bodhicaryāvatāra* (Tib. byang chub kyi spyod pa la 'jug pa), while the shorter Tunhuang version as well as most Indian commentaries say *Bodhisattvacaryāvatāra* (Tib. byang chub sems dpa'i spyod pa la 'jug pa).

2 There is a short presentation of the Nyingma position on Madhyamaka in Düdjom Rinpoche's *The Nyingma School of Tibetan Buddhism* (1991). We have two studies on Mipham Rinpoche's (1846–1912) presentation of Prāsaṅgika-Mādhyamika by Williams (1998b) and Pettit (1999) as well as a translation of his commentary on Candrakīrti's *Madhyamakāvatāra* (Padmakara 2002). Some positions of Sakya masters are known through Sato (1983), Jackson (1994), Dreyfus (1997), Śākya mchog ldan (2000), and especially through Della Santina's (1986a) detailed study of an early Tibetan outline of Madhyamaka by the Sakya master Sönam Senge (Tib. bsod nams seng ge, 1429–1490). Ruegg (2000) presents various Tibetan positions on whether Centrists have a thesis or not. Finally, there is a series of papers on the Svātantrika-Prāsaṅgika distinction in Dreyfus and McClintock 2003.

3 It is generally accepted by now that the terms "Autonomists" (Skt. *Svātantrika, Tib. rang rgyud pa; an asterisk before a Sanskrit word indicates that it is reconstructed from another language, usually Tibetan) and "Consequentialists" (Skt. *Prāsaṅgika, Tib. thal 'gyur pa) are Tibetan inventions that did not exist in India (this is also explicitly acknowledged by Tibetan masters, such as Butön, Tsongkhapa, and Śākya Chogden). Over the centuries, this distinction has become the standard Tibetan subdivision of the Madhyamaka school. In many Tibetan doxographies, one finds extremely detailed elaborations of this distinction (logical, epistemological, and even ontological), which often entail a number of problems as well as questionable hierarchies of philosophical systems. However, since most people who study Tibetan Buddhism in both the East and the West keep referring to these terms, for the sake of following common consensus I will use them too, but only in a provisional way and with certain clarifications to follow (for more details on the distinction between Autonomists and Consequentialists, see Chapter 3).

4 Of course, the Gelugpa tradition itself is not monolithic in terms of doctrinal issues. However, especially with regard to Centrism, Tsongkhapa's positions are for the most part strictly followed and never questioned. From this perspective, the Gelugpa school is the most univocal among the Tibetan traditions.

5 There are even a considerable number of Tibetan masters (both past and present) who deny that the Gelugpa version qualifies as Madhyamaka at all, let alone as Consequentialism.

6 The topic has been touched on by Williams (1983) and Ruegg (1988). The latter has translated the first part of the Eighth Karmapa's introduction to his commentary on the *Madhyamakāvatāra*. There are also several draft translations of some sections in this commentary that directly comment on Candrakīrti's root verses. However, the vast portions of this commentary that treat Madhyamaka in general and address various other interpretations of it, such as those of Tsongkhapa, Dölpopa, and Śākya Chogden, are not accessible in any other languages.

Hookham's study (1991) is primarily focused on the teachings on Buddha nature and "Shentong-Madhyamaka."

7 Tib. bka' 'gyur. This is the collection of the Buddhist sūtras and tantras translated into Tibetan.

8 Tib. bstan 'gyur. This is the translated collection of commentaries on the Buddha's teachings, independent treatises, rituals, and practice texts written by Indian Buddhist masters.

9 Tib. sgam po pa.

10 Tib. bka' gdams pa.

11 This text belongs to the Tibetan genre of *lam rim* (graded path), laying out the entire Buddhist path from the level of a beginner up through the fruition of Buddahood. For the Sanskrit and Tibetan names of texts from the *Tengyur*, as well as for details on Tibetan works, see the Bibliography.

12 Tib. dus gsum mkhyen pa.

13 Tib. phyva pa chos kyi seng ge.

14 Tib. pa tshab lo tsā ba nyi ma grags.

15 The Second Pawo Rinpoche's *History of the Dharma* reports that during his time (the sixteenth century), sixteen of these volumes were still existent (Dpa' bo gtsug lag phreng ba 1986, p. 1313).

16 Tib. rang byung rdo rje.

17 Tib. zab mo nang don. This is a general commentary on the tantras, emphasizing the topics of nādi, prāṇa, and bindu.

18 Tib. rnam shes ye shes 'byed pa'i bstan bcos.

19 Tib. snying po bstan pa'i bstan bcos.

20 Tib. rol pa'i rdo rje.

21 Tib. mthong ba don ldan.

22 Tib. rong ston shes bya kun rig.

23 Tib. bshad grva.

24 Tib. dvags po legs bshad gling.

25 Tib. za dam nyin byed gling.

26 Kong sprul blo gros mtha' yas 1982, vol. I, pp. 505–07.

27 Tib. chos grags rgya mtsho.

28 Tib. rigs gzhung rgya mtsho.

29 Tib. mi bskyod rdo rje.

30 These are Abhidharma, Vinaya, Pramāṇa (valid cognition), Prajñāpāramitā, and Madhyamaka. From among these, the Eighth Karmapa did not write a commentary of his own on valid cognition but restored and supplemented *The Ocean of Texts on Reasoning.*

31 Tib. dbang phyug rdo rje.

32 These are *The Ocean of Definitive Meaning* (Tib. nges don rgya mtsho), *Eliminating the Darkness of Ignorance* (Tib. ma rig mun sel), and *Pointing a Finger at the Dharma Body* (Tib. chos sku mdzub tshugs).

33 Unfortunately, only his commentaries on Vasubandhu's *Treasury of Abhidharma* and Candrakīrti's *Entrance into Centrism* have survived to the present.

34 Tib. ris med.

35 Tib. dkon mchog yan lag.

36 Tib. chos kyi dbang phyug.

37 Tib. karma phrin las pa phyogs las rnam rgyal.

38 Tib. dpa' bo gtsug lag phreng ba.

39 Tib. dvags po bkra shis rnam rgyal.

40 Tib. chos kyi 'byung gnas.

41 Tib. 'jam mgon kong sprul blo gros mtha' yas.

42 For more details, see *The Treasury of Knowledge,* Pawo Rinpoche's *History of the Dharma* (esp. pp. 1310–11), Situ Chökyi Jungnay's *Moon Crystal Jewel* (Chos kyi 'byung gnas 1972) *The History of the Sixteen Karmapas of Tibet* (Karma Thinley 1980), and *Karmapa: The Black Hat Lama of Tibet* (Douglas and White 1976).

43 Tib. dpal spungs.

44 Tib. rang byung rig pa'i rdo rje.

45 The five texts that cover the traditional fivefold curriculum of Tibetan monastic colleges in terms of sūtra studies are the *Abhidharmakoṣa, Vinayasūtra, Pramāṇavārttika, Abhisamayālaṃkāra,* and *Madhyamakāvātara* plus their main commentaries by the Seventh and Eighth Karmapas. The three texts in terms of tantra studies are the *Mahāyānottaratantraśāstra, The Profound Inner Reality* (Tib. zab mo nang don; by the Third Karmapa), and the *Hevajratantra,* plus their respective main commentaries by Jamgön Kongtrul Lodrö Taye.

46 A more literal—and better—translation of the essential Buddhist term *duḥkha* (Tib. sdug bsngal) would be "unsatisfactoriness." However, since the common consensus on rendering it as "suffering" has become firmly established, I will follow it.

47 The original meaning of the Sanskrit term *kleśa* is "defilement," "pollution," or "impurity," which is amply attested by the Buddhist canon. Its interpretation as "affliction" is a later development, from which the Tibetan standard translation *nyon mongs* results. *Pṛthivībandhu's commentary (P5569) on Vasubandhu's *Discourse on the Five Aggregates* (Skt. Pañcaskandhaprakaraṇa, Tib. phung po lnga'i rab byed; P5560) explains both: "They make body and mind uneasy and afflicted and render the mind stained. Therefore, they are called 'afflictions.'" Tibetan Tripitaka, Peking Edition (Tokyo-Kyoto: Suzuki Research Foundation, 1956); hereafter cited in notes as P), P5569.
Here, "affliction" is used, in conformity with the majority of modern Buddhist authors.

48 See Bibliography.

49 Batchelor (1987) uses Dngul chu thogs med's commentary *Byang chub sems dpa'i spyod pa la 'jug pa'i 'grel pa legs bshad rgya mtsho.*

50 Śāntideva 1997. This includes a translation of the ninth chapter of Kun bzang dpal ldan's commentary *Byang chub sems dpa'i spyod pa la 'jug pa'i 'grel pa 'jam dbyangs bla ma'i zhal lung bdud rtsi'i thig pa.*

51 See Bibliography.

52 The full title is: *The Exposition of The Entrance into Centrism That Represents the Excellent Words of the Glorious Tüsum Khyenba, Called The Chariot of the Tagbo Siddhas.* This title also points back to the starting point of the general transmission of Madhyamaka in the Kagyü lineage, since the First Karmapa Tüsum Khyenba extensively studied with Patsab Lotsāwa, as described further later on.

53 Tib. tsong kha pa blo bzang grags pa.

54 Tib. rgod tshang pa mgon po rdo rje (1189–1258), one of the early Drugba Kagyü (Tib. 'brug pa bka' brgyud) masters.

55 Tib. 'jig rten gsum mgon rin chen dpal (1143–1217). He was the founder of the Drikung Kagyü (Tib. 'bri gung bka' brgyud) lineage.

56 Tib. sangs rgyas mnyan pa bkra shis dpal 'byor.

57 Tib. kun mkhyen padma dkar po.

58 Tib. dbu ma yang dag par brjod pa.

59 In particular, since both the Eighth Karmapa and Pawo Rinpoche repeatedly write about the same or related subjects in different parts of their texts, I often put such miscellaneous information together under the topic at hand.

60 For example, sheerly to save space, I provide the sources of translated quotations but not the actual Sanskrit, Pāli, Tibetan, or Chinese text. Also, I usually do not go into the details of critically analyzing different editions. The interested reader is referred to the originals.

61 *The Perfection of Wisdom in 8,000 Lines*, p. xix. Of course, this statement applies not only to American society, but to all so-called "modern societies."

62 See Vimalakīrtinirdeśasūtra (Tib. dri med grags pa'i nges bstan gyi mdo), Chapter IX, "The Dharma-Door of Nonduality."

63 Dpa' bo gtsug lag phreng ba, n.d., p. 888. Thurman (1997) elaborates:

> This is the most famous moment of the Scripture: Vimalakīrti's moment of silence on the subject of non-duality, i.e., the ultimate. It is noteworthy, however, that Vimalakīrti talks a great deal about the ultimate on many other occasions; his silence here is given its special impact by the series of profound statements preceeding it, which culminate in the statement of Mañjuśrī to the effect that silence is itself the best explanation of non-duality. Hence all silence is not to be exaggeratedly taken as the profoundest teaching, but only such a silence in the special context of profound thought on the ultimate. For example, the silences of the disciples in Chap. III, as they became speechless when confronted by the eloquent criticism of Vimalakīrti, are not taken to be profound; nor is the silence of Śāriputra when questioned by the goddess in Chap. 8 accepted as anything extraordinary.
>
> Candrakīrti, in his *Prasannapadā* (p. 57, I.7–8), has this to say in regard to the question as to whether the Enlightened Ones employ logical arguments or not: "Who can say if the Holy Ones (employ logical arguments) or not? The ultimate is inherent (even) in the 'Keeping Silent of the Holy Ones.' What then would cause us to imagine whether

they employ logical arguments or do not employ logical arguments?" It is important to note that equating the ultimate with the "Keeping Silent of the Holy Ones" in no way precludes the ultimacy of their speech. As the Goddess says to Śāriputra (p. 59): " . . . do not point to liberation by abandoning speech! Why? The holy liberation is the equality of all things!"

Thus, to imitate the Scripture's pattern of expression: "Silence" and "speech" are dualistic. Just as speech is ultimately meaningless, so silence exists only in contrast with speech. Penetration into the equality of silence and speech is the entrance. (pp. 131–32)

64 Lit. "expansion, proliferation" (usually translated as "elaborations" or "fabrications"). This term covers the entire range of the many-layered mental flux of setting up and relating to reference points, in terms of both subject and object. In this sense, "discursiveness" represents the subjective side of this process, while "reference points" are its objective aspect. (Thus, according to the context, I will use either one or both of these terms.) Discursiveness and reference points are found in ordinary sentient beings and to a lesser degree in noble ones who do not rest in meditative equipoise. Discursiveness ranges from coarse thoughts down to even the most subtle dualistic tendencies of a separate perceiver and perceived. For example, these tendencies manifest in such a way that it still appears to the senses as if there were objects out there that are perceived by a mind different from them, even when it is realized that there are no outer objects different from mind and no really existing mind either. (For an excellent and detailed description of this term and its range, see Schmithausen 1969b, pp. 137ff.)

65 XXV.24.

66 XXIV.10.

67 Tib. rnal 'byor spyod pa. In India, this school was also called Vijñaptivāda (Tib. rnam rig smra ba). Its proponents are also called Yogācāra(s), while the presently popular Sanskritization "Yogācārin" is not used in Indian texts. Tibetans usually refer to this school as "Mere Mentalism" (Tib. sems tsam, mostly translated as "Mind Only"). However, in India, the corresponding term *cittamātra* was not used as a name for this school but only for one of its key concepts. Likewise, the followers of this school were not called "Mere Mentalists" (Tib. sems tsam pa), since neither the popular (but wrong) Sanskritization "Cittamātrin" nor the more probable term "Caittamātrika" appears in any Indian texts. For more details, see chapter 4.

68 For more details, see Chapter 1.

69 There is some debate among Western scholars as to whether the Prajñāpāramitā sūtras already existed at the time of Nāgārjuna, whether he really commented on them, and whether he was a Mahāyānist at all. I do not address these issues here.

Both Tāranātha's *History of Buddhism in India* (1980, p. 102-103) and *The Treasury of Knowledge* (Kong sprul blo gros mtha'yas 1982, vol. I, p. 403) report that the first ones to teach Madhyamaka were Rāhulabhadra and eight of his contemporaries, such as *Kamalagarbha, *Ghanasa, and Prakāśadharmamaṇi. This Rāhulabhadra was Nāgārjuna's teacher and also ordained him. Traditionally, he is often equated with the siddha Saraha.

70 Skt. śūnyavāda, Tib. stong par smra ba.

71 This master is variously referred to as Bhavya, Bhāvi(n), Bhāviveka, Bhāviviveka, or Bhāvaviveka. From the scriptures, it seems that Bhavya is the most proper form. However, since Bhāvaviveka is the most commonly used name in Western literature on Centrism, I will follow this common consensus.

72 Tib. dbu ma snga rabs pa.

73 As an aside—and, again, this is not meant to be sectarian in any way—in the context of the transmission of the teachings from India to Tibet, it seems of interest to note that all founders of the Kagyü, Nyingma, and Sakya schools knew Sanskrit, had access to the original texts, and were engaged in direct teacher-student relationships with many Indian masters. On the other hand, Tsongkhapa, the founder of the Gelugpa school, relied exclusively on Tibetan translations and had no contact with Indian masters.

74 For details of these lineages, see Chapter 1.

75 "Middle way" would be *madhyamā pratipat* (Tib. dbu ma'i lam).

76 In Sanskrit, *-ma* is a tadhita-affix and *-ka* a kṛt-affix.

77 Skt. Samādhirājasūtra, Tib. ting nge 'dzin gyi rgyal po'i mdo, IX.27.

78 In translating the Sanskrit *pāramitā*, I follow the Sanskrit etymology, which primarily suggests "perfection." Nearly all Tibetan commentaries identify "gone to the other side or shore" as the contextual etymology.

79 Skt. Ratnacūḍaparipṛcchāsūtra, Tib. gtsug na rin chen gyis zhus pa'i mdo (P47, fol. 219b).

80 Skt. Kāśyapaparivartasūtra, Tib. 'od srung gi le'u (§§ 56–7, 60).

81 XI.2ab.

82 Skt. Dharmadhātusaragīti, Tib. chos kyi dbyings lta ba'i glu, verse 46.

83 Tib. bsdus pa'i rigs pa (quoted in Vol. II, pp. 243–44). This is a text of the same genre as what is called *Collected Topics* in the Gelugpa tradition, which introduces basic terminology and reasoning for beginning students at the Tibetan monastic colleges. Unfortunately, the text quoted is now lost.

84 Dpa' bo gtsug lag phreng ba, n.d., p. 309.

85 Ibid., p. 321. About the use of the term "identitylessness" and other details, see the section in chapter 2 entitled "The Two Types of Identitylessness."

86 This is clearly expressed in all Centrist reasonings, since they always negate all theoretical possibilities in relation to phenomena through the structure of the fourfold logical approach known as the tetralemma: For example, it is refuted that something is existent, nonexistent, both, or neither.

87 See, for example, the *Dhammacakkapavattanasutta* (the first teaching that the Buddha gave in the Deer Park at Sarnath).

88 Verses 51, 58–59.

89 VI.118.

90 For an elaboration on this knowledge and its relation to wisdom (Skt. jñāna, Tib. ye shes), see the section in chapter 2 entitled "From Knowledge to Wisdom."

91 These teachings on the subjective aspect of prajñāpāramitā are called "the hidden meaning of the Prajñāpāramitā sūtras," which are systematically elucidated in Maitreya's *Ornament of Clear Realization* and its many commentaries. In all four schools of Tibetan Buddhism, they are studied even more extensively than the Madhyamaka teachings, which mainly emphasize the objective aspect of the prajñāpāramitā teachings, i.e., emptiness. Together, these two complementary topics reflect the entire scope of the Prajñāpāramitā sūtras.

92 *Webster's New International Dictionary* defines this term as "the process or result of regarding as a thing; convert mentally into something concrete or objective; give definite form or content to; materialize." This corresponds very well to the Sanskrit *bhāvagrāha* and the Tibetan *dngos 'dzin.* Thus, when I use the term "reification," it refers to the tendency to solidify our experiences and the world around us, to operate with the resulting "solid things," and to cling to them as being real.

93 Skt. Lalitavistarasūtra, Tib. rgya cher rol pa'i mdo, XXV.1 (P783, p. 238.5.6).

94 It should be clear that this does not mean simply to take the nature of the mind as the final reference point. Not only is this not possible precisely because of the nonreferential nature of the mind, but if one were to take it as a reference point, that would be a sure sign that whatever one might have realized at this point is not mind's nature.

95 Skt. Aṣṭāsāhasrikaprajñāpāramitāsūtra, Tib. sher phyin brgyad stong pa (ACIP KD0012@03A).

96 P47, fols. 219b–220a.

97 In ancient India, there were techniques to produce fireproof garments by using certain minerals (probably asbestos).

98 Verses 20–22. As for "basic element" as a synonym for Buddha nature, especially in the case of Nāgārjuna, it should be more than clear that this does not refer to the only absolutely existing nature that is left as something identifiable after everything else has been refuted.

99 V.93–114.

100 This is Bhāvaviveka's commentary on Nāgārjuna's *Fundamental Verses* (ACIP TD3853@190A).

101 Skt. ārya, Tib. 'phags pa. The four types of noble ones in Buddhism are the Buddhas as well as all hearers, solitary realizers, and bodhisattvas from their respective paths of seeing onward.

102 This is Candrakīrti's word commentary on Nāgārjuna's *Fundamental Verses on Centrism* (ACIP TD3860@163B).

103 Ibid., @184A.

104 ACIP TD3862@255A. Many people think that Centrism is concerned only with emptiness and that wisdom is dealt with only by the Yogācāra or Shentong tradition. However, in Candrakīrti's texts (especially his autocommentary on *The Entrance into Centrism*), he indeed deals with the exegesis of wisdom too. He definitely does not treat it as a non-Centrist subject. For example, he describes the Dharma Body as "the body whose nature is wisdom" (@331B). (The same is true of the Yogācāras' treatment of emptiness.)

105 Verses 9–12ab. This text is listed under Candrakīrti's (6th/7th century) works in the *Tengyur* and appears as an appendix to his autocommentary on *The Entrance into Centrism.* Its colophon says that it is authored by the great master Candrakīrti, but also that it was translated into Tibetan by the author himself and the translator 'Gos khug pa lha btsas, who lived in the eleventh century. There was an eleventh-century master by the name Candrakīrti (Tibetan tradition calls him "the lesser Candrakīrti") who was a disciple of Jetāri (10th/11th century), one of the teachers of Atiśa.

106 Mi bskyod rdo rje 1996, p. 27.

107 Dpa' bo gtsug lag phreng ba, n.d., p. 874.

108 There are different interpretations as to the meaning of the term "dharmas" here. Some schools say that it refers to all phenomena of cyclic existence and nirvāṇa. Others take it to mean the enlightened qualities of Buddhahood that are intrinsic to the nature of mind or Buddha nature and thus describe this expanse as the source of all qualities of the noble ones.

109 Often a threefold division of awareness is presented:

(1) awareness of something other (mind being aware of something other than itself, such as outer objects)

(2) self-awareness (mind being aware of itself)

(3) awareness of the lack of nature.

"Awareness of the lack of nature" means to directly realize the true nature of all phenomena, i.e., that they are without nature. Such realization occurs from the path of seeing onward and is also called "the wisdom that realizes identitylessness," "yogic valid perception," or "personally experienced wisdom." The latter term emphasizes that this wisdom is a unique, immediate, and alive experience, not just some imagined idea of something of which one has heard or read. Mind realizing the nature of all phenomena includes mind being aware of its own ultimate nature, which is the unity of awareness and emptiness. Such realization is free from the triad of something that is aware, something of which it is aware, and the act of being aware, while at the same time being a vivid and transformative experience in the noble ones' own minds (Skt. pratyātmāryajñāna, Tib. 'phags pa'i so so rang gi ye shes). It is in this sense that many Tibetan masters, such as the Seventh Karmapa, have explained this wisdom as the most sublime expression of the principle that mind is able to be aware of itself in a nondual way, i.e., free from subject and object. However, this is to be clearly distinguished from the ordinary notion of self-awareness (2), which is that all beings are aware of their own direct experiences, such as being happy or sad.

This difference is reflected in the Sanskrit words *svasaṃvedana* (Tib. rang rig; self-awareness) and *pratyātmavid* (so so rang rig; personal experience) and its derivatives, such as *pratyātmavedanīya*. More literally, *pratyātmavedanīyajñāna* (Tib. so so rang rig pa'i ye shes) means "the wisdom of what is to be personally experienced (i.e., the true nature of phenomena)." (In themselves, the corresponding Tibetan expressions *rang rig* and *so so rang rig* do not mirror this distinction.)

In the Tibetan tradition, the meaning of *so so* in *so so rang rig pa'i ye shes* is explained in two ways. First, it refers to the fact that the final, immediate realization of the nature of our mind can only be accomplished by our mind's wisdom itself and not by anything extrinsic to it, such as the teacher's instructions or blessings. In other words, the only way to really personally *know* what a Buddha's or bodhisattva's wisdom is like is to experience it in our own mind. In this sense, such wisdom is truly inconceivable and incommunicable, which is part of what the term "personally experienced wisdom" indicates, since it is one's very own "private" experience unshared with others. (In this context, it should be clear that "personal" or "private" does not refer to an individual person, since the wisdom of the noble ones encompasses the very realization that there is no such person or self. Nevertheless, it is an experience that occurs only in certain distinct mind streams that have been trained and not in others.) The second explanation of *so so* is that, just like a mirror, this wisdom clearly sees all phenomena in a distinct way without mixing them up.

110 Dpa' bo gtsug lag phreng ba, n.d., p. 647.

111 Ibid., pp. 833–34.

112 Ibid., pp. 831–32.

113 In this respect, Mikyö Dorje's efforts here are very similar to Mipham Rinpoche's demonstration in his *Lamp of Certainty* (Tib. nges shes sgron me) three hundred years later that the

view of Consequentialism is in full accord with and essential for the teachings on Mahāsandhi (Tib. rdzogs chen).

114 *Saṃyutta Nikāya* II.17ff., specifically:
"That entities have existence, O Kaccāna, is one extreme. That entities have no existence is another extreme. These extremes are avoided by the Thus-Gone One, and he teaches the dharma from the middle."

115 In their more general sense, the terms "entity" and "nonentity" translate *bhāva/abhāva*, which are equivalents for "existent/nonexistent." As for the more specific sense of these terms when translating *vastu*, "entity" is a technical term that is defined as "something that is able to perform a function." This refers not only to material things but includes mind and its various expressions. Conversely, "nonentities" in this sense (such as empty space) cannot perform any function.

116 XV.7.

117 *Saṃyutta Nikāya* II.19ff.

118 Skt. avyākṛta, Tib. lung du ma bstan. These fourteen questions are as follows:
(a) the four wrong views of whether the Thus-Gone One (1) exists after death, (2) does not exist, (3) both, or (4) neither;
(b) the four wrong views of whether the world is (5) eternal, (6) not eternal, (7) both, or (8) neither;
(c) the four wrong views of whether the world (9) has an end, (10) has no end, (11) both, or (12) neither; and
(d) the two wrong views of whether the soul (or the self) and the body are (13) one or (14) different.
For all the references in the Pāli canon, see Della Santina 1986a, p. 15.

119 *Majjhima Nikāya* 72, *Aggi-Vaccagottasutta* 1.484.

120 Ibid., 1.486 (both quotes as translated in Lord Chalmers, *Further Dialogues of the Buddha*, vol. 1 (London: 1926)).

121 XXV.17 on views (a); XXVII.29 on views (b); XXVII.21–22 on views (c); XXVII.15–18 on views (d).

122 For example, see his *Precious Garland* II.4–6 on views (c).

123 For further references from the Pāli canon, see also Gómez 1976, Harris 1991, Sutton 1991, and Nayak 2001.

124 *Saṃyutta Nikāya* II.267.

125 *Saṃyutta Nikāya* IV (*Salāyatana-Vagga*, 54).

126 *Majjhima Nikāya* III.106–108.

127 Pāl. suññatassānimittassa lābhinī (*Therīgāthā* 46).

128 Skt. Ratnakūṭa, Tib. dkon brtsegs.

129 Skt. Pitāputrasamāgamasūtra, Tib. yab sras mjal ba'i mdo.

130 Skt. Saddharmapuṇḍarīkasūtra, Tib. dam chos pad ma dkar po'i mdo.

131 Skt. Laṅkāvatārasūtra, Tib. lang kar gshegs pa'i mdo. See Lindtner 1992 for very illuminating parallels between this sūtra and the early Madhyamaka texts by Nāgārjuna and

Āryadeva. Among later Madhyamaka works, frequent reference to this sūtra is mainly made in Kamalaśīla's *Stages of Meditation.*

132 Skt. Saṃdhinirmocanasūtra, Tib. dgongs pa nges par 'grel pa'i mdo.

133 a.k.a. Ācārya Śūra (Tib. rta dbyangs; slob dpon dpa' bo).

134 Tib. gzhung phyi mo'i dbu ma. Śāntideva is usually considered a Consequentialist.

135 For details on the Autonomist-Consequentialist distinction, see Chapter 3.

136 In the Tibetan translation of the only extant Indian commentary on Candrakīrti's *Entrance into Centrism,* Jayānanda's *Madhyamakāvatāraṭīkā* (P5271), the terms "Autonomist" (rang rgyud pa) and "Autonomist Centrist" (dbu ma rang rgyud pa) are mentioned a few times (ACIP TD3870-1@281A–282B). However, there is no reference to "Consequentialists" (thal 'gyur pa). There is also an anonymous, incomplete Sanskrit palm-leaf manuscript (**Lakṣaṇaṭīkā*) with short notes on Candrakīrti's *Lucid Words* and his autocommentary on *The Entrance into Centrism* that was preserved in Tibet. It refers to Bhā(va)viveka as a "proponent of autonomous proofs" (*svatantrasā[dha]navādin,* fol. 10b.6). The first (Tibetan) scholar who is reported to have made an explicit distinction by using both these names was Patsab Lotsāwa.

137 This refers to the classical Indo-Tibetan doxographical classification of four Buddhist philosophical systems: the Followers of the Great Exposition, the Sūtra Followers, the Yoga Practitioners (or Proponents of Cognizance), and the Centrists. This classification seems to have first appeared in the works of Bhāvaviveka and is later used in Bodhibhadra's *Jñānasārasamucchayanibandhana* (P5252), Mokṣākaragupta's *Tarkabhāṣā (P5762),* Maitrīpa's *Tattvaratnavāli* (P3085; which, however, includes the Sūtra Followers in the great vehicle), and Sahajavajra's *Sthitasamucchaya* (P3071). The names of the four schools are also found in the texts of Candrakīrti, Śāntarakṣita, and Kamalaśīla. In Tibet, this fourfold classification already appears in the ninth-century Sanskrit-Tibetan dictionary *Mahāvyutpatti* (Tib. bye brag tu rtogs par byed pa chen po) and became the standard doxographical classification of Buddhist philosophical systems. However, this set of four schools should be understood more as a pedagogical summary of the many strands and views of Buddhist schools in India. For example, what is called the Vaibhāṣika school here actually refers to at least eighteen schools that moreover never thought of themselves as belonging to a single main school. Strictly speaking, "Vaibhāṣikas" are only those among these schools who follow the *Mahāvibhāṣā,* a huge compendium on Abhidharma that was compiled by several arhats. As for the Sūtra Followers, from all that we know, there seem to have been only a handful of them (making the notion of a distinct school questionable), and none of their original texts have survived.

138 When these two masters are called Autonomists, it is only in retrospect and just refers to their approach of formulating Centrist reasonings. As for the contents of their system, they propagated a synthesis of Yogācāra and Madhyamaka that is quite different from, for example, Bhāvaviveka's presentation of Centrism. Therefore, it is not unproblematic to call all these masters Autonomists. (For more details, see Chapter 3.)

139 For example, during the early ninth century, Nāgārjuna's *Mūlamadhyamakakārikā* was already translated (later revised by Kanakavarman, Mahāsumati, and Patsab Lotsāwa) as well as Buddhapālita's and Bhāvaviveka's commentaries on this text. There were also translations of Nāgārjuna's *Yuktiṣaṣṭikā, Śūnyatāsaptati, Vigrahavyāvartanī,* and *Ratnāvalī,* along with Candrakīrti's commentaries on the first two of these texts. Of course, the early translations included the texts by Śāntarakṣita, Kamalaśīla, and Jñānagarbha. Śāntideva's *Bodhicaryāvatāra* also was translated at that time. All of these texts were then included in the first Tibetan catalogue of translations (Tib. dkar chag ldan dkar ma).

140 Tib. rngog lo tsā ba blo ldan shes rab.

141 His only surviving text is the *Dbu ma'i shar gsum gyi stong thun.* He was also well versed in the teachings on valid cognition and relied on them very much in his presentation of Madhyamaka. In fact, he considered Dharmakīrti to be a Mādhyamika. Obviously, Chaba was the first one to explain emptiness as a nonimplicative negation. Both this and his explanations on valid cognition were later adopted by Tsongkhapa and his followers (for more details, see the sections below on reasoning and Tsongkhapa's system).

142 Tib. 'brom ston pa rgyal ba'i 'byung gnas.

143 Tib. nag tsho lo tsā ba tshul khrims rgyal ba.

144 Tib. po to ba.

145 Madhyamaka lineage II from Atiśa and lineage III from Patsab Lotsāwa are transmitted not only in the Kagyü school but also in all other Tibetan schools.

146 This lineage is commonly known as the transmission of the Six Dharmas of Nāropa and thus is not specifically a Madhyamaka lineage.

147 There is a gap of about five hundred years between Nāgārjuna and Candrakīrti. One traditional account has it that Nāgārjuna had a life span of six hundred years, and Candrakīrti is then often presented as his direct disciple. The Eighth Karmapa quotes another version from an old manuscript about the history of the four transmission lineages of the Kagyüs that Marpa brought to Tibet. This text reports a prophecy by many ḍākiṇīs right after the passing-away of Nāgārjuna that he would be reborn as Candrakīrti five hundred years later. (Western scholarship assumes instead that there were two Nāgārjunas, an earlier one and a later one.) As for the transmission of the Madhyamaka lineage between Nāgārjuna and Candrakīrti according to Tāranātha, see below under the lineage from Atiśa.

148 Tib. 'gro mgon ras chen.

149 Tib. spom brag pa.

150 Tib. rgyal ba g.yung ston pa.

151 Tib. mkha' spyod dbang po.

152 Tib. de bzhin gshegs pa.

153 Tib. 'jam dpal bzang po.

154 Tib. dpal 'byor don grub.

155 Tib. snye mo go shri dkon mchog 'od zer.

156 Tib. rje btsun ras pa chen po. This is what the Eighth Karmapa calls his main teacher, the First Sangye Nyenba Rinpoche.

157 For the continuation of this lineage to the present day, see for example Douglas and White 1976.

158 Tib. yid la mi byed pa'i chos skor nyi shu rtsa lnga (the Sanskrit for "mental nonengagement" is *amanasikāra*). These twenty-five texts are P3073–3097. Their topic is not only "mental nonengagement" or Centrism; they treat a great variety of subjects pertaining to the great vehicle and the vajra vehicle.

159 Verse 2.

160 Fols. 179b.1–185a.4.

161 In Indian philosophy in general, Aspectarians, or Real Aspectarians (Skt. Sākāravādin/Satyākāravādin, Tib. rnam bcas pa/rnam bden pa), are those who assert that mind apprehends its objects via a mental aspect of the object that appears to consciousness. Buddhist Aspectarians are the Sūtra Followers and certain Yogācāras. Non-Aspectarians (Skt. Nirākāravādin, Tib. rnam med pa) are those who deny that there is such an aspect. Buddhist Non-Aspectarians are the Followers of the Great Exposition and certain Yogācāras who do not deny the mere appearance but the actual reality of such a mental, objective aspect ("False Aspectarians," Skt. Alīkākāravādin, Tib. rnam brdzun pa). In Tibet, these two kinds of Yogācāras are called "Real Aspectarian Mere Mentalists" (Tib. sems tsam rnam bden pa) and "False Aspectarian Mere Mentalists" (Tib. sems tsam rnam brdzun pa), because they either assert or deny that the objective aspect that appears to consciousness is really existent as mind.

Specifically, in his commentary, Sahajavajra identifies all the above schools as well as those Centrists whom he regards as asserting or denying aspects (Skt. Sākāramādhyamika/ Nirākāramādhyamika, Tib. rnam bcas dbu ma pa/rnam med dbu ma pa) as the persons who do not realize true reality.

162 In this context, it is interesting that the early Gelugpa scholar Sera Jetsünba Chökyi Gyaltsen (Tib. se ra rje btsun pa chos kyi rgyal mtshan, 1469–1546) has also affirmed that Maitrīpa, Marpa, and Milarepa are in accord with Candrakīrti (Gsung lan klu sgrub dgongs rgyan. New Delhi: Champa Chogyal, 1969, fols. 20b.3ff.). Also the later Gelugpa master Janggya Rölpay Dorje (Tib. lcang skya rol pa'i rdo rje, 1717–1786) in his *Presentation of Philosophical Systems* (Tib. grub pa'i mtha'i rnam par bzhag pa) says the same, using the above quote from Maitrīpa and explicitly adding Nāropa (see Lopez 1987, pp. 264–66).

163 Skt. *Alīkākāra-Cittamātra-Madhyamaka, Tib. sems tsam rnam rdzun gyi dbu ma (for the meaning and translation of the term "Mere Mentalism," see Chapter 4). Mikyö Dorje elaborates: This system explains that the actual meaning of the dohās of the siddhas lies in the ultimately established, self-aware, and self-luminous consciousness empty of apprehender and apprehended. This view has been widely represented in India and Tibet by master Vajrapāṇi (born 1017), Asu from Nepal, Kor Nirupa (1062–1162), and others. *The Blue Annals* (pp. 855–60) says that "the upper tradition of Mahāmudrā" (Tib. phyag chen stod lugs) comes from this Vajrapāṇi, who was a direct disciple of Maitrīpa. Asu is reported to have spent most of his life in the province of Ü (Tib. dbus) in central Tibet. From him comes "the lower tradition of Mahāmudrā" (Tib. phyag chen smad lugs).

164 Tib. 'gos lo tsā ba gzhon nu dpal. He was a translator and scholar who studied with many different masters from all schools of Tibetan Buddhism. His *Blue Annals* (Tib. deb ther sngon po) is one of the standard historical works in Tibet. Most of what Mikyö Dorje says in his introduction is also found in *The Blue Annals*. For details, see Ruegg 1988.

165 'Gos lo tsā ba gzhon nu dpal 1996, p. 724.

166 Tib. tha mal gyi shes pa mngon byed.

167 Different schools interpret the meaning of this term in various ways. As for its etymology, *The Treasury of Knowledge* quotes Ajitamitra's *Commentary on the Instructions for the King*: "The Body of Dharmatā is the Dharma Body. It is [called] 'body' for the following reasons: Since it is the 'body' of all dharmas, it does not go beyond the nature of the suchness of all beings. It is the support for all mundane and supramundane qualities."

Thus, in general, the word *dharma* in this term is understood to refer to all phenomena, to the nature of phenomena (Skt. dharmatā, Tib. chos nyid) or to the infinite and excellent qualities of enlightenment. Thus, *The Treasury of Knowledge* defines the Dharma Body as follows: "It is the very expanse of dharmas that is completely pure by nature and endowed with all uncontaminated qualities. By having become free from all adventitious stains as well, it is the very essence that is endowed with twofold purity. This is the Essence Body or Dharma Body." (Kong sprul blo gros mtha' yas 1982, vol. II, pp. 595–96).

168 Skt. dauṣṭhulya, Tib. gnas ngan len.

169 The text repeats several times that another name of Mother Prajñāpāramitā is Mahāmudrā (fols. 51a.8, 57b.3, 59b.4, and 65a.3) and also equates emptiness with Mahāmudrā.

170 P4532, fols. 43b.5; 45b.8; 46a.2–3; 47b.5–6.

171 Kong sprul blo gros mtha' yas 1982, vol. III, p. 378.

172 'Gos lo tsā ba gzhon nu dpal 1996, p. 725.

173 As in *The Blue Annals* ('Gos lo tsā ba gzhon nu dpal 1984, vol. II, pp. 847–48; misrepresented as a quote in slightly different form on p. 725 in the English translation) and *The Treasury of Knowledge* (Kong sprul blo gros mtha' yas 1982, vol. III, p. 381). Gö Lotsāwa's *Commentary on The Sublime Continuum* repeats this very same statement several times, relating it to both Sahajavajra (pp. 17.7–9, 137.15–23) and the Indian siddha Padampa Sangye's (d. 1117) instructions called *The Pacification of Suffering* (pp. 5.18–9; 53.2–4).

174 'Gos lo tsā ba gzhon nu dpal 2003, p. 137 (I am indebted to Klaus-Dieter Mathes for drawing my attention to these passages).

175 Fol. 176a.5.

176 Fol. 190a.5–7.

177 Fol. 189a.2–4.

178 Fols. 192a.8–192b.1. There are several other places in Sahajavajra's text that speak about the connections between Prajñāpāramitā, emptiness, Madhyamaka, and Mahāmudrā.

179 This means the nirvāṇa of a Buddha that does not abide either in cyclic existence or in the one-sided nirvāṇic peace of arhats.

180 Skt. Padminīnāmakālacakrapañjikā, Tib. dus 'khor kyi dka' 'grel padma can zhes bya ba, P1350 (quoted in Khro ru mkhan po tshe rnam 1989, p. 236).

181 Skt. Saptaśatikaprajñāpāramitāsūtra, Tib. sher phyin bdun bgrya pa.

182 ACIP KD0012@167B.

183 Skt. Sāgaramatiparipṛcchāsūtra, Tib. blo gros rgya mtshos zhus pa'i mdo.

184 P5324, fol. 106a.3–6.

185 Dpa' bo gtsug lag phreng ba, n.d., p. 325.

186 P5324, fol. 190b.1–2.

187 ACIP TD3915@34A–35B, TD3916@050A, and TD3917@62A–B. For more details, see the section on Madhyamaka meditation in Chapter 2.

188 Skt. amanasikāra/manasikārābhāva, Tib. yid la mi byed pa/yid la byed pa med pa.

189 Just Like *Tathāgatagarbha* (Tib. de gshegs snying po), this term is usually translated as "Buddha nature." In its original meaning, the Sanskrit term *garbha* signifies the space within some enclosure or sheath (it also came to mean "embryo," "seed," and, later, "essence"). This fits very well with a nonreifying understanding of Buddha nature as the open, luminous space of the nature of mind within the adventitious stains that obscure it. The term *tathāgatagarbha* can also be found in the Prajñāpāramitā sūtras. The *Adhyardhaśatikaprajñāpāramitā* says, "all

sentient beings contain the Heart of the Thus-Gone Ones" (Skt. sarvasattvās tathāgatagarbhāḥ; see Zimmermann 2002, p. 90). It does not appear in the Hīnayāna sūtras or other early texts of the Mahāyāna, but "the luminous mind defiled by and then cleansed of adventitious stains" can already be found in these scriptures (for example, *Aṅguttara Nikāya* I.10: *pabhassaraṃ idaṃ bhikkhave cittaṃ taṃ ca kho āgantukehi upakkilesehi upakkiliṭṭhaṃ*; *Aṣṭasāhasrikā* (ACIP KD0012@142B), *Pañcaviṃśatisāhasrikā* (ACIP KD0009-1@169A/KD0009–2@253A), *Samādhirājasūtra* (Dutt, ed. 1941–54 Vol. II.2, pp. 300.9–10); see also Ruegg 1969, pp. 411ff.).

190 Tib. phag mo gru pa, one of the three main disciples of Gampopa.

191 This text had apparently disappeared in India from about the seventh to the eleventh century. It is said to have been recovered by Maitrīpa from an old stupa.

192 'Gos lo tsā ba gzhon nu dpal 1996, p. 724. On Sūtra Mahāmudrā, see also pp. 840–41 and 976–77.

193 Tib. phyag rgya chen po man ngag gi bshad sbyar rgyal ba'i gan mdzod.

194 In Tibet, this name has become a pejorative stereotype, identified with the exclusive cultivation of a thought-free mental state—as representing realization of the ultimate—along with a complete rejection of the aspect of means, such as the accumulation of merit and proper ethical conduct. (However, there are at least two Tibetan versions of the debate at Samye, and the more verifiable one gives quite a different account of what Hvashang said. See Karmay 1988, the *Bsam gtan mig sgron*, and the *Sba bzhed* chronicle.)

195 Tib. bsam yas. This was the first Tibetan Buddhist monastery, which was established by King Trisong Detsen in the eighth century.

196 Tib. sdug bsgnal zhi byed.

197 Tib. pha dam pa sangs rgyas.

198 Tib. khro phu lo tsā ba byams pa'i dpal. According to *The Blue Annals*, he studied in Nepal and India and invited the three great paṇḍitas Mitrayogin, Buddhaśrī, and Śākyaśrībhadra to Tibet. He also received instructions on Mahāmudrā from two direct disciples of Gampopa and Pamo Truba, thus establishing one of the eight lesser Kagyü subschools, the Tropu Kagyü. He also received instructions on Mahāmudrā from two direct disciples of Gampopa and Pamo Truba ('Gos lo tsā ba gzhon nu dpal 1996, pp. 709–11).

199 a.k.a. Mitradzoki.

200 Tib. 'jam ba gling pa.

201 Tib. khrims khang lo chen.

202 Vanaratna visited for several years between 1433 and 1454.

203 In a recent edition of four Mahāmudrā texts written by Dzünba Chöle (Tib. btsun pa chos legs, 1437–1521) from the Bodong (Tib. bo dong) lineage in western Tibet, the author specifically mentions that his texts treat the sahajayoga (Tib. lhan cig skyes sbyor), which is another name for Gampopa's Mahāmudrā system. Dzünba Chöle's autobiography reports that it was from the Sakya master Paljor Sangbo (Tib. dpal 'byor bzang po) that he received both the Mahāmudrā teachings of Lama Shang (Tib. bla ma zhang yu brag pa brston 'grus grags pa, 1122–1193) and the cycle *Richö Korsum* (Tib. ri chos skor gsum) by Gyalwa Yanggönba (Tib. rgyal ba yang dgon pa, 1213–1258), a disciple of Götsangba Gönbo Dorje. See Btsun pa chos legs 2000.

There is also a Gelugpa Mahāmudrā lineage, which equally makes a distinction between Sūtra and Tantra Mahāmudrā. For details, see H. H. Dalai Lama 1997 and R. Jackson 2001.

204 Tāranātha's *History of Buddhism in India* (Tāranātha 1980) says that the Madhyamaka lineage after Āryadeva continued with the latter's disciple Rāhulabhadra (of the caste of śūdras, pp. 126, 136), Rāhulamitra, Nāgāmitra (p. 148), and Saṃgharakṣita (p. 151). The latter was the Madhyamaka teacher of both Buddhapālita and Bhāvaviveka (p. 186). Candrakīrti learned Nāgārjuna's works from some unnamed disciples of Bhāvaviveka and from Kamalabuddhi, a student of Buddhapālita (p. 198).

*The Blue Annals* ('Gos lo tsā ba gzhon nu dpal 1996, pp. 35, 344) as well as Tāranātha's and Butön's historical works also speak about the earlier Brahman Rāhulabhadra (the author of the *Prajñāpāramitāstotra*), who was the teacher of Nāgārjuna and ordained him as a monk.

205 Tib. rig pa'i khu byug.

206 Later, the Eighth Karmapa also mentions Nagtso Lotsāwa as being part of this lineage. He was sent to India by King Jangchub Ö (Tib. byang chub 'od) to invite Atīśa to Tibet and received this transmission from him. He did the first translation of Candrakīrti's *Entrance into Centrism* into Tibetan and was also instrumental in translating many other Madhyamaka texts.

207 Tib. spyan lnga ba tshul khrims 'bar.

208 Tib. bya yul ba.

209 Tib. sha ra ba.

210 This means that one negates the existence of something without affirming or implying anything about it, such as saying, "Purple flying rabbits do not exist." The other main type of negation in Indo-Tibetan logic is an implicative negation, in which something is implied or affirmed as a remainder after negating certain factors. For more details on these, see the section in chapter 2 on reasoning in Centrism.

211 Tib. stong nyid shor sa bzhi. These are four pitfalls to be avoided in advanced Mahāmudrā meditation: deviating from emptiness through grasping at it as the fundamental nature of knowable objects (Tib. shes bya'i gshis la shor ba), deviating from emptiness through sealing things and experiences as empty (Tib. rgyas 'debs su shor ba), deviating from emptiness through taking it as the remedy that annihilates the afflictions (Tib. gnyen por shor ba), and deviating from emptiness through taking meditation on emptiness as the only path that leads to the later attainment of Buddhahood (Tib. lam du shor ba).

212 *The Blue Annals* says that the disciples of Patsab Lotsāwa trace their lineage back to the Brahman Rāhulabhadra as the teacher of Nāgārjuna ('Gos lo tsā ba gzhon nu dpal 1996, pp. 35, 344).

213 He is said to have been one of the teachers of Atīśa. (Obviously, there is a gap of about two hundred years between Mañjuśrīkīrti and Devacandra. No further information on this seems to be available.)

214 This Kashmiri Brahman was the teacher of the translator Rinchen Sangbo (Tib. rin chen bzang po, 958–1055). He was the grandfather of Sajjana, who was a teacher of the translators Ngog Lotsāwa, Dsen Kawoche (Tib. btsan kha bo che, born 1021), and Zu Gaway Dorje (Tib. gzu dga' ba'i rdo rje, 11th century).

215 a.k.a. Hasumati.

216 According to *The Blue Annals* ('Gos lo tsā ba gzhon nu dpal 1996, p. 475) and Pawo Rinpoche's *History of the Dharma* (Dpa' bo gtsug lag phreng ba 1986, vol. II, p. 3), he also studied Centrism (particularly the texts by "the three Eastern Centrists" Jñānagarbha, Śāntarakṣita, and Kamalaśīla) with Chaba Chökyi Senge and Gyamarba Jangchub Tra (Tib. stod lungs pa

rgya dmar pa byang chub grags; a student of Ngog Lotsāwa and teacher of Chaba Chökyi Senge).

217 Patsab Lotsāwa had four main disciples: Tsangba Sarbö (Tib. gtsang pa sar sbos), Majaba Jangchub Yeshe (Tib. rma bya pa byang chub ye shes), Ngar Yönten Tra (Tib. ngar yon tan grags), and Shang Tangsagba Yeshe Jungnay (Tib. zhang thang sag pa ye shes 'byung gnas). Thus, in terms of this Madhyamaka transmission, one often speaks of "Patsab and his four sons" (Tib. pa tshab bu bzhi).

Note that Majaba Jangchub Yeshe is not to be confused with Majaba Jangchub Dsöndrü (Tib. rma bya pa byang chub brtson 'grus), who died around 1185. Often, however, the latter instead of the former is listed as one of the four sons of Patsab. In any case, Jangchub Dsöndrü first was a student of Chaba Chökyi Senge. Later, he became Patsab's disciple, thus following the Consequentialist approach and being an important figure in the early dissemination of this system in Tibet. He was also a disciple and collaborator of two of Patsab's contemporaries, the Kashmiri Centrist Jayānanda and his disciple Khu Lotsāwa Dode Bar (Tib. khu lo tsā ba mdo sde 'bar).

218 Tib. 'brom dbang phyug grags pa.

219 Tib. shes rab rdo rje.

220 Tib. bstan tshul and grags ldan.

221 Tib. bde ba'i lha.

222 Tib. jo btsun dbu ra pa (in *The Blue Annals*, jo btsun and dbu ra pa figure as two persons).

223 Tib. shes rab dpal.

224 Tib. dar ma shes rab.

225 Tib. bang ston shes rab rin chen.

226 Tib. bsod nams seng nge.

227 Tib. bang ston bsam gtan zang po.

228 Tib. bang ston gzhon nu bsam gtan.

229 Tib. thang nag pa.

230 Tib. bkra shis seng ge.

231 Tib. gzhon nu bzang po.

232 Tib. gsas khang pa chos grags.

233 Tib. thang sag pa gzhon nu rgyal mtshan. Starting with this name, the subsequent names in this lineage in *The Blue Annals* differ, the last one mentioned being Lodrö Balrinba (Tib. blo gros dpal rin pa). All of them are said to have expounded Centrism on the basis of Candrakīrti's *Lucid Words* and his autocommentary on *The Entrance into Centrism* ('Gos lo tsā ba gzhon nu dpal 1996, p. 344).

234 Tib. rgyal mo rong pa chen po.

235 Tib. byams chen rab 'byams pa sang rgyas 'phel.

236 Tib. 'bum phrag gsum pa. This is Paṇḍita Trilakṣa, a.k.a. Sthirapāla (Tib. brtan skyong).

237 Tib. lo chen skyabs mchog dpal bzang po, a Sakya master (1257-1310).

238 Tib. red mda' ba gzhon nu blo gros, one of the most famous Sakya masters (1348-1412). He was also the early Madhyamaka teacher of Tsongkhapa before the latter developed his own approach.

In his *Grub mtha' kun shes* (1999, p. 170), Dagtsang Lotsāwa says that, starting with the four sons of Patsab Lotsāwa, the transmission of Consequentialism reached Rendawa via the early Sakya masters, Bang Lotsāwa Lodrö Denba (Tib. dpang lo tsā ba blo gros brtan pa, 1276-1342), Shongtön Dorje Gyaltsen (Tib. shong ston rdo rje rgyal mtshan), Jamsar Sherab Öser (Tib. 'jam gsar shes rab 'od zer, both 13th-14th c.), Butön (1290-1364), and Kyabcho Balsangbo. For another, more detailed, lineage of Consequentialism from Patsab Lotsāwa to Rendawa, see Jackson 1985 (p. 31).

239 Tib. stag tshang lo tsā ba shes rab rin chen, another Sakya master (1405–?) who was one of the most severe critics of Tsongkhapa.

240 It may be added that Rongtön Sheja Künrig (considered to be a reincarnation of Kamalaśīla) is sometimes said to have tended toward the Autonomist approach. However, he belongs to two Consequentialist lineages from Patsab Lotsāwa within the Sakya school. In several of his Centrist works, he himself states that he follows the unbroken transmission from Patsab through Shang Tangsagba (whom he called "a new Candrakīrti") and also mentions Majaba Jangchub Dsöndrü as one of his sources. For details, see Jackson 1985 (pp. 26, 31), Yoshimizu 1993 (p. 213), and Ruegg 2000 (pp. 66–68).

241 ACIP KD0012@03A.

242 Tib. dol po pa shes rab rgyal mtshan (1292–1361).

243 These two masters are considered the main Indian commentators on the hidden meaning of the Prajñāpāramitā sūtras.

244 There is a play on the Tibetan words in the text, since it just says *dbu ma*. This can mean both Madhyamaka and the central channel in the body, which is "central" in Vajrayāna practice.

245 Dvags po bkra shis rnam rgyal, p. 153.3–4. The author of this classic Mahāmudrā text in the Kagyü tradition is considered to be an incarnation of Gampopa.

246 Ibid., pp. 155.5–156.2.

247 Skt. Prajñāpāramitāhṛdayasūtra, Tib. shes rab snying po'i mdo.

248 Skt. rūpa, Tib. gzugs. In its more specific sense, this term refers to visible forms—color and shape—but it is also used as an equivalent for matter in general. In the latter case, it includes the four great material elements as well as all five sense objects and their sense faculties, thus representing the first of the five aggregates. Here, the term is used in this second sense.

249 Skt. utpattikrama, Tib. bskyed rim.

250 Skt. saṃpannakrama, Tib. rdzogs rim.

251 Tib. shākya mchog ldan (1428–1507). He was a famous Sakya master and also a disciple of the Seventh Karmapa.

252 Quoted in *The Treasury of Knowledge* (Kong sprul blo gros mtha' yas 1982, vol. II, p. 553).

253 These are one-pointedness (Tib. rtse gcig), freedom from discursiveness (Tib. spros bral), one taste (Tib. ro gcig), and nonmeditation (Tib. sgom med).

254 Tib. nges don rgya mtsho (Rumtek ed., n.d., fol. 101a.3–b.2).

255 Tib. phyag rgya chen po khrid yig chen mo gnyug ma'i de nyid gsal ba (Tibetan text in *Clarifying the Natural State*. Hong Kong: Rangjung Yeshe Publications, 2001, p. 52).

256 Skt. Prajñāpāramitopadeśa, Tib. shes rab kyi pha rol tu phyin pa'i man ngag (P5579) by Ratnākaraśānti. (There is another text with the same name in the *Tengyur* by Kambala (P5314), but it is more like a very brief sādhana of Prajñāpāramitā.)

257 P5310–5312.

258 P5324 and P5325. For details on Atīśa's and Kamalaśīla's texts, see the section in Chapter 2 on Madhyamaka meditation and the Bibliography. Dvags po bkra shis rnam rgyal, *Moonbeams*, pp. 333.6–334.2.

259 Ibid., p. 359.1–2.

260 Ibid., pp. 402.1–403.1.

261 Ibid., pp. 394.6–395.2.

262 The ten perfections are the usual six of generosity, ethics, patience, vigor, meditative stability, and knowledge plus the four of means, aspiration prayers, power, and wisdom. Each of these ten perfections correponds to one of the ten grounds of bodhisattvas and represents the main practice on its respective ground.

263 This term is usually translated as "postmeditation," which at best seems to be too neutral a word and has the connotation of just taking a break. Subsequent attainment refers to the level of realization of emptiness that is attained as a result of having rested in meditative equipoise. Subsequent to rising from such equipoise, the realization of emptiness that has been gained while resting in it informs and enhances the seeing of the illusionlike nature of all appearances and experiences while practicing the six perfections during the time between the formal sessions of meditative equipoise. Actually, a synonym for subsequent attainment is "illusionlike samādhi."

264 VI.23.

265 1988, p. 54.

266 In the same vein, "the four realities of the noble ones"—usually translated as "the four noble truths"—do not really indicate some truths that are in themselves noble. Rather, they are described as the ways in which suffering, its origin, its cessation, and the path are clearly seen from the perspective of noble ones. From the perspective of ordinary deluded beings, these are neither true nor real. And even when ordinary beings gain some understanding that they are true, they do not at all experience the full scope of these four as their reality (see also *Bod rgya tshig mdzod chen mo*. Beijing: Mi rigs dpe skrun khang, 1985, pp. 1371, 1777).

267 Dpa' bo gtsug lag phreng ba, n.d., p. 644.

268 XXIV.10.

269 Skt. Dharmadhātuprakṛtisaṃbhedanirdeśasūtra, Tib. chos kyi dbyings kyi rang bzhin dbyer med par bstan pa'i mdo.

270 Dpa' bo gtsug lag phreng ba, n.d., pp. 645–46.

271 Lit. "children." This is an expression for ordinary beings who do not look beyond the immediate experiences of this life.

272 Dpa' bo gtsug lag phreng ba, n.d., pp. 646–47.

273 Skt. timira, Tib. rab rib. There is usually a wide range of translations of this term (such as "cataract" or "ophthalmia"). Judging by the symptoms of this visual impairment that are described in Tibetan texts, it must primarily refer to what—in Western terms—is called "floaters" or "mouches volantes." These are congealed proteins in the gel of the vitreous body of the eye that appear as floating, out-of-focus threads in the visual field. They are set into motion through eye movements, and when the eyes are kept still, they pass through one's visual field or sink down slowly, which can give the impression of slowly sinking hairs or a hair-net (Skt. keśa/keśoṇḍuka, Tib. skra shad). Sometimes they also appear as little dark dots. Such appearances can also just show as hazy spots in the visual field etc. They usually increase with age and can be seen best against bright backgrounds. All of this is not really considered as a disease in the West, since—to a varying degree—the same process happens in everybody's eyes. Some Tibetan texts mention also the symptom of double vision—such as seeing two moons—which can be a symptom of cataracts (degeneration of the eye-lens). Double vision does not appear though due to the above changes in the vitreous body, whereas patients with cataracts do not report "floating hairs" or the like. However, the analogy of the example that is given here—the scalpel that removes a membrane—would typically refer to operating on cataracts (the changes in the vitreous body cannot be operated on). Thus, one could describe "rab rib" as a general term for "blurred vision" due to turbidities in the eyes, be it in the vitreous body or the lens.

274 ACIP TD3860@13A.

275 Ibid., @14A

276 Lines 35ab.

277 Verse 4.

278 *Saṃyutta Nikāya* XXII, 94 (quote abbreviated).

279 IX.3–4ab.

280 Lit. "proponents of really existing entities."

281 For further explanations of the terms "nominal ultimate" and "nonnominal ultimate," see the section below entitled "Dividing Space: Divisions of the Ultimate."

282 ACIP TD3860@163B.

283 ACIP TD3856@56B.

284 In light of the above meanings of the term *saṃvṛti*, to translate it as "relative" seems far too vague and neutral. Moreover, both seeming and ultimate reality are relative for two reasons. First, as was shown, both do not exist on their own but only in mutual dependence. Second, the seeming appears only in relation to ordinary sentient beings and the ultimate only in relation to noble ones. In light of what was said about "truth" and "reality," the popular compound "relative truth" does not make things any better.

285 ACIP TD3856@59B.

286 Technically speaking, in Sanskrit, this is a *karmadhāraya* compound.

287 In this case, the compound is read as a *tatpuruṣa* compound.

288 This would be a *bahuvrīhi* compound, literally meaning "that which has or entails the ultimate object."

289 ACIP TD3860@163B.

290 To translate *paramārtha* as "absolute" is highly misleading, since it turns the Centrist approach upside down. The whole point of Centrism is to demonstrate again and again that there is nothing absolute; there is not something that exists inherently on its own and independently of any circumstances. It should be very clear that ultimate reality is no exception to that. Thus, something absolute is precisely the object of negation throughout the Centrist view and is not its ultimate reality.

291 Dpa' bo gtsug lag phreng ba, n.d., p. 644.

292 VI.28.

293 This type of ignorance belongs to the afflictive obscurations, which mainly obstruct liberation from cyclic existence. Unafflicted ignorance constitutes the cognitive obscurations, which mainly obstruct the omniscience of Buddhahood.

294 Skt. Prajñāpāramitāsaṃcayagāthā, Tib. shes rab kyi pha rol tu phyin pa sdud pa tshigs su bcad pa (abbr. mdo sdud pa).

295 Verses 7–9.

296 Verse 5.

297 ACIP TD3882@04A-04B.

298 III.282. This is what is meant by the expression "the center free from extremes" (Tib. mtha' bral dbu ma).

299 Skt. Dvayasatyāvatārasūtra, Tib. bden pa gnyis la 'jug pa'i mdo.

300 Verse IX.2cd.

301 Roughly speaking, this term refers here to the process of exhaustively eliminating every mistaken mental reference point, which results in the recognition that there is no reference point to be seen.

302 This refers to the process of ascertaining something that remains after the exclusion of certain features of this something, such as eliminating the wrong notion that a tree in the dark is a robber and thus ascertaining that the tree is just a tree.

303 Skt. bhūtakoṭi, Tib. yang dag mtha'.

304 In this explanation of dharmadhātu, "dharmas" are not understood as phenomena but as all the positive qualities in terms of the realization and relinquishment of the noble ones.

305 Mi bskyod rdo rje, n.d., vol. I, p.357.

306 The detailed presentation of these eight flaws makes up the sūtra's third chapter, called "The Questions of Suviśuddhamati" (ACIP KL0107@10A–14B).

307 This term refers to conceptual objects by indicating the process through which they appear for the thinking mind. For example, impermanent phenomena and phenomena that arise from causes and conditions are not different in nature, since all impermanent phenomena arise from causes and conditions, and all phenomena that arise from causes and conditions are impermanent. However, when we think "impermanent phenomena," a different mental image or notion comes to mind than when we think "phenomena that arise from causes and conditions." It is said that we select the specific notion of "impermanent phenomena" through the conceptual exclusion of everything that is not an impermanent phenomenon. In this way, a certain notion is isolated from all other notions, and this is why it is called an isolate.

308 Quoted in Mi bskyod rdo rje 1996, pp. 256–57.

309 Ibid., p. 258.

310 Skt. Ratnakaraṇḍasūtra, Tib. dkon mchog za ma tog gi mdo.

311 Skt. Mahābherīhārasūtra, Tib. rnga bo chen po'i mdo.

312 XXII.16, XXV.19.

313 In order to truly realize his teachings, the Buddha advised, one should rely not on persons but on the dharma; not on words but on the meaning; not on consciousness but on wisdom; and not on the expedient meaning but on the definitive meaning.

314 Tib. dus gsum mkhyen pa'i zhus lan, fol. 81b.4.

315 Tib. grags pa rgyal mtshan.

316 Lit. "those with or at a ford" (also Tīrthakara—"ford-builder"). Originally, this was a neutral term, meaning "follower of a spiritual system." Specifically, the Jainas refer to their founding gurus by the name Tīrthakara. In Buddhist texts, this is a general—and rather pejorative—term for non-Buddhist schools and practitioners in India. In his *Treasury of Knowledge*, Jamgön Kongtrul Lodrö Taye explains this term in a more positive way as referring to those who dwell within a part (*mu*) of liberation or on a stepping-stone (*stegs*) toward it, although their paths are not sufficient to grant actual release from saṃsāra. (Kong sprul blo gros mtha' yas 1982, vol. II, p. 335).

317 Quoted in Mi bskyod rdo rje 1996, p. 260.

318 In India, the teachings on mind training were only transmitted orally and were brought to Tibet by Atīśa. The first one to write them down in the presentation of seven topics was Geshe Chekawa Yeshe Dorje (Tib. dge bzhes 'chad ka ba ye shes rdo rje, 1101–1175). The quote is slogan III.14.

319 Padma dkar po, pp. 111–12.

320 ACIP TD3862@255A.

321 VI.24–25.

322 Verses 2–3.

323 VI.79.

324 For more details and scriptural evidence, see Chapter 3.

325 For example, ACIP KD0012@23A and KL0009-2@11B.

326 IX.32, 34.

327 Kong sprul blo gros mtha' yas 1982, vol. III, pp. 28–29. For more details on the distinction between nominal and actual ultimate reality, see Chapter 3.

328 On the topic of translating these terms and other details, see the section below entitled "The Two Types of Identitylessness."

329 Skt. vimokṣadvāra, Tib. rnam par thar pa'i sgo. In brief, the nature of phenomena is emptiness; causes lack any signs or defining characteristics; and the appearance of results is not bound to expectations or wishes.

330 Skt. anabhisaṃskāradvāra, Tib. mngon par 'du mi byed pa'i sgo.

331 For further details, see the section below entitled "The Emptiness of Emptiness."

332 VI.23.

333 This is the highest type of meditative absorption within the fourth meditative stability of the form realm, during which primary minds and mental events with an unstable continuum—i.e., the five sense consciousnesses, the mental consciousness, and their accompanying mental events—temporarily cease. However, the latent tendencies for the arising of these consciousnesses are not eliminated. Thus, mistaken appearances will occur again, once one rises from this meditative absorption. When performed for a long time, it leads to rebirth in the highest level of the gods of the form realm.

334 Verses 10, 13b–d, 14 (Bhavya is another name of Bhāvaviveka. His statement is found in *The Heart of Centrism*, III.285).

335 VI.23b.

336 XXV.13.

337 XXIV.9–10.

338 V.10 and VIII.19.

339 VI.80ab.

340 Kong sprul blo gros mtha' yas 1982, vol. II, p. 534.

341 Tib. sor mo'i phreng ba la phan pa'i mdo.

342 Skt. Hīnayāna, Tib. theg pa chung ngu/dman pa. The terms "lesser vehicle," "inferior vehicle," and "lower vehicle" are in no way meant to disparage the practitioners of this path. Rather, the teachings of this most basic vehicle are as essential for the practice of all other Buddhist vehicles as a house's lowest part—its foundation—is for its higher stories. In the sūtras of the great vehicle, these terms are often used by the Buddha himself to indicate the differences in view, path, and fruition between this vehicle and the great vehicle.

343 Skt. Brahmāviśeṣacintisūtra, Tib. tshangs pa khyad par sems kyis zhus pa'i mdo.

344 Skt. Tathāgatajñānamudrāsamādhisūtra, Tib. de bzhin gshegs pa'i ye shes kyi phyag rgya'i ting nge 'dzin gyi mdo.

345 1960, p. 15.

346 ACIP TD3854@260B. The traditional ascription of this text to *the* Bhāvaviveka is disputed. For an overview of the reasons to confirm his authorship, see Lindtner 1982b.

347 Verses IX.9ab, 39, 76–77.

348 Etymologically, the Sanskrit word *śūnyatā* stems from the root *śvi-/śū-* ("to swell"), which implies the notion of hollowness. In this way, the phenomena of seeming reality outwardly appear to be real and solid, while actually resembling empty balloons, only inflated by ignorance.

349 In both cases, "nature" translates the Sanskrit term *svabhāva* (Tib. rang bzhin/ngo bo nyid), which literally means "own-being," "self-existence," or "intrinsic state of being."

350 XV.1–2.

351 ACIP KL0176@341B.

352 Verse 53.

353 VI.184–185.

354 ACIP TD3862@315A.

355 XXIV.18.

356 Biologically speaking, a banana or plantain "tree" is not a tree but a species of grass. Thus, very much like an onion, it consists only of several layers of leaves without a core.

357 I.88–92.

358 These are the four immeasurables (Skt. caturapramāṇa, Tib. tshad med bzhi).

359 These are the four means of attracting those to be trained (Skt. catursaṃgrahavastu, Tib. bsdu ba'i dngos po bzhi).

360 The preceding seven sets constitute the thirty-seven dharmas that concord with enlightenment.

361 P47, fols. 216b–218a.

362 ACIP TD3916@51B and TD3917@67B.

363 I.16.

364 ACIP KL0107@034B.

365 Skt. Śatasāhasrikaprajñāpāramitāsūtra, Tib. shes rab kyi pha rol tu phyin pa stong phrag brgya pa.

366 Skt. Pañcaviṃśatisāhasrikāprajñāpāramitāsūtra, Tib. mdo le'u brgyad ma. In this version, Haribhadra has inserted the names of the chapters and topics of *The Ornament of Clear Realization* before the corresponding sections of the sūtra.

367 This is a summary of *The Prajñāpāramitā Sūtra in Eight Thousand Lines.*

368 In his commentary on *The Ornament of Clear Realization*, he enumerates and compares all three sets of sixteen, eighteen, and twenty emptinesses in detail (Mi bskyod rdo rje n.d., vol. II, pp. 363–73).

369 Verse 23.

370 This refers to the attainment of arhathood while still being alive in one's physical body. Thus, there is some remainder of the five aggregates.

371 This is the attainment of arhathood right after death without any remainder of the five aggregates.

372 Skt. prakṛtiśūnyatā, Tib. rang bzhin stong pa nyid.

373 Skt. svalakṣaṇaśūnyatā, Tib. rang gi mtshan nyid stong pa nyid. Usually, specifically characterized phenomenon is an equivalent for conditioned phenomenon, i.e., a concrete phenomenon that has its own specific and unique characteristics, such as a blue cup in front of us. It is unique in that there is no other cup in the world that is its exact likeness. This contrasts with generally characterized phenomena, such as the concept "blue cup," which is a general category that covers many specific instances of blue cups. Moreover, the blue cup in front of us performs the function of holding water, while the concept "blue cup" does not.

374 Skt. anupalambhaśūnyatā, Tib. mi dmigs pa stong pa nyid.

375 Skt. abhāvasvabhāvaśūnyatā, Tib. dngos po med pa'i ngo bo nyid stong pa nyid.

376 Skt. bhāvaśūnyatā, Tib. dngos po stong pa nyid.

377 Skt. abhāvaśūnyatā, Tib. dngos po med pa stong pa nyid.

378 Skt. svabhāvaśūnyatā, Tib rang gi ngo bo stong pa nyid. Here, I translated *svabhāva* as "self-entity" (instead of just "entity" or "nature") in order to highlight the contrast between this emptiness and the following one.

379 Skt. parabhāvaśūnyatā, Tib. gzhan gyi ngo bo/gzhan gyi dngos po stong pa nyid.

380 ACIP TD3862@324B.

381 P5192, fols. 69b.2–71a.8.

382 Skt. adhimukticaryā, Tib. mos pas spyod pa. In general, the term "engagement through devoted interest" stands for the level of bodhisattva practice on the two paths of accumulation and junction. Since the nature of phenomena has not been seen directly, one engages in the path with a conceptual mind motivated by the devoted interest to see this nature. In particular, in the Prajñāpāramitā sūtras, this term refers mostly to the path of junction alone, which is how it is used by Haribhadra here.

383 Skt. dharmottara, Tib. chos mchog. This is the fourth and highest level of the path of junction.

384 Skt. svayaṃbhūta, Tib. rang 'byung nyid.

385 "Yogic valid perception" refers to directly realizing the nature of phenomena on the path of seeing and above.

386 *The Treasury of Knowledge* presents both sets, while Pawo Rinpoche's commentary presents only the latter.

387 In Buddhism, the physical sense faculties are regarded as a kind of subtle matter. They are located in, but are distinct from, the gross physical sense organs, such as the eyeballs.

388 Haribhadra's *Illumination of The Ornament of Clear Realization* gives a similar explanation: "Also the emptiness of the primordial nature of the wisdom that focuses on the emptiness of the internal and so on through the emptiness of all phenomena is emptiness. Therefore, it is the emptiness of emptiness. The mere wisdom that all phenomena are emptiness is the emptiness of all phenomena. Also this [fourth emptiness] here teaches emptiness, because it relinquishes conceptions that cling to [this wisdom] as such." (P5192, fol. 69b.5–7)

389 This is a term for Buddha nature.

390 This does not mean that hearers and solitary realizers also meditate on the four emptinesses of the conditioned phenomena of the path, the unconditioned phenomena of nirvāṇa, the middle way, and cyclic existence. However, they engage in the path, attain nirvāṇa, practice the middle way free from the extremes of ascetism and indulgence, and relinquish cyclic existence. On the other hand, they do not engage in dedications and so on in order to render all that is positive inexhaustible. They also do not deal with Buddha nature, a Buddha's major and minor marks, or the Buddha qualities.

391 The terms "imaginary form" (Skt. parikalpitarūpa, Tib. kun tu brtags pa'i gzugs), "conceived form" (Skt. vikalpitarūpa, Tib. rnam par brtags pa'i gzugs), and "perfect form" (Skt. pariniṣpannarūpa, yongs su grub pa'i gzugs), or "form in terms of the nature of phenomena" (Skt. dharmatārūpa, Tib. chos nyid kyi gzugs) appear quite frequently in the Prajñāpāramitā sūtras, most prominently in the chapter of Maitreya in *The Prajñāpāramitā Sūtra in Twenty-five Thousand Lines.* These terms can be equated with the three natures: the imaginary nature, the other-dependent nature, and the perfect nature respectively.

392 In addition, in the eighth chapter of *The Sūtra That Unravels the Intention* (The Questions of Maitreya), the Buddha describes how these sixteen emptinesses serve to eliminate the different kinds of clinging to the various signs of realizing suchness.

393 In the presentation of sixteen emptinesses, the emptiness of emptiness (A4) switches places with the emptiness of the great (A5), while the emptiness of specifically characterized phenomena (A13) does the same with the emptiness of all phenomena (A14). The emptiness of nonentities (A17/B15) and the emptiness of the nature of nonentities (A18/B16) are also found in different places.

394 Obviously, this does not mean that Buddha nature is something that can be pinned down as having some intrinsic nonempty nature of its own.

395 Compare, for example, with Latin *anima* and German *Atem.*

396 ACIP TD3865@190B.

397 When it is clear from the context that the single term *ātman* indeed *is* of a personal nature, for the sake of convenience, I still mostly use the word "self."

398 Often translated as "the views about the transitory collection." For an explanation of this term, see the section below entitled "Personal Identitylessness."

399 VI.44.

400 Actually, personal identitylessness is just an instance of phenomenal identitylessness. As will be explained below, it is nevertheless taught separately for a specific purpose.

401 I.35.

402 II.219cd–220ab.

403 I.3ab and VI.120.

404 II.223ab.

405 I.29–30.

406 XIV.25cd.

407 VI.165.

408 For details, see Appendix II.

409 For more details, see Chapter 5.

410 However, as will be explained below, when actually practicing the progressive stages of meditation on emptiness, one begins with personal identitylessness, since it is the object of the coarser form of the general clinging to identity.

411 Originally, the first aggregate just referred to one's body. Later, it became an equivalent for matter in general.

412 Skt. Saṃmitīya, Tib. mang pos bkur ba. This is one of the eighteen subschools of the Followers of the Great Exposition.

413 Skt. Vātsīputrīya, Tib. gnas ma bu pa. Vātsīputra was a disciple of Śāriputra, and his followers represent another one of the eighteen subschools.

414 VI.179ab. For further explanations on the relation between personal and phenomenal identitylessness and how this pertains to the realizations of hearers, solitary realizers, and bodhi-

sattvas, see the section in Chapter 3 entitled "Do Hearers and Solitary Realizers Realize Emptiness?"

415 These two words are cognate with the Sanskrit root *jñā* in both *prajñā* and *jñāna.*

416 The four major common sciences are (1) linguistics, (2) epistemology, (3) medical science, and (4) arts and crafts. The five minor are (1) calculation (which includes astronomy, astrology, and mathematics), (2) poetry, (3) prosody, (4) expression and style, and (5) dance and drama.

417 Skt. Saptaśatikaprajñāpāramitā, Tib. sher phyin bdun bgrya pa.

418 Verse 48.

419 Verse 1.

420 Mi bskyod rdo rje, n.d., vol. I, p.4..

421 ACIP TD3860@163B.

422 Ibid., @184A.

423 ACIP TD3862@255A.

424 Skt. Sarvabuddhaviṣayāvatārajñānālokālaṃkārasūtra, Tib. sangs rgyas thams cad kyi yul la 'jug pa'i ye shes snang ba'i rgyan gyi mdo.

425 Skt. Gaganagañjaparipṛcchāsūtra, Tib. nam mkha'i mdzod kyis zhus pa'i mdo.

426 P5324, fol. 106a.3–6.

427 XI.17.

428 ACIP TD3862@331B.

429 Mi bskyod rdo rje 1996, p. 673.

430 Verse V.21/I.154.

431 Skt. Vajrasamādhisūtra, Tib. rdo rje'i ting nge 'dzin gyi mdo.

432 Soteriological questions are surely relevant in Jewish, Christian, and Islamic ideologies or mysticism. However, usually, these systems only talk about liberating human beings. Also, they are considered religious systems more than philosophies.

433 1979, p. 12.

434 Verses 69cd–70. There is dispute among Western scholars about Nāgārjuna's authorship. For positive evidence, see Lindtner (1982a, 1992), who is criticized by Dragonetti (*WZKS* 1986).

435 Dpa' bo gtsug lag phreng ba, n.d., p. 831.

436 Tib. nges shes sgron me; translated by Pettit (1999) as *Mipham's Beacon of Certainty.*

437 VI.4–5. These verses are also found in the *Subhāṣitasaṃgraha,* an anonymous compilation of extracts from Buddhist texts (Sanskrit edition by C. Bendall 1903–4, p. 387).

438 Kong sprul blo gros mtha' yas 1982, vol. III, p. 37.

439 VIII.15.

440 XXII.11.

441 Verses 9–12ab.

442 Tib. mnyam med dvags po bka' brgyud kyi lta sgom la nges pa cha tsam rnyed pa'i glu gnyug ma rang shar, lines 12–13.

443 Tib. phyag chen sngon 'gro.

444 In order to avoid confusing formal Indo-Tibetan rhetorical reasonings (Skt. prayogavākya, Tib. sbyor ba'i ngag) with Aristotelian syllogistics, I do not use the Western term "syllogism." Specifically, Dharmakīrti-type formal inferences for one's own benefit and for the benefit of others both have different formats from Aristotelian syllogisms. Moreover, the arguments for the benefit of others are not primarily deductive formats (they do not include the thesis), while Aristotelian syllogisms definitely are (one of their three members is the thesis). For the differences, see the comparison of the formats of these two inferences with the well-known three-part Aristotelian syllogism below.

445 In this limited context, I deliberately do not touch upon the many technicalities, such as specific terms, logical fallacies, and the issues of deduction and induction, that are related to the presentation of the three modes. Rather, I choose a simplified description in terms of set theory in order to facilitate a basic understanding of Centrist reasonings. Thus, instead of speaking of logical "entailment" (Skt. vyāpti, Tib. khyab pa), I explain the three modes here in terms of "inclusion" of one set in another. (May great logicians bear with me!) If one lacks a basic understanding of the three modes, the intricacies of Centrist reasonings are very often difficult to penetrate. Readers who wish to go into detail may refer to the vast specific literature on Buddhist reasoning and logic. See, for example, Dreyfus 1997 and Perdue 1993.

446 This is also called a formal probative argument (Skt. prayogavākya, Tib. sbyor ba'i ngag).

447 Compare the above two formats of reasoning with the classical Aristotelian syllogism:
All men are mortal.
Socrates is a man.
Therefore, Socrates is mortal.
The format of the inference for others is not to be confused with the classical five-membered Indian probative argument developed by the non-Buddhist school of the Logicians (see chapter 3).

448 Skt. adṛśyānupalabdhihetu, Tib. mi snang ma dmigs pa'i gtan tshigs.

449 Skt. dṛśyānupalabdhihetu, Tib. snang rung ma dmigs pa'i gtan tshigs.

450 Skt. saṃbhandhānupalabdhihetu, Tib. 'brel zla ma dmigs pa'i gtan tshigs.

451 For example, in "At this restaurant, there is no elephant," what is to be negated is that there *is* an elephant at the restaurant. The predicate of what is to be negated is just the phrase "there is an elephant." ("At this restaurant" is the subject in question, i.e., the specific place of the nonexistence of an elephant.)

452 Skt. viruddhopalabdhihetu, Tib. 'gal zla dmigs pa'i gtan tshigs.

453 Examples are provided only for the obvious ones of the various types of pseudoreasons, because the others would require too much explanation as to exactly how they do not apply or are contradictory or uncertain. For details, see Dreyfus 1997 and Perdue 1993.

454 Verse 22.

455 There is no room here to elaborate on this greatly relevant issue. A detailed presentation can be found in, for example, the second chapter of Dharmakīrti's *Commentary on Valid Cognition* that establishes the Buddha as the ultimate source of valid cognition (translated in R. Jackson 1993). It includes an account of the mind-body problem, i.e., that in Buddhism, mind

is not just a "self-emerging quality" or an epiphenomenon of the body or the brain. For this, see also the explanation of the last part of the vajra sliver reasoning that negates arising without any cause in the section below entitled "The Five Great Madhyamaka Reasonings."

456 Western science refers to this and many other kinds of behavior as "instinct," which is a very convenient category to subsume any behavior that is inexplicable through learning or other conditions in this life, without, however, explaining much. In Buddhism, "instinct" is explained as the ripening of habitual tendencies from past lifetimes.

457 In addition, it does not deny the existence of heaven in the first place.

458 Space is defined as the mere absence of anything that has the capacity to obstruct.

459 The four extremes are existence, nonexistence, both, and neither. The eight reference points are four pairs that are listed in the opening verse of *The Fundamental Verses on Centrism*: arising and ceasing, permanence and extinction, coming and going, and unity and multiplicity.

460 Verse 59.

461 IX.32–34.

462 Tib. bsod nams rtse mo.

463 This is a technical term for a mental image as the object of a conceptual consciousness.

464 Bsod nams rtse mo 1994, p. 1143.

465 VI.118.

466 VI.117.

467 Ngog Lotsāwa seems to have tended in that direction too.

468 ACIP KD0012@23A and KL0009-2@11B.

469 Tib. gtsang nag pa brtson 'grus seng ge, a disciple of Chaba Chökyi Senge.

470 Here, "worldly" refers to the conceptual inferential cognitions of practitioners on the paths of accumulation and junction before they attain a direct realization of ultimate reality on the path of seeing, which is the first supramundane path.

471 Verses 28–30.

472 VI.185.

473 ACIP TD3862@315A.

474 Ch. LIII, fol. 279.

475 Technically speaking, these conceptual mental images are called "object generalities" or "term generalities," depending on whether they are triggered by the perception of their referent object or by just hearing or reading a term. For example, we may give rise to the mental image "chair" upon seeing the shape and color of what we consider a chair. Such an image may also appear in our mind when reading the word "chair" in a book or hearing it from someone else.

476 In Buddhism, the term "substance" can refer to either material or mental substance.

477 I.3ab and VI.120.

478 Verses 10, 13b–d, 14.

479 Verses 31–33 (Unless otherwise indicated, all subsequent quotations in this section are from this text.)

480 ACIP TD3832@129A–129B.

481 This is a summary of verses 40–51. It is to be noted that especially this part of *The Rebuttal of Objections* about the rejection of valid cognition is almost never quoted or dealt with in Gelugpa texts. Obviously, this text by Nāgārjuna does not really support the Gelugpa emphasis on entities being established through conventional valid cognition. Usually, mainly verse 29 on "no thesis" is quoted and then interpreted as just referring to Centrists' having no "autonomous or really existing thesis" (Tsongkhapa's *Essence of Good Explanations* quotes verse 41 on valid cognition not being established through itself but interprets it as just refuting self-aware consciousness; see Thurman 1989, p. 321).

482 Verses 1–2, 17–19.

483 Verse 24.

484 Ruegg (2002) quotes *The Sūtra of the Arrival in Laṅka* to the same effect: "that the statement 'all entities/dharmas are unoriginated' should not be made a thesis (*pratijñā*) because the deconstruction of the thesis thus ensues (*pratijñāhāniḥ prasajyate*)." (p. 113).

485 Verse 23.

486 IX.138–140.

487 VI.175.

488 Verses 26, 61–62.

489 ACIP TD3832@127B–128A.

490 Verses 63–64.

491 ACIP TD3832@135A–135B.

492 To be sure, in terms of ethics, conduct, karmic causes and results, and such on the level of seeming reality, their words are clearly not noncommittal.

493 IX.109–110.

494 XXIV.11. Awareness-mantras (Skt. vidyāmantra, Tib. rig sngags) can be used to propitiate mundane and supramundane deities in order to partake of their activity. If these mantras are used improperly, however, these deities might turn against the person who supplicates them.

495 This statement represents claims of a partial kind of emptiness (such as that there must exist some basis for appearances) and attempts to establish seeming reality in its own right.

496 ACIP TD3860@164B.

497 Verse 82.

498 Verses 58ab, 88, 101.

499 XXIV.1.

500 XXIV.16–17, 20.

501 ACIP TD3860@109A–109B.

502 IX.33.

503 IX.25.

504 Verse 67.

505 Lines 28cd.

506 ACIP TD3832@128A.

507 ACIP TD3860@023B.

508 Ibid., @164A.

509 XXIV.10.

510 These texts include his *Commentary on the Mind of Enlightenment, The Precious Garland,* and *A Letter to a Friend.*

511 I could not locate this quote in Āryadeva's texts.

512 ACIP TD3854@261B–262A.

513 XVIII.5.

514 ACIP TD3860@162A–162B.

515 Verses 70–71.

516 1983, pp. 150–51.

517 Verses 29–30.

518 Verse 50.

519 XVI.25. This verse mentions only three of the four extreme positions. However, implicitly, it also includes the fourth possibility of being neither existent nor nonexistent, as can be seen in such verses as XIII.20 and XIV.21.

520 Verse 68. In his autocommentary, Śāntarakṣita makes it clear that this verse also includes the fourth possibility of neither existence nor nonexistence (ACIP TD3885@072A).

521 ACIP TD3860@05B. Often, autonomous inferences are explained as entailing the three modes of a correct reason, which must be established through valid cognition. There is, however, a wide range of different understandings of what exactly "autonomous reasoning" means. For details, see Chapter 3.

522 Ibid., @08A.

523 XVIII.9, see also XXIV.8–10, 18.

524 Lines 24ab.

525 IX.53ab.

526 ACIP TD3856@60B. Technically, in Indian debate language, plain destructive caviling for the mere sake of arguing, without having and trying to prove a thesis of one's own, is called *vitaṇḍā* (Tib. khyad gsod byed pa). Almost all Indian schools of thought regard such an approach as a fallacy in debate.

527 IV.8–9.

528 Interestingly, the same issue is treated in detail in *The Sūtra of the Arrival in Laṅka* (ACIP KL0107@193B-194B).

529 VI.173.

530 ACIP TD3862@311A.

531 Quoted in Mi bskyod rdo rje 1996, p. 569.

532 Ibid., pp. 569–70.

533 Ibid., pp. 469–70.

534 For example, both in the first chapter of his *Lucid Words* (ACIP TD3860@05A) and in his autocommentary on *The Entrance into Centrism* (ACIP TD3862@247A) Candrakīrti uses the term "position" (Skt. pratijñā, Tib. dam bca') for the four negative statements in verse I.1 of Nāgārjuna's *Fundamental Verses* (i.e., that entities do not arise from themselves, nor from others, and so on). *The Lucid Words* also applies this term to what Nāgārjuna says in other verses, such as VIII.1 (ACIP TD3860@061A) and XX.19 (@131B). However, he makes it clear that all of these are just "mere positions" in the sense of what conforms with reasoning. None of them involves any ontological or other commitment on the part of Centrists.

535 See the section above entitled "Freedom Is the Nature of Not Having a Nature."

536 As Ruegg 2000 (pp. 159-60) points out, this statement is found in both Gorampa's (1429–1489) and Majaba Jangchub Dsöndrü's commentaries on *The Fundamental Verses*, with the first explicitly presenting it as Patsab's view. The same is expressed in Rongtön Sheja Künrig's commentary on *The Entrance into Centrism.*

537 Padma dkar po, n.d., p. 114.

538 1983, pp. 157–59.

539 Verses 51, 59.

540 I.72.

541 Tib. mkhas pa rnams 'jug pa'i sgo.

542 Verses 70–72.

543 Verses 9–11. The last two lines of the quote refer to Vimalakīrti's famous silence in the *Vimalakīrtinirdeśasūtra*, when Mañjuśrī had a dialogue with him about ultimate reality.

544 Lines 7, 18–20.

545 III.282.

546 ACIP TD3853@48B-49A.

547 Ibid., @227B.

548 ACIP TD3889@286A.

549 ACIP TD3915@35A.

550 In particular, the issues of whether Centrists have a philosophical system and thesis of their own and in what sense, in the light of their treatment by Tsongkhapa and his followers, assume a dimension that goes far beyond methodology or reasoning. The Gelugpa school presents these points as being of fundamental ontological and epistemological significance. For more details, see Chapter 3.

551 Theoretically, one could add the last two possibilities to the reasoning of the freedom from unity and multiplicity too, and investigate whether really existing things can be both a unity and a multiplicity or neither. The main reason these options are not explicitly investigated in this reasoning is that the impossibility of something being both a unity and a multi-

plicity or neither is just so much more obvious than the impossibility of things arising from both themselves and others or neither.

552 For details, see the explanation of the vajra sliver reasoning in the section below entitled "The Detailed Explanation of the Five Great Reasonings."

553 See the explanation of the vajra sliver reasoning in the section below entitled "The Detailed Explanation of the Five Great Reasonings."

554 This is also called "the argument that negates arising from the four extremes" (Skt. *caturantotpādapratiṣedhahetu, Tib. mtha' bzhi skye 'gog gi gtan tshig).

555 ACIP KL0107, for example @284A.

556 Skt. Śālistamebhavasūtra, Tib. sa lu ljangs pa'i mdo.

557 Skt. Anavataptanāgārājaparipṛcchāsūtra, Tib. klu'i rgyal po ma dros pas zhus pa'i mdo.

558 Skt. Pratītyasamutpādasūtra, Tib. rten cing 'brel bar 'byung ba'i mdo.

559 For example, in verses 1, 61–62.

560 Verses 7, 32.

561 In Chapter XIV, particularly XIV.19.

562 ACIP TD3915@30A.

563 IX.116–142.

564 ACIP TD3915@28B–29B.

565 XX.21–22.

566 It is taught in the context of refuting the second extreme of the vajra sliver reasoning, i.e., arising from something other.

567 IX.143–150.

568 Verse 4.

569 Verse 14.

570 ACIP TD3882@07A–09A.

571 ACIP TD3883@29A–35A.

572 1932–35, pp. 970–76.

573 ACIP TD3887@138A.

574 ACIP TD3889@280Bf.

575 Verses 22, 66.

576 Verses 18–19, 45, 48.

577 For example, it is used in verses VII.17, XII.2, XVIII.10, XXIV.18–19, 21, and 36.

578 It appears in the sixth chapter at the end of the refutation of phenomenal identity (VI.107–116).

579 ACIP TD3948@279A–280A. (Atiśa refers to what is called above "the reasoning that negates an arising of existents and non-existents" as "the reasoning that negates arising from the four possibilities.")

580 ACIP TD3887@136B–138B.

581 As we know, this conclusion through mental analysis accords very well with the experimental findings of modern physics.

582 This highlights the fact that Centrist reasonings do not usually present "the heterologous set," i.e., the opposite of what is equivalent to the predicate (not really existing, not arising, lacking a nature, and so on), because there is nothing that really exists, arises, or has a nature of its own. Thus, the third mode—the absence of the reason in the heterologous set—does not have a basis to be established. Nevertheless, as formulated above, if there *were* something really existent, it would have to exist as either one or many. Thus, this is not considered a flaw in such reasonings.

583 I.1.

584 The latter are mainly the texts of Dignāga and Dharmakīrti and their commentaries.

585 Easy to remember: Buddhapālita's commentary bears the same name as its author (ACIP TD3842@161B).

586 In particular, the position of arising from something other has traditionally been connected with the Logicians (*ārambhavāda*) and certain Ābhidhārmikas.

587 These are the causal condition, the object condition, the dominant condition, and the immediate condition. Chapter I of *The Fundamental Verses* explains in detail that things in general do not really arise from these four conditions.

588 VI.14.

589 This obviously does not refer to certain findings of modern physics where the result is said to precede the cause, but to our ordinary experience of the relation between cause and effect.

590 This refers to the third of the five Centrist reasonings—the negation of an arising of existents and nonexistents—which is explained below.

591 ACIP TD3860@011B.

592 I.3cd.

593 Ibid., I.2–3ab.

594 Ibid., I.4.

595 Ibid., I.5–6.

596 Ibid., I.7.

597 Ibid., I.9.

598 ACIP TD3860@013A.

599 I.11–12.

600 Ibid., I.13–14.

601 The following is a rather simplified description of the more complex position (*nayavāda*) of the Jainas.

602 ACIP TD3860@012A.

603 Ibid., @012A–012B. These two lines are a quote from *The Entrance into Centrism* (VI.100ab).

604 This view originated with Ajita Keśakambala, an elder contemporary of Buddha Śākyamuni. This shows that the modern idea of mind as an epiphenomenon is not really so new.

605 This refers to a story from ancient India that illustrates that there is often much ado about nothing: In the dusty roads of a town, a man produced some fake footprints that looked like those of a wolf and then proclaimed everywhere that there was a dangerous wolf in town, thus terrifying everybody.

606 See the section above entitled "Reasons and Negations."

607 This is just a very brief sketch of some major arguments for the existence of past and future lives and for matter or the body not being the cause for the mind. Buddhist texts present detailed explanations of many more reasons that relate to these issues. Obviously, the latter topic corresponds to the current popular scientific claim that mind is just an epiphenomenon of the body or matter in general. However, from the Centrist point of view, since all these questions of other lifetimes and the body-mind issue only pertain to seeming reality, they are not dealt with in the context of the five great Centrist reasonings. These reasonings exclusively pertain to the ultimate nonexistence of body, mind, and other lifetimes. Obviously, the function of such reasonings is not to give reasons for the real existence of anything, nor to address the question of whether body and mind have a causal relationship. Hence, this is not the place to elaborate on these issues, which are greatly disputed in both the East and the West. For their detailed presentation, see the chapter of Dharmakīrti's *Commentary on Valid Cognition* that establishes the Buddha as the ultimate source of valid cognition (translated in R. Jackson 1993).

608 VI.32.

609 The name of this school comes from its main scripture, called *The Great Detailed Exposition* (Skt. Mahāvibhāṣa, Tib. bye brag tu bshad pa chen mo). The school asserts that all things in the three times exist as distinct, substantial entities right now. Thus, it proposes a kind of backwards chronology of cause and result: All things that are to come already exist in a substantial way in the future. They just transit into the present, while those things that exist in the present pass into the past, all of them maintaining their substantial existence throughout this process.

610 VII.17.

611 Ibid., VII.19cd.

612 ACIP TD3882@07A–09A.

613 I.48.

614 Of course, about these causes and conditions, Centrists say neither that they really exist nor that they are the same as or other than their results.

615 XXIV.18–19.

616 Skt. gandharva, Tib. dri za. These are the celestial musicians of Indra who live in the air and the heavenly waters.

617 ACIP TD3865@220B.

618 VI.113, 170cd.

619 XXIV.36.

620 VI.115.

621 VI.71cd, 96.

622 VIII.16.

623 Here this term specifically refers to the opposite of real entities. Such an entity is defined as that which is able to perform a function. For example, water from a spring performs the function of quenching our thirst, but the mere concept of water does not.

624 "Term generality" is a technical term for a purely conceptual mental image that is triggered by a word or term and is not in itself an outer object; for example, the conceptual image that is triggered by the term "chair" does not perform the functions of an actual chair on which one can sit. A term generality may refer to an actual object, as in this example, or it may not correspond to any object at all, such as the mental image that is triggered by the expression "purple flying tigers" or "my self."

625 See the section above entitled "The Two Types of Identitylessness."

626 See the section above entitled "Personal Identitylessness."

627 Verse 49.

628 ACIP TD3916@048B.

629 XVIII.1.

630 The same applies for nonconceptual mental perception (Skt. mānasapratyakṣa, Tib. yid kyi mngon sum).

631 This is, for example, the position of the Buddhist school of the Vātsīputrīyas (Tib. gnas ma bu pa).

632 XVIII.2ab.

633 For example, *Saṃyutta Nikāya* I.135. It is also found in *The Questions of King Milinda (Milindapañha).* (Ed. Trenckner. London: Pali Text Society, 1962, pp. 26–28).

634 VI.151.

635 Points 2–5 of this sevenfold analysis correspond to the above negation of the twenty views about a real personality.

636 There are many other reasonings to negate a self, such as the ten ways of competence (Tib. mkhas pa bcu) as the remedy for the tenfold view about a personal self that are described in Maitreya's *Distinction between the Middle and Extremes* (III.15–23). This is a very detailed description as to how various imputed features of a hypothetical self are contradictory to the features of the aggregates and such. (1) The competence in knowing the aggregates serves as the remedy for regarding the self as something singular, since it is the nature of the aggregates to contain a great variety of many things. (2) The competence in the eighteen constituents is the remedy for regarding the self as a cause, since the constituents exhaustively contain all possible causes. (3) The competence in the twelve sources serves as the remedy for thinking that the self is the experiencer, since all objects are experienced through the interdependence of the twelve sources. (4) The competence in interdependence serves as the remedy for seeing the self as a creator, because things are not created by a self but originate in dependence on various causes and conditions. (5) The competence in what is the case and what is not the case serves as the remedy for thinking that the self wields some power, since the self has no power over things, which are solely under the power of specific causes and results. (6) The competence in the faculties serves as the remedy for regarding the self as a ruler, since there are only the twenty-two faculties that dominate all things. (7) The competence in time serves as the rem-

edy for holding the self to be permanent, since arising and ceasing happen within the context of the three times. (8) The competence in the four realities of the noble ones functions as the remedy for assuming the self as the matrix or support for afflicted phenomena and purified phenomena, because the first two realities are the matrix of afflicted phenomena and the latter two are the matrix of purified phenomena. (9) The competence in the vehicles serves as the remedy for the belief that the self is that which practices yoga, since the qualities of the respective vehicles appear only through the consciousnesses that cultivate them. (10) The competence in conditioned and unconditioned phenomena serves as the remedy for conceiving of the self as that which is first bound and later liberated, since bondage comes from conditioned and afflicted causes and results, while unconditioned liberation means being free from such causes and results.

637 VI.117, 118ab, 119.

638 IX.34.

639 Skt. Ratnameghasūtra, Tib. dkon mchog sprin gyi mdo.

640 ACIP TD3915@30B.

641 ACIP TD3916@046B–047A.

642 Ibid., @046A.

643 Skt. pratisaṃkhyāvipaśyanā, Tib. so sor rtog pa'i lhag mthong.

644 These two terms represent one of the standard Tibetan subdivisions of the sūtra teachings of the great vehicle, the former lineage starting with Mañjuśrī (continued by Nāgārjuna and his followers) and the latter with Maitreya (continued by Asaṅga and his followers). In this classification, the tantric Buddhist teachings are referred to as "the lineage of experiential practice and blessings" (Tib. nyams len byin rlabs kyi brgyud pa).

645 Dpa' bo gtsug lag phreng ba, n.d., p. 327.

646 Tib. paṇḍita'i dpyad sgom.

647 Tib. kusāli'i 'jog sgom.

648 IX. 110.

649 P5324, fol. 106a.3–6.

650 Verse 44.

651 Verse 59.

652 ACIP TD3915@034B–035A.

653 Ibid., @033B.

654 Dpa' bo gtsug lag phreng ba, n.d., p. 326.

655 For more details on this issue, see the section below entitled "Mental Nonengagement in Meditation."

656 Verse 45.

657 Tib. sems gnas dgu.

658 Skt. avikalpapratibimba, Tib. rnam par mi rtog pa'i gzugs brnyan.

659 Skt. savikalpapratibimba, Tib. rnam par rtog pa dang bcas pa'i gzugs brnyan.

660 VI.175a–c.

661 Tib. gzung ba la mi dmigs pa'i rnal 'byor.

662 Tib. 'dzin pa la mi dmigs pa'i rnal 'byor.

663 Skt. animittayoga, Tib. mtshan ma med pa'i rnal 'byor.

664 ACIP TD3916@049B–050A.

665 ACIP TD3916@050B–051A.

666 These are the four applications of mindfulness, the four correct exertions (Skt. catvāri samyakprahāṇāni, Tib. yang dag spong ba bzhi), the four limbs of miraculous powers (Skt. catvāra ṛddhipādāḥ, Tib. rdzu 'phrul gyi rkang pa bzhi), the five faculties (Skt. pañcendriyāṇi, Tib. dbang po lnga), the five powers (Skt. pañcabalāni, Tib. stobs lnga), the seven branches of enlightenment (Skt. saptasaṃbodhyaṅgāni, Tib. byang chub kyi yan lag bdun), and the eightfold path of the noble ones (Skt. āryāṣṭāṅgamārga, Tib. 'phags pa'i lam yan lag brgyad). As for the four correct exertions, while *prahāṇa* can mean either "relinquishment" or "exertion," it is always rendered as the former in Tibetan (spong ba). However, here, the term clearly refers to four activities in which one exerts effort.

667 For more details on this fourfold practice of mindfulness, see the translation of Pawo Rinpoche's commentary below (3.2. Phenomenal Identitylessness).

668 P5325, fol. 107a.6–107b.2.

669 Skt. śūnyatābhāvanākrama, Tib. stong nyid sgom rim.

670 As Lindtner (1997, p. 164) reports, all the verses of this text are found in Chapter X of *The Sūtra of the Arrival in Laṅka.*

671 P4532 (fols. 69a.7-74b.4).

672 P5334. In terms of both layout and content, this text can be considered as an abbreviated version of Kamalaśīla's three-volume *Stages of Meditation.* As a counterpart, Vimalamitra also wrote *The Topics of Instantaneous Nonconceptual Meditation* (Skt. *Sakṛtprāveśikanirvikalpabhāvanāpada, Tib. cig car 'jug pa rnam par mi rtog pa'i sgom don, P5306).

673 Even if Nāgārjuna's authorship is disputed, the text is clearly written from a Centrist point of view and outlines the typical sequence of the progressive stages of meditation as found in all the other Centrist texts on this topic listed above (see the more detailed presentation in Kamalaśīla's *Stages of Meditation* below).

674 Verses 22–24.

675 Verse 25.

676 VI.96.

677 Verse 27. He elaborates on this in the next verses by stating that the three natures—the imaginary nature, the other-dependent nature, and the perfect nature—are nothing but enumerations of emptiness in relation to labeling our mind as being without nature. Furthermore, he refutes a ground consciousness and self-awareness as ultimately existing real entities. For more details on the Centrist interpretation and use of the teachings on "mere mind," see Chapter 4.

678 Verse 46.

679 Tib. chos kyi grags pa.

680 Chos kyi grags pa 2001, p. 94.

681 Verses 49–51.

682 These two lines are again a quote from Smṛti's commentary.

683 Chos kyi grags pa 2001, pp. 95–97.

684 Verses 69–70.

685 X. 256–258 (ACIP KL0107@270A). The first two verses are also found in Nāgārjuna's *Stages of Meditation* (verses 54–55).

686 ACIP TD3915@033A–033B, 037B. The above three verses are also quoted in Śāntarakṣita's *Commentary on The Ornament of Centrism* (ACIP TD3885@79B) and explained in Kamalaśīla's subcommentary (fols. 137a–138a). Just as an aside, the above quote and many others from *The Sūtra of the Arrival in Laṅka* show clearly that it is highly inappropriate to categorically characterize this whole sūtra as just teaching "Mind Only" in the sense of a really existing mind that is ultimate reality.

687 P5324, fols. 105b.4–106a.7.

688 Here this term refers to the philosophical systems of the Followers of the Great Exposition and the Sūtra Followers.

689 For more details on this, the problem of a "Mind Only school," and whether there is a Shentong school, see Chapters 3 and 4.

690 See mainly the works by Khenpo Tsultrim Gyamtso Rinpoche in the Bibliography.

691 See also the section above entitled "The Two Types of Identitylessness" for more ideas on similar questions (such as what happens to our self when we lose some parts of our body or how we use language when referring to "I" and "mine").

692 Skt. sahopalambhaniyama, Tib. lhan cig dmigs par nges pa.

693 Tib. snang ba dang sems gsal tsam gyi ngo bor gcig par nges pa (in Western scholarship, following Iwata (JIBS 1984), often referred to as "the *saṃvedana* inference"). These two reasonings are found, for example, in Dignāga's *Compendium of Valid Cognition* (I.9-10) and its autocommentary as well as in Dharmakīrti's *Ascertainment of Valid Cognition* (*Pramānaviniścaya* I.55bff). The first one also appears in his *Commentary on Valid Cognition* (v. 388-391) and the latter in Śāntarakṣita's *Synopsis of True Reality* (lines 2001, 2003, and 2029-2033).

694 Tib. sdom gsum rab dbye (*Sa skya pa'i bka' 'bum,* vol. 5, Tokyo: 1968, p. 311.2.5).

695 Dvags po bkra shis rnam rgyal, n.d., p. 357.3–6.

696 Ibid., pp. 359.1–4.

697 There are at least two Tibetan versions of this debate, and the more verifiable one presents quite a different account of what Hvashang actually said. For details, see Karmay 1988, the *Bsam gtan mig sgron* by Nubchen Sangye Yeshe (Tib. gnubs chen sangs rgyas ye shes ) from the eighth/ninth century, and the *Sba bzhed* chronicle. Chinese sources refer to this debate but do not elaborate on any of its issues, obviously not considering them as problems to be addressed.

698 Dpa' bo gtsug lag phreng ba, n.d., p. 325.

699 Skt. Sāgaramatiparipṛcchāsūtra, Tib. blo gros rgya mtshos zhus pa'i mdo.

700 ACIP KD0012@167B.

701 ACIP TD3948@285A.

702 P5501, for example, fols. 156b.4–157b.7 and 158a.4.

703 Skt. Avikalpapraveśadhāraṇī, Tib. rnam par mi rtog pa la 'jug pa'i gzungs (P810). This text describes how bodhisattvas enter the expanse of nonconceptuality by gradually relinquishing all coarse and subtle characteristics and conceptions in terms of nature, remedy, true reality, and attainment. It is also referred to as one of the major sūtra sources for the Dzogchen teachings in the *Bsam gtan mig sgron.*

704 ACIP TD3915@034A–034B.

705 Skt. asmṛti, Tib. dran pa med pa. *Smṛti* is usually translated as "mindfulness." Here, however, the point does not so much concern not being mindful of phenomena as not paying any attention to them in the sense of not having any notions about them so that the mind stays completely detached from all dualistic appearances.

706 ACIP TD3917@061B–064A.

707 Skt. arthasāmānya, Tib. don spyi.

708 Tib. stong nyid med dgag la 'dzin stangs.

709 For example, he explains this in great detail in the section on superior insight in his *Great Stages of the Path* (Tib. lam rim chen mo). For an example of common critiques of Tsongkhapa's approach to identifying the object of negation in analytical meditation (in terms of both a personal self and the real existence of phenomena), as illustrated by Gendün Chöpel, see Lopez 2001.

710 Verse 59.

711 Verses 44, 49–50.

712 VI.117.

713 Verses 7–8ab.

714 Mi bskyod rdo rje 1996, p. 637.

715 Ibid., p. 481.

716 Skt. Daśabhūmikasūtra, Tib. sa bcu pa'i mdo.

717 XI.11, 43.

718 XI.14-40. There are already many books that describe the qualities of the Dharma Body (such as the ten powers, the four fearlessnesses, and the eighteen unique qualities) and the two Form Bodies as well as their enlightened activities in detail (see, for example, *Buddha Nature*, Snow Lion, 2000). Hence, rather than repeating these descriptions, I try to highlight a few general key points on wisdom and the enlightened bodies from the Centrist point of view.

719 Dpa' bo gtsug lag phreng ba, n.d., pp. 685–86.

720 XI.17.

721 ACIP TD3862@331B.

722 Tib.'og min. There are three kinds of Akaniṣṭha: (1) the ultimate Akaniṣṭha, i.e., the formless state of the Dharma Body; (2) the Richly Adorned Akaniṣṭha (Skt. ghandavyūhākaniṣṭa, Tib. 'og min rgyan stug po bkod pa), which is the sphere in which Bodies of Complete Enjoy-

ment manifest; and (3) the highest pure level of the form realm, which is a natural sphere of Emanation Bodies. Only the middle one is referred to here.

723 X.4ab, 36.

724 For a number of details in this section, I am greatly indebted to Ruegg (1981, 2000).

725 ACIP TD3854@280A.

726 Besides Śāntarakṣita's main disciple, Kamalaśīla, this group includes masters such as Jñānagarbha, Śrīgupta, Haribhadra, Vidyākaraprabha (c. 800), Jetāri (10-11th c.), and the Nepalese Paṇḍita Nandaśrī.

727 ACIP TD3885@78B.

728 Fol. 136b.

729 Commenting on *The Synopsis*' lines 1916–17.

730 It is true that Śāntideva mainly uses consequences in his *Entrance to the Bodhisattva's Way of Life*, but neither this text nor his *Compendium of Training* refers to this way of reasoning as being an issue, let alone as a feature that divides Centrists. Moreover, to varying degrees, Nāgārjuna and all other Centrists likewise employ consequences.

731 Fol. 114a.

732 ACIP TD3852@ 44A–B. (*The Compendium of the Heart of Wisdom* is by Āryadeva.)

733 He is said to have been a disciple of Āryadeva and is best known for his praises of the Buddha (such as *Varṇarhavarṇastotra*, *Mahārājakanikalekha*, and *Śatapañcāśatka*), whose style resembles the praises by Nāgārjuna.

734 These texts are *Maṇḍalavidhi*, *Prajñāpāramitopadeśa*, *Navaślokī*, and *Ālokamālā* ("Garland of Light"). Kambala is mostly considered a Yogācāra, but his above texts are certainly in perfect accord with Centrism. In his *Ālokamālā*, he moreover displays quite a unique early synthesis of Centrism and Yogācāra. Thus, Atīśa's identification of Kambala's Centrist texts as belonging to the model texts of Centrism is remarkable and further supports the impression that the demarcation lines of different Buddhist "schools" in India were not as hard and fast as many later Tibetan authors assumed.

735 He wrote a now lost commentary on *The Fundamental Verses*.

736 P5325, fols. 126a.5–126b.2.

737 Verse 15.

738 Verses 2–3.

739 ACIP TD3948@282B. To eliminate doubts, he adds that his subsequent statement "For meditating on the ultimate, valid cognition is not needed" was made in another context and thus does not apply to the presentation at hand.

740 Ibid., @280A. Dreyfus (2003) refers to this passage as Atīśa using the distinction between Centrists who conventionally accept outer objects and those who interpret seeming reality according to Yogācāra. He says, "Even as late an author as Atīśa (11th century) uses it, classifying on its basis both Candrakīrti and Bhāvaviveka as authoritative interpreters of Nāgārjuna." (p. 3) However, this passage does not make *any* distinction between Centrists, nor does Atīśa use this distinction elsewhere. The mere fact that this text does not mention Śāntarakṣita and Kamalaśīla can hardly be regarded as Atīśa using this particular distinction. Nor is it indicated by the fact that his *Centrist Pith Instructions* does not include the works of Śāntarakṣita and

Kamalaśīla under the Centrist model texts, especially since Bhāvaviveka's texts are not so included either.

741 Tib. dge bsnyen zla ba (Upāsaka Candra), a common way to refer to Candragomī who was a layman. That he is added here is remarkable, since he is usually considered to be a Yogācāra.

742 ACIP TD3948@285A.

743 Fol. 129a.4/8.

744 Tibetans mostly use the term "those who speak of establishing illusion through reasoning" (sgyu ma rigs grub smra ba).

745 I could not find Maitrīpa's quote for the second approach in the texts of Nāgārjuna, Āryadeva, Buddhapālita, Candrakīrti, Śāntideva, or any later Autonomists.

746 ACIP TD3901@68B, 71A.

747 Verses 19–24.

748 Kong sprul blo gros mtha' yas 1982, vol. II, p. 513.

749 Skt. Pañcakramaṭīkā, Tib. rim lnga'i grel pa.

750 Tib. mdo sde dbu ma.

751 Tib. rnal 'byor spyod pa'i dbu ma.

752 Fols. 180a.6–182b.1.

753 Skt. Sākāramādhyamika, Tib. rnam bcas dbu ma.

754 Skt. Nirākāramādhyamika, Tib. rnam med dbu ma.

755 Tib. ye shes sde.

756 Tib. lta ba'i khyad par (P5847, fol. 252b).

757 For example, the *lTa ba'i rim pa'i man ngag* (P5843, fol. 140a–b) by the translator Gawa Paldse (Tib. ka ba dpal brtsegs), the *lTa ba'i bye brag* by Nyima Ö (Tib. nyi ma 'od; probably identical with *lTa ba'i rim pa*, Dunhuang Ms. BL/IOL Stein 607), and several other Dunhuang manuscripts. (Some texts say *rnal 'byor (pa'i) dbu ma* and others *rnal 'byor spyod pa'i dbu ma*).

758 Tib. phyi'i dbu ma.

759 Tib. nang gi rnal byor gyi dbu ma (Ms. BN Pelliot tibétain 842, fols. nga b.7ff).

760 Tib. bye brag tu rtogs par byed pa chen po.

761 Tib. rong zom paṇḍita chos kyi bzang po.

762 *Collected Works*: *lTa ba'i brjed byang* (fols. 11b–12a), *Grub mtha'i brjed byang* (fols. 5a–6a), and *Man ngag lta ba'i phreng ba zhes bya ba'i 'grel pa* (fol. 28b).

763 In his *Lamp of Certainty*, Mipham Rinpoche says that Rongzom and Candrakīrti share the same view of emptiness (Pettit 1999, p. 196).

764 Tib. rog bande shes rab 'od (*Grub mtha' chen po bstan pa'i sgron me*. Leh, Ladakh: 1977, fol. 83b f.).

765 *Tshogs chos legs mdzes ma* (in Sgam po pa 1975, vol. I, fol. 85a).

766 Tib. zung 'jug rab tu mi gnas pa.

767 Tib. rgyun chad rab tu mi gnas pa.

768 The quote is a summary of more extensive passages in the *Prajñāpāramitā Sūtras in 8,000 Lines* and *25,000 Lines* (ACIP KD0012@23A, KD0009-2@05B-11B).

769 Padma dkar po, n.d., p. 41.

770 As mentioned in the introduction, in the Tibetan translation of Jayānanda's *Madhyamakāvatāraṭīkā* (P5271), the terms "Autonomist Centrist" (dbu ma rang rgyud pa) and "Autonomist" (rang rgyud pa) are mentioned a few times (ACIP TD3870-1@281A–282B) as being opposed to Candrakīrti. However, there is no reference to "Consequentialists." Instead, Jayānanda speaks of himself merely as "Centrist."

771 *Sa skya pa'i bka' 'bum* (Tokyo: 1968), vol. 2, pp. 495.4.2, 496.1.3, and elsewhere.

772 Mi bskyod rdo rje 1996, p. 14. Judging from the nonhonorific style of the Karmapa's presentation, this Majaba is probably not Majaba Jangchub Dsöndrü (whom he usually calls "the great master Majaba"), but rather Patsab Lotsāwa's direct disciple Majaba Jangchub Yeshe.

773 Tib. don sgrub byed.

774 Tib. tha snyad sgrub byed.

775 Tib. rang rgyud du smra ba'i dbu ma pa (Rma bya ba byang chub brston 'grus 1975, pp. 41–45).

776 Tib. grags pa rgyal mtshan.

777 *rGyud kyi mngon par rtogs pa rin po che'i ljon shing* (fol. 30a).

778 Tib. 'ba' ra ba rgyal mtshan dpal bzang.

779 On the Autonomist-Consequentialist distinction, Rendawa's commentary on *The Entrance into Centrism* (Red mda' ba gzhon nu blo gros 1993, p. 28) only says that he has written about the differences in their assertions "elsewhere." The most probable sources should be his *sTong thun chen mo* on Candrakīrti's *Lucid Words* and/or his commentary on a number of such *stong thun*, called *Tshig gsal stong thun rnams kyi ṭikka* (A khu shes rab rgya mtsho's list of rare texts, no. 11350).

In general, Rendawa clearly favors Candrakīrti's approach, but without further research, it is impossible to determine his opinion on the nature and the scope of the Autonomist-Consequentialist distinction. However, the publisher's foreword to Rendawa's commentary states the Sakyapa stance on this as follows: "The division into Autonomists and Consequentialists is not made through the view of the ultimate, but they are divided through the way of formulating reasonings that serve as means of proof. There is no difference in their view, since both are fully qualified Centrists" (p. ga). Appearing in the foreword to Rendawa's highly revered commentary, such a statement cannot but be expected to accord with his view. (Besides, it is almost literally the same as what the Eighth Karmapa says.)

780 Bu ston rin chen grub 1931, vol. II, p. 135.

781 See Nagasawa 1962.

782 This is reported in Mipham Rinpoche's *Ketaka Jewel* ('Ju mi pham rgya mtsho 1979, p. 10).

783 In *mDzod bdun: The Famed Seven Treatises of Vajrayāna Buddhist Philosophy*. Gangtok, Sikkim: Sherab Gyaltsen and Khentse Labrang, 1983 (*Yid bzhin mdzod*, p. 536; *Grub mtha'i mdzod*, pp. 201–12; and *Theg mchog mdzod*, p. 91).

784 Tib. dbus pa blo gsal (in his *Grub pa'i mtha' rnam par bshad pa)*. For details, see Mimaki 1983.

785 That this is not unjustified can be seen from Jñānagarbha's autocommentary on verse 21 of *The Distinction between the Two Realities* (see below; see also Eckel in Dreyfus and McClintock 2003, pp. 190–92). In most later Tibetan doxographies, Jñānagarbha is regarded as an Autonomist Centrist Following the Sūtras. However, in terms of content, his writings show quite a close affinity with those of Śāntarakṣita and Kamalaśīla. For further problems with classifying this master in terms of Tibetan doxographic categories, see also Eckel 1987 and Lopez 1987.

786 Tib. bo dong paṇ chen phyogs las rnam rgyal. He has written more than one hundred volumes.

787 For the confirmation of this fact with regard to the first text, I am indebted to Klaus-Dieter Mathes.

788 'Go lo tsa ba gzhon nu dpal 1996, p. 334.

789 Ibid., pp. 341–44.

790 Tib. bon sgo gsal byed by Tre ston rgyal mtshan dpal.

791 Tib. dbu ma dgongs pa rab gsal (written in 1418). There, Tsongkhapa contrasts "Centrists of Yoga Practice" with "Autonomists who accept outer referents."

792 Tib. mkhas grub dge legs dpal bzang. He says that there are two kinds of Autonomists: Those like Bhāvaviveka and Jñānagarbha hold that form, sound, and so on are external objects other than mind. Those like Śāntarakṣita hold that form and such are not objects other than mind and that neither external objects nor a real basis (of cognition) exist (see Eckel 1987, p. 19).

793 Tib. mdo sde spyod pa'i dbu ma rang rgyud pa. This was later rendered by Western scholars into Sanskrit as *Sautrāntika-Svātantrika-Mādhyamika (a more literal retrotranslation would be *Sūtr(ānt)ācāra-Svātantrika-Mādhyamika).

794 Tib. rnal 'byor spyod pa'i dbu ma rang rgyud pa, *Yogācāra-Svātantrika-Mādhyamika.

795 Avalokitavrata's *Prajñāpradīpaṭīkā* briefly mentions Candrakīrti but without addressing his critique of Bhāvaviveka. Prajñākaramati's *Bodhicāryāvatārapañjikā* on verses VI.23, 25, and 28–29 also refers to him. Apart from Atiśa's mere mentioning of Candrakīrti as stated above, he quotes verse VI.80 of the latter's *Entrance into Centrism* as verse 19 of his *Entrance into the Two Realities.* Not without irony, apart from Jayānanda's commentary, the text that most favorably mentions Candrakīrti quite often (and quotes him six times) is Bhāvaviveka's *Jewel Lamp of Centrism* (for details, see Lindtner 1982b).

Jñānagarbha refutes some opponents who say that, if entities do not arise in actuality, just like the child of a barren woman, they do not even arise on the level of the seeming (ten stanzas of refutation in his autocommentary on verse 25 of his *Distinction between the Two Realities*). Some modern scholars (Eckel, Lindtner, Ruegg) regard this as probably being directed against Candrakīrti's understanding of seeming reality as presented in his *Entrance into Centrism* VI.36–38. There, however, Candrakīrti uses the example of a reflection for seeming phenomena and says that empty entities such as reflections *do* arise from other empty entities. More important, in verses VI.108–113 and their autocommentary (ACIP TD3862@ 288A–290B), Candrakīrti himself extensively refutes precisely the above position of Jñānagarbha's opponents, explaining why the phenomena of seeming reality are not like the child of a barren woman. Ultimately, both such phenomena and the child of a barren woman are empty and do not arise, but from the perspective of ordinary beings, the former—including dreams and illusions—appear due to certain equally illusory conditions, while the latter never does. As explained before, in his works, Candrakīrti repeatedly objects to plain nihilism.

796 The colophon of this commentary says that it was not even written in India but during Jayānanda's stay in the borderlands between Tibet and China near Mañjuśrī's five-peaked mountain (Chin. Wu-t'ai-shan).

797 All of this is also highlighted by the fact that both the major Tibetan historians Tāranātha (1980, pp. 198–99) and Butön (1931, vol, II, pp. 134–35) in their historical works dedicate less than one page to Candrakīrti, saying only that he followed Buddhapālita and not even mentioning Candrakīrti's critique of Bhāvaviveka. Tāranātha also writes very briefly on Buddhapālita and Bhāvaviveka (pp. 186–87), but nowhere does he refer to the Autonomist-Consequentialist distinction. He states that Bhāvaviveka "composed a commentary refuting the views of the earlier *ācārya-s* as expressed in their expositions of the *Madhyamakamūla*" and that, unlike Buddhapālita, "because he had thousands of monks as his followers, his views were more extensively spread." In comparison, both Tibetan historians write at length about other Centrists such as Nāgārjuna, Āryadeva, and Śāntideva as well as Yogācāras such as Asaṅga, Vasubandhu, Dignāga, and Dharmakīrti.

798 Except for some additional considerations, quotations, and a few insertions from *The Treasury of Knowledge*, the remaining sections of this chapter are for the most part (at times abridged) paraphrases of Mikyö Dorje's commentary (Mi bskyod rdo rje 1996, pp. 135–218).

WARNING: If your resistance to Centrist reasoning has not sufficiently built up through the vaccination of the preceding chapters, the remaining parts of this chapter may prove hazardous to your sanity.

799 Tib. tshur mthong, lit. "those who see just this side."

800 Also called circularity of argument or same predicament.

801 Skt. svatantrapratijñā, Tib. rang rgyud kyi dam bca'.

802 ACIP TD3856@60A–B.

803 Verse 33.

804 Verses 33–34.

805 III.360, 209.

806 The most common Tibetan explanation of autonomous reasoning is that it entails the three modes of a correct reason, which have to be established from their own side. This means that they are established through a valid cognition that operates through the power of entities and is acknowledged from the perspectives of both proponent and opponent. However, as will be shown in detail below, this is obviously not the indigenous understanding of autonomous reasonings by those very Indian masters who became designated as Autonomists later (see also the essays of McClintock and Eckel in Dreyfus and McClintock 2003, pp. 125–71 and 173–203).

807 As we saw, they do not consider such valid cognitions as part of their own Centrist system either.

808 VIII.104. The meaning of this verse is exactly the same as that of the famous verse IX.34 of Śāntideva's *Bodhicaryāvatāra*:

Once neither entities nor nonentities  
Remain before the mind,

There is no other mental flux [either].
Therefore, it is utter nonreferential peace.

809 Verses 9cd–11.

810 Lines 71ab.

811 Mikyö Dorje adds here that he has treated the above claims of three features of the valid cognition of Autonomists together for the sake of simplicity. He clarifies that, by doing so, he does not mean to misrepresent the various positions of those who claim such features as saying that all Autonomists accept all three of these features, since some claim that there are also Autonomists who seem to just accept one or two.

812 In Buddhist texts, "verbal testimony" is usually called "scriptural authority" (Skt. āgama, Tib. lung). This set of four kinds of valid cognition came from the non-Buddhist school of the Logicians and was the most widely accepted in India. Thus, again just following common consensus, Candrakīrti provisionally employs this set of four kinds of valid cognition as the most common, conventional model of our ways of knowing on the level of seeming reality. He does not refer to the set of only two valid cognitions (perceptual and inferential) as asserted by Buddhist logicians such as Dignāga and Dharmakīrti.

813 ACIP TD3860@081A.

814 Ibid., @025B.

815 This is obviously an interpretation of the term "autonomous" (*svatantra/rang rgyud*) that is different from the Gelugpa understanding (the latter requiring the three modes in relation to phenomena that are established through their own specific characteristics and a corresponding valid cognition). Mikyö Dorje's explanation of the term "autonomous" seems furthermore to hinge on the double meaning of *svatantra/rang rgyud*, since this can also mean "one's own continuum." Inasmuch as all reasonings employed by Consequentialists arise and are pronounced within their own personal continua, such reasonings are "autonomous" in this sense, since they clearly do not arise or are pronounced within the continua of others. Thus, the above passage could also be read, " . . . these three modes are stated as such by the first debater's own continuum (*rang rgyud*) and not by the continuum of others (*gzhan rgyud*)."

816 In Buddhism, there are only two possible types of sounds: those that are brought about by the efforts of sentient beings (such as speech or music) and those that are not (such as the sound of the wind or a river).

817 The explanations under (2c) correspond very much with Candrakīrti's and Rongtön Sheja Künrig's understanding of autonomous reasoning and to what extent Consequentialists can use it (see Yoshimizu and Cabezón in Dreyfus and McClintock 2003, pp. 257–88 and 298–301). To simplify somewhat, one could say that autonomous reasoning in this sense generally means any probative argument with the correct three modes (for or by whomever these may be established) that says "how it is" (either conventionally or ultimately). According to Rongtön's commentary on *The Entrance into Centrism* (*Nges don rnam nges*), Consequentialists employ, for example, "inferences acknowledged by others" (Tib. gzhan grags kyi rjes dpag), which can be seen as the Consequentialist equivalent of autonomous reasoning (Rong ston shes bya kun rig, n.d., pp. 77–78). He further explains: "What is the difference between 'inferences acknowledged by others' and autonomous inferences? In a probative argument that establishes an autonomous thesis, the three modes are ascertained. [In inferences] acknowledged by others, it is for the sake of eliminating the wrong ideas of opponents that one states as the reason what these others accept, without however establishing any thesis in an independent way (rang dbang du)." (pp. 83–84).

"Autonomous reasons are rejected, but we do not deny 'what is to be proven' and 'the means to prove' as mere imputations. . . . Thus, a reason (which is like [the reflection of] the moon in water) makes an opponent (who is like an illusion) realize what is to be proven (which is like a dream)." (pp. 74–75).

As for the difference between autonomous reasonings and mere absurd consequences (as was said above), the latter do not have to involve the correct three modes. This means that they are just unwanted consequences that follow from another position that was wrong in the first place. Thus, they are logically correct, but their explicit meaning must be false, since it is just an absurd outgrowth of a previous false statement. If these consequences (such as "if things arose from themselves, then it would follow that they arise endlessly and pointlessly") are supplemented with a reason that is the opponent's explicit or implicit position (such as "because these things exist already"), the second and third modes usually do apply (at least for the opponent).

818 ACIP TD3886@88A.

819 ACIP TD3865@146A–B.

820 Since the subject in question is in fact a nonexistent, there is nothing that can be attributed to it (such as being impermanent, permanent, a cause, or a result) and also nothing in it that could be established in common for both debaters. Thus, any attempts at proving or invalidating based on this must be defective.

821 ACIP TD3865@232B.

822 Skt. prasaṅgasādhana, Tib. thal ba sgrub pa/sgrub pa'i thal gyur.

823 Dharmakīrti's general explanation on the implicit proof by a consequence appears very briefly in his *Pramāṇavārttika* IV.12cd. The details including the above example are found in *Pramāṇaviniścaya* III.2 (P5710, fol. 286a.5ff.) and its commentaries in the context of refuting the Differentiators and other non-Buddhist schools who claim that a generality (held to be a unitary, permanent entity apart from its instances) is actually connected to the multiplicity of its particulars. (As for their connection, they assert a so-called "connection of possession," such as between a vessel and a juniper tree in it). This type of reasoning is a rather formal way of stating the unwanted consequence that "a generality would then not be a unity, because it is connected to the multiplicity of its instances." The implied contraposition of this consequence (Skt. prasaṅgaviparyaya, Tib. thal bzlog) as a probative argument is, "A generality is not connected to the multiplicity of its instances, because—according to you—it is a unity." Thus, either a generality is a unity, or, it is connected to a multiplicity, but both is impossible. (Dharmakīrti's final point in this debate is that any connection between a generality and its particulars is not between actual entities, but purely through conceptual imputation.)

Logically speaking, the above consequence and its contraposition say the same. However, in terms of their formats, it is just the latter that corresponds exactly to an inference acknowledged by others (see the examples with regard to the four possibilities of arising right below).

824 For an example, see *Pramāṇavārttika* IV.12–13.

825 Skt. dūṣaṇābhāsa, Tib. sun 'byin ltar snang. This is an attempt to invalidate someone's position through a defective argument that is in fact incapable of doing so.

826 Kong sprul blo gros mtha' yas 1982, vol. II, p. 528.

827 I.e., if something is present at the time of its cause, this does not entail that its arising is meaningless.

828 This means that all the above absurd consequences of its arising being pointless and so on apply to the vase as a lump of clay in the earth too, since it is claimed to exist and thus does

not have to arise again. Therefore, to bring this nonmanifest vase into play does not improve the position of the Enumerators in any way.

829 For the justification of this reason, see the section in Chapter 2 entitled "The Five Great Madhyamaka Reasonings."

830 P3099, fols. 178b.7–179a.3.

831 Mi bskyod rdo rje 1996, pp. 272–75.

832 ACIP TD3853@189A.

833 Verses 12, 34.

834 ACIP TD3882@06B.

835 ACIP TD3883@27A.

836 ACIP TD3915@037A.

837 ACIP TD3860@10A–B. For details, see the section below entitled "The Origin of the Controversy between Autonomists and Consequentialists."

838 ACIP TD3882@10A–B.

839 Verse 64.

840 ACIP TD3892@41B.

841 ACIP TD3854@260A.

842 Verses 2–3. Especially for Gelugpas, the classification of the seeming as correct and false is distinctively Autonomist. Therefore, it should necessarily follow for them from these verses that Atīśa is an Autonomist. However, since they definitely regard him as a Consequentialist, they are left with an obvious contradiction here.

843 ACIP TD3862@347A–B.

844 Mi bskyod rdo rje 1996, p. 705. As mentioned above, Tragba Gyaltsen and Bodong Paṇchen Choglay Namgyal also speak of those Centrists who accord with the Followers of the Great Exposition and those who accord with the Sūtra Followers. Bodong Paṇchen identifies Āryavimuktisena as an example of the first type and Bhāvaviveka as belonging to the second type.

845 This refers to the Followers of the Great Exposition, the Sūtra Followers, and the Yogācāras.

846 See in particular the section in Chapter 2 entitled "Do Centrists Have a Thesis or Position?"

847 III.245cd–246.

848 III.261.

849 III.266–267. The last two lines play on the etymology of "Buddha," i.e., awakened and unfolded.

850 Sometimes, one also finds the two supplementary criteria of not just being a mental imputation and of appearing within its own specific class in a way that accords with this class.

851 P5431, verses 19–21, 23–24.

852 ACIP TD3901@71A.

853 Tib. rang rgyud (or sgrub byed) 'phen pa'i thal 'gyur. In an autonomous reasoning impelled by a consequence, both the predicate and the reason of the consequence are reversed into their negatives and their positions are switched. A simple example is the consequence "It follows that sound is not produced, because it is permanent." The impelled reasoning is: "Sound is impermanent, because it is produced." An example of a consequence that does not impel autonomous reasoning is: "It follows that sound is impermanent, because it is produced."

854 pratijñā, liṅga, udāharaṇa, upanaya, nigamana. This is the standard format of reasoning employed by the Indian non-Buddhist school of the Logicians. Candrakīrti gives such probative arguments, for example, when unpacking Buddhapālita's commentary on *Fundamental Verses* I.1 through consequences (ACIP TD3860@07A), when providing an alternative argument against things arising from themselves (@07B), and when explaining *Fundamental Verses* III.2cd (@011A). For details, see the section below entitled "The Origin of the Controversy between Autonomists and Consequentialists."

855 ACIP TD3860@05B.

856 I.84–86.

857 Commenting on lines 586–587 of Śāntarakṣita's *Synopsis.*

858 For details, see Dreyfus and McClintock 2003, pp. 145–46.

859 ACIP TD3842@244A (commenting on *Fundamental Verses* XVIII.8ab).

860 Mi bskyod rdo rje 1996, p. 163.

861 Skt. āśrayāsiddha, Tib. (chos can) gzhi ma grub pa.

862 If there is a reason that really has the capacity to prove that all things are without nature, then this very reason is the exception that is not without nature and thus by itself disproves what it is supposed to prove.

863 The same point is made in Śāntarakṣita's *Synopsis of True Reality*, lines 2736–2738.

864 ACIP TD3885@074B–075B on verses 76–78.

865 ACIP TD3882@09B–10A on verses 18–19.

866 This refers to the fourteen undecided questions that the Buddha refused to answer.

867 Tib. rgyal tshab dar ma rin chen.

868 Tib. yul rang gi sdod lugs nas rang gi mtshan nyid kyis grub pa'i gzhal bya.

869 Such an explanation is, for example, given in detail in Kedrub Je's *sTong thun chen mo* (Delhi ed.), pp. 317–18; translated in Cabezón 1992).

870 In Dreyfus and McClintock 2003, p. 134 (McClintock's italics).

871 See Dar ma rin chen 1980, topic four on the rejection of autonomous reasoning.

872 This means that they accept that whatever is established through either the reasoning consciousness that evaluates the ultimate or the wisdom of the meditative equipoise of noble ones is necessarily ultimate reality.

873 VI.81–83.

874 ACIP TD3862@312B.

875 ACIP TD3860@19A.

876 Ibid., @270A.

877 VI.30–31ab.

878 VI.35.

879 ACIP TD3860@025B.

880 Verse 1.

881 Verse 8.

882 ACIP TD3860@19A–B.

883 Ibid., @19B.

884 In Dreyfus and McClintock 2003, p. 113 (Tillemans's italics).

885 Ibid., p. 84. For more details on how Tsongkhapa substantially shifted from Candrakīrti's original critique of Bhāvaviveka, see the section below entitled "The Origin of the Controversy between Autonomists and Consequentialists."

886 Tsong kha pa 1990–1991, Delhi ed., pp. 577–78 (Bhāvaviveka's words are found in ACIP TD3853@242A–B).

887 Ibid., p. 579.

888 ACIP TD3853@48B, 62A, 153B, 154A, 247A; ACIP TD3856@59B (commentary on *Heart of Centrism* III.26).

889 ACIP TD3853@242B.

890 For further reasons that Bhāvaviveka did not hold such a position and would have resisted it, see also Eckel's essay in Dreyfus and McClintock 2003 (pp. 173–203). I would add here that when I point to instances of Tsongkhapa employing out-of-context quotes, I do not mean to imply that he is the only one in Tibetan Buddhism (or Buddhism in general) who does so. Unfortunately, he is not. My point is that all those who do this are far from furthering their own case.

891 For details, see Hopkins 1983 and Tauscher in Dreyfus and McClintock 2003.

892 Dreyfus and McClintock 2003, pp. 95–96.

893 1989, pp. 12–13.

894 Dpa' bo gtsug lag phreng ba, n.d., p. 821.

895 Tsong kha pa blo bzang grags pa 1990–1991, p. 132.13–16.

896 Hopkins (1989, p. 13) also quotes the above passage by Tsongkhapa and the following by Candrakīrti, without, however, addressing this obvious discrepancy.

897 Having clarified at the beginning of his *Entrance into Centrism* that this text is a commentary on the meaning of Nāgārjuna's (main) Centrist treatise *The Fundamental Verses*, Candrakīrti uses the term "the Centrist treatise" (Tib. dbu ma'i bstan bcos) throughout to refer to Nāgārjuna's text.

898 ACIP TD3862@347A.

899 Ibid., @347B.

900 Dreyfus and McClintock 2003, pp. 341–42. To be fair, it should be noted that Dreyfus continues here: "This does not mean, however, that we should go to the other extreme and

reject his views altogether. In particular, his second suggestion that there are other substantial philosophical differences between the two traditions is important. Whether or not Tsong kha pa is right on all the 'eight difficult points,' it appears quite probable that he is onto something significant."

901 ACIP TD3856@B072B (commentary on *Heart of Centrism* III.71; except for the last line, the last verse is literally *Saṃyutta Nikāya* III.141–42).

902 ACIP TD3856@073B (III.73ab).

903 Ibid., @073B–074A (III.73cd).

904 Ibid., @074A (III.74).

905 Ibid., @074A–B (III.75).

906 Ibid., @074B (III.76).

907 Skt. svātmaka, Tib. rang gi bdag nyid. This is often used as an equivalent for "nature" (Skt. svabhāva, Tib. rang bzhin) and "specific characteristic" (Skt. svalakṣaṇa, Tib. rang gi mtshan nyid).

908 ACIP TD3853@53B (commenting on *Fundamental Verses* I.3).

909 Tib. lta ba ngan sel, fol. 41a.3–5.

910 ACIP TD3854@260B.

911 Ibid., @260A–261A.

912 That there are many good reasons not to doubt the Tibetan canon's attribution of this text to Bhāvaviveka is explained in detail in Lindtner 1982b.

913 ACIP TD3885@58A (commentary on verse 8).

914 In Dreyfus and McClintock 2003, pp. 145, 147–48 (McClintock's italics). See the above quote from Śāntarakṣita's own *Commentary on The Ornament of Centrism*, verses 76–78.

915 For details, see Lipman 1979.

916 Dreyfus and McClintock 2003, pp. 107–08 (Tillemans's italics).

917 Skt. bhikṣu (lit. "beggar"), Tib. dge slong.

918 Tsong kha pa 1990–1991, p. 187.14–18.

919 ACIP TD3842@161B.

920 This is the brief version of what Candrakīrti says below about this issue in detail.

921 ACIP TD3853@049A.

922 The Tibetan here is *glags yod pa'i tshig* (which usually translates *sāvakāśavacana*), while the same passage in *The Lucid Words* reads "a statement that is a consequence" (Skt. prasaṅgavākya, Tib. thal bar 'gyur ba'i tshig). Avalokitavrata's commentary on Bhāvaviveka's text explains the latter term as "a statement that affords an opportunity for objections by another debater" (rgol ba gzhan gyi klan ka'i glags yod pa'i tshig).

923 ACIP TD3853@49A–B.

924 For a translation of this, see Ames in Dreyfus and McClintock 2003, pp. 47–48.

925 In meaning, this corresponds to what is called reductio ad absurdum in the West, which is normally used to prove the opposite of what is shown to be absurd. The Indian school of

the Logicians (Naiyāyika) uses a similar approach in what they call *tarka*. Also Dharmakīrti uses such consequences to implicitly prove something (Skt. prasaṅgasādhana, Tib. sgrub pa'i thal 'gyur).

As will be shown below, Bhāvaviveka usually emphasizes that both his own negations and Nāgārjuna's consequences do *not* imply anything at all. He obviously treats Buddhapālita differently in this matter.

926 Mi bskyod rdo rje 1996, pp. 181–218. I do not highlight Candrakīrti's own words as they appear in the Karmapa's explanations. More literal and complete English translations of the first chapter of *The Lucid Words* from both Sanskrit and Tibetan are available elsewhere, for example, Ruegg 2002 and Hopkins 1983. I will, however, indicate the original passages from *The Lucid Words* in both La Vallée Poussin's Sanskrit edition (abbr. LVP) and the Tibetan ACIP version, since the latter is more easily accessible to most people. For the detailed Sanskrit references, see Ruegg 2000.

927 This heading covers LVP 14.1–16.2 (ACIP TD3860@05B–06A). Candrakīrti does not give a definition of autonomous reasoning, but judging from his following discussion, for him this obviously means a reasoning that demonstrates one's own position, whose elements (subject, predicate, and reason) and their relations (the three modes) are established in common for both parties in a debate. This means that when Centrists like Bhāvaviveka use autonomous reasoning in this sense, its elements and their relations must be accepted by the Centrists themselves (which is precisely Candrakīrti's main critique). Note that Candrakīrti's understanding of autonomous reasoning substantially differs from that of Tsongkhapa and his followers as described above (i.e., that the reasoning's elements and relations as well as the valid cognition that establishes them must be conventionally established through their own specific characteristics from the perspective of the object's own way of being).

928 As mentioned above, even a renowned Autonomist like Kamalaśīla (ACIP TD3886@88A) makes the same point of adapting the use of consequences and probative arguments to the situation at hand.

929 Here, the Karmapa approves of some old manuscripts that comment that Consequentialists, for the sake of revealing the Enumerators' self-contradictions, challenge them by formulating arguments and examples that are acknowledged by the Enumerators and result in negating that entities arise from themselves.

930 LVP 16.2–16.11 (ACIP TD3860@06A).

931 XVI.25.

932 Verses 29–30.

933 LVP 16.11–18.5 (ACIP TD3860@06A–B).

934 LVP 18.5–23.3 (ACIP TD3860@06B-7B).

935 The phrase "out of the wish . . . their own certainty" is literally found in Dignāga's *Compendium of Valid Cognition* (IV.6ab). That Candrakīrti uses it here is not to be seen as an approval of it on his side, but rather as a way of confronting Bhāvaviveka with a scriptural source by the Buddhist logician on whom he so strongly relies.

936 For examples of how the Enumerators may reply to the first Centrist consequence and how this does not help their position, see the section above entitled "Refutation of Mistaken Assumptions about Autonomists and Consequentialists."

937 Apart from Candrakīrti's rejection of the ontological foundations of Dignāga's and Dharmakīrti's approach to reasoning, it may be seen as another sign of him strictly following common worldly consensus that he explicitly uses the format of the general five-membered probative argument that was commonly used by both non-Buddhists and Buddhists before Dignāga and Dharmakīrti.

938 Candrakīrti adds that the negation of "arising" also applies to the Enumerators' own terminology of "manifestation," since "arising" and "manifestation" are alike in that something is not observable first and becomes observable later.

939 Skt. puruṣa, Tib. skyes bu.

940 Skt. prakṛti, Tib. rang bzhin. For more details, see Appendix II.

941 LVP 23.3–24.7 (ACIP TD3860@07B–08A).

942 As Ruegg (1991, 2002) has pointed out, Hopkins (1983) does not just present the reversed meaning of Buddhapālita's consequence (*prasaṅgaviparīta*) as Bhāvaviveka himself formulates it in the context of the third flaw that he attributes to Buddhapālita. By relying on the Gelugpa literature on the reversal/contraposition of consequences (*thal bzlog* and *thal ba 'phen pa*), Hopkins first presents two consequences that Bhāvaviveka is claimed to have seen in Buddhapālita's own consequence:

"It follows that the subject, things, are produced senselessly because of being produced from self.

It follows that the subject, things, are produced endlessly because of being produced from self."

Then, it is claimed that Bhāvaviveka saw *these* consequences (and not Buddhapālita's own) as implying their opposite meaning:

"The subject, things, are not produced from self because their production is not senseless. The subject, things, are not produced from self because their production is not endless." (pp. 490-1)

The first two consequences amount to contrapositions of Buddhapālita's own consequence (*prasaṅgaviparyaya*), which are then treated as "consequences that impel an autonomous reasoning" (Tib. *rang rgyud 'phen pa'i thal 'gyur*), i.e., the latter two statements. However, Bhāvaviveka said that it follows from Buddhapālita's own consequence that entities *do arise* from something *other* (and not that they do not arise from themselves), because their arising is fruitful and because it comes to an end. In this, the predicate and the reasons are simply reversed in meaning and stay in their places, without being turned into the negatives of the predicate and the reason that then switch their positions (contraposition). Thus, the contraposition of an implicit inference by a consequence (as it is known and used by Buddhist logicians like Dignāga and Dharmakīrti) has per se nothing to do with Bhāvaviveka's simple reversal, which was obviously also how Candrakīrti treated the issue in his *Lucid Words*.

To make a complicated matter worse, the Tibetan translation for both contraposition (*prasaṅgaviparyaya*) and reversal of a consequence (*prasaṅgaviparīta*) is *thal bzlog*. A further source for confusion is that *prasaṅgāpādana* and *prasaṅgāpatti* on the one hand ("adducing a consequence," as found in the above passages of *The Lucid Words*) and *prasaṅgasādhana* on the other ("implicit proof by a consequence," as found in Dharmakīrti's *Pramāṇaviniścaya* III.2) are all translated as *thal ba sgrub pa*. Tibetan literature on *thal bzlog* then tends to use the term *thal ba 'phen pa* instead of *thal ba sgrub pa* in the first sense. However, inasmuch as *thal ba 'phen pa* involves contraposition (*prasaṅgaviparyaya*), it is *not* the same as *thal ba sgrub pa* as found in *The Lucid Words*. Despite the confusing and conflating Tibetan terminology here, it is impossible to assume that Tsongkhapa was not aware of the differences in meaning. However, treating the topics of reversal and contraposition in the joined way that he does serves as one of his toeholds to weave the system of Dignāga and Dharmakīrti into his version of Consequentialism. For more details, see Ruegg 2002 (pp. 250-265) and Iwata 1987.

943 LVP 24.7–25.7 (ACIP TD3860@08A–B).

944 V.1, IV.2, XXV.4.

945 XIII.1.

946 ACIP TD3860@81A.

947 Ibid., @98A.

948 As it stands, this statement by Candrakīrti is somewhat problematic, since both the *Rebuttal of Objections* and its autocommentary do in fact use quite a number of probative arguments. To be sure, the Karmapa glosses Candrakīrti's answer as "has not formulated *autonomous* probative arguments . . . ," thus indicating that Candrakīrti obviously meant that Nāgārjuna did not use probative arguments as Bhāvaviveka understands them.

Examples of Nāgārjuna's use of probative arguments in his *Rebuttal of Objections* and its autocommentary include verse 21cd:

> However, entities are established as being empty,
> Because they are without nature.

His autocommentary explains:

> However, my words are established as being empty, because they are without nature. Just as my words are empty because they are without nature, also all entities are empty, because they are without nature.

Verse 22 says:

> The dependent origination of entities
> Is what is called "emptiness."
> What is dependent origination
> Is being without nature.

His autocommentary explains:

> Dependently originating entities are emptiness. Why? Because they are without nature. . . . Why? Because they are dependent on causes and conditions. . . . Therefore, it is justified to say, "They are empty, because they are without nature." Likewise, also my words are dependently originating. Therefore, they are without nature. Therefore, it is justified to say, "They are empty, because they are without nature." Just as a vase, yarn, and so on—which are naturally empty, because they are dependently originating—can hold . . . water . . . and protect from the cold . . . , likewise also my words (which are without nature, because they are dependently originating) can very well prove that entities are without nature. (ACIP TD3832@126B–127A; other examples are verses 24, 63, and 67–69).

Not only does Nāgārjuna here formulate quite a number of probative arguments of the format A is B because of C, but even all the members of a five-membered probative argument are found:

> [1, thesis] My words are empty, [2, reason] because they are without nature. All entities that are without nature are empty, [3, example] just like a vase or yarn. Likewise, [4, application] my words are without nature. [5, conclusion] Therefore, because of being without nature, my words are empty.

As for the *Akutobhayā* (P5229), the earliest commentary on *The Fundamental Verses*, it is traditionally attributed to Nāgārjuna himself, but this is not accepted by the followers of Tsongkhapa, many Sakya masters and some modern scholars. This text is not even mentioned by Buddhapālita, Bhāvaviveka, and Candrakīrti, while being identified as Nāgārjuna's autocommentary by Avalokitavrata. Be that as it may, as Huntington (1995) and Walser (1998) have pointed out, this commentary does not much more than persistently incorporate Nāgārjuna's text into the format of either—mostly abridged—versions of the above probative arguments or absurd consequences. Even if the *Akutobhayā* is not by Nāgārjuna himself, it clearly shows that such an approach was nothing unusual in early Centrist commentaries. Moreover, as Huntington extensively shows, Buddhapālita's own commentary "incorporates lines, passages, and almost entire chapters from the Akutobhayā." Thus, he says, the *Akutobhayā* certainly existed in the mainstream of early Madhyamaka exegesis and, via Buddhapālita's text, exerted a considerable influence upon later commentators as well. Hence, a more thorough study of the contents of the *Akutobhayā* and how it influenced the Centrist approach to reasoning seems to be very necessary, especially in the context of the later Autonomist-Consequentialist controversy.

949 ACIP TD3853@048B, 62A, 153B, 154A, 247A (see also his *Blaze of Reasoning,* ACIP TD3856@59B).

950 ACIP TD3862@05A, 093B.

951 See Bhāvaviveka's *Lamp of Knowledge* on verses II.19, VI.1, X.1–2 and 5.

952 There seems to be a single further, more content-oriented critique of Buddhapālita by Bhāvaviveka, involving the closely related questions of whether phenomenal identitylessness is taught in the sūtras of the hearers and whether hearers and solitary realizers realize phenomenal identitylessness. For details, see the section below entitled "Do Hearers and Solitary Realizers Realize Emptiness?"

953 LVP 25.7–26.2 (ACIP TD3860@08B).

954 LVP 26.2–31.1 (ACIP TD3860@08B–10A).

955 ACIP KD0095@145A.

956 XVIII.10.

957 It is to be noted that, in his *Heart of Centrism,* Bhāvaviveka himself explicitly states that arising from itself is not justified even on the seeming level (III.139).

958 Most commentators understand the opponents here to be the Differentiators. However, if one considers the reasoning at hand as a whole (sound is impermanent, because it is produced), since the Differentiators also say that sound is impermanent (despite being a property of space), Buddhists would not have to prove its impermanence to them. Thus, one may identify the opponent here as the Analyzers, who say that sound is a property of space and permanent.

959 The latter is Mikyö Dorje's identification.

960 The Tibetan says *mngon par gsal ba,* which is used throughout for the Sanskrit *abhivyakti* as a typical term of the Enumerators (thus Mikyö Dorje's identification of the opponent here as the Enumerators). However, the Sanskrit here is *vyaṅgya,* which is similar in meaning but the typical term of the Analyzers.

961 Verse 30.

962 For example, Williams (1985) has demonstrated that the views ascribed by Jamyang Shayba (1648–1722) to Majaba Jangchub Dsöndrü do not correspond at all to what the latter says himself. In her detailed study of the views of early Tibetan Centrists that are considered false by the Gelugpas, Yoshimizu (1993) comes to the conclusion that Jamyang Shayba's "attribution of the 'false interpretations' of the Prāsaṅgika-Madhyamaka theory to the early Centrist masters related to Pa tshab and Jayānanda is by no means reliable. One may even suspect

him of having intentionally discredited them . . ." (p. 216). She says that Tsongkhapa attributes these theories to his contemporaries, without specifying any names. However, when investigated, they do not apply to masters such as Gorampa or Rendawa (p. 218).

963 LVP 31.1–34.1 (ACIP TD3860@10A-11A).

964 I.7.

965 ACIP TD3853@58B–59A.

966 Ibid., @49B.

967 Ibid., @63A.

968 Ibid., @68B.

969 Ibid., @66B–67A.

970 III.39ab.

971 III.27ab.

972 LVP 34.1–36.2 (ACIP TD3860@11A–B).

973 Notice that here again Candrakīrti may be said to follow the format of the five-membered probative argument (and not just an absurd consequence without a reason), the content of which corresponds to *Fundamental Verses* III.2. Explicitly, Candrakīrti only states the last three members of such a probative argument. However, in general, the combination of the fourth and fifth member says exactly the same thing as the first and the second together, so either set is often dropped.

974 The Karmapa identifies the passage quoted as coming from Vasubandhu. I could not locate it in Vasubandhu's *Vādavidhi* (his treatise on reasoning), the most likely source.

975 Skt. Nyāyamukha (Taisho 1628; Sanskrit in G. Tucci, *The Nyāyamukha of Dignāga*, p. 15).

976 VIII.19.

977 ACIP TD3860@199B.

978 This approach is similar to Tsongkhapa's identification and subsequent negation of the object of negation in Centrism, where one also wonders about his point in first defining something nonexistent and then going on to refute it at length (for details, see Chapter 6).

979 The following is based on her article in Dreyfus and McClintock 2003, pp. 257–88.

980 In his correction of a previous misreading due to an incorrect Tibetan translation, Tsongkhapa is found again to have misread a crucial passage in *The Lucid Words* to make it fit his own interpretation (Ibid., pp. 267–68).

981 These two points are discussed at length in Chapter 2 in the section entitled "Do Centrists Have a Thesis or Position?"

982 ACIP TD3842@197B–198A.

983 ACIP TD3853@113A–B.

984 Except for the last line ("Thus spoke the friend of the sun."), this is literally *Saṃyutta Nikāya* III.141–2.

985 It is more than doubtful that Bhāvaviveka himself believed in his—obviously rhetorical—claim of the great vehicle being without purpose, just because the lesser vehicle already teaches phenomenal identitylessness. Especially in the first three chapters of his *Blaze of Reasoning*, he amply demonstrates that he does not regard the teaching on phenomenal identitylessness as the only feature that distinguishes the great vehicle from the lesser and accounts for its superiority.

986 ACIP TD3853@184B–185B.

987 ACIP TD3856@146A–147A and @161B–163A (commenting on *Heart of Centrism* IV.4–5 and IV.24–27, especially IV.27cd).

988 Skt. śrotāpanna, Tib. rgyun zhugs. This is the name for practitioners who have attained the path of seeing as the first major result in the vehicle of the hearers.

989 The knowledge that and how karma and afflictions have been exhausted and will never arise again.

990 ACIP TD3915@26B (Rahder ed., p. 65).

991 Ibid., @28A.

992 Skt. Saṃvṛtiparamārthasatyanirdeṣasūtra, Tib. kun rdzob dang don dam pa'i bden pa bstan pa'i mdo (Ibid., @34A–35B).

993 ACIP TD3886@86B.

994 His *Sarvadharmaniḥsvabhāvasiddhi* also agrees with these statements (ACIP TD3889 @289Bf.).

995 ACIP TD3915@033B–036A.

996 ACIP TD3917@57B.

997 ACIP TD3865@190B.

998 ACIP KD0012@03B.

999 ACIP TD3860@114A–B.

1000 I.8.

1001 ACIP TD3862@266A-268A/Mi bskyod rdo rje 1996, pp. 72–86.

1002 It is remarkable that neither Candrakīrti nor the Karmapa adduces the above passage from *The Sūtra of the Ten Grounds* quoted by Kamalaśīla, since it is so much more explicit in expressing that hearers and solitary realizers realize emptiness.

1003 This refers to practitioners of other spiritual paths who may gain some temporal freedom from attachment by way of suppressing or weakening its manifest expression but do not eradicate its latent tendencies.

1004 XXIII.14.

1005 VI.131, 140–141.

1006 In several other verses among those in the sixth chapter of *The Entrance into Centrism* that refute a personal self (VI.117–165), Candrakīrti elaborates further on the indispensability of realizing the emptiness of the aggregates for liberation from cyclic existence.

1007 The three paths are the twelve links of dependent origination, grouped in three categories: affliction (links 1, 8, 9), action (2, 10), and arising (the remaining seven links).

1008 I.35–37.

1009 IV.57–-65.

1010 IV.66.

1011 ACIP TD3864@028A (on verse 51).

1012 VI.28.

1013 Verse 64.

1014 The Consequentialists' distinction between afflictive and cognitive obscurations is sometimes summarized as the former consisting of the afflictions plus the clinging to reality and the latter consisting of the latent tendencies of the former two plus the clinging to characteristics. The Karmapa's commentary on *The Entrance into Centrism* XI.40 says that both this verse and its autocommentary by Candrakīrti clearly explain the latent tendencies of the afflictions as being cognitive obscurations. As the autocommentary says: "The latent tendencies of ignorance are the obstruction to the complete analysis of all knowable objects. The existence of latent tendencies of desire and such is the cause for such [strange] physical and verbal behaviors [even in arhats]. The latent tendencies of ignorance, desire, and so on only cease in omniscient Buddhas, but not in others." (ACIP TD3862@342B–343A).

Thus, the Karmapa says, the claim by some Tibetans that "Consequentialists do not present the latent tendencies of the afflictions as cognitive obscurations" can only mean that they did not make the effort to read this even once (Mi bskyod rdo rje 1996, p. 693).

Apart from the Consequentialists' distinction between afflictive and cognitive obscurations, there are a number of other—more or less differing—ways of making this distinction. Most of them are based on the system of Maitreya/Asaṅga. There it is said that the afflictive obscurations are just the manifest afflictions, including the afflicted kind of ignorance, understood as ignorance about and clinging to an "I" (as a real personal self). The cognitive obscurations are constituted by the latent tendencies of the afflictions and unafflicted ignorance. The latter is again described in various ways. Some say that it has three degrees of subtlety: clinging to reality (Tib. bden 'dzin), clinging to characteristics (mtshan 'dzin), and clinging to duality (gnyis 'dzin). *The Sublime Continuum* (V.14ab) says that the cognitive obscurations (as equivalent to unafflicted ignorance) are the conceptions about the three spheres (agent, object, and action). Maitreya's *Distinction between the Middle and Extremes* (II.14–16) describes them as tenfold in correspondence with what is relinquished on the ten grounds of bodhisattvas. The most detailed description of the cognitive obscurations is found in *The Ornament of Clear Realization* and its commentaries, which speak about "the one hundred eight conceptions about the apprehender and the apprehended." (There are two sets of nine misconceptions about both the apprehender and the apprehended, thus making thirty-six. These are further related to each of the three realms, thus resulting in one hundred eight.) The factors to be relinquished on the paths of junction, seeing, and meditation respectively are equally constituted by this same set of misconceptions, the difference lying merely in their degrees of subtlety.

1015 IV.86.

1016 XV.7.

1017 IV.90, 93.

1018 This represents a brief list of the classic sets of criteria for whether the perfections, such as generosity, are the actual perfections leading to Buddhahood or just conditioned positive actions leading only to better rebirths within cyclic existence. For details, see *The Treasury of Knowledge* (Kong sprul blo gros mtha' yas 1982, vol. II, pp. 492–96) and Maitreya's *Distinc-*

*tion between the Middle and Extremes* V.1–10 with the commentary by Mipham Rinpoche (Mi pham c. 1990, vol. pa, pp. 747–54).

1019 Verse 27.

1020 III.284–286.

1021 Dpa' bo gtsug lag phreng ba, n.d., p. 883.

1022 *The Treasury of Knowledge* adds that Autonomists do not present the seeming by just following worldly conventions, since they see possibilities for mistakenness in such an approach. For worldly people simply use conventions without any analysis through reasoning whatsoever. Thus, Autonomists prefer to present seeming reality in accordance with either the Sūtra Followers or the Yogācāras, who know how to apply reasonings. Consequentialists do not follow other proponents of philosophical systems, but just the conventions used by worldly people; Consequentialists say that the noble ones are the sole authorities on the valid cognition of ultimate reality, while worldly people are the sole authorities on what is conventionally considered the valid cognition of seeming reality. (Kong sprul blo gros mtha' yas 1982, vol. II, pp. 519–20).

1023 Skt. yāvatjñāna, Tib. ji snyed pa mkhyen pa. Together with the wisdom that knows suchness (Skt. yathājñāna, Tib. ji lta ba mkyen pa), this wisdom comprises the supreme knowing or omniscience of a Buddha in its two main aspects of knowing the true nature of phenomena just as it is and the extent of that nature as it is reflected in the manifold display of all phenomena.

1024 *The Treasury of Knowledge* explains: Some Autonomists say that Buddhas possess an illusionlike wisdom that has undergone a complete change of state. Thus, for them, an illusionlike seeming reality appears, but this is not mistakenness, because they have no clinging to its reality. This means that impure karmic appearances exist for Buddhas. Consequentialists say that since appearances originate from the latent tendencies of unafflicted ignorance, they are mistaken. However, since Buddhas have relinquished all mistakenness without exception, the manifestation of such appearances has completely subsided. Thus, there are no karmic appearances that exist for them. (Kong sprul blo gros mtha' yas 1982, vol. II, p. 523).

1025 Dpa' bo gtsug lag phreng ba, n.d., pp. 884–85.

1026 Kong sprul blo gros mtha' yas 1982, vol. II, pp. 541–42.

1027 Particularly in the vehicle of the hearers, the path of seeing is variously explained as having sixteen, fifteen, twelve, or four moments.

1028 XI.45cd.

1029 Quoted in ACIP TD3862@345A.

1030 2000, pp. 71–72.

1031 Tib. rigs bsdus 'phrul gyi lde mig. In *Blo rtags kyi rnam bzhag rigs gzhung rgya mtsho'i snying po dang rigs bsdus 'phrul gyi lde mig* (Sikkim, India: Karma Shri Nalanda Institute, Rumtek, 1989), pp. 130–31, 156.

1032 A good example is his "Perfect Expression of Centrism" (Tib. dbu ma yang dag par brjod pa) in *Milarepa's Life Story and Enlightened Songs* (Tib. rnal 'byor gyi dbang phyug chen po mi la ras pa'i rnam mgur. Mtsho sngon mi rigs dpe skrun khang, 1989, p. 482).

1033 This term is used in a number of different ways in different contexts and also for different schools. To avoid confusion, it is helpful to keep the following main usages in mind. In its most general sense, in all Buddhist schools, it just refers to the practice of yoga, i.e., meditation practice as opposed to study and reflection (in this sense it is also used in the title and content of Āryadeva's *Four Hundred Verses on the Yogic Practice of Bodhisattvas*). As can be seen from the early texts of the Yogācāra school, such notions as "mere mind" or "mere cognizance"—in the sense that all that we experience happens nowhere other than in our mind—originated in the context of meditation practice with its various mental images, before they became systematically extended into a denial of external objects altogether. Second, Yogācāra stands for the other major school of the great vehicle besides the Centrists, and in particular for the system of Maitreya and Asaṅga. Third, this term appears in the term "*Yogācāra-Svātantrika-Madhyamaka" (a retrotranslation into Sanskrit of a term coined by Tibetans), which is a designation for the system of such masters as Śāntarakṣita and Kamalaśīla. Fourth, it is also found in the combination "Yogācāra-Madhyamaka," which can stand for a number of syntheses between Yogācāra and Madhyamaka, including the systems of Śāntarakṣita and Ratnākaraśānti. In the Kagyü and Nyingma schools, this term is mostly taken to be a synonym for the lineage of vast activity, which came to be called the system of other-emptiness. In this case, often the name "Great Yogācāra-Madhyamaka" is used.

1034 Many proponents of other-emptiness also adduce additional sources of the meaning of Shentong in the tantras, but the systematic presentation of their system is primarily founded on the texts of Maitreya, Asaṅga, and Vasubandhu.

1035 To translate *cittamātra* as "Mind Only" is very common but highly misleading, since this wrongly implies some kind of absolute idealism, i.e., the notion that mind is the only entity that really or ultimately exists. In particular, when used for Asaṅga's Yogācāra, it completely distorts his view, since there is no connotation of an absolute or sole existence of mind in his system at all (this is discussed in more detail below). In general, the use of *-mātra* in Buddhist texts is a demeaning, restrictive term, not a reifying honorific. That is how it is invariably used by Buddhists, be it in the Centrist "mere seeming" (saṃvṛtimātra) or in other common terms used by both Centrists and Yogācāras, such as "mere name" (nāmamātra), "mere designation" (prajñaptimātra), or "mere delusion" (bhrāntamātra). All of these are notions or problems to be overcome and not to be reified, thus making any idealist and ontological interpretation of the terms *cittamātra* or *vijñaptimātra* all the more obsolete. Otherwise, one could equally absurdly call the Centrists "Proponents of Name Only" or "Proponents of Designation Only" and claim that names and designations are the only ultimately existing entity for them, since they repeatedly say that all phenomena are "mere names" (nāmamātra) or "mere designations" (prajñaptimātra) (see, for example, Nāgārjuna's *Acintyastava*, verse 36, as well as Candrakīrti's *Lucid Words* and autocommentary on *The Entrance into Centrism*).

1036 A detailed presentation of the tremendous vastness and diversity of Yogācāra and its development into the Shentong system in Tibet is beyond the scope of this book. For more details, see especially the works by Griffiths, Harris, Hookham, Keenan, Lindtner (1997), Mathes, Schmithausen, Stearns, and Willis.

1037 In fact, when looking at the meaning rather than merely the words, there are hardly any proponents of Shentong who make any ontological claim of an inherently existing entity, be it Buddha nature or the perfect nature (not even Dölpopa, if he is read properly). Karma Trinlayba, one of the main disciples of the Seventh Karmapa, summarizes the exemplary position of the Third Karmapa Rangjung Dorje on this. Karma Trinlayba defines Shentong as meaning that the unchanging nature of mind as such—which is free from distinctions and bias, naturally luminous, and the unity of expanse and awareness—is Buddhahood, once it becomes free from adventitious stains. That this primordial ground is not affected by any stains is the meaning of Shentong. The fact that this very mind as such is unaware of itself is called "adventitious stains." (Paraphrase of a quote in the introduction to *Dbu ma gzhan stong skor bstan bcos phyogs bsdus deb dang po*, p. ga.)

1038 In his *Chariot of the Tagbo Siddhas*, he refutes all kinds of reifying interpretations of what is taught in the lineage of vast activity. However, on the conventional level, he accepts nonreifying presentations of the three natures. He even says that it is very much in accord with Centrism, when this lineage presents the three natures as the threefold lack of nature, thus implying that they come down to the same essential point (Mi bskyod rdo rje 1996, p. 443). For more details, see chapter 5.

1039 The same is clearly stated in the Seventh Karmapa's *Ocean of Texts on Reasoning* (Chos grags rgya mtsho 1985, vol. I, p. 196) and in Padma Karpo's *Cutting Through Doubts about the Threefold Progression of the Wheels of Dharma* (Tib. chos 'khor rim pa gsum gyi dogs gcod), (1973, p. 338).

The question of the "final view" of the Eighth Karmapa—if there is such a thing—is a rather complex one. In his *History of the Dharma*, Pawo Rinpoche says that the Seventh Karmapa had prophesied that, since he could only comment on valid cognition and the Prajñāpāramitā sūtras in this life, he would comment further on the other traditional topics of Buddhist studies, such as Madhyamaka, in his next incarnation (Dpa' bo gtsug lag phreng ba 1986, p. 1276). Thus, the Eighth Karmapa's major commentaries on Abhidharma, Vinaya, and Prajñāpāramitā, and his latest commentary on the sūtra teachings, *The Chariot of the Tagbo Siddhas*, are regarded as the fulfillment of this prophecy. Pawo Rinpoche states that the Eighth Karmapa considered Saraha and Nāgārjuna as the final authorities to clarify the view (Ibid., pp. 1254–55). This accords with what the Karmapa himself says in his *Chariot*. Pawo Rinpoche also reports that, upon being fully ordained as a monk, Mikyö Dorje received extensive instructions on the view of "other-emptiness" by his preceptor and early teacher Chödrub Senge (Tib. chos grub seng ge), who then requested the Karmapa to uphold this view (Ibid., p. 1236). Thus, before his outspoken rejection of a Shentong-Madhyamaka in *The Chariot*, his first great commentary (on *The Ornament of Clear Realization*) uses the term "other-emptiness" frequently, but explains it in a way that is very different from what one would ordinarily expect. In fact, this commentary mainly presents the hidden meaning of the Prajñāpāramitā sūtras in terms of the view of the Seventh Karmapa, i.e., the unity of the lineages of profound view and vast conduct. The commentary also makes it very clear that "Mere Mentalism" is not the lineage of vast activity. The Eighth Karmapa also wrote a short text on other-emptiness (Tib. *dbu ma gzhan stong smra ba'i srol legs par phye ba'i sgron me*). However, in both texts, one looks in vain for any reifying or absolutist interpretation of other-emptiness. One is rather tempted to call the Karmapa's presentation "Shentong Lite" in comparison with other texts, since it very much accords with and uses the Centrist approach. In addition, Pawo Rinpoche reports the Karmapa to have said that it is not reasonable that the view of all teachings on valid cognition, Abhidharma, Madhyamaka, and the Vajrayāna is other-emptiness (Ibid., p. 1240).

In general, it is regarded as one of the signs of a commentator of the highest caliber to expound each scripture according to its own system and context, without mixing different traditions or imposing one's own "highest" view. Pawo Rinpoche says that this approach is reflected in all commentaries by the Eighth Karmapa, since he always taught in accordance with the propensities of his disciples and by keeping to the principles that apply to the specific texts of sūtras and tantras and not by just clinging to a single meaning throughout (Ibid., p. 1254). That one has to treat the systems of Madhyamaka and Yogācāra independently in their own contexts is also expressed by Mikyö Dorje himself.

So far, the works of Karmapa Mikyö Dorje have hardly been studied by Western scholars. Instead, unfounded claims about him are often repeated, such as that he was one of the greatest proponents of the system of other-emptiness in the Kagyü lineage. From the perspective of his texts, this is definitely not the case. That the Karmapa's works are often hard to read and require careful examination in order to determine exactly what his points in highly complex matters are does not make it any easier to gain a well-founded picture of his view. What is certain, though, is that he went to considerable pains to employ the language and technique of debate used by his opponents (often from the Gelugpa school) in good Consequentialist style, flinging their own approach back at them so as to refute their positions.

1040 Skt. parabhāvaśūnyatā, Tib. gzhan gyi ngo bo/gzhan gyi dngos po stong pa nyid. This is the twentieth of the twenty emptinesses described earlier.

1041 This is very similar to Asaṅga's description of the other-dependent nature as a term for the compound of the imaginary nature and the perfect nature, as he illustrates it in *The Synopsis of the Great Vehicle* through the example of gold ore being nothing more than the compound of ordinary stone and pure gold (II.29, fols. 22a.7–22b.6; for details, see in the section below entitled "The System of the Lineage of Vast Activity.").

1042 Mi bskyod rdo rje, n.d., vol. I, pp. 347–48..

1043 This can be clearly seen in the different approaches in his commentaries on *The Entrance into Centrism* and *The Ornament of Clear Realization.*

The above explanations are found in Mikyö Dorje's commentary on *The Entrance into Centrism* (Mi bskyod rdo rje 1996, pp. 634–36). The commentary on the same text by the Ninth Karmapa Wangchug Dorje also agrees on this issue.

1044 This refers to Dölpopa and his followers. The following passage comes from Dölpopa's *Fourth Council* (Tib. bka' bsdu bzhi pa), in which the two realities are compared to two opposing kingdoms.

1045 XXII.12, 15.

1046 Ibid., XXII.16.

1047 In Yogācāra texts, there are a number of different ways to describe the three natures and their relation. The main difference lies in whether one looks more at the subjective or the objective side of the process of how mind is deluded, how this manifests, and how purification takes place. For more details, see the section below entitled "The System of the Lineage of Vast Activity."

1048 Skt. Mahāparinirvāṇasūtra, Tib. mya ngan las 'das pa chen po'i mdo.

1049 Skt. Brahmāparipṛcchāsūtra, Tib, tshang pas zhus pa'i mdo (quoted in *The Lucid Words*, ACIP TD3860@182A).

1050 XXIV.11 The above explanations are found in Pawo Rinpoche's commentary on *The Entrance to the Bodhisattva's Way of Life* (Dpa' bo gtsug lag phreng ba, n.d., pp. 273ff.).

1051 Mi bskyod rdo rje 1996, pp. 432–34. It is to be noted that this is not the same as saying that the entirety of the teachings on Buddha nature per se are of expedient meaning. Thus, the classification as expedient meaning does not apply to Buddha nature when understood as a nonreifying equivalent of the expanse of dharmas, the ultimate luminous nature of mind, or the emptiness endowed with the supreme of all aspects. It also does not mean that Buddha nature is altogether nonexistent. In his commentary on *The Ornament of Clear Realization*, the Eighth Karmapa clarifies that Buddha nature refers to the aspect of the natural purity of the Dharma Body, which is "the luminous nature of the mind" (Mi bskyod rdo rje, n.d., vol. I, pp. 250–51). For more details, see the section below entitled "The System of the Lineage of Vast Activity."

1052 ACIP TD3862@281A–282A (the passage in the sūtra is ACIP KL0107@135B–136A).

1053 Skt. amalavijñāna, Tib. dri ma med pa'i rnam shes. This term was coined by the Yogācāra Paramārtha (500–569).

1054 I.28. The Karmapa's commentary on *The Ornament of Clear Realization* shows in detail that, when analyzed, none of these three reasons can be established to prove what they supposedly prove, which is that Buddha nature actually *exists in* sentient beings or that they *possess* it. Thus, these reasons have to be taken as teaching an expedient meaning (Mi bskyod rdo rje, n.d., vol. I, pp. 248–50).

1055 III.94.

1056 V.10.

1057 I.156cd–157.

1058 Skt. Mahāparinirvāṇasūtra, Tib. mya ngan la 'das pa chen po'i mdo.

1059 Skt. Śrīmālādevīsiṃhanādasūtra, Tib. lha mo dpal phreng gi seng nge'i sgra'i mdo.

1060 Skt. upacāra, Tib. nyer brtags.

1061 I.27.

1062 ACIP KL0107@239B.

1063 For details, see the Bibliography, especially the works of Anacker, Harris, Keenan, Lusthaus, Schmithausen, Sutton, and Willis.

1064 As Harris and others point out, it is quite obvious that the idea of belonging to a distinct school of thought was a very late development in Indian Buddhism. From all that we know, neither Nāgārjuna nor Asaṅga and Vasubandhu considered themselves in such a manner. Individual masters had their distinct views on certain matters but did not think in terms of different schools. For example, Centrists such as Bhāvaviveka and Candrakīrti did not see themselves as belonging to distinct subschools within Centrism, and the same goes for individual Yogācaras. Even the very late Indian master Atīśa had both Yogācāras and Centrists as his personal teachers without seeing any contradiction. For the most part, the categorization of these masters in terms of certain schools was only made later by others, especially by Tibetan doxographers.

1065 In fact, both Asaṅga and Sthiramati wrote commentaries on Nāgārjuna's *Fundamental Verses*, now extant only in Chinese translations (Taisho 1565, 1567). Atīśa even mentions the latter as one of the eight standard commentaries on Nāgārjuna's text used in his day, another one (now lost) having been composed by Guṇamati (ACIP TD3948@280B).

As can be seen from the developments of both the Madhyamaka and the Yogācāra schools in India, they influenced each other to a considerable degree. There were even syntheses of Yogācāra and Madhyamaka, such as by Śāntarakṣita, Kamalaśīla, and Ratnākaraśānti (for more details, see Harris 1991 and Ruegg 1981, 2000).

1066 For example, both Asaṅga and Vasubandhu wrote commentaries on *The Diamond Cutter Sūtra* (Skt. Vajracchedika). Moreover, Vasubandhu composed a vast commentary on the *Prajñāpāramitā Sūtras* in 100,000, 25,000, and 18,000 lines (Skt. Āryaśatasāhasrikapañcaviṃśatisāhasrikāṣṭādaśasāhasrikaprajñāpāramitābṛhaṭṭīkā, P5206). He also wrote commentaries on the *Daśabhūmikasūtra* (P5494) and the *Akṣayamatinirdeśasūtra* (P5495). Dignāga wrote a summary of the sūtra in 8,000 lines (Skt. Prajñāpāramitārthasaṃgraha, a.k.a. Prajñāpāramitāpiṇḍārtha).

1067 For example, Asaṅga's *Commentary on The Sūtra That Unravels the Intention.*

1068 ACIP TD3948@280A.

1069 For example, the three natures appear not only in the *Laṅkāvatārasūtra* and the *Saṃdhinirmocanasūtra*, but also in several Prajñāpāramitā sūtras. They are also mentioned by Nāgārjuna in his *Acintyastava* and *Bodhicittavivaraṇa*. (Here, I do not consider the claims that certain "later" sūtras do not come from the Buddha but were written by Centrists or Yogācāras.)

1070 X.368a.

1071 1991, p. 31.

1072 For more details and the sources, see the following section.

1073 1997, p. 169 (words in brackets added).

1074 Up to the present day, the whole curriculum related to the Prajñāpāramitā sūtras in Tibetan monastic colleges is entirely based on this text by Maitreya/Asaṅga.

1075 As for the different developments of the Yogācāra after Vasubandhu, there are several ways to distinguish various schools or lineages. In *The Essentials of Buddhist Philosophy* (pp. 83–84), Takakusu identifies three main streams: (1) the line of Dignāga, Agotra, and Dharmapāla at Nālandā University; (2) the line of Guṇamati and Sthiramati at Valābhi University; and (3) the line of Nanda, whose tenets were later followed by Paramārtha.

1076 In general, most Western scholars have finally come to agree that it is completely wrong and misleading to refer to the Yogācāra school as "idealist" in the sense that this term has in Western philosophy (for more details, see, for example, Harris 1991, Keenan 1989 and 1997, and Willis). In fact, this is a particularly obvious example of mistakenly trying to match specific terms of Western philosophy with Indian systems of thought. When I use "idealist" here, it is only in the sense in which Tillemans uses it: "2. If we wish to satisfactorily answer the question as to whether Yogācāras, like Dharmapāla, were idealists, we must change our usual understanding of that term. A Buddhist idealist does not just accept mind-dependence or a reduction of existence to mind, but also that mind has a preferred ontological status and is more real than external objects. 3. While Dharmapāla's acceptance of the reality of mind *qua paratantra* does seem to make him an idealist in our revised sense, the structure of his system guarantees that any attempt to conceptualize or formulate what that mind is like or how it exists is impossible." (1990, p. 68)

1077 As for Dignāga and Dharmakīrti, the difficult question of where exactly they fit in is much disputed and beyond the scope of this work. Various interpretations cast them as Sautrāntikas, as Yogācāras of different types, and, in their final intention, as Yogācāra-Mādhyamikas in the sense of Shentong-Madhyamaka (as the Seventh Karmapa holds in his *Ocean of Texts on Reasoning* that comments on the texts of these two masters).

1078 These are the following texts:
—The Five Dharma Works by Maitreya (Tib. byams chos sde lnga; see Bibliography)

—The Five Works on the Grounds (Tib. sa sde lnga) by Asaṅga:

1) *The Grounds of Yoga Practice*, a.k.a. as *The Main Corpus of the Many Grounds* (Skt. Bahubhūmivastu, Tib. sa mang dngos gzhi) P5536-8.
2) *The Synopsis of Ascertainment* (Skt. Viniścayasaṃgrahaṇī, Tib. gtan la dbab pa bsdu ba) P5539.
3) *The Synopsis of Bases* (Skt. Vastusaṃgrahaṇī, Tib. gzhi bsdu ba) P5540.
4) *The Synopsis of Specifications* (Skt. Paryāyasaṃgrahaṇī, Tib. rnam grangs bsdu ba) P5542.
5) *The Synopsis of Exposition* (Skt. Vivaraṇasaṃgrahaṇī, Tib. rnam bshad bsdu ba) P5543.

Actually, these five form the five chapters of the encyclopedic work *The Treatise on the Grounds of Yoga Practice* (Skt. Yogācārabhūmiśāstra, Tib. rnal 'byor spyod pa'i sa'i bstan bcos). The first chapter—*The Grounds of Yoga Practice*—expounds the Yogācāra system and includes seventeen "grounds," among them the Śrāvakabhūmi, the Pratyekabuddhabhūmi, and the Bodhisattvabhūmi ("grounds" 13–15). The *Viniścayasaṃgrahaṇī* is a commentary on this first chapter.

—The Two Summaries ( Tib. sdom pa rnam gnyis) by Asaṅga:
1) *The Compendium of Abhidharma.*
2) *The Synopsis of the Great Vehicle.*

—The Eight Discourses (Tib. pra ka ra ṇa sde brgyad) by Vasubandhu:
1) *Commentary on The Ornament of Sūtras* (Skt. Mahāyānasūtrālaṃkārabhāṣya, Tib. theg pa chen po'i mdo sde rgyan gyi 'grel pa) P5527.
2) *Commentary on The Distinction between the Middle and Extremes.*
3) *Commentary on The Distinction between Phenomena and Their Nature.*
4) *The Principles of Exegesis* (Skt. Vyākhyāyukti, Tib. rnam bshad rigs pa) P5562.
5) *The Discourse on Establishing Karma* (Skt. Karmasiddhiprakaraṇa, Tib. las sgrub pa'i rab byed) P5563.
6) *The Discourse on the Five Aggregates* (Skt. Pañcaskandhaprakaraṇa, Tib. phung po lnga'i rab byed) P5560.
7) *The Twenty Verses.*
8) *The Thirty Verses.*

From among Vasubandhu's other works, one may add his *Instruction on the Three Natures* and his *Commentary on The Synopsis of the Great Vehicle* to this list.

1079 Literally, the Tibetan says *sems tsam* ("Mere Mentalism"). However, here, I translate this term as *Yogācāra*, because that is what it means in this context and also in order to avoid the usual confusion associated with the term "Mere Mentalism" or Mind Only.

1080 Mi bskyod rdo rje 1996, p. 40.

1081 Mipham Rinpoche says that all five dharma works of Maitreya had already been translated during the early translation period in Tibet. Thus, obviously, there were already some teachings available on them.

1082 Tib. gzu dga' ba'i rdo rje.

1083 Tib. btsan kha bo che.

1084 According to Kongtrul Lodrö Taye's introduction to his *Commentary on The Sublime Continuum*, Zu Gaway Dorje composed a now lost commentary on this text (fol. 9b). Some of the teachings of Dsen Kawoche are recorded in a text called *Gzhan stong gi lta khrid* by Jonangpa Kunga Drölchog (Tib. kun dga' grol mchog, 1507–1566), who was one of the successors of Dölpopa. His presentations of the three natures follow the explanations given by Yogācāra masters such as Asaṅga very closely (for details, see Stearns 1999, pp. 88ff.).

1085 Particularly his interpretation of *The Sublime Continuum* was later adopted in most points by the Gelugpa school.

1086 Tib. lcang ra ba.

1087 Tib. dar ma brtson 'grus.

1088 Tib. phyogs mdo sde sbug.

1089 Tib. yu mo ba mi bskyod rdo rje. In terms of the view, he is considered the founder of the Jonang school (Tib. jo nang). His main works are the recently rediscovered *Four Cycles of the Luminous Lamp* (Tib. bstan bcos gsal sgron skor bzhi). They deal with the correct practice of the six-branch yoga of the *Kālacakra Tantra* and treat some of the topics on which Dölpopa later elaborated, without, however, using his specific terminologies, such as "other-empty." Tāranātha says that "he is the founder of the philosophical system of mantric other-empty [Centrism]." (*The Collected Works of Jo-nang rje-btsun Tāranātha*, vol. II, p. 16. Leh, Ladakh: Smanrtsis Shesrig Dpemdzod, 1983.).

1090 *The Blue Annals* mentions the existence of an anonymous Tibetan commentary on *The Sublime Continuum* that includes pith instructions on practice related to this text, as well as several short treatises, such as the *Repository of Wisdom* (Tib. ye shes kyi bzhag sa), that contain pith instructions of the school of Dsen ('Gos lo tsā ba gzhon nu gzhon nu dpal 1996, p. 348). The great Kashmiri Paṇḍita Śākyaśrībhadra (1140s–1225) is also reported to have given pith instructions on the *Five Dharma Works of Maitreya* on Mount Sinpori near Gyantse (Ibid., p. 349).

1091 As Stearns (1999, pp. 50ff.) informs us, the term "other-empty" seems to have occurred in a few texts predating Dölpopa. However, the latter definitely was the first one to use it in an extensive way as the cornerstone in his presentation of the dharma.

1092 In his *Triyānavyavasthāna* (P4535, fol. 114a), the late Indian Centrist Ratnākaraśānti (11th century) was the first to make the distinction between Real Aspectarians and False Aspectarians with regard to Centrists. (This distinction is better known in the Yogācāra system.)

1093 Tib. zab gsal dbu ma.

1094 He also refers to the first three texts of Maitreya as "the Centrism of Yoga Practice" (Tib. rnal 'byor spyod pa'i dbu ma) and to the last two as "the Centrism of Complete Certainty about the Ultimate" (Tib. don dam rnam nges kyi dbu ma).

1095 Tib. tā ra nā tha kun dga' snying po. Together with Dölpopa, he was the best-known proponent of the Jonang school.

1096 Tib. ka thog rig 'dzin tshe dbang nor bu.

1097 Tib. 'jam dbyangs mkhyen brtse dbang po, the famous Sakya master who was one of the founders of the Rime movement in eastern Tibet.

1098 There are people, both inside and outside the Nyingma tradition, who claim him as a proponent of Shentong, while others see him as favoring the Consequentialist approach of the great Longchen Rabjampa (Tib. klong chen rab 'byams pa, 1308-13). Mipham's own *Dam chos dogs sel* ('Ju mi pham rgya mtsho 1992, p. 521), a reply to criticism on his commentary on the *Ornament of Centrism*, says:

> I do also not have the burden of [having to] establish Shentong,
> [Since] both Rong[zom] and Long[chenpa] accord with the texts of Nāgārjuna
> And also someone inferior like me is one-pointedly inclined towards them.

He continues by saying that he wrote his reply only due to being forced by the words of others who regard the Shentong like an enemy. A similar approach of trying to eliminate misconceptions of what is actually intended by the Shentong view can be found in his *gZhan stong khas len seng ge nga ro* (translated in Pettit 1999). For more details on Mipham's view, see Pettit and Kapstein 2000.

1099 For more details, see Hookham 1991 and Stearns 1995, 1999.

1100 Tib. gsal ba gzhan stong.

1101 Tib. dbyings gzhan stong.

1102 These teachings are largely based on his commentary on *The Sublime Continuum* and his presentation of other-emptiness in *The Treasury of Knowledge*. Apart from these, he also wrote a number of independent shorter texts on the subject.

1103 Further sources are the Seventh Karmapa Chötra Gyamtso's *Ocean of Texts on Reasoning* (vol. I), Pawo Rinpoche's commentary on *The Entrance to the Bodhisattva's Way of Life*, and *The Treasury of Knowledge*.

1104 1981, p. 200.

1105 Lit. "imagination of what is unreal." This term is not to be confused with the "imaginary nature." In fact, it is an equivalent of the other-dependent nature in its impure aspect, i.e., when it imagines the imaginary nature. Put simply, the imaginary nature refers to all the objects that are imagined by false imagination as their subject.

1106 I.1–2. In terms of the content, there is an interesting parallel between lines 1cd ("Emptiness exists within false imagination and false imagination also exists within emptiness") and the famous phrases in *The Heart Sūtra*: "Form is emptiness; emptiness also is form." In lines 1a–c and again in line 2d, the dialectic process of insight proceeds from acknowledging the seeming existence of false imagination via the realization of the nonexistence of the duality of apprehender and apprehended, to an altogether different sense of existence of emptiness in that emptiness is not some entity but the actual mode of being of all phenomena. This pattern finds its parallel in the Prajñāpāramitā sūtras. For example, The *Diamond Cutter Sūtra* says: "Subhūti, as for the arrangements of Buddha-fields, called 'the arrangements of Buddha-fields,' the Thus-Gone One said that these arrangements do not exist. Therefore, they are called 'the arrangements of Buddha-fields.'" (ACIP KD0016@221B).

1107 In general, when Maitreya and Asaṅga refer to "nature," this does not mean that they did not understand the teachings on emptiness and the lack of nature. Rather, they are explicit in saying that all notions of nature are nothing but mental constructs, i.e., the imaginary "nature." Similar to the Centrists, they use the term "nature" but do not attach any claim of real or ultimate existence to it.

1108 ACIP KD0106@22A.

1109 Ibid., @35B.

1110 Again, this is not to be understood in any reifying sense (see also the presentation of the sixteen emptinesses in Chapter 2).

1111 nirvikārapariniṣpanna, Tib. 'gyur med yongs grub.

1112 aviparyāsapariniṣpanna, Tib. phyin ci ma log pa'i yongs grub.

1113 Skt. śrutavāsanā, Tib. thos pa'i bag chags. These are the latent tendencies resulting from having listened to the dharma and thus listening to it again. Primarily, the Buddhist teachings are seen as the natural outflow of the expanse of dharmas. Indirectly, the latent tendencies that are accumulated in the minds of those who listen to or study these teachings are also called the natural outflow of the expanse of dharmas.

1114 Skt. niṣyanda, Tib. rgyu mthun pa.

1115 Skt. vimuktikāya, Tib. rnam par grol ba'i sku. As for this distinction between the Dharma Body and the Body of Complete Release, the latter designates the removal of merely the afflictive obscurations, as it is attained by the arhats of the hearers and solitary realizers too. The Dharma Body refers to the removal of the cognitive obscurations. (Without relating these two bodies to the distinction between bodhisattvas and arhats, *The Supreme Continuum* describes both of them as aspects of Buddha enlightenment. In discussing the Dharma Body as the actual state of Buddhahood in general, it is understood that both types of obscurations have been relinquished in it. In this sense, it includes the Body of Complete Release.)

1116 Skt. haṃsa, Tib. ngang pa. Often, this term is translated as "swan,"as this obviously seems to fit better with our sense of poetry. However, there lived no swans in India in ancient times, and the Sanskrit clearly refers to a species of white wild goose common in India. (Such a goose is also considered to be the riding animal of the god Brahmā.) These geese are said to be able to filter milk from a mixture of milk and water, leaving just the water behind.

1117 I.45, 46, 48, 49 (P5549, fols. 11b.2–12a.6).

1118 These are the five physical sense faculties and the mental sense faculty, which includes all types of consciousness.

1119 Skt. ṣaḍāyatanaviśeṣa, Tib. skye mched drug gi khyad par.

1120 For the relationship between the three natures, see also the very illuminating comparison with the example of a holographic image in Kaplan 1990. Such an image appears as something external to and distinct from the perceiver, but there is no such image independent of someone's experience of it as a three-dimensional object over there. The image does not exist on the film, and there is also no conglomeration of light waves that makes up this image. How it appears is only imagined. Still, there is an experience of this image. Once the light that triggers this image is turned off, the image disappears. What is left on the subjective level is the experience of seeing that there is no such image.

1121 III.10bc–11ab.

1122 Verse 23.

1123 ACIP KD0106@27A–B.

1124 XIV.34.

1125 The claim that the other-dependent nature is ultimately existing obviously was known in India, as is shown by the first chapter of Sthiramati's *Subcommentary on The Distinction Between the Middle and Extremes.* Sthiramati presents four alternative models of interpreting verse I.1, without, however, providing their sources. The first model says that false imagination (as an equivalent of the other-dependent nature) exists ultimately by its nature (P5534, fol. 24b.6–8). This is not, however, Sthiramati's own position.

1126 Besides the *Daśabhūmikasūtra* and the *Laṅkāvatārasūtra*, in which this famous sentence appears rather isolated and somewhat out of context, its earliest source is the *Bhadrapālasūtra* (P760, fol. 15b.1). In the latter, this statement appears as the culmination of a long section that explains that appearances within meditative equipoise as well as all that appears as external objects are nothing but appearances in the mind. Following this sentence, the text also gives a reason for it: "[All of] this appears in just the ways in which oneself individually imagines/conceives it."

As for the system of "Mere Mentalism," Tibetan doxographies elaborate on many more details and subschools, such as Real Aspectarians and False Aspectarians (see, for example, Kong sprul blo gros mtha' yas 1982, vol. II, pp. 497–510). However, the above points are the main issues that are relevant here in terms of Centrist critique.

1127 ACIP TD4038-1@77A-B.

1128 P5528, ACIP TD4027@03A (commentary on verses I.6–7).

1129 P5534, fols. 35b–36b.

1130 VII.8.

1131 Chapter X.256–258 (ACIP KL0107@270A), as quoted in Kamalaśīla's *Stages of Meditation* (ACIP TD3915@33A). For his detailed explanation of this quote, see the section in chapter 2 entitled "The Progressive Stages of Meditation on Emptiness."

1132 Lines 264–275. The same is also expressed in lines 182–185, which treat "the four applications."

1133 Verses 35cd–36.

1134 Sometimes, Yogācāras differentiate between *cittamātra* and *cittamātratā, vijñaptimātra* and *vijñaptimātratā,* and so on, the latter indicating the actual nature of the former, i.e., the perfect nature.

1135 Verses 28–30.

1136 P5534, fol. 35a.2–3.

1137 VI.96. The argument that there is no apprehender without something apprehended is also used in VI.71cd and by Nāgārjuna (for example, *Bodhicittavivaraṇa,* verse 39 and *Lokātītastava,* verse 10).

1138 Chapter X (verses 359–360, 362–363), ACIP KL0107@275B–276A.

1139 This is the same as what Nāgārjuna's *Commentary on the Mind of Enlightenment* says (see the section on Madhyamaka meditation in Chapter 2).

1140 These two terms refer to dualistic mind (the six or eight consciousnesses) and mental events (such as feelings and discrimination).

1141 Quoted and translated in Lusthaus 2002, p. 465 (Taisho 1585.6c; Ch.2:4B).

1142 Verse 34.

1143 Verses 22–23 and 25. As an aside, in the light of such explicit statements, Tsongkhapa's claim that Nāgārjuna and the Consequentialists *assert* the existence of outer objects is all the more unbelievable (especially since he fails to provide proper scriptural support for his claim). Further evidence to the contary includes *Fundamental Verses* V.7:

Thus, space is neither an entity nor a nonentity,
Neither what is to be characterized
Nor a defining characteristic.
The other five elements are analogous to space.

1144 ACIP TD3915@30A. Similar statements are found in Śāntarakṣita's texts.

1145 P5481, fols. 3a.8–3b.2.

1146 VII.1

1147 ACIP KD0106@20B–21A.

1148 Ibid., @21B.

1149 P5481, fol. 8a.7–8.

1150 The same is said in Vasubandhu's *Thirty Verses* 18.

1151 I.61, fol. 13b.7–8.

1152 Verse 5a.

1153 Skt. acittikābhūmi, Tib. sems med pa'i sa.

1154 ACIP TD4035@160B–161A.

1155 P5539, fols. 9a.4-10a.4.

1156 I.48.

1157 Lines 223–227. These five aspects are also described in Vasubandhu's commentary on this text (P5529, fols. 41a.3–41b.4), *The Synopsis of the Great Vehicle,* VIII.2 (P5549, fols. 39b.5–8), its commentary by Asvabhāva (P5552, fol. 322b.4–8), *The Compendium of Abhidharma* (P 5550, fol. 138a.4–6), and *The Synopsis of Ascertainment* (P5539, fols. 29a.5–29b.5).

1158 X.25.

1159 IX.26, ACIP KD0106@74A.

1160 Fol. 334a.7–8.

1161 Taisho 1595 (see Griffiths 1989, p. 37).

1162 For example, I.143, II.3, 38–39.

1163 IX.15, XIV.19.

1164 II.26, fols. 21a.5–21b.4.

1165 II.27, fols. 21b.5–22a.4.

1166 III. 8–9, fols. 28a.5–29a.7.

1167 II. 132 (verse 198), ACIP KL0107@276B.

1168 Fol. 180b.6–7.

1169 Fol. 180a.6–7/fol. 282b.1–2.

1170 Fol. 180b.4–6.

1171 ACIP KD0012@02A–B.

1172 X.81.

1173 The term *āśrayaparivṛtti* (Tib. gnas yongs su gyur pa) is usually translated as "transformation." In general, there are a great number of scriptures (from the Pāli canon up through the tantras) in which this term is used with reference to quite different things or processes (see Davidson 1985). In some of them, the word "transformation" might be appropriate, but the whole point in terms of the expanse of dharmas, natural purity, or the luminous nature of the mind is that there is no transformation of something into something else. Rather, the revelation of mind's wisdom nature as fruitional enlightenment is just a change of its state as seen by a deluded mind, but does not refer to any change in its entity, just like the sun first being covered by clouds and then being free from clouds. However, as an expedient meaning, this process of uncovering mind's fundamental nature may often be described as if there were a transformation of something impure, such as mental afflictions, into something pure, such as wisdom.

1174 Fol. 180a.7–8.

1175 II.29, fols. 22a.7–22b.6.

1176 II.17, fol. 18b.5–8.

1177 II.28, fol. 22a.6–7.

1178 The very same approach is also adopted in Nāgārjuna's *Praise to the Expanse of Dharmas.*

1179 I.154-155.

1180 The last two sentences are a quote form the *Cūlasuññatasutta* (*Majjhimanikāya* 121), one of the few sūtras from the Pāli canon that were also included in the Tibetan *Kangyur.* There it is called *Śūnyatānāmamahāsūtra* (Tib. mdo chen po stong pa nyid ces bya ba, P956, fol. 275a.2-3), which is not to be confused with the *Mahāsuññatasutta* (*Majjhimanikāya* 122, P957).

1181 P5526, fols. 118a.4-118b.6. Just as an aside, like many other passages in Asaṅga's commentary, the above should make it more than evident why the usual Gelugpa doctrine of Buddha nature being nothing but emptiness as a non-implicative negation (and Asaṅga being a Consequentialist in the Gelugpa sense) can only be forced upon this text by far-fetched and long-winded reinterpretations.

1182 I.156–157.

1183 In *Dbu ma gzhan stong skor bstan bcos phyogs bsdus deb dang po* 1990, pp. 45–46.

1184 What follows is explained in Rang byung rdo rje, n.d., pp. 25ff.

1185 This is also called "the emptiness endowed with the supreme of all aspects." Jamgön Kontrul Lodrö Taye's *Commentary on The Profound Inner Reality* (Kong sprul blo gros mtha' yas 1970) says: "Here, the Omniscient [Seventh Karmapa] Chötra Gyamtso states that "emptiness endowed with the supreme of all aspects" and "the Heart of the Blissfully Gone Ones" are equivalent. That the Heart of the Blissfully Gone Ones actually possesses the sixty-four superior qualities of freedom and maturation means to be endowed with the supreme of all aspects. That these [qualities] do not exist as something identifiable or as [real] characteristics is the meaning of emptiness. Therefore, he taught that the practice of this—to cultivate luminosity without conceptions—is Mahāmudrā meditation." (fol. 110a).

The thirty-two qualities of freedom are the ten powers, the four fearlessnesses, and the eighteen unique qualities of the Dharma Body. The thirty-two qualities of maturation are the thirty-two major characteristics of the Form Bodies.

1186 Mi bskyod rdo rje, n.d., vol. I, pp. 248, 250–251.

1187 II.69 (ACIP KL0107@130A).

1188 Tāranātha 1980, pp. 98-101.

1189 Kong sprul blo gros mtha' yas 1982, vol. I, pp. 401-403.

1190 Tib. rnal 'byor spyod pa sems tsam pa. S.C. Das's *Tibetan-English Historical Buddhist Glossary* (Sri Satguru Publications, Delhi, 1990, p. 137) also refers to Avitarka as a Yogācāra master.

1191 Kong sprul blo gros mtha' yas 1982, vol. II, pp. 508-509.

1192 In the Chinese transmission of Yogācāra, Dharmapāla's interpretation continued mainly through Hsüan-tsang, while Asaṅga's tradition was transmitted there through Paramārtha. (The latter even speaks about two kinds of vijñaptimātratā. The first refers to the second step in a progressive sequence of realization, i.e., that—without outer objects—there is only the apprehending mind as the subject. The next step is then to realize that this apprehender equally does not exist and thus gives way to the luminous non-dual expanse of dharmas.) Besides

Paramārtha, further Indian masters involved in transmitting this lineage to China and translating its texts include Buddhasānta, Bodhiruci, Dharmagupta, and Prabhākaramitra.

1193 ACIP TD3853@234B–249A. This controversy is also dealt with in Avalokitavrata's subcommentary on Bhāvaviveka's text (ACIP TD3859-1@048Aff).

In fact, as indicated above by Tillemans (1990), despite this claim by Dharmapāla, the latter's overall position is rather complex and subtle. For example, in his commentary on *The Four Hundred Verses,* he says that the other-dependent nature *does* really exist (in the sense of not being totally nonexistent like the horns of a rabbit), but that it is not itself the ultimate. Furthermore, he is found there to say such things as, "One should be convinced of the voidness of all dharmas"; "The principle of voidness is free from all characters of dharmas, such as existence, [nonexistence,] etc." (Tillemans 1990, p. 93); and "So, thus all dharmas are likened to illusions: in them not the slightest substance whatsoever can be found. . . . Thus, dharmas are produced by causes and conditions; their natures are all void, like an illusion." (Ibid., p. 171) Indeed, many passages of his commentary might as well have been written by a Centrist. Like Centrists in general, he emphasizes the framework of the two realities. For him too, existence and nonexistence pertain to seeming reality, while ultimate reality lies beyond these as well as all other kinds of duality. Like Bhāvaviveka, he was also concerned with validating seeming reality.

Bhāvaviveka's position with regard to Yogācāra also is not as clear-cut as it might seem at first. For example, in this very chapter of *The Lamp of Knowledge,* he accepts the other-dependent nature to be included in conventional reality (ACIP TD3853@243A). In his *Jewel Lamp,* he even elaborates on "mere mind" as "the subtle, inner yoga" in the progressive stages of meditation in Centrism (ACIP TD3854@280A). In his *Blaze of Reasoning* (on *Heart of Centrism* V.78cd), he explains that outer objects are produced by karma which is generated by consciousness (ACIP TD3856@220B).

In fact, often the controversy between these two masters—as well as between other Centrists and Yogācāras—represented more certain differences in terms of contexts of meaning than in terms of content per se. In addition, accounting for scholarly rivalries among the major Buddhist universities at the time, one often finds a distinct flavor of misrepresentation and polemics in such controversies. As Eckel (1985) says: "Nagao has pointed out how difficult it is to interpret the Yogācāra position in a way that does full justice to the complexity of these existence-terms. . . . But Bhāvaviveka was free to do something that a modern interpreter might find indefensible: he could take the words at face value and treat the Yogācāra formulas as an affirmation of both an 'absence' and a 'presence.' . . . In its own terms, the system gives a consistent answer . . . . But when Bhāvaviveka takes the Yogācāra concepts and projects them onto a Madhyamaka system with Madhyamaka presuppositions, they give rise to certain obvious anomalies." (pp. 36, 39).

1194 Like Sthiramati's text, Dharmapāla's work is available only in Chinese translation, called *T'a-ch'eng Kuang Pai-lun Shih* (Taisho 1571).

1195 The first seven verses of this fifth chapter present the position of Bhāvaviveka's opponents, with the fourth one corresponding to verse I.6 from *The Distinction between the Middle and Extremes.*

1196 These arguments are a summary of those found in Dignāga's *Ālambanaparīkṣā.* The same issues are also briefly addressed in Bhāvaviveka's *Karatalaratna* (Taisho 1578).

1197 ACIP TD3856@199A.

1198 For more details, see Lindtner 1986a and Keenan 1997.

1199 1980, p. 187. The debate between Candragomī and Candrakīrti is explained just below.

1200 In this context, Candrakīrti also quotes lines I.9cd from *The Distinction between the Middle and Extremes* (ACIP TD3860@022A), but *in support* of his refutation of an opponent.

1201 Skt. śakti, Tib. nus pa.

1202 See Schmithausen 1967, p. 126.

1203 ACIP TD3862@347B.

1204 For example, see Tāranātha 1980, pp. 204–06.

1205 Lines Ib–d.

1206 ACIP TD3883@016B–017A.

1207 As found in his commentary on Dharmakīrti's *Pramāṇavārttika* I.4.

1208 ACIP TD3883@039B.

1209 For example, a detailed refutation is found in Kamalaśīla's *Madhyamakāloka* (P5287, fols. 180b.6–181a.3, 182b.3–8, 200b.2–6). Similar refutations are found in his *Madhyamakālaṃkārapañjika*, *Sarvadharmaniḥsvabhāvasiddi*, and *Bhāvanakrama* I, as well as in Jñānagarbha's *Satyadvayavibhāgavṛtti*, Śāntarakṣita's *Madhyamakālaṃkāravṛtti*, and Haribhadra's *Abhisamayālaṃkārāloka.* (For further details, see Moriyama 1984 and Ichigo 1989.) Just as an aside, the fact that Śāntarakṣita refutes both the Real Aspectarian and the False Aspectarian approaches makes the claims of some scholars that he is a Real Aspectarian Centrist obsolete. He says that all minds—including the wisdom of a Buddha—entail some aspect or image that is not real. This, however, does not make him a False Aspectarian either, since they usually claim that Buddha wisdom is without aspects.

1210 For details and sources, see Moriyama 1991.

1211 Besides the Yogācāras mentioned above, there are a number of other commentators on the texts of Maitreya, Asaṅga, and Vasubandhu and/or authors of independent texts, such as Guṇaprabha, Jinaputra, Jñānaśrī, Kambala, Sāgaramegha, Sumatiśīla, and Vinītadeva. Their texts remain to be studied, so it is not clear at this point whether some of them were included among Centrist opponents. Thus, the above listing of opponents in Centrist texts is not meant as an exhaustive presentation but more as an outline of general trends.

1212 This text was most probably written some decades before Bhāvaviveka's Yogācāra critique. It is interesting to note that Atīśa's *Centrist Pith Instructions* includes Kambala's Centrist works side by side with those of Nāgārjuna, Āryadeva, Mātṛceṭa, and Candrakīrti under the model texts for all Centrists (P5325, fol. 126b.1–2).

1213 Tāranātha also remarks that before Bhāvaviveka the followers of the great vehicle shared the same dharma, whereas thereafter they "were split into two groups and started having controversies." (1980, p. 187)

1214 See also the earlier remarks on the very subtle differences in the dispute between Dharmapāla and Bhāvaviveka.

1215 1997, p. 21.

1216 1991, p. 68.

1217 Quoted in Kong sprul blo gros mtha' yas 1982, vol. II, p. 555.

1218 II.123 (ACIP KL0107@116A).

1219 ACIP TD3882@013A.

1220 Verses 25, 27.

1221 P3099, fols. 180a.3–6, 181b.2–7.

1222 V.28ab.

1223 Chapter XXV (ACIP TD3853@245B).

1224 ACIP TD3856@207Bff.

1225 ACIP TD3862@276B–277A.

1226 ACIP KL0107@136A. It should be noted, however, that this very sūtra also provides a wide range of other meanings of "mere mind" that can hardly be interpreted in this way, such as:

> Having relinquished examination and what is to be examined
> With regard to putting an end to all views,
> Nothing to be observed, and nonarising:
> These I explain as mere mind.
> Neither the lack of entities nor nonentity,
> Relinquishment of entities and nonentities,
> Likewise, being released from mind:
> These I also explain as mere mind.
> Suchness, the empty end,
> Nirvāṇa, the expanse of dharmas,
> And the variety of mental bodies:
> These I also explain as mere mind (Ibid., @185A–B).

1227 VI.96.

1228 ACIP TD3862@282A–B.

1229 ACIP TD3882@012B. As an aside, this is one of the most striking passages that renders the classification of Jñānagarbha as a Sautrāntika-Mādhyamika more than doubtful.

1230 Ibid., @013A.

1231 Verse 92.

1232 P5287, fols. 170b.8–171a.1. Compare also his detailed explanations on this topic in *The Stages of Meditation* (see the section in Chapter 2 entitled "The Progressive Stages of Meditation on Emptiness").

1233 1932–35, p. 594.18–25.

1234 This text is considered as reflecting the system of *Yogācārā-Svātantrika-Madhyamaka.

1235 This one-sided prioritization of Consequentialism (in a moreover very uncommon form) with a simultaneous deprecation of so-called Mind Only is associated with an almost total neglect, if not denial, of the Yogācāra system of Maitreya and Asaṅga. More recently, an increasing number of modern Western scholars agree that such presentations are merely based on the scriptures of Tsongkhapa and his followers, with little if any basis in the original texts. See, for example, Hookham 1991, Kapstein 2000, Sparham 1993, 2001, and Stearns 1995, 1999.

1236 The approach of the Kagyü curriculum differs to some extent, since the Seventh Karmapa's *Ocean of Texts on Reasoning* treats Dignāga and Dharmakīrti as Yogācāras and elaborates on this system. The curriculum also includes *The Sublime Continuum* as a bridge between the views of sūtra and tantra; it is studied as the first text of the Vajrayāna curriculum.

1237 See below for Dölpopas's own qualifications of such statements.

1238 1999, pp. 23, 48.

1239 In the writings of Longchenpa, the term "other-empty" is mentioned just once without connecting it to how Dölpopa used it (see Stearns 1999, p. 51). As mentioned above, Mipham Rinpoche's position is far from being clearly "other-empty," and he himself said that he was a Consequentialist.

1240 This is especially obvious from Rendawa's writings. For example, in his commentary on *The Entrance into Centrism*, contrary to Tsongkhapa, he clearly says that Centrists do not have any thesis whatsoever. Even the "positions" of negating arising from the four extremes are pronounced merely from the perspective of others with wrong ideas. They are not the Centrists' own system, because for them there is nothing to be negated and thus no negation (Red mda' ba gzhon nu blo gros 1993, pp. 104–05). Throughout, Rendawa uses the term "the center free from extremes" (Tib. mtha' bral dbu ma) as an expression for the correct Centrist view, which is vehemently rejected by the Gelugpa school. (In general, Rendawa's commentary accords significantly with the Eighth Karmapa's *Chariot of the Tagbo Siddhas.*) Further differences between Rendawa and Tsongkhapa are listed by the authoritative Sakya doxographer Ngawang Chötra (Tib. ngag dbang chos grags, 1572–1641) in his *Grub mtha'i shan 'byed* (fols. 106b–110a; quoted in Ruegg 2000, pp. 63–64).

Quite tellingly, despite it being widely known that Rendawa was Tsongkhapa's first and long-time teacher of Centrism, the latter does not list Rendawa at all (!) in his own records on the lineages for his studies (Tib. gsan yig) of Nāgārjuna's texts including Candrakīrti's *Lucid Words.* Ironically, Tsongkhapa *does* list Majaba Jangchub Dsöndrü and Majaba Jangchub Yeshe, who were both (falsely) accused of wrong views on Centrism by later Gelugpas.

For some features of Sakya Paṇḍita's understanding of Madhyamaka, such as Centrists having no thesis or tenet of their own, see Jackson 1985 and Ruegg 2000, pp. 169–71.

1241 Tib. legs bshad rgya mtsho.

1242 Line 19a.

1243 Verses 44–45.

1244 Verses 88 and 101.

1245 Verse 22.

1246 XXV.10; see also XVIII.10.

1247 II.30, fols. 23a.6–23b.1. The last two verses are also found almost identically in *The Ornament of Sūtras* (XII.50–51).

1248 This is not only the view of the Tibetan Kagyü and Nyingma schools but also agreed upon by several modern scholars, such as the leading Western authority on Yogācāra, Prof. L. Schmithausen. In two of his articles (1971, 1973), he shows in precise detail that, from the point of view of the Indian texts on Buddha nature, the interpretation of Buddha nature as presented in the Gelugpa school is untenable. Further similar references include Hookham 1991, Mathes 1996, 2002, Stearns 1999, and Zimmermann 2002.

1249 See H. H. Dalai Lama 1997, pp. 230–31.

1250 Tib. chos nyid gzhan stong.

1251 Tib. chos can gzhan stong.

1252 ACIP KL0107@034B.

1253 Verse 53.

1254 ACIP KL0107@208B–209A.

1255 I.155.

1256 ACIP KL0107@186B.

1257 2000, pp. 80–81.

1258 Tib. ri chos nges don rgya mtsho.

1259 Mi bskyod rdo rje, n.d., vol. I, p. 348.

1260 2000, p. 122.

1261 In Dreyfus and McClintock 2003, p. 71.

1262 Skt. ṛṣi, Tib. drang srong. Originally a name for Hindu sages, it is used here for the Buddha.

1263 V.18–19.

1264 Kong sprul blo gros mtha' yas 1982, vol. II, pp. 555–56.

1265 XV.10.

1266 Skt. vikalpavikṣepa, Tib. rnam g.yeng gi rtog pa (II. 21, fol. 19b.6–7).

1267 I.2ab.

1268 For example, Asaṅga's *Compendium of Abhidharma* says: "The meaning of dependent origination: It means that there is no creator, it means causality, it means that there is no sentient being, it means other-dependence, . . ." (P5550, fol. 77b.6).
Nāgārjuna agrees in his *Praise to the Inconceivable*:

> The seeming is other-dependent
> And originating from causes and conditions.
> It has been called "the other-dependent" [by you].
> The ultimate, however, is not artificial.
> It [may] also [be called] "nature, primordial nature, true reality,
> Substance, entity, and what is real."
> Neither does an imaginary entity exist,
> Nor is there something other-dependent. (44–45)

Jñānagarbha's *Distinction between the Two Realities* says:

> Mere dependently originating entities
> Devoid of anything imagined
> Should be understood as the correct seeming.
> The imaginary is the false [seeming]. (8)

Kamalaśīla's *Illumination of Centrism* states:

> The other-dependent nature refers to those entities that are common consensus when not examined, accord with the way they appear, and dependently originate, just like illusions. (P5287, fol. 162b.6–7).

His commentary on *The Ornament of Centrism* (ACIP TD3886@107A) also equates the other-dependent nature with dependent origination, as does Śāntarakṣita's commentary on *The Distinction between the Two Realities* (ACIP TD3883@046A). The Eighth Karmapa says the same (see Chapter 5). Most modern Western scholars, such as Nagao 1991, Harris 1991, King 1994, and Keenan 1997, agree.

One could also say that the imaginary and other-dependent natures correspond to the two aspects of dependent origination, or what is called "nominal establishment in mutual dependence" (Tib. ltos grub) and actual dependent origination itself, i.e., seeming appearances that depend on causes and condition. The imaginary nature is just nominally established as mere names and superimpositions—such as existent and nonexistent, good and bad, large and small—which all exist only nominally and in mutual dependence, not on their own. The perfect nature is nothing other than identitylessness or emptiness.

1269 VII.2d, 5ab.

1270 I.4a/d.

1271 XVI.10, XVIII.4–5.

1272 ACIP TD4027@023B-025B.

1273 Kāśyapaparivartasūtra §§ 52–71.

1274 ACIP TD4027@024A–025A.

1275 Ibid., @02B.

1276 P5481, fols. 3a.8–3b.2.

1277 VII.1.

1278 I.9ab.

1279 II.69.

1280 XVIII.9.

1281 Verses 20–22. "Basic element" (Skt. dhātu, Tib. khams) is a synonym for Buddha nature. Especially in the writings of Nāgārjuna, it should be more than clear that this does not refer to the only absolutely existing nature that is left as something identifiable after everything else has been refuted.

1282 XI.43.

1283 See Chapter 1.

1284 Chos grags rgya mtsho 1985, vol. I, pp. 196–97.

1285 Isn't that what we all somehow want: not to have to exert ourselves but to have the guru do all the work for us—get up, go to the grocery store, buy the candy bar (of course, with her or his own money), bring it back to us, unwrap it, put it in our mouths, and even move our jaws up and down?

1286 I.e., the tantras.

1287 Quoted in Kong sprul blo gros mtha' yas 1982, vol. II, p. 553.

1288 Skt.: nāpaneyam ataḥ kimcit prakṣeptayaṃ na kiṃcana
draṣṭavyaṃ bhūtato bhūtaṃ bhūtadarṣī vimucyate.

1289 Sgam po pa 1990, p. 289.

1290 Gaganagañjaparipṛcchāsūtra, Tib. nam mkha'i mdzod kyis zhus pa'i mdo.

1291 Pratītyasamutpādahṛdayakārikā, Tib. rten cing 'brel bar 'byung ba'i snying po'i tshig le'ur byas pa (P5467).

1292 Skt. Kāyatrayastotranāmasyavivaraṇa, Tib. sku gsum la bstod pa zhes bya ba'i rnam 'grel (P2016, fol. 83a.7). Dragonetti (1979) identifies four more sources: Aśvaghoṣa's *Saundarananda* (XIII.44) and *Śuklavidarśana* (a summary of the *Śālistambasūtra* that begins with this verse), Sthiramati's *Madhyāntavibhāgaṭīkā* (P5534, fol. 36a.5), and the *Nāmasaṃgītiṭīkā* ad VI.5 (which attributes it to Nāgārjuna).

1293 Dpa' bo gtsug lag phreng ba, n.d., p. 874.

1294 This is not a classification in terms of their sequence in time, but rather a thematic classification of what is taught in the sūtras. In other words, it is not that the Buddha first taught only and all sūtras on the four realities of noble ones for the hearers and solitary realizers, then only and all Prajñāpāramitā sūtras on emptiness, and finally only and all the sūtras of the third turning. Rather, to different disciples at different times, he taught what he deemed appropriate for them. It is through their main topics that these discourses can be classified as the three wheels of dharma.

The term "wheel" is used here, since, in some of its features, the teachings of the Buddha correspond to a wheel. For example, it is compared to the mighty wheel of a Cakravartin king in that it can overcome adverse factors and obstacles. Through the teachings, one leaves certain paths behind and travels on others with the vehicles taught by the Buddha. As on wheels, traveling on these paths is swift. Another similarity to a wheel is that the teachings possess the spokes of the eightfold path of the noble ones.

1295 ACIP KD0106@38A–B. The traditions of the Pāli canon do not accept the latter two wheels as the teachings of the Buddha. They say that the Buddha only taught the wheel of dharma of the four realities of noble ones, repeating it three times in terms of the nature, function, and completion of the four realities, thus presenting them in twelve aspects.

In the Prajñāpāramitā sūtras, after having referred to this very format, their own teachings on emptiness are identified as the second wheel of dharma: "Then, many thousand sons of the gods residing in the sky above . . . showered down flowers of divine substances . . . and spoke the following words: 'Oh, through the teachings of this perfection of knowledge, many thousand sons of the gods have attained endurance with regard to the dharma of nonarising. We see the turning of the second wheel of dharma in Jambudvīpa.'" (Naturally, the Buddha answers that, precisely because of emptiness, there are no two wheels of dharma and such. See *Prajñāpāramitā Sūtras in Eight Thousand Lines* and *Twenty-five Thousand Lines*: ACIP KD0012@113B and KL0009-2@289B.)

1296 Skt. Dhāraṇīśvararājaparipṛcchāsūtra, Tib. gzungs kyi dbang phyug rgyal pos zhus pa'i mdo (P814, pp. 300.5.4ff.). This passage is also quoted in Asaṅga's *Exposition of The Sublime Continuum* (P5526, fols. 77a.5-77b.6) and Nāgārjuna's *Compendium of Sūtras* (ACIP TD 3934@189B–190A).

1297 II.57–59.

1298 VIII.15.

1299 Dpa' bo gtsug lag phreng ba, n.d., pp. 888–89.

1300 Quoted in *The Treasury of Knowledge*, Kong sprul blo gros mtha' yas 1982, vol. III, p. 24.

1301 XXV.24cd.

1302 In Chapter 7, "The Questions of Paramārthasamudgata" (ACIP KD0106@038A–039A).

1303 Quoted in *The Treasury of Knowledge*, Kong sprul blo gros mtha' yas 1982, vol. III, pp. 19–20.

1304 Skt. Akṣayamatinirdeśasūtra, Tib. blo gros mi zad pas bstan pa'i mdo.

1305 Skt. manuja, Tib. shed las skyes.

1306 Skt. mānava, Tib. shed bu. These latter two terms are names for sentient beings in general and human beings in particular. They stem from the Vedic myths about the creation of the world, in which it is said that Manu was the first human, out of whom the universe arose.

1307 P842, fols. 155b.5–156a.7.

1308 Most of the following statements by the Eighth Karmapa are from his section on distinguishing the expedient and the definitive meaning (Mi bskyod rdo rje 1996, pp. 435–44).

1309 As quoted in ACIP TD3862@282B.

1310 Verses 56–57.

1311 ACIP TD3859-1@07B.

1312 ACIP TD3860@13A-14A.

1313 VI.97.

1314 ACIP TD3862@282B.

1315 ACIP TD3870-1@211A-216B.

1316 This refers to the introductory verses of Nāgārjuna's *Fundamental Verses.*

1317 Vol. III, pp. 20-21.

1318 P5539 (for example, Ḥi fol. 17b.8ff. and 60a.2ff.). This text quotes *The Sūtra That Unravels the Intention* almost in its entirety. Also, as mentioned earlier, Asaṅga's *Exposition of The Sublime Continuum* (P5526, fols. 77a.5-77b.6) extensively quotes the passage from *The Sūtra Requested by King Dhāraṇīśvara* that compares the three turnings of the wheel of dharma to the progressive cleansing of a precious stone.

1319 However, Vasubandhu also wrote a commentary on *The Sūtra of the Teaching of Akṣayamati* (P5495), following the distinction made in this sūtra.

1320 Here, *The Treasury of Knowledge* even says that Vasubandhu's *Principles of Exegesis* (Skt. Vyākhyāyukti, Tib. rnam bshad rigs pa, P5562) and its commentary (P5570, by Guṇamati) specifically state that the second turning is of definitive meaning. I could not find any such statement in either of these texts. Rather, the fourth and only chapter in Vasubandhu's text that deals with this issue says that statements in the Prajñāpāramitā sūtras such as, "All phenomena are without nature" are "the guiding meaning" (Tib. bkri ba'i don) within the great vehicle and do not explain the definitive meaning (fol. 116b.6). Vasubandhu repeatedly states that such statements are not to be taken literally (Tib. sgra ji bzhin ma yin pa), but are made with certain intentions (Tib. dgongs pa can; see fols. 116b.8, 118a.2, 122a.7) in order to dispel certain wrong views. He quotes the great vehicle's *Sūtra of the Arising of Great Confidence* (Tib. theg pa chen po la dad pa skye ba'i mdo; the *Kangyur* contains a Theg pa chen po la dad pa rab tu sgom pa'i mdo, P812), which gives a detailed presentation of twenty-eight wrong views that arise from erroneously taking statements with certain intentions literally. These twenty-eight are said to be worse than the sixty-two wrong ideas based on the views about a real personality (119a.7-122a.7) that are well-known in the sūtras of the hearers, such as the *Brahmajālasūtra.* Then, Vasubandhu's text explicitly identifies the threefold lack of nature

(Tib. ngo bo nyid med pa gsum) as presented in *The Sūtra That Unravels the Intention* as the great vehicle's definitive meaning of the above statement in the Prajñāpāramitā sūtras (123b.1-124a.6). He accordingly differentiates how existence is to be understood on the seeming and the ultimate level (127b.6ff.). Guṇamati's commentary follows all of this and also relates the term "non-arising" to the three natures (fol. 150b.3-7). The suchness of all phenomena is said to be the identitylessness of persons and phenomena, which lies beyond mind's imaginative activity (156a.7-156b.3).

It is to be well noted here that all of the above is said to defend the great vehicle against charges by the hearers and so on that it is not the word of the Buddha and is mere nihilism. It is obviously not designed as a debate among followers of the great vehicle.

1321 Kong sprul blo gros mtha' yas 1982, vol. III, pp. 20–21.

1322 For further examples, see Chapter 1.

1323 VI.72.

1324 Chapter 4 (The Questions of Subhūti), ACIP KD0106@18A.

1325 Ibid., @27A.

1326 ACIP TD3887@135A.

1327 Verse 28.

1328 XIV.34.

1329 Verse 23.

1330 P5481, fols. 8b.7–9a.3.

1331 Ibid., fol. 11a.6 (the passage in the sūtra is ACIP KD0106@053A–053B).

1332 This refers to the four fearlessnesses, which are part of the thirty-two major marks of a Buddha.

1333 II.14.

1334 1973, pp. 336–38.

1335 Skt. Tathāgatakośasūtra, Tib. de bzhin gshegs pa'i mdzod kyi mdo (quoted in *Blaze of Reasoning*, ACIP TD3856@163B–164A).

1336 II.3, III.94–97.

1337 XVIII.6.

1338 VIII.20.

1339 ACIP KD0106@037A–038A.

1340 Quoted in the autocommentary on *The Entrance into Centrism* (ACIP TD3862@282B).

1341 Verses 98–99.

1342 V.20.

1343 Fol. 175b. Here, it is interesting to note that the early Tibetan Consequentialist Majaba Jangchub Dsöndrü in his commentary on *The Fundamental Verses* (Tib. 'thad pa'i rgyan) states that the scriptures that explain the intention of the final turning as Madhyamaka are such texts as Maitreya's *Sublime Continuum* and Candrakīrti's *Entrance into Centrism* (Rma bya ba byang chub brtson 'grus 1975, fols. 4b–5a).

1344 Quoted in Kong sprul blo gros mtha' yas, n.d., fol. 151a.

1345 Dpa' bo gtsug lag phreng ba 1986, p. 1254.

1346 In this paragraph and the following, the Karmapa evidently plays with the terms for the three natures (imaginary, other-dependent, and perfect).

1347 XV.2cd.

1348 VI.72–78.

1349 ACIP KD0106@026B.

1350 As was explained in Chapter 2 in the section on the two realities, to be actually undeceiving is the definition of ultimate reality.

1351 This is the phrase from Candrakīrti's autocommentary (ACIP TD3862@283A) on which Jayānanda comments.

1352 ACIP TD3870-1@216B.

1353 Verse 34 (see also 35).

1354 Verse 69 (see also 97).

1355 Verse 23.

1356 Verse 25.

1357 Skt. kalpanāmātra, Tib. rtog pa tsam. This is frequently used as one of the equivalents of "mere mind" (Skt. cittamātra, Tib. sems tsam) in the Yogācāra school.

1358 Verse 36.

1359 Verse 44.

1360 Verse 3.

1361 The same is very clearly expressed in Asaṅga's *Synopsis of the Great Vehicle* (X.32, fols. 49a.8–49b.1).

1362 Verse 21.

1363 XI.45.

1364 Ibid., XI.46–47.

1365 I.93.

1366 Dreyfus and McClintock 2003, p. 307.

1367 For example, the Eighth Karmapa usually refers to "the great Tsongkhapa" and even wrote a praise of him. The Fourth Karmapa Rölpay Dorje, who gave lay ordination to Tsongkhapa as a boy, said about him: "This is a holy child who will be of great benefit to people. Therefore, he is like a second Buddha come to Tibet." Later, Tsongkhapa wrote in a letter to the Fifth Karmapa Teshin Shegba: "You are like a second Buddha. I would like to see you but I am in a three year retreat. So I am sending you a statue of Maitreya which belonged to Atīśa." (Karma Thinley 1980, pp. 66, 75).

1368 Bdud 'joms 'jigs bral ye shes rdo rje 1991, vol. I, pp. 929–30.

1369 In this context, it is quite interesting to see that Tsongkhapa's Madhyamaka system as found in his so-called "mature texts" (i.e., after his visionary exchanges with Mañjuśrī) exhibits clear signs of development and even radical shifts. On the other hand, later Gelugpa orthodoxy persistently tries to explain away any traces of development or shift in Tsongkhapa's "mature period." Besides Tsongkhapa's non-Gelugpa critics, more recently, even someone like Thupten Jinpa (1998, 2000), who has been thoroughly trained in the traditional Gelugpa educational system, pointed to definite signs of change in Tsongkhapa's views.

1370 See his commentaries on *The Entrance into Centrism* and *The Ornament of Clear Realization* and elsewhere. Specifically, he includes mistaken Kagyü followers of Mahāmudrā and the Nyingmapas in his critique (see also Kong sprul blo gros mtha' yas 1982, vol. III, p. 25).

1371 See Dpa' bo gtsug lag phreng ba 1986, pp. 1324–26.

1372 This is one of Sakya Paṇḍita's most famous texts.

1373 Bdud 'joms 'jigs bral ye shes rdo rje 1991, vol. I, pp. 931, 933.

1374 In addition, to be innovative or creative is one thing, but to work out elaborate theories on the basis of the slimmest or nonexistent scriptural evidence and to proclaim these theories as the only correct interpretation of Nāgārjuna and Candrakīrti is quite another (especially when such theories are often found to contradict a more straightforward reading of what these masters actually said). It seems that the claims in this particular interpretation of Centrism are sometimes uncritically taken over by certain modern authors as being Centrism per se, without considering the fact that it is just one version among others.

1375 Mi bskyod rdo rje 1996, pp. 119–21.

1376 ACIP KL0107@180B–181A.

1377 Tib. zhig pa dngos po yin pa; often abridged as zhig pa('i) dngos po/zhig dngos.

1378 Tsong kha pa blo bzang grags pa 1973, p. 226.

1379 Tib. dka' gnad brgyad kyi rjes byang/zin bris.

1380 The latter point refers to the claim that the wisdom of a Buddha possesses dualistic appearances with regard to seeming reality while *simultaneously* not possessing dualistic appearances with regard to emptiness.

Later Gelugpa commentators enumerate even more unique points (for example, Jamyang Shayba's *Great Exposition of Tenets* lists sixteen).

1381 Tsong kha pa blo bzang grags pa 1975–79, pp. 442–89.

1382 Tib. 'gal ba'i khur chen bco brgyad. These are found in detail in his *Grub mtha kun shes* (Stag tshang lo tsā ba 1976, fols. 213-241) as well as in the First Paṇ chen Lama's reply *sGra pa Shes rab rin chen pa'i rtsod lan* (for a list of all eighteen points, see Cabezón 1992, pp. 391-92).

Moreover, in his *Rig gnas kun shes* (A khu shes rab rgya mtsho's list, no. 13092, recently edited by K. Mimaki), Dagtsang Lotsāwa criticizes Tsongkhapa for mistakenly including the teachings on valid cognition (one of the four common, traditional branches of knowledge) in the Buddhist teachings proper (the uncommon field of knowledge).

1383 Go rams pa bsod nams seng ge 1968–69, fol. 40a.4.

1384 Śākya mchog ldan 1975, p. 559.

1385 For details, see especially Dreyfus and McClintock 2003, Śākya mchog ldan 2000, Pettit 1999 (especially pp. 128–30), Tauscher 1995, Williams 1998b, and Yoshimizu 1993.

1386 See Chapter 3.

1387 VI.38.

1388 For further objections to "establishment through conventional valid cognition," see the section in Chapter 2 entitled "A Critical Analysis of Some Other Tibetan Views on the Two Realities in Centrism."

1389 ACIP TD3860@164B.

1390 IX.139ab.

1391 P6143, fol. 71b.1–4.

1392 One can recognize the traits of Tsongkhapa's variant interpretation of this verse already in his own commentary on the ninth chapter of Śāntideva's text (*Shes rab le'u'i ṭikā blo gsal ba*) and in Gyaltsab Je's commentary too. It is, however, the above quote from *The Elucidation of the Intention* that makes the most explicit connection to his unique understanding of the object of negation.

1393 One of the standard Gelugpa definitions of ultimate reality is "what is found from the perspective of the final reasoning consciousness." Also, as said above by Tsongkhapa, conventionally established phenomena are not invalidated through a reasoning consciousness.

1394 Tib. lcang skya rol pa'i rdo rje.

1395 Tib. bstan dar lha ram pa.

1396 Tib. lta mgur a ma ngos 'dzin, lines 35–42. "The Mother" stands for Prajñāpāramitā.

1397 Ch. LIII, fol. 279.

1398 ACIP TD3862@315A.

1399 VI.141.

1400 ACIP KL0107@034B.

1401 For more details, see the end of the section in Chapter 3 entitled "The Actual Distinction between Autonomists and Consequentialists."

1402 Except for 5) (svalakṣaṇasiddha) and 6) (svabhāvasiddha), none of these six terms is attested in Sanskrit.

1403 It was shown in Chapter 3 that this claim is unfounded.

1404 Tib. rang kya ba.

1405 This chart is based on Hopkins 1983, p. 299 (terminology adapted).

1406 These considerations apply not only to the special object of negation of Consequentialists as opposed to Autonomists but also to "real existence" as the general Centrist object of negation as identified by Tsongkhapa.

1407 For further details, see the section in Chapter 2 entitled "What Is the Object of Negation in Centrist Reasonings?"

1408 *Fundamental Verses* XV.10.

1409 Verses 10, 13b–d, 14 (Bhāvaviveka's statement is *Heart of Centrism* III.285).

1410 IX.2cd.

1411 VI.23.

1412 Tib. bcad shes.

1413 IX.32, 34.

1414 In Buddhist epistemology, these are the only two types of connection admitted. They apply only to entities that perform a function, not to nonentities that do not perform a function.

1415 1975–79, fol. 409b. (The same is explained in *Essence of Good Explanations*, 1975–79, pp. 700ff.) As explained before, the former term refers to eliminating certain features of something, whereas the latter stands for affirming something that remains after the exclusion of certain features of this something, such as eliminating the wrong notion that sound is permanent and consequently ascertaining that it is impermanent.

1416 Since nonimplicative negations are nonentities, they are by definition permanent.

1417 *Fundamental Verses* XXII.12ab.

1418 Skt. prāpti, Tib. thob pa. This is held by certain Followers of the Great Exposition to be the "factor of continuity" for karmic actions.

1419 XXV.13d.

1420 ACIP TD3860@059B.

1421 Ibid., @178B.

1422 The usual Buddhist understanding of notions such as arising, being present, and ceasing is that they do not refer to the abstract ideas of "arising," "presence," or "cessation" but to *something*—a functional entity—that arises, is present, and ceases. The same goes for "disintegrating." This means that something that is in the process of disintegrating is a momentarily impermanent but still existent entity. However, after this something *has* disintegrated, it is simply gone and not an existent entity anymore. Conventionally, it may be said that what is "left" is the absence of the entity that has disintegrated, but there is no question that this absence of an entity is not an entity itself. Rather, any absence that we may refer to is by definition just an object of a conceptual consciousness, not an object of direct perception. For example, when we smash a vase, the vase has disintegrated as a vase. We cannot see or perceive the absence of this vase per se; it is only something that we can think of when comparing the state of an existent vase before with there being no vase now (in fact, without having perceived an existent vase before, such as when simply looking into the empty sky, we do not even think of the absence of a vase, let alone perceive such an absence). All that we can directly perceive after a vase has been smashed are the shards of the vase, which in themselves, however, are neither a vase nor the absence of a vase. In the philosophical systems of the lower vehicle, the notions of arising and so on may also refer to the observable *process* of arising and such, also being understood as a functional entity. As a technical term, this is called a "nonassociated formation" (Skt. viprayuktasaṃskāra, Tib. ldan min 'du byed). Centrists, however, do not accept the notion of nonassociated formations, nor do they use the term.

Connected to this is the status of the three times—past, present, and future—or rather entities in the three times. The Karmapa explains that, conventionally, only phenomena in the present can be said to exist, while the past and future do not exist. In other words, if something exists, it has to be right now, otherwise it is either no longer existent or not yet existent. In contrast, Tsongkhapa holds that all three times exist.

1423 Many of the twelve links do not refer to a strict, linear causality but are rather meant as mere conditionality in a very literal sense, as the Buddha himself put it: "Without this happening, that does not occur." Thus, without dying there could be no next life, but the continuity of assuming a rebirth is fundamentally based on and caused by ignorance. So one cannot say that dying itself "causes" one's next life.

1424 ACIP TD3860@188A.

1425 XVII.6, 21.

1426 ACIP TD3842@236B.

1427 ACIP TD3862@279A.

1428 Ibid., @260A.

1429 VII.29, 33.

1430 *Rebuttal of Objections*, verse 70.

1431 *Fundamental Verses* XXIV.20.

1432 Reprint in *rJe'i gsung lta ba'i skor* (Dharamsala: 1975, vol. I, p. 83).

1433 All Tibetan schools, including the Gelugpas, regard Chaba Chökyi Senge as an Autonomist Centrist.

1434 For details, see his essay in Dreyfus and McClintock 2003, especially pp. 235–37.

1435 In no way do I mean to insinuate that Tsongkhapa and his followers did not strive for such liberation.

1436 1989, p. 143.

1437 1981, p. 158.

1438 Newland remarks: "In such situations, the individual's sense of identity hinges upon magnifying and preserving very subtle differences. Thus, . . . disputes on Mādhyamika between scholars . . . often turn on differences so thin that one hesitates to call them 'philosophical.' Nevertheless, debating and analyzing such differences plays an enormous role in the textbooks and the lives of those who use them." (1992, p. 24)

1439 Tib. zhen pa bzhi bral.

1440 *Majjhima Nikāya* 63, I. 429 (quotation abbreviated).

1441 *Studies in the Laṅkāvatāra Sūtra* (London: 1930), pp. 162—63.

1442 *Aṅguttara Nikāya* III.65.

1443 This account is based on Tāranātha 1980 as well as Dpa' bo gtsug lag phreng ba 1986 and n.d.

1444 Skt. Sūtrasamucchaya, Tib. mdo kun las btus pa (text now lost).

1445 Maybe he recited the homage once again, since it was added to the text later.

1446 Tib. nyams len byin rlabs kyi brgyud pa.

1447 Tib. lta spyod zung 'jug gi brgyud pa.

1448 I am well aware that, in a general sense, "intellect" can also mean one's basic power or faculty of knowing, which would fit the meaning of *buddhi* quite nicely. However, these days, the word "intellect" usually connotes mere conceptual engagement in abstract ideas that are far removed from "real life" and one's experience, and in this sense, it has a pejorative flavor for many people. Hence, I think that using the word "intellect" rather distorts the issue at hand. Also, in terms of the verse's content, it is rather trivial that ultimate reality as it is cannot be grasped by mere intellect in this sense. So it would be surprising if this were all that Śāntideva had in mind here.

1449 IX.3ab.

1450 Dpa' bo gtsug lag phreng ba, n.d., p. 645; see also the corresponding quote from Prajñākaramati's commentary in the translation part.

1451 Skt. Ghandavyūhasūtra, Tib. rgyan stug po bkod pa'i mdo.

1452 Verse 14.

1453 IX.23.

1454 Skt. Dvayasatyāvatārasūtra, Tib. bden pa gnyis la 'jug pa'i mdo.

1455 ACIP TD@193B.

1456 The equivalence of "cognition" and "consciousness" as well as the definition of "knowable object" is, for example, stated in texts such as *The Classifications of Mind* (Tib. blo rig) and *The Collected Topics* (Tib. bsdus grva).

1457 These are texts such as those mentioned in the previous note.

1458 ACIP KD0106@04B–05A.

1459 IX.25.

1460 The Chinese Buddhist canon does not contain any commentaries on Śāntideva's text.

1461 This text is not a distinct commentary, but just the eighth chapter of P5274. In the Tohoku catalogue (T3877), it is called *A Commentary on the Difficult Points of the Knowledge Chapter and on the Dedication* (Skt. Bodhisattvacaryāvatāraprajñāparicchedapariṇamapañjikā, Tib. byang chub sems dpa'i spyod pa la 'jug pa'i shes rab le'u dang bsngo ba'i dka' 'grel).

1462 This is not the earlier Yogācāra teacher by the same name (530–561), but the later master from Suvarṇadvīpa (Sumatra) who is also often referred to as Dharmakīrti from Suvarṇadvīpa. He was one of the teachers of Atiśa and wrote P5280 and P5281 at the latter's request.

1463 The Padmakara Translation Group (Śāntideva 1997) lists two more texts as Indian commentaries on the *Bodhicaryāvatāra*:

Dhārmikasubhūtighoṣa. *Bodhisattvacaryā[saṃgraha]pradīparatnamālā* (Byang chub sems dpa'i spyod pa bsdus pa'i sgron ma rin po che'i phreng ba). T3936.

Dīpaṃkaraśrījñāna (Atiśa). *Bodhisattvacaryāvatārasūtrīkṛitāvāda* (Byang chub sems dpa'i spyod pa la 'jug pa'i mdo tsam gdams ngag tu byas pa). P5348.

However, these two texts are not commentaries on Śāntideva's text but short outlines of bodhisattva conduct in general.

Hopkins (1983) lists Atiśa's *Bodhisattvacaryāvatārabhāṣya* (Byang chub sems dpa'i sypod pa la 'jug pa'i bshad pa) P5872. This text too is not an actual commentary on the *Bodhicaryāvatāra* but just links the names of its ten chapters to the stages of the path of bodhisattvas as these are outlined in the Prajñāpāramitā literature.

1464 For short descriptions of these Indian commentaries, see Williams (1998a) and Dietz (1999).

1465 Reportedly, there were earlier Tibetan commentaries that are now lost, for example, by Ngog Lotsāwa, his disciple Shang Tsebongwa Chökyi Lama (Tib. zhang tshe spong ba chos kyi bla ma), and Chaba Chökyi Senge.

1466 Tib. dngul chu thogs med.

1467 Tib. 'ju mi pham rgya mtsho.

1468 Tib. kun bzang dpal ldan.

1469 Tib. rdza dpal sprul o rgyan 'jigs med chos kyi dbang po.

1470 The text regularly and extensively quotes P5273, P5275, P5278, and P5282. It also refers to P5274, P5280, and P5281.

1471 Tib. sa bzang ma ti pan chen 'jam dbyangs blo gros. He was a disciple of Dölpopa Sherab Gyaltsen and one of the teachers of Rendawa.

1472 Tib. mtsho sna pa chen po shes rab bzang po.

1473 Dpa' bo gtsug lag phreng ba, n.d., p. 831.

1474 Ibid., p. 874.

1475 This is commentary P5282 (ACIP TD3880@256A). In general, many passages from other commentaries that are quoted in this text are not verbatim but more or less paraphrased versions of the originals that are available now. It may also be that Pawo Rinpoche used different editions from the present ones. Often, however, the variants in this text are just scribal errors, misspellings, or omissions. Therefore, I do not always indicate these in the notes, but my translation follows the available originals.

1476 This is commentary P5275 (ACIP TD3874@65B).

1477 This refers to Prajñākaramati's commentary (P5273, ACIP TD3872@185B).

1478 This is commentary P5278 (ACIP TD3876@159A). In Pawo Rinpoche's commentary, it is just called *shes rab le'u kho na'i dka' 'grel chung ngu.*

1479 I.e., a circular argument.

1480 Numbers in brackets refer to the page numbers of the Tibetan text.

1481 Skt. nirvedhabhāgiyamārga, Tib. nges 'byed cha mthun gyi lam. This is another name for the path of junction.

1482 Generally, wherever there are variants in the Tibetan editions of Śāntideva's text or when the Tibetan differs from the Sanskrit, I have followed the Sanskrit (La Vallée Poussin 1902–14) without specifying the different readings in each case, as these can be found in Wallace and Wallace 1997. Among Tibetan commentators, it seems that only Bu ston, Pawo Rinpoche, and Mipham Rinpoche explicitly address such differences.

1483 This is an epithet for the Prajñāpāramitā sūtras.

1484 I could not locate this quote in *The Precious Garland* by Nāgārjuna. However, there is a nearly identical verse in Āryadeva's *Four Hundred Stanzas* (VIII.5).

1485 An utpala is a type of blue lotus flower.

1486 IX.23.

1487 Verse 19 (quoted in ACIP TD3872@197A).

1488 Verse 33.

1489 It is to be remembered that both Śāntideva's text and its commentaries were originally addressed to purely male monastic audiences. In general, of course, statements such as the above about the bodies of women equally pertain to males too.

1490 Skt. sadbhāva, Tib. dngos yod.

1491 This refers to the creation of magical displays through certain incantations and rituals, which was quite common in ancient India.

1492 From page 656 in the Tibetan original onward, all the root verses under each heading are presented as one set and followed by a section that gives an outline of the topics discussed in the individual verses. After that, the commentary on the whole set is given. In the translation, I have continued to follow the format that was used up to this point, in which the individual root verses are immediately followed by their respective outlines and commentaries.

1493 In other words, the Mere Mentalists say themselves that external objects and—even more so—illusions do not really exist. Therefore, one can equally fling their objection ("Once there is no subject, what would observe the object?") back at them: "Once there is no object, what would be observed?"

1494 This is one of the two subschools of the Mere Mentalists, the other being the False Aspectarians.

1495 As quoted in Candrakīrti's *Lucid Words* (ACIP TD3860@021A).

1496 X.335 (gātha 568). The same appears in prose right after the above sentence in *The Sūtra Requested by Crown Jewel.*

1497 VII. 9.

1498 Ibid., VII.12.

1499 I.e., a circular argument in the sense that both counterparts would mutually depend on each other. Thus, none of them can be established inherently by itself alone.

1500 There is no commentary for verse 22. The corresponding passage of Künzang Pelden's commentary says:

> Is that which knows that consciousness is illuminated by itself this consciousness itself, or is it a consciousness other than this one? The first case is not justified: This does not apply here, since it is the given object of analysis. If it needed to be known through a consciousness other than this [illuminating] consciousness itself, then there would be an infinite regress of that which knows it, and it could not possibly be known. If these [two consciousnesses] were not simultaneous, then objects of the past that have ceased or future ones that have not yet arisen could not be known. Since there is no mutual dependence in something simultaneous in the present, it could not possibly be known then either. Therefore, **once** other-dependent consciousness **is** not seen either by itself or by something other than itself, and **not seen by anything** else either, an analysis of [its] distinctive features, such as "**illuminating**" **and** "**not illuminating**," is meaningless. A presentation of distinctive attributes with respect to a basis of attribution that was never seen is **like** saying, "**The looks** and the physical condition **of a barren woman's daughter** are such and such." **Even if described, they are meaningless.** (Kun bzang dpal ldan 1994, pp. 641–62)

1501 In his commentary on *The Entrance into Centrism,* Karmapa Mikyö Dorje says the following on this issue of self-awareness and recollection:

> Self-awareness is not even conventionally established through recollection. For, if there were certainty about a causal connection between self-awareness and recollection as there is between fire and smoke, [self-awareness] would be established [through recollection] in this way. However, such a causal connection is not established [for them]. If self-awareness is not only not established as the cause for recollection but not even [established] in itself, recollection as the [assumed] result for which this [unestablished self-awareness] functions as a cause is not established either. Thus, conventionally, though

there is no self-awareness, mere recollection occurs, since it arises as such from the conditions from which recollection arises, . . . just as water [in a river] comes from rain and fire from rubbing [two] sticks. (Mi bskyod rdo rje 1996, p. 400).

1502 In different commentaries, the example of the rat's poison is explained in various ways (for the most common version, see Vibhūticandra's commentary in the section below entitled "The Synopsis of Other Commentaries" as well as Pelden and Sönam 1993, p. 159).

1503 ACIP TD3874@071A.

1504 This seems to have been a rather commonly used technique in ancient India to heighten one's visual capacity. Here, Minyak Künzang Sönam points out that the example of the eye lotion not only does not prove self-awareness but it actually invalidates the existence of self-awareness: Since the eye lotion is an example of something that is very close but not seen, it exactly illustrates that one's own mind does not see itself, and not the opposite (Pelden and Sönam 1993, p. 159).

1505 Most other commentaries say that line 25a indicates three cognitions: "How something is known" refers to conceptual consciousness as opposed to perception ("seen") and information from others ("heard").

1506 Here this term is used as a synonym for False Aspectarians.

1507 These are P5280 (ACIP TD3878@192B) and P5281 (ACIP TD3879@191A).

1508 ACIP TD3872@190B–191A.

1509 Ibid., @191A.

1510 Verse 23.

1511 III.282. This quote is also found in a number of other texts, such as Āryadeva's *Compendium of the Essence of Wisdom* (verse 28; ACIP TD3851@27B). Pawo Rinpoche's text quotes only the first line.

1512 ACIP TD3872@191B.

1513 XXIV.8c.

1514 ACIP TD3872@192A–192B.

1515 Ibid., @192B.

1516 This text has "dharma" (chos) instead of "meaning" (don).

1517 ACIP TD3872@193A–193B.

1518 The quote in this text ends at "mind."

1519 ACIP TD3872@193B–194A.

1520 This version of the rat example corresponds to the detailed explanation in Pelden and Sönam 1993 (p. 159).

1521 Verse 45.

1522 ACIP TD3872@207B.

1523 ACIP TD3880@258A.

1524 Ibid., @258B.

1525 Ibid., @260A.

1526 Ibid., @262B.

1527 Ibid., @263A.

1528 Ibid., @263B.

1529 Ibid., @264A.

1530 Tib. dka' 'grel chung ngu. In the *Tengyur*, there are five pañjikās (Tib. dka' 'grel) on the *Bodhicaryāvatāra*:

Prajñākaramati's *Bodhicaryāvatārapañjikā* (P5273, 281 fols.)
an anonymous *Bodhisattvacaryāvatāravivṛttipañjikā* (P5274, 72 fols.)
Vairocanarakṣita's *Bodhisattvacaryāvatārapañjikā* (P5277, 75 fols.)
an anonymous *Bodhisattvacaryāvatāraprajñāparicchedapañjikā* (P5278, 25 fols.)
Vibhūticandra's *Bodhisattvacaryāvatāratātparyapañjikāviśeṣadyotanī* (P5282, 115 fols.).

Pawo Rinpoche's text calls P5273 *The Great Commentary*; P5282 is always referred to as "Vibhūti"; and P5278 is explicitly called *The Small Commentary on the Knowledge Chapter Only*. Moreover, all the quotes from these texts can be clearly located. This leaves P5274 and P5277 as the possible sources for quotes from what Pawo Rinpoche calls *The Small Commentary on the Difficult Points*. The first short quote from this text (p. 127 in Pawo Rinpoche's commentary) accords pretty much with a corresponding passage in P5274. However, none of the other quotes can be found in either of these two commentaries, nor in any of the remaining ones in the *Tengyur*. Unanimously, all further available sources, such as Butön's *History of Buddhism* (Lokesh Chandra ed., vol 24, p. 949) and his commentary on the *Bodhicaryāvatāra*, as well as all Western authors list only the ten commentaries as found in the Bibliography.

None of the Tibetan or Western scholars whom I consulted could resolve this issue either. There is some possibility that Pawo Rinpoche still had access to one of the numerous lost Indian commentaries. (It seems to be ruled out that he was just quoting from a very different edition or translation of P5274 and P5277, since most of the passages quoted in his text are much longer than and quite different in content from what these two commentaries say on the corresponding verses.) There is also an anonymous, fragmentary commentary in Sanskrit that was found in the Durbar Library in Kathmandu, Nepal, by Cecil Bendall. L. de La Vallée Poussin used this as yet unpublished and unanalyzed manuscript for his edition of Prajñākaramati's *Bodhicaryāvatārapañjikā*, referring to it as *Bodhicaryāvatāraṭippānī*. In any case, style and context of the passages from the *Small Commentary* in question suggest a translated Indian commentary, thus ruling out the possibility that Pawo Rinpoche refers to the now lost commentary by Ngog Lotsāwa (A khu shes rab rgya mtsho's list, no. 11077).

1531 The former are the Enumerators. Akṣapāda (Tib. rkang mig pa, lit. "Eye-Feet") is better known under the name Gautama and was the founder of the Nyāya school (he wrote the *Nyāyasūtra*). He was a follower of the god Śiva (Tib. dbang phyug) and received his name in the following way: Śiva appointed him as attendant for his consort, the goddess Uma, who became very attracted to this handsome man and displayed all kinds of seductive physical expressions in front of him. Since she was the consort of his god, he considered it completely inappropriate to respond to her flirtations. Thus, he kept directing his gaze to his feet and meditated in that way. This pleased Śiva so much that he gave him the name Eye-Feet.

1532 ACIP TD3876@163B.

1533 Tib. legs bshad sdud pa. This is a commentary on *The Entrance to the Bodhisattva's Way of Life* by the fourteenth-century Kadampa master Tsonaba Chenbo Sherab Sangbo (Tib. mtsho sna pa chen po shes rab bzang po).

1534 Verses 46, 51.

1535 In other words, it is not necessarily the case that everything whose nature is not established is not an object of meditation.

1536 Verse 23.

1537 The large general section on Buddhahood in this commentary (pp. 677–792) is not translated here.

1538 Sanskrit has not only a singular and a plural but also a "dual," which specifically indicates two in number.

1539 Skt. niḥśreyasa, Tib. nges legs. This is another term for liberation from cyclic existence.

1540 Prajñākaramati's commentary refers here to a wooden pillar consecrated with mantras.

1541 Skt. Puṣpakūṭadhāraṇi, Tib. me tog brtsegs pa'i gzungs.

1542 Skt. Bodhisattvapiṭakānāmasūtra, Tib. byang chub sems dpa'i sde snod ces bya ba'i mdo. This is a part of the vast sūtra collection known as *The Jewel Mound Sūtra* (Skt. Ratnakūtasūtra, Tib. dkon mchog brtsegs pa'i mdo).

1543 Tib. 'dul ba lung sman gyi gzhi. This is one of the four texts of the Hīnayāna's Vinaya that were taught by Buddha Śākyamuni.

1544 Lines 391cd.

1545 V.20.

1546 ACIP TD3874@072A–073A.

1547 ACIP TD3880@264B–265B.

1548 IV.83.

1549 ACIP TD3876@165B.

1550 Sabsang is the native area of the Tibetan Centrist master Sabsang Mati Panchen Jamyang Lodrö. For his commentary, see Sa bzang ma ti pan chen 'jam dbyangs blo gros 1975.

1551 I could not locate these notes in Atiśa's texts.

1552 The four aspects of the reality of suffering are: impermanence, suffering, emptiness, and identitylessness.
The four aspects of the reality of the origin of suffering are: cause, origin, intense arising, and condition.
The four aspects of the reality of cessation are: cessation, peace, excellence, and definite emergence.
The four aspects of the reality of the path are: path, adequacy, accomplishment, and definite deliverance.

1553 This is an epithet for the Prajñāpāramitā sūtras.

1554 Skt. Samatāpravṛttisūtra, Tib. mnyam pa nyid la 'jug pa'i mdo.

1555 These are cultivated during the four applications of mindfulness (for details, see section 3.2.1. The General Topic below).

1556 Sūtra, Abhidharma, and Vinaya.

1557 This refers to the actual qualities of realization and relinquishment in the mind streams of true practitioners on the path.

1558 Skt. Mahāmeghasūtra, Tib. sprin chen po'i mdo.

1559 This refers to the Centrist view that in Tibet was called "the center free from extremes" (Tib. mtha' bral dbu ma), another name for the view of "the earlier Centrists." As mentioned in the introduction on the lineages of Centrism, this view was proclaimed by Patsab Lotsāwa Nyima Tra and his four main disciples (specifically Shang Tangsagba); the Sakya masters Rendawa, Gorampa Sönam Senge, and Dagtsang Lotsāwa; the Eighth Karmapa; Pawo Rinpoche, and others. This view uses Madhyamaka analysis that results in an unqualified negation of all four positions of the typical Centrist tetralemma without asserting anything instead in order to completely overcome all conceptualizations. In this way, it is certainly an accurate characterization of the Indian Prāsaṅgika Madhyamaka approach.

This is also what is understood by "the view of neither existence nor nonexistence" when this expression is used by its advocates as solely pertaining to ultimate reality, i.e., that "the center" in the sense of ultimate reality is "neither the existence of a nature nor the nonexistence of a nature." Starting with Tsongkhapa (1357–1419), the tradition of "the later Centrists"—the Gelugpa school—criticized this view by saying that "nonexistence of a nature" is the correct Centrist view and thus not to be negated (for details, see Chapter 6). In addition, in order to discredit the above understanding of Centrism, its critics linked "the view of neither existence nor nonexistence" with the notorious stereotype of Hvashang Mahāyāna, through which this understanding, in their eyes, assumed a pejorative meaning.

Mipham Rinpoche's *Lamp of Certainty* says that this term is also used as a pejorative for the system of the Great Perfection. See Pettit 1999, p. 297.

1560 An expression for the practice of the Great Seal, as exemplified in the Ninth Karmapa's *Ocean of Definitive Meaning* (Tib. nges don rgya mtsho). The Eighth Karmapa calls the Madhyamaka lineage of Maitrīpa "the center without mental engagement" (see the Introduction).

1561 This also refers to the teachings of the Great Seal, as it says in the Kagyü tradition's *Short Prayer to Vajradhara*: "The essence of thoughts is dharmakāya."

1562 This expression can be found in the teachings of the Great Seal, the Great Perfection, the tantras, and even many sūtras, such as the Prajñāpāramitā sūtras.

1563 I.e., they mistakenly considered themselves to be the brilliant suns among scholars who dispel the darkness of others' wrong views.

1564 The Tibetan is not clear here: It could either be *rdo rta* (stone horse) or *rngo rta* (mangy horse). From the context, it is certain that the sense of the word is pejorative. The Dzogchen Ponlop Rinpoche said that this is some local jargon of the area where Pawo Rinpoche came from.

1565 There are disputes as to the proper order of verses 42–51 and whether verses 49–51 are the authentic words of Śāntideva or were inserted later by others. The translation follows the order of the root verses as they are presented in this commentary (with verses 49–51 inserted between lines 42b and 42c according to the context of establishing the great vehicle). See also below after the commentary to verse 51.

1566 The Tibetan here is *gal ste ma brtags gcig gis ni* (Skt. ekenāgamyamānena sakalaṃ yadi doṣavat). Most other Tibetan editions read *gal ste ma gtogs gcig gis ni* (If by a single one that is not included . . .). Also *gal ste ma rtogs gcig gis ni* (If by a single one that is not realized . . .) can be found.

1567 In the first sentence (the objection), all three modes of a correct reason are not established. However, the second proof sentence neither attempts to attack the first mode nor tries to give the "right" answer (with a correct second mode). Rather, in good Consequentialist style, it is an absurd consequence that only shows that the opponents' way of formulating the reason can equally be used to prove exactly the opposite, i.e., what they are trying to negate.

The basic problem with this objection of the hearers is that they pick just one of their own criteria for belonging to the sūtras of the hearers (which for them are equivalent to Buddha's speech) and claim that the lack of this single criterion invalidates all the sūtras of the great vehicle as Buddha's speech. (To claim the lack of this criterion in the scriptures of the great vehicle—teaching impermanence—is wrong in itself, since in fact these scriptures also teach impermanence. However, this is not the point that is attacked here.) What is pointed out here is: If the lack of just a single criterion were enough to exclude all sūtras of the great vehicle from what constitutes the Buddha's speech, then it absurdly follows that finding a single criterion of the hearers' sūtras in the sūtras of the great vehicle is also enough to include the latter in what is Buddha's speech.

1568 In Pawo Rinpoche's text, there appears a fifth line of this verse (*de ni theg dman la yang mtshungs*: "this would apply in the same way to the inferior vehicle too"). This line is neither found in any of the other editions of Śāntideva's text nor the commentaries available to me. See also in the following synopsis of other commentaries the discussion as to whether the whole verse is part of Śāntideva's original work.

1569 Skt. abhiprāya, Tib. dgongs pa.

1570 Skt. abhisaṃdhi, Tib. ldem dgongs.

1571 Mahākāśyapa was one of the foremost disciples of the Buddha. He inherited the leadership of the saṅgha after the Buddha had passed into nirvāṇa. Śāriputra was praised by the Buddha as foremost among the wise (with respect to the teachings of the hearers).

1572 See *The Sūtra of the Prophecy of the Young Lady Excellent Moon* (Skt. Candrottarādārikāvyākaraṇasūtra, Tib. bu mo zla mchog lung bstan pa'i mdo).

1573 Skt. Bahuśrutīya, Tib. mang thos pa. This is one of the eighteen Vaibhāṣika subschools.

1574 The teachings of this Buddhist school are thus compared to a story in ancient India that illustrates that there is often a lot of ado about nothing: In the dusty roads of a town, a man produced some fake footprints that looked like those of a wolf and then proclaimed everywhere that there was a dangerous wolf in town, thus terrifying everybody.

1575 Skt. Mūlasarvāstivādin, Tib. gzhi thams cad yod par smra ba. This is another of the eighteen Vaibhāṣika subschools.

1576 Skt. Saṃmitīya, Tib. mang bkur ba, also one of the sects of the Vaibhāṣikas. For various charts of all eighteen schools, see Hopkins 1983, p. 340. For an illuminating discussion of this topic, see Dalai Lama 1988, pp. 45–49.

1577 Skt. pañjikopādhyāya, Tib. 'grel chen mkhan po. This is an epithet of Prajñākaramati, one of the main Indian commentators on this text.

1578 ACIP TD3872@224A and ACIP TD3880@267A.

1579 I could not find any such statement in Kalyāṇadeva's commentary. Dānaśrī was one of the Indian paṇḍitas who were involved in the early period of translation in Tibet. The *Tengyur* contains two texts by him, but neither of them deals directly with the *Bodhicaryāvatāra.*

1580 The Sanskrit word *śloka* indicates a unit of 32 syllables, which can be either in prose or in verse. Here, it refers to verse 51.

1581 As explained earlier, this line is only found in Pawo Rinpoche's commentary.

1582 ACIP TD3874@073B.

1583 ACIP TD3876@166A.

1584 All following quotations from *The Ornament of Sūtras* are found in its second chapter, "Establishing the Great Vehicle."

1585 Ibid., II.12.

1586 Skt. māra, Tib. bdud.

1587 *The Ornament of Sūtras*, II.1.

1588 He is the third of 1,002 Buddhas who appear during this "excellent eon" in which we live (Buddha Śākyamuni is the fourth).

1589 Skt. Kṛkin. This king—a sponsor of the former Buddha Kāśyapa—had ten visions in a dream. The ninth among these visions was explained by the Buddha as follows: "O great monarch, in thy dream thou hast seen how 18 men were pulling at a piece of cloth. This means that the Teaching of the Buddha Śākyamuni will be split into 18 sects. But the cloth, that is (the Doctrine of) Salvation, will not be torn asunder." This is found in the *Svapnanirdeśanāmasūtra* (Tib. rmi lam nges bstan pa zhes bya ba'i mdo), quoted in Bu ston rin chen grub's *History of Buddhism* (1931, II.98).

1590 *The Ornament of Sūtras*, II.2.

1591 This refers to the Buddha's first teaching on this earth to his first five human disciples in the Deer Park in Sarnath.

1592 Tib. dga' ldan. This is one of the six heavens of the desire realm in which the enjoyment of the dharma is also present. It is the place where the Buddhas of this eon dwell before they appear on earth.

1593 Skt. Buddhāvataṃsakasūtra, Tib. sangs rgyas phal po che'i mdo; also called *The Flower Ornament Sūtra.*

1594 *The Ornament of Sūtras*, II.6.

1595 Tib. rdzogs smin sbyang. This refers to the perfection of aspiration prayers, the ripening of sentient beings, and the purification of Buddha-fields.

The full extent of the perfection of aspiration prayers is the complete perfection of the power of the positive roots that are the causes for the ability to effortlessly and spontaneously promote the welfare of others while one-pointedly resting in meditative equipoise within the nature of phenomena.

The full extent of the ripening of sentient beings is the complete perfection of the power of the positive roots that are the causes for the ability to display millions of physical manifestations in millions of Buddha-fields and to establish the retinue in front of each such manifestation—countless sentient beings—on the path of the noble ones due to teaching them just a single verse of dharma.

The full extent of the purification of Buddha-fields is the complete perfection of the power of the positive roots that are the causes for accomplishing the particular Buddha-field in which one will become enlightened, just as the full extent of the ripening of fruits is their being ready to be enjoyed.

1596 *The Ornament of Sūtras*, II.3.

1597 Ibid., II.4.

1598 Ibid., II.5.

1599 Ibid., II.7.

1600 Ibid., II.9.

1601 Ibid., II.10a–c.

1602 V.22. Here, the term "arhat" refers to fully enlightened Buddhas and not to those who attained the fruition of the vehicles of the hearers and solitary realizers.

1603 Skt. pañcānantarya, Tib. mtshams med lnga. Often translated as the "five immeasurably negative actions": killing one's father, one's mother, or an arhat; creating a schism in the saṅgha; and intentionally causing blood to flow from the body of a Buddha. They are called "without interval" because their result is rebirth in a hell realm immediately after death, without the interval of an intermediate state (bardo) before the next rebirth.

1604 V.24.

1605 Skt. Sarvavaidalyasaṃgrahasūtra, Tib. rnam par 'thag pa thams cad bsdus pa'i mdo. In general, the term "collection of complete pulverization" is another name for the "very vast scriptural collection" (Skt. vaipulyam, Tib. shin tu rgyas pa'i sde) in the twelvefold classification of the sūtras of the Buddha (Skt. dvadaśadharmapravacana, Tib. gsung rab yan lag bcu gnyis). This collection is the scriptural collection of bodhisattvas and teaches the great vehicle only. It bears the name "complete pulverization" because it completely pulverizes all obscurations. (Kong sprul blo gros mtha' yas 1982, vol. I, p. 349).

1606 An epithet of Maitreya.

1607 This refers to Buddha Śākyamuni in one of his previous lifetimes.

1608 Skt. dvadaśadhūtaguṇa, Tib. sbyangs pa'i yon tan bcu gnyis: (1) wearing the dress of a dung sweeper (i.e., only clothes that other people have thrown away), (2) owning only three robes, (3) only wearing clothes made out of one kind of material, such as wool, (4) begging for alms, (5) eating only while sitting at one's eating place (i.e., not getting up and returning to eat), (6) not eating food after noon, (7) living in isolated places, (8) living under trees, (9) living in places without a roof, (10) living in charnel grounds, (11) sleeping in a sitting position, and (12) being content to stay anywhere (i.e., without manipulating the ground in any way to make it more comfortable).

1609 Skt. Sarvadharmāpravṛttinirdeśasūtra, Tib. chos thams cad 'byung ba med par bstan pa'i mdo.

1610 In a general sense, this refers to being mentally ready for the dharma of nonarising, i.e., emptiness (Skt. anutpattidharmakṣānti, Tib. mi skye ba'i chos la bzod pa). Thus, here "endurance" does not mean passively enduring or bearing something but rather indicates an active openness and receptiveness to integrate the experience of emptiness into one's mind stream. In a more specific sense, "endurance" stands for reaching the level of endurance among the four levels—heat, peak, endurance, and supreme dharma—of the path of junction. Here, the practitioner newly attains some degree of endurance—or readiness in the sense of lack of fear—with respect to profound emptiness. Strictly speaking, the complete form of this kind of endurance is only attained from the path of seeing onward when one directly sees the nature of phenomena and then familiarizes oneself with this realization.

1611 *The Ornament of Sūtras,* II.15b–d.

1612 This obviously refers to a proclamation by Tsongkhapa. In addition, *The Blue Annals* reports a very similar statement by Tsang Nagba Dsöndrü Senge, another earlier Consequentialist in thirteenth-century Tibet: "A man similar to me, able through study to ascertain the meaning of texts according to the method of Śrī Candrakīrti, will not appear henceforth." ('Go lo tsā ba gzhon nu dpal 1996, p. 334).

1613 Skt. tīrthakara, Tib. mu stegs byed pa.

1614 ACIP KL0107@214B.

1615 I could not locate this verse in the ACIP version of the sūtra (which, however, contains incomplete sections).

1616 V.2–5.

1617 Ibid., V.6.

1618 Skt. Bodhisattvacaryopadeśasūtra, Tib. byang chub sems dpa'i spyod pa bstan pa'i mdo.

1619 Skt. cakravartin, Tib. 'khor los bsgyur ba'i rgyal po. Universal monarchs who travel wherever they want on huge wheels that are made out of gold, silver, copper, or iron. They rule on up to all four continents of the world-system containing Mount Meru and the four continents as presented in ancient Indian cosmology.

1620 Skt. Mañjuśristhānasūtra, Tib. 'jam dpal gnas pa'i mdo.

1621 Tib. chos kyi phyag rgya'i mdo.

1622 Skt. upasaṃpadā, Tib. bsnyen par rdzogs pa (lit. "approaching, entering").

1623 This refers to the formal ritual of being fully ordained as a monk, which starts with the candidate's own request for ordination, followed by three formalized repetitions of this request by his preceptor (Skt. upadhyāya, Tib. mkhan po)—one of the elder fully ordained monks who conduct the ceremony—to these other monks. The ritual is concluded by means of questions to rule out impediments to ordination (such as being sick or not yet twenty years old).

1624 ACIP KD0113@78B (Pawo Rinpoche's commentary quotes only the first line.)

1625 Ibid., @117B (The second line as quoted here reads, "I taught three vehicles for the sake of guidance.")

1626 Skt. Parivrājaka, Tib. kun tu rgyu ba. This is the general name for wandering mendicants of Brahmanic origin, following orthodox Vedic teachings or heterodox paths (the name for mendicants from other castes on heterodox paths was Śramaṇa). Some of these mendicants were mere sophists, some Ājīvikas (see Appendix II), but most of them experimented with a wide range of gurus and spiritual methods.

1627 Ibid., @40A-B.

1628 I.93.

1629 Here "endurance" refers to the third part of the path of junction.

1630 All these examples refer to stories in the Vinaya scriptures about such arhats. For example, Maudgalyāyana—who was renowned for his miraculous powers—went to the hell realms and met a hell-being who was suffering in a very particular way and told him that such suffering had befallen him because—during his human lifetime as a non-Buddhist spiritual teacher—he had propagated certain wrong views. The hell-being requested Maudgalyāyana to tell his students that their teacher urged them to renounce their wrong views because of such karmic results. When Maudgalyāyana returned to the surface of the earth and told the teacher's students what he had seen and heard, they did not believe him but took his words as an insult to their deceased guru and beat him to death.

Udāyin still had some attachment and preferred to teach dharma in the neighborhood brothel. The local robber chief caught him alone with his own favorite prostitute and chopped his head off.

The arhat Little Kubja had the problem that everything that was given to him as alms did not stay in his begging bowl but fell out immediately. So he finally tried some broth made of mud, which stayed in his bowl but led to his passing away.

Nanda used to stare at the women in the audience when giving a dharma talk.

There are other stories (quoted in Crosby and Skilton 1995): High-caste Mahākāśyapa could not rid himself of habitual snobbery and—despite his renown for ascetism—could not help jigging to a tune because of his former lives spent as a monkey. Likewise, Gavāmpati—because of his many lifetimes as an ox—habitually regurgitated his food to chew the cud. Madhuvasiṣṭha—another ex-monkey—could not resist climbing walls and trees. Reportedly, even a pratyekabuddha—who had been a courtesan in past lives—still dressed "like a coquette."

Pūrṇa(maitrāyaṇīputra) was noted for his abilities in expounding the dharma and his skill in training novice monks.

1631 Skt. Sarvapuṇyasamuccayasamādhisūtra, Tib. bsod nams thams cad bsdus pa'i ting nge 'dzin gyi mdo.

1632 Skt. Drumakinnararājaparipṛcchāsūtra, Tib. mi'am ci'i rgyal po ljon pas zhus pa'i mdo.

1633 Skt. poṣada, Tib. gso sbyong. This is a regular ceremony required for all ordained persons to restore and purify their vows.

1634 I.39.

1635 Lines I.11ab.

1636 Skt. vrata, Tib. brtul zhugs.

1637 ACIP TD3874@073B.

1638 Ibid., @073B–074A.

1639 ACIP TD3880@266B.

1640 Ibid., @267A–267B.

1641 ACIP TD3876@166A.

1642 Skt. vāyu, Tib. rlung; lit. "wind."

1643 ACIP KD0106@21B.

1644 Skt. puruṣa, Tib. skyes bu. For more details on this system, see Appendix II.

1645 Skt. rajas, tamas, sattva; Tib. rdul, mun pa, snying stobs.

1646 Skt. prakṛti, Tib. rang bzhin (also called "primal substance," Skt. pradhāna, Tib. gtso bo).

1647 Skt. jagat, Tib. 'gro ba. This is a synonym for the whole universe, indicating its dynamic character.

1648 Skt. mahat/buddhi, Tib. chen po/blo.

1649 Skt. ahaṃkāra, Tib. nga rgyal.

1650 Skt. pañcatanmātra, Tib. de tsam lnga.

1651 The main point that is refuted here is that the permanent self—the individual—is consciousness. See also section 4.2.2.1.3.1. The Refutation of the Primal Substance of the Enumerators below.

1652 The example of labeling one person as both father and son comes from the Enumerators. What they try to illustrate with this is as follows: Whatever is perceived—sound, form, and so on—is basically nothing other than the permanent and single "nature," which becomes perceptible as various "manifestations" (Skt. vikāra, Tib. rnam 'gyur) due to the desire of the individual. This nature actually is the equilibrium of the three "constituents" lightness, motility, and darkness. Here the Centrists' refutation starts: Unlike a person who is labeled in different ways in dependence on other persons, something permanent is something that by definition does not depend on anything, otherwise it would be conditioned and thus impermanent. Hence, the three constituents cannot be something that is qualified in dependence on something else. This entails moreover that they cannot be a cause for anything, since they are permanent, i.e., unchanging and unceasing.

1653 In the way that Pawo Rinpoche comments on lines 64cd, the term "nature" (Skt. svabhāva, Tib. rang bzhin) can be understood on two levels. First, the Enumerators' assertion is that the three constituents of darkness, lightness, and motility are what manifest as "cognition" (Skt. buddhi, Tib. blo) and enable actual perception by the self or the "individual," which is the only factor in their system that is considered sentient or conscious. However, even if this assertion is accepted, the three constituents do not per se have a nature that would allow them to perceive sound (since they are unconscious matter).

On a more specific level, the phrase "at the time of not being dependent" refers to the equilibrium of the three constituents. This state is just what makes up the primordial "nature" (Skt. prakṛti, Tib. rang bzhin), which in itself is not a permanent perception of sound but just undifferentiated primal matter. Moreover, it is said to be imperceptible at all times, whereas the perception of sound is definitely something that is experienced. Thus, these two—the primordial nature and the perception of sound—cannot be the same.

1654 These are two of the five Pandava sons, the heroes in the ancient Indian epic *Mahābhārata.*

1655 Mipham Rinpoche's *Ketaka Jewel* says here: "If you think that there is an apprehension of sound even when form is apprehended, all manifestations would be apprehended [simultaneously] whenever any one [of them occurs], or sound would not be apprehended even when [there is] sound. Since all manifestations are of [this] single nature, it is impossible that certain [manifestations] are [only] apprehended at certain times and not apprehended at the times when others [of them occur]. . . . If what is seen as something distinct [perception of sound and perception of form] is nevertheless one, then it follows that everything is one." ('Ju mi pham rgya mtsho 1979, pp. 91–92)

1656 Skt. pradhāna, Tib. gtso bo (another name for prakṛti).

1657 ACIP TD3874@075A.

1658 Ibid., @075B.

1659 Ibid., @075B–076B.

1660 ACIP TD3880@267B. I could not locate the quote in this passage.

1661 Ibid., @268B–269A.

1662 ACIP TD3876@167B.

1663 Ibid., @168B.

1664 Tib. ba men. An Indian species of deer that has features similar to an ox.

1665 ACIP TD3876@168B.

1666 ACIP TD3872@230A.

1667 Ibid., @231A.

1668 The *Ketaka Jewel* adds that this is as impossible as it is to paint space ('Ju mi pham rgya mtsho 1979, p. 96).

1669 Tib. gzegs zan pa ("Husk-Eater"). Kāṇāda was the founder of the non-Buddhist school of the Differentiators and received his name because he was able to meditate for a long time while sustaining himself by eating only grain husks. He was also called Owl (Skt. Ulūka, Tib. 'ug pa) because, upon his accomplishment of Īśvara, the deity alighted on a stone liṅgam in his meditation cave in the form of an owl, who was then asked by Kāṇāda for confirmation of his attainment.

1670 The *Ketaka Jewel* says: "Bodhisattvas see that there is no self, but the objects of their compassion—all sentient beings—do not realize this. Hence, they continuously and unnecessarily experience the appearances of suffering as if they had a self. Since there are such [beings], [bodhisattvas] develop compassion when they observe them, for the following reason: [Bodhisattvas] are not attached to a personal self and see that others suffer [through their clinging to] such a self despite the fact that they do not have one. Thus, mental states of cherishing others more than oneself blossom naturally, and they also see that it is possible to dispel the suffering of others just like deep sleep." ('Ju mi pham rgya mtsho 1979, p. 101)

1671 The *Ketaka Jewel* gives the following example: "This is just like people who are afflicted by evil spirits. These persons live in the same surroundings as other people. However, from their perspective, deluded appearances, such as the forms of demons, exist. Thus, [for them,] also the suffering caused by these [appearances] and the relief of being free from such suffering exist." (Ibid., p. 102)

1672 Traditionally, these eight qualities define how good drinking water should be: cool, sweet, light, soft, clear, pleasant, wholesome, and soothing.

1673 Skt. māna, Tib. nga rgyal. Usually, this is the word for "pride," but it can—as in this case—also refer to the clinging to a personal self or "me" which leads to desire for what seems pleasant and aversion to what seems unpleasant. The actions that are motivated by such afflictions then cause the various sufferings of cyclic existence.

1674 ACIP TD3874@077B.

1675 Verse 101 of this text says:

When a banana tree together with
The entirety of its parts has been dissected,
There is nothing [left] whatsoever.
Similarly, also persons with their constituents, when dissected, are like this.

1676 ACIP TD3880@269B.

1677 Ibid., @270A.

1678 Ibid., @270B.

1679 Skt. Tathāgataguhyasūtra, Tib. de bzhin gshegs pa'i gsang ba'i mdo.

1680 ACIP TD3872@241B–242A.

1681 "Higher abhidharma" refers to Asaṅga's *Compendium of Abhidharma* (P 5550, fols. 114b.3–4). In the great vehicle, the presentations in Vasubandhu's *Treasury of Abhidharma* are considered the "lower abhidharma."

1682 ACIP TD4089@21A.

1683 Skt. dharmadhātu, Tib. chos kyi khams.

1684 Skt. dharmāyatana, Tib. chos kyi skye mched.

1685 IV.1.

1686 XVIII.42.

1687 XVIII.43–44.

1688 The Tibetan says "eight," because the Tibetan translation of verse 79 has five lines.

1689 This statement refers to the view of Tsongkhapa and his followers that there is a common basis for the various perceived objects of different sentient beings. For example, what is wet and moistening is seen as water by humans, as nectar by gods, as pus and blood by hungry ghosts, and so forth. In his *Chariot of the Tagbo Siddhas*, the Eighth Karmapa too refutes this position.

1690 What is refuted in verses 80 and 81 are the two possibilities of how a body could theoretically exist in its parts: It must be the case either that one body with all its parts pervades the entirety of our body parts by being an exact one-to-one match or that an entire body with all its parts is present in each and every one of its parts (thus implying a multiplicity of bodies).

1691 Of course, either this is just redundant or else the consequence would be that there are two versions of each body part: the actual and the one that belongs to this extra body.

1692 Here, some Sanskrit versions say *kāya* (body, figure) and others *kāśthama* (wooden pile, trunk). Pawo Rinpoche and Padma Karpo read *tho yor* (pile of stones). Most other Tibetan versions of this line read *lus ni skye bu ltar snang ba* (the body appears like a person). The commentaries of Ngülchu Togme and Minyak Künzang Sönam simply ignore this and comment in the same way as Pawo Rinpoche does. Most Indian and Tibetan commentaries available to me explain here that the body appears as a person as long as the conditions for such an appearance are present; i.e., it does not appear as a person when it is an embryo in its earliest stages or when it is cremated and only ashes remain. Kalyāṇadeva and Mipham Rinpoche refer to both Sanskrit versions and, accordingly, give two different explanations (see the following synopsis of other commentaries).

1693 ACIP TD3874@078B.

1694 This must refer to the unidentified *Small Commentary on the Difficult Points.* Mostly, Pawo Rinpoche also calls Prajñākaramati's *Great Commentary on the Difficult Points* just *Great Commentary.* Moreover, just as in the case of *The Small Commentary on the Difficult Points,* none of the quotes of this text here can be located in any of the commentaries on the *Bodhicaryāvatāra* in the *Tengyur* either, and it seems quite unlikely that there is yet another unidentifiable *Small Commentary.*

1695 In Buddhism, the term "feeling" has a much more limited meaning than in Western thinking generally. It only refers to direct, nonconceptual experiences—physical sensations or mental feelings—on their most basic level; these can be pleasurable, unpleasurable, or neutral. All the elaborated "feelings" and "emotions" of our Western internal landscape are simply considered the subsequent conceptualization of our direct experiences.

1696 Pawo Rinpoche's version of lines 90bc has *'di yis* instead of *'di yi* and *gzhan 'ga' tsam* instead of *gzhan dga' tsam.* Thus, his commentary refers to the following reading:

You might say, "Suffering exists in a subtle form."
Isn't it that this removes the gross form [of pleasure]?
If it is merely something other,
Any subtlety must still pertain to this.

1697 As can be seen, the text of verses 90 and 91 is somewhat rearranged in the commentary, which is partly due to the variants in lines 90bc.

Padma Karpo's commentary shows the same variants but gives a different explanation: "**You might say,** 'At the time of pleasure, **suffering exists in a subtle form.** However, **isn't it that** this gross pleasure **removes** the **gross form** [of suffering]? Then, **it is merely something other;** i.e., its gross form has subsided and its subtle form becomes manifest.' **Any subtlety must still pertain to** its respective type. Since it cannot go beyond [its type], it is still suffering or pleasure [respectively]." (p. 157)

Almost all other commentators explain this verse by taking the first three lines as the statement of the opponent. Ngülchu Togme's commentary may exemplify this: "**You might say,** 'Since the experience of **suffering in a subtle form exists**, it is definitely a feeling. However, **isn't it that its gross form is removed** by powerful pleasure? It surely is. The nature of **this** subtle [suffering] **is a joy different from that** gross pleasure, i.e., a **mere** slight pleasure.' **Any** experience of [such] **subtlety** would not be suffering, since it **must still pertain to this** type of pleasure." (p. 344)

See also Künzang Pelden's commentary (Kun bzang dpal ldan 1990, pp. 90–91), which—as so often—corresponds almost exactly to Mipham Rinpoche's *Ketaka Jewel.*

1698 When the text says here "coming into contact," this refers to all-inclusive mutual contact in all dimensions. If infinitesimal particles (or anything else, for that matter) were to touch like two folded hands, they would come into contact on just the palm sides, but not on the back sides, for example. Consequently, they would not be partless. Moreover, one could not say that the two particles—or hands—have contact, since only one of their respective sides—the palm side—has contact. Thus, in order to have full mutual contact on all sides, the particles would have to completely interpenetrate each other. This is not possible either, since they are all equal in having no spatial extension whatsoever that could accommodate something else inside. For this reason, they cannot intermingle; i.e., they could at most exist side by side without overlapping. Strictly speaking, their very quality of being partless and dimensionless excludes any contact at all (let alone 100 percent mutual contact), since they do not have the slighest surface that could have contact.

1699 This refers to verse VIII.101ab:

What is called "continuum" and "collection"
Is not real, just like a rosary, an army, and such.

Some commentators identify the preceding verses about examining the body and its parts (particularly verses IX.85–86) as that "which was already analyzed earlier."

1700 There appears no commentary for line 97d. The corresponding passage of Künzang Pelden's commentary reads: "There is no pleasure to be strived for or to be accomplished. **And which** person **would be afflicted by what** suffering? They are mere illusory appearances of a mistaken mind." (Kun bzang dpal ldan 1990, p. 696)

1701 Here, only the first and the last among the objects of the five senses are explicitly mentioned, but this implicitly includes also the remaining three, i.e., sounds, smells, and tastes.

1702 In other words, if object and experiencer did not have a relationship of being cause and result respectively, the experiencer would be something without a cause. On the other hand, causal connection requires that the cause precedes the result. Thus, simultaneity of two things that are substantially separate and distinct entities that are not related at all—like a mountain in the east and a mountain in the west—excludes a causal connection (as well as the second possible type of connection, i.e., a connection of identity). So how could the one experience the other?

1703 This is analogous to the refutation of self-awareness (verses 17ff.).

1704 ACIP TD3874@079B.

1705 I.e., the non-Buddhist school of the Differentiators.

1706 ACIP TD3874@080B.

1707 Skt. rasāyana, Tib. bcud len. This refers to various practices for extracting the essence of minerals and so on, which sustains the body without other food.

1708 ACIP TD3880@272A.

1709 Skt. mana indriya, Tib. yid dbang.

1710 Skt. manokalpanā, Tib. yid rtog.

1711 See lines 99cd.

1712 All commentators agree here that "inside" refers to the sense faculties. However, in the case of the comment that is criticized here, lines 102ab and lines 102cd would come to mean exactly the same thing, i.e., that mind dwells neither in the sense faculties (inside), nor in form (outside), nor in between (anywhere else). However, Pawo Rinpoche's point here seems to be that mind does not only *not dwell somewhere in* the sense faculties, in outer objects, or in between, but that lines 102cd say in addition that mind *is also not identical with* these faculties, objects, or anything other than these.

1713 ACIP TD3874@081A–081B.

1714 ACIP TD3876@172B.

1715 XXIV.14 (the text quotes only the last two lines).

1716 XXIV.20.

1717 Skt. Candrottarādārikāvyākaraṇasūtra, Tib. bu mo zla mchog lung bstan pa'i mdo.

1718 Skt. kalpaka, Tib. rtog pa pa.

1719 Verse 30.

1720 ACIP TD3874@081B–082A.

1721 I could not locate this quote.

1722 ACIP TD3880@274A–274B.

1723 ACIP TD3876@172B–173A.

1724 The gist of this is as follows: In the example, the existence of the seed is not revealed merely by the material sprout (it neither perceives nor infers its own cause). Rather, our mind has to first perceive the sprout (the result) and then infer the existence of the seed (its cause) based on this perception (which, moreover, requires a proper understanding of causality in general and in this specific case; for example, mere observation of a sprout by a baby without such an understanding would not reveal the existence of the seed to this baby). Thus, this is a process that is more complex than the example suggests.

On the other hand, the implication when the opponent's example is applied to consciousness and knowable object is that—just as the perception of a sprout may lead to an inference about the seed—consciousness itself (the result) should be perceived (a) and thus lead to an inference (b) about the real existence of objects (its cause). However, such two extra consciousnesses (a) and (b) are not observed and moreover are superfluous. Conventionally speaking, unlike a sprout, consciousness in itself is what reveals its perceived object (though not its real existence). Thus, there is no need for this mere perception of an object to lead to a further perception of itself plus to some inference about the existence of an object that it already perceived. Even if one assumes such further consciousnesses, what would they look like? It was already refuted in the section on self-awareness that a given consciousness itself can perceive its own existence (verses 17ff.). If it were another consciousness that perceives the existence of the first one, this would result in the fallacy of infinite regress. Thus, a (really existing) perception of this first consciousness is impossible, not to mention an ensuing inference that is based on such a perception. Consequently, the (real) existence of objects cannot be inferred by reason of a consciousness that perceives them. If the perception of objects were proof of their real existence, this would moreover lead to the absurd consequence that the objects that are perceived in a dream are really existent outside referents, because they are perceived.

1725 ACIP TD3874@082A–082B.

1726 Ibid., @082B.

1727 Verse 48.

1728 These four possibilities are (1) a single result arising from a single cause, (2) a single result arising from multiple causes, (3) multiple results arising from a single cause, and (4) multiple results arising from multiple causes. Thus, "the refutation of arising from the four possibilities" is not to be confused with "the refutation of arising from the four extremes," which is another name for the vajra sliver reasoning.

1729 This refers to the explanation of the vajra sliver reasoning below.

1730 This reasoning is taught in detail in verses 116–142.

1731 I.1.

1732 Skt. Cārvāka, Tib. tshu rol mdzes pa pa.

1733 Skt. Nirgrantha, Tib. gcer bu pa. This is another name of one of the two subsects of Jainism, i.e., the Digambaras ("Sky-Clad Ones").

1734 This refers to Pawo Rinpoche's guru, the Eighth Karmapa Mikyö Dorje.

1735 Verses 70–72 (the present text does not quote lines 71cd and 72cd).

1736 Verses 9–11. The last two lines refer to Vimalakīrti's famous silence in his dialogue with Mañjuśrī about ultimate reality in the *Vimalakīrtinirdeśasūtra.*

1737 *The Treasury of Knowledge* adds: "The Autonomists do not present the seeming by just following worldly conventions, since they see possibilities for mistakenness in such an approach. For, worldly people simply use conventions without any analysis through reasoning whatsoever. Thus, they prefer to present seeming reality in accordance with either the Sūtra Followers or the Yogācāras who know how to apply reasonings. The Consequentialists do not follow other proponents of philosophical systems but just the conventions used by worldly people. For Consequentialists, the noble ones are the sole authorities on the valid cognition of ultimate reality, while worldly people are the sole authorities on what is conventionally considered the valid cognition of seeming reality." (Kong sprul blo gros mtha' yas 1982, vol. II, pp. 519–20)

1738 Quoted in ACIP TD3860@05B (the passage in Buddhapālita's text is ACIP TD3842 @161B).

1739 Ibid., @08B (the passage in Bhāvaviveka's text is ACIP TD3854@49A).

1740 Ibid., @08B–09A.

1741 Tib. dvangs ma.

1742 Tib. snyigs ma.

1743 As for the pure essence and the dross, Jamgön Kongtrul Lodrö Taye's commentary on *The Profound Inner Reality* explains: "In each one of all phenomena of the aggregates, sources, and constituents, there is the pure essence (the aspect of wisdom) and the dross (the aspect of [mistaken] consciousness). By taking the collection of both the pure essence and the dross as the basis for purification and the dross as that which is to be purified, the means for purification—maturation and liberation—accord with the gradations of the basis for purification, and thus the result of purification—the three enlightened bodies—is revealed." (Sikkim, India: Rumtek, 1970, fol. 25b)
As Pawo Rinpoche states below, when misinterpreting this, one may cling to the nonexistence of ordinary, mistaken consciousness and the real existence of wisdom.

1744 ACIP TD3860@012A.

1745 Ibid., @011B.

1746 VI.14.

1747 I.2.

1748 Ibid., I.3ab.

1749 Ibid., I.3cd.

1750 Ibid., I.4a–c.

1751 Ibid., I.5–6.

1752 Ibid., I.7.

1753 Ibid., I.8.

1754 Ibid., I.9.

1755 ACIP TD3860@013A.

1756 I.10–12.

1757 Ibid., I.13–14.

1758 *Fundamental Verses* XII.9ab.

1759 Ibid., VIII.4ab.

1760 ACIP TD3860@012A–012B. The last two lines are taken from Candrakīrti's own *Entrance into Centrism* (VI.100ab).

1761 This reasoning is taught in verses 143–150.

1762 As mentioned before, the followers of this school assert that all things in the three times exist as substantial entities right now. Thus, the things that exist in the future right now come into the present in the next moment and appear as what we call "results," while the things that exist in the present right now (the causes of these results) pass into the past, remaining existent there.

1763 VII.17.

1764 Ibid., VII.19cd.

1765 VI.117.

1766 Tib. dbang phyug. This refers to the supreme godhead in Hinduism since the time of the Vedas, who is mostly identified as the personal god who creates the universe. Later, this supreme godhead often became synonymous with the god Śiva. Several philosophical systems claim the existence of Īśvara, such as the Differentiators and some subschools of the Enumerators. (In Śaṅkara's *Advaitavedānta*, Īśvara is understood as the impersonal, primordial nature of the universe, thus being identical with the Brahman.)

1767 It is said that Īśvara creates the world through his mental activity.

1768 Here, all other commentaries that I consulted say: The opponents claim that Īśvara creates the self and the particles of earth and such. However, since they also claim that all these are permanent, there cannot be a relationship of cause and result between them. How could a permanent Īśvara ever create something, i.e., change his state by creating various things? And how could a self or particles ever be created, since their state of eternity does not allow them to be created or influenced by anything in the first place?

1769 The point here is that if there were a permanent cause that created everything since the infinite past and lasts into the infinite future, there would be no results at all, because their cause has not ceased and will never cease. Or, alternatively, the results—just like their cause—should exist infinitely too. Both consequences are disproved by the fact that we see newly arisen results as well as their cessation everywhere around us. Thus, there cannot be a permanent cause like Īśvara.

1770 Verses 123–125 show that any activity of creation by a creator god, such as Īśvara, is impossible, whether it is considered to be independent of other factors or dependent on them. If such activity were independent of anything, nobody else would have to exert any effort at anything, such as producing food by farming, since there could be nothing that was not created by Īśvara. Thus, even if one made one's own effort, it would be completely in vain and superfluous. Strictly speaking, any actions and even any thinking by sentient beings would be impossible, since these would not come from Īśvara. Thus, the whole idea of karma or any ethics would collapse too.

If it is said that Īśvara is the creator of everything and yet depends on other causes and conditions for this, then it follows that, once the causes and conditions for a result are complete, he could not but "create" this result—whether he wants to or not—because it becomes manifest at this point and thus must have been created by him. On the other hand, it follows that, as long as these causes and conditions are not complete, he obviously does not have the power of creation, because the result is not manifest, even if he wants it to be.

Thus, in both cases, Īśvara is fully under the control of other factors. This not only contradicts the claim of his absolute power to create or not create but moreover makes him completely superfluous in the process of producing results altogether: Once the other causes are complete, they are fully sufficient to manifest the result. Therefore, an additional creator is not needed, nor could he prevent the arising of the result even if he wished to. As long as other causes are incomplete, such a creator is of no use either, since he cannot produce the result without them. Thus, in any case, he cannot influence the result in the slightest.

1771 Verse 12.

1772 ACIP TD3874@083A–083B.

1773 ACIP TD3880@276A.

1774 The primal substance is the first of the twenty-five factors of the Enumerators that comprise all phenomena. For Sanskrit terms and more details, see Appendix I.

1775 It is to be noted that this cognition itself is not sentient, since it derives from primal matter. Rather—just like a mirror in which one sees one's face—it serves as a support for the sentient self to experience objects. Thus, perception comes about only through the combination of the self and cognition.

1776 The following arguments relate to the Enumerators' position that all manifestation or universal flux comes from or has the nature of the three constituents. At the same time, these constituents are equated with pleasure, suffering, and dullness respectively. Thus, it follows that all manifestations must possess these three feelings.

1777 Here, most other commentaries explain: If you say that pleasure arises from cloth, since things like cloth do not actually exist, the pleasure that arises from them does not exist either.

1778 Moreover, this means that pleasure is both the cause for cloth and its result, which is like saying, "This one person is both my mother and my daughter." If the Enumerators were to say that this refers to two different pleasures—one being the cause and the other being the result—they would contradict their own basic claim that the constituents, such as lightness/pleasure, are something single.

1779 This refers back to the Enumerators' thesis that, for example, subtle suffering exists at the time of intense pleasure but is not experienced (verses 88–91).

1780 On the other hand, if the grossness of pleasure were something different from pleasure (and thus totally disconnected), it would follow that pleasure has to be experienced in just the same way all the time, even when its grossness has changed into subtlety.

1781 These two lines could also be read as follows: "You might assert, 'A nonexistent cannot arise from total nothingness.'" However, among the Indian commentaries, only Kalyāṇadeva's commentary supports this reading, while all others seem to understand the Sanskrit ablative (*kiṃcidasattvād*) as indicating a reason. The Tibetan commentaries all follow this, since the translations of this verse agree in saying "because" (*phyir*).

1782 To recall, the Enumerators basically say that if the result does not exist at the time of the cause, it cannot arise later, since it is impossible for something to arise from nothing. They use the example of sesame oil, which is already present within sesame seeds and just becomes manifest when one grinds them. On the other hand, if one grinds sand, no oil is produced. Moreover, there are no other causes that could make a result that does not exist in the first place into an existent result later. Thus, they say, the result must exist at the time of the cause. However, if entities arise from themselves alone, it implicitly follows that they need no other factors for their arising, such as farming or grinding the sesame seeds. Also, if the result already exists at the time of the cause, there is no need for it to arise or become manifest again, or it would arise endlessly.

Most other commentaries explain lines 135ab in the following way: The Enumerators do not explicitly assert that the clearly manifest result as such does not exist at the time of the cause, but that is what follows from their claim that it becomes clearly manifest only later. So they deny that the result is entirely nonexistent at the time of the cause and arises completely newly. However, implicitly, this is exactly what their position comes down to, because, by claiming that the result exists as a potential, they just obscure the distinction between the nonexistence of the result at the time of the cause and its existence later. Saying that it is not manifest at the time of the cause amounts to saying that it does not exist. Otherwise, it would have to be perceptible in some way at this time, which it clearly is not.

1783 Some commentaries give the following reason: The knowledge that the result exists in the cause is a particular result within the consciousnesses of the Enumerators. Therefore, such resultant knowledge must also exist in worldly beings, because they also have consciousness, i.e., its cause.

1784 In all Tibetan translations of this verse, the last two lines read as follows:

| | |
|---|---|
| *de nyid du ni stong pa nyid* | In true reality, meditation on emptiness |
| *sgom pa de phyir mi 'thad 'gyur* | Is therefore unjustified. |

In Sanskrit, this would be *tattvataḥ śūnyatā tasmād bhāvanā nopapadyate.* However, what these lines actually say is *tattvataḥ śūnyatā tasmād bhāvānāṃ nopapadyate,* which is confirmed by all Indian commentaries and their Tibetan translations. Thus, the Tibetan should read: *de nyid du ni dngos rnams kyi/ stong nyid de phyir mi 'thad 'gyur.* Pawo Rinpoche seems to comment on both possibilities, with an unusual gloss of *de nyid du ni.* Except for Bu ston, who explicitly refers to both versions, all other Tibetan commentators comment on the first version only, which seems to result from a certain emphasis on the practical application of one's understanding of emptiness in meditation.

1785 The usual reading of lines 139ab refers to the fact that a negation of something has to depend on a preceding notion of this thing; for example, one cannot talk or think about the nonexistence of a vase without having the notion of a vase in the first place. Pawo Rinpoche seems to focus on the necessity of using and communicating with conventional notions or terms—which are always imputations—in order to demonstrate what they refer to.

1786 ACIP TD3874@084B.

1787 Ibid., @084B–085A. In the last sentence, Pawo Rinpoche's commentary quotes line 133b: "Being gross or subtle means nothing but impermanence." However, Kalyāṇadeva's commentary clearly refers to lines 134ab.

1788 Ibid., @085A.

1789 ACIP TD3876@175A.

1790 Ibid., @176A. There are some textual variants after "It is that which is superimposed as the nature [of all phenomena], . . . (Tib. ngo bo nyid du sgro btags pa ste)." In the present text, this quote continues with: *dogs pa dang bcas pa 'gog pa yin no zhes* (which does not make much sense; I assume *dogs pa* is just a misspelling of *dgos pa*). P5278 says: *dgag par bzung bar mi nus pa'i phyir ro.* ACIP and D3876 both read: *dgos par bya ba la dgos par byed pa yin no.* (Here, the passage in P5278 above follows after a few more sentences, which suggests that these are missing in P5278.) Thus, my translation follows ACIP and Derge.

1791 Some Indian non-Buddhist schools say that results come about through time as their ripening cause.

1792 ACIP TD3876@176A–176B.

1793 Most other commentaries relate verses 143–144 to the reasoning of dependent origination.

1794 It seems that Pawo Rinpoche deemed verses 145–146ab to be self-explanatory, since he gives no further comment. The corresponding part of Künzang Pelden's commentary says: "If the result is analyzed, is what is to be produced an existent or a nonexistent? **What use is a cause for** a result that is **an entity**, i.e., something **that exists already** by its nature? These two are not suitable as cause and result for each other. You might say, 'The result is something nonexistent that is produced by the cause.' **What use is a cause, if** the result's own entity is a mere **nonexistent?** [There is no need for a cause], since, in general, a nonexistent does not have a cause and such a [nonexistent] remains within its nature of being a nonexistent. You might think, 'A mere nonexistent is not something that is produced by a cause. However, it is the cause that makes this nonexistent result into an existing entity.' No [cause] is capable [of this]: **Even** the combined efforts of **billions of causes cannot alter the lack of an entity** (i.e., [the lack of] a phenomenon)—or the nonexistence of a nature of its own—into an entity. This is just as the horns of a rabbit cannot be transformed into an existent, no matter how many causes are combined. A nonexistent will never turn into something that has to depend on something [else]. Another reason the lack of an entity cannot be transformed into an entity is: It is not justified either that [this lack of an entity] turns into [an entity] without discarding its nature (i.e., being the lack of an entity) or that it turns into [an entity] by discarding [this nature]." (Kun bzang dpal ldan 1990, pp. 724–25)

1795 ACIP TD3874@087A.

1796 ACIP TD3876@176B.

1797 This refers to Buddha Śākyamuni's miracle at Śrāvastī, where he displayed such feats.

1798 Unlike the Sanskrit, the Tibetan translation of this verse switches the first two and the last two lines. Thus, the Tibetan commentaries also give the reverse order of rebirth in pleasant and unpleasant states. The Indian commentaries confirm the order that is given here.

1799 This refers to the golden ground at the very bottom of a four-continent world with Mount Meru.

1800 The Sanskrit for this line is *sukhopakareṇaiḥ svakaiḥ*. The Tibetan says *rang gi bde ba'i tshogs char kyis* ("with the rains of my own happiness") instead of *rang gi bde ba'i tshogs chas kyis*. This is the common variant of this line in most Tibetan translations. Pawo Rinpoche addresses the difference in his synopsis of other commentaries below.

1801 Skt. Bhūmipālaputra, Tib. sa srung gi bu. This is the elephant on whom the god Indra rides.

1802 The Sanskrit of this verse reads:

*kadopalambhadṛṣṭibhyo deśayiṣyāmi śūnyatām*
*saṃvṛttyānupalambhena puṇyasaṃbhāramādarāt*

The Tibetan says:

| | |
|---|---|
| *nam zhig dmigs pa med tsul du* | Having carefully gathered the accumulation of merit |
| *gus pas bsod nams tsogs bsags te* | In a nonreferential manner, |
| *dmigs pas phung bar gyur rnams la* | When will I teach emptiness |
| *stong pa nyid ni ston par 'gyur* | To those who are ruined by being referential? |

The English translation primarily follows Prajñākaramati's commentary. He explains that the accumulation of merit is not gathered in a random way, but by very carefully employing the expedient conventions of seeming reality, without which ultimate emptiness cannot be taught. The accumulation of merit consists of the perfections, such as generosity, which are all practiced in a nonreferential manner, that is, by not conceptualizing the triad of giver, recipient, and the act of generosity. Those who have referential views are the realists, that is, those who cling to really existing entities. (ACIP TD 3872@287A–B).

1803 Skt. kṛtayuga, Tib. rdzogs ldan dus. According to ancient Indian cosmology, this is the first of four phases in an eon—the "golden age"—in which human beings have an extremely long life span. At this time, wealth, wishes, happiness, and dharma are spontaneously provided in vast abundance.

1804 The second version seems to be a freer translation of "offerings" (Skt. upakareṇa, lit. "help, service, instrument"), which fits the context of this metaphor nicely. Originally, it might well have been just a scribal error, since, in Tibetan, the difference between these two versions is just a single letter (*char* instead of *chas*). All Indian commentaries refer to the first version (as does Mipham Rinpoche), whereas most Tibetan commentaries explain the latter.

1805 ACIP TD3874@087A.

1806 Ibid., @087A.

1807 Ibid., @087A–088A.

1808 ACIP TD3880@280A-281B.

1809 Skt. Rājadeśasūtra, Tib. rgyal po la gdams pa'i mdo. In the *Kangyur*, there are three sūtras by this name, which are taught for different kings. It is usually the sūtra taught for King Prasenajit of Kosala that is referred to.

1810 ACIP TD3880@281B–282A.

1811 Sources: Mi nyag dgon po 1999 (pp. 237–42), Ko zhul grags pa 'byung gnas dang rgyal ba blo bzang mkhas grub 1992 (pp. 995–96), Dpa' bo gtsug lag phreng ba 1986 (pp. 1528–31), and Chos kyi 'byung gnas 1972 (vol. II, pp. 55–63).

1812 Tib. dbu ru ṣnye thang, an area in central Tibet near Lhasa.

1813 Tib. gnyags dznyā na ku mā ra.

1814 Tib. bla ma dar.

1815 Tib. lam rnyed sgrol ma.

1816 Tib. chos dbang lhun grub.

1817 Tib. dge bsynen cha lung.

1818 Tib. lho brag gro bo lung gi dgon pa. Trowo Lung is a region in Lhotrag in southern Tibet.

1819 Tib. dge 'dun rgya mtsho.

1820 Tib. mi pham chos kyi rgyal po.

1821 Tib. paṇḍita ngag dbang grags pa.

1822 Tib. dvags po paṇḍita chos rgyal bstan pa'i rgyal mtshan.

1823 Tib. dbus smyon he ru ka kun dga' bzang po. He is not to be confused with the well-known Tsang Nyön Heruka, who lived from 1452–1507.

1824 Tib. legs bshad gling.

1825 Tib. bka' chen bzhi.

1826 Tib. zhva lu lo chen chos skyong dpal bzang po.

1827 Tib. kong po, a region in southern Tibet.

1828 Tib. zing po 'bum pa sgang.

1829 This means "Glorious Garland of Holy Scriptures." Literally, the Tibetan word *gtsug lag* means "[to touch one's] crown of head [with one's] hands." Thus, it is a reverential word for scriptures, especially for the teachings of the Buddha.

1830 Tib. tsa ri'i gnas nang rong chung. Tsari is a region in southern Tibet, and Naynang is the area where the main seat of the line of Pawo tulkus is situated.

1831 Tib. gzhu gru bzhi'i mkha' 'gro gsang phug.

1832 Tib. mkha' ro'i gsang phug.

1833 Tib. mtsho dkar khyung rdzong.

1834 Tib. rgyal tshab grags pa don grub, another one of the four regents of the Karmapas.

1835 Tib. grags pa dpal 'byor.

1836 Tib. phag mo rnam bshad chen mo.

1837 Tib. rtsis kyi bstan bcos rin chen gter mdzod.

1838 Tib. gso ba rig pa'i rgyud bzhi rnam bshad.

1839 Tib. sman dpyad zin bris snying po bsdus pa.

1840 For more details, see, for example, Frauwallner 1956 and Hiriyanna 1973.

1841 Skt. varṇa.

1842 Skt. bhedābheda.

1843 Skt. pramāṇa, Tib. tshad ma.

1844 Skt. pratyakṣa, anumāṇa, śabda, upamāṇa; Tib. mngon sum, rjes dpag, sgra, dpe nyer 'jal.

1845 Skt. prameya, Tib. gzhal bya.

1846 The claim that the legendary sage Kapila (Tib. ser skya pa, "The Blond One") is the founder of this system is historically unfounded. That this name is mentioned in the Vedas (*Sagāthakam* 784) more probably refers to Kaphila who wrote verses 547–556 of the verse collection *Theragāthā.*

1847 Tib. rang bzhin.

1848 Tib. skyes bu.

1849 Skt. guṇa, Tib. yon tan.

1850 Skt. rajas, tamas, sattva. Tib. rdul, mun pa, snying stobs.

1851 Skt. jagat, Tib. 'gro ba.

1852 Skt. vikāra, Tib. rnam 'gyur.

1853 Skt. buddhi or mahat, Tib. blo or chen po. Cognition is also called "the great one" because all further manifestations evolve from it and because it is the only factor that is capable of bringing about a liberating realization.

1854 Skt. ahaṃkāra, Tib. nga rgyal.

1855 Skt. pañcatanmātra, Tib. de tsam lnga.

1856 Skt. jīva, Tib. srog.

1857 For reasons of space, the sūtras quoted are not listed here again.

# Index